T5-CQC-549

VOLUME II CHAPTERS 15-26

INTERMEDIATE ACCOUNTING

VOLUME II CHAPTERS 15-26

INTERMEDIATE ACCOUNTING

Sixth Canadian Edition

Thomas R. Dyckman
Ann Whitney Olin Professor of Accounting
Cornell University

Morton Nelson
Wilfrid Laurier University

Roland E. Dukes
University of Washington

Michael Zin
University of Windsor

Charles J. Davis
California State University—Sacramento

Joan E. D. Conrod
Dalhousie University

IRWIN

Burr Ridge, Illinois
Boston, Massachusetts
Sydney, Australia

Cover photo courtesy of Loblaw Companies Limited

Material from the Examinations and Unofficial Answers,
copyright © 1955, 1960-1990 by the American Institute of
Certified Public Accountants, the Canadian Institute of Chartered
Accountants, the Certified General Accountants Association
of Canada, and from the Society of Management Accountants
of Canada, is adapted or reprinted with permission.

© RICHARD D. IRWIN, INC., 1974, 1978, 1982, 1986, 1989, and 1992

All rights reserved. No part of this publication may be
reproduced, stored in a retrival system, or transmitted, in
any form or by any means, electronic, mechanical,
photocopying, recording, or otherwise, without the prior
written permission of the publisher.

Senior sponsoring editor: Roderick T. Banister
Project editor: Jean Lou Hess
Production manager: Ann Cassady
Designer: Laurie Entringer
Art manager: Kim Meriwether
Compositor: Beacon Graphics Corporation
Typeface: 10/12 Times Roman
Printer: The Maple-Vail Book Manufacturing Group

ISBN 0-256-09967-7 (Main Text)
ISBN 0-256-15629-8 (Vol. I)
ISBN 0-256-15630-1 (Vol. II)

Library of Congress Catalog Number: 91-77506

Printed in the United States of America
1 2 3 4 5 6 7 8 9 0 VB 0 9 8 7 6 5 4 3

PREFACE

◆

PHILOSOPHY AND PURPOSE
◆

Financial reporting plays a unique role in the process of allocating resources in our economy. The subject matter of this text, *Intermediate Accounting,* Sixth Canadian Edition, is the development of the principles underlying that reporting process.

This revision represents a major reorganization and rewriting effort. Our aim is to improve the text as a learning tool while continuing the comprehensiveness and technical quality of previous editions.

The text is completely current as to the date of publication and includes discussion of the most recent statements by the accounting standard setting bodies. In particular, we have incorporated *CICA Handbook,* section 3060, "Capital Assets," section 1000, "Financial Statement Concepts," section 3480, "Extraordinary Items," section 3830, "Non-monetary Transactions," and the latest pronouncements on accounting for income taxes into the text. Every attempt has been made to assure the accuracy of this material.

Each of us has taught intermediate accounting for many years. In doing so we have developed an awareness of the issues and applications most difficult for the student to master and have exercised special care in those areas to make the presentation as clear, understandable, and stimulating as possible.

Before embarking on this revision, we surveyed the marketplace to solicit views on topics to be included in the intermediate accounting course, chapter sequencing, desirability of real-world examples, and degree of comprehensiveness. The answers to our surveys and questionnaires were exceptionally helpful in providing overall direction for this revision. In addition, the panel of eight reviewers was a tremendous source of information about the education process and our proposed changes in pedagogy. The insights and recommendations of these reviewers helped shape the final form and substance of the text.

Objectives and Overall Approach of the Sixth Canadian Edition This sixth Canadian edition has several objec-

tives. The primary objective is to provide comprehensive coverage of financial accounting topics, both their application and rationale. The text emphasizes the reasons for specific accounting principles, along with clear discussions and illustrations of their applications. We believe that continual integration of theory and practice is the most efficient way to present the subject matter. When the student discovers there is a reason for a procedure, much less is relegated to pure memorization. Consequently, this text does not rely on large and complex exhibits as the sole explanation for accounting procedures.

A secondary objective is to bring the subject to life and increase the student's interest in the material. To accomplish this, we have greatly increased the text's real-world emphasis. The text has literally hundreds of real-world reporting examples and frequent discussions of the financial reporting experiences of actual firms.

Throughout the text, we discuss the process by which specific accounting principles are developed, thus reinforcing the real-world nature of financial reporting standards. The impact of lobbying and the need for compromise by standard setters is discussed in several chapters affected by the more controversial pronouncements. One aim of this emphasis is to develop the student's ability to critically evaluate particular reporting standards. We want the student to address the question: Is a particular accounting principle successfully fulfilling the primary objective of financial statements, namely to provide information useful for decision making? A second aim is to acquaint the student with the political setting in which standard setting takes place.

The topical sequencing of material within each chapter is designed to present the important reporting issues and the reasons financial statement users and preparers are concerned about them. This approach leads to a discusssion of the current GAAP solution to the issue with appropriate rationale. In the more controversial areas, we consider other potential solutions and why these may have been rejected by the relevant standard-setting body. As a result, the student is frequently reminded of the dynamic and interactive nature of the standard-setting process and the inherent difficulties facing standard setters in reaching a consensus.

We also emphasize the areas in which the accounting standards provide a choice from among several alternative methods. In related discussions, the text probes the incentives for choosing from among alternative accounting methods.

Curriculum Concerns This revision is responsive to the concerns of accounting academics. These concerns suggest a new orientation for accounting education. With this new direction, students should be encouraged "to learn how to learn." Curricula should emphasize the underlying concepts, rather than memorization of rules and regulations. The focus is on the process of inquiry in which the student learns to identify problem situations, to search for relevant information, to analyse and interpret the information, and to reach a well-reasoned conclusion.

With these goals in mind, this edition frequently asks questions and presents important contemporary issues in a manner that compels the student to think about the appropriate solution to a reporting problem. We believe that the discussions of the more controversial and involved issues will lead the student to his or her own position on these issues. To this end, the text often focusses on the process of inquiry, rather than encouraging memorization of the standards and procedures. What information would the user find more useful in making a decision? What would the student do in this situation?

We view the current GAAP solutions to reporting problems as one step in the continuing evolutionary process of attempting to provide the most cost-effective and useful information possible. The text involves the student in that process. For example, many of the cases require students to identify and solve unstructured problems and to consider multiple data sources. In addition, by weaving theory and application together throughout the text, students are encouraged to apply their knowledge to new situations.

Writing Style and Exposition The text mixes a clear, direct, and concise writing style with an active voice to maintain the positive flow of the material and the student's attention. The text is well outlined and provides considerable structure and good transition between topics. We have clarified and simplified many of the application examples without sacrificing completeness.

The text makes generous use of outlining by using distinctive captions to provide a structure for the reader. We have attempted to minimize the number of pages without any visual "break." We believe that

frequent use of examples, headings, and new pedagogical devices increases understandability and ease of reading, while maintaining the student's interest. A greater use of visual aids is apparent in this edition. Furthermore, the new pedagogical features enhance the learning experience for students.

An increased use of summary tables and exhibits helps to synthesize the more complex areas, and gives the student an opportunity to evaluate progress. Many of the exhibits and illustrations were class-tested to fine tune them.

To increase the conversational tone and use of current terminology, certain terms were changed. For example, "balance sheet" replaces "statement of financial position," "income statement" replaces "statement of income," and "payment" replaces "rent" in present value discussions. Also, in the text and the end-of-chapter material, the sixth edition uses actual year designations such as 1992, rather than 19A, for increased realism.

The text assumes completion of a basic introductory course in financial accounting and is intended primarily for schools covering intermediate accounting in two semesters. For example, one logical sequencing for a two-semester course is Chapters 1–14 in the first course, followed by Chapters 15–26.

REVISION APPROACH AND ORGANIZATION
◆

Financial accounting is concerned with measurement of economic attributes and their recognition in asset, liability, owners' equity, and income accounts. Income determination and disclosure also are important goals of financial reporting. The sixth edition reflects a new sequencing of chapters. After considering the conceptual framework of the CICA and a review of the accounting process, the chapters in this book are grouped into modules corresponding to the major balance sheet account classifications, in natural balance sheet order. Within each is a consideration of the related income and disclosure issues. The text concludes with a series of chapters on specialized accounting topics. These chapter groupings are:

	Part	Chapters
I	Foundation and Review	1–6
II	Asset Recognition and Measurement	7–14
III	Liabilities	15–19
IV	Owners' Equity	20–22
V	Special Topics	23–26

Changes in Chapter Order The sixth edition significantly changes chapter sequencing. The major changes in chapter order are:

Chapter 2, "Financial Statement Concepts and Principles" (Chapter 6 in the previous edition) now appears earlier. We believe this is preferable because it allows the instructor to discuss theory before covering the financial statements in the review chapters. The reviewers responded to this major organizational change very favourably.

Chapter 7, "Revenue and Expense Recognition" (Chapter 13 in the previous edition) appears as the first chapter in the section of the text devoted to asset measurement. The chapter ties back to the conceptual framework (when to recognize assets), thereby linking theory with the practical issues of when to record revenues and expenses. The earlier presentation also allows the instructor to cover certain topics without first having to explain recognition criteria.

Chapter 14, "Investments: Temporary and Long Term" (Chapter 18 in previous edition) is now sequenced as part of the asset section of the text. This grouping allows completion of revenue recognition issues (in this chapter, for intercompany investments) before taking up accounting issues related to liabilities.

Chapter 17, "Accounting for Income Taxes" (Chapter 23 in the previous edition) is now sequenced as part of the liability section of the text. In this way, the liability issues are completed before turning to owners' equity.

Chapter 22, "Earnings per Share" (part of Chapter 22 in the previous edition) is now a stand-alone special topics chapter given the overall importance and complexity of the topic.

Chapter 25, "Financial Statement Analysis and Changing Prices" (part of Chapter 22 and Chapter 25 in the previous edition) are now combined in the sixth edition. Adjustments for the effect of changing prices are no longer required, yet many financial statement users continue to make such adjustments when analysing statements. Hence, adjusting for price-level changes is considered as part of financial statement analysis.

Chapter 26, "Special Topics: Disclosure, Interim Reporting, and Segment Reporting" is a new chapter that combines parts of chapters from the previous edition along with new material on disclosure issues.

Flexibility in Use

In reordering the chapters, we had definite objectives in mind. The topical chapters are grouped to provide a more clear and logical transition within major parts of the text. The commonality of issues and principles within each part reinforces similar principles and enhances their understanding.

However, instructors are not bound by this order. For example, some instructors prefer to cover current liabilities immediately after current assets. This text provides the flexibility to accomplish this and virtually any other ordering desired. The chapters following Chapter 6 are topical in nature, and all rely on the first five chapters for conceptual grounding, and the "big-picture" review in Chapters 3 through 5. Given that the topical chapters are self-contained, a considerable degree of flexibility in chapter sequencing is maintained.

Also, liberal use of appendixes increases the flexibility of topical coverage for the instructor. This additional flexibility is important given the ever-increasing scope of topics in the intermediate accounting course.

Real-World Emphasis

This text makes extensive use of financial reporting examples from actual companies when discussing specific reporting areas. We also make frequent use of the CICA's *Financial Reporting in Canada* for information on trends in financial reporting. In addition, many references to reporting decisions and consequences from the businesses world are taken from the financial press, and many other sources. Loblaw Companies Limited graciously permitted us to reproduce their entire 1990 financial statements and accompanying notes.

Using actual companies in examples helps show how reporting is carried out in practice. References to well-known corporations capture and hold the student's interest as well and reflect the tremendous variety of current accounting practices. The real-world examples also help to convince the student of the importance of many abstract concepts and procedures.

Ethics

A topic of continuing interest in business schools, ethical issues are treated in several chapters through an ethics case in the end-of-chapter material. Ethics cases are included in Chapters 3, 6, 8, 9, 11, 12, 16, 19, 23, and 24. In addition, implicit references are made to the ethics of financial reporting throughout the text.

End-of-Chapter Material

Numerous changes and revisions were made to the end-of-chapter material. Older and more repetitive items were deleted, and many new items were added. These additions supplement the already considerable inventory of homework assignments. Professional accounting examination questions continue to be used in this edition; many were updated.

The **questions** at the end of each chapter provide a context for in-class discussion; **exercises** are generally structured applications of specific issues in the chapter; **problems** tend to be longer and less structured applications of one or more specific issues in the chapter; and **cases** often require the student to integrate several issues in the chapter and provide an opinion on a reporting problem or situation.

The cases and some problems provide an opportunity for students to practice their analytical and written communication skills. Furthermore, they frequently place the student in an unstructured setting requiring a broad view to be taken of a business reporting problem. The context in which financial reporting is used must be considered in these instances.

To help the instructor choose appropriate items, each exercise, problem, and case is titled to indicate the primary issue involved. In addition, each is keyed to one or more learning objectives to allow instructors to select those areas they wish to emphasize.

The quantity and variety of items, both in substance and level of difficulty, allow an instructor to vary the homework items from term to term. The end-of-chapter material was checked for accuracy by faculty colleagues.

NEW PEDAGOGICAL FEATURES
◆

Several new pedagogical features have been added to this edition. They are designed to make learning easier and, in general, to make this text more user-friendly.

Learning Objectives

Done in list form, a set of proactive learning objectives opens each chapter to provide the student with learning goals and a preview of upcoming topics.

Introductions

Immediately after the list of learning objectives are the introductions or "stage setters" that discuss events and reporting by actual companies relevant to the chapter and provide a transition to the upcoming chapter topics. These introductions are attention-grabbing and help the reader understand the significance of the area about to be studied.

Concept Reviews

Throughout the chapters, usually at the end of major sections, students are asked to respond to a brief list of questions. These questions are answerable directly from the text and help students check their understanding of the section's basic concepts or message. These questions also provide a break from the reading and reinforce the major ideas. In addition, the concept reviews give the readers an idea of how well they comprehended the material before moving ahead. The questions are analogous to a short quiz after a lecture on a particular part of a chapter. The answers to the concept review questions are provided at the end of the solutions manual for the convenience of the instructor.

Summary of Key Points

Each chapter concludes with a recap of the main ideas presented. The summaries are now done in list format rather than a paragraph style. The list format better highlights the chapter's content by making the most important ideas more easily identifiable. Each point is keyed to the relevant learning objective.

Review Problem with Solution

Immediately after the summary of key points, a review problem illustrates several of the chapter's main concepts, followed by the solution. The review problems also provide additional practice for the student and a self-test for evaluating progress.

Key Terms

Just before the end-of-chapter material, a list of the chapter's most important new terms appears. Page references indicate where the terms were defined and initially discussed. The key terms are printed in bold for emphasis, allowing the student to easily locate them, and to review their meanings in the context of the chapter.

Comprehensive Problems

In many chapters, one or more problems in the end-of-chapter material cover several of the chapter's learning objectives. Their objective is to integrate the more important ideas into a single situation. They are identified by this symbol in the margin:

COMPREHENSIVE PROBLEM
◆

Ethics Case

Many chapters include a case in the end-of-chapter material that emphasizes the ethical implications of particular actions and reporting decisions. The student often is placed in a situation requiring a decision that has ethical ramifications. These cases are identified by this symbol in the margin:

Loblaw Cases

Many chapters also include a case based on the 1990 annual statements of Loblaw Companies Limited. This case provides an up-to-date application of the chapter material to an actual company. These problems are identified by the Loblaw logo.

KEY CHAPTER REVISIONS
◆

The changes to the sixth edition were very extensive. The following list highlights the major revisions made in each chapter.

Chapter 1, "The Environment of Accounting"
- The basic accounting model has been moved to Chapter 3.
- The 1986 Allied and Federated Stores takeover is used to illustrate the value and limitations of financial reporting.

Chapter 2, "Financial Statement Concepts and Principles"
- The major parts of the CICA's Financial Statement Concepts, as they reflect the development of accounting principles, are discussed and compared to the FASB's conceptual framework.

Chapter 3, "Review: The Accounting Information Processing System"
- The more general systems approach to the accounting cycle is discussed in the chapter, while an appendix that includes **acetate transparencies** illustrates the worksheet.
- Greater emphasis is placed on adjusting and reversing entries.
- A new discussion comparing two methods of reporting operating payments that precede recognition of

revenue and expense helps the student to understand adjustments and reversals.

Chapter 4, "Review of the Income Statement"
- New and detailed discussion of the measurement and reporting guidelines for discontinued operations results in comprehensive coverage of this topic.
- The coverage of intraperiod tax allocation parallels the greater emphasis on items below income from continuing operations.
- The new emphasis on the issue of current operating performance versus the all-inclusive approach to income measurement complements the discussion of comprehensive income.

Chapter 5, "Review: The Balance Sheet and the Statement of Changes in Financial Position"
- The balance sheet and statement of changes in financial position of Alcan Aluminum Limited are used to present and illustrate many of the concepts in this chapter.
- The various valuation approaches used in the balance sheet, the usefulness of the balance sheet, and the limitations of the balance sheet are stressed.
- Both direct and indirect forms of the statement of changes in financial position are discussed.

Chapter 6, "Interest Concepts of Future and Present Value"
- Symbols for future and present value calculations are now more user-friendly.
- Use of summary tables and time-line exhibits simplifies the presentation.
- The interest tables now appear in an appendix.

Chapter 7, "Revenue and Expense Recognition"
- The earlier coverage of revenue recognition will assist the discussion of asset recognition in later chapters.
- The fundamental concepts of revenue recognition are emphasized throughout the chapter.
- The conceptual discussion leads to the general criteria for revenue recognition.

Chapter 8, "Cash and Receivables"
- Different formats for bank reconciliations are covered and emphasis is placed on proof of cash.
- The in-depth discussion on using receivables for financing reflects the complexities in this area.
- New coverage on notes receivable exchanged for cash and other privileges demonstrates the variety of uses for notes and resulting accounting issues.

Chapter 9, "Inventory Measurement and Cost of Goods Sold"
- Coverage of consignments is expanded.
- The chapter now distinguishes between cost-flow assumptions under both the periodic and perpetual systems.

- A new section discussing the alternatives emphasizes the importance of judgment in this area.

Chapter 10, "Alternative Inventory Valuation Methods"

- The LCM material has been rewritten to clarify the steps in the calculation and includes additional situations.
- The discussion of the gross margin and retail methods is rewritten to emphasize calculational steps.
- The discussion of effects of inventory errors has been rewritten to include clearer examples.

Chapter 11, "Capital Assets: Acquisition, Disposal, and Exchange"

- This discussion of the issue of what to capitalize includes the *CICA Handbook* material on donations.
- The substantially greater emphasis on capitalization of interest includes both theory and application.
- A generalized approach to valuing property acquired in an exchange helps to simplify this area.

Chapter 12, "Capital Assets: Depreciation and Impairment"

- Considerably greater emphasis is placed on the nature of depreciation, incentives for choice of methods, and what depreciation means to the financial statement user.
- Depreciation policy is discussed in terms of its effect on dividend policy and cash flows.
- A section on impairment of value considers the decade-long trend of corporations to take large write-offs of operational assets.

Chapter 13, "Intangible Assets and Natural Resources"

- The accounting for all intangibles other than goodwill, research and development, and computer software costs is reorganized.
- In-depth treatment of goodwill estimation emphasizes concepts and examples.
- The oil and gas controversy complements a complete discussion of accounting for natural resources.

Chapter 14, "Investments: Temporary and Long Term"

- Changing between the cost and equity methods is discussed and illustrated.
- Consolidations discussion is shorter and has been moved to an appendix.
- Also moved to an appendix are special purpose funds, cash surrender value of life insurance, and futures contracts.

Chapter 15, "Short-Term Liabilities"

- New coverage of bonus payments is added.
- The chapter now includes refinancing of short-term debt and the reporting of debt as short-term.
- The sections on taxes collected for third parties and conditional payments are extensively revised.

Chapter 16, "Long-Term Liabilities"

- Greater emphasis is placed on theory discussion and rationale for positions on such controversial topics as troubled debt restructuring, debt extinguishment, and valuation of debt issued with equity securities.
- There is new coverage of troubled debt restructuring, which now appears in an appendix.
- The CICA financial instruments project is discussed in terms of project financing relationships, unconditional purchase obligations, zero-coupon bonds, and creative financial instruments.

Chapter 17, "Accounting for Income Taxes"

- The chapter is reorganized with coverage of concepts made clearer and simpler.
- Accounting for operating losses precedes interperiod tax allocation.

Chapter 18, "Accounting for Leases"

- Accounting for lessor and lessee is covered in series rather than in parallel fashion; the lessee is considered first (emphasis on liabilities).
- Greater emphasis is placed on special issues including different interest rates, bargain renewal offers, and the use of guaranteed residual values to secure off-balance-sheet financing.
- An appendix covers real estate and tax issues of leases.

Chapter 19, "Accounting for Pensions"

- The chapter is totally reorganized using a modularized approach to emphasize the basics and to ease into the complexities.
- New coverage on pension termination enhances the real-world flavour of the subject.
- Two new appendixes appear: settlements, curtailments, and termination benefits; and accounting for the pension plan.

Chapter 20, "Corporations: Contributed Capital"

- Material on par value shares and treasury stock is contained in appendixes. This reflects the pervasiveness of CBCA legislation and provides flexibility for the instructor.
- Greater emphasis is placed on the issues underlying redeemable preferred shares.

Chapter 21, "Corporations: Retained Earnings and Stock Options"

- Fractional share rights and stock appreciation rights and spin-offs receive greater emphasis.
- The discussion of quasi reorganizations is moved to an appendix.

Chapter 22, "Earnings per Share"

+ EPS is given its own chapter to allow for more detailed discussion.
+ Basic, fully diluted, adjusted, and pro forma EPS are fully explained.
+ Extensive examples are now provided.

Chapter 23, "Statement of Changes in Financial Position"

+ The importance of cash flow information for financial statement users is examined.
+ The indirect method, prevalent in Canadian practice, is emphasized.
+ A complete explanation of the direct method is given in both simple and complex examples.
+ Three approaches to preparing the statement are illustrated: a format-free approach, the spreadsheet, and the T-account.
+ The spreadsheet is simplified to allow a simultaneous solution of the statement under both direct and indirect methods.

Chapter 24, "Accounting Changes and Error Corrections"

+ Accounting for changes in accounting principles retroactively, on a current basis, and prospectively are thoroughly examined.
+ The issues affecting accounting changes and alternative views and motivations for changes are stressed, including a review of positive theory implications and income smoothing.
+ Prior period adjustments and error corrections are explained in a thorough treatment.

Chapter 25, "Financial Statement Analysis and Changing Prices"

+ The inclusion of both financial statement analysis and accounting for changing prices is a major organizational change aimed at streamlining the coverage of these two related topics.
+ New ratios used in financial statement analysis are discussed, and used to analyse a real life set of financial statements.
+ Four models reporting the effects of price level changes are discussed, the advantages and disadvantages of each are reviewed, and a brief example highlighting the nature of each model is examined.

Chapter 26, "Special Topics: Disclosure, Interim Reporting, and Segment Reporting"

+ The first section is an all new discussion of standards and information overload and the principle of full disclosure.
+ A complete review of the nature and content of the notes to the financial statements highlights their role and function.

+ A more straight-forward presentation of interim and segment disclosure is included in this chapter.

ANCILLARIES AND SUPPLEMENTARY MATERIALS
◆

FOR THE PROFESSOR

INTERMEDIATE ACCOUNTING, Sixth Edition, offers numerous teaching aids to assist the instructor.

Solutions Manual, Chapters 1–14 and 15–26—Done in two volumes, this comprehensive solutions manual provides complete solutions and explanations for all end-of-chapter questions, exercises, problems, and cases. The estimated completion time for each item is given in the assignment assistance schedule at the beginning of each chapter. Answers to the concept review questions are included at the end of the manual.

Solutions Transparencies—Acetate transparencies of solutions to selected exercises and problems are free to adopters. Now increased in clarity, these transparencies are especially useful when covering problems in large classroom settings.

FOR THE STUDENT

Several support materials have been designed especially for the student.

Study Guides—The study guide provides the student with a summarized look at each chapter's issues. Included are outlines, chapters overviews, key concepts, and review questions and exercises. The study guide was prepared by Rosita Chen and Sheng-Der Pan, both of California State University-Fresno and Frank Reichardt and Henry Funk, both of Red River Community College.

Manual Practice Set—Video One, a manual practice set, can be assigned after Chapter 6 as a review of the accounting cycle.

Cases—Canadian Cases in Financial Accounting, prepared by Joan E. D. Conrod and Carol E. Dilworth, contains 90 cases that provide a variety of practical situations where professional judgment is necessary. The casebook is accompanied by an instructor's manual.

Computer Supplement—Kellogg Business Systems by Leland Mansuetti and Keith Weidkamp, both of Sierra College, is a computerized simulation that can be used after Chapter 6. It is available on 5.25″ and 3.5″ disks.

Check Figures—A list of check figures for selected end-of-chapter material is available.

ACKNOWLEDGMENTS

◆

The text in its present form would not have been possible without the contributions of a great many people. We recognize and appreciate all of their efforts.

Our thanks and gratitude are extended to the outstanding faculty reviewers who provided criticism and constructive suggestions during the preparation of this edition. They spent a great deal of time on both the previous edition, letting us know of the areas needing modification, and with the first draft of the sixth edition. Their comments and suggestions were instrumental in making this text more complete and understandable. They were also crucial to the text's accuracy and clarity. Each recommendation was considered, and many incorporated, to make this edition the most comprehensive and thorough edition to date. The reviewers were:

Joel Amernic
University of Toronto

Robert Bell
*British Columbia
Institute of Technology*

Ron Davidson
Simon Fraser University

Carol Dilworth
*Professional Educator
and Author*

John Glendenning
Centennial College of Applied Arts and Technology

George Gorelik
University of British Columbia

Peter Morgan
*George Brown College of
Applied Arts and Technology*

Frank Reichardt
Red River Community College

Nicola Young
*Mount Saint Vincent
University*

Ildiko Tiszovszky and Lisa Voll at Wilfrid Laurier University, Mark Waddington at Dalhousie University, and Carol Dilworth, Professional Educator and Author, provided valuable assistance by checking the solutions to the end-of-chapter material. The accounting professors at Wilfrid Laurier University, the University of Windsor and John R. E. Parker of Dalhousie University provided general moral support. To numerous other colleagues and users whose constructive comments and suggestions have led to the improvements reflected in this latest edition, our thanks. We sincerely appreciate comments and suggestions from all sources. We also appreciate the permissions granted by several firms and organizations including the Canadian Institute of Chartered Accountants, the Certified General Accountants Association of Canada, the Society of Management Accountants of Canada, and Loblaw Companies Limited.

We are grateful to the people at Irwin for their never-ending support: Rod T. Banister, sponsoring editor; Karen Morgan and Nancy Lanum, developmental editors; Jean Lou Hess, project editor; Clare Wulker and Pat O'Hayer, copy editors; Laurie Entringer, designer; Ann Cassady, production manager; and Judy Besser, secretary—editorial.

We welcome your ideas and comments as you use this text and look forward to hearing from you.

TO THE STUDENT

◆

Accounting has been described as the language of business. If this is so, your introductory course has given you an understanding of some fundamental building blocks: the nouns, verbs, adjectives, prepositions, and so forth. In accounting terms, these are the concepts of assets, liabilities, owners' equity, expenses, revenues, income, and others. Intermediate accounting is designed to extend these concepts to form phrases, sentences, paragraphs, and chapters. Intermediate accounting allows us to tell the financial story of an organization. As such, intermediate accounting is essential to your education in accounting and, therefore, to your mastery of the language of business.

We believe accounting at this level is an exciting subject and have structured this text in a way that captures the excitement and realism. You will be learning about actual situations faced by companies and how accounting plays a role in the decisions. These examples are extracted from the financial press, as well as from our personal experiences. We feel they are important and illustrate the challenges that await you.

We expect that many of you will be considering a career in financial accounting either with a public accounting firm, in business, or in government. Intermediate accounting is a key educational experience to have in preparing for that choice. Your instructor has selected this text from a number of alternatives because of the belief that this text will help you master the material needed in your career. Together, the instructor, the text, and your classmates provide the ingredients for a successful learning experience. Use each wisely.

We urge you to read the assigned material carefully. Sometimes two readings will be necessary. Learning is an active process. Keep paper and pencil handy. Work through each example; highlight important ideas. Ac-tually write down answers to the concept review questions located at strategic points in the text. Work all assigned problems, particularly the comprehensive ones, and, if possible, check your answers. If your instructor permits, work with a classmate and share ideas. Remember, you are not finished until you not only have a satisfactory answer, but you know why it is the best answer. Learn by doing.

It may be useful to think of an accounting issue or problem as a puzzle or mystery. Try asking what is going on and why. This will make your reading and learning more fun. In accounting, sometimes the answer depends on what is acceptable, what the rules are, or what is politically or operationally feasible.

If you find it difficult to master a chapter and to sort out what is important, try concentrating on the learning objectives given at the start of each chapter. Then, after reading the chapter, review the summary of key points and solve the review problem located at the end of each chapter. In working the review problem, do not look at the answer until you have tried to solve the problem. When checking your answer, do not stop with noting what the authors did. Rather, ask why each step in the solution was made. Then work the problems, exercises, and cases assigned by your instructor. If you still have difficulties, talk to your instructor. Your instructor wants to help you and can do so.

We think learning in general and accounting in particular can and should be both fun and exciting. We have worked many hours to achieve these goals in this text. When you finish your course, we sincerely hope you agree. We hope that you will have as much fun studying this text as we had in preparing it and the related materials, and that you find the study of accounting as interesting and challenging as we have. Our very best wishes to you in your studies and future career.

Morton Nelson
Michael Zin
Joan Conrod

CONTENTS

◆

PART II

ASSET RECOGNITION AND MEASUREMENT 269

CHAPTER 11

Capital Assets: Acquisition, Disposal, and Exchange 477

CHAPTER 12

Capital Assets: Depreciation and Impairment 537

CHAPTER 13

Intangible Assets and Natural Resources 595

CHAPTER 17

Accounting for Income Taxes 817

CHAPTER 18

Accounting for Leases 863

CHAPTER 19

Accounting for Pensions 923

INTERMEDIATE
ACCOUNTING

LIABILITIES

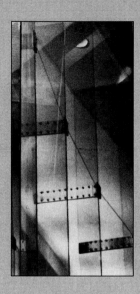

C H A P T E R
15

Short-Term Liabilities

LEARNING
OBJECTIVES
◆

After you have studied this chapter, you will be able to:

1. Define a liability and specify its characteristics.

2. Distinguish between short-term (current) and long-term liabilities.

3. Explain when it is appropriate to recognize a liability in a firm's accounts and how to measure the value attached to the liability.

4. Properly account for interest-bearing and noninterest-bearing current liabilities as well as for notes with unrealistic interest rates.

5. Explain why cash collected in advance of delivery of a good or service creates a liability for the firm.

6. Properly account for the incurrence and payment of short-term liabilities.

7. Define contingent and estimated liabilities and appropriately account for or provide disclosure.

◆

INTRODUCTION

◆

On Thursday, August 26, 1982, Manville Corporation, a supplier of asbestos insulation, and its principal U.S. and Canadian affiliates voluntarily filed for reorganization under Chapter 11 of the U.S. bankruptcy laws in New York. In an interview published in *The Wall Street Journal* as an advertisement on August 27, John A. McKinney, Manville's chief executive officer, answered questions about this action:

Question: Why did you file [for reorganization under the bankruptcy laws] now?

McKinney: We're a public company. We are required to comply with certain accounting requirements. Under these rules we're supposed to estimate the costs of current and probable litigation wherever possible and create a reserve for the liability in an amount equal to the estimate. When the asbestos cases began to proliferate, we couldn't estimate their probable number or cost, and our auditors qualified their opinion about our financial statements....We hired epidemiologists and other professionals to develop an estimate of probable future disease cases. On the basis of their work so far, we forecast that we could get at least 32,000 more lawsuits on top of the 20,000 already asserted.

Question: A total of 52,000 lawsuits at a cost of $40,000 a piece could mean a total cost of $2 billion....Could Manville afford it?

McKinney: Not on our own....The booking of a large reserve [liability] now for current and future asbestos health liabilities would wipe out most of our net worth. Without showing a good sized net worth on our balance sheet, affordable credit would have dried up, and we simply could not have operated. So, when our board of directors learned this morning of the probable need for a large reserve, it considered the options and concluded we had to file for relief under Chapter 11.[1]

In the interview, McKinney further asserts that Manville's "businesses are in good shape," it "will not go out of business," not "a single employee will lose a job, pay, or benefits," there is "no significant problem in making full, timely payment [to suppliers]," and that there will be no effect on customers. Yet, Manville filed for reorganization under Chapter 11. Moreover, not to have done so, in McKinney's words, "would have strangled the Company slowly, by deferring maintenance and postponing capital expenditures, and would also have led to cannibalizing good businesses just to keep going." And all of this would not have happened at least not on August 26, 1982, if it hadn't been for the accounting standards on contingent liabilities.

◆

WHAT IS A LIABILITY?

◆

On the surface, the answer may seem rather simple. A liability is something a company owes and must pay to someone else. Generally, this description will do quite well, but it is not sufficient for certain difficult situations. A good example is provided by the interview with Manville's McKinney. Should a liability be recorded for potential health claims, arising from potential lawsuits that have not even been submitted to the firm or to the courts for consideration?

Manville's case is not unique. A. H. Robins Company experienced a similar situation regarding the use of the company's Dalkon Shield. Problems with this intrauterine

---

[1] The impact on net worth alluded to by McKinney is caused by the following entry needed to establish the expected liability under future litigation of the alleged injuries caused by asbestoses (the reserve mentioned in the quote):

Shareholders' equity (or retained earnings) XXX
    Liability under litigation   XXX

Debiting shareholders' equity or, equivalently, retained earnings reduces the company's net worth.

device surfaced by the mid-1970s; yet a liability was not recorded until 1984, and this liability was only about 25% of the final amount required.

For other situations where accountants wrestle with whether a liability exists and, if so, in what amount, consider these issues:

- Coupons that have not been presented for redemption.
- Frequent flier miles earned by airline travelers.
- Potential requirements to clean up toxic dumps.
- Company promises to pay post-retirement health benefits.
- Preferred stock with cumulative dividends, nonparticipating as to voting, and callable by either issuer or holder on demand.

The AcSB has defined a **liability** as the "obligation of an entity arising from past transactions or events, the settlement of which may result in the transfer or use of assets, provision of services or other yielding of economic benefits in the future."[2] Thus a liability possesses three essential characteristics:

- An obligation exists that can be satisfied only by the transfer of an asset or a service to another entity.
- The obligation must be unavoidable.
- The event that gave rise to the obligation has occurred.

When a liability is incurred in conformity with the definition, it should be immediately recognized and recorded. The *Handbook* definition of a liability is important because it is specific about the essential distinctions defining a debt. The amount of a liability conceptually should be measured as the present value of all future cash payments (or the cash equivalent of non-cash assets and services), discounted at an interest rate consistent with the risks involved. A liability involves a principal amount that is subject to interest, whether specified or not, and interest on the principal amount, which is incurred as time passes.

Accounting recognition of a liability should take place on the date the liability is incurred. The transaction that creates a liability usually identifies the date when the obligation comes into existence. However, the recognition date of a liability is not always clear cut, such as in the case of an injury to an employee, or outsider, when the final determination of the existence of a liability depends on the legal decision of a court of law.[3]

Furthermore, current liabilities can influence operations in a way that long-term liabilities generally do not because current liabilities represent a claim on current resources that are thereby unavailable for day-to-day operations. These claims differ from long-term liabilities, such as bonds, that mature years into the future. The distinction is critical to the classification of liabilities as either current or long-term.

Measurement of the amount of a liability sometimes is difficult. The transaction that creates a liability usually provides the basis for measuring its amount. Measuring the amount of a liability is directly related to its cause. The cause, in the following examples, is reflected by a debit to:

Type of Account Debited	Example
An asset.	Inventory purchased on account.
Another liability.	A note signed for trade payables that are presently indicated on the balance sheet as current accounts payable.
Retained earnings.	Cash dividends declared.

[2] *CICA Handbook,* paragraph 1000.28, "Financial Statement Concepts."

[3] From an auditing standpoint, identification of existing liabilities is a critical problem because many liabilities are easy to hide or overlook. This issue—determining the existence of liability—is precisely the one faced by Manville in deciding whether to record the liability for asbestos-related health claims, discussed in the introduction to this chapter.

Type of Account Debited	Example
An expense.	Repair services rendered, creating a liability to be paid.
A loss.	A litigation award against the company.
Cash collected in advance of service.	Cash collected for magazine subscriptions to be delivered over the coming year.

For example, when an asset is acquired on credit, the asset and related liability are recognized at cost under the cost principle. The cost of the asset received measures the amount of the liability. Sometimes, the relationship between the cost of the asset and the valuation of the liability is not clear-cut. Assume a company acquired a machine and promised to pay the quoted price (a single amount) of $10,000 at the end of one year from date of purchase, with no separate interest payments specified. The amount of the liability and the cost of the machine are not $10,000. The liability, and the cost of the asset, should be measured as the present value of the future cash payment. If the market interest rate for this level of risk is 15%, the present value is

$$\$10,000(PV1, 15\%, 1) = \$10,000(.86957) = \$8,696 \text{ (rounded)}$$

The appropriate journal entries are as follows:

Purchase date:

```
Machine . . . . . . . . . . . . . . . . . . . . . . . . . . . . .   8,696
    Note payable, 15% (face, $10,000). . . . . . . . . . . . .          8,696
```

Payment date:

```
Note payable ($10,000 − $1,304). . . . . . . . . . . . . . . .   8,696
Interest expense ($8,696)(.15). . . . . . . . . . . . . . . .    1,304
    Cash. . . . . . . . . . . . . . . . . . . . . . . . . . . . .        10,000
```

Implicit interest on short-term liabilities (particularly those involving accrued liabilities and accounts payable of one to three months) need not be recognized separately in accounting. The requirements to account separately for interest does not apply to receivables and payables arising from transactions with customers or suppliers in the normal course of business which are due in customary trade terms not exceeding approximately one year. This is an application of the materiality and cost-benefit constraints discussed in Chapter 2.

Companies usually measure, record, and report short-term liabilities at their maturity amount because the cost of the asset received and the maturity amount of the liability coincide, and the stated interest rate on the liability is the same as the effective interest rate. When the stated and effective rates are the same, the maturity amount and the present value of the liability are the same.

Aside from the materiality and cost-benefit constraints, short-term liabilities should be recorded and reported at their present value when they are acquired.

Although exchange transactions usually establish the amount and maturity date of a liability, in some situations a definite liability is known to exist, or it is likely that one exists, but the exact amount or the maturity date are not known precisely. One section of this chapter devoted to this problem discusses the recording and reporting of what are called *estimated liabilities* and *loss contingencies*.

The classification of liabilities as current or long-term can have serious ramifications for the accounting entity. In some cases, legal or contractual arrangements may stipulate certain levels of working capital or quick asset ratios. Users of financial statements could be affected by levels of current or long-term liabilities and improper classification could affect their decisions. Therefore, proper classification of liabilities is yet another instance where professional judgment must be exercised.

CONCEPT REVIEW

1. What are the three essential characteristics of a liability?
2. What is the typical time when a liability should be recognized?
3. Most accountants would agree that the extent of a liability incurred is the present value of the future payment. Why, then, is the gross amount to be paid at the future date typically recorded for short-term liabilities?

WHAT IS A CURRENT LIABILITY?

Current (short-term) liabilities are defined as "amounts payable within one year from the date of the balance sheet or within the normal operating cycle, where this is longer than a year."[4] Current assets are those assets expected to be converted to cash or used in normal operations during the operating cycle of the business, or one year from the balance date, whichever is longer.[5] Because of the association between current assets and current liabilities, the time dimension that applies to current assets also generally applies to current liabilities. Liabilities that do not conform to this definition are called *long-term,* or noncurrent, liabilities. Long-term liabilities are discussed in Chapter 16.

The usual types of current liabilities are

- Accounts payable.
- Short-term notes payable.
- Cash and property dividends payable.
- Accrued liabilities related to expenses.
- Advances and returnable deposits.
- Unearned revenues (cash collected in advance of rendering service such as rent paid in advance).
- Taxes (income, sales, property, and payroll).
- Compensated-absence liabilities.
- Conditional payments.
- Current maturities of long-term debt.
- Obligations callable on demand by the creditor.

Special accounting problems related to these current liabilities are discussed in the following sections.

Accounts Payable

Accounts payable—more descriptively trade accounts payable— is a designation reserved for recurring trade obligations. These obligations arise from the firm's ongoing operations including the acquisition of merchandise, materials, supplies, and services used in the production and sale of goods or services.[6] Other current payables that do not conform to the definition of trade accounts (such as income taxes and the current portion of long-term debt) should be reported separately from accounts payable.

---

[4] *CICA Handbook,* paragraph 1510.03, "Current Assets and Current Liabilities."

[5] The normal operating cycle of a business is the average period of time between the expenditure of cash for goods and services and the time that those goods and services are converted back to cash. This cash-to-cash cycle is illustrated by the following sequence: cash expenditure to buy inventory, inventory fabricated to finished product, product sold on account, account collected in cash.

[6] In determining the amount of the liability, the accountant must adjust for purchase discounts, allowances, and returns. (See Chapter 9 for a discussion of these topics.)

Short-Term Notes Payable

A short-term note might be a trade note payable that arises from the same source as an account payable, or a nontrade note payable that arises from some other source, or the current maturity of a long-term liability, which arises when the next debt payment will be made out of current assets. A short-term note is either secured by a mortgage or any other type of lien that specifies particular assets pledged as security or unsecured, if the creditor's repayment is based on the general creditworthiness of the debtor. Disclosure for a secured note payable should include an examination of primary terms of the debt agreement, including the identity of any pledged assets.

A note payable may be designated as either interest-bearing or noninterest-bearing. An interest-bearing note explicitly contains a rate of interest. This rate is called the *stated rate*. Notes designated as noninterest-bearing do not contain explicit interest but, instead, implicitly reflect a rate of interest called the *effective rate* or *yield*. In other words, regardless of designation, all commercial debt instruments implicitly or explicitly require the debtor to pay interest. This is because the cost of using money over time cannot be avoided. The amount of periodic interest on a debt is

Principal amount × Interest rate × Time = Interest amount

The **stated rate of interest** is the interest rate specified on a debt instrument. The stated rate determines the amount of cash interest that will be paid on the principal amount of the debt. In contrast, the **effective rate of interest (yield)** on a debt is the market interest rate based on the actual cash, or cash-equivalent, amount that was borrowed. The effective rate is used to discount the future cash payments on a debt to the cash equivalent borrowed. The cash or cash equivalent amount received by the debtor is the amount that is subject to the effective interest rate. The maturity amount of a debt is the amount to be paid on the maturity date, excluding any separate interest payments due on that date. These two types of notes are discussed in more detail next.

Interest-Bearing Notes   Interest-bearing notes specify the principal amount of the note as the face amount. In addition, the note specifies a stated rate of interest. For an interest-bearing note, the debtor receives cash, other assets, or services equal to the face amount and pays back that amount plus interest at the stated rate on one or more interest dates. Under these conditions, the stated and effective interest rates are the same. This is the usual case.

To illustrate an interest-bearing note, assume that on October 1, 1991, Banff Company borrowed $10,000 cash on a one-year note with 12% interest payable at the maturity date. Banff Company received cash equal to the face amount of the note, $10,000.[7] The accounting year ends December 31, and the maturity date of the note is September 30, 1992. This transaction requires the following accounting and reporting:

Entries during 1991:

October 1, 1991—To record the interest-bearing note at its present value:

Cash 10,000
    Note payable, short-term   10,000

December 31, 1991—Adjusting entry for accrued interest:

Interest expense ($10,000) (12%) (³⁄₁₂)   300
    Interest payable.   300

---

[7] It may be useful to demonstrate that under the conditions specified the present value of this interest-bearing note will be equal to the cash borrowed as well as the principal, face, and maturity amounts of the debt:

Face: $10,000 (*PV* 1, 12%, 1) = $10,000(.89286) = $ 8,929
Interest: $1,200 (*PVA*1, 12%, 1) = $1,200(.89286) =   1,071
Total present value $10,000

Reporting at December 31, 1991—Interest-bearing note payable:

```
Income statement:
    Interest expense . . . . . . . . . . . . . . . . . .$   300
Balance sheet:
    Current liabilities:
        Note payable, short-term . . . . . . . . . . .   10,000
        Interest payable . . . . . . . . . . . . . .      300
```

Entry at maturity date:

September 30, 1992—payment of face amount plus interest at maturity:[8]

```
Interest payable . . . . . . . . . . . . . . . . . . . . . . .     300
Interest expense ($10,000) (.12) (⁹⁄₁₂) . . . . . . . . . . . . .   900
Note payable, short-term . . . . . . . . . . . . . . . . . .      10,000
    Cash . . . . . . . . . . . . . . . . . . . . . . . . . . .          11,200
```

Noninterest-Bearing Notes *Noninterest bearing* is not a good descriptive designation for this type of note because such notes do, in fact, bear interest. The face amount of this kind of note includes both the amount borrowed and interest as a single amount to be paid back at the maturity date. The borrower does not receive cash or other resources equal to the face amount of the note; rather, the borrower receives the difference between the face amount and the interest on the note. The amount on the note designated as the cash to be received is the discounted value of the face amount using the effective interest rate. The remainder, the difference between the discounted cash value and the face amount of the note, is the interest. The effective interest rate is determined by reference to market rates for instruments of similar risk. The effective rate is not specified on the note but for a short-term noninterest-bearing note with a specified term, the rate can be determined.[9]

Consider an example. Brite Lite Company signed an $11,200, one-year, noninterest-bearing note and received $10,000 cash. The note was discounted at 10.714% interest ($1,200 ÷ $11,200). However, Brite Lite Company received only $10,000 cash; therefore, the effective rate of interest was 12% ($1,200 ÷ $10,000). The present value of this note is $10,000; that is:

$$\$11,200(PV\,1, 12\%, 1) = \$11,200(.89286) = \$10,000$$

This debt should be recorded at its present value which can be done by recording the note on a net basis, or by recording it on a gross basis at its face value and offsetting this account with a discount account. Both approaches are illustrated next.

---

[8] The entry given in the text assumes no reversing entry on January 1, 1992. If a reversing entry were made on January 1, 1992, the entry would be:

```
Interest payable . . . . . . . . . . . . . . . . . . . . . . . . . . . . . 300
    Interest expense . . . . . . . . . . . . . . . . . . . . . . . . . . . . .      300
```

Then on September 30, 1992, the required entry is:

```
Interest expense . . . . . . . . . . . . . . . . . . . . . . . . . . . 1,200
Note payable, short-term . . . . . . . . . . . . . . . . . . . . . . .10,000
    Cash . . . . . . . . . . . . . . . . . . . . . . . . . . . . . . .      11,200
```

Reversing entries simplify the process of recognizing interest expense in the next period particularly in computerized accounting systems. The determination of interest on noninterest-bearing notes is also known as imputing interest.

[9] A noninterest-bearing note is also called a *discounted note* because the cash received is less than the face amount of the note.

Accounting entries and reporting (net basis):

Entries during 1991:

October 1, 1991—To record the noninterest-bearing note payable at its net present value (i.e., net) amount:

Cash 10,000
      Note payable, short-term (noninterest-bearing)*   10,000

* The note was recorded at its present value (i.e., principal amount) rather than at its face amount of $11,200. The interest entries will increase the $10,000 initially recorded to $11,200, which is the payment required at maturity.

December 31, 1991—Adjusting entry to record accrued interest:

Interest expense ($10,000) (.12) ($\frac{3}{12}$)   300
      Note payable, short-term*   300

* The carrying value of the note after this entry is $10,300 ($10,000 + $300). An alternative would be to credit interest payable.

Reporting at December 31, 1991:

Income statement:
  Interest expense . . . . $ 300
Balance sheet:
  Current liabilities:
    Note payable, short-term ($10,000 + $300) $10,300

Entries at maturity date:

September 30, 1992—To record (*a*) accrued interest to date and (*b*) payment of the face amount of the note at maturity:

Interest expense ($10,000) (.12) ($\frac{9}{12}$)   900
      Note payable, short-term   900

Note payable ($10,000 + $300 + $900) 11,200
      Cash   11,200

Accounting entries recorded (gross basis)

Entries during 1991:

October 1, 1991—To record a noninterest-bearing note payable at its gross (face) amount:[10]

Cash 10,000
Discount on note payable, short-term   1,200
      Note payable, short-term   11,200

December 31, 1991—Adjusting entry for accrued interest:

Interest expense ($1,200) ($\frac{3}{12}$)   300
      Discount on note payable, short-term   300

Reporting at December 31, 1991—Noninterest-bearing note payable:

Income statement:
  Interest expense . . . . $ 300
Balance sheet:
  Current liabilities:
    Note payable $11,200
    Less: Unamortized discount   900   10,300

---

[10] The amount of interest expense and the liability balances are the same, regardless of whether the note is recorded at net or gross.

Entries at maturity date:

September 30, 1991—Payment of the face amount of the note:

```
Interest expense ($1,200) (9/12) . . . . . . . . . . . . . . . . .      900
Note payable, short term  . . . . . . . . . . . . . . . . . . . . 11,200
     Discount on note payable, short-term . . . . . . . . . . .             900
     Cash . . . . . . . . . . . . . . . . . . . . . . . . . . . .        11,200
```

Accounting for Short-Term Notes Payable that Have an Unrealistic Interest Rate

Sometimes a non-cash asset is acquired and a note payable is given that has a stated rate of interest less than the current market rate (the effective rate) of interest for the level of risk involved. When this happens the cost of the asset is the present value of the future cash payments discounted at the current market rate of interest rather than at the stated interest rate. Assume, for example, that a machine is purchased on January 1, 1991, with a one-year, $1,000, 6% interest-bearing note. The current market rate of interest for obligations with this level of risk is 12%.

1. Cost of the machine:

$$(\$1,000 + \$60)\,(PV\,1, 12\%, 1) = (\$1,060)\,(.89286) = \$946.43.$$

2. Entries (net method):

   January 1, 1991—Acquisition date:

```
Machine . . . . . . . . . . . . . . . . . . . . . . . . . . 946.43
     Note payable . . . . . . . . . . . . . . . . . . . . . . .        946.43
```

   December 31, 1991—Payment date:

```
Note payable . . . . . . . . . . . . . . . . . . . . . . . 946.43
Interest expense ($946.43) (.12) . . . . . . . . . . . . . . 113.57
     Cash ($1,000 + $60) . . . . . . . . . . . . . . . . . .        1,060.00
```

This example uses the current market interest rate for similar notes with the same risks for the effective rate. This rate may be difficult to estimate reliably. Alternatively if the competitive cash price of the non-cash asset received is known, it should be used to establish the effective rate of interest.

Cash and Property Dividends Payable

After declaration by the board of directors, cash or property dividends payable should be reported as a current liability if they are to be paid within the coming year or operating cycle, whichever is longer. Cash and property dividends payable are reported as a liability between the date of declaration and payment on the legal basis that declaration gives rise to an enforceable contract.[11]

Liabilities are not recognized for undeclared dividends in arrears on preferred stock or for any other dividends not yet formally declared by the board of directors. Dividends in arrears on cumulative preferred stock should be disclosed in notes to the financial statements. Scrip dividends payable are reported as a current liability unless there is no intention to make payment in the near future.[12]

---

[11] Technically, dividends are not current liabilities because they are distributions to owners. Stock dividends payable also are not current liabilities but rather merely a division of the assets into more ownership shares.

[12] A dividend payable in scrip is a promise by the corporation to pay the dividend at a later date. Scrip dividends are declared when the corporation wishes to keep its record of continuous dividend payments uninterrupted, has the necessary retained earnings to legally declare the dividend, but is currently short of cash.

Accrued Liabilities

Accrued liabilities include wages earned by employees and interest earned by creditors but not as yet paid. Accrued liabilities are recorded in the accounts by making adjusting entries at the end of the accounting period. For example, any wages that have not yet been recorded or paid at the end of the accounting period must be recorded by debiting wage expense and crediting wages payable. Recognition of accrued liabilities is consistent with the definition of a liability and the matching principle.

Advances and Returnable Deposits

A special liability arises when a company receives cash deposits from customers and employees. Deposits may be received from customers as guarantees for payment of obligations that may be incurred in the future or to guarantee performance of a contract or service. For example, when an order is taken, a company may require an advance payment to cover losses that would be incurred if the order is canceled. Such advances create liabilities for the company receiving the cash until the underlying transaction is completed. Advances are recorded by debiting cash and crediting an account such as liability, customer deposits.

Deposits frequently are received from customers as guarantees in case of noncollection or for possible damage to property left with the customer. For example, deposits required from customers by gas, water, light, and other public utilities are liabilities of such companies to their customers. Also, employees may make returnable deposits to ensure the return of keys and other company property, for locker privileges, and for club memberships. Deposits should be reported as current or long-term liabilities depending on the time involved between the date of deposit and expected termination of the relationship. If the advances or deposits are interest-bearing, an adjusting entry is required to accrue interest expense and to increase the related liability.[13]

Unearned Revenues (Revenues Collected in Advance)

Cash collected in advance of the delivery of the good or service creates a liability. The cash does not yet qualify for recognition as revenue in conformity with the revenue principle. Examples of revenues collected in advance include gift certificates, college tuition, rent, ticket sales, and magazine subscriptions. Such transactions are recorded as debits to cash and credits to appropriately designated current liability accounts. Often titled "unearned revenues" this account may be given a modifying adjective, for example, unearned subscription revenues in the case of subscriptions. Other titles for this account include "prepaid subscription revenue" and "subscription revenue collected in advance." Although the phrase *deferred revenues* is also occasionally encountered in this type of account title, it is not an adequate description of the account.

Subsequently, when the product or service is delivered and the revenue is earned, the liability account is decreased and the appropriate revenue account is credited. This latter entry often is one of the year-end adjusting entries (see Chapter 3 on adjusting entries).

To illustrate, on November 1, 1991, Zorex Company collected rent of $6,000 for the next six months. The accounting period ends December 31. The entries are

November 1, 1991—Rent collected in advance:

```
Cash . . . . . . . . . . . . . . . . . . . . . . . . . . . . . . . . . . 6,000
    Rent revenue collected in advance
        (or unearned rent revenue) . . . . . . . . . . . . . . . .        6,000
```

---

[13] Employees also have portions of their wages withheld for saving bond purchase programs, share purchase plans, medical insurance premiums, and retirement programs. These withholdings constitute liabilities until the amounts are either delivered to a trustee or the service (delivery of the savings bond, for example) is completed.

December 31, 1991—Adjusting entry for the portion earned:

```
Rent revenue collected in advance
   (or unearned rent revenue) . . . . . . . . . . . . . . . . . . . . .  2,000
      Rent revenue ($6,000) (⅔). . . . . . . . . . . . . . . . . .           2,000
```

The remaining prepaid rent revenue of $4,000 is reported as a current liability because Zorex has an obligation to render future occupancy services during the following four months.

Another example of an obligation to render future service is a television cable subscription for which the cash has been collected prior to delivery of service. This liability is illustrated in the 1989 financial statements of Rogers Communications Inc. The company includes an account called *prepayments for services* in its liabilities.

Taxes

Provincial and federal laws require businesses to collect certain taxes from customers and employees for remittance to designated governmental agencies. These taxes include sales taxes, income taxes withheld from employee paycheques, property taxes, and payroll taxes. Similar collections also are made on behalf of unions, insurance companies, and employee-sponsored activities. When collections are made for third parties, cash and current liabilities both increase. The collections represent liabilities that are settled when the funds are remitted to the designated parties. Three typical situations are illustrated. They involve:

◆ Sales taxes.
◆ Federal income taxes withheld.
◆ Payroll taxes.

Sales Taxes   In most provinces retail businesses are required to collect a sales tax at the time of sale and to remit the tax to the taxing authority. Typical entries, assuming a 9% sales tax and $500,000 of sales, are

1. At date the tax is assessed (point of sale):

```
Cash and accounts receivable . . . . . . . . . . . . . . . . . 545,000
   Sales revenue . . . . . . . . . . . . . . . . . . . . . . . . . . .        500,000
   Sales tax payable ($500,000) (.09) . . . . . . . . . . . . .         45,000
```

2. At date of remittance to taxing authority:

```
Sales tax payable . . . . . . . . . . . . . . . . . . . . . .  45,000
   Cash . . . . . . . . . . . . . . . . . . . . . . . . . . . . .          45,000
```

The preceding entries assume the sales tax is separately recognized at the point of sale. Some companies simply include the sales tax in sales revenue. In this case, an adjusting entry is required at the end of the accounting period debiting sales revenue and crediting sales tax payable (or cash).

Goods and Services Tax   The Goods and Services Tax (GST) is another tax collected for a third party—in this case, the federal government. The Emerging Issues Committee of the CICA has indicated that revenues should be recorded net of the GST collected. Purchases of goods or services should be recorded net of any GST recoverable and the net amount of the GST payable or receivable should be carried as a liability or asset, as appropriate.

Any GST that is not recoverable should be accounted for as a component of the cost of the goods or services to which it relates. If it is paid and is not recoverable in relation to a capital asset, GST is included in the asset's capital cost. If it relates to current costs, it will be included in the determination of net income for the period.

Payroll Deductions

Income Taxes Withheld   Federal and most provincial laws require employers to withhold from the pay of each employee an estimate of the income taxes payable on the income of the employee earned in the period.[14] The estimates are provided in tax tables available from Revenue Canada. Income taxes withheld must be remitted within a specified time period to the Receiver General. The amounts withheld are current liabilities of the employer until remitted.

Canada Pension Plan (CPP)   The Canada Pension Plan Act provides a number of income and death benefits to qualified participants in the CPP and to their families.[15] Employers are obligated to match employees' deductions and remit the sum of the two to the Receiver General of Canada. The amount to be deducted is specified in the act and is subject to an annual maximum.

Unemployment Insurance (UI)   Under the federally legislated Unemployment Insurance Act, any employee engaged in what the act defines as insurable employment must make a contribution each pay period to the Unemployment Insurance Commission. The employer must remit 1.4 times this deduction.

Hospital Insurance   Several provinces have revised their hospitalization plans and now tax the employers' payrolls. Instead of deducting hospitalization premiums from employees, employers are assessed a percentage of the total monthly payroll. These amounts, which are equivalent to a payroll tax, are remitted monthly to the respective provincial treasurers.

Workers' Compensation   Under provincial legislation, hospital and medical expenses and partial salaries are paid for employees injured while working. The benefits provided by the Workers' Compensation Board (WCB) are financed by premiums paid by employers. The employers' obligation is determined by the size of their payrolls subject to WCB assessment and the past history of the industry and entity. Payments to the WCB are semiannual on January 31 and July 1, based on estimated assessable wages. As a consequence, frequently an accrued liability exists on the entity's books of account for the difference between the amounts based on the estimated and actual payrolls.

Other Payroll Deductions   Other common payroll deductions include union dues, medical insurance premiums, life or disability insurance premiums, charitable donations, and employee-sponsored activities. The amounts deducted are simply carried as current liabilities until they are remitted to the appropriate agencies.

Illustration of Payroll Deductions   Thor Company paid January 1991 salaries of $100,000. Other payroll deductions are as follows:

Gross wages		$100,000
Income taxes	$20,000	
Canada Pension Plan	2,250	
Unemployment insurance	2,100	
Union dues	1,400	
Donations	1,600	27,350
Net pay		$ 72,650

---

[14] The federal government has agreed with all provinces, except Quebec, to serve as collector of personal income taxes levied in the province. The federal government then redistributes funds collected to the provinces. Employers in the Province of Quebec must make separate payroll deductions for federal and provincial income taxes levied on employees' income.

[15] The Canada Pension Plan exists in all provinces except Quebec. The Quebec provincial government has enacted the Quebec Pension Plan Act, the provisions of which are similar to those of the CPP.

To record salaries and employee deductions:

Salary expense	100,000	
Employee income taxes payable		20,000
CPP payable		2,250
UI payable		2,100
Union dues payable		1,400
Employee donations payable		1,600
Cash		72,650

To record payroll expenses payable by the employer:

Salary expense	7,190	
CPP payable		2,250
UI payable ($2,100 × 1.4)		2,940
Hospitalization tax payable—rate assumed ($100,000 × 2.0%)		2,000

To record remittance of payroll deductions (composite entry):

Employee income taxes payable	20,000	
CPP payable	4,500	
UI payable	5,040	
Union dues payable	1,400	
Employee donations payable	1,600	
Hospitalization tax payable	2,000	
Cash		34,540

Property Taxes Companies pay property taxes directly to the taxing authority. These taxes are based on the assessed value of real property and are levied at the local governing level to support school, city, county, and other designated activities. The tax assessed must be paid; if not, it constitutes a lien on the property being taxed.

Property taxes for the current year usually are assessed near the end of the year and billed early in the next year. In this situation, the accounting period during which these taxes should be recognized precedes the period in which the taxes are paid. Correct matching of the property tax expense with the period benefited means that the expense must be accrued before the actual amount of the tax is known. Therefore, estimates often must be used. In local communities, the typical sequence of assessing property taxes is as follows: by midyear, tentative taxable valuations are developed along with estimated tax rates; by year-end, each property owner receives the actual taxable valuation, tax rate, and the resulting property tax; and during the early part of the following year, payment is made to the taxing authority. Therefore, 1991 property taxes typically would be assessed late in 1991 and paid in 1992. Most businesses accrue property tax expense based on best estimates and handle revisions as changes in estimates. At year-end, the estimated amounts that have been recorded in the related expense and liability accounts are adjusted to agree with the actual amount assessed, which must be used for annual accounting and reporting purposes.

To illustrate accounting for property taxes, consider a situation that involves quarterly recognition of property taxes during 1991. The following sequence of events and their accounting treatment are appropriate:

1. January 1991—Estimate of 1991 property tax based on an expected 20% increase over the 1990 actual tax ($2,061):

    ($2,061 × 1.20) ÷ 4 = $618; use $600 per quarter as the estimate.

    March 31, 1991—Accrue tax for first quarter:

Property tax expense	600	
Property tax payable		600

    Entry made in March and June; total, $1,200.

2. July 1991—Received the following from taxing authority:

$$\begin{array}{c}\text{Tentative 1991} \\ \text{taxable valuation,} \\ \$190,076\end{array} \times \begin{array}{c}\text{Estimated 1991} \\ \text{tax rate per} \\ \$100 \text{ valuation,} \\ \$1.4470\end{array} = \begin{array}{c}\text{Estimated 1991} \\ \text{property tax,} \\ \$2,750:\end{array}$$

$$\begin{array}{c}\text{September 30, 1991} \\ \text{(change in estimate)}\end{array} = (\$2,750 - \$1,200) \div \begin{array}{c}\text{2 quarters} \\ \text{remaining}\end{array} = \begin{array}{c}\$775; \text{ use } \$780 \\ \text{per quarter} \\ \text{as the estimate}.\end{array}$$

Property tax expense . . . . 780 ⎫ Entry made in
Property tax payable . . . .   780 ⎭ September.

3. December 29, 1991—Received actual 1991 tax assessment:

$$\begin{array}{c}\text{1991 taxable valuation,} \\ \$197,076\end{array} \times \begin{array}{c}\text{1991 tax rate per} \\ \$100 \text{ valuation } (\$1.45)\end{array} = \$2,858$$

December 31, 1988:

Property tax expense ($2,858 − $1,200 − $780) 878
Property tax payable   878

4. 1991 financial statements:

Income statement:
   Property tax expense $2,858
Balance sheet:
   Current liabilities:
      Property tax payable 2,858

5. January 1992—Payment of 1991 property tax:

Property tax payable 2,858
Cash   2,858

Regardless of the respective tax and accounting fiscal periods, this accounting approach can be adapted to conform to GAAP.[16]

Conditional Payments

Some liabilities are established on the basis of a firm's periodic income. Two primary examples are certain bonuses or profit-sharing plan payments to employees and income taxes based in part on taxable income. These items can be established at year's end, but the liability often must be estimated quarterly. Until paid, they usually represent current liabilities of the organization.[17]

Corporate Income Taxes Payable   Federal and provincial income taxes are based on federal and provincial tax legislation. Differences are inevitable between taxable income computed for financial reporting purposes and taxable income used to determine provincial and federal tax liabilities. Indeed, these differences have increased in recent years. Because the interpretation of the Income Tax Act often depends on the courts and since quarterly reports require a provision for the tax liability, estimates are required. The estimated liability should be reported as a current liability based on the firm's best current estimates. Periodic payments, which change through the year as the estimated tax changes, are required.

---

[16] In a situation where property taxes are levied in advance of the taxing jurisdiction's fiscal year, the appropriate accounting would use the deferral method. Cash (or a liability) is credited, and deferred (or prepaid) property tax expense is debited. The prepayment is written off to expense over the period covered by the assessment.

[17] Royalty agreements are another example of a conditional payment based on a percentage of income leading to a current liability.

Bonuses   Many companies pay cash bonuses to selected employees based on earnings. Accountants should insist that any agreement be specific. For example, if earnings are involved, it should be clear whether the earnings are before or after taxes. Further, when earnings are involved, the adjusting entry to recognize the bonus cannot be established until all other adjusting entries have been made.

Bonus payments to employees should be considered additional wages in the year earned. As such, bonuses increase the period's wage expense and establish a concurrent liability. The liability is usually payable within a short time and, hence, is properly considered a current liability.

Computation of the bonus and the accompanying entries is complex because the bonus is an expense and hence deductible from income. In addition, the bonus affects the computation of the company's tax expense and, thereby, also income. Consider this example:

Suppose Aldar Limited has income of $500,000 in 1991 before establishing the year's bonus. Suppose, further, that the bonus agreement specifies the employees are to be paid 10% of income as this year's bonus. Now if the bonus were not a taxable expense, the bonus amount would be ($500,000)(.10), or $50,000. However, the bonus is an expense and must be deducted in determining the income on which the bonus is to be paid. To properly establish the bonus, assume for the moment there is no tax effect. Then the bonus is 10% of income with income first reduced by the bonus.

In symbols:

$$\text{Bonus} = .10(\$500{,}000 - \text{Bonus})$$

and solving

$$\text{Bonus} = \$50{,}000 - .1(\text{Bonus})$$

$$1.1(\text{Bonus}) = \$50{,}000$$

$$\text{Bonus} = \$45{,}455\,.$$

Unfortunately, this is only a partial solution because the effect of the bonus on the company's tax expense has, so far, been ignored. Fortunately, a similar argument resolves the problem. The argument proceeds as follows, assuming a 40% tax rate. If the bonus were known, the tax expense would be:

$$\text{Tax} = .40(\$500{,}000 - \text{Bonus})$$

And if the tax were known, the bonus would be:

$$\text{Bonus} = .10(\$500{,}000 - \text{Bonus} - \text{Tax})\,.$$

These two equations, involving two unknowns, can be solved simultaneously to yield both the bonus and the tax expense. Simplifying these two equations:

$$\text{Tax} = \$200{,}000 - .4\text{Bonus}$$

$$\text{Bonus} = \$50{,}000 - .1\text{Bonus} - .1\text{Tax}$$

Now substituting this expression for tax into the simplified expression for the bonus gives:

$$\text{Bonus} = \$50{,}000 - .1\text{Bonus} - .1[\$200{,}000 - .4(\text{Bonus})]$$

or:

$$\text{Bonus} = \$50{,}000 - .1\text{Bonus} - \$20{,}000 + .04(\text{Bonus})$$

and:

$$1.06\text{Bonus} = \$30{,}000$$

giving:

$$\text{Bonus} = \$28{,}302$$

Using this figure for the bonus:

$$\text{Tax} = \$200,000 - .4(\$28,846)$$

$$\text{Tax} = \$188,462.$$

The calculation of the bonus and the tax requires that all other adjusting entries be completed first. Once this has been done, the bonus can be calculated as illustrated and entered into the accounts as follows:

Employee bonus expense	28,846	
Bonus payable		28,846

Compensated-Absence Liabilities

The Canada Labour Code requires that employees normally be granted two weeks' vacation or the equivalent per year. On a 52-week year, each employee is thus entitled to a vacation equivalent to 4% of a 50-week work period. In addition, the Labour Code provides for several statutory holidays such as Canada Day and New Year's Day. Union contracts or company policies often provide vacation and holiday entitlements more generous than those in the statutes. GAAP require that we account for these compensated absences.

When salaries and wages are paid during these absences from work, the expense is recognized in the current year. However, when the employees can retain and carry over unused time for these events to future years, the question arises as to when the expense for this unused time should be recognized: in the prior year in which it was earned or the later year(s) in which it is taken? To date, the AcSB has not issued any guidance on compensated-absence liabilities. However, the FASB has issued *Statement 43*, "Accounting for Compensated Absences." *SFAS No. 43* requires that any expense due to compensated absences must be recognized (accrued) in the year in which it is earned, provided:

- The absence from work relates to services already rendered.
- The carryover accumulates (or vests).
- The payment is probable (the absence will occur).
- The amount (i.e., cost) can be reliably estimated.[18]

Implementing *SFAS No. 43* involves an adjusting entry at the end of each fiscal year to accrue all of the compensation cost for the vacation and holiday time that is to be carried over. This is done by recognizing an expense and a current liability. When the vacation or holiday time is taken, the liability account is debited at the time the employee is paid. These entries recognize the cost of compensated absences as an expense in the period earned rather than when taken.

For example, consider a situation that involves the carryover of vacation time. Conway Company has 500 employees; each employee is granted three weeks' vacation time each year with full pay. Vacation time, up to a maximum accumulation of four weeks, may be carried over to subsequent years prior to termination of employment. At the end of 1991, the end of the annual accounting period, personnel records revealed the following information concerning carryover vacation times and amounts:

Number of Employees	Weeks per Employee	Carryover from 1991*	
		Total Weeks	Total Salaries
10	2	20	$30,000
3	1	3	6,000

* There are no carryovers from years prior to 1991.

---

[18] In the case of accumulated rights to receive nonvesting (employees are not entitled to non-vesting benefits if employment ceases) sick pay benefits, accrual is not required but is permitted. A strong case can be made that the illness (when it occurs) is the major event rather than when the employee worked.

Disregarding payroll taxes, the indicated entries are as follows:

December 31, 1991—Adjusting entry to accrue vacation salaries not yet taken or paid:

```
Salary expense . . . . . . . . . . . . . . . . . . . . . . . . .  36,000
    Liability for compensated absences . . . . . . . . . . .            36,000
```

During 1992—Vacation time carryover is taken and the salaries paid (one person did not take two weeks of carryover, $3,000):

```
Liability for compensated absences . . . . . . . . . . . . .  33,000
    Cash ($36,000 − $3,000) . . . . . . . . . . . . . . . .            33,000
The balance remaining in the liability account is $3,000.
```

This illustration assumed that there was no change in the rate of pay from 1991 to 1992 (when the carryover was used) for those employees who had the carryover. If there were rate changes, the pay difference would be debited (if an increase) or credited (if a decrease) to wage expense during 1992. The change is considered a change in estimate.[19] For example, if the 1992 wages relating to the employees who used their carryovers during 1992 increased by $1,000, the 1992 entry would be

```
Liability for compensated absences . . . . . . . . . . . . .  33,000
Wage expense (1992) . . . . . . . . . . . . . . . . . . . .   1,000
    Cash ($36,000 + $1,000 − $3,000). . . . . . . . . . . .            34,000
The balance remaining in the liability account remains $3,000.
```

Current Maturities of Long-Term Debt

How should a debt that is part current and part non-current be reported? The problem arises when periodic payments are made on a debt. A payment is due in the next accounting period while additional payments will be made in later accounting periods. If the next payment is to be made from current assets, that portion of the debt should be reported as a current liability. For example:

```
Current liabilities:
    Current payment on bond issue . . . . . . . . . . . . . . .  $100,000
Long-term liabilities:
    Bonds payable (less current portion, $100,000) . . . . . . . . . $400,000
```

The portion in parentheses is often not reported separately.

Obligations Callable on Demand by the Creditor

The kinds of debt illustrated in the following cases must be included in the current liability classification:

Case 1—obligations that are payable on demand (i.e., callable), or will be due on demand within one year from the balance sheet date, or the operating cycle, if longer, even though liquidation within that period is not expected.

Case 2—long-term obligations that are, or will be, callable by the creditor either: because of a violation of the terms of the debt at the date of the balance sheet, or because the violation, if not cured within a specified grace period, will make the debt callable.

The concept that supports these current liability classifications is that the debtor of a long-term obligation or a callable note meeting the preceding specifications cannot control the payment date.

---

[19] In practice, many firms would simply recalculate the liability at the next year-end and adjust it through salary expense.

CONCEPT REVIEW

1. What are the different categories of current liabilities?
2. What is the difference between the nominal and the effective rate of interest?
3. How is a liability for a bonus based on income calculated?

SHORT-TERM OBLIGATIONS EXPECTED TO BE REFINANCED

A company may be motivated to reclassify liabilities from current to long term to improve its reported working capital position. One reason given for such reclassifications is that because the company intends to refinance the debt, it does not expect to be making any payments on the debt from current assets. The following guidelines prevent abuses and provide that current liabilities expected to be refinanced can be reclassified as long-term liabilities only if the debtor fully intends to refinance the specific short-term debt and shows an ability to refinance the debt by actually refinancing it on a long-term basis before the financial statements are issued, or by entering in good faith into a long-term, noncancelable refinancing agreement that is supported by a viable lender. The maximum amount that may be classified as long term cannot exceed the amount irrevocably refinanced less the effect of all refinancing restrictions.

Firms, for example, often finance new plant and equipment with short-term commercial paper expecting to finance it later on a long-term basis and then report the debt as long term.

When a financing agreement is relied on to classify current obligations as long-term debt, it should meet the following criteria:

1. The agreement must be noncancelable by all parties (except for violations by the debtor) and extend beyond one year from the balance sheet date or from the start of the operating cycle, whichever is longer.
2. At the balance sheet date and the issue date, the company must not be in violation of the agreement.
3. The lender must be financially capable of honouring the agreement.

The amount of the short-term debt that can be classified as long term cannot exceed the amount available under the agreement, must be adjusted for any limitations in the agreement, and cannot exceed a reasonable estimate of the minimum amount expected to be available (if the amount available for refinancing will fluctuate). If any of these three amounts cannot be estimated, the entire amount of the short-term debt should remain a current liability. Current obligations liquidated after the balance sheet date but before the statement issue date must be reported as current obligations if the funds used in refinancing were short-term. This is the case even if long-run financing is ultimately obtained before the financial statement issue date.

If a short-term obligation is to be excluded from current liabilities under a financing agreement, footnote disclosure is required and should include:

1. A general description of the financing agreement.
2. The terms of any new obligation to be incurred.
3. The terms of any equity security to be issued.

If the long-term financing is expected to be accomplished using equity financing, the short-term obligations must remain as current liabilities. Short-term obligations that satisfy the requirements to be shown as long term can be given a specific and distinct caption if desired such as "short-term debt expected to be refinanced."

CONCEPT REVIEW

1. Why might a company be motivated to reclassify a liability from short to long term?
2. Under which conditions can a current liability be reclassified as a long-term liability?
3. When a short-term obligation is excluded from current liabilities under a financing agreement, what footnote disclosure is required?

CONTINGENCIES AND ESTIMATED LIABILITIES

The central issue here is the definition of a debt when one or more specific events have not occurred. Liabilities often must be estimated because a known liability exists but the ultimate amount is uncertain or a loss contingency exists. A **contingency** is defined in the *CICA Handbook,* paragraph 3290.02, as

> an existing condition, or situation, involving uncertainty as to possible gain (hereinafter, "gain contingency") or a loss (hereinafter, "loss contingency") to an enterprise that will ultimately be resolved when one or more future events occur or fail to occur. Resolution of the uncertainty may confirm the acquisition of an asset or the reduction of a liability or the loss or impairment of an asset or the incurrence of a liability.

Section 3290, "Contingencies," is the basic pronouncement on contingencies and estimated liabilities and is the basis for this discussion. This section is divided into three parts:

- Contingent liabilities (loss contingencies) that must be accrued and reported at estimated dollar amounts in the body of the financial statements.
- Contingent liabilities that are reported only in the notes to the financial statements.
- Gain contingencies.

Paragraph 3290.06 delineates contingencies and specifies particular accounting treatments on the basis of whether the contingency is:

1. **Likely.** The chance of the occurrence (or non-occurrence) of the future event is high.
2. **Unlikely.** The chance of the occurrence (or non-occurrence) of the future event is slight.
3. **Not determinable.** The chance of the occurrence (or non-occurrence) of the future event cannot be determined.

The provisions of section 3290 relating to contingencies are summarized as shown in Exhibit 15–1.

Loss Contingencies that Must Be Accrued and a Liability Recognized

Paragraph 3290.12 requires that a loss contingency should be accrued in the financial statements by charging income when both of the following conditions are met:

- It is likely that a future event will confirm that an asset had been impaired or a liability incurred at the date of the financial statements.
- The amount of the loss can be reasonably estimated.

This situation corresponds to statement 1 in Exhibit 15–1. Notice, also, that this situation is similar to many liabilities that are estimated in compliance with the matching principle. Loss contingencies that must be considered for appropriate disclosure include estimated losses on receivables (allowance for doubtful accounts); estimated warranty obligations; litigations, claims, and assessments; and anticipated losses on the disposal of a segment of the business. If the amount of the loss can vary considerably,

EXHIBIT 15–1   Summary of Accounting for Contingencies

Probabilistic Nature of the Occurrence of the Contingent Event	Amount Can Be Reasonably Estimated	Amount Cannot Be Reasonably Estimated
	Loss Contingency	
Likely	1. Accrue both a loss and a liability, and report them in the body of the statements.	2. Do not accrue; report as a note in the financial statements.
Unlikely	3. No accrual or note required; however, a note is permitted.	4. No accrual or note required; however, a note is permitted.
	Gain Contingency	
Likely	5. No accrual except in very unusual circumstances. Note disclosure required.	6. Note disclosure required; exercise care to avoid misleading inferences.
Unlikely	7. Disclosure not recommended.	

no amount should be accrued unless there is substantial certainty that at least some minimum amount will be paid. In this case, the minimum amount is accrued. Footnote disclosure is appropriate, however.

A loss contingency that meets both of the previously noted criteria, in addition to being accrued in the accounts, must be reported on the balance sheet as a liability, and on the income statement as an expense or loss in the period in which the two criteria are first met. Three examples illustrate the accrual of a loss contingency and recognition of a liability.

Case A—Product Warranty Liability   Roll Company sold merchandise for $200,000 cash during the current period. Experience has indicated that warranty and guarantee costs will approximate 0.5% of sales. The indicated entries are

1. In year of sale:

   As sales take place (total to end of year):

Cash	200,000	
Sales revenue		200,000

   At year-end (or periodically):

Warranty expense	1,000	
Warranty liability		1,000

2. Subsequently, actual warranty expenditures of $987 were made during the warranty period:

Warranty liability	987	
Cash (and other resources used)		987

3. Instead, if the actual expenditure was $1,100, the entry would be:

Warranty liability	1,000	
Warranty expense	100	
Cash (and other resources used)		1,100

The preceding entries assume that Roll estimates the warranty expense as a ratio of sales dollars and that the expense will be 0.5% of sales, or more if the actual expenditures are greater. Another approach would be to charge the actual expenditures to the expense account as they are incurred. Then, at the end of the accounting period, an estimate of the warranty liability would be made and accrued as follows:

1. Actual warranty expenditures of $987 were made during the accounting period:

Warranty expense.	987	
Cash (and other resources used).		987

2. At the end of the accounting period, goods which sold for $30,000 are still under warranty, and it is estimated that the associated warranty costs on these goods may amount to 0.3% of the selling price. This entry sets up the liability:

Warranty expense ($30,000 × .3%)	90	
Warranty liability.		90

In subsequent periods, the actual warranty costs would continue to be charged to the warranty expense account as incurred. At the end of each accounting period, the warranty liability account would be increased or decreased according to the estimate of the level of the liability desired. The other side of the entry would be debits or credits to the expense account as appropriate.

For an example of the type of disclosure provided, Mountain Medical Equipment's 1989 financial statements include the following note related to warranties:

Estimated Liability for Future Warranty Claims

The Company provides customers with warranties ranging from one to three years primarily covering the cost of parts. The liability for future warranty claims reflects the estimated cost of warranty repairs on products previously sold.

Case B—Liability from Premiums, Coupons, and Trading Stamps   As a promotional device, many companies offer premiums to customers who turn in coupons, UPC codes, and so on. At the end of each accounting period, a portion of these response devices will be outstanding (unredeemed by the customers), some of which ultimately will be turned in for redemption. These outstanding claims for premiums represent an expense and an estimated liability that must be recognized in the period of sale of the merchandise. The amounts may not be trivial. In a recent set of financial statements Canadian Tire Corporation Ltd. reported accrued liabilities and coupons outstanding of $104 million.

To illustrate the accounting, Baker Coffee Company offered its customers a premium—a special coffee cup free of charge (cost to Baker, 75 cents each) with the return of 20 coupons. One coupon is placed in each can of coffee when packed. The company estimated, on the basis of past experience, that only 70% of the coupons would be redeemed. The following additional data for two years are available:

	First Year	Second Year
Number of coffee cups purchased at $.75.	6,000	4,000
Number of cans of coffee sold	100,000	200,000
Number of coupons redeemed	40,000	120,000

These entries are indicated:

1. To record purchases of cups:

	First Year	Second Year
Premium inventory	4,500	3,000
Cash	4,500	3,000

2. To record the estimated liability and premium expense based on sales:

Premium expense* 2,625		5,250
Premium claims payable	2,625	5,250

* Computations:
Year 1: (100,000 ÷ 20) ($.75) (.70) = $2,625.
Year 2: (200,000 ÷ 20) ($.75) (.70) = $5,250.

3. To record redemption of coupons:

Premium claims payable* 1,500		4,500
Premium inventory	1,500	4,500

* Computations:
Year 1: (40,000 ÷ 20) ($.75) = $1,500.
Year 2: (120,000 ÷ 20) ($.75) = $4,500.

Case C—Liability from Litigation   Assume Solon Company was sued during the last quarter of the current year because of an accident involving a vehicle owned and operated by the company. The plaintiff is seeking $100,000 damages. If, in the opinion of management and company counsel, it is likely that damages will be assessed and a reasonable estimate is $50,000, this is the indicated entry:[20]

Estimated loss from pending lawsuit 50,000	
Estimated liability from pending lawsuit	50,000

Imasco Limited gives an example of such disclosure in its 1989 statements.

> **Notes to the Consolidated Financial Statements (in part):**
>
> 17. Other information
>
> f. The Corporation and its subsidiaries are parties to claims and suits brought against them in the ordinary course of business. In addition, certain of the subsidiaries acquired as part of the Genstar transaction are subject to numerous claims and suits, some of which are asbestos related. Certain of these claims and suits allege significant damage. In the opinion of management, all such claims and suits are adequately covered by insurance or are provided for in the financial statements, or if not so covered or provided for, the results are not expected to materially affect the Corporation's financial position.

Estimated liabilities, such as those just illustrated, may ultimately require expenditures that differ from the amount estimated to satisfy the actual liability. When the estimated liability varies from the actual, the difference is accounted for as a change in estimate under the provisions of *CICA Handbook*, section 1506. The expense is increased or decreased if the total amount is known in the same year. If the total amount is known only in a later year, an expense or gain is recognized, as appropriate.

Loss Contingencies that Are Disclosed Only in Notes

Potential loss contingencies, such as guarantees of indebtedness, accommodation endorsements, threat of expropriation of assets, standby letters of credit (guarantees of the credit of a third party), and risks due to fire, flood, and other hazards, also must be assessed and accounted for in conformity with *CICA Handbook*, section 3290.

In Exhibit 15–1, statement 1, a loss contingency and the related liability are accrued and reported only when the loss is likely and the amount can be reasonably estimated.

---

[20] It is unlikely that legal counsel and management would disclose a belief that a contingent loss is probable and can be reliably estimated. This situation would suggest that it may be advisable to settle out of court. To disclose a tacit expectation of loss in advance may prejudice the outcome of the trial. For this reason, lawyers vehemently object to such disclosures. The information appears, if at all, in the notes to the financial statements. Even then, it is extremely unusual for the firm to mention specific amounts unless court judgments have already been rendered.

In contrast, Exhibit 15–1 indentifies three situations involving loss contingencies for which disclosures in the notes are required or permitted. The note describes the nature of the contingency and gives an estimate of the possible loss or range of loss, or it states that a reasonable estimate of the possible loss cannot be made.

Examples of two contingent liability disclosures follow from the 1989 annual report of Cineplex Odeon. The first is an example of a guarantee of a loan while the second is an example of a potential loss from a legal action.

15. Commitments and Contingencies (in part)

(D) A subsidiary of the Corporation has been engaged in a joint venture with a subsidiary of New Visions Entertainment Corporation. The New Visions joint venture entity is involved in the production and distribution of films. The Corporation has given notice of its intention to discontinue participation in this joint venture after the completion of the first five pictures. Production of these pictures has been substantially completed.

The Corporation is contingently responsible for the repayment of approximately $17,500,000 of the joint venture entity's bank financing with respect to the production of the first five pictures and for 50% of any prints and advertising expenditures not funded by third parties with respect to these films. The bank financing is collateralized by third party distribution contracts which, upon the release of the remaining four pictures, will provide for aggregate payments approximately equal to the total outstanding joint venture bank indebtedness. The Corporation intends to meet its print and advertising funding obligations with respect to the first five pictures.

The co-venturer and others have disputed the Corporation's right to terminate its involvement in the joint venture, have commenced arbitration proceedings and seek damages and other relief with respect thereto. The Corporation considers its withdrawal to be proper under the agreement.

(E) Four class action and/or derivative lawsuits have been filed and subsequently consolidated into one action in the U.S. District Court for the Central District of California against the Corporation and certain of its directors and former directors. The consolidated action seeks compensatory damages on behalf of all persons who purchased shares of the Corporation's common stock between May 14, 1987, and June 14, 1989, alleging violations of certain securities laws, and claims with respect to fraud and misrepresentation. The lawsuit further seeks compensatory and punitive damages derivatively for the benefit of the Corporation, alleging breach of fiduciary duty. The Corporation and the directors named believe that they have meritorious defenses to the claims alleged and intend to defend vigorously the lawsuit.

The Corporation and its subsidiaries are also involved in certain litigation arising out of the ordinary course and conduct of its business. Certain litigation results from activities in acquired companies which pre-dated the purchase by the Corporation. In certain cases the vendor of the business has agreed to indemnify the Corporation to the extent of losses, if any, incurred. The outcome of other litigation is not currently determinable. However, although such matters cannot be predicted with certainty, management does not consider the Corporation's exposure to litigation to be material to these financial statements.

Gain Contingencies

For a gain contingency to arise, the characteristics of a contingency must be present. A gain contingency implies an increase in assets or a decrease in liabilities, depending on future events.

Contingent gains are rarely accrued; however, they are accorded note disclosure, provided the note does not give misleading implications. The different treatment accorded gain contingencies, compared with loss contingencies, is justified by the conservatism constraint.

Executory Contracts

Executory contracts or agreements occur when two parties agree to transfer resources or services but neither party has yet performed. For example, a purchase agreement may have been made, but no assets have been received and no payments have been made. Other examples include lines of credit, pensions, leases, and promises of future compensation prior to any transfer of resources. When a transfer of resources occurs, the contract or agreement is no longer executory. Executory contracts usually are not recorded because a transfer of assets or liabilities has not yet occurred. However, if the anticipated considerations are material, full disclosure should be made.

CONCEPT REVIEW

1. When must a loss contingency be accrued?
2. When is it necessary to report a loss contingency in the notes? What value, if any, should be reported?
3. How are executory contracts treated in the accounting records?

SUMMARY OF KEY POINTS

(L.O. 1)   1. A liability possesses three essential characteristics:
   • The existence of an obligation that can only be satisfied by the transfer of an asset or a service to another entity.
   • The obligation is unavoidable.
   • The event which gave rise to the obligation has occurred.

(L.O. 2)   2. Current liabilities are those whose liquidation is reasonably expected to require the use of existing resources properly classified as current assets, or the creation of other current liabilities.

(L.O. 3)   3. A liability should conceptually be measured as the present value of all future cash payments discounted at an interest rate consistent with the risks involved.

(L.O. 4)   4. All obligations explicitly or implicitly involve interest.

(L.O. 5)   5. Cash or other assets received in advance of the delivery of goods or services create a liability for the receiving firm.

(L.O. 3, 6)   6. Short-term obligations expected to be refinanced on a long-term basis may be classified as long-term liabilities if the debtor (a) fully intends to refinance and (b) shows an ability to refinance by so doing or entering a noncancelable refinancing agreement supported by a viable lender.

(L.O. 7)   7. A loss contingency must be accrued if (a) prior to issuance of the financial statements, information suggests that it is likely an asset has been impaired or a liability incurred and (b) the amount of the loss can reasonably be estimated.

(L.O. 7)   8. Loss contingencies for guarantees of indebtedness, stand-by letters of credit, and related events are reported in the notes if they are likely but cannot be reasonably estimated.

(L.O. 7)   9. Gain contingencies are usually not accrued but rather reported in the notes if likely to occur.

REVIEW PROBLEM

◆

In the introduction to this chapter, the situation faced by the Manville Company in 1982 was described. React to the following issues:

1. Does Manville face a contingent liability?
2. If so, must it be accrued?
3. If not, is footnote disclosure appropriate?
4. If accrual or footnote disclosure is appropriate, what amount should be shown?

REVIEW SOLUTION

◆

The authors believe a loss is likely and that an amount can be reasonably estimated. The minimum, which would appear from the limited published data to be at least $2 billion, should be accrued. Further, an estimate of the upper end of the possible loss range should be disclosed in a footnote.

KEY TERMS

Contingency (731)
Current (short-term) liabilities (717)
Effective rate of interest (yield) (718)

Liability (715)
Stated rate of interest (718)

QUESTIONS

1. Give a conceptual definition of a liability.
2. Conceptually, how should a liability be measured?
3. Relate the measurement of a liability to its cause.
4. Why are most liabilities recognized at maturity value at the beginning of the term?
5. Compute the present value of a $10,000, one-year note payable that specifies no interest, although 10% would be a realistic rate. What is the amount of the principal and the interest?
6. In evaluating a balance sheet, some bankers say the liability section is one of the most important parts. What are the primary reasons for their position on this point?
7. Some liabilities are reported at their maturity amount. In general, when should liabilities, prior to maturity date, be reported at less than their maturity amount?
8. How is the cost principle involved in accounting for current liabilities?
9. Define a current liability.
10. Differentiate between secured and unsecured liabilities. Explain the reporting procedures for each.
11. Distinguish between the stated rate of interest and the effective rate of interest (yield) on a debt.
12. Briefly define the following terms related to a note payable: principal, face, and maturity amounts.
13. Distinguish between an interest-bearing note and a noninterest-bearing note.
14. Assume $4,000 cash is borrowed on a $4,000, 10%, one-year note payable that is interest-bearing and that another $4,000 cash is borrowed on a $4,400 one-year note that is noninterest-bearing. For each note give the following:
    a. Face amount of the note.
    b. Principal amount.
    c. Maturity amount.
    d. Interest paid.
15. Are all declared dividends a liability between declaration and payment dates? Explain.
16. Why is a deferred revenue classified as a liability?
17. What is a compensated absence? When should the expense related to compensated absences be recognized?
18. What is the accounting definition of a contingency? What are the three characteristics of a contingency? Why is the concept important?
19. How does the accountant measure the likelihood of the outcome of a contingency? In general, how does this affect the accounting for and reporting of contingencies?
20. Briefly explain the accounting and reporting for loss contingencies.

EXERCISES

E 15–1
Characteristics of
Liabilities
(L.O. 1)

The following five characteristics may be associated with any liability:

a. The transfer of an asset or the obligation to provide a service is assured.
b. The magnitude of the obligation must be of material size relative to the firm's assets.
c. The obligation to transfer assets or provide services must be unavoidable if the existence of the obligation is at least likely.
d. The obligation arises from a past event.
e. An explicit interest rate must be stated as attaching to the obligation.

Required:

Indicate which of the preceding are necessary characteristics for the item to be a liability. Explain.

E 15–2
Identifying Liabilities and
Current Liabilities
(L.O. 1, 2)

These four items were noted in the chapter:

a. Coupons that may be redeemed for merchandise or service.
b. Frequent flier miles earned by airline travellers.
c. Probable requirements to clean up toxic wastes.
d. Preferred stock that is cumulative as to dividends, non-participating as to voting, and callable by either issuer or holder on demand.

Required:

Which of these items, if any, should be considered liabilities and recognized on the balance sheet? Should any of them or portions thereof be recognized as current liabilities? Explain.

E 15–3
Identifying Current
Liabilities
(L.O. 2)

Following are six items:

a. Bank overdraft.
b. Retained earnings.
c. Long-term debt.
d. Dividends declared but not paid.
e. Customer payments for magazine subscriptions not yet delivered.
f. Corporate income taxes payable.

Required:
Identify the current liabilities among these six items.

E 15–4
Identifying a Current
Liability
(L.O. 2)

Suppose a firm has an obligation that requires it to pay another organization $500,000 two years from today.

Required:

Normally such a liability would be considered long term and not current. Is there any situation in which this obligation could be considered a current liability? Explain.

E 15–5
Interest-Bearing and
Noninterest-Bearing Notes
Compared
(L.O. 4)

a. On January 1, 1991, a heavy-duty truck was purchased that had a listed price of $33,500. Payment in full was: cash, $8,500, and a two-year, noninterest-bearing note of $25,000 (maturity date, December 31, 1992). A realistic rate for this level of risk was 12%. The accounting period ends December 31. Assume that this note is a current liability in this company.
b. On January 1, 1991, a small truck was purchased and full payment was made as follows: cash, $5,000, and a one-year, 6%, interest-bearing note of $10,000, maturity date December 31, 1991 (which also is the end of the accounting period). A realistic interest rate for this level of risk was 12%.

Required:

Give all entries for each case from purchase date through maturity date of each note. Disregard depreciation. Round to the nearest dollar.

E 15–6
Interest-Bearing Note:
Entries and Reporting
(L.O. 4)

On May 1, 1991, Murray Meters borrowed $100,000 cash and signed a one-year, 12% interest-bearing note for that amount. Murray's accounting period ends December 31.

Required:

1. Give all of the required entries from May 1, 1991, through the maturity date of the note. Disregard reversing and closing entries.
2. Show how all amounts related to the note should be reported on the debtor's balance sheet at December 31, 1991, and the 1991 income statement.

E 15–7
Analysis of Two
Noninterest-Bearing
Notes—One Has an
Unrealistic Rate
(L.O. 4)

On March 1, 1991, Lasorda Lumber borrowed $60,000 cash from SP Bank and signed a one-year note for $70,650 (designated Note A); no interest was specified in the note. On June 1, 1991, Lasorda borrowed additional cash and signed a one-year note, face amount, $17,775 (designated Note B). No interest was specified in the note; however, the going rate of interest for this level of risk was 18.5%. The accounting period ends December 31. Table 6A–2; $n = 1$; $i = 18.5\% = 1.18500$.

Required:

	Note A	Note B
a. How much cash was received?	$_____	$_____
b. What was the face amount of the note?	$_____	$_____
c. What was the principal of the note?	$_____	$_____
d. How much interest expense should be reported in:		
1991?	$_____	$_____
1992?	$_____	$_____
e. What was the stated interest rate?	_____%	_____%
f. What was the yield or effective interest rate?	_____%	_____%

E 15–8
Analysis and Comparison
of Interest-Bearing and
Noninterest-Bearing Notes
(L.O. 4)

On September 1, 1991, Dyer Company borrowed cash on a $10,000 note payable due in one year. Assume the going rate of interest was 12% per year for this particular level of risk. The accounting period ends December 31.

Required:

Complete the following tabulation; round to the nearest dollar.

	Assuming the note was—	
	Interest-Bearing	Noninterest-Bearing
a. Cash received	$_____	$_____
b. Cash paid at maturity date	$_____	$_____
c. Total interest paid (cash)	$_____	$_____
d. Interest expense in 1991	$_____	$_____
e. Interest expense in 1992	$_____	$_____
f. Amount of liabilities reported on 1991 balance sheet:		
Note payable (net)	$_____	$_____
Interest payable	$_____	$_____
g. Principal amount	$_____	$_____
h. Face amount	$_____	$_____
i. Maturity value	$_____	$_____
j. Stated interest rate	_____%	_____%
k. Yield or effective interest rate	_____%	_____%

E 15–9
Noninterest-Bearing Note:
Entries and Reporting
(L.O. 4)

On April 1, 1991, Martin Manufacturing purchased a heavy machine for use in operations by paying $10,000 cash and signing a $40,000 (face amount) noninterest-bearing note due in one year (on March 31, 1992). The going rate of interest for Martin on this type of note was 14% per year. The company uses straight-line depreciation. The accounting period ends on December 31. Assume a five-year life for the machine and 10% residual value.

Required:

1. Give all entries from April 1, 1991, through March 31, 1992 (round amounts to the nearest dollar).
2. Show how all of the related items would be reported on the 1991 income statement and balance sheet.

E 15–10
Current Liabilities:
Original and Adjusting
Entries
(L.O. 4, 5, 6)

Voss Company, a large retail outlet, completed the following selected transactions during 1991 and 1992.

a. At the end of 1991, accrued wages that have not yet been recorded amounted to $34,000. These accrued wages were paid in the January 15, 1992, payroll, which amounted to $173,000 (disregard payroll taxes).
b. On November 1, 1991, rent revenue for the following six months was collected, $8,400.
c. On October 1, 1991, Voss received $800 as a deposit from a customer for some special containers that are to be returned on or about March 31, 1992. Voss agreed to "give the customer credit at an annual rate of 6% interest on the deposit." The containers were returned on April 1, 1992.

Required:

Give all of the required entries (omit closing and reversing entries) during 1991 and 1992 for each of the preceding transactions. The accounting period of Voss ends on December 31.

E 15–11
Reporting Liabilities:
Dividends and Secured
Notes
(L.O. 4, 6)

The records of the Fisk Corporation provided the following information at December 31, 1991:

a. Notes payable (trade), short-term (includes a $4,000 note given on purchase of equipment that cost $20,000; assets were mortgaged in connection with purchase)	$ 30,000
b. Bonds payable ($30,000 due each April 1)	120,000
c. Accounts payable (including $3,000 owed to president of the company)	50,000
d. Accrued property taxes (estimated)	1,000
e. Stock dividends issuable on March 1, 1992 (at par value)	26,000
f. Cash dividends declared, payable March 1, 1992	20,000
g. Long-term note payable, maturity amount (unamortized amount, $14,500)	16,000
h. Accrued interest on all bonds and notes	13,500

Required:

Assuming the fiscal year ends December 31, show how each of these items should be reported on the balance sheet at December 31, 1991.

E 15–12
Entries to Record Payroll
and Related Deductions
(L.O. 6)

Ryan Company paid salaries for the month amounting to $120,000. CPP deductions were $3,200 and UIC deductions were $3,460. Income taxes withheld were $38,000 and $1,200 was withheld for union dues under the collective agreement. Hospitalization taxes are 1.8% of gross salaries.

Required:

Give entries to record the (1) salary payment and the liabilities for the deductions, (2) employer payroll expenses, and (3) remittance of the taxes and deductions.

E 15–13
Recording Payroll and
Related Deductions
(L.O. 6)

Smiley Limited paid salary and wages of $143,800. Of this amount, $43,800 was deducted for income taxes, $5,470 was deducted for CPP, $5,820 was deducted for UIC, $3,600 for life insurance premiums, and $3,480 for extended health care benefits. Provincial hospitalization taxes are 1.8% of gross payroll.

Required:

Give the entries to record liabilities for payroll deductions, payroll expenses, and remittance of the deductions.

E 15–14
Compensated Absences:
Entries and Reporting
(L.O. 6)

Langston Mowers allows each employee to earn 15 paid vacation days each year with full pay while on vacation. Unused vacation time can be carried over to the next year; if not taken during the next year it is lost. By the end of 1991, all but 3 of the 30 employees had taken their earned vacation time; these three carried over to 1992 a total of 20 vacation days, which represented 1991 salary of $5,000. During 1992, each of these three used their 1991 vacation carryover; none of them had received a pay change from 1991 to the time they used their carryover. Total cash wages paid were: 1991, $700,000; 1992, $740,000.

Required:

1. Give all of the entries for Langston related to vacations during 1991 and 1992. Disregard payroll taxes.
2. Compute the total amount of wage expense for 1991 and 1992. How would the vacation time carried over from 1991 affect the 1991 balance sheet.

E 15–15
Estimated Warranty
Expense: Recording and
Reporting
(L.O. 7)

Franco Furniture sells a line of products that carry a three-year warranty against defects. Based on industry experience, the estimated warranty costs related to dollar sales are first year after sale—1% of sales; second year after sale—3% of sales; and third year after sale—5%. Sales and actual warranty expenditures for the first three-year period were as follows:

	Cash Sales	Actual Warranty Expenditures
1991	$ 80,000	$ 900
1992	110,000	4,100
1993	130,000	9,800

Required:

1. Give entries for the three years for the (*a*) sales, (*b*) estimated warranty expense, and (*c*) the actual expenditures.
2. Which amount should be reported as a liability on the balance sheet at the end of each year?

E 15–16
Liability for Premiums:
Entries and Reporting
(L.O. 7)

Van Slyke Stereos has initiated a promotion program whereby customers are given coupons redeemable in $25 special savings certificates. Each certificate can be turned in to the savings company for its face amount at the end of the third year from its issuance to the customer. One coupon is issued for each dollar of sales. On the surrender of 500 coupons, one $25 savings certificate (cost $20) is given. It is estimated that 25% of the coupons issued will never be presented for redemption. Sales for the first period were $400,000, and the number of coupons redeemed totaled 210,000. Sales for the second period were $440,000, and the number of coupons redeemed totaled 300,000. The savings certificates are acquired as needed.

Required:

Prepare journal entries (including closing entries) relative to the premium plan for the two periods. Show amounts that should be reported in the balance sheet and income statement for the two periods. *Hint:* Use the following accounts: cash, premium expense, estimated premium claims payable, and income summary.

E 15–17
Loss Contingency—Three
Cases: Entries and
Explanation
(L.O. 7)

Canseco Company is preparing the annual financial statements at December 31, 1992. During 1992, a customer fell while riding on the escalator and has filed a lawsuit for $40,000 because of a claimed back injury. The lawyer employed by the company has carefully assessed all of the implications. If the suit is lost, the lawyer's reasonable estimate is that the $40,000 will be assessed by the court.

Required:

How should the contingency be handled during 1992 in each of the following cases? Give all necessary entries and/or any notes:

1. Assume that the lawyer and the management concluded that it is reasonably likely that the company will be liable, and it is reasonably estimated that the amount will be $40,000.
2. Assume, instead, that the lawyer, the independent accountant, and management have reluctantly concluded that it is likely that the suit will be successful.
3. Assume that the conclusion of the legal counsel and management is that it is unlikely that there will be a contingency loss. They believe the suit is without merit.

E 15–18
Property Taxes: Recording
(L.O. 7)

Tudor Company is located in a relatively small town that has recently restructured its property tax procedures. During the past year (1991) the company experienced a significant increase in the property appraisal for taxes. The company paid property taxes of $120,000. However, it expects the tax for the current year, 1992, to decrease some because of citizen complaints. Both the city tax year and Tudor's accounting year end on December 31. The following events occurred during 1991:

January 20—paid the 1991 property taxes.

January 30—estimated a 10% decrease in property taxes for 1992. The company accrues property taxes each month.

July 10—received a tentative tax notice assessment for taxes, $2,280,000; preliminary tax rate per $100 valuation, $5.00. The company will revise its estimate to these assessments.

December 29—received final tax notice, 1992 tax assessed, $111,000, payable by January 15, 1993.

January 25, 1993—paid the 1992 property tax.

Required:

Give the journal entries related to property taxes from January 1, 1992, through January 1993.

PROBLEMS

P 15–1
Interest-Bearing and
Noninterest-Bearing Notes
Compared: Entries,
Reporting
(L.O. 4)

Herzog Company borrowed cash on August 1, 1991, and signed a $15,000 (face amount), one-year note payable, due on July 31, 1992. The accounting period ends December 31. Assume a going rate of interest of 11% for this company for this level of risk.

Required:

Round amounts to nearest dollar.

1. How much cash should Herzog receive on the note assuming: Case A, an interest-bearing note, and Case B, a noninterest-bearing note?
2. Give the following entries for each case:
   a. August 1, 1991, date of the loan.
   b. December 31, 1991, adjusting entry.
   c. July 31, 1992, payment of the note, assuming no reversing entry was made.
3. What liability amounts should be shown in each case on the December 31, 1991, balance sheet?

P 15–2
Interest-Bearing and
Noninterest-Bearing Notes
Compared: Entries
(L.O. 4)

On October 1, 1991, Uribe Company borrowed $30,000 cash and signed a one-year note payable, due on September 30, 1992. The going rate of interest for this level of risk was 16%. The accounting period ends on December 31.

Required:

1. Compute the face amount of the note assuming:
   a. Case A—An interest-bearing note.
   b. Case B—A noninterest-bearing note.
2. Complete a tabulation as follows:

	Case A: Interest-Bearing	Case B: Noninterest-Bearing
a. Total cash received	$30,000	$30,000
b. Face amount of note	$____	$____
c. Total cash paid	$____	$____
d. Total interest paid	$____	$____
e. Interest expense, 1991	$____	$____
f. Interest expense, 1992	$____	$____
g. Amount of liabilities reported on the 1991 balance sheet:		
Note payable	$____	$____
Interest payable	$____	$____
h. Principal amount	$____	$____
i. Stated interest rate	____%	____%
j. Yield or effective interest rate	____%	____%
k. Time to maturity:		
October 1, 1991	Months____	Months____
December 31, 1991	Months____	Months____

3. Give entries indicated for each case from October 1, 1991, through maturity date (assume reversing entries were not made).
4. Show how the liability and expense amounts should be reflected for each case on the December 31, 1991, balance sheet and the 1991 income statement.

P 15–3
Noninterest-Bearing Note,
Two-Year: Entries and
Reporting
(L.O. 4)

On January 1, 1991, Gagne Company acquired a machine (an operational asset) that had a list price of $35,000. Because of a serious cash problem, Gagne paid $5,000 cash and signed a two-year note with a maturity amount of $30,000 due on December 31, 1992. The note did not specify interest. Assume the going rate of interest for this company for this level of risk was 15%. The accounting period ends December 31.

Required:

Round amounts to nearest dollar.

1. Give the entry to record the purchase of the machine.
2. Complete the following tabulation related to the note:

   a. Cash equivalent received . . . . $_____
   b. Face amount . . . . $_____
   c. Total interest to be paid . . . . $_____
   d. Interest expense:
       1991 . . . . $_____
       1992 . . . . $_____
   e. Liabilities on the 1991 balance sheet . . . . $_____
   f. Depreciation expense (on cost) (10-year estimated
       life; no residual value; straight-line) . . . . $_____
   g. Effective interest rate . . . . _____%
   h. Stated interest rate . . . . _____%

3. Give all entries (exclude closing and reversing entries) from January 1, 1991, through the end of 1992.
4. Show how the liabilities and expenses would be reported on the 1991 and 1992 financial statements (assume the company has a two-year operating cycle).

P 15–4
Noninterest-Bearing Note,
Two-Year: Entries and
Reporting
(L.O. 4)

On January 1, 1991, Lyle Company purchased a large used machine for operations; the asking price was $46,000. Payment was made by $6,000 cash and a $40,000 (maturity value), two-year, noninterest-bearing note payable due on December 31, 1992. The note did not specify interest; however, for Lyle, the rate for this level of risk was 13%. Assume straight-line depreciation, a five-year life, and no residual value. The accounting period ends on December 31.

Required:

Round amounts to nearest dollar.

1. Give the entry to record the purchase of the machine.
2. Complete the following tabulation related to the note:

   a. Cash equivalent received . . . . $_____
   b. Face amount of note . . . . $_____
   c. Cash to be paid at maturity . . . . $_____
   d. Total interest expense . . . . $_____
   e. Interest expense:
       1991 . . . . $_____
       1992 . . . . $_____
   f. Depreciation expense . . . . $_____
   g. Effective interest rate . . . . _____%
   h. Stated interest rate . . . . _____%

3. Prepare a debt amortization schedule for this note. Use the following column headings: date, interest expense, and carrying value of the liability (also refer to Chapter 6).
4. Give all entries (except closing and reversing entries) from January 1, 1991, through the end of 1992.
5. Show how the liabilities and expenses should be reported on the 1991 and 1992 financial statements (assume the current operating cycle is two years).

P 15–5
Property Tax and Sales
Tax: Recording and
Reporting
(L.O. 6)

Santiago Department Store has asked you to assist in improving its accounting for taxes. The following selected transactions that were completed during 1992 have been presented to you for analysis; the accounting period ends on December 31.

a. Property taxes—Property taxes for 1991 amounted to $24,000. During January 1992 Santiago estimated that the property tax would increase approximately 10% for 1992. During June 1992, the company received a tentative property tax appraisal that indicated a property valuation of $2.1 million and an estimated 1992 tax rate per $1,000 of $13.10. The final tax assessment notice was received December 19, 1992, and specified a 1992 property tax of $30,000. The 1992 property taxes were paid in full on January 17, 1993.

b. Sales revenue for 1992 amounted to $8 million; the sales tax rate is 6%, and 98% of all sales were subject to tax. Unremitted sales tax at the end of 1992 amounted to $18,000.

Required:

Round to the nearest dollar.

1. Give all entries indicated for (a) the accrual of property tax (during 1992 on a monthly basis) and the payment on January 17, 1993, and (b) the sales tax (for 1992) transactions.
2. Show how the effects of the preceding tax transactions should be reported on the 1992 financial statements.

P 15–6
Compensated Absences:
Entries and Reporting
(L.O. 6)

Alomar Company has a personnel policy that allows each employee with at least one year's employment 20 days' vacation time and 2 holidays with regular pay. Unused days are carried over to the next year; if not taken during the next year, the vacation and holiday times are lost. Alomar's accounting period ends December 31.

At the end of 1992, the personnel records showed the following:

Vacations Carried over to 1993		Holidays Carried over to 1993	
Total Days	**Total Salaries**	**Total Days**	**Total Salaries**
70	$8,400	10	$1,280

During 1993, all of the 1992 vacation time, and eight days of the holiday time, which were carried over, were taken. Salary increases in 1993 for these employees relating to the days carried over amounted to $800. Total cash wages paid were 1992, $890,000; 1993, $920,000.

Required:

1. Give all of the entries for Alomar Company related to vacations and holidays during 1992 and 1993. Disregard payroll taxes.
2. Show how the effects of the preceding transactions should be reported on the 1992 and 1993 financial statements of Alomar.

P 15–7
Contingency Losses, Five
Events: Explanations,
Entries, Reporting
(L.O. 7)

Davis Corporation is preparing its first set of financial statements at December 31, 1991, along with the appropriate adjusting entries. Among the contingent losses under consideration are the following transactions and events:

a. Sales revenue for 1991 was $960,000. Unpaid credit sales at year-end amounted to $22,000, and it is likely that $1,000 of that amount will result in a loss.

b. Two of the major product lines sold during the year carry a two-year warranty for defects (both labour and parts cost). Sales of these items amounted to $40,000. On the average, warranty expenditures approximate 4% of sales price.

c. During 1991, Davis issued 5,000 "DC orange coupons." Each 10 coupons held can be turned in, within one year from the date on the coupon, for a $15 credit on any item sold by Davis that costs more than $50. Davis estimates that 25% of the coupons will be redeemed.

d. Davis was sued by a shopper for $50,000 damages due to an accident in the retail store. The shopper asserts a permanent back injury, characterized primarily by pain and stiffness. Legal counsel is of the opinion that it is likely that the plaintiff will prevail in court and that Davis will have to pay 10% of the claim; it is anticipated that the insurance company will pay the balance. The suit, or the claim otherwise, is expected to be resolved in mid-1992.

e. Davis Corporation endorsed and guaranteed a $25,000, 15%, one-year mortgage note given by a local supplier (of merchandise) to Davis. The bank required a guarantor. The bank indicated that the probability of default by the supplier was reasonably possible.

f. The comprehensive liability insurance policy carried by Davis Corporation covers all claims for damages to individuals or groups due to accident, negligence, and other injuries relating to the legitimate operations of the company. However, the insurance policy carries an escape clause that states: "When the insured is willfully negligent, as determined by an independent third party, 10% of the loss must be paid by the insured."

Required:

1. Evaluate each of the preceding transactions and events and recommend appropriate accounting and reporting actions. Give any entry or note required for each item.
2. Identify each liability and the amount that should be reported on the 1991 balance sheet.

P 15–8
Redeemable Coupons:
Accounting and Reporting
(L.O. 7)

For the purpose of stimulating sales, Carter Cereal Company places a coupon in each box of cereal sold; the coupons are redeemable in chinaware. Each premium costs the company 90 cents (the cost of printing the coupons is negligible). Ten coupons must be presented by the customers to receive one premium. The following data are available:

Month	Boxes of Cereal Sold	Premiums Purchased	Coupons Redeemed
January	650,000	25,000	220,000
February	500,000	40,000	410,000
March	560,000	35,000	300,000

Management estimates that only 50% of the coupons will be presented for redemption.

Required:

1. Prepare entries for each of the following events for each of the three months:
   a. Premiums purchased.
   b. Premium expense and related liability.
   c. Coupons redeemed.
2. Complete the following schedule for each month:

Accounts	Ending Account Balances		
	January	February	March
Premiums—Chinaware inventory			
Estimated premium claims payable			
Premium expense (monthly)			

P 15–9
Estimated Warranty Costs:
Entries and Reporting
(L.O. 7)

Hrbek Hardware, Inc., provides a product warranty for defects on two major lines of items sold since the beginning of Year 1. Line A carries a two-year warranty for all labour and service (but not parts). The company contracts with a local service establishment to service the warranty (both parts and labour). The local service establishment charges a flat fee of $60 per unit payable at date of sale.

Line B carries a three-year warranty for parts and labour on service. Hrbek purchases the parts needed under the warranty and has service personnel who perform the work and are paid by the job. On the basis of experience, it is estimated that for Line B, the three-year warranty costs are 3% of dollar sales for parts and 7% for labour and overhead. Additional data available are as follows:

	Year		
	1	2	3
Sales in units, Line A.	700	1,000	
Sales price per unit, Line A.	$ 610	$ 660	
Sales in units, Line B.	600	800	
Sales price per unit, Line B.	$ 700	$ 750	
Actual warranty outlays, Line B:			
Parts.	$3,000	$ 9,600	$12,000
Labour and overhead	$7,000	$22,000	$30,000

Required:

1. Give entries for annual sales and expenses for Year 1 and Year 2 separately by product line. Assume all sales were for cash.
2. Complete a tabulation as follows:

		Year-End Amounts	
Accounts	Year 1	Year 2	Year 3
a. Warranty expense (on income statement)	$____	$____	
b. Estimated warranty liability (on balance sheet)	$____	$____	$____

P 15–10
Recording and Reporting Liabilities, Including Payroll Deductions (L.O. 6)

The following selected transactions of Mattingly Company were completed during the accounting year just ended, December 31, 1991.

a. Merchandise was purchased on account; a $10,000, one-year, 16% interest-bearing note, dated April 1, 1991, was given to the creditor. Assume a perpetual inventory system.
b. Cosigned an $8,000 note payable for another party (no entry required).
c. On July 1, the company borrowed cash; a one-year, noninterest-bearing note with a face amount of $28,750 was signed. Assume a going rate of interest at 15%.
d. Payroll records showed the following (assume amounts given are correct):

Gross Wages	Employee				Employer	
	ITD	UIC	CPP	Union Dues	UIC	CPP
$50,000	$15,000	$3,100	$2,900	$500	$4,340	$2,900

Remittances were ITD, $14,350; UIC, $7,250; CPP, $5,720; Union dues, $480.
e. The company was sued for $150,000 in damages. It appears a court judgment against the company that is reasonably estimated to be $125,000 is likely. For problem purposes, assume this is an extraordinary item.
f. On November 1, 1991, the company rented some office space in its building to Ildiko Company and collected rent in advance for six months; total, $2,400.
g. Cash dividends declared but not yet paid, $14,000.
h. Accrued interest on the notes at December 31.

Required:

1. Give the entry or entries for each of the preceding transactions and events.
2. Prepare a list (title and amount) of the disclosures related to the liabilities at December 31, 1991.

P 15–11
Contingencies and Warranty Costs (L.O. 7)

Cope Company is a manufacturer of household appliances. During the year, the following information became available:

a. Warranty costs on its household appliances are estimated to be 1% of sales.
b. One of its manufacturing plants is located in a foreign country. There is a threat of expropriation of this plant. The threat of expropriation is deemed to be reasonably possible. Any compensation from the foreign government would be less than the carrying amount of the plant.
c. Cope is likely to receive damages next year as a result of a lawsuit filed this year against another household appliances manufacturer.

Required:

In answering the following, do not discuss deferred income tax implications:

1. How should Cope report the warranty costs? Why?
2. How should Cope report the threat of expropriation of assets? Why?
3. How should Cope report this year the damages that may be received next year? Why?

(AICPA adapted)

P 15–12
Contingencies and
Warranty Costs
(L.O. 7)

Spackenkill Company is a manufacturer of household appliances. During the year, the following information became available:

a. Potential costs due to the discovery of a safety hazard related to one of its products—These costs are likely and can be reasonably estimated.
b. Potential costs of new product warranty costs—These costs are likely but cannot be reasonably estimated.
c. Potential costs due to the discovery of a possible product defect related to one of its products— These costs are reasonably possible and can be reasonably estimated.

Required:
1. How should Spackenkill report the potential costs due to the discovery of a safety hazard? Why?
2. How should Spackenkill report the potential costs of warranty costs? Why?
3. How should Spackenkill report the potential costs due to the discovery of a possible product defect? Why?

(AICPA adapted)

P 15–13
Compensated Absences
(L.O. 6)

Carol Company has many long-time employees who have built up substantial employee benefits. These employee benefits include compensation for future vacations.

Required:
What conditions must be met for Carol to accrue compensation for future vacations? Include in your answer the theoretical rationale for accruing compensation for future vacations.

(AICPA adapted)

P 15–14

COMPREHENSIVE PROBLEM
♦

Overview: Liabilities,
Contingency Losses,
Recording, and Reporting
(L.O. 4, 6, 7)

The following selected transactions of Gaetti Company were completed during the current accounting year ended December 31, 1991:

a. March 1, 1991, borrowed $20,000 on a two-year, 12%, interest-bearing note.
b. April 1, 1991, borrowed cash and signed an $18,838, two-year, noninterest-bearing note (no interest was specified) due March 31, 1993. The market rate of interest for this level of risk was 16%.
c. June 1, 1991, purchased a special truck with a list price of $29,000. Paid $9,000 cash and signed a $20,000, one-year, noninterest-bearing note (no interest was specified). The market rate of interest for this level of risk was 16%.
d. During 1991, sold merchandise for $40,000 cash that carried a two-year warranty for parts and labour. A reasonable estimate of the cost of the warranty is 1½% of sales revenue. By December 31, 1991, actual warranty costs amounted to $250.
e. June 1, 1991, Gaetti cosigned and guaranteed payment of a $60,000, 14%, one-year note owed by a local supplier to City Bank. The bank required a cosignature; however, they believe that default by the debtor is only reasonably likely.
f. October–November 1991, to promote sales during these two months, Gaetti gave its customers 10,000 premium certificates based on cash sales. Each certificate turned in during December 1991 and January 1992 will reduce the price by 50 cents on all single items that sell for more than $20. A reasonable estimate is that 75% of the certificates will be redeemed. By December 31, 1991, 60% of those issued had been redeemed.
g. Year 1991, property taxes to be recorded monthly:
   1. Prior year property taxes, $2,087; expected to increase by 15% during 1991.
   2. December 10, 1991—Final tax assessment received, $2,500; paid on February 1, 1992, the latest payment date without penalty.
h. December 1991, dividends declared (not yet paid or issued):
   1. Cash, $18,000 (use payable account).
   2. Stock, $12,000 (use issuable account).
i. December 1991—Sales revenue (excluding sales taxes collected) for the month, $300,000. Sales tax 5%, applicable to 98% of the sales. No unpaid sales tax carried over from November 1991.
j. December 31, 1991, accrual of interest payable.

Required:

Round to the nearest dollar.

1. For each of the 10 transactions, give all entries that Gaetti should make in 1991 based on the data given.
2. List each current liability (account title and the amount) that should be reported on the 1991 balance sheet of Gaetti Company.

CASES

C 15–1
Evaluation of a Liability:
Recommendations
(L.O. 3)

Evans Equipment Company sells new and used earth-moving equipment. It uses a perpetual inventory system, and its accounting period ends December 31. On December 28, 1990, Evans purchased a used backhoe for resale, at an agreed price of $40,000. Terms of the purchase were: cash down payment, $10,000, plus a note payable, face amount, $30,000, maturity date, December 28, 1992. The company bookkeeper entered the equipment in the perpetual inventory account at $40,000 and reported no interest expense for 1990 because the note did not specify that any interest would be paid. In answer to a question by the newly engaged independent auditor, the bookkeeper said that the entry on maturity date of the note would be a debit to notes payable and a credit to cash of $30,000. The transaction was recorded on January 5, 1991, because it was on that date that Evans received the equipment and the cheque was drawn.

Required:

1. Evaluate the accounting treatment of the purchase of the equipment. Consider both theoretical and GAAP issues. State any assumptions that you make.
2. If the company's accounting seems in error, give recommendations for what should be done including reasons. Also provide the necessary journal entries. State any factual assumptions made.

C 15–2
Contingencies; Four
Situations
(L.O. 7)

Unlucky Company is preparing its annual financial statements at December 31, 1991, and is concerned about application of *CICA Handbook,* section 3290, "Accounting for Contingencies." Four unrelated situations are under consideration:

a. During 1992, a shopper sued the company for $500,000 for a claimed injury that occurred on the premises owned by Unlucky. No date for the trial has been set; however, the lawyer employed by Unlucky has completed a thorough investigation. Because it can be proven that the customer did fall on the premises, the legal counsel believes it will not be difficult for the plaintiff to prove injury. There is some evidence that it was due, at least partially, to negligence by the plaintiff. The attorney believes that it is not likely, but is reasonably possible, that the suit will be successful (for the plaintiff), but for a significantly smaller amount that cannot be reasonably estimated at this time.

b. The company had a $10,000, 8%, one-year note receivable from a customer. Unlucky discounted the note, with recourse, at the bank to obtain cash before its due date (June 1, 1992). If the maker does not pay the bank by the due date, Unlucky will have to pay it. The customer has an excellent credit rating (having never defaulted on a debt).

c. An outside party has filed a claim against Unlucky for $25,000 claiming that certain actions by Unlucky caused the party to lose a contract on which the estimated profit was this amount. In the opinion of the legal counsel engaged by Unlucky, it is unlikely that the claim will be successful. Counsel does not believe it will ever be brought to trial. If necessary, Unlucky will defend itself in court.

d. The company owns a small plant in a foreign country; the plant has a book value of $3 million and an estimated market value of $4 million. The foreign government has indicated its unalterable intention to expropriate the plant during the coming year and to reimburse Unlucky for 50% of the estimated market value.

Required:

For each situation, respond to the following:

1. What accounting recognition, if any, should be accorded each situation at the end of 1991? Explain why and give journal entries.
2. Indicate how each situation should be reported on the balance sheet and income statement.

C 15–3
Analysis of Actual
Financial Statements
(L.O. 2, 7)

Refer to the 1990 financial statements of Loblaw Companies (see the appendix at the end of the text) and respond to the following questions.

Required:

1. What current liabilities does Loblaw list on its balance sheet? Indicate the type of liability from the list under "What Is a Current Liability?" on page 717 of the text.
2. Does Loblaw discuss any of its current liabilities in the notes to its financial statements? If so, describe.
3. Does Loblaw have any contingent liabilities? If so, what are they?

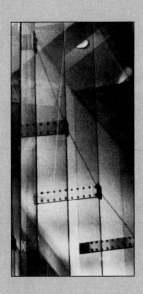

Long-Term Liabilities

After you have studied this chapter, you will be able to:

1. Define long-term liabilities and value them for financial reporting purposes.

2. Describe the characteristics of bonds and compute the price of a bond at issuance.

3. Account for basic and more complex bond situations from the viewpoints of both the issuer and investor.

4. Discuss the accounting issues surrounding long-term debt instruments issued with equity rights.

5. Describe the different ways long-term debt may be extinguished.

6. Calculate the value of long-term notes and measure periodic interest.

7. Account for serial bonds (refers to Appendix 16A).

8. Discuss the issues underlying accounting for troubled debt restructuring (refers to Appendix 16B).

◆

INTRODUCTION
◆

In 1989 business debt in Canada equaled $397,500 million or 56.2% of GDP. This is in comparison to total 1989 corporate after-tax profits of $35,955 million. Consumer debt rose from $46,620 million in 1981 to $92,820 million in 1989.[1]

In 1988 the average total debt to equity ratio was 75%.[2] Clearly, debt is providing and consuming through payments of principal and interest a large portion of corporate resources.

Debt, in particular long-term debt, is an increasingly important component of corporate financial structure. Long-term debt represents significant claims of outside parties on corporate assets and cash flows extending far into the future. The results of measurement, recognition, and disclosure of long-term debt (and related interest costs) are crucial to the assessment of a corporation's ability to survive and to provide cash flows to shareholders.

For example, many companies are facing a potentially devastating liability for toxic-waste cleanup. Although these liabilities have seldom been reported, section 3060 of the *CICA Handbook* requires companies to state on their balance sheets the estimated liability for restoring capital assets to environmentally sound conditions.

Deregulation of the airline industry and the resulting increased competition prompted the airlines to develop creative programs to lure passengers. The frequent-flier plan is a popular example. Passengers accrue credits for distances flown. These credits can be converted into free airline tickets. In 1988, it was estimated that the total value of such credits for all airlines exceeded $1.7 billion. Some accountants argue that disclosure of these liabilities in the balance sheet should be required.

The following outline highlights this chapter's major topics in accounting for long-term debt:

◆ Characteristics and valuation of long-term liabilities.
◆ Bonds payable: characteristics, valuation, accounting principles for issuer and investor, bonds issued with equity rights.
◆ Debt extinguishment: by open-market purchase, by call, by refunding, by in-substance defeasance.
◆ Long-term notes and mortgages.
◆ Additional issues and disclosures.
◆ Accounting for serial bonds (Appendix 16A).
◆ Troubled debt restructure (Appendix 16B).

Income taxes, pensions, and leases are topics that also involve long-term liabilities; they are discussed in later chapters.

◆

CHARACTERISTICS AND VALUATION OF LONG-TERM LIABILITIES
◆

CICA Handbook, paragraph 1000.28, defines liabilities as:

> obligations of an entity arising from past transactions or events, the settlement of which may result in the transfer or use of assets, provision of services or other yielding of economic benefits in the future.

A long-term liability is an obligation that fulfills this definition and that extends beyond one year from the current balance sheet date or the operating cycle of the debtor (borrower), whichever is longer.

Debt capital is an attractive means of financing for the debtor. Creditors do not acquire voting privileges in the debtor company. Debt capital is obtained more easily than

---

[1] The Financial Post Company, *Report on the Nation* (Toronto: October 1990)

[2] Statistics Canada, *Financial Flow Accounts, 1989.*

equity capital for some new and risky firms. In some cases, the overall cost of debt financing is lower than equity financing. Interest expense, unlike dividends, is tax deductible. Furthermore, a successfully leveraged firm earns a rate of return on borrowed funds which exceeds the rate it must pay in interest.[3]

Debt financing often supplies the capital for expansion and takeover activities when issuance of new stock is difficult. The potential increase in profits from expansion can be sufficiently attractive to induce firms that traditionally shun debt to increase liability levels. For example, Adolph Coors Company planned the first major debt issue in its 117-year history to expand and increase its market share.[4]

However, leverage is dangerous if sales or earnings decline. Under these circumstances, interest expense becomes an increasing percentage of earnings. Business failures frequently are caused by incurring too much debt on unfulfilled expectations of high sales and profits. For example, Campeau Corporation reported significant financial difficulties in its 1990 annual report primarily due to assuming excessive debt.

In addition, debt agreements often restrict the operations and financial structure of the debtor company. The purpose of restrictions is to reduce the risk of default. Restrictions may include ceilings on dividends and future debt, requirements that specific income and liquidity levels be maintained and creation of **sinking funds** to ensure that adequate funds are available to extinguish the debt. A sinking fund is a cash fund restricted for a specific purpose; it is classified as an investment. Violation of restrictions places the debtor in technical default, meaning that the debt is due at the creditor's discretion.

From the investor's point of view, creditors enjoy the increased security of legally enforceable debt payments, eventual return of principal, and prior claim to assets on corporate liquidation. Although debt investments provide, on average, a lower overall return to investors than equity investments, they are generally less risky. Debt securities with claims on specific assets reduce the risk further.

An example of sinking fund debt is included in the 1990 financial statements of John Labatt Limited:

Sinking fund debentures (in millions)	1990	1989
7⅜% Series F to mature April 15, 1992	$—	$ 2
9½% Series G to mature September 1, 1990	10	10
8½% Series H to mature March 1, 1993	10	10
9¼% Series I to mature March 15, 1994	12	13
11⅜% Series J to mature October 1, 1999	31	32

Maturities and sinking fund requirements for the years ending April 30, 1991, through 1995 are $27 million, $109 million, $113 million, $17 million, and $6 million, respectively.

The sinking fund debentures are secured by a floating charge on the undertaking, property, and assets of John Labatt Limited. At April 30, 1990, the company had satisfied all of the covenants under the trust deed relating to the sinking fund debentures.

Three General Valuation and Measurement Principles These measurement and valuation principles, discussed in Chapter 8, apply to long-term liabilities as well as long-term notes receivable. Three general principles are emphasized:

◆ First, long-term liabilities are recorded at the fair value of goods or services obtained by incurring debt. The market rate of interest is the rate implicit in the transaction and equates the present value of the required future cash payments to the fair value of goods and services.[5]

---

[3] Chapter 25 discusses financial leverage in more detail.

[4] "Adolph Coors Might Offer Millions in Debt," *The Wall Street Journal*, March 16, 1990, p. C21.

[5] If the fair value of goods and services cannot be determined, the liability is recorded at the present value of required future cash payments discounted at the market interest rate for similar debt instruments.

♦ Second, periodic interest expense is based on the market interest rate on the date of debt issuance, and the liability balance at the beginning of the reporting period.

♦ Third, the book value of long-term debt at a balance-sheet date is the present value of all remaining cash payments required, discounted at the market interest rate at issuance. The rate of interest used for this purpose is not changed during the term of the debt.

These three principles are the foundation for measuring and recording long-term debt and interest expense.

BONDS PAYABLE

A **bond** is a debt security issued by companies and government units to secure large amounts of capital on a long-term basis. Bonds are legal documents representing a formal promise by the issuing firm to pay principal and interest in return for the capital invested by the bondholders (investors).

A formal bond agreement, or **bond indenture,** specifies the terms of the bonds and the rights and duties of issuer and bondholder. The indenture specifies any restrictions on the issuing company, the dollar amount authorized for issuance, the interest rate and payment dates, the maturity date, conversion and call privileges, and the responsibilities of an independent trustee appointed to protect the interests of both the issuer and the investors. The trustee, usually a financial institution, maintains the necessary records and disburses interest and principal. The investors receive bond certificates, representing the contractual obligations of the issuer to the investors.

Bonds normally are issued in small denominations such as $1,000 and $10,000. The small denominations increase the affordability of the bonds and allow investors greater diversification in their portfolios which in turn reduces overall investment risk.

Bonds may be marketed in several ways. Typically, an entire bond issue is sold to investment bankers. Investment bankers may underwrite (assist in selling and assume all or part of the risk) the bond issue at a specified price to individual investors, thus realizing underwriter's compensation. Alternatively, the underwriting firm may purchase the bond issue outright, guarantee a price to the issuing firm, and risk selling the bonds at a greater price. Private direct placement with financial institutions and individual investors is an alternative to underwriting.

Many bond issues are offered through a **prospectus.** A prospectus is a document that includes audited financial statements of the issuer and states the offering price; it also describes (1) the securities offered, (2) the issuing company's business, and (3) the conditions under which the securities will be sold. To announce the bond issue, an advertisement similar to the one in Exhibit 16–1, which indicates the details of the bond issue and includes a list of the underwriters, typically appears in the financial press.

Many actively traded bond issues are listed on a daily basis by exchanges. Trades between investors are not recorded by the issuing company. Newspapers such as Toronto's *Globe and Mail* daily publish information about listed bonds (see Exhibit 16–1).

Information about the risk of bond issues is available from Standard & Poor's Corporation, Moody's Investor Services, and other rating services. These services use the following quality designations and rating symbols:

	Rating Symbols	
Quality Designation	**Standard & Poor's**	**Moody's**
Prime . . . . AAA		Aaa
Excellent . . . . AA		Aa
Upper medium . . . . A		A
Lower medium . . . . BBB		Baa
Marginally speculative . . . . BB		Ba
Very speculative . . . . B		B, Caa
Default . . . . D		Ca, C

EXHIBIT 16-1   Example of an Ontario Hydro Advertisement for a New Bond Issue

FINANCIAL NOTICES

These Securities having been sold, this announcement appears as a matter of record only.

New Issue

April 1991

Canadian $3,990,000,000

(aggregate principal amount at maturity for all series)

Ontario Hydro

Zero Coupon Canadian Dollar Bonds

with Serial Maturities From April 11, 1992 to April 11, 2031

Irrevocably and unconditionally guaranteed by

Province of Ontario
(Canada)

Merrill Lynch & Co.	Nomura International	ScotiaMcLeod Inc.
Nesbitt Thomson Deacon Inc.		RBC Dominion Securities Inc.

Burns Fry Limited	Deutsche Bank Capital Markets Limited
Goldman Sachs International Limited	IBJ International Limited
Morgan Stanley International	Salomon Brothers International Limited
UBS Phillips & Drew Securities Limited	Wood Gundy Inc.

Source: *Globe and Mail*, April 19, 1991, p. B14.

The bond rating reflects the issuing company's perceived ability to pay principal and interest and is affected by the firm's recent financial statements. For example, the medium and long-term obligations of Citibank Canada and Citicorp Ltd. were downgraded in 1990 to reflect the increased risk and earnings volatility in the commercial real estate sector. Dominion Bond Rating Service Ltd. also cited Citicorp's exposure to highly leveraged transactions and loans to developing countries.[6] A firm's bond rating affects the bond price and the ability of the company to raise additional debt capital.[7]

Classification of Bonds

Investors have a wide variety of investment goals, preferences, and policies. As a result, many different types of bonds are issued. The following classification of bonds reflects this diversity.

1. Issuing entity.
   a. Industrial bonds: issued by private companies.
   b. Government bonds: issued by public entities.
2. Collateral.
   a. Secured bonds: supported by a lien on specific assets; bondholders have first claim on proceeds from sale of secured assets.
   b. Debenture bonds: unsecured; backed only by issuer's credit; on bankruptcy of issuer, bondholders become general creditors for distribution of issuer's assets.[8]
3. Purpose of issue.
   a. Purchase money bonds: issued in full or part payment for property.
   b. Refunding bonds: issued to retire existing bonds.
   c. Consolidated bonds: issued to replace several existing issues.
4. Payment of interest.
   a. Ordinary (term) bonds: provide cash interest at a stated rate.
   b. Income bonds: interest is dependent on issuer's income.
   c. Registered bonds: pay interest only to the person in whose name the bond is recorded or registered.
   d. Coupon bonds: pay interest on receipt of coupons detached from bonds.
5. Maturity.
   a. Ordinary (term) bonds: mature at a single specified date.
   b. Serial bonds: mature on several installment dates.
   c. Callable bonds: issuer can retire bonds before maturity date.
   d. Redeemable bonds: bondholder can compel early redemption.
   e. Convertible bonds: bondholder can convert bonds into equity securities of the issuer.

Valuation of Bonds Payable

Several bond features contribute to the valuation of, and accounting for, a bond issue. To illustrate, assume that late in 1990, Randolph Company plans to issue $100,000 of 10%, $1,000 face value debentures dated January 1, 1991.[9] The bonds mature

---

[6] *Globe and Mail*, "Report on Business," November 24, 1990, p. B6.

[7] Some argue that bond rating agencies are too slow to react to changes in risk. For example, Moody's did not reduce the rating of the bonds of Integrated Resources until their value declined 50% in market value. See "Guess Who's Talking Tough on Junk. Staid Moody's," *The Wall Street Journal*, February 23, 1990, p. C1.

[8] Junk bonds are high-interest rate, high-risk, unsecured bonds. They were used extensively in the 1980s to finance leveraged buyouts.

[9] Debenture bonds are used for the example, but the general valuation principles apply to most bond issues.

December 31, 2000, and pay interest on June 30 and December 31. These five features are generally noted in the bond indenture, appear on the bond, and do not change:

1. The face (maturity, principal, or par) value of a bond is the single amount payable when the bond is due ($1,000 per bond for Randolph).
2. The maturity date is the end of the bond term and the due date for the face value (December 31, 2000, for Randolph). The length of the bond term reflects the issuer's long-term cash needs, the purposes for which the funds will be used, and the expected ability to pay principal and interest.
3. The stated (coupon, nominal, contractual) interest rate is the rate applied to face value to determine periodic interest payments (10% for Randolph). This rate is normally set to approximate the rate of interest on bonds of a similar risk class.
4. The interest payment dates are the dates the periodic interest payments are due (June 30 and December 31 for Randolph). Semiannual interest payments are common.[10] Randolph pays $50 interest on these dates for each bond ($1,000 × 10% × ½), regardless of issue price or market rate of interest at date of issue.
5. The bond date is the earliest date the bond may be issued and represents the planned issuance date of the bond issue (January 1, 1991, for Randolph).

Two other features necessary for valuation do not appear on the bond and are dependent on market factors:

6. The market (effective yield) interest rate is the true compounded rate that equates the price of the bond issue to the present value of the interest payments and face value. This rate is not necessarily the same as the stated rate. (Assume this rate is 12% for the Randolph issue.)
7. The bond issue date is the date the bonds are actually sold to investors. Bonds are often issued after the bond date. (Assume the issue date is July 1, 1991, for the Randolph issue.)

The process of issuing bonds often requires more time than expected, causing the bonds to be issued after the bond date. The process includes registration with the appropriate securities commission, negotiations with underwriters, printing, and other clerical tasks. Changes in the firm and in the economy can increase the difficulty of marketing bonds. The issuing company may also delay issuance to take advantage of declining interest rates.

The market interest rate depends on several interrelated factors including the general rate of interest in the economy, the perceived risk of the bond issue, yields on bonds of similar risk, inflation expectations, the overall supply of and demand for bonds, and the bond term.

Bond Prices If the market and stated interest rates are equal, bonds sell at face value. In this case, the interest payments yield a return equal to the market rate for bonds of similar duration and risk. However, the stated and market rates are frequently not the same. Changes in the market rate and issue price are inversely related. If the market rate (12%) exceeds the stated rate (10%), the issue price of the Randolph bonds must be below face value to give the investor a return equal to the market rate. Investors are not willing to pay the $1,000 face value per bond (a price that yields 10%) because competing debt securities yield 12%.

When the market interest rate exceeds the stated rate, bonds sell at a **discount** (below face value). For example, the Randolph bonds sold at a discount. When the stated rate exceeds the market rate, the reverse is true and the bonds sell at a **premium**

---

[10] The decision to pay interest twice per year represents a trade off between investors' desire for more frequent cash payments and the issuing company's desire to reduce clerical costs.

(above face value). In this case, the bonds offer a stated rate above the market rate, making them more attractive. The price of the bonds increases until the yield decreases to the market rate. The terms *discount* and *premium* do not imply negative or positive qualities of the bond issue. They are the result of adjustments to the selling price to bring the yield rate in line with the market rate on similar bonds.

The investor buys two different types of cash flows when purchasing a bond: principal and interest. The price of a bond issue (and valuation at issuance) equals the present value of these payments discounted at the market rate of interest:

Present value of principal
$100,000(PV1, 6\%^a, 19^b) = \$100,000(.33051)$ $33,051
Present value of interest payments
$100,000(.10)(\frac{1}{2})(PVA, 6\%, 19) = \$5,000(11.15812)$ 55,791
Price of Randolph bonds, July 1, 1991 . . . . $88,842

Discount on bonds ($100,000 − $88,842). $11,158

^{a} Market rate of interest: 12% (6% per semiannual period).

^{b} Bond term: July 1, 1991, through December 31, 2000; 19 semiannual periods.

Investors who purchase the Randolph bonds at a discount and hold them for the entire term earn 6% compounded semiannually on their original investment of $88,842. Although issuers usually attempt to set the stated rate close to the expected market rate at issuance (which minimizes the discount or premium), deep discount bonds and zero coupon bonds are exceptions.

Deep discount bonds sell for a small fraction of face value because the stated interest rate is much lower than the market rate. Zero coupon bonds pay no interest whatsoever. The investor receives only one payment: face value at maturity. For example, if the Randolph bonds were zero coupon bonds, they would sell for $33,051, the present value of the maturity payment.

Deep discount bonds and zeros are issued for a variety of reasons.[11] The issue price is small relative to face value and this attracts investors. Zeros, and all bonds issued at a discount, increase in value each year as they approach maturity. Although the annual increase in value of a zero is taxable, investors can structure their investment to defer taxes until maturity (e.g., through an individual retirement account). When so structured, zeros are a popular investment for parents wishing to save for their children's college education. Issuing companies find the reduced or nonexistent interest payments attractive.

After issuance, bond prices and interest rate changes are inversely related. Firm-specific factors such as changes in income, financial position, and risk also affect bond prices.

Bond prices are quoted as a percentage of face value to accommodate all denominations. For example, a $1,000 bond quoted at 97 sells for $970 (.97 × $1,000). Exhibit 16–2 is an excerpt from a table of bond prices in the *Globe and Mail*.

Bond prices exclude accrued interest at the stated rate. Total proceeds on bonds sold between interest dates include accrued interest since the last interest date. If the Randolph bonds sell on August 1, 1991, at 90, for example, total proceeds are computed as follows:

Price [.90($100,000)]. $90,000
Accrued interest from July 1, 1991
    [$100,000(.10)(\frac{1}{12})].   833
Proceeds $90,833

---

[11] Zero coupon bonds were first conceived in 1973 during the Arab oil embargo. Investment bankers worried that selling interest-bearing bonds would be difficult to market in the Middle East because the Koran prohibits interest. See "A Strange Breed of Bond," *Forbes*, May 25, 1981, p. 142.

EXHIBIT 16-2 Canadian Bond Prices

Explanation: the listed bond issue of Alcan Aluminum Limited (ALCAN) has a stated interest rate of 12.45%, matures November 7, 1997, and has a current yield, or effective interest rate, of 11.034% if purchased at the close of business on March 19, 1991, for the closing price of 106.5 (106.5% × face value). The current yield, as listed, is a one-year approximation to the true compounded rate.

The Globe and Mail, Tuesday, March 19, 1991

CANADIAN BONDS

Selected quotations, with changes since the previous day, on actively traded bond issues, provided by RBC Dominion Securities. Yields are calculated to full maturity, unless marked C to indicate callable date. Price is the midpoint between final bid and ask quotations Mar. 18, 1991.

Issuer	Coupon	Maturity	Price	Yield	$ Chg
GOVERNMENT OF CANADA					
CANADA	9.25	5 MAR 93	99.700	9.417	-0.200
CANADA	9.50	1 SEP 93	99.925	9.530	-0.200
CANADA	10.25	1 FEB 94	101.550	9.610	-0.300
CANADA	9.25	1 OCT 94	99.250	9.504	-0.350
CANADA	10.00	1 MAR 95	101.175	9.630	-0.400
CANADA	9.25	1 MAY 96	98.675	9.580	-0.600
CANADA	9.75	1 OCT 97	100.425	9.660	-0.700
CANADA	9.50	1 OCT 98	98.925	9.704	-0.850
CANADA	9.25	1 DEC 99	97.125	9.744	-1.000
CANADA	10.50	1 JUL 00	104.075	9.815	-0.950
CANADA	10.50	1 MAR 01	104.175	9.830	-1.000
CANADA	9.75	1 JUN 01	100.075	9.734	-0.950
CANADA	9.50	1 OCT 01	98.275	9.765	-1.000
CANADA	10.00	1 MAY 02	100.925	9.858	-1.000
CANADA	11.75	1 FEB 03	111.450	10.070	-1.000
CANADA	10.25	1 FEB 04	102.500	9.899	-1.000
CANADA	10.00	1 JUN 08	99.625	10.043	-1.250
CANADA	9.50	1 JUN 10	96.125	9.953	-1.375
CANADA	9.00	1 MAR 11	92.250	9.896	-1.375
CANADA	10.25	15 MAR 14	102.000	10.025	-1.375
CANADA	11.25	1 JUN 15	109.750	10.157	-1.375
CANADA	10.50	15 MAR 21	104.075	10.066	-1.350
PROVINCIAL					
ALBERTA	10.75	15 JAN 96	102.100	10.179	-0.550
ALBERTA TEL	9.50	8 JUL 97	97.050	10.139	-0.700
B C	11.00	20 JUN 95	102.750	10.175	-0.450
B C	11.25	16 AUG 00	104.950	10.408	-0.950
B C	10.75	21 FEB 11	100.950	10.632	-1.200
HYDRO QUEBEC	11.25	10 OCT 00	102.475	10.826	-0.950
HYDRO QUEBEC	11.00	15 AUG 20	99.125	11.099	-1.400
MANITOBA	11.25	17 OCT 00	104.350	10.515	-0.950
MANITOBA	10.50	5 MAR 31	97.400	10.783	-1.250
NEW BRUNSWIC	11.25	18 OCT 95	102.525	10.535	-0.450
NEW BRUNSWIC	11.25	13 DEC 00	102.775	10.776	-0.900
NEWFOUNDLAND	10.13	22 NOV 14	89.850	11.366	-1.200
NFLD&LAB HYD	9.88	15 JUL 96	96.775	10.679	-0.550
N S POWER	11.85	24 OCT 95	104.475	10.586	-0.450

Issuer	Coupon	Maturity	Price	Yield	$ Chg
N S POWER	11.00	26 FEB 31	99.225	11.085	-1.250
ONTARIO HYD	11.50	16 JUN 92	102.000	9.703	-0.100
ONTARIO HYD	10.00	16 JUN 93	100.450	9.755	-0.200
ONTARIO HYD	10.75	19 NOV 95	102.000	10.192	-0.450
ONTARIO HYD	10.88	8 JAN 96	102.325	10.240	-0.550
ONTARIO HYD	9.63	3 AUG 99	96.150	10.319	-1.000
ONTARIO HYD	10.00	19 MAR 01	97.900	10.342	-0.950
ONTARIO HYD	9.25	6 JAN 04	91.400	10.482	-1.000
ONTARIO HYD	10.00	17 OCT 14	94.600	10.627	-1.150
ONTARIO HYD	11.00	1 OCT 20	103.700	10.588	-1.250
ONTARIO	10.75	1 MAY 96	101.900	10.257	-0.550
ONTARIO	10.88	10 JAN 01	102.750	10.415	-0.950
P E I	11.00	14 MAR 11	97.825	11.275	-1.100
QUEBEC	10.75	12 MAR 96	100.925	10.504	-0.600
QUEBEC	10.00	26 APR 00	95.525	10.781	-0.850
SASKATCHEWAN	10.50	15 APR 94	100.775	10.193	-0.250
SASKATCHEWAN	10.75	21 FEB 96	101.100	10.453	-0.550
SASKATCHEWAN	11.00	9 JAN 01	101.825	10.689	-0.900
SASKATCHEWAN	10.25	10 APR 14	93.950	10.975	-1.200
TORONTO -MET	10.25	20 MAR 01	98.700	10.462	-0.900
CORPORATE					
ALCAN	12.45	7 NOV 97	106.500	11.034	-0.750
BELL CANADA	10.50	15 MAY 98	100.625	10.369	-0.875
BELL CANADA	11.45	15 APR 10	104.750	10.853	-1.250
BC TELEPHONE	10.50	12 JUN 00	99.625	10.559	-0.875
BC TELEPHONE	11.90	22 NOV 15	107.625	10.993	-1.375
CDN IMP BANK	10.38	31 JAN 00	97.625	10.793	-0.750
CDN UTIL	11.77	30 NOV 20	106.750	10.992	-1.375
HOUSEHOLD FN	12.40	1 NOV 95	103.625	11.359	-0.500
IMPERIAL OIL	9.88	15 DEC 99	96.750	10.446	-0.875
IMASCO LTD	11.85	15 FEB 96	103.500	10.901	-0.500
ROYAL BANK	11.00	11 JAN 02	101.500	10.756	-0.875
ROYAL BANK	10.50	1 MAR 02	98.750	10.694	-0.875
SEARS CANADA	11.75	5 DEC 95	102.500	11.043	-0.375
TRANSALTA UT	11.50	15 DEC 00	105.000	10.656	-1.000
TRANSCDA PIP	11.90	20 AUG 15	104.875	11.306	-1.125
UNION GAS	11.50	28 AUG 15	101.500	11.316	-1.375

Source: *Globe and Mail*, March 19, 1991, p. B10.

An investor who purchases the bonds on August 1 and holds the bonds five months to December 31 earns only five months' worth of interest. Yet the investor receives six months' worth of interest on December 31. Therefore, the investor must pay one month of interest at purchase. This system facilitates trading of bonds.

Fundamental Bond Accounting Principles for Issuer and Investor

Although the primary focus of this chapter is on accounting for the debtor company, accounting for the bondholder (investor) is also illustrated. The accounting concepts and procedures are essentially the same. A long-term liability for the debtor is usually a long-term investment (or receivable) for the creditor. At issuance, both parties record the same amounts and use the same interest rate.[12] Chapter 14 discussed accounting for investments in short-term debt securities.

To demonstrate accounting for bonds, several case examples are used which illustrate different reporting situations. In Case 1, bonds are issued on the bond date and at the beginning of the fiscal year. Three different effective interest rates are illustrated.

Case 1: Common information: bonds issued on bond date, the beginning of fiscal year.

On January 1, 1991, Gresham Company issues $100,000 of 7% debentures dated January 1, 1991, which pay interest December 31. The bonds mature on December 31, 1995. Elmhurst Company purchased the entire bond issue. Both companies have calendar years.

Part A: effective interest rate = 7%

Part B: effective interest rate = 6%

Part C: effective interest rate = 8%

Case 1, Part A: Bonds sell at face value; effective and stated rate = 7%

$$\text{Price} = \$100,000(PV1, 7\%, 5) + \$100,000(.07)(PVA, 7\%, 5)$$

$$= \$100,000(.71299) + \$7,000(4.10020) = \$100,000$$

When a bond is issued, the issuer records the maturity value of the bond in bonds payable, a long-term liability account. The investor records the cash equivalent paid for the bond in an investment account. In this case, the maturity value equals the amount paid. The following entries are made during the bond term assuming Elmhurst holds the bonds to maturity.

Gresham Company (Issuer)		Elmhurst Company (Investor)	

January 1, 1991—Issue bonds:

Cash	100,000		Bond investment	100,000	
Bonds payable		100,000	Cash		100,000

December 31, 1991 to 1995—Interest payment:

Interest expense	7,000		Cash	7,000	
Cash			Interest revenue		7,000
($100,000 × .07)		7,000			

December 31, 1995–Bond maturity:

Bonds payable	100,000		Cash	100,000	
Cash		100,000	Bond investment		100,000

Interest expense for bonds issued at face value equals the amount of the interest payment. The book value of the bonds remains $100,000 to maturity for both firms. Subsequent changes in the market rate of interest are ignored for journal entry purposes.[13] At maturity, bonds payable and the investment account are closed as shown in the last preceding entry. Matured bonds are canceled to prevent reissuance.

---

[12] However, transaction costs can cause the rates used by the investor and the issuer to differ.

[13] Some accountants argue that the market interest rate should be incorporated into accounting for bonds. Otherwise, the book value of the debt does not equal its market value. However, it is assumed that the bond will be carried to maturity, in which case the market rate at issuance reflects the true interest rate over the bond term.

Case 1, Part B: Bonds sell at a premium, effective rate = 6%

$$Price = \$100,000(PV1, 6\%, 5) + \$100,000(.07)(PVA, 6\%, 5)$$

$$= \$100,000(.74726) + \$7,000(4.21236) = \$104,213$$

The bonds sell at a premium because they pay a stated rate that exceeds the yield rate on similar bonds. The $4,213 premium is recorded in premium on bonds payable, an adjunct valuation account. The premium increases the net bond liability. The present value (which equals book value) at issue date ($104,213) is the amount which, if invested by the issuing company at the effective interest rate, satisfies all payments required on the bond issue including the face value. The following entry records the issue:

Gresham Company			**Elmhurst Company**	
(Issuer)			**(Investor)**	

January 1, 1991—Issue bonds:

Cash	104,213		Bond investment 104,213	
Bonds payable		100,000	Cash	104,213
Premium on bonds				
payable		4,213		

Investors typically do not use premium or discount accounts (the gross method) to account for long-term investments in bonds. In contrast, issuers tend to use the gross method as just illustrated. If the investor does not intend to hold bonds for a long period, separate disclosure of the premium or discount has little value.[14]

Total interest expense for a bond issue equals total cash payments required by the bond (face value and interest) less the aggregate issue price. Total interest expense is not equal to total cash interest over the term for a bond sold at a premium or discount, as shown for Gresham Company:

Face value	$100,000
Total cash interest [.07($100,000)(5 years)]	35,000
Total cash payments required by bond.	135,000
Issue price	104,213
Total interest expense for bond term	$ 30,787

Elmhurst paid $4,213 more than face value but will receive only face value at maturity, and the effective rate is less than the stated rate. Therefore, total interest expense for Gresham over the bond term is less than total interest paid.

Subsequent to acquisition, the premium or discount is amortized over the bond term by the issuer. An amortized premium reduces periodic interest expense relative to interest paid, and amortized discount increases interest expense. The net bond liability equals face value plus the remaining unamortized bond premium or less the remaining unamortized bond discount. The discount or premium is completely amortized by the end of the bond term. Therefore, net book value equals face value at maturity.

Interest Method   Two amortization methods are in use: the interest method and the straight-line method. The interest method is preferable because it applies the correct yield rate to the liability balance at the beginning of each period. That liability balance represents the true present value of the obligation at that date. The straight-line method amortizes an equal amount of premium or discount per month. In certain situations

---

[14] Under the gross method, Elmhurst would record:

Bond investment	100,000	
Premium on bond investment	4,213	
Cash		104,213

(discussed later), the straight-line method is not appropriate. The interest method is illustrated first, in the entries for the first two years:

Interest Method

Gresham Company (Issuer)	Elmhurst Company (Investor)

December 31, 1991—Interest payment:

Interest expense	6,253*		Cash.	7,000
Premium on bonds			Bond investment.	747
payable	747		Interest revenue	6,253
Cash				
($100,000 × .07)		7,000		

*$6,253 = $104,213(.06)

December 31, 1992—Interest payment:

Interest expense	6,208*		Cash.	7,000
Premium on bonds			Bond investment.	792
payable	792		Interest revenue	6,208
Cash				
($100,000 × .07)		7,000		

*$6,208 = ($104,213 − $747) (.06)

GRESHAM COMPANY
Partial Long-Term Liability Section of Balance Sheet
December 31, 1992

Bonds payable	$100,000
Unamortized premium on bonds payable	
($4,213 − $747 − $792)	2,674
Net book value of bonds payable	$102,674

Interest expense under the interest method is the product of the effective interest rate (6%) and net liability balance at the beginning of the period. Interest expense is, therefore, a constant percentage of beginning book value. The investor receives part of the original investment back with each interest payment.[15] In 1991, this amount is $747, which reduces the net bond liability at the beginning of 1992. Consequently, 1992 interest expense is less for 1991. The book value of the bonds at December 31, 1992, is the present value of remaining cash flows:

$$\$102,674 = \$100,000(PV1, 6\%, 3) + \$100,000(.07)(PVA, 6\%, 3)$$

$$= \$100,000(.83962) + \$7,000(2.67301)$$

The *CICA Handbook*, paragraph 3070.02, recommends that debt discount and expense be included as part of deferred charges on the balance sheet. In practice, many firms do not disclose the unamortized premium or discount as a separate line item in the balance sheet. The unamortized discount or premium is typically disclosed in a footnote or parenthetically in the balance sheet.

An **amortization table** often is prepared by the issuer to support bond journal entries. The table gives all the data necessary to make the journal entries over the term of the bond, and each year's ending net liability balance. An amortization table for Gresham is shown in Exhibit 16–3. This table repeats the information recorded in the earlier 1991 and 1992 entries.

Straight-Line Method This popular alternative to the interest method directly determines the amortization of premium or discount. An equal amount of discount or

---

[15] The amortization period for the issuer runs from date of sale to maturity date (the bond term); for the investor, it runs from the purchase date to maturity date. The example assumes Elmhurst holds the bonds to maturity.

EXHIBIT 16–3   Amortization Table for Gresham Company Bonds Sold at Premium—
Interest Method

Date	(a) Interest Payment	(a) Interest Expense	(b) Premium Amortization	(c) Unamortized Premium	(d) Net Bond Liability
January 1, 1991				$4,213	$104,213
December 31, 1991	$ 7,000	$ 6,253	$ 747	3,466	103,466
December 31, 1992	7,000	6,208	792	2,674	102,674
December 31, 1993	7,000	6,160	840	1,834	101,834
December 31, 1994	7,000	6,110	890	944	100,944
December 31, 1995	7,000	6,056	944	0	100,000
	$35,000	$30,787	$4,213		

a. (Previous net liability balance) (.06): $104,213(.06) = $6,253

b. (Interest payment) − (Interest expense): $7,000 − $6,253 = $747

c. (Previous unamortized premium) − (Current period amortization): $4,213 − $747 = $3,466

d. $100,000 + (Current unamortized premium): $100,000 + $3,466 = $103,466

premium is amortized each interest period. Interest expense equals the cash interest paid less premium amortized or plus the discount amortized. This method produces a stable dollar amount of interest expense each period rather than a constant rate of interest each period. The following entry is recorded each period by Gresham (premium example) under this method:

Straight-Line Method

<table>
<tr><td colspan="2" align="center">Gresham Company
(Issuer)</td><td colspan="2" align="center">Elmhurst Company
(Investor)</td></tr>
</table>

December 31, 1991–1995—Interest payment:

Interest expense 6,157		Cash. 7,000	
Premium on bonds		Bond investment	843
payable 843*		Interest revenue	6,157
Cash			
($100,000 × .07) 7,000			

*$843 = $4,213 ÷ 5 years

The straight-line method recognizes the average amount of interest each year ($6,157 = $30,787/5), while the interest method reflects the changing debt balance. The straight-line method is allowed when interest expense is not materially different under the two methods (*APB Opinion No. 21*, par. 15).

The use of the straight-line method is questionable when the discount or premium is significant, or when the bond term is exceptionally long. For example, the method seriously misstates interest expense early in the term of a zero coupon bond. Similarly, very long bond terms magnify the differences between the two methods because the initial net liability can be considerably smaller or larger than face value.[16]

Case 1, Part C: Bonds sell at a discount, effective rate = 8%

$$\text{Price} = \$100,000(PV1, 8\%, 5) + \$100,000(.07)\,(PVA, 8\%, 5)$$

$$= \$100,000(.68058) + \$7,000(3.99271) = \$96,007$$

The Gresham bonds sell at a discount because the stated rate is less than the yield rate on similar bonds. The discount is recorded in the discount on bonds payable

---

[16] For example, under the interest method, the issuer of 15%, $1,000, 25-year bonds yielding 10% ($1,454 issue price) recognizes $145 of interest expense in the first year per bond, 10% more than the $132 under the straight-line method.

EXHIBIT 16–4   Amortization Table for Gresham Company Bonds Sold at Discount—
Interest Method

Date	Interest Payment	(a) Interest Expense	(b) Discount Amortization	(c) Unamortized Discount	(d) Net Bond Liability
January 1, 1991				$3,993	$ 96,007
December 31, 1991	$ 7,000	$ 7,681	$ 681	3,312	96,688
December 31, 1992	7,000	7,735	735	2,577	97,423
December 31, 1993	7,000	7,794	794	1,783	98,217
December 31, 1994	7,000	7,857	857	926	99,074
December 31, 1995	7,000	7,926	926	0	100,000
	$35,000	$38,993	$3,993		

a. (Previous net liability balance) (.08): $96,007(.08) = $7,681

b. (Interest expense) − (Interest payment): $7,681 − $7,000 = $681

c. (Previous unamortized discount) − (Current period amortization): $3,993 − $681 = $3,312

d. $100,000 − (Current unamortized discount): $100,000 − $3,312 = $96,688

account. This account is a contra liability valuation account, which is subtracted from bonds payable to yield the net liability at present value. The entries for the first two years follow, along with an amortization table for the entire bond term (see Exhibit 16–4).

Gresham Company (Issuer)	Elmhurst Company (Investor)

January 1, 1991—Issue bonds:

Cash 96,007		Bond investment 96,007	
Discount on bonds		Cash	96,007
payable 3,993			
Bonds payable	100,000		

Interest Method

December 31, 1991—Interest expense:

Interest expense 7,681*		Cash. 7,000	
Discount on bonds		Bond investment 681	
payable	681	Interest revenue	7,681
Cash			
($100,000 × .07)	7,000		

* $7,681 = $96,007(.08)

December 31, 1992—Interest expense:

Interest expense 7,735*		Cash. 7,000	
Discount on bonds		Bond investment 735	
payable	735	Interest revenue	7,735
Cash			
($100,000 × .07)	7,000		

* $7,735 = ($96,007 + $681) (.08)

GRESHAM COMPANY
Partial Long-Term Liability Section of Balance Sheet
December 31, 1992

Bonds payable	$100,000
Unamortized discount on bonds payable	
($3,993 − $681 − $735)	(2,577)
Net book value of bonds payable	$ 97,423

EXHIBIT 16–5   Summary Table: Accounting for Bonds

Assume semiannual interest payments.

> Price of bond issue = Present value of principal and interest payments
>
> = (Face value) $(PV1, e, n)$ + (face value) (s) (PVA, e, n)

Where: e = effective interest rate per six-month period.
s = stated interest rate/2.
n = number of semiannual periods in bond term.

> Initial discount = Face value − Price of bond issue
> (effective rate exceeds stated rate)
>
> Initial premium = Price of bond issue − Face value
> (stated rate exceeds effective rate)
>
> Net book value of bonds = Face value + Unamortized premium, or
> Face value − Unamortized discount

	Premium	Discount
As maturity approaches:		
Unamortized	Declines	Declines
Net book value	Declines	Increases
Annual interest expense*	Declines	Increases

* Under interest method

Two Methods of Amortizing Premium and Discount

	Straight-Line Method	Interest Method
Annual interest expense	Constant over term	Changes each year
Annual interest expense as a percentage of beginning book value	Changes each year	Constant over term

The amortization of the discount increases the net liability causing interest expense to increase each year. As maturity approaches, the net liability increases to face value. The investor receives only $7,000 cash each year, but the value of the bond increases by the amount of the discount amortization. Discount amortization is the second component of interest expense. In 1991, this amount is $681, which increases the net bond liability at the beginning of 1992. Consequently, 1992 interest expense exceeds that of 1991. As Exhibit 16–4 illustrates, total interest expense for Gresham exceeds total cash paid by the amount of the initial discount.

Exhibit 16–5 summarizes several aspects of bond accounting.

CONCEPT REVIEW

1. How does a premium on bonds payable occur, and what does it represent?
2. Why is interest expense increased by the amount of discount amortized?
3. Why is the straight-line method of amortization not appropriate for deep discount bonds?

ADDITIONAL ISSUES IN ACCOUNTING FOR BONDS
◆

Accounting for bonds becomes somewhat more complex when the issue date or bond date does not coincide with the first day of the fiscal year, or with an interest payment date. However, the same basic principles already discussed are applicable. For Case 2, assume the Gresham Company bonds are issued during the fiscal year on an interest payment date.

Case 2: Interest payment date does not coincide with fiscal-year-end; bonds issued on interest payment date

Information for Gresham bond issue:

1. The bond date is March 31, 1991, and the maturity date is March 31, 1996.
2. The issue date is September 30, 1991.
3. The bonds pay interest on a semiannual basis: September 30 and March 31.
4. The stated interest rate is 8% (4% per semiannual period) and the effective interest rate is 6% (3% per semiannual period).
5. Face value: $100,000.
6. Both Gresham and Elmhurst have calendar years.

Therefore:

Bond term: $4\frac{1}{2}$ years, or 9 semiannual periods.

Price $= \$100,000(PV1, 3\%, 9) + \$100,000(.04)(PVA, 3\%, 9)$.

$= \$100,000(.76642) + \$4,000(7.78611) = \$107,786$.

Typically, the end of the accounting period does not coincide with an interest date. In this situation, the issuer and investor accrue interest on the bond issue from the last interest date in the accounting period to the end of the accounting period. The issuance entry, the adjusting entry, and the first two interest payment entries for Gresham and Elmhurst are recorded as follows under the interest method:

Gresham Company (Issuer)			Elmhurst Company (Investor)		

September 30, 1991—Issue bonds:

Cash	107,786		Bond investment	107,786	
Premium on bonds			Cash		107,786
payable		7,786			
Bonds payable		100,000			

Interest method

December 31, 1991—Recognize interest expense:

Interest expense	1,617*		Interest receivable	2,000	
Premium on bonds			Bond investment		383
payable	383		Interest revenue		1,617
Interest payable		2,000†			

* $\$1,617 = \$107,786(.06)(\frac{3}{12})$
† $\$2,000 = \$100,000(.08)(\frac{3}{12})$

GRESHAM COMPANY
Portion of Liability Section of Balance Sheet
December 31, 1991

Current liabilities:		
Interest payable		$ 2,000
Long-term liabilities:		
Bonds payable	$100,000	
Unamortized premium on bonds payable	7,403*	
Net book value of bonds payable		$107,403

* $\$7,403 = \$7,786 - \$383$

Under the interest method, when fiscal and interest periods do not coincide, interest expense is allocated on a proportional basis within interest periods. For example, the December 31, 1991, entry recognizes one half of the first semiannual interest expense amount.[17]

The March 31 entry, which follows, settles the interest payable from the previous year and recognizes the last half of the first semiannual interest expense amount. Assume reversing entries are not recorded.

Interest Method

Gresham Company (Issuer)		Elmhurst Company (Investor)	

March 31, 1992—Interest payment:

Interest expense	1,617*		Cash.	4,000
Premium on bonds payable	383		Bond investment	383
Interest payable.	2,000		Interest revenue	1,617
Cash ($100,000 × .08/2) . . .		4,000	Interest receivable	2,000

* $1,617 = $107,786(.06)($\frac{3}{12}$)

Only one quarter of a year's interest expense is recognized on this date. The $4,000 cash payment is comprised of the interest receivable from 1991, three months' interest in 1992, and a return of the original investment (premium amortization). For completeness, this is the September 30 entry:

Interest Method

Gresham Company (Issuer)		Elmhurst Company (Investor)	

September 30, 1992—Interest payment:

Interest expense	3,211*		Cash.	4,000
Premium on bonds payable	789		Bond investment	789
Cash ($100,000 × .08/2) . . .		4,000	Interest revenue	3,211

* $3,211 = ($107,786 − $383 − $383)(.06)($\frac{6}{12}$)

Amortization tables in this situation are based on interest periods rather than reporting periods. The information to compute the amounts in the preceding entries is found in the following partial amortization table for the interest method:

Date	Interest Payment	Interest Expense	Premium Amortization	Unamortized Premium	Net Bond Liability
Sept. 30, 1991				$7,786	$107,786
March 31, 1992	$4,000	$3,234	$766	7,020	107,020
Sept. 30, 1992	4,000	3,211	789	6,231	106,231

For example, the $383 of premium amortized on December 31, 1991, is one half of the $766 amount shown in the amortization column for March 31, 1992.

Bond Issue Costs Several costs are incurred in preparing and selling a bond issue. **Bond issue costs** include legal, accounting, underwriting, commission, engraving, printing, registration, and promotion costs. These costs are paid by the issuer and reduce the net proceeds from the bond issue, thus raising the effective interest rate for the issuer.

Bond issue costs are classified as a deferred charge (long-term asset) rather than a reduction of the premium or increase in the discount (*CICA Handbook*, paragraph 3070.02). Bond issue costs contribute to the financing of operations that produce revenue. Under the matching principle, bond issue costs are expensed against

---

[17] If Gresham used the straight-line method, $433 of premium ($7,786 × $\frac{1}{9}$ × $\frac{1}{2}$) is amortized, and $1,567 of interest expense ($2,000 − $433) is recognized on December 31.

revenues during the bond term. The straight-line method of amortization generally is used for expedience.

Derlan Industries disclosed the following information in its 1989 annual report related to debt issue costs:

(*Dollars in thousands*)	**1989**	**1988**
Other assets:		
Debentures and senior note issue expenses. . .	$749	$676

Note 1 (in part): Summary of Significant Accounting Policies:
Other assets:
> Issue costs of debentures and US$ Series A and B Unsecured Senior Notes are amortized over the 10-year life of the debentures and notes using the straight-line method.

To illustrate accounting for bond issue costs, assume $3,600 of bond issue costs are incurred to issue the bonds in Case 2 (4½-year bond term). The bond issue costs are amortized at the rate of $400 per semiannual period ($3,600/9 semiannual periods). Gresham makes the following entries in addition to those recorded for Case 2.

Gresham Company
(Issuer)

September 30, 1991—Record bond issue cost:

Bond issue cost	3,600	
Cash		3,600

December 31, 1991—Amortize bond issue cost:

Bond issue expense ($3,600 × ⅑ × ½)	200	
Bond issue cost		200

Effects on Gresham Company's 1991:

Income statement: Bond issue expense	$ 200
Balance sheet: Long-term deferred charge balance	$3,400

March 31, 1992—Amortize bond issue cost:

Bond issue expense	200	
Bond issue cost		200

According to some accountants, bond issue costs are not assets because they provide no future benefit. Rather, they reduce the funds derived from the bond issue. Treatment as an adjustment to the premium or discount, or as an expense of the borrowing period is appropriate according to this view. It appears, however, that the AcSB, in their discussions of this issue, will be adopting the view that these costs should be deferred (i.e., placed on the balance sheet) and amortized over the life of the related financial instrument.[18]

Bonds Issued between Interest Dates   In the previous two cases, bonds are issued on an interest date. The objective of these cases is to emphasize the principles underlying bond accounting. However, bonds typically are not issued on an interest date for the same reasons that the issue date is usually not the bond date. Two new problems arise: accounting for accrued interest since the most recent payment date, and computing the issue price.

---

[18] If the methods of amortizing premium or discount and bond issue costs are the same, deferral and amortization of bond issue costs yield the same income as does treating bond issue costs as a reduction of the proceeds. Only the classification of expense is different (interest expense versus bond issue expense). However, deferral and amortization (present GAAP) cause an asset to be recorded rather than a liability to be reduced.

Case 3: Bonds issued between interest payment dates

Information for Gresham bond issue:

1. The bond date is March 31, 1991, and the maturity date is March 31, 1996.
2. The issue date is June 1, 1991 (between interest dates).
3. The bonds pay interest each September 30 and March 31.
4. Face value: $100,000.
5. The stated rate is 8% and the effective interest rate is 10%.
6. Both Gresham and Elmhurst have calendar fiscal years.

The calculation of the price of a bond issued between interest payment dates must include the partial period between the issue date and the first interest payment date (June 1, 1991, to September 30, 1991, for Case 3), as follows:

```
Price of bond at immediately preceding interest date
  (March 31, 1991):
    Face value $100,000(PV1, 5%, 10) = $100,000(.61391) . . . . . .  $61,391
    Interest $100,000(.08/2)(PVA, 5%, 10) = $4,000(7.72173) . . . .   30,887
                                                                     ─────────
      Total present value . . . . . . . . . . . . . . . . . . . .            $92,278
Growth in bond value at yield rate, from March 31, 1991,
  to June 1, 1991: $92,278(.05)(⅖) . . . . . . . . . . . . . . . .             1,538
Cash interest at stated rate from March 31, 1991, to
  June 1, 1991: $100,000(.04)(⅖) . . . . . . . . . . . . . . . .              (1,333)
                                                                            ─────────
    Price of bond at June 1, 1991 . . . . . . . . . . . . . . . . .          $92,483
```

The $1,538 growth component is the normal interest return on the bond from March 31 to June 1 and is added for bonds issued at either a discount or premium. The cash interest is the portion of that return actually due September 30 as a separate payment. Therefore it is deducted from the bond price. Stated bond prices are exclusive of accrued interest at the stated rate.

Interpolation, using the bond prices at the two interest payment dates bordering the issue date, also can be used to determine the issue price:

```
Price at March 31, 1991 (from previous calculation):              $92,278

Price at September 30, 1991:
  Face value
    [$100,000(PV1, 5%, 9) = $100,000(.64461)] . . . . . .  $64,461
  Interest
    [$100,000(.08/2)(PVA, 5%, 9) = $4,000(7.10782)] . . .   28,431
                                                           ─────────
      Total present value . . . . . . . . . . . . . . . .           $92,892
```

Interpolated price at June 1, 1991:

$$\$92,278 - \tfrac{2}{6}(\$92,278 - \$92,892) = \$92,483$$

OR

$$\$92,892 + \tfrac{4}{6}(\$92,278 - \$92,892) = \$92,483$$

The bond issue date (June 1) is two months, that is, $\tfrac{2}{6}$ of a semiannual period after March 31. Therefore, $\tfrac{2}{6}$ of the difference between the March 31 and September 30 prices is subtracted from the March 31 price in the first interpolation. In the second interpolation, $\tfrac{4}{6}$ of the difference is added to the September 30 price to account for the additional four months the bond is outstanding. This approach is followed independently of whether the bond is issued at a premium or discount.[19]

---

[19] The two methods of computing the price of a bond between interest dates are equivalent because the difference in bond prices at adjacent interest dates equals the growth in bond value at the yield rate less the cash interest for an interest period. The first method applies the appropriate fraction of the partial interest period to the growth at the yield rate and subtracts the stated interest rate. The second method focusses only on the prices exclusive of accrued interest; therefore, no subtraction of accrued interest is necessary.

Accrued interest at the stated rate from March 31 to June 1 is collected from the investor. The initial discount or premium amount is independent of accrued interest and equals face value less the bond price, as usual. The following entry records the bond issuance:

Gresham Company (Issuer)			Elmhurst Company (Investor)	

June 1, 1991—Issue bonds:

Cash 93,816*			Bond investment 92,483	
Discount on bonds payable . . . . . 7,517†			Interest receivable 1,333	
Interest payable	1,333‡		Cash	93,816
Bonds payable	100,000			

* $92,483 + $100,000(.08)^{2/12}$

† $100,000 − $92,483

‡ $100,000(.08)^{2/12}$; two months' accrued interest from the bond date to the issue date is collected from the investor and then is reimbursed on the first interest payment date.

The entry to record the first interest payment after issuance (September 30) takes into account the partial interest period. The amortization table constructed for the same bond but assuming issuance on March 31, 1991, the interest date immediately preceding the actual issue date, is used as the basis for this entry under the interest method. Part of this table, as well as the September 30, 1991, interest entry, is as follows:

Partial Amortization Table for Gresham Company Bonds
Sold at Discount on June 1, 1991—Interest Method
Under the Assumption of Issuance on March 31, 1991

Date	Interest Payment	Interest Expense	Discount Amortization	Unamortized Discount	Net Bond Liability
Mar. 31, 1991				$7,722	$92,278*
Sept. 30, 1991	$4,000†	$4,614‡	$614§	7,108‖	92,892#
Mar. 31, 1992	4,000	4,645	645	6,463	93,537

* Price if sold on March 31, 1991, to yield 10%.

† $100,000(.08)^{6/12}$

‡ $92,278(.10)^{6/12}$

§ $4,614 − $4,000

‖ $7,722 − $614

$92,278 + $614, or $100,000 − $7,108

Interest Method

Gresham Company (Issuer)			Elmhurst Company (Investor)	

September 30, 1991—Interest payment:

Interest payable. 1,333			Cash. 4,000	
Interest expense 3,076*			Bond investment 409	
Discount on bonds payable	409†		Interest receivable	1,333
Cash ($100,000 × .08/2)	4,000		Interest revenue	3,076

* The interest for four months based on the March 31 issue price: $3,076 = $92,278(.10) (4/12). Also, $3,076 = $4,614(4/6).

† The amortization for four months based on the March 31 issue price: $409 = $614(4/6). Also the growth in bond value from June 1 to September 30: $409 = $92,892 − $92,483.

After the first interest payment entry, the preceding amortization table (based on issuance at March 31) is used for the remaining entries during the bond term.

Under the straight-line method of amortization, the bond discount is amortized over the 58-month bond term at $129.60 per month ($7,517/58). The September 30 entry under the straight-line method follows:

Straight-Line Method

Gresham Company (Issuer)			Elmhurst Company (Investor)		

September 30, 1991—Interest payment:

Interest payable.	1,333		Cash.	4,000	
Interest expense	3,185		Bond investment	518	
Discount on bonds payable		518*	Interest receivable		1,333
Cash ($100,000 × .08/2)		4,000	Interest revenue		3,185

* ($7,517/58-month bond term) (four months)

CONCEPT REVIEW

1. What new accounting issues arise when bonds are issued between interest dates.
2. If bonds issued May 1 pay interest on June 30 and December 31, how many months of accrued interest does the issuer receive from the investor? What interest rate is used to compute the accrued interest?
3. Are bond issue costs an asset or a reduction of a liability? Defend both points of view.

DEBT SECURITIES WITH EQUITY RIGHTS

Firms issue debt securities that include rights to acquire capital stock. Rights to acquire equity securities enhance marketability and improve the terms to the issuer. The investor receives a potential right to become a shareholder and participate in stock price appreciation in addition to principal and interest payments. Two common examples of this hybrid security are non-convertible bonds with detachable stock warrants and bonds convertible into capital stock.

Non-convertible Bonds with Detachable Stock Purchase Warrants A stock warrant conveys the option to purchase from the issuer a specified number of shares of common stock at a designated price per share, within a stated time period (the exercise period). The warrant is valuable because it enables the holder to buy shares for less than market value if the market value is more than the designated price. Warrants generally increase the bond price on the expectation that the common stock price will increase and create a market for the warrant.[20]

For example, BMC Industries, Inc., disclosed the following information related to detachable warrants in its 1989 annual report:

> Additionally, detachable warrants to purchase 960,000 shares of the Company's common stock at $7.00 per share were issued to the purchasers of the subordinated notes. . .$1,526,000 of the proceeds of the subordinated notes was allocated to the detachable warrants and included in common stock.

If the warrants are detachable, a portion of the bond price should be allocated to the warrants. The warrant market value is sufficiently objective to justify the separate

---

[20] Warrants are detachable or non-detachable. If detachable, the warrants are traded as separate securities. If non-detachable, the debt security is surrendered to obtain the stock.

valuation for warrants. The allocation is credited to a contributed capital (owners' equity) account and is based on the market values of the two securities on the date of issuance (the proportional method). If only the warrants, for example, have a readily determinable market value, the bonds are valued at the difference between the total bond price and the market value of the warrants (the incremental method).

In contrast, if the stock purchase warrants are not detachable, no separate market for them exists and the entire bond price is allocated to the bonds.

After the issue price is allocated to the bonds and detachable warrants, bond accounting is not affected by the warrants. Therefore, the following example of accounting for non-convertible bonds with detachable stock purchase warrants does not illustrate interest recognition.

> Embassy Limited issues $100,000 of 8%, 10-year, non-convertible bonds with detachable stock purchase warrants to Nuvolari Limited.
>
> Each $1,000 bond carries 10 warrants. Each warrant entitles Nuvolari to purchase one share of common stock for $15. The bond issue therefore includes 1,000 warrants (100 bonds × 10 warrants per bond).
>
> The bond issue sells for 105 exclusive of accrued interest. Shortly after issuance, the warrants traded for $4 each.

1. *Incremental method* (only one security has a market value; no market value is determined for the bonds as separate securities).

	Embassy Limited (Issuer)		Nuvolari Limited (Investor)	
Issuance entry:				
Cash	105,000	Investment in bonds	101,000	
Bonds payable		100,000	Investment in	
Detachable stock			detachable stock	
warrants.		4,000*	warrants	4,000	
Premium on bonds			Cash		105,000
payable		1,000†		

* (1,000 warrants) ($4); detachable stock warrants is a contributed capital account (owners' equity).
† Value allocated to bonds − Face value of bonds [($105,000 − $4,000) − $100,000].

The warrants are credited at market value. The remaining or incremental portion of the proceeds ($101,000) is allocated to the bonds. The amount of premium recorded is consistent with the previous discussion and equals the amount allocated to the bonds and their face value. Nuvolari classifies its two investment accounts as current or long-term depending on the intended holding period.

2. *Proportional method* (both securities have market values)—Shortly after issuance, the warrants traded for $4 each and the bonds were quoted at 103 ex-warrants (without warrants attached).

Market value of bonds [$100,000(1.03)].	$103,000
Market value of warrants [$4(1,000)]	4,000
Total market value of bonds and warrants	$107,000
Allocation of proceeds to bonds [$105,000 × $103,000 ÷ $107,000].	$101,075
Allocation of proceeds to warrants [$105,000 × $4,000 ÷ $107,000].	3,925
Total proceeds allocated.	$105,000

	Embassy Limited (Issuer)		Nuvolari Limited (Investor)	

Issuance entry:

Cash	105,000		Investment in bonds 101,075	
Bonds payable		100,000	Investment in	
Detachable stock			detachable stock	
warrants.		3,925	warrants 3,925	
Premium on bonds			Cash	105,000
payable		1,075*		

* $101,075 – $100,000

The entries to account for exercise and expiration using the incremental method example follow:

Warrant Exercise and Expiration: Data from Incremental Method Example

	Embassy Limited (Issuer)		Nuvolari Limited (Investor)	

Entry to account for exercise of 900 warrants:

Cash (900 × $15).	13,500		Investment in common stock 17,100	
Detachable stock warrants. . .	3,600*		Investment in	
Common stock		17,100†	detachable stock warrants. . .	3,600
			Cash	13,500

* $4 (900 warrants)

† ($15 + $4)900

Entry to account for expiration of remaining 100 warrants:

Detachable stock warrants	400*		Loss on investment 400	
Contributed capital from			Investment in detachable	
expiration of detachable			stock warrants.	400
stock warrants.		400		

* $4 (100 warrants).

The entry to record the shares issued on exercise is not affected by the market price. The warrant conveys the right to purchase stock for $15 per share regardless of the current market price. A detachable stock warrant is reduced by the original amount allocated to it ($4 per warrant); the $3,600 worth of resources allocated to warrants is allocated to the share capital account. Under the facts of the proportional method example, the debit to detachable stock warrants is $3,532.50 ($3,925 × 900/1,000) with a corresponding adjustment to the share capital account credit.

The expiration entry is recorded at the end of the exercise period for any warrants that remain outstanding. Warrants are not exercised by the end of the expiration period through oversight or because of an unfavourable stock price. The issuing company retains the portion of the bond price originally allocated to the expired warrants. Firms may choose to credit premium on bonds payable instead of contributed capital from expiration of detachable stock warrants if the bonds are outstanding.

Convertible Bonds   A **convertible bond** is exchanged for capital stock (usually common stock) of the issuer at the option of the investor. Typically, convertible bonds also are callable at a specified redemption or call price, at the option of the issuer. If the bonds are called, the holders either convert the bonds or accept the call price. Convertible bonds often are marketable at lower interest rates than conventional bonds because investors assign a value to the conversion privilege. Convertible bonds typically are not issued with stock warrants.

The bond indenture of convertible bonds specifies a conversion ratio or conversion price. The conversion ratio is the number of shares of common stock issued on conversion of one bond. The conversion price is the quotient of bond face value and conversion ratio.

For example, assume Manitoba Limited issues 5,000 convertible bonds, each convertible into 10 shares of Manitoba common stock and callable at $1,020. Face value is $1,000 per bond. Conversion can occur at the option of the holder on any date two years after issuance. The conversion ratio is 10 and the conversion price is $100 ($1,000 face value/10). The conversion price is the dollar amount of face value exchanged for each share of stock. The conversion price approximates the cost per share and typically is set 10% to 20% above the stock price at issuance.[21]

This example of a convertible bond was in the footnotes to the 1989 Stelco Inc. annual report:

> On August 23, 1988, the Corporation issued $150,000,000 principal amount of Convertible Subordinated Debentures bearing interest at a rate of 7¾ percent payable semi-annually commencing February 28, 1989.
>
> The Debentures are convertible at the option of the holder at any time after November 23, 1988...into the Corporation's Series A Convertible Common Shares at a conversion price of $28.50 per share.

Convertible bonds offer certain advantages to the issuer. The bonds often sell at a lower interest rate (or a higher price) and with fewer restrictions than non-convertible bonds. The convertibility feature improves prospects for raising debt capital. Companies also use convertibles as a means of securing equity financing at a lower cost. By setting the conversion price above the prevailing stock price, fewer shares must be issued to obtain the same amount of capital. Furthermore, if the bonds are converted, the face value is never paid.

The call option protects the issuer from being forced to issue stock with an aggregate value greatly in excess of the call price. In the Manitoba example, if the stock price is $104 and rising a year after issuing the convertible bonds, Manitoba can call the bonds at $1,020 before the stock price rises much higher. In this case, the investors can choose to convert and receive stock worth $1,040 per bond ($10 \times 104) rather than accept the call price.[22]

Convertible bonds are not without disadvantages, however. If the share price does not rise, the firm must service the debt. Stable or declining share prices indicate financial problems that can be compounded by the interest on convertible debt. In the opposite case, if the issuing company is very successful and its stock price increases significantly after issuing convertible bonds, the company incurs the opportunity cost of foregoing the sale of converted shares at a higher price.

The primary advantage of convertible bonds to the investor is the potential for increased wealth if the shares appreciate. If not, the investor continues to receive interest (although most likely at a lower rate than on non-convertible bonds) and face value at maturity.

Accounting for the issuance of convertible bonds poses a conceptual problem. A popular view holds that the economic value of the conversion feature, reflected in the bond price, should be recorded as shareholders' equity. However, current GAAP specifies that the convertible bonds are recorded as debt only, with no value assigned to the conversion privilege. Accountants reasoned that the debt and equity features of a convertible bond are inseparable and do not exist independently of each other.

A separate market does not exist for either the bond standing alone or the conversion privilege. There is no objective basis (e.g., a market or an exchange transaction)

---

[21] Otherwise the bonds would be converted immediately, if allowed by the indenture, to the detriment of the issuing corporation.

[22] Investors often do not convert at the earliest date on which the market value of stock to be received on conversion exceeds the market value of the bonds. Expectations of further stock price increases may convince them to wait longer.

for allocating the bond price to the bond and conversion feature. The value of the conversion feature is contingent on a future share price, which cannot be predicted.

Accounting for interest expense and amortization of premium and discount is not affected by convertibility. The bond term is used as the amortization period because conversion cannot be predicted. Accounting for interest is omitted in the following example:

Tollen Limited sells $100,000 of 8%, convertible bonds for $106,000 to Menton Limited.

At the option of the investor, each $1,000 bond is convertible to 10 shares of Tollen Limited common stock on any interest date after the end of the second year from date of issuance.

	Tollen Limited (Issuer)			Menton Limited (Investor)	
Issuance entry:					
Cash	106,00		Bond investment. . . .	106,000	
Premium on bonds payable		6,000	Cash		106,000
Bonds payable		100,000			

When the bonds are converted, the issuer and investor update interest expense (revenue) and amortization of premium or discount to the date of conversion. Then, bonds payable and bond investment are closed. Two methods are acceptable for valuing the shares issued on conversion:

1. *Book value method:* record the shares at the book value of the convertible bonds; recognize no gain or loss.
2. *Market value method:* record the shares at the market value of stock or debt, whichever is more reliable. A gain or loss equal to the difference between the market value and the book value of debt is recognized.

The following entries illustrate both methods:

Menton converts the bonds on an interest date. Both firms record interest in the usual way.

The stock price is $110 per share and $3,000 of premium remains unamortized for both firms after updating the premium account.

	Book Value Method	Market Value Method
Tollen Limited (Issuer)		
Entry for conversion of bonds:		
Bonds payable	100,000	100,000
Premium on bonds payable	3,000	3,000
Loss on conversion of bonds.		7,000[†]
Common stock	103,000*	110,000

* Amount needed to complete entry; book value of bonds is $103,000.

[†] Market value of shares issued (1,000 shares × $110 = $110,000) less book value of bonds ($103,000) equals loss of $7,000.

	Book Value Method	Market Value Method
Menton Limited (Investor)		
Entry for conversion of bonds:		
Investment in stock	103,000	110,000
Bond investment	103,000	103,000
Gain on conversion of bonds . .		7,000

Under the book value method, the owners' equity accounts replace the bond accounts for the issuer. Under the market value method, the owners' equity accounts are credited at full market value, as if the issued shares were sold on the date of conversion. The gain or loss on conversion is not classified as extraordinary because the investor initiated the conversion. Tollen's $7,000 loss is the cash forgone by issuing shares on bond conversion. However, the loss is not necessarily equal to the economic loss (or gain) because the market value of the bonds is not considered in the accounting.

The book value method appears to be more popular. Many accountants view the conversion as the culmination of a single transaction that started when the convertible bonds were issued. The valuation of issued stock is restricted to the actual resources received on the bond issue, adjusted for amortization to date of conversion. Furthermore, this view holds that the gain (loss) under the market value method is not supported by the value of resources originally received on the bond issue. Others prefer the market value method because it uses current value to measure the investment. The valuation of the shares issued is based on the value received if the shares were sold.

Induced Conversion of Convertible Debt   Issuers of convertible debt sometimes change the conversion provisions after the issuance date to induce prompt conversion. The inducement is an incentive beyond the original shares issued on conversion. Common inducements include an increase in the conversion ratio, issuance of stock rights, and payment of cash or other consideration. Decreasing interest rates and a preference for lower debt levels prompt an induced conversion.

GAAP requires that the issuer recognize an expense equal to the fair value of consideration transferred in excess of the fair value of the securities issuable under the original conversion terms. The expense is not classified as an extraordinary item because the original debt agreement remains in effect during the inducement period, and the debt is extinguished at the bondholder's option rather than the issuer's.

The expense is recognized only for bonds converted during the limited time period. The market value of consideration transferred is measured at the date the inducement is accepted. The following is an example of induced conversion:

Cologne Limited holds 500, 6% convertible bonds payable issued at face value ($1,000) by Berlin Limited. Each bond is convertible into 10 shares of common stock.

Berlin offers two additional shares of common stock for each bond as an inducement to convert. The offer is open for a two-month period.

The bondholders accept the inducement within the required period. The market price of the common stock on the conversion date (also an interest date) is $110.

Berlin Limited (Issuer)   **Cologne Limited** (Investor)

Book Value Method

Conversion entry:

Berlin Limited (Issuer)		Cologne Limited (Investor)	
Bonds payable 500,000		Investment in stock 500,000	
Debt conversion expense 110,000*		Bond investment	500,000
Common stock	610,000		

* (12 − 10) 500 ($110) market value of 2 additional shares per bond.

Market Value Method

Conversion entry:

Berlin Limited (Issuer)		Cologne Limited (Investor)	
Bonds payable 500,000		Investment in stock 660,000	
Debt conversion expense . . . 110,000		Bond investment	500,000
Loss on conversion . . . . . . 50,000†		Gain on conversion. . . .	160,000
Common stock	660,000*		

* Market value of stock issued: $110(12) (500) = $660,000
† $660,000 − $610,000 (book value of conversion)

The issuer recognizes the market value of the two additional inducement shares per bond as an expense under both methods. Under the book value method, the expense is effectively capitalized as an increase in owners' equity reflecting the issuance of additional common shares without proceeds.[23] Under the market value method, part of the loss on conversion is reclassified as debt conversion expense. The increase to owners' equity is measured at the total market value of shares issued. If cash is the inducement, the debt conversion expense equals the amount of cash paid.

One view of induced conversions holds that expense recognition is inappropriate for transactions involving a firm and its equity investors. Others believe the inducement is an extinguishment, implying that market values should be recorded. Another view holds that the cost of the inducement should be treated as a reduction of the equity capital provided. However, in *SFAS No. 84,* paragraph 27, the FASB reasoned that a firm incurs a cost not expected under the original agreement when inducing conversion:

> In exchange for the assets or securities given up in excess of those it was already committed to pay or issue, the enterprise receives performance. In the absence of such consideration, the conversion would not have occurred at that time. The Board believes that this type of an exchange of consideration for performance is a transaction that should be recognized as a cost of obtaining that performance.

The FASB opinion is that the cost of an inducement not contemplated in the original conversion agreement should be recognized as a separate cost.

CONCEPT REVIEW

1. Why is a value recorded for detachable warrants, but not for the conversion feature of convertible bonds?
2. How is the premium (discount) computed for bonds issued with detachable warrants?
3. What is the rationale for the market value method of accounting for conversion of convertible bonds? And what does the gain or loss on conversion represent?

DEBT EXTINGUISHMENT
◆

Firms typically use the proceeds of most bond issues and other long-term debt instruments for the entire debt term. At the maturity date all discount or premium is fully amortized; gains and losses are not recognized on normal retirement. However, it is not uncommon for firms to retire debt before or after maturity. Early retirement of debt decreases the debt-equity ratio and can facilitate future debt issuances.

Another major incentive to retiring bonds before maturity occurs when interest rates increase enough to cause bond prices to decrease below book value. This enables the issuer to retire bonds at a gain. When interest rates decrease, firms use the opportunity to retire more expensive bonds and issue lower interest rate bonds. However, a loss occurs in this case because bond prices increase above book value.

Accounting for debt retirement has not yet been addressed by the AcSB. Therefore, the tendency in Canada is to look toward U.S. practice. The main reporting issues are (1) determining when a debt extinguishment occurs and (2) classifying the gain or loss on extinguishment. The gain or loss is the difference between the book value and market value of the debt on the date of extinguishment. The relevant pronouncements are summarized as follows:

1. *APB Opinion No. 26,* "Early Extinguishment of Debt" (1972), defines early extinguishment of debt as any retirement of debt before scheduled maturity (except

---

[23] The additional shares issued are similar to a stock dividend. A stock dividend is the issuance of shares to existing shareholders without proceeds to the issuing firm. Stock dividends reduce retained earnings. In the Berlin example, debt conversion expense also reduces retained earnings.

through conversion by holder) and requires recognition of the difference between market value and book value of debt retired as an ordinary gain or loss in the year of extinguishment.

2. *SFAS No. 4,* "Reporting Gains and Losses from Extinguishment of Debt" (1975), amends *APB Opinion No. 26* by requiring that gains and losses from extinguishment of debt (whether early, at maturity, or after maturity) be classified as extraordinary and disclosed net of tax effect. Gains and losses from cash purchases of debt made to satisfy sinking-fund requirements are exempt from classification as extraordinary.

3. *SFAS No. 64,* "Extinguishments of Debt Made to Satisfy Sinking-Fund Requirements" (1982), amends *SFAS No. 4* by restricting the exemption from extraordinary classification to those gains and losses from sinking-fund purchases that must be made within one year of the date of the extinguishment. Also, such classification is determined without regard to the means used to retire the debt.

4. *SFAS No. 76,* "Extinguishment of Debt" (1983), amends *APB Opinion No. 26* by re-defining debt extinguishment for financial reporting purposes. Paragraph 3 includes only these three circumstances:

   a. The debtor is relieved of all obligations associated with the debt through direct payment or purchase of its own debt securities on the market, by replacement (refunding) of debt with another issue, or by calling debt.

   b. The debtor is legally released from the debt judicially or by the creditor and it is probable (as defined in *SFAS No. 5,* "Accounting for Contingencies") that the debtor will not be required to make future payments on the debt. This occurs, for example, when mortgage debt secured by an asset is assumed by another firm purchasing that asset.

   c. The debtor irrevocably places cash or other assets in trust solely to satisfy the scheduled payments under the debt, and the possibility that the debtor will be required to make future payments on the debt is remote. This is **in-substance defeasance** of debt. However, the debtor remains legally liable for the debt.

Debt extinguishments occur before, at, or after maturity. These provisions apply only to debt with fixed payment schedules and specified maturities. Except for in-substance defeasance, they apply regardless of the means used to extinguish the debt.

Gains and losses on debt extinguishment are classified as extraordinary items in the United States even though they might be frequent occurrences. (Given the provisions in the revised section 3480 of the *CICA Handbook,* it is unlikely that these gains and losses would be classified as extraordinary in Canada.) In many instances, extinguishment gains are significant in relation to operating income. Classification as extraordinary brings the gains into the open. Firms no longer are able to report a large extinguishment gain as a component of ordinary income.

Extinguishment of debt is now broadly defined and is not restricted to early retirement, nor to cash reacquisitions of debt.[24] Normal conversion of and induced conversion of convertible bonds are not debt extinguishments for purposes of classifying the gain or loss because retirement occurs at the option of the investor. However, retirement of debt accomplished through issuance of equity securities is a debt extinguishment for purposes of applying *SFAS No. 76.*[25]

Accounting for debt extinguishment involves:

♦ Updating interest expense, discount or premium, and related issue costs to the retirement date.

♦ Removing the liability accounts.

♦ Recording the transfer of cash, other resources, or debt securities.

♦ Recording a gain or loss.

---

[24] Some troubled debt restructures, discussed in Appendix 16B, result in debt retirement but are not considered debt retirements.

[25] *FASB Technical Bulletin No. 80–1.*

EXHIBIT 16–6   Data for Open Market Extinguishment: Previous Gresham Company Bonds, Case 1, Part B (Premium)

Issue date: January 1, 1991			Total face value: $100,000		
Stated interest rate: 7%			Bond date: January 1, 1991		
Interest payment date: December 31			Yield rate at issuance: 6%		
Maturity date: December 31, 1995			Bond issue costs: $3,600*		

Amortization Table for Gresham Company Bonds
Sold at Premium Interest Method

Date	Interest Payment	Interest Expense	Premium Amortization	Unamortized Premium	Net Bond Liability
Jan. 1, 1991				$4,213	$104,213
Dec. 31, 1991	$7,000	$6,253	$747	3,466	103,466
Dec. 31, 1992	7,000	6,208	792	2,674	102,674

* New information.

Required disclosures for extraordinary gains and losses from extinguishment include:

- A description of the transaction including the means used for extinguishment.
- The income tax effect of the gain or loss.
- The per share amount of the aggregate gain or loss net of related tax effect (*SFAS No. 4,* par. 9).

The following examples use bonds to illustrate debt extinguishment.

Extinguishment of Bonds by Open Market Purchase

In an open-market purchase of bonds, the issuer pays the current market price as would any investor purchasing the bonds. As a basis for our example, Exhibit 16–6 repeats a portion of the amortization table for the Gresham bonds.

Interest rates increased since these bonds were issued and on March 1, 1992, Gresham purchases 20% ($20,000 face value) of the bonds on the open market at 90. The price declined reflecting the increased interest rates.[26] The entries to record the extinguishment under effective interest and straight-line methods follow:

	Interest Method		Straight-Line Method	
March 1, 1992—Update interest and premium amortization:				
Interest expense	207*		205	
Premium on bonds payable	26		28†	
Interest payable.		233‡		233

* .06($103,466) (²⁄₁₂) (.20)
(Market rate at issue) (Book value on January 1, 1992) (²⁄₁₂ of year) (Portion of bond issue retired)

† $4,213(²⁄₆₀) (.20)
(Original premium) (2 months/60-month bond term) (Portion of bond issue retired)

‡ $20,000(.07) (²⁄₁₂)
(Accrued interest from January 1, 1992)

	Interest Method		Straight-Line Method	
March 1, 1992—Update bond issue expense:				
Bond issue expense	24*		24	
Bond issue cost.		24		24

* $3,600(²⁄₆₀) (.20)
(Total issue cost) (2 months/60-month bond term) (Portion of bond issue retired)

[26] The price equals the present value of all remaining payments at the current market rate. For simplicity, the market price is given, but could be computed as in Case 3, bonds issued between interest dates.

	Interest Method	Straight-Line Method

March 1, 1992—Remove relevant accounts, recognize gain:

Bonds payable	20,000		20,000
Premium on bonds payable	667*		646[†]
Interest payable	233		233
Cash		18,233[‡]	18,233
Bond issue cost		552[§]	552
Gain on bond extinguishment		2,115[‖]	2,094[#]

* \$3,466(.20) − \$26
(Unamortized premium January 1, 1992) (Portion of bond issue retired) − (Amount of premium amortized through March 1, 1992)

[†] \$4,213($^{46}/_{60}$) (.20)
(Original premium) (46 months remaining/60-month bond term) (Portion of bond issue retired)

[‡] \$20,000(.90) + \$233 interest payable

[§] \$3,600($^{46}/_{60}$) (.20)
(Total issue cost) (46 months remaining/60-month bond term) (Portion of bond issue retired)

[‖] Book value of bonds retired (\$20,000 + \$667 = \$20,667) less price of bonds (\$18,000) less unexpired bond issue cost on bonds retired (\$522) equals the gain of \$2,115.

[#] Calculation similar to interest method.

Extinguishment does not affect accounting for the remaining 80% of the bond issue; 80% of the values in the amortization table are used for the remaining bond term as well as 80% of the bond issue costs.

The first entry under the interest method employs the most recent book value for the entire bond issue as the basis for computing interest expense for the two-month period ending March 1, 1992, (\$103,466) for 20% of the bond issue. Amortization of premium and bond issue cost is recorded as usual, but only for 20% of the bond issue.

Under the interest method, on January 1, 1992, \$693 (\$3,466 × .20) of unamortized premium remains on the portion of the issue retired; \$26 of that amount is amortized on March 1. Therefore, the remaining \$667 (\$693 − \$26) is removed from the accounts.

Under the straight-line method, the fraction of the bond term remaining on March 1, 1992, is $^{46}/_{60}$, which is used to determine the amount of bond issue cost and premium to remove. Only 20% of the total remaining on March 1, 1992, is removed from the two accounts.

The Nature of the Gain The gain is the difference between the total market price and book value of the bonds, decreased by the unexpired portion of the bond issue costs relating to the retired bonds. The remaining bond issue costs generate no future benefit. Brokerage fees and other costs of retiring the bonds also decrease the gain (increase the loss).

The gain occurs because the market value of the bonds decreases below book value. GAAP requires the use of the market rate at issuance for measuring the book value of the bond. However, the gain fails to reflect economic reality.[27] For example, some would argue that the bond extinguishment did not alter Gresham's economic position because the debt was retired at market value. A more profitable alternative might be to apply the \$18,000 to a higher yield investment. Retiring low-cost debt when interest rates rise is questionable, particularly if additional debt issuances are contemplated.

Sinking-Fund Retirements: Ordinary Gain and Loss Classification Early retirement of bonds fulfills the sinking-fund requirements of some bond issues. Under *SFAS No. 64,* gains and losses from such extinguishments, which must be made within one year of

---

[27] Financial statement and footnote disclosures often do not provide sufficient information to completely analyze the economic effect of a bond retirement on the company. The economic gain or loss depends on the discount rate chosen. Only coincidentally will the reported gain equal the computed economic gain. See J. Dietrich and J. Deitrick, "Bond Exchanges in the Airline Industry: Analyzing Public Disclosures," *The Accounting Review,* January 1985, pp. 109–26.

the extinguishment, are treated as ordinary income items, without regard to the means used to retire the debt.

For example, if Gresham is required by the bond indenture to purchase the $20,000 of bonds it retired on March 1, 1992, within one year of that date to satisfy a sinking-fund requirement, the gain is reported as ordinary income. In contrast, if the sinking-fund retirement deadline is May 1, 1993, the gain is classified as extraordinary because retirement did not occur within one year of the required date.

This exemption recognizes the difference between required and discretionary extinguishments and allows one year to complete the necessary arrangements for bond retirement. If an issuer must retire bonds under the indenture and does so within a year of the deadline, it is difficult to argue that the purpose of the retirement is to manipulate income. However, if bonds are retired two years ahead of schedule, the issuer could have motivations other than meeting a distant deadline.[28]

Treasury Bonds   Regardless of the form extinguishment takes, if the issuer does not cancel its bonds after reacquisition but contemplates reissue at a later date, treasury bonds is debited in lieu of bonds payable. Treasury bonds is a contra bond payable account. When the bonds are reissued, treasury bonds is credited rather than bonds payable, and a new discount or premium is recorded. If canceled, treasury bonds is credited and bonds payable is debited. Like bonds payable, treasury bonds is debited or credited only with face value.

Retirement of Convertible Debt   When convertible bonds are converted, the gain or loss is classified as ordinary. Occasionally, firms retire convertible bonds through open-market purchase or other methods. Gains and losses on these retirements are classified as extraordinary, consistent with the intent of *SFAS No. 4*.

Extinguishment by Exercise of Call Privilege by Issuer

Bonds frequently carry a call privilege allowing the issuer to retire the debt by paying the call price during a specified period. The call price places a ceiling on the market price. Investors who purchase callable bonds are thus placed at a disadvantage if interest rates decline because they may have to surrender bonds that pay higher interest than non-callable bonds. For these reasons, callable bonds are often issued with higher interest rates than non-callable bonds. In addition, the call price typically exceeds face value by the call premium, which can decline each year of the bond term.

Issuers account for callable and non-callable bonds in the same way because exercise of the call privilege is not a certainty. The full bond term is used for amortization and interest recognition. When bonds are called, the usual procedures for recording debt extinguishment are followed. A loss is more likely than a gain because callable bonds are normally issued below the call price.

To illustrate the exercise of a call privilege, assume that Pana Company calls all $100,000 of its five-year, 10% bonds callable at 101 on June 30, 1991, an interest payment date. After the entry to record the interest payment, interest expense, and amortization of discount, $1,200 of discount remains unamortized. The remaining bond term is three and a half years. Pana spent $2,000 to issue the bonds, and $600 to call them. The following entry records the extinguishment:

Entry to exercise call privilege:

Bonds payable	100,000	
Loss on bond extinguishment	4,200	
Discount on bonds payable		1,200
Cash (1.01 × $100,000 + $600)		101,600
Bond issue cost ($2,000 × 3.5/5)		1,400

---

[28] Some bond indentures specify serial retirement of bonds. These scheduled maturities are preplanned and do not qualify as early retirements for the purpose of exemption from extraordinary classification under *SFAS No. 64*.

Extinguishment of Bonds by Refunding

When a **refunding** occurs, a bond issue is replaced with another bond issue. One way of refunding is to issue new bonds in exchange for the old bonds. Cash is involved if the bond issues have different market values. More frequently, however, the proceeds from a new bond issue are used to retire the old issue because the holders of the old issue do not necessarily become the new creditors. In both cases, the accounting or refunding is similar to all other forms of debt extinguishment. The following information illustrates the two situations involving refunding:

1. *Refunding — by direct exchange of debt securities:* On January 1, 1991, WestCal Limited issues $100,000 of 10-year, 5% bonds at face value with interest payable each June 30 and December 31. On January 1, 1995, the bondholders agreed to accept $90,000 of 20-year, 8% bonds with the same interest dates as the 5% bonds. The market rate of interest on similar bonds is 8%.

Analysis:

a. The bondholders receive 10% less principal but a 60% increase in the interest rate.
b. *PV* (market value) of new bonds $90,000
  PV (market value) of old bonds (12 semiannual periods remain in the old issue):
    Principal: $100,000 (*PV* 1, 4%, 12) = $100,000(.62460) $62,460
    Interest: $2,500(*PVA*, 4%, 12) = $2,500(9.38507)   23,463   85,923

  Difference: Economic loss to WestCal . . . . $ 4,077

January 1, 1995 — Refunding entry:

    Bonds payable, 5% 100,000
        Bonds payable, 8%   90,000
        Gain on bond extinguishment.   10,000

WestCal accepts the economic loss to extend the maturity 20 years and to avoid the costs of issuing the new bonds for cash. The creditors receive $2,200 more in interest each year ($7,200 − $5,000). WestCal records a $10,000 accounting gain yet sustains an economic loss of $4,077 because increases in interest rates allow new bonds with a lower face value but higher present value to replace the old bonds. By refunding the old bonds, WestCal has promised a new stream of future cash payments with an increased present value.

This is yet another example of the problems that arise from using the market rate at issuance to measure the book value of bonds. WestCal could invest $85,923 at 8% and satisfy the remaining payments on the 5% bonds. Many accountants view this value as a more appropriate valuation of the 5% bonds, particularly if WestCal intends to extinguish bonds early.

2. *Refunding — by issuing new debt and purchasing old debt:* On January 1, 1991, WestCal Limited issues $100,000 of 10-year, 5% bonds at face value with interest payable each June 30 and December 31. On January 1, 1995, WestCal issues at face value $86,000 of 20-year, 8% bonds with the same interest dates as the 5% bonds. The market price of the old bonds is 86.

January 1, 1995 — Issue 8% bonds:

    Cash 86,000
        Bonds payable   86,000

January 1, 1995 — Retire 5% bonds:

    Bonds payable 100,000
        Cash   86,000
        Gain on bond extinguishment.   14,000

The accounting gain is $14,000, but no economic gain or loss because the 5% bonds were extinguished at market value.

Extinguishment by In-Substance Defeasance

SFAS No. 76 expands the concept of debt extinguishment to include in-substance defeasance: irrevocable placement of assets into a trust for the sole purpose of paying interest and principal on the debt. The debtor does not actually pay the creditor but, instead, surrenders assets sufficient to cover all future debt payments. The FASB reasoned that the economic position of the debtor under in-substance defeasance is equivalent to immediate retirement of the debt. Both the liability and assets placed in trust are removed from the accounts.

Firms extinguish debt by in-substance defeasance for several reasons. Recognition of a gain is one incentive. The gain on extinguishment may be larger if recognized earlier (through in-substance defeasance), depending on interest rate changes. The debt rating of the extinguished debt may be improved, and the general perception of the riskiness of the debtor consequently reduced. Debt to equity and other ratios are improved. Prepayment penalties from direct payments to creditors are avoided. The call premium on callable bonds is also avoided by in-substance defeasance.

Certain requirements must be met to fulfill in-substance defeasance (*SFAS No. 76,* paragraph 4):

1. Qualifying assets include only monetary assets that are essentially risk-free as to the amount and timing of interest and principal collection. The assets must be denominated in the currency in which the debt is payable. Examples of qualifying assets for debt payable in U.S. dollars are (*a*) direct obligations of the U.S. government and (*b*) obligations guaranteed by the U.S. government.
2. The assets placed in trust must provide cash flows (interest and principal) that approximately coincide, as to timing and amount, with payments required on the debt.
3. The probability that the debtor will be required to make future payments on the debt is remote.
4. Assets placed in trust to be used for trustee fees and other associated costs do not qualify as assets to be used to satisfy the debt payments.
5. Footnote disclosure of the extinguishment arrangements and the amount of the debt extinguished is required until the debt is legally retired.[29]

The intent of the in-substance defeasance requirements is to eliminate essentially all risk that funds will be unavailable to meet the required debt payments. Only those basically risk-free assets that yield scheduled cash flows can supply the assurance that all debt payments will be satisfied. Investments in equity securities do not qualify for this reason. No other provision in the debt agreement can call for a future payment that could not be fulfilled by the assets placed in trust by the debtor.

SFAS No. 76 applies only to debt with specified maturities and fixed payment schedules. In-substance defeasance extinguishment is not available to variable interest rate debt. The second and third requirements listed above could not be fulfilled for such debt. For example, the trust assets would be insufficient to cover all debt payments if interest rates increased.

To illustrate in-substance defeasance:

Example On January 1, 1989, the Eugene Company issues 100, 7%, $1,000 bonds dated January 1, 1989, to yield 6%. The bonds pay interest each January 1 and mature January 1, 1994.

On January 1, 1991, Eugene purchases $100,000 (face value) of 7% treasury bonds maturing in three years for $97,400 to yield approximately 8%. Eugene irrevocably transfers these bonds to a trust for the sole purpose of satisfying the remaining interest and principal payments on its 7% bonds.

---

[29] Some respondents to the exposure draft preceding *SFAS No. 76* considered this disclosure requirement to contradict the substance of the statement and to cast doubt on the extinguishment. They reasoned that if debt is in-substance extinguished, further disclosure serves no purpose.

The market rate of interest on the 7% bonds is 9% on January 1, 1991. The book value of the bonds is $102,673 [$100,000(PV1, 3, 6%) + $7,000($PVA$, 3, 6%)]. The current price of the bonds is $94,937 [$100,000(PV1, 3, 9%) + $7,000($PVA$, 3, 9%)].

After purchasing the treasury bonds and recording the January 1, 1991, interest payment, Eugene records the following entry to extinguish the bonds:

January 1, 1991—In-substance defeasance:

Bonds payable	100,000	
Premium on bonds payable	2,673	
Investment in treasury bonds		97,400
Extraordinary gain, bond extinguishment		5,273

The Eugene extinguishment fulfills the requirements of in-substance defeasance. The treasury bonds are essentially risk-free, and their scheduled principal and interest payments closely coincide with those of the Eugene bonds.

The extraordinary gain equals the difference between the book value and market value of the consideration used to extinguish the debt. The yields are not the same for the treasury bonds and the Eugene bonds; therefore, the market values are somewhat different. If Eugene purchased the treasury bonds before January 1, 1991, the market value may be different from book value. In this case, a gain or loss equal to the difference between these two values is recognized on disposal of the investment. This gain or loss does not affect the extraordinary gain on extinguishment.

The Eugene example illustrates the importance of coinciding schedules of interest and principal payments. If the treasury bonds pay significantly less (or more) interest than the Eugene bonds or if the timing of cash flows is significantly different, the trust experiences periods of cash deficiency (or surplus). Cash deficiencies contradict the intent of in-substance defeasance, and surpluses require an assumption about reinvestment.

Consequently, *SFAS No. 76* contains no provision for assumptions about reinvestment of surplus assets. After the assets are placed into the trust, interest rate changes in the market are irrelevant. Only the schedule of cash flows is meaningful.

Partial in-substance defeasance is also allowed under *SFAS No. 76* (paragraph 36). A pro rata portion of all remaining principal and interest payments on a debt instrument with a specified maturity can be extinguished in this manner. A firm cannot partially extinguish only interest or only principal.

SFAS No. 76 prompted some firms to instantaneously retire debt by investing in essentially risk free securities yielding a higher rate than newly issued debt and placing the securities into irrevocable trusts. Immediate gains were recognized because of the lower present value of the securities. *FASB Technical Bulletin No. 84–4* ruled that such transactions are counter to the intent of in-substance defeasance. The FASB did not wish to create an incentive for income manipulation. Consequently, in-substance defeasance applies only to existing debt, not to newly issued debt.

The Debate over In-Substance Defeasance   The four-to-three vote with which *SFAS No. 76* was adopted reveals the controversial nature of in-substance defeasance. Those in opposition to the statement maintain that unless the debtor is legally released from debt, the liability should remain on the books. They argue that the resulting gains erode the quality of earnings and benefit managers whose compensation contracts are tied to reported income.

The issue of violation of a debt agreement remains to be addressed. Debt previously extinguished through in-substance defeasance becomes immediately payable if the indenture agreement is violated. For example, the ending current ratio for a reporting period may fall below the required level. In this case, should the debit be reinstated and trust assets placed on the books? The trust assets also may be insufficient to cover the debt because not enough interest has been earned by the fund.

EXHIBIT 16–7   Summary of Gain and Loss Classification on Debt Settlement

Method of Settlement*	Classification of Gain or Loss†
1. Conversion of convertible bonds	Ordinary
2. Induced conversion of convertible bonds (gain, loss, and conversion expense)	Ordinary
3. Direct payment to creditors	Extraordinary
4. Sinking-fund purchases made within one year of the date of the extinguishment	Ordinary
5. Use of equity securities to settle debt	Extraordinary
6. Retirement of convertible debt	Extraordinary
7. Call	Extraordinary
8. Refunding	Extraordinary
9. Legal release from obligation	Extraordinary
10. In-substance defeasance	Extraordinary

* The word *settlement* includes any means of debt retirement except for troubled debt restructuring (see Appendix 16B). *Extinguishment* has more specific connotations under *SFAS No. 76*.

† These classifications are based on the FASB recommendations. It is likely that all or some of the items listed as extraordinary would be treated as ordinary in Canada.

Another potential problem is default by the trustee for the government securities. Defaults have involved trustees and firms dealing in government securities, including Drysdale Government Securities, Lombard-Wall, and Lion Capital Associates.[30] In addition, if the debtor declares bankruptcy, is the trust fund a secured asset, or is it available to all creditors?

Summary of Gain and Loss Classification

Exhibit 16–7 is a summary of gain and loss classification for debt extinguishments and retirements.

CONCEPT REVIEW

1. If gains and losses on debt extinguishment are not particularly unusual, why are they classified as extraordinary?
2. Why is the gain or loss on a debt retirement made June 30, 1991, to fulfill sinking fund requirements that must be made by January 1, 1992, classified as ordinary?
3. What is the main justification for treating in-substance defeasance as a debt extinguishment when the debt is not legally liquidated?

LONG-TERM NOTES AND MORTGAGES
◆

A long-term note is a formal document that specifies the terms of a debt. Notes often are used for specific asset acquisitions or loans for particular purposes. In contrast, bonds are used to raise large amounts of capital for several purposes. Notes generally have shorter maturities than bonds and typically are not traded in organized exchanges or markets.

Chapter 8 discussed notes at length, and their accounting from the creditor's perspective. The accounting for the debtor applies the same three general valuation and

---

[30] B. Gaumnitz and J. Thompson, "In-Substance Defeasance: Costs, Yes; Benefits, No," *Journal of Accountancy*, March 1987, p. 105.

measurement principles cited at the beginning of this chapter. The *CICA Handbook,* section 1000, recognizes that present value techniques can be used for valuation of assets and liabilities. *APB Opinion 21* uses discounting for all notes except the following:

1. Payables from ordinary business transactions due in one year or less.
2. Payables arising from advances and deposits not requiring repayment but which will be applied to the price of goods and services in the future.
3. Payables arising from security deposits.
4. Payables arising from cash lending and demand or savings deposits of financial institutions.
5. Payables whose interest rates are affected by the tax attributes or legal restrictions prescribed by government.
6. Payables between a parent company and its subsidiary, or between subsidiaries of a common parent company.

The following examples illustrate accounting for notes by the debtor firm.

Example 1: Long-Term Note, Stated Rate = Market Rate   On April 1, 1991, Baylor Company borrowed $12,000 from Lionel Company and issued a three-year, 10% note. Interest is payable each March 31, and the principal is payable at the end of the third year. The stated and market interest rates are equal. The entries for Baylor, a calendar fiscal year company, follow:

April 1, 1991—Issue note:

Cash	12,000	
Long-term note payable		12,000

December 31, 1991, 1992, 1993—Adjusting entries:

Interest expense ($12,000 × .10 × $\frac{9}{12}$)	900	
Interest payable		900

March 31, 1992, 1993—Interest payment:

Interest expense ($12,000 × .10 × $\frac{3}{12}$)	300	
Interest payable	900	
Cash ($12,000 × .10)		1,200

March 31, 1994—Note maturity:

Interest expense	300	
Interest payable	900	
Long-term note payable	12,000	
Cash		13,200

This example poses no significant measurement issues because the market and stated interest rates are the same and cash is received in exchange for the note.

Example 2: Long-Term Note, Stated and Market Rates Different   Fema Company purchased goods on January 1, 1991, and issued a two-year, $10,000 note receivable with a 3% stated interest rate. Interest is payable each December 31, and the entire principal is payable December 31, 1992. The merchandise does not have a ready market value. The market rate of interest appropriate for this note is 10%. The present value of the note and its recorded value is computed as follows:

Present value of maturity amount [$10,000(*PV*1, 10%, 2) = $10,000(.82645)]	$8,265
Present value of the nominal interest payments [$10,000(.03) (*PVA*, 10%, 2) = $300(1.73554)]	520
Present value of the note at 10%	$8,785

The present value of the note is less than its face value because the note pays less interest than is available elsewhere in the market. For that reason, a higher maturity (face value) must be paid to compensate the seller for the lower interest rate. The difference between face value and present value is the discount on the note. The $1,215 discount ($10,000 − $8,785) is the interest beyond the 3% cash payments that will be paid at maturity. The following entry records the note and purchase (assuming a periodic inventory system) and reflects the gross method of recording:

January 1, 1991—Issue note:

Inventory	8,785	
Discount on long-term notes payable.	1,215	
Long-term notes payable		10,000

The January 1, 1991, long-term liability section of Fema Company balance sheet includes the following:

Long-term notes payable.	$10,000
Discount on long-term notes payable	1,215
Net long-term notes payable	$ 8,785

(Under the net method, $8,785 is recorded in the notes payable account; a discount account is not used.)

December 31, 1991—Interest payment:

Interest expense ($8,785 × .10)	879	
Discount on long-term notes payable		579
Cash		300

Interest expense exceeds the cash payment, reflecting recognition of part of the discount as interest expense. The amortization of the discount account increases the net long-term note payable as the following balance sheet disclosure reveals:

Balance Sheet at January 1, 1992

Long-term notes payable	$10,000
Discount on long-term notes payable.	636*
Net long-term notes payable.	$ 9,364

* $1,215 − $579

The straight-line method is acceptable if it yields results not materially different from the interest method. Under the straight-line method, Fema amortizes $607 ($1,214/2) of the discount and recognizes $907 of interest expense ($300 + $607) each period. The remaining entries for Fema follow under the interest method:

December 31, 1992—Interest payment:

Interest expense ($9,364 × .10)	936*	
Discount on long-term notes payable		636
Cash		300

* Slight rounding error from truncation of present value factors.

December 31, 1992—Note maturity:

Long-term notes payable	10,000	
Cash		10,000

Example 3: Long-Term Note Issued for Noncash Consideration, Payments Include Interest and Principal On January 2, 1991, Bellow Company purchased equipment by paying $5,000 down and issuing a $10,000, 4% note payable in four equal annual installments starting December 31, 1991. The current market rate on notes of a similar nature and risk is 10%. The market value of the equipment is not readily determinable.

The payment (P) and present value of the note are determined as follows:

$$\$10,000 = P(PVA, 4\%, 4) = P(3.62990)$$

$$\text{Payment} = \$10,000 \div 3.62990 = \$2,755$$

Present value of note:

$$\$2,755(PVA, 10\%, 4) = \$2,755(3.16987) = \$8,733$$

January 2, 1992—Issue note (net method):

Equipment ($5,000 + $8,733)	13,733	
Cash		5,000
Long-term notes payable		8,733

December 31, 1991—Interest expense:

Interest expense ($8,733 × .10)	873	
Long-term notes payable	1,882	
Cash		2,755

The entries for the remaining term of the note parallel Example 2. The main difference between Examples 2 and 3 is the payment structure.

In response to high and unstable interest rates, innovative debt arrangements were developed to supplement notes with traditional terms. These notes include point-system mortgages, shared-appreciation mortgages, and variable-rate mortgages.

Point-System Mortgages   A point is 1% of the face value of a point-system mortgage note. Proceeds are reduced (held back) on the note by the product of points and face value. Consequently, the effective interest rate exceeds the stated rate on the note.

For example, assume that Jasper National Bank assesses Elkhorn Company five points on a $100,000, 12%, five-year mortgage note used to purchase a building. The note requires annual (for simplicity) mortgage payments, which include interest and principal. Proceeds equal $95,000 ($100,000 × .95) However, the debtor agreed to pay five mortgage payments, which reflect 12% on a $100,000 face value. The mortgage payment and effective rate is computed as follows:

$$\$100,000 = (PVA, 12\%, 5) \text{ (Mortgage payment)}$$

$$\text{Mortgage payment} = \$100,000/(3.60478) = \$27,741$$

Let e be the effective rate for the mortgage agreement:

$$\$95,000 = \$27,741(PVA, e, 5)$$

$$\$95,000/\$27,741 = 3.42453$$

From Table 6A–4, the rate is between 14% and 15% and is approximated by interpolation:

$$e = 14\% + \frac{3.43308 - 3.42453}{3.43308 - 3.35216}(15\% - 14\%) = 14.1\%$$

The effective rate of interest exceeds the 12% stated rate specified on the note payable and reflects the true interest rate paid by Elkhorn over the term of the mortgage. Elkhorn records the note for $95,000, the amount received. The $5,000 excess of face value over proceeds represents interest recognized over the note term (a discount).

The complete amortization table for the Elkhorn point-system mortgage follows:

Date	Payment	(a) Interest Expense	(b) Principal Reduction	(c) Principal Balance
January 1, 1991				$95,000
December 31, 1991	$ 27,741	$13,395	$14,346	80,654
December 31, 1992	27,741	11,372	16,369	64,285
December 31, 1993	27,741	9,064	18,677	45,608
December 31, 1994	27,741	6,431	21,310	24,298
December 31, 1995	27,741	3,443*	24,298	0
	$138,705	$43,705	$95,000	

a. Previous principal balance (.141); $13,395 = $95,000(.141)
b. Payment − Interest expense; $14,346 = $27,741 − $13,395
c. Previous principal balance − Principal reduction; $80,654 = $95,000 − $14,346
* Rounded up $17 to compensate for rounding effective interest rate.

Shared-Appreciation Mortgage (SAMs)   Under the terms of a SAM, the lender charges a lower stated interest rate in return for a share of market value appreciation on property financed with the note. Decreases in market value are not shared. Appreciation also can include a share of the earnings in an investment project financed by the mortgage note.

The effective interest rate on shared-appreciation mortgages equates the net proceeds with the future cash payments on the note. The forecasted amount of property appreciation accruing to the lender reduces the loan proceeds for this purpose. However, the borrower receives the full amount of the loan initially and pays the appreciation on sale of the property. Modifying the previous Elkhorn example, assume a lower rate of 8% on the $100,000 loan. Elkhorn receives the entire $100,000 and agrees to the annual payments implied by these terms. In return for the lower interest rate, Jasper National Bank expects to receive approximately $10,000 of appreciation (at present value) on the property. The payments and effective rate are computed as follows:

$$\$100,000 = (PVA, 8\%, 5) \times \text{Mortgage payment}$$

$$\text{Mortgage payment} = \$100,000/(3.99271) = \$25,046$$

Let e be the effective rate for the mortgage agreement:

$$\$100,000 - \$10,000 = \$25,046(PVA, e, 5)$$

$$\$90,000/\$25,046 = 3.59339$$

The value for e falls between 12% and 14%.

A close approximation to the effective rate of 12.13% can be found by using a business calculator. Interpolation can also be used.

Adjustable Rate Mortgages (ARMs)   The stated rate of interest on ARMs (also called *floating-rate,* or *variable-rate,* mortgages) changes periodically to correspond to market rate changes. ARMs shift the risk of changing interest rates from the lender to the borrower. The interest rate on long-term notes usually is changed quarterly, semiannually, or annually, although three-year intervals are not uncommon. In contrast, the floating rate charged on short-term notes often is changed when the prime interest rate changes. The prime rate is the rate charged by commercial banks to preferred corporate customers.

When interest rates are adjusted, a new payment is computed which equates the note's principal balance to the present value of all remaining payments using the new interest rate. No other accounting complications arise.

CONCEPT REVIEW

1. Payments on regular mortgages include both interest and principal. Under the interest method, what effect does the amount of principal reduction in Period 1 have on the interest expense recognized in Period 2?
2. What is the general principle guiding valuation of notes payable when the contractual rate of interest does not represent the rate of interest agreed to by debtor and creditor?
3. When interest rates are changed on an adjustable mortgage, how is interest expense computed for the first payment after the change?

ADDITIONAL ISSUES AND DISCLOSURES FOR LONG-TERM LIABILITIES
◆

Unconditional Purchase Obligations, Project Financing Arrangements, and R&D Arrangements

Firms often contract with suppliers to guarantee a long-term source of goods and services. An **unconditional purchase obligation** is a future obligation to transfer funds for fixed or minimum quantities of goods and services. Technically, until goods and services are received by the buyer, no liability exists. Nevertheless, the entity has made an unrevocable commitment to transfer funds at a future date. However, information about unconditional long-term purchase commitments and other project financing relationships may be important to financial statement users attempting to assess the future obligations and cash flows of the business. Neither Canadian nor U.S. GAAP requires that these obligations be recorded as liabilities. However, FASB requires note disclosure.

A **project financing arrangement** is an agreement through which the debt of a newly created venture is guaranteed by two or more investing entities. For example, Companies A, B, and C may jointly invest in mineral exploration Company X by providing initial funds. Company X then borrows substantial funds on the market promising to repay these loans out of the proceeds of the venture once the mine is in production. To allow X to receive the borrowings needed at reasonable rates, Companies A, B, and C guarantee the loans. To complicate matters even further, A, B, and C often promise to purchase a certain proportion of the production from Company X. The problem arises because the sponsoring companies are not required to report the debt of Company X on their balance sheets. GAAP does require, however, that these companies disclose their commitments to Company X in the notes to their financial statements. It could be possible that these arrangements would be viewed as joint ventures, in which case section 3055 of the *CICA Handbook* would apply.

Special **research and development arrangements** have been devised to avoid the rule that research and most development costs must be expensed as incurred (*CICA Handbook,* section 3450) and to avoid the reporting of a liability. For example, assume that Electro-Nucleonics entered into an agreement with Pru-Tech, a limited partnership. The agreement specified that Pru-Tech would advance $7 million to Electro for rights to royalties from the sales of products developed by Electro. Pru-Tech was able to raise its own funds, which it advanced to Electro. The impetus for Electro to enter into this arrangement was to avoid (1) expensing research and development expenditures and (2) recognizing a liability for funding the activities.

The *CICA Handbook* does not deal with R&D under such an arrangement. The FASB in *SFAS No. 68* requires Electro to record a liability if it is obligated to repay any of the funds advanced (in any form) regardless of the outcome of the activity. If this is the case, Electro has not transferred the risk of the venture to Pru-Tech. In addition, Electro recognizes R&D expense as incurred. In contrast, if the financial risk of the project is transferred because repayment of funds provided by the other party depends solely on the project results, then Electro accounts for the arrangement as a contract to perform R&D services and does not record a liability.

The importance of long-term liability measurement and disclosure as a measure of the risk and financial strength of companies is unquestioned. However, as the discussion of unconditional purchase obligations and other arrangements implies, the criteria for recognizing liabilities are imprecise. The definition of a liability in section 1000 allows considerable latitude in interpretation. As discussed in the next section, creative financial instruments are increasing the complexity of liability recognition and measurement. Creative financial instruments increase the opportunity for **off-balance sheet financing.** Through off-balance sheet financing, firms can raise debt capital without reporting liabilities.

THE AcSB FINANCIAL INSTRUMENTS PROJECT
◆

The 1980s ushered in an enormous number of new and creative financial instruments.

> A Rip Van Winkle who fell asleep in 1979 and just woke up would hardly recognize today's financial landscape . . . Arthur Andersen & Company has kept a list of new financial products since 1986; it now . . . totals more than 600.[31]

Internationalization, deregulation, increased competition, inflation, changes in the financial services industry, tax law changes, and interest rate volatility contributed to the explosion in the number and variety of financial instruments issued by firms. Many of these new securities are debt instruments. Debt is favoured by firms unwilling to issue more shares for fear of reducing earnings per share.

Exchangeable debentures are an example of an innovative debt instrument. InterNorth Company issued 10.5% callable debentures, due 2008, exchangeable for the shares of Mobil Corporation owned by InterNorth. The exchange provision lowered the interest rate for InterNorth. Until the exchange, InterNorth receives Mobil dividends. The bondholders stand to benefit from Mobil stock price appreciation. Several accounting issues arise: (1) Is this one instrument or two? (2) Does the exchangeability provision affect the reporting of the investment in Mobil stock? (3) How is the income statement affected?

Another example is an interest rate swap, an arrangement between two companies that agree to trade interest payments. One company with variable-rate debt may desire the security of fixed-rate debt but cost and low debt rating prohibit issuance. Another company willing to risk interest rate fluctuation may exchange its fixed interest payments for the variable payments of the first company. For example, the footnotes to CT Financial Services Inc.'s 1989 financial statements included the following note:

> The company enters into swap contracts as a principal to reduce exposure to movement in interest and foreign exchange rates, which contracts are not reflected in the consolidated statement of condition. . . . The swap contracts give rise to credit risk measured by determining the replacement cost, should counterparties default on their original contractual obligations. The notional principal amount of these obligations was $1,804,340,000 at December 31, 1989. . . . Management moniters credit risk regularly and does not anticipate any material losses will result from these contracts.

Interest rate swaps create a number of accounting issues. Should the agreement be recorded in the accounts and if so how are they measured? Is cash exchanged between the two parties an adjustment to interest expense? Over what period should gains and losses be recognized?

---

[31] "Is Financial Product Explosion Perilous for Investors?" *The Wall Street Journal,* December 21, 1989, p. C1.

The incentives to issue imaginative financial instruments are diverse. Firms may wish to: (1) reduce interest rate risk, (2) increase the flexibility and attractiveness of financial instruments in a period of increased competition for capital, (3) lower the overall cost of financing, and (4) seek tax advantages.

Accounting for many of these instruments is not yet specified under GAAP. Therefore, until definitive guidelines are promulgated, accountants employ existing pronouncements where relevant.

The CICA, IASC, and FASB are considering the many issues related to financial instruments to supply guidance in accounting for these instruments. The historical cost, transaction-based traditional accounting model has created an incentive to develop financial instruments that allow the recognition of income earlier than traditional instruments, the deferral of losses, and the avoidance of disclosure of risks and liability recognition (off-balance sheet financing).

The projects affect many different areas of financial accounting. Some of the issues concern long-term liabilities with respect to: (1) disclosure, (2) recognition and measurement, and (3) distinguishing between liabilities and equity.

The 1990 Statement of Principles, which applies to all entities (as opposed to only financial institutions) defines a financial instrument as "any contract that gives rise to both a (recognized or unrecognized) financial asset of one entity and a (recognized or unrecognized) financial liability of another entity."

The approach to the development of accounting standards for recognition and measurement is to analyze each type of instrument in terms of fundamental building blocks. This reflects the belief that all financial instruments, regardless of complexity, can be broken down into understandable parts. The approach also recognizes the impossibility of writing accounting standards for every instrument and may reduce the need for the current piecemeal approach to GAAP.

Six fundamental financial instruments have been tentatively identified: (1) unconditional receivable or payable; (2) receivable or payable conditional on the occurrence of an event beyond the control of either party; (3) forward contract, an unconditional right and obligation to exchange financial instruments; (4) option, a right or obligation to exchange other financial instruments conditional on the occurrence of an event within the control of one party to the contract; (5) guarantee, a right or obligation to exchange financial instruments conditional on an event outside the control of either party; and (6) equity instrument.

A callable bond is a common example of a compound security. The security is comprised of an unconditional payable and an option to call the bonds.

Accounting for instruments that have both equity and liability attributes would have special impact on accounting for liabilities. The questions of accounting for convertible debt, debt with warrants attached, and stock options need to be considered. For example, does a company that grants its executives the option to purchase its stock at a fixed price incur a liability?

The CICA and the IASC are working on the project together. It is expected that both a Canadian and an international set of standards will come from the project.

Classifications of Short-Term Liabilities to Be Refinanced

In an effort to reduce current liabilities, some firms refinance them on a long-term basis. The *CICA Handbook,* paragraph 1510.06, stipulates that "Obligations, otherwise classified as current liabilities, should be excluded from the current liability classification to the extent that contractual arrangements have been made for settlement from other than current assets." This guideline is important to creditors who rely on accurate classification of liabilities between current and non-current. Firms seeking short-term credit have an incentive to reclassify obligations to non-current status. In particular, the current ratio (current assets to current liabilities) is improved by reclassifying short-term liabilities as non-current.

EXHIBIT 16–8   Long-Term Liability Disclosures, Stelco Inc.

(Dollars in thousands)	1989	1988
Long-term debt (Note 8).	$855,453	$822,413
8 Long-Term Debt		
5⅞% sinking fund debentures due May 1, 1990	$ 22,043	$ 23,361
9¼% sinking fund debentures due November 1, 1990	35,253	36,746
10⅞% sinking fund debentures due September 15, 1994.	38,880	40,817
9¾% sinking fund debentures due April 1, 1995	58,983	64,028
10¼% sinking fund debentures due April 30, 1996	63,817	67,937
10¾% sinking fund notes due November 20, 1995		
(1989—US $50 million, 1988—US $58 million)*	57,925	69,606
13½% sinking fund debentures due October 1, 2000	69,210	76,910
7¾% convertible subordinated debentures due August 31, 1998	150,000	150,000
10.40% retractable debentures due November 30, 2009	125,000	—
	$621,111	$529,405
Capital lease (expiring January 1, 2000)	40,594	42,873
Notes payable	270,000	269,554
	$931,705	$841,832
Less amount due within one year, net of prepayments.	76,252	19,419
	$855,453	$822,413

* Long-term debt payable in United States fund has been translated at the December 31 rates of exchange. This translated amount is not necessarily indicative of the amount which will be repaid when the obligations are retired.

Short-term obligations, as discussed in Chapter 15, are those liabilities scheduled to mature within one year of the balance sheet or operating cycle whichever is longer. These may be classified as long-term only if the firm has made a contractual arrangement for long-term refinancing or a contractual arrangement has been made to settle the liability by the issue of share capital.

Current Portion of Long-Term Debt

The portion of long-term debt paid from current assets during the year following the balance sheet or the operating cycle, if longer, is reported as a current liability. For example, the December 31, 1994, balance sheet classifies the net Gresham bond payable liability in Case 1 as current because the bonds mature one year later.

Derlan Industries Limited reported the following in the current liabilities section of its 1989 balance sheet:

	1989	1988
(Dollars in thousands)		
Current portion of long-term debt	$2,990	$5,159

If debt is paid from non-current sources such as a bond sinking fund, the debt remains classified as a long-term liability for the entire bond term.

General Long-Term Liability Disclosures

Exhibit 16–8 is a portion of the 1989 Stelco Inc. annual report. It provides a comprehensive illustration of long-term liability disclosures.

CICA Handbook section 3210 requires disclosure of the aggregate amount of maturities and sinking fund requirements for all long-term debt in each of the five years following the balance sheet date (par. 3210.02). For example, Alcan Aluminium Limited included the following in the footnotes to its 1989 financial statements:

> Based on rates of exchange at year-end, debt repayment requirements over the next five years amount to [in millions of US$] $64 in 1990, $68 in 1991, $76 in 1992, $100 in 1993, and $77 in 1994.

SUMMARY OF KEY POINTS

(L.O. 1) 1. Long-term liabilities are those fulfilling the definition of a liability and having a term exceeding one year or the operating cycle, whichever is longer.

(L.O. 1) 2. Three basic principles are used for valuing long-term liabilities. The recorded value at issuance is the present value of all future cash flows discounted at the current market rate of interest for debt securities of equivalent risk. Interest expense is the product of the market rate at issuance and the balance in the liability at the beginning of the reporting period. And the book value of long-term debt at a balance sheet date is the present value of all remaining cash payments required, using the market rate at issuance.

(L.O. 2) 3. Bonds are long-term debt instruments that specify the face value paid at maturity and the stated interest rate payable according to a fixed schedule. Bonds are a significant source of capital for many firms; many different types of bonds are issued to appeal to investor preferences.

(L.O. 2) 4. The price of a bond at issuance, which excludes accrued interest at the stated rate, is the present value of all future cash flows discounted at the current market rate of interest for bonds of a similar risk class.

(L.O. 3) 5. Bonds are sold at a premium if the stated rate exceeds the market rate, and vice versa for bonds sold at a discount. The premium or discount is amortized over the remaining life of the security. Bond premiums and discounts are amortized under the straight-line method (acceptability depends on the materiality constraint) or the interest method (conceptually preferable because it is based on present value concepts).

(L.O. 3) 6. Accounting for bonds depends on the features inherent in the particular bond issue. Bonds issued between interest dates require payment of accrued interest by the investor, and the bond price using present value techniques. Bonds were discussed from the viewpoint of both issuer and investor.

(L.O. 4) 7. Certain long-term debt instruments are issued with equity rights, including bonds issued with detachable stock warrants and convertible bonds. The equity feature is recorded by the issuer only if a separate market exists for the equity feature. Convertible bonds are treated similarly to non-convertible bonds until they are converted because the value of the conversion feature cannot be estimated reliably.

(L.O. 5) 8. Extinguishment of debt can occur before, at, or after the maturity date. Extinguishment is accomplished by direct payment or replacement with another debt instrument, by obtaining a release from the creditor, or by placing assets in an irrevocable trust to pay the debt.

(L.O. 5) 9. The gain or loss from extinguishment, which is the difference between market value of consideration used for extinguishment and book value of debt extinguished, is included in the calculation of net income.

(L.O. 6) 10. Long-term note valuation follows the general principles for valuing long-term liabilities. Notes are formal promises by a debtor to pay principal and interest. Many types of notes are in common use.

(L.O. 7) 11. Serial bonds mature according to a schedule rather than at one date. Accounting for serial bonds parallels regular bonds, although certain computational complexities arise. The bonds outstanding method simplifies the accounting for interest and amortization of premium and discount.

(L.O. 8) 12. A troubled debt restructure (TDR) occurs when the debtor cannot meet the required debt payments, and the creditor makes a concession to the debtor such as reduced or deferred interest or principal payments. TDRs are settlements or modifications of debt terms.

(L.O. 8) 13. Restructured debt is recorded at the lower of the sum of restructured flows and book value of the old debt. Gains recognized by the debtor on restructure are classified as extraordinary.

REVIEW PROBLEM

◆

On August 1, 1992, Pismo Corporation, a calendar-year corporation that records adjusting entries only once a year, issued bonds with the following characteristics:

1. $50,000 total face value.
2. 12% stated rate.
3. 16% yield rate.
4. Interest dates are February 1, May 1, August 1, and November 1.
5. Bond date is October 31, 1991.
6. Maturity date is November 1, 1996.
7. $1,000 of bond issue costs are incurred.

Required:

1. Provide all entries required for the bond issue through February 1, 1993, for Pismo assuming the interest method.
2. On June 1, 1994, Pismo retired $20,000 of bonds at 98 through open market purchase. Provide the entries to update the bond accounts for this portion of the bond issue and to retire the bonds assuming the interest method.
3. Provide the entry required on August 1, 1994, under the:
   a. Interest method.
   b. Straight-line method.

REVIEW SOLUTION

◆

1. August 1, 1992—Issue bonds and incur issue costs:

Bond issue cost	1,000	
Cash		1,000

Cash	43,917*	
Discount on bonds payable	6,083	
Bonds payable		50,000

* Four and one quarter years, or 17 quarters, remain in the bond term.
$43,917 = $50,000(PV1, 4\%, 17) \times .03($50,000) (PVA, 4\%, 17)$
     $= $50,000(.51337) + $1,500(12.16567)$

November 1, 1992—Interest payment date:

Interest expense	1,757*	
Discount on bonds payable		257
Cash		1,500†

Bond issue expense	59‡	
Bond issue cost		59

* $1,757 = $43,917(.04)$

† $1,500 = $50,000(.03)$

‡ $59 = $1,000/17$

December 31, 1992—Adjusting entry:

Interest expense 1,178*		
Discount on bonds payable		178
Interest payable.		1,000†
Bond issue expense	39‡	
Bond issue cost.		39

*$1,178 = ($43,917 + $257) (.04) (⅔ of quarter)

† $1,000 = $1,500(⅔)

‡ $39 = $59(⅔)

February 1, 1993—Interest payment date:

Interest expense	589*	
Interest payable.	1,000	
Discount on bonds payable		89
Cash		1,500
Bond issue expense	20†	
Bond issue cost.		20

* $589 = ($43,917 + $257) (.04) (⅓ of quarter)

† $20 = $59(⅓)

2. On May 1, 1994, the remaining term of the bonds is two and one half years or 10 quarters, and the $20,000 of bonds to be retired have the following book value:

$$BV = \$20,000(PV\,1, 4\%, 10) + \$20,000(.03)\,(PVA, 4\%, 10)$$

$$= \$20,000(.67556) + \$600(8.11090) = \$18,378$$

On May 1, 1994, the remaining discount on the portion of bonds to be retired is therefore $1,622 ($20,000 − $18,378).

June 1, 1994—Update relevant bond accounts before retirement:

Interest expense	245*	
Discount on bonds payable		45
Cash		200†
Bond issue expense	8‡	
Bond issue cost.		8

June 1, 1994—Remove relevant bond accounts:

Bonds payable	20,000	
Loss on bond extinguishment	1,404	
Discount on bonds payable		1,577§
Bond issue costs		277‖
Cash .98 × $20,000		19,600

* $245 = $18,378(.04) (⅓ of quarter)

† $200 = $20,000(.03) (⅓)

‡ $8 = $1,000(1/17) (⅓) (.40 of issue retired)

§ $1,577 = $1,622 − $45

‖ At June 1, 1994, 9⅔ quarters remain in bond term: $227 = $1,000(.40) (9⅔)/17

3. On May 1, 1994, the remaining term of the bonds is two and one half years or 10 quarters, and the remaining $30,000 of bonds have the following book value.:

$$BV = \$30,000(PV\,1, 4\%, 10) + \$30,000(.03)\,(PVA, 4\%, 10)$$

$$= \$30,000(.67556) + \$900(8.11090) = \$27,567$$

On May 1, 1994, the remaining discount is therefore $2,433 ($30,000 − $27,567).

a. August 1, 1994—Interest payment date:

Interest expense		1,103*
Discount on bonds payable	203	
Cash	900†	
Bond issue expense	35	
Bond issue cost	35‡	

* $1,103 = $27,567(.04)

† $900 = $30,000(.03)

‡ $35 = (.60 of issue remaining)$1,000/17

b. Under the SL method, discount is amortized $358 ($6,083/17) per quarter on the entire bond issue.

August 1, 1994—Interest payment date:

Interest expense		1,115
Discount on bonds payable	215*	
Cash	900	
Bond issue expense	35	
Bond issue cost	35	

* $215 = 358(.60)

APPENDIX 16A: *Accounting for Serial Bonds*

A **serial bond** issue matures in a series of installments, rather than in one maturity amount. The advantages of serial bonds to the issuer include:

* Less need for a sinking-fund.
* Lower perceived risk of the issue.
* Improved marketability.
* Less burdensome debt retirement schedule.

Price of Serial Bonds, Accounting Considerations

Serial bonds are sold either as separate issues or as one aggregate issue. If the bonds are sold separately, it is possible to identify the yield rate on each, which normally increases with the length of the term to compensate for increased risk. If sold in the aggregate, the entire bond issue carries a single average yield rate. Either way, the price of serial bonds is the sum of the present values of each issue using the appropriate yield rate. Serial bond valuation is consistent with ordinary bond issues.

Three methods of accounting for serial bonds are available:

Interest method: If the yield rate on each issue is known, each issue is treated as an individual bond issue. If not, the entire issue is treated as one bond issue, and the average yield rate is used to recognize interest. The book value of serial bonds payable is reduced by the face amount of serial bonds retired at each maturity date. Otherwise, procedures for amortizing discount and premium are identical to ordinary bonds.

Straight-line method: An equal amount of premium or discount is allocated to each reporting period for each separate issue. Then the amounts for each issue are totaled by reporting period. Total amortization for a reporting period reflects each separate issue outstanding that period. This method is permitted only if it produces results not materially different from the interest method.

Bonds outstanding method: The discount or premium for each separate issue need not be identified under this method. A constant rate of discount or premium per dollar of bond outstanding per period is used for amortization. This modified straight-line method is permitted only if it produces results not materially different from the interest method.

All three methods relate the premium or discount to the total face value of bonds outstanding during the period. This amount decreases by the face value of each maturing issue. Consequently, relative to an ordinary bond, discounts and premiums are amortized more quickly.

Serial Bond Amortization, Early Retirement, and Maturity

The following examples illustrate accounting for serial bonds and early retirement. An unrealistically short bond term simplifies the presentation.

Example Michael Limited issues $100,000 of 8% serial bonds on January 1, 1991. The bonds are sold as one issue to yield 10%. The bonds pay interest each December 31 and mature according to the following schedule:

Maturity Date	Maturity Amount
January 1, 1992	$ 20,000
January 1, 1993	50,000
January 1, 1994	30,000
	$100,000

On January 1, 1992, Michael retired $10,000 of the issue scheduled to mature January 1, 1994, by open-market purchase at 99.

Issue Price of Serial Bonds

	Serial Bond Price	Discount*
Bonds due January 1, 1992		
Face value [$20,000($PV$1, 10%, 1) = $20,000(.90909)]	$18,182	
Interest [$1,600($PVA$, 10%, 1) = $1,600(.90909)]	1,455	
	$19,637	$ 363
Bonds due January 1, 1993 (similar computations)	48,265	1,735
Bonds due January 1, 1994 (similar computations)	28,508	1,492
Total serial bond price	$96,410	
Total serial bond discount		$3,590

* Face value minus price of individual issue.

January 1, 1991—Issue serial bonds:

Cash	96,410	
Discount on serial bonds	3,590	
Serial bonds payable		100,000

Selected Entries under the interest method follow.

Interest Method:

December 31, 1991—Interest payment:

Interest expense (.10 × $96,410)	9,641	
Discount on serial bonds		1,641
Cash (.08 × $100,000)		8,000

January 1, 1992—Retire bonds due January 1, 1992:

Serial bonds payable	20,000	
Cash		20,000

January 1, 1992—Retire $10,000 of bonds due January 1, 1994:

Serial bonds payable	10,000	
Loss on bond extinguishment	247	
Discount on bonds payable		347*
Cash (.99 × $10,000)		9,900

* $10,000 less the book value of retired bonds (two years before scheduled): $10,000 − [$10,000(PV1, 10%, 2) + $800($PVA$, 10%, 2)] = $10,000 − [$10,000(.82645) + $800(1.73554)] = $10,000 − $9,653 = $347

After the early retirement, the book value of the remaining serial bonds equals:

Book value of serial bonds January 1, 1991	$ 96,410
Amortization of discount on December 31, 1991	1,641
Book value of bonds maturing January 1, 1992	(20,000)
Book value of bonds retired early on January 1, 1992	(9,653)
Book value of $70,000 remaining bonds January 1, 1992	$ 68,398*

* This value is also the present value of remaining cash flows.

December 31, 1992—Interest payment:

Interest expense (.10 × $68,398)	6,840	
Discount on serial bonds		1,240
Cash (.08 × $70,000)		5,600

The remaining entries under the interest method are consistent with the previous ones and follow the same principles. These entries are the maturity of bonds on January 1, 1993, and January 1, 1994, at face value, and the interest payment on December 31, 1993.

Straight-Line Method The following table illustrates this method for the Michael issue:

Amortization Table—Straight-Line Method

Bond Maturity January 1	Discount on Issue	Bond Term (Years)	Amortization per Period	Amortization Recognized in		
				1991	1992	1993
1992	$ 363	1	$363	$ 363		
1993	1,735	2	868	868	$ 868	
1994	1,492	3	497	497	497	$497
Total amortization recognized in				$1,728	$1,365	$497

When bonds are retired early, the amount of discount remaining on those bonds can be read directly from the preceding table.

December 31, 1991—Interest payment:

Interest expense	9,728	
Discount on serial bonds		1,728
Cash (.08 × $100,000)		8,000

January 1, 1992—Retire bonds due January 1, 1992:

Serial bonds payable	20,000	
Cash		20,000

January 1, 1992—Retire $10,000 of bonds due January 1, 1994:

Serial bonds payable	10,000	
Loss on bond extinguishment	231	
Discount on bonds payable		331*
Cash (.99 × $10,000)		9,900

* ($497 + $497) ($10,000/$30,000) = $331
Discount remaining at January 1, 1992, on the January 1, 1994, issue × Fraction retired

December 31, 1992—Interest payment:

```
Interest expense  . . . . . . . . . . . . . . . . . . . . . . . . . .   6,799
    Discount on serial bonds . . . . . . . . . . . . . . . . .           1,199*
    Cash (.08 × $70,000) . . . . . . . . . . . . . . . . . . .           5,600
* $868 + ($497) ($20,000/$30,000)
```

Bonds Outstanding Method: Under the **bonds outstanding method,** the amount of premium or discount allocated to each reporting period is the product of three amounts:

1. A constant rate of amortization per dollar of bond per period.
2. The dollar amount of bonds outstanding (at face value) during the period.
3. The length of the period.

The following table develops the rate of amortization:

Bonds Outstanding Method
Computation of Amortization Rate

Face Value of Bonds Outstanding during		
1991	$100,000	
1992	80,000*	
1993	30,000	
Sum	$210,000	

$$\text{Rate of discount amortization per dollar of face value per year} = \frac{\text{Initial discount}}{\text{Sum of bonds outstanding}}$$

$$= \frac{\$3,590}{\$210,000} = \$.0171$$

* On January 1, 1992, $20,000 of bonds mature; therefore $80,000 of bonds are outstanding during 1992.

The amortization rate indicates that $.0171 of discount is associated with each dollar of face value per year. The following entries complete our example:

December 31, 1991—Interest payment:

```
Interest expense  . . . . . . . . . . . . . . . . . . . . . . .   9,710
    Discount on serial bonds (.0171 × $100,000 × 1 year) . . . .        1,710
    Cash (.08 × $100,000) . . . . . . . . . . . . . . . . . .            8,000
```

January 1, 1992—Retire bonds due January 1, 1992:

```
Serial bonds payable  . . . . . . . . . . . . . . . . . . . .   20,000
    Cash . . . . . . . . . . . . . . . . . . . . . . . . . .             20,000
```

January 1, 1992—Retire $10,000 of bonds due January 1, 1994:

```
Serial bonds payable  . . . . . . . . . . . . . . . . . . . .   10,000
Loss on bond extinguishment . . . . . . . . . . . . . . . . .      242
    Discount on bonds payable . . . . . . . . . . . . . . . .              342*
    Cash (.99 × $10,000) . . . . . . . . . . . . . . . . . . .           9,900
* (.0171 × $10,000 × 2 years remaining in bond term) = $342
```

December 31, 1992—Interest payment:

```
Interest expense  . . . . . . . . . . . . . . . . . . . . . .   6,797
    Discount on serial bonds (.0171 × $70,000 × 1 year). . . . .        1,197
    Cash (.08 × $70,000) . . . . . . . . . . . . . . . . . . .           5,600
```

The amortization rate is applied to any amount of face value or any period length without further complication. For example, if the bonds scheduled to mature January 1, 1994, are retired March 1, 1992, rather than on January 1, 1992, the amount of discount to be removed is $314 (.0171 × $10,000 × $1\frac{10}{12}$ years).

The complications arising when serial bonds are issued during a fiscal year are minimized by the bonds outstanding method. For example, assume that $100,000 of serial bonds are issued March 31, 1991, at a premium and that the amortization rate is $.02. If $25,000 of bonds mature on March 31, 1992, the total amount of premium amortized during 1992 is $1,625:

$$(.02 \times \$100,000 \times \tfrac{3}{12}) + (.02 \times \$75,000 \times \tfrac{9}{12}) = \$1,625$$

APPENDIX 16B: Troubled Debt Restructure

With increasing frequency during the 1980s, debtor firms (and many nations) were unable to make interest and principal payments on long-term debt. Others experienced a related problem: violation of debt indentures. Rising interest rates, non-performing loans, poor management, unsatisfactory returns on investments, and lack of demand for the products and services provided by firms contributed to troubled debt.

Faced with non-performing investments in debt securities or receivables, creditors frequently agree to a debt restructure allowing the debtor to remain in operation. The following terms are typical of restructure agreements:

♦ Elimination of interest and principal payments.
♦ Reduction of interest rates and principal amounts.
♦ Extension of debt terms.
♦ Settlement of debt through cash payment or transfer of equity securities.

Creditors agree to such provisions in the hope that the debtor can resolve its financial difficulties. Creditors usually receive more on restructured debt than through bankruptcy by the debtor.[32]

Because the CICA has not yet addressed the issue of troubled debt restructure, a summary of *SFAS No. 15,* "Accounting by Debtors and Creditors for Troubled Debt Restructurings," is provided. **Troubled debt restructure** (TDR) is defined as follows in paragraph 2:

> A restructuring of a debt constitutes a troubled debt restructuring . . . if the creditor for economic or legal reasons related to the debtor's financial difficulties grants a concession to the debtor that it would not otherwise consider.

For a debt restructure to be troubled, the creditor must accept new debt or assets with an economic value less than the book value of the original debt. An example of a TDR is the acceptance by a creditor of $10,000 in full payment of a $15,000 receivable. The creditor must make a concession, which can arise from an agreement between the creditor and the debtor or can be imposed by a law or court.

A creditor normally makes no concession in an ordinary refinancing of debt; therefore, refinancings are usually not TDRs.[33] Although debt is settled in some TDRs, the provisions of *SFAS No. 76,* "Extinguishment of Debt," do not apply.

The accounting issues arising from the creditor's concession include the measurement of the new liability and receivable (or consideration transferred in settlement), and the reporting of any gain or loss on restructure.

Types of TDRs

TDRs are accomplished in two fundamentally different ways:

1. Settlement of debt by transfer of assets or equity interest of the debtor to the creditor. The market value of the assets or equity securities must be less than the book value (including accrued interest) of the debt or receivable.[34]
2. Continuation of debt with modification of debt terms. TDRs effected by modifying terms fall into two categories:
   a. Total restructured payments are less than or equal to the book value (including accrued interest) of the debt or receivable.
   b. Total restructured payments exceed the book value (including accrued interest) of the debt or receivable.

---

[32] Some debtors intentionally default on debt to force a consideration of restructure. Robert Campeau, a Toronto retailer, deliberately defaulted on $705 million worth of loans from two major secured creditors in 1990 in an attempt to obtain favourable restructuring terms. See "Campeau Wins Pact to Defer Late Payments," *The Wall Street Journal,* March 6, 1990, p. A8.

[33] Nor does a TDR occur if the creditor reduces the effective interest rate on debt to match a decrease in market rates to maintain a relationship with a debtor that can readily obtain debt financing from other sources at the market rate.

[34] A transfer of equity securities pursuant to the existing terms of convertible debt does not qualify as a transfer of an equity interest.

Accounting Provisions of *SFAS No. 15*

Accounting for Settlements   The main provisions of *SFAS No. 15* relating to settlements follow:

Debtor:
1. The debtor recognizes an extraordinary gain equal to the difference between debt book value and market value of consideration received.
2. The accounts related to the debt are removed.
3. A gain or loss on disposal is recognized equalling the difference between market value and book value of consideration transferred (no gain or loss if the debtor issues stock) and is classified in conformity with *APB Opinion No. 30*.

Creditor:
1. The creditor records the consideration received at market value and recognizes an ordinary, unusual or infrequent, or extraordinary loss in conformity with *APB Opinion No. 30*. The loss equals the difference between the recorded value of the investment or receivable less the market value of consideration received.
2. The accounts related to the investment or receivable are removed.

KEY TERMS

Amortization table (762)
Bond (754)
Bond indenture (754)
Bond issue costs (767)
Bonds outstanding method (800)
Convertible bond (773)
Discount (757)
In-substance defeasance (778)
Off-balance sheet financing (791)
Premium (757)

Project financing arrangement (790)
Prospectus (754)
Refunding (782)
Research and development arrangements (790)
Serial bonds (797)
Sinking fund (753)
Troubled debt restructure (801)
Unconditional purchase obligation (790)

QUESTIONS

1. List and briefly explain the primary characteristics of long-term debt securities.
2. What are the primary distinctions between a debt security and an equity security?
3. Explain the difference between the stated rate of interest and the effective rate on a long-term debt security.
4. Briefly explain point-system mortgages, SAMs, and variable-rate mortgages.
5. Briefly explain the effects on interest recognized when the stated and effective rates of interest are different.
6. What are the primary characteristics of a bond? What distinguishes it from capital stock?
7. Contrast the following classes of bonds: (*a*) industrial versus governmental, (*b*) secured versus unsecured, (*c*) ordinary versus income, (*d*) ordinary versus serial, (*e*) callable versus convertible, and (*f*) registered versus coupon.
8. What are the principal advantages and disadvantages of bonds versus common stock for (*a*) the issuer and (*b*) the investor?
9. Distinguish between the par amount and the price of a bond. When are they the same? When different? Explain.
10. Explain the significance of bond discount and bond premium to (*a*) the issuer and (*b*) the investor.
11. Assume a $1,000, 8% (payable semiannually), 10-year bond is sold at an effective rate of 6%. Explain how to compute the price of this bond.
12. Explain why and how bond discount and bond premium affect (*a*) the balance sheet and (*b*) the income statement of the investor.

13. What is the primary conceptual difference between the straight-line and interest methods of amortizing bond discount and premium?
14. Under GAAP, when is it appropriate to use the (*a*) straight-line and (*b*) interest method of amortization for bond discount or premium?
15. When the end of the accounting period of the issuer is not on a bond interest date, adjusting entries must be made for (*a*) accrued interest and (*b*) discount or premium amortization. Explain in general terms what each adjustment amount represents.
16. When bonds are sold (or purchased) between interest dates, accrued interest must be recognized. Explain why.
17. What are convertible bonds? What are the primary reasons for their use?
18. Why is the accounting different for non-convertible bonds with detachable stock purchase warrants and non-convertible bonds with non-detachable stock purchase warrants?
19. Define extinguishment of debt.
20. When may extinguishment of debt occur? List the various ways that extinguishment of debt occurs.
21. Explain how an accounting gain or loss to the debtor may occur when a call privilege is exercised.
22. When the issuer purchases its own debt securities in the open market to extinguish the debt, two entries usually must be made. Explain.
23. What is meant by refunding?
24. What is meant by in-substance defeasance?
25. What effect does in-substance defeasance have on the balance sheet?
26. What is meant by troubled debt restructuring? What are some of the features of typical restructuring arrangements?
27. Explain the income classification of gains and losses from troubled debt restructuring.
28. Differentiate between a debt restructure in which debt is settled and one in which it continues after the restructure.

EXERCISES

E 16–1
Bonds—Issue above, at, and below Par: Effective Rates and Interest Expense
(L.O. 2, 3)

Rowe Corporation authorized $600,000, 8% (interest payable semiannually), 10-year bonds payable. The bonds were dated January 1, 1991; interest dates are June 30 and December 31.

Assume four different cases with respect to the sale of the bonds: *Case A*—Sold on January 1, 1991, at par; *Case B*—Sold on January 1, 1991, at 102; *Case C*—Sold on January 1, 1991, at 98; *Case D*—Sold on March 1, 1991, at par.

Required:

1. For each case, what amount of cash interest will be paid on the first interest date, June 30, 1991?
2. In what cases will the effective rate of interest be (*a*) the same, (*b*) higher, or (*c*) lower than the stated rate?
3. After sale of the bonds, and prior to maturity date, in what cases will the carrying or book value of the bonds (as reported on the balance sheet) be (*a*) the same, (*b*) higher, or (*c*) lower than the maturity or face amount?
4. After the sale of the bonds, in Cases A, B, and C, which case will report interest expense (*a*) the same, (*b*) higher, or (*c*) lower than the amount of cash interest paid each period?

E 16–2
Bonds: Compute Four Bond Prices
(L.O. 2)

Compute the bond price for each of the following situations (show computations and round to nearest dollar):

a. A 10-year, $1,000 bond; annual interest at 7% (payable 3½% semiannually) purchased to yield 6% interest.
b. An eight-year, $1,000 bond; annual interest at 6% (payable annually) purchased to yield 7% interest.
c. A 10-year, $1,000 bond; annual interest at 6% (payable semiannually) purchased to yield 8% interest.
d. An eight-year, $1,000 bond; annual interest at 6% (payable annually) purchased to yield 6% interest.

E 16–3
Issue above, at, below Par, Straight-Line: Issuer and Investor Entries
(L.O. 2, 3)

Yale Corporation issued to Zepher Corporation a $30,000, 8% (interest payable semiannually on June 30 and December 31), 10-year bond dated and sold on January 1, 1991. Assumptions: Case A—sold at par; Case B—sold at 103; and Case C—sold at 97.

Required:

In parallel columns for the issuer and the investor (assume a long-term investment), give the appropriate journal entries for each case on (1) January 1, 1991, and (2) June 30, 1991 (use the gross method). Assume the difference between the interest method and the straight-line method of amortization is not material; therefore, use staight-line amortization.

E 16–4
Compute Bond Price, Interest Method, Straight-Line, Issuer and Investor Entries
(L.O. 2, 3)

New Corporation sold and issued to Old Corporation a $10,000, 9% (interest payable semiannually on June 30 and December 31), 10-year bond, dated and sold on January 1, 1991. The bond was sold at an 8% effective rate (4% semiannually).

Required:

1. Compute the price of the bond.
2. In parallel columns for the issuer and the investor (assume a long-term investment), give the appropriate journal entries on (*a*) January 1, 1991, and (*b*) June 30, 1991 (use the gross method). Assume the difference between the interest method and the straight-line method of amortization is material; therefore, use the interest method.

E 16–5
Bonds at a Premium, Accrued Interest: Straight-Line, Gross, and Net Methods
(L.O. 3)

On September 1, 1991, Golf Company sold and issued to Youngblood Company $60,000, five-year, 9% (payable semiannually) bonds for $64,640 plus accrued interest. The bonds were dated July 1, 1991, and interest is payable each June 30 and December 31. The accounting period for each company ends on December 31.

Required:

In parallel columns, give entries, using the gross method for the issuer and the net method for the investor (a long-term investment) for the following dates: Setpember 1, 1991; December 31, 1991; January 1, 1992; and June 30, 1992. Assume the difference between the interest method and straight-line method amortization amounts is not material; therefore, use straight-line amortization.

E 16–6
Bonds, Accrued Interest, Issuer Entries: Straight-Line, Gross
(L.O. 3)

Ryan Corporation sold and issued $300,000, three-year, 8% (payable semiannually) bonds payable for $312,800 plus accrued interest. Interest is payable each February 28 and August 31. The bonds were dated March 1, 1991, and were sold on July 1, 1991. The accounting period ends on December 31.

Required:

1. How much accrued interest should be recognized at date of sale?
2. How long is the amortization period?
3. Give entries for Ryan Corporation through February 1992 (including reversing entries). Use straight-line amortization and the gross method.
4. Would the preceding amounts also be recorded by the investor? Explain.

E 16–7
Compute Bond Price: Amortization Schedule, Interest Method, Entries, Issuer Gross, Investment
(L.O. 2, 3)

Radian Company issued to Seivers Company $30,000, four-year, 8% bonds dated June 1, 1991. Interest is payable semiannually on May 31 and November 30. The bonds were issued on March 1, 1992, for $28,371 plus accrued interest. The bonds would have sold at the effective rate on the next interest date for $28,478. The accounting period ends December 31 for both companies. The effective interest rate was 10%.

Required:

Round to the nearest dollar.

1. Verify the bond price. Use straight-line interpolation between interest dates.
2. Prepare a bond amortization schedule starting on March 1, 1992, and continuing to maturity, May 31, 1995. Use interest-method amortization.
3. In parallel columns, give entries for the issuer and the investor (as a long-term investment) for the following dates: March 1, 1992, and May 31, 1992. Use interest-method amortization, the gross method for issuer, and the net method for the investor.

E 16–8
Non-convertible Bonds
with Detachable Warrants:
Entries, Issuer and Investor
(L.O. 4)

Hardware Corporation issued $150,000, 6%, 10-year, non-convertible bonds with detachable stock purchase warrants. Each $1,000 bond carried 20 detachable warrants, each of which was for one share of Hardware common stock with a specified option price of $60. The bonds sold at 102 including the warrants (no bond price ex-warrants was available), and, immediately after date of issuance, the detachable stock purchase warrants were selling at $4 each. The entire issue was acquired by Software Company as a long-term investment.

Required:

1. Give entries for both the issuer and the investor at date of acquisition of the bonds. Use the gross method.
2. Give the entry for the investor assuming a subsequent sale of all of the warrants to another investor at $5.50 each.
3. Disregard (2). Give the entries for the issuer and the investor assuming subsequent tender of all of the warrants by the investor for exercise at the specified option price. At this date, the stock was selling at $75 per share.

E 16–9
Convertible Bonds:
Entries, Issuer and
Investor, Conversion
(L.O. 4)

Stonewall Corporation issued $40,000, 5%, 10-year convertible bonds. Each $1,000 bond was convertible to 10 shares of common stock of Stonewall Corporation at any interest date after three years from issuance. The bonds were sold at 105 to Mason Corporation as a long-term investment.

Required:

1. Give the entry for both the issuer and the investor at the date of issuance. Use the gross method.
2. Give entries for both the issuer and the investor assuming that the conversion privilege is subsequently exercised by Mason Corporation immediately after the end of the third year. Assume that 30% of any premium or discount has been amortized and that, at date of conversion, the common stock was selling at $125 per share.

E 16–10
Debt Issuance and Early
Retirement
(L.O. 3, 5)

On January 1, 1991, Quaid Company issued $100,000 of 10% debentures. The following information relates to these bonds:

Bond date: January 1, 1991.

Yield rate: 8%

Maturity date: January 1, 1996.

Interest payment date: December 31.

Bond issue costs incurred: $2,000.

On March 1, 1992, Quaid retires $10,000 (face value) of the bonds when the market price is 110.

Required:

Provide entries for Quaid on the following dates under both the interest and straight-line methods of amortization.

1. January 1, 1991, bond issuance.
2. December 31, 1991, first interest payment.
3. March 1, 1992, entries to update the portion of the bond issue retired and to extinguish the bonds.

E 16–11
Bond Issuance, Interest,
and Early Retirement
(L.O. 2, 3, 5)

This exercise has three independent situations.

a. On April 1, 1991, Felly Company issued 400 of its 10%, $1,000 bonds at 97 plus accrued interest. The bonds are dated January 1, 1991, and mature on January 1, 2001. Interest is payable semiannually on January 1 and July 1.
b. On July 1, 1991, Centre Company issued 9% bonds in the face amount of $1 million, which mature on July 1, 2001. The bonds were issued for $939,000 to yield 10%, resulting in a bond discount of $61,000. Centre uses the interest method of amortizing bond discount. Interest is payable annually on June 30.
c. On July 1, 1992, Fondue Company issued 2,000 of its 9%, $1,000 callable bonds for $1,920,000. The bonds are dated July 1, 1992, and mature on July 1, 2002. Interest is payable semiannually on January 1 and July 1. Fondue uses the straight-line method of amortizing bond

discount. The bonds can be called by the issuer at 101 at any time after June 30, 1997. On July 1, 1998, Fondue called in all the bonds and retired them.

Required:

1. Compute the proceeds on the Felly bond issue.
2. Compute the unamortized discount on the Centre bond issue on July 1, 1993.
3. Give the entry to record the extinguishment of the Fondue bond issue.

(AICPA adapted)

E 16–12
Extinguishment by Call:
Issuance and
Extinguishment Entries
(L.O. 5)

On January 1, 1991, Radar Company issued $100,000 bonds payable with a stated interest rate of 12%, payable annually each December 31. The bonds mature in 20 years and have a call price of 103, exercisable by Radar Company after the fifth year. The bonds originally sold at 105.

On December 31, 2002, the company called the bonds. At that time, the bonds were quoted on the market at a price to yield 10%. Radar Company uses straight-line amortization; its accounting period ends December 31.

Required:

1. Give the issuance entry for Radar Company required on January 1, 1991. Use the gross method.
2. Give the entry for extinguishment of the debt.

E 16–13
Extinguishment by Call:
Update, Issuance, and
Extinguishment Entries
(L.O. 5)

On January 1, 1991, Sty Company issued $200,000 bonds payable with a stated interest rate of 5%, payable annually each December 31. The bonds mature in 10 years and are callable after the 4th year at 101. The bonds originally sold on January 1, 1991, at 104.

On June 30, 1996, the bonds were called. The company uses straight-line amortization, and the accounting period ends December 31.

Required:

1. Give the issuance entry on January 1, 1991. Use the gross method.
2. Give any entries on the extinguishment (i.e., call) date.

E 16–14
Extinguishment by
Refunding: Issuance and
Extinguishment Entries
(L.O. 5)

On January 1, 1991, Rocket Corporation issued $500,000, 6%, 20-year bonds at 98. The interest is payable each December 31. Rocket uses straight-line amortization and the gross method. Its accounting period ends December 31.

On January 1, 2002, Rocket issued $500,000, 9%, 20-year, refunding bonds at par. On this date, the old 6% bonds could be purchased in the open market at their present value based on the current effective rate of 9%. Rocket immediately purchased all of the 6% debt.

Required:

Round to the nearest dollar.

1. Give the entry for issuance of the 6% bonds.
2. Give the entry for issuance of the 9% bonds.
3. Give the entry to record the extinguishment of the old debt by refunding.
4. What effect did the refunding have on the working capital of Rocket Corporation?

E 16–15
Extinguishment by
Purchase in the Open
Market: Entries
(L.O. 5)

On January 1, 1991, Nue Corporation issued $100,000, 10%, 10-year bonds at 98. Interest is paid each December 31, which also is the end of the accounting period. The company uses straight-line amortization and the gross method. On July 1, 1996, the company purchased all of the bonds at 101 plus any accrued interest.

Required:

1. Give the issuance entry.
2. Give the interest entry on December 31, 1991.
3. Give the related entries on July 1, 1996.

E 16–16
Extinguishment by
In-Substance Defeasance
(L.O. 5)

On January 1, 1991, Slick Corporation borrowed cash on a $900,000, 5%, seven-year, note payable. Interest is payable semiannually on each June 30 and December 31. On January 1, 1995, the company entered into an agreement with the creditors to irrevocably transfer the note to an independent trustee for payment of 10% interest each interest period and the principal at maturity. Slick transmitted to the trustee cash equal to the present value of the note so that the trustee can pay each of the six remaining interest payments and the note principal on the maturity date. Cash in the amount of $704,010 was paid to the trustee to invest so that there will be sufficient cash to make the payments. Slick's accounting period ends December 31.

Required:

1. Give the entry for Slick Corporation on January 1, 1991.
2. Give the related entries on June 30 and December 31, 1991.
3. Give the extinguishment entry on January 1, 1995.
4. Show how the $704,010 was computed assuming an expected net earning rate by the trust of 10%.
5. What conditions must be met to qualify the transaction, on January 1, 1995, as an extinguishment of the $900,000 debt?

E 16–17
Long-Term
Noninterest-Bearing Note
(L.O. 6)

Fox purchases goods on January 1, 1991, and issues a $10,000 noninterest-bearing note requiring $5,000 to be paid on December 31 of 1991 and 1992. Each payment includes principal and interest. The market rate of interest is 10%.

Required:

1. Compute the amount to be recorded in purchases.
2. Give the entry to record the purchase.
3. Give the entry to record the 1991 payment on the note.
4. Give the entry to record the 1992 payment on the note.

E 16–18
Long-Term Note: Borrower
and Lender, Entries and
Reporting
(L.O. 6)

On May 1, 1991, Watt Company borrowed $24,000 cash from Tandy Bank on a $24,000, 10%, three-year note. Interest is payable each April 30, and the principal is payable on April 30, 1994. The accounting period ends on December 31 for each party.

Required:

1. Give all current and adjusting entries through April 30, 1992, for both the borrower and the lender.
2. Show how this note and the related items would be shown on the 1991 financial statements of each party.

E 16–19
Long-Term Note: Borrower
and Lender, Effective
Rate, Amortization
Schedule, Entries
(L.O. 6)

On January 1, 1991, Derek Company borrowed cash from Patricia Finance Company on a $30,000, 12%, two-year note. The note will be paid off in two equal installments each December 31. Patricia assessed Derek two points. The accounting period for each company ends December 31.

Required:

1. Compute the amount of each annual payment.
2. Show how the effective rate of 13.55% was computed.
3. Prepare a debt amortization schedule for the two parties.
4. Give all entries for each party from January 1, 1991, through the maturity date.

E 16–20
Long-Term Note: Borrower
and Lender, Amortization
Schedule, Entries
(L.O. 6)

The following data are available: on January 1, 1991, a borrower signed a long-term note, face amount, $100,000; time to maturity, three years; stated rate of interest, 8%. The effective rate of interest of 10% determined the cash received by the borrower. The note will be paid in three equal annual installments on each December 31 (also, this is the end of the accounting period for both parties).

Required:

1. Compute the cash received by the borrower and prepare a debt amortization schedule.
2. Give the required entries for both the borrower and lender for each of the three years.

E 16–21
Long-Term Note: Borrower
and Lender Entries,
Effective Rate,
Amortization Schedule
(L.O. 6)

The following information is known: on January 1, 1991, a borrower signed a long-term note, face amount, $100,000; time to maturity, three years; stated interest rate, 12%; and cash proceeds from the loan, $96,661. The note will be paid in equal annual installments on each December 31 (also, this is the end of the accounting period for both parties).

Required:

1. Prepare a debt amortization schedule.
2. Give the required entries for both the borrower and lender for each of the three years.

E 16–22
Long-Term Note:
Unrealistic Rate,
Amortization Schedule,
Entries for Debtor and
Creditor
(L.O. 6)

Cathy Company purchased a machine at the beginning of 1991 with a three-year, $2,000, 5% note, payable in three equal annual payments of $734 (including principal and interest) at each year-end. The current market rate of interest for this level of risk was 12%.

Required:

1. What was the cost of the machine to Cathy Company?
2. Give the entry by Cathy to record the purchase. Use the net approach.
3. Prepare the amortization schedule for the note.
4. Give the entries for both the debtor and the creditor at the end of each year (assuming the accounting year-end for the debtor and creditor coincides with the note's year-end).

PROBLEMS

P 16–1
Bonds: Price Computation,
Amortization Schedule,
Gross, Interest Method,
Entries, and Reporting
(L.O. 2, 3)

Alpha Corporation sold and issued to Beta Corporation $400,000, 8% (payable semiannually on June 30 and December 31), three-year bonds. The bonds were dated and sold on January 1, 1991, at an effective interest rate of 10%. The accounting period for each company ends on December 31.

Required:

1. Compute the price of the bonds.
2. Prepare a debt amortization schedule for the life of the bonds (use the interest method and round to the nearest dollar).
3. Prepare, in parallel columns, entries for the issuer and the investor (as a long-term investment) through December 31, 1991. Use the gross method.
4. Show how the issuer and the investor would report the bonds on their respective balance sheets at December 31, 1991.
5. What would be reported on the income statement for each party for the year ended December 31, 1991?

P 16–2
Bonds: Accrued Interest,
Straight-Line, Gross,
Entries, Reporting
(L.O. 3)

Foyt Corporation sold and issued to Mears Corporation $50,000 of bonds on June 1, 1991, for $51,320 plus any accrued interest. The bond indenture provided the following information:

Maturity amount	$50,000
Date of bonds	April 1, 1991
Maturity date	March 31, 1993 (2 years)
Stated interest rate	6½%, payable semiannually
Interest payments.	March 31 and September 30

Required:

1. In parallel columns, give entries for the issuer and investor (as a long-term investment) from date of sale to maturity. Assume the difference between the amortization amounts is not material; therefore, use straight-line amortization. Also assume the accounting period for each company ends on December 31. Use the gross method.
2. Show how the bonds would be reported on the balance sheet of each company at December 31, 1991.
3. What would be reported on the income statement for each company for the year ended December 31, 1991?

P 16–3
Bonds: Interest Method,
Adjusting Entries
(L.O. 3)

Jones Corporation issued bonds, face amount $100,000, three-year, 8% (payable semiannually on June 30 and December 31). The bonds were dated January 1, 1991, and were sold on November 1, 1991, for $100,739 (including interest of $2,667 and a bond price of $98,072) at an effective interest rate of 9%. The bonds would have sold at the effective rate on December 31, 1991, for $98,206. The bonds mature on December 31, 1993. The bonds were purchased as a long-term investment by Smith Corporation.

Required:

1. Construct a time scale that depicts the important dates for this bond issue.
2. In parallel columns, give the entries at November 1, 1991, for the issuer and the investor.
3. Prepare a bond amortization schedule using the interest method.
4. In parallel columns, give the entries for both the issuer and investor for interest and amortization at the interest date, December 31, 1991. Use the interest method of amortization.
5. Compute and verify the balance in the interest accounts of the two parties to the transaction immediately after (4).

6. Assume the accounting period for each party ends on February 28. In parallel columns, give the adjusting entries for each party on February 28, 1992. Assume the interest method of amortization.
7. Compute the amount of amortization per month for each party, assuming straight-line amortization is used (i.e., the difference between the amortization amounts is not material).

P 16–4
Bonds: Price Computation, Interest Method, Entries for Both Parties
(L.O. 2, 3)

Randy Corporation issued $200,000, 8% (payable each February 28 and August 31), four-year bonds. The bonds were dated March 1, 1991, and mature on February 28, 1995. The bonds were sold on August 1, 1991, to yield 8½% interest. The bonds were purchased by Voss Corporation as a long-term investment. The accounting period for each company ends on December 31. The bonds were sold for $196,967 plus accrued interest of $6,667. They would have sold on August 31, 1991, for $197,027.

Required:

1. Diagram a time scale depicting the important dates for this bond issue.
2. Prepare an amortization schedule using the interest method of amortization.
3. In parallel columns, give entries for the issuer and the investor from date of sale through February 28, 1992. Base amortization on (2).
4. Compute the amount of amortization per month for each party, assuming the straight-line method is used (because the difference between the amortization amounts is not material).

P 16–5
Bonds: Bond Price Computation, Straight-Line, Entries to Issuer (Gross) and Investor (Net)
(L.O. 2, 3)

Koy Corporation sold and issued to Lott Corporation (as a long-term investment) $100,000, four-year, 11% bonds on September 1, 1991. Interest is payable semiannually on February 28 and August 31. The bonds mature on August 31, 1995, and were sold to yield 10% interest. The accounting period for both companies ends on December 31. Use the gross method for the issuer and the net method for the investor.

Required:

1. Compute the price of the bonds (show computations and round to nearest dollar).
2. In parallel columns, give all entries required through February 1992 (including reversing entries) in the accounts of the issuer and the investor. Assume the difference between the interest method and the straight-line method of amortization is not material; therefore, use straight-line amortization.

P 16–6
Case A, Convertible Bonds: Entries; Case B, Detachable Stock Warrants
(L.O. 4)

This problem involves two independent cases:

Case A
On January 1, 1991, when its common stock was selling for $80 per share, Ancil Corporation issued $5 million of 4% convertible debentures (i.e., bonds) due in 10 years. The conversion option allowed the holder of each $1,000 bond to convert the bond into five shares of the corporation's no par value common stock. The debentures were issued for $5.5 million. The present value of the bond payments at the time of issuance was $4.25 million, and the corporation believes the difference between the present value and the amount paid is attributable to the conversion feature. On January 1, 1992, the corporation's no par value common stock was split 3 for 1. On January 1, 1993, when the corporation's common stock was selling for $90 per share, holders of 40% of the convertible debentures exercised their conversion options. For convenience, assume the corporation uses the straight-line method for amortizing any bond discount or premium.

Required:

1. Give the entry to record the original issuance of the convertible debentures.
2. Give the entry to record the exercise of the conversion option, using the book value method. Show supporting computations.

Case B
On July 1, 1993, Alberta Ltd. issued $1 million of 7% bonds payable in 10 years. The bonds pay interest semiannually. Each $1,000 bond includes a detachable stock purchase right. Each right gives the bondholder the option to purchase for $30, one share of no par value common stock at any time during the next 10 years. The bonds were sold for $1 million. The value of the stock purchase rights at the time of issuance was $50,000.

Required:

Prepare the entry to record the issuance of the bonds.

(AICPA adapted)

P 16–7
Bonds: Detachable Stock Warrants, Entries for Issuer and Investor
(L.O. 4)

Friendly Corporation issued $1 million, 6%, non-convertible bonds with detachable stock purchase warrants. Each $1,000 bond carried 20 detachable stock purchase warrants, each of which called for one share of Friendly common stock at the specified option price of $60 per share. The bonds sold at 106, and the detachable stock purchase warrants were immediately quoted at $1 each on the market.

Goode Company purchased the entire issue as a long-term investment.

Required:

1. Give the following entries for Friendly Corporation (the issuer):
   a. To record the issuance of the bonds.
   b. To record the subsequent exercise by Goode of the 20,000 stock purchase warrants.
2. Assuming Goode did not exercise the 20,000 stock purchase warrants in requirement (1), give the following entries for Goode Company (the investor):
   a. Acquisition of the bonds (including the stock purchase warrants).
   b. Subsequent sale to another investor of half of the stock purchase warrants at $1.50 each.
   c. Subsequent exercise of the remaining half of the stock purchase warrants (by tendering them to Friendly Corporation). The market value of the stock was $62 per share.

P 16–8
Induced Conversion of Convertible Bonds
(L.O. 4)

Convee Company issued $75,000 of 12% convertible bonds at face value on an interest payment date several years ago. The face value of each bond is $1,000, and each bond is convertible into 15 shares of no par value common stock of Convee. Convee has embarked on a program of debt reduction; interest rates have declined during the term of the convertible bonds. Consequently, Convee offers the convertible bondholders $50 cash per bond as an inducement to convert. The market price of Convee stock is currently $70 per share. The bonds must be converted within a three-month period to receive the cash inducement. The bondholders accept the inducement and convert within the required period.

Required:

1. Why did the bondholders convert?
2. Record the conversion; assume that Convee uses the book value method to record conversions of convertible bonds.
3. Record the conversion, but assume Convee uses the market value method to record conversions of convertible bonds.
4. Explain why induced conversion is not treated as debt extinguishment for purposes of classifying the inducement cost.

P 16–9
Extinguishment by Using In-Substance Defeasance
(L.O. 5)

Dusty Corporation borrowed $2 million cash on a 6% note payable on January 1, 1991. This five-year note is payable in five equal annual installments of $474,793 starting on December 31, 1991. On January 1, 1993, the company entered into an agreement with the three creditors to irrevocably transfer the government securities (held by Dusty as a long-term investment) to a trustee. The trustee will make the three remaining equal interest payments on each payment date and will pay the principal on December 31, 1995. The government securities cost Dusty $1.1 million, and they will be valued at their current market value based on a 9% effective rate.

Required:

1. Give the entry that Dusty Corporation made on January 1, 1991.
2. Give the entries that Dusty Corporation made on December 31, 1991 and 1992.
3. Give the extinguishment entry on January 1, 1993.
4. What conditions must be met by Dusty Corporation to qualify the transaction on January 1, 1993, as an extinguishment of the debt.

P 16–10
Extinguishment: Debtor Entries, Purchase in the Open Market
(L.O. 5)

On July 1, 1991, Coputer Corporation issued $600,000, 5% (payable each June 30 and December 31), 10-year bonds payable. The bonds were issued at 97, and issue costs of $2,000 were paid from the proceeds. Assume straight-line amortization of discount and bond issue costs.

Due to an increase in interest rates, these bonds were selling in the market at the end of June 1994 at an effective rate of 8%. Because the company had available cash, $200,000 (face amount) of the bonds were purchased in the market and retired on July 1, 1994.

Required:

1. Give the entry by Coputer Corporation to record issuance of the bonds on July 1, 1991.
2. Give the entry by Coputer Corporation to record the extinguishment of part of the debt on July 1, 1994. How should the gain or loss be reported on the 1994 financial statements of Coputer Corporation?
3. Was the extinguishment economically favourable to the issuer, investor, or neither? Explain.

P 16–11
Extinguishment by
Refunding: Debtor Entries
(L.O. 5)

Davis Corporation issued $200,000, 4½% (payable each December 31), 10-year bonds on January 1, 1991. The issuer may call them at any time after 1994 at 104. The bonds sold on January 1, 1991, at 98. Straight-line amortization is used.

Due to a large increase in interest rates, the bonds were being sold in the market at the end of 1995 at 86 (i.e., at an effective rate of 8%). In view of this situation, Davis decided to issue a new series of bonds (a refunding issue) in the amount of $150,000 (8% payable annually, five-year term) on January 1, 1996; the new issue was sold at par. Davis had cash on hand sufficient for the remaining cost of retirement of the old bonds. Disregard income tax effects.

Required:

1. Give the entry for Davis Corporation to record issuance of the bonds at 98 on January 1, 1991.
2. Assume the $150,000 refunding issue was sold at par; give the required entry for Davis.
3. Assume all of the old bonds were immediately purchased in the open market at 86 on January 2, 1996. Give the required entry for Davis. How should the gain or loss be reported on the financial statements?
4. What was the economic gain or loss to the issuer and the investor?

P 16–12
Extinguishment with
Equity Securities; Call,
Refunding, Entries
(L.O. 5)

On January 1, 1991, Grand Corporation issued $100,000, 9% (payable each June 30 and December 31), 10-year bonds payable (convertible and callable) at a 10% effective rate of interest. Each $1,000 bond is convertible, at the option of the holder, into Grand no par value common stock as follows: first five years—25 shares for each bond tendered; second five years—20 shares for each bond. The bonds can be called, at the option of Grand, after the fifth year at 101.

On July 1, 1997, the market interest rate on comparable bonds is 8%, and the common stock is quoted on the market at $52 per share.

Required:

1. Give the entry to record the issuance of bonds on January 1, 1991. Show computation of the bond issue price. Use the gross method.
2. Give the entry to record payment of bond interest and the amortization of bond premium or discount on June 30, 1991. Use the interest method.
3. Prepare the journal entries at July 1, 1997, to record each of the following separate assumptions (use straight-line amortization):

   Assumption A—All of the bondholders converted their bonds to common stock. Use the market value method to record the conversion.

   Assumption B—Grand called all of the bonds at the stipulated call price.

   Assumption C—Grand refunded all of the outstanding 9% bonds by purchasing them in the open market at the current yield rate of interest. Cash for the refunding was obtained by issuing new 8% bonds (interest payable semiannually) at par; cash proceeds were $103,000 (face amount of bonds sold).

4. Which of the three above alternative means of retiring the old 9% bond payable is most likely to occur? Why?

P 16–13
Three Transactions:
Bonds, Detachable
Warrants,
Extinguishment—Entries
(L.O. 3, 4, 5)

This problem involves three independent situations.

a. On January 1, 1995, Hopewell Company issued its 8% bonds that had a par value of $1 million. Interest is payable at December 31 each year. The bonds mature on December 31, 2004. The bonds were sold to yield a rate of 10%.

b. On September 1, 2004, Junction Company issued at 104 (plus accrued interest), 4,000 of its 9%, 10-year, $1,000 par value, non-convertible bonds with detachable stock purchase warrants. Each bond carried two detachable warrants; each warrant was for one share of common stock, at a specified option price of $15 per share. Shortly after issuance, the warrants were quoted on the market for $3 each. No market value can be determined for the preceding bonds. Interest is payable on December 1 and June 1. Bond issue costs of $40,000 were incurred, and deducted from the proceeds.

c. On December 1, 1991, Cone Company issued its 7%, $2 million par value bonds for $2.2 million, plus accrued interest. Interest is payable on May 1 and November 1. On July 1, 1994, Cone purchased and retired the bonds at 98, plus accrued interest. Cone uses the straight-line method for the amortization of bond premium because the results do not materially differ from the interest method; the total amortization period at the date of issuance was 50 months.

Required:

1. Give the entry to record the issuance of the bonds by Hopewell Company. Show supporting computations.
2. Give the entry to record the issuance of the bonds by Junction Company. Show computations.
3. Give the entries required by Cone Company:
   a. At issue date.
   b. At reacquisition date.

(AICPA adapted)

P 16–14
Long-Term Note: Borrower and Lender Entries, Amortization Schedule, Adjusting Entry
(L.O. 6)

On January 1, 1991, Baker Company borrowed cash from Alter Finance Company and signed a three-year, $30,000 note. Interest is payable each December 31 at a stated interest rate of "floating prime at January 1 of each year plus 2%." The principal is due on December 31, 1993. The following actual prime rates were used by Alter: January 1, 1991, 13%; January 1, 1992, 12%; and January 1, 1993, 15%. The accounting period for each company ends on December 31.

Required:

1. Compute the total amount of interest paid, by year.
2. What was the difference between the stated and effective rates? Explain.
3. Give all entries for each company through maturity date.
4. Give the 1991 adjusting entry that would have been necessary had the accounting periods for each company ended on August 31 instead of December 31.

P 16–15
Note with Share Appreciation: Amortization Schedule, Entries and Reporting for Borrower and Lender
(L.O. 6)

On January 1, 1991, Cantral Company borrowed cash from Tenor Financing Company on a $60,000, 14%, three-year note. Interest is payable each December 31, and the principal is payable December 31, 1993. This note is designated as Note A.

On the same date, Cantral Company also borrowed cash from Tulare Commercial Loan Company on a $200,000, 9%, five-year note. This note, designated as Note B, will be paid with five equal annual payments each December 31. Tulare granted a low 9% stated rate in exchange for a 10% share appreciation in an office building under construction. The current best estimate of the present value of the share appreciation at January 1, 1991, was $52,754. The accounting period for each company ends on December 31.

Required:

1. What is the amount of each annual payment on Note B?
2. For each note, what is (a) the stated interest rate and (b) the effective interest rate?
3. Prepare a debt amortization schedule for Note B.
4. For each note separately, give all entries for both the borrower and the lenders through December 31, 1991.
5. Show the items and amounts that would be reported on the December 31, 1991, financial statements, by each company under the captions: revenues, expenses, assets, liabilities, and shareholders' equity (current and non-current classifications are not required).

P 16–16
Note with Unrealistic Interest Rate: Entries and Reporting for Both Parties, Gross Method
(L.O. 6)

Sable Company purchased merchandise for resale on January 1, 1991, for $5,000 cash plus a $20,000, two-year note payable. The principal is due on December 31, 1992; the note specified 8% interest payable each December 31.

Assume Sable's going rate of interest for this type of debt was 15%. The accounting period ends December 31.

Required:

1. Give the entry to record the purchase on January 1, 1991. Show computations (round to nearest dollar).

2. Complete a tabulation as follows:

    a. Amount of cash interest payable each December 31 . . . . $_____
    b. Total interest expense for the two-year period . . . . $_____
    c. Amount of interest reported on income statement for 1991. . . . . $_____
    d. Amount of liability reported on the balance sheet at
       December 31, 1991 (excluding any accrued interest) . . . . $_____

3. Give the entries at each year-end for the debtor.
4. Give the entries at each year-end for the creditor.
5. Show how the debtor and creditor should report or disclose the data related to the note on the income statement and balance sheet at each year-end.

P 16–17
Serial Bonds
(L.O. 7)

A $700,000 issue of serial bonds dated April 1, 1991, was sold on that date for $707,600. The interest rate is 8%, payable semiannually on March 31 and September 30. Scheduled maturities are as follows:

Serial	Date Due	Amount
B	March 31, 1992	$100,000
C	March 31, 1993	200,000
D	March 31, 1994	200,000
E	March 31, 1995	200,000

Required:

1. Prepare an amortization schedule for the issuer; use the bonds outstanding method.
2. Give all entries for the issuer relating to the bonds, including reversing entries, through March 31, 1992. The issuing company adjusts and closes its books each December 31.

P 16–18
Serial Bonds
(L.O. 7)

On January 1, 1991, Tobin Corporation sold serial bonds (dated January 1, 1991) due as follows: serial A, $10,000, December 31, 1995; serial B, $15,000, December 31, 1996; and serial C, $25,000, December 31, 1997. The bonds carried a 3% coupon (stated) interest rate per semi-annual period (each June 30 and December 31) and were sold to yield 4% interest per semiannual period.

Required:

Round to the nearest dollar.

1. Compute the selling price of the bond issue.
2. Prepare an amortization schedule for Tobin for the life of the bond issue, assuming the interest method is used. (Hint: Discount amortization is June 30, 1991, $306; June 30, 1996, $352.)
3. Give Tobin's entry to record retirement of half of Serial C at 99½ on June 30, 1997. Assume the accounting period ends December 31.

P 16–19

COMPREHENSIVE PROBLEM
♦

Bond Issuance and
Retirement
(L.O. 2, 3, 5)

Westlawn Company issues $200,000 of 10% bonds on March 1, 1991. Additional information on the bond issue is as follows:

Bond date: January 1, 1991.

Maturity date: January 1, 2001.

Yield rate: 12%.

Interest payment dates: June 30, December 31.

Required:

1. Record the bond issue and the first interest payment for Westlawn under the interest method.
2. On August 1, 1996, Westlawn purchased 30% of the bonds on the open market for 103. Record the necessary entries to update the portion of the bond issue retired and to record the extinguishment.
3. Have interest rates risen or fallen between the issuance of the bonds and the early extinguishment? (Assume no significant change in Westlawn's risk.)
4. Discuss the nature of the gain or loss you recorded in (2). In explaining this item to a financial statement user, what cautions would you include in your discussion?

CASES

C 16–1
Convertible Bonds versus Detachable Stock Warrants (L.O. 4)

Seton Corporation is considering the issuance of $100,000, five-year bonds. These two alternatives are under consideration:

Alternative A—At the beginning of 1991, issue convertible bonds which would specify that each $1,000 bond can be tendered for conversion to 15 shares of Seton's no par value common stock, at any time after the second year from issue date of the convertible bonds. Seton's best estimate is that the convertible bonds can be sold to Investor X for $108,000 cash at the beginning of 1991, provided the common stock is selling at that time for not less than $65 per share.

Alternative B—At the beginning of 1991, issue 100 non-convertible $1,000 bonds with 15 detachable stock purchase warrants per bond. Each warrant can be tendered at any time after 1992 for one share of Seton's no par value common stock at an option price of $60 per share. Seton's best estimate is that the non-convertible bonds can be sold to Investor XX for $108,000 cash at the beginning of 1991, if the common stock is selling at that time for not less than $65 per share. The warrants are expected to have a market value of $2 each immediately after issuance of the bonds; the bonds do not have a listed market price.

Seton's management is considering which alternative to select. The management is concerned about several issues that may influence the decision. One such issue is the comparative impact of the two alternatives on the financial statements. Your assistance in selecting an alternative has been requested.

Required:

1. Using Seton's best estimate, give the journal entries for each alternative that each party would make at the beginning of 1991. Use the gross method. Explain any differences in accounting values between the two alternatives.
2. Give the entries for each alternative that each party would make at the beginning of 1994, assuming all of the bonds in Alternative A are tendered for conversion and all of the warrants are turned in for shares in Alternative B. Seton's common stock is selling for $75 per share. Use the market value method for Alternative A. Assume straight-line amortization.
3. Complete the following schedule, assuming the transactions in (1) and (2) have taken place.
4. Outline your response to management's request for assistance in choosing between the two alternatives. Consider the results of (2).

Items	A—Convertible bonds		B—Detachable warrants	
	Issuer	Investor	Issuer	Investor
Gain (loss) conversion				
Investments:				
Bonds				
Common stock				
Liabilities:				
Bonds payable				
Shareholders' equity:				
Common stock				
Cash:				
Inflow				
Outflow				

C 16–2
Zero Coupon Bonds and Amortization Methods (L.O. 3)

The Shelby Company issues $10 million worth of bonds maturing 25 years after issuance. The bonds yield 16% but pay no interest.

Required:

1. Why would Shelby issue bonds paying no interest?
2. Why would investors buy them?
3. Compute the issue price (assume annual compounding periods and that issue date and bond date are the same).
4. Compute interest expense for the 1st, 16th, and 25th years under the interest method.

5. Compute interest expense for the 1st, 16th, and 25th years under the straight-line method.

6. Comment on your findings in (4) and (5). Why is the straight-line method inappropriate for the Shelby bonds?

C 16–3
Ethical Considerations:
Reporting Liabilities
(L.O. 1, 2)

Discuss the following two situations from an ethical and financial reporting viewpoint. (Note: (b) requires knowledge of material from Chapter 15.)

a. Canuck Airlines has accumulated a liability of 4 billion kilometers due to its frequent-flier program. Its estimated liability for free flights amounts to $270 million but could be $40 million higher if the opportunity cost of lost revenue from displaced passengers is considered.

   The airlines argue that the actual cost of each free flight is only approximately $8—for food, insurance, and other miscellaneous costs. That is, the cost of filling an otherwise empty seat. Furthermore, flyers with free tickets often bring along a paying customer, which more than offsets the negligible cost. Consequently, the average liability disclosed is only a fraction of the amount industry analysts insist exists.

b. In December, Jim Wilson, the controller of Fargo Company, a calendar-year company, was faced with a tough situation. The bond indenture of a major issue of Fargo bonds required maintaining a 3 to 1 current ratio as measured at each balance sheet date. Fargo has recently experienced cash shortages caused by a downturn in the general economy and demand for Fargo's products. However, leading economic indicators suggest that an upturn is expected.

   A substantial account payable would be due in January. Fargo did not have the cash to pay the debt. Furthermore, the January cash budget based on a realistic estimate of sales and collections from accounts receivable indicated a cash shortage requiring short-term financing. The payable due in January was large enough to cause the current ratio at December 31 to fall below 3.0. The controller began the search for a financial institution willing to refinance the payable on a long-term basis. If successful, the payable would be reclassified as long-term, allowing Fargo to comply with the bond indenture. Several financial institutions were willing to refinance the payable, but none would agree to do so on a non-cancelable basis.

   The controller was quite stressed by the situation. Non-compliance with the bond indenture could lead to technical default. If the bondholders exercise their right and call the bonds, Fargo may be forced into bankruptcy. The controller was confident that Fargo could rebound in the coming year and reasoned that more harm would come to the company, its employees, and shareholders if he did not take action that would result in compliance with the bond indenture. Wilson therefore decided to refinance the payable on a long-term basis, reclassify the payable as long-term, and include in the footnotes a statement that the refinancing agreement complies with GAAP.

C 16–4
Analysis of Actual
Financial Statements
(L.O. 1)

Refer to the 1990 financial statements of Loblaw (see the appendix immediately following Chapter 26) and respond to the following questions.

1. What was the total interest expense for the year?
2. What percent of total interest in 1990 is related to long-term debt?
3. For 1990, what percent of income before taxes is total interest expense?
4. At the end of 1990, what is the ratio of total debt to total assets?
5. How would you characterize the market's perceived riskiness of this company? Explain.

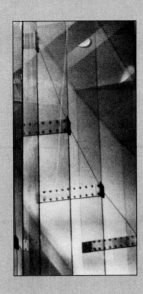

C H A P T E R

17

Accounting for Income Taxes

LEARNING OBJECTIVES

◆

After you have studied this chapter, you will be able to:

1. Explain the concepts of income tax allocation.

2. Explain and account for interperiod income tax allocation.

3. Explain and account for intraperiod income tax allocation.

4. Account for loss carryback tax benefits.

5. Account for loss carryforward tax benefits with and without the condition of virtual certainty.

◆

In its 1989 annual report, Bell Canada reported deferred income taxes of $2,037 million. Bell's retained earnings in the same statement was $2,129 million. Stelco Inc. reported deferred income taxes of $282 million and retained earnings of $615 million in its 1989 balance sheet.

In many cases such as these, deferred income taxes are significant amounts on the balance sheets of Canadian companies. What do these amounts represent? Are they liabilities? Or, as some financial analysts claim, should they be treated as part of shareholders' equity?

◆

ACCOUNTING FOR INCOME TAX EXPENSE
◆

There are two fundamental views of income tax expenses. One view is that income tax should be accounted for on a current expense basis. The other view is that income tax should be accounted for on the allocation basis.

Proponents of the current expense basis hold that the amount of income tax expense for a period should be measured as the amount of income tax actually payable for that period. They argue that the amount of tax payable determines the tax expense because income tax is determined by law and the legal amount of tax for a period is the amount currently payable.

Proponents of the allocation basis argue that in accordance with the matching principle, income tax expense should be based on the enterprise's reported net income and not on taxable income which is determined by applying the provisions of the Income Tax Act.

One of the major causes of the difference between income for accounting purposes (statement income) and income for tax purposes (taxable income) is depreciation. The Income Tax Act provides for **capital cost allowance** (CCA) that is depreciation for tax purposes and is a variation of the double-declining-balance method of depreciation. Because most companies use straight-line depreciation, there can be significant differences between statement and taxable income. Exhibit 17–1 presents an example of differences between statement and taxable income caused by depreciation.

Under the current expense basis, income tax expense would equal income tax payable in 1991–95. However, under the allocation basis, income tax expense would be $152 ($380 × 40%) each year. In the opinion of the Accounting Standards Board of the CICA, **income tax allocation** is the more appropriate method.

The use of the allocation method, however, raises another issue. Income tax expense in 1991 (using Exhibit 17–1) would be $152 while income tax payable would be $120. What, then, does the $32 difference represent and how should it be accounted for?

Exhibit 17–1 illustrates an example of a **timing difference**. In accounting for income taxes, timing differences arise because revenues and/or expenses are recognized in one period for accounting purposes but are recognized in a different period(s) for taxation purposes. In Exhibit 17–1, accounting depreciation in 1991 is $120 while CCA is $200. The $80 difference is a timing difference. The tax effect of this timing difference is $32 ($80 × 40%) and would be recorded as a deferred credit (deferred income tax) on the 1991 balance sheet. Therefore, the 1991 income tax entry would be:

```
Income tax expense ($380 × .4) . . . . . . . . . . . . . . . . . . . . . 152
    Income tax payable . . . . . . . . . . . . . . . . . . . . . . . . .      120
    Deferred income tax . . . . . . . . . . . . . . . . . . . . . . . .       32
```

EXHIBIT 17–1   Financial Information, Chicopee Limited

Assets subject to depreciation:
  Cost January 1, 1991: $600
  Life: 5 years, no salvage value.
Depreciation for statement purposes: straight-line
Depreciation for tax purposes: assume sum-of-the-years' digits*
Income before depreciation and taxes, 1991–1995: $500
Income tax rate: 40%

	1991	1992	1993	1994	1995
Income statement					
Income before depreciation and taxes	$500	$500	$500	$500	$500
Depreciation	120	120	120	120	120
Income before taxes	$380	$380	$380	$380	$380
Tax return					
Income before depreciation and taxes	$500	$500	$500	$500	$500
Capital cost allowance	200	160	120	80	40
Taxable income	$300	$340	$380	$420	$460
Taxes payable (40%)	$120	$136	$152	$168	$184

* Although the sum-of-the-years'-digits method of depreciation is not allowed for tax purposes, it provides a reasonable surrogate for capital cost allowances for illustrative purposes.

Another aspect of timing differences is that their impact on income tax accounting eventually reverses as illustrated in the following table (data are taken from Exhibit 17–1).

	Income Tax		Deferred
Year	Expense	Payable	Tax Balance
1991	$152	$120	$32
1992	152	136	48
1993	152	152	48
1994	152	168	32
1995	152	184	—
Total	$760	$760	

Over the five-year period, the total tax paid equals the total tax expense. The differences on a year-by-year basis arise because of the manner in which the depreciation is recognized for tax purposes as opposed to how it is recognized for accounting purposes; that is, the timing of the recognition.

Other timing differences may result in deferred tax debits because, instead of delaying the payment of income taxes, the timing difference initiates a prepayment of the tax. A more comprehensive discussion of tax allocations follows.

CONCEPTS OF INCOME TAX ALLOCATION
◆

Fundamental Views of Income Tax Expense

Under current GAAP, income tax expense is viewed as a deduction on the income statement similar to cost of goods sold, salary expense, and depreciation expense (and, where appropriate, as an offset to an extraordinary item). In this view, income tax expense is measured on the allocation basis and is reported along with all other expenses. This means that income tax expense of a period is based on the pretax income of the period, regardless of when the income tax will be paid. Thus, it causes the reporting of deferred income tax. Proponents of the current GAAP view of interperiod income tax allocation acknowledge the uncertainties involved in the accrual amounts of income tax expense; however, they point out that certain other accounting valuations are inherently uncertain (e.g., depreciation). They believe the accounting model is sufficiently robust to handle the uncertainties involved in interperiod income tax allocation. Moreover, they note that empirically most deferred tax amounts are credit balances (i.e., liabilities). They argue that failure to report deferred income tax and the concomitant higher income tax expense would bias reported amounts of net income upward for the majority of companies (a non-conservative practice).

Different Interpretations of Deferred Income Tax Debits and Credits

Interperiod income tax allocation causes deferred income tax amounts which are reported on the balance sheet. The amounts may be debits or credits. Are such debits assets (i.e., prepaid expenses or deferred charges) and are such credits liabilities, or are they contingencies? Alternatively, are deferred tax debits and credits valuation adjustments (i.e., contra accounts) to the accounts to which they relate? Each of these possible interpretations is discussed next.

Deferred Tax Amounts Viewed as Assets and Liabilities   Deferred tax debits may be viewed as assets because they can be viewed as prepayments of future income tax expense. Such debits arise when the income tax must be paid before the related revenue is recognized as earned. Thus, the deferred debit amount can be viewed as an estimated asset.

Deferred tax credits can be viewed as liabilities because such credits arise when the income tax is paid after the related expense is recognized as incurred. Viewed this way, the deferred tax credit is an estimated liability.

Deferred Tax Amounts Viewed as Contingencies   Deferred tax amounts can be viewed as contingencies because their ultimate realization depends on (1) the tax rates during the periods when they reverse; (2) future amounts of reported income; and (3) future changes in tax laws or accounting concepts. *CICA Handbook,* section 3290, "Contingencies," was not in effect in 1967 when interperiod tax allocation was mandated, and it is not currently applied to interperiod income tax allocation. However, if it were applied to interperiod tax allocation, it would provide a conceptual basis for viewing deferred tax amounts as contingencies. That is, the section requires that if (1) it is probable that a contingent loss (or expense) will occur and (2) the amount of the loss can be reasonably estimated, companies must accrue the loss. These conditions appear to be met for many companies with tax deferrals. The specifications of section 3290 for deferred tax debits also could be applied; however, the results would not be parallel with losses, because of a reluctance to recognize contingent assets, and this poses a substantive conceptual issue.

In summary, the *Handbook* leaves the interpretation of tax deferrals open as to whether they are assets and liabilities or contingencies. If we conform to the accounting model (i.e., Assets = Liabilities + Owners' equity) it follows that deferred tax debits are assets and deferred tax credits are liabilities, even though they are uncertain as to amount at the time they are initially recorded.

Which Tax Rate to Use in Recording Deferred Taxes?

Two different views have been proposed as to what tax rates should be applied in computing deferred income taxes. One view holds that the beginning rate should be used (i.e., the deferral method); the other view opts for estimated future tax rates (i.e., the liability method).

Deferral Method   This view is that the current income tax rate when the timing difference originated is the apropriate rate on which to base the tax deferral. Under the deferral method, recorded deferred tax amounts are not adjusted for subsequent changes in tax rates. Currently, the *CICA Handbook* requires the **deferral method** as stated in paragraph 3470.20 on the basis that it is the most practical and useful method.

Liability Method   This view is that amounts of deferred tax should be based on estimates of the future tax rates which will be in effect when the timing differences reverse. Thus, the **liability method** provides for adjustment of deferred tax amounts due to changes in tax rates or other factors in periods subsequent to initial recording of the tax deferral. Proponents of this view argue that ultimate realization of the amount of the tax deferral depends on the tax rates in effect when the timing differences reverse and thus the amounts to be realized bear no necessary relationship to the tax rates in effect when they originate.

Comprehensive versus Partial Income Tax Allocation

Some accountants favour **comprehensive tax allocation**, in which all timing differences are recognized.[1] Other accountants favour partial allocation under the theory that, in principle, the income tax expense of a period should be the amount of income tax payable for the period.

In contrast to comprehensive allocation, proponents of **partial tax allocation** base their view on the inherent uncertainty of deferred tax amounts. They also note that many companies indefinitely postpone the payment of deferred tax amounts. This postponement occurs for companies with stable or growing investments in depreciable assets and which use accelerated depreciation for tax purposes and straight-line depreciation for accounting purposes (this is perhaps the most important timing difference). Under partial allocation, indefinite postponement is viewed as virtually synonymous with a permanent difference, so that interperiod tax allocation should not apply. Thus, proponents of partial allocation would not record income tax expense for taxes indefinitely postponed in this way. They would apply interperiod income tax allocation only to specific short-term timing differences that would cause material misstatements of reported income if tax allocation were not applied. The *CICA Handbook* requires comprehensive allocation.

CONCEPT REVIEW

1. What are the main reasons for income tax allocation?
2. What are the different alternatives for the treatment of deferred income tax debits or credits?
3. Explain the differences between the deferral method and the liability method of income tax allocation.

---

[1] For a discussion of differing views, see Christina S. R. Drummond and Seymour L. Wigle, "Let's Stop Taking Comprehensive Tax Allocation for Granted," *CA Magazine*, October 1984, pp. 56–61; J. Alex Milburn, "Comprehensive Tax Allocation: Let's Stop Taking Some Misconceptions for Granted," *CA Magazine*, April 1982, pp. 40–46; and Thomas H. Beechy, "Partial Allocation: Variations on a Theme," *CA Magazine*, March 1985, pp. 82–86.

TYPES OF INCOME TAX ALLOCATION

Section 3470 of the *CICA Handbook* provides the basic guidelines for income tax allocation for financial accounting purposes. This section recognizes two types of income tax allocation:

1. **Interperiod income tax allocation**—the allocation of income tax expense among two or more accounting periods. The basic principle is to report income tax expense in the period in which the income that caused the tax effect is reported. Interperiod income tax allocation (*a*) requires certain accounting entries and (*b*) is reflected on the financial statements.
2. **Intraperiod income tax allocation**—the allocation of the current year's income tax amount to the subclassifications of the statements of income and retained earnings that caused the tax expense. Intraperiod income tax allocation is a reporting requirement only; it does not require accounting entries.

Next, the principles and application of interperiod income tax allocation are discussed.

PRINCIPLES OF INTERPERIOD INCOME TAX ALLOCATION

Interperiod income tax allocation conforms to the matching principle; that is, income tax expense should be matched with the income that caused the income tax effect. Income tax allocation is necessary because some transactions affect the determination of income for financial accounting purposes (i.e., in the income statement) in one period and the computation of income tax payable (i.e., in the income tax return) in another period. Because of these transactions, income tax expense and income tax payable often are different amounts for a particular accounting period. Interperiod income tax allocation specifically deals with this difference, called **deferred income tax**. Deferred income tax may be an asset (i.e., prepaid income tax; a debit) or a liability (i.e., income tax to be paid in the future; a credit).[2]

Two special accounting terms are used when discussing interperiod income tax allocation:

1. **Accounting income**—net income for the period shown in the financial statements before the provision for income taxes and after excluding any items that are permanently non-taxable or non-deductible for income tax purposes. An accounting loss is the converse of accounting income. The accounting income/loss is used to compute **income tax expense**.
2. **Taxable income**—the amount used to compute income tax payable, which is determined on the income tax return. Taxable income is based on the revenues and gains less the expenses and losses that must be reported on the income tax return in conformity with income tax law and the tax regulations. Accounting income often is used as the starting point to compute taxable income.

Interperiod income tax allocation involves application of the appropriate corporate **income tax rates** to (*a*) accounting income to determine income tax expense and (*b*) taxable income to determine income tax payable. The difference between the expense and payable amounts—deferred income tax—is recorded in the accounts and reported in the financial statements.

---

[2] The discussion in this part does not consider the income tax effect of a prior period adjustment because (*a*) it is reported on the statement of retained earnings, and (*b*) it is reported on the tax return and in the financial statements for the same period.

Income Tax Differences

Interperiod income tax allocation requires identification of transactions that cause differences between accounting income and taxable income. Such a transaction causes either a timing difference or a permanent difference.

Timing Differences Timing differences arise as differences between the periods in which transactions affect taxable income and the periods in which they enter into the determination of pretax accounting income. Timing differences originate in one period and reverse or turn around in one or more subsequent periods. Some timing differences reduce income taxes that would otherwise be payable currently; others increase income taxes that would otherwise be payable currently. Timing differences represent taxable items that are included in computing income tax expense in one period but are included in computing income tax payable in a prior or later period.

For example, on July 1, 1992, Brandon Corporation collected $12,000 rent in advance for the following 12-month period. Pretax accounting income for 1992 would include half of this amount, $6,000. However, under the tax requirement Brandon Corporation would have to report $12,000 of revenue for 1992. Therefore, pretax accounting income for 1992 would be $6,000 less than taxable income. In this situation, the 1992 entry to record income tax and deferred income tax would be (pretax accounting income, $30,000; taxable income, $36,000; tax rate, 40%):

```
Income tax expense ($30,000 × 40%) . . . . . . . . . . . . . . 12,000
Deferred income tax [($36,000 − $30,000) × 40%] . . . . . . . . 2,400
    Income tax payable ($36,000 × 40%) . . . . . . . . . . .        14,400
```

The deferred income tax amount reverses or turns around in 1993. At that time, pretax accounting income will include the remaining $6,000 of rent revenue. However, none of the rent revenue will be included in 1993 taxable income. That is, in 1993, pretax accounting income will be $6,000 more than taxable income. The entry to record income tax for 1993 and the reversal, or turn around, would be (pretax accounting income, $40,000; taxable income, $34,000; tax rate, 40%):

```
Income tax expense ($40,000 × 40%) . . . . . . . . . . . . . . 16,000
    Deferred income tax [($40,000 − $34,000) × 40%]. . . . . .        2,400
    Income tax payable ($34,000 × 40%) . . . . . . . . . . .        13,600
```

A timing difference always causes deferred income tax (either a debit or credit). It always reverses or turns around in one or more subsequent accounting periods. Four different types of transactions cause timing differences:

1. Revenues or gains that are included in taxable income one or more periods after they are included in accounting income; for example, gross profit on installment sales.
2. Expenses or losses that are deducted in determining taxable income one or more periods after they are deducted in determining accounting income; for example, estimated (accrued) warranty costs.
3. Revenues or gains that are included in taxable income before they are included in accounting income; for example, rent collected in advance.
4. Expenses or losses that are deducted in determining taxable income before they are deducted in determining accounting income; for example, capital cost allowance claimed for tax purposes in excess of the depreciation written for accounting income purposes.

To emphasize, timing differences (a) relate only to items recognized on both the income statement and the tax return, but in different reporting periods; (b) always cause a deferred income tax debit or credit to be recorded; and (c) always reverse (i.e., turn around) in one or more future reporting periods.

Permanent Differences   A permanent difference arises when a transaction causes pretax accounting income and taxable income to be different, and the effect will not reverse or turn around in future periods. **Permanent differences** are not subject to income tax allocation. Permanent differences arise in two situations:

1. Revenues and expenses that are included in **pretax income** but are never included in taxable income. For example, dividends from other Canadian corporations are included in pretax income. However, they are specifically excluded from taxable income and never will be subject to income tax. In such a situation there is no income tax to allocate.
2. Revenues and expenses that are included on the income tax return but never included in pretax income. For example, in the oil and gas industry, accumulated depletion based on cost for accounting purposes cannot exceed total asset cost less residual value. However, for income tax purposes, statutory depletion is permitted whereby accumulated depletion may exceed cost (the usual case). The excess of statutory depletion over cost depletion is not recognized for accounting purposes. Thus, statutory depletion in excess of cost depletion has no effect on income tax expense. It creates a tax saving that does not reverse.

In summary, income tax allocation never is applied to permanent differences because they do not cause income tax differences that will subsequently reverse or turn around. Income tax expense is calculated on pretax income plus or minus permanent differences (i.e., accounting income).

Illustration of Interperiod Income Tax Allocation

The pretax data given in Exhibit 17–2 illustrate the principles of interperiod income tax allocation. Notice that Ildiko Corporation has three different types of revenue, three different types of expense, and a resulting pretax income of $30,000 for 1992, and $40,000 for 1993.

The following four independent cases are analyzed:

Case A—no timing or permanent tax differences.

Case B—a timing difference that causes a deferred tax debit.

Case C—a timing difference that causes a deferred tax credit.

Case D—a permanent tax difference only.

Case A—no timing or permanent differences:

Assumption relating to Exhibit 17–2. The revenues and expenses for each year also were included in taxable income.

Analysis—pretax income, accounting income, and taxable income are the same each year because there are no timing or permanent differences.

Entries to record income tax:

1992:

```
Income tax expense ($30,000 × 40%) . . . . . . . . . . . . . . 12,000
    Income tax payable ($30,000 × 40%) . . . . . . . . . . .        12,000
```

1993:

```
Income tax expense ($40,000 × 40%) . . . . . . . . . . . . . . 16,000
    Income tax payable ($40,000 × 40%) . . . . . . . . . . .        16,000
```

No deferred income tax is reported for either year. Both income tax expense and income tax payable are the same for each period.

EXHIBIT 17-2   Data to Illustrate Interperiod Income Tax Allocation

ILDIKO CORPORATION
Pretax Statements of Income
For Year Ended December 31

	1992	1993
Revenues:		
Sales revenue $100,000		$120,000
Rent revenue 6,000		6,000
Investment revenue 1,000		1,000
Total revenues.	$107,000	$127,000
Expenses:		
Cost of goods sold. 65,000		75,000
Depreciation expense 10,000		10,000
Interest expense. 2,000		2,000
Total expenses	77,000	87,000
Pretax income.	$ 30,000	$ 40,000

Average income tax rate, 40%.

Case B—a timing difference that causes a deferred income tax debit:

Assumption related to Exhibit 17–2. On July 1, 1992, rent revenue of $12,000 was collected in full for the following 12 months. For income tax purposes, the $12,000 is taxable in 1992.

Analysis—The rent revenue causes a timing difference so that (a) pretax income and accounting income are the same, but taxable income is different for each of the two periods, and (b) the deferred tax effect that originates in 1992 reverses or turns around in 1993.

Computation of taxable income:

	1992	1993
Pretax income (given)	$30,000	$40,000
Taxable income:		
1992: ($30,000 + $6,000)	$36,000	
1993: ($40,000 − $6,000)		$34,000

Entries to record income tax:

1992:

```
Income tax expense ($30,000 × 40%) . . . . . . . . . . . . . 12,000
    Deferred income tax [($36,000 − $30,000) × 40%] . . . . . . . .   2,400
    Income tax payable ($36,000 × 40%) . . . . . . . . . . .         14,400
```

The 1992 income statement reports income tax expense of $12,000. The balance sheet for 1992 reports (a) income tax payable, $14,400 (assuming no prepayments); and (b) a current asset (a debit) for deferred income tax, $2,400. The $2,400 is an asset because it is viewed as prepaid income tax expense.

1993:

```
Income tax expense ($40,000 × 40%) . . . . . . . . . . . . . 16,000
    Income tax payable ($34,000 × 40%) . . . . . . . . . . .         13,600
    Deferred income tax [($40,000 − $34,000) × 40%]. . . . .          2,400*
        * Now has a zero balance because the tax effect has reversed.
```

The 1993 income statement reports income tax expense of $16,000. The balance sheet for 1993 reports income tax payable of $13,600 (assuming no prepayments). Deferred income tax will not be reported because it has a zero balance. That is, it was debited for $2,400 in 1992 and credited for the same amount in 1993. Notice that at the end of 1993, the deferred income tax amount of $2,400 from 1992 reversed or turned around. At that time, for this particular transaction, the total (for the two years combined) pretax accounting income and total taxable income amounts are the same. In summary, the income tax expense (not income tax payable) was allocated to the respective periods in which the related rent revenue was reported for accounting purposes, regardless of when the rent revenue was reported on the tax return.

Case C—a timing difference that causes a deferred income tax credit:
Assumption relating to Exhibit 17–2. Ildiko Corporation uses straight-line depreciation on its statement (as shown in Exhibit 17–2). However, it claims the maximum capital cost allowance (CCA) available for tax purposes for machinery that has an undepreciated capital cost (UCC) balance of $100,000 on January 1, 1992.

Analysis—Pretax income and accounting income are the same, but taxable income is different each year because depreciation expense causes a timing difference and the tax effect reverses or turns around over the 10-year life of the asset.

Analysis of depreciation:

	1992	1993
Straight-line	$10,000	$10,000
Capital cost allowance:		
1992: ($100,000 × 20%)	20,000	
1993: [($100,000 − $20,000) × 20%]		16,000
Computation of taxable income:		
Pretax income (straight-line depreciation)	30,000	40,000
Taxable income (capital cost allowance):		
1992: ($30,000 + $10,000 − $20,000)	20,000	
1993: ($40,000 + $10,000 − $16,000)		34,000

Entries to record income tax:

1992:

```
Income tax expense ($30,000 × 40%) . . . . . . . . . . . . . . 12,000
    Income tax payable ($20,000 × 40%) . . . . . . . . . . .        8,000
    Deferred income tax [($20,000 − $10,000) × 40%]. . . . . .      4,000
```

The income statement for 1992 reports income tax expense of $12,000. The balance sheet reports (*a*) a liability for income tax payable of $8,000 (assuming no prepayments) and (*b*) another liability, deferred income tax, of $4,000. In this case, deferred income tax is a liability because the tax expense related to it has been reported on the income statement. The tax must be paid in later periods when declining-balance depreciation expense becomes less per period than straight-line depreciation. Thus, the deferred tax (a credit) completely reverses or turns around by the time the asset is fully depreciated. (see Exhibit 17–1).

1993:

```
Income tax expense ($40,000 × 40%) . . . . . . . . . . . . . . 16,000
    Income tax payable ($34,000 × 40%) . . . . . . . . . . .       13,600
    Deferred income tax [($16,000 − $10,000) × 40%]. . . . . .      2,400
```

The income statement for 1993 reports income tax expense of $16,000. The balance sheet reports (*a*) a liability for income tax payable of $13,600 (assuming no prepayments) and (*b*) another liability, deferred income tax, of $6,400 (i.e., $4,000 + $2,400).

Over time, this $6,400 credit will be offset by debits because straight-line depreciation expense then will be greater than CCA (i.e., the deferred tax amounts will completely reverse or turn around).

Case D—a permanent tax difference only:

Assumption relating to Exhibit 17–2. The investment revenue of $1,000 each year was from dividends from Canadian corporations. This means that it will never be subject to income tax.

Analysis—Dividend revenue that is not subject to income tax must be reported on the income statement. However, no income tax expense should be computed on it because it will never be included in taxable income. Dividend revenue in this case is a permanent difference because it will never turn around. In this case, **pretax income** and accounting income differ while accounting income and taxable income are the same.

Computation of accounting income and taxable income:

	1992	1993
Accounting income (only for computing income tax expense):		
1992: ($30,000 − $1,000)	$29,000	
1993: ($40,000 − $1,000)		$39,000
Taxable income:		
1992: ($30,000 − $1,000)	29,000	
1993: ($40,000 − $1,000)		39,000

Entries to record income tax:

1992:

| Income tax expense ($29,000 × 40%) . . . . | 11,600 | |
| Income tax payable . . . . | | 11,600 |

1993:

| Income tax expense ($39,000 × 40%) . . . . | 15,600 | |
| Income tax payable . . . . | | 15,600 |

Comprehensive Illustration of Interperiod Income Tax Allocation

When numerous timing differences occur, an organized approach is needed to determine pretax income, accounting income, taxable income, income tax expense, income tax payable, and deferred income tax. Different application approaches may be used to resolve this problem.

One common approach useful in most problem situations is illustrated in Exhibit 17–3. The worksheet in this exhibit combines several timing differences into a single entry to record income tax for the period. To emphasize the efficiency of this worksheet, the data given in Exhibit 17–2 are used with the assumptions of cases B, C, and D (all repeated in Exhibit 17–3 for convenience). Exhibit 17–3 is organized by year in the following format: Case data for 1992 and 1993; worksheet and income tax entry for 1992; financial reporting, 1992; worksheet and entry to record income tax expense for 1993; and financial reporting, 1993.

The explanations and analyses just given for cases B, C, and D, based on Exhibit 17–3, are not repeated. Study Exhibit 17–3 because it presents an efficient problem-solving approach for situations that involve more than one tax allocation issue.

Changes in Income Tax Rates

Timing differences give rise to deferred income taxes which are computed on the basis of tax rates in effect when the timing difference occurred. Subsequently the deferred taxes recognized reverse over the cycle of the timing difference. On this point the *CICA Handbook,* paragraph 3470.18 states:

Where the difference between accounting and taxable income in a period gives rise to a transfer to income from the tax allocation balance accumulated in prior periods, such

EXHIBIT 17–3   Comprehensive Illustration—Interperiod Income Tax Allocation

ILDIKO CORPORATION
Pretax Income Statements
For Years Ended December 31

	1992	1993
Revenues:		
Sales revenue	$100,000	$120,000
Rent revenue	6,000	6,000
Investment revenue	1,000	1,000
Total revenues	107,000	127,000
Expenses:		
Cost of goods sold	65,000	75,000
Depreciation expense (straight-line)	10,000	10,000
Interest expense	2,000	2,000
Total expenses	77,000	87,000
Pretax income	$ 30,000	$ 40,000

Average income tax rate, 40%.

Additional data:
Case B—July 1, 1992, collected $12,000 rent in advance for the following 12 months. This full amount is subject to income tax in the year collected.
Case C—On January 1, 1992, machinery has a UCC balance of $100,000; the CCA rate is 20%; and straight-line depreciation is used for financial reporting purposes.
Case D—Investment revenue of $1,000 was a dividend from a Canadian corporation.

1992—Income Tax Worksheet and Entry to Record Combined Income Tax Effect

Item	Income Tax Expense	Income Tax Payable
Pretax income	$ 30,000	$ 30,000
Case D—Deduct investment revenue dividends from Canadian corporations (a permanent difference)	(1,000)	(1,000)
Case A—Add rent revenue taxed in current year ($12,000 − $6,000)		6,000
Case C—Deduct CCA claimed in excess of depreciation ($10,000 − $20,000)		(10,000)
Accounting income	29,000	
Taxable income		25,000
Income tax rate	× .40	× .40
Income tax expense	$ 11,600	
Income taxes payable		$ 10,000

Deferred income taxes $11,600 − $10,000 = $1,600 credit

Entry to record combined effect of income tax for 1992:

Income tax expense	11,600	
Deferred income tax, short-term (rent revenue) ($6,000 × .40)	2,400	
Income tax payable		10,000
Deferred income tax, long-term (depreciation) ($10,000 × .40)		4,000

EXHIBIT 17–3 *(continued)*

Ildiko Corporation—Financial Statements, Including Income Tax, 1992

Income statement for the year ended December 31, 1992:

Revenues:

Sales revenue	$100,000	
Rent revenue	6,000	
Investment revenue	1,000	$107,000

Expenses:

Cost of goods sold	65,000	
Depreciation expense	10,000	
Interest expense	2,000	
Income tax expense	11,600	88,600
Net income		$ 18,400

Balance sheet at December 31, 1992 (partial):

Current assets:	
Deferred income tax*	$ 2,400
Current liabilities:	
Income tax payable (assuming no prepayments)	10,000
Long-term liabilities:	
Deferred income tax*	4,000

1993—Income Tax Worksheet and Entry to Record Combined Income Tax Effect

Item	Income Tax Expense	Income Tax Payable
Pretax income	$ 40,000	$ 40,000
Case D—Deduct investment revenue dividends from Canadian corporations (a permanent difference)	(1,000)	(1,000)
Case A—Deduct rent revenue taxed in prior year ($6,000 − $12,000)		(6,000)
Case C—Deduct additional depreciation (CCA) ($10,000 − $16,000)		(6,000)
Accounting income	39,000	
Taxable income		27,000
Income tax rate	× .40	× .40
Income tax expense	$ 15,600	
Income taxes payable		$ 10,800

Deferred income taxes $15,600 − $10,800 = $4,800 credit

Entry to record combined effect of income tax for 1993:

Income tax expense	15,600	
Income tax payable		10,800
Deferred income tax, short-term (rent revenue) ($6,000 × .40)		2,400
Deferred income tax, long-term (depreciation) ($6,000 × .40)		2,400

---

* These amounts net to $1,600 (credit); see discussion of following section, "Classification of Deferred Income Tax."

EXHIBIT 17-3   (*concluded*)

Ildiko Corporation—Financial Statements, Including Income Tax, 1993		
Income statement for the year ended December 31, 1993:		
Revenues:		
Sales revenue	$120,000	
Rent revenue	6,000	
Investment revenue	1,000	$127,000
Expenses:		
Cost of goods sold.	75,000	
Depreciation expense	10,000	
Interest expense.	2,000	
Income tax expense	15,600	102,600
Net income		$ 24,400
Balance sheet at December 31, 1993 (partial):		
Current liabilities:		
Income tax payable (assuming no prepayments)		$ 10,800
Long-term liabilities:		
Deferred income tax*		6,400

* Balance in the long-term deferred income tax account, $4,000 + $2,400 = $6,400, credit; credit balance in the short-term deferred income tax account, $2,400 − $2,400 = $-0-. See discussion of following section, "Classification of Deferred Income Tax."

transfer will be computed at the rate of accumulation. Where there are practical difficulties in identifying the specific components, the transfer may be calculated at the effective average rate of accumulation; that is, the proportion that the accumulated deferred credit or charge bears to the accumulated difference between taxable and accounting income. This calculation might be made either by types of differences or in the aggregate.

Ideally, the company is able to identify the rate of accumulation for a particular situation and use that rate to transfer the amount(s) out of the deferred tax balance. The following illustration assumes that the rate of accumulation cannot be determined and thus, an average rate is calculated.

To illustrate the accommodation of a change in the tax rates during the timing cycle, assume Voll Company had the following data:

	1990	1991	1992
Pretax income	$20,000	$25,000	$30,000
Capital cost allowance	15,000	12,000	9,000
Depreciation.	10,000	10,000	10,000
Income tax rate	40%	45%	50%

The entries to record income taxes would be as follows:

1990:

Income tax expense ($20,000 × .40)	8,000	
Income taxes payable [($20,000 + $10,000 − $15,000) × .40]		6,000
Deferred income taxes [($15,000 − $10,000) × .40].		2,000

1991:

Income tax expense ($25,000 × .45)	11,250	
Income taxes payable [($25,000 + $10,000 − $12,000) × .45]		10,350
Deferred income taxes [($12,000 − $10,000) × .45].		900

1992:

Income tax expense ($15,500 − $414) 15,086
Deferred income taxes [($10,000 − $9,000) × .414*]   414
    Income taxes payable [($30,000 + $10,000 − $9,000) × .50].   15,500
    * ($2,000 + $900) ÷ ($5,000 + $2,000) = .414

In the preceding sequence of entries, the timing differences which arose in 1990 and 1991 begin to reverse in 1992. In 1990, 1991, and 1992 the tax liability was based on the tax rate then in effect as required by law. The drawdown of deferred taxes in 1992 is based on the average rate of accumulation up to 1992; that is, the deferred tax balance of $2,900 divided by the accumulated timing difference of $7,000. This ensures that a deferred tax debit does not arise because the reversals are taken out of the deferred tax credit balance at a faster rate than the rate of accumulation when income tax rates change.

Classification of Deferred Income Tax on the Balance Sheet

Deferred income taxes must be reported on the balance sheet (*a*) if a debit, as a current or non-current asset; and (*b*) if a credit, as a current or long-term liability. On this point the *CICA Handbook* states:

> Accumulated tax allocation credits and/or debits should be segregated in the balance sheet as between current and non-current according to the classification of the assets and liabilities to which they relate [paragraph 3470.24].
>   Current accumulated tax allocation debits or credits should be shown in current assets or current liabilities [paragraph 3470.26].
>   Non-current accumulated tax allocation debits or credits should be shown as a deferred charge or as a deferred credit outside shareholders' equity [paragraph 3470.27].

Therefore, current debits and credits are offset, and non-current debits and credits are offset; however, current and non-current debits and credits are not offset. To illustrate the classification of deferred tax amounts, the classifications shown in Exhibit 17–3 were based on the following analysis of individual items:

	Balance Sheet	
	Current	Non-current
Year 1992: Balance in the deferred income tax account, $1,600 credit comprised of:		
Debits:		
Rent revenue collected in advance, a current item because the related liability, unearned rent revenue, is a current liability ($6,000 × .40) . . .	$2,400	
Credits:		
Depreciation of machinery, a non-current item because the related asset, machinery, is a non-current asset ($10,000 × .40).		$4,000
Year 1993: Balance in the deferred income tax account, $6,400 credit comprised of:		
Debits:		
None		
Credits:		
Depreciation of machinery, a non-current item because the related asset, machinery, is a non-current asset ($10,000 + $6,000) × .40		$6,400

INTRAPERIOD INCOME TAX ALLOCATION

◆

GAAP specifies two distinctly different types of income tax allocation: (*a*) interperiod income tax allocation, caused by timing differences among accounting periods resulting from differences between the income statement and the tax return (discussed earlier); and (*b*) intraperiod income tax allocation, which relates total income tax for the

EXHIBIT 17–4   Intraperiod Tax Allocation

Data for Five Comparative Cases

1. Pretax income:

	Case A	Case B	Case C	Case D	Case E
Income before extraordinary items (loss).	$30,000	$30,000	$(30,000)	$ 30,000	$ 30,000
Extraordinary gain (loss)	10,000	10,000*	40,000	(10,000)	(40,000)
Pretax income (loss).	$40,000	$40,000	$ 10,000	$ 20,000	$(10,000)†
Total income tax expense	$16,000	$14,000	$ 4,000	$ 8,000	$ (4,000)

2. Tax rates assumed: 40%; and 20% (i.e., ½ × 40%) on capital gains.

* Capital gain

† Involves a tax loss carryback (discussed later).

period to the various statement components that caused the tax. It is important to understand that both types of income tax allocation must be applied; one is not an alternative to the other.

The concept of intraperiod allocation is to report the income tax (or tax saving) associated with a particular kind of item along with that item in the financial statements (i.e., tax expense must follow the item that caused it). A gain increases taxes payable because it increases income. A loss creates a tax saving because it reduces the total income on which taxes are paid. Therefore, the tax effect on extraordinary gains and losses, and prior period adjustments is a reduction of the gain or loss. To illustrate intraperiod income tax allocation, assume the following for Abco Limited:

Pretax income before extraordinary items	$40,000
Extraordinary gain (pretax)	10,000
Total income tax expense, average tax rate 40% [($40,000 + $10,000) × .40].	20,000

Abco Limited would report the results of intraperiod tax allocation of the $20,000 total income tax expense as follows:

Income before income tax and before extraordinary items.		$40,000
Less: Income tax expense ($40,000 × .40)		16,000
Income before extraordinary items		24,000
Extraordinary gain (specified)	$10,000	
Less: Applicable income tax ($10,000 × .40)	4,000	6,000
Net income.		$30,000

In this example, as in most of the examples in this textbook, average tax rates are used to illustrate the particular discussion without laborious income tax computations.

Exhibit 17–4 presents five separate cases to illustrate how total income tax expense for the period is allocated to the several components of income which caused a tax expense (or a tax saving). Note that in each case the allocations always sum to the total tax amount.

Income tax, with intraperiod tax allocation, would be reported as follows for five independent cases. Computations are given to show how the allocated amounts were derived. In all five cases, income (loss) before income tax and before extraordinary items is $30,000 and is associated with income tax expense (saving) of $12,000. The following discussion focusses on the application of intraperiod tax allocation to the extraordinary item.

In **Case A,** the extraordinary gain produced tax expense of $4,000, which is computed at the 40% tax rate.

Case A:

Income before income tax and before extraordinary gain.		$ 30,000
Less: Income tax expense. . . . . $30,000 × .40 =		12,000
Income before extraordinary gain.		$ 18,000
Extraordinary gain (specified)	$10,000	
Less: Applicable income tax expense . . . . $10,000 × .40 =	4,000	6,000
Net income.		$ 24,000

Total tax: $12,000 + $4,000 = $16,000 expense.

Case B is like Case A, except that the extraordinary gain is taxed at 20% because it is a capital gain (assumed tax rate); if the extraordinary item in Case B had been a loss, it would also have been subject to the same 20% tax rate.

Case B:

Income before income tax and before extraordinary gain.		$ 30,000
Less: Income tax expense. . . . . $30,000 × .40 =		12,000
Income before extraordinary gain.		$ 18,000
Extraordinary gain (specified)	$10,000	
Less: Applicable income tax expense (capital gain) . . . . $10,000 × ½ × .40 =	2,000	8,000
Net income.		$ 26,000

Total tax: $12,000 + $2,000 = $14,000 expense.

In **Case C,** the first $30,000 of the extraordinary gain offsets the $30,000 loss before tax and before extraordinary item. The remainder of the extraordinary gain (i.e., $10,000) is taxed at 40%.

Case C:

Income (loss) before income tax and before extraordinary gain.		$(30,000)
Less: Income tax saving. . . . . $30,000 × .40 =		12,000
Income (loss) before extraordinary gain.		$(18,000)
Extraordinary gain (specified)	$40,000	
Less: Applicable income tax expense . . . . $40,000 × .40 =	16,000	24,000
Net income.		$ 6,000

Total tax: $16,000 − $12,000 = $4,000 expense.

In **Case D,** the $10,000 extraordinary loss offsets $10,000 of income before tax and before extraordinary items.

Case D:

Income before income tax and before extraordinary loss		$ 30,000
Less: Income tax expense. . . . . $30,000 × .40 =		12,000
Income before extraordinary loss		$ 18,000
Extraordinary loss (specified).	$10,000	
Less: Applicable income tax saving . . . . $10,000 × .40 =	4,000	6,000
Net income.		$ 12,000

Total tax: $12,000 − $4,000 = $8,000 expense.

In **Case E,** the extraordinary loss (i.e., $40,000) exceeds income before tax and before extraordinary items (i.e., $30,000). The $30,000 extraordinary loss offsets all of income before tax and before extraordinary items. The remainder of the extraordinary loss (i.e., $10,000) must be carried back to preceding years or forward to future years under tax loss carryback and carryforward provisions discussed later. In this case, a tax loss carryback to preceding years is assumed.

Case E:

Income before income tax and before extraordinary loss			$ 30,000
Less: Income tax expense.	$30,000 × .40 =		12,000
Income before extraordinary loss			$ 18,000
Extraordinary loss (specified).		$40,000	
Less: Applicable income tax saving	$40,000 × .40 =	16,000	(24,000)
Net loss			$ 6,000

Total tax: $12,000 − $16,000 = $4,000* tax saving.

* Assume a tax loss carryback to preceding years.

Intraperiod income tax allocation involves only the reporting phase of accounting and seldom, if ever, the recording phase except in the cases where prior period adjustments are involved (see the following section). Therefore, it seldom gives rise to entries in the accounts and does not modify the entries to record income tax as illustrated in the prior discussion of interperiod income tax allocation.

INCOME TAX EFFECTS OF PRIOR PERIOD ADJUSTMENTS
◆

Paragraph 3600.05 of the *CICA Handbook* states in part that "The financial statements of prior periods presented for comparative purposes are restated as necessary to reflect the retroactive application of a prior period adjustment, including any related income tax effect." Where the adjustment relates to a period earlier than that presented for comparative purposes, the adjustment is made to the opening balance of retained earnings.

If an error caused a misstatement of reported income of a prior period and if the misstated item had an income tax effect, the prior period adjustment would also need to correct for the income tax effect of the error. In such a case, the company most likely would file an amended tax return to claim a refund or to pay additional taxes, as the case may be.

To illustrate, assume SASK Corporation inadvertently understated depreciation expense on both the financial statements and the tax return in 1992 by $10,000 when the income tax rate was 40%.[3] In 1994, the company discovered this error when the income tax rate was 45% (there was no error in 1993 or 1994). Two entries (or a single combined entry) would correct the error in 1994:

Prior period adjustment (expense correction)	10,000	
Accumulated depreciation.		10,000
Receivable for refund of 1992 income tax ($10,000 × 40%)	4,000	
Prior period adjustment (tax refund on expense correction)		4,000

Notice that the tax rate in effect during the year when the error was made (i.e., 40%) was used, rather than the tax rate of the correction year (i.e., 45%). Any interest and/or penalties related to the extra income tax, and any interest related to any tax refunds also would affect the net amount of the prior period adjustment.

---

[3] For the purpose of this example, assume that the CCA for tax purposes is the same as the depreciation expense.

THE INVESTMENT TAX CREDIT

The **investment tax credit** is a provision in the income tax laws designed to encourage investments in new productive assets, such as plant, machinery, and equipment. Currently, the law provides that taxpayers who acquire qualified assets can receive an investment tax credit as a direct offset to income tax expense and tax payable. This tax credit is important to investors because they can reduce their income tax payable for the year of purchase of the qualified asset by a portion of its full cost.[4] The nature of a tax credit, as opposed to a tax deduction, is that a tax credit causes a direct dollar-for-dollar tax reduction, whereas a tax deduction decreases income tax only by the deduction amount multiplied by the income tax rate. However, the amount of the investment tax credit deducted from the taxes payable must also be deducted from the capital cost of the asset for tax purposes thus reducing the amount of CCA for tax purposes over the useful life of the asset.

The full amount of the investment tax credit is received through a decrease in income tax payable in the year in which the qualified asset is purchased; however, it relates to the acquired asset which contributes to revenue generation over its useful life. Consequently, the question is posed, in terms of the matching principle, whether the income statement effect of the investment tax credit should be (a) recorded and reported only in the period of purchase, or (b) allocated over the useful life of the related asset.

In July 1984, the CICA issued section 3805 of the *Handbook,* "Investment Tax Credits," which recommends that investment tax credits should be accounted for using the cost reduction approach (paragraph 3805.12).

Under this method the total amount of the investment tax credit is either

1. Deducted from the related assets with any depreciation or amortization calculated on the net amount.
2. Deferred and amortized to income on the same basis as the related assets (paragraph 3805.13).

Thus, the investment tax credit amount is allocated over the estimated useful life of the assets to which it relates. This method relates the investment tax credit to use rather than to the purchase of the asset. The primary argument often given for this method is that it conforms better to the matching principle and, therefore, better measures both periodic income and asset values.

The accounting entries for the investment tax credit would be similar to those needed for accounting for government assistance (see Chapter 11). To the extent that depreciation for accounting purposes is different than CCA for tax purposes, a debit or credit to the deferred tax account could also arise. Exhibit 17–5 demonstrates the relevant accounting procedures.

DISCLOSURE OF INCOME TAX

Full disclosure of the components of income tax expense (including deferred income tax) is required. In respect to the income statement, paragraph 3470.29 states that "The amount by which the current income tax provision has been increased or decreased as a result of tax deferrals should be disclosed" either by showing the current and deferred portions of the income tax provision separately on the income statement or by means of a note to the financial statements (see Exhibit 17–3).

---

[4] Depending on the type of capital expenditure and the location of the enterprise, the investment tax credit may be from 7% to 35%.

EXHIBIT 17–5 Recording and Reporting the Investment Tax Credit

Illustrative Data:

January 1, 1991:
  Purchased eligible transportation equipment (30% CCA rate) costing $100,000 to be depreciated over 10 years, no residual value.
December 31, 1991:
  Pretax income (after $9,300 depreciation on new equipment), $150,000.
  Income tax expense ($150,000 × 40% tax rate), $60,000.
  Investment tax credit ($100,000 × 7%; not included in previous amounts), $7,000.

Entries for 1991

a. January 1—Purchase qualified equipment:

Equipment	100,000	
Cash		100,000

b. December 31—Record depreciation expense:

Depreciation expense	10,000	
Accumulated depreciation		10,000

c. December 31—Record income tax and investment tax credit:

Income tax expense (40% × $150,000)	60,000	
Deferred investment tax credit (7% × $100,000)		7,000
Income tax payable		53,000

d. December 31—Record amortization of investment tax credit for 1991:

Deferred investment credit ($\frac{1}{10}$ × $7,000)	700	
Depreciation expense		700

e. December 31—Record deferred tax credit on timing difference for new equipment:

Income tax payable ($4,650* × 40%)	1,860	
Deferred income tax, long-term (depreciation)		1,860

Reporting for 1991

Income statement:

Depreciation expense		$ 9,300
Pretax income		$150,000
Income tax expense—current	$ 58,140	
—deferred	1,860	60,000
Net income		$ 90,000

Balance sheet:

Equipment (at cost)		$100,000
Accumulated depreciation	$ 10,000	
Deferred investment tax credit	6,300	16,300
Carrying value		$ 83,700
Income tax payable		$ 51,140†
Deferred income taxes		$ 1,860

* Timing difference calculation:

Capital cost of equipment	$100,000
Less investment tax credit at 7%	7,000
Net capital cost	$ 93,000
CCA for 1991: 30% × $93,000 × ½ᵃ	$ 13,950
Depreciation expense for 1991: $10,000 − $700	9,300
Timing difference	$ 4,650

ᵃ Half-year rule requires that only one half of normal capital cost allowance be taken in year of acquisition

† Reconciliation of income tax payable:

Accounting income	$150,000
Add: depreciation expense (net)	9,300
Deduct: capital cost allowance	(13,950)
Taxable income	$145,350
Income tax at 40%	$ 58,140
Deduct: investment tax credit	7,000
Income tax payable	$ 51,140

The balance sheet should disclose separately the current and non-current accumulated tax allocation credits and/or debits according to the assets and liabilities to which they relate. The current accumulated tax allocation debits or credits should be included in current assets or current liabilities. The non-current accumulated tax allocations should be shown as a deferred charge or as a deferred credit outside shareholders' equity (see Exhibit 17–3).

Effective January 1988, the *CICA Handbook* also requires that a company with shares that trade publicly or one required to file financial statements with a securities commission "disclose in its financial statements the components of the variation from the basic income tax rate" (paragraph 3470.33). The purpose of this disclosure is to facilitate both intercompany and interperiod comparisons. The following excerpts illustrate the disclosure of the variation from the basic income tax:

DERLAN INDUSTRIES LIMITED

Notes to Consolidated Financial Statements
For the Years Ended December 31, 1989 and 1988

9. Income taxes

a. Provision for income taxes comprises:

(*thousands of dollars*)	**1989**	**1988**
Current.	4,014	8,737
Deferred	1,440	1,068
	5,454	9,805

b. The company's effective income tax rate has been determined as follows:

(*percentages*)	**1989**	**1988**
Canadian statutory income tax rate	43.5	47.0
Manufacturing and processing allowance.	(1.1)	(0.8)
Lower effective foreign tax rates.	(10.5)	(7.9)
Federal surtax.	0.6	0.9
Non-taxable dividend income	(1.5)	(1.0)
Other.	(.3)	(2.9)
	30.7	35.3

JOHN LABATT LIMITED

Notes to the Consolidated Financial Statements
April 30, 1990

4. Income taxes

The effective income tax rate is comprised of the following:

	1990	1989
Combined basic federal and provincial income tax rates.	43.8%	45.4%
Less:		
Manufacturing and processing deduction.	(2.8)	(3.0)
Capital gains and non-taxable income	(9.8)	(11.8)
	31.2%	30.6%

CONCEPT REVIEW

1. What is the difference between a permanent difference and a timing difference?
2. Explain interperiod and intraperiod tax allocation.
3. How is the income tax on a prior period adjustment presented in the financial statements?

EXHIBIT 17–6   Quebec Company—Loss Carryback Data for Years Ending December 31

	1989	1990	1991	1992
Accounting income (loss)	$10,000	$ 8,000	$ 5,000	$(15,000)
Timing difference:				
Depreciation	$ 3,000	$ 3,000	$ 3,000	$ 3,000
Capital cost allowance.	6,000	5,000	4,000	3,500
	$ (3,000)	$(2,000)	$(1,000)	$ (500)
Taxable income (loss)	$ 7,000	$ 6,000	$ 4,000	$(15,500)
Income tax rate: 40%				

INCOME TAX LOSS CARRYBACKS AND CARRYFORWARDS

◆

Federal tax laws allow taxpayers to carry back and to carry forward operating losses. The effect is that a corporation may secure a refund of taxes paid in the three years preceding the loss and, if the loss is so large that it is not absorbed when carried back, it may be carried forward and applied against future taxable income for up to seven years.

Loss Carryback

In a period when an operating loss follows periods of net income sufficient to offset the loss, the resultant **loss carryback** gives rise to a refund of income taxes paid in prior periods. The loss is carried back and deducted from the taxable incomes of the prior periods; this results in a reduction of the tax. Amended tax returns are filed for the affected period(s) and the refund is claimed. The refund is both realizable and measurable in the period (year) of the loss and is, therefore, recognized in the loss period. Paragraph 3470.40 of the *CICA Handbook* states: "Where the loss for tax purposes gives rise to a recovery of income taxes of the previous period, such recovery should be reflected in the income statement for the period of the loss."

Exhibit 17–6 illustrates the accounting for loss carryback. The data for 1989 to 1992 includes depreciation expense and capital cost allowances for each year as well as reconciliations between accounting and taxable income (loss).

These journal entries record the income taxes for 1989 to 1991:

December 31:	1989		1990		1991	
Income tax expense	4,000		3,200		2,000	
Income taxes payable		2,800		2,400		1,600
Deferred income taxes . . .		1,200		800		400

These entries reflect the income tax expense based on accounting incomes, income tax payable based on taxable incomes, and the deferred tax credit based on the timing difference for each year.

Accounting income for 1992 is a loss of $15,000. Because of the difference between depreciation and CCA, the loss for tax purposes is $15,500; this may be carried back against the taxable incomes reported for the previous three years. All of the taxes paid for 1989 and 1990 would be refundable and $1,000 [($4,000 − $1,500) × .4] of the taxes of $1,600 payable for 1991 would be refundable. The journal entry to record income taxes in 1992 follows:

December 31, 1992:

<pre>
Tax refund receivable ($15,500 × .4). 6,200
    Income tax expense ($15,000 × .4)   6,000
    Deferred income tax ($500 × .4)   200
</pre>

Once the amended 1989–91 tax returns reflecting the loss carryback are filed, the receipt of the tax refund is assured. Therefore, it is appropriate to show the asset (refund receivable) on the 1992 balance sheet. Because income tax expense is based on accounting income, the benefit of the loss (i.e., the refund of income taxes) is also based on the accounting income (loss). In this case, the entire benefit is realizable. Therefore, it is recognizable and there is a negative tax expense of $6,000 ($15,000 × .4). The $200 credit to deferred income tax recognizes the effect of the timing difference caused by depreciation and capital cost allowance.

The lower portion of Quebec Company's income statement would show the following:

QUEBEC COMPANY
Income Statement (in part)
For the Year Ended December 31, 1992

Loss before income taxes $15,000
Deduct: Recovery of prior years'
   income taxes due to loss carryback . . . . . <u>6,000</u>
Net loss . . . . $ 9,000

Loss Carryforward

When a company has experienced an operating loss which cannot be absorbed by the profits of the previous three years, it may carry the loss forward and apply it against the profits of the following seven years. This **loss carryforward** creates a recognition problem. The loss carryforward can convey a benefit in the form of a reduction in future income taxes provided that sufficient income is earned in the carryforward period. The determination of the extent of this benefit to be recognized in the year of the loss is the major concern of this section.

Virtual Certainty To recognize the entire benefit of the loss carryforward, the *CICA Handbook* requires that there be **virtual certainty**. Paragraph 3470.43 of the *Handbook* states:

> A corporation which has incurred a loss for tax purposes may be virtually certain of realizing the tax benefit resulting from the loss or a portion thereof in the carryforward period prescribed by the tax laws. Virtual certainty of realizing the tax benefit on a loss other than a capital loss requires all three of the following conditions to be present:
> (i) the loss results from an identifiable and nonrecurring cause;
> (ii) a record of profitability has been established over a long period by the corporation, or a predecessor business, with any occasional losses being more than offset by income in subsequent years; and
> (iii) there is assurance beyond any reasonable doubt that future taxable income will be sufficient to offset the loss carryforward and will be earned during the carryforward period prescribed by the tax laws. In assessing its ability to earn sufficient future taxable income to offset the loss, a corporation may recognize that it can maximize its taxable income during the loss carryforward period by not claiming certain deductions allowable for tax purposes (e.g., capital cost allowances). This will result either in a reduction of accumulated deferred income tax credits or in the recording of deferred income tax debits during the carryforward period.

The recognition of the loss carryforward benefit in the year of the loss depends on the assurance that the benefit will be realized within the seven-year carryforward

EXHIBIT 17-7   Partial Income Statement for Years Ending December 31, Elora Company

	1991	1992
Accounting income (loss)	$ 50,000	$(55,000)
Timing difference:		
Depreciation	$ 15,000	$ 15,000
Capital cost allowance.	(25,000)	(22,000)
	(10,000)	(7,000)
Taxable income (loss)	$ 40,000	$(62,000)

Other data:
1. Income tax rate: 40%
2. Allocation of taxable loss for 1992:

Total loss available	$ 62,000
Carryback to 1991	40,000
Carryforward available	$ 22,000

period. This criterion of realization is the same as that used for the recognition of any asset or benefit and is consistent with the principles recommended in section 1000, "Financial Statement Concepts," of the *CICA Handbook* (see Chapter 2).

Exhibit 17–7 presents the data for accounting for a loss carryback and a loss carryforward with virtual certainty. The Income Tax Act allows loss carrybacks to be applied to any or all of the three preceding years. For simplicity, Exhibit 17–7 assumes that the loss in 1992 may be carried back only to 1991 and that conditions for virtual certainty exist. Therefore, the entire benefit of the available loss carryforward may be recognized in 1992, the year of the loss.

The entry to record income taxes for 1992 would appear as follows:

December 31, 1992:

Tax refund receivable ($40,000 × .4).	16,000	
Income tax benefit available ($22,000 × .4)	8,800	
Deferred income tax ($7,000 × .4)		2,800
Income tax expense ($55,000 × .4)		22,000

The tax refund receivable arises because $40,000 of the taxable loss is carried back and applied against the taxable income of 1991 reducing it to zero. The 1991 taxes paid will thereby be refunded. Because the criteria of virtual certainty were assumed to be satisfied, the balance of the 1992 loss will be carried forward and used to reduce future taxable income and taxes payable. Therefore, the benefit of the loss carried forward $8,800 ($22,000 × .4) may be included as an asset on the balance sheet at the end of 1992. The credit to deferred income tax records the effect of the timing difference in 1992 and the credit to income tax expense records the overall reduction in income taxes as a result of the 1992 operating loss.

The partial financial statements presented in Exhibit 17–8 reflect the disclosures arising out of the preceding example.

Timing Difference Reversals   The Income Tax Act regulates the use of capital cost allowances (CCA) by defining the maximum claimable. Therefore, the amount of CCA a firm wishes to use may vary from nil to the maximum allowed. Most profitable firms usually claim the maximum CCA allowable to reduce their taxable income as much as possible.

Unlike loss carryforwards, CCA does not have a time limit. In some cases, a firm may wish to maximize the **benefits of loss carryovers** particularly when its future profitability might be questionable. In the previous example, Elora could reduce its loss for tax purposes to $40,000 by not claiming any CCA in 1992. Then the entire taxable loss

EXHIBIT 17–8   Partial Financial Statements for 1992, Elora Company

Partial income statement:		
Net loss before income taxes		$55,000
Recovery of income taxes:		
Recovery of prior years' taxes.	$16,000	
Recognition of loss carryforward benefit	$ 8,800	
	$24,800	
Less deferred income tax	2,800	22,000
Net loss		$33,000
Partial balance sheet:		
Current assets:		
Tax refund receivable.		$16,000
Other assets:		
Tax benefit available for application against		
future years' income taxes		$ 8,800

Deferred income taxes—$2,800 credited to the existing balance.

of $40,000 could be absorbed by carrying it back to 1991. This is accomplished by reversing previously built up timing differences. The journal entry in 1992 to reflect this would be:

December 31, 1992:

```
Tax refund receivable ($40,000 × .4). . . . . . . . . . . . . .   16,000
Deferred income taxes ($15,000 × .4) . . . . . . . . . . . . .    6,000
    Income tax expense ($55,000 × .4) . . . . . . . . . . . .             22,000
```

The $6,000 debit to deferred taxes arises because depreciation expense is $15,000 more than the CCA claimed, which is zero. This represents a $15,000 reversal of the timing difference and the tax effect at 40% is $6,000.

Another method for achieving the same result is to amend the previous years' tax returns to claim less CCA which would increase taxable income in those years allowing more of the loss to be carried back. While this would not increase the refund, which is limited to the actual tax paid, it decreases the amount of tax carryforward thus reducing the dependence on future earnings. Remember that CCA may be claimed at any time so that the time limitation on loss carryforwards may make this strategy advantageous. An illustration of this point is included in the following section.

Without Virtual Certainty   As shown earlier, when there is virtual certainty, the benefit of the loss carryforward (i.e., the reduction of future income taxes) may be recorded as an asset on the assumption that the company will earn sufficient profits in the upcoming fiscal years to absorb the loss carryforward before the seven-year time limit expires. When the conditions of virtual certainty cannot be met, the value of the loss carryforward benefit as an asset becomes questionable because of the possibility that it will not be realized. As with any other asset, the degree to which it will be realized in future periods affects the value of the asset in the current period.

Where virtual certainty does not exist, paragraph 3470.47 of the *CICA Handbook* states that:

> . . . accumulated deferred income tax credits, which have arisen because of timing differences in prior periods, may nevertheless exist and may be reduced or eliminated in the carry-forward period prescribed by the income tax laws by claiming less capital cost allowances than depreciation recorded, or making other similar adjustments which have the effect of increasing taxable income or reducing losses for tax purposes. In these cases, such reductions or eliminations provide a means of realizing the tax benefit, and

EXHIBIT 17-9   Partial Income Statements for Years Ended December 31, Estevan Company

	1990	1991	1992	1993
Accounting income (loss)	$ 70,000	$(290,000)		
Timing difference:				
Depreciation	$ 20,000	$ 20,000		
Capital cost allowance.	50,000	—		
	$(30,000)	$ 20,000		
Taxable income (loss)	$ 40,000	$(270,000)		

Other data:
1. The credit balance of deferred taxes is solely due to timing differences in the depreciation of long-lived assets. The timing difference at December 31, 1990, is $190,000 arising from a net book value of $460,000 and an undepreciated capital cost of $270,000.
2. The 1990 tax return will be amended to increase the amount of the loss carryback.
3. Conditions for virtual certainty do not exist.
4. The income tax rate is 40%.

it is therefore appropriate to recognize the tax benefit of the loss carry-forward as a reduction of accumulated deferred income tax credits to the extent that such credits could be reduced within the carry-forward period.

When more depreciation (CCA) has been claimed for tax purposes than has been charged to expense in the accounting records, an **accumulated timing difference** arises. The accumulated timing difference (ATD) may also be measured as the difference between the net book value and the undepreciated capital cost of a long-lived asset. The tax effect of the accumulated timing difference is represented by the balance in the deferred tax account. The accumulated timing difference is the most common reason for deferred tax credits.

When conditions of virtual certainty do not exist, the *CICA Handbook* does not allow tax carryforward benefits to be set up as an asset. However, the *Handbook* allows the recognition of the carryforward benefit to the extent that deferred tax credits may be reduced. Therefore, the loss carryforward benefit that may be recognized in the year of the loss is limited to the least of the following three amounts:

1. The tax carryforward benefit itself.
2. The credit balance in the deferred tax account after adjusting for current period and/or amendment of previous period timing differences.
3. The total of the available timing difference drawdown during the carryforward period.

The company may use up the available loss carryforward more assuredly by claiming less capital cost allowances than depreciation recorded (or by making other adjustments of similar effect) thus increasing taxable income during the loss carryforward period.

Exhibit 17-9 presents the basic data for an example of loss carryovers when virtual certainty does not exist. The information is first presented for 1990 and 1991. The 1992 and 1993 results are added to the illustration as it progresses.

The following sets of journal entries and calculations present the accounting for income taxes and the loss carryovers for 1990 and 1991. Although losses may be carried back for three years, it is assumed, for simplification, that only one year's carryback is available.

The entry to record the income tax for 1990 follows:

December 31, 1990:

```
Income tax expense ($70,000 × .4) . . . . . . . . . . . . . . . 28,000
    Income tax payable ($40,000 × .4). . . . . . . . . . . . .        16,000
    Deferred income tax ($30,000 × .4) . . . . . . . . . . . .        12,000
```

The tax expense is based on the accounting income of $70,000 and the difference between the expense and the tax payable is the tax effect of the timing difference of $30,000.

Because virtual certainty does not exist at the end of 1991, the year of the loss, it is to the company's advantage to carry back as much of the loss as possible so as to minimize the loss carryforward. Therefore, the 1990 tax return would be amended and refiled without a claim for CCA. The revised taxable income for 1990 thus becomes $90,000 ($40,000 + $50,000) and this is the amount of the loss carryback. The loss carryforward available is $180,000 ($270,000 − $90,000).

The amount of the loss carryforward benefit which may be recognized in the year of the loss (1991) is calculated by determining the least of the following three amounts:

1. The tax carryforward benefit itself:

$$\$180,000 \times .4 = \$72,000$$

2. The credit balance in the deferred tax account after adjusting for current period and/or amendment of previous period timing differences:

	ATD	Deferred Tax
Balance, December 31, 1990	$190,000	$76,000cr
Amendment to 1990 tax return (CCA)	(50,000)	20,000dr
1991 timing difference	(20,000)	8,000dr
Balance, December 31, 1991	$120,000	$48,000cr

Adjusted credit in the deferred tax account $48,000

3. The total of the available timing difference drawdown during the carryforward period:

The loss carryforward period is seven years. Assuming that depreciation expense would continue at $20,000 per year, the drawdown and the tax effect would be:

$$\$20,000 \times 7 \text{ years} \times 40\% = \$140,000 \times .4 = \$56,000$$

Therefore, the amount of the tax carryforward benefit which may be recognized in 1991 (i.e., the least of the three amounts calculated) is $48,000 which represents a reversal to the accumulated timing difference (ATD) of $120,000. In the following journal entry to record the taxes for 1991, the tax carryforward benefit recognized of $48,000 is also part of the debit to the deferred tax account.

To record income taxes—December 31, 1991:

Income tax refund receivable ($40,000 × .4)	16,000	
Deferred income taxes ($50,000 + $20,000 +		
$120,000) × .4	76,000	
Income tax expense ($290,000 − $60,000) × .4		92,000

The credit to income tax expense may be reconciled as follows:

Tax loss available—1991	$270,000
Carried back to 1990 ($40,000 + $50,000)	90,000
Loss carryforward available.	$180,000
Maximum recognizable in period of loss	
($48,000/.4) from (2)	120,000
Unrecognized loss carryforward	$ 60,000
Loss carryforward recognized in 1991:	
Accounting loss 1991.	$290,000
Unrecognized loss carryforward	60,000
Loss carryforward recognized in 1991.	$230,000
Loss carryforward benefit recognized	
($230,000 × .4)	$ 92,000

EXHIBIT 17-10   Partial Income Statements for Years Ended December 31, Estevan Company

	1990	1991	1992	1993
Accounting income (loss)	$ 70,000	$(290,000)	$ 80,000	
Timing difference:				
Depreciation	$ 20,000	$ 20,000	$ 20,000	
Capital cost allowance.	50,000	—	—	
	$(30,000)	$ 20,000	$ 20,000	
Taxable income (loss)	$ 40,000	$(270,000)	$100,000	

The $92,000 credit to income tax expense in 1991 may also be broken down as follows:

> Refund of the 1990 taxes paid ($40,000 × .4) $16,000
> Amendment to 1990 tax return: the CCA not
>   claimed ($50,000 × .4).   20,000
> 1991 timing difference reversal: 1991 depreciation
>   ($20,000 × .4).   8,000
> Maximum carryforward benefit recognizable as
>   per the calculation in (2) ($120,000 × .4).   48,000
> Credit to income tax expense $92,000

The unrecognized loss carryforward at the end of 1991 is $60,000 which will result in a benefit of $24,000 ($60,000 × .4). Unlike the situation where virtual certainty exists, this amount does not appear as an asset on the balance sheet. Instead, the amount would be explained in the notes to the financial statements to inform readers that this future benefit is available. The benefit is then recognized in future periods when the tax loss carryforward is utilized.

As a result of the 1991 entry, the deferred tax account would have a nil balance, as shown next. Columns have been added to illustrate the relationship between **net book value** (NBV) and **undepreciated capital cost** (UCC) to the accumulated timing difference (ATD) and deferred income tax balance (DT).

Schedule of Accumulated Timing Differences and Deferred Tax

	NBV	UCC	ATD	DT
Balance, December 31, 1990	$460,000	$270,000	$190,000	$76,000cr
Amendment to 1990 tax return (CCA). . .		50,000	(50,000)	20,000dr
1991 depreciation.	(20,000)		(20,000)	8,000dr
1991 benefit recognition				48,000dr
Balance, December 31, 1991	$440,000	$320,000	$120,000	NIL

Income taxes—1992   Exhibit 17–10 presents the additional data for 1992.

To prepare the income tax journal entries when loss carryforwards are involved, it is often simpler to begin by ignoring the loss carryforward. Thus, this entry records income taxes for 1992, ignoring the loss carryforward:

December 31, 1992:

> Income tax expense ($80,000 × .4) 32,000
> Deferred income tax ($20,000 × .4) 8,000
>   Income tax payable ($100,000)   40,000

Recall that $90,000 of the 1991 taxable loss of $270,000 was carried back to 1990. Therefore, $180,000 is available to carry forward to 1992 and beyond. The second entry for 1992 illustrates the utilization of $100,000 of the $180,000 to reduce the 1992 taxable income to zero.

EXHIBIT 17–11   Partial Income Statements for Years Ended December 31, Estevan Company

	1990	1991	1992	1993
Accounting income (loss)	$ 70,000	$(290,000)	$ 80,000	$150,000
Timing difference:				
Depreciation	$ 20,000	$ 20,000	$ 20,000	$ 20,000
Capital cost allowance.	50,000	—	—	45,000
	$(30,000)	$ 20,000	$ 20,000	$(25,000)
Taxable income (loss)	$ 40,000	$(270,000)	$100,000	$125,000

December 31, 1992:

```
Income tax payable ($100,000 × .4) . . . . . . . . . . . . . . 40,000
     Loss carryforward benefit recognized
        ($60,000 × .4). . . . . . . . . . . . . . . . . . . . . .        24,000
     Deferred income tax . . . . . . . . . . . . . . . . . . . .        16,000
```

The $40,000 debit to income tax payable is simply the reversal of the credit in the first entry because the loss carryforward is applied against the 1992 taxable income.

The credits may be explained as follows: Recall that the total loss carryforward benefit from 1991 was $72,000 ($180,000 × .4), and that a benefit of only $48,000 ($120,000 × .4) was allowed to be recognized in 1991. The remaining loss carryforward benefit of $24,000 results from the unrecognized loss carryforward of $60,000 (i.e., $60,000 × .4). Because a loss carryforward of $100,000 was utilized (realized) in 1992, the unrecognized benefit is now recognized. The $16,000 credit to deferred taxes is a partial reversal of the $48,000 debit to that account which was made in 1991 to enable us to recognize the loss carryforward benefit in the year of the loss. The updated schedule of timing differences and deferred tax follows:

Schedule of Accumulated Timing Differences and Deferred Tax

	NBV	UCC	ATD	DT
Balance, December 31, 1990	$460,000	$270,000	$190,000	$76,000cr
Amendment to 1990 tax return (CCA). . .		50,000	(50,000)	20,000dr
1991 depreciation.	(20,000)		(20,000)	8,000dr
1991 benefit recognition				48,000dr
Balance, December 31, 1991	$440,000	$320,000	$120,000	NIL
1992 depreciation.	(20,000)		(20,000)	8,000dr
1992 reversal				16,000cr
Balance, December 31, 1992	$420,000	$320,000	$100,000	$ 8,000cr

Income taxes—1993   The partial income statements for 1993 have been added in Exhibit 17–11 to the previous data and the results for 1990 through 1993 follow.

As was done for 1992, the first income tax entry for 1993 ignores the presence of a loss carryforward. The second entry accounts for the utilization of the remaining tax loss carryforward of $80,000 ($270,000 − $90,000 − $100,000).

December 31, 1993:

```
Income tax expense ($150,000 × .4) . . . . . . . . . . . . . . 60,000
     Deferred income tax ($25,000 × .4) . . . . . . . . . . . .        10,000
     Income tax payable ($125,000 × .4) . . . . . . . . . . . .        50,000

Income tax payable ($80,000 × .4). . . . . . . . . . . . . . . 32,000
     Deferred income tax . . . . . . . . . . . . . . . . . . . .        32,000
```

The schedule of deferred income tax and accumulated timing differences, updated to the end of 1993, follows.

Schedule of Accumulated Timing Differences and Deferred Tax

	NBV	UCC	ATD	DT
Balance, December 31, 1990	$460,000	$270,000	$190,000	$76,000cr
Amendment to 1990 tax return (CCA). . .		50,000	(50,000)	20,000dr
1991 depreciation	(20,000)		(20,000)	8,000dr
1991 benefit recognition				48,000dr
Balance, December 31, 1991	$440,000	$320,000	$120,000	NIL
1992 depreciation	(20,000)		(20,000)	8,000dr
1992 reversal				16,000cr
Balance, December 31, 1992	$420,000	$320,000	$100,000	$ 8,000cr
1993 depreciation	(20,000)	(45,000)	25,000	10,000cr
1993 reversal				32,000cr
Balance, December 31, 1993	$400,000	$275,000	$125,000	$50,000cr

By the end of 1993, several events have taken place. First, total benefit of the accounting loss, $116,000 ($290,000 × .4), has been recognized in two stages: $92,000 in 1991 which was comprised of the $16,000 refund of the 1990 income taxes and the $76,000 January 1, 1991, balance in the deferred tax account; and $24,000 in 1992 as a result of utilizing the loss carryforward in 1992.[5] Second, the recognition of a portion of the loss carryforward in 1991 caused the debit of $48,000 to the deferred tax account. This debit was later reversed in two stages: $16,000 in 1992 and $32,000 in 1993. Third, the $48,000 debit to deferred taxes in 1991 causes a necessary distortion in the relationship between the accumulated timing differences (ATD) and the deferred tax balance—that is, deferred taxes are no longer 40% of the ATD. However, this relationship is re-established by the end of 1993 once the tax loss carryforwards have been completely utilized.

The income statements for 1991, 1992, and 1993 are presented next to show the reporting of the loss benefits.

ESTEVAN COMPANY

Partial Income Statement

For Year Ended December 31, 1991

Net loss before income taxes		$290,000
Provision for income taxes:		
Recovery of prior year's taxes	$16,000	
Deferred income taxes	76,000	92,000
Net loss after income taxes		$198,000

Note to financial statement:

The company has not recorded in its financial statements the effect of losses which have not been claimed for tax purposes and which amount to $60,000.

ESTEVAN COMPANY

Partial Income Statement

For Year Ended December 31

	1992		1993	
Net income before income taxes		$80,000		$150,000
Income tax expense:				
Current	$ 40,000		$50,000	
Deferred	(8,000)		10,000	
Benefit of loss carryforward	(24,000)	8,000	—	60,000
Net income		$72,000		$ 90,000

[5] The figure $76,000 is comprised of the tax effects of the amendment to the 1990 tax return, $20,000; the 1991 timing difference, $8,000; and the maximum carryforward benefit recognizable, $48,000.

Varity Corporation provided the following information in its 1990 financial statements with respect to income taxes and the realization of the tax benefit of prior years' losses:

VARITY CORPORATION

Notes to Consolidated Financial Statements (in part)

Years Ended January 31

(Dollars in millions)	1990	1989	1988
Income tax provision at the combined statutory rate	$ 45.4	$ 43.6	$ 0.9
Increase (decrease) in income tax provision attributable to:			
Net effect of income subject to foreign tax rates	(3.2)	(5.0)	(6.0)
Tax benefit of losses not recognized.			20.8
Non-taxable capital items.	(2.6)	(4.2)	(11.9)
Permanent differences resulting from purchase accounting.	3.9	3.1	2.5
Other non-taxable items	(2.2)	(0.4)	(3.8)
Exchange adjustments	2.4	4.6	4.1
Realization of the tax benefit of prior years' losses.	(25.2)	(28.5)	0.0
Income tax provision	$ 18.5	$ 13.2	$ 6.6

At January 31, 1990, the Company had tax losses for financial reporting purposes aggregating approximately $1 billion available to be carried forward for which potential recoveries have not been recognized in the accounts. These loss carryforwards...expire as follows: January 31, 1991, $18 milliion; 1992, $52 million; 1993, $67 million; 1994, $120 million; 1995 and beyond, approximately $753 million.... Relevant tax laws...may limit the use of these tax losses.

CONCEPT REVIEW

1. Why are loss carryback benefits fully recognizable in the year of the loss?
2. Why is there a limitation on the recognition of loss carryforward benefits?
3. Explain what is meant by "no virtual certainty."

SUMMARY OF KEY POINTS

(L.O. 1) 1. For most companies, deferred tax debits or credits arise on the balance sheet because of timing differences.

(L.O. 1) 2. The *CICA Handbook* advocates the use of comprehensive income tax allocation.

(L.O. 2) 3. Timing differences occur because revenues and/or expenses may be recognized for accounting purposes in different periods than for taxation purposes.

(L.O. 2) 4. Permanent differences occur when an item is included for accounting purposes but is permanently excluded for taxation purposes, or vice versa.

(L.O. 2, 3) 5. Interperiod tax allocation refers to items allocated between accounting periods while intraperiod allocation refers to items allocated within an accounting period.

(L.O. 4) 6. Tax losses may be carried back and used to reduce taxable incomes of the three years prior to the loss year.

(L.O. 4) 7. The benefit of the loss carryback (i.e., the refund of previously paid taxes) may be recognized in the year of the loss.

(L.O. 5) 8. If the loss is not absorbed by carryback, the remainder of the loss available may be carried forward and applied to future earnings for a period of seven years after the loss.

(L.O. 5) 9. Because of the uncertainty of future profits, the *CICA Handbook* places restrictions on the amount of the loss carryforward benefits which may be recognized in the year of the loss.

REVIEW PROBLEM

◆

Deszca Development Limited is a Canadian-controlled company with an average tax rate of 40%. The company has a December 31 year-end and has provided the following information:

	1991	1992	1993	1994
Operating income (loss) before the following:.	$ 70,000	$ 55,000	$ 80,000	$(430,000)
Investment income	1,000	1,500	1,200	1,800
Depreciation expense.	(30,000)	(30,000)	(30,000)	(30,000)
Pretax income (loss)	$ 41,000	$ 26,500	$ 51,200	$(458,200)

Additional information:

Capital cost allowance claimed	$ 40,000	$ 50,000	$ 60,000	NIL

Net book value of depreciable assets—January 1, 1994 . . . . $ 570,000
Undepreciated capital cost—January 1, 1994. . . . . $ 310,000
Deferred income tax balance—January 1, 1994 . . . . $ 104,000cr

Investment income consists of dividends from tax-paying Canadian corporations.

Required:

Prepare the journal entry to record income taxes for 1994 assuming that conditions for virtual certainty do not exist and that the tax returns for 1991–1993 are amended to maximize the amount of loss carryback.

REVIEW SOLUTION

◆

1. Schedule of accounting and taxable income (loss):

	1991	1992	1993	1994
Pretax income (loss)	$ 41,000	$ 26,500	$ 51,200	$(458,200)
Permanent difference:				
Investment income	1,000	1,500	1,200	1,800
Accounting income (loss)	40,000	25,000	50,000	(460,000)
Timing difference:				
Depreciation	30,000	30,000	30,000	30,000
Capital cost allowance	40,000	50,000	60,000	—
	(10,000)	(20,000)	(30,000)	30,000
Taxable income (loss).	$ 30,000	$ 5,000	$ 20,000	$(430,000)

2. Calculation of loss carryback and carryforward available:

Taxable loss—1994		$430,000
Loss carrybacks and CCA adjustment:		
1991—$30,000 + $40,000	$70,000	
1992—$5,000 + $50,000	55,000	
1993—$20,000 + $60,000	80,000	205,000
Loss carryforward available		$225,000

3. Calculation of maximum loss carryforward benefit recognizable:

Actual loss carryforward benefit: $225,000 × .4 . . . . $90,000

Balance of deferred tax credit after adjustments:

	ATD	DT
Balance, January 1, 1994.	$ 260,000	$104,000cr
1994 timing difference.	(30,000)	12,000dr
CCA adjustment for 1991–93.	(150,000)	60,000dr
Balance after adjustments	$ 80,000	$ 32,000cr

Credit balance in deferred tax account $32,000

Available timing difference drawdown in the carryforward period:
$30,000 × 7 years × .4. . . . . $84,000

Therefore, the loss carryforward benefit recognizable in 1994 is $32,000

4. Income tax journal entry—December 31, 1994:

Income tax receivable ($55,000 × .4).	22,000	
Deferred income tax ($30,000 + $150,000 + $80,000) × .4	104,000	
Income tax expense.		126,000

5. Detail of credit to income tax expense—1994:

Refund of taxes paid 1991–93 ($55,000 × .4).	$ 22,000
Amendment of 1991–93 tax returns (CCA) claimed ($40,000 + $50,000 + $60,000) × .4	60,000
1994 timing difference reversal in 1994 ($30,000 × .4)	12,000
Maximum loss carryforward benefit recognizable ($80,000 × .4)	32,000
Credit to income tax expense	$126,000

KEY TERMS

Accounting income (822)	Investment tax credit (835)
Accumulated timing difference (842)	Liability method (821)
Benefit of loss carryovers (840)	Loss carryback (838)
Capital cost allowance (CCA) (818)	Loss carryforward (839)
Comprehensive tax allocation (821)	Net book value (844)
Deferral method (821)	Partial tax allocation (821)
Deferred income tax (822)	Permanent difference (824)
Income tax allocation (818)	Pretax income (824)
Income tax expense (822)	Taxable income (822)
Income tax rate (822)	Timing difference (818)
Interperiod tax allocation (822)	Undepreciated capital cost (UCC) (844)
Intraperiod tax allocation (822)	Virtual certainty (839)

QUESTIONS

1. What are the two types of income tax allocation? Briefly distinguish between the two.
2. Relate the matching principle to interperiod income tax allocation.
3. Explain when deferred income tax can be either an asset or a liability.
4. Briefly define pretax accounting income and taxable income.
5. Define an income tax difference. Identify and briefly define the two types of differences.
6. XT Corporation (a) uses straight-line depreciation in its accounting and accelerated depreciation on its income tax return, and (b) receives tax-free dividends from another Canadian corporation. What kind of tax difference is caused by each of these items? Explain.
7. Does the "deferred" caption in deferred income taxes mean that deferred income tax is always a long-term (non-current) item? Explain.
8. What is the nature of a permanent difference? Do permanent differences give rise to deferred income taxes? Give two examples of permanent differences that arise in accounting for income taxes.
9. What is intraperiod income tax allocation? How does it differ from interperiod income tax allocation?
10. On January 1, 1991, CD Corporation purchased an asset that cost $42,000; it has a seven-year life (no residual value). For accounting purposes it will be depreciated on the straight-line basis. For income tax purposes the machine will be depreciated straight-line over a three-year period. The income tax rate is 35%. Compute the following amounts: (a) depreciation each year for accounting purposes and tax purposes, (b) temporary difference at the end of 1991, and (c) the related amount that would be reflected in the entry to record income taxes at the end of 1991.
11. Explain the difference between a deferred income tax credit and a deferred income tax debit.
12. Define an investment tax credit. How does it differ from a tax deduction?
13. Explain the situation on recognizing a deferred income tax asset in interperiod income tax allocation.

14. RV Corporation's accounting and income tax records provided the following data at the end of 1991: Pretax accounting income, $60,000; taxable income, $51,000; and temporary differences, $9,000. Prepare a reconciliation of pretax income and taxable income.

15. Bye Corporation is preparing its 1991 financial statements. Pretax amounts are income before extraordinary items, $300,000; extraordinary gain, $20,000; and prior period adjustment, $16,000 (a loss). Interperiod income tax computations showed income tax expense (including the prior period adjustment) of $104,880. How much income tax should be allocated to each of the three amounts assuming the average method of intraperiod income tax allocation is used?

16. Define income tax loss carrybacks and carryforwards. Briefly explain the two options available to taxpayers.

17. In respect to loss carrybacks and loss carryforwards, which can be recorded with greater certainty of realization of the benefit therefrom? How does this difference in certainty affect the accounting treatment accorded loss carrybacks and carryforwards?

EXERCISES

E 17–1
Analysis of Interperiod Income Tax Deferrals
(L.O. 1)

The following six independent situations require interperiod income tax allocation. For each item indicate with a check (√) whether the balance in the deferred income tax account would be a debit or a credit.

Item	Beginning Balance in the Deferred Income Tax Account Would Be a	
	Debit	Credit
a. Construction contracts, percentages of completion for accounting and completed contract for income tax	_____	_____
b. Estimated warranty costs, accrual basis for accounting and cash basis for income tax	_____	_____
c. Straight-line depreciation for accounting and accelerated depreciation for income tax	_____	_____
d. Unrealized gain (i.e., loss recovery), LCM recognized for accounting; and gain recognized only on disposal of the asset for income tax	_____	_____
e. Rent revenue collected in advance, accrual basis for accounting, cash basis for income tax	_____	_____
f. Unrealized loss, LCM recognized for accounting and loss recognized only on disposal of the asset for income tax	_____	_____

E 17–2
Terminology Overview
(L.O. 1)

Some terms frequently used in the *CICA Handbook,* section 3470, are listed in the left column. Brief definitions are listed to the right. Match the definitions with the terms by entering the appropriate letters in the blanks.

Term	Brief Definition
_____ 1. Deferred tax debit.	A. Income tax payable plus net deferred tax amounts.
_____ 2. Accounting income.	B. An amount used to compute income tax payable.
_____ 3. Permanent difference.	C. An income tax provision intended to encourage investments in new product-line assets.
_____ 4. Schedule of temporary differences.	D. May result in a cash refund or a reduction of income tax payable.
_____ 5. Temporary difference.	E. An amount used to compute income tax expense.
_____ 6. Taxable income.	F. A deferred tax that has a net debit reported as an _____.
_____ 7. Investment tax credit.	G. A deferred tax amount that has a debit balance.
_____ 8. Income tax expense.	H. A tax difference that does not reverse or turn around.
_____ 9. Asset.	I. An allocation of tax among the components in the financial statement.
_____ 10. Loss carryback.	J. A computation that is essential to compute the deferred tax amounts.
_____ 11. Intraperiod income tax allocation.	K. A pretax amount that represents a difference between financial accounting and tax return amounts that reverse or turn around.

E 17–3
Analyze a Tax Difference: Entries and Reporting (L.O. 2)

Voss Corporation reported pretax accounting income of: 1991, $75,000, and 1992, $88,000. Taxable income for each year would have been the same as pretax accounting income except for the tax effects of $3,600 rent revenue collected in advance on October 1, 1991, for six months (not included in the preceding amounts). Rent revenue is taxable in the year collected. The tax rate for 1991 and 1992 is 30%, and the year-end for both accounting and tax purposes is December 31.

Required:

1. Is this a timing difference or a permanent difference? Why?
2. Give the entries at the end of 1991 and 1992 to record income tax.
3. Prepare partial income statements starting with pretax accounting income.
4. Show how any deferred income tax would be reported on the 1991 and 1992 balance sheets.

E 17–4
Reporting Deferred Income Tax on the Balance Sheet (L.O. 2)

At the end of 1992, Raleigh Corporation's deferred tax account had a $90,000 credit balance. The income tax rate was 30%. This credit balance was due only to the following pretax temporary differences:

a. Depreciation for accounting purposes, $200,000; for income tax purposes, $300,000. The related asset has a five-year remaining life.
b. Installment sale revenue; for accounting purposes, $600,000; for income tax purposes, $400,000. The collection period is the following four years with equal amounts each year.

Required:

Show how the deferred tax amounts should be reported on the 1992 balance sheet. Show computations.

E 17–5
Recording and Reporting Income Tax Consequences for a Two-Year Period (L.O. 2)

The records of Star Corporation provided the following data related to income tax allocation:

	1991	1992
Pretax income.	$200,000	$220,000
Taxable income	220,000	200,000
Income tax rate	34%	34%

The deferred tax account showed a zero balance at the start of 1991. There was only one temporary difference, a revenue, which was taxable in 1991 but was recorded for accounting purposes in 1992. There are no carrybacks or carryforwards.

Required:

1. Give the journal entry to record the income tax consequences for each year.
2. Show how income tax expense, income tax payable, and deferred income tax should be reported on the financial statements each year.

E 17–6
Analyze a Tax Difference: Entries and Reporting (L.O. 2)

Stacy Corporation would have had identical income before taxes on both its income tax returns and income statements for the years 1991 through 1994 were it not for the fact that for tax purposes an operational asset that cost $120,000 was depreciated by the sum-of-the-years'-digits (SYD) method (assumed for problem purposes to be acceptable for income tax), whereas for accounting purposes, the straight-line method was used. Both the accounting and tax periods end December 31. The operational asset has a four-year estimated life and zero residual value. Income before depreciation and income taxes for the years concerned are as follows:

	1991	1992	1993	1994
Pretax income (excluding depreciation)	$60,000	$80,000	$70,000	$70,000

Assume the average income tax rate for each year was 30%.

Required:

1. Is this a timing difference or a permanent difference? Why?
2. Prepare a partial income statement, starting with pretax accounting income, for each year to reflect interperiod tax allocation.
3. Give journal entries at the end of each year to record income taxes.
4. Give the amount of deferred income tax that would be reported on each of the four balance sheets.

E 17–7
Analyze Four Deferred
Tax Items: Entries and
Reporting
(L.O. 2)

The pretax income statements for Victor Corporation for two years (summarized) were as follows:

	1991	1992
Revenues	$180,000	$200,000
Expenses	150,000	165,000
Pretax income	$ 30,000	$ 35,000

For tax purposes, the following income tax differences existed:

a. Expenses on the 1992 income statement include membership fees of $10,000, which is not deductible for income tax purposes.
b. Revenues on the 1992 income statement include $10,000 rent, which is taxable in 1991 but was unearned at the end of 1991.
c. Expenses on the 1991 income statement include $8,000 of estimated warranty costs, which are not deductible for income tax purposes until 1992.

Required:

1. Compute (*a*) income tax expense and (*b*) income tax payable for each period. Assume an average tax rate of 40%.
2. Give the entry to record income taxes for each period.
3. Recast the preceding income statements to include income taxes as allocated.
4. What amount of deferred income tax will be reported on the balance sheet at each year-end?

E 17–8
Deferred Income Tax,
Change in Tax Rate
(L.O. 2)

Moon Corporation's accounts and related records revealed the following data for the first two years of its operations:

	1991	1992
Pretax income	$100,000	$110,000
Rent collections one year in advance	9,000	
Rent revenue allocated (included in pretax income)	6,000	3,000

Moon had no other complicating income tax factors in 1991 and 1992.

Required:

1. Does the rent revenue cause a timing difference or a permanent difference? Why?
2. Record income taxes for the company for 1991 and 1992, assuming the income tax rate for each year was 30%.
3. Record the income taxes for the company for 1991 and 1992, assuming the income tax rate was 30% for 1991 and it changed to 40% for 1992. Explain the impact of the change in the tax rate from 1991 to 1992.
4. What amounts would be reported on the 1991 and 1992 income statements and balance sheets for both (2) and (3)?

E 17–9
Deferred Income Tax,
Change in Tax Rate
(L.O. 2)

The accounts of Star Corporation provided the following data: pretax income: 1991, $150,000 and 1992, $135,000; a $10,000 expense was properly included in the 1992 pretax income. This expense must be included in the 1992 tax return. The company has no other income tax differences.

Required:

1. Is the $10,000 expense a timing difference or a permanent difference? Why?
2. Record income tax assuming the income tax rate is 30% each year.
3. Record income tax assuming the income tax rates were: 1991, 40% and 1992, 30%.
4. What amounts would be reported on the 1991 and 1992 income statements and balance sheets for (2) and (3) (assuming taxes for a given year are paid early in the next year)?

E 17–10
Classification of Timing Differences on the Balance Sheet
(L.O. 2)

The following five different transactions cause timing differences. For each independent item, indicate with a check mark (√) in the appropriate column how the related deferred tax should be initially classified on the balance sheet.

Transaction (timing difference)	Asset		Liability	
	Current	Non-current	Current	Non-current
1. Rent revenue collected in advance	———	———	———	———
2. Estimated warranty costs.	———	———	———	———
3. Depreciation on operational assets (straight-line for accounting, accelerated for tax)	———	———	———	———
4. Long-term construction contracts (percentage of completion for accounting, completed contract for tax)	———	———	———	———
5. Installment sales (sales revenue recognized for accounting before inclusion in taxable income).	———	———	———	———

E 17–11
Interperiod Tax Allocation: a Revenue and an Expense
(L.O. 2)

The records of TN Corporation, at the end of 1991, provided the following data related to income taxes:

a. Gain on disposal of a special asset, $50,000; recorded for accounting purposes at the end of 1991; reported for income tax purposes at the end of 1993.

b. Estimated expense, $30,000, accrued for accounting purposes at the end of 1991; reported for income tax purposes when paid at the end of 1992.

c. Taxable income (from the tax return) at the end of 1991, $100,000; the enacted income tax rate is 34%.

Required:

1. Did the gain and expense cause temporary differences? Explain why. Classify each item as deductible or taxable and explain why.

2. Prepare the following for 1991: (a) reconciliation of taxable income with pretax income and compute income taxes payable and (b) entry to record income taxes at the end of the year.

3. Show the amounts that will be reported on the (a) income statement and (b) balance sheet for 1991.

E 17–12
Carryback—Carryforward Options: Entries and Reporting
(L.O. 4, 5)

Tyson Corporation reported pretax income from operations in 1991 of $80,000 (the first year of operations). In 1992, the corporation experienced a $40,000 pretax loss from operations. Assume an average income tax rate of 45%. Realization of future income cannot be estimated beyond reasonable doubt.

Required:

1. Assess Tyson's income tax situation for 1991 and 1992 separately. How should Tyson elect to handle the loss in 1992?

2. Based on your assessments in (1), give the 1991 and 1992 income tax entries that Tyson should make.

3. Show how all tax-related items would be reported on the 1991 and 1992 income statements and balance sheets.

E 17–13
Carryback—Carryforward Options, Choice Required: Entries
(L.O. 4, 5)

Toner Corporation reported the following taxable income and loss: 1991, income, $10,000 (tax rate 20%), and 1992, $40,000 loss (tax rate 20%). At the end of 1992, Toner made the following estimates: 1993 income, $4,000 (tax rate 20%); 1994 income, $11,000 (tax rate 20%); and 1995 income, $50,000 (tax rate 30%). On the basis of these estimates, which the company considered to be conservative, Toner elected the carryforward-only option.

Required:

1. Give the income tax entry for 1991.

2. Give the income tax entry for 1992. Explain the basis for your response.

3. Give the income tax entry for 1993, assuming the actual income was $6,000 (tax rate, 20%).

4. Give the income tax entry for 1994, assuming the actual income was $13,000 (tax rate, 20%).

5. Give the entry for 1995, assuming the actual income was $45,000 (tax rate 35%).

6. Did Toner make a wise choice? Explain.

E 17–14
Intraperiod Income Tax
Allocation
(L.O. 3)

P.W.M. Ltd. manufactures sawmill machinery and a quality line of machinery used in the production of furniture.

For the fiscal year ended November 30, 1991, P.W.M. Ltd. reported accounting and taxable income before income taxes of $840,000. Included in this amount was a fully taxable extraordinary gain of $95,000. Also included was a fully deductible loss of $90,000 which arose as a result of the disposition of some assets in 1991 after the company had closed a part of its plant. Income tax rates are 46% of taxable income, and the rates have not changed for the last three years.

The annual audit has disclosed a $70,000 overstatement of income for the previous fiscal year. This overstatement should be treated as a prior period adjustment, and the company will file an amended income tax return.

Required:

1. Using intraperiod income tax allocation procedures, prepare the journal entries to record the income taxes.
2. Prepare a partial income statement in good form for the fiscal year ended November 30, 1991, starting with the line "Income before income tax and extraordinary items."

(SMA)

E 17–15
Correction of Accounting
Error Including Income
Tax Consequences
(L.O. 3)

On January 1, 1991, Cooper Corporation purchased a patent for $6,300. The patent had an estimated remaining economic life of seven years. During January 1993, the newly employed accountant discovered that the full cost of the patent was debited to patent expense on the purchase date (for both accounting and income tax purposes). The income tax rate for 1991 and 1992 was 40%, and 1993, 34%. The annual accounting and tax periods end on December 31. Assume that the patent is amortized over the useful life, straight-line, for both accounting and tax purposes.

Required:

Give any entry that should be made during January 1993 to correct the error including the income tax consequences. Use an account titled "Accumulated Amortization, Patent."

PROBLEMS

P 17–1
An Overview of Income
Tax Allocation,
Depreciation
(L.O. 1, 2)

The financial statements of Dakar Corporation for a four-year period reflected the following pretax amounts:

	1991	1992	1993	1994
Income statement (summarized):				
Revenues	$110,000	$124,000	$144,000	$ 164,000
Expenses	(80,000)	(92,000)	(95,000)	(128,000)
Depreciation expense (straight-line)	(10,000)	(10,000)	(10,000)	(10,000)
Balance sheet (partial):				
Machine (four-year life, no residual value),				
at cost	$ 40,000	$ 40,000	$ 40,000	$ 40,000

Dakar has an average tax rate of 40% each year and uses accelerated depreciation for income tax purposes as follows: 1991, $16,000; 1992, $12,000; 1993, $8,000; and 1994, $4,000.

Required:

1. Is this a temporary difference? Explain why.
2. Prepare the following for each year: (*a*) schedule to reconcile pretax and taxable incomes, (*b*) schedule to compute income tax payable, (*c*) schedule to compute deferred income tax, and (*d*) journal entry at each year-end to record income taxes.
3. For each year show the deferred income tax amount that should be reported on the balance sheet.

P 17–2
Analyze Three Income Tax Items: Entries and Reporting
(L.O. 1, 2)

The income statements for Victor Corporation for two years are summarized as follows:

	1991	1992
Revenues	$360,000	$400,000
Expenses	284,000	362,000
Pretax income before permanent and temporary differences	$ 76,000	$ 38,000
Taxable income	$112,000	$ 22,000

Income tax rate, 40%.

For tax purposes, the following income tax differences existed:

a. Expenses on the 1991 income statement include a membership fee of $20,000, which is not deductible for income tax purposes.
b. Revenues on the 1992 income statement include $20,000 rent revenue, which is taxable in 1991 but was unearned at the end of 1991.
c. Expenses on the 1991 income statement include $16,000 of estimated warranty costs, which are not deductible for income tax purposes until 1992.

There were no other differences.

Required:

1. Is each one of the three income tax consequences given above a temporary difference? Explain why.
2. Prepare the following for each year: (*a*) schedule to reconcile pretax and taxable incomes, (*b*) schedule to compute income tax payable, (*c*) schedule to compute deferred income tax, and (*d*) journal entry at each year-end to record income taxes.
3. Show how the deferred income tax would be reported on the income statements and balance sheets.

P 17–3
Recording and Reporting the Income Tax Consequences of a Deferred Debit and a Deferred Credit
(L.O. 1, 2)

The records of IW Corporation provided the following income-tax related information:

	1991	1992	1993	1994
Pretax income	$90,000	92,000	95,000	98,000
Taxable income	63,000	101,000	104,000	107,000

Income tax rate, 30%.

The preceding amounts include only two temporary differences as follows (no other changes occurred):

a. Installment sales—for accounting purposes in 1991, $30,000; included in the tax return, $10,000 each year, 1992 through 1994.
b. Cost of warranties—for accounting purposes, $4,000 in 1991; deducted for income tax $1,000 each year, 1991 through 1994.

Required:

1. Prepare the following for each year: (*a*) schedule to reconcile pretax and taxable income and to compute income taxes payable, (*b*) schedule of temporary differences, (*c*) schedule to compute deferred income taxes, and (*d*) journal entry at the end of each year to record income taxes.
2. Show how income tax expense, deferred income tax, and income taxes payable should be reported on the financial statements for each year.

P 17–4
Interperiod Tax Allocation: Depreciation and Dues Considered
(L.O. 2)

Fox Corporation purchased a machine on January 1, 1991, that cost $40,000. The machine had an estimated service life of five years and no residual value. Fox uses straight-line depreciation for accounting purposes and accelerated depreciation for the income tax return as follows: 1991, 30% of asset cost; 1992, 25%; 1993, 20%; 1994, 15%; and 1995, 10%. Taxable income on the tax return for 1991 was $150,000. The 1991 income statement showed a $15,000 deduction for country club dues; income tax regulations do not permit the deduction of dues for income tax purposes. There were no other factors to complicate the company's income tax computations during 1991. The income tax rate is 40%.

Required:

1. Identify any temporary differences and explain the basis for your decisions. Also, identify any taxable amounts and deductible amounts and explain their effects on the analysis of the income tax differences.
2. Prepare the following at the end of 1991: (*a*) schedule to reconcile pretax income and taxable income and to compute income tax payable and (*b*) journal entry to record income taxes at year-end.
3. Show the amounts for 1991 that should be reported on the income statement and balance sheet.

P 17–5
Recording and Reporting Income Tax Consequences for Temporary Differences
(L.O. 2)

The records of LA Corporation provided the following information: Taxable income based on tax return: 1991, $47,600; income tax rate, 30%. There were two temporary differences as follows:

a. December 1, 1991, collected $2,400 rent in advance for 1992. The $2,400 must be included on the 1991 tax return.
b. On December 1, 1991, the company recorded a $10,000 estimated expense that will be paid in 1992 and included in the 1992 income tax return.

Required:

1. Prepare a reconciliation of taxable income with pretax income for 1991.
2. Prepare a schedule of temporary differences for 1991.
3. Give the entry to record income taxes at the end of 1991. Show computations for each amount.
4. Show how the income tax consequences should be reported on the three required financial statements for 1991 assuming 75% of the income tax payable was paid by the end of 1991.

P 17–6
Analysis of Three Temporary Differences
(L.O. 2)

Triple Corporation started operations on January 1, 1991. At the end of 1991, the following income tax related data were available:

	1991
Taxable income	$116,500
a. Gross margin on installment sales:	
Accounting	175,000
Tax return	65,000
b. Rent revenue collected in advance:	
Accounting	6,000
Tax return	4,000
c. Estimated warranty expense:	
Accounting (accrued)	15,000
Tax return	12,000
Income tax rate	30%

Required:

1. What kind of tax difference is represented by each of these three income tax consequences? Explain.
2. Prepare the following schedules related to income tax allocation for 1991:
    a. Schedule to reconcile pretax income and taxable income.
    b. Schedule of temporary differences.
3. Give the entry at the end of 1991 to record income taxes; show computations.
4. Show the items that should be reported on the 1991 financial statements assuming 75% of taxes payable were paid.

P 17–7
Interperiod Tax Allocation,
Timing Differences,
Schedule
(L.O. 2)

Triple X Corporation's accounts and related records revealed the following data for the first two years of its operations:

	1991	1992
Pretax income.	$160,000	$180,000
Income tax differences:		
1. Estimated warranty expense (included in		
pretax income)	15,000	16,000
Cash payments on warranties arising in—		
1991 (deductible for tax purposes)	12,000	2,000
1992 (deductible for tax purposes)		15,000
2. Rent revenue collected one year in advance		
(taxable in year collected)	6,000	
Rent revenue allocated on accrual basis		
(included in pretax income)	4,000	2,000
3. Gross margin on installment sales recognized		
on sales basis (amount included in		
pretax income)	175,000	230,000
Gross margin reportable for income tax purposes		
(amount included on tax return; cash collection		
basis) on installment sales made in—		
1991	65,000	110,000
1992		75,000
Income tax rate	30%	30%

Required:

1. What kind of tax differences are represented by the preceding three transactions? Explain.
2. Give separate entries to record income tax for 1991 and 1992. Combine the three items previously detailed in each entry; therefore, you are to prepare a schedule for each year.
3. Show how the tax effects should be reported in the 1991 and 1992 financial statements. Assume income tax payable is paid early in the next year.

P 17–8
Interperiod Tax Allocation,
Comprehensive—Six Items,
Schedule
(L.O. 2, 3)

The following data for X Corporation are available for a two-year period:

	1992	1993
Income before extraordinary item (pretax).	$100,000	$120,000
Extraordinary loss, pretax	(15,000)	(17,000)
Prior period adjustment, gain, pretax.	7,000	
Timing differences included in above amounts:		
a. Revenue on income statement, taxable		
in following period	5,000	
b. Revenue on income statement, taxable in		
preceding period and not included in 1992		
income statement		7,000
c. Expense on income statement, tax		
deductible in following period	8,000	
d. Expense on income statement, tax		
deductible in subsequent period		6,000
e. 1992 extraordinary loss of $15,000 previously		
shown; tax deductible as follows	10,000	5,000
1993 extraordinary loss; fully deductible		
in 1993		17,000
f. Prior period gain on statement of retained		
earnings, taxable in next period	4,000	
Retained earnings, beginning balance	30,000	55,000

Use an average income tax rate of 35% on all items. Item (*f*) requires an amended tax return.

Required:

1. Compute income tax expense and income tax payable that should be reported on the income statement for each year. Show (*a*) operating income, (*b*) extraordinary items, and (*c*) prior period adjustments separately. Use a schedule similar to Exhibit 17–4.

2. Give one entry each year to record income tax. To check your entry, detail the items and amounts that comprise the deferred income tax amount.

3. Prepare a partial income statement, partial statement of retained earnings, and partial balance sheet for each year to show how income tax should be reported. Include both interperiod and intraperiod allocations.

P 17–9
Comprehensive: Four Differences (L.O. 2)

BG Corporation began operations in 1991. The accounting and income tax periods end on December 31. The records of the company provided the following income tax-related data (in thousands) at the end of 1991:

Pretax income each year:

1991	1992	1993	1994	1995
$11	$327	$360	$450	$470

Income tax rate is 30%.
Temporary differences:

a. A $500,000 estimated litigation loss was accrued (i.e., recognized) at the end of 1991 for accounting purposes; expected settlement date, end 1994 for income tax purposes.

b. A $200,000 gain on a special installment sale, recognized for accounting purposes at the end of 1991; included in income tax return as collected in equal amounts for 1992 through 1995.

c. A depreciable asset that cost $100,000 (estimated useful life five years and no residual value) is depreciated as follows (thousands):

	1991	1992	1993	1994	1995
Accounting purposes	$ 20	$ 20	$ 20	$ 20	$ 20
Income tax purposes	(33)	(27)	(20)	(13)	(7)
Difference	$(13)	$ (7)	$ 0	$ 7	$ 13

d. Rent revenue collected in advance at the end of 1991, $32,000; recognized for accounting purposes in 1992 and 1993. The full amount must be included in the 1991 income tax return.

Required:

1. Prepare the following schedules for each year: reconciliation of taxable income and pretax income, and timing differences.

2. Give the entry to record income taxes at the end of each year. Show computations.

3. Show the amounts that should be reported on the three required financial statements at the end of each year. Assume that the income tax liability is paid at the beginning of the following year.

P 17–10
Loss Carryforward: Entries and Reporting (L.O. 4)

The pretax financial statements of Gibson Limited for the first two years of operations reflected the following amounts:

	1991	1992
Revenues	$275,000	$330,000
Expenses	320,000	315,000
Pretax income (loss)	$(45,000)	$ 15,000
Depreciation expense (included in expenses)	$ 30,000	$ 30,000
Capital cost allowance claimed	NIL	NIL

Income tax rate for 1991 and 1992: 40%

Required:

1. Gibson will have to apply loss carryforward because there are no prior earnings. Estimates of future earnings are uncertain. Prepare the journal entries to record income taxes for 1991 and 1992.

2. How much should Gibson claim in capital cost allowance in 1992 to reduce its tax liability?

P 17–11
Loss Carryback-
Carryforward: Entries
(L.O. 4, 5)

Decker Limited began operations in 1991 and reported the following information for the years 1991 to 1995:

	1991	1992	1993	1994	1995
Pretax income.	$ 8,000	$15,000	$ 9,000	$(95,000)	$ 6,000
Depreciation	10,000	10,000	10,000	10,000	10,000
Capital cost allowance	10,000	18,000	14,000	NIL	NIL

Income tax rate: 40%
Assume that Decker's only depreciable assets were purchased in 1991 and cost $100,000.

Required:

Prepare the journal entries for income taxes for 1994 and 1995. Assume Decker amends and re-files the 1991, 1992, and 1993 tax returns. In 1994 Decker's long-range profitability was doubtful. Provide all necessary schedules.

P 17–12
Loss Carryforward: With
and Without Virtual
Certainty
(L.O. 5)

Prince Corporation pretax financial statements for the first two years of operations reflect the following amounts:

	1991	1992
Revenues	$295,000	$330,000
Expenses	320,000	315,000
Pretax income (loss)	$(25,000)	$ 15,000

Assume an average tax rate of 40% and no timing or permanent differences.

Required:

1. Assume future income during the next seven years is unpredictable (i.e., uncertain):
   a. Restate the preceding financial statements incorporating the income tax effects appropriately allocated. Show computations.
   b. Give entries to record the income tax effects for each year. Explain the basis for your entries.
2. Assume instead that future income of $10,000 is reasonably certain during the next seven years. Complete (1a) and (1b).

P 17–13
Carryback-Carryforward
Options: Entries,
Discussion
(L.O. 4, 5)

The financial statements of Bayshore Corporation for the first four years of operations reflected the following pretax amounts.

	1991	1992	1993	1994
Income statement (summarized):				
Revenue	$125,000	$155,000	$180,000	$230,000
Expense	120,000	195,000	160,000	200,000
Pretax income (loss).	$ 5,000	$(40,000)	$ 20,000	$ 30,000

Assume an average income tax rate of 40%, and that future incomes are uncertain at the end of each year. Management of Bayshore Corporation elects the carryback-carryforward option to lock in the immediate cash refund on the carryback.

Required:

1. Recast the previous statements to incorporate the income tax effects. Show computations.
2. Give entries to record the income tax effects for each year.
3. Explain the alternate option that Bayshore might have considered. What are the primary considerations that Bayshore should assess in making its choice?

P 17–14
Loss Carryovers: Entries
(L.O. 4, 5)

The results for Simon Ltd. are as follows:

	1991	1992	1993
Pretax income (loss)	$47,000	$(77,000)	$34,000
Depreciation	7,000	7,000	7,000
Capital cost allowance	9,000	NIL	8,000

There are no profits available for loss carryback prior to 1991.

Net book value of depreciable assets at January 1, 1991: $85,000. Undepreciated capital cost at January 1, 1991: $69,000.

The tax rate is 40% and is not expected to change. There are no other sources of timing differences.

Required:

1. Prepare a schedule calculating taxable income for 1991, 1992, and 1993. The tax return is *not* amended for revised capital cost allowance.
2. Prepare journal entries recording income taxes for 1992 and 1993 assuming the conditions for virtual certainty do not exist.
3. Prepare a schedule showing the balance in the deferred tax account and the accumulated timing differences.
4. Redo (2) assuming conditions for virtual certainty do exist.

P 17–15
Loss Carryovers: Entries,
No Virtual Certainty
(L.O. 4, 5)

The Village Company, which began operations in 1991, manufactures and sells television sets. The company estimated that warranty expenses would be 2% of sales.

The following information is taken from the company's books:

	($000)				
	1991	1992	1993	1994	1995
Sales	$3,000	$6,000	$8,000	$10,000	$15,000
Actual warranty costs	60	80	200	90	75
Accounting income (loss)					
before taxes	NIL	(980)	NIL	2,000	4,000
Depreciation.	600	600	600	600	600
Capital cost allowance	600	NIL	500	450	400
Dividends received from taxable					
Canadian corporation.	NIL	20	20	NIL	NIL

Net book value of depreciable assets at December 31, 1991: $7,600,000. Undepreciated capital cost at December 31, 1991: $5,600,000.

The tax rate is 40% and there are no other sources of timing differences. Assume conditions for virtual certainty as defined in the *Handbook* do not exist in 1992.

Required:

Journal entries to record income taxes for 1992 to 1995 inclusive. The tax return for 1991 is not amended.

P 17–16
Loss Carryovers: Entries,
No Virtual Certainty
(L.O. 4, 5)

The XY Company presents the following data for the first four years of operations:

	1991	1992	1993	1994
Pretax income (loss).	$ 70,000	$(240,000)	$100,000	$135,000
Timing difference:				
Depreciation	$ 20,000	$ 20,000	$ 20,000	$ 20,000
Capital cost				
allowance	50,000	NIL	NIL	45,000
	$(30,000)	$ 20,000	$ 20,000	$ (25,000)
Taxable income (loss)	$ 40,000	$(220,000)	$120,000	$110,000

Timing differences are solely due to the difference between net book value and undepreciated capital cost of operating assets. At December 31, 1991:

> Net book value = $415,000
> Undepreciated capital cost = $270,000
> Deferred taxes = $58,000 CR.
> Tax rate = 40%

Required:

1. Journal entries to record income taxes for 1992, 1993, and 1994 assuming conditions for virtual certainty exist and the tax return for 1991 is not amended for revised CCA.
2. Journal entries to record income taxes for 1992, 1993, and 1994 assuming conditions for virtual certainty do *not* exist and that the tax return for 1991 is amended to maximize the loss carryback.

P 17–17

COMPREHENSIVE PROBLEM
♦

Interperiod and
Intraperiod Tax Allocation
(L.O. 3, 4, 5)

Concorde Ltd. prepared the following income statement:

CONCORDE LTD.
Income Statement
For the Year Ended December 31, 1992

Revenue.		$1,210,000
Cost of goods sold.		730,000
Gross profit.		$ 480,000
Less:		
Depreciation	$115,000	
Advertising	85,000	
Other.	60,000	260,000
Net income before extraordinary item		$ 220,000
Less:		
Extraordinary item		94,000
Net income		$ 126,000

Concorde is uncertain as to how to proceed regarding income tax. You have discovered the following information:

a. Revenue includes $80,000 rental income which is properly accrued for accounting purposes but will be included in taxable income next year.
b. The undepreciated capital cost available at the beginning of the year is $847,000 and the class has a 20% maximum capital cost allowance.
c. Revenue includes dividends received ($52,000) which are not taxable at any time.
d. Advertising includes $40,000 which is not deductible at any time.
e. There is a loss carryforward of $48,000 available to be used this year. There was no virtual certainty at the time of the loss and the tax effect of the loss carryforward has not been journalized.
f. The extraordinary item was the loss on disposal of a fixed asset. The cash received was $12,000, the cost was $243,000 and accumulated depreciation was $137,000. The asset was one of the class mentioned in (*b*).
g. The tax rate is 40% and has not changed since the company was formed.

Required:

1. Prepare journal entries to record the preceding adjustments regarding income tax.
2. Prepare a reconciliation starting with net income before income tax and ending with net income.

(CGAAC)

P 17–18
Loss Carryovers: Timing
Differences
(L.O. 4, 5)

Zap Ltd. has the following information:

a. Tax rates for all years up to and including 1996 = 40%.
b. The balance of the deferred income tax account as of January 1, 1992, was $450,000 *credit*.
c. The depreciation and CCA were as follows:

	Depreciation	CCA
1992	$60,000	$0
1993	60,000	0
1994	60,000	0
1995	60,000	0
1996	65,000	0

d. The net income/(loss) before income tax was:

1992	$ 20,000
1993	30,000
1994	140,000
1995	(830,000)
1996	170,000

e. There were no other differences between net income before income tax and taxable income.
f. There was no virtual certainty regarding the using up of the loss for tax purposes within the allotted time.
g. There is reasonable assurance that the temporary timing differences will reverse.

Required:

1. Prepare the journal entries to record the tax effects of these events for 1995 and 1996.
2. If, in point (b), the deferred income tax account had a balance of $450,000 debit, but all other information remained the same, indicate how the journal entries in (1) for 1995 only would change.

(CGAAC adapted)

P 17–19
Loss Carryovers: Entries
(L.O. 4, 5)

Master Manufacturing is a Canadian-controlled corporation with an average income tax rate of 45%. Because Master operates in a very technical and volatile industry, there is no certainty with respect to future earnings. The company has a December 31 year-end and has provided the following information:

	1991	1992	1993	1994
Operating income (loss) after depreciation	$10,000	$20,000	$30,000	$(460,000)
Depreciation	40,000	40,000	40,000	40,000
Capital cost allowance.	50,000	40,000	60,000	NIL

Net book value of depreciable assets—January 1, 1994	$530,000
Undepreciated capital cost allowance—January 1, 1994	$310,000
Balance of deferred income taxes—January 1, 1994	$99,000 cr.

Required:

1. Explain the significance of the certainty/no virtual certainty distinction as stipulated in the *CICA Handbook* with respect to its effect on accounting for loss carryforwards.
2. Prepare the appropriate journal entry to record income taxes for 1994. Show all calculations.

CASE

C 17–1
Analysis of Actual
Financial Statements
(L.O. 2)

Refer to the 1990 financial statements of Loblaw (see the appendix immediately following Chapter 26) and respond to the following questions.

1. What was Loblaw's income tax expense for 1990, 1989, and 1988?
2. How much income tax did Loblaw pay in 1990, 1989, and 1988?
3. What caused Loblaw's tax rate to change from the basic income tax rate in 1990? By how much?

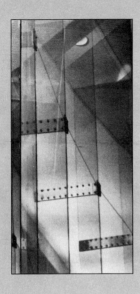

C H A P T E R

18

Accounting for Leases

After you have studied this chapter, you will be able to:

1. Explain the nature of a lease and why the lessee wishes to keep the lease off the balance sheet, while the lessor prefers to remove the leased asset from its records by considering the lease transaction as a sale or transfer.

2. Distinguish between a capital lease and an operating lease for the lessee and the lessor.

3. Account for operating leases for the lessee and lessor.

4. Account for capital leases for the lessee.

5. Account for sales-type and direct-financing leases for the lessor.

6. Account for the special problems relating to leases, including bargain purchase offers; residual value guarantees; different interest rates used by the lessee and lessor; depreciation of the leased asset by the lessee; executory and initial direct costs; and classification of lease receivables and payables.

7. Describe the requirements and account for sale-leaseback arrangements.

8. Describe lease disclosure requirements.

9. Explain the rules for accounting for leases involving real estate (Appendix 18A).

10. Explain the additional tax issues involved in leases (Appendix 18B).

◆

INTRODUCTION
◆

W ell over \$100 billion in business assets will be leased this year by large and small companies alike. Assets such as construction equipment, computer mainframes, delivery vehicles, office furnishings, real estate, commercial aircraft, communications systems—even entire manufacturing plants, equipment included—will be leased at some point during the year. Although leasing, rather than buying, business assets has always been fairly common, in the late 1960s, many companies discovered leasing in a big way, changing the face of asset leasing forever.

From the relatively simple idea of renting space or equipment, the concept of leasing expanded and became a complex proposition in which leasing is now used to finance asset acquisitions, usually involving both economic and tax benefits. To understand this new face of leasing, consider the following situations: A major fast-food pizza chain had to revise the debt it was reporting on its balance sheet from \$30 million up to \$156 million.[1] That's a 520% increase in debt! The chain had been growing by leaps and bounds, seemingly without having to borrow money to finance its growth, which mystified a number of people. But it was no mystery to astute investors and accountants who knew what was going on. The firm used leases to finance its growth. Everything was leased—stores, baking ovens, restaurant seating, delivery trucks, everything! The problem was that none of the liabilities incurred in conjunction with these leases was being reported on the balance sheet. Then the accounting rules were changed. Before the change, the fast-food chain's total shareholder's equity was only \$46 million, and with \$30 million in debt, the debt-to-equity ratio was about 40% to 60% (2:3), which many analysts would consider less than satisfactory debt coverage. With debt now reported at \$156 million, the ratio reversed to 75% to 25% (3:1), a rather frightening ratio by anyone's standards.

On another front, it is not widely known that many banks and investment firms have been active in the lease investment market for the past two decades. Rather than investing in stocks or bonds, some investors prefer something a little more exotic—such as a \$250,000 pooled participation investment in a Boeing 767, leased and operated by Air Canada, but owned jointly by 25 or more private investor-lessors. Or instead of a jet airliner, it might be a string of railroad freight cars, or a 3-million-gallon liquid storage tank. Lease investments may be arranged in any of these plus many more.

In addition to investor lease services, investment firms also work with noninvestor lessees and lessors. For example, a major rail shipper, or even a railroad itself, may need freight cars. If so, agents will, for a fee, put shippers in touch with investors who lease out freight cars.

◆

BASIC LEASE ACCOUNTING ISSUES
◆

The *CICA Handbook,* paragraph 3065.03(n), defines a **lease** as "the conveyance, by a lessor to a lessee, of the rights to use a tangible asset usually for a specified period of time in return for rent".[2] In the commonly used sense of the term, a lease is a fee-for-usage contract between an owner of property and a renter. The owner of the property is referred to as the **lessor** and the renter is the **lessee**. The lease specifies the terms under which the lessee shall have the right to use the owner's property and the compensation to be paid to the lessor in exchange. The lessee is obligated to make periodic

---

[1] See S. Pulliam, "Beating FAS-13," *Corporate Finance,* December 1988, p. 31.

[2] This definition does not include "leasing agreements concerning the rights to explore for or to exploit natural resources, nor licensing agreements for items such as motion pictures, videotapes, plays, manuscripts, patents, and copyrights."

rent payments to the lessor in accordance with a schedule of lease payments normally included as a provision of the lease.

In a leasing context, property includes both real and personal assets. Personal property includes both tangible assets (such as machinery, equipment, or transportation vehicles) and intangibles (such as patents, licenses, or copyrights).

Accounting for leases in the basic sense of the term is not complicated. The lessee makes periodic rent payments to the lessor and accounts for these as normal expense items. Meanwhile, the lessor collects the rent payments, crediting an income account such as leasing revenue (or "other income" if leasing is not one of the company's mainstream business activities).

Lessee's Books: Entry to record payment of monthly rent expense:

Rent expense 000
    Cash   000

Lessor's Books: Entry to record receipt of monthly rent payment as income:

Cash 000
    Leasing income   000

The Lease from the Lessee's Viewpoint

Leasing has evolved from being a relatively simple business activity to being a complex one with financing issues and multiple business motives. As the popularity of leasing grew, lessee companies were pleasantly surprised to find that leasing could afford them special economic and tax advantages if the lease were structured properly.[3] Specifically, lessees were quick to discern the key distinction between a capital lease and an operating lease.

Capital Lease Section 3065 of the *CICA Handbook* defines a **capital lease** as one in which substantially all the risks and benefits of ownership in the leased asset are transferred from the lessor to the lessee. The lessee records the leased property on the balance sheet. The fair value of the property involved is capitalized and reported as a balance sheet asset, and the debt obligation incurred in signing the lease is recorded as a liability on the balance sheet. From an accounting standpoint, this is much the same as if the property was purchased, with the acquisition being made possible by 100% debt financing. The lessee even records depreciation expense on the leased asset.

Operating Lease All leases that do not transfer substantially all the risks and benefits of ownership from the lessor to the lessee are **operating leases**. The lessee does not account for the property on the balance sheet. The lessee rents the property, with rent payments charged to expense as they come due.

The specific provisions of the lease contract, rather than the characteristics of the leased asset, determine whether the lease is a capital lease or an operating lease. An example of a lease provision that indicates a capital lease is the transfer of title to the leased asset from the lessor to the lessee at the conclusion of the lease term. Ownership risk involves the responsibility for casualty loss, wear and tear, obsolescence, and maintenance. Ownership rewards involve benefits such as the right to use, increases in the value of the leased asset, and ultimate transfer of title. Section 3065 provides specific criteria (discussed shortly) for identifying a capital lease. All leases failing to meet these criteria are considered operating leases. Distinctions between capital and

---

[3] Leasing activity can also change rapidly due to business conditions and to changes in the tax law. For example, legislation that allowed and later changed the investment tax credit had immediate effects on the amount of leasing activity in the country.

EXHIBIT 18-1   Summary of Basic Lease Accounting Issues for Lessees and Lessors

Lessee	Lessor
Operating lease	Operating lease
♦ Lessee is considered to be renting (not owning) the asset from the lessor.	♦ Lessor continues to own the asset that is leased to the lessee.

♦ Lessee makes periodic rent payments to the lessor; these are accounted for as current operating expenses:
Rent expense 000
  Cash   000
	♦ Lessor collects periodic rent payments that are accounted for as current operating income:
	Cash 000
	  Leasing income 000

♦ At end of lease term, the asset is returned to the lessor.	♦ At end of lease term, the asset is returned to the lessor.
♦ Lessee does not record depreciation expense.	♦ Lessor records depreciation on the asset.
Capital Lease	Direct Financing Lease
♦ Lessee is considered to own the asset for accounting purposes.	♦ Asset is considered to be sold to the lessee at the inception of the lease.

♦ Lease is capitalized on lessee's books as follows:
Leased asset 000
  Lease liability   000
	♦ Asset is removed from lessor's books and replaced by receivable as follows:*
	Lease receivable. 000
	  Asset. 000

♦ Lessee recognizes periodic payment as part interest and part reduction of principal:
Interest expense 000
Lease liability. 000
  Cash   000
	♦ Lessor recognizes periodic collection of rent as part interest and part as reduction of principal:
	Cash 000
	  Interest revenue. 000
	  Lease receivable 000

♦ At the end of the lease term, the asset generally is retained by the lessee.	♦ At the end of the lease period, the asset is generally retained by the lessee.
♦ Depreciation expense is recorded on the asset.	♦ No depreciation expense is taken during the time the asset is out on lease.

* If an immediate profit is involved, the lease is called a sales-type lease, and the accounting entry is:

> Lease receivable   000
> Cost of goods sold   000
>   Sales revenue   000
>   Asset.   000

operating leases and the basic accounting treatments for both lease classifications are summarized in Exhibit 18–1.[4]

In earlier times, the criteria for determining whether a lease transaction should be accounted for as a capital or operating lease were rather ambiguous. The central issue then and now is management's intent when it acquires the asset for use. Consider two situations:

Leasing situation No. 1: In conjunction with a one-time-only major building project, a construction company leases bulldozers for a period of two years to supplement its own equipment. Following this two-year period, the company intends to return the equipment to the lessor. This lease should be accounted for as an operating lease.

Leasing situation No. 2: Working in close contact with a lending institution, a group of physicians arranges to have a medical clinic custom designed and constructed for their medical practice. Their intention is to lease the property from the lending institution holding title to the property using a lease contract for a period of 30 years. This lease should be accounted for as a capital lease.

---

[4] The material in Exhibit 18–1 suggests a symmetry in the lessor and lessee entries. This symmetry is prevalent in other transactions such as credit sales between a seller and buyer. But such symmetry is not always present in leasing. In some cases, a lease may be classified differently by the lessor and the lessee. Later in this chapter, cases are discussed in which the lessor records a capital lease while the lessee records the same lease as an operating lease.

Off-Balance-Sheet Financing   By structuring leasing transactions as operating leases rather than capital leases (in situations where management's intent points to capital lease accounting treatment), lessees are able to take possession of and make full use of assets without either capitalizing them or reporting the attending lease payment obligations as balance sheet debt. This accounting treatment is referred to as **off-balance-sheet financing**. Because most companies routinely take on financing debt in conjunction with asset acquisitions (unless they are cash rich), off-balance-sheet financing is attractive to lessee companies for two primary reasons:

◆ Debt-equity ratio. Adding more debt to a company's capital structure causes the debt part of the ratio to increase, which is an adverse development if the debt-equity ratio is already considered high. As a result, shareholders might sell their shares, causing the stock price to decline, and creditors may refuse to extend credit (or might call in loans).[5]

◆ Existing debt covenants. If there are bondholders, the bond indenture agreement may include restrictive covenants designed to protect the bondholders' investments. One such covenant prohibits a company from taking on additional debt without the consent of the present bondholders. Bank loans frequently carry similar debt restrictions. Thus, a company may be prohibited from using capital leases.

The accounting profession has had concerns over the accounting for leases dating back at least to 1949. Lease accounting continued to be a matter of private interpretation and a case-by-case approach to the application of the rules then in existence.

Section 3065 of the *CICA Handbook* is the foundation for this chapter; it includes a set of tightly defined criteria for determining when and how a lessee must account for a leasing transaction as either an operating lease or a capital lease. These same pronouncements also set forth specific criteria for lessor accounting treatments.

The Lease from the Lessor's Viewpoint

The widespread popularity of business leasing is underscored by the fact that a CICA survey of 300 companies in 1989 disclosed that 210 of these companies (70%) engaged in leasing activities in one form or another.[6] On the lessor side, the largest share of the market is represented by banks, other lending institutions, and commerical leasing companies.[7] The other major portion of the lessor market is made up of manufacturers and dealer/distributors of industrial products that offer business buyers a choice of either buying their products outright or leasing them.[8]

Financial institutions and commercial leasing companies generally engage in lease transactions structured as either operating leases or direct-financing leases. Direct-financing leases are the preferred arrangement, and they account for the majority of leasing transactions.

Operating Lease: In an operating lease the lessor acquires an asset and leases it to a lessee in two separate transactions. The asset stays on the lessor's books throughout the term of the lease, and is accounted for in the same way that other revenue-producing assets are accounted for on the balance sheet. When the asset is leased (which may or

---

[5] The appearance of more debt on the balance sheet can create the perception to the statement reader that the firm faces larger periodic interest charges and, hence, greater risk when business conditions deteriorate. The perception may hold even though there would be no change in the firm's interest payments if it had borrowed the money from a bank rather than financing the acquisition under a lease.

[6] CICA, *Financial Reporting in Canada, 1989* (Toronto: CICA, 1989), Table 2.8, p. 129.

[7] Some of these non-bank commercial lessors are tiny one-person shops while others are organizations such as Bramalea Limited.

[8] In many cases, manufacturers set up subsidiary companies to handle leasing and other product financing arrangements. GMAC (General Motors Acceptance Corporation) and General Electric Capital Corporation are two such finance subsidiaries.

may not coincide with its acquisition), the lessor sets up a lease revenue (income account) to record and account for rent receipts from the lessee. No lease receivable (asset account) is used. The lessor depreciates the asset in the normal manner.

Direct-Financing Capital Lease   In a **direct-financing lease**, the lessor typically purchases an asset (only to accommodate the leasing transaction) and immediately leases it to the lessee. The purchased asset resides on the lessor's books only momentarily. The lease transaction removes the asset from the books, replacing it with a receivable. Conceptually, accounting for a direct-financing lease is identical to accounting for a sale on credit. But rather than reporting an account receivable, the lessor reports a lease receivable on the balance sheet. Because the asset itself is considered sold, no asset depreciation is taken by the lessor. The lessor's profit is derived entirely from interest.

Sales-Type Capital Lease   **Sales-type leases,** used by manufacturers and dealer/distributors, are first cousins to direct-financing leases. Unlike a direct-financing lease, in which the asset is purchased and immediately leased, a sales-type lease does not necessarily involve a prior purchase. The manufacturer leases (sells) the asset directly out of finished goods inventory, or a dealer/distributor leases (sells) the asset out of its inventory account. The key distinction to this type of lease—which is symmetrical with a lessee's capital lease—is the way the lessor accounts for the transaction. As shown at the end of Exhibit 18–1, a lease receivable account is opened with entries made to cost of goods sold, sales revenue, and the asset. The lessor's profit is derived partially from selling the asset and partially from interest. A precise, technical definition of a sales-type lease is found later in this chapter.

Advantages of Leasing

In general, leasing affords the following primary advantages for lessees, which contribute to the demand for leasing transactions:

- Leasing may resolve cash problems by making financing available for up to 100% of the leased asset value. Bank loans typically are limited to 80% of the asset's value.[9] Also, interest rates on leases may be negotiated at fixed rates, while many bank loans feature variable rates.
- Leasing transactions can be structured as operating leases, allowing the lessee to achieve off-balance-sheet financing when debt restrictions or limitations exist.
- In the case of industrial equipment that frequently must be built to order and can require lengthy asset-implementation delays, leasing ready-to-use equipment can be attractive.
- If assets are needed only temporarily, seasonally, or sporadically, leasing may avoid the problem of owning assets that cannot be kept in full-time productive use.
- Leasing assets for relatively short lease periods rather than owning them affords the lessee protection from state-of-the-art product and high-tech equipment obsolescence.
- Leasing may provide income tax advantages derived from accelerated depreciation, interest expense, and investment tax credits in some cases.[10]
- In general, lease payment schedules are flexible and can be tailored to dovetail with the lessee's expected cash inflows from operations.

---

[9] An important issue to the lessee is determination of whether to lease or buy the needed asset using bank financing. Finance texts consider this issue in great detail.

[10] Lease agreements are sometimes drawn up to shift tax advantages to the party (lessee or lessor) in the higher tax bracket. In exchange, the benefiting party compensates the forfeiting party in the form of either higher lease payments to the lessor (if the lessee gains the tax benefits) or lower payments (if the lessor gains the benefits).

On the lessor side of the market, manufacturers and dealers/distributors of industrial equipment use leasing to facilitate sales.[11] For lending institutions and commercial lessors, leasing is simply another addition to their financial services product line.

Disadvantages of Leasing

Leasing has disadvantages as well as advantages; the following is a list of drawbacks, loosely tracking the previously stated advantages of leasing:

- The 100% financing of leased assets also means higher interest in total dollar cost.
- Off-balance-sheet financing merely masks the fact that new layers of debt are being assumed.
- Leasing ready-to-use equipment (as opposed to custom built) may result in quality control problems and lost sales.
- With seasonal leasing, there is no guarantee that equipment will be available when needed. Also, leasing interest rates may be based on whatever the traffic will bear.
- Short-term leases may avoid protection from product obsolescence, but short-term leasing rates are normally set at a premium over longer-term rates (to compensate the lessor for assuming the obsolescence risk).
- Tax benefits may be temporary. A new tax provision can be enacted at any time, counteracting the old provision. This is a danger with all long-term leases featuring tax benefits.
- Long-term leases at fixed rates expose the lessor-lender to the risk of losses if interest rates increase.[12]

CONCEPT REVIEW

1. What is the basic difference between a capital lease and an operating lease to the lessee?
2. What is the basic difference between a direct financing capital lease and a sales-type capital lease?
3. List three advantages and three disadvantages of leasing.

ACCOUNTING FOR OPERATING LEASES

The following example illustrates the characteristics of an operating lease. Assume Grafixs, Ltd. (lessee) leases a computer from Comfast Ltd. (lessor) for two years beginning March 1, 1991. Grafixs agrees to pay Comfast $4,800 a year, payable in advance on March 1 of each year. Comfast is responsible for ownership (executory) costs, such as maintenance, property taxes, and insurance. In this lease, the lessee incurs only one risk, payment of the rentals, and obtains only one benefit, temporary use of the asset. Because the risks and benefits of ownership are not transferred, this is an operating lease.

---

[11] Due to the high cost of such equipment, purchase financing is often a virtual necessity. To ensure sales, many manufacturers offer product financing options, including leasing programs, in what has come to be known as full-service selling strategies. Today, this approach is becoming a common means, for example, of selling new automobiles.

[12] This risk applies to financial institutions and commercial lessors that participate in direct-financing leases and also to manufacturers and dealer/distributors that engage in sale-type leases. The latter are susceptible to rising interest rates because most use bank borrowings or issue commercial paper (both are sensitive to interest rates) to finance lease sales.

Assume both firms' accounting periods end on December 31. Entries for the lessor (Comfast) to recognize receipt of the lease payments for 1991 are as follows:

March 1, 1991—To record receipt of initial rent payment:

Cash	4,800	
Unearned revenue		4,800

December 31, 1991—To recognize revenue earned and depreciation of the asset:

Unearned rent revenue	4,000	
Rent revenue ($4,800 × $^{10}\!/_{12}$)		4,000
Depreciation expense*	500	
Accumulated depreciation		500

* Amount based on an assumed cost of $5,000, 10 year life, no salvage value, and straight line depreciation.

Unearned rent revenue is a liability of the firm and reflects the lessor's obligation to make the asset available in the future.

Entries for the lessee (Grafixs) are:

March 1, 1991—To record receipt of initial rent payment:

Prepaid rent	4,800	
Cash		4,800

December 31, 1991—To recognize rent expense:

Rent expense ($4,800 × $^{10}\!/_{12}$)	4,000	
Prepaid rent		4,000

The prepaid rent of $4,800 initially represents an asset for services due.

In some cases, an operating lease provides that, in addition to the periodic rent, a non-refundable down payment is made at the inception of the lease agreement. In this case, the lessor debits cash and credits unearned rent revenue when the down payment is received. The lessee debits an asset account called "leasehold" (or "prepaid rent expense") and credits cash. Each party then amortizes the prepayment over the life of the lease on a systematic and rational basis.

For example, suppose Grafixs also makes a non-refundable down payment March 1, 1991, of $720 to Comfast to cover both years. The lessor's entries would be:

March 1, 1991—To record receipt of non-refundable payment:

Cash	720	
Unearned rent revenue		720

December 31, 1991—To recognize rent revenue:

Unearned rent revenue	300	
Rent revenue ($720 × $^{10}\!/_{24}$)		300

The non-refundable payment is recognized as additional rent when earned. The straight-line method is used here to recognize revenue as time passes. While an interest method is theoretically justified, it is unlikely to be employed in practice. Simplicity and materiality would prevail.

The lessee's entries are:

March 1, 1991:

Prepaid rent	720	
Cash		720

December 31, 1991:

Rent expense	300	
Prepaid rent		300

ACCOUNTING FOR CAPITAL LEASES

Prior to the issuance of *CICA Handbook* section 3065, most lessees accounted for all leases as operating leases. Proponents of lease capitalization contended that in many cases the operating lease approach was improper because it resulted in off-balance-sheet financing; that is, obtaining financing without recording the contractual debt. In their view, a lease that transfers a material equity interest in the leased property creates an asset for the lessee that is more than a temporary right to use the leased property. Hence, they argued that the lessee should recognize this material interest by capitalizing as an asset the present value of the future lease rentals. Further, they reasoned that such a lease creates a liability equal to the present value of the future rents, which also should be recognized by the lessee. Similar reasoning led to the conclusion that, where a material equity interest in the property is transferred, the lessor should recognize a sale of the asset. Thus, the lessor would both record a receivable and remove the cost of the asset from its records. Thereafter, the asset should be depreciated by the lessee rather than by the lessor. Moreover, the lease rental payments should be accounted for by both parties in the same manner as periodic payments on a long-term liability for which each rental payment is a combination of interest and reduction of debt.

The proponents of lease capitalization also pointed out that recognition of an asset and a liability on the lessee's financial statements would make their statements comparable with those of firms that purchased assets and financed the purchase price with long-term debt. They argued that a lessee company that leased properties under long-term leases and a company that owned similar properties financed by long-term debt were in the same economic position. Both companies were committed to a series of regular payments over a long term; lessees paid rents, while owners paid interest and principal on the debt. Both had exclusive rights to use similar assets over most or all of the useful lives of the assets. Also, in many long-term lease contracts, the lessee is committed to pay repairs and maintenance, taxes and insurance, and similar executory costs associated with assets over their useful lives. If lessees could avoid recognition of assets and liabilities while owners could not, their fininacial statements would not be comparable even though they were in similar economic and, to some extent, similar legal positions.

Opposition to the capitalization of lease rentals arose because lessees were reluctant to recognize a lease-related liability. They pointed out that various other long-term contracts were not recognized under GAAP, and that lease contracts should not be singled out for different treatment.[13] Lessees argued that sudden recognition of large, previously unrecorded long-term lease liabilities could cause some lessees to be in technical default on other long-term debt covenants, which limited their indebtedness to a certain amount or required a certain ratio of assets to debt. These loan covenants based on financial ratios often did not consider the possible recognition of liabilities related to lease contracts because at the time the loan was negotiated, GAAP did not require such recognition. In effect, altering accounting rules for leases caused some companies to change existing debt agreements. The CICA moved ahead because it did not accept the opposition's arguments as persuasive.

The major consideration in distinguishing between a capital and operating lease is whether the lease arrangement "transfers substantially all of the benefits and risks of ownership of the leased property from the lessor to the lessee" (paragraph 3065.09). The criteria listed in Exhibit 18–2 are common to the lessor and lessee; they are designed to enable accountants to determine if the risks and rewards are being transferred. That is, if the lessee will eventually obtain ownership or most of the economic benefits and, if the lessor will recover the cost of, and earn a return on, the investment,

---

[13] Employment contracts whereby employers agreed to pay certain salaries for future services, purchase commitments that do not involve probable losses, and most post-employment benefits including pensions were but a few of the types of executory contracts for which an asset and corresponding liability were not recognized under GAAP at this time.

EXHIBIT 18–2   Criteria for Identifying a Capital Lease for the Lessee

The lease must meet any one of the following four criteria:*

1. The lease transfers ownership of the leased asset to the lessee by the end of the lease term.
2. The lease contains a bargain purchase option.
3. The lease term is equal to 75% or more of the total estimated economic life of the leased asset.
4. The present value of the minimum lease payments at the inception of the lease is at least 90% of the market value of the leased asset at that time.†

* Criteria 3 and 4 do not apply if the beginning of the lease term falls within the last 25% of the total economic life of the leased asset, land is the only asset leased, or the lease involves both land and building(s).

† The term *minimum lease payments* is a technical one and is discussed and defined later in the chapter.

the risks and rewards are being transferred. Thus, the lessee is effectively financing a purchase of the lease asset and should recognize the asset and the liability on the balance sheet.

Accounting for Capital Leases: Lessee

Capital leases are broadly defined in the prior sections. (Leases involving land, building, and equipment together are discussed in Appendix 18A.) Because of the significant differences between accounting for operating and capital leases and the difficulty in determining when substantially all the risks and rewards of ownership have been transferred, section 3065 of the *CICA Handbook* specifies detailed criteria that qualify a lease contract as a capital lease. These criteria are outlined in Exhibit 18–2 for lessees. Four criteria apply to lessees; if any one of these four criteria is met by the lessee, the lease qualifies as a capital lease for the lessee.

Transfer of Ownership (Criterion No. 1)   If a lease explicitly states that ownership of the asset transfers to the lessee at the end of the lease term, without payment of additional compensation to the lessor, the lease is nothing more than a purchase financing arrangement, similar to an installment purchase.

Bargain Purchase Option (BPO) (Criterion No. 2)   A **bargain purchase option (BPO)** is an inducement designed to ensure that the lessee buys the asset being leased at the end of the lease term. BPOs are often found in leases that contain no explicit transfer of ownership provision. Essentially, the BPO serves the same purpose. A BPO requires comparing the offer's purchase price to the leased asset's residual value at the end of the lease term. If an asset's residual value is expected to be $10,000, for example, the BPO price might be $5,000, or even less. The lessee is not expected to pass up these savings, and the probability is high that the lessee will buy the asset at the BPO date.

Lease Term Equals 75% of Asset's Useful Service Life (Criterion No. 3)   If the estimated useful economic life of an asset is 30 years, for example, and the term of the lease is 25 years, the lessee will have possession and unrestricted use of the asset for five sixths (83.4%) of its life. This control is equivalent to ownership. A bargain renewal offer (BRO) lengthens the lease life to be used in the comparison.

Minimum lease payments (at present value) equal 90% of the asset's fair value (Criterion No. 4)   **Minimum lease payments** is a technical term for the total dollars the lessee is obligated to pay the lessor over the course of the lease—including the BPO, if any. The bulk of the minimum lease payments take the form of periodic rental payments, meaning the amount to be paid each year for the use of the asset. For a complete definition of minimum lease payments and their components, refer to Exhibit 18–3.

EXHIBIT 18-3 Minimum Lease Payment Components

Minimum lease payments are the payments that the lessee is obligated to make or can be required to make in connection with the leased property. These components make up minimum lease payments:

♦ **Periodic rental payments (minimum rental payments):** The periodic rental payments are the base component. They are the total amount paid to the lessor for use of a leased asset, computed at present value. In business leasing situations, periodic rental payments are ordinarily made annually, with the first payment at the inception of the lease, and subsequent payments on the lease anniversary date. *Because lease payments are made at the front end of each lease period, when computing present values of such payments, present value annuity due (PVAD) tables are used rather than ordinary annuity tables.*

♦ **Executory costs:** Insurance, routine maintenance, and taxes due on the leased asset are the main items that make up executory costs. Lease contracts typically require the lessee to pay these costs to the lessor in conjunction with the periodic rental payments. For lease computation purposes, executory costs are deducted from periodic rental payments. *Unless otherwise noted, periodic rental payment amounts included in all examples and illustrations in this text are assumed to be net of executory costs.*

♦ **Bargain purchase option (BPO):** A BPO is an inducement offered to ensure that the lessee buys the leased asset at the end of the lease period. If a bargain purchase option is offered, the dollar amount, at present value, is included in the minimum lease payments computation. *Because a BPO is a one-time-only payment at the end of the lease term, its present value is computed using present vlaue of 1 (PV 1) tables.*

Leases that do not feature BPOs (and do not provide for transfer of ownership as a provision of the lease) may contain one or the other of the lease provisions that follow—both of which are intended to protect the lessor's investment in the asset's residual value.

♦ **Guaranteed residual value:** The lessee may be required to guarantee to the lessor the leased asset's residual value at the end of the lease term. If so, the present value of the guaranteed amount is included in the minimum lease payments, *using present value of 1 (PV 1) tables.*

♦ **Failure to renew penalty:** Some leases feature a base lease term plus term extensions. At the end of the base term, the lessee has the option to renew or terminate the lease. In certain instances, failure to renew the lease may impose a penalty on the lessee, which compensates the lessor for the loss of leasing income and recalculation of the asset's residual value. If a penalty clause is present in the lease, the present value of the penalty is included in the minimum lease payments *using present value of 1 (PV 1) tables.* The assumption is that the renewal option will be rejected by the lessee.

To illustrate the application of Criterion No. 4, assume that an asset is being leased for five years at a periodic rental payment of $25,000 each year. The interest rate on the lease is 10%. The present value of $25,000 annual payments at 10% for five years is $104,247 = $25,000 (*PVAD*, 10%, 5) = $25,000 (4.16987). Next assume that the fair value of the leased asset is $110,000. In this case, the present value of the $104,247 minimum lease payments equals 94.8% of the asset's fair market value ($104,247 ÷ $110,000), meeting Criterion No. 4 and requiring capital lease accounting treatment.

If *any one* of the four criteria is met, the leased asset is considered to be purchased from the lessor at the inception of the lease; therefore, the asset must be capitalized on the lessee's books (capital lease). If none of the criteria is met, the transaction is accounted for as an operating lease.

The lessee records a capital lease, at the date of inception of the lease at the lower of the asset's fair market value or the present value of the rental payments.[14] The lessee

---

[14] Section 3065 of the *CICA Handbook* requires that the recorded value of the leased asset may not exceed its market value; that is, if the present value of the lease payments is greater than the market value of the leased asset at the lease inception date, both the asset and liability must be recorded at the market value of the leased asset. In this case, the implied interest rate would have to be computed. For example, if the market value of the lease asset in the example was $96,375 instead of $110,000, the implicit interest rate would be computed as follows: $96,375 ÷ $25,000 = 3.8550; reference to Table 6A–6 for $n = 5$, shows that the implicit interest rate is almost exactly 15%. The entries for the lessee would change to reflect the 15% rate.

records the lease by a debit to an asset account, with a title such as "leased property," and a credit to lease liability for the present value of all future rents required in the lease agreement. Thus, the lessee's basic approach to lease valuation can be expressed as:

$$\begin{pmatrix} \text{Valuation of leased} \\ \text{asset and related} \\ \text{liability at lease inception} \end{pmatrix} = \begin{pmatrix} \text{Periodic lease} \\ \text{payments} \end{pmatrix} \begin{pmatrix} \text{Present value of} \\ \text{annuity of } n \text{ rents} \\ \text{at } i \text{ rate of interest} \end{pmatrix}$$

Example Consider the following:

1. On January 1, 1991, Lessor Company and Lessee Company sign a three-year lease for an asset with an estimated useful life of three years.
2. The agreement involves no collection uncertainties, and the lessor's performance is complete.
3. The three rental payments are $36,556 each, payable January 1, 1991, 1992, and 1993.
4. The fair market value of the asset at the inception of the lease is $100,000, which is also the carrying value (cost) on the lessor's books.
5. The lease contains no renewal or bargain purchase option and the asset reverts to the lessor at the end of the three-year lease period.
6. The lessee's incremental borrowing rate is 10%.
7. Lessee Company and Lessor Company depreciate the asset using the straight-line method for book purposes. The asset's residual value is estimated to be nil.
8. The accounting year ends December 31 for each party.
9. The lessor's implicit interest rate (target rate of return) is 10%.

Because of (1), the lease described in the example meets Criterion 3 of Exhibit 18–2, and that is sufficient to classify it as a capital lease. (The lease also meets Criterion 4, but this is not necessary to classify it as a capital lease because Criterion 3 is met.) Criteria 1 and 2 are not met since there is neither a provision for transfer of ownership nor a bargain purchase offer; the lease is still a capital lease because only one of the criteria needs to be satisfied.

Using the lessee's incremental borrowing rate, (6) in the example, the lessee's computation of the valuation of the leased asset and the related lease liability is:[15]

$$\$36,556(PVAD, 10\%, 3) = \$36,556(2.73554) = \underline{\underline{\$100,000}}$$

The lessee's journal entries and reporting based on the rentals specified in the lease contract and the $100,000 cost of the asset for the first year are:

January 1, 1991—To record the lease:

Leased asset	100,000	
Lease liability		100,000
Lease liability.	36,556	
Cash		36,556

December 31, 1991—To recognize interest and depreciation expense:

Interest expense (see Exhibit 18–4)	6,344	
Lease liability		6,344
Depreciation expense $100,000(⅓).	33,333	
Accumulated depreciation.		33,333

---

[15] Throughout this section, lease payments are assumed to be made on the first day of each period; thus, the present value of an annuity due is used. If the payments are not in the form of an annuity, each payment would need to be discounted separately.

EXHIBIT 18–4 Lease Amortization Schedule (Annuity Due Basis)

Date	Annual Lease Payments	Annual Interest at 10%	Decrease (Increase) in Lease Receivable/ Liability	Lease Receivable/ Liability Balance
January 1, 1991				$100,000
January 1, 1991	$ 36,556	—	$ 36,556	63,444
December 31, 1991	—	$6,344	(6,344)	69,788
January 1, 1992	36,556	—	36,556	33,232
December 31, 1992	—	3,324	(3,324)	36,556
January 1, 1993	36,556	—	36,556	–0–
	$109,668	$9,668	$100,000	

Only the entries for 1991 are shown. The entries for each of the next two years are identical except for the accrual of interest expense. The amortization schedule for the lease is shown in Exhibit 18–4. Interest expense for 1992 is $3,324 as shown in column 3 of the amortization schedule in Exhibit 18–4.

Lessee's Interest Rate Determining the appropriate interest rate to use in the present value discounting by the lessee is important. The rate directly affects the valuation of the leased asset and the related lease liability recorded at the inception of the lease. The higher the interest rate, the lower the amount capitalized for the asset and recorded for the liability, and vice versa.

The lessee must compute the valuation of the asset leased and the lease liability by discounting the lease payments using the lower of the lessee's incremental borrowing rate, or the discount rate used by the lessor (also called the lessor's **implicit interest rate**) if known to the lessee.[16] If the lessor's implicit interest rate is not known, or cannot be estimated reliably, the lessee's incremental borrowing rate must be used. The lessee's incremental borrowing rate is the rate that, at lease inception date, the lessee would have incurred to borrow (over a similar term) the funds necessary to purchase the leased asset. The choice of a specific interest rate by the lessee does not affect total expenses (interest expense plus depreciation expense). However, the timing of the recognition of each of these two expenses is affected.

Lessee's Depreciation Section 3065 states that the lessee should depreciate the asset cost in a manner consistent with the lessee's normal depreciation policy. The residual value, any bargain purchase options, and any guaranteed residual value may affect depreciation by the lessee. These topics are discussed later in this chapter.

The lessee's entries parallel those that would be recorded for an actual purchase on a credit basis involving periodic payments that are part principal and part interest. For the current example, the lessee reports on December 31, 1991:

1. Leased property at cost of $100,000 with accumulated depreciation of $33,333.
2. A lease liability of $69,788: ($100,000 − $36,556) plus accrued interest payable of $6,344.
3. Interest expense of $6,344.
4. Depreciation expense of $33,333.

---

[16] The problem of whose rate to use is typically resolved by the limitation of market value. Only in the case of an unguaranteed residual value (discussed later under special problems) does a substantive recording issue emerge.

CONCEPT REVIEW

1. What entries does a lessee make for an operating lease?
2. What are the four criteria used to determine whether a lease must be recognized on the balance sheet of a lessee?
3. What is the most important difference between the accounting for an operating lease and a capital lease? What is the meaning of the term *off-balance-sheet financing?*

Accounting for Capital Leases: Lessor

The criteria for determining whether the lessor must capitalize a lease include the criteria given in Exhibit 18–2. If the lease meets any one of the four criteria in Exhibit 18–2 and both of the following criteria, the lease must be capitalized by the lessor:

1. Collectibility of the minimum lease payments is reasonably assured.
2. No important uncertainties surround the amount of unreimbursable costs yet to be incurred by the lessor under the lease.[17]

These two additional criteria provide for risks that might make the first four criteria inoperative for the lessor. In addition to making a careful distinction between operating and capital leases, section 3065 further defines capital leases for the lessor as either direct-financing leases or sales-type leases. In the most simple terms, a sales-type lease involves a profit to the lessor; a direct-financing lease does not.[18]

The lessor classifies a lease as a direct-financing lease if there is no manufacturer's or dealer's profit or loss. In this situation, the lessor's cost (or carrying amount, if different) of the leased asset is assumed to equal its market value at the inception date; therefore, this value is used by the lessor to compute the lease rentals. Typically, leasing companies (as opposed to manufacturers and dealers) have only direct-financing leases, rather than sales-type leases, because they purchase property for lease and not for resale. The lessor's profit objective is to set the periodic lease rentals at a level sufficiently high to yield the target (implicit) rate of return on the lessor's investment in the leased asset. Expressed as a formula, the lessor's basic approach is to compute the amount of the periodic lease rentals as follows:

$$\text{Periodic lease rental} = \frac{\text{Lessor's investment (cost or carrying amount, if different) in leased asset}}{\text{Present value of annuity of } n \text{ payments at } i \text{ rate of interest}}$$

Direct-Financing Lease   The lease in the previous example is a capital lease to the lessor because it meets Criterion 3 from Exhibit 18–2 (see item 1 of the example) and both lessor's criteria (see Item 2 of the example). It is a direct-financing lease because (under item 2 in the example) the fair market value is equal to the cost on the lessor's books implying there is no dealer profit. The lessor's incentive comes from the interest revenue earned in financing the transaction. The lessor's implicit interest rate is in item 9 of the example. Therefore, the lessor computes the periodic lease rental as follows:

$$\text{Rent} = \$100,000 \div (PVAD, 10\%, 3) = \$100,000 \div (2.73554)$$

$$= \underline{\$36,556}$$

---

[17] Important uncertainties might include commitments by the lessor to guarantee performance of the leased asset in a manner more extensive than the typical product warranty or to protect the lessee from obsolescence of the leased asset. However, the necessity of estimating executory costs, such as insurance, maintenance, and taxes to be paid by the lessor, does not by itself constitute an important uncertainty under this provision.

[18] There is no distinction between a direct-financing lease and a sales-type lease for the lessee.

The lessor's entries for the annuity-due payment lease are:

January 1, 1991—To record the lease:

```
Lease receivable . . . . . . . . . . . . . . . . . . . . . . . . 100,000
    Asset. . . . . . . . . . . . . . . . . . . . . . . . . . .           100,000
```

January 1, 1991—First rental:

```
Cash . . . . . . . . . . . . . . . . . . . . . . . . . . . . . 36,556
    Lease receivable . . . . . . . . . . . . . . . . . . . .            36,556
```

December 31, 1991—To recognize interest earned:

```
Lease receivable ($100,000 − $36,556) × .10 . . . . . . . . .   6,344
    Interest revenue. . . . . . . . . . . . . . . . . . . . .            6,344
```

Sales-Type Lease The basic distinction between direct-financing leases and sales-type leases is that in a sales-type lease, a manufacturer's or dealer's profit or loss is recognized by the lessor at inception of the lease. This means that in a sales-type lease the market value of the leased asset at the inception of the lease is greater or less than the lessor's cost (or carrying amount, if different).

Sales-type leases typically arise when a manufacturer or dealer uses a leasing arrangement as a secondary means of marketing its products. The objectives of a company that either sells or leases its products are to earn a profit on the sale of the leased asset and also to earn interest on the related lease receivable. Thus, for a sales-type lease, two different profits are recognized during the lease term:

1. Manufacturer's or dealer's profit (gross margin or gross profit) is recognized in full at date of inception of the lease. Profit is computed as follows:

$$
\begin{array}{ccc}
\text{Normal sales price} & \text{Cost (or carrying} & \text{Manufacturer's or} \\
\text{(market value)} \quad - & \text{amount, if different)} \ = & \text{dealer's profit or} \\
\text{of the leased asset} & \text{of the leased asset} & \text{loss}
\end{array}
$$

2. Interest revenue on the lease receivable is recognized over the term of the lease. The total amount of interest is computed as follows:

$$
\begin{array}{ccc}
\text{Gross lease} & \text{Normal sales price} & \\
\text{receivable (includes} \ - & \text{(market value)} \quad = & \text{Total interest} \\
\text{the interest charge)} & \text{of the leased asset} & \text{revenue}
\end{array}
$$

The example to this point has involved a direct-financing lease. A new example is needed to illustrate the accounting for a sales-type lease. This is easily done by changing item 4 in the example to read:

4. The fair market value of the asset at the inception of the lease is $100,000, while the carrying value (cost) on the lessor's books is $80,000.

With this one change, a dealer's profit of $20,000 is introduced. The same calculation is used for the periodic rental payment. The payment is:

$$\$100,000 \div (PVAD, 10\%, 3) = \$100,000 \div 2.73554 = \$36,556$$

The accounting entries for the lessor are:

January 1, 1991—Inception of lease:

```
Lease receivable . . . . . . . . . . . . . . . . . . . . . . . 100,000
Cost of goods sold . . . . . . . . . . . . . . . . . . . . . .  80,000
    Sales revenue . . . . . . . . . . . . . . . . . . . . . .            100,000
    Asset. . . . . . . . . . . . . . . . . . . . . . . . . . .            80,000
```

EXHIBIT 18–5   Lease Amortization Schedule (Annuity Due Basis)

Date	Annual Lease Payments	Annual Interest at 10%	Decrease (Increase) in Lease Receivable/ Liability	Lease Receivable/ Liability Balance
January 1, 1991				$100,000
January 1, 1991	$ 36,556	—	$ 36,556	63,444
December 31, 1991	—	$6,344	(6,344)	69,788
January 1, 1992	36,556	—	36,556	33,232
December 31, 1992	—	3,324	(3,324)	36,556
January 1, 1993	36,556	—	36,556	–0–
	$109,668	$9,668	$100,000	

EXHIBIT 18–6   Lease Classification: Lessor

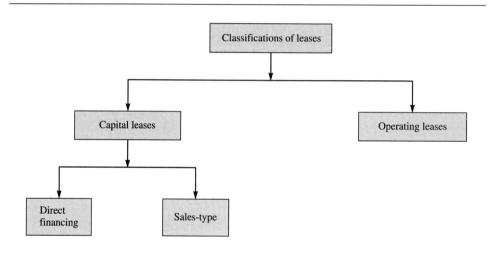

January 1, 1991—First rental:

Cash (see Exhibit 18–5). 36,556
    Lease receivable 36,556

December 31, 1991—Accrual of 1991 interest:

Lease receivable ($100,000 − $36,556) × .10. 6,344
    Interest revenue. 6,344

December 31, 1991—Depreciation expense for one year:

Not applicable.

The related amortization schedule from which the entries for future years can be obtained is given in Exhibit 18–5.

In the December 31, 1991, financial statements the lessor reports:

1. A lease receivable of $69,788.
2. Sales revenue of $100,000; cost of sales of $80,000; and interest revenue of $6,344.

The lessor's entry at the date of inception of a sales-type lease is similar to the entry that would be made if the leased asset had been sold outright on credit. That is, the lessor debits lease receivable and credits sales revenue for the sale price of the leased

EXHIBIT 18-7 Lease Classification by Lessors and Lessees

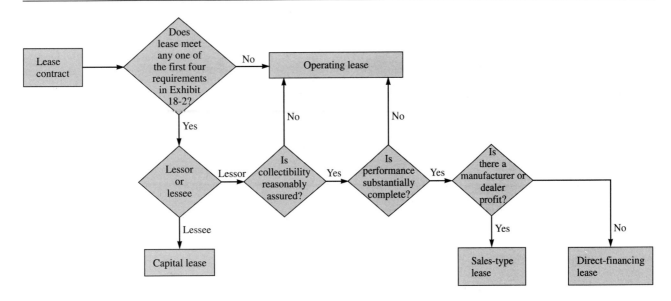

asset ($100,000). This amount is the same as the present value of the payments to be received. At the same time, the lessor debits cost of goods sold and credits the leased asset for its cost or carrying amount (as inventory), $80,000. The difference of $20,000 ($100,000 − $80,000) measures the lessor's manufacturer's or dealer's profit on the sale. The subsequent entries by the lessor to record collections of periodic rent, interest revenue, and reduction of the lease receivable are the same as the lessor's entries under a direct-financing lease.

The classification of leases to the lessor is diagramed in Exhibit 18–6. A flowchart for classifying leases for both the lessee and the lessor is provided in Exhibit 18–7. (Exhibit 18–7 does not cover leases involving real estate; this is discussed in Appendix 18A.)

Termination of Lease Agreements

A capital lease agreement may terminate due to a change of provisions in the lease, renewal or extention of the original lease, or expiration of the lease term. When a lease is terminated, the entries by the lessee and lessor are as follows:

By lessor: On termination, the net carrying value of the lease receivable is removed from the accounts, and the leased asset is recorded at the lower of its original cost or present market value. Any difference is recognized as gain or loss in the period of termination.

By lessee: On termination, both the net carrying value of the leased asset and the lease liability are removed from the accounts. A gain or loss is recognized in the period of termination for any difference.

For an example, suppose the lease situation given earlier (see Exhibit 18–5) is terminated on December 31, 1991. Assume the fair market value of the leased asset on this date is $61,000. The entries are:

Lessor			**Lessee**		
Asset.	61,000		Lease liability	69,788	
Loss on lease			Accumulated depreciation	33,333	
termination	8,788		Leased asset.		100,000
Lease receivable		69,788	Gain on lease		
			termination		3,121

Lease Entries under an Ordinary Annuity

While it is common for the rental payments to be in the form of an annuity due as is true in the example used in this chapter, the rents can be in the form of an ordinary annuity. This would be true in the example if the payments were due December 31, 1991, 1992, and 1993. In this case, the payments, assuming they were unchanged at $36,556, imply a valuation for the leased asset of $36,556 (*PVA,* 10%, 3) = $36,556 (2.48685) = $90,909.

If the lease had involved an ordinary annuity, the lessor's entries for 1991 would have been:

January 1, 1991—Inception of lease:

Loss on lease transaction	9,091	
Lease receivable	90,909	
Asset		100,000

December 31, 1991—Accrual of interest:

Lease receivable $90,909(.10)	9,091	
Interest revenue		9,091

December 31, 1991—First rental:

Cash	36,556	
Lease receivable		36,556

The lessor does not record depreciation because the asset is considered sold. The entries for the following years are identical to those for 1991 except for the interest revenue, which is $6,344 ($63,444 × .10) for 1992. On December 31, 1991, the lessor would report:

1. A lease receivable of $63,444 ($100,000 − $36,556).
2. Interest revenue of $9,091.
3. Loss on lease transaction of $9,091.

The entries for 1991 on the lessee's books would be:

January 1, 1991—Inception of lease:

Leased asset	90,909	
Lease liability		90,909

December 31, 1991—Accrual of interest:

Interest expense $90,909(.10)	9,091	
Lease liability		9,091

December 31, 1991—First rental:

Lease liability	36,556	
Cash		36,556

December 31, 1991—Record depreciation:

Depreciation expense $90,909(⅓)	30,303	
Accumulated depreciation		30,303

To avoid confusion, annuities due are used throughout the rest of the discussion.

CONCEPT REVIEW

1. Which two additional criteria must be met before a lease is capitalized by a lessor?
2. What is the difference between a sales-type lease and a direct-financing lease to a lessor?
3. Does the lessor recognize depreciation on a sales-type lease or a direct-financing lease?

SPECIAL ISSUES IN ACCOUNTING FOR LEASES

◆

Up to this point, the discussion has illustrated the fundamentals of accounting and reporting for leases by lessees and lessors. Now, the following additional issues in accounting for leases that make the accounting more complex are considered.

1. Bargain purchase options in capital leases.
2. Bargain renewal options.
3. Residual value in capital leases.
4. Different interest rates.
5. Depreciation of a leased asset by the lessee.
6. Executory and initial direct costs.
7. Sale-leaseback arrangements.
8. Classification of lease receivables and payables.
9. Lease disclosure requirements.

Exhibit 18–8 presents a list of technical lease terms and their definitions as set forth in section 3065 of the *CICA Handbook*. These terms are used extensively in the remainder of this chapter.

Bargain Purchase Options in Capital Leases

A bargain purchase option (BPO) permits a lessee to purchase the leased property, during a specified period of the lease term, at a price below the expected market value at that time. This price is sufficiently low to reasonably assure that the lessee will take advantage of the bargain. In effect, a BPO is viewed as a sale and transfer of ownership of the leased asset to the lessee at the specified bargain price. The definition of minimum lease payments in Exhibit 18–8 states that if the lease contains a BPO, only the rental payments over the lease term and the BPO payment are included in the minimum lease payments. This means that when there is a BPO, any residual values are disregarded when computing the lease rent amount. In this case, the residual value is used only to determine whether the purchase option is a bargain.

Including a BPO in a capital lease contract means that there are two cash flows to the lessor from the lessee: one is from the periodic rentals and the other is from the BPO price. Thus, a BPO affects the amount of the annual rentals required to meet the lessor's target rate of return and the lessee's capitalizable cost of the leased asset. Compared with the example used earlier, in which the leased asset had no residual value and no BPO, the annual rental in a lease with a BPO is less than in a lease without a BPO. This occurs because the lessor recovers part of the investments in the leased asset through the BPO price. The recovery reduces the amount that must be received from the periodic rentals. Therefore, the lessor includes the BPO amount in computing the amount of each annual rental. The lessee includes the BPO in computing the cost of the leased asset to be capitalized.

To adapt the original, continuing example to a BPO situation, Items 1, 5, and 7 are changed as follows:

1. The estimated life of the asset is four years.
5. There is a BPO of $10,000 exerciseable at the end of the three-year lease term.
7. The estimated residual value of the leased asset is $15,000 at the BPO exercise date. The asset's residual value at the end of the fourth year is nil.

The lease continues to be a direct-financing lease to the lessor and a capital lease to the lessee. The lease payment is calculated to be:

Carrying value of leased asset	$100,000
Less: present value of the BPO	
$10,000($PV$1, 10%, 3) = $10,000(.75131)	7,513
Net asset cost to be recovered through rentals	$ 92,487

EXHIBIT 18-8   Technical Lease Definitions

1. **Fair [market] value of the leased property** is "the price for which the leased property could be sold in an arm's-length transaction."
2. A **bargain purchase option** is a "provision allowing the lessee, at its option, to purchase the leased property for a price which is sufficiently lower than the expected fair [market] value of the property, at the date the option becomes exercisable, that exercise of the option appears, at the inception of the lease, to be reasonably assured."
3. A **bargain renewal option** is a "provision allowing the lessee, at its option, to renew the lease for a rental which is sufficiently lower than the fair rental of the property, at the date the option becomes exercisable, that exercise of the option appears, at the inception of the lease, to be reasonably assured."
4. The **residual value** of the leased property is "the estimated fair [market] value of the leased property at the end of the lease term." Depending on the provisions of the lease agreement, estimated residual value may not be guaranteed; or it may be guaranteed in full or in part by the lessee or by a third-party guarantor. If it is not guaranteed in full, the unguaranteed residual value is "the estimated residual value which is not guaranteed."
5. **Executory costs** are costs related to the operation of the leased property (e.g., insurance, maintenance, and property taxes).
6. **Initial direct costs** are those costs incurred by the lessor; they are directly associated with negotiating and executing a specific leasing transaction such as commissions, legal fees, and costs of preparing and processing documents.
7. The **interest rate implicit in the lease** is "the discount rate that, at the inception of the lease, causes the aggregate present value of:
   i. the minimum lease payments, from the standpoint of the lessor, excluding that portion of the payments representing executory costs to be paid by the lessor and any profit on such costs; and
   ii. the unguaranteed residual value accruing to the benefit of the lessor;
   to be equal to the fair value of the leased property to the lessor at the inception of the lease." [This definition applies to both the lessor and the lessee.]
8. The **lease term** is "the fixed noncancelable period of the lease plus [*a*] all periods, if any, covered by bargain renewal options . . . and [*b*] all periods, if any, covered by ordinary renewal options preceding the date on which a bargain purchase option is exercisable; . . . provided that the lease term does not extend beyond the date a bargain purchase option becomes exercisable."
9. The **lessee's incremental borrowing rate** is "the rate that, at the inception of the lease, the lessee would have incurred to borrow, over a similar term and with similar security for the borrowing, the funds necessary to purchase the leased asset."
10. **Minimum lease payments.**
    a. "From the point of view of the lessee minimum lease payments comprise:
       i. the minimum rental payments called for by the lease over the lease term:
       ii. any partial or full guarantee, by the lessee or a third party related to the lessee, of the residual value of the leased property at the end of the lease term. When the lessee agrees to make up a deficiency in the lessor's realization of the residual value below a stated amount, the guarantee to be included in the minimum lease payments would be the stated amount rather than an estimate of the deficiency to be made up; and
       iii. any penalty required to be paid by the lessee for failure to renew or extend the lease at the end of the lease term; provided that if the lease contains a bargain purchase option, only the total of the minimum rental payments over the lease term and the payment called for by the bargain purchase option would be included in minimum lease payments.
    b. From the point of view of the lessor, minimum lease payments comprise:
       i. minimum lease payments for the lessee as described in (*a*) and
       ii. any residual value or rental payments beyond the lease term guaranteed by a third party unrelated to either the lessee or lessor, provided that the guarantor is financially capable of discharging the obligations under the guarantee." [Note: When there is a bargain purchase option, residual value is of no future concern to the lessor because the leased asset will be retained by the lessee at the end of the lease term.]
11. Lessor's **gross investment in the lease** [only for direct-financing and sales-type leases] is the minimum lease payments, net of executory costs, plus the unguaranteed residual value retained by the lessor.
12. Lessor's **net investment in the lease** [only for direct-financing and sales-type leases] is the gross investment less unearned interest revenue included therein.

Annual rental:

$$\$92,487 \div (2.73554) = \$33,809\,.$$

Exhibit 18–9 illustrates lessor and lessee accounting for a BPO. The lessor must consider two different cash inflows in computing the lease payments. They are the cash to be received when the BPO is exercised and the annual rentals. This two-stage computation by the lessor is based on the lease specifications, the lessor's carrying value of the leased asset, and the lessor's implicit interest rate (the target rate of return) on the investment. The BPO is discounted from the first exercise date of the BPO to the lease inception date. Often this period of time is less than the lease term.

The lessee knows the lease specifications, including the annual rental of \$33,809 and the BPO of \$10,000 at the end of the third year. The lessee also knows that the implicit

EXHIBIT 18-9   Accounting for a Direct-Financing Lease with a Bargain Purchase Option

Lessor			**Lessee**		
January 1, 1991—inception of lease:*					
Cash	33,809		Leased asset[‡]	100,000	
Lease receivable[†]	66,191		Lease liability		66,191
Asset		100,000	Cash		33,809
December 31, 1991—adjusting entries:					
Lease receivable	6,619		Interest expense[†]	6,619	
Interest revenue[†]		6,619	Lease liability		6,619
			Depreciation expense	25,000	
			Accumulated depreciation		25,000
			($100,000 ÷ 4 = $25,000).		
December 31, 1993—exercise of BPO					
Cash	10,000		Lease liability	10,000	
Lease receivable		10,000	Cash		10,000

Lease Amortization Schedule with Bargain Purchase Option (Annuity Due Basis)

Date	Annual Lease Payments	Annual Interest at 10%	Decrease (Increase) in Lease Receivable/Liability	Lease Receivable/Liability Balance
January 1, 1991	Initial value			$100,000
January 1, 1991	$ 33,809	—	$ 33,809	66,191
December 31, 1991	—	$ 6,619	(6,619)	72,810
January 1, 1992	33,809	—	33,809	39,001
December 31, 1992	—	3,900	(3,900)	42,901
January 1, 1993	33,809	—	33,809	9,092
December 31, 1993	—	908	(908)	10,000
December 31, 1993	10,000	—	10,000	–0–
	$111,427	$11,427	$100,000	

* This entry records the $10,000 BPO in the receivable account. Alternatively, the entry could be made to record the BPO amount in the asset account, leased asset.

† Computation: See schedule below.

‡ Lessee's computation of cost of leased asset (the lessee capitalizes the BPO):

PV of rentals: $33,809 (*PVAD*, 10%, 3) = $33,809(2.73554) = $ 92,487
PV of BPO: $10,000(*PV*1, 10%, 3) = $10,000(0.75131) =   7,513

Valuation of leased asset to be capitalized (rentals plus BPO) = $100,000

interest rate on the lease is 10% based on the asset's market value or because the lessor informed the lessee of the rate in this example.[19] With these data, the lessee can compute the capitalizable cost of the leased asset:

$$\$33,809(PVAD, 10\%, 3) +$$
$$\$10,000(PV1, 10\%, 3) = \$33,809(2.73554) + \$10,000(0.75131)$$
$$= \$100,000$$

(This calculation is also shown in Exhibit 18-9).

Exhibit 18-9 also presents representative entries for the lessor and lessee. Notice that only the lessee records depreciation expense on the leased asset because under a capital lease a purchase of the leased asset by the lessee is assumed. When there is a BPO, the lessee depreciates the leased asset over its total expected useful life (less any estimated residual value at the end of that time) rather than the lease term of three

---

[19] Assumed to be equal to the incremental borrowing rate of the lessee.

years. It always is assumed that the BPO will be exercised which causes the lessee to receive title and permanent ownership of the leased asset.

If, on December 31, 1993 (the BPO date), the lessee lets the bargain purchase option lapse, the lessor and the lessee would remove from their respective accounts all remaining balances related to the lease contract and recognize a loss. The following entries on December 31, 1993, would replace those in Exhibit 18–9 assuming:[20]

1. A new estimated residual value of $8,000 instead of $15,000.
2. The lease was not renewed.

Lessor:

Asset (new residual value)	8,000	
Loss on lapse of lease purchase option	2,000	
Lease receivable		10,000

Lessee:

Lease liability	10,000	
Loss on lapse of lease purchase option	15,000	
Accumulated depreciation ($25,000 × 3)	75,000	
Leased asset		100,000

Bargain Renewal Option

Criterion 3 in Exhibit 18–2 requires that a lease be a capital lease if the lease term is at least 75% or more of the estimated economic life of the leased asset. Determining an asset's **lease term** is not a simple matter.[21] For example, the lease term is generally fixed. However, this period can be extended by a **bargain renewal option (BRO)**. A BRO allows the lessee to renew the lease for a rental that is less than the expected fair market rental at the time the option is exercisable.

If it can be established at the inception of the lease that the difference between the rent under the renewal option is sufficiently less than the expected fair market rental amount at the option's exercise date, the lease life is extended to cover the additional period. Under similar reasoning, the lease life would also be extended if substantial penalties were incurred by the lessee for failure to renew or extend the lease, for renewal periods preceding a BPO, for renewal periods during which the lessee is a guarantor of the lessor's debt, and for periods representing renewals or extensions of the lease at the lessor's option. The lease term never extends beyond the date when a BPO becomes exercisable.

Residual Value in Capital Leases

Residual values can affect the accounting of the lessor and lessee in several ways including: the computation of the minimum lease payments, the amount to be capitalized by the lessee, and the periodic depreciation expense. Furthermore, when the lease term is less than the estimated useful economic life of the leased property, two different **estimated residual values** need to be considered: the value at the end of the lease term and the value at the end of the property's estimated useful life. In the continuing example as depicted in Exhibit 18–9, the estimated residual value at the end of the three-year lease term is $15,000, while the estimated residual value at the end of the asset's four-year life is nil.

---

[20] The lessor has a loss of $2,000 because the estimated $8,000 residual value on the BPO date, December 31, 1993, is less than the balance in the lease receivable account of $10,000. If there were no change in the original estimate of residual value of $15,000, the lessor would record a gain of $5,000.

[21] Determining the economic life is also not simple particularly for specialized assets. This issue is covered in Chapter 11.

When the leased asset has economic value at the end of the lease term, that residual value must be incorporated into the accounting for the lease. Therefore, it is necessary to determine which party (lessor or lessee) the lease agreement specifies shall own the leased asset (and therefore the residual value) at the end of the lease term.

The accounting impact of an estimated residual value at the end of the lease term in a capital lease is as follows:

If the lessee gets the residual value:

- The leased property and its residual value at the end of the lease term belong to the lessee at no additional cost (above the annual lease rentals). In this situation, the residual value does not affect the lessor's computation of the periodic lease payments nor the lessor's accounting, or the lessee's cost to be capitalized. However, the lessee should depreciate the asset over its total useful life less any estimated residual value at the end of that total life.
- The estimated residual value at the end of the lease term is sold by the lessor and purchased by the lessee through a BPO. In this situation, the BPO amount is included in the lease accounting by both the lessor and lessee as discussed earlier and illustrated by Exhibit 18–9.

If the lessor retains the residual value:

- When the lessor retains the residual value by getting the leased assets back at the end of the lease term, there is a risk that the lessee will not properly maintain the leased asset, in which case the residual value is either low or zero. To minimize this risk, the lease agreement may require the lessee to guarantee all or part of the estimated residual value. Thus, the estimated residual value retained by the lessor at the end of the lease term may be:
  - Unguaranteed by the lessee.
  - Guaranteed in full by the lessee.
  - Guaranteed in part by the lessee.
  - Guaranteed by a third party for a fee depending on the provisions of the lease agreement. These four cases are discussed next.

Unguaranteed Residual Value Retained by Lessor

When the lease agreement provides that the lessor retains the leased asset at the end of the lease term, any residual value is owned by the lessor. When that residual value is unguaranteed by the lessee, the lessor should compute the periodic rentals by deducting the present value of the estimated residual value from the total amount to be recovered under the lease agreement because the residual value is not sold. The lessee capitalizes only the lease payments, which excludes any amount for residual value because the lessee does not buy the residual value. This means that the lessee does not capitalize the unguaranteed residual value retained by the lessor. (This creates a situation in which the entries by lessee and lessor are not symmetrical).

Exhibit 18–10 illustrates a direct-financing lease with a $10,000 **unguaranteed residual value** at the end of the lease term. The lessor's computation of the annual rentals in which the present value of the unguaranteed residual value is deducted yields $33,809, the same amount as was calculated for the lease when a $10,000 BPO was involved. However, since the $10,000 residual value is not guaranteed by the lessee, the lessee only capitalizes the net asset cost of $92,487 = $100,000 − $10,000(PV1, 10%, 3). Exhibit 18–10 gives selected entries for the lessor and lessee and the lessee's computation of the cost of the leased asset, which does not include the unguaranteed residual value because it is owned by the lessor. Thus, the entries (and the amortization schedules) of the lessor and lessee differ (even though they use the same implicit interest rate) because the estimated unguaranteed residual value is retained in the lessor's accounts but is not capitalized in the lessee's accounts. The lessor's entry on January 1,

EXHIBIT 18-10   Accounting for a Direct-Financing Lease with Unguaranteed Residual Value

Lessor		Lessee	
Lease receivable. 100,000*		Leased asset . . . . 92,487†	
Asset	100,000	Lease liability.	92,487

January 1, 1991—First rental:

Lessor		Lessee	
Cash 33,809		Lease liability. 33,809	
Lease receivable.	33,809	Cash	33,809

December 31, 1991—Adjusting entries:

Lessor		Lessee	
Lease receivable. 6,619		Interest expense. 5,868	
Interest revenue	6,619	Lease liability.	5,868
See lessor's amortization schedule below.		See lessee's amortization schedule below.	
		Depreciation expense 30,829	
		Accumulated depreciation	30,829
		($92,487 ÷ 3 = $30,829).	

Lessor		Lessee	
December 31, 1993—End of lease term—to remove the residual value from the lease receivable account:		To remove the asset from the accounts:	
Asset 10,000		Accumulated depreciation 92,487	
Lease receivable.	10,000	Leased asset	92,487

Lease Amortization Schedule (Annuity Due Basis)

		Lessor			Lessee		
Date	Lease Payments	Interest at 10%	Receivable Decrease (Increase)	Receivable Balance	Interest at 10%	Liability Decrease (Increase)	Liability Balance
January 1, 1991	Initial value			$100,000			$92,487
January 1, 1991	$ 33,809	—	$33,809	66,191	—	$33,809	58,678
December 31, 1991. . . .	—	$ 6,619	(6,619)	72,810	$5,868	(5,868)	64,546
January 1, 1992	33,809	—	33,809	39,001	—	33,809	30,737
December 31, 1992. . . .	—	3,900	(3,900)	42,901	3,072	(3,072)	33,809
January 1, 1993	33,809	—	33,809	9,092	—	33,809	–0–
December 31, 1993. . . .	—	908	(908)	10,000 (RV)			
	$101,427	$11,427	$90,000		$8,940	$92,487	

* This entry records the $10,000 residual value in the lease receivable account. The entry could have been made to record the residual value in an asset account, Leased Property.

† Lessee's computation of cost of leased asset (the unguaranteed residual value is not capitalized by the lessee): $33,809(*PVAD*, 10%, 3) = $33,809(2.73554).

1991, the date of inception of the lease, removes the cost of the leased asset and records the receivable, which includes the $10,000 residual value. The last entry, made at the termination of the lease, removes the residual value ($10,000) from the receivable account and returns it to its original asset account.[22]

The lessor's amortization schedule, shown in Exhibit 18–10, leaves an ending asset balance of $10,000 (the residual value) in the lessor's lease receivable account. The initial value in the lease receivable account for the lessor is the lessor's cost of the leased asset, $100,000, because the lessor plans to recover the total cost from the lessee's payments and the asset is returned to the lessor at the end of the lease term. In contrast, the lessee's amortization schedule starts with the lease liability amount of $92,487,

[22] Some accountants prefer to leave the present value of the residual value in its original asset account for amortization during the lease term because it will not be "collected for" during that term. Both approaches produce the same end results. Section 3065 states that the unguaranteed residual value of the leased asset accruing to the lessor should be included in the investment in the lease. This specification relates more fundamentally to computation of the lease payments by the lessor and not to the details of a specific journal entry.

EXHIBIT 18–11   Accounting for a Sales-Type Lease with Unguaranteed Residual Value

Lessor		Lessee	

January 1, 1991—Inception of lease:

Lease receivable	100,000		Leased asset	92,487[†]	
Cost of goods sold	72,487*		Lease liability.		92,487
Sales revenue		92,487**			
Asset		80,000			

January 1, 1991—First rental:

Cash	33,809		Lease liability.	33,809	
Lease receivable.		33,809	Cash		33,809

December 31, 1991—Adjusting entries:

Lease receivable	6,619		Interest expense	5,868	
Interest revenue		6,619	Lease liability.		5,868
See lessor's amortization schedule below.			See lessee's amortization schedule below.		
			Depreciation expense	30,829	
			Accumulated depreciation		30,829
			($92,487 ÷ 3 = $30,829).		

December 31, 1993—End of lease term—
to remove the residual value:

			To remove the asset from the accounts:		
Asset residual value	10,000		Accumulated depreciation	92,487	
Lease receivable.		10,000	Leased asset		92,487

Lease Amortization Schedule (Annuity Due Basis)

		Lessor			Lessee		
Date	Lease Payments	Interest at 10%	Receivable Decrease (Increase)	Receivable Balance	Interest at 10%	Liability Decrease (Increase)	Liability Balance
January 1, 1991	Initial value			$100,000			$92,487
January 1, 1991	$ 33,809	—	$33,809	66,191	—	$33,809	58,678
December 31, 1991. . . .	—	$ 6,619	(6,619)	72,810	$5,868	(5,868)	64,546
January 1, 1992	33,809	—	33,809	39,001	—	33,809	30,737
December 31, 1992. . . .	—	3,900	(3,900)	42,901	3,072	(3,072)	33,809
January 1, 1993	33,809	—	33,809	9,092	—	33,809	–0–
December 31, 1993. . . .	—	908	(908)	10,000 (RV)			
	$101,427	$11,427	$90,000		$8,940	$92,487	

* Lessor's cost of goods sold is the carrying value of the asset less the present value of the unguaranteed residual value ($80,000 − $7,513 = $72,487), because the residual value was not sold.

** Lessor's sales revenue: $100,000 − $7,513 = $92,487.

[†] Lessee's computation of leased asset cost excluding the unguaranteed residual value is: $33,809 × (PVAD, 10%, 3) = $33,809(2.73554) = $92,487.

which excludes the present value of the residual value and ends with a zero balance. The lessee depreciates the leased asset over the lease term and disregards the unguaranteed residual value.

At the end of the lease term, the $10,000 residual value of the leased asset, which is retained by the lessor in this case, is transferred by the lessor from the lease receivable account to the original asset account. The lease receivable account will then have a zero balance. In contrast, all of the lessee's lease account balances will be zero already.

For a sales-type lease with an unguaranteed residual value, CICA paragraph 3065.43 requires that the lessor deduct the present value of the unguaranteed residual value from both sales revenue and cost of goods sold. The main purpose of this rule is to avoid overstating sales revenue. Notice that the manufacturer's or dealer's profit, lease receivable, or annual interest revenue is not changed. Exhibit 18–11 shows the case of the sales-type lease used earlier (Exhibit 18–5) but now with an unguaranteed residual value of $10,000. Both sales revenue ($92,487) and cost of goods sold ($72,487) are computed by deducting the present value of the unguaranteed residual value [$10,000 $(PV\,1, 10\%, 3) = \$10,000\,(0.75131) = \$7,513$] from the cash equivalent price ($100,000) and carrying value ($80,000), respectively. This approach results in the same manufacturer's or dealer's profit as when residual value is guaranteed. However, both sales revenue and cost of goods sold are reduced because the residual value is not sold but rather reverts to the lessor.

Residual Value Guaranteed by Lessee and Retained by Lessor

When the lessor retains the residual value of the leased asset, the lease agreement may require the lessee to guarantee all or part of the estimated residual value at the end of the lease term. Such guarantees are made to motivate the lessee to take better care of the leased asset.

Residual Value Fully Guaranteed by the Lessee   In this case, the residual value estimated at the inception of the lease is fully guaranteed by the lessee, which means that the lessee must pay the cash equivalent to make up any residual value deficiency. The deficiency is based on an appraisal (usually by an independent party) at the end of the lease term. To continue the extended example used in Exhibit 18–10, assume the actual residual value at the end of the lease term determined in accordance with the lease contract is $9,000, rather than the previously estimated $10,000. Assuming a fully guaranteed residual value, the lessee must pay the lessor $1,000 cash.

To compute the periodic lease payments when the residual value is fully guaranteed, the lessor deducts the present value of the total residual value from the total amount to be recovered under the lease agreement because at the inception of the lease the lessor expects to realize the full amount of the residual value at the end of the lease term.

A capital lease with a fully guaranteed residual value by the lessee is illustrated in Exhibit 18–12. The lessor deducts the present value of the guaranteed residual value to compute the periodic rentals. The lessee capitalizes $100,000 (the same amount recognized by the lessor), which is the "net cost to be recovered through rentals" of $92,487 plus the present value of the fully guaranteed residual value of $7,513. The lessee capitalizes the sum of these two amounts because the lease liability is the total present value guaranteed to be transferred from the lessee to the lessor. The guaranteed residual value is added by the lessee; in contrast, an unguaranteed residual value is excluded from the capitalized lease value.

At termination of the lease on December 31, 1993, the actual residual value is determined (independently as specified in the lease agreement). This residual value then is compared with the guaranteed residual value to determine whether the lessee owes the lessor additional consideration. If, as assumed, the actual residual value at the end of 1993 is determined independently to be $9,000, then the lessee is obligated to pay the lessor $1,000 cash ($10,000 − $9,000). If the guaranteed value had been less than the actual value, the lessor would have no obligation to make a refund to the lessee.

The estimated residual value on an asset under a capital lease must be reviewed annually to determine whether it is realistic (*CICA Handbook,* paragraph 3065.41 and .49). If the estimate is revised by a material amount, a change in estimate should be recognized and the subsequent lease entries (and schedules) revised accordingly. A fully guaranteed residual value is accounted for in the same way for both direct and sales-type leases. Finally, since there is neither a transfer of title at the end of the lease nor a BPO (neither condition (1) nor (2) of Exhibit 18–2 is met), depreciation is again based on the life of the lease, three years.

Residual Value Partially Guaranteed by the Lessee   When the lessee guarantees only a part of the estimated residual value of the leased asset, the lessor bases the computation of

EXHIBIT 18-12   Accounting for a Direct-Financing Lease with a $10,000 Residual Value Guaranteed by the Lessee

Lessor		Lessee	
January 1, 1991—Inception of lease:			
Lease receivable. 100,000*		Leased asset* 100,000	
Asset	100,000	Lease liability.	100,000
January 1, 1991 First rental:			
Cash 33,809		Lease liability. 33,809	
Lease receivable.	33,809	Cash	33,809
December 31, 1991—Adjusting entries:			
Lease receivable. 6,619		Interest expense. 6,619	
Interest revenue	6,619	Lease liability.	6,619
		Depreciation expense 30,000	
		Accumulated depreciation	30,000
		($100,000 − $10,000) ÷ 3 = $30,000.	
December 31, 1993—Lease termination; assuming an actual residual value of $9,000:			
		Accumulated depreciation 90,000	
Asset (market value). 9,000		Lease liability. 10,000	
Cash ($10,000 − $9,000) 1,000		Loss on lease contract 1,000	
Lease receivable.	10,000	Leased asset	100,000
		Cash	1,000

Lease Amortization Schedule (Annuity Due Basis)

Date	Lease Payments	Interest at 10%	Decrease (Increase) in Receivable/Liability	Lease Receivable/Liability Balance
January 1, 1991	Initial value			$100,000
January 1, 1991	$ 33,809	—	$33,809	66,191
December 31, 1991.	—	$ 6,619	(6,619)	72,810
January 1, 1992	33,809	—	33,809	39,001
December 31, 1992.	—	3,900	(3,900)	42,901
January 1, 1993	33,809	—	33,809	9,092
December 31, 1993.	—	908**	(908)	10,000 (guaranteed residual value)
	$101,427	$11,427	$90,000	

* $33,809(PVAD, 10\%, 3) + \$10,000(PV1, 10\%, 3) = \$33,809(2.73554) + \$10,000(0.7531)$
** rounded

the periodic lease payments (and the related amortization schedule) on the estimated residual value. In contrast, to compute the amount to be capitalized, the lessee adds only the partially guaranteed amount to the lessor's lease payments. Therefore, the amounts recorded by the lessor and lessee would not be the same. This procedure is the same for direct and sales-type leases.

Residual Value Guaranteed by Third Party and Retained by Lessor

The residual value of a leased asset may be guaranteed in full or in part by a third party guarantor, usually retained by the lessor for a fee. In this case, the lessor would deduct the amount of the guarantee to compute the lease payments because the cash for any residual value deficiency will come from a different source. The lease receivable includes both sources, the present value of both the rental payments and the guaranteed residual value. The lessee does not include the present value of the guaranteed residual value in the cost of the leased asset because the residual value is guaranteed by a third party (not the lessee). This again results in asymmetrical entries between the lessor and lessee. To illustrate this case, assume now that the $10,000 residual value is

EXHIBIT 18-13   Accounting for a Direct-Financing Lease with Guaranteed Residual Value of $20,000 by a Third Party

Lessor (Direct Financing Lease)		**Lessee (Operating Lease)**	
January 1, 1991—Inception of lease:			
Lease receivable 100,000		No entry.	
Asset	100,000		
January 1, 1991—First rental:			
Cash 31,063		Rent expense 31,063	
Lease receivable	31,063	Cash	31,063
December 31, 1991—Adjusting entries:			
Lease receivable 6,894		No entry.	
Interest revenue	6,894		
See lessor amortization schedule below.			

Lessor's Lease Amortization Schedule (Annuity Due Basis)

Date	Lease Payments	Interest at 10%	Decrease (Increase) in Receivable	Lease Receivable Balance
January 1, 1991	Initial value			$100,000
January 1, 1991	$31,063	—	$31,063	68,937
December 31, 1991.	—	$ 6,894	(6,894)	75,831
January 1, 1992	31,063	—	31,063	44,768
December 31, 1992.	—	4,477	(4,477)	49,245
January 1, 1993	31,063	—	31,063	18,182
December 31, 1993.	—	1,818	(1,818)	20,000 (guaranteed
	$93,189	$13,189	$80,000	residual value)

guaranteed by a third party. The entries are shown in Exhibit 18–12. The calculations once again lead to rental payments of $33,809 by the lessee because the lessor is assured of the $10,000 from a third party (not the lessee).

The lessor includes the present value of the residual value as part of the lease payments, resulting in a lease receivable of $92,487 + $7,513 = $100,000. This amount is greater than 90% of the leased asset's market value, $100,000 (.90) = $90,000, at the inception of the lease. Therefore, for the lessor the lease satisfies Criterion 4 in Exhibit 18–2 for a capital lease in this case. Since the present value of the lease payments, excluding the residual value, is $92,487, which also exceeds 90% of the leased asset's market value of $100,000, the lessee also treats the lease as a capital lease.

An interesting result occurs if the lessee has a third party guarantee $20,000 for the residual value. In this situation, the lessor reduces the rentals to $31,063 in recognition of the larger receivable guaranteed for the residual value:

$$[\$100,000 - \$20,000(PV1, 10\%, 3)] \div$$

$$(PVAD, 10\%, 3) = [\$100,000 - \$20,000(.75131)] \div (2.73554)$$

$$= (\$100,000 - \$15,026) \div 2.73554 = \$31,063$$

The lessor capitalizes the value of the lease payments plus the present value of the residual value to obtain $100,000: $31,063(2.73554) + $20,000(.75131). This amount exceeds 90% of the leased asset's fair market value (.9 × $100,000 = $90,000) and hence the lease satisfies Criterion 4 in Exhibit 18–2 for a capital lease. However, the guaranteed residual value by a third party is excluded from the minimum lease payments for the lessee. The lessee computes only the present value of the $31,063 payments obtaining $84,974 = $31,063(PVAD, 10%, 3) = $31,063(2.73554). This amount is less than 90% of the market value of the asset at lease inception (.90 × $100,000 = $90,000). Because of this result, and the fact that no other requirement for a capital lease is met in this case (no transfer of ownership at the end of the lease term, no bargain purchase

EXHIBIT 18-14 Summary of Residual Value Accounting (Assuming the Lessor and Lessee Use the Same Interest Rate)

Situation	Symmetrical Entries and Schedules?	Reason
1. No residual value	Yes	No residual value effect on either party
2. Unguaranteed residual value (Exhibits 18–10 and 18–11)	No	Lessor includes (deducts) the present value of the residual value in lease rental computation. Lessee excludes (does not add) residual value in cost computation.
3. Residual value fully guaranteed by lessee (Exhibit 18–12)	Yes	Lessor includes (deducts) total residual value in lease rental computations. Lessee includes (adds) fully guaranteed residual value in cost computation.
4. Residual value partially guaranteed by lessee	No	Lessor includes (deducts) total residual value in lease rental computations. Lessee includes (adds) the portion of residual value that is partially guaranteed in cost computation.
5. Full or part residual value guarantee by third party (Exhibit 18–13)	No	Lessor includes (deducts) residual value guarantee in lease rental computations. Lessee excludes (does not add) residual value in cost computation (because the residual value is guaranteed by a third party).

option, and a lease term that is less than 75% of the lease asset's life) the lessee treats the lease as an operating lease. The entries for this special case are given in Exhibit 18–13.

Thus, by using a third-party guarantor, a lessor may record a lease as a capital lease while the lessee may record the lease as an operating lease, thereby circumventing the CICA's attempt to ensure accounting symmetry between lessor and lessee (equivalent accounting treatment of a lease contract between contracting parties). The introduction to this chapter described how investment banking and securities firms are in the leasing service business. One of the leasing services they provide is professional assistance in structuring leases so that lessees are able to keep them off their balance sheets, while lessors account for them as direct-financing leases. The use of third party guarantor is one of the means used to accomplish this result.

Exhibit 18–14 summarizes the complex implications of residual values in lease accounting when the lessor and lessee use the same implicit interest rate.

Different Interest Rates

To this point in the chapter, all leasing examples and illustrations have been based on the assumption that the lessor's implicit interest rate and the lessee's incremental borrowing rate were equal. For convenience and math ease, a 10% rate was used in most of the illustrations. Suppose, instead, that the lessor's implicit interest rate was 9%

while the lessee's incremental borrowing rate remained at 10%. If so, which rate should be used?

The question of which rate to use applies only to the lessee. The lessor is in the driver's seat and sets whatever rate is considered reasonable and competitive. The rate used by the lessee, however, is the one of concern to the CICA; paragraph 3065.16 instructs lessees to use their incremental borrowing rate, unless the lessor's implicit interest rate is known to the lessee and that rate is lower than the lessee's own borrowing rate.

The phrase *if it is known* as used in section 3065 of the *CICA Handbook* may conger up images of the lessor playing cat and mouse games, keeping the lessee in the dark about the interest rate being charged. In truth, most leasing transactions are conducted completely in the open. Although the lessor's interest rate is not explicitly stated in the lease contract, it usually is communicated orally and also may be found in business documents accompanying the lease. In fact, the rate charged by the lessor is frequently subject to negotiation. Thus, in most cases, the lessee simply uses the lower of the incremental borrowing rate or the lessor's implicit interest rate.

In some cases, however, even though the implicit interest rate may be known to the business executive who negotiated the lease, the company's accounting staff (or external accountants) may not be fully briefed on the terms of the lease transaction and, therefore, must rely on the lease itself for accounting detail information. Also, in many instances, lessee-companies use independent business brokers to negotiate leases, subject to review and approval by legal counsel. These outside representatives may be unavailable for detailed information gathering, or not attuned to the information needs of accountants.

The true target audience for section 3065 is those lessees who persist in treating lease transactions as operating leases rather than capital leases. Here's how interest rates fit into their plans.

The higher the interest rate assigned to a leasing transaction, the lower the dollar amount capitalized as a leased asset. This is because, from the lessee's point of view, the total dollar amounts of the minimum lease payments are fixed. Thus, if the capitalized portion can be kept below 90% of the leased asset's cost, the lessee can treat the transaction as an operating lease, substituting rental expense for capital expenditures.

To illustrate, assume that a lessee—for whatever reason—wishes to account for a leasing transaction as an operating lease rather than a capital lease. The same $100,000 example asset used throughout this chapter is also involved in this instance. Again, the lease term is three years, and the asset here is assumed to have a $10,000 residual value at the lease's end point. The minimum lease payments are $33,809 for three years, which everyone, except for the lessee, knows is based on an implicit interest rate of 10%.[23]

The lessee knows only two facts: The cost of the asset being rented is $100,000 and the annual rental payments will be $33,809. The residual value is unknown to the lessee. Suppose the lessee claims that the incremental borrowing rate is 14%. The lessee will then compute the present value to be:

$$\$33,809(PVAD, 14\%, 3) = \$33,809(2.64666) = \$89,481$$

The calculations for both interest rates are:

Rate	Minimum Lease Payments		Present Value Annuity Due Factor		Present Value of Lease Payments	Percent of Asset Cost
10%	$33,809	×	2.73554	=	$92,487	92.487%
14	33,809	×	2.64666	=	89,481	89.481

[23] This example assumes that the lease contains neither a transfer of ownership provision nor a bargain purchase option, and that the lease term is less than 75% of the asset's total useful economic life.

If left unchallenged, the lessee would account for the transaction as an operating lease, and the lessor would account for it as a direct-financing lease.

Lessees are normally well aware of the fair market cost of the assets they lease and they know the minimum lease payments and term of the lease. But they may not know the leased asset's residual value as of the end of the lease term (a value whose future amount is discounted by lessors), because lessees are not interested in buying this portion of the asset's value. If the residual value is not known, it can be further argued that the implicit interest rate used by the lessor may be impossible for the lessee to determine, in which case lessees use their incremental borrowing rate as described earlier.

The illustration here allowed the lessee to use a higher discount rate than the lessor's rate. If the lower lessor rate were known to the lessee, section 3065 requires the lessee to use the lower rate. Not only does this make it more likely the lessee will capitalize the lease, but it also prevents the lessee from understating the liability in the accounts if capitalization is required.

DEPRECIATION OF A LEASED ASSET BY THE LESSEE: CAPITAL LEASE

◆

The depreciable life and estimated value used by the lessee in computing periodic depreciation expense on a leased asset in a capital lease arrangement depend on the terms of the lease contract. If the lease does not contain a BPO or transfer ownership to the lessee at the end of the lease term (Criteria 1 and 2 in Exhibit 18–2), the period of depreciation must be the lease term rather than the total useful life of the leased property. In this case, the residual value must be ignored by the lessee if no residual value is guaranteed by the lessee. However, if the lessee does guarantee a residual value amount (either in total or in part), the guaranteed amount must be used by the lessee as the residual value.

If ownership of the leased asset is transferred from the lessor to the lessee at the end of the lease term or the lease contains a BPO, the lessee depreciates the capitalized cost over the total useful life of the leased asset to the lessee (rather than over the term of the lease). In this case, the lessee uses the estimated residual value as of the end of the asset's useful life (rather than as of the end of the lease term). The longer useful life and lower residual value are used in such cases because the parties assumed that the lessee will retain the asset after the end of the lease term. This assumption is required by section 3065 of the *CICA Handbook* when the lease contains a BPO or transfers ownership of the leased asset from the lessor to the lessee at the end of the lease term.

EXECUTORY AND INITIAL DIRECT COSTS

◆

Two kinds of lease costs incurred by the lessor are given special accounting treatment. They are executory costs and initial direct costs.

Executory Costs

Executory costs are expenses of ownership and use that include insurance, property taxes, and maintenance. In the case of an operating lease, the executory costs, typically, are paid by the lessor and are recovered by the lessor in the periodic lease rentals. In the case of a capital lease, a major part, if not all, of the executory costs usually are shifted by the lease contract for direct payment by the lessee. Therefore, they are not included in the periodic rentals. However, to the extent that the executory costs are incurred by the lessor and then added each year to the current lease payment, they should be excluded by the lessee in computing the present value of the periodic rentals for capitalization purposes. Instead, they should be reported by the lessee as an expense when incurred. If such executory costs are not known by the lessee at the time the current lease payment is made, they should be estimated.

Assume that the lessor in the original example agreed to insure the leased asset at a cost of $1,000 per year and then to bill the lessee. The current lease payment should then be $37,556. This amount is equal to the minimum lease rentals required to yield a 10% rate of return to the lessor ($36,556) plus the annual executory cost ($1,000). The executory costs are excluded by the lessee in computing the amount capitalized.

The interest revenue accruing to the lessor and the interest expense of the lessee are unaffected by the inclusion of executory costs since the $1,000 is paid directly to the insurer; thus, discounting would be inappropriate. Journal entries to reflect the annual executory costs incurred by the lessor on the date of the first rental are as follows:

January 1, 1991—First rental received:

Lessor:

Cash 37,556		
Lease receivable	36,556	
Insurance payable (or prepaid insurance if already paid) . . .	1,000	

Lessee:

Lease liability. 36,556		
Insurance expense (or prepaid insurance) 1,000		
Cash	37,556	

Initial Direct Costs

Initial direct costs are incremental costs incurred by the lessor in negotiating and consummating a lease agreement. They include legal fees, cost of credit and other investigations, commissions and employees' compensation directly related to initiating the lease, and clerical costs of preparing and processing the lease documents. These costs have no effect on the lessee's accounting.

In the case of an operating lease, the initial direct costs should be apportioned by the lessor over the lease term on a reasonable basis (usually straight-line) to match them with revenues that they helped earn. In the case of a direct-financing lease, initial direct costs, according to paragraph 3065.40 of the *CICA Handbook,* "should be expensed as incurred and a portion of the unearned income equal to the initial direct costs should be recognized in income in the same period." The remaining income is deferred and recognized over the lease term to produce a constant rate of return.

For instance, suppose the lease in the continuing example involved initial direct costs of $6,000. The lease is a direct financing lease to the lessor. The investment to be recovered is now $100,000 plus $6,000, or $106,000. The lessor's entries for the first year would be:

January 1, 1991—To record the lease:

Lease receivable 100,000		
Deferred expenses 6,000		
Asset.	100,000	
Cash	6,000	

January 1, 1991—First rental:

Cash 36,556		
Lease receivable	36,556	

December 3, 1991—To recognize interest earned and amortization of initial indirect expenses using the straight-line method:

Lease receivable 6,344		
Direct lease expense 2,000		
Interest revenue.	6,344	
Deferred expenses	2,000	

In the case of a sales-type lease, the initial direct costs should be expensed by the lessor in the year in which the lease is initiated (as an offset to manufacturer's or dealer's profit) because they are considered to be a selling expense in the year in which the manufacturer's or dealer's margin is recognized.

CONCEPT REVIEW

1. Explain why a (discounted) residual value fully guaranteed by a lessee is added to the lease obligation by the lessee but excluded if the guarantee is by a third party.
2. Under what conditions must the lessee use the lessor's implicit interest rate? Why does this requirement exist?
3. What are executory costs and why does the lessee exclude them from the present value calculation of the lease liability?

SALE-LEASEBACK ARRANGEMENTS
◆

When the owner of an asset sells it and immediately leases it back from the buyer, the transaction is called **sale-leaseback**. The use of the property continues without interruption. These transactions are subject to the provisions of paragraph 3065.65 to 3065.70 of the *CICA Handbook*. The characteristics of a typical sale-leaseback arrangement may be diagrammed for the seller-lessee and the buyer-lessor as follows:

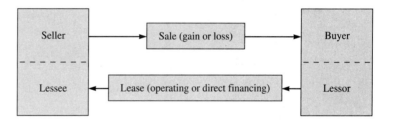

Typically, a sale-leaseback transaction involves a sale of the property at the approximate current market value and a long-term lease. The periodic rents are set to earn a realistic rate of interest on the sale price. The seller-lessee usually pays the executory costs.

The first advantage offered by a sale with a leaseback arrangement is that it allows the lessee to take a tax deduction for lease payments on leased assets. The inducements to lessors also are tax related, due to the investment tax credit (if provided in the income tax regulations) and early tax deductions for accelerated depreciation and interest expense on any debt used to finance the purchase of the asset for leasing.

A second advantage to the seller-lessee is the immediate cash inflow from the sale. Third, the sale may produce a gain, particularly if the asset is fully depreciated, that increases the seller-lessee's reported earnings. Fourth, the seller-lessee's lease payments may be reduced by the advantage of the new depreciation charges available to the buyer-lessor on the asset. (This amount may also be reflected in the purchase price.)

Under the provisions of section 3065, the lessor and lessee in a sale with a leaseback arrangement identify the lease as an operating or capital lease by applying the criteria listed in Exhibit 18–2. If the lease provisions satisfy one of the four criteria, the lease must be classified as a direct-financing lease (a sales-type lease is not permitted by section 3065). All other leases are classified as operating leases. Once the determination is made that the leaseback is an operating lease or a direct-financing lease, the accounting by the lessor is the same as illustrated earlier in this chapter. Sale with a leaseback arrangement poses a problem for the seller-lessee (they pose no special

EXHIBIT 18–15   Accounting for Sale-Leaseback: Operating Lease

Seller-Lessee			Buyer-Lessor		
January 1, 1991—Sale of warehouse:			January 1, 1991—Purchase of warehouse:		
Cash	95,000		Warehouse	95,000	
Warehouse (net).		80,000	Cash.		95,000
Unearned gain on SLB sale		15,000			
January 1, 1991—To record first lease payment:			January 1, 1991—To record first lease receipt:		
Rent expense	23,530		Cash.	23,530	
Cash		23,530	Rent revenue.		23,530
December 31, 1991—To record amortization of unrecognized gain:*			December 31, 1991—To record depreciation expense:		
Deferred gain on SLB sale	3,000		Depreciation expense.	19,000	
Rent expense		3,000	Accumulated depreciation		19,000
$15,000 ÷ 5 = $3,000.			$95,000 ÷ 5 = $19,000.		

* Straight-line method is used because equal payments are made each year.

problem for the buyer-lessor) in accounting for any gain or loss on the sale of the asset to the buyer-lessor. The problem arises because there is a high probability that the sale transaction and the leaseback transaction are not independent because the same two parties structure the two transactions. Without constraints, the seller-lessee could sell the asset to the buyer-lessor for an unrealistically high (or low) price purposely to report a gain (or loss) on the sale. The seller-lessee could then lease the asset back under an agreement with a present value equal to the sale price of the asset. On completion of both transactions, the seller-lessee would be in the same economic position if neither the sale nor the leaseback had occurred. However, a phantom gain or loss on the sale would have been reported. Because of these and other possibilities, the *CICA Handbook* specified detailed guidelines for seller-lessees.

Section 3065 treats sale-leaseback arrangements as though the two transactions were a single financing transaction in which any gain or loss on the sale is deferred and amortized by the seller-lessee. In this regard, paragraph 3065.68 states: "when the leaseback is classified as a capital lease, any profit or loss arising on the sale should be deferred and amortized in proportion to the amortization of the leased asset." An example to illustrate the deferral and amortization follows. It is based on these facts:

1. On January 1, 1991, the seller-lessee sells a warehouse to the buyer-lessor for $95,000; the warehouse had a carrying value on the seller-lessee's books of $80,000, an estimated remaining useful life of five years, and no residual value.
2. Both parties signed a five-year lease with a 12% implicit interest rate.
3. Annual lease payments start January 1, 1991.

First, it is assumed that the lease qualifies as an operating lease, and second, to the contrary, that the lease is a direct-financing capital lease for the lessor. These are the lease payments in either case:

$$\$95,000 \div (PVAD, 12\%, 5) = \$95,000 \div (4.03735) = \$23,530.$$

Exhibit 18–15 shows the seller-lessee's basic entries for a sale-leaseback arrangement for both parties assuming an operating lease. Exhibit 18–16 gives the entries and lease amortization schedule for a direct-financing lease for the lessor. In both cases the seller-lessee must defer recognition of the $15,000 gain on the sale of the asset. The gain is amortized with a year-end adjusting entry. Under the operating lease, the seller-lessee credits rent expense for the amortized portion of the deferred gain ($15,000 ÷ 5 years = $3,000). Under the direct-financing lease, the seller-lessee records the periodic amortization as a credit to depreciation expense. A credit to an

EXHIBIT 18–16   Accounting for Sale-Leaseback: Direct-Financing Lease for the Lessor and a Capital Lease for the Lessee

Seller-Lessee			Buyer-Lessor		
January 1, 1991—Sale of warehouse:			January 1, 1991—Purchase of warehouse:		
Cash	95,000		Warehouse	95,000	
Warehouse		80,000	Cash		95,000
Unearned gain on SLB sale		15,000			
January 1, 1991—To record capital lease:			January 1, 1991—To record direct financing lease:		
Leased asset	95,000		Lease receivable	95,000	
Lease liability		95,000	Warehouse (on lease)		95,000
January 1, 1991—Payment of first lease payment (see amortization schedule below):			January 1, 1991—Receipt of first lease payment:		
Lease liability	23,530		Cash	23,530	
Cash		23,530	Lease receivable		23,530
December 31, 1991—Adjusting entries: To record depreciation expense:					
Depreciation expense	19,000				
Accumulated depreciation ($95,000 ÷ 5)		19,000			
To record amortization of unrecognized gain:					
Unearned gain on SLB sale	3,000				
Depreciation expense		3,000	December 31, 1991—To record accrued interest on lease receivable:		
$15,000 ÷ 5 = $3,000.					
To record accrued interest on lease liability:*					
Interest expense	8,576		Lease receivable	8,576	
Lease liability		8,576	Interest revenue		8,576

*Lease Amortization Schedule (Annuity Due Basis)

Date	Annual Lease Payment	Annual Interest at 12%	Lease Receivable/Liability Decrease (Increase)	Receivable/Liability Balance
January 1, 1991				$95,000
January 1, 1991	$ 23,530		$23,530	71,470
December 31, 1991		$ 8,576	(8,576)	80,046
January 1, 1992	23,530		23,530	56,516
December 31, 1992		6,782	(6,782)	63,298
January 1, 1993	23,530		25,530	39,768
December 31, 1993		4,772	(4,772)	44,540
January 1, 1994	23,530		23,530	21,010
December 31, 1994		2,520	(2,520)	23,530
January 1, 1995	23,530		23,530	–0–
	$117,650	$22,650	$95,000	

expense account, rather than to a gain account, is consistent with the CICA's view that a sale-leaseback transaction essentially is a single transaction. Thus, deferral and amortization of the unearned gain usually is viewed as an adjustment to the seller-lessee's expense or revenue associated with the leased asset. Aside from these entries, the lessee accounts for the lease in the same way as previously illustrated.

Under a direct-financing lease, if there is a loss on the sale, the seller-lessee must recognize the loss on the date of sale. The loss is recognized immediately because the market value of the leased asset was less than the seller-lessee's carrying value, which is considered compelling evidence that the seller-lessee sustained a loss in value. The lessee's entries for the direct-financing lease are the same as previously illustrated. See Exhibit 18–16.

CLASSIFICATION OF LEASE RECEIVABLES AND PAYABLES

◆

When a lessor has lease receivables (and the lessee has lease payables) extending beyond one year (or the operating cycle of the business, if longer), the amount of the lease to be reported as a current asset by the lessor and as a current liability by the lessee must be determined. The lessor's total lease receivable, as well as the lessee's payable, should be reported, at their present value using the interest rate applied to the lease. The issue is to separate the current portion. There are two approaches: The first approach recognizes the present value of the next year's payment as the current portion. The second approach records the current year's decline in the lease receivable (payable) as the current portion.

To illustrate the classification of lease receivables (payables) for reporting purposes involving an annuity due, refer to the amortization schedule in Exhibit 18–4. The lease classification is illustrated from the perspective of the lessor's lease receivable. The same conclusions also apply to classification of the lessee's lease payable.

The first approach would report on December 31, 1991, the current receivable of $36,556, which is due January 1, 1992, as the current portion of the lease and $33,232 as the long-term portion. The second approach would report the decline in the lease during 1992, namely, $33,232 ($69,788 − $36,556), as the current portion. The latter method is the more common but the former is not proscribed under GAAP and may be found in financial reports.[24] The argument contained in the next paragraph may help explain why $33,232 is the portion of the lease treated as current for reporting.

At December 31, 1991, assuming the operating cycle is one year or less, the lessor has an upcoming lease receivable on January 1, 1992, of $36,556, collectible on January 1, 1992. The last receivable of $36,556 is collectible on January 1, 1993. These amounts must be reduced by any unearned interest included therein because interest is earned over the next period. For example, in 1992, $3,324 of interest revenue will be recognized and this amount must be deducted from the current portion of the 1991 lease receivable. The net lease receivable (current portion) after deducting unearned interest at December 31, 1991, is $33,232 ($36,556 − $3,324).

LEASE DISCLOSURE REQUIREMENTS

◆

CICA Handbook, section 3065 requires disclosure of many details concerning leasing arrangements in the financial statements or the accompanying notes. The primary lease disclosures are:

Lessee disclosures:

1. For capital leases (para. 3065.21–.28)
   a. *The gross amount of assets under capital leases and related accumulated amortization should be disclosed.* Disclosure of leased property and accumulated amortization by major category; for example, land, buildings, machinery, may be desirable.
   b. *Obligations related to leased assets should be shown separately from other long-term obligations. Particulars of obligations related to leased assets, including interest rates and expiry dates, should be shown separately from other long-term obligations. Significant restrictions imposed on the lessee as a result of the lease agreement should be disclosed.* It may be desirable to disclose the existence and

---

[24] For a discussion of these issues, see R. Swieringa, "When Current Is Noncurrent and Vice Versa!" *The Accounting Review,* January 1984, pp. 123–30, and A. Richardson, "The Measurement of the Current Portion of Long-Term Lease Obligations—Some Evidence from Practice," *The Accounting Review,* October 1985, pp. 744–52.

terms of renewal or purchase options that are not included in the computation of minimum lease payments.

    c. Any portion of lease obligations payable within a year out of current funds should be included in current liabilities.

    d. Disclosure should be made of the future minimum lease payments in aggregate and for each of the five succeeding years. A separate deduction should be made from the aggregate figures for amounts included in the minimum lease payments representing executory costs and imputed interest. The resultant net amount would be the balance of the unpaid obligation.

    e. The amount of amortization of leased property included in the determination of net income should be disclosed separately or as part of depreciation and amortization expense for fixed assets. Disclosure should also be made of methods and rates of amortization.

    f. Interest expense related to lease obligations should be disclosed separately, or as part of interest on long-term indebtedness. It may be desirable to disclose separately the amount of contingent rentals included in the determination of net income and to disclose the basis of determination of such rentals.

    g. To permit an assessment of commitments under lease obligations, it may be appropriate to disclose the amount of future minimum rentals receivable from noncancelable subleases.

2. For operating leases (par. 3065.32–.33)

    a. Disclosure should be made of the future minimum lease payments, in the aggregate and for each of the five succeeding years under operating leases. The nature of other commitments under such leases should also be described. Leases with an initial term of one year or less may be excluded from this disclosure requirement.

    b. It may be desirable to disclose the amount of operating lease rentals included in the determination of net income, the basis of determination of any contingent rentals, type of property leased, remaining term of lease, and existence and terms of renewal options and to segregate minimum rentals, contingent rentals, and sublease revenue.

Lessor disclosures (par. 3065.51–.54)

1. For sales-type and direct-financing leases:

    a. The net investment in the lease is considered to be distinct from other assets and disclosed separately.

    b. For purposes of statement presentation, the lessor's net investment in the lease would include:

        i. The minimum lease payments receivable, less any executory costs and related profit included therein; plus

        ii. Any unguaranteed residual value of the leased property accruing to the lessor; less

        iii. Unearned finance income remaining to be allocated to income over the lease term.

    c. When income tax factors have been considered in accounting for a direct-financing or sales-type lease, any unamortized investment tax credit would either be deducted in computing the net investment in the lease or shown as a deferred credit. Deferred income taxes, if any, relating to the net investment in the lease would be presented separately from the net investment.

    d. The lessor's net investment in direct-financing and sales-type leases should be disclosed and, in a classified balance sheet, segregated between current and long-term portions. Finance income from direct-financing or sales-type leases should be disclosed. Disclosure should be made of how the investment in leases has been computed for purposes of recognizing income. It may be desirable to disclose the aggregate future minimum lease payments receivable, unguaranteed residual value, unearned finance income, and executory costs included in minimum lease payments. Further desirable disclosure includes total contingent rentals taken into income, lease term, and amount of minimum lease payments receivable for each of the five succeeding years.

2. For operating leases (par. 3065.58–.59)

   a. *Disclosure should be made of the cost of property held for leasing purposes and the amount of accumulated depreciation.*

   b. *Rental income from operating leases should be disclosed.* Desirable disclosure with respect to operating leases may include minimum future rentals, in the aggregate and for each of the five succeeding years, and total contingent rentals included in income.

Firms usually provide information on their leases in the notes to financial statements section of the annual report. The information may differ depending on the extent of the leasing activity in which the enterprise engages. Two examples follow:

ELECTROHOME LIMITED

Notes to Consolidated Financial Statements

Year Ended December 29, 1989

9. Fixed assets	1989	1988
	(*in thousands*)	
Land	$ 2,358	$ 2,358
Buildings	20,620	12,652
Machinery and equipment	38,787	38,558
Tooling	1,692	1,497
	63,457	55,065
Accumulated depreciation	34,434	31,655
	$29,023	$23,410
Included in the amounts are assets under capital leases as follows:		
Cost	$ 3,362	$ 3,342
Accumulated depreciation	2,042	1,771
	$ 1,320	$ 1,571

11. Bank advances and long-term debt (in part)

The following is a schedule of future minimum lease payments under capital and operating leases together with the present value of the net lease payments at December 29, 1989:

	Capital leases	Operating leases
	(*in thousands*)	
1990	$ 457	$ 841
1991	402	615
1992	154	473
1993	102	389
1994	55	370
1995 to 2004	467	838
Total minimum lease payments	1,637	$3,526
Less amount representing interest	399	
Present value of net minimum lease payments	$1,238	

Of the present value of net minimum lease payments $341,000 is due in 1990 and is included in principal due within one year on long-term debt.

INTERNATIONAL SEMI-TECH MICROELECTRONICS INC.

Notes to Consolidated Financial Statements January 31, 1990

3. Fixed Assets

At January 31, fixed assets were comprised of (in thousands):

	1990	1989
Land and buildings	$ 27,288	$ 20,917
Machinery and equipment	33,182	43,975
Other equipment	4,963	4,511
Furniture and fixtures	4,162	5,299
Leasehold improvements	3,490	13,465
	73,085	88,167
Accumulated depreciation and amortization	(21,197)	(14,228)
	$ 51,888	$ 73,939

Included in machinery and equipment are capitalized leases for equipment with a cost of $12,570,000 (1989—$13,687,000) and accumulated amortization of $5,982,000 (1989—$3,827,000).

6. Long-Term Debt

(b) Obligations under capital and operating leases

The following is a schedule by year of future minimum lease payments together with the balance of the obligations under leases (in thousands):

Fiscal Year	Capital Leases	Operating Leases
1991	$ 3,526	$25,920
1992	2,733	17,274
1993	1,555	8,771
1994	581	5,488
1995	131	3,046
Thereafter	—	6,344
	8,526	66,843
Amount representing interest	(1,167)	—
	7,359	$66,843
Less: current portion	(2,877)	
	$ 4,482	

An Unresolved Issue Many financial institutions have structured leases so the lessor could treat the transaction as a sale or financing lease while the lessee could treat the lease as an operating lease, keeping the debt an off-balance-sheet item.[25] The effect on lessee debt equity ratios can be substantial as indicated at the start of this chapter. Capitalization also increases expenses because book depreciation plus interest exceed the operating lease payment in the early years of the lease, generally without any mitigating tax benefit.

Just how this works was covered in the discussion of residual values and interest rates. It is relatively easy to avoid any mention of transferring asset ownership, Criterion 1. To avoid selling the property at a bargain price, Criterion 2, the lessor amortizes the debt incurred to buy the asset at the same rate that its value is expected to decline. To ensure that the asset fails the 75% test, Criterion 3, the lessee usually signs a short-term lease.

---

[25] Banks and other financial institutions, when acting as lessors, normally prefer (if not insist) that leases be structured as direct-financing leases and not operating leases. The logic behind this preference is the fact that banks are in the business of financing the acquisition of business assets (direct-financing lease) and not owning assets rented out to businesses (operating leases). Also, direct-financing leases tend to be more profitable for banks and other lenders than is the case with operating leases. This is due primarily to the simpler, cleaner nature of the lease-servicing work involved in a direct-financing lease.

The most difficult criterion to overcome is Criterion 4, which requires that the present value of the payments exceed 90% of the asset's fair value. This criterion requires ingenuity to defeat. Use of a guaranteed residual value put up by a third party and assured use of the lessee's incremental borrowing rate by keeping the lessor's interest rate unknown to the lessee are the primary means of keeping the lease payments under the 90% level and, hence, keeping the lease off the lessee's books.[26] Third party guarantees of residual values are included in the payment calculations by the lessor (but are excluded by the lessee) and thereby lower the lessor's implicit interest rate. However, if the guaranteed residual value by the third party is unknown to the lessee, the lessee will not be able to calculate the lessor's implicit rate. A higher discount rate for the lessee lowers the present value of the rental payments; thus, the 90% test can be circumvented.

Whenever very specific rules have been set down by accounting policy makers, the game has become how to beat the rules. Usually clever individuals can devise means of doing so, and the lease situation is an example. Many accountants believe that most, if not all, leases should be capitalized. In general, they do not agree with the current situation. Businesspeople, on the other hand, see no advantage in changing the current rules under which they have grown accustomed to operating.[27] Indeed, businesses can be expected to resist recording additional lease liabilities on their financial statements.

Professional judgment must be used by accountants when they encounter innovative lease contracts. The form of the contract may indeed indicate an operating lease for the lessee. However, if the substance of the contract is, in fact, a capital lease, the lease should be accounted for as such. This substance over form argument is not uncommon when the provisions of the *CICA Handbook* are interpreted and applied by professional accountants.

CONCEPT REVIEW

1. Why would the owner of an asset be interested in selling the asset and then leasing it back?
2. Is the discounted value of the next year's payment typically shown as the current portion of a lessee's liability? Why or why not?
3. What are the main disclosure requirements for capital and operating leases?

SUMMARY OF KEY POINTS

◆

(L.O. 1)   1. A lease is an agreement that conveys the right from the lessor to a lessee to use property, plant, or equipment, usually for a stated period of time.

(L.O. 1)   2. Leasing is popular because it conserves cash, protects against obsolescence and interest rate changes, and may provide a means of excluding the liability from the balance sheet.

(L.O. 1)   3. Lessees prefer to keep leases off their balance sheets to minimize the extent of their reported liabilities on the balance sheet. Doing so also makes their debt ratios (such as debt to equity) appear smaller. Lessors, on the other hand, prefer to treat

---

[26] Third party guarantors, in effect, insure the market value of a leased asset. For a fee, they assume the risk that, for whatever reason, the asset's residual value at the end of the lease term will fall short of the original estimate made at the outset of the lease. Insurance losses for third party guarantors can be substantial, as Lloyd's of London (a consortium of insurance companies) found out with its guarantee business in the computer-leasing field.

[27] See R. Abdel-khalik, "The Economic Effects on Lessees of *FASB Statement 13, 'Accounting for Leases,'*" Research Report (Norwalk, Conn.: FASB, 1981).

leases as sale or financing capital leases. In other words, lessees prefer to follow the accounting for operating leases, while lessors prefer to follow the accounting for capital leases. This preference for a lack of accounting symmetry was what the CICA wished to avoid. However, clever structuring of leases leads to this asymmetric result.

(L.O. 2)   4. For accounting purposes, a lease agreement is considered to be either an operating lease or a capital lease.

(L.O. 3)   5. An operating lease is equivalent to a rental agreement. The lessee pays a periodic fee for use of the asset. This fee is revenue to the lessor. The asset remains the property of the lessor, who depreciates the asset's cost.

(L.O. 3)   6. The lessee treats a lease as a capital lease if it meets any one of the following four criteria: (1) the lease transfers ownership, (2) the lease contains a bargain purchase offer, (3) the lease term equals or exceeds 75% of the estimated economic life of the asset, and (4) the present value of the minimum lease payments equals or exceeds 90% of the fair market value of the leased asset.

(L.O. 3)   7. The lessor treats the lease as a capital lease if in addition to satisfying any one of the criteria for the lessee (see Key Point 6), it meets two additional criteria: (1) collectibility of all rentals is reasonably assured, and (2) future costs are reasonably predictable or the lessor's performance is substantially complete.

(L.O. 3)   8. The lessor treats a capital lease as a sale if a profit accrues (the present value of the receivable obtained exceeds the carrying value of the transferred asset). Otherwise, the lease is accounted for as a financing agreement, and the lessor recognizes only interest revenue.

(L.O. 4)   9. A capital-asset lease is a means of financing an asset acquisition that ultimately belongs to the lessee. The asset is removed from the books of the lessor and entered on the books of the lessee. The lessee also recognizes a liability for the contract lease payments and recognizes depreciation on the asset. The asset is removed from the lessor's books. The periodic payment by the lessee represents payment on principal and interest of the loan to the lessor. Present values are used.

(L.O. 5)   10. A direct-financing lease for the lessor results in removing the asset from the lessor's books. Revenue is earned through interest over the lease life.

(L.O. 5)   11. A sales-type lease to the lessor results in removing the asset from the lessor's books. Revenue is earned at the inception of the lease equal to the difference between the value of the lease and the carrying value of the leased asset on the lessor's books. Interest revenue is also earned over the lease life.

(L.O. 6)   12. Since lessees capitalize only the residual values they guarantee while lessors capitalize all residual values, provisions for guarantees of the residual value by a third party can result in a lease being accounted for as an operating lease by the lessee and as a capital lease by the lessor. This asymmetric result can also be obtained if the lessee uses a different (and higher) interest rate than the lessor.

(L.O. 7)   13. A sale-leaseback arrangement is an agreement in which the seller-lessee sells an asset and then continues to use the asset. The seller-lessee obtains cash while incurring a tax-deductible lease payment. The buyer-lessor receives the lease payments, depreciates the asset for tax purposes, and also may deduct for purposes any interest on debt used to finance the asset purchase. The seller-lessee accounts for the transaction as a sale and for the lease as a capital lease. The buyer-lessor accounts for the transaction as a purchase and the lease as a direct-financing lease.

(L.O. 8)   14. The portion of a lessee's lease liability typically reported as current is the decline in the present value of the total lease obligation that occurs during the operating period.

(L.O. 8)   15. Lease disclosure requirements for both lessees and lessors are extensive and include data on payments to be made and descriptions of lease agreements for both capital and operating leases.

**REVIEW
PROBLEM**

◆

Orion leased a computer to the Lenox Silver Company on January 1, 1991, under these terms:

1. Lease term (fixed and noncancelable) . . . . 3 years
2. Estimated economic life of the equipment . . . . 5 years
3. Fair market value at lease inception $5,000
4. Lessor's cost of asset $5,000
5. Bargain purchase offer. . . . . None
6. Transfer of title . . . . No
7. Guaranteed residual value by lessee (excess to lessee)
   January 1, 1994. . . . . $2,000
8. Lessee's normal depreciation method. . . . . Straight-line
9. Lessee's incremental borrowing rate 11%
10. Executory costs . . . . None
11. Initial indirect costs . . . . None
12. Collectibility of rental payments . . . . Assured
13. Peformance by lessor . . . . Complete
14. Annual rental (1st payment, January 1, 1991). $1,620
15. Lessor's implicit interest rate. . . . . Unknown
                                                              to lessee
16. Unguaranteed residual value (known only to lessor). . . . . None

Required:

1. Determine what type of lease this is for the lessee.
2. Determine what type of lease this is for the lessor.
3. Provide entries for the lessee and the lessor from January 1, 1991, through January 1, 1992.
4. Provide entries for the lessee and the lessor if the asset is disposed of for $2,100 by the lessee on January 1, 1994. Assume interest has been accrued on December 31.

**REVIEW
SOLUTION**

◆

1. Discounting the minimum lease payments, which include the guaranteed residual value of $2,000, yields:

$$\$1,620(PVAD, 11\%, 3) + \$2,000(PV1, 11\%, 3)$$

$$= \$1,620(2.71252) + \$2,000(.73119) = \$5,857$$

The lease qualifies as a capital lease to the lessee because the present value of the minimum lease payments, $5,857, exceeds 90% of the fair value of the leased property at the time of the lease inception (Criterion 4). It does not satisfy any of the first three criteria. In this case, the lessor's implicit rate could not be used because it is unknown to the lessee. But even if it were known (or were estimated, assuming the lessee knew there was no unguaranteed residual value) and, to be used by the lessee, it was lower than 11%, the present value of the minimum lease payments would be even greater. (Lower discount rates increase present values.) Thus, this lease would still qualify as a capital lease to the lessee.

2. The lessor is constrained to record the lease at the asset's fair market value at the time of the lease's inception, $5,000. This is also the revenue to the lessor. Because in this case the revenue recognized equals the carrying cost of the asset on the lessor's books, there is no immediate profit on the transaction. This is a direct-financing lease to the lessor.

3. **Lessee entries:**

January 1, 1991—Inception of lease:

Leased asset 5,000
  Lease liability   5,000

The lessee is also constrained to enter the lower of the discounted payments or the fair market value.

December 31, 1991—Accrual of interest:

Interest expense ($5,000 − $1,620)(.2455)   830
    Lease liability   830

The interest rate used here is 24.55% and is found by solving:

$$\$1,620(PVAD, i, 3) + \$2,000(PV1, i, 3) = \$5,000$$

for the interest rate.

The lessee must use the rate that equates the lease payments to the recorded value of the leased asset, here constrained to the market value of $5,000 because it is less than $5,857, the discounted minimum lease payments.

December 31, 1991—To recognize depreciation expense:

Depreciation expense 1,000
    Accumulated depreciation [($5,000 − $2,000) ÷ 3]   1,000

Because the lease is a capital lease due to Criterion 4, and the asset reverts to the lessor, the asset is depreciated over the life of the lease.

January 1, 1992—second rental payment:

Lease liability. 1,620
    Cash   1,620

Lessor entries:

January 1, 1991—To record sale:

Lease receivable 5,000
    Assets   5,000

January 1, 1991—To record first payment:

Cash 1,620
    Lease receivable   1,620

December 31, 1991—To record interest earned:

Lease receivable   830
    Interest revenue.   830

January 1, 1992—To record second payment:

Cash 1,620
    Lease receivable   1,620

4. Entries on disposal of asset:
  Lessee:
  January 1, 1994—To recognize disposal of asset:

Cash   100
Lease liability. 2,000
Accumulated depreciation. 3,000
    Leased asset   5,000
    Gain on disposition.   100

The lessee is assumed to sell the asset for $2,100 and to retain the $100 excess.

Lessor:

January 1, 1994—To recognize receipt of payment:

Cash 2,000
    Lease receivable   2,000

While the question did not ask what entries would be made if the lease had been an operating lease, so as not to imply the answers to requirements (1) and (2), they are shown next for 1991 only.

Lessee:

January 1, 1991 — To record the first payment:

Rent expense	1,620	
Cash		1,620

Although the lessee is owed the rent service at this moment, the service will be fulfilled by year's end and thus the amount may be debited to the expense now.

Lessor:

January 1, 1991 — To record the first payment:

Cash	1,620	
Lease revenue		1,620

Although the lessor has not earned the revenue as of January 1, it will be earned by the end of the fiscal year and thus may be credited to revenue now. The lessor would also recognize depreciation at this time. Data to establish the depreciation amount were not provided.

APPENDIX 18A: Leases Involving Real Estate

Leases involving real estate are subject to several special accounting rules. These leases can be separated into three categories: (1) land only, (2) land and buildings, and (3) equipment as well as real estate.

Leases Involving Land Only

If land only is leased, and either (*a*) ownership transfers to the lessee at the end of the lease term, or (*b*) the lease contains a bargain purchase option (Criterion 1 or 2 in Exhibit 18–2), the lessee must account for it as a capital lease. If collectibility of the minimum lease payments is reasonably assured and no important uncertainties remain regarding the unreimbursable costs to be incurred by the lessor, the lessor also must account for it as a capital lease (either sales-type or direct-financing, depending on the circumstances). Criteria 3 and 4 of Exhibit 18–2 are not involved in determining the nature of a lease for land only.

Leases Involving Land and Buildings

If a lease that involves both land and buildings satisfies either Criterion 1 or 2 of Exhibit 18–2, the lessee must account for it as a capital lease and allocate the capitalized value of the minimum lease payments between the land and buildings based on their relative market value at the inception of the lease. If the lease also meets the additional criteria for the lessor, the lessor must account for it as a single unit (and thus does not allocate the capitalized value of the lease payments) either as a direct-financing or sales-type lease, depending on the circumstances.

The accounting for a lease involving land and buildings that does not meet either criterion 1 or 2 depends on the relative market values of the land and buildings at the inception of the lease. This situation involves either: Case A (the market value of the land is an insignificant proportion of the total market value of the leased property), or Case B (the market value of the land is a significant proportion of the total market value of the leased property.)

Case A—If the market value of the land is an insignificant proportion of the total market value of the property leased, both lessor and lessee must consider the land and buildings as a single unit in applying criteria 3 and 4 of Exhibit 18–2. If either of these criteria is met, the lessee treats the lease as a capital lease; otherwise, it is treated as an operating lease. If the lease meets either criterion 3 or 4 and both criteria for the lessor, the lessor treats the lease as a single capital lease.

Case B—If the market value of the land is a significant proportion of the value of the leased property, both lessee and lessor consider land and building separately when applying criteria 3 and 4. Lease payments associated with land are determined by applying the lessee's incremental borrowing rate to the market value of the land. The remaining lease payments are allocated to the buildings. If the lease associated with the building meets criterion 3 or 4, the lessee accounts for it as a capital lease. If, in addition, it meets the criteria for the lessor, the lessor also accounts for it as a capital lease. The land portion of the lease is accounted for as an operating lease because it satisfies neither criterion 1 nor 2.

Leases Involving Real Estate and Equipment

If a lease involves both equipment and real estate, the portion of the lease payments applicable to the equipment is estimated by whatever means are appropriate in the circumstances. The equipment portion of the lease then is separately subject to Criteria 1 through 4 for the lessee and all six criteria for the lessor. The real estate portion of the lease is accounted for as described under the two immediately preceding captions.

APPENDIX 18B: *More on Tax Considerations*

Although this is not a course in taxation, a few additional remarks are appropriate because tax considerations are an important factor in many leasing arrangements.

For any number of reasons the lessee may be unable to use the tax benefits provided in purchasing an asset—namely, depreciation, interest on debt incurred in connection with the acquisition, and the investment tax credit when available. While such a company may be in the market to acquire new assets, it may be that the company is in a growth phase and has little or no taxable income against which tax benefits could be applied. Chances are that such a company probably has operating losses being carried forward from previous years. Also, such companies tend to be short on cash and must borrow heavily to finance new asset acquisitions. If so, the company has ample internal means for sheltering future taxable income; tax benefits from leasing would go to waste.

But tax benefits that the lessee can't use might be extremely valuable to some other company that has a large cash position and is reporting high levels of taxable income. Such a company is probably in the market for tax savings. The solution, of course, is to match the cash-poor company (in the market to acquire assets) with the cash-rich company (in the market for tax savings). Then the task is structuring a lease transaction that meets both parties' needs. The wealthy company with high taxable income becomes the lessor and retains the tax benefits that otherwise would be passed on to the lessee. The needy company benefits by negotiating lease rental terms below the going market rate. Generally, the lessor-company is happy to accommodate the lessee company in exchange for retention of the tax benefits involved.

By allowing the use of accelerated depreciation methods (i.e., capital cost allowances), some accountants point out that Revenue Canada makes tax incentives more attractive and thereby encourages leasing transactions. Similarly, the existence and extent to which the Income Tax Act allows investment tax credits to be taken also works in favour of leasing. These are just two examples of the many ways in which Revenue Canada influences economic activity levels and promotes tax-oriented business transactions, some of which have little meaningful economic gain attached to them.

KEY TERMS

Bargain purchase option (BPO) (872)	Lessee (864)
Bargain renewal option (884)	Lessee's incremental borrowing rate (882)
Capital lease (865)	Lessor (864)
Direct-financing lease (868)	Minimum lease payments (872)
Estimated residual value (884)	Off-balance-sheet financing (867)
Executory costs (893)	Operating lease (865)
Implicit interest rate (875)	Sale-leaseback (895)
Initial direct costs (894)	Sales-type lease (868)
Lease (864)	Unguaranteed residual value (885)
Lease term (882)	

QUESTIONS

1. Match the following items with the numbered statements by entering one letter in each blank space.

   A. Lessor; B. Capital lease; C. Operating lease; D. Lessee.
   _____ (1) Contract in which lessor finances property leased.
   _____ (2) Lender in a lease contract transaction.
   _____ (3) Tenant in a lease contract transaction.
   _____ (4) Type of lease that requires capitalization.
   _____ (5) Type of lease that does not require capitalization.
   _____ (6) Property owner in a lease contract transaction during the lease term.

   Questions 2 and 3 are based on the following information (briefly explain your choices):
      Marne Company purchased a machine for leasing purposes on January 1, 1991, for $1 million. The machine has a 10-year life, no residual value, and will be depreciated on a straight-line basis. On March 1, 1991, Marne leased the machine to Dal Company for $400,000 a year for a five-year period ending February 28, 1996. During the year ended December 31, 1991, Marne incurred normal maintenance and other related expenses of $25,000 under the provisions of this assumed operating lease. Dal paid $400,000 to Marne on March 1, 1991.
2. Assuming an operating lease, what was the income before income taxes derived by Marne from this lease for the year ended December 31, 1991?
   a. $229,167.   c. $160,000.
   b. $291,667.   d. $225,000.
3. What was rent expense for Dal from this lease for the year ended December 31, 1991?
   a. $225,000.   c. $400,000.
   b. $120,000.   d. $333,333.
4. Give the primary GAAP concepts of accounting for an operating lease by lessors and lessees.
5. Advance rental payments often are received under operating lease contracts that extend well beyond a single fiscal year. Give the acceptable accounting procedures that should be used for advance rentals.
6. What is meant by capitalization of a lease from the view of the lessee?
7. From a lessee's standpoint, leases are classified as capital or operating leases. Which criteria identify a capital lease?
8. From a lessor's view, a capital lease involves two types of leases. Identify the types and distinguish between them.
9. Briefly define the following terms related to capital leases (refer to the technical definitions):
   a. Lease term.
   b. Bargain purchase option.
   c. Bargain renewal option.
   d. Minimum lease payments from the standpoint of the lessee.
   e. Minimum lease payments from the standpoint of the lessor.
   f. Interest rate implicit in the lease.
10. How does a lessee determine what interest rate is appropriate for capitalization of a lease?
11. How does an unguaranteed residual value in a sales-type lease affect the lessor's accounting in recording the entries at date of inception of the lease?
12. Briefly explain how inclusion of a provision of residual value guaranteed by a third party in a capital lease can result in asymmetric accounting by lessor and lessee.
13. Define initial direct costs.
14. Define executory costs.
15. When computing annual depreciation, what residual value should the lessee use for a leased asset under a capital lease? Briefly explain each alternative.

EXERCISES

E 18–1
Operating Lease:
Leasehold Costs, Entries
(L.O. 3)

Arrow Company signed an operating lease contract effective for five years from January 1, 1991. Arrow is to pay $40,000 at the start of the lease plus $6,000 monthly rentals throughout the lease term. During January 1991, Arrow spent $20,000 renovating the property leased and also built an addition to the leased property with the lessor's consent at a cost of $80,000. The estimated life of the addition is 20 years, and its residual value is zero. The lease contract does not contain a renewal option and may be terminated by the lessee with six months' notice.

Required:

Give all entries on Arrow's books to reflect the renovation outlays, leasehold, and rental payments for 1991 and entries at the end of 1991, assuming Arrow's accounting year is the calendar year. The straight-line method of amortization is to be used.

E 18–2
Explain Distinctions:
Capital versus Operating,
Direct-Financing versus
Sales-Type Leases
(L.O. 1, 2)

Part A

Capital leases and operating leases are the two classifications of leases described in the *CICA Handbook,* from the standpoint of the lessee.

Required:

1. Describe how a capital lease would be accounted for by the lessee both at the inception of the lease and during the first year of the lease; assume the lease transfers ownership of the property to the lessee by the end of the lease term.
2. Describe how an operating lease would be accounted for by the lessee both at the inception of the lease and during the first year of the lease; assume equal monthly payments are made by the lessee at the beginning of each month of the lease. Do not discuss the criteria for distinguishing between capital leases and operating leases.

Part B

Sales-type leases and direct-financing leases are two of the classifications of leases described in the *CICA Handbook,* from the standpoint of the lessor.

Required:

Compare and contrast a sales-type lease with a direct-financing lease as follows:

1. Net investment in the lease.
2. Recognition of interest revenue.
3. Manufacturer's or dealer's profit.

Do not discuss the criteria for distinguishing between the leases described earlier and operating leases.

E 18–3
Lease: Apply Lease
Criteria, Entries for Lessor
and Lessee
(L.O. 2, 4, 5)

Kim Leasing Company agreed with Lee Corporation to provide the latter with equipment under lease for a three-year period. The equipment cost Kim $40,000 and will have no residual value when the lease term ends. Kim expects to collect all rentals from Lee and has no material cost uncertainties. The carrying value of the equipment was $40,000 at the inception of the lease. The three equal annual rents (amount to be determined) are to be paid each January 1, starting January 1, 1991, at which time the equipment was delivered. Lee has agreed to pay taxes, maintenance, and insurance throughout the lease term as well as any other ownership costs. Kim expects a 20% return (known to Lee). The accounting year of both companies ends December 31.

Required:
Round to the nearest dollar.

1. What kind of lease is this to Lee? To Kim?
2. Compute the annual rentals and prepare an amortization schedule reflecting the interest and principal elements of Lee's payments over the three-year term of the lease. Give all journal entries relating to the lease for Lee Corporation for 1991 including year-end adjusting entries.
3. Give all journal entries for Kim Leasing Company relating to the lease for 1991 including year-end adjusting entries.

E 18–4
Lease: Financing or Sales
Type, Schedule, Entries for
Lessor
(L.O. 2, 5)

Brown Company uses leases as a secondary means of selling its products. The company contracted with Blue Corporation to lease a machine to be used by Blue as an operational asset. The retail market value of the asset at the inception of the lease was $50,000; it cost Brown $40,000 and is carried in its inventory at that value. Payments of $11,231 are to be made by Blue at the end of each of five quarters following inception of the lease. Brown's implicit interest rate is 4% per quarter, which is known by Blue. The lease qualified as a capital lease for both parties.

Required:

Round to the nearest dollar.

1. Classify the lease and show how the $11,231 rental payment was computed and prepare an amortization schedule for use by Brown covering the five-quarter term of the lease.
2. Give Brown's journal entries at the inception of the lease and on receipt of the first payment. Assume the first receipt coincides with the end of Brown's accounting year.

E 18–5
Lease: Financing or
Sales-Type, Schedule and
Entries, Lessor and Lessee
(L.O. 2, 4, 5)

MPI Corporation (lessor) and JRD Company (lessee) agreed to a noncancelable lease. The following information is available regarding the lease terms and the leased asset:

a. MPI's cost of the leased asset, $60,000. The asset was new at lease inception date.
b. Lease term, four years, beginning January 1, 1991. Lease rental payments are made each January 1, beginning January 1, 1991.
c. Estimated useful life of leased asset, four years. Estimated residual value at end of lease, zero.
d. Sales price of leased asset on January 1, 1991, $66,000.
e. MPI's implicit interest rate, 15% on retail price (known to JRD).
f. MPI expects to collect all rentals from JRD, and there are no material cost uncertainties.

Required:

1. What kind of lease is this to MPI? To JRD?
2. Compute the annual lease rentals.
3. Prepare an amortization schedule for the lease.
4. Give the journal entries for both parties on January 1, 1991, and December 31, 1991. Do not make closing entries.

E 18–6
Lease: Analysis of Dealer's
Profit or Loss
(L.O. 2, 4, 5)

Hardin Company is an equipment dealer who sometimes uses leasing as a means to sell its products. On January 1, 1991, Hardin leased equipment to Wesley Corporation. The lease term was four years, with annual lease payments of $6,769 to be paid on each December 31. The equipment has an estimated zero residual value at the end of the lease term. The equipment was carried on Hardin's accounts at a cost of $24,000. Hardin expects to collect all rentals from Wesley, and there were no material cost uncertainties at inception of the lease. The implicit interest rate on the lease was 11% on the selling price (known to Wesley).

Required:

1. What kind of lease is this to Hardin? To Wesley?
2. What is the cost of the equipment to Wesley?
3. What is the dealer's profit or loss recognized by Hardin?
4. Assume the implicit interest rate is 4% (not 11%). What is the dealer's profit or loss recognized by Hardin?
5. Give the entries (based on the 11% rate) at date of inception of the lease for each party.

E 18–7
Overview of Special Lease
Cases: Provide
Explanations
(L.O. 6, 8)

Select the best answer in each of the following. Justify each choice that you make.

1. On the first day of its accounting year, Lessor, Inc., leased certain property at an annual rental of $100,000 receivable at the beginning of each year for 10 years. The first payment was received immediately. The leased property, which is new, cost $550,000 and has an estimated useful life of 12 years and no residual value. Lessor's implicit rate is 12%. Lessor had no other costs associated with this lease. Lessor should have accounted for this lease as a sales-type lease but mistakenly treated the lease as an operating lease. What was the effect on net income during the first year of the lease by having treated this lease as an operating lease rather than as a sales-type lease?
   a. No effect.
   b. Overstated.
   c. Understated.
   d. The effect depends on the accounting method selected for income tax purposes.
2. The appropriate valuation of leased assets under an operating lease on the balance sheet of a lessee is as follows:
   a. Zero.
   b. The absolute sum of the lease payments.

    c. The sum of the present values of the lease payments discounted at an appropriate rate.

    d. The market value of the asset at the date of the inception of the lease.

3. What are the three types of expenses that a lessee experiences with capital leases?

    a. Lease expense, interest expense, amortization expense.

    b. Interest expense, amortization expense, executory costs.

    c. Amortization expense, executory costs, lease expense.

    d. Executory costs, interest expense, lease expense.

4. When measuring the present value of future rentals to be capitalized in connection with a capital lease, identifiable payments to cover taxes, insurance, and maintenance should be accounted for as follows:

    a. Included with the future rentals to be capitalized.

    b. Excluded from future rentals to be capitalized.

    c. Capitalized, but at a different rate and recorded in a different account than future rentals.

    d. Capitalized, but at a different rate and during a different period from the rate and period used for the future rental payments.

5. GAAP requires that certain lease agreements be accounted for as purchases. The theoretical basis for this treatment is that a lease of this type:

    a. Effectively conveys most of the benefits and risks incident to the ownership of property.

    b. Is an example of form over substance.

    c. Provides the use of the leased asset to the lessee for a limited time.

    d. Must be recorded in accordance with the concept of cause and effect.

6. Your client constructed an office building at a cost of $500,000 and then sold this building to Jones for a large gain. The client leased it back from Jones for a stipulated annual rental. How should this gain be treated?

    a. Recognized in full as an ordinary item in the year of the transaction.

    b. Recognized in full as an extraordinary item in the year of the transaction.

    c. Amortized as an adjustment of the rental cost, an ordinary item, over the life of the lease.

    d. Amortized as an extraordinary item over the life of the lease.

(AICPA adapted)

E 18–8
Direct-Financing Lease with BPO: Schedule, Entries for Lessor
(L.O. 5, 6)

Lessor Santi and Lessee Thomas contract for the lease of a machine for six rentals of $6,000 each. The first $6,000 rental is to be paid at the inception of the lease, and $6,000 is to be paid at the start of each of five quarters thereafter. They also agree that at the time of the sixth payment, for an added $6,930 bargain purchase option payment, Thomas can buy the property. The interest rate is 2.5% per quarter. The lease qualifies as a direct-financing lease.

Required:
Round to the nearest dollar.

1. Calculate the lease payments and prepare an amortization schedule for the lease covering the six-quarter term.
2. Give the lessor's entries at the inception of the lease and at the time of the sixth payment if the lessee exercises the purchase option. Assume a direct-financing lease.

E 18–9
Direct-Financing Lease with BPO
(L.O. 4, 5)

Flint Company leased a computer to Land Company for a five-year period. Flint paid $46,965 for the computer (estimated useful life five years, no residual value). The lease started on January 1, 1991, and qualifies as a direct-financing lease to the lessor and a capital lease to the lessee. Flint uses a target rate of return of 14% in all lease contracts. The first rental payment was on January 1, 1991, and the accounting periods end on December 31.

Required:

1. Compute the annual rental for the lessor and the amount to be capitalized for the lessee. The computer reverts to the lessor at the end of the lease term.
2. Now assume, instead, that the lease contract contains a BPO which states that Land Company can purchase the computer on December 31, 1994, for $14,000, at which time its estimated residual value is $17,500. Compute the annual rental for the lessor and the amount to be capitalized for the lessee. Show whether the BPO is really a bargain.
3. Give the entries at the inception date under (1) and (2) for the lessor and lessee.

E 18–10
Financing Lease:
Unguaranteed Residual
Value, Schedules, Ordinary
and Annuity Due
(L.O. 5)

The present value to a lessor of a lease on which the lessee is obligated to make a $20,000 payment at the end of each of the next three years and on which there is an unguaranteed residual value of $4,000 at the end of the lease term is $49,133 if the lessor's implicit interest rate is 14%. The lease qualifies as a direct-financing lease.

Required:
Round amounts to the nearest dollar.

1. Prepare an amortization schedule for the lessor covering the three-year lease term.
2. Compute the present value of a similar lease, assuming the lessor's implicit rate is 12%. Prepare an amortization schedule similar to the one required in (1).
3. Assume instead that each of the three $20,000 annual payments is paid at the beginning of each year, in advance, and that the $4,000 residual value is expected at end of the lease term of three years. What is the present value of the lease payments at 14%? Prepare the lessor's amortization schedule for this lease.

E 18–11
Sales-Type Lease:
Unguaranteed Residual
Value, Inception Entries
(L.O. 2, 4, 5, 6)

On January 1, 1991, ABC Company signed a lease contract with Abel Company. The leased asset cost ABC $45,000 and had a normal selling price of $55,000. Three annual rentals, based on selling price, are payable by Abel on January 1, beginning in 1991. The asset reverts to ABC at the end of the lease term, December 31, 1993, and is estimated to have an unguaranteed residual value on that date of $3,000. ABC's implicit interest rate is 12%, which is known to Abel.

Required:
1. What type of lease is this for ABC?
2. Compute the annual lease rentals.
3. Give the lessor's entry on January 1, 1991.
4. Give the lessee's entry on January 1, 1991.

E 18–12
Guaranteed Residual Value
by Third Party: Lessor,
Direct-Financing, and
Lessee, Operating
(L.O. 2, 6)

Mike Leasing Company (lessor) and Ash Corporation (lessee) signed a four-year lease on January 1, 1991. The leased property cost Mike $50,000, which was also its carrying value at inception of the lease. The leased asset had an estimated useful life of six years and the property reverts to Mike at the end of the lease term. Lease payments of $12,830 are payable on January 1 of each year and were set to yield Mike a return of 12%, which was known to Ash. The estimated residual value at the end of the lease term is $10,000 and is guaranteed by a third party. The lease contains no bargain purchase option, and Mike is reasonably certain of the collectibility of lease rentals and there are no additional costs to be incurred. The lease qualifies as a direct-financing lease to the lessor, but an operating lease to the lessee.

Required:
1. What evidence supports this as a direct-financing lease for the lessor? Give Mike's journal entries at inception of the lease and to record the first lease payment.
2. What evidence supports this as an operating lease for Ash? Explain. Give Ash's journal entries at inception of the lease and to record the first lease payment.

E 18–13
Direct-Financing Lease:
Residual Value Partially
Guaranteed by the Lessee
(L.O. 4, 5, 6)

Davis Company leased a large copier to Gore Company for a three-year period. Davis paid $15,000 for the copier and immediately placed it on this lease on January 1, 1991 (estimated useful life of four years and an estimated residual value at the end of the lease term of $3,000). Davis used an expected rate of return of 16% on cost (known by Gore). Because of inadequate maintenance, the lessee agreed to guarantee two thirds (i.e., $2,000) of the residual value. The lease qualifies as a direct-financing lease for the lessor and a capital lease for the lessee. The lessee uses straight-line depreciation. The first lease payment is on January 1, 1991; the accounting periods for both parties end on December 31. At the lease termination date, an independent appraiser provided an estimated residual value of $1,500. The lessee immediately paid the difference of $500 ($2,000 guaranteed residual value minus $1,500, the actual residual value).

Required:
1. Compute the minimum lease payment for the lessor and the amount to be capitalized by the lessee.
2. Give the entries for the lessor and lessee on January 1, 1991.
3. Give the entries for the lessor and lessee to record the lease termination.

E 18–14
Accounting for Executory Costs
(L.O. 4, 5, 6)

On January 1, 1991, Lessor Foxtrot leased a machine to Lessee Tango on a three-year direct-financing lease to the lessor and a capital lease to the lessee. The machine cost the lessor $42,000 and was immediately placed on lease at a 12% target rate of return (known by both parties). The lease did not contain a BPO and there is no residual value. The rentals are payable each year starting on January 1, 1991. The accounting period ends December 31. All executory costs are to be paid by the lessee. However, insurance coverage was provided, at a cost of $87 per year, under the lessor's blanket policy. This amount is billed each year along with the lease rental.

Required:

1. Compute the annual lease rental.
2. Give the entry for the lessor and lessee to record the inception of the lease (do not include the first rent payment).
3. Give the entry for the lessor and lessee to record the first rent payment.

E 18–15
Sale-Leaseback, Direct-Financing Lease
(L.O. 7)

Grumpy Grocery owns the building it uses; it has current carrying value on January 1, 1991, of $900,000, a 10-year remaining life, and no residual value. On this date it was sold to Investor Brown for $1 million cash. Simultaneously, the two parties executed a 10-year direct-financing lease with a 12% implicit interest rate; each annual rent is payable on December 31 (end of the accounting periods).

Required:

1. Compute the annual rents to be paid by Grumpy to Brown.
2. Give the entries for the seller-lessee (Grumpy Grocery) for 1991. Use straight-line depreciation.

E 18–16
Operating Lease: Amortization, Interest Method
(L.O. 2, 3)

Valley Company paid $50,000 on January 1, 1991, to Hill Properties as an advance lease bonus to secure a three-year lease on premises it will occupy starting from that date. Additionally, $60,000 will be paid as rent on December 31 throughout the term of the lease. The lease contains no specific renewal agreement. Valley's accounting period ends December 31. Hill will maintain the property and pay taxes and other ownership costs.

Required:

Round to the nearest dollar.

1. What type of lease contract is involved? Explain.
2. Develop an interest method schedule to amortize the advance lease bonus using a 14% rate (assume an ordinary annuity).
3. What is Valley's total occupancy cost for 1991 under the interest method used in your response to (2)? What is the total occupancy cost using the straight-line basis for 1991?
4. What lease-related items should Valley's financial statements report as of December 31, 1991, if the amortization schedule developed in (2) is used?

PROBLEMS

P 18–1
Lease: Determine Type, Entries for Lessor and Lessee
(L.O. 2, 3)

Fox leases a limo to Cine Productions for four years on January 1, 1991, requiring equal annual payments on each January 1, and, in addition, a single lump-sum prepayment of $3,000. The leased asset, recently purchased new, cost the lessor $50,000. Estimated value of asset at end of lease term is $20,000.

The annual lease payments were computed to yield Fox a 12% yield (the implicit interest rate after considering residual value is known to Cine Productions). The leased asset has an eight-year life with zero residual value at the end of Year 8. There is no bargain purchase option, and the asset is retained by Fox at the end of the lease term. Depreciation will be on the straight-line basis. The accounting period for both lessor and lessee ends December 31.

Required:

1. Compute the annual lease payment.
2. What type of lease is this? Explain.
3. In parallel columns for the lessor and lessee, give the following:
   a. Entries at the inception of the lease, including the initial advance payment.
   b. Adjusting and closing entries for the year ended December 31, 1991. Use straight-line amortization for the prepayment.

P 18–2
Operating Lease: Down Payment, Entries for Both Parties
(L.O. 3, 8)

On July 1, 1991, Staley Company leased a small building and its site to West Company on a five-year contract. The lease provides for an advance rental at $5,000 plus an annual rental of $18,000 payable each July 1 starting in 1991. The lease can be terminated at any year-end by the lessee with a six-month advance notice. There is no renewal agreement. On July 8, 1991, West Company spent $8,000 on internal changes and painting. Staley's accounts showed the following data on January 1, 1991: Initial cost of the building, $125,000 (accumulated depreciation, $30,000); estimated remaining life, 15 years; and estimated residual value, $5,000. The accounting period for each company ends December 31.

Required:

1. Give the entries for the lessor and lessee for 1991, 1992, and through July 1, 1993. Both companies will use straight-line depreciation and amortization of the advance rental. Use reversing entries; closing entries not required.
2. Give the amounts that each party should report on their respective 1991 and 1992 income statements and balance sheets.

P 18–3
Direct-Financing Lease: Ordinary versus Annuity Due, Schedules, Entries for Both Parties
(L.O. 4, 5)

On January 1, 1991, Armor Leasing Company leased to Hogg Service Company a new machine that cost $91,000. The lease is a direct-financing lease to Armor and a capital lease to Hogg, who agreed to pay all executory costs and assume other risks and costs of ownership. Armor computed the periodic rents at an amount that will yield an annual return on cost of 10%, and the lessee, being aware of this rate, also uses it to record the lease and calculate interest expense. The property is expected to have no residual value at the end of the four-year lease term. There are no collection or cost uncertainties. Both lessor and lessee have accounting years ending December 31.

Required:
Round all amounts to the nearest dollar.

1. If the annual rents are payable at the end of each year, provide the following: (*a*) the amount of the periodic rental payments and (*b*) an amortization schedule for the lessor reflecting interest and recovery of investment throughout the four-year lease term.
2. Assume, instead, that the annual rentals are payable at the start of the lease and annually thereafter. Provide the answers to (*a*) and (*b*) that were required in (1).
3. Hogg depreciates all assets using the straight-line method. Give entries under (1) for both lessor and lessee relating to the lease for 1991, including adjusting and closing entries.

P 18–4
Sales-Type Lease: Amortization Schedules, Entries for Both Parties
(L.O. 4, 5)

Key Company uses leases as a secondary means of selling its products. On January 1, 1991, it contracted with Lock Corporation to lease machinery for six years that had a sales price of $90,000 and that cost Key $60,000 (its carrying value in inventory). Equal annual lease payments of $18,786 are to be made each January 1, starting on January 1, 1991. Key's implicit interest rate, based on the sales price, is 10% (known to Lock). This lease qualifies as a capital lease for both parties. The accounting period for both companies ends on December 31.

Required:
Round to the nearest dollar.

1. Prepare an amortization schedule for Key and Lock covering the six-year lease term.
2. Give the lessor's and lessee's entries at the inception of the lease. The lessee uses straight-line depreciation and zero residual value of the asset after six years. Also, give the adjusting and closing entries for both parties at December 31, 1991.

P 18–5
Direct-Financing and Sales-Type Leases Compared: Entries for Both Parties
(L.O. 4, 5)

On January 1, 1991, Sun Company leased to Marfa Corporation new equipment. The equipment cost Sun $38,000. The lease agreement specified that Marfa is to make five equal annual lease payments (on December 31, beginning December 31, 1991) to yield Sun a 14% return. The equipment has a five-year useful life with no residual value. Ownership of the leased asset transfers to Marfa at the end of the lease term. Marfa is aware of the implicit interest rate used by Sun. Straight-line depreciation will be used. Sun expects to collect all rentals from Marfa, and there are no material cost uncertainties at inception of the lease. The accounting period for both Sun and Marfa ends December 31.

Required:

1. If the equipment has a sales price of $42,000 on January 1, 1991, and the lease rentals are based on this amount, what type of lease is this to the lessor? To the lessee? Explain. Compute the annual rental payments and prepare an amortization schedule for the lessor and lessee. Give all journal entries associated with this lease for the lessor and the lessee for the year ended December 31, 1991, including adjusting and closing entries.
2. If the equipment has a cost or carrying value of $38,000 on January 1, 1991, and the lease rentals are based on this amount, what type of lease is this to the lessor? To the lessee? Explain. Compute the annual rental payments and prepare an amortization schedule for the lessor and the lessee. Give all journal entries associated with this lease for the lessor and the lessee for the year ended December 31, 1991, including adjusting and closing entries.

P 18-6
Direct-Financing Lease:
Different Interest Rates
Used by Lessor and
Lessee, Entries
(L.O. 4, 5, 8)

On January 1, 1991, Lessor Alexa leased a machine to Lessee Baker on a three-year lease that qualifies as a direct-financing lease. The machine cost Alexa $240,000 immediately prior to the lease. The machine has a three-year estimated useful life and no residual value. The lessor used an 11% target rate of return. The three annual lease payments start on January 1, 1991. The lessee uses straight-line depreciation, will retain the machine at the end of the lease term, and has a borrowing rate of 10%. The lessee must use the lower of the two interest rates. The accounting period for each company ends on December 31.

Required:

1. Compute the equal annual rentals that the lessor will receive.
2. Prepare an amortization schedule for the lessor and give the related entries through December 31, 1991.
3. Compute the lease capitalization amount and prepare an amortization schedule for the lessee and give the related entries through December 31, 1991.
4. Complete the following 1991 comparative tabulation for the lessor and lessee and explain any differences:

Items	Lessor	Lessee
Income statement:		
Interest revenue		
Interest expense		
Depreciation expense		
Balance sheet:		
Lease receivable		
Lease liability		
Leased asset		
Accumulated depreciation		

P 18-7
Sales-Type Lease: BPO,
Entries for Both Parties
(L.O. 4, 5, 6)

On January 1, 1991, Lessor Ray and Lessee Evans signed a four-year lease that qualifies as a sales-type lease. The equipment cost Ray $900,000 and the cash sale price is $1.4 million. The equipment has a six-year estimated useful life. Estimated residual values were end of year 4, $200,000; and end of year 6, $80,000. The lease gives Evans an option to buy the equipment at the end of year 4 for $150,000 cash. The lease requires four equal annual rents starting on January 1, 1991. Ray's expected rate of return on the lease is 15% and the incremental borrowing rate of Evans is 16%. On December 31, 1994, the lessee exercised the purchase option, at which time a new estimate of residual value was $180,000.

Required:

1. Compute the annual rent and the amount the lessee should capitalize.
2. Prepare a lease amortization schedule for the lessor and lessee.
3. Give the entries for the lessor and lessee from the date of inception through the lease termination date.

P 18–8

COMPREHENSIVE PROBLEM
◆

Analysis to Classify Lease:
Capital versus Operating,
Unguaranteed Residual
Value, Entries for Both
Parties
(L.O. 1, 2, 3, 4, 5, 6)

Lessor Sales Company and Lessee Manufacturing Company agreed to a noncancelable lease. The following information is available regarding the lease terms and the leased asset:

a. Lessor's cost of the leased asset, $30,000. The asset was new at the inception of the lease term.

b. Lease term, four years starting January 1, 1992.

c. Estimated useful life of the leased asset, six years. Estimated residual value at end of six years, zero.

d. On January 1, 1992, estimated unguaranteed residual value of the leased asset one day after the end of the lease term is $4,000.

e. Depreciation method for the leased asset, straight-line.

f. Lessee's incremental borrowing rate on January 1, 1992, 18%. The lessee is considered a high-risk borrower.

g. Bank prime rate of interest on January 1, 1992, 10%.

h. Purchase option price of leased asset exercisable one day after the end of the lease term, $4,500.

i. Title to the leased asset retained by the lessor unless the purchase option is exercised.

j. Sales price of leased asset on January 1, 1992, $40,000.

k. Lessor's unreimbursable cost uncertainties, none.

l. Four annual lease rentals due on January 1 of each year during the lease term, with the first payment due at inception of the lease term, $11,643.

m. The accounting period for the lessor and lessee ends on December 31.

Both the lessor and lessee knew all of the preceding information.

Required:
Round to the nearest dollar.

1. What was the lessor's implicit interest rate in this lease?
2. What type of lease was this to the lessee? To the lessor? Explain.
3. In parallel columns for the lessor and lessee, record the following:
    a. Entry, or entries, at inception of the lease on January 1, 1992, if appropriate.
    b. Adjusting and closing entries on December 31, 1992.

P 18–9
Lease Classification:
Entries for Lessor and
Lessee
(L.O. 2, 4, 5)

The following data are available about a noncancelable lease that involves a leased asset that was new at the inception date of the lease term:

Lease term . . . . 6 years
Interest rate implicit in the lease 12%
Lessee's incremental borrowing rate 14%
Amount of each lease payment $3,648
Lessor's cost of asset (market value) $15,000
Lessee has no way of knowing the interest rate implicit in the lease.
Each lease payment occurs at the end of each period (i.e., an ordinary annuity).
Unreimbursable cost uncertainties of lessor . . . . None
Credit standing of lessee . . . . Excellent
Depreciation method, if needed . . . . Straight-line
Estimated useful life of asset . . . . 6 years
Estimated residual value at end of lease term . . . . $–0–
Accounting period for both parties ends on December 31.

Required:
Round to the nearest dollar.

1. What type of lease is this to the lessee? To the lessor? Explain.
2. Give entries in parallel columns for lessor and lessee to record:
    a. The inception of the lease on January 1, 1991.
    b. All entries needed at year-end, December 31, 1991, for both parties to record lease payment (receipt), interest, depreciation, and so forth, including closing entries.

P 18–10

Direct-Financing Lease: Unguaranteed Residual Value, Entries for Lessor (L.O. 5, 6)

Jinx, Incorporated, purchased a machine (for leasing purposes) on January 1, 1991, for $270,000. By prior agreement the machine was delivered to Pine Company (lessee) under a direct-financing lease whereby Pine paid the first lease rental of $73,516 on January 1, 1991, and agreed to pay three more such annual rentals.

At the end of the four-year lease term, the machine will revert to the lessor, at which time it is expected to have a residual value of $20,000 (none of which was guaranteed by the lessee). The lessor's implicit interest rate was 10% on cost.

Required:
Round amounts to the nearest dollar.

1. Show how the lessor computed the annual rental.
2. Prepare a lease amortization schedule for the lessor.
3. Give all of the entries for the lessor on the following dates:
   January 1, 1991—Purchase and other transactions.
   December 31, 1991—End of the accounting period.
   1994—Return of the machine by the lessee at the termination of the lease. At this date the machine has an actual market value of $14,000 (instead of the $20,000 estimated residual value).
4. How would the lessor's entries differ at the end of the lease term if the actual market value of the machine turned out to be $23,000 (instead of the estimated residual value of $20,000)?

P 18–11

Capital Lease: Residual Value, Third Party Guarantee, Schedules and Entries for Both Parties (L.O. 2, 4, 5, 6)

The following data are available regarding a noncancelable lease:

a. Lease term, five years, beginning January 1, 1991.
b. The leased property cost the lessor $400,000 on January 1, 1991.
c. Estimated useful life of the asset, six years; residual value at the end of the six-year useful life, $20,000.
d. On January 1, 1991, the estimated residual value of the leased asset at the end of the lease term, $50,000. This residual value is guaranteed in full by a third party guarantor (not the lessee).
e. Depreciation method for the leased asset, straight-line.
f. No bargain purchase option available to the lessee. Ownership retained by lessor at the end of the lease term.
g. Five annual lease payments are payable on January 1 of each year (starting January 1, 1991) to yield the lessor a 14% return (implicit interest rate). Lessee does not know, and cannot reliably estimate, the lessor's yield rate. Lessee's incremental borrowing rate is 16%.
h. Lessor's unreimbursable cost uncertainties, none. Lessee's credit rating, excellent.
i. Lessor and lessee accounting year-end, December 31.

Required:
Round to the nearest dollar.

1. Compute the annual rentals by the lessor.
2. What type of lease is this to the lessor? To the lessee? Explain.
3. Prepare an amortization schedule for the lessor. Give the following entries for the lessor:
   a. At the inception of the lease and for the initial lease rental on January 1, 1991.
   b. Adjusting and closing on December 31, 1991.
4. Prepare an amortization schedule for the lessee. Give the following entries for the lessee:
   a. At the inception of the lease and for the initial lease rental on January 1, 1991.
   b. Adjusting and closing on December 31, 1991.

P 18–12

Direct-Financing Lease: Change in Residual Value, Amortization Schedule (L.O. 6)

On January 1, 1991, Klondike Leasing Company leased equipment to a lessee for an eight-year term whereby $45,000 rents are payable each January 1, starting on January 1, 1991. The unguaranteed residual value of the equipment at the end of the lease term is $20,000. The interest rate implicit in the lease is 15%. The accounting period for both the lessor and lessee ends on December 31. The lease qualifies as a direct-financing lease.

Required:

Round to the nearest dollar.

1. Compute the initial investment value (i.e., cost to the lessor) of the leased property and the total amount of interest to be earned by Klondike over the lease term.
2. Immediately after the fifth annual payment, the lease amortization schedule shows a lease receivable balance of $114,181. Prepare the amortization schedule for the lessor, using the value determined in (1) to prove the correctness of that amount. For problem purposes, stop the amortization schedule after the January 1, 1995, payment.
3. Immediately after the fifth payment, Klondike determined that the expected unguaranteed residual value of $20,000 probably will be zero. This change in accounting estimate will decrease the unrecovered investment value by the present value of the previously estimated residual value. Prepare the journal entry to record this change. After adjusting the January 1, 1995, receivable balance, complete the lease amortization schedule developed in (2) from the $114,181 value in view of this new determination.

P 18–13
Sales-Type Lease:
Schedule, Entries for
Lessor
(L.O. 5, 6)

On December 31, 1991, a lessor leased a machine that cost $70,000. The machine was leased on January 1, 1992, for five years under a sales-type lease, which required annual payments of $28,199 at the end of each year. At inception of the lease, the sales value of the leased asset was $110,000. At the end of the lease term, the machine will revert to the lessor, at which time the estimated residual value will be $5,000 (none of which is guaranteed by the lessee). The lessor's implicit rate of interest was 10% on the investment.

Required:

Round amounts to the nearest dollar.

1. Show how the lessor computed the annual rental of $28,199.
2. Prepare a lease amortization schedule for the lessor.
3. Give the following entries for the lessor:
   a. To record acquisition of the machine on December 31, 1991.
   b. To record the inception of the lease on January 1, 1992.
   c. To record collection of the first rental and recognition of interest revenue on December 31, 1992 (end of the accounting period).
   d. To record, at termination of the lease on December 31, 1996, the last rental, interest revenue, and return of the asset, assuming the estimate of residual value is confirmed.
4. How would the lessor's entries differ at the end of the lease term, assuming the market value of the returned machine was $4,000 (instead of the $5,000 estimated residual value).

P 18–14
Sales-Type Lease:
Amortization Schedules,
Entries for Both Parties
(L.O. 2, 4, 5)

Lessor Company entered into a lease with Lessee Company on January 1, 1994. The following data relate to the leased asset and the lease agreement:

a. Asset leased—large construction crane.
b. Cost to Lessor, $150,000.
c. Estimated useful life, 10 years.
d. Estimated residual value at end of useful life, $10,000.
e. Lessor's normal selling price, $200,000.
f. Lease provisions:
   (1) Noncancelable; the asset will revert to Lessor at the end of the lease term.
   (2) Estimated residual value at end of lease term, $20,000 (none guaranteed).
   (3) Ownership does not transfer to Lessee by the end of the lease term.
   (4) No bargain purchase option is included.
   (5) Lease term, six years starting January 1, 1994.
   (6) Lease payment at each year-end, starting December 31, 1994, $43,329.
g. Lessor's implicit rate of return, 10% (assume Lessee knows this rate).
h. Lessee's incremental borrowing rate, 12% (assume this is evidence of a good credit rating).
i. Lessor has no material cost uncertainties.

Required:

Show computations and round to the nearest dollar.

1. What kind of lease was this to Lessee Company? Give the basis for your response.
2. What kind of lease was this to Lessor Company? Give the basis for your response.
3. For Lessor Company, give the entries to record (*a*) the lease at inception date and (*b*) the first rental.
4. For Lessee Company, give the entries to record (*a*) the lease at inception date and (*b*) the first rental.

P 18–15
Determine the Kind of
Lease: Schedule, Entries
for Both Parties
(L.O. 2, 4, 5, 8)

Lessor and lessee agreed to a noncancelable lease for which the following information is available:

a. Lessor's cost of the asset leased, $25,000. The asset was new at the inception of the lease term.
b. Lease term, four years starting January 1, 1993.
c. Estimated useful life of the leased asset, six years.
d. On January 1, 1993, lessor and lessee estimated that the residual value of the leased asset on the purchase option date [see (*h*)] will be $6,000 and zero at the end of its useful life. The residual value is not guaranteed.
e. Depreciation method for the leased asset, straight-line.
f. Lessee's incremental borrowing rate, 10%. Lessee has an excellent credit rating.
g. Lessor's interest rate implicit in the lease, 10%.
h. Purchase option price of leased asset exercisable on January 2, 1996, $5,000.
i. Title to the leased asset retained by the lessor unless the purchase option is exercised.
j. Sale value of leased asset on January 1, 1993, $30,000.
k. Lessor's unreimbursable cost uncertainties, none.
l. Four annual lease rentals payable each January 1 during the lease term, with the first payment due at inception of the lease term, $7,526.

Required:

Round to the nearest dollar.

1. Show how the annual rental was computed.
2. Is this an operating lease or a capital lease to the lessee? Explain. Compute the lessee's capitalizable cost of the leased asset.
3. What type of lease is this to the lessor? Explain.
4. Prepare an amortization schedule. In parallel columns for the lessee and lessor, record the inception of the lease on January 1, 1993 (if appropriate), and the adjusting and closing entries on December 31, 1993.
5. Prepare the financial statement presentation of all lease-related accounts as they would appear in the financial statements of the lessee at December 31, 1993, for the year then ended. Disclosures are not required.

P 18–16
Direct-Financing Lease:
Executory Cost, Partially
Guaranteed Residual
Value, Entries
(L.O. 4, 5, 6)

Stockton Leasing Company (lessor) entered into a four-year noncancelable, direct-financing lease with Acme Corporation (lessee) on January 1, 1991. The leased asset has a six-year life, with zero residual value at the end of the six years. On January 1, 1991, both lessor and lessee estimated the residual value of the asset at the end of the lease term to be $30,000, of which Acme guaranteed $20,000. The leased asset cost $500,000 (same as its market value). Lease payments are to be made on December 31 of each year, starting December 31, 1991, and are set to yield 16% to Stockton (implicit interest rate). This interest rate is known to Acme, which has an 18% incremental borrowing rate. Straight-line depreciation is used. Stockton agreed to pay annual executory costs of $3,000 and included this amount in the lease rentals. There is no bargain purchase option, and ownership is retained by Stockton at the end of the lease term. The accounting period for both companies ended on December 31.

Required:

Round to the nearest dollar.

1. Compute the annual lease rentals.
2. Prepare amortization schedules for the lessor and lessee.

3. Record the following for the lessor and lessee:
   a. Entry at the inception of the lease.
   b. Adjusting and closing entries at December 31, 1991.
4. Assuming that the acutal residual value of the leased asset on December 31, 1994 (end of lease term), was $15,000, prepare entries for lessor and lessee on December 31, 1994, to record the return of the asset to the lessor.
5. Ignore (4). Assuming that the actual residual value of the leased asset on December 31, 1994, was $25,000, prepare entries for lessor and lessee on December 31, 1994, to record the return of the asset to the lessor.

P 18–17
Accounting for Initial Direct Lease Costs
(L.O. 5)

On January 1, 1991, Lessor Smith leased equipment to Lessee Thomas. The equipment cost the lessor $400,000 and the lessor's expected rate of return was 15%. The three annual payments are to start on December 31, 1991. The lease has no BPO and there is no residual value. The lessor incurred, and paid, initial direct costs of $6,000 consummating the lease. The lessor recorded these costs as a credit to cash and a debit to a temporary holding account called "Initial Direct Leasing Costs." The rent payments were indirectly set to cover such costs.

Required:

1. Compute the annual rent (ordinary annuity basis) set by the lessor assuming the following cases:

Case A

An operating lease (including the initial direct leasing costs).

Case B

A direct-financing lease (including the initial direct leasing costs).

Case C

A sales-type lease (including the direct leasing costs). The normal or regular selling price of the leased asset is $600,000.

2. Give the lessor's entries for (*a*) the inception of the lease and (*b*) the payments related to the lease at the end of the first year, for each case.
3. Give any entry needed for each case that the lessor should make during the first year for the initial direct costs. (The lessee's entries are unaffected.)

P 18–18
Sale-Leaseback: Operating and Direct-Financing Leases Compared
(L.O. 7)

On January 1, 1991, Supergrocery, Inc., sold the building currently used to Diversified Investors for $9 million, its current market value. Prior to the sale, the carrying value of the building was $7 million. The estimated remaining useful life of the building is 10 years and no residual value at that time; straight-line depreciation is used.

On January 1, 1991, Supergrocery signed a 10-year noncancelable leaseback agreement that has a 15% implicit rate of return for the lessor. The lessee's incremental borrowing rate also is 15%. The annual rent payments start on January 1, 1991. During 1991, Supergrocery would pay $10,000 for executory costs (e.g., insurance, taxes, maintenance), if this transaction qualifies as a direct-financing lease. Alternatively, if this qualifies as an operating lease, this $10,000 would be paid by the buyer-lessor. For problem purposes only, two cases are assumed about the lease: Case A—an operating lease; Case B—a direct-financing lease.

Required:
For practical reasons give all amounts in 000s.

1. Compute the annual lease payments and the gain or loss on the sale of the building.
2. Give the 1991 entries for the seller-lessee and the buyer-lessor in parallel columns for Case A—operating lease.
3. (*a*) Prepare the lease amortization schedule through 1992 for Case B—direct-financing lease.
   (*b*) Give the 1991 entries for the seller-lessee and the buyer-lessor in parallel columns for Case B—direct-financing lease.

P 18–19
Operating Lease: Advance Payments, Ordinary Annuity Basis
(L.O. 3)

In lieu of making four $10,000 rent payments spaced at one-year intervals with the first payment due at the end of the first year of the lease term, the lessee and lessor agree that the lessee can make a lump-sum initial payment, the amount to be computed, at the start of the four-year lease term. This amount was calculated on the basis of an agreed 16% annual interest rate.

Required:
Round all amounts to the nearest dollar.

1. Compute the lump-sum initial payment amount.
2. On the assumption that the lessee amortizes the prepayment on a straight-line basis, give the lessee's entries to record the initial payment and year-end adjustments if the lease year and lessee accounting year coincide.

P 18–20
Operating Lease: Advance Payment, Annuity Due Basis
(L.O. 3)

A lessor and a lessee began negotiations that would have provided that the lessee pay six semiannual $8,000 rents for the use of property with the first payment to be at the beginning of the lease term. However, after agreeing that money was worth 14% per year at the time, the parties finally agreed that the lessee would instead pay $? at the outset and that this single advance payment would be in lieu of all other rents for the three-year term. Assume an operating lease.

Required:
Round to the nearest dollar.

1. Show how the advance payment was calculated and prepare an amortization schedule covering the entire term of the lease.
2. Assume that the lessor and lessee amortize the advance payment computed in (1) by the straight-line method. Give entries for both parties to record amortization at the end of the year if the lease year and accounting year of the parties coincide.

CASES

C 18–1
Implementing Section 3065 of the *CICA Handbook*— Interest Rate
(L.O. 6)

Pertinent provisions of section 3065 concerning the interest rate to be used in capitalizing leases are as follows:

> the discount rate used by the lessee in determining the present value of minimum lease payments would be the lower of the lessee's rate for incremental borrowing and the interest rate implicit in the lease, if practicable to determine.

Required:
Evaluate the foregoing criteria in light of the following assertions:

1. Asking a lessor what interest rate is inherent in a lease transaction would be similar to asking a farmer what rate is implicit in the price the farmer can expect now for next fall's wheat crop. There are varying degrees of risk in any operation having a distant future; the higher the farmer's future risks are thought to be, the higher the farmer will set his or her rate and, likewise, for the lessor.
2. The assumption that a lease has an implicit interest rate, in many cases, represents circular reasoning in that the market value of the leased asset itself (i.e., the benchmark value used in determining the implicit rate) is determined by market forces. The value of the property stems from the rentals it will command rather than the rentals stemming from the value of the property.
3. One determinant of the implicit interest rate in a lease is the residual value of the property to be leased. This is a subjective judgment, which, depending on the property, can be substantially in error. Lessors will not disclose what this guess is.

C 18–2
Concern about
Debt-Equity Ratio and
Third Party Residual Value
Guarantees
(L.O. 1, 2, 8)

Speedware Corporation has entered into a debt agreement that restricts its debt-to-owners'-equity ratio to less than two to one. The corporation is planning to expand its facilities, which creates a need for additional financing. The board of directors is considering leasing the additional facilities but is concerned that leasing may violate its existing debt agreement, which would place the corporation in default. The potential lessor insists that the lease be structured such that it can be accounted for as a capital lease by the lessor (the lessor is a dealer and wants to recognize the dealer's profit on the transaction immediately). In addition, the lessor requires that the residual value of the leased asset be guaranteed when it reverts to the lessor at the end of the lease term. Speedware's board has asked you to analyze the following alternatives:

Alternative A—Speedware would enter into a lease that qualifies as a capital lease (to Speedware). If this alternative is selected, Speedware's reported debt-to-owners'-equity ratio would be 1.9, and its ability to issue debt in the future would be seriously constrained.

Alternative B—Speedware would enter into a lease and pay a third party to guarantee the residual value of the leased property. The lease would be structured such that it would qualify as an operating lease to Speedware and a capital lease to the lessor. In this case, Speedware's reported debt-to-owners'-equity ratio would be unaffected by the lease contract.

Required:

Analyze and explain the consequences of each of the preceding alternatives. Are there any ethical considerations to be evaluated?

C 18–3
Analysis of Actual
Financial Statements
(L.O. 2, 3, 4, 8)

Refer to the 1990 financial statements of Loblaw (see the appendix immediately following Chapter 26) and respond to the following questions.

Required:

1. Does Loblaw Companies Limited have any capitalized leases? How do you know?
2. If the firm has capitalized leases, is the firm a lessee or lessor?
3. If the firm has capitalized leases, where do the liabilities appear on the balance sheet and in what amounts?
4. Does Loblaw have any operating leases? How do you know? How are these rentals accounted for by the firm?
5. Does Loblaw lease a substantial portion of its buildings, machinery, and equipment under capital leases?
6. Assuming Loblaw depreciates its leased property using the same method as is used principally to depreciate its other fixed assets, what criteria (Exhibit 18–2) caused the company to capitalize these leases?

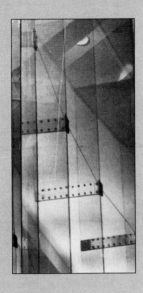

CHAPTER

19

Accounting for Pensions

After you have studied this chapter, you should be able to:

1. Explain the fundamental pension concepts.

2. Explain the basic nature of pension expense and compute the components of pension expense not subject to delayed recognition.

3. Distinguish between projected benefit obligation and accrued pension cost.

4. Explain unrecognized pension costs and their effect on pension expense.

5. Compute and record pension expense and balance sheet pension accounts.

6. Prepare a reconciliation of funded status and the balance in the reported pension account.

7. Explain the concepts of pension plan settlements, curtailments, and termination benefits (refers to Appendix 19A).

8. Explain the concepts for accounting for pension plans (refers to Appendix 19B).

◆

INTRODUCTION
◆

In 1988 the Accumulated Reserves of Employer-Sponsored Pension Plans amounted to $272.4 billion, up from $15.6 billion in 1970. There were 21,239 such plans with 4,845,107 members.[1] The increase in the assets controlled by pension funds means that the funds exercise increasing power in corporate boardrooms.

The size of corporate pension funds reflects the substantial expense resulting from employers' promises to pay retiree pension benefits. This expense is a significant percentage of total expenses for many companies. For example, MacMillan Bloedel's expense was 7.4% of pretax income in 1989. Bell Canada's was 4.5% of pretax income in 1989.

A company promises to pay estimated retirement benefits in partial payment of services provided by its employees each year. How should the cost of the benefits earned in a period be measured if payable at a much later date? Should the entire liability for promised benefits be recognized immediately? If not, are the financial statements misleading?

The need to estimate a variety of factors over a long time horizon compounds the difficulty of these questions. If future salaries are used to estimate benefits, should reported costs also reflect future salaries? How many employees will be working for the company in 20 years? How long will they draw retirement benefits? To what extent can these estimates be relied on for financial reporting? This chapter considers these and other issues in accounting for pensions.

◆

PENSION PLAN FUNDAMENTALS
◆

Since the early 1900s public and private retirement programs have provided pension benefits for employees. These programs include the Canada Pension Plan, company retirement programs for employees, and tax-sheltered savings plans. Companies establish pension plans to increase employee motivation and productivity, to reduce current demands for pay increases, to comply with union demands, and to be competitive in the labour market. Pension costs are a substantial percentage of total compensation costs, and pension benefits are a significant portion of total income for many retirees.

Through **pension plans,** employers agree to make payments into a fund for future retirement benefits, in return for current and past services. A **pension plan participant** is any current or former employee (or beneficiaries of these individuals) for whom the pension plan provides benefits. Pension plans provide participants with a degree of retirement security not otherwise possible. Pension plans can also purchase insurance benefits at rates lower than those available to individuals. Pension plans discourage turnover because participants may lose a portion of their accumulated **pension benefits** if they change jobs.

Most pension plans conform to Income Tax Act requirements to qualify for the following tax advantages:

◆ Employers deduct contributions to the pension fund, subject to certain limitations.
◆ Employers exclude pension fund earnings from taxable income.
◆ Employees exclude employer contributions from taxable income, subject to certain limitations.
◆ Employees defer tax on benefits until retirement.[2]

---

[1] Statistics Canada, *Trusteed Pension Funds, 1988* (Ottawa: Statistics Canada, 1990), Tables A and B, pp. 10 and 11.

[2] This deferral of tax provides two benefits to employees: (1) the pension fund grows much faster during the years of employment and (2) employees may be in a lower tax bracket when they retire.

Types of Pension Plans Employers establish two types of pension plans: defined benefit and defined contribution pension plans. This chapter is primarily concerned with defined benefit plans.

In a **defined contribution plan,** the contributions are defined by formula or contract; the benefits are not specified. For example, some defined contribution plans require the employer to contribute an amount equal to a percentage of the employee's salary each month into an employee-directed investment fund. The employer makes no promise about the amount of retirement benefits. The employee bears the risk of pension fund performance in a defined contribution plan.

In a **defined benefit plan,** the sponsor commits to specified retirement benefits. The benefits are defined by a **pension benefit formula;** the contributions are not specified. The employer bears the risk of pension fund performance. Fund shortages caused by poor investment performance increase the employer's liability.

The primary variables in a defined benefit formula generally include the number of qualified years of service credited to the employee, compensation levels, and age. The following is an example of a final-pay pension benefit formula for a defined benefit plan:

Annual benefit payment during retirement

$$= 2.5\%(\text{Number of year's service})(\text{Final salary})$$

An employee with a $100,000 final salary who retires after 25 years of service receives $62,500 (2.5% × 25 × $100,000) each year of retirement. The annual benefit amount helps determine the investment required to satisfy the obligation, and the cost of the pension plan. The 2.5% component implies that 40 years of service be rendered to receive a pension equal to the employee's final salary.

Vesting of Benefits The right to receive earned pension benefits is **vested** when it is no longer contingent on continued employment. Most plans require a minimum employment term before benefits vest. Vesting provisions are especially important in a mobile labour force. Without vesting, workers who change jobs lose all their accumulated benefits. Vesting also may guarantee benefits to the spouse of an employee who dies before retiring.

Pension Plan Funding A pension fund is an accumulation of cash and other assets restricted to the payment of retiree benefits. Funding sources include employer contributions, fund earnings, and employee contributions. Pension fund earnings generally supply a significant portion of total required funding. Pension plans are contributory or noncontributory. A plan is **contributory** if the employees must pay part of the funding needed to provide the specified benefits, or if the employees voluntarily make payments to increase retirement benfits. A plan is **non-contributory** if only the employer provides funding.

Firms fund pension plans in three ways:

1. The firm maintains and administers the pension fund internally.
2. A bank or trust company, serving as the fund trustee, invests the employer contributions, makes retirement payments, and provides the employer with periodic information about the plan and investment performance.
3. The firm purchases a retirement annuity from an insurance company that accepts the responsibility for paying the pension benefits to the retirees.

The examples in this chapter assume an outside trustee. The trustee takes over ownership of the assets and bears the obligation for retirement payments in a defined contribution plan. The trustee and employee are legally separate. Exhibit 19–1 summarizes the relationships among the parties to a pension plan when an outside trustee is used.

EXHIBIT 19-1   Relationships among Entities in a Pension Plan

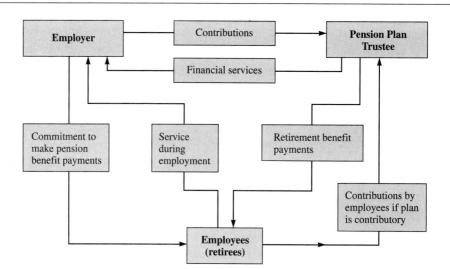

Defined benefit pension plans are fully funded or overfunded if the market value of plan assets equals or exceeds the present value of all benefits promised to participants. Otherwise the plan is underfunded. Tax law, pension regulations, general economic conditions, current period pension benefits earned, cash flow constraints, and past fund performance all affect the amount contributed each year by employers to pension funds.

Importance of Actuaries   Actuaries—professionals trained in a specific branch of mathematics and statistics—develop the estimates of future retirement benefit payments needed to compute the employer's pension expense and pension obligation. Actuaries use statistical models incorporating several variables, including turnover, inflation, future compensation levels, life expectancy, the interest rate used for discounting benefit payments, final retirement age, and administrative costs.

The actuary works with the employer to develop the historical data and expected changes in the employee population for this estimation process. Actuaries also give advice on the attributes of the plan most appropriate to the employer.

CONCEPT REVIEW

1. What is the main difference between defined contribution and defined benefit plans?
2. What role does a pension benefit formula play in a defined benefit pension plan?
3. What is the significance of an overfunded or underfunded pension plan?

CURRENT PENSION ACCOUNTING

Accounting for a defined contribution plan does not involve new measurement or recognition issues. The employer debits pension expense for the required amount, credits cash for the amount paid, and credits a liability for underpayments or debits a prepaid asset for overpayments.

The major issues encountered in pension accounting involve defined benefit plans and include how to measure and recognize pension expense and pension liabilities.

Measuring Pension Expense in Defined Benefit Plans   Pension expense is measured under the concept of **attribution**, the process of assigning pension benefits to periods of employee service as defined by the pension benfit formula.[3] Pension expense includes the cost of pension benefits earned in the period, the effects of previous overfunding or underfunding, return on the pension fund, and changes in the plan and underlying assumptions.

Pension expense reflects future compensation levels if they are a factor in the benefit formula. However, only benefits attributable to services rendered through the reporting date are included in the measurement of pension expense and liabilities.

Recognizing Pension Liabilities   The *CICA Handbook,* paragraph 1000.28, defines liabilities as follows:

> Liabilities are obligations of an entity arising from past transactions or events, the settlement of which may result in the transfer or use of assets, provisions of services or other yielding of economic benefits in the future.

The obligation to pay retirement benefit payments arises from past service by employees and the pension agreement. The existence of a future pension obligation is evident, although the amount is not certain until retirement.

Many accountants maintain, however, that the employer's pension liability is satisfied to the extent that the present value of future benefits is funded. Under this view, the sponsoring firm does not own the assets contributed to the fund, and it has a liability only for underfunded pension benefits. This view is consistent with in-substance defeasance (see Chapter 16). The arrangement between the employer and trustee further supports this view. The trustee is a separate legal entity having title to the plan assets. Normally, the assets are restricted. The employer has access to the assets only on termination of the plan.

An alternative view holds that the employer extinguishes its liability only when benefit payments are made. This view requires recognition of the total obligation (present value of unpaid benefits) and pension fund assets in the balance sheet. Otherwise, the sponsor has significant off-balance-sheet debt, and sponsor assets are greatly understated. In addition, the economic substance, rather than the legal form, of the sponsor-trustee relationship suggests that the sponsor, rather than the trustee, is in debt to employees for pension benefits. The ability of the employer to terminate the plan and reclaim surplus assets supports this view. Furthermore, the employer is liable for any underfunded amounts.

The profession adopted a modified version of the latter view. Both the fund asset balance and several liability measures are disclosed in the financial statements. But the AcSB stopped short of recognizing the total liability in the accounts, favouring footnote disclosure.

Section 3460 of the *CICA Handbook,* "Pension Costs and Obligations"   The original *CICA Handbook* pronouncement on pensions was issued in December 1968 and revised in October 1973. It offered employers significant latitude in the methods of determining pension expense and required only minimal disclosure. In January 1974, the CICA Accounting Standards Board recognized that section 3460 no longer met the needs of the users of the financial statements. Realizing that an in-depth study was needed, the CICA commissioned a research study, *Pension Costs and Obligations,* by T.R. Archibald. Serious deliberations on the new *Handbook* recommendations began in 1980 after the study was published.

---

[3] The term *pension expense* designates the pension cost recognized in a period. Manufacturing firms capitalize part of total periodic pension cost to inventory for the portion relating to manufacturing personnel.

The FASB also began its own deliberations on pension cost accounting in 1974. The significant U.S. pronouncements are *SFAS No. 35,* a standard for pension plan reporting; *SFAS No. 36,* a standard for employers' disclosures; *SFAS No. 81,* on accounting for the costs of post-retirement health benefits and life insurance; and *SFAS No. 91,* a standard on settlements, curtailments, and termination benefits.

After some fine-tuning based on comment letters to the exposure drafts, *SFAS No. 87,* "Employers' Accounting for Pensions," was approved and issued in December 1985 by FASB; the CICA approved and issued the revised section 3460, "Pension Costs and Obligations," in April 1986. The provisions of section 3460 are considered in the remainder of this chapter.

The employer and the trustee are separate and independent entities. Each one maintains its own accounting system. The employer records cash contributions to the pension fund, periodic pension expense, and pension liabilities and assets. Accounting for the pension plan itself concerns the investment of pension fund assets and pension payments to retirees. *CICA Handbook* section 4100, "Pension Plans," published in March 1990, addresses financial reporting by pension plans as separate entities. Section 4100 is not concerned with issues relating to financial statement disclosures by employers regarding the plans they initiate. Accounting for pension plans is briefly discussed in Appendix 19B.

Section 3460 retained the basic idea that the periodic pension be recognized before the actual payment of benefits to retirees and significantly changed accounting for pensions in three ways:

- The cost of a pension plan is more directly related to the terms of the plan. A projected-benefit method prorated on services for defined benefit plans must be used to determine the retirement benefit.
- Employers now recognize a liability equal to the underfunded obligation based on current compensation levels.
- The recommendations expanded disclosure including the actuarial present value of accrued pension benefits attributed to services rendered up to the reporting date, and the value of plan assets (paragraph 3460.60).

MEASURING PENSION EXPENSE AND PENSION OBLIGATIONS
◆

Let's consider the pension plan of the Lone Pine Corporation, a hypothetical software development company. This example focusses on one employee, Nicole Whitney, a software engineer; it develops the concepts of pension expense and liability for pension benefits.[4] Exhibit 19–2 gives the initial data for the example.

Discount Rate   Employers use a discount rate to compute the actuarial present value of benefits, pension expense, and the obligation of the sponsor under the plan. The **discount rate** is the rate at which pension obligations could be settled if sufficient funds were invested at that rate. The **actuarial present value** considers not only the time value of money but also factors affecting the probability of payment, including life expectancy, turnover, and disability.

Section 3460 requires that the discount rate and other assumptions be based on the best estimates of management. The employer changes the discount rate periodically to

---

[4] In practice, the actuary analyzes data for the employee group and develops estimates of life expectancy, turnover, and other factors. It is generally not possible to predict the benefits payable to an individual employee. However, the example uses one individual to simplify the presentation and focus on the concepts. Actuarial models are beyond the scope of this text.

EXHIBIT 19–2 Information for Lone Pine Pension Plan and Employee Nicole Whitney

Pension plan: Non-contributory, defined benefit plan
Pension plan inception: January 1, 1991
Date Nicole Whitney joined Lone Pine: January 1, 1991
Starting salary: $45,000 per year
Whitney's age on January 1, 1991: 40 years old
Whitney's expected retirement date: December 31, 2015 (25 years of employment service expected)
Whitney's expected salary at retirement: $150,000
Pension benefit formula:
   Annual retirement benefit payment = 2%(Number of service years)(Final salary)
Discount rate and expected long-term rate of return on pension plan assets (assume expected equals actual return): 10%
Whitney's expected retirement period: 10 years; payments are made at the end of each calendar year during retirement
Time line depicting service and retirement periods for Whitney:

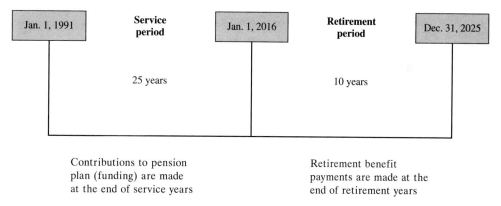

Contributions to pension plan (funding) are made at the end of service years		Retirement benefit payments are made at the end of retirement years	
First contribution:	Dec. 31, 1991	First payment:	Dec. 31, 2016
Last contribution:	Dec. 31, 2015	Last payment:	Dec. 31, 2025

reflect changing economic conditions. When choosing the discount rate, firms consider the following factors:

- Rates implicit in annuity contracts offered by insurance companies.
- Information on interest rates from Statistics Canada.
- Returns on high-quality fixed-income investments expected during the accumulation period.

Firms also consider the average age of employees. For example, the discount rate for a plan covering workers close to retirement might reflect a portfolio of investments with shorter maturities than those of a plan covering a younger work force.[5]

Pension Expense

Pension expense is the net cost of these six components:

1. *a.* Service cost (SC).
   b. Interest cost.
   c. Actual return on plan assets.
2. Amortization of unrecognized prior service cost.

---

[5] Minor changes in discount rates can dramatically affect the measurement of the employer's obligation. For example, a 1% decrease in the discount rate can increase pension liabilities 10% to 15%. See "The Surplus Vanishes," *Forbes,* November 17, 1986, p. 94.

3. Amortization of gains or losses from changes in actuarial assumptions.
4. Amortization of experience gains or losses.
5. Transition asset or liability.
6. Gains or losses on plan settlements or curtailments (Appendix 19A).

Service Cost (Component 1*a* of Pension Expense)

Service cost is the actuarial present value of pension benefits attributed to employee service in a period based on the pension benefit formula. The service cost for Whitney in 1991 is computed as follows:

$$\text{Annual retirement benefit earned in 1991} = .02 \times 1 \text{ service year} \times \$150,000$$
$$= \$3,000$$

$$\text{Service cost, 1991} = \text{Present value of benefit payments earned in 1991}$$
$$= \$3,000 \times (PVA, 10\%, 10^*)$$
$$\times (PV1, 10\%, 24^\dagger)$$
$$= \$3,000 \times 6.14457 \times .10153$$
$$= \underline{\underline{\$1,872}}$$

* 10 years of retirement payments.

† Retirement in 24 years.

Whitney earned a retirement benefit of $3,000 per retirement year by working for Lone Pine during 1991. To receive the entire benefit, she must continue with Lone Pine until the benefits vest. However, section 3460 states that vesting should not serve as a basis for recognizing pension costs. Therefore, the cost of providing benefits is recognized in the periods in which the employee renders the services to which the benefits relate.

Service cost for Whitney in 1991 is $1,872, the investment required at December 31, 1991, to settle the obligation of Lone Pine for her future retirement payments earned in 1991. Service cost is not related to the amount contributed to the fund in 1991.[6]

For the first year only (assuming no amendments or transition gain or loss, and funding at the end of the year), pension expense equals service cost. No other components are involved. If Lone Pine contributes only $1,500 to the pension fund trustee because of liquidity problems, the following entry records pension expense:

December 31, 1991—To record pension expense:

Pension expense	1,872	
Accrued/prepaid pension cost		372
Cash		1,500

Accrued/Prepaid Pension Cost Account   The $372 balance in accrued/prepaid pension cost represents a liability, the amount by which the pension plan is underfunded. This account title is used to indicate that the plan can be underfunded (liability) or overfunded (asset). If Lone Pine plans to increase funding in 1992 to cover the deficiency, the liability is classified as current.

If Lone Pine contributes $1,900 (rather than $1,500) to the fund in 1991, accrued/prepaid pension cost has a debit balance (asset) of $28, the amount by which the fund is overfunded. The balance in accrued/prepaid pension cost equals the difference between cumulative pension expense recognized to date and cumulative funding to date.

---

[6] In practice, the determination of service cost considers productivity, seniority, promotion, turnover, life expectancy, and disability.

EXHIBIT 19-3 Reconciliation of Funded Status and Accrued/Prepaid Pension Cost, Lone Pine Corporation, December 31, 1991

Projected benefit obligation.	($1,872)
Plan assets at fair value.	1,500
Underfunded PBO (funded status)	($ 372)
Balance in (accrued)/prepaid pension cost	($ 372)

This account is referred to as accrued pension cost if it has a credit (liability) balance, and prepaid pension cost if it has a debit (asset) balance. It is not uncommon for firms to report a pension asset. For example, Bell Canada Limited reported $20.2 million prepaid pension cost in 1988 and $7.1 million accrued pension cost in 1989.

Employer Pension Obligations The **projected benefit obligation** (PBO) is the actuarial present value of the benefits attributed to employee service rendered to date, as measured by the pension formula. Service cost increases PBO, while benefit payments reduce PBO.

PBO at the end of the first year of a pension plan (without amendments) equals service cost ($1,872 for Whitney), because service cost is also the present value of benefits earned in the first year. The AcSB believes that PBO is the most representationally faithful measure of the pension obligation because it is an estimate of a present obligation to make future cash payments as a result of past transactions. The going-concern assumption supports the use of future compensation levels in calculating PBO.

Plan Assets Plan assets are exclusively restricted for the payment of pension benefits. Except for plan terminations, the employer should not have access to plan assets. Otherwise, a plan's funded status is very uncertain. Plan assets include investments (primarily stocks, bonds, and other securities) and operational assets used in administering the pension fund.

Investment assets are valued at market value or market-related value. The market value is the amount realizable through normal sale. **Market-related value** equals market value or a calculated value that is adjusted to market value of plan investments over a period not exceeding five years. The use of market-related value reduces the volatility of periodic pension expense.

For simplicity, this chapter assumes that the pension fund consists entirely of investments and that market (or fair) value and market-related value are equal.

Funded Status, 1991 The funded status of a plan is the difference between PBO and the plan assets at fair value; it indicates whether the plan is underfunded or overfunded. Funded status is the critical measure of a pension plan. Lone Pine's plan is underfunded because PBO exceeds the pension fund's fair value, as indicated in Exhibit 19–3.

At the end of 1991, the pension fund holds $1,500, the first contribution made by Lone Pine. PBO and fund assets describe separate characteristics of the pension plan and are not related. However, they have two attributes in common: Neither is recorded in the accounts of the employer and both are reduced by benefit payments. Benefit payments are paid from plan assets and extinguish the employer's liability. They are recorded by the trustee rather than by the employer.

PBO and plan assets are not recorded in the employer's accounts. This is an example of off-balance-sheet financing. The disclosure of funded status is an example of offsetting, one of three fundamental aspects of prior pension accounting retained by section 3460. In this example, the plan's funded status equals the balance in the accrued pension cost account. Therefore, Lone Pine's plan assets are offset against PBO

EXHIBIT 19-4   New Information and Initial Pension Calculations, Lone Pine Corporation, 1992

1992 compensation for Nicole Whitney: $47,250 (a 5% raise for 1992)
Estimated salary at retirement: $150,000 (unchanged)
Funding for 1992: $2,000 (increased)
Service cost for 1992:
    Annual retirement benefit earned in 1992 = 2% × 1 service year × $150,000 = $3,000
                Service cost, 1992 = $3,000 × (PVA, 10%, 10) × (PV1, 10%, 23*)
                          = $3,000 × 6.14457 × .11168 = $2,059

    PBO, December 31, 1992 = $6,000† × (PVA, 10%, 10) × (PV1, 10%, 23) = $4,117

* 23 years from December 31, 1992, to retirement.
† Whitney has earned two years of retirement benefits or $6,000 according to the formula:
$$2\% \times 2 \text{ years} \times \$150,000 = \$6,000$$

for balance sheet reporting. There are no reconciling items. Later in this chapter, the reconciling items that result from certain compromises made by the AcSB are discussed.

Non-recognition of PBO is controversial. The AcSB was sensitive to concerns that recognition of PBO in the balance sheet would greatly increase many companies' debt levels. For example, in 1984, a large corporation's unfunded pension liability was 148% of the total market value of its outstanding shares.

1992: Components 1b and c of Pension Expense   Information and pension calculations appear in Exhibit 19–4 for 1992.

Interest Cost (Component 1b of Pension Expense)

The second component of pension expense, interest cost, is the growth in PBO during a reporting period. At December 31, 1991, PBO equals $1,872. Therefore, interest cost for 1992 equals $187 ($1,872 × .10). The amount of the liability for Whitney's first year benefits only is $2,059, computed in two ways:

$$\$2,059 = \$1,872 \times 1.10 \text{ (interest for one year)}$$

Or

$$\$2,059 = \$3,000 \times (PVA, 10\%, 10) \times (PV1, 10\%, 23)$$

$$= \$3,000 \times 6.14457 \times .11168$$

Lone Pine must have $1,872 invested at December 31, 1991, to provide the benefits promised in 1991, and must have $2,059 invested at December 31, 1992, for the same benefits. The $187 difference is interest cost, PBO ($2,059 − $1,872). The current year service cost is not part of interest cost.

PBO ($4,117 in Exhibit 19–4) is the present value of benefit payments earned through that date. An alternative method to compute PBO highlights the relationship of pension expense components and PBO:

PBO, December 31, 1992:
Service cost through December 31, 1992 = $1,872 + $2,059 = $3,931
Interest cost through December 31, 1992 . . . . =   187
Benefits paid to Whitney through December 31, 1992 . . . =   –0–
PBO, December 31, 1992 . . . . $4,118

($1 discrepancy is due to rounding of present value factors)

Actual Return on Plan Assets (Component 1c of Pension Expense)

The actual return on plan assets, Component 1c of pension expense, is the increase or decrease in plan assets at fair value, adjusted for contributions and benefit payments.

The following equation shows the changes in the fund during a period:

Beginning fund balance
+ Actual return
+ Employer contributions
− Benefit payments
Ending fund balance

Return on plan assets reduces pension expense by partially or wholly offsetting the interest cost component and increasing the pension fund assets. Actual return on fund assets includes dividends and interest, and realized and unrealized changes in the fair value of plan assets.

The example assumes, for simplicity, that the actual return is 10% of the beginning fund balance, and that it equals the expected return. The fund balance at the beginning of 1992 is $1,500 (contribution in 1991). Therefore, the actual return in 1992 is $150 (10% × $1,500). Pension expense in 1991 does not reflect an actual return component because no fund existed at the beginning of 1991.

Pension expense for 1992 is computed as follows:

Service cost . . . . $2,059 (from Exhibit 19–4)
Interest cost   187
Actual return . . . .   (150)
Pension expense, 1992 . . . . $2,096

Lone Pine funds $2,000 in 1992 (Exhibit 19–4) and records the following entry to recognize pension expense:

December 31, 1992 — To record pension expense:

Pension expense 2,096
    Accrued/prepaid pension cost   96
    Cash   2,000

Pension expense increased in 1992 because service cost reflects a shorter period to retirement, interest cost increases pension expense, and actual return is less than interest cost. The balance in accrued/prepaid pension cost at December 31, 1992, is $468 ($372 from 1991 + $96). The $96 increase represents a further funding deficiency. Full funding required a contribution of $2,468 ($2,096 + $372 previous accrued/prepaid pension cost balance) in 1992.

Funding levels and pension expense are inversely related because actual return reduces pension expense. For example, if the plan were fully funded in 1991 ($1,872 contribution), pension expense in 1992 is $2,059 (1992 service cost) because interest cost and actual return exactly offset. Early full funding results in smaller subsequent pension expense.

The fund balance at the end of 1992 is as follows:

Fund balance, January 1, 1992 . . . . $1,500
Actual return, 1992   150
Sponsor contributions, 1992 2,000
Benefits paid, 1992 . . . .   –0–
Fund balance, December 31, 1992 . . . . $3,650

In practice, the discount rate and actual earnings rate may differ appreciably in any given year. For example, assume both PBO and the fund balance at the beginning of a year is $100,000, and the discount rate is 10%. If the actual interest rate earned during the year is only 7%, pension expense is increased by $3,000, the actual return ($7,000)

EXHIBIT 19–5   Reconciliation of Funded Status and Accrued/Prepaid Pension Cost, Lone Pine
Corporation, December 31, 1992

Projected benefit obligation.	($4,118)
Plan assets at fair value.	3,650
Underfunded PBO (funded status)	($ 468)
Balance in (accrued)/prepaid pension cost	($ 468)

EXHIBIT 19–6   Summary of Relationships among Pension Items

	Effect On:		
Item	**Pension Expense**	**Projected Benefit Obligation**	**Plan Assets**
Service cost	Increase	Increase	No effect
Interest cost	Increase	Increase	No effect
Actual return	Decrease	No effect	Increase
Contributions	No effect*	No effect	Increase
Benefit payments	No effect	Decrease	Decrease

* Contributions indirectly reduce future pension expense by increasing plan assets and, therefore, actual return.

falls short of the interest cost ($10,000). The shortfall is the employer's responsibility, and is therefore part of the employer's expense.

Exhibit 19–5 shows the reconciliation of funded status for 1992. Relationships among several new terms introduced in this section are summarized in Exhibit 19–6.

Pension Spreadsheet   The spreadsheet in Exhibit 19–7 brings together the reports of the actuary and trustee, emphasizing the relationship among pension variables.

The spreadsheet reinforces certain pension relationships listed in Exhibit 19–6. For example, service cost and interest cost appear in the PBO and pension expense columns as an addition. Actual return increases assets but is entered as a negative item in the pension expense column. The contribution is a positive entry in the assets column, and is a decrease in the accrued/prepaid pension cost column.

Pension Expense Based on Funding Levels   The belief that an exchange takes place between employer and employee supports attribution as the basis for expense recognition. In exchange for services provided by the employee, the employer provides a pension. Pension benefits are deferred compensation recognized during periods worked by the employees. The amount funded by the employer is not the primary factor in the measurement of pension expense. Funding is a financing issue; expense recognition is a measurement issue.

The AcSB rejected the cost approach, an alternative to attribution, as the basis for recognizing pension expense. The cost approach projects the estimated total benefit at retirement and determines the annual contribution (funding) necessary to provide that benefit. Under this approach, pension expense equals the necessary contribution. For the Nicole Whitney example, this approach recognizes only $208 of pension expense in 1991, computed as follows:

$$P \times (FVA, 10\%, 24) = \$3,000 \times (PVA, 10\%, 10)$$

$$P \times 88.49733 = \$3,000 \times 6.14457$$

$$P = \$208$$

EXHIBIT 19–7   Pension Spreadsheet

	PBO (Actuary)	Plan Assets (Trustee)	Pension Expense	(Accrued)/ Prepaid Pension Cost
	LONE PINE COMPANY			
	Pension Plan Spreadsheet, 1992			
Beginning balances, 1992	$1,872	$1,500		$ (372)
Service cost	2,059		$2,059	
Interest cost	187		187	
Actual return		150	(150)	
Contributions		2,000		2,000
Benefits paid	0	0		
Ending balances:				
PBO	$4,118			
Plan assets		$3,650		
Underfunded PBO		$468		
Pension expense			$2,096	(2,096)
Accrued pension cost				$ 468

where:

P. = the annual payment required to fulfill the expected retirement annuity

The left side of the preceding equation is the accumulation of an annuity of $208 each year for 24 years, Whitney's remaining service period. That accumulation is necessary to fund the retirement annuity of $3,000 each year to Whitney. Lone Pine need only contribute $208 annually for 24 years to fulfill the benefits promised Whitney based on her service in 1991.

However, as Whitney provides more years of service, the necessary payment increases. For example, the required payment needed to fulfill the benefits earned in Whitney's last service year alone is $18,434 computed as [$3,000 × (*PVA, 10%, 10*)]. Furthermore, this amount adds to the required annual payments for earlier years of service. The cost approach would have provided an incentive to maintain very low funding levels early in the pension plan, to the possible detriment of the participants.

According to the AcSB, the cost approach focusses on the financing, rather than the accrual aspects of the pension plan. The benefit formula is a more relevant basis for determining pension cost. In addition, the attribution approach is more consistent with *CICA Handbook* section 1000 which defines liabilities as obligations. The employer's obligation for a defined benefit pension plan is determined by the benefit formula, rather than by the necessary funding amount.

Future compensation levels   Many benefit formulas incorporate future compensation levels. In these cases, pension expense reflects these estimated higher compensation levels before they are conferred. Service cost is therefore based on (1) service to the measurement date and (2) compensation levels associated with periods after the measurement date. The AcSB perceived a major difference between promising to pay 2% of final pay and 2% of current pay.

In practice, in addition to future compensation levels, service cost considers expected inflation, productivity, seniority, and automatic cost of living increases and promotion. Although future salaries are contingent on future events, service cost reflects estimates of turnover, life expectancy, and disability, thus considering only those likely to reach that salary.

Delayed Recognition   *CICA Handbook* section 3460 postpones the recognition of certain changes in the employer's pension obligations and plan assets. Delayed recognition is a fundamental aspect of current pension accounting. The changes are recognized systematically over subsequent periods. The unamortized (unrecognized) amounts are carried forward to the next accounting period.

One effect of delayed recognition is that the balance in accrued/prepaid pension cost does not equal the plan's funded status. Reconciling items are required in the funded status report. For example, an increase in PBO resulting from a plan amendment is recognized only gradually in pension expense. Therefore, the balance in the accrued/prepaid pension cost reflects only the portion of the increase in PBO amortized to date. Delayed recognition is an example of accounting for estimate changes. As new information becomes available, the economic effects are treated currently and prospectively.

The primary purpose of delayed recognition is to reduce the volatility of pension reporting by spreading changes in the pension plan over a number of years. Delayed recognition increased the acceptance of the revisions in section 3460 by the business community. Investors consider increased volatility in expenses and income a symptom of increased risk.

Many groups criticize delayed recognition on the basis that it materially understates both assets and liabilities over the long term. Pension expense does not reflect the true economic cost of the pension plan under this view. However, footnote disclosure of the unrecognized items partially mitigates this problem. The remaining pension expense components and additional liability are discussed in the next sections.

CONCEPT REVIEW

1. How is the benefit formula used in the calculation of service cost for a period?
2. Why are pension expense, service cost, and projected benefit obligation equal to each other for the first year of Lone Pine's pension plan?
3. Why are PBO and plan assets not recorded in the accounts?

PRIOR SERVICE COST (COMPONENT 2 OF PENSION EXPENSE)

◆

Prior service cost (PSC) results from plan amendments granting employees and retirees pension benefits attributable to service rendered before the pension plan was initiated or from later plan amendments that granted increased pension benefits attributable to service rendered before the amendment.

Retroactive increases in pension benefits are a common result of collective bargaining agreements. For example, if an employer initiates a pension plan in 1992, employees who started in 1980 suffer severe injustice if not granted pension benefits for services rendered before 1992. Almost all plans recognize service rendered before the inception of the plan.[7]

PSC, the present value of increased benefits under the amendment, is an increase in PBO. An expanded expression of PBO follows:

$$
\begin{array}{l}
\ \text{Sum of service cost to measurement date} \\
+\ \text{Sum of interest cost to measurement date} \\
+\ \text{PSC (present value at measurement date)} \\
-\ \underline{\text{Benefits paid to measurement date}} \\
=\ \underline{\underline{\text{PBO at measurement date}}}
\end{array}
$$

---

[7] Mark Warshawsky, *The Funding of Private Pension Plans* (New York: Board of Governors of the Federal Reserve System, 1987), p. 3.

EXHIBIT 19–8 Information for Example

SIERRA COMPANY
Information for Example of PSC Amortization

Date of amendment: January 1, 1991
Amendment grant: Increased benefits to all active employees through retroactive increase in benefits per service year.*
PSC: Present value of increased benefits at January 1, 1991, is $48,000
Active employees and remaining estimated service years at January 1, 1991: Five employees with a total of 12 years.

Employee	Employee Service Years				
	1991	**1992**	**1993**	**1994**	**Total**
Jim	1				1
Frank†	1	1			2
Susan	1	1			2
Kate	1	1	1		3
Bill	1	1	1	1	4
Service years per fiscal year	5	4	2	1	12

Note: Average remaining service period: 12 total years/five employees = 2.4 years.

* The present value of these benefits and PBO are computed in a similar fashion.

† Frank has two years of service remaining: 1991 and 1992.

Assume that on January 1, 1992, Lone Pine Company (from Exhibit 19–2) amends its plan to award Whitney an additional annual $500 retirement benefit, for service rendered in 1991. Nicole has 24 years of service remaining, and she expects to draw 10 retirement payments. PSC is computed as follows:

PSC, January 1, 1992 = Present value of increased benefits granted by amendment

$$= \$500 \times (PVA, 10\%, 10) \times (PV1, 10\%, 24)$$

$$= \$500 \times 6.14457 \times .10153 = \$312$$

Employers who increase pension benefits attributable to prior periods receive benefits in future periods through improved employee productivity and morale, reduced turnover, and reduced demands for pay raises.[8] For this reason, and because immediate recognition is too great a departure from past pension accounting, the AcSB decided to require delayed recognition of PSC. Therefore, PSC is amortized in periods after the grant and PSC is not recorded in an account.

Amortization (recognition) of PSC is the fourth component of pension expense and generally increases pension expense.[9] PSC is amortized over the expected average remaining service life of the employee group at the date of the amendment. Employees hired after that date do not affect the amortization. The number of years used for amortization is not subsequently changed, except for a curtailment (discussed in Appendix 19A). Amortization of PSC is limited to amounts known at the beginning of the year.

Amortizing Prior Service Cost

The straight-line method which amortizes PSC over the average remaining service period of employees covered under the plan is illustrated in the next section. Although

---

[8] It is difficult to support retroactive recognition of PSC. The quality of their service could not have been affected by an unknown future grant.

[9] A plan amendment may reduce PBO by reducing future benefits on a retroactive basis. The reduction is first used to reduce any existing unrecognized PSC. The amortization of the excess reduces pension expense.

EXHIBIT 19–9 Reconciliation of Funded Status

SIERRA COMPANY
Summary Pension Plan Information and
Reconciliation of Funded Status and Accrued/Prepaid Pension Cost
December 31, 1991

PSC information applies from Exhibit 19–8
Unrecognized PSC, December 31, 1991: $28,000
Service cost, 1991: $300,000
Interest cost, 1991: $80,000
Actual return on plan assets: $90,000
PBO, December 31, 1991: $1,200,000 (includes PSC granted January 1, 1991)
Plan assets at fair value: $962,000
Accrued/prepaid pension cost, December 31, 1991: $210,000 cr. (after recording pension expense)

Pension Expense, 1991:

Service cost	$300,000
Interest cost.	80,000
Actual return	(90,000)
Amortization of PSC	20,000
Pension expense.	$310,000

Reconciliation of Funded Status, December 31, 1991

Projected benefit obligation	($1,200,000)
Plan assets at fair value	962,000
Underfunded PBO (funded status).	($ 238,000)
Unrecognized PSC	28,000
Balance in (accrued)/prepaid pension cost.	($ 210,000)

other methods of amortization might be appropriate, straight-line has the advantage of being simple. Exhibit 19–8 presents the information for an example.

Straight-Line Method The average remaining service period for the employee group is 2.4 years, as indicated in Exhibit 19–8. The following table illustrates the results of the straight-line method:

Year	Amortization Recognized	Unrecognized PSC at December 31
1991	$48,000/2.4 = $20,000	$48,000 − $20,000 = $28,000
1992	$48,000/2.4 = $20,000	$28,000 − $20,000 = $ 8,000
1993	Remainder $ 8,000	$ 8,000 − $8 ,000 = –0–

The straight-line method related total PSC to the average service period of employees under the plan. The method fully amortizes PSC before the last covered employee retires, a violation of the matching concept. However, frequent plan amendments may imply that the benefit period of each amendment is shorter than the entire service period of active employees. The straight-line method is particularly suited to these circumstances.

Because the cost of the amendment was known at the beginning of 1991, amortization of the PSC began in 1991. Section 3460 allows that the amortization may commence in the period following the determination of the adjustment arising from the initiation or amendment (paragraph 3460.41).

Reconciliation of Funded Status and Accrued/Prepaid Pension Cost

Unrecognized PSC is a reconciling amount in the funded status and report. Exhibit 19–9 presents summary information for Sierra Company's pension plan and the reconciliation for 1991.

Sierra's plan is underfunded by $238,000. However, $28,000 of unrecognized PSC remains unrecognized. Until recognized, it does not affect pension expense, and therefore does not affect accrued/prepaid pension cost. The unrecognized PSC explains why funded status and accrued/prepaid pension cost are not equal.

CONCEPT REVIEW

1. What are the two sources of prior service cost? How is prior service cost computed?
2. Explain the effect of prior service cost on the projected benefit obligation.
3. What is the rationale for amortizing PSC in current and future periods?

UNRECOGNIZED GAINS AND LOSSES (COMPONENTS 3 AND 4 OF PENSION EXPENSE)

Pension accounting is greatly dependent on estimates that must be updated as new information becomes available. For example, PBO reflects estimates of employee turnover. If turnover is greater than expected, PBO is reduced because the estimate of benefit payments is decreased.

Two Sources of Gains and Losses A gain occurs when a change in actuarial estimate or experience decreases the PBO, or when actual return on plan assets exceed expected return. The opposite holds true for pension losses. Pension gains decrease pension expense when recognized because gains reduce the cost of the pension plan to the employer. Pension losses conversely increase pension expense.

PBO gains and losses are subdivided into adjustments arising from changes in assumptions and experience gains and losses. An experience gain (loss) occurs when actual results are more (less) favourable than planned. The previous turnover example caused an experience gain. An actuarial gain (loss) occurs when changes in assumptions about future events reduce (increase) PBO. Increasing the discount rate reduces the present value of future payments and causes an actuarial gain.

In each accounting period, the actuary provides information about PBO gains and losses, and the trustee provides information about asset gains and losses. The gains and losses from both sources are combined to form a net gain or loss for accounting purposes. The employer amortizes the net gain or loss to periodic pension expense in a rational and systematic manner, usually over the expected average remaining service life of the employee group.

Unrecognized gains and losses are accounted separately from PSC although both may represent increases in PBO. Unrecognized gains and losses have more than one source and may offset each other to some extent. PSC is not offset against other pension items because it is unique. Furthermore, the employee group to which unrecognized gains and losses relate may change over time. PSC pertains to one specific employee group. For these reasons, PSC and unrecognized gains and losses warrant separate accounting treatment.

To illustrate the calculation of an actuarial loss, reconsider the Nicole Whitney example from Exhibit 19–4. In that example, Lone Pine used a 10% discount rate to compute PBO at December 31, 1992, as follows:

$$PBO, \text{ December 31, 1992} = \$6,000 \times (PVA, 10\%, 10) \times (PV1, 10\%, 23)$$

$$= \$6,000 \times 6.14457 \times .11168 = \underline{\underline{\$4,118}}$$

EXHIBIT 19–10   Information for White Mountain Company: Calculation of Experience Gains or Losses, 1991

Plan assets (from plan trustee):
    Actual market value January 1, 1991 . . . . $220,000
    Contributions—1991   40,000
    Return on plan assets—1991   24,000
    Expected value—December 31, 1991 . . . . $284,000
    Actual market value December 31, 1991 292,000
    Experience gain—1991 . . . . $ 8,000
Projected benefit obligation (from actuary):
    PBO January 1, 1991 . . . . $260,000
    Interest on accrued benefits   26,000
    Service cost—1991   48,000
    Contributions—1991. . . . . (40,000)
    Expected value December 31, 1991 . . . . $294,000
    Actual PBO December 31, 1991 299,000
    Experience loss—1991 . . . . $ 5,000

EXHIBIT 19–11   Information for White Mountain Company: Component 4 of Pension Expense, 1991

Service cost, 1991: $48,000
Interest cost, 1991: $26,000
Actual return on plan assets, 1991: $24,000
Amortization of PSC, 1991 (assumed): $7,000
Amortization of change in assumption, 1991 (assumed): $(600)
Net experience gain, 1991 ($8,000 − $5,000): $3,000
Expected average remaining service life (assumed): 10 years

At the beginning of January 1993, on the advice of its actuary, Lone Pine decides to reduce the discount rate to 8%, based on changing market conditions. PBO is recalculated as follows:

$$PBO, \text{ January 1, 1993} = \$6,000 \times (PVA, 8\%, 10) \times (PV1, 8\%, 23)$$
$$= \$6,000 \times (6.71008) \times (.17032) = \underline{\$6,857}$$

The resulting $2,739 actuarial loss is the difference between the original and adjusted PBO ($6,857 − $4,118).

Similar to PSC, unrecognized gains and losses are subject to delayed recognition because gains and losses are subject to offset by future gains and losses. For example, future PBO increases from changing life expectancy and turnover can offset previous PBO decreases.

The AcSB was sympathetic to exposure draft respondents who maintained that immediate recognition of gains and losses produces unacceptable volatility in pension expense. Ultimately, total pension expense equals total contributions made by the firm to the fund. Recognition of all short-term gains and losses under the periodicity assumption does not necessarily provide relevant information about long-run pension costs.

Many firms strive to reduce pension expense volatility. For example, immediate recognition of the huge losses suffered by many pension funds from Black Monday (October 19, 1987) would have unnecessarily increased pension expense for many firms, because the market has since recovered much of its loss.

EXHIBIT 19–12   Unamortized Pension Costs, Chicopee Company, 1991–1992

Unamortized Pension Costs	January 1, 1991	Years Remaining
PSC.	$180,000	15
Net gain—1988	32,000	12
Net loss—1989.	16,000	14
Net loss—1990.	26,000	13
December 31 results		**EARSL***
Net gain—1991	$ 11,000	11
Net loss—1992.	14,000	12

General Example of Components 3 and 4

Component 3—Gains and losses arising from changes in assumptions are amortized to pension expense over the expected average remaining service life of the employee group. Therefore, in the Nicole Whitney case, the actuarial loss of $2,739 will be amortized over the next 23 years at $119 ($2,739/23) per year beginning in 1993, the year the change was made.

Component 4—Experience gains and losses arise because period-end expected values for either the plan assets or the PBO differ from actual period-end values. Exhibit 19–10 illustrates the determination of experience gains or losses for plan assets and the PBO for White Mountain Company.

The experience gains and losses are thus determined by using the actual balances at the beginning of the period, adding or subtracting the transactions during the period to arrive at the expected values, and comparing the actual values as determined by the trustee and actuary, respectively, to the expected values.

Exhibit 19–11 contains information to illustrate the effect of Component 4 on pension expense. The objective of this example, which assumes several values discussed later, is to present a picture of pension expense using the components described to this point. Pension expense for 1991 is therefore computed as follows:

Service cost.	$ 48,000
Interest cost.	26,000
Actual return on assets	(24,000)
Amortization of PSC	7,000
Amortization of change in assumptions	(600)
Amortization of net experience gain ($3,000/10)	(300)
Pension expense, 1991.	$ 56,100

Unamortized PSC, Change in Assumptions, and Experience Gains and Losses

In the determination of the preceding pension expense, the net experience gain determined in 1991 is amortized in 1991. Although this may appear appropriate, section 3460 of the *CICA Handbook* allows that the amortization of any adjustments for changes in assumptions or experience gains and losses may commence in the period following their determination.

The adjustments do not appear on the balance sheet. As shown earlier, however, their amortization enters into the calculation of pension expense for the period. Therefore, it is necessary to maintain a schedule of the total adjustments, the amounts amortized, and the remaining balances to be amortized into the determination of pension expense. Exhibit 19–12 provides an example of unamortized pension costs.

The PSC arose through a revision to the pension plan prior to 1988. The net gains and losses arose in the years indicated. The costs are being amortized over the

EXHIBIT 19-13   Amortization Schedule for Unamortized Pension Costs, Chicopee Company, December 31

	1991	1992
Opening balance*	$190,000	$166,524
Net (gain) loss 1991	(11,000)	
Net (gain) loss 1992		14,000
Amortization of PSC ($180,000/15)	(12,000)	(12,000)
Amortization of 1988 gain ($32,000/12)	2,667	2,667
Amortization of 1989 loss ($16,000/14)	(1,143)	(1,143)
Amortization of 1990 loss ($26,000/13)	(2,000)	(2,000)
Amortization of 1991 gain ($11,000/11)		1,000
Closing balance	$166,524	$169,048

* From Exhibit 19–12 ($180,000 − $32,000 + $16,000 + $26,000).

expected average remaining service life (EARSL) of the employee group established at the time the gains or losses were determined. The years remaining column indicates the number of years left in the amortization period.

Exhibit 19–13 illustrates an amortization schedule for unamortized costs using the information from Exhibit 19–12. The amortization is assumed to commence in the year following the determination of adjustments.

The 1991 opening balance in Exhibit 19–13 represents the unamortized portion of the pension costs as of January 1, 1991. The amortization of these amounts in 1991 would increase pension expense by $12,476 ($12,000 − $2,667 + $1,143 + $2,000). The amortization of the 1991 net gain does not begin until 1992, as indicated. Similarly, the 1992 net loss would not begin to be amortized until 1993.

CONCEPT REVIEW

1. What is the rationale for delayed recognition of pension gains and losses?
2. Explain how the computation of pension expense may be affectd by past service costs. What adjustments are necessary for components 3 and 4 of pension expense?
3. Explain how amortization of unrecognized pension costs reduces volatility in pension expense.

UNRECOGNIZED TRANSITION ASSET OR LIABILITY (COMPONENT 5 OF PENSION EXPENSE)

In an effort to reduce the impact of the accounting changes, *CICA Handbook* section 3460 established a phase-in period for adjustment to the new requirements. With some exceptions, employers of all affected plans were to comply with the provisions of section 3460 for reporting years beginning after December 1, 1986.

Under the previous pension pronouncement, employers frequently reported a pension asset or liability account similar to accrued/prepaid pension cost. The transition asset or liability bridges the gap between the two pronouncements.

The concept of delayed recognition is applied to this pension item, the fifth and final component of pension expense. Similar to the amortization of unrecognized net gains or losses, amortization of unrecognized transition assets or liabilities may increase or decrease pension expense.

The fifth component is unique because it results from a transition asset or liability which occurs only once; after it is fully amortized, the fifth component is no longer an ingredient of pension expense.

Transition Asset or Liability The transition asset or liability equals the difference, at date of transition, between the actuarial present value of the accrued pension benefits, and the value of pension fund assets. The transition asset or liability affects neither PBO nor plan assets. The transition item includes unrecognized gains and losses and unrecognized prior service cost from accounting under the earlier version of section 3460.

When a liability, the transition item is similar to PSC. It is that part of underfunded PBO resulting from benefits promised before transition to the new accounting principles, and may result from past retroactive grants. The amortization of a transition asset is a gain and reduces pension expense.

The transition asset or liability is amortized on a straight-line basis over the average remaining service period of employees expected to receive benefits under the plan.

Rationale for Present Accounting Treatment The unrecognized transition item is actually the result of several components: (1) unrecognized costs of past retroactive plan amendments, (2) unrecognized net gain or loss from previous periods, and (3) the cumulative effect of past accounting principles which were different from the current section 3460. Although the AcSB considered treating this element as a change in accounting principle, it decided that separation of the several components is not practical. Consequently, the unrecognized transition item is treated as a change in estimate, currently and prospectively through delayed recognition amortization. This treatment provides yet another source of income smoothing.

Other factors contributed to the adoption of delayed recognition. Many firms with underfunded plans have large transition liabilities. Respondents to the exposure draft preceding the *Handbook* section argued that immediate recognition of both the liability and resulting expense would adversely affect the perception of these firms in the marketplace. Current and prospective treatment is counter to the common retroactive treatment afforded new accounting principles that significantly alter previous accounting.

CONCEPT REVIEW

1. Explain how the transition asset or liability is computed. What does it represent?
2. How is the transition asset or liability unique among the three pension items subject to delayed recognition?
3. Why does amortization of a transition asset reduce pension expense?

COMPREHENSIVE CASE AND GENERAL PENSION DISCLOSURES

The following case provides an illustration of the interrelationships among pension accounts and unrecognized items as they change over three accounting periods.

On January 1, 1989, the Owens Valley Company converts to section 3460 of the *CICA Handbook* for its non-contributory, defined benefit pension plan. On that date, Owens Valley has a $10,000 accrued pension liability. Exhibit 19–14 provides the basic information to account for pensions for 1989, 1990, and 1991.

The actuary and trustee provide most of the information necessary for the accounting. Their reports reveal the components and balances of PBO and plan assets. The accounting entries and other disclosures are provided for each year and the disclosures required by section 3460 are presented at the end of the case.

1989 The beginning balances across the top of the spreadsheet in Exhibit 19–15 originate from several sources. The actuary provides the beginning amount of PBO, and the trustee's report is the source of plan assets at fair value. The employer's informal record supplies the unrecognized transition liability.

EXHIBIT 19–14   Pension Plan Information

OWENS VALLEY COMPANY
Pension Plan Information

Transition date: January 1, 1989
Transition liability January 1, 1989: $20,000

From Actuary's Report	1989	1990	1991
Discount rate used by actuary	10%	10%	10%
Average remaining service period of employees (years)	10	10	12
PBO, January 1	$100,000	$150,000	$195,000
Service cost	40,000	50,000	60,000
Interest cost (10% of PBO at January 1)	10,000	15,000	19,500
PSC (determined January 1)*		20,000	
Actuarial loss (December 31)[†]	30,000		
Experience gain (December 31)[‡]			(12,000)
Benefit payments to retirees	(30,000)	(40,000)	(40,000)
PBO, December 31	$150,000	$195,000	$222,500

From Trustee's Report			
Plan assets at fair value, January 1	$ 80,000	$ 95,000	$116,000
Return on plan assets	8,000	8,550	9,280
Contributions by Owens Valley	36,000	50,000	55,000
Benefit payments to retirees	(30,000)	(40,000)	(40,000)
Expected asset value, December 31	$ 94,000	$113,550	$140,280
Experience gain (loss)	1,000	2,450	(1,080)
Plan assets at fair value, December 31	$ 95,000	$116,000	$139,200

Company Assumptions

Unrecognized PSC is amortized over average remaining service period at date of grant.
Unrecognized net gain or loss is amortized over the average remaining service period, beginning in the following year.
Transition item is amortized over 15 years beginning in 1989.

* Change in coverage.

[†] Increase in life expectancy estimates.

[‡] Increase in actual turnover, relative to previous expectations.

The pension expense column is always empty at the beginning of the year because pension expense is closed at the end of the previous year. The pension expense column has three entries corresponding to pension expense Components 1a, b, and c, as well as the amortization of the transition cost. The last column, accrued/prepaid pension cost, begins with a nil balance. This is the only column affecting the employer's balance sheet.

The transition liability is amortized beginning in 1989 because the amount was known at the beginning of the year. The unrecognized gain is not amortized until 1990. The large actuarial loss increases PBO; amortization of this item begins in 1990. Owens Valley makes the following entry to record pension expense for 1989:

December 31, 1989 — To record pension expense:

```
Pension expense  . . . . . . . . . . . . . . . . . . . . . . . . 43,333
    Cash . . . . . . . . . . . . . . . . . . . . . . . . . .        36,000
    Accrued pension cost . . . . . . . . . . . . . . . . . .         7,333
```

The spreadsheet automatically reflects the reconciliation between funded status and the balance in accrued pension cost, at both the beginning and end of the period. For

EXHIBIT 19–15 Pension Plan Spreadsheet

OWENS VALLEY COMPANY

Pension Plan Spreadsheet, 1989, 1990, 1991

Transition liability, January 1, 1989:

	PBO under revised section 3460	$100,000
	Fair value of plan assets	80,000
	Transition liability	$ 20,000

	Memorandum Record			Statement Accounts	
	PBO (Actuary)	**Plan Assets (Trustee)**	**Unrecognized Pension Cost**	**Pension Expense**	**Accrued/ Prepaid Pension Cost**
1989:					
Balance, January 1	$100,000	$ 80,000	$	$	$
Transition liabilities			20,000		
Service cost	40,000			40,000dr	40,000cr
Interest cost	10,000			10,000dr	10,000cr
Actual return		8,000		8,000cr	8,000dr
Benefit payments	(30,000)	(30,000)			
Contribution.		36,000			36,000dr
Actuarial loss	30,000		30,000		
Experience gain		1,000	(1,000)		
1989 amortization:					
Transition—15 years			(1,333)	1,333dr	1,333cr
Balance, December 31	$150,000	$ 95,000	$47,667	$43,333dr	$ 7,333cr
1990:					
Service cost	50,000			$50,000dr	50,000cr
Interest cost	15,000			15,000dr	15,000cr
Actual return		8,550		8,550cr	8,550dr
Benefit payments	(40,000)	(40,000)			
Contribution.		50,000			50,000dr
PSC.	20,000		20,000		
Experience gain		2,450	(2,450)		
1990 amortization:					
Transition.			(1,333)	1,333dr	1,333cr
PSC—10 years.			(2,000)	2,000dr	2,000cr
Actuarial loss 1989—10 years			(3,000)	3,000dr	3,000cr
Gain 1989—10 years.			100	100cr	100dr
Balance, December 31	$195,000	$116,000	$58,984	$62,683dr	$20,016cr
1991:					
Service cost	60,000			$60,000dr	60,000cr
Interest cost	19,500			19,500dr	19,500cr
Actual return		9,280		9,280cr	9,280dr
Benefit payments	(40,000)	(40,000)			
Contribution.		55,000			55,000dr
Net experience gain	(12,000)	(1,080)	(10,920)		
1991 Amortization:					
Transition.			(1,333)	1,333dr	1,333cr
PSC.			(2,000)	2,000dr	2,000cr
Actuarial loss 1989			(3,000)	3,000dr	3,000cr
Gain 1989.			100	100cr	100dr
Gain 1990—10 years.			245	245cr	245dr
Balance, December 31	$222,500	$139,200	$42,076	$76,208dr	$41,224cr

example, underfunded PBO ($55,000) less net unrecognized pension cost ($47,667) yields the ending accrued pension cost balance ($7,333) at the end of 1989.

1990   The ending balances from 1989 carry over to 1990. The total unrecognized pension cost is not a part of the formal accounting record but helps explain the difference between off-balance-sheet amounts and the recorded pension liability. The prior service cost is determined at the beginning of 1990 and its amortization begins in 1990. Owens Valley records pension expense as follows:

December 31, 1990 — To record pension expense:

Pension expense	62,683	
Cash		50,000
Accrued pension cost		12,683

1991   The experience gain on the PBO and the experience loss on the plan assets may be offset against one another for the unrecognized pension costs. Thus, the net gain of $10,920 is to be amortized over 12 years beginning in 1992. The other items are similar to those in 1989 and 1990. Owens records the following entry at the end of 1991:

December 31, 1991 — To record pension expense:

Pension expense	76,208	
Cash		55,000
Accrued pension cost		21,208

Financial Statement Disclosures

Section 3460 of the *CICA Handbook* requires that an enterprise disclose "separately the actuarial present value of accrued pension benefits attributed to services rendered up to the reporting date and the value of the pension fund assets" (paragraph 3460.60).

Paragraph 3460.61 lists other pension information which an enterprise may wish to disclose. The list of other possible disclosures and an indication of how many of the 300 companies surveyed made these disclosures is presented in Exhibit 19–16.

Owens Valley would include the information regarding the accrued pension benefits and the plan assets in the notes to the financial statements section of its annual report in a manner similar to the following:

> Notes to the Financial Statements
> *Pension Information*

	1991	1990	1989
Accrued pension benefits	$ 222,500	$195,000	$150,000
Pension fund assets	139,200	116,000	95,000

Other information with respect to the pension would be included in the financial statements and may or may not be disclosed separately. Therefore, the income statement and balance sheet would include pension expense and the accrued pension cost figures (taken from Exhibit 19–15) although the figures may be aggregated with other expenses and liabilities, respectively.

	1991	1990	1989
Income statement:			
Pension expense (a component of an operating expense such as cost of goods sold, or wages and salaries)	$76,208	$62,683	$43,333
Balance sheet:			
Accrued pension costs (shown separately or as a component of other liabilities)	$41,224	$20,016	$ 7,333

Exhibit 19–17 presents the pension disclosure from the 1989 annual report of Alcan Aluminum Limited.

EXHIBIT 19-16   Other Disclosures

Other disclosures are suggested but not required by new section 3460. For both defined benefit and defined contribution pension plans, disclosure of the following information is suggested:

- The pension expense for the period.
- A general description of the pension plan(s).
- The nature and effect of significant matters affecting comparability of information presented.

For defined benefit plans, additional suggested disclosures are:

- The amount of the deferred charge or accrual for pension costs.
- The basis of valuing pension fund assets.
- The salary and interest rate assumptions used in determining the pension expense and actuarial present value of accrued pension benefits.
- The method and period used to amortize adjustments arising from plan initiation or amendment, changes in assumptions, and experience gains and losses.
- The date of the most recent actuarial valuation performed for accounting purposes.

Disclosure by the survey companies of the additional suggested information was as follows:

	Number of Companies		
	1988	**1987**	**1986**
Basis of valuing pension fund assets	166	124	18
General description of the pension plan(s)	160	125	48
Pension expense for the period	81	75	69
Disclosed in balance sheet or note thereto:			
◆ Deferred charge	46	40	14
◆ Accrual	30	25	9
◆ Both deferred charge and accrual	4	3	1
Amortization of amounts arising from changes in plan's benefits, changes in assumptions, and/or experience gains or losses:			
◆ Period	40	29	54
◆ Method and period	39	17	6
Date of the most recent actuarial valuation	38	46	59
Salary and interest rate assumptions used	34	33	14
Nature and effect of significant matters affecting comparability	30	89	29

Most of the disclosures of the nature and effect of significant matters affecting comparability were in connection with a change in accounting policy on accounting for pension costs.

Source: CICA, *Financial Reporting in Canada, 1989* (Toronto: CICA, 1989), p. 194.

Defined contribution plans have the following disclosure requirements: the present value of required future contributions in respect of past service (paragraph 3460.74). The *CICA Handbook* indicates that enterprises may wish to disclose additional information such as the pension expense for the period, a general description of the pension plan, and the nature and effect of significant matters affecting comparability of information presented (paragraph 3460.75).

For example, Fleetwood Enterprises disclosed the following in its 1988 annual report:

Note 6. Retirement Plans:

The Company has defined contribution retirement plans covering substantially all employees. There are no prior service costs associated with these plans. The Company follows the policy of funding retirement plan contributions as accrued. Contributions to these plans are summarized as follows:

Amounts in thousands

1988	$10,467
1987	9,469
1986	8,779

EXHIBIT 19-17   Alcan Aluminum Limited Pension Disclosure

Notes to Consolidated Financial Statements

15. *Pension Plans*

Alcan and its subsidiaries have established pension plans in the principal countries where they operate, for the greater part contributory and generally open to all employees. Most plans provide pension benefits that are based on the employee's highest average eligible compensation during any consecutive 36-month period before retirement. Plan assets consist primarily of listed stocks and bonds.

Alcan's funding policy is to contribute the amount required to provide for benefits attributed to service to date with projection of salaries to retirement and to amortize unfunded actuarial liabilities for the most part over periods of 15 years or less.

Pension Cost ($ in millions)	1989	1988	1987
Service cost for the year	$ 83	$ 76	$ 63
Interest cost on projected benefit obligations	169	153	130
Actual return on assets	(474)	(222)	(84)
Variance of actual return from expected long-term rate of 8.3% (8.1% in 1988 and 8.0% in 1987) being deferred, and amortization of other gains and losses	251	22	(111)
Net cost for the year	$ 29	$ 29	$ (2)
The plans' funded status at December 31 was:			
Actuarial accumulated benefit obligation which is substantially vested	$2,119	$1,771	$1,571
Plan assets at market value	$2,880	$2,468	$2,204
Actuarial projected benefit obligation based on average compensation growth of 6.2% (6.2% in 1988 and 6.1% in 1987) and discount rate of 8.0% (8.2% in 1988 and 8.1% in 1987)	2,506	2,080	1,879
Plan assets in excess of projected benefit obligation	374	388	325
Unamortized actuarial gains—net*	(466)	(218)	(139)
Unamortized prior service cost*	360	134	150
Unamortized portion of actuarial surplus at January 1, 1986*	(249)	(301)	(329)
Pension asset in balance sheet	$ 19	$ 3	$ 7

* Being amortized over the expected average remaining service life of employees, generally 15 years.

Revising Section 3460

The revised section 3460 issued in 1986 became effective only after lengthy debate. Earlier in this chapter we presented two views of the pension liability: (1) the liability is extinguished to the extent of funded pension benefits and (2) the liability is extinguished when retirement payments are made. The Accounting Standards Board chose a compromise position.

The board rejected the notion that the pension plan bears the obligation for pension benefits and retained the idea that plan assets are controlled by the employer. The AcSB noted the frequent raiding of excess assets by employers as support for this view. However, the AcSB was unwilling to mandate recognition of the projected benefit obligation and assets in the balance sheet.

During the exposure draft phase, considerable support was voiced for disclosure. However, fear of the detrimental effect of PBO recognition in the balance sheet caused respondents to strongly oppose recognition. To a degree, the requirement of footnote disclosure placated those arguing for full liability recognition and appeased those opposing the use of future compensation levels for liability recognition.

The use of future compensation levels for the measurement of a present obligation was opposed by some accountants. In their view, dependence on estimates of factors including compensation levels, inflation, promotion, productivity, and life expectancy, was excessive. Nevertheless, the AcSB believed that PBO is the correct measure of the employer's liability at the balance sheet date.

Certain committee members believed the use of a market-related asset value and the expected rate of return allow too much flexibility in the measurement of pension expense. The result is lack of comparability and uniformity, one of the objectives of section 3460. The AcSB decided that the market or market-related approach was more appropriate.

The AcSB acknowledged that delayed recognition, one of the major ideas underlying the revisions to section 3460, excludes the most current and most relevant information from the employer's balance sheet. The committee noted, however, that immediate recognition of unrecognized pension items is impractical and too great a departure from previous accounting principles, and might cause adverse economic consequences.

The AcSB also noted that to a degree accrued pension cost and expanded footnote disclosures mitigate the effects of delayed recognition. At a minimum, the underfunded pension liability is disclosed in the balance sheet. Furthermore, delayed recognition reduces the volatility of pension expense but does not affect disclosure of PBO or plan assets.

Some plans with assets in excess of PBO may disclose a liability. For example, if the pension fund assets increase in value faster than expected, gains are recognized only on a delayed basis. Therefore, pension expense is larger than under immediate recognition. Under these circumstances, the firm may reduce its contributions; thus, accrued pension cost increases. Pension expense also incorporates an unrecognized net asset at transition as a reducing component only gradually, contributing to liability recognition.

Section 3460 still has its critics. For example, the recommendations allow considerable opportunity for income manipulation. The use of future salaries to measure service cost and the flexibility in choosing the discount rate are two variables an employer can manage for income effect. One study found that the profitability of a company and the rate used for discounting pension obligations are inversely related.[10] Firms with lower profitability chose higher discount rates resulting in lower pension obligations. Although section 3460 reduces that latitude somewhat, the problem of comparability and consistency remains.

SUMMARY OF KEY POINTS

(L.O. 1)   1. There are two basic types of pension plans. Employers bear the risk of providing the specified retirement benefit in a defined benefit plan. A benefit formula defines the amount of retirement benefit. Vested benefits are not contingent on future employment. The employer's responsibility ends with the contribution in defined contribution plans.

(L.O. 1)   2. An overfunded plan is one with assets in excess of the benefit obligation. In an underfunded plan, the pension obligation exceeds assets. The actuary provides much of the data for measuring pension expense and liabilities. The actuary uses present value analysis and estimates of life expectancy, turnover, retirement age, future compensation levels, interest rates, and other variables in measuring a plan's costs and obligations.

(L.O. 2)   3. Pension expense is based on the attribution of benefits to periods of employee service as measured by the benefit formula. The elements of pension expense are service cost, interest cost, actual return, amortization of prior service cost, gain or loss to the extent recognized, and amortization of an unrecognized transition asset or liability.

---

[10] Zvi Bodie, Jay Light, Randal Morck, and Robert Taggart, Jr., "Corporate Pension Policy: An Empirical Investigation," *Financial Analysts Journal*, September–October 1985.

(L.O. 3)   4. Service cost, component 1*a* of pension expense, is the actuarial present value of pension benefits attributed by the benefit formula to services rendered in a period. It is the increase in projected benefit obligation during the period, exclusive of plan amendments, interest cost, and gains or losses.

(L.O. 4)   5. Interest cost, component 1*b* of pension expense, is the growth in projected benefit obligation due to the passage of time. It is the product of the discount rate and beginning projected benefit obligation.

(L.O. 4)   6. Actual return on plan assets, component 1*c* of pension expense, generally reduces pension expense. Actual return, and employer and employee contributions are the sources of plan assets, measured at fair value. Actual return consists of interest, dividends, and realized and unrealized changes in the value of plan assets.

(L.O. 5)   7. Projected benefit obligation is the actuarial present value of all benefits attributed by the formula to employee service rendered to date, and reflects future compensation levels if incorporated by the benefit formula. Projected benefit obligation is the fundamental measure of the pension liability. The difference between projected benefit obligation and fair value of plan assets is the plan's funded status.

(L.O. 6)   8. The change for the period in the balance sheet account, accrued/prepaid pension cost, is the difference between the amount funded and pension expense. The balance in accrued/prepaid pension cost usually does not equal the plan's funded status.

(L.O. 7)   9. Prior service cost, gains and losses, and transition assets or liabilities are not recognized immediately in pension expense or in recorded balance sheet accounts. Rather, to reduce volatility in the measurement of pension expense and liabilities, they are gradually recognized through amortization.

(L.O. 7)   10. Prior service cost is the present value of benefits granted for service rendered before the plan's inception or before a plan amendment date. Gains and losses result from changes in projected benefit obligation and differences between actual and expected return. A transition asset or liability is the difference between the pension asset or liability and the plan's funded status, at the date of adopting section 3460 as revised.

(L.O. 8)   11. The reconciliation of funded status and the balance in accrued/prepaid pension cost highlights the delayed recognition concept in pension accounting. The funded status is critically important for the evaluation of a pension plan. The reconciliation explains why the balance sheet account does not equal funded status, and discloses the remaining unrecognized pension cost amounts.

(L.O. 9)   12. Pension plan settlements, curtailments, and termination benefits are events that require immediate recognition of gains or losses.

(L.O. 10)   13. Pension plans are subject to separate accounting and reporting guidelines. The accumulated benefits of participants are treated as the equity of the pension plan, and equal the plan assets at fair value less plan liabilities.

REVIEW PROBLEM
◆

Each of the following independent cases illustrates a different aspect of pension accounting:

1. *Present value: computation of pension expense, projected benefit, and accumulated benefit.* Raymond is a participant in a pension plan. Information on the plan and Raymond's involvement follow:

Plan inception: January 1, 1991
Funding: $3,000 per year for the first three years
Raymond's first day with the company: January 1, 1991
Raymond's expected service period: 20 years
Raymond's expected final salary: $100,000
Retirement period: 10 years
Raymond's salary for 1991, 1992: $30,000
Discount rate, expected return rate, actual return rate: 10%
Pension benefit formula: Yearly benefit during retirement = (Number
  of years worked) × (Final salary)/25

Required:

a. Compute pension expense for 1991.

b. Compute projected benefit obligation at December 31, 1992.

2. *Components of pension expense.* The following data relate to a defined benefit pension plan:

PBO January 1, 1991, not including any of the following items.	$20,000
Actuary's discount rate	8%
PSC from amendment dated January 1, 1991 (10 years is the amortization period).	$10,000
Unrecognized transition liability, original initial value: $5,000 at January 1, 1989, the transition date unrecognized amount at January 1, 1991	4,000
Gain from change in actuarial assumptions, computed as of January 1, 1991, straight-line amortization, 15-year period	3,000
Actual return on plan assets, 1991.	2,000
Fair value of plan assets January 1, 1991.	16,000
Fair value of plan assets December 31, 1991	15,500
Contributions to plan assets in 1991.	4,000
Benefits paid to retirees in 1991.	5,000
Service cost for 1991	9,000

Required:

a. Compute pension expense for 1991.

b. Compute PBO at January 1, 1992.

c. Compute experience gain or loss on plan assets at December 31, 1991.

3. *Unrecognized gains and losses.* Mountain Oak Company presents the following information related to its pension plan, for 1991, before recording pension expense.

Projected benefit obligation, January 1, 1991	$300,000
Unrecognized gain, January 1, 1991	12,000
Actuarial loss, determined at December 31, 1991	4,000
Plan assets at fair value, January 1, 1991	280,000
Expected long-term rate of return	10%
Plan assets at fair value, December 31, 1991	$295,000
1991 contribution to pension fund	10,000
Benefits paid in 1991	15,000
Average remaining service life of employees:	
January 1, 1991	20 years
January 1, 1992	16 years
Projected benefit obligation, December 31, 1991	$325,000

Required:

a. Determine the amortization of the unrecognized gain for 1991, using straight-line amortization based on average remaining service life.

b. Determine the unrecognized pension costs at January 1, 1992, assuming straight-line amortization.

c. Amortization of unrecognized pension costs, for 1992, assuming straight-line amortization.

REVIEW SOLUTION

◆

1. *a.* Benefit based on future salary levels, earned in 1991:

$$1 \times \$100,000/25 = \$4,000$$

Pension expense, 1991 = service cost, 1991

$$= \$4,000 \times (PVA, 10\%, 10) \times (PV1, 10\%, 19)$$

$$= \$4,000 \times 6.14457 \times .16351 = \$4,019$$

   b. Benefits based on future salary levels, earned through 1992:

$$2 \times \$100,000/25 = \$8,000$$

$$\text{Projected benefit obligation} = \$8,000 \times (PVA, 10\%, 10) \times (PV1, 10\%, 18)$$

$$= \$8,000 \times 6.14457 \times .17986 = \$8,841$$

2. a. Pension expense, 1991:

Service cost	$ 9,000
Interest cost (8% × $27,000*).	2,160
Actual return.	(2,000)
Amortization of PSC $10,000/10	1,000
Amortization of unrecognized gain $3,000/15 . . .	(200)
Amortization of transition liability	500†
Pension expense, 1991	$10,460

* $27,000 = $20,000 + $10,000 (PSC) − $3,000 (gain)

† From the information given, amortization is $500/year.

Amortization of 1991 experience loss begins in 1992.

   b. PBO, January 1, 1992:

PBO, January 1, 1991:	$20,000
PSC.	10,000
Actuarial gain	(3,000)
Revised PBO, January 1, 1991	27,000
Interest cost [8% × $27,000]	2,160
Service cost, 1991	9,000
Benefits paid, 1991	(5,000)
PBO, January 1, 1992	$33,160

   c. Experience gain/loss on plan assets for 1991:

Plan assets at fair value, January 1, 1991	$16,000
Actual return, 1991	2,000
Contributions, 1991	4,000
Benefits paid, 1991	(5,000)
Expected value of plan assets, December 31, 1991 . . .	17,000
Plan assets at fair value, December 31, 1991	15,500
Experience loss, 1991	$ 1,500

3. *a.* Straight-line amortization based on average service life = $12,000/20 = $600, decreases pension expense
   b. Expected return = 10% × $280,000 = $28,000
   Actual return is determined as follows:

$$\$280,000 + \text{Actual return} + \$10,000 - \$15,000 = \$295,000$$

$$\text{Actual return} = \$20,000$$

Experience loss on plan assets: $28,000 − $20,000 = $8,000
Calculation of unrecognized pension costs at January 1, 1992:

Unrecognized gain, January 1, 1991	$(12,000)
1991 amortization of unrecognized gain	600
Actuarial loss, December 31, 1991.	4,000
Experience loss, 1991	8,000
Unrecognized loss, January 1, 1992 . . . . . $	600

c. Amortization of unrecognized pension costs in 1992:

Unrecognized gain, January 1, 1991: $12,000/20 . . . $(600)
Actuarial loss, December 31, 1991: $4,000/16.   250
Experience loss, 1991: $8,000/16.   500
Amortization, 1992—increases expense . . . . $ 150

APPENDIX 19A: *Settlements and Curtailments of Defined Benefit Plans, and Termination Benefits (Component 6 of Pension Expense)*

Employers occasionally make changes to defined benefit plans causing immediate recognition of certain items subject to delayed recognition under section 3460. Paragraphs 3460.53–.55 provide guidelines to account for these events.

For example, plan termination or a plant closing resulting in a significant reduction of personnel may require immediate recognition of unrecognized pension items. Future benefit payments and, therefore, projected benefit obligations (PBO) are reduced. The rationale for delayed recognition no longer applies under these circumstances.

Pension plan curtailments, pension plan settlements, and termination benefits are planned changes, as opposed to actuarial or experience gains and losses.

Pension Plan Settlements   A **settlement** is an irrevocable transaction that relieves the employer (or the plan) of primary responsibility for a pension plan obligation and that eliminates significant risk related to the obligation and assets used to effect the settlement.

Examples include lump-sum cash payments to replace future pension benefits and the purchase of an annuity to cover pension benefits. Employers may partially or completely settle a plan. For example, an employer may settle only the vested benefits and continue the plan. Accumulation of resources in an investment for future payment of pension benefits does not constitute a settlement. The investment is reversible and does not relieve the employer of the pension obligation.

Pension Plan Curtailments   A **curtailment** is an event which either reduces the expected years of future service of present employees, or eliminates, for a significant number of employees, the accrual of defined benefits for some or all of their future services.

Curtailments can occur through termination of employee service earlier than expected, or through a business contraction. The termination or suspension of a plan is also a curtailment if employees do not earn additional defined benefits for future service. Curtailments often decrease PBO, causing a gain. If the benefit formula is based on projected final (or average-final) compensation levels, the curtailment reduces PBO because benefits are reduced. A curtailment may also increase PBO, causing a loss.

Settlements and curtailments can occur simultaneously. For example, a plan termination may cause both a curtailment and a settlement. The employer is relieved of the pension obligation, and there are no expected years of future service.

Termination Benefits   **Termination benefits** are (1) special termination benefits offered for only a short period of time, or (2) contractual termination benefits required by the pension plan only if a special event, such as a plant closing, occurs.

Termination benefits are often provided to employees when their employment is terminated before their expected retirement dates. Termination benefits are also used to encourage employees to voluntarily retire or seek employment elsewhere. For example, a typical offer may be early-retirement incentives to managers as part of a cost-cutting program. Pension payments may be increased by 15% for five years or until age 65, whichever occurs first.

Termination benefits are lump-sum payments, periodic future payments, or both. Termination benefits may be associated with plan termination, although the two are not necessarily related.

EXHIBIT 19A–1   Pension Plan Settlement

HAVASU COMPANY
Accounting for Pension Plan Settlement

Reconciliation schedule, December 31, 1991, after all adjusting entries are completed:
(Dollars in thousands)

Projected benefit obligation	($2,000)
Plan assets at fair value	2,100
Overfunded PBO	100
Unrecognized transition asset	(200)
Unrecognized net gain	(200)
Accrued pension cost	($ 300)
Vested benefit obligation	($1,200)

On December 31, 1991, Havasu settles the vested benefit obligation by purchasing with pension plan assets an annuity contract that transferred the obligation to an insurance company.

Accounting for Settlements

The partial or complete settlement of a pension plan reduces PBO. One justification for delayed recognition of gains and losses is to allow offsetting against future gains and losses. To the extent that PBO is settled, the ability of future gains and losses arising from changes in PBO and asset value is reduced. In addition, settlement of the PBO is viewed as the realization of the net gain or loss at date of settlement.

The gain or loss recognized in a settlement is the net sum of unrecognized gain or loss and the unrecognized transition amounts. The gain or loss is recognized in full if the entire projected benefit obligation is settled. If only part of the projected benefit obligation is settled, a pro rata portion of the amount is recognized. For example, if 25% of the projected benefit obligation is settled, 25% of the gain or loss is recognized.

Therefore, the recognized gain or loss equals:

$$\text{Pro-rata portion of PBO settled} \times \left(\text{Unrecognized net gain or loss} + \text{Unrecognized transition amount}\right)$$

An unrecognized gain is added to the unrecognized transition asset, and an unrecognized loss offsets the unrecognized transition asset. The unrecognized transition asset is included because transition assets are more likely to result from gains before transition than from plan amendments (which usually increase PBO and cause losses).

Exhibit 19A–1 supplies the information for a settlement example. Havasu is settling 60% of its projected benefit obligation ($1,200/$2,000); therefore the recognized gain is $240 ($400 × 60%). Havasu records the gain as follows:

December 31, 1991—To record settlement gain:

Accrued pension cost 240,000
    Settlement gain   240,000

Havasu reports the settlement gain as an operating gain. The debit to accrued pension cost reflects the realization of a previously unrecognized gain. Exhibit 19A–2 illustrates the effect of the settlement on the reconciliation schedule.

The Havasu settlement is not a termination because the plan continues. The assets and PBO are reduced by the settlement. The remaining unrecognized pension items are subject to amortization in future periods.

Accounting for Curtailments

Curtailments reduce the expected future service of some or all employees, and they may increase or decrease PBO. The recognized curtailment gain or loss is the net sum of the change in the PBO and the portion of any unrecognized gains or losses attributable to those employees whose

EXHIBIT 19A-2 Pension Plan Settlement Analysis

HAVASU COMPANY

Analysis of the Effects of Pension Plan Settlement

		Settlement	
(*Dollars in thousands*)	**Before**	**Effects**	**After**
Projected benefit obligation	$(2,000)	$ 1,200	$(800)
Plan assets at fair value	2,100	(1,200)	900
Overfunded PBO	100	0	100
Unrecognized transition asset*	(200)	(120)	(80)
Unrecognized net gain*	(200)	(120)	(80)
Accrued pension cost	$ (300)	$ (240)	$ (60)

* 60% is recognized.

EXHIBIT 19A-3 Pension Plan Curtailment

AMADOR COMPANY

Information for Two Independent Curtailment Cases

1. On January 1, 1991, Amador Company significantly reduces its operations and terminates a number of employees.
2. The curtailment reduces Amador's PBO by $500 and the expected future years of employee service by 50%.
3. Reconciliation schedules for the two cases:

(*Dollars in thousands*)	Case I	Case II
Projected benefit obligation	$(1,000)	$(1,000)
Plan assets at fair value	1,100	900
(Underfunded) overfunded PBO	100	(100)
Unrecognized PSC	40	40
Unrecognized transition (asset), liability	(100)	90
Unrecognized net (gain), loss	(150)	150
(Accrued) prepaid pension cost	$ (110)	$ 180

future services are being reduced. The PBO gain or loss is offset against the unrecognized loss or gain because the change in PBO caused by the curtailment may not be independent of previously unrecognized gains and losses. A part of the PBO, for example, may be related to actuarial assumptions concerning increases in compensation levels that produced currently unrecognized losses. A reduction in future service levels (and therefore a PBO gain) caused by the curtailment is considered to reverse part of the previously unrecognized loss. Hence, the offsetting of PBO gain (loss) with the unrecognized loss (gain). The net gain or loss is recognized immediately.

Exhibit 19A-3 provides information for the next two examples. Exhibits 19A-4 and 19A-5 illustrate the accounting for the curtailments.

In contrast to settlements, plan assets are often not affected by curtailments. In both situations, however, assuming continuation of the plan, the remaining unrecognized pension items are carried forward for future amortization.

Accounting for Termination Benefits

Employers who offer special termination benefits must recognize a loss and a related liability when the employees accept the offer, and termination benefits are estimable. Employers who provide contractual termination benefits must recognize a loss and a related liability when (1) it is probable that employees are entitled to benefits and (2) the amount is estimable.

EXHIBIT 19A-4   Accounting for Curtailment—Case I

AMADOR COMPANY
Accounting for Effects of Curtailment—Case I

Effects on Reconciliation Schedule

		Curtailment	
(*Dollars in thousands*)	**Before**	**Effects**	**After**
Projected benefit obligation	$(1,000)	$500	$ (500)
Plan assets at fair value	1,100		1,100
(Underfunded) overfunded PBO	100		600
Unrecognized PSC*	40	(20)	20
Unrecognized transition (asset) liability*	(100)	50	(50)
Unrecognized net (gain), loss*	(150)	75	(75)
(Accrued) prepaid pension cost.	$ (110)	$605	$ 495

January 1, 1991—To record curtailment gain:

Accrued (prepaid) pension cost 605
  Gain from curtailment   605
(The accrued pension cost liability is now prepaid pension cost.)

* Reduced by 50% by curtailment.

EXHIBIT 19A-5   Accounting for Curtailment—Case II

AMADOR COMPANY
Accounting for Effects of Curtailment—Case II

Effects on Reconciliation Schedule

		Curtailment	
(*Dollars in thousands*)	**Before**	**Effects**	**After**
Projected benefit obligation	$(1,000)	$500	$(500)
Plan assets at fair value	900		900
(Underfunded) overfunded PBO	(100)		400
Unrecognized PSC*	40	(20)	20
Unrecognized transition (asset) liability*	90	(45)	45
Unrecognized net (gain), loss*	150	(75)	75
(Accrued) prepaid pension cost	$ 180	$360	$ 540

January 1, 1991—To record curtailment gain:

Accrued (prepaid) pension cost . . . . — 360
  Gain from curtailment   360

* Reduced by 50% by curtailment.

The cost of termination benefits includes lump-sum payments and the present value of any expected future payments. Termination benefits are paid from company assets or pension plan assets.

Disclosure

For settlements, curtailments, and termination benefits, the employer discloses the following information: (1) a description of the event and (2) the amount of gain or loss recognized. When the gain or loss from settlements, curtailments, or termination benefits is directly related to the disposal of a business segment, it is included in the total gain or loss reported from discontinued operations (discussed in Chapter 4).

APPENDIX 19B: Financial Reporting by Pension Plans

The diversity of reporting practices and the significance of pension assets and benefits prompted the CICA to consider reporting standards for pension plans. The resulting recommendations, section 4100 titled "Pension Plans," establishes standards of financial accounting and reporting for the annual statements of the plan and applies to both defined benefit and defined contribution pension plans.[11]

The financial statements of a pension plan are separate from those of the employer. Pension plan statements report on the amounts available for payment of benefits. Participants of the plan, advisors to participants, investors and creditors of the employer, and government are the main consumers of plan financial statements.

The main objective of plan financial statements is to provide information useful in assessing the present and future ability of the plan to pay benefits when due. To fulfill this objective, information about assets and benefits must appear in pension plan financial statements.

Financial Statement Components

To accomplish the objective of pension plan financial statements, the following three categories of information, measured under the accrual basis of accounting, are required:

1. Net Assets Available for Benefits   The difference between a plan's assets and its liabilities, or net assets available for benefits, is the participants' equity, that amount available to plan participants. Participant benefits are not liabilities of the plan because the plan exists for the benefit of the employees. Liabilities include normal operating liabilities for plan operations.

The assets of a plan include contributions receivable from the employer (and employees if the plan is contributory), investments, and operating assets. Contributions receivable are included in assets if a formal commitment is made by the employer to make a future contribution. Investments are measured at fair value (not a forced or liquidation sale value).[12] Operating assets are measured at cost less accumulated depreciation or amortization.

2. Changes during the Year in the Net Assets Available for Benefits   Minimum disclosure includes:

- Investment income by type of investment, excluding changes in market values of investment assets.
- Changes during the period in the market value of investment assets.
- Contributions from employer and participants.
- Administrative expenses.
- Benefit payments.
- Refunds and transfers.
- Net assets available for benefits at the beginning and the end of the period.

This category provides a much more detailed picture of pension plan assets than is required of the employer.

3. The Actuarial Present Value of Accumulated Plan Benefits   Accumulated plan benefits are the future benefit payments attributable to employee service rendered, to the financial statement date, as measured under the plan's provisions. The present value of benefits is another measure of the total obligation of the employer. Both the time value of money and probability of payment are considered in this measurement.

Changes in actuarial assumptions and experience are treated as estimate changes. For example, if the discount rate used to measure the present value of benefits is decreased, the

---

[11] Section 4100 does not require financial statements to be prepared by the plan. Rather, it establishes principles applying to financial statements when they are prepared and purport to be in accordance with GAAP.

[12] This major departure from the historical cost principle is particularly appropriate in light of the objective of financial statements for pension plans.

EXHIBIT 19B-1   Net Assets Available

INYO COMPANY PENSION PLAN
Statement of Net Assets Available for Benefits
December 31, 1991

Assets

Investments at fair value:

Canadian government securities	$ 400,000	
Investments in corporate bonds	600,000	
Investments in common stock	1,900,000	
Mortgages	700,000	
Real estate	2,100,000	
		$5,700,000
Receivables:		
Employee contributions	300,000	
Accrued interest and dividends	90,000	
		390,000
Cash		250,000
Total assets		$6,340,000

Liabilities

Accounts payable	160,000	
Accrued payables	210,000	
Total liabilities		370,000
Net assets available for benefits		$5,970,000

actuarial present value of accumulated benefits increases. Information about factors causing changes in the actuarial present value of accumulated plan benefits should also be disclosed. This information explains why the present value of accumulated benefits changed during the period and includes plan amendments, changes in actuarial assumptions, benefits earned in the period, and benefits paid. This facilitates an assessment of the plan's ability to pay benefits on a continuing basis, and supplements the disclosures as of a particular date.

Additional required disclosures to supplement the financial statements include the methods used to determine investment fair value, assumptions used to determine the actuarial present value of accumulated benefits, including changes in assumptions, the plan agreement including vesting and benefit provisions, and plan amendments.

Example of Financial Statement Disclosures   The following statements in Exhibits 19B–1 through 19B–4 illustrate the required disclosures for pension plans. Other formats are also acceptable.

In Exhibit 19B–1, the net of plan assets and plan liabilities is referred to as *net assets available for benefits.* Employee benefits are not listed as liabilities because they are the liability of the employer, not the plan.

The statement in Exhibit 19B–2 explains why net assets available increased or decreased. Investment income distinguishes appreciation in market value, interest, and dividends. Contributions also increase the assets available. Benefit payments are the main deduction. The contributions from employees include the receivable $300,000 at year-end listed in the statement of net assets available for benefits. The end of year balance in net assets is the same value for the statements in Exhibits 19B–1 and 19B–2. The present value of accumulated pension benefits is presented in the statement in Exhibit 19B–3.

The term *liability* is not used in the statement in Exhibit 19B–3. The plan is not liable to participants. Rather, the present value of accumulated benefits is one measure of the unpaid benefits earned to date. The statement of net assets available for benefits and the statement of accumulated plan benefits are used to determine the plan's funded status; it may be overfunded or underfunded using current compensation levels to determine the present value of benefits.

EXHIBIT 19B–2   Changes in Net Assets Available

INYO COMPANY PENSION PLAN
Statement of Changes in Net Assets Available for Benefits
For the Year Ended December 31, 1991

Investment income:

Net appreciation in fair value, investments	$ 230,000	
Interest	100,000	
Dividends	150,000	
Rents	80,000	
		$ 560,000
Less: Investment expenses		30,000
		530,000
Contributions:		
Employer	1,500,000	
Employee	450,000	
		1,950,000
Total additions		2,480,000
Benefits	1,300,000	
Administrative expenses	450,000	
Total deductions		1,750,000
Net increase		730,000
Net assets available for benefits:		
Beginning of year		5,240,000
End of year		$5,970,000

EXHIBIT 19B–3   Accumulated Plan Benefits

INYO COMPANY PENSION PLAN
Statement of Accumulated Plan Benefits
December 31, 1991

Actuarial present value of accumulated plan benefits:

Vested benefits:	
Of participants currently receiving payments	$1,100,000
Other participants	3,200,000
	4,300,000
Nonvested benefits	2,200,000
Total actuarial present value of accumulated plan benefits	$6,500,000

The final statement in Exhibit 19B–4 explains why the actuarial present value increased during 1991.

The increase in benefit percentage affects all future retirement benefits and increases the accumulated benefit total. An increase in average retirement age decreases expected total benefits. Benefits paid reduce both the accumulated plan benefit and assets available. The ending actuarial value ($6 million) appears in the statements in Exhibits 19B–3 and 19B–4. Appropriate footnotes to fulfill the additional information requirements outlined earlier normally accompany the financial statements.

The four pension plan statements in this appendix are not articulated as a balance sheet and income statement would be. However, the second and fourth categories of required information explain the change from the previous period in the first and third categories. The assets available and accumulated benefits measure separate attributes of the plan. They are analogous to, but not the same as, plan assets at fair value.

EXHIBIT 19B–4   Changes in Accumulated Plan Benefits

INYO COMPANY PENSION PLAN
Statement of Changes in Accumulated Plan Benefits
For the Year Ended December 31, 1991

Actuarial present value of accumulated plan benefits, beginning of year.	$4,900,000
Increase (decrease) during the year attributable to:	
Plan amendment (increase in benefit percentage) . . . . $ 470,000	
Change in actuarial assumption (increase in average assumed retirement age). . . . . (560,000)	
Benefits earned in 1991 2,990,000	
Benefits paid in 1991 . . . . (1,300,000)	
Net increase.	1,600,000
Actuarial present value of accumulated plan benefits, end of year . .	$6,500,000

Pension plan financial statements provide information not available from the employer. Plan liabilities, net assets available for benefits, and benefits earned and paid during the year are examples. Furthermore, plan financial statements provide detailed information about the actual return on fund assets and about plan expenses. By focussing on different aspects of the pension plan, pension plan financial statements and employers' pension disclosures supply a broad range of disclosures for the assessment of a pension plan.

KEY TERMS

Actuarial present value (928)
Attribution (927)
Contributory pension plan (925)
Curtailment (953)
Defined benefit pension plan (925)
Defined contribution pension plan (925)
Discount rate (928)
Market-related value of pension plan assets (931)
Non-contributory pension plan (925)

Pension benefit formula (925)
Pension benefits (924)
Pension plan (924)
Pension plan participant (924)
Prior service cost (936)
Projected benefit obligation (931)
Service cost (930)
Settlement (953)
Termination Benefits (953)
Vested benefits (925)

QUESTIONS

1. Distinguish between a defined contribution pension plan and a defined benefit pension plan.
2. Distinguish between the three parties involved in accounting and reporting for a pension plan.
3. What are the primary actuarial factors related to a penison plan?
4. Explain the three funding approaches that the employer can use for pension plans.
5. Distinguish between a contributory pension plan and a non-contributory pension plan.
6. Employer X has a defined benefit pension plan. The estimated pension expense for 1991 is $100,000. Explain and give the 1991 journal entry for each of the following cases: Case A—X pays 100% of the pension expense; Case B—X pays 80% of the expense; Case C—X pays 120% of the expense.
7. Employee X will receive an annual pension benefit of $12,000 for five years, starting on December 31, 1992. Assuming an interest rate of 8%, how much must be in the pension fund on January 1, 1992? Explain why the answer is not $60,000.
8. Employer W must build a pension fund of $50,000 by December 31, 1997. Five equal annual payments are made into the fund starting on December 31, 1993. The fund will earn 8%. What is the amount of each payment? Explain why it is not $10,000.
9. Explain why pension accounting must be based on assumptions and estimates.
10. What is the pension benefit formula?
11. Explain the application of the matching principle in accounting for pensions.

12. What does attribution mean in pension accounting?
13. Three special features of pension accounting are (a) delayed recognition, (b) net cost, and (c) offsetting. Explain each feature.
14. What is the vested benefit obligation?
15. List and define the components of net periodic pension expense.
16. Define and explain the projected benefit obligation (PBO).
17. What information would typically be found in the report from the trustee on plan assets?
18. Explain what is meant by the "underfunded (overfunded) PBO."
19. Explain the primary approaches (i.e., rules) for amortizing unrecognized pension costs.
20. In the case of the unrecognized pension costs, such as prior service cost, which are first incurred during 1991, amortization may or may not be appropriate at the end of 1991. Explain why.
21. Explain a pension plan curtailment.
22. Explain a pension plan settlement.
23. Explain termination benefits.

EXERCISES

E 19–1
Understanding Pension Terminology
(L.O. 1, 2)

Match the brief definitions with the terms by entering one letter in each space provided.

Terms

_____ 1. Projected benefit obligation
_____ 2. Expected return on plan assets
_____ 3. Amortization of gains and losses
_____ 4. Pension plan assets
_____ 5. Net periodic pension expense
_____ 6. Fair market value (of plan assets)
_____ 7. Amortization of prior service costs
_____ 8. Actual return on plan assets
_____ 9. Prepaid pension cost
_____ 10. Accumulated benefit obligation
_____ 11. Interest cost
_____ 12. Discount rate
_____ 13. Service cost (pensions)
_____ 14. Amortization of transition cost
_____ 15. Vested benefit obligation

Brief Definition

A. Amount reported as total pension expense for the period; comprised of six components
B. Allocation to periodic expense of the cost of retroactive pension benefits
C. Actuarial present value of all future pension benefits excluding the effects of expected future compensation levels
D. Beginning market-related value of pension plan assets multiplied by the expected rate of return on plan assets
E. Cost of future pension benefits earned during the current accounting period
F. The interest rate used by the actuary to adjust for the time value of money
G. Present value of the employee's benefits not contingent on remaining an employee
H. Allocation to periodic expense of the difference between expected and actual return on plan assets and changes in actuarial assumptions
I. Cumulative fund assets plus unrecognized pension costs in excess of the PBO
J. Difference between plan assets at fair market value at the beginning and ending of the period minus contributions and plus distributions during the accounting period
K. The value of plan assets between a willing buyer and a willing seller (not a forced sale)
L. Attribution (allocation) to accounting periods of the costs recognized when revised section 3460 is first applied
M. Actuarial present value of all future pension benefits, including the effects of current and future compensation levels
N. Projected benefit obligation at the beginning of the current accounting period multiplied by the actuary's discount rate
O. Resources set aside to provide future pension benefits to retirees

Choose the best answer from among the multiple choice alternatives.

1. Service cost for 1991 for a pension plan whose pension benefit formula considers estimates of future compensation levels is
   a. The present value of benefits earned by employees in 1991 based on current salary levels.
   b. The increase in PBO for 1991 less interest cost on the beginning balance in PBO.
   c. The nominal value of benefits earned by employees in 1991 based on future salary levels.
   d. The present value of benefits earned by employees in 1991 based on future salary levels.
2. The following statements describe some aspect of accounting for defined benefit pension plans. Choose the incorrect statement.
   a. When only the first three components of pension expense have occurred to date for a plan, and actual return has always equaled expected return, underfunded PBO at a reporting date equals the balance in the accrued pension liability.
   b. When only the first three components of pension expense have occurred to date for a plan, and actual return has always equaled expected return, pension expense reflects the true annual cost to the company of providing future benefits earned in the current period, assuming all the actuarial assumptions are correct.
   c. Because the last three components of pension expense are derived from amortizing initial present values on a straight-line or similar basis, the true total cost of these items is not reflected in pension expense.
   d. Pension expense can be negative.
3. Choose the correct relationship among off-balance-sheet values and values reported in a balance sheet, relative to a pension plan.
   a. Underfunded PBO less amortization of unrecognized PSC equals the balance in accrued pension cost.
   b. Unrecognized PSC is an item which reconciles the balance in accrued pension cost and overfunded PBO.
   c. Sum of pension expense to date = PBO.
   d. PBO − Pension expense = Balance in accrued pension cost.
4. For external reporting purposes, assuming an underfunded PBO, the liability that must be reported in the balance sheet is
   a. PBO − Plan assets at fair value.
   b. Balance in accrued pension cost.
   c. Unamortized pension costs.
   d. Pension expense.
5. Defined contribution plans and defined benefit plans are two common types of pension plans. Choose the correct statement concerning these plans.
   a. The required annual contribution to the plan is determined by formula or contract in a defined contribution plan.
   b. Both plans provide the same retirement benefits.
   c. The retirement benefit is usually determinable well before retirement in a defined contribution plan.
   d. In both types of plans, pension expense is generally the amount funded during the year.
6. PBO and plan assets at fair value are two values critical to the determination of the financial status of defined benefit plans. Choose the correct statement regarding items to be included in each (none of these statements is necessarily complete).
   a. Ending PBO includes total service cost to date, interest cost to date, net initial unamortized actuarial gain or loss to date, and initial PSC.
   b. Ending PBO includes total service cost to date, interest cost to date, net initial unamortized actuarial gain or loss to date, initial PSC, and initial transition cost.
   c. Ending fair value of plan assets includes funding to date, expected return to date, reduced by benefits paid to date.
   d. Ending PBO includes service cost to date, gross differences between expected and actual returns to date, net initial unamortized actuarial gain or loss to date, less contributions to date.
7. Which of the following is not one of the components of pension expense (or part of a component)?
   a. Initial transition asset.
   b. Amortization of unrecognized gain or loss.
   c. Actual return on plan assets.
   d. Growth (interest cost) in PBO since the beginning of the period.

E 19–3
Prepaid Pension Cost
(L.O. 5)

Rico Corporation adopted a defined benefit pension plan on January 1, 1986. The plan does not provide any retroactive benefits for existing employees. The pension funding payment is made to the trustee on December 31 of each year. The following information is available for 1986 and 1987:

	1986	1987
Service cost.	$150,000	$165,000
Funding payment (contribution).	170,000	185,000
Interest on projected benefit obligation		15,000
Actual return on plan assets.		18,000

Required:

What amount of prepaid pension cost should Rico report in its December 31, 1987, balance sheet? (Prepare the journal entry to record pension expense for 1987.)

(AICPA adapted)

E 19–4
Amortization of Transition Amount
(L.O. 5)

As of December 31, 1987, these were the projected benefit obligation and plan assets of a non-contributory, defined benefit plan sponsored by Neeni, Inc.:

Projected benefit obligation	$780,000
Plan assets at fair value	600,000

Neeni elected to apply the provisions of section 3460 in its financial statements for the year ended December 31, 1988. As of December 31, 1987, all amounts accrued as net periodic pension cost had been contributed to the plan. The average remaining service period of active plan participants expected to receive benefits was estimated to be 10 years at the date of transition. Some participants' estimated service periods are 20 and 25 years.

Required:

What amount of amortization of the transition amount should Neeni amortize?

(AICPA adapted)

E 19–5
Pension Plan, One Employee: Compute Funding Payment
(L.O. 2)

Fisher Company initiated a non-contributory, defined benefit pension plan on January 1, 1991. The accounting period ends December 31. This exercise relates to one employee, V. R. Able. The pension formula specifies that Able will receive five annual retirement benefits of $50,000 at the end of each year, starting on December 31, 2001. Fisher Company will fully fund the pension plan by contributing 10 equal annual amounts starting on December 31, 1991. The pension fund will earn 8% annual interest during Able's service period and 7% during the retirement (payment) period.

Required:

Compute the equal annual funding payment that must be made by Fisher Company. Round to the nearest $1.

E 19–6
Pension Plan, Five Employees: Compute Funding Payment
(L.O. 2, 3)

Plans are being made to fund the prospective pension benefits of a group of employees of Farr Company due to retire in nine years and to be paid amounts from one to five years after retirement as shown here:

End of year 1	$ 90,000
End of year 2	50,000
End of year 3	30,000
End of year 4	15,000
End of year 5	5,000
Thereafter.	–0–
Total of pension payments	$190,000

Funds deposited with the pension fund trustee will earn 6% per annum. The pension plan contract calls for deposit of an amount sufficient to fund all of the expected payments from the fund by the date the employees retire.

Required:

Compute the amount required by the trustee on the employees' retirement date, assuming the first pension payment is one year after retirement, and prepare a proof schedule reflecting the 6% earnings on unsued funds and pension payout by the trustee. Round amounts to nearest dollar.

E 19–7
Understanding the PBO, Plan Assets, and Underfunding or Overfunding
(L.O. 2, 3)

BV Company has a non-contributory, defined benefit pension plan. Data available for 1991 were:

Projected benefit obligation (PBO):
Balance, January 1, 1991 . . . . $164,000
Balance, December 31, 1991. 214,000

Plan assets (at fair value):
Balance, January 1, 1991 . . . . $ 80,000
Balance, December 31, 1991. 140,000

Required:

1. How much did the PBO increase during 1991? Give six items that could have caused the PBO to change.
2. How much did the pension plan assets change during 1991? Give three items that could have caused the change in plan assets.
3. Compute the amount of the underfunded or overfunded PBO at (*a*) January 1, 1991, and (*b*) December 31, 1991. Explain what these amounts mean.

E 19–8
Understanding the Relationships between the Actuary's Report and the Trustee's Report
(L.O. 2, 3, 4)

The following items may appear on the 1992 PBO, actuary's report (AR), or the trustee's report, status of plan assets (TR). Enter one check mark to the left for each item to indicate the report on which each one would appear. However, if a single item appears in both reports, enter two check marks. If the item does not appear on either report, do not enter a check mark on that line.

AR	TR	Items (1992 unless Stated Otherwise)
_____	_____	1. December 31, 1991, ending pension obligation
_____	_____	2. Interest cost
_____	_____	3. Loss (gain) related to changes in actuarial assumptions
_____	_____	4. Unrecognized pension costs
_____	_____	5. Cash funding by the employer
_____	_____	6. Prior service cost (increase)
_____	_____	7. Net periodic pension expense
_____	_____	8. Actual return on plan assets
_____	_____	9. Accrued/prepaid pension costs
_____	_____	10. Underfunded or overfunded PBO
_____	_____	11. December 31, 1991, balance of pension plan asset
_____	_____	12. Pension benefits paid to retirees
_____	_____	13. Transition cost (increase or decrease)
_____	_____	14. PBO balance, January 1, 1993
_____	_____	15. Expected return on plan assets
_____	_____	16. Pension plan assets, January 1, 1993
_____	_____	17. Service cost
_____	_____	18. Accumulated benefit obligation

E 19–9
Prepare Trustee's Report: Analysis, Prepare Employer's Entries
(L.O. 2, 3)

Mason Company has a non-contributory, defined benefit pension plan. On December 31, 1991 (end of the accounting period and the measurement date), information about the pension plan included the following:

a. Projected benefit obligation (actuary):
January 1, 1991 . . . . $ 40,000
Service cost 60,000
Interest cost. 3,600
Pension benefits paid . . . . (–0–)
December 31, 1991 . . . . $103,600

[Interest (discount) rate used by actuary, 9%.]

b. The trustee's report on plan assets showed a beginning balance of $50,000, cash received from the employer of $37,000, and an actual return on plan assets of $10,000.

c. Unamortized prior service cost, gains and losses, transition costs, and additional minimum liability— none (from company records).

Required:

1. Prepare the trustee's report on the status of the plan assets (i.e., a listing of the beginning asset balance, changes, and ending balance).
2. Compute the amount of the underfunding or overfunding of the PBO on the beginning and ending dates.
3. Give the 1991 entry for Mason Company to record net periodic pension expense.
4. Give the same entry, assuming cash funding of $55,000 (instead of $37,000).
5. Show how the interest of $3,600 was computed.

E 19–10
Compute Net Periodic Pension Expense and Underfunded or Overfunded PBO, Entries (L.O. 4, 5)

The 1991 records of Jax Company provided the following data related to its non-contributory, defined benefit pension plan (amounts in 000s):

a. Projected benefit obligation (report of actuary):

Balance, January 1, 1991	$1,500
Service cost	600
Interest cost	120
Pension benefits paid	(200)
Balance, December 31, 1991	$2,020

Discount rate used by actuary, 8%.

b. Plan assets at fair value (report of trustee):

Balance, January 1, 1991	$1,204
Actual return on plan assets	84
Contributions, 1991	508
Pension benefits paid, 1991	(200)
Balance, December 31, 1991	$1,596

c. January 1, 1991, balance of unrecognized prior service cost, gains and losses, and transition cost, zero.

Required:

1. Compute the 1991 net periodic pension expense. Show the correct amount for each of the six components.
2. Give the 1991 entry(s) for Jax Company to record pension expense and funding.
3. Compute the underfunded or overfunded PBO at the beginning and end of 1991.

E 19–11
Compute Net Periodic Pension Expense and Underfunding or Overfunding of the PBO, Entries (L.O. 2, 3, 4)

Fox Company has a non-contributory, defined benefit pension plan. On December 31, 1991 (end of the accounting period and measurement date), the following data were available:

a. Projected benefit obligation (actuary's report):

Balance, December 31, 1990	$180,000
Prior service cost (due to plan amendment on January 1, 1991)	20,000
Balance, January 1, 1991	200,000
Service cost	130,000
Interest cost	16,000
Pension benefits paid	(–0–)
Balance, December 31, 1991	$346,000

Interest (discount) rate used by actuary, 8%.

b. Funding report of the trustee:

Balance, January 1, 1991	$210,000
Actual return on plan assets*	10,000
Cash received from employer	100,000
Pension benefits paid to retirees	(–0–)
Balance, December 31, 1991	$320,000

* Same as the expected return.

Required:

1. Show how the interest cost was computed.
2. Compute net periodic pension expense. Assume prior service cost will be amortized over a 10-year average remaining service period. Show the correct amounts for each component.
3. Give the 1991 entry for Fox Company to record net periodic pension expense.
4. Give the same entry assuming cash funding from the employer of $142,000, and no other changes.
5. Compute the underfunding or overfunding of the PBO for (3) and (4).

E 19–12
Compute Net Periodic Pension Expense and Underfunded or Overfunded PBO, Entries
(L.O. 2, 3, 4)

New Company started a non-contributory, defined benefit pension plan on January 1, 1990. Data available for 1991 were:

a. Projected benefit obligation, 1991 (actuary's report):

Balance, January 1, 1991	$60,000
Service cost	20,000
Interest cost (interest rate, 10%)	6,000
Prior service cost	–0–
Losses (gains) due to change in actuarial assumptions (amortization to start in 1992)	(4,000)
Pension benefits paid	(1,000)
Balance, December 31, 1991	$81,000

b. Status of fund assets (trustee's report):

Balance, January 1, 1991	$55,000
Actual earnings on plan assets (same as expected return)	5,000
Payments received from employer during 1991	30,000
Pension benefits paid	(1,000)
Balance, December 31, 1991	$89,000

c. Company records: Unamortized gain from 1990 due to changes in assumptions, $3,000 (this amount was included in the 1990 PBO). There are no gains or losses on plan assets. Unamortized (unrecognized) prior service cost and transition cost from 1990 are zero.

Required:

1. Compute net periodic pension expense for 1991 assuming the 1990 losses (gains) are amortized for 1991 over a 15-year average remaining service period.
2. Give the 1991 pension expense and funding entry for New Company.
3. Give the same entry assuming the 1991 cash payment by employer was $18,000 instead of $30,000.
4. Compute the underfunded or overfunded PBO for (2) and (3).

E 19–13
Pension Spreadsheet: Underfunded and Accrued Pension Cost, Entries
(L.O. 2, 3, 4)

GEE Company has a defined benefit pension plan. At the end of the current reporting period, December 31, 1995, the following information was available:

a. Projected benefit obligation (actuary's report):

Balance, January 1, 1995	$600
Service cost	78
Interest cost ($600 × 7%, actuary's rate)	42
Loss (gain) change in actuarial assumptions*	18
Pension benefits paid	(40)
Balance, December 31, 1995	$698

b. Status of fund assets (trustee's report):

Balance, January 1, 1995	$500
Actual return on plan assets (same as expected)	30
Cash received from employer company	70
Pension benefits paid to retirees	(40)
Balance, December 31, 1995	$560

c. From company records, unamortized pension cost from prior years
(amortize over remaining service periods, as indicated):

Transition cost (3 years)	$ 18
Prior service cost (9 years).	27
Losses (gains) (12 years).	36
Total	$ 81

* Amortization to start in 1996.

Required:

1. Set up and complete a spreadsheet or format of your choice to develop the pension data required at the end of 1995.
2. Give the employer's pension entry at December 31, 1995.

E 19–14
Pension Spreadsheet:
Underfunded and Accrued
Pension Cost, Entry
(L.O. 2, 3, 4)

Avis Company has a defined benefit pension plan. At the end of the current reporting period, December 31, 1991, the following information was available:

a. Projected benefit obligation (actuary's report):

Balance, January 1, 1991.	$750
Service cost	80
Interest cost ($750 × 10%, actuary's rate).	75
Loss (gain) change in actuarial assumptions*	(7)
Pension benefits paid	(34)
Balance, December 31, 1991	$864

b. Status of fund assets (trustee's report):

Balance, January 1, 1991.	$600
Actual return on plan assets (same as expected)	54
Cash received from employer company	150
Pension benefits paid to retirees	(34)
Balance, December 31, 1991	$770

c. From company records, unamortized pension cost from prior years
(amortize over a 10-year average remaining service period):

Transition cost	$100
Prior service cost	30
Losses (gains).	(20)
Total	$110

* Amortization to start in 1992.

Required:

1. Set up and complete a spreadsheet or format of your choice to develop the pension data required at the end of 1991.
2. Give the employer's pension entry at December 31, 1991.

E 19–15
Understanding Pension
Accounting Terminology
(L.O. 2, 3, 4, 5)

Match the following items with the financial statements by entering the appropriate letter in each blank.

Items	**Reported on the Financial Statements**
_____ 1. Accumulated benefit obligation	A. Income statement, expense
_____ 2. Unrealized pension cost	B. Income statement, gains and losses
_____ 3. Unrecognized gains (losses)	C. Balance sheet, assets
_____ 4. Prepaid pension cost	D. Balance sheet, liabilities
_____ 5. Unrecognized prior service cost	E. Balance sheet, owners' equity
_____ 6. Pension benefits paid	F. None of the above
_____ 7. Expected return on pension plan assets	
_____ 8. Unrecognized transition cost	
_____ 9. Accrued pension cost	
_____ 10. Net periodic pension expense	
_____ 11. Pension plan assets used in operations of the plan (i.e., furniture and fixtures)	
_____ 12. Unfunded accumulated benefit obligation	
_____ 13. Pension plan assets at fair value	

E 19–16
Unrecognized Gains and
Losses
(L.O. 4)

On January 1, 1991, a company reported a $6,000 unrecognized gain in the informal record of its pension plan. This gain is being amortized over 12 years. During 1991, the following events occurred:

a. There was an experience loss on plan assets of $2,000 for 1991.
b. A gain of $4,000 was determined by the actuary at December 31, 1991, based on changes in actuarial assumptions.

The company amortizes unrecognized gains and losses on the straight-line basis over the average remaining service life of active employees (20 years) beginning in the year after the loss. Further information on this plan follows:

	Values at	
	January 1, 1991	**December 31, 1991**
PBO	$50,000	$56,000
Fair value of plan assets	30,000	34,000

Required:
Compute amortization of unrecognized gain or loss for 1991 and 1992.

E 19–17
Transition Asset or
Liability
(L.O. 4)

Maxfield Corporation made its transition to the revised section 3460 for its pension plan on January 1, 1991. At that date, its PBO was $120,000, and plan assets at fair value were $140,000. Accounting for pensions prior to 1991 produced an accrued pension liability of $30,000 as of January 1, 1991.

Required:

1. Determine the transition asset or liability for Maxfield on January 1, 1991.
2. If the transition item relates to an employee group with an average remaining service life of 10 years, how is pension expense in 1991 affected by the amortization of the item?

E 19–18
Prepare Pension
Spreadsheet: Entries
(L.O. 2, 3, 4, 5)

Fox Company has a non-contributory, defined benefit pension plan. The following data are available at December 31, 1991, which is the end of the accounting period and the measurement date:

a. Projected benefit obligation (actuary):
   Balance, January 1, 1991 . . . .$223,000
   Service cost 80,000
   Interest cost . . . .   ?
   Prior service cost . . . .   –0–
   Losses (gains) due to changes in assumptions
     (begin amortizing in 1992)   8,000
   Pension benefits paid . . . . (30,000)
   Balance, December 31, 1991 . . . .$?

   Average remaining service period, 10 years.
   Actuary's discount rate, 8%.
   Accumulated benefit obligation, $292,000.
b. Pension plan assets (trustee):
   Balance, January 1, 1991, at fair value $200,000
   Contributions to the pension plan by Fox. 70,000
   Actual return on plan assets 10,000
   Benefits paid to retirees . . . . (30,000)
   Balance, December 31, 1991 . . . .$250,000

   Fair value of plan assets, December 31, 1991 = $240,000.
c. Other balances at December 31, 1990: Unrecognized pension costs (total), $3,000; only prior service has a balance; accrued pension cost, $20,000.

Required:

1. Prepare a spreadsheet or format of your choice to develop the required pension data.
2. Give the annual pension entry for Fox.

E 19–19
Prepare Spreadsheet:
Entries
(L.O. 2, 3, 4, 5)

Saxon Company has a non-contributory, defined benefit pension plan. The accounting period ends December 31, 1991 (also the pension measurement date). Pension plan data for 1991 are as follows:

a. Projected benefit obligation:

Balance, January 1, 1991	$5,000
Service cost	3,000
Interest cost	400
Loss (gain) due to change in actuarial assumptions,	
January 1, 1991	30*
Pension benefits paid	(60)
Balance, December 31, 1991	$8,370

Actuary's discount rate, 8%.
Average remaining service period, 10 years.

b. Pension plan assets:

Balance, January 1, 1991, at fair value	$4,000
Actual return	150
Contribution to the pension fund by Saxon	3,200
Benefits paid to retirees	(60)
Balance, December 31, 1991	$7,290

c. Company records:
January 1, 1991, Unamortized amounts:

Unrecognized prior service cost	$ 500
Unrecognized gain/loss	300 (gain)
Unrecognized transition cost	200

* Begin amortizing in 1991.

Amortize all unrecognized items over the average service period (for problem purposes).

Required:

1. Prepare a spreadsheet or other format of your choice for the pension plan for 1991.
2. Based on (1), give the December 31, 1991, entry to record pension expense and funding for Saxon.

E 19–20
Understanding Pension
Accounting Terminology
(L.O. 7)

Match the following brief descriptions with the terminology by entering appropriate letters in the blanks.

Terminology	Brief Description
_____ 1. Curtailment	A. Vested benefit obligation—for pension benefits retained regardless of employment to retirement date
_____ 2. Accrued/prepaid pension cost	
_____ 3. Termination benefits	B. An irrevocable event (or transaction) that (1) relieves the employer of a primary pension obligation and (2) reduces the employer's risks
_____ 4. Settlement	
_____ 5. Interest expense	C. The effects of a curtailment gain or loss are recorded in this account
_____ 6. Loss, termination benefits	
_____ 7. None of the above	D. Special or contractual benefits paid to employees who retire early
	E. An event that either (1) reduces expected years of future service or (2) reduces the number of employees
	F. This account is debited when it is probable that early retirees will be entitled to special benefits and the amount can be reasonably estimated
	G. When termination benefits are paid over an extended time, this account must be periodically debited

E 19–21
Pension Curtailment:
Analysis, Entry
(L.O. 7)

CT Company has a non-contributory, defined benefit pension plan. On June 1, 1991, the company reduced its operations and, as a consequence, terminated 150 of its regular employees. As of that date the actuary provided the following information (000s):

	Total	Related to Terminations
Projected benefit obligation	$1,000	$100
Additional data as of June 1, 1992:		
Plan assets at fair value	$ 875	
Unrecognized PSC	50	
Unrecognized gains	70	

Unrecognized pension costs are reduced in proportion to the reduction in PBO.

Required:

1. Complete a schedule to indicate the effect of the curtailment.
2. Prepare the journal entry to record the curtailment.

E 19–22
Pension Settlement:
Analysis, Entry
(L.O. 7)

Stacy Company has a non-contributory, defined benefit pension plan. On December 31, 1991 (end of the accounting period and pension measurement date), the company settled a portion of its PBO obligation. Settlement was made by purchasing, with pension plan assets, non-participating annuity contracts that cost $248. Relevant pension plan data on this date were (all amounts in 000s):

a. Actuary's report, December 31, 1991 (before the settlement):

Projected benefit obligation	$400
Benefit obligation settlement	248

b. Trustee's report (before the settlement):

Pension plan assets at fair value	$415

c. Company records (before the settlement):

Unrecognized net assets at transition	$ 50
Unrecognized net gain subsequent to acquisition	60
Accrued/prepaid pension cost (a credit)	95

Required:

1. What percent of the PBO was settled?
2. Complete an analysis of the pension plan settlement to determine its effects (similar to the one shown in the chapter).
3. Give the entry to record the settlement.

E 19–23
Pension Termination:
Entries
(L.O. 7)

On January 1, 1991 (accounting period ends December 31), Fox Company reduced its payroll by terminating 40 employees. Each terminated employee was given (*a*) a lump-sum payment of $1,000, on January 1, 1991, and (*b*) six monthly payments of $100 starting January 31, 1991. The payments were made from company assets. All of the terminated employees accepted the termination benefits as of January 1, 1991.

Required:

1. Compute the cost of the termination benefits as of January 1, 1991. Use a 2% interest rate, compounded monthly.
2. Give the following entries for Fox Company:
   (*a*) January 1, 1991—to record the termination.
   (*b*) January 1, 1991—to record the lump-sum cash payment.
   (*c*) January 31, 1991—to record the first monthly payment.

PROBLEMS

P 19–1
Present Value: PBO
(L.O. 3)

Felco Company sponsors a pension plan with the following pension benefit formula:

$$\text{Benefit paid at} \atop {\text{end of each year} \atop \text{of retirement}} = \left(\text{Number of} \atop \text{years worked}\right)\left(\text{Annual salary} \atop \text{at retirement}\right)\Big/25$$

Credit for service began January 1, 1981, Bob Johnson's first day with the company. Johnson is expected to work a total of 30 years with an annual salary at retirement of $100,000. He is expected to draw 10 years of retirement benefits. The discount rate is 10%.

Required:
Compute PBO on January 1, 1991, if Johnson's current salary is $30,000.

P 19–2
Prior Service Cost
Amortization
(L.O. 4)

On January 1, 1991, Oracle Company amended its pension plan by granting retroactive pension benefits for work performed prior to that date. The present value of those benefits was determined to be $100,000 at that date. The following employees expect to receive benefits under the plan; they have the following years remaining in their careers at January 1, 1991:

Bob: three years

Joe: five years

Required:
Determine the amortization of prior service cost to be recognized in 1995.

P 19–3
Pension Expense
(L.O. 2, 4)

The following data relate to a pension plan:

PBO, January 1, 1991	$30,000
Initial total PSC awarded January 1, 1989 (relates to an employee group with an average remaining service period of 10 years, use SL method)	10,000
Initial total transition liability (transition occurred January 1, 1989, use SL method, 15 years)	8,000
Discount rate	8%
Unrecognized gain (use SL method, 15 years), January 1, 1991	$ 5,000
Service cost	7,000
Contributions	9,000
Actual return	3,000
Average remaining service period	15 years

Required:
Provide the entry to record pension expense for 1991.

P 19–4
Unrecognized Gains and
Losses
(L.O. 4)

Information for a pension plan follows:

Unrecognized gain January 1, 1990	$ 2,000
Years used to amortize unrecognized gain or loss	10
Fair value of plan assets January 1, 1990	$50,000
Expected rate of return on plan assets	12%
Fair value of plan assets December 31, 1990	$55,000
1991 funding.	10,000
Benefits paid in 1991	8,000
Actuarial loss computed December 31, 1990	2,000

Required:
Compute the net unrecognized gain or loss at January 1, 1991.

P 19–5
Pension Expense
(L.O. 2, 4)

The following information pertains to a pension plan for a company that always recognizes only the minimum amortization of unrecognized gains and losses.

Unrecognized gain or loss, January 1, 1990	$ 0
PBO, January 1, 1990, not considering the following items	30,000
Discount rate	10%
Fair value of plan assets, January 1, 1990	$12,000
Initial PSC value, from a grant in 1986	20,000
Unrecognized PSC, January 1, 1990	4,000
Average remaining service life of employees covered under	
initial PSC grant	10 years
Actuarial loss, January 1, 1990	$ 6,000
Expected rate of return on fund assets	12%
Average remaining service life used to amortize	
unrecognized gain or loss	12 years
Service cost, 1990	$ 6,000
Service cost, 1991	7,000
Funding amount, end of 1990	8,000
Funding amount, end of 1991	10,000
Actual return on fund in 1990	900
Actual return on fund in 1991	1,200

No benefits were paid in either year.

Required:

Compute pension expense for 1990 and 1991.

P 19–6
Pension Spreadsheet:
Overfunded and a Prepaid
Pension Cost, Entry
(L.O. 2, 3, 4)

Waters Company has a defined benefit pension plan. At the end of the current reporting period, December 31, 1991, the following information was available:

a. Projected benefit obligation (actuary's report):

Balance, January 1, 1991	$ 75,000
Service cost	20,000
Interest cost ($75,000 × 10%, actuary's rate)	7,500
Loss (gain) change in actuarial assumptions*	(200)
Pension benefits paid	(21,000)
Balance, December 31, 1991	$ 81,300

Average remaining service period, 10 years.[†]

b Status of fund assets (trustee's report):

Balance, January 1, 1991	$ 80,000
Actual return on plan assets (same as expected)	8,000
Cash received from employer company	15,000
Pension benefits paid to retirees	(21,000)
Balance, December 31, 1991	$ 82,000

c. From company records—Unrecognized pension costs:

Transition cost	$ 5,000
Prior service cost	10,000
Losses (gains)	(1,000)
Total	$ 14,000
Accrued (prepaid) pension cost	$(19,000)

* At December 31, 1991.

[†] Assume this is appropriate for all amortizations.

Required:

1. Set up and complete a spreadsheet or other format of your choice to develop the pension data required at the end of 1991.
2. Give the employer's pension entry at December 31, 1991.

P 19–7
Prepare a Spreadsheet and Respond to a Query about the Use of Cash
(L.O. 2, 3, 4)

Stoney Company first applied the provisions of section 3460 to its non-contributory, defined benefit program on January 1, 1991. The annual accounting period ends on December 31. Data about the pension plan for 1992 follow:

a. Projected benefit obligation (actuary's report):

Balance, January 1, 1992	$16,000
Service cost	1,920
Interest cost ($16,000 × 8% actuary's rate)	1,280
Loss (gain) change in actuarial assumptions*	660
Pension benefit paid to retirees	(1,600)
Balance, December 31, 1992	$18,260
Actuary's estimated discount rate	8%
Average remaining service period (assumed appropriate for all amortizations)	11 years

b. Status of fund assets (trustee's report):

Balance, January 1, 1992	$12,600
Actual return on plan assets	1,000
Cash received from employer company	3,000
Pension benefits paid to retirees	(1,600)
Balance, December 31, 1992 (same as fair value)	$15,000

c. Company data on January 1, 1992:

Unrecognized transition cost	$ 660
Unrecognized prior service cost	1,980
Unrecognized losses (gains)	(440)
Total unrecognized	$ 2,200
(Accrued)/prepaid pension cost	$ (1,200)

* At December 31, 1992.

Required:

1. Prepare a pension spreadsheet or other format of your choice and give Stoney's 1992 journal entry for the pension plan.
2. The company president asked the following question: We paid $3,000 cash to the pension fund, but the pension liability was reduced by only $598. Why? Prepare your response with data and explanation.

P 19–8
Comparative Cases: Prepare Two Spreadsheets and Employer's Entry
(L.O. 2, 3, 4)

Art Company first applied the provisions of section 3460 to its non-contributory, defined pension plan in 1991. The annual accounting period ends December 31. Data about the pension plan for 1992 follow for two comparative cases to emphasize how losses versus gains affect the results.

	Case A	**Case B**
a. Actuary's PBO report at December 31, 1992:		
Projected benefit obligation (actuary's report):		
Balance, January 1, 1992	$500	$500
Service cost	100	100
Interest cost ($500 × 10%), actuary's rate	50	50
Loss (gain) change in actuarial assumptions*	8	(8)
Pension benefits paid to retirees	(10)	(15)
Balance, December 31, 1992	$648	$627
Actuary's estimated interest rate	10%	10%
Average remaining service period†	8 years	8 years
b. Status of fund assets (trustee's report):		
Balance, January 1, 1992	$450	$450
Actual return on plan assets	20	20
Cash received from employer company	150	120
Pension benefits paid to retirees	(10)	(15)
Balance, December 31, 1992	$610	$575
Market value of plan assets*	$615	$580

	Case A	Case B
c. Company data on January 1, 1992:		
Unrecognized transition cost.	$ 8	$ 8
Unrecognized prior service cost	16	16
Unrecognized losses (gains)‡.	24	(24)
Total unrecognized	$ 48	$ –0–
(Accrued)/prepaid pension cost.	$ (2)	$ (50)

* At December 31, 1992; amortizations start in 1993.

† Assume eight years is appropriate for all amortizations.

‡ Due only to changes in actuarial assumptions.

Required:

Prepare a spreadsheet or other format of your choice and give the employer's journal entry for the pension plan for Case A and Case B. When preparing these two spreadsheets, focus on the effects of losses versus gains.

P 19–9
Spreadsheet: Entries
(L.O. 2, 3, 4, 5)

Frazier Company has a non-contributory, defined benefit pension plan. The company must record its pension expense for the year ended December 31, 1991. The following data are available (in 000s):

a. Actuary's report:

Balance, January 1, 1991.	$ 300
Service cost	30
Interest cost (at 8%).	24
Loss (gain) actuarial changes*	10
Pension benefits paid to retirees	(100)
Balance, December 31, 1991	$ 264

b. Fund trustee's report:

Balance, January 1, 1991 (at fair value)†	$ 200
Actual return on plan assets	18
Payments received from Frazier	60
Pension benefits paid	(100)
Balance, December 31, 1991 (at fair value)	$ 178

c. Data from company records:

Unrecognized transition cost (January 1, 1991)	$ 27
Unrecognized prior service cost (January 1, 1991)	36
Unrecognized loss (January 1, 1991)	4
Total unrecognized	$ 67

Amortization periods, for problem purposes only:
   Transition cost, nine years; prior service cost,
   nine years; and losses (gains), four years.
   (Accrued)/prepaid pension cost, January 1, 1991, $(33).

* At December 31, 1991.

† Same as market-related value.

Required:

Prepare a pension spreadsheet or other format of your choice and give the 1991 entry for Frazier Company.

P 19–10
Spreadsheet: Entries
(L.O. 2, 3, 4, 5)

Jacks Company has a non-contributory, defined benefit pension plan. The company must record its pension expense for the year ended December 31, 1991. The following data are available (in 000s):

a. Actuary's report: PBO

Balance, January 1, 1991.	$ 300
Service cost	50
Interest cost (at 8%)	24
Loss (gain) actuarial changes (December 31, 1991)	(10)
Pension benefits paid to retirees	(124)
Balance, December 31, 1991	$ 240

b. Fund trustee's report:

Balance, January 1, 1991 (at fair value)*	$ 170
Actual return on plan assets	27
Payments received from Jacks	110
Pension benefits paid	(124)
Balance, December 31, 1991	$ 183
Market value of plan assets, December 31, 1991	$ 163

c. Data from company records:

Unrecognized transition cost (January 1, 1991)	$ 60
Unrecognized prior service cost (January 1, 1991)	40
Unrecognized loss (gain) (January 1, 1991)	–0–
Total unrecognized	$ 100

Average remaining service period is 10 years (for problem purposes use this for
amortizing each of the three unrecognized pension costs).

Accrued/prepaid pension cost, January 1, 1991, $30 accrued.

* Same as market-related value.

Required:

Prepare a pension spreadsheet or other format of your choice and give the 1991 entry for Jacks
Company.

P 19–11

COMPREHENSIVE PROBLEM
◆

Prepare Pension
Spreadsheet for Two
Consecutive Years
(L.O. 2, 3, 4, 5)

AAP Company has a non-contributory, defined benefit pension plan. This case focusses on the
accounting required at December 31, 1991 and 1992, with emphasis on the PBO, plan assets, unrecognized pension costs, net periodic pension expense, and accrued/prepaid pension cost. The
data for the two years are as follows (in 000s):

	1991	1992
a. Actuary's (PBO):		
Projected benefit obligation, beginning	$1,700	$2,196
Service cost	180	210
Interest cost	136	198
Prior service cost	240	
Loss (gain), actuarial changes, December 31	20	5
Pension benefits paid	(80)	(125)
Projected benefit obligation, ending	$2,196	$2,484
Average remaining service period, December 31,	10 years	9 years
Actuary's interest rate	8%	9%
b. Trustee's report (plan assets at fair value):*		
Balance at beginning	$1,000	$1,230
Actual return on plan assets	90	110
Contributions from employer	200	440
Pension benefits paid to retirees	(80)	(125)
Balance at ending	$1,210	$1,655
Market value of plan assets	$1,230	$1,640
c. AAP Company records:		
Unrecognized cost at January 1, 1991		
Prior service cost	$ –0–	
Transition cost (12 years)	300	
Loss (gain) (10 years)	150	
Total	$ 450	

* Same as market-related value.

Required:

Prepare a pension spreadsheet or format of your choice and give the related pension entry for
AAP Company for 1991 and 1992.

P 19–12
Pension Curtailment:
Analysis and Entry
(L.O. 7)

Hardy Company experienced financial difficulties in 1991. In response, one action taken by Hardy's management was to offer special termination benefits to certain employees. Each employee was offered $10,000 in a lump-sum cash payment to resign. One hundred employees accepted the offer. The special termination benefits were paid from Hardy's assets, not from pension plan assets.

In addition, Hardy's pension plan obligation was curtailed. The amount of the reduction in Hardy's projected benefit obligation due to the curtailment was $500,000. None of this amount was vested; therefore, Hardy did not reduce pension plan assets. Expected future years of employee service were reduced by 25% due to the curtailment. Details of Hardy's pension plan obligation, assets, and recognized and unrecognized amounts as of December 31, 1991 (termination date), follow (amounts in thousands):

Projected benefit obligation (PBO)	$(2,800)
Plan assets at fair value	2,000
	(800)
Add (deduct) unamortized items:	
Unrecognized transition cost	400
Unrecognized net gain	(200)
Unrecognized prior service cost	100
Accrued (prepaid) pension cost	$ (500)

Required:

1. Prepare an analysis of the effects of the curtailment, showing your computations.
2. Give the entry to reflect the curtailment and special termination benefits.

P 19–13
Pension Curtailment:
Analysis and Entries
(L.O. 7)

Casey Company has had a non-contributory, defined benefit pension plan for its employees since 1991. Faced with declining demand for its products, Casey reduced its operations in 1995. Because of the reduced level of operations, a number of employees were terminated, and Casey's pension obligations were curtailed. The impact of the curtailment was to reduce Casey's projected benefit obligation by $200,000 and the expected future years of employee service by 20 percent, as of January 1, 1995. The following pension plan information is based on two independent cases as of January 1, 1995 (amounts in thousands):

	Case A	Case B
Projected benefit obligation (PBO)	$(1,200)	$(1,500)
Plan assets at fair value	1,000	2,000
	(200)	500
Add (deduct) unamortized items:		
Unrecognized transition (cost) gain	50	(80)
Unrecognized net gain (loss)	100	(120)
Unrecognized prior service cost	30	40
Accrued (prepaid) pension cost	$ (20)	$ 340

Required:

1. Prepare an analysis of the effects of the curtailment for each case, showing your computations.
2. Give the entry to reflect the curtailment for each case.

P 19–14
Pension Settlement:
Analysis and Entries
(L.O. 7)

On December 31, 1991, Watson Corporation reduced its pension obligations by purchasing non-participating annuity contracts with pension plan assets. The annuity contracts were designed to provide Watson's employees with future pension benefits in return for a fixed payment of $500,000 by Watson. A summary of Watson's pension plan obligation, assets, and recognized and unrecognized components immediately before the settlement for two independent cases (amounts in thousands) follows:

	Case A	Case B
Projected benefit obligation (PBO).	$(2,500)	$(2,000)
Plan assets at fair value	2,200	2,200
	(300)	200
Add (deduct) unamortized items:		
Unrecognized transition (cost) gain	50	(70)
Unrecognized net gain (loss).	120	(130)
Unrecognized prior service cost	40	40
Accrued (prepaid) pension cost	$ (90)	$ 40

Required:

Round to the nearest thousand.

1. Prepare an analysis of the effects of the settlement for each case. Show computations. The analysis should have column headings as follows:

Item	Before Settlement	Effects of Settlement	After Settlement

2. Give the entry to reflect the settlement for each case.

P 19–15
Pension Plan Financial Statements
(L.O. 8)

The following information (which is in no particular order) relates to the Bamson Company pension plan. Some of the values refer to account balances as of December 31, 1991. Others refer to changes in amounts during 1991:

Interest earned on plan investments	$ 20,000
Vested benefits:	
Of participants currently receiving payments	80,000
Other participants.	400,000
Investments at fair value	500,000
Cash	230,000
Accrued and account payables	440,000
Net appreciation in fair value, investments	50,000
Contributions:	
Employer.	850,000
Employee.	300,000
Change in actuarial assumption (decrease in average assumed retirement age)	60,000
Benefits paid.	800,000
Nonvested benefits.	200,000
Dividends.	5,000
Investment expenses	10,000
Benefits earned	950,000
Administrative expenses	150,000
Employee contributions	200,000
Accrued interest and dividends.	20,000

Required:

1. Prepare the statements of net assets available for benefits, statement of changes in net assets available for benefits, statement of accumulated plan benefits, and statement of changes in accumulated plan benefits, for the Bamson plan. Use the format suggested in Appendix 19B.
2. What does the total actuarial present value of accumulated plan benefits represent?
3. Is the plan overfunded or underfunded at December 31, 1991?
4. By how much has the plan changed its funded status during 1991?

CASES

C 19–1
Ethical Considerations and
Opportunities for
Managing Pension Expense
and Liabilities
(L.O. 2, 3, 4, 5)

You are the senior auditor for the audit of a client firm in considerable financial difficulty. In particular, debt covenants may be violated if liabilities are increased. In addition, the client's balance in retained earnings is minimal as a result of artificially high dividends and diminished earnings in the past several years.

The client is dominated by its CEO, a person who has worked his way up the ladder and has served the firm for 30 years. The CEO makes most of the major decisions in the firm. This person is the primary firm representative working with the audit staff. At present, there is no organized audit committee. The CEO is very aggressive with respect to earnings.

Reading the company's minutes, you have discovered that extreme emphasis has been placed on meeting earnings projections. Department officers have been fired for not meeting earnings goals for two successive years. The firm uses FIFO, straight-line depreciation, and other accounting techniques that reduce or delay expense recognition. The firm has resisted using the installment sales method for customers with questionable credit ratings.

You know that part of your responsibility as an auditor is to develop an audit plan that is sensitive to audit risk. Audit risk is the probability that you may unknowingly fail to modify your audit report on financial statements that are materially misstated. Your audit plan should be designed to provide reasonable assurance that material errors and irregularities are detected.

Required:

You understand that the pressures faced by this firm from both within and without may create pressures for unethical and fraudulent financial reporting. What aspects of pension accounting should you inspect with special care? What pension-related variables might be changed, and in what direction, to achieve reduced pension expense and liabilities? Include in your discussion reasons why you chose these variables.

C 19–2
Loblaw Companies
Limited: Analysis of
Actual Financial
Statements
(L.O. 4)

Refer to the 1990 financial statements of Loblaw (see the appendix immediately following Chapter 26) and respond to the following questions.

Required:

1. How large are pension plan assets relative to total assets listed in the balance sheet?
2. Are the pension plans underfunded or overfunded as at December 31, 1990 and 1989? By how much?
3. What was Loblaw's pension expense for 1989?
4. Which pension plan optional disclosures are included or missing from Loblaw's financial statements?

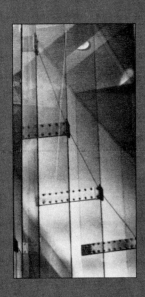

OWNERS' EQUITY

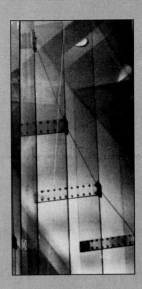

C H A P T E R

20

Corporations: Contributed Capital

After you have studied this chapter, you will be able to:

1. Explain the characteristics, advantages, and disadvantages of the corporate form of business organization.

2. Describe the different types of shareholders' investments and the various rights that attach to each.

3. Describe and demonstrate accounting and reporting practices for the issuance of various forms of share capital, both for cash and for non-cash consideration (refer to the chapter and Appendix 20A).

4. Apply prescribed accounting and reporting practices for the issuance of subscribed shares.

5. Apply accounting and reporting practices for the retirement of shares, including callable and redeemable shares, and for the conversion of convertible preferred shares.

6. Apply accounting and reporting practices for treasury shares (refer to Appendix 20B).

◆

INTRODUCTION
◆

In previous chapters, we have focussed our discussion on understanding the content and application of generally accepted accounting principles applied primarily to assets and liabilities. The principles we covered were applicable to all forms of business organization, whether sole proprietorship, partnership, or corporation. Because of the legal requirements and complex contracts that can be developed under the corporate form of organization, we will now separately consider the accounting and reporting requirements for owners' equity for corporations. The term **shareholders' equity** will be used to refer to the owners' equity section of a corporation's financial statements.

The corporation is the dominant form of business organization measured in terms of total contributed capital invested in the economy. It will, in all likelihood, continue to be dominant because:

1. The corporate form of business organization allows for the accumulation of large amounts of capital in organizations such that economies of scale can be achieved.
2. The corporate form of business organization limits the liability of the shareholders.
3. Ownership interests of corporations can generally be transferred more readily than can other forms of ownership.

This chapter concentrates on the transactions that affect contributed capital of the corporation. Chapter 21 covers the accounting and reporting issues that affect earnings retained in the organization.

◆

CONTRIBUTED CAPITAL AT FORMATION
◆

Formation of a Corporation

Federal and provincial legislation provide for the formation and operation of **corporations**. With the passage of the federal Canada Business Corporations Act, 1975, Canada has on its statute books the most modern, clear, practical, and comprehensive corporation law in the English-speaking world.

This act recognizes that incorporation is a right and not a privilege as it was previously viewed. The act creates a practical balance of interests among, and protection with maximum flexibility to, shareholders, creditors, management, and the public. Historically, corporation laws have varied in many respects; however, since 1975 the trend has been to model provincial legislation on the Canada Business Corporations Act. The discussion in this text is therefore based on the federal act with occasional references to provincial legislation where provisions result in substantially different accounting treatment of like transactions.

Corporations (federal) are brought into existence when the director, Corporations Branch, Department of Consumer and Corporate Affairs, issues a certificate of incorporation after the applicant has submitted the articles of incorporation and certain other documents to the director. The articles of incorporation and bylaws adopted by shareholders constitute the framework within which a corporation operates.

Classification of Corporations

Corporations may be classified as follows:

1. *Federally incorporated entities:* corporations incorporated under the Canada Business Corporations Act, 1975, as amended. Constitutionally, there is no particular

reason to prefer federal over provincial incorporation, as either type may engage in business throughout Canada. Federal incorporation may be viewed as more prestigious and is generally preferred by those doing significant business abroad.

2. *Provincially incorporated entities:* corporations created under the relevant provincial companies act. Some jurisdictions (e.g., Ontario) allow for two subclassifications:

   a. *Private corporations,* which have restricted rights to transfer shares, are allowed only a limited number of shareholders, and may not sell shares or securities to the public. Private corporations are not subject to rigid reporting requirements.

   b. *Other corporations,* which have no such restrictions or special exemptions.

3. *Crown corporations:* entities that are ultimately accountable through a Minister of the Crown to Parliament or a legislature for the conduct of their business. These can be governmental units or business operations owned by government. Examples include Canada Post, Air Canada, and Canadian National Railways (CNR).

4. *Not-for-profit corporations:* entities formed for social, charitable, or educational purposes. Normally, ownership is not transferable and members and contributors do not receive economic gain. The unique accounting and reporting problems associated with these organizations are covered in advanced accounting courses.

Characteristics of Share Capital

Share capital, represented by share certificates, evidence *ownership* in a corporation. Shares may be bought, sold, or otherwise transferred by the shareholders without the consent of the corporation unless there is an enforceable agreement to the contrary. Ownership of shares usually entitles the holder to certain basic rights:

1. The right to influence the *management* of the corporation through participating and voting in shareholder meetings.
2. The right to participate in the *earnings* of the corporation through dividends declared by the board of directors.
3. The right to share in the distribution of *assets* of the corporation at liquidation or through liquidating dividends.

These basic rights are shared proportionately by all shareholders of each share class unless the articles of incorporation or bylaws (and as noted on the share certificates) specifically provide otherwise. Additional rights may be provided for in the articles of incorporation, for example, the right to purchase shares on a *pro rata,* or proportionate, basis when shares represent additional share capital issues. This right is designed to protect the proportionate interest of each shareholder.

If the corporation has only common shares outstanding, all holders enjoy the basic rights. In the case of two or more share classes, the holders of the other share class(es) have rights that are favourable or unfavourable as compared with the common.

Fundamental Concepts and Distinctions

The fundamental concepts that underlie the accounting and reporting of shareholders' equity may be summarized as follows:

1. *Separate legal entity*—According to the law, a corporation is a non-personal entity that may own assets, owe debts, and conduct operations as an independent entity separate from each shareholder. Thus, it is a *separate accounting entity,* independent of the shareholders.[1]

---

[1] The issue of what constitutes a separate legal entity becomes more complex when one corporation is the majority shareholder of a second corporation, or when there are reciprocal holdings of shares. Complex ownership structures are covered in advanced accounting courses.

2. *Sources of shareholders' equity*—The primary *sources* of shareholders' equity are organized, accounted for, and reported separately on the balance sheet to provide useful data for financial statement users. Sources of shareholders' equity include the following:

 a. **Contributed capital** (often referred to as *paid-in capital*):
   (1) Share capital:
    (*a*) Preferred shares.
    (*b*) Common shares.[2] Normally, the entire value of proceeds obtained or assets received for *nopar* shares is recorded as share capital. If *par value* shares are allowed in the incorporating jurisdiction, proceeds are divided between share capital and other contributed capital.
   (2) Other contributed capital or *additional paid-in capital* (an obsolete term, *capital surplus,* sometimes is used):
    (*a*) From share transactions: Contributed capital from share retirement transactions, that is, shares retired for a price lower than the original issue price. If par value shares are allowed in the incorporating jurisdiction, the excess of issue proceeds over par value is recorded as other contributed capital. If treasury stock transactions are allowed, any contributed capital arising from these transactions is also classified here.
    (*b*) Other: Contributed capital from donation of assets.
 b. **Retained earnings:**
   (1) Appropriated retained earnings (sometimes inappropriately called *reserves*). This is defined and discussed in Chapter 21.
   (2) Unappropriated retained earnings.
 c. **Unrealized capital**—In *rare* circumstances, corporations have been allowed to value assets at market value rather than cost. The offsetting capital increment is unrealized until the assets are sold or used in operations, and is classified as contributed capital. Mutual funds and insurance companies, required to record assets at market values, will record unrealized capital as well.

Exhibit 20–1 illustrates a typical shareholders' equity section in a balance sheet. Notice that shareholders' equity is reported by *source,* that is, contributed capital, retained earnings, and unrealized capital.

3. *Issuance of share capital*—The issuance of share capital is recorded in conformity with the *cost principle.* That is, the issue price recorded should be the cash consideration received plus the market value of all non-cash considerations received.

4. *Sale and repurchase of shares*—Transactions of a corporation involving the sale, purchase, or resale (if allowed) of its own shares do not create "gains" or "losses" that are reported on the income statement. Rather, any difference between the market value of the consideration paid/received by the corporation and the average share capital is regarded as an adjustment to shareholders' equity.

5. *Equity versus debt*—Shareholders' equity should be clearly separated from the liabilities of the corporation.

6. *Form of business organization*—Aside from owners' equity, the accounting and reporting practices for a business are not affected in principle by its status as a corporation, partnership, or sole proprietorship. The legal form of a business can materially influence the financial (tax) consequences of various decisions for the business. The principles applied, however, are consistent across alternative forms of business entity.

7. *Terminology*—The word *capital* is used differently in accounting, finance, and the business world. For example, the word *capital* sometimes is used to mean *total* owners' equity. For precision and clarity, this text uses the word *capital* to identify that portion of shareholders' equity that relates to share capital plus additional contributed

---

[2] Share capital is also referred to as *Class A, Class B, Class C,* and so on, rather than as *preferred* or *common.*

EXHIBIT 20–1   Shareholder's Equity Section of a Balance Sheet

Shareholders' Equity

Contributed capital:

  Share capital:

Preferred shares, nopar value, $.60 dividend, cumulative and non-participating, unlimited shares authorized; 15,000 issued and outstanding*	$162,000	
Preferred shares subscribed, 100 shares	1,200	
Total preferred shares outstanding and subscribed	163,200	
Common shares, nopar value, unlimited shares authorized; 8,000 shares issued and outstanding	43,000	$206,200
Additional contributed capital:**		
Retirement of common shares	10,000	
Donation of plant site	5,000	15,000
Total contributed capital		221,200
*Retained earnings:***		
Appropriated for bond sinking fund	50,000	
Unappropriated	170,000	
Total retained earnings		220,000
Unrealized capital:		
Appraisal increase credit, increased value of land and buildings, market-value adjustment recorded in 1985 on change of control		120,000
Total shareholders' equity		$561,200

* In jurisdictions that permit the issuance of par value shares, any excess proceeds over par value would appear as a premium under additional contributed capital.

** The additional contributed capital accounts often are aggregated into a single amount on the balance sheet with detailed disclosure in the notes or a supporting schedule (see Exhibit 20–7).

***Total retained earnings often is reported on the balance sheet with disclosure of the appropriations in a supporting note.

capital. It excludes retained earnings and unrealized capital. We use the generic terms *contributed capital* and *paid-in capital* interchangeably.

Prior to discussing share capital, it may be useful to define the following terms:

1. **Authorized share capital**—the maximum number of shares that can be legally issued. Under the Canada Business Corporations Act, a corporation is entitled to issue an unlimited number of shares. The corporation may choose to place a limit on authorized shares. Such a limit must be stated in the articles of incorporation. Certain provincial incorporation acts impose authorized share limits on corporations.

2. **Issued share capital**—the number of shares that have been issued to shareholders to date.

3. **Unissued share capital**—the number of shares of authorized share capital that have not been issued; that is, the difference between authorized and issued shares.

4. **Outstanding share capital**—the number of shares that have been issued and are currently owned by shareholders.

5. **Treasury stock**—shares issued and later reacquired by the corporation and that are still held by the corporation; that is, the difference between issued shares and outstanding shares. Under the Canada Business Corporations Act and most provincial legislation, shares reacquired by a corporation must be *retired,* and treasury stock cannot exist. In these jurisdictions, issued and outstanding shares will be equal.

6. **Subscribed shares**—unissued shares set aside to meet subscription contracts (i.e., shares sold on credit and not yet paid for). Subscribed shares are usually not issued until the subscription price is paid in full.

Advantages and Disadvantages of the Corporate Form of Organization

The corporate form of business has both advantages and disadvantages when compared with a partnership or sole proprietorship. The primary advantages:

1. *Limited liability*—the liability of each shareholder is limited to his or her proportionate share of total shareholders' equity, which is represented by the number of shares owned. In case of dissolution or insolvency, shareholders may lose an amount limited to their investment, or the book value of the shares they own, whichever is greater. The creditors of a corporation have no recourse to the personal assets of shareholders.
2. *Capital accumulation*—large accumulations of funds from investors with diverse investment objectives are possible, as well as access to the investment markets (e.g., stock exchanges). This allows a firm to invest in large, expensive capital equipment or make other capital investments in order to achieve manufacturing or other efficiencies.
3. *Ease of ownership transfer*—the continuity, transfer, expansion, and contraction of ownership interests are facilitated by the nature of share capital.

The primary disadvantages of the corporate form of business include:

1. *Increased taxation*—corporate earnings are subject to double taxation in that they are taxed, first, as earned by the corporation and, again, after distribution in the form of dividends to shareholders. The tax system involves a series of tax credits, both for corporations and individuals, to reduce this effect, but some residual double taxation remains.
2. *Difficulties of control*—the large and impersonal characteristics of a corporation may cause problems for shareholders who wish to control the corporation. Since ownership is usually separated from management and can become quite dispersed, owners may be unable to exercise active and frequent control over management actions.

CONCEPT REVIEW

1. How is a federally incorporated corporation different from a provincially incorporated corporation? What is a private corporation? A crown corporation?
2. Explain the differences between authorized share capital, issued share capital, outstanding share capital, subscribed share capital, and treasury stock.
3. Most corporations will have two primary sources of shareholders' equity. What are they? How are they distinguished on the balance sheet?

DIFFERENT KINDS OF EQUITY SECURITIES
◆

Equity securities include all of the classifications of a corporation's share capital. Specifically, share capital includes two basic types of shares: common and preferred. More than one class of common or preferred shares may be issued by a corporation, and their contractual characteristics can vary greatly. Indeed, in the extreme, some preferred shares have many of the characteristics of debt.

The different features or contractual rights that may be attached to an issue of common or preferred shares are considered next. After covering these contractual features, accounting for equity securities with various features, regardless of classification, is covered in detail.

Par Value Shares

Some jurisdictions provide for the issuance of **par value shares,** that is, shares with a designated dollar amount per share as stated in the articles of incorporation and as printed on the face of the share certificates. Par value shares may be either common or preferred.

Par value shares sold initially at less than par are said to have been issued at a *discount*. Par value shares sold initially above par are said to have been issued at a *premium*. Today, the issuance of par value shares at a discount is not permitted by legislation.[3]

In the early history of corporations, only par value shares were permitted. Because the owners of a corporation were not personally liable to the corporation's creditors, statutes were intended to afford a measure of protection to creditors. In this respect, the courts tended to hold that shareholders of a corporation who paid *less* than par value for their shares could be assessed an additional amount equal to the discount if it was deemed necessary to satisfy creditors' claims.

Since 1975, the trend in Canada has been to model provincial legislation on the Canada Business Corporations Act, which only allows nopar shares. Consequently, the concept of par value in Canada has all but disappeared. Transactions involving par value shares are illustrated in Appendix 20A.

Nopar Value Shares

Nopar value shares do not carry a designated or assigned value per share—nor is such provided for in the articles of incorporation. This allows for all the consideration received on sale of the securities to be classified in the share capital account, and it avoids the need to divide the consideration into two artificial components: par value and excess over par. It also means that the entire proceeds on the sale of shares are available as a measure of protection to the corporations' creditors.

Common Shares

Common shares are the residual issue of shares, and normally carry certain basic rights: voting power, the right to dividends as declared, and the residual right to assets on liquidation. When there is only one class of shares, all of the shares are common shares, whether so designated or not.

The common shareholders are the residual owners of the corporation. As such, their position is more risky than the positions of creditors and preferred shareholders. The corporation owes its creditors legally enforceable principal and interest amounts on specified dates, and preferred shares usually specify a priority as to dividend and liquidation amounts per share. Consequently, the common shareholders are exposed to the risks and the benefits of corporate success or failure because their right to cash flows comes after creditor and preferred shareholder claims have been met.

Preferred Shares

Preferred shares are so designated because they confer certain *preferences,* or differences, over common shares.

The most common preference for preferred shares is a priority claim on dividends, usually at a stated rate or amount. In exchange for this preference, the preferred

---

[3] Despite laws that forbid issuance of par value shares at a discount, it sometimes happens *de facto* when promoters and others receive shares in exchange for non-cash assets or services that are overvalued.

shareholder often sacrifices voting rights and the right to dividends beyond the stated rate or amount. In general, however, preferences may involve one or more of the following:

1. Voting rights.
2. Dividends.
   a. Cumulative or non-cumulative.
   b. Non-participating, partially participating, or fully participating with common shareholders, in dividends in excess of the stated preferred dividend.
3. Assets in liquidation.
4. Convertibility to other securities.
5. Call features, under specified conditions.
6. Redemption or retraction.

The dividend rate on preference shares must be specified, usually as a dollar amount per share, such as $1.20 per preferred share. This preference does not guarantee a dividend but means that, when the board of directors declares a dividend, preferred shareholders must get their $1.20 preferred dividend before common shareholders receive *any* dividends.

Voting Privileges on Preferred Shares   The Canada Business Corporations Act requires only that *one* class of shares have voting power—usually, the common shares. The corporation may specify alternative voting rights and arrangements in its articles of incorporation. Usually, preferred shares do not have voting rights, although a corporation may choose to deviate from this norm. One possibility is that the preferred shares will be non-voting except in certain circumstances, such as when preferred dividends have not been paid or during a vote on a takeover bid.

Cumulative Dividend Preferences on Preferred Shares   *Cumulative* preferred shares provide that dividends not declared in a given year accumulate at the specified rate on such shares. This accumulated amount must be paid in full if and when dividends are declared in a later year, before any dividends can be paid on the common. If cumulative preference dividends are not declared in a given year, they are said to have been passed and are called *dividends in arrears* on the cumulative preferred shares. If only a part of the preferred dividend is met for any year, the remainder of the cumulative dividend is in arrears. Cumulative preferred shares carry the right, on dissolution of the corporation, to dividends in arrears to the extent the corporation has retained earnings. However, different provisions for dividends in arrears may be stipulated in the articles of incorporation and bylaws. Dividends in arrears are recorded with a memo entry, not as liabilities. Since preferred shareholders cannot force the board of directors to declare dividends, dividends in arrears do not meet the definition of a liability. The *CICA Handbook* requires that arrears of dividends for cumulative preference shares be disclosed, usually in the notes to the financial statements.

Participating Dividend Preferences on Preferred Shares   *Participating* preferred shares provide that the preferred shareholders participate above the stated preferential rate on a *pro rata basis* in dividend declarations with the common shareholders. First, preferred shareholders receive their preference rate. Second, the common shareholders receive a specified *matching* dividend. Then, if the declared dividend is larger than these two amounts, the excess is divided on a pro rata basis between the two share classes. Participation must be specified in the articles of incorporation and stated on the share certificates. In Canada, public companies have rarely, if ever, issued participating preferreds. Private companies may be more creative, recognizing that it is often more difficult for them to raise share capital.

Preferred shares may be *fully participating* or *partially participating*. If partially participating, preferred shares may participate in dividend declarations in excess of their preference rate, but the participation is capped off at a certain level. Dividends above this level accrue solely to the common shareholders. Fully participating shares, on the other hand, share in the full extent of dividend declarations.

For example, a corporation may issue preferred shares, entitled to a preference dividend of 50 cents with participation up to 70 cents after common shareholders receive 25 cents per share. In this case, participation with the common shareholders would be limited to the additional 20 cents above the regular 50-cent rate. The 25-cent dividend to the common shareholder is the *matching* dividend, and it is specified in the articles of incorporation. It is meant to provide the same rate of return on the common shares in the initial allocation and acknowledges that the share classes are of different relative size and value.

The following cases, A through E, illustrate various combinations of cumulative/non-cumulative rights and of participating/non-participating rights. Assume that Mann Corporation has the following share capital outstanding:[4]

Preferred shares; nopar value; dividend entitlement, 50 cents;
  10,000 shares outstanding $100,000
Common shares, nopar value, 40,000 shares outstanding 200,000

Case A   Preferred shares are cumulative and non-participating; dividends are two years in arrears; dividends declared, $28,000.

	Preferred	Common
Step 1—Preferred in arrears (50 cents × 10,000 × 2)	$10,000	
Step 2—Preferred, current (50 cents × 10,000)	5,000	
Step 3—Common (balance).		$13,000
	$15,000	$13,000

Preferred shares receive their dividends in arrears and the current dividend before the common shares receive any dividend.

Case B   Preferred shares are non-cumulative and non-participating; dividends have not been paid for two years; dividends declared, $28,000.

	Preferred	Common
Step 1—Preferred, current (50 cents × 10,000)	$5,000	
Step 2—Common (balance).		$23,000
	$5,000	$23,000

Preferred shares may only receive dividends for the current year regardless of the fact that dividends were missed in two previous years.

Case C   Preferred is non-cumulative, partially participating up to 70 cents after common shares have received 25 cents per share. Dividends declared, $28,000.

	Preferred	Common
Step 1—Preferred, current (10,000 × 50 cents)	$5,000	
Step 2—Common, matching (40,000 × 25 cents).		$10,000
Step 3—Preferred, participating.	2,000*	
Step 4—Balance to common ($28,000 − $5,000 − $10,000 − $2,000) . . .		11,000
	$7,000	$21,000

* Dividend available: $13,000   ($28,000 − $5,000 − $10,000).
  Preference share: $ 4,333   [$13,000 × $5,000/($10,000 + $5,000)].
  Limit (maximum): $ 2,000   (10,000 × 20 cents).

---

[4] Dividends are discussed substantively in Chapter 21. Cases A, B, C, D, and E are given here only to help you to understand the definition and features of preferred shares. The declaration of a dividend is much more involved than selecting a total amount.

Notice that the return on investment after the first two steps is equal: a $5,000 (5%) return on a $100,000 investment for the preferred shares and a $10,000 (5%) return on a $200,000 investment for common shares. The returns are carefully contrived, and they help determine market value for shares. Step 3 involves the calculation of the amount that preferred shares participate in the "excess" dividend declaration. The $28,000 declaration is $13,000 above the required $15,000 preference dividend and matching amounts. Preference shares get their pro rata share of this amount, subject to any limitation for partial participation. The pro rata share here is based on the minimum dividend: the $5,000 preference dividend and a $10,000 matching dividend produce a $15,000 base. The preference share is $5,000/$15,000, while the common would receive $10,000/$15,000. Thus, if there were no limitation on participation, preference shares would receive another $4,333. As it is, they are limited to $2,000 (10,000 × 20 cents). The pro rata allocation was based on minimum dividend entitlements. Articles of incorporation may state that pro rata allocations may be based on the total par value of shares or on assigned values. This simply changes the composition of the fraction used to allocate the excess dividend.

Case D   Exactly the same as Case C, except total dividends declared are $16,000:

	Preferred	Common
Step 1—Preferred, current (10,000 × 50 cents)	$5,000	
Step 2—Common, matching (40,000 × 25 cents).		$10,000
Step 3—Preferred, participating.	333*	
Step 4—Balance to common ($16,000 − $5,000 − $10,000 − $333)		667
	$5,333	$10,667

* Dividend available: $1,000   ($16,000 − $5,000 − $10,000).
  Preference share: $ 333   [$1,000 × $5,000/($10,000 + $5,000)].
  Limit (maximum): $2,000   (10,000 × 20 cents).

Case E   Exactly the same as Case C, except preferred shares are two years in arrears, *cumulative,* and *fully participating.* Dividends declared are $37,000.

	Preferred	Common
A: Preferred, in arrears ($5,000 × 2).	$10,000	
B: Step 1—Preferred, current (10,000 × 50 cents)	5,000	
Step 2—Common, matching (40,000 × 25 cents)		10,000
Step 3—Preferred, participating*	4,000	
Step 4—Balance to common		
($37,000 − $10,000 − $5,000 − $10,000 − $4,000)		8,000
	$19,000	$18,000

* Dividend available: $12,000   ($37,000 − $10,000 − $5,000 − $10,000).
  Preference share: $ 4,000   [$12,000 × $5,000/($10,000 + $5,000)].
  Limit (maximum):   none   (fully participating).

In the absence of an expressed stipulation in the articles of incorporation or bylaws, courts have taken the view that preferred shareholders have *no* right to participate with common shares.

Asset Preference on Preferred Shares   Preferred shares that have a liquidation preference provide that the preferred shareholders, in case of corporate dissolution, have a priority over the common shareholders on the assets of the corporation up to a stated amount per share. After the preferred shareholders' asset preference is satisfied, the remainder of the assets are distributed to the common shareholders. The liquidation preference of the preferred shares is disclosed in the financial statements.

Preferred Shares Convertible to Other Securities   Preferred shares may carry a *convertibility* provision: at the *option of the preferred shareholder,* the preferred shares owned may be exchanged for (converted to) other securities, usually common shares. Because the conversion privilege offers the preferred shareholder the option of holding the original preferred shares or converting them to another specified security, convertible preferred shares are favoured by investors. Convertibility privileges should be disclosed in the financial statements of the issuing corporation, either on the balance sheet or in the disclosure notes.

Callable Preferred Shares Preferred shares may be *callable,* which means that at the *issuer's option,* the preferred shares can be called in for cancellation at a specified price and date(s). When callable shares are called by the issuer, the shareholder has no option but to forward the shares (usually through a stockbroker) to the issuer and receive payment as specified in the call agreement. All dividends in arrears on cumulative preferred shares must be paid prior to the call date. The call price is usually above the original issue price. Call provisions must be disclosed in the financial statements.

Redeemable Preferred Shares Some corporations issue preferred shares with the unique feature of *redemption,* either (1) mandatory redemption at a specified date and price or (2) redemption at the option of the shareholder, who has a right to redeem the shares at a specified date and at a specified redemption price. The latter feature allows the shareholder to sell the shares back to the issuing corporation, and the issuing corporation must purchase them. Mandatory redemption is a stronger situation. The corporation has no choice but to redeem all shares of such an issue at the specified date and price. These shares may also be called *retractable* or *term-preferred shares.*

Redeemable preferred shares have financial characteristics of both debt and equity. They are similar to debt in that they must be either retired or refunded at the option of the holder at a specified date. On the other hand, they have several characteristics of equity:

1. If a dividend is passed, the shareholder does not have the right to initiate default proceedings as would a debtholder whose interest payments were passed.
2. Redeemable preferred shares are subordinate to debt in the event of liquidation.

Some accountants believe that preferred shares with extensive characteristics of debt should be reported as debt rather than as shareholders' equity. Recently, we have seen more and more issues of preferred shares with mandatory redemption over a relatively short time period of 5 to 10 years. Such issues carry a commitment to use the firm's future cash flows to redeem the preferreds and as such are more like debt than equity. Current GAAP, however, does not directly recognize preferred shares as debt. An Accounting Guideline from the Accounting Standards Steering Committee on term preferred shares specifies that such shares would normally be included in shareholders' equity, separately and clearly disclosed. On the other hand, the U.S. SEC has a rule prohibiting the inclusion of redeemable preferred shares in the general category of shareholders' equity.[5] Amounts for redeemable preferred shares, non-redeemable preferred shares, and common shares cannot be combined in financial statements filed with the SEC. It is likely that there will be increasing pressure on standard setters to change the requirements to allow accounting for such issues as debt rather than as equity.

Exhibit 20–2 is an illustration of the reporting and disclosure of redeemable preferred shares by Ranger Oil Ltd. in 1988. Compare this treatment to the disclosure of BFGoodrich Company, a U.S. company (see Exhibit 20–3). They exclude the redeemable preferred shares from shareholders' equity.

If redeemable preferred shares are debt, why don't corporations just issue debt in the first place? From the issuing firm's perspective, preferred dividends are not tax deductible, whereas interest payments normally would be. The answer may lie in the use

---

[5] *SEC Release No. 33-6097.*

EXHIBIT 20-2   Disclosure of Redeemable Preferred Shares, Ranger Oil Ltd.

Balance Sheet — Shareholders Equity	1988	1987
Capital Stock (note 5):		
Authorized:		
Preferred and common shares without par value		
in unlimited number		
Issued:		
596,900 redeemable preferred shares	$ 14,923	$ 14,923
74,634,896 (1987—74,611,474) common shares	145,084	144,987

Note to Financial Statements

5. Capital Stock
Redeemable Preferred Shares
The Company's 9.25% Cumulative Redeemable Retractable Preferred Shares, Series A, are retractable at the option of the holder on April 10, 1991, at $25.00 U.S. per share. The shares will be redeemable at the option of the Company on and after April 11, 1990, at $25.75 U.S. per share and on and after April 11, 1991, at $25.00 U.S. per share. Commencing April 1, 1991, the Company is obliged to purchase in each calendar quarter 0.75% of the total outstanding preferred shares at prices not exceeding $25.00 U.S., with such obligation to carry over to succeeding calendar quarters in the same calendar year.

of the debt-to-equity ratio or other similar measures of debt capacity in debt agreements and covenants. Debt covenants are usually based on financial statements generated using GAAP. If a borrower could circumvent a possible debt covenant violation by issuing redeemable preferred shares instead of straight debt, the management of the borrowing firm may be inclined to do so.

A second motivation for issuing redeemable preferred shares rather than debt occurs when the buyer is another corporation: the issue may be offered at a dividend rate lower than the interest rate on equivalent debt. An investing corporation might accept this lower rate because corporations can exclude dividend income from taxable income, but will receive no such exemption for interest income. There are also certain tax advantages for individuals who receive dividend income, although they are not as significant as those enjoyed by corporations. The result of these tax rules is that the issuing company may be able to raise capital at a lower after-tax cash cost through an equity issue rather than a debt issue.

CONCEPT REVIEW

1. What are the fundamental differences between common and preferred shares? What are some reasons why a firm might issue preferred shares?
2. A firm has issued and outstanding 1,000 shares of nopar cumulative, non-participating shares of $5 preferred shares, and 20,000 of nopar common shares. Dividends are in arrears for one year (not including the current year). The board of directors declares dividends of $25,000 to be paid to shareholders at the end of the current fiscal year. How will the $25,000 be shared between the preferred and common shareholders?

ACCOUNTING FOR VARIOUS EQUITY TRANSACTIONS
◆

Accounting for the Issuance of Nopar Value Shares

Accounting for shareholders' equity emphasizes *source;* therefore, if a corporation has more than one share class, separate accounts should be maintained for each. If there is only one share class, an account titled "share capital" usually is used. In cases where there are two or more classes, account titles such as "common shares," "preferred

EXHIBIT 20-3 Disclosure of Redeemable Preferred Shares, BFGoodrich

(in millions)	December 31	
	1988	1987
Redeemable preferred stocks.	$ 11.3	$ 14.4
Shareholders' equity:		
$3.50 cumulative convertible preferred stock:		
Series D (stated at involuntary liquidation value of $50 per share)		
2,200,000 shares issued and outstanding.	110.0	110.0
Common stock—$5 par value:		
Authorized 100,000,000 shares; issued 25,554,627 shares	127.8	127.8
Additional capital.	382.9	382.2
Income retained in the business	548.9	405.3
Cumulative unrealized translation adjustments	(2.6)	(19.8)
Common stock held in treasury, at cost (352,396 shares in 1988		
and 417,511 shares in 1987).	(12.4)	(14.6)
Total shareholders' equity	1,154.6	990.9

Abridged Notes to Consolidated Financial Statements

Note Q: *Preferred Stock*

There are 10,000,000 authorized shares of Series Preferred Stock—$1 par value. Shares of Series Preferred Stock which have been redeemed are deemed retired and extinguished and may not be reissued. As of December 31, 1988, 534,174 shares of Series Preferred Stock have been redeemed. The Board of Directors establishes and designates the series and fixes the number of shares and the relative rights, preferences and limitations of the respective series of the Series Preferred Stock.

Whenever dividends on Cumulative Series Preferred Stock are in arrears six quarters or more, holders of such stock (voting as a class) have the right to elect two Directors of the Company until all cumulative dividends have been paid.

Dividends on outstanding Series Preferred Stock must be declared and paid or set apart for payment, and funds required for sinking-fund payments, if any, on Series Preferred Stock, must be paid or set apart for payment before any dividends may be paid or set apart for payment on the Common Stock.

Redeemable Preferred Stock—Series A (stated at involuntary liquidation value of $100 per share): BFGoodrich has issued 250,000 shares of $7.85 Cumulative Preferred Stock, Series A. In order to comply with sinking-fund requirements, each year on August 15, BFGoodrich must redeem 12,500 shares of the Series A Stock. The redemption price is $100 per share, plus dividends accrued at the redemption date. BFGoodrich may redeem, at such price, up to an additional 12,500 shares in each year. The sinking-fund requirements may also be satisfied with shares acquired on the open market. At December 31, 1988 and 1987, BFGoodrich held 12,050 and 12,500 shares, respectively, for future sinking-fund requirements. After giving effect to the shares held for future sinking-fund requirements, there were 112,950, 125,000 and 150,000 shares of Series A Stock outstanding at December 31, 1988, 1987 and 1986, respectively. The aggregate amount of redemption requirement for the Series A Stock is $.1 for 1989 and $1.3 in each of the years 1990, 1991, 1992, and 1993.

Redeemable Preferred Stock—Series B (stated at involuntary liquidation value of $10 per share): BFGoodrich had issued 372,838 shares of $.975 Cumulative Preferred Stock, Series B. Sinking-fund requirements required BFGoodrich to redeem 30,000 shares of the Series B Stock on July 15 of each year at a redemption price of $10 per share, plus dividends accrued at the redemption date. On July 15, 1988, BFGoodrich redeemed the 192,838 outstanding shares of Series B Cumulative Preferred Stock at $10.24 per share plus accrued dividends.

shares, $5," or "preferred shares, $1.25" are used. The dollar amounts listed with nopar preferred shares indicate the dividend entitlement. The sequence of transactions related to the issuance of shares is:

1. Authorization of shares.
2. Sale for cash or subscription (i.e., the sale of shares on credit).
3. Collection of subscriptions when applicable.
4. Issuance of shares.

Authorization—The articles of incorporation will authorize an unlimited (or, less frequently, a limited) number of shares. This authorization may be recorded as a memo entry in the general journal and in the ledger account by the following notation:

Common Shares—Nopar Value
(Authorized: Unlimited Shares)

Nopar Value Shares Issued for Cash   When shares are issued, a *share certificate,* specifying the number of shares represented, is prepared for each shareholder. An entry reflecting the number of shares held by each shareholder is made in the *shareholder ledger,* a subsidiary ledger to the share capital account.

In most cases, shares are sold and issued for cash rather than on a subscription (i.e., credit) basis. The issuance of 10,000 common shares, nopar, for cash of $10.20 per share would be recorded as follows:

```
Cash . . . . . . . . . . . . . . . . . . . . . . . . . . . . . 102,000
        Common shares, nopar (10,000 shares) . . . . . . . . .          102,000
```

The common shares account is credited for the total proceeds received.

Shares Sold on a Subscription Basis

When a corporation is first organized, prospective shareholders often sign a contract to purchase a specified number of shares *on credit* with payment due at one or more specified future dates. Also, a corporation may sell its shares on credit subsequent to incorporation. Such contractual agreements are known as *stock subscriptions,* and the shares involved are called **subscribed share capital**. Because finanical statement elements are created by a legal contract, accounting recognition is necessary. The purchase price is debited to stock subscriptions receivable, and share capital subscribed is credited.

To illustrate, assume 120 common shares of BT Corporation, nopar value, are subscribed for at $12 by J. Doe. The total is payable in three installments of $480 each. The entry by BT Corporation would be as follows:

```
Stock subscriptions receivable—common shares (Doe) . . . . . . .1,440*
        Common shares subscribed, nopar (120 shares) . . . . . . .          1,440
        * Payable in three installments of $480 each.
```

The credit balance in common shares subscribed reflects the corporation's obligation to issue the 120 shares on fulfillment of the terms of the agreement by the subscriber. This account is reported on the balance sheet similarly to the related share capital account (see Exhibit 20–1). There are two ways to present stock subscriptions receivable. Some argue it should be classified as a *current* asset if the corporation expects current collection; otherwise, it is reported as a *non-current* asset under the category "other assets."

Others argue it should be *offset* against the common shares subscribed account in the shareholders' equity section of the balance sheet. Some accountants believe that all subscriptions receivable should be reported as a contra account to the related share account. This is the preferred approach, as it maintains the integrity of the equity elements of financial statements.

In some cases, subscription contracts call for installment payments. In such cases, separate "call" accounts may be set up for each installment. If the corporation has a number of subscriptions, it is usually desirable to maintain a *subscribers' ledger* as a subsidiary record to the share subscriptions receivable account similar to that maintained for trade accounts receivable.

Collections on subscriptions receivable may be in cash, property, or services. The appropriate account is debited, and subscriptions receivable is credited. If a non-cash asset or a service is received, the amount recorded would be based on the rules for non-cash sales of share capital.

Share certificates are not usually issued until the subscription price is fully paid. As the last collection is received, the issuer makes two entries. To illustrate, assume the third and last collection on the above subscription is received. The entries would be as follows:

To record the collection:

```
Cash . . . . . . . . . . . . . . . . . . . . . . . . . . . . . . .   480
        Stock subscriptions receivable—common shares (Doe). . . . .         480
```

To record issuance of shares:

```
Common shares subscribed, nopar (120 shares) . . . . . . . . . . 1,440
        Common shares, nopar (120 shares). . . . . . . . . . . . .       1,440
```

Default on Subscriptions

When a subscriber *defaults* after partial fulfillment of the subscription contract, certain complexities arise. In case of default, the corporation may decide to (1) return all payments received to the subscriber; (2) issue shares equivalent to the number of paid for in full, rather than the total number subscribed; or (3) keep the monies received. The first two options involve no disadvantage to the subscriber, although the corporation may incur an economic loss if share prices have dropped. The third option is not a norm, although legislation generally does not prevent it. Most legislation covers the contingency where the corporation elects this alternative. Such laws vary considerably; two contrasting provisions are as follows:

1. The subscribed shares are *forfeited,* and all payments made by the defaulting subscriber are forfeited by the subscriber. Therefore, the forfeited amount is credited to the contributed capital of the corporation. Further, the corporation is free to resell the shares. Provisions of this type favour the corporation and seldom occur. To illustrate, assume that J. Doe had subscribed for 120 common shares for $1,440 and that one payment had been made by Doe prior to default. All related account balances would be removed as follows:

```
Common shares subscribed (120 shares) . . . . . . . . . . . . . . 1,440
        Stock subscriptions receivable—common shares (Doe). . . . . .       960
        Contributed capital from defaulted subscriptions
        (amount paid in by Doe). . . . . . . . . . . . . . . . . . .       480
```

2. The shares are forfeited, but the corporation must resell the shares under a *lien* whereby the original subscriber must be reimbursed for the amount that the net receipts for the shares (i.e., the total cash collected from both the sale to the subscriber and subsequent resale of the shares to another investor, less the costs incurred by the corporation in making the later sale) exceed the *original subscription price*. To avoid an incentive to default, the refund to the defaulting subscriber cannot exceed the amount paid to the date of default less resale costs. Exhibit 20–4 illustrates the accounting for this provision.

Non-Cash Sale of Share Capital

Corporations sometimes issue shares for non-cash assets. A corporation might make a private placement of preferred shares and common shares in exchange for real estate. A private placement occurs when an issuer of securities arranges to sell an issue to a limited number of specific buyers; the issue is not sold in a public market. Usually, a private placement can occur without the issuer meeting all the onerous public disclosure requirements of a public offering.

When a corporation issues its shares for *non-cash* assets or services or to settle debt, the transaction should be recorded at the fair value of that which is *given up*— the shares—unless the fair value of the asset or service *received* is more clearly

EXHIBIT 20-4   Default on Subscriptions—Shares Resold under Lien

1. BT Corporation received from subscriber Doe a subscription for 120 shares of nopar preferred shares at $12 per share:

     Subscription receivable, preferred shares, Doe (120 shares × $12) $1,440
         Preferred shares subscribed, 120 shares $1,440

2. BT Corporation received a $480 installment on the subscription from subscriber Doe:

     Cash 480
         Subscription receivable, preferred shares, Doe   480

3. Subscriber Doe defaults on the subscription. BT Corporation records the default under the lien provision:

     Preferred shares subscribed, 120 shares 1,440
         Subscription receivable, preferred shares, Doe ($1,440 − $480) . . .   960
         Payable to subscriber Doe (pending resale of
            formerly subscribed shares)   480

4. BT Corporation resells the formerly subscribed shares for $15 per share. BT Corporation paid the cost of resale, $50, and debited the amount to the payable to subscriber Doe account:

     Resale of shares:
         Cash [(120 shares × $15) − $50] 1,750
         Payable to subscriber Doe (resale costs) 50
            Preferred shares, nopar (120 × $15)   1,800

5. BT Corporation pays stipulated amount to subscriber Doe:

     Payable to subscriber Doe* 430
         Cash   430

* Computation:
   Amount to be paid to subscriber Doe based on lien provisions:
     Net receipts for the shares:
       Cash collected from subscriber Doe . . . . $ 480
       Cash collected from resale of shares   1,800
       Less: Cost of resale . . . .   (50)
         Net receipts $2,230
     Original subscription price   1,440
     Remainder payable to subscriber Doe, subject to limitation . . . . $ 790
     Limitation—total actual payments made by subscriber Doe, less resale costs
       (i.e., $480 − $50) . . . . $ 430

   Therefore, pay $430 to subscriber Doe.

established. If this is the case, then the value of the asset received is used. It is sometimes difficult to determine an objective and reliable value for the shares issued, especially if they are infrequently traded, or if the issuance in question is a very large or very small block of shares compared to the norm. It is often far easier to assess the value of the consideration received, and this will become the value recorded.[6] If the current market value of neither the shares issued nor the non-cash consideration received can be reliably determined, appraised values are used. Further, if market values or appraisals are not reliably determinable, the values must be established by the governing authority of the company (i.e., the board of directors and management). If a reliable market value for the shares is established within a reasonable time after such a transaction, then the

---

[6] *CICA Handbook,* Section 3830, "Non-Monetary Transactions," (Toronto: CICA).

originally recorded appraised value, or the value set by the corporation's governing authority, may be revised.

The issuance of shares for non-cash consideration sometimes involves questionable valuations. Some companies have disavowed market values and independent appraisals in order to permit the governing authority of the company to set arbitrary values in these non-cash transactions. In some such cases, companies are motivated to overvalue the assets received, and, as a consequence, overvalue shareholders' equity. This condition is often referred to as *watered stock:* the value of the resources received for the issued shares is less than the value of the shares issued (i.e., they are watered down). On the other hand, some companies are motivated to undervalue the assets received. As a consequence, they understate shareholders' equity—a condition often called *secret reserves.* Secret reserves are also created intentionally and in error by depreciating or amortizing a properly recorded asset over a period less than its useful life.

Special Sales of Share Capital

A corporation usually sells each class of its share capital separately. However, a corporation may sell two or more classes for one lump-sum amount (often referred to as a *basket sale*). In addition, a corporation may issue two or more classes of its share capital in exchange for non-cash consideration.

When two or more classes of securities are sold and issued for a single lump sum, the total proceeds must be allocated logically among the several classes of securities. Two methods used in such situations are (1) the *proportional method,* in which the lump sum received is allocated proportionately among the classes of shares on the basis of the relative market value of each security, and (2) the *incremental method,* in which the market value of one security is used as a basis for that security and the remainder of the lump sum is allocated to the other class of security.

The method selected should produce the most reliable results based upon the data available at the transaction date. To illustrate, assume VW Corporation issued 1,000 common shares, nopar, and 500 preferred shares, nopar, in three different situations as follows:

Situation 1—Proportional Method Applied The common shares were selling at $40 per share and the preferred at $20. Assume the total cash received was $48,000. Because reliable market values are available, the proportional method is preferable as a basis for allocating the lump-sum amount as follows:

Proportional allocation:

Market value of common (1,000 shares × $40)	$40,000	(⅘)
Market value of preferred (500 shares × $20)	10,000	(⅕)
Total market value	$50,000	(5/5)

Allocation of the lump-sum sale price of $48,000:

Common ($48,000 × ⅘)	$38,400
Preferred ($48,000 × ⅕)	9,600
Total	$48,000

The journal entry to record the issuance is:

Cash	48,000	
Common shares, nopar (1,000 shares)		38,400
Preferred shares, nopar (500 shares)		9,600

Situation 2—Incremental Method Applied   The common shares were selling at $40; a market for the preferred has not been established. Because there is no market for the preferred shares, the market value of the common is used as a basis for the following entry:

```
Cash . . . . . . . . . . . . . . . . . . . . . . . . . . . . . . 48,000
    Common shares, nopar (1,000 shares) . . . . . . . . . . .        40,000
    Preferred shares, nopar (500 shares) ($48,000 − $40,000). . .     8,000
```

Situation 3—Arbitrary Allocation   When there is no established market for either class of shares, neither the proportional method nor the incremental method of allocation can be used. In this case, an arbitrary allocation is used. In the absence of any other logical basis, a *temporary* allocation may be made by the board of directors. Should a market value be established for one of the securities in the near future, a correcting entry based on such value would be made.

Share Issue Costs

Corporations often incur substantial expenditures with major public share issues. These expenditures include registration fees, underwriter commissions, legal and accounting fees, printing costs, clerical costs, and promotional costs. These expenditures are called *share issue costs*. While share issue costs are usually not large compared with the total funds received, they are large enough to require careful accounting. Two methods of accounting for share issue costs are used:

1. *Offset method*—Under this method, share issue costs are treated as a reduction of the amount received from the sale of the related share capital. The rationale to support this method is that these are one-time costs that cannot be reasonably assigned to future periodic revenues and that the *net* cash received is the actual appropriate measure of capital raised. Therefore, under this method, share issue costs are debited to the share capital account.
2. *Deferred charge method*—Under this method, share issue costs are recorded as a deferred charge and are then amortized over a reasonable period. The rationale for this method is that these costs create an intangible asset that contributes to the earning of future revenues. They are allocated against future periodic revenues in conformity with the matching principle.

Although the offset method dominates, both methods are used. Subsequent to the issuance of share capital, costs required to maintain shareholder records, transfer costs, and dividend payment costs (clerical only) are expensed when incurred. Organization costs are discussed in Chapter 13.

Unrealized Capital

Unrealized capital, as a category of shareholders' equity, is not widely used in practice. It arises when assets are written up above cost or net book value. Because of adherence to the cost principle and the concept of conservatism, assets rarely are written up from cost to fair market value. In the past, the most common example of such write-ups was writing up capital assets from cost to market values in *unusual* circumstances, like a change in control. An upward adjustment of the asset account requires an offsetting credit to unrealized capital increment. This is called an appraisal increase credit (see Exhibit 20–1). Starting in 1991, this is no longer permitted by the *CICA Handbook*.

Life insurance and mutual fund companies, required to carry certain assets at market value, will report an unrealized capital increment.

Donated Capital

Sometimes a corporation may receive a donation of assets—**donated capital**. An example would be a donation of land from a city in order to induce a corporation to locate some of its operations in the city. In this case, the corporation records the donated asset at its fair market value, with a corresponding credit to donated capital. The donation is viewed by the accounting profession as a capital contribution rather than as an earnings item. No gain or loss is recorded for the transaction. Donated capital appears in the shareholders' equity section of the balance sheet among the additional paid-in capital items or, on occasion, as a separate category between contributed capital and retained earnings. It must be described as to source.

CONCEPT REVIEW

1. When shares are sold on a subscription basis, what are the arguments for and against accounting for the subscription receivable as an asset? As a contra to shareholders' equity? Why is the transaction recorded at all?
2. A bundle of securities, consisting of one common share and one share of a new issue of preferred, is sold for $50. This is 50% more than the current market price of the firm's publicly traded common shares. Describe how to account for the issue. What amount will be credited to which of the various shareholders' equity accounts?

CHANGES IN CONTRIBUTED CAPITAL
◆

Redemption or Cancellation of Shares

At the option of the corporation, statutes provide conditions for the purchase and cancellation of the corporation's outstanding shares. A corporation may decide to acquire its own shares for any of the following reasons:

1. To provide cash flow to shareholders in lieu of dividends. Acquisition may provide a tax advantage to the selling shareholder because any resulting gain on sale of the shares is generally given preferential capital gain treatment for tax purposes. Some corporations regularly acquire their own shares; others do so only when they have excess cash and few investment opportunities.
2. To acquire shares when they appear to be "undervalued." A corporation with excess cash may feel that buying undervalued shares for cancellation will benefit the remaining shareholders. These transactions also help make a market (i.e., provide a buyer) for the shares.
3. To buy out one or more particular shareholders and to thwart takeover bids.
4. To increase earnings per share by reducing the shares outstanding.
5. To reduce dividend payments by reducing the shares outstanding.

Companies must exercise extreme care in transactions involving their own shares because of the opportunity the corporation (and its management) has to use insider information to the detriment of a shareholder from whom the corporation is acquiring its own shares. For example, an oil company (or members of its management) with inside knowledge of a profitable oil discovery could withhold the good news and acquire shares at an artifically low market price. This would unfairly deprive the selling shareholder of the true market value. For these reasons, securities law prohibits corporations from engaging in deceptive conduct, including acts related to transactions involving their own shares.

When shares are purchased and immediately retired, all capital items relating to the specific shares are removed from the accounts. If the shares are cumulative preferred and there are dividends in arrears, such dividends are paid and charged to retained earnings in the normal manner. Where the cost of the acquired shares is different from the average original issuance price, the CICA recommends that the cost be allocated as follows for nopar shares:[7]

1. When the reacquisition cost is *higher* than the average price per share issued to date:
   a. To share capital, in the amount of the average price per share credited to the share capital account to date.
   b. Any excess, to contributed capital if contributed capital has been created by any prior reacquisition transaction of the same class of shares.
   c. Any excess, to retained earnings.
2. When the reacquisition cost is *lower* than the average price per share issued to date:
   a. To share capital, in the amount of the average price per share credited to the capital account to date.
   b. Any excess, to contributed capital.

The effect of these rules is to ensure that a corporation records no income effect (i.e., no gain or loss on the income statement) on buying back its own shares. If this were not the case, the potential for income manipulation is obvious. To illustrate the application of these rules, assume that SC Corporation has 200,000 nopar common shares outstanding, and that there is $1,000,000 in the common share account. The contributed capital account from previous retirement transactions of common shares has a $7,200 credit balance. The corporation acquired and retired 10,000 shares at a price of $6.25 per share. The shareholder who sold these shares back to SC Corporation had originally bought them for $4.00 per share. The transaction would be recorded as follows:

```
Common shares (10,000 shares) ($1,000,000/200,000) × 10,000. .  50,000
Contributed capital, common share retirement . . . . . . . . .   7,200
Retained earnings ($62,500 − $50,000 − $7,200). . . . . . . . .   5,300
    Cash (10,000 × $6.25)  . . . . . . . . . . . . . . . . .            62,500
```

The first step in constructing this journal entry is to compare the cost to retire the shares ($62,500) with the *average* initial issuance price to date ($50,000). The specific issue price of these shares ($4.00) is irrelevant. Since the corporation paid $12,500 more to retire these shares than their original proceeds, the net resources of the corporation are reduced by this amount. The $12,500 is debited first to contributed capital from prior share retirements until that account is exhausted. Retained earnings is debited for the balance. The effect of this transaction is to reduce paid-in capital by $57,200, and total shareholders' equity by $62,500.

If the shares were reacquired for $4.25 per share, the entry to record the transaction would be:

```
Common shares (10,000 shares) ($1,000,000/200,000) × 10,000. .  50,000
    Contributed capital, common share retirement
      ($50,000 − $42,500) . . . . . . . . . . . . . . . . . . .          7,500
    Cash (10,000 × $4.25)  . . . . . . . . . . . . . . . . . .           42,500
```

Total shareholders' equity and paid-in capital go down only by $42,500 ($50,000 less $7,500), reflecting the fact that the corporation paid *less* to repurchase the shares than the average issuance price to date.

---

[7] *CICA Handbook,* Section 3240, "Share Capital," (Toronto: CICA).

Retirement of Callable and Redeemable Shares

Corporations often issue *callable* preferred shares, which provide that the corporation, *at its option* after a certain date, can call in the shares at a specified price for formal retirement. In contrast, redeemable shares provide that *at the option of the shareholder or on a specific date,* and under certain conditions, the shares will be retired at a specified price per share. The same cost allocation process is followed as was described in the previous section. If the preferred shares are cumulative and there are dividends in arrears, such dividends must be paid and debited to retained earnings at the time of the call or redemption. This is usually part of the redemption terms. The *CICA Handbook* specifies that the financial statements must disclose the redemption price of redeemable shares, details concerning the number of shares redeemed in the period, and the amount of consideration given in the redemption.

To illustrate, assume a corporation had 2,500 callable preferred shares outstanding, $260,000; and retained earnings, $45,000. Assume the corporation called and formally retired all of the preferred shares. Two different assumptions as to the call and retirement are illustrated below:

Assumption 1 The preferred shares are callable at $110 per share — $6 per share above the original issue price of $104 ($260,000/2,500). Dividends are up to date:

Preferred shares (2,500 shares at $104)	260,000	
Retained earnings.	15,000	
Cash (2,500 shares × $110)		275,000

Assumption 2 The preferred shares are cumulative and entitled to a yearly dividend of $5; three years' dividends are in arrears. The shares are callable at $101 plus the dividends in arrears, which must be paid:

Retained earnings (2,500 × $5 × 3 years)	37,500	
Cash		37,500

Preferred shares (2,500 shares × $104)	260,000	
Contributed capital from retirement of preferred shares		
($104 − $101) × 2,500 shares		7,500
Cash (2,500 shares × $101)		252,500

Restriction on Reacquisition of Shares

When shares are purchased, assets of the corporation are disbursed to the owners of the particular shares purchased. If a corporation has a free hand, creditor interests or the interests of another class of shareholders may be jeopardized through the distribution of corporate assets via share repurchases. To prevent such situations, legislation restricts purchases by requiring a solvency test or restriction or appropriation of retained earnings equal to the cost of the shares. For example, the Canada Business Corporations Act, Section 32, provides that:

A corporation shall not make any payment to purchase or otherwise acquire shares issued by it if there are reasonable grounds for believing that
a. the corporation is, or would after the payment be, unable to pay its liabilities as they become due; or
b. the realizable value of the corporation's assets would after the payment be less than the aggregate of its liabilities and stated capital of all classes.

Restriction or appropriation of retained earnings equal to the cost of the purchased shares is based on the view that the purchase of shares has the same impact as the payment of a cash dividend. Therefore, the retained earnings should be appropriated or frozen.

Shares Received by Donation

Shareholders occasionally donate shares back to the corporation. For example, a donation may constitute recognition of an overvaluation of assets originally given in exchange for the shares. When donated shares are received and retired, the share capital account is reduced by the average price per share credited to the account to date, and a contributed capital account, "donated capital," is created.

For example, assume a corporation has 100,000 nopar common shares outstanding, originally issued (on average) for $17.50 per share. If 1,000 shares were donated to the corporation, the following journal entry would be made:

Common shares (1,000 shares) (1,000 × $17.50) 17,500
    Contributed capital on share donation   17,500

Conversion of Convertible Preferred Shares

Corporations sometimes issue *convertible* preferred shares, which are similar to convertible bonds, discussed in Chapter 16. These shares give the shareholder an option, within a specified time period, to exchange the convertible preferred shares currently held for other classes of share capital, usually common shares, at a specified rate. The accounting treatment for conversion of preferred shares is analogous to the book value method for convertible bonds. The converted shares are formally retired when received by the corporation. Conversion privileges require the issuing corporation to set aside a sufficient number of units of the other security to fulfill the conversion privileges until they are exercised or expire.

At date of conversion, all account balances related to the converted shares are removed and the new shares issued are recorded at the same amount. To illustrate, assume the following data:

Preferred shares; convertible; non-cumulative; nopar; shares outstanding, 100,000 . . . . . $220,000
Common shares; nopar; shares outstanding, 150,000 200,000

The conversion privilege specifies the issuance of one common share for each preferred share turned in for conversion. Assume shareholders turn in 10,000 preferred shares for conversion. The following entry would record the event:

Preferred shares (10,000 shares) ($220,000/100,000) × 10,000 . . 22,000
    Common shares (10,000 shares)   22,000

The market value of the common shares on the date of conversion is not considered when recording the transaction. For instance, the 10,000 common shares issued could have a market value of $3.50 each, or a $35,000 total market value. This conversion has clearly entailed an opportunity cost to the corporation's existing shareholders, who would have been better off if the common shares could have been sold in the open market for their full market value. The accounting model does not capture this aspect of the conversion.

When bonds are converted to common shares, the corporation may use the market value of the common shares *or* the book value of the bond liability to value the common shares issued. This was discussed in Chapter 16.

Additional Contributed Capital

Contributed capital is created by a number of events that involve the corporation and its shareholders. Several accounts for additional contributed (paid-in) capital were introduced in this chapter, such as contributed capital on share repurchase or donations. Exhibit 20–5 summarizes some of the transactions that may cause increases or decreases in additional contributed capital.

EXHIBIT 20–5 Some Transactions that May Affect Additional Contributed Capital

Increase in Additional Contributed Capital	Decrease in Additional Contributed Capital
1. Receipt of donated shares or assets (Chapter 20).	1. Retirement of shares at a price greater than average issue price to date, when previous contributed capital has been recorded (Chapter 20).
2. Retirement of shares at a price less than average issue price to date (Chapter 20).	2. Issue of par value shares at a discount—a rare event (Appendix 20A).
3. Issue of par value shares at a price or assigned value higher than par (Appendix 20A). Shares may be issued for cash, non-cash consideration, or by subscription (Chapter 20); on bond conversion (Chapter 16); on conversion of preferred shares (Chapter 20); and as a stock dividend (Chapter 21).	3. Treasury stock transactions, shares issued below cost, when previous contributed capital has been recorded (Appendix 20B).
4. Treasury stock transactions, shares reissued above cost (Appendix 20B).	4. On a quasi reorganization (Appendix 21A).

EXHIBIT 20–6 Consolidated Statement of Shareholders' Equity, The Seagram Company

THE SEAGRAM COMPANY LTD. AND SUBSIDIARY COMPANIES
January 31, 1988, 1989, and 1990

(U.S. dollars in thousands, except per share amounts)	Shares without Par Value		Share Purchase Warrants	Cumulative Currency Translation Adjustments	Retained Earnings
	Number	Amount			
January 31, 1987	95,494,856	$257,368	$ 27,679	$(228,456)	$3,898,969
Twelve months ended January 31, 1988:					
Net income					521,088
Dividends—$1.05 per share					(100,279)
Change in translation adjustments				122,534	
Shares issued—conversion of debt	347,344	19,977			
—exercise of share purchase warrants	51,025	2,293	(404)		
Shares purchased and cancelled	(1,107,000)	(3,221)			(60,033)
January 31, 1988	94,786,225	276,417	27,275	(105,922)	4,259,745
Twelve months ended January 31, 1989:					
Net income					589,460
Dividends—$1.175 per share					(113,219)
Change in translation adjustments				(69,690)	
Shares issued—exercise of share purchase warrants	3,443,198	138,259	(27,275)		
Shares purchased and cancelled	(15,000)	(44)			(734)
January 31, 1989	98,214,423	414,632	—	(175,612)	4,735,252
Twelve months ended January 31, 1990:					
Net income					710,578
Dividends—$1.40 per share					(134,978)
Change in translation adjustments				17,379	
Shares issued—exercise of stock options	291,285	18,056			
—conversion of debt	273,741	18,367			
Shares purchased and cancelled	(3,324,318)	(14,416)			(231,908)
January 31, 1990	95,455,131	$436,639	$ —	$(158,233)	$5,078,944

STATEMENT OF SHAREHOLDERS' EQUITY

◆

Corporations must disclose the changes in their equity accounts that take place during the year. Often these changes are presented and summarized in one schedule. One example, which shows the numerous changes reported by the Seagram Company Ltd. over a three-year period, is shown in Exhibit 20–6. The "translation adjustments" reflect unrealized capital increases or decreases that result from translating financial statements of independent or self-sustaining foreign subsidiaries into the reporting currency. Accounting for foreign currency translation is a topic covered in advanced accounting courses.

CONCEPT REVIEW

1. Why might a corporation choose to repurchase and retire its own shares?
2. A corporation retires 5,000 of its preferred shares for $20 per share. The balance in the preferred share account is $700,000, representing 100,000 outstanding shares. Record the journal entry to reflect this transaction. How would your answer change if the price paid was $3.00 per share?
3. Assume instead that the preferred shares in Question 2 were converted into 20,000 nopar common shares. Would total shareholders' equity change? Would paid-in capital?

SUMMARY OF KEY POINTS

◆

(L.O. 1)   1. For corporations, owners' equity is called *shareholders' equity.* Claims to ownership are represented by share capital. Different types of claims are represented by shares with differing contractual rights for the holder. Shareholders' equity arises from two sources: contributed capital and capital arising from earnings of the corporation not paid out to shareholders. The latter is called *retained earnings.*

(L.O. 1)   2. The principal advantages of the corporate form of organization over proprietorships and partnerships include: (1) the ability to accumulate large amounts of capital, (2) limited liability for the shareholders, and (3) ease of ownership transfer. The principal disadvantages of the corporate form are: (1) the possibility of double taxation and (2) difficulties of control. Double taxation is caused because the earnings of the corporation are normally taxed, and dividends received by shareholders, representing distributions of corporate earnings, are taxed again.

(L.O. 2)   3. Two basic types of shares are common and preferred. Common shares generally have the residual claim and the residual risk of the corporation. Preferred shares have one or more contractually specified preferences over common shares. These preferences involve one or more of the following rights: voting rights, dividend rights, preference in liquidation rights, conversion rights, call rights, and redemption rights.

(L.O. 2)   4. Preferred share features can vary from one extreme, where the shares have almost the same risks and opportunity for returns as common shares, to the opposite extreme, where the risks and returns are such that the shares are essentially a form of debt. An example of the former would be convertible, fully participating preferred shares. The latter would be represented by cumulative preferred shares, redeemable at the option of the shareholder.

(L.O. 3)   5. Authorized capital represents the total number of shares that legally can be issued. Issued shares are the number of shares that have been sold or otherwise issued to shareholders. Treasury stock exists when outstanding shares are reacquired by the corporation and are held pending resale. Outstanding shares equal issued shares less treasury shares. Subscribed shares are unissued shares that must be used to meet subscription contracts. Subscription contracts are legal contracts between the corporation and a purchaser of shares, stating the number of shares the purchaser has agreed to purchase, an agreed price, and the period of payment for the shares.

(L.O. 3)   6. In conformity with legislative requirements, most shares issued are nopar shares. The entire amount of consideration received on the issuance of nopar shares is recorded in the share capital account itself.

(L.O. 3)   7. Par value shares may be issued under a few provincial companies acts. Whether for preferred or common shares, par value is accounted for at issuance by first crediting the appropriate share capital account with the par value of the shares issued. Any additional amount by which the proceeds of the issuance exceeds par value is credited to an additional paid-in capital account. (See Appendix 20A.)

(L.O. 3)   8. When a corporation issues shares for assets or for services rendered to the corporation, the accounting difficulty often is how to determine the appropriate amount at which to record the transaction. The market value of the shares issued is used to value the transaction. If this value is not readily determinable, then the market value of the goods or services received is used.

(L.O. 3)   9. Share issue costs either are offset against the proceeds received, resulting in the net proceeds being recorded in shareholders' equity, or are treated as a deferred charge on the balance sheet. The deferred charge is amortized over future periods. Both methods are acceptable under GAAP, but the offset method (net proceeds) is the more commonly used method.

(L.O. 4)   10. Stock subscriptions are contractual agreements specifying a certain number of shares that are to be acquired by specified buyers. Subscribed stock receivables are generally not viewed as an asset of the corporation. They are treated as a contra to shareholders' equity.

(L.O. 5)   11. When shares are retired, either through a call or redemption, or simply through open market acquisition, all capital balances relating to the specific shares are first removed. Any remaining balance is either debited to a paid-in capital account or to retained earnings, as appropriate, or credited to an additional paid-in capital account.

(L.O. 5)   12. Upon conversion of convertible preferred shares, all account balances related to the converted shares are removed, and newly issued shares are recorded at the book value of the converted shares.

(L.O. 6)   13. Treasury stock is accounted for using the single-transaction method. The acquisition cost of the shares acquired is debited to a contra shareholders' equity account titled "treasury stock, at cost." When the stock is resold, the difference between the acquisition price and the resale price is debited to a paid-in capital account or to retained earnings, as appropriate, or credited to an additional paid-in capital account. (See Appendix 20B.)

REVIEW PROBLEM
◆

On January 2, 1991, Greene Corporation was incorporated in the province of Ontario. It was authorized to issue an unlimited number of nopar value common shares, and 10,000 shares of nopar, $8, cumulative and non-participating preferred. During 1991 the firm completed the following transactions:

Jan.   8   Accepted subscriptions for 40,000 common shares at $12 per share. Down payment on the subscribed shares totaled $150,000.

      30   Issued 4,000 preferred shares in exchange for the following assets: machinery with a fair market value of $35,000, a factory with a fair market value of $110,000, and land with an appraised value of $295,000.

Mar. 15   Machinery with a fair market value of $55,000 was donated to the company.

Apr. 25   Collected the balance of the subscriptions receivable and issued the shares.

June 30   Purchased 2,200 common shares at $18 per share. The shares were retired.

Dec. 31   Closed the income summary to retained earnings. The income for the period was $88,000.

Required:

1. Prepare the journal entries to record the above transactions.
2. Prepare the shareholders' equity section of the balance sheet for Greene Corporation at December 31, 1991.

**REVIEW
SOLUTION**

◆

Account for subscription of common shares:

Cash	150,000	
Stock subscriptions receivable	330,000	
Common shares subscribed (40,000 shares)		480,000

Issue preferred shares in exchange for assets; recorded at fair market value of the assets in the absence of a value for the preferred shares:

Machinery	35,000	
Factory	110,000	
Land	295,000	
Preferred shares (4,000 shares)		440,000

Record receipt of donated assets:

Machinery	55,000	
Contributed capital, donation of machinery		55,000

Record receipt of cash for subscribed shares and issuance of shares:

Cash	330,000	
Stock subscriptions receivable		330,000
Common shares subscribed (40,000 shares)	480,000	
Common shares (40,000 shares)		480,000

Record acquisition and retirement of common shares:

Common shares $\left(\dfrac{\$480,000}{40,000}\right) \times 2,200$	26,400	
Retained earnings	13,200	
Cash ($18 \times 2,200$)		39,600

Closed the income summary:

Income summary	88,000	
Retained earnings		88,000

GREENE CORPORATION
Shareholders' Equity at December 31, 1991

Contributed capital:
  Common shares, nopar (unlimited shares authorized,
    37,800 shares issued and outstanding) . . . . $ 453,600
  Preferred shares, nopar, $8, cumulative and non-participating
    (10,000 shares authorized, 4,000 shares issued) 440,000
  Donation of machinery 55,000
Total contributed capital . . . . $ 948,600
Retained earnings 74,800
Total shareholders' equity $1,023,400

Note: Preferred dividends are one year in arrears.

APPENDIX 20A: *Par Value Shares*

A corporation that is permitted under its enabling legislation to issue par value shares must specify the par value in its articles of incorporation and on the share certificates.

    Par value has no particular relationship to market value. Its significance is that:

1. It represents the minimum price that must be paid at the initial sale of the shares.
2. In the case of insolvency, as long as the par value of all outstanding shares was fully paid in (or capitalized in the case of a stock dividend), shareholders cannot be held personally liable

to creditors. If shares are issued for less than par, or at a discount, the courts have required shareholders to make up the difference in the event of insolvency.

3. Par value is often used as the basis for preferred dividends.

To avoid a real or implied discount, many corporations use a very low par value, such as $1 per share, and sell shares at a much higher price.

Issuance of Shares

To illustrate share transactions concerning par value shares, assume the following authorized capital:

Preferred shares, par $10, 5%, cumulative, and non-participating, 20,000 shares authorized.

Common shares, par $1, 100,000 shares authorized.

The preferred dividend entitlement is expressed as 5%, which means 5% of par value, or 50 cents per share. Assume that the corporation sold 5,000 preferred shares at $12.50 per share, and 50,000 common shares at $7 per share. These transactions would be recorded as follows:

```
Cash (5,000 × $12.50). . . . . . . . . . . . . . . . . . . . .  62,500
     Preferred shares, par $10 (5,000 shares) (5,000 × $10) . . .          50,000
     Contributed capital in excess of par, preferred
       ($62,500 − $50,000) . . . . . . . . . . . . . . . .                 12,500

Cash (50,000 × $7) . . . . . . . . . . . . . . . . . . . . . 350,000
     Common shares, par  $1 (50,000 shares) (50,000 × $1). . .             50,000
     Contributed capital in excess of par, common
       ($350,000 − $50,000) . . . . . . . . . . . . . . . .               300,000
```

Only the par value may be credited to the share capital account. Any excess is recorded in the other contributed capital accounts.

The par value is the legal, or stated, capital of the corporation and is regarded as the permanent investment of the shareholders. By law, it cannot be reduced without special permission. Other contributed capital, on the other hand, may be returned to the shareholders by means of a liquidating dividend, as long as the corporation meets solvency tests specified by legislation (liquidating dividends will be discussed in more detail in Chapter 21).

In the rare instances that shares are issued below par value, a *discount* is created. Shareholders would be required to pay in the amount of a discount in the event of insolvency.

Assume a corporation sold 1,000 common shares, par $1, for 75 cents per share:

```
Cash (1,000 × 75 cents). . . . . . . . . . . . . . . . . . .    750
Discount on common shares ($1,000 − $750). . . . . . . . . . .    250
     Common shares, $1 par (1,000 shares) (1,000 × $1) . . . . .            1,000
```

The discount would be shown as a negative element of other contributed capital.

Instead, assume the corporation received subscriptions for 10,000 common shares at $7.25 per share:

```
Stock subscriptions receivable—common shares
   (10,000 × $7.25). . . . . . . . . . . . . . . . . . . . . 72,500
     Common shares subscribed, par $1 (10,000 shares)
       (10,000 × $1) . . . . . . . . . . . . . . . . . . . .               10,000
     Contributed capital in excess of par, common shares
       ($72,500 − $10,000) . . . . . . . . . . . . . . . .                 62,500
```

Notice that the full premium is recorded on subscription and only the par value is segregated as "subscribed." When the subscription is collected, the following two entries would be necessary:

```
Cash . . . . . . . . . . . . . . . . . . . . . . . . . . . . 72,500
     Stock subscriptions receivable—common shares . . . . . . .            72,500

Common shares subscribed, par $1 (10,000 shares). . . . . . . 10,000
     Common shares, par $1 (10,000 shares) . . . . . . . . . .             10,000
```

Generally, the only difference between recording a transaction involving par value shares compared to nopar value shares is that par value shares involve a contributed capital account in addition to the par account.

Basket Proceeds

Assume that NW Corporation's common shares were selling at $40 per share and the preferred at $20. The corporation issued 1,000, $10 par common shares and 500, $8 par preferred shares for the lump sum of $48,000. As was previously illustrated, the proceeds would be allocated by relative market value:

	Market Value	Fraction of Total	Allocation of $48,000
Common (1,000 shares at $40)	$40,000	⅘	$38,400
Preferred (500 shares × $20)	10,000	⅕	9,600
Total	$50,000	⁵⁄₅	$48,000

The journal entry to record the issuance of par value shares is as follows:

```
Cash . . . . . . . . . . . . . . . . . . . . . . . . . . . . . .  48,000
        Common shares, par $10 (1,000 shares) . . . . . . . . . .         10,000
        Preferred shares, par $8 (500 shares) . . . . . . . . . .          4,000
        Contributed capital in excess of par,
          common ($38,400 − $10,000) . . . . . . . . . . . . . .          28,400
        Contributed capital in excess of par,
          preferred ($9,600 − $4,000) . . . . . . . . . . . . . .           5,600
```

Remember that if the shares were nopar value, *all* the allocated proceeds, not just the par value, would go to the share capital account itself.

Retirement

When shares are retired, the relevant portion of the par value must be eliminated. If the reacquisition cost is *higher* than the average issuance price per share, cost is allocated as follows:

1. To share capital, in an amount equal to par.
2. Any excess to contributed capital, to the extent contributed capital was created by prior retirement transactions in this class of shares.
3. Any excess to contributed capital, in an amount equal to the pro rata share of contributed capital that arose on sale of this class of shares.
4. Any excess, to retained earnings.

If shares are redeemed for less than par value, cost is assigned:

1. To share capital, in an amount equal to par.
2. Any excess, to contributed capital.

Assume that a corporation had 55,000, $5 par value preferred shares outstanding, and $150,000 in the "contributed capital in excess of par, preferred" account. First, the corporation retired 5,000 of these shares at $4 per share, as reflected in the following journal entry:

```
Preferred shares, $5 par (5,000 shares) (5,000 × $5) . . . . . .  25,000
        Cash (5,000 × $4) . . . . . . . . . . . . . . . . . . . .          20,000
        Contributed capital, preferred share retirement . . . . .           5,000
```

One month later, 25,000 shares were retired for $9 per share:

```
Preferred shares, $5 par (25,000 shares) (25,000 × $5) . . . . . 125,000
Contributed capital, preferred share retirement . . . . . . . .   5,000
Contributed capital in excess of par,
  preferred ($150,000 × 25/50). . . . . . . . . . . . . . . . .  75,000
Retained earnings ($225,000 − $125,000 − $5,000 − $75,000) .  20,000
        Cash (25,000 × $9). . . . . . . . . . . . . . . . . . . .         225,000
```

First, the par value is reduced. Second, any contributed capital created by previous preferred share retirements is eliminated. The reduction to contributed capital in excess of par is the pro rata share of the account at the date of the transaction: 25,000 of 50,000 *outstanding* shares were eliminated. Finally, if a further debit is needed, retained earnings is part of the journal entry.

If the shares had been redeemed for $7, the following entry would have been made:

```
Preferred shares, $5 par (25,000 shares) . . . . . . . . . . . 125,000
Contributed capital, preferred share retirement  . . . . . . . .   5,000
Contributed capital in excess of par,
    preferred ($175,000 − $125,000 − $5,000)  . . . . . . . . .  45,000
        Cash (25,000 × $7) . . . . . . . . . . . . . . . . . .            175,000
```

Only a portion of contributed capital in excess of par is eliminated and no reduction to retained earnings is necessary.

Conversion

On conversion, the average book value of converted shares is transferred from the capital accounts of one class of shares (both par and other contributed capital) to the capital accounts of the newly issued class. Assume a corporation has 75,000, $10 par value preferred shares convertible to par value $2 common shares on a ratio of five-for-one (i.e., five preferred shares can be converted to one common share). There is $15,000 in the "contributed capital in excess of par, preferred" account. If 10,000 preferred shares are converted, the following journal entry would be made:

```
Preferred shares, par $10 (10,000 shares) (10,000 × $10) . . . .   100,000
Contributed capital in excess of par,
    preferred ($15,000 × 10/75) . . . . . . . . . . . . . . . .     2,000
        Common shares, par $2 (2,000 shares)
            (10,000 × 1/5 × $2) . . . . . . . . . . . . . . . .              4,000
        Contributed capital in excess of par, common . . . . . . .          98,000
```

Remember that transactions involving par value shares generally involve two accounts to record value changes to equity accounts: par value, and contributed capital in excess of par.

Changing Par Value

Companies sometimes want to increase the number of shares outstanding. One reason is to reduce the market price per share, as this may increase market activity of the shares. One way to do this is to reduce the par value per share and yet keep total legal capital the same. A corporation, if it conforms with the applicable corporate legislation, may amend the articles of incorporation to change the par value (and/or the number of authorized shares) of one or more classes of authorized shares.

To record changes in par value, all capital account balances that relate to the old shares retired are removed from the accounts, and the new shares issued are recorded. If an additional credit is needed, an appropriately designated contributed capital account is credited; if an additional debit is needed, retained earnings is debited.

A stock split is a special case involving a change in par value. In a stock split, the par value per share is reduced and the number of shares outstanding is increased proportionately. Therefore, the balance in the share capital account is unchanged. Only a memorandum entry in the original share capital account is needed to reflect the new par value per share and the number of shares outstanding after the split (see Chapter 21).

CONCEPT REVIEW

1. What types of corporations have par value shares authorized? In what way are the shares different from nopar shares?
2. If you were forming a corporation and expected shares to trade for around $5, would you set par value at $5? Why?
3. If 10,000, $10 par value preferred shares that originally sold for $12 per share were converted to 20,000, $1 par value common shares, what amount would be credited to the common shares account? Contributed capital in excess of par, common shares?

Treasury stock is a corporation's own share capital (preferred or common) that (a) has been is-sued, (b) subsequently is reacquired by the issuing corporation, and (c) after acquisition has not yet been resold or formally retired. Thus, the purchase of treasury stock does not reduce the number of *issued* shares but does reduce the number of *outstanding* shares. Treasury shares sub-sequently may be resold and then are classified as outstanding shares.

In Canada, the federal Canada Business Corporations Act (and provincial legislation modeled after the Act) provides that corporations that reacquire their own shares must immediately *retire* those shares. Thus, corporations may not hold and subsequently reissue their own shares (i.e., engage in treasury stock transactions) in most Canadian jurisdictions.

Some provincial corporations acts do allow treasury stock transactions, but such transactions are increasingly rare in Canada. They are far more common in the United States, where corpo-rations regularly engage in treasury stock transactions, subject to insider trading rules of the various stock exchanges.

A company that is permitted to acquire treasury stock may do so for any of the reasons a company normally would reacquire its own shares (e.g., to provide return to shareholders, make a market, buy back undervalued shares, thwart a takeover bid, etc.). The key to a treasury stock acquisition is that the shares may be reissued. The company may use the shares to raise addi-tional capital—a process far faster through the issuance of treasury stock than a new share issue. The shares may also be used for stock dividends, employee stock option plans, and so on. A cor-poration allowed to engage in treasury stock transactions has additional flexibility over one not so permitted.

The purchase of treasury stock decreases both assets and shareholders' equity, whereas a sale of treasury stock increases both assets and shareholders' equity. Treasury stock may be obtained by purchase, by settlement of an obligation, or through donation. Except on rare occasion, treasury stock does not carry voting, dividend, or liquidation rights. Treasury stock is accounted for as a *contra* to shareholders' equity, *and is not an asset*. Treasury stock transactions will not affect the income statement.

Accounting for Treasury Stock

There are two methods of accounting for treasury stock. These are (1) the single-transaction method and (2) the two-transaction method. The difference between these methods rests on whether the acquisition and subsequent resale are regarded as a single transaction or as two separate transactions.

Under the single-transaction method, a *treasury stock account* is debited for the *cost* of the shares acquired upon the purchase of treasury stock. When the shares are resold, the treasury stock account is credited for the cost, and the difference, which is the gain or loss, affects vari-ous equity accounts. The single-transaction method is based on the view that the purchase and subsequent resale are one continuous transaction. Purchase is the initial step, involving the use of assets to effect a temporary contraction of total capital. The final step in the transaction is the resale of treasury shares and a consequent expansion of assets and total capital. Under this method, the balance in the treasury stock account is logically shown as a deduction from the to-tal of shareholders' equity.

When treasury stock is resold at a price in excess of its cost, and the single-transaction method is used, the excess should be recorded as contributed capital in a special contributed capital account. Where the shares are sold at less than their cost, the deficiency should be charged as follows:

1. First, to capital arising from prior resale or cancellation of shares of the same class.
2. Second, to retained earnings after the balance in (1) above has been exhausted.

Under the two-transaction method, the objectives to be accomplished are:

1. To make a final accounting with the retiring shareholders from whom the treasury shares were acquired.
2. To record precisely the capital contributed by the new shareholder, the purchaser of trea-sury shares.

The final accounting with the retiring shareholder involves removal of the amount originally invested by the shareholder, computed on an average basis for all shares issued. When the shares are resold, the entire proceeds of the sale are treated as capital invested by the new shareholder, that is, as if the shares were an original issue. Any balance in treasury stock is a reduction to share capital.

With respect to acquisition and resale of the company's own shares, the CICA recommends (*CICA Handbook*, paragraph 3240.10):

> The Committee is of the opinion that the single-transaction method as set out above is the preferable method of accounting for the acquisition by a company of its own shares.

The following entries illustrate both methods of accounting for treasury stock.

Recording Treasury Stock—Single-Transaction Method

1. To record the initial sale and issuance of 10,000 common shares at $26 per share:

Cash (10,000 shares at $26)	260,000	
Common shares (10,000 shares).		260,000

2. To record the acquisition of 2,000 shares of common treasury shares at $28 per share:

Treasury stock, common (2,000 shares at $28)	56,000	
Cash		56,000

Note: Under the single-transaction method, the cash price paid is always the amount debited to the treasury stock account.

3. To record sale of 500 shares of the treasury shares at $30 per share (above cost):

Cash (500 shares, at $30)	15,000	
Treasury stock, common (500 shares at cost, $28)		14,000
Contributed capital from treasury stock		
transactions, common		1,000

Note: Had this sale been at cost [$28 per share], no amount would have been entered in the contributed capital account.

4. To record the sale of another 500 shares of the treasury stock at $19 per share (below cost):

Cash (500 shares at $19)	9,500	
Contributed capital from treasury stock		
transactions, common*	1,000	
Retained earnings.	3,500	
Treasury stock, common (500 shares at cost, $28)		14,000

* Debit limited to the current balance in this account (see Entry 3); any remainder is allocated to retained earnings.

Assuming Transactions 1 through 4 above, and a beginning balance in retained earnings of $40,000, the balance sheet would reflect the following:

Shareholders' Equity
(Single-Transaction Method for Treasury Stock)

Contributed Capital:	
Common shares, authorized 50,000 shares,* issued 10,000 shares,	
of which 1,000 are held as treasury stock	$260,000
Retained earnings ($40,000 − $3,500)	36,500
Total contributed capital and retained earnings	296,500
Less: Treasury stock, 1,000 shares at cost, $28.	28,000
Total shareholders' equity	$268,500

*Assumed.

Recording Treasury Stock—Two-Transaction Method

1. To record the initial sale and issuance of 10,000 common shares at $26 per share:

Cash (10,000 shares at $26)	260,000	
Common shares (10,000 shares).		260,000

2. To record acquisition of 2,000 shares of treasury common stock at $28 per share:

```
Treasury stock, common (2,000 shares at $26) . . . . . . . . . 52,000*
Contributed capital from treasury stock transactions,
   common . . . . . . . . . . . . . . . . . . . . . . . . . . . . . . . . . –0– †
Retained earnings . . . . . . . . . . . . . . . . . . . . . . . . . . . 4,000
      Cash (2,000 shares at $28) . . . . . . . . . . . . . . . .            56,000
* Average per share paid in.
† No balance is available to absorb a debit.
```

Alternatively, had the 2,000 shares been acquired for $46,000 cash, the following entry would be made:

```
Treasury stock, common . . . . . . . . . . . . . . . . . . 52,000
   Cash . . . . . . . . . . . . . . . . . . . . . . . . . . . . . . .          46,000
   Contributed capital from treasury stock
      transactions, common . . . . . . . . . . . . . . . . . . .          6,000
```

3. To record the sale of 500 shares of treasury stock at $30 per share (above cost):

```
Cash (500 shares at $30) . . . . . . . . . . . . . . . . . . 15,000
   Treasury stock, common (500 shares at $26) . . . . . . . . .          13,000
   Contributed capital from treasury stock
      transactions, common . . . . . . . . . . . . . . . . .          2,000
Note: Had this sale been at cost ($28 per share), a credit of $1,000 would have been made to con-
tributed capital from treasury stock transactions, common.
```

4. To record the sale of another 500 shares of treasury stock at $19 per share (below cost):

```
Cash (500 shares at $19) . . . . . . . . . . . . . . . . . . 9,500
Contributed capital from treasury stock
   transactions, common* . . . . . . . . . . . . . . . . . . . . . . 2,000
Retained earnings . . . . . . . . . . . . . . . . . . . . . . . . . . 1,500
      Treasury stock, common (500 shares at $26) . . . . . . . .          13,000
* Debit limited to the current balance in this account.
```

Shareholders' equity, assuming Transactions 1 through 4 above and a beginning balance in retained earnings of $40,000, would be reported as follows:

Shareholders' Equity
(Two-Transaction Method for Treasury Stock)

Contributed capital:
Common shares, authorized 50,000 shares, issued 10,000 shares $260,000
Less: Treasury stock, 1,000 shares at $26   26,000

   Total common shares outstanding, 9,000 shares $234,000
Retained earnings ($40,000 − $4,000 − $1,500)   34,500

   Total shareholders' equity $268,500

Observe that the *total* amount of shareholders' equity reported under the single-transaction method and the two-transaction method is the same ($268,500); the basic difference between the two methods is reflected only in the detailed accounts constituting shareholders' equity.

Accounting for Par Value Treasury Stock

In the case of shares with par value, the single-transaction method can be applied almost exactly as for nopar value stock, as discussed above. When the two-transaction method is used with par value shares, the par value is reflected in the share capital account and is used as the "basic value," replacing the $26 used in the nopar example. With par value shares, there is always an entry to an account for contributed capital in excess of par; other than this difference, the accounting for par value shares under the two-transaction method would be as illustrated above.

Treasury Stock Received by Donation

Shareholders sometimes donate a corporation's shares back to the corporation. Shares received by donation are classified as treasury stock unless formally retired. Neither total assets nor total equity is changed by the donation of treasury stock. Three methods have been employed in recording the receipt of donated treasury stock:

1. When the donated shares are received, debit the treasury stock account for the current market value of the shares and credit "contributed capital, donated treasury stock" for the same amount. Upon subsequent sale, any gains or losses (i.e., net asset increases or decreases) would be accounted for as illustrated above for the single-transaction method.
2. When the donated shares are received, debit the treasury stock account for the average paid in (or in the case of par value shares, the par) and credit an appropriately designated donated capital account. Subsequent sales would be recorded as illustrated above for the two-transaction method.
3. When donated shares are received, a memorandum entry is made on the basis that there was no cost. Subsequent sales amounts would be credited to contributed capital for the full sales price. This method is seldom used.

CONCEPT REVIEW

1. Describe two methods of accounting for treasury shares. How do they differ with respect to the treatment of amounts in the individual contributed capital accounts in the shareholders' equity section of the balance sheet? What effect does choosing one method over the other have on the total balance reported in shareholders' equity?
2. A firm buys 100 of its common shares for $140 each. The average issuance price of its common shares to date has been $110 per share. The shares are held as treasury stock, then resold for $150 each. Show two ways to account for this transaction. Assume this is the first treasury stock transaction for this company.

KEY TERMS

Authorized share capital (985)
Callable preferred shares (991)
Common shares (987)
Contributed capital (984)
Corporation (982)
Cumulative dividend preferences (988)
Donated capital (999)
Issued share capital (985)
Nopar value shares (987)

Par value shares (987)
Participating dividend preferences (988)
Preferred shares (987)
Redeemable preferred shares (991)
Shareholders' equity (982)
Subscribed share capital (985)
Treasury stock (985)
Unissued share capital (985)
Unrealized capital (998)

QUESTIONS

1. Define crown corporations, private corporations, and not-for-profit corporations. Why might a corporation choose federal incorporation over provincial incorporation?
2. What are the basic rights of all shareholders? How may one or more of these rights be withheld from the shareholders?
3. Explain each of the following: authorized share capital, issued share capital, unissued share capital, outstanding share capital, subscribed shares, and treasury stock.
4. In accounting for corporate capital, explain what it means to report by source, and the significance of doing so.
5. Explain how the cost principle relates to the issuance of shares.
6. Define the term *capital* as it is usually applied in accounting.

7. Why do few Canadian companies have treasury stock transactions?
8. Distinguish between par and nopar shares.
9. Distinguish between common and preferred shares.
10. Explain the difference between cumulative and non-cumulative preferred shares.
11. Explain the difference between non-participating, partially participating, and fully participating preferred shares.
12. Explain asset preference as it relates to preferred shares.
13. Define redeemable preferred shares.
14. Under what circumstances should stock subscriptions receivable be reported (*a*) as a current asset, (*b*) as a non-current asset, and (*c*) as a deduction in the shareholders' equity section of the balance sheet?
15. Explain the terms *secret reserves* and *watered stock*.
16. How should a premium or discount on par value shares be accounted for and reported?
17. How are assets valued when shares are given in payment?
18. Briefly explain the two methods of accounting for share issue costs.
19. What is an unrealized capital increment?
20. Why do corporations reacquire their own shares for retirement? Why must they exercise caution in these transactions?
21. Explain how the purchase price is allocated when shares are reacquired and retired at a cost *higher* than average issuance price to date. What changes if average issuance price is higher?
22. What is the effect on shareholders' equity when shares are retired? On share capital?
23. Is it possible to record a gain or loss on share retirement? Explain.
24. When shares are retired, is the original issue price of those individual shares relevant? Why or why not?
25. What are convertible shares? Why might an investor decide to exercise a conversion option?
26. How is shareholders' equity effected by the conversion of preferred shares to common shares?
27. What is the significance of par value?
28. When a company has par value shares, how is the total average original issuance price determined?
29. When outstanding par value shares are retired, what equity accounts may be affected?
30. Define treasury stock.
31. What is the effect on assets, liabilities, and shareholders' equity of the (*a*) purchase of treasury stock and (*b*) sale of treasury stock?
32. Explain the theoretical difference between the single-transaction method and the two-transaction method in accounting for treasury stock.
33. When comparing the single- and two-transaction methods of accounting for treasury stock, total shareholders' equity is unaffected, yet some components of shareholders' equity are affected. Is this statement correct? Explain.
34. In recording treasury stock transactions, why are gains recorded in a contributed capital account, whereas losses may involve a debit to retained earnings?
35. How is treasury stock reported on the balance sheet (*a*) under the single-transaction method and (*b*) under the two-transaction method?

EXERCISES

E 20–1
Share Issuance: Effects on the Balance Sheet
(L.O. 3)

NIC Corporation was incorporated with unlimited nopar value shares authorized. During the first year, 120,000 shares were sold at $8 per share. One thousand additional shares were issued in payment for legal fees. At the end of the first year, NIC reported net income of $46,000. Dividends of $20,000 were paid on the last day of the year. Liabilities at the year-end amounted to $60,000.

Required:

Complete the following tabulation (show calculations); state any assumptions that you make.

Item	Amount	Assumptions
a. Total assets	$	
b. Owners' equity	$	
c. Contributed capital	$	
d. Issued share capital	$	
e. Outstanding share capital	$	
f. Unissued share capital.	$	

E 20–2
Prepare Shareholders'
Equity: Two Share Classes,
Subscribed Shares
(L.O. 2, 3, 4)

RAE Corporation was incorporated with 100,000 nopar common shares authorized, and an authorized maximum of 20,000 nopar shares of 60-cent, cumulative and non-participating preferred. Shares issued to date: 40,000 shares of common sold at $220,000 and 10,000 preferred shares sold at $21 per share. In addition, subscriptions for 2,000 preferred shares have been taken, and 30% of the purchase price of $21 has been collected. The shares will be issued upon collection in full. The retained earnings balance is $288,000. At year-end, there was a $10,000 unrealized appraisal increase credit on long-term assets.

Required:
Prepare the shareholders' equity section of the balance sheet.

E 20–3
Shareholders' Equity,
Subscriptions, Donation,
and Unrealized Capital
(L.O. 2, 3, 4)

Prepare, in good form, the shareholders' equity section of the balance sheet for Warren Corporation.

Retained earnings	$ 390,000
Preferred shares subscribed, but not yet issued (3,000 shares)	33,000
Preferred shares nopar, 60 cents, authorized unlimited shares (15,000 shares issued)	177,000
Common shares, no par, authorized unlimited shares (110,000 shares issued)	2,240,000
Stock subscriptions receivable, preferred.	4,000
Donation of plant site.	50,000
Appraisal increase credit on capital assets	10,000

E 20–4
Analysis of Shareholders'
Equity: Prepare Statement
(L.O. 2, 3, 4)

The following data were provided by the accounts of Mitar Corporation at December 31, 1993:

Subscriptions receivable (non-current).	$ 5,000
Retained earnings, January 1, 1993	450,000
Common shares, nopar, authorized, unlimited shares; issued 50,000 shares	688,000
Future site for office (donated to Mitar).	15,000
Common shares subscribed, 1,000 shares (to be issued upon collection in full)	22,000
Subscriptions receivable, share capital (due in three months).	2,000
Bonds payable	100,000
Net income for 1993 (not included in retained earnings above)	95,000
Dividends declared and paid during 1993	40,000

Required:

1. Respond to the following (state any assumptions that you made):

   a. Total retained earnings at end of 1993 is . . . . $_____
   b. Retained earnings on January 1, 1993 was. . . . . $_____
   c. Number of shares outstanding is . . . . $_____
   d. Total shareholders' equity is . . . . $_____
   e. Number of shares issued is. . . . . $_____
   f. Average selling price per share including any shares subscribed was . . . . . . $_____
   g. Number of shares sold including any shares subscribed was. . . . . $_____

2. Prepare the shareholders' equity section of the balance sheet at December 31, 1993. Use good form, complete with respect to details.

E 20–5
Compute Dividends:
Preferred Shares,
Cumulative and Partially
Participating
(L.O. 2)

Darby Corporation has the following shares outstanding:

Preferred, nopar, 60 cents, cumulative and partially participating up to an additional 20 cents; 5,000 shares outstanding. No dividends were declared during the prior two years.
Common shares, nopar, 10,000 shares outstanding; participating matching dividend, $1.50 per share.

The board of directors has just declared a cash dividend of $33,000.

Required:
You have been requested to complete the following journal entry to record the dividend declaration (show computations):

    Dividends declared, preferred* . . . . _____
    Dividends declared, common* . . . . _____
        Dividends payable . . . .   _____
    * Closed to retained earnings.

E 20–6
Compute Dividends:
Preferred Shares,
Comprehensive, Six Cases
(L.O. 2)

AB Corporation has the following shares outstanding:

   Common, nopar—6,000 shares.
   Preferred, nopar, $6—1,000 shares.

Matching dividend, if applicable, $3 per share.

Required:
Compute the amount of dividends payable in total and per share on the common and preferred shares for each separate case:

Case A

Preferred is non-cumulative and non-participating; dividends declared, $20,000.

Case B

Preferred is cumulative and non-participating; two years in arrears; dividends declared, $34,000.

Case C

Preferred is non-cumulative and fully participating; dividends declared, $24,000.

Case D

Preferred is non-cumulative and fully participating; dividends declared, $40,000.

Case E

Preferred is cumulative and partially participating up to an additional $3; three years in arrears; dividends declared, $60,000.

Case F

Preferred is cumulative and fully participating; three years in arrears; dividends declared, $50,000.

E 20–7
Compute Dividends:
Preferred Shares, Four
Cases
(L.O. 2)

Davis Corporation reported net income during four successive years as follows: $1,000, $2,000, $1,000, and $23,000. Share capital outstanding consisted of 3,500 nopar value common shares and 3,000, nopar, 50-cent preferred shares.

Required:
If net income in full were declared and paid as dividends each year, determine the amount to be paid on each share class for each of the four years, assuming:

Case A

Preferred is non-cumulative and non-participating.

Case B

Preferred is cumulative and non-participating.

Case C

Preferred is non-cumulative and fully participating. The matching dividend for common shares is $1.00 per share.

Case D

Preferred is cumulative and fully participating. The matching dividend for common shares is $1.00 per share.

E 20–8
Compute Dividends:
Preferred Shares, a Legal
Constraint
(L.O. 2)

PT Corporation has the following account balances:

Common shares, nopar, 40,000 shares outstanding $280,000
Preferred shares, nopar, $1.80 cumulative and non-participating, 5,000
  shares outstanding 115,000
Retained earnings (total cash dividends limited to the balance in retained
  earnings; no dividends were paid during the two prior years) 220,000

Required:

1. The average issue price per share for (*a*) common was $_____ and (*b*) preferred was $_____.
2. Compute dividends for each share class under each of the following proposals:
    a. The dividend declaration is $50,000.
    b. The dividend declaration specifies that the same amount of dividends per share will be paid for each share class and all preferences of the preferred shares are met. Does this situation pose a problem? Explain.

E 20–9
Share Issuance:
Subscriptions
(L.O. 3, 4)

New Corporation has unlimited common shares authorized. Give the journal entries for the following transactions during the first year.

a. To record authorization (memorandum).
b. Sold 100,000 shares at $7; collected in full and issued the shares.
c. Received subscriptions for 10,000 shares at $7 per share; collected 60% of the subscription price. The shares will not be issued until collection is in full.
d. Issued 200 shares to a lawyer in payment for legal fees related to incorporation. Treat the legal fees as a deferred charge.
e. Issued 10,000 shares and paid $190,000 cash in total payment for a building.
f. Collected balance on subscriptions receivable in (*c*).

State and justify any assumptions you make. Assume all transactions occurred within a short time span.

E 20–10
Share Issuance:
Subscriptions, Default
(L.O. 3, 4)

The charter of Maly Corporation authorized unlimited nopar value common shares. A. B. Cook subscribed for 500 shares at $25 per share, paying $2,500 down, the balance to be paid $1,000 per month. The shares will not be issued until collection in full. After paying for three months, Cook defaulted. Six months later, the corporation sold the shares for $33 per share.

Required:

1. Give all journal entries related to the 500 shares originally subscribed for by Cook, assuming Maly refunded all collections made to date of default.
2. Give the journal entry for the default, assuming shares equivalent to the collections were issued to Cook (at $25 per share). Also give the entry for the sale of the remaining shares at $33 six months later.
3. Give the journal entries, assuming the subscriber paid in full as scheduled over the 10-month period.

E 20–11
Non-Cash Sale of Shares:
Three Cases
(L.O. 3)

The charter for Kay Manufacturing Corporation authorized unlimited nopar common shares and 10,000 nopar preferred shares. The company issued 600 common shares and 100 preferred shares for used machinery. In the absence of other alternatives, the board of directors is willing to place a stated value of $10 and $50 on the common and preferred shares, respectively.

Required:

For each separate situation, give the entry to record the purchase of the machinery: Case A—the common shares are currently selling at $70 and the preferred at $80; Case B—the common shares are selling at $70, and there have been no recent sales of the preferred and no reliable value can be placed on the used machinery; and Case C—there is no current market price for either share class; however, the machinery has been independently appraised at $44,000.
State and justify any assumptions made.

E 20–12
Share Retirement: Entries
and Account Balances
(L.O. 5)

The accounting records of Crouse Corporation showed the following:

Preferred Shares, 2,000 shares outstanding, nopar . . . . $ 72,000
Common Shares, 10,000 shares outstanding, nopar 235,000
Retained earnings 75,000

The following transactions took place during the year:
Jan. 15   Acquired and retired 1,000 common shares for $17,000.
    30   Acquired and retired 500 shares of preferred at $39.50 per share.
Feb. 16   Acquired and retired 1,000 common shares for $26.00 per share.
    18   Acquired and retired 100 shares of preferred at $22.00 per share.

Required:

1. Give the journal entries to record the above transactions.
2. Calculate the resulting balance in each account in shareholders' equity.

E 20–13
Changes in Shareholders'
Equity—Overview
(L.O. 3, 4, 5)

Each numbered item in the tabulation given below changes the amount of owners' equity. Some (*a*) affect retained earnings directly and appear on the retained earnings statement, others (*b*) affect retained earnings indirectly because they are reported on the statement of income, others (*c*) affect share capital accounts directly, and others (*d*) affect donated, unrealized, or other contributed capital equity accounts.

Item	(a)	(b)	(c)	(d)
1. Donation of a plant site to the company.				
2. Purchased and retired common shares at a price less than average issue price to date.				
3. Declaration of cash dividend payable next period.				
4. Unrealized capital increment on writing up capital assets to market value.				
5. Sale of additional common shares of the corporation.				
6. Sold the company's common shares on credit.				
7. Corrected an accounting error (expense) from a prior period.				
8. Default on a share subscription.				
9. Conversion of preferred shares to common shares.				
10. Declared and paid a cash dividend.				
11. Exchanged the corporation's share capital for land.				
12. Purchased and retired common shares at a price greater than the average issue price to date.				

Required:

Indicate with a check mark where each of the numbered items should be reported. Be prepared to discuss any questionable items. If more than one category is appropriate, put a check mark in all appropriate boxes.

E 20–14
Preferred Shares Converted
to Common Shares:
Three Cases
(L.O. 5)

The records of Lawrence Corporation reflected the following:

Preferred shares, 1,000 shares outstanding, nopar, 10,000 shares $105,000
Common shares, 1,000 shares outstanding, nopar, 1,000 shares   52,000
Retained earnings   50,000

The preferred shares are convertible into common shares. Give the entry, or entries, required in each of the following cases:

Case A

The preferred shares are converted to common shares, share for share.

Case B

The preferred shares are converted to common shares on a one-for-three basis; that is, three shares of common are issued for each share of preferred.

Case C

The preferred shares are converted to common shares on a one-for-five basis (i.e., five shares of common are issued for each share of preferred) plus a cash payment by the holders of the preferred in the amount of $35 per share of common received.

E 20–15
Share Retirement: Analysis
(L.O. 5)

During 1992, Veech Corporation had several changes in shareholders' equity. The comparative balance sheets for 1991 and 1992 reflected the following amounts in shareholders' equity:

	Balances December 31	
	1991	**1992**
Common shares	$700,000	$600,000
Preferred shares	230,000	180,000
Contributed capital, retirement of preferred shares	0	27,000
Retained earnings	120,000	130,000

In 1992, the only transactions affecting common and preferred share accounts were the retirement of 2,000 common shares and 1,000 preferred shares, respectively. Net income was $50,000 in 1992, and dividends declared, $20,000.

Required:

1. What was the original issue price of the common shares? The preferred?
2. What amount was paid for the common shares retired? The preferred? (*Hint:* Reconstruct the journal entries to record the retirement.)

E 20–16
Share Issuance: Par Value,
Subscriptions
(L.O. 2, 3, 4)

The charter of Voss Corporation authorized the issuance of 400,000 shares of par value common shares. Give journal entries for the following transactions, assuming, for Case A, the par value is $1 per share, and for Case B, the shares have a par value of $4 per share. Set up two columns so that Case A is to the left and Case B is to the right. Explain and justify any assumptions that you made. Assume all transactions occurred within a short time span.

a. Authorization recognized (memorandum).
b. Sold 150,000 shares at $5 and collected in full; the shares were issued.
c. Received subscriptions for 12,000 shares at $5 per share; collected 40% of the subscription price. The shares will be issued upon collection in full.
d. Issued 500 shares for legal services related to incorporation. Use the deferred charge method.
e. Issued 2,000 shares and paid $80,000 cash for some used machinery.
f. Collected balance of subscriptions in (c).

E 20–17
Prepare Shareholders'
Equity: Par Value
(L.O. 2, 3, 4)

Prepare, in good form, the shareholders' equity section of the balance sheet for Tipler Corporation as of December 31, 1992.

Retained earnings	$ 690,000
Premium on common shares	80,000
Preferred shares subscribed, but not yet issued (3,000 shares)	15,000
Preferred shares, 6%, par $5, authorized 50,000 shares (30,000 shares issued)	150,000
Common shares, par $20, authorized 500,000 shares (110,000 shares issued)	2,200,000
Stock subscriptions receivable, preferred	4,000
Donation of plant site	110,000
Contributed capital on retirement of common shares	25,000
Premium on preferred shares	30,000

E 20–18
Share Redemption and
Cancellation: Entries
(L.O. 5)

Scotia Corporation has the following account balances on January 1, 1992:

Common shares, par $5, 40,000 shares outstanding	$200,000
Preferred shares, par $20, 9%, cumulative and non-participating, 5,000 shares outstanding	100,000
Contributed capital in excess of par:	
Common	80,000
Preferred	5,000
Contributed capital on retirement of common shares	10,000
Retained earnings	210,000

During the year, the following transactions took place, in chronological order:
a. Acquired and retired 1,000 preferred shares at $15.
b. Acquired and retired 5,000 common shares at $10.

    c. Acquired and retired 2,000 preferred shares at $22.
    d. Acquired and retired 1,000 common shares at $6.

Required:

1. Prepare journal entries to record the above transactions.
2. Give the resulting balance in each shareholders' equity account.

E 20–19
Treasury Stock—
Single-Transaction:
Entries and Reporting
(L.O. 6)

Fisher Corporation had 10,000 shares of nopar preferred shares outstanding, which sold initially at $14 per share, and 10,000 nopar common shares, sold initially for $20 per share. The retained earnings balance was $81,600. The corporation purchased 200 shares of its preferred at $25 per share and 500 shares of its common at $30 per share. Subsequently, 100 shares of the common treasury shares were sold for $26 per share.

Required:

1. Give entries to record the treasury stock transactions, assuming the single-transaction method is used.
2. Prepare the shareholders' equity section of the balance sheet subsequent to the above transactions.

E 20–20
Treasury Stock—Two-
Transaction Method:
Entries and Account
Balances
(L.O. 6)

Minnesota Corporation had the following shares outstanding:

Common shares, nopar, 20,000 shares	$300,000
Preferred shares, nopar, 6,000 shares	150,000

    The following treasury stock transactions were completed:

a. Purchased 50 common shares at $17 per share.
b. Purchased 20 preferred shares at $27 per share.
c. Sold 30 common shares at $14 per share.
d. Sold 10 preferred shares at $35 per share.

Required:

1. Give entries for all of the above transactions, assuming the two-transaction method is used for treasury stock.
2. Give resulting balances in each shareholders' equity account; assume a beginning balance in retained earnings of $80,000.

E 20–21
Treasury Stock—
Single-Transaction Method:
Entries and Account
Balances
(L.O. 6)

On January 1, 1991, Simon Corporation issued 10,000 shares of nopar common shares at $50 per share. On January 15, 1994, Simon purchased 50 shares of its own common at $55 per share to be held as treasury stock. On March 1, 1994, 20 of the treasury shares were resold at $58. On March 31, 10 of the treasury shares were sold for $52. The balance in retained earnings was $25,000 prior to these transactions.

Required:

1. Give all entries indicated, using the single-transaction method.
2. Give the resulting balance in each of the shareholders' equity accounts.

PROBLEMS

P 20–1
Shareholders' Equity:
Donation, Appropriation,
and Unrealized Capital
(L.O. 2, 3, 4)

Use appropriate data from the information given below to prepare the shareholders' equity section of a balance sheet for CT Corporation.

Stock subscriptions receivable, preferred.	$ 8,000
Retained earnings appropriated for bond sinking fund	40,000
Appraisal increase credit	44,000
Preferred shares, nopar value, $6, unlimited number authorized, cumulative and	
fully participating, 9,000 shares outstanding	105,000
Bonds payable, 7%	200,000
Common shares, nopar, unlimited number authorized, 5,000 shares outstanding.	250,000
Donation of future plant site to CT	6,000
Discount on bonds payable	1,000
Retained earnings, unappropriated	250,000
Preferred shares subscribed (to be issued upon collection in full).	10,000

P 20–2
Entries and Reporting: Subscriptions
(L.O. 2, 3, 4)

Don Corporation was authorized to issue unlimited preferred shares, 60 cents, nopar value, and unlimited common shares, nopar value. During the first year, the following transactions occurred:

a. 20,000 common shares were sold for cash at $12 per share.
b. 2,000 preferred shares were sold for cash at $25 per share.
c. Subscriptions were received for 2,000 preferred shares at $25 per share; 20% was received as a down payment, and the balance was payable in two equal installments. The shares will be issued upon collection in full.
d. 5,000 common shares, 500 preferred shares, and $37,500 cash were given as payment for a small plant facility that the company needed. This plant originally cost $40,000 and had a depreciated value on the books of the selling company of $20,000.
e. The first installment on the preferred subscriptions was collected.

Required:

1. Give journal entries to record the above transactions. State and justify any assumptions you made.
2. Prepare the shareholders' equity section of the balance sheet at year-end. Retained earnings at the end of the year amounted to $121,500.

P 20–3
Default on Subscriptions, Two Assumptions: Entries
(L.O. 3, 4)

Ace Corporation was authorized to issue an unlimited number of nopar value common shares. A. B. Rye subscribed for 10,000 shares at $20 per share and paid a 30% cash down payment. The remaining 70% was payable in four equal quarterly amounts. After paying the first quarterly amount, Rye defaulted. The shares were issuable at date of full payment.

Required:

1. Give the journal entries to record (a) the subscription and (b) collection of the first quarterly payment.
2. Assumption A—Give the journal entries to record (a) the default by Rye and the issuance to Rye of shares equivalent to the cash paid by Rye and (b) the sale of the remaining subscribed shares to another party for cash at $22 per share (the cost of reselling was 40 cents per share).
3. Assumption B—Give the journal entries to record (a) the default by Rye and (b) resale under lien of all of the subscribed shares to another party for cash at $22 per share (the cost of reselling was 40 cents per share), including any cash refunded to Rye.

P 20–4
Subscriptions, Non-Cash Sale: Entries and Reporting
(L.O. 3, 4)

Day Corporation operates a manufacturing business. Day is authorized to issue unlimited common shares, nopar value, and 50,000 shares of 60-cent nopar preferred shares, which are cumulative and non-participating. During the early part of the first year, the following transactions occurred:

a. Each of the six incorporators of Day Corporation subscribed to 1,000 common shares at $18 per share and 500 preferred shares at $12 per share. Half the subscription price was paid. Shares will be issued on payment in full.
b. Another individual purchased 500 shares of Day common and 100 shares of preferred, paying $9,280 cash.
c. One of the incorporators purchased a used machine for $40,000 and immediately transferred it to the corporation for 2,000 common shares, 200 preferred shares, and a one-year, 15% interest-bearing note for $8,000.
d. The investors paid the balance of the subscriptions, and the shares were issued.

Required:

1. Give all journal entries indicated for Day Corporation
2. Prepare the shareholders' equity section of the balance sheet. Assume retained earnings of $53,320 at year-end.

P 20–5
Subscriptions, Deferred Charge: Entries and Reporting
(L.O. 3, 4)

Koke Corporation was authorized to issue an unlimited number of 60-cent cumulative, non-participating nopar preferred shares, and an unlimited number of common shares, nopar value. During the first year of operations, the following transactions affecting shareholders' equity were completed:

a. The company sold for cash 9,000 shares of the preferred at $25 per share; the shares were issued.

b. Subscriptions were received for an additional 1,000 preferred shares at $25 per share; 20% was collected. The balance is to be paid in four equal installments; the shares will be issued upon collection in full.

c. Each of the three promoters was issued 1,000 common shares (only the common has voting privileges) at $20 per share; each paid one fifth in cash. The remainder was considered to be appropriate reimbursement for promotional activities; the shares were issued. Use the deferred charge method.

d. An individual purchased 100 preferred shares and 100 common shares and paid a single sum of $4,400. The shares were issued. Assume a current market price of $25 for the preferred and that, at this date, no current market price for the common was established.

e. Collected cash from the subscribers, (b) above, for the first installment.

f. Issued 5,000 common shares for a used plant. The plant had been independently appraised during the past month at $110,000 and was reported by the seller at a book value of $60,000. Assume that, at this date, no current market price for the common was established.

Required:

1. Prepare journal entries to record the above transactions. State and justify any assumptions you make.
2. Prepare the shareholders' equity section of the balance sheet, assuming retained earnings at year-end of $32,200 and an appraisal increase credit of $6,600.

P 20–6

COMPREHENSIVE PROBLEM
◆

Reconstruct Entries Based on Shareholders' Equity (L.O. 3, 4)

The shareholders' equity section of the balance sheet for the Star Corporation at the end of its first accounting year was reported as follows:

Contributed capital:
  Share capital:
    Preferred, $6, cumulative, non-participating, nopar value,
      redeemable at $125 per share, authorized unlimited shares;
      issued and outstanding, 4,185 shares . . . . $ 432,000
      Preferred shares subscribed, 465 shares . . . . 48,000 $ 480,000

    Common shares, nopar value, authorized unlimited shares;
      issued and outstanding, 954,000 shares. 7,651,080
      Common shares subscribed, 106,000 shares 850,120   8,501,200
Retained earnings 110,000
Total shareholders' equity. $9,091,200

Required:

Prepare journal entries during the first year as indicated by the above report. Use the memorandum approach to record the authorization and assume that all shares were purchased through subscriptions under terms of 30% cash down payment and 70% payable six months later. Also assume that of the 70%, all but 10% of the subscribers had paid in full by year-end. Shares are not issued until full collection from the subscriber.

P 20–7
Compute Dividends, Preferred Shares: Three Cases (L.O. 2)

Zapata Corporation reported net income during five successive years as follows: $20,000, $30,000, $9,000, $5,000, and $48,000. The share capital consisted of 15,000, nopar value common, and 20,000, 60-cent nopar preferred shares.

Required:

For each separate case, prepare a tabulation showing the amount each share class would receive in dividends if (1) the entire net income was distributed each year, and (2) 60% of each year's earnings were distributed that year.

Case A

Preferred shares are non-cumulative and non-participating.

Case B

Preferred shares are cumulative and non-participating.

Case C

Preferred shares are cumulative and fully participating. The matching dividend for common shares is $1.20 per share.

P 20–8
Compute Dividends,
Comprehensive: Five Cases
(L.O. 2)

Ace Corporation is authorized to issue unlimited $1.20 nopar preferred shares, and unlimited nopar common shares. There are 5,000 preferred and 8,000 common shares outstanding. In a five-year period, annual dividends paid were $4,000, $40,000, $32,000, $5,000, and $36,000, respectively.

Required:

Prepare a tabulation (including computations) of the amount of dividends that would be paid to each share class for each year under the following separate cases. Where applicable, the matching dividend per common share is $3.00.

Case A

Preferred shares are non-cumulative and non-participating.

Case B

Preferred shares are cumulative and non-participating.

Case C

Preferred shares are non-cumulative and fully participating.

Case D

Preferred shares are cumulative and fully participating.

Case E

Preferred shares are cumulative and partially participating up to an additional 40 cents; assume the dividend for Year 5 was $42,000 instead of $36,000.

P 20–9
Retired Shares: Entries
and Shareholders' Equity
(L.O. 5)

On January 1, 1992, Cada Corporation reported the following in shareholders' equity:

Preferred shares, nopar value, 70 cents, cumulative; authorized, 100,000 shares; issued, 40,000 shares.	$ 386,000
Common shares, nopar value; authorized, 500,000 shares; issued, 40,000 shares.	642,000
Contributed capital on retirement of preferred shares	9,000
Retained earnings	1,250,000

During 1992, certain shares were reacquired. In accordance with the regulations in Cada's incorporating legislation, all reacquired shares were retired. Transactions were as follows:

Jan. 15   Bought 5,000 preferred shares for $10 per share.
Feb. 12   Bought 1,000 common shares for $20 per share.
     25   Bought 2,000 preferred shares for $12.30 per share.
Apr. 26   Bought 1,000 preferred shares for $14 per share.
July 16   Bought 4,000 common shares for $14 per share.

Required:

1. Prepare journal entries to reflect the above transactions.
2. Restate shareholders' equity to reflect the entries.

P 20–10
Retired and Donated
Shares: Entries and
Shareholders' Equity
(L.O. 5)

Monet Corporation had 30,000 shares of nopar value common shares authorized, of which 20,000 shares were issued three years ago at $15 per share. During the current year, the corporation received 500 shares as a bequest from a deceased shareholder; in addition (at approximately the same date), 1,000 shares were purchased at $14 per share. All 1,500 shares were retired. At the end of the year, a cash dividend of 85 cents per share was paid; prior to the dividend, retained earnings amounted to $40,000.

Required:

1. Prepare entries to record all of the transactions.
2. Prepare the shareholders' equity section of the balance sheet at year-end.

P 20–11
Shares Retired: Entries
(L.O. 5)

The records for Maryville Corp. provided the following data on shareholders' equity:

a. Preferred shares, nopar, issued 2,000 shares for $52.
b. Preferred shares reacquired, 200 shares (cost $54 per share).
c. Common shares, nopar, issued 3,000 shares for $103.
d. Common shares reacquired, 300 shares (cost $98 per share).

The corporation immediately retired all reacquired shares. Management also decided to purchase for retirement another 400 common shares that could be purchased currently at $125 per share.

Required:

Give entries for the following transactions:

1. Acquisition and retirement of all reacquired shares. Give separate entries for the preferred and common.
2. Purchase of the 400 common shares and their immediate retirement.

P 20-12
Shareholders' Equity: Par Value, Donation, Appropriation, and Unrealized Capital (L.O. 2, 3, 4)

Use appropriate data from the information given below to prepare the shareholders' equity section of the balance sheet for PT Corporation.

Stock subscriptions receivable, preferred.	$ 8,000
Retained earnings appropriated for bond sinking fund	40,000
Appraisal increase credit	44,000
Preferred shares, 6%; authorized, 1,000 shares; par $100 per share; cumulative and fully participating	90,000
Bonds payable, 7%	200,000
Common shares, $1 par, 5,000 shares authorized and outstanding	5,000
Donation of future plant site to PT	6,000
Premium on preferred shares	15,000
Discount on bonds payable	1,000
Retained earnings, unappropriated	250,000
Preferred shares subscribed (to be issued upon collection in full).	10,000
Premium on common shares	245,000

P 20-13
Subscriptions, Non-Cash Sale: Entries and Reporting, Par and Nopar Compared (L.O. 2, 3, 4)

Vance Corporation was authorized to issue unlimited common shares. During the first year, the following transactions affecting shareholders' equity were completed:

a. Immediately after incorporation, sold 80,000 shares at $25 per share for cash.
b. Near year-end, received a subscription for 1,000 shares at $25 per share, collected 60% in cash, balance due in two equal installments within one yar. The shares will be issued upon collection in full.
c. Near year-end, issued 500 shares for a used machine that would be used in operations. The machine cost $20,000 new and was carried by the seller at a book value of $11,000. It was appraised at $15,000 six months previously by an independent appraiser.
d. Collected half of the unpaid subscriptions in (b).

Required:

1. Give the journal entries for each of the above transactions. Assume the following: Case A—the shares have a par value of $10 per share; Case B—the shares have nopar value; and Case C—the shares have a par value of $1 per share. Set up parallel columns for each case. State and justify any assumptions you make.
2. Prepare the shareholders' equity section of the balance sheet at the end of the first year for each case. Assume a balance in retained earnings of $462,500 at year-end.

P 20-14
Retired Shares, Par Value, Entries and Shareholders' Equity (L.O. 3, 5)

On January 1, 1992, Bonn Corporation reported the following in shareholders' equity:

Preferred shares, par value $8.00, 6%, cumulative; authorized, 100,000 shares; issued, 40,000 shares.	$ 320,000
Common shares, par value $1.00; authorized, 500,000 shares; issued, 40,000 shares	40,000
Contributed capital on issuance of preferred shares	66,000
Contributed capital on issuance of common shares.	602,000
Contributed capital on retirement of preferred shares	9,000
Retained earnings	1,250,000

During 1992, certain shares were reacquired. In accordance with the requirements of Bonn's incorporating legislation, all reacquired shares were retired.

Jan. 15   Bought 5,000 preferred shares for $10 per share.
Feb. 12   Bought 1,000 common shares for $20 per share.
      25   Bought 2,000 preferred shares for $12.30 per share.
Apr. 26   Bought 1,000 preferred shares for $14 per share.
July 16   Bought 4,000 common shares for $14 per share.

Required:

1. Prepare journal entries to reflect the above transactions.
2. Restate shareholders' equity to reflect the entries.

P 20–15
Treasury Stock, Single- and Two-Transaction Methods Compared: Entries and Account Balances
(L.O. 6)

At January 1, 1991, the records of Frazer Corporation provided the following:

Common shares, nopar value, 60,000 shares outstanding $840,000
Retained earnings 160,000

During the year, the following transactions affecting shareholders' equity were recorded:

a. Purchased 500 shares of treasury stock at $20 per share.
b. Purchased 500 shares of treasury stock at $22 per share.
c. Sold 600 shares of treasury stock at $25.
d. Net income for 1991 was $45,000.

Required:

1. Give entries for the initial issuance of shares and for each of the above transactions, in parallel columns, assuming application of (*a*) the single-transaction method and (*b*) the two-transaction method.
2. Give the resulting balances in each capital account.

P 20–16
Treasury Stock: Entries and Reporting, Par and Nopar, Single-Transaction and Two-Transaction Methods
(L.O. 6)

Fibber Corporation reported the following summarized data prior to the transactions given below:

Assets $660,000
Less: Liabilities 100,000
                                                                            $560,000

Shareholders' equity:
  Preferred shares, $10 par $300,000
  Common shares, nopar value; outstanding, 30,000 shares. 150,000
  Contributed capital in excess of par, preferred. 30,000
  Retained earnings 80,000
                                                                            $560,000

The following transactions affecting shareholders' equity were recorded:
a. Purchased preferred as treasury stock, 600 shares at $15.
b. Purchased common as treasury stock, 1,000 shares at $20.
c. Sold preferred treasury stock, 100 shares at $17.
d. Sold common treasury stock, 400 shares at $14.

Required:

1. Give entries in parallel columns for the treasury stock transactions (*a*) through (*d*), assuming application of (1) the single-transaction method and (2) the two-transaction method.
2. Prepare the resulting balance sheet for each method with emphasis on shareholders' equity.

P 20–17
Treasury Stock: Reconstruction
(L.O. 2, 3, 6)

At the end of 1992, the comparative balance sheet for Sandford Corporation reported the following shareholders' equity amounts:

	Balances December 31	
	1991	1992
Preferred shares, par $10; shares authorized, 20,000	$150,000	$200,000
Common shares, nopar; shares authorized, 100,000; issued near the end of 1991, 30,000; 1992, 31,000	210,000	218,000
Contributed capital in excess of par, preferred.	74,000	155,600
Treasury stock, preferred	2,000	1,000
Treasury stock, common	2,100	3,500*
Retained earnings	60,074	97,974†

Restriction on retained earnings at the end of 1991 equal to the cost of treasury shares held: Preferred, $5,124; common, $1,950 (300 shares).

* Increased by 200 shares during 1992 at $8 per share.
† No dividends were declared during 1992.

Required:

1. What method is being used to account for the treasury stock? Explain.
2. At the end of 1991, what had been the average selling price per share (by the corporation) of the (*a*) preferred and (*b*) common shares?
3. Complete the following tabulation for the treasury stock held at December 31, 1991 (show computations):

	Number of Treasury Shares Held	Average Cost per Share
Preferred	_____	_____
Common	_____	_____

4. How many shares were outstanding at December 31, 1991, for (*a*) preferred and (*b*) common?
5. What was the total amount of shareholders' equity at December 31, 1991?
6. Give the required entry for each transaction that affected shareholders' equity during 1992 (exclude consideration of net income). The preferred shares sold for $26 per share in 1992.

CASES

C 20–1
Issuance of Share Capital to Organizers: Valuation (L.O. 1, 3, 4)

C. Banfield, an engineer, developed a special safety device to be installed in backyard swimming pools that, when turned on, would set off an alarm should anything (e.g., a child) fall into the water. Over a two-year period, Banfield's spare time was spent developing and testing the device. After receiving a patent, three of Banfield's friends, including a lawyer, considered plans to produce and market the device. Accordingly, a company was formed, which was authorized to issue an unlimited number of nopar value common shares. Each of the four organizers contributed $20,000, and each received in return 2,000 shares. They also agreed that, for other considerations, each would receive 5,000 additional shares. Each organizer made a proposal as to how his additional 5,000 shares would be paid for. These individual proposals were made independently; then the group considered them as a package. The four proposals were as follows:

> **Banfield:** The patent would be turned over to the corporation as payment for the 5,000 shares. An independent appraisal of the patent could not be obtained.

> **Lawyer:** 1,000 shares would be received for legal services already rendered during organization, 1,000 shares would be received as advance payment for legal retainer fees for the next three years, and the balance would be paid for in cash at $10 per share.

> **Friend No. 2:** A small building, suitable for operations, would be given to the corporation for the 5,000 shares. It was estimated that $20,000 would be needed for renovation prior to use. The owner estimates that the market value of the building is $750,000, and there is a $580,000 loan on it to be assumed by the corporation.

> **Friend No. 3:** To pay $10,000 cash for the shares plus a 12% (the going rate) interest-bearing note for $40,000 (subscriptions receivable) to be paid out of dividends over the next five years.

Required:

You have been engaged as an independent public accountant to advise the group. Specifically, you have been asked the following questions:

1. How would the above proposals be recorded in the accounts? Assess the valuation basis for each, including alternatives.
2. What are your recommendations for an agreement that would be equitable to each organizer? Explain the basis for such recommendations.

C 20–2
A Reporting Issue Concerning Preferred Shares: Equity versus Debt (L.O. 2, 3)

Onray Corporation reported the following items on its balance sheet dated December 31, 1992.

Liabilities:	
Long-term note payable, 12% interest payable each June 30 and December 31 (maturity date December 31, 1997)	$ 500,000
Shareholders' equity:	
Common shares, nopar, 175,000 shares outstanding	6,000,000
Preferred shares; nopar value, $9; non-voting, cumulative, non-participating, mandatory redemption at $100 no later than December 31, 1997; 4,000 shares outstanding	400,000
Retained earnings	800,000

Required:

1. Critically evaluate the reporting classifications applied by Onray. Did Onray violate current GAAP? Explain.
2. Disregarding all current accounting "rules," how do you think Onray should report the four items shown above? Explain why.

C 20–3
Equity versus Debt
Agreements: Asset
Purchased
(L.O. 2, 3)

Ellis Corporation purchased equipment having a cash price of $144,000, for $107,000 cash and a promise to deliver an indeterminate number of shares of its nopar common shares, with a market value of $15,000, on January 1 of each year for the next four years. Hence, $60,000 in market value of shares will be required to discharge the $37,000 balance due on the equipment.

Required:

1. Discuss the propriety of recording the equipment at:
    a. $107,000 (the cash payment).
    b. $144,000 (the cash price of the equipment).
    c. $167,000 (the $107,000 cash payment plus the $60,000 market value of common shares that must be transferred to the vendor in order to settle the obligation according to the terms of the agreement).
    Assume an ordinary annuity.
2. Discuss the arguments for treating the balance due as:
    a. A liability.
    b. Common shares subscribed.

(AICPA adapted)

C 20–4
Conceptual: Classification
of Treasury Stock
(L.O. 6)

Arguments are made that treasury stock is an asset because it is purchased, owned, and paid for in cash like any other asset. Further, as with other assets, it can be sold for cash at any time in an established market. Conclusion: because treasury stock has the overriding attributes of an asset, it should be reported and classified on the balance sheet as an asset.

Required:

1. Assuming you have no GAAP constraints to consider, should treasury stock be classified on the balance sheet with assets or with shareholders' equity?
2. Justify your position indicated in (1) above.
3. Assume the issuing company has a bond sinking fund, being accumulated to retire outstanding bonds payable at the maturity date. It is administered by an independent outside trustee in accordance with the bond agreement. Assume the sinking fund investments include shares of the issuing company. How should those particular shares be classified? Explain the basis for your conclusions.

C 20–5
Reporting Shareholders'
Equity: Actual Case
(L.O. 2, 3, 4, 5)

The 1990 annual report of Loblaw Companies Limited is shown in an appendix immediately following Chapter 26. You are to respond to the following questions related to 1990 unless stated otherwise:

a. What types of share capital does the company use? Give the dividend per share. List the rights or features of each class.
b. Are any of the preferred share classes more like debt than equity? Explain.
c. At the end of 1990, how many shares were in each share class?
d. By share class, what is the average amount paid in for the shares outstanding at the end of 1990? Compare this to the redemption price, if applicable, and dividend rate.
e. What percentage of total assets was provided by the shareholders overall at the end of 1990?
f. Reconstruct the changes that occurred in the common share account in 1990. (Hint: prepare journal entries for the conversion of junior preferred shares and the exercise of stock options).

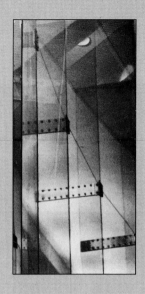

C H A P T E R

21

Corporations: Retained Earnings and Stock Options

LEARNING
OBJECTIVES
◆

After you have studied this chapter, you will be able to:

1. Explain the nature of retained earnings and dividends.

2. Prepare the proper accounting entries for cash dividends, property dividends, liquidating dividends, and scrip dividends.

3. Account for stock dividends and stock splits.

4. Explain the nature of an appropriation of retained earnings and how it should be reported.

5. Apply the appropriate accounting and reporting standards for stock option plans, rights, and warrants.

6. Apply the appropriate accounting treatment for stock appreciation rights.

7. Recognize a quasi reorganization, explain when it is appropriate, and apply the proper accounting procedures (see Appendix 21A).

◆

The 1990 annual report of Goodyear Canada Inc. shows that nearly 99% of its share-holders' equity is one item—retained earnings:

(in thousands of dollars)		December 31	
Shareholders' Equity		**1990**	**1989**
Capital stock:			
Common shares:			
Authorized, 2,906,600 shares; issued and			
outstanding, 2,572,600 shares.	$ 129	$ 129
Capital surplus	584	584
Retained earnings.	131,635	148,954
		$132,348	$149,667

Since its inception, Goodyear Canada has retained over $131 million of its earnings. Why did Goodyear do this? Were shareholders likely to have been upset that these earnings were not distributed to them in the form of dividends? What did the company do with these retained earnings? If management wanted to distribute these earnings by declaring $131 million as dividends at the end of 1990, is it likely that they would have been able to do so?

When a corporation earns a profit, management of the corporation advises the board of directors on two alternative uses of the earnings:

1. Reinvest the earnings in assets of the firm.
2. Distribute the earnings to shareholders in the form of a dividend.

If the company has investment and growth opportunities with which it expects to earn profits in the future, management may well advise that earnings be retained and used as a source of capital for financing these investment opportunities. Retaining earnings are a common way for a firm to provide capital for growth. Goodyear Canada has financed a large portion of its growth over the years simply by retaining earnings and reinvesting them in the business. Generally, investors are not disappointed to have a firm retain earnings and reinvest them in the business, so long as the retained earnings earn a high return. When the decision is to pay out the earnings as a dividend, there must be some form of asset, usually cash, which is distributed. Cash dividends basically depend on the income earned by the corporation *and* available cash.

Once the earnings are reinvested, however, they are generally not available for distribution to shareholders. For example, the $131 million in retained earnings for Goodyear Canada could not easily be distributed to shareholders—the earnings have been invested in property and equipment, in inventory and accounts receivable, and in other forms of assets. Many of these would have to be liquidated in order to raise the cash that would be needed to distribute a $131 million dividend.

There is a great deal of controversy concerning how dividend levels affect the market value of shares outstanding. For our purposes, it is sufficient to note that there is a wide range of practice. Some firms never pay dividends, while others pay out a significant portion of their earnings. There appear to be many strategies, individually tailored, that maximize shareholder wealth and the market value of shares.

The purpose of this chapter is to discuss the application of concepts and procedures used in measuring, recording, and reporting retained earnings, stock rights, and options. We begin with a discussion of retained earnings and the various transactions that influence this item. The second half of this chapter discusses the rationale for, and the accounting treatment of, stock rights and options.

◆

CHARACTERISTICS OF RETAINED EARNINGS

◆

Retained earnings represent accumulated net income or net loss (including all gains and losses), and prior period adjustments of a corporation, less its accumulated cash dividends, property dividends, stock dividends, and other amounts transferred to contributed capital accounts. If the accumulated losses and distributions of retained earnings exceed the accumulated gains, a *deficit* will exist (i.e., a debit balance) in retained earnings. Income (net of any losses) of the corporation that is not distributed as dividends increases retained earnings and thus increases total shareholders' equity.

As explained in Chapter 20, a distinction is maintained between *contributed* or *paid-in capital* and *retained earnings* to delineate the primary sources of total shareholders' equity. Total retained earnings may include two categories: appropriated or restricted retained earnings and unappropriated retained earnings. When these two categories are recorded separately in the accounts, the retained earnings account (if not designated otherwise) represents the unappropriated portion of retained earnings (i.e., it has not been set aside, appropriated, or restricted for specific reasons). The second category, appropriated retained earnings, includes specially designated amounts in separate accounts, such as retained earnings appropriated for a bond sinking fund. The reporting of appropriated and unappropriated retained earnings is discussed later in this chapter.

Increases and decreases in total retained earnings can be summarized as follows:

Retained Earnings

Decreases (Debits)	Increases (Credits)
• Net loss (including extraordinary items)	• Net income (including extraordinary items)
• Prior period adjustments (primarily correction of accounting errors of prior periods)	• Prior period adjustments (primarily correction of accounting errors of prior periods)
• Cash dividends	• Removal of deficit by quasi reorganization
• Property dividends	
• Scrip dividends	
• Stock dividends	
• Share retirement transactions	

NATURE OF DIVIDENDS

◆

Dividends are distributions of cash, non-cash assets, or the corporation's own shares to shareholders in proportion to the number of outstanding shares of each class of share held by each shareholder. A dividend requires a credit to the account that represents the item distributed (i.e., cash, non-cash asset, or share capital) and a debit to retained earnings (some exceptions are explained later). The types of dividends encountered frequently are:

1. *Usual*
   a. Cash dividends (cash disbursed).
   b. Property dividends (non-cash assets disbursed).
   c. Stock dividends (corporation's own shares issued).
2. *Special*
   a. Liquidating dividends (return of contributed capital).
   b. Scrip dividend (creation of a long-term liability, a dividend is declared to be paid at a specific future date).

Corporations are not *required* to pay dividends. They rarely distribute all their earnings as cash or property dividends for a number of economic, legal, and contractual reasons. The corporation may want to:

1. Conserve cash for other immediate uses.
2. Expand, grow, and modernize by investing the assets received when income was earned.

3. Provide a cushion of resources to minimize the effect of a recession or other unforeseen contingencies.

Some corporate legislation and bond covenants place restrictions on the amount of retained earnings that may be used for cash and/or property dividends. These constraints recognize the effects of cash and property dividends; that is, such dividends require (1) a disbursement of assets and (2) a reduction in retained earnings by the same amount. Cash and property dividends cannot be paid without this dual effect.

For example, Westcoast Transmission Company Limited reported the following in the notes to the 1987 financial statements:

9. Dividend Restriction:
The First Mortgage and the indentures relating to the Company's long term debt and preferred shares contain restrictions as to the declaration or payment of dividends, other than stock dividends, on common shares. Under the most restrictive provision, the amount available for dividends at December 31, 1987, was $146,000,000 (December 31, 1986—$132,000,000; December 31, 1985—$143,000,000).

Retained earnings totalled $273,049,000 on December 31, 1987, so $127,049,000 ($273,049,000 − $146,000,000) was not available for dividend distribution.

Relevant Dividend Dates

Prior to payment, dividends must be formally declared by the board of directors of the corporation. Four dates are important in accounting for dividends: (1) date of declaration, (2) date of record, (3) ex-dividend date, and (4) date of payment.

Date of Declaration   On this date, the corporation's board of directors formally announces the dividend declaration. In the case of a cash or property dividend, the declaration is recorded on this date as a debit to retained earnings and a credit to dividends payable. In the absence of fraud or illegality, the courts have held that formal declaration of a cash, property, or liability (i.e., scrip) dividend constitutes an enforceable contract between the corporation and its shareholders. Therefore, on the dividend declaration date, such dividends are recorded and a liability (i.e., dividends payable) is recognized.

In the case of a **stock dividend,** no corporate assets are involved, directly or indirectly, because the corporation's shares are issued in the dividend distribution. The courts have held that a stock dividend declaration is revocable up to the date of issuance. Because there is no liability, an entry is not required on the declaration date. However, accountants sometimes prefer to make an entry on the declaration date to recognize the intention to issue additional shares (i.e., credit stock dividends distributable, which is reported as a positive item under shareholders' equity since it is not a liability). If the stock dividend is not recorded, it would be disclosed in the notes to the financial statements.[1]

Under revenue recognition rules, the investor's dividend revenue is earned on the declaration date, not the date of record, the ex-dividend date, or the date of payment. The promise of payment, which is legally enforceable, confers a future economic benefit on the recipient.

Date of Record   This date is selected by the board of directors and is stated in the declaration. Usually it follows the declaration date by two to three weeks. The date of

---

[1] See the subsequent section on stock dividends.

record is the date on which the list of *shareholders of record* is prepared. Individuals holding shares at this date, as shown in the corporation's shareholders' record, receive the dividend, regardless of sales or purchases of shares after this date. No dividend entry is made in the accounts on this date. The time between the declaration and record dates is provided so that all changes in share ownership can be registered with the transfer agents.

Ex-Dividend Date Technically, the ex-dividend date is the day after the date of record. However, to provide time for transfer of shares, the stock exchanges advance the effective ex-dividend date by three or four days. Thus, one who holds shares on the day prior to the stipulated ex-dividend date receives the dividend.

Between the declaration date and the ex-dividend date, the market price of the shares includes the dividend. On the stipulated ex-dividend date, the price of the shares usually drops because the recipient of the dividend already has been identified, and succeeding owners of the shares will not receive that particular dividend. Dividends are followed carefully by the stock markets, and are regularly published, for example, in a section called, "Dividends Declared," in *The Financial Post*.

Date of Payment This date also is determined by the board of directors and usually is stated in the declaration. The date of payment typically follows the declaration date by four to six weeks. At the date of payment of cash or property dividends, the liability recorded at date of declaration is debited and the appropriate asset account is credited. A stock dividend distribution usually is recorded on the date of its issuance as illustrated in a subsequent section.

A cash or property dividend is a non-reciprocal transfer, which is defined as a transfer of assets or services in one direction. In this case, the transfer is from an enterprise to its owners, with no assets or services coming from the other direction.

Types of Dividends

Cash Dividends Cash dividends are the usual form of distributions to shareholders. The declaration first meets the entitlements of the preferred shares, if any, and then extends to the common shares.

To illustrate a cash dividend, assume the following announcement is made: The board of directors of Bass Company, at their meeting on January 20, 1993, declared a dividend of 50 cents per share, payable March 20, 1993, to shareholders of record on March 1, 1993. Assume that 10,000 nopar common shares are outstanding.

At date of declaration (January 20, 1993):

```
Retained earnings* (10,000 shares × 50 cents) . . . . . . . . . . . 5,000
    Cash dividends payable . . . . . . . . . . . . . . . . . . .          5,000
    * Or cash dividends declared, which is later closed to retained earnings.
```

At date of record (March 1, 1993): No Entry. The list of dividend recipients is prepared as of this date.

At date of payment (March 20, 1993):

```
Cash dividends payable . . . . . . . . . . . . . . . . . . . . . 5,000
    Cash . . . . . . . . . . . . . . . . . . . . . . . . . . .          5,000
```

Cash dividends payable is reported on the balance sheet as a current liability if the duration of the dividend liability is current; otherwise, it is a long-term liability.

part, to the shareholders, as when a corporation is reducing its permanent capital. Under corporate legislation, this cannot be done if such a distribution will jeapardize creditors' positions.

Mining companies sometimes pay dividends on the basis of earnings computed prior to the deduction for depletion. This would be an intentional liquidating dividend equal to the amount of depletion. A mining company might pay such a liquidating dividend when it is exploiting a non-replaceable asset that would no longer exist after it is fully mined. Shareholders should be informed of the portion of any dividend that represents a return of capital. Such dividends are not investor income and usually are not taxable to shareholders as income. Rather, they reduce the *cost* of the investment.

In accounting for liquidating dividends, an additional contributed capital account, rather than retained earnings, is debited because a portion of contributed capital is returned. Before debiting the share capital accounts, as would be done if shares were being retired, any other contributed capital accounts would be debited and eliminated. In some cases, it may be desirable to set up a special account, capital repayment, which would be reported as a deduction (contra account) in the contributed capital section of the balance sheet. For example, assume Dako Corporation declared a cash dividend of $40,000 and informed shareholders that 75% of it was a liquidating dividend. The entries would be:

At the declaration date:

```
Retained earnings ($40,000 × 25%) . . . . . . . . . . . . . . .  10,000
Capital repayment ($40,000 × 75%) . . . . . . . . . . . . . . .  30,000
    Dividends payable  . . . . . . . . . . . . . . . . . . . . . . . .      40,000
```

At the payment date:

```
Dividends payable. . . . . . . . . . . . . . . . . . . . . . . . .  40,000
    Cash . . . . . . . . . . . . . . . . . . . . . . . . . . . . . . . . .      40,000
```

Unintentional liquidating dividends may occur when the balance of retained earnings is overstated because of overstatement of income or other inappropriate accounting. For example, any error that overstated revenues or understated expenses would cause retained earnings to be overstated. In such cases, if reported retained earnings (prior to correction) was used in full for dividends, part of the dividend would be a liquidating dividend. Unintentional liquidating dividends paid, and later discovered, would require an error-correcting entry to correct the retained earnings account and any other accounts that were affected.

Scrip Dividends   Sometimes a corporation that has a temporary cash shortage will declare a dividend to maintain its continuing dividend policy by issuing a scrip dividend. A **scrip dividend** (also called a *liability dividend*) occurs when the board of directors declares a dividend and issues promissory notes, called *scrip,* to the shareholders. This declaration means that a comparatively long time (e.g., six months or one year) will elapse between the declaration and payment dates. In most cases, scrip dividends are declared when a corporation has sufficient retained earnings as a basis for dividends but is short of cash. A shareholder may hold the scrip until the due date and collect the dividend, or sell (i.e., discount) the scrip to a financial institution to obtain immediate cash. When scrip is used, the due date and rate of interest are specified. Scrip usually is payable at a specified future date, and the interest period usually is specified as the time from the declaration date to the payment date. However, if the dividend is payable part cash and part scrip, the interest period usually starts on the dividend payment date. A scrip or liability dividend is recorded as a debit to retained earnings and a credit to a liability account such as scrip dividends payable or notes payable to shareholders. On payment, the liability account is debited and the cash account is credited. Because interest paid on a liability dividend is not a part of the dividend, any interest payments should be debited to interest expense, rather than directly to retained earnings as a part of the dividend. In other respects, accounting for a liability dividend is the same as for a cash dividend.

Assume Baton Corporation declared a 1992 dividend of 25 cents per share on its 200,000 outstanding nopar common shares. Scrip was issued in full for the dividend that specified a 10% interest rate and a maturity date six months after declaration.

At the declaration date:

Retained earnings (200,000 shares × 25 cents). 50,000	
Scrip dividends payable (or notes payable	
to shareholders)	50,000

At the scrip payment date:

Scrip dividends payable 50,000	
Interest expense ($50,000 × 10% × %12) 2,500	
Cash	52,500

Stock Dividends

A **stock dividend** is a proportional distribution to shareholders of additional common or preferred shares of the corporation. *A stock dividend does not change the assets, liabilities, or total shareholders' equity of the issuing corporation. It does not change the proportionate ownership of any shareholder.* For instance, assume Early Broadcasting Ltd. has 120,000 common shares outstanding. One shareholder, J. S. Brown, owns 12,000 shares, or one tenth of the shares. The corporation declares and issues a 10% stock dividend. This has the following effect on share capital:

	Before		After	
Total shares outstanding	120,000	100%	132,000*	100%
Brown's shareholding	12,000	10%	13,200*	10%
* Previous outstanding total × 110%.				

Brown's relative ownership percentage has not changed. If the shares sold for $20 per share before the dividend, what will happen to that market value after the split? Logically, it should decline:

	Before	After
Total market value of the		
company (120,000 × $20)	$2,400,000	$2,400,000 (no change)
Shares outstanding	120,000	132,000
Price per share	$20 ($2,400/120)	$18.18 ($2,400/$132)
Brown's total market value:		
12,000 × $20	$ 240,000	
13,200 × $18.18		$ 240,000

What will really happen to the market price of the shares in this situation? The answer is unclear. Often, there is no decrease in market value, or a smaller decrease than the size of the stock dividend would seem to dictate. Some believe that this is a market reaction to other factors (e.g., an anticipated increase in cash dividends that historically follows a stock dividend). Because of the complexity and sophistication of the stock markets, it is very difficult to determine why a share price does or does not change. However, it is generally recognized that if a company doubles its outstanding shares through a stock dividend, the market price will reduce by one half.

A stock dividend causes the transfer of an amount from retained earnings to the contributed, or paid-in, capital accounts (i.e., share capital). Therefore, it only changes the *internal* account balances of shareholders' equity. If additional contributed capital accounts are debited in full for a stock dividend, retained earnings is unaffected.

When a stock dividend is of the same class as that held by the recipients, it is called an *ordinary stock dividend*. When a class of share capital other than the one already held by the recipients is issued, such a dividend is called a *special stock dividend* (e.g., preferred shares issued to the owners of common).

Numerous reasons exist for a company to issue a stock dividend:

1. To reveal that the firm plans to permanently retain a portion of earnings in the business. The effect of a stock dividend, through a debit to retained earnings and offsetting credits to permanent capital accounts, is to raise the contributed capital and thereby shelter this amount from future declaration of cash or property dividends.
2. To increase the number of shares outstanding, which reduces the market price per share and which, in turn, tends to increase trading of shares in the market. A stock dividend should not create value: it takes the "pie"—the value of the company—and cuts it into smaller pieces, each of which sells for a lower price. This is an important reason for the issuance of stock dividends. More investors can afford investments in equity securities if the unit cost is low.
3. To continue dividend distributions without disbursing assets (usually cash) that may be needed for operations. This action may be motivated by a desire to please shareholders; they may be willing to accept a stock dividend representing accumulated earnings because shareholders can sell these additional shares. Note that shareholders who sell their stock dividend shares are in reality selling part of their original investment, which has simply been subdivided into smaller units. The effect of a stock dividend may be purely psychological: the shareholders feel they have received something of value. Ordinary stock dividends are not subject to income tax to shareholders. Instead, they reduce the *per share* investment cost.

Accounting Issues Related to Ordinary Stock Dividends   The three primary issues in accounting for stock dividends are the value that should be recognized, the accounts and dates that should be used, and the manner of disclosure in the financial statements.

There is disagreement among accountants about the value that should be used in recognizing stock dividends. The shares issued for the dividend could be recorded at market value, at stated (or par) value, or at some other value.

The CICA has made no recommendation on the matter; however, the Canada Business Corporations Act, 1975, requires shares to be issued at fair market value. In Ontario, on the other hand, legislation permits the board of directors to capitalize any amount it desires. In the United States, small stock dividends (i.e., less than 20% to 25% of the outstanding shares) must be recorded at market value, while large stock dividends are recorded only as a memo entry.

We will examine three alternatives: market value, stated value, and memo disclosure.

Situation 1 — Market Value Method   Consistent with the Canada Business Corporations Act, a corporation's board of directors should require capitalization of the current market value of the additional shares issued. The market value of the stock dividend should be measured on the basis of the market price per share immediately after the stock dividend is issued. This method can be rationalized as follows:

Many recipients of stock dividends look upon them as distributions of corporate earnings and usually in an amount equivalent to the [market] value of the additional shares received. Furthermore, it is to be presumed that such views of recipients are materially strengthened in those instances, which are by far the most numerous, where the issuances are so small in comparison with the shares previously outstanding that they do not have any apparent effect upon the share market price and, consequently, the market value of the shares previously held remains substantially unchanged. The committee therefore believes that where these circumstances exist the corporation should in the public interest account for the transaction by transferring from [retained earnings] to the category of permanent capitalization ... an amount equal to the [market] value of the additional shares issued [i.e., the market value immediately after issuance].[2]

The difficulty with this method is that it is inconsistent with the view that shareholders have received nothing new of value, just a repackaging of their existing ownership interest. It may help foster the impression that the dividend is worth something.

The issue is complicated by evidence that the market price per share may *not* drop proportionately to the increased number of shares outstanding after the dividend. In any event, if the stock price does not drop proportionately after a stock dividend, the shareholders receive a real increase in their wealth and market value treatment is logical.

Situation 2 — Stated Value Method   The board of directors in certain jurisdictions may decide to capitalize a stated amount per share—average paid in per share to date, or par value, if applicable. This method can be rationalized based on the evidence of market value figures available. For instance, if the market price is proportionately reduced by the stock dividend, then it is clear that the shareholders have received nothing of value and should not be encouraged to believe that they have. In these circumstances, capitalization should be limited to legal requirements.

Strong arguments are made for some sort of stated value because (1) the corporation's assets, liabilities, and total shareholders' equity are not changed, and (2) the shareholders' proportionate ownership is not changed. Arguments based on market value changes lack persuasive validity because of measurement problems.

Situation 3 — Memo Entry   Since a large stock dividend may be issued for the primary purpose of reducing market price per share, it is obvious that the shareholder has received nothing of value. A memo entry should be recorded to identify the number of shares issued, outstanding, and subscribed. No change is made in any capital account. This parallels the treatment of a stock split, to be discussed later in this chapter. Large stock dividends are often called *stock splits effected as a stock dividend*.

The Toronto Dominion Bank reported a 100% stock dividend in the 1989 annual report:

> On May 25, 1989, the Bank declared a stock dividend of one common share on each common share outstanding at the close of business on July 10, 1989. The numbers of common shares outstanding have been restated accordingly.

The corporation used the memo entry approach; that is, no amount was capitalized for the stock dividend.

Recording a Stock Dividend   Fundamentally, a stock dividend is recorded as a debit to retained earnings and a credit to the share capital issued. As we noted earlier, the declaration of a stock dividend is revocable prior to issuance date. Thus, many companies do not make an originating journal entry on declaration date, but rather they record the dividend only on the issuance date. Moreover, whether or not the originating entry is made on the declaration or issuance date, a disclosure note is needed for financial

---

[2] AICPA, *Accounting Research Bulletin 43,* "Restatement and Revision of Accounting Research Bulletins" (New York, 1953), Chapter 7, Section B, par. 10.

statements prepared *between* these two dates. Either recording approach can be used, as follows:

Declaration date—declared a 10% common stock dividend; issued 10,000 shares, nopar; market value, $5 per share.

	Orginating Entry Date	
	Declaration	Issuance
Declaration date:		
Retained earnings	50,000	None
Stock dividends distributable*	50,000	
* Reported as a credit under shareholders' equity until issuance.	Also use disclosure note	Use disclosure note
Issuance date:		
Retained earnings		50,000
Stock dividends distributable	50,000	
Common shares, no par	50,000	50,000

The differences between these two approaches are trivial; either one satisfies GAAP in all respects. The stock dividends distributable account is not a liability, for it does not involve settlement by the future transfer of assets (cash, etc.). It is an obligation to issue equity and is properly classified in shareholders' equity.

Southam Inc. reported stock dividends in their 1989 annual report:

Consolidated Statement of Reinvested Earnings

	Year Ended December 31		
(thousands of dollars)	**1989**	**1988**	**1987**
Balance at beginning of year	$507,531	$339,329	$287,752
Net income.	90,466	205,238	82,682
	597,997	544,567	370,434
Deduct:			
Dividends on common shares:			
Cash—$.76 per share (1988—$.62; 1987—$.52 per share) . . .	42,904	35,030	29,878
Stock—56,792 (1988—102,224; 1987—56,399 shares)	1,875	2,006	1,227
	44,779	37,036	31,105
Premium on redemption of common shares for cancellation. . .	74,127		
Balance at end of year	$479,091	$507,531	$339,329

From the notes to the financial statements:

7. Capital Stock

Common shares

The directors may determine whether to pay dividends in cash or by issuing fully paid common shares and which shareholders have the right to elect to receive such dividends in shares. The directors have determined that shareholders who come within the "constrained class" or who are indebted in respect of shares included in the Employee Stock Investment Plans are ineligible to receive stock dividends on such shares.

Summary of Share Transactions

	1989		1988		1987	
	Shares	Amount	Shares	Amount	Shares	Amount
Issued at January 1	63,616,230	$226,644	64,106,053	$236,246	63,688,170	$231,237
Stock dividends.	56,792	1,875	102,224	2,006	56,339	1,227
Employee stock investment plans.	735,907	22,521	362,424	7,196	1,588,269	27,967
Contribution of capital . . .				1,250		
	64,408,929	251,040	64,570,701	246,698	65,332,778	260,431
Shares purchased for cancellation	2,541,917	9,550	954,471	20,054	1,226,725	24,185
Issued at December 31 . . .	61,867,012	$241,490	63,616,230	$226,644	64,106,053	$236,246

Southam capitalized $1,875,000 in 1989 as a result of the stock dividend, although it is not clear whether this represents market or stated value.

CONCEPT REVIEW

1. What four dates are important in the accounting for dividends, and what does each represent?
2. What are liquidating dividends? How are they accounted for?
3. Describe the three alternative methods of accounting for stock dividends. Which method is appropriate under the Canada Business Corporations Act?

Special Stock Dividends

In the case of *special* stock dividends, such as a stock dividend in preferred shares issued to owners of common, the market value of the dividend (i.e., the preferred) shares should be capitalized by the issuing corporation. Issuance of the dividend shares usually would not be expected to have much impact on the market value of the other (i.e., the common) shares. In this instance, shareholders would appear to receive a dividend equal to the market value of the dividend shares received.

Exhibit 21–1 provides examples of the issuance of ordinary stock dividends and of special stock dividends: Case A—stock dividend, market value method; Case B—stock dividend, stated value method; Case C—stock dividend, memo entry; and Case D—a special stock dividend.

To conclude the discussion of stock dividends, we reemphasize that an important aspect of such dividends is that an amount of retained earnings is transferred to contributed (permanent) capital (i.e., capitalized). This transfer reveals that the company has "grown through earnings" by permanently removing such earnings from dividend availability. For many corporations, this represents a large amount of contributed capital.

Dividends and Treasury Stock

Dividends are not paid on treasury stock. However, treasury stock occasionally is used for the issuance of a stock dividend. If treasury stock is used for this purpose, the stock dividend should be recorded by a debit to retained earnings (or other appropriate account) for the *market value* of the treasury stock issued and a credit to treasury stock for the *book value* of the treasury stock issued, and any credit difference increases contributed capital. A debit difference would reduce contributed capital or retained earnings.

In respect to treasury stock, a stock dividend usually is not deemed to increase the number of shares of treasury stock held. However, should the opposite view prevail, the amount of retained earnings that should be capitalized is a critical issue.

Fractional Share Rights

When a small stock dividend is issued, not all shareholders are going to own exactly the number of shares needed to receive whole shares. For example, when a firm issues a 5% stock dividend and a shareholder owns 30 shares, the shareholder is entitled to one and one-half shares (30 × .05). When this happens, the firm can issue *fractional share rights* for portions of shares to which individual shareholders are entitled.

To demonstrate, suppose Moon company has 1,000,000 outstanding common shares, nopar value. Moon issues a 5% stock dividend. The market value of the common shares

EXHIBIT 21-1   Stock Dividend Entries—Counter Corporation

Case Data Prior to Dividend (Same for Each Case):

Preferred shares, no par, unlimited shares authorized,
    5,000 shares outstanding $110,000
Common shares, no par, unlimited shares authorized,
    10,000 shares outstanding. 115,000
Retained earnings 150,000
Total shareholders' equity $375,000

Market price per share immediately before issuance of dividend shares:
Preferred, $25; Common, $24.

Stock Dividend Entry at Date of Issuance of Dividend Shares (Each Situation Is Independent):

Case A—market value method: A 10% common stock dividend (i.e., one additional common share is issued for each 10 shares already held) is declared and issued on the common shares. The market price remains $24 per share. The stock dividend is capitalized at market value.

    Retained earnings (1,000 shares at market, $24) 24,000
        Common shares (1,000 shares)   24,000

Case B—stated value method: A 20% common stock dividend (i.e., one additional common share for each five shares already held) is declared and issued on the common shares. The market value per share drops immediately to $20. The stock dividend is capitalized at $11.50 per share, the average paid in to date ($115,000/10,000).

    Retained earnings (2,000 shares at $11.50) 23,000
        Common shares (2,000 shares)   23,000

Case C—memo method: A 200% common stock dividend (i.e., two additional common shares for each share already held) is declared and distributed on the common shares. The market value per share drops to $8.

    Memo: 200% common share dividend distributed, 20,000 shares.

        30,000 shares are now issued and outstanding.

Case D—A special stock dividend: A 20% common stock dividend (i.e., one additional share for each five shares already held) is issued to both common and preferred shareholders. The market price per common share does not change appreciably after issuance from $24:

    Retained earnings (3,000 shares* at $24) 72,000
        Common shares (3,000 shares)   72,000
    * Computation: (10,000 + 5,000 shares) × 20% = 3,000 shares.

---

after the stock dividend is $80 per share. The number of shares to be issued is 5% times the number of shares outstanding (1,000,000 × .05), or 50,000 shares. Suppose the firm's share ownership is such that 42,000 whole or complete shares can be issued. The firm would issue fractional share rights for the remaining shares to be issued. Each fractional share right would entitle the holder to acquire 5%, or one twentieth of a share. Since there are 8,000 shares yet to be issued, there would be 8,000 times 20, or 160,000 fractional share rights issued. A market would develop for the fractional share rights, with each having a market value of approximately one twentieth of a whole share ($80/20), or $4. Shareholders could buy or sell fractional share rights to the point where whole shares could be acquired. A holder would have to turn in 20 fractional share rights to receive one common share.

The entries for recording the issuance of the above stock dividend and fractional share rights would be as follows:

To record the 42,000 shares issued as a stock dividend (at market value):

    Retained earnings (42,000 × $80) 3,360,000
        Common shares, nopar   3,360,000

To record the issuance of 160,000 fractional share rights:

> Retained earnings (8,000 × $80). 640,000
>   Common share fractional share rights.   640,000

Notice that the price per right is $4 ($640,000/160,000).

When rights are turned in to the company for redemption in common shares the common share fractional share rights account is debited, and common shares are credited. Suppose, for example, that 150,000 fractional share rights are turned in for 7,500 common shares (150,000/20). The entry to record the transaction would be:

> Common share fractional share rights
>   (150,000 × $4). 600,000
>   Common shares, nopar   600,000

If the remaining rights are allowed to lapse, the corporation would record contributed capital:

> Common share fractional share rights (10,000 × $4) 40,000
>   Contributed capital, lapse of share rights   40,000

Share rights are issued in a variety of circumstances which are examined in more depth later in this chapter. An alternative to the issuance of fractional share rights is to make a cash payment to shareholders for any fractional shares to which they are entitled. The firm would sell enough shares to represent fractional ownership, then distribute the proceeds to shareholders as appropriate. Moon would sell 8,000 shares at a market price of $80:

> Cash (8,000 × $80) 640,000
>   Common shares, nopar (8,000 shares)   640,000

Shareholders with fractional shareholdings would receive a cash dividend in lieu of fractional share rights. Thus, our shareholder above who owned 30 shares and thus was entitled to 1.5 shares would receive one share from the firm and a cash payment of $40 ($80 per share × .5 shares), representing the value of the one-half share at current market value. The entry to record the cash payment is a debit to retained earnings and a credit to cash. This procedure is simpler for the shareholder, as there is no need to buy or sell fractional shares.

LEGALITY OF DIVIDENDS
◆

The requirement that there be retained earnings or certain elements of contributed capital before dividends can be declared has already been mentioned. Precise identification of the elements of shareholders' equity that are available for cash, property, and stock dividends, respectively, would require study of the provisions of the particular incorporating legislation. However, at least two provisions appear to be uniform: (1) dividends may not be paid from *legal capital* (usually represented in the share capital accounts) and (2) retained earnings are available for dividends unless there is a contractual or statutory restriction. Under the Canada Business Corporations Act, a liquidity test must also be met: dividends may not be declared or paid if the result would be that the coporation was unable to meet its liabilities as they came due, or if the dividend resulted in the realizable value of assets being less than liabilities plus stated capital.

The accountant has a responsibility when the legality or accounting treatment of dividends is at issue to ensure that such matters are referred to a lawyer and to ascertain that the financial statements disclose all material facts concerning such dividends.

STOCK SPLITS
◆

A **stock split** is a change in the number of shares outstanding with no change in the recorded capital accounts. A stock split is implemented by either calling in all of the old shares and concurrently issuing the split shares, or by issuing the additional split shares with notification to the shareholder of the change in outstanding shares. The primary purpose of a stock split is to increase the number of shares outstanding and decrease the market price per share. In turn, this will often increase the market activity of the shares. By increasing the number of shares outstanding, a stock split also reduces earnings per share. In a normal stock split, no accounting entry is needed because there is no change in the dollar amounts in the share capital accounts, additional contributed capital, or retained earnings. No consideration has been received by the corporation for the issued shares, and since market value is directly affected by the split, shareholders receive nothing of direct value. Therefore, in a stock split, the following dollar amounts are *not changed:* (1) share capital account, (2) additional contributed capital accounts, (3) retained earnings, and (4) total shareholders' equity. Shares issued, outstanding, and subscribed are changed, as is par value, if any.

To illustrate a 200% or two-for-one stock split (two new shares for each old share called in), and to compare it with a 100% stock dividend (one additional share for each share already outstanding), assume Split Corporation is authorized to issue 200,000 common shares, nopar, of which 40,000 shares were issued initially at $10, and has retained earnings with a current balance of $450,000. The different effects of a 100% stock dividend capitalized at $10 per share and a 200% stock split may be contrasted as shown below:

Split Corporation — Stock Dividend and Stock Split Compared

Transaction	Total Shares Outstanding		Issue Price		Prior to Stock Dividend or Stock Split	After 100% Stock Dividend	After 200% Stock Split
Initial issue	40,000	×	$10	=	$400,000		
100% stock dividend	80,000	×	10	=		$800,000*	
Two-for-one stock split	80,000	×	5	=			$400,000
Total contributed capital					400,000	800,000	400,000
Retained earnings					450,000	50,000*	450,000
Total shareholders' equity.					$850,000	$850,000	$850,000

* Retained earnings capitalized: 40,000 shares × $10 = $400,000; entry: Debit retained earnings, $400,000; credit contributed capital accounts, $400,000.

The stock dividend changes both contributed capital and retained earnings. The stock split, however, changes neither of these amounts. Total shareholders' equity was unchanged by both the stock dividend and the stock split. Notice that the shareholder is left in the same position whether there is a 200% stock split or a 100% stock dividend — two shares will be owned for every one share previously held. Similarly, the market price of the shares should be the same whether the transaction is described as a split or a dividend. This makes the different accounting methods, used for transactions that are basically the same, suspect. It hardly seems to promote the concept of "substance over form." Thus, the memo treatment of a large stock dividend is preferable because it produces the same result as the memo treatment for a stock split.

A reverse stock split decreases the number of shares. It also involves a proportional *increase* in the par or stated value per share, if any, and reduction in the number of shares issued and outstanding.

APPROPRIATIONS AND RESTRICTIONS OF RETAINED EARNINGS

From time to time, retained earnings may be *appropriated* as a result of management action or *restricted* by contract or law. **Appropriated retained earnings** and **restricted retained earnings** involve a constraint on a specified portion of accumulated earnings for a specific purpose. Such specific appropriations and restrictions nevertheless represent a part of *total* retained earnings. Thus, retained earnings comprises two subcategories: (1) appropriated and restricted retained earnings, and (2) unappropriated retained earnings. In general, the term *appropriations* is used for voluntary divisions and *restrictions* for those that are required by law or contract.

Appropriations and restrictions of retained earnings usually are recorded as debits to the retained earnings account (i.e., unappropriated retained earnings) and credits to descriptively designated appropriation or restriction of retained earnings accounts. For instance, a $100,000 appropriation for future contingencies would be created as follows:

```
Retained earnings. . . . . . . . . . . . . . . . . . . . . .100,000
    Retained earnings appropriated for contingencies . . . . .        100,000
```

For reporting purposes on the financial statements, the appropriations and restrictions may be reported in any one of three ways:

1. Report each appropriation or restriction as a separate item on the statement of retained earnings.
2. Report appropriations or restrictions parenthetically on the statement of retained earnings.
3. Disclose appropriations or restrictions in the notes to the financial statements.

All these methods satisfy GAAP requirements and are found in practice.

When the need for an appropriation or restriction no longer exists, the appropriated balance is returned to the unappropriated retained earnings account. This is done by making an entry reversing the initial appropriation.

Retained earnings are appropriated and restricted primarily to allow shareholders and other financial statement users to assess the amount of unappropriated retained earnings available for dividend declaration. Appropriations and restrictions of retained earnings arise in the following situations:

1. To fulfill a *legal requirement,* as in the case of a restriction by law on retained earnings equivalent to the cost of treasury stock held.
2. To fulfill a *contractual agreement,* as in the case of a debt covenant that stipulates a restriction on the use of retained earnings for dividends that require the disbursement of assets.
3. To report a discretionary appropriation by the board of directors to constrain a specified portion of retained earnings as an aspect of financial planning.
4. To report a discretionary appropriation by the board of directors of a specified portion of retained earnings in anticipation of possible future losses.

The appropriation or restriction of retained earnings by transferring an amount from retained earnings to an appropriated retained earnings account has no effect on assets, liabilities, or total shareholders' equity. An appropriation is a clerical identification for information purposes only. It does not set aside specific assets, such as cash. Assets may be set aside as a separate action, for instance, cash invested in a separate fund, such as a bond sinking fund.

Types of Appropriations and Restrictions Illustrated

Restriction Required by Law   Some jurisdictions that allow corporations to hold treasury stock place a restriction on retained earnings equal to the cost of treasury stock held to protect creditors.

Restriction Required by Contract   To offer security to lenders, credit agreements often include various provisions restricting payment of cash and property dividends. One type of provision calls for the periodic restriction of a specific amount of retained earnings. Another common provision, called funding, requires (1) the periodic deposit of a specific amount of cash in a fund, held by a trustee, and (2) a restriction of retained earnings to match the funding.

To illustrate the latter situation, assume that Sinclair Corporation issued $500,000 10-year bonds payable, and the bond indenture required the issuer to restrict $50,000 of retained earnings annually, in addition to depositing $35,000 cash each year in a bond sinking fund. The entries at inception would be:

To establish the restriction:

Retained earnings.	50,000	
Retained earnings restricted for bonds payable		50,000

To establish the bond sinking fund:

Bond sinking fund	35,000	
Cash		35,000

The balance sheet would report the bond sinking fund as an asset under "investments and funds." It would also report the $50,000 restriction using one of the three approaches previously named. When the bonds mature, the cash accumulated in the bond sinking fund would be used to help pay the maturity amount. The "retained earnings restricted for bonds payable" account balance then would be returned to the unrestricted retained earnings account:

Retained earnings restricted for bonds payable.	500,000	
Retained earnings		500,000
Total restriction, $50,000 × 10 = $500,000.		

Appropriated Retained Earnings for Financial Planning   Many corporations grow by retaining a large portion of their earnings in the business. In such cases, it may be desirable to capitalize a portion of accumulated earnings by issuing stock dividends. Alternatively, the board of directors may disclose their intention not to use a specific amount of retained earnings for cash or property dividends by establishing discretionary appropriation accounts such as the following:

Retained earnings appropriated for investment in plant.
Retained earnings appropriated for working capital.

Appropriation for Possible Future Losses   In case of possible future losses, the board of directors will sometimes direct that a portion of retained earnings be appropriated and identified with titles such as the following:

Retained earnings appropriated for possible future inventory cost declines.[3]
Retained earnings appropriated for possible loss in pending lawsuit.
Retained earnings appropriated for self-insurance.

Even if the event does happen, any actual loss arising therefrom should be recorded as an ordinary, unusual or infrequent, or extraordinary item. This would be done whether or not there is a related appropriation account. Such losses should not be debited to the appropriation account. After the loss is recognized as a deduction to net income, the appropriation should be returned to unappropriated retained earnings. Thus, the effect of having reported the appropriation prior to the loss was (a) to hold back an equivalent amount of retained earnings from dividend declarations, and (b) to report unappropriated retained earnings at the same balance that would exist if the event occurred during the current year and was reported on the income statement.

The primary purpose of appropriations is communication to financial statement users by removing specific amounts from availability to be paid as current dividends. Once an appropriation or restriction is returned to unappropriated retained earnings,

---

[3] An appropriation for possible future inventory cost decline is not the same account used with respect to the valuation of inventory at LCM (allowance to reduce inventory to lower-of-cost-or-market). The allowance is related to a cost decline that has *already* materialized. The appropriation account relates to a possible cost decline in the future.

EXHIBIT 21–2   Statement of Retained Earnings: Reporting Prior Period Adjustments and Appropriations

---

Basic Case Data, Bradfield Corporation

1. For the year ended December 31, 1993, Bradfield Corporation reported the following:
   a. Retained earnings balance, December 31, 1992, $158,000.
   b. Net income, $52,000.
   c. Dividends declared and paid, $30,000.
2. Total opening retained earnings included a $25,000 appropriation for investment in plant and a $15,000 restriction for a bond sinking fund. Both these amounts were increased by $10,000 during the year 1993.
3. During 1993, it was discovered that 1992 depreciation expense was understated by $20,000 (the applicable tax rate during 1992 was 30%).

Reporting Retained Earnings:

BRADFIELD CORPORATION

Statement of Retained Earnings
For Year Ended December 31, 1993

Balance in retained earnings, January 1, 1993	$158,000
Adjustments applicable to prior periods (a debit):	
Correction of accounting error in 1992, net of $6,000 income tax saving (see Note 4)	(14,000)
Balance in retained earnings, January 1, 1993, as corrected	144,000
Add: Net income for 1993	52,000
Total	196,000
Deduct: Dividends for 1993	(30,000)
Balance in retained earnings, December 31, 1993 (see Note 5)	$166,000

Note 4: During 1992, the company inadvertently understated depreciation expense by $20,000. This accounting error caused an overstatement of the reported income of 1992, and of the balance in retained earnings at December 31, 1992 (January 1, 1993), by $14,000, which reflects the $6,000 tax effect of the error. The error was detected and corrected during 1993 by debiting retained earnings for a prior period adjustment in the after-tax amount of $14,000. To correct other affected accounts, deferred taxes was reduced for the $6,000 tax saving and accumulated depreciation was increased by $20,000.

Note 5: Appropriations and restrictions:

Appropriation for investment in plant	$ 15,000
Restriction for bond sinking fund	25,000
Unappropriated retained earnings	106,000
Total retained earnings	$166,000

---

the full amount once again becomes available for dividends, should the board of directors decide to declare them.

REPORTING RETAINED EARNINGS
◆

The statement of retained earnings may include the following:

1. Beginning balance of retained earnings.
2. Restatement of beginning balance for prior period adjustments.
3. Restatement of beginning balance for retroactively applied accounting changes.
4. Net income or loss for the period.
5. Dividends.
6. Appropriations and restrictions of retained earnings.
7. Adjustments made pursuant to a quasi reorganization.
8. Adjustments resulting from some share retirements.
9. Ending balance of retained earnings (the result).

Exhibit 21–2 illustrates the reporting of a retained earnings statement. Appendix 21A discusses quasi reorganizations.

CONCEPT REVIEW

1. Does a shareholder receive anything of value in a stock dividend? Why?
2. What is the difference to the shareholder, if any, between receiving a four-for-one stock split and a 300% stock dividend? How would each be accounted for?
3. When are fractional share rights issued? What value does the corporation assign to them?
4. What are appropriated retained earnings? Why would management want to appropriate a portion of the firm's retained earnings?

STOCK RIGHTS AND WARRANTS

◆

Corporations often issue *stock rights* that provide the holder with an option to acquire a specified number of shares in the corporation under prescribed conditions and within a stated future time period. When rights are issued to current shareholders, the corporation normally issues one right for each share owned. However, it may take more than one right to acquire an additional share. When more than one right is required to obtain one share, the rights represent fractional shares and are called *fractional share rights.*

Evidence of ownership of one or more stock rights is a certificate called a *stock warrant.* Stock rights sometimes are simply referred to as stock warrants. A stock warrant typically specifies (1) the number of rights represented by the warrant, (2) the option price (which may be zero) per share of the specified shares, (3) the number of rights needed to obtain a share, (4) the expiration of the rights, and (5) instructions for exercising the rights.

Three dates are important regarding stock rights: (1) *announcement date* of the rights offering, (2) *issuance date* of the rights, and (3) *expiration date* of the rights. Between the announcement date and the issuance date of the rights, the related shares will sell *rights on.* That is, the price of the shares will include the value of the rights because the shares and the rights are not separable during that period of time. After the issuance date of the rights and until expiration of the rights, the shares and rights sell separately. That is, the shares sell *ex rights* during this period of time. The rights will have a separate market price.

Stock rights received by a shareholder may be (1) *exercised* by purchasing additional shares, as specified, from the corporation, (2) *sold* at the market value of the rights, or (3) allowed to *lapse* on the expiration date.

Corporations issue stock rights and options for the following reasons:

1. To give existing shareholders the first chance to buy additional shares when the corporation decides to raise additional equity capital by selling a large number of unissued shares. Stock rights are evidence of shareholders' preemptive right to maintain their existing level of ownership in the firm even if new shares are issued.
2. As compensation to outsiders (such as underwriters, promoters, and professionals) for services provided to the corporation.
3. As a "poison pill" to make the corporation less attractive as a takeover target.
4. To represent fractional shares when a stock dividend is declared and issued.
5. As additional compensation to officers and other employees of the corporation. These rights often are referred to as stock options or stock incentive plans.
6. To enhance the marketability of other securities issued by the corporation. These include issuing common stock rights with convertible bonds payable (discussed and illustrated in Chapter 16).

ACCOUNTING FOR STOCK RIGHTS

♦

The issuance of stock rights causes accounting problems for both the recipient (i.e., the investor) and the issuing corporation. Stock rights received on shares held by an investor have no additional cost. Therefore, the current carrying value of the shares already owned is allocated by the investor between the original shares and the rights received, based on the then-current market values. Accounting for rights received by investors is discussed in Chapter 14.

Accounting for stock rights by the issuing corporation involves either a memorandum entry or a regular journal entry on each of the three relevant dates defined above: (1) announcement date, (2) issuance date, and (3) expiration date. The accounting treatment appropriate for rights depends on the circumstances under which stock rights are issued.

Case 1—Issuance of Stock Rights Related to a Planned Sale (Primarily to Existing Shareholders) of Unissued Shares   In this case, rights may be issued in advance of the planned sale date to give current shareholders the first chance to purchase the new shares being offered for sale. These are preemptive rights.

Case data:
Marley Corporation account balances prior to the decision to issue rights:

	Amount
Common shares, nopar, authorized unlimited shares; issued and outstanding, 30,000 shares.	$450,000
Retained earnings.	70,000

Decision of Marley Corporation:

♦ To increase the outstanding shares by 50% (i.e., to issue 15,000 additional shares).
♦ Issue price per share to current shareholders—$30 plus two stock rights.
♦ Announcement date: January 1, 1993.
♦ Issue date for rights: March 1, 1993. One right is to be issued per share.
♦ Expiration date for rights: September 1, 1993.

Market prices:

Rights—Between issuance and expiration dates, average $3 per right.

Shares—At announcement date, $30 per share.

Shares—At issue date, $30 per share.

Shares—At expiration date, $34 per share.

Journal entries by Marley Corporation:

January 1, 1993—announcement date—no entry because there is no completed transaction.

March 1, 1993—Issuance date—memorandum only because there is no flow of resources; there is only a commitment to issue shares. The memo expresses that commitment:

Memo—Issued 30,000 stock rights to current shareholders for 15,000 common shares to be sold. Each share will be sold for $30 cash plus the receipt of two stock rights. After September 1, 1993, all outstanding rights will expire and the remaining shares will be sold in the market at the then-current market price.

July 1, 1993—exercise date—1,000 stock rights exercised by one shareholder (a completed transaction with resource flows):

    Cash (1,000 rights ÷ 2 = 500 shares) × $30 15,000
        Common shares (500 shares)   15,000
        (Remaining rights outstanding, 29,000 for 14,500 common shares.)

Case 2—Rights for Services Rendered   A corporation sometimes needs to conserve cash during the early part of its life and, as a consequence, issues its own shares for professional services rendered. In some instances, stock rights rather than shares are issued. To illustrate, assume that at the end of 1992, its first year of operations, Jones Corporation issued 600 stock rights to a lawyer for legal services when the rights were selling at $2 each. The rights specify that, for each three rights tendered, one common share will be issued for $60 cash at any time up to the end of the fifth year of the life of the corporation. The indicated entries on the books of the issuing corporation would be as follows:

Year 1992—date of issuance of stock rights:

    Expense—legal services (600 rights at $2)* 1,200
        Stock rights outstanding (600 rights for
        200 common shares)   1,200
    * Observe that the rights are valued at their current market price. If no market price for shares
    is available, the market value of the legal services must be used.

Note that, unlike Case 1, there is a completed transaction at the issuance date, since legal services were rendered. Thus, the rights are recorded.

Year 1996—the 600 stock rights are tendered by the lawyer and 200 shares (600 ÷ 3 = 200) are issued:

    Cash (200 shares at $60) 12,000
    Stock rights outstanding (600 rights). 1,200
        Common shares (200 shares)   13,200

During the period the stock rights are outstanding, the item "stock rights outstanding (for 200 shares), $1,200" should be reported under shareholders' equity along with the share capital account to which it relates.

Case 3—Rights Issued as a Poison Pill   Corporations, trying to make themselves less attractive as a takeover target, will sometimes issue rights that would make it far more expensive for an outsider to gain control. Sherritt Gordon Limited describes the following rights plan in its 1989 annual report:

> Shareholder Rights Plan—In November 1989, the Board of Directors announced the adoption of a Shareholder Rights Plan, providing for the issue of one Right for each outstanding common share of the company at an Exercise Price of $41.00. The Rights expire on November 23, 1999, unless exchanged or redeemed on an earlier date. Such Rights can only be exercised on the occurrence of certain triggering events, which include (*i*) a person (an "Acquiring Person") acquiring 20% or more of the common shares of the company (except through a permitted bid or certain other limited exceptions) or (*ii*) the company merging or amalgamating with or into any other person (other than a wholly owned subsidiary) or (*iii*) the company or one or more of its subsidiaries selling or transferring more than 50% of the company's assets to another person. Upon the occurrence of the events described above each Right entitles the holder, other than an Acquiring Person, to purchase that number of common shares of the company or other person, as the case may be, having an aggregate market price equal to twice the Exercise Price for an amount in cash equal to the Exercise Price. The Plan will be submitted for confirmation to the next annual meeting of shareholders.

In the event of a takeover, the shareholders would be allowed to buy shares at half the going market price. This would greatly increase the shares outstanding, and severely dilute the value of the shares held by the "Acquiring Person" (who is not entitled to exercise rights). Since these rights are contingent on certain future events—a takeover—they are not formally recorded in the financial statements. Disclosure, however, is critical to the purpose of the rights.

Case 4—Stock Rights Issued with a Stock Dividend This case was illustrated in the discussion of fractional shares.

Case 5—Stock Rights Issued with Employee Incentive Compensation Plans This is a complex case; it is discussed in more detail in the next section.

Case 6—Stock Rights Issued to Enhance the Marketability of Other Securities This case was illustrated in Chapter 14.

STOCK OPTION INCENTIVE PLANS FOR EMPLOYEES

The discussion of corporations is concluded with stock option plans because they usually involve the issuance of share capital. Corporations often establish stock option plans whereby shares in the company are issued to employees over a period of time. The purposes of stock option plans are varied. They may be used to help recruit and retain outstanding employees, to encourage ownership in the company by employees, and to encourage managers to make decisions that will maximize the value of the firm.

Plans for the issuance of share capital to employees are designated with a variety of terms, none of which have been accorded standard usage. For instance, the terms *stock option plan, stock incentive plan, stock incentive program, stock awards plan,* and *stock purchase plan* are all found in practice. In stock option plans, the issuing corporation is designated as the *grantor,* and the employee recipient is designated as the *grantee.*

The most important accounting issue associated with a stock option plan is whether the plan causes additional expense to the company. Thus, for accounting purposes, the distinction is between the following two basic categories of stock option incentive plans for employees:

1. *Non-compensatory plans*—These plans specify the issuance of company shares to employees at a price that is not significantly less than the market price. Thus, (1) no additional cost to the company and (2) no additional compensation to the employee are recognized. For example, the Royal Bank of Canada allows certain groups of employees to buy common shares of the bank, through payroll deductions and cash deposits, at 95% of the market value of the shares at the time of purchase. There are no charges to income in connection with the plan.
2. *Compensatory plans*—These plans involve both (1) compensation expense to the grantor and (2) compensation income to the grantee. Such plans usually specify the issuance of shares to designated employees at a set price per share (to be paid by the employee) that is significantly less than the current market price of the shares at measurement date (defined later). In some cases, the employee receives the shares under specified conditions at no cost.

The *CICA Handbook,* except for recommending descriptive disclosure (paragraphs 3240.03–.04), has not issued recommendations with regard to stock options. In the United States, accounting for stock options is governed by *Accounting Research Bulletin (ARB) No. 43,* Chapter 13B, as amended and supplemented by *APB Opinion No. 25,* "Accounting for Stock Issued to Employees." The discussions that follow are based on these two pronouncements.

Accounting for Non-Compensatory Stock Option Plans for Employees

Non-compensatory stock options involve no expense to the company and no compensation to the employees. Therefore, they cause no special accounting problems. A non-compensatory stock plan is one that possesses at least the following four characteristics:

1. Substantially all full-time employees meeting limited employment criteria are included.
2. The shares are offered to eligible employees equally or are based on a uniform percentage of salary or wages.
3. The time permitted for exercise of an option or purchase right is limited to a reasonable period.
4. The discount from the market price of the shares is no greater than would be reasonable in an offer of shares to shareholders or others. Discounts up to 15% are currently being permitted in actual practice.

Accounting for a non-compensatory stock option plan involves recording the issuance (i.e., sale) of the shares in conformity with the cost principle. The option price per share is the issue price. To illustrate accounting for non-compensatory stock options, assume Nichi Corporation has a stock purchase plan. The employees may acquire shares from the company at a discount of 4% from the market price through payroll deductions. Typical entries for a non-compensatory plan, including $7,200 of voluntary payroll deductions for employee share purchases, would be (amounts assumed):

1. To record the monthly payroll of $90,000 and related deductions:

```
Salary and wage expense . . . . . . . . . . . . . . . . . . .  90,000
    Withholding income tax payable. . . . . . . . . . . . .          18,400
    Payroll taxes payable . . . . . . . . . . . . . . . . .           6,500
    Liability—employee stock purchase plan* . . . . . . . . .         7,200
    Cash (or salary and wages payable) . . . . . . . . . . .          57,900
* Per payroll deductions authorized in advance by employees.
```

2. To record issuance of the required number of shares to employees (market price per share, $18.75):

```
Liability—employee stock purchase plan. . . . . . . . . . . .   7,200
    Common shares, nopar (400 shares)* . . . . . . . . . . .           7,200
* $7,200 ÷ ($18.75 × 96%) = 400 shares.
```

Notice that the shares are recorded at their issuance price, not fair market value. The shares would have raised $7,500 ($18.75 × 400) had they been sold on the open market. The $300 opportunity cost is not recorded.

Accounting for Compensatory Stock Option Incentive Plans for Employees

A stock option plan for employees that does not meet all four of the characteristics of a non-compensatory plan must be classified and accounted for as a *compensatory* stock option incentive plan. A compensatory stock option incentive plan for employees almost always involves (1) an expense to the grantor corporation in addition to the regular wage and salary expense and (2) additional compensation income to the grantee. In some instances, the option price might be more than the market price of the shares on the measurement date; in these instances, no compensation (or expense) is recorded.

Accounting for compensatory stock option plans requires (1) application of the cost principle to measure and record the total amount of compensation cost during the relevant service period and (2) application of the matching principle to allocate the total compensation cost as a periodic expense throughout the service period of the grantee (from date of grant).

Many diverse and complex specifications are included in the numerous types of compensatory stock option plans that exist. Measurement, recording, and reporting are complex. The discussions and illustrations that follow present the basic distinctions and recording requirements that must be used for all plans. For practical reasons, we do not comprehensively discuss each possibility in the wide range of compensatory plans.

EXHIBIT 21-3   Data for Compensatory Stock Option Plan—Robinson Corporation

---

Plan Specifications and Actual Data for Stock Option Transactions of Executive Corkum:

1. Robinson Corporation—plan specifications—executive stock options:
   a. Options approved for each of 10 designated executives.
   b. 5,000 common shares, no par, for each executive.
   c. Non-transferable, exercisable (i.e., it vests) 5 years after grant and prior to expiration date, which is 10 years from date of grant. Exercise of option requires continuing employment to date exercised.
   d. Option price, $20 per share.
2. On January 1, 1992, Executive Corkum was granted an option for 5,000 shares:
   a. For services to be performed from date of grant to first exercise date (i.e., vesting date) at December 31, 1996 (approximately equal services each year).*
   b. At January 1, 1992, the quoted market price was $30 per share.
   c. The option was exercised by Executive Corkum on December 31, 1996, when the quoted market price per share was $60 (a steady increase during 1992 through 1996).

---

* The vesting date is important because on that date the employee can exercise the option to acquire the shares with no constraints as to continued employment or disposition of the shares.

The various stock option incentive plans may be classified as:

1. **Stock options**—These options give the grantee (i.e., the employee) the right to buy a specified number of common shares of the grantor (i.e., the issuing company) at a specified price per share.
2. **Stock appreciation rights (SARs)**—These rights provide a cash bonus to the employee (grantee) based upon the change in the market value of a specified class of share capital from the date of grant to the exercise date.
3. **Combination plans**—Typically, these plans give the grantee the option to select one alternative from among two or more alternatives, such as to select either stock options or cash (SARs).

To account for any stock option plan, five basic questions must be resolved. To illustrate resolution of these basic questions, a simplified stock option plan for Robinson Corporation is presented in Exhibit 21-3.

Question 1: Is the plan compensatory?

Any plan that fails to meet *one* of the four characteristics of a non-compensatory plan is classified as a compensatory plan.

◆ Robinson Corporation's plan is compensatory because, according to the data given in Exhibit 21-3, it is limited to only 10 executives (not substantially all of the full-time employees), and the discount from the market price of the shares is 33⅓% [i.e., ($30 − $20) ÷ $30]. Discounts associated with non-compensatory plans may range no higher than 15%. Either factor would make the plan compensatory.

Question 2: When should the total compensation cost be measured?

Conceptually, total compensation cost should be measured when the *grantor* forgoes alternative uses (e.g., sale) of the optioned shares. This date is called the *measurement date* under GAAP, as specified by *APB Opinion No. 25* (par. 10). It is "the first date on which are known both (1) the number of shares that an individual employee is entitled to receive and (2) the option price...if any." Both of these specifications are necessary to measure total compensation cost. The measurement date is usually the date of grant. However, a compensation plan may have provisions that cause the measurement date to be later than the date of grant, which introduces accounting complexities.

◆ For Robinson Corporation, the measurement date is the date of grant. On that date, January 1, 1992, both (1) the number of optioned shares (5,000 per executive) and (2) the option price per share ($20) are known (see Exhibit 21-3).

Question 3: What is the amount of total compensation cost?

Total compensation cost for one executive, Mr. Corkum, is determined on the measurement date. It is the difference between the market value of the shares on that date and the option price per share, multiplied by the number of optioned shares.[4] If the market value of the shares is less than the option price on the measurement date, no compensation cost is recorded. If the quoted market price is unavailable, the best estimate of the market value of the shares should be used to measure compensation.

♦ For Robinson Corporation (Exhibit 21–3), total compensation cost on the measurement date (date of grant, January 1, 1992) was $50,000 per executive. That is, the market value of the shares on measurement date, $30, minus the option price, $20, times optioned shares, 5,000, equals $50,000.

Question 4: To what service period should total compensation cost be assigned as periodic expense?

Under the matching principle, total compensation cost should be allocated as periodic expense over a service period that extends from the date of grant to the date on which the employee has no further service obligations or constraints imposed by the stock option incentive plan. Usually, the service period will end at the first date that the option is exercisable (i.e., the vesting date). From that date forward, if the option is exercised, the employee controls the disposition of the shares. Sometimes the compensation plan specifies the service period. If the termination of the service period is not known at the date of grant, the grantor must use a best estimate. The assignment of total compensation cost to periodic expense must begin in the first year and extend through the end of the service period. The service period is not reduced in length by early exercise of the options. When estimates of the service period are used, revisions are accounted for prospectively, as a change in accounting estimate.

♦ For Robinson Corporation, the total compensation cost of $50,000 should be allocated as expense equally to each year of the five-year service period from date of grant (January 1, 1992) to the first exercise date (December 31, 1996). Executive Corkum is required to work for the company during that period.

Question 5: What journal entries should be made by the grantor?

The journal entries to record the effects of a compensatory stock option plan will vary depending upon whether the:

1. measurement date is *on* the date of grant, or
2. measurement date is *after* the date of grant.

Measurement Date on Date of Grant   If the measurement date is on the date of grant, the number of optioned shares, the option price, and the market price of the shares are known. Therefore, total compensation cost can be calculated. Total compensation cost is recorded on the date of grant as a debit to deferred compensation cost and a credit to executive stock options outstanding. These two accounts are reported on the balance sheet under shareholders' equity as follows:

```
Contributed capital:
    Executive stock options outstanding  . . . . . . . . . .  $XXX
    Less: Deferred compensation cost  . . . . . . . . . . .    XX    $X
```

Stock options are reported in the financial statements because the stock options have been issued to the employee but the shares have not been issued. However, the

---

[4] Conceptually, compensation cost should be the market value of stock rights (not the shares themselves). The value of the stock rights cannot be known since there is no market in the options, so the difference between the market price and the option price per share is used as a surrogate valuation.

employee has not yet earned the stock options, and consequently, no owners' equity has been created for the unearned stock options.[5]

For each subsequent period in the employee's service period, total compensation cost is allocated on a straight-line basis. Straight-line allocation is used because it is reasonable to assume that the employee will provide equal service each period.

Exhibit 21–4 illustrates accounting for Robinson Corporation when the measurement date is on the grant date. The exhibit restates the case data and gives the entries required (1) on the measurement date, (2) at each year-end to record the assignment of periodic expense, and (3) on the exercise date. The related reporting is also presented.

Note in Exhibit 21–4 that the "actual incentive compensation earned" by the grantee, Executive Corkum, was ($60 − $20) × 5,000 shares = $200,000. The total additional compensation expense reported by the grantor, Robinson Corporation, was ($30 − $20) × 5,000 shares = $50,000. This comparison shows a basic flaw in the accounting for stock option plans. The total opportunity cost to the corporation of issuing the options is not acknowledged in the financial statements. That is, Robinson could have sold the shares on the open market for $300,000, but was committed to sell them for $100,000. Keep in mind, though, that this opportunity cost of $150,000 [($300,000 − $100,000) − $50,000] is only ascertainable when the options are exercised. The corporation views the transaction at the earlier measurement date, when they have a firm commitment to issue shares at the executive's option.

Measurement Date after Date of Grant If on the date of grant either the number of optioned shares or option price is not known, or if the appropriate market price is not known, total compensation expense cannot be computed. This means that the measurement date must be after the date of grant. Nevertheless, periodic compensation expense must be recorded for each service year from the date of grant. Therefore, between the date of grant and the later measurement date, best estimates of total compensation cost must be used for accounting purposes. At the end of each service year from the date of grant to the later measurement date, the best estimate must be revised. This is done by using the latest year-end share price because this price is considered to be the new best estimate.[6] Also, new estimates may have to be made for either the number of optioned shares or the option price or both. Although changes in accounting estimates are supposed to be spread prospectively over the current and future periods, *FASB Interpretation No. 28,* Appendix B, uses the catch-up method. Application of this method means that when the estimated share price changes, the amount recorded in the prior year must be updated in full in the current year with a catch-up amount.

Exhibit 21–5 illustrates the accounting for Robinson Corporation when the measurement date is later than the date of grant. The exhibit gives the changes assumed in the option plan and the entries at (1) date of grant, January 1, 1992, (2) year-end, to record periodic expense (for the periods of service between the grant date and the later measurement date for which the estimates were made), and (3) exercise date. The *measurement date* is the first date that the options can be exercised, December 31, 1994. The exhibit concludes with the related reporting. Notice that Robinson Corporation had to estimate total compensation cost at the end of 1992 and 1993. To compute

---

[5] *APB Opinion No. 25* (par. 14) also states: "If stock is issued in a plan before some or all of the services are performed, part of the consideration recorded for the stock issued is unearned compensation and should be shown as a *separate reduction of stockholders' equity.* The unearned compensation should be accounted for as expense of the period or periods in which the employee performs service" (italics added).

[6] *FASB Interpretation No. 28,* "Accounting for Stock Appreciation Rights and Other Variable Stock Option or Award Plans" (Stamford, Conn., December 1978). There is some misunderstanding of this interpretation because in par. 18 it prescribes "prospective application" (which is how a change in estimate is treated), but in Appendix B the catch-up (retroactive approach) is illustrated. The change-in-estimate approach spreads the catch-up amounts over the remaining periods on a straight-line basis. The change-in-estimate approach appears to be conceptually and practically preferable, especially when significant increases followed by significant decreases in market prices occur.

EXHIBIT 21–4   Accounting for Compensatory Stock Options, Robinson
Corporation—Measurement Date Is Date of Grant

Case Data:

1. Robinson Corporation—executive stock option incentive plan:
   a. Options approved for each of 10 designated executives.
   b. 5,000 common shares, nopar, for each executive.
   c. Non-transferable, exercisable 5 years after grant and prior to expiration date, which is 10 years from date of grant. Exercise of options requires continuing employment to first exercise date.
   d. Option price, $20 per share.
2. On January 1, 1992, Executive Corkum was granted an option for 5,000 shares:
   a. For services to be performed from date of grant to first exercise (i.e., vesting) date, December 31, 1996 (approximately equal services each year).
   b. At January 1, 1992, the quoted market price was $30 per share.
   c. The option was exercised by Executive Corkum on December 31, 1996, when the quoted market price per share was $60 (a steady increase during 1992 through 1996).

Entries of Robinson Corporation for Stock Option Transactions of Executive Corkum:

1. January 1, 1992—date of grant; to record total deferred compensation expense and the issuance of stock options to Executive Corkum:

Deferred compensation expense		
[($30 − $20) × 5,000 shares]	50,000	
Executive stock options outstanding		
(for 5,000 shares)		50,000

2. December 31, 1992, through 1996—to record the annual allocation of deferred compensation expense to compensation expense (equal amount for each of the five years):

Compensation expense	10,000	
Deferred compensation expense.		10,000
$50,000 ÷ 5 years = $10,000 per year (straight-line because		
approximately equal services each year).		

3. December 31, 1996–exercise date, to record the stock rights tendered by Executive Corkum and issuance of the 5,000 shares:

Cash (5,000 shares × $20 option price)	100,000	
Executive stock options outstanding (for 5,000 shares)	50,000	
Common shares (5,000 shares)		150,000

Reporting in the Financial Statements of 1992

Income Statement:		
Compensation expense		$ 10,000
Balance sheet:		
Contributed capital:		
Common shares, nopar value, authorized no limit, issued		
and outstanding 200,000 shares (assumed).		$2,000,000
Executive stock options outstanding (for		
5,000 common shares)	$50,000	
Less: Deferred compensation expense	40,000	10,000
Other contributed capital (etc.)	(not illustrated)	

Note: For additional disclosures required, see the last section of the chapter.

estimated total compensation expense at the end of 1992 and 1993, the grantor had to use the year-end market price of the shares as the best estimate and a best estimate for the option price. The expense amounts for 1993 and 1994 were computed using the catch-up method. Study Exhibit 21–5 carefully to understand the use of estimates to record periodic compensation expense.

Exhibit 21–6 recaps the approach used to account for stock option plans.

EXHIBIT 21–5 Accounting for Compensatory Stock Options, Robinson Corporation—Measurement Date Subsequent to Date of Grant

Case Data

1. Basic data as given in Exhibit 21–4, except the option price is unspecified.
2. Date of grant to Executive Keaton—January 1, 1992:
    a. A stock option for 5,000 common shares is granted to Executive Keaton, exercisable after 5 years from date of grant and within 10 years from date of grant at which time the option expires.
    b. Option price—to be established on December 31, 1994, by reducing the basic option price of $20 by the percentage increase in net income for 1992 through 1994 (a three-year period).
    c. Additional compensation will be for services rendered from date of grant, January 1, 1992, to the first exercise date, December 31, 1996, assuming approximately equal services each year.
    d. Market price per share on date of grant, $20.
3. Estimates made on December 31, 1992, and December 31, 1993, of the amounts for December 31, 1994, measurement date:
    a. Percentage increase in net income for 1992 through December 31, 1994: 15%.
    b. Resulting estimated option price on December 31, 1994, measurement date: $20 × (1 − .15) = $17 per share.
    c. Market price estimated for December 31, 1994, measurement date: for 1992, use the actual market price on December 31, 1992—$22 per share; for 1993, use the actual market price on December 31, 1993—$24 per share.
4. Actual amounts on December 31, 1994, the measurement date:
    a. Percentage increase in net income for 1992 through December 31, 1994: 10%.
    b. Resulting actual option price: $20 × (1 − .10) = $18 per share.
    c. Market price per share quoted on December 31, 1994: $28.
5. December 31, 1996—Executive Keaton exercised the option on December 31, 1996, when the quoted price per share was $60.

Entries of Robinson Corporation for Stock Option Transactions of Executive Keaton

1. January 1, 1992 (date of grant to Executive Keaton):
    No entry—measurement and recording of compensation expense will begin on December 31, 1992, and will be based on estimated amounts until the measurement date.
2. December 31, 1992—end of period; to record stock options and compensation earned by Executive Keaton during 1992—based on estimated future market price (use actual current market price, $22) and estimated future option price (i.e., $17):

Deferred compensation expense, estimated		
[($22 − $17) × 5,000 shares]	25,000	
Executive stock options outstanding		25,000
Compensation expense [straight-line;		
($25,000 ÷ 5 years)]	5,000	
Deferred compensation expense		5,000

3. December 31, 1993—end of period; to record stock options and compensation earned by Executive Keaton during 1993—based on estimated future market price (use actual current market price, $24) and estimated future option price (i.e., $17):

Deferred compensation expense [($24 − $17) ×		
5,000 shares = $35,000] − $25,000	10,000*	
Executive stock options outstanding		10,000
Compensation expense [($25,000 + $10,000 −		
$5,000) ÷ 4 years]	7,500	
Deferred compensation expense		7,500

4. December 31, 1994—measurement date; to record stock options and compensation earned by Executive Keaton, during 1994—based on actual current market price (i.e., $28) and actual option price (i.e., $18) on the measurement date:

Deferred compensation expense	15,000	
Executive stock options outstanding ([($28 − $18) ×		
5,000 = $50,000] − $25,000 − $10,000)		15,000
Compensation expense [($25,000 + $10,000 + $15,000) −		
($5,000 + $7,500) ÷ 3 years]	12,500	
Deferred compensation expense		12,500

EXHIBIT 21-5   (concluded)

5. December 31, 1995 and 1996—end of period; to record compensation earned by Executive Keaton during 1995 and 1996:

Compensation expense (same as 1994). 12,500
    Deferred compensation expense.   12,500

6. December 31, 1996—exercise date; to record the stock rights tendered by Executive Keaton and the issuance of the 5,000 shares:

Cash ($18 × 5,000 shares). 90,000
Executive stock options outstanding (for 5,000 shares) 50,000
    Common shares (5,000 shares)   140,000

Reporting on 1993 and 1994 Financial Statements

	1993		1994	
Income Statement:				
Compensation expense	$ 7,500		$ 12,500	
Balance Sheet:				
Contributed capital:				
Common shares, nopar, authorized no limit, issued and outstanding 80,000 shares (assumed).	$600,000		$600,000	
Executive stock options outstanding (for 5,000 shares).	$ 35,000**		$ 50,000‡	
Less: Deferred compensation expense	(22,500)†	12,500	(25,000)§	25,000
Other contributed capital, etc. (not illustrated here)				

* Alternate computation:
  Balance required [($24 − $17) × 5,000 shares = $35,000] − $5,000 = $30,000
  Current balance in the account ($25,000 − $5,000) . . . . = 20,000
  Increase needed in account balance $10,000

** $25,000 + $10,000 = $35,000.
† $25,000 − $5,000 + $10,000 − $7,500 = $22,500.
‡ $35,000 + $15,000 = $50,000.
§ $22,500 + $15,000 − $12,500 = $25,000.

Lapse of Stock Options

Employee stock options outstanding may be allowed to *lapse* due to:

1. Failure of an employee to fulfill the option obligations due to severance, disability, or death (i.e., the options now are not exercisable). Such situations should be accounted for as a change in accounting estimates. The credit balance relating to the particular lapsed option carried in the stock options outstanding account, and any related debit balance carried in the deferred compensation cost account, should be removed. The difference should be accounted for as a reduction of compensation expense in the period of forfeiture.
2. Failure to exercise because the option price is higher than the quoted market price of the shares (i.e., it would not be rational to exercise the options). In this situation, the employee has fulfilled the obligations (i.e., services) of the option plan. For example, assume Executive Keaton (Exhibit 21–5) did not exercise the stock rights by the time they were to lapse, December 31, 2001. All compensation expense has been

EXHIBIT 21-6   Shares Issued to Employees—Summarized

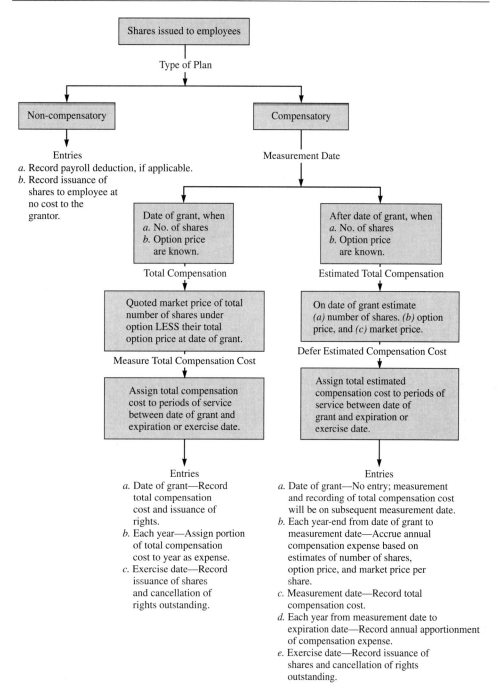

recorded. However, there is a remaining credit balance of $50,000 in executive stock options outstanding. What should be the disposition of this balance on the date of lapse, December 31, 2001? There are no specific standards to cover this situation.

Two approaches are used:

1. Transfer the credit balance of executive stock options outstanding to an appropriately designated account, such as "contributed capital from lapsed stock options." This approach increases permanent capital by the amount of compensation expense on the basis that the employee made a contribution of permanent capital.

2. Allocate the credit balance of executive stock options outstanding to compensation expense of the current period and a reasonable number of future periods as a change in estimate. This approach does not assume that the employee made a contribution to permanent capital. Rather, it assumes that the prior debits to compensation expense (which decreased retained earnings) should be corrected as a change in estimate. This method increases retained earnings rather than permanent capital. This approach is conceptually preferable.

STOCK APPRECIATION RIGHTS

Stock appreciation rights (as previously defined) were developed primarily to provide cash incentives to employees and to take advantage of certain income tax provisions. These plans involve the issuance of *stock appreciation rights* (SARs) that, upon exercise, require the grantor to pay cash (in some cases, either cash or common shares) to the grantee. The amount of cash to be paid is based on the difference between the grant price and the market price of the company's common shares on the exercise date.

From the point of view of the employee, stock appreciation rights have two potential advantages over stock options. First, with SARs the employee does not have to purchase shares as is required with stock options. If a large number of shares are involved, coming up with the cash necessary to exercise a stock option may be a problem for the employee. Second, under a stock option plan, the difference between the market price and the exercise price for the newly acquired shares is considered taxable income for the employee when the shares are acquired. The employee must have the resources to pay the resulting income tax, which presents another cash flow problem, especially if the employee wishes to hold the newly acquired shares. SARs do not require the employee to come up with cash to acquire shares. Rather, cash is paid to the employee. As with stock options, this receipt of cash is immediately considered taxable income for the employee, but the employee has cash in hand to pay the income tax.

SAR plans involve dates similar to stock option incentive plans—grant date, measurement date, exercise date, and year-ends during the service period. Total compensation cost must be allocated to years within the service period, from the date of grant. Neither the market price nor the exercise date is known in advance; estimates must be used each year to record annual compensation expense. Also, because cash will be paid, a liability account labeled "stock appreciation plan liability" replaces the "executive stock options outstanding" equity account that usually is used with stock incentive plans.[7]

To illustrate accounting for SARs, the following simplified example is presented:

On January 1, 1991, Soker Corporation began a stock appreciation rights plan. It specifies that for each SAR, the grantee will receive cash for the difference between the market value per share of the company's common shares on the date the SARs are exercised and the market price per share on the measurement date, which is the date the SARs are granted. The rights require continuing employment and may be exercised at any time between the end of the fourth year after the grant date and the expiration date, at the end of the sixth year after the grant date or when employment is terminated, whichever is earlier. The service period is from the grant date to the earliest exercise date (i.e., the vesting date), or in this case, four years.

On January 1, 1992, the company's common shares have a market price of $10 per share, and Executive Killian is granted 5,000 SARs under the above incentive plan.

---

[7] The entries used for stock option incentive plans usually are set up on the deferral basis (see Exhibit 21–4). In contrast, SARs usually are set up on the accrual basis as illustrated here. Either approach may be used in either situation because the entries can be made so that their net effects (but not detailed effects) are the same.

Killian exercises the SARs on December 31, 1995. Relevant year-end market prices of Soker common shares are as follows:

Year-end	Price per Share
1992	$11.00
1993	13.50
1994	12.00
1995	14.00
1996	12.00

First, we must determine whether this a compensatory plan or a non-compensatory plan. Since the plan does not apply to all employees, it is a compensatory plan. Therefore, it will create compensation expense for the grantor and additional compensation income for the grantee. Next, the earliest possible measurement date must be determined in order to establish a service period. Since the earliest exercise date is four years after the grant date, the service period is four years, and the earliest measurement date is December 31, 1995. Since this is the date that Executive Killian exercises the SARs, we can compute the total actual compensation to be 5,000 SARs times the difference between the price on the exercise date ($14 per share) less the price on the grant date ($10 per share), or $5,000 \times (\$14 - \$10)$ equals $20,000.

To compute the compensation expense for each year we need to know the year-end market price of common shares and the portion of the service period that has expired. With this information we can compute the total amount of compensation expense that must be accrued to the end of the current year, which will be labeled as "stock appreciation rights liability":

$$\begin{matrix} \text{Stock appreciation} \\ \text{rights liability} \\ \text{(to date)} \end{matrix} = \begin{matrix} \text{No. of} \\ \text{SARs granted} \end{matrix} \times \left[\begin{matrix} \text{Market price} \\ \text{per share at} \\ \text{end of} \\ \text{current year} \end{matrix} - \begin{matrix} \text{Market price} \\ \text{per share at} \\ \text{grant date} \end{matrix} \right] \times \begin{matrix} \text{Percent of} \\ \text{period of} \\ \text{service} \\ \text{completed} \\ \text{to date} \end{matrix}$$

After computing the amount to be accrued as the SAR liability for the end of the current year, the current year compensation expense equals the accrual at the end of the current year less the accrual at the end of the prior year. A schedule of these computations for Soker Company is as follows:

(1) Year	(2) Year-End Market Price	(3) Difference from Grant Date Price	(4) Aggregate Compensation to Date (Col. 3 × No. of SARs Granted)	(5) Percent Accrued (Percent of Service Period Expired)	(6) SAR Liability Accrued to Year-End (Col. 4 × Col. 5)	(7) Annual Compensation Expense (Current Liability Minus Prior Year Liability)
1992	$11.00	$1.00	$5,000	25%	$1,250	$1,250
1993	$13.50	$3.50	$17,500	50%	$8,750	$7,500
1994	$12.00	$2.00	$10,000	75%	$7,500	$(1,250)
1995	$14.00	$4.00	$20,000	100%	$20,000	$12,500

The annual compensation expense is equal to the SAR liability at the end of the current year less the SAR liability at the end of the prior year. When the market price of common shares declines as it does in this example in 1994, the total accrued liability is reduced. In this year, there will be a credit to compensation expense and a debit entry to the SAR liability. In the extreme event that the market price falls below the market price at the grant date, the stock appreciation plan liability account would be reduced to zero with an offsetting credit to compensation expense.

The journal entries to record the compensation expense resulting from the SARs for the four years would be:

1992:

Compensation expense	1,250	
Stock appreciation plan liability		1,250

1993:

Compensation expense	7,500	
Stock appreciation plan liability		7,500

1994:

Stock appreciation plan liability	1,250	
Compensation expense		1,250

1995:

Compensation expense	12,500	
Stock appreciation plan liability		12,500

SARs require use of yearly common share market values and result in the accrual of the entire value of the SAR to the employee, and the cash cost to the grantor. This is inconsistent with the rules for stock option plans—the latter identify a cost only on the measurement date. This inconsistency is troubling, as with essentially the same economic effects, the company may report significantly different (1) total compensation expense, (2) patterns of compensation expense for each year in the service period, and (3) amounts and items on the balance sheet.

ADDITIONAL DISCLOSURES REQUIRED FOR STOCK OPTION PLANS (NON-COMPENSATORY AND COMPENSATORY)

◆

Grantor companies must disclose certain information about their stock option plans. The purpose of these disclosures is to inform existing and potential investors and creditors of the company's obligation to make such shares available to employees under existing option plans. This information would be important, for example, to an investor contemplating the purchase of a controlling interest in the company. Based on the full-disclosure principle, the required disclosures are:

1. The status of the option plan at the end of the period.
2. The number of shares under option.
3. The option price.
4. The number of shares into which options are exercisable.
5. The number of shares exercised during the period and the option price thereof.

Hayes Dana reported the following information on its compensatory stock option plan for the year ended December 31, 1989:

Stock options: The Corporation has a stock option plan through which options have been granted to officers and other key employees for the purchase of common shares. Options may be granted at prices equal to the market value at the date of the grant and are exercisable during periods of ten years from such date.

The following options to purchase were outstanding as at December 31:

Expiry date	Option price per share	Number of Shares 1989	1988	1987
June 3, 1988	$ 6.125	—	—	56,500
July 10, 1995	12.000	84,475	107,900	110,000
July 10, 1997	12.000	85,813	98,100	100,100
July 12, 1999	15.125	99,350	—	—
		269,638	206,000	266,600

Stock option transactions for the respective years were as follows:

	1989	1988	1987
Outstanding at beginning of year:.	**206,000**	266,600	195,650
Granted	**99,650**	—	100,350
Exercised	**(31,012)**	(54,200)	(23,250)
Cancelled	**(5,000)**	(6,400)	(6,150)
Outstanding at end of year	**269,638**	206,000	266,600
Cash consideration received on options exercised . . .	**$372**	$332	$142
Shares reserved for future stock option grants. . . .	**198,975**	293,625	289,525

Of the options outstanding at December 31, 1989, 97,000 (1988—76,000; 1987—82,000) share options were held by nine officers, of whom one is a director.

CONCEPT REVIEW

1. When is a stock option plan compensatory?
2. A corporation issued 1,000 options to buy one common share at $10. The market value of a common share was $11 at the grant date and $100 at the exercise date, 10 years later. How much compensation expense would be recorded by the corporation over the 10-year period? How much did the employee benefit from the plan?

SUMMARY OF KEY POINTS

◆

(L.O. 1)   1. Retained earnings, also occasionally called *earnings invested in the business,* generally represents the accumulated net income or net loss and prior period adjustments of a corporation, less the sum of dividends declared since the inception of the corporation.

(L.O. 1)   2. Retained earnings are either appropriated or unappropriated.

(L.O. 2)   3. Dividends are distributions of cash, non-cash assets, or the corporation's own shares, distributed to shareholders in proportion to the number of outstanding shares of each class of shares held by each shareholder.

(L.O. 2)   4. The relevant dates for dividends are:
   a. The declaration date—the date the corporation's board of directors formally announces the dividend.
   b. The date of record—the date on which the list of shareholders entitled to a dividend will be prepared.
   c. The ex-dividend date—the date after the date of record on which the shares will trade without the right to receive the declared dividend.
   d. The date of payment—the date on which distribution of dividends to the list of shareholders of record actually occurs.

(L.O. 2)   5. The declaration of cash or property dividends other than stock dividends by the board of directors creates a liability for the corporation as of the date of declaration.

(L.O. 2)   6. Liquidating dividends are a return of capital rather than a return on capital. They represent a reduction of the paid-in capital of the corporation.

(L.O. 2)   7. Scrip dividends are a declaration of the intention of the corporation to pay a cash dividend at some specified date in the future. Scrip in the form of a promissory note is issued by the corporation to shareholders at the date of declaration. Interest expense accrues on the scrip dividend amounts between the declaration date and the payment date.

(L.O. 3)   8. Stock dividends are proportional issuances of additional share capital to shareholders. Stock dividends may be recorded at the market value of the shares, at a stated amount approved by the board of directors, or in a memo entry. In general, small stock dividends (less than 20 or 25%) are recorded at market value, while large dividends are recorded in a memo entry.

(L.O. 3)   9. A stock split is a change in the number of shares outstanding. There is no resulting change in the corporation's share capital accounts. A memo entry reflects the larger number of outstanding shares.

(L.O. 4)   10. Appropriations of retained earnings are the result of the corporation's voluntary action to constrain a portion of retained earnings for some specific purpose. Restrictions of retained earnings result from contractual or legal agreements wherein a portion of retained earnings cannot be paid out in dividends.

(L.O. 5)   11. Stock rights are privileges awarded to various individuals or shareholders to acquire a specified number of shares at a specified price during a specified period of time.

(L.O. 5)   12. Many corporations have stock option incentive plans for employees. Such plans are either compensatory or non-compensatory. If the plans are compensatory, they result in compensation expense for the grantor and income for the grantee. Non-compensatory plans do not result in compensation expense or income to the recipient.

(L.O. 5)   13. Non-compensatory plans must have several characteristics:
a. Substantially all employees must be included.
b. Shares are offered to all eligible employees essentially equally or based on a percentage of salary or wages.
c. The time for exercising the option is of reasonable length.
d. The discount on the purchase price is small, generally 15% or less.

(L.O. 5)   14. Compensation expense for stock options is allocated over the service period from the grant date to the date at which the employee has no further service obligations or constraints under the stock option plan. For any given period within the service period, a best estimate of total compensation expense is used to determine the allocation. As this estimate changes from period to period, a catch-up method is used to determine the current period allocation.

(L.O. 6)   15. Stock appreciation rights require the grantor to pay cash or common shares to the grantee based on the difference between the grant price and the market price of the common shares on the exercise date. SARs are usually compensatory, and as such result in compensation expense for the corporation and income to the recipient.

(L.O. 7)   16. A quasi reorganization is a procedure in which a corporation, usually one that has a deficit in retained earnings, can establish a new basis of accounting for its assets, liabilities, and shareholders' equity, and in the process have a fresh accounting start with a retained earnings balance of zero immediately after the quasi reorganization (see Appendix 21A).

REVIEW PROBLEM

◆

The Bionic Company has the following shareholders' equity section as of December 31, 1992:

Shareholders' Equity

Contributed capital:
Preferred shares, nopar, $8, cumulative, voting; unlimited
   shares authorized, 10,000 shares issued and outstanding $1,050,000
Common shares, nopar; unlimited shares authorized,
   70,000 shares issued and outstanding 2,150,000

   Total paid-in capital. 3,200,000
   Retained earnings. 3,000,000

Total shareholders' equity $6,200,000

There are no dividends in arrears on the preferred shares.

1. Earnings during 1993 were $600,000. The board of directors declared a cash dividend totaling $280,000 to be paid as appropriate to preferred and common shareholders. In addition, a stock dividend of 10% is declared on the common shares. The market value of common shares is $68 per share.
2. In order to familiarize shareholders with one of the company's new products and to reduce inventory, the board declares and distributes a property dividend of one ounce of a new perfume the company produces for every outstanding common share before the above stock dividend. The cost of the perfume is $6.00 per ounce, and it has an established wholesale market value of $10.00 per ounce.
3. Subsequent to the end of 1993 and the above transactions, the board declares a 3 for 2 stock split. The market value of common shares is $75 per share at the time.

Required:
1. Show all computations and entries to record the above transactions.
2. Show the shareholders' equity section as of December 31, 1993.

**REVIEW
SOLUTION**
◆

1. Computations and entries:
   a. To close the 1993 earnings to retained earnings:

   Income summary 600,000
        Retained earnings   600,000

   b. To compute and record cash dividends payable to preferred and common shareholders:

Total amount of dividends to be paid	$280,000
Preferred shareholder dividends: 10,000 × $8	(80,000)
Common dividends	$200,000

   The entry to record dividends payable:

   Retained earnings. 280,000
        Dividends payable (preferred).   80,000
        Dividends payable (common)   200,000

   c. To compute and record stock dividend: The number of shares to be issued as a stock dividend is:

   70,000 shares outstanding × .10 = 7,000 shares.

   Since the stock dividend is small, it is to be recorded at market value. The amount to be capitalized as permanent capital is:

   7,000 shares × $68 per share = $476,000

   The entry is:

   Retained earnings. 476,000
        Common shares, nopar (7,000 shares)   476,000

2. Computations and entries to record the property dividend: The property dividend is to be recorded at market value, with the gain being recorded for the amount by which the market value of the perfume exceeds the book value:

Market value of property dividend (70,000 × $10)	$700,000
Cost of property dividend (70,000 × $6).	(420,000)
Gain on disposal of inventory.	$280,000

The entries to record the property dividend are:

a. Record the gain when dividend declared:

Inventory held for property dividend. 700,000		
Inventory, at cost	420,000	
Gain on disposal of inventory		
(closed to retained earnings).	280,000	

b. Record declaration of dividend:

Retained earnings. 700,000	
Property dividend payable.	700,000

c. When property dividend is distributed:

Property dividend payable 700,000	
Inventory held for property dividend.	700,000

3. The three-for-two stock split occurs after all the above transactions; therefore, the number of common shares to be split is 70,000 plus the 10% stock dividend (7,000 shares), or a total of 77,000 shares. Every two shares outstanding will become three new shares; hence, there will be 77,000 times $\frac{3}{2}$, or 115,500 new shares outstanding after the split. The stock split is recorded in a memo entry as follows:

Three-for-two split authorized by board of directors; outstanding shares increased from 77,000 to 115,500.

There is no change in paid-in capital and no capitalization of retained earnings for this transaction. Paid-in capital, $2,626,000 ($2,150,000 + $476,000) equalled $34.10 per share ($2,626,000/77,000) before the split and is $22.73 ($2,626,000/115,500) per share after the split. One would expect a corresponding decline in market price per share.

The Bionic Company has the following shareholders' equity section as of December 31, 1993:

Shareholders' Equity

Contributed capital:	
Preferred shares, nopar, $8, cumulative, voting; unlimited	
shares authorized, 10,000 shares issued and outstanding	$1,050,000
Common shares, nopar; unlimited shares authorized,	
115,500 shares issued and outstanding.	2,626,000
Total paid-in capital.	3,676,000
Retained earnings*	2,424,000
Total shareholders' equity	$6,100,000

*($3,000,000 + $600,000 − $280,000 − $476,000 − $700,000 + $280,000).

It is assumed that the earnings figure of $600,000 does not include the $280,000 gain on disposal of inventory connected with the property dividend.

APPENDIX 21A: *Quasi Reorganization*

If a corporation has sustained heavy losses over an extended period of time that cause a significant *deficit* in retained earnings, and there are unrealistic carrying values for assets, a quasi reorganization may be desirable.

Quasi reorganization is a procedure whereby a corporation, without *formal* court proceedings of dissolution, can establish a new basis of accounting for assets, liabilities, and shareholders' equity. In effect, a quasi reorganization is an accounting reorganization in which a fresh start is reflected in the accounts with respect to certain assets, liabilities, legal capital, and retained earnings. For example, Argyl Energy Corporation eliminated its deficit position as of January 1, 1987:

Consolidated Statement of Deficit

	Year Ended December 31	
	1987	**1986**
Retained earnings (deficit) at beginning of year	$(3,572,998)	$ 4,817,460
Reduction of stated capital	3,572,998	—
Loss for the year	(178,432)	(8,225,052)
Dividends on Series 1 Preference shares	(175,910)	(165,406)
Deficit at end of year	$ (354,342)	$(3,572,998)

The $3,572,998 transfer came from Class A non-voting shares, which were reduced by $3,105,178, and Class B voting shares, which were reduced by $467,820. No asset values were changed.

The Committee on Accounting Procedure of the AICPA recognized the procedure, provided it is properly safeguarded.[8] The Securities and Exchange Commission also recognized quasi reorganization and listed certain associated safeguards or conditions:

1. Retained earnings immediately after the quasi reorganization must be zero.
2. Upon completion of the quasi reorganization, no deficit shall remain in any corporate capital account.
3. The effects of the whole procedure shall be made known to all shareholders entitled to vote and appropriate approval in advance obtained from them.
4. A fair and conservative balance sheet shall be presented as of the date of the reorganization, and the readjustment of values should be reasonably complete, in order to obviate as far as possible future readjustments of like nature.[9]

Creditor approval must also be obtained in most jurisdictions.

The accounting guidelines to record a quasi reorganization are (1) the recorded values relating to appropriately selected assets are restated; (2) the capital accounts (and occasionally the liabilities) are restated, and the retained earnings account is restated to a zero balance; and (3) the corporate entity itself is unchanged.[10] Subsequent to a quasi reorganization there must be full disclosure in the financial statements for the year of reorganization of the reorganization procedure and its effects. Also, the retained earnings amount must be "dated" for a period of 3 to 10 years after the reorganization date, as illustrated in Exhibit 21A–1.

In the case data presented in Exhibit 21A–1, the company could consider two alternatives (note the $400,000 debit balance in retained earnings). First, the corporation could be *dissolved,* pay creditors, and then form a new corporation. The new corporation would receive the remaining assets and report their total amount as the shareholders' equity of the new corporation.

Alternatively, the corporation may undergo a *quasi reorganization* (without dissolution). This would be less cumbersome and less expensive than legal reorganization. By complying with the conditions set forth above, including creditor and shareholder approval, the quasi reorganization may be effected without paying off the creditors at this time. The entries needed are reflected in Exhibit 21A–1. That exhibit also shows the restated balance sheet amounts immediately after the quasi reorganization. The quasi reorganization restatements of specific account balances are transferred to retained earnings. Retained earnings then is restated to a zero balance, and legal capital is reduced accordingly.

In general, a quasi reorganization is justified when (1) a large deficit from operations exists, (2) there is approval from shareholders and creditors, (3) the cost basis of accounting for operational assets becomes unrealistic in terms of going-concern values,[11] (4) a break in continuity of the historical cost basis clearly is needed so that realistic financial reporting is possible, (5) the retained earnings balance is totally inadequate to absorb an obvious decrease in going-concern

---

[8] *ARB No. 43,* Chapter 7, Section A.

[9] Securities and Exchange Commission, *Accounting Series Release 25.*

[10] For a detailed treatment of quasi reorganization, see J. S. Schindler, *Quasi-Reorganization* (Michigan Business Studies, vol. 13, no. 5) (Ann Arbor: Bureau of Business Research, University of Michigan, 1958).

[11] The *CICA Handbook,* Section 3060, "Capital Assets," specifies that such assets are to be recorded at cost. If the net book value exceeds recoverable amounts, a write-down is necessary.

EXHIBIT 21A-1   Accounting for a Quasi Reorganization

Case Data

1. At January 1, 1995, immediately prior to quasi reorganization:

Balance sheet:

Current assets.	$ 200,000
Operational assets.	1,300,000
	$1,500,000
Liabilities.	$ 300,000
Share capital	1,600,000
Retained earnings.	(400,000)
	$1,500,000

2. The inventories are overvalued by $50,000, and the carrying value of the operational assets should be reduced by $350,000.

Entries and Balances:

Accounts	Balances before Quasi Reorganization	Entries to Record Quasi Reorganization*				Balances after Quasi Reorganization
Current assets	$ 200,000			(a)	$ 50,000	$ 150,000
Operational assets	1,300,000			(b)	350,000	950,000
Total assets	$1,500,000					$1,100,000
Liabilities	$ 300,000					$ 300,000
Share capital	1,600,000	(c)	$800,000			800,000
Retained earnings (deficit)	(400,000)	(a)	50,000			(Note 1)
		(b)	350,000	(c)	800,000	
Total liabilities and shareholders' equity	$1,500,000					$1,100,000

Note 1 (on balance sheet): Retained earnings represents accumulations since January 1, 1995, at which time a $400,000 deficit was eliminated as a result of quasi reorganization.

* Explanation of entries:

(a) To write down a current asset (inventory) by $50,000.

(b) To write down an operational asset by $350,000.

(c) To bring retained earnings up to a zero balance and to restate share capital by the same amount (i.e., $400,000 + $50,000 + $350,000 = $800,000). This leaves share capital at $800,000, the amount necessary to reconcile the basic accounting model after quasi reorganization.

asset values, and (6) a fresh start, in the accounting sense, appears to be desirable or advantageous to all parties who are concerned with the corporation. A quasi reorganization usually is supervised by a court to assure adequate protection of the interests of all parties. Because contributed capital, as measured in the accounts, is reduced in a quasi reorganization, all concerned parties seek equity through court supervision to avoid future litigation.

KEY TERMS

Appropriated retained earnings (1044)	Restricted retained earnings (1044)
Cash dividend (1033)	Scrip dividend (1036)
Compensatory stock option plans (1051)	Spin-off (1034)
Liquidating dividends (1035)	Stock appreciation rights (1060)
Non-compensatory stock option plans (1051)	Stock dividend (1037)
	Stock rights (1048)
Property dividend (1034)	Stock split (1043)
Quasi reorganization (1066)	

QUESTIONS

1. Explain what an appropriation of retained earnings is, and why it is done.
2. What are the principal sources and uses of retained earnings?

3. Differentiate between total retained earnings and the balance of the retained earnings account.
4. What are the four important dates relative to dividends? Explain the significance of each.
5. Distinguish between cash dividends, property dividends, and liability or scrip dividends.
6. What is a liquidating dividend? What are the responsibilities of the accountant with respect to such dividends?
7. Explain the difference between intentional and unintentional liquidating dividends.
8. What is the difference between a cash or property dividend and a stock dividend?
9. When property dividends are declared and paid, a loss or gain often must be reported. Explain this statement. How is a spin-off treated?
10. Explain how interest paid on a liability or scrip dividend is recorded.
11. Contrast the effects of a stock dividend (declared and issued) versus a cash dividend (declared and paid) on assets, liabilities, and total shareholders' equity.
12. Contrast the effects of a typical small stock dividend (declared and issued) versus a typical cash dividend (declared and paid) on the components of shareholders' equity.
13. Explain why the amount of retained earnings reported on the balance sheet often is not the net amount of all accumulated earnings (and losses) less all accumulated cash and property dividends.
14. Distinguish between a stock dividend and a stock split.
15. What should happen to the market price of a common share after a stock dividend? Is this always the case?
16. Explain the distinction between (a) a bond sinking fund and (b) an appropriation of retained earnings for bond retirement.
17. What items are properly reported on the statement of retained earnings?
18. Is the following statement correct? "Retained earnings was reduced by the $10,000 appropriated for plant expansion." Explain.
19. Does a bond sinking fund cause a restriction on retained earnings? Explain.
20. What is the difference between stock rights and stock warrants?
21. Can stock rights usually be bought and sold? Explain.
22. List the three important dates with respect to stock rights. When will the related shares sell (a) rights on and (b) ex rights?
23. List the primary situations when stock rights are used.
24. Explain how the following account should be reported: "Stock rights outstanding (for 100 shares), $3,000."
25. Stock option incentive plans for employees may be either non-compensatory or compensatory. Briefly explain each.
26. Give the two primary accounting principles that underlie the accounting for compensatory stock option incentive plans for employees. Identify their application.
27. What is the measurement date for a compensatory stock option incentive plan? Why is it sometimes later than the date of grant?
28. How is the amount of total compensation expense in a stock option plan calculated?
29. Why are estimates necessary when the measurement date is later than the date of grant of a compensatory stock option?
30. What are stock appreciation rights?
31. What is a quasi reorganization? What accounts normally change?

EXERCISES

E 21–1
Overview:
Subclassifications of
Shareholders' Equity
(L.O. 1)

Shareholders' equity has the following subclassifications:

A. Share capital.
B. Additional contributed capital (excluding donated capital).
C. Donated capital.
D. Retained earnings.
E. Retained earnings appropriated.
F. Unrealized capital.
G. Unallocated deduction.

Match each item below with the letter above that corresponds to its proper classification within shareholders' equity. Use NA if the above classifications are not applicable (give explanations if needed):

1. _____ Net loss.
2. _____ Restriction on retained earnings.
3. _____ Goodwill.
4. _____ Extraordinary item.
5. _____ Cash dividends declared, not paid.
6. _____ Bond sinking fund.
7. _____ Excess of retirement price over original issue proceeds, retired shares.
8. _____ Plant site given by Twin City.
9. _____ Net income.
10. _____ Correction of accounting error.
11. _____ Excess of original issue proceeds over retirement price, retired shares.
12. _____ Proceeds on share issuance.
13. _____ Subscribed stock.
14. _____ Stock dividends declared, not issued.
15. _____ Prior period adjustment.

E 21–2
Property Dividend Recorded: Common and Preferred Shares (L.O. 2)

The records of Frost Corporation showed the following at the end of 1993:

Preferred shares, $1.20, cumulative, non-participating, nopar value
 (10,000 shares issued and outstanding) $230,000
Common shares, nopar value (50,000 shares issued and outstanding) 240,000
Retained earnings 125,000
Investment in shares of Ace Corporation (500 shares at cost). 10,000

The preferred shares are in arrears for 1991 and 1992. On January 15, 1993, the board of directors approved the following resolution: "The 1993 dividend, to shareholders of record on February 1, 1993, shall be $1.20 on the preferred and $1.00 per share on the common; the dividends in arrears are to be paid on March 1, 1993, by issuing a property dividend using the requisite amount of Ace Corporation shares. All current dividends for 1993 are to be paid in cash on March 1, 1993." On January 15, 1993, the shares of Ace Corporation were selling at $60 per share and at $62 on March 1, 1993.

Required:

1. Compute the amount of the dividends to be paid to each class of shareholder, including the number of shares of Ace Corporation and the amount of cash required by the declaration. Assume that divisibility of the shares of Ace Corporation poses no problem.
2. Give journal entries to record all aspects of the dividend declaration and its subsequent payment.

E 21–3
Cash Dividend Recorded: Return of Capital, Entries (L.O. 2)

On December 1, 1992, the board of directors of Jax Mining Company declared the maximum cash dividend permitted by their articles of incorporation. The company had never declared a dividend prior to this time. There were 100 shareholders, each holding 200 shares with nopar value. The articles provided that "dividends may be paid equal to all accumulated profits prior to the depletion amount." Retained earnings showed a correct balance of $60,000; depletion for the year amounted to $12,000 (accumulated depletion was $20,000). The dividend was payable 60 days after declaration date.

Required:

1. Give all entries related to the dividend through the payment date.
2. What special notification, if any, should be given the shareholders?
3. What items related to the dividend declaration would be reported on a balance sheet dated December 31, 1992, assuming net income for 1992 of $15,000 (included in the $60,000 balance of retained earnings given above)? Write any note that may be needed to fully disclose the dividend.

E 21–4
Cash and Scrip Dividend: Entries (L.O. 2)

On September 1, 1994, Fox Corporation declared a cash dividend of $2 per share on its 400,000 outstanding common shares. The dividend is payable on December 1, 1994, to shareholders of record as of October 1, 1994, as follows: one-fourth cash and the balance with scrip, which will be paid on June 30, 1995, plus 12% annual interest starting on the cash payment date. The annual accounting period ends December 31. The amount in the retained earnings account is adequate for payment of the dividend.

Required:

Give all required journal entries, through final payment, directly related to this dividend.

E 21–5
Stock Dividend Recorded:
Dates Cross Two Periods
(L.O. 3)

The records of Round Corporation showed the following balances on November 1, 1992:

Share capital, nopar, 30,000 shares $402,000
Retained earnings   200,000

On November 5, 1992, the board of directors declared a stock dividend to the shareholders of record as of December 20, 1992, of one additional share for each five shares already outstanding; issue date, January 10, 1993. The market value of the shares was $18 per share. The annual accounting period ends December 31. The stock dividend is recorded on the distribution date.

Required:

1. Give entries in parallel columns for the stock dividend assuming: *Case A*— market value is capitalized; *Case B*— $10 per share is capitalized; and *Case C*— average paid in is capitalized.
2. Explain when each value should be used.
3. In respect to the stock dividend, what should be reported on the balance sheet at December 31, 1992?

E 21–6
Stock Dividend with
Fractional Share Rights:
Entries and Reporting
(L.O. 3)

The accounts of WP Corporation provide the following data at December 31, 1993:

Share capital, nopar; authorized shares, 100,000;
  issued and outstanding, 20,000 shares. $180,000
Retained earnings.   150,000

On May 1, 1994, the board of directors of WP Corporation declared a 50% stock dividend (i.e., for each two shares already outstanding, one additional share is to be issued) to be issued on June 1, 1994. The stock dividend is to be recorded at distribution and capitalized at the average of contributed capital per share at December 31, 1993.

On June 1, 1994, all of the required shares were issued for the stock dividend, except for those required by 1,300 fractional share rights (representing 650 full shares) issued.

On December 1, 1994, the company honoured 1,000 of the fractional share rights by issuing the requisite number of shares. The remaining fractional share rights were still outstanding at the end of 1994.

Required:

1. Give the required entries by WP Corporation at each of the following dates:
   a. May 1, 1994.
   b. June 1, 1994.
   c. December 1, 1994.
2. Prepare the shareholders' equity section of the balance sheet at December 31, 1994, assuming net income for 1994 was $30,000.
3. Assume instead that the fractional share rights specified that (*a*) two such rights could be turned in for one share without cost or (*b*) each right could be turned in for $2.50 cash. As a result, 900 rights were turned in for shares, 200 rights for cash, and the remainder (200 rights) lapsed. Give the entry to record the ultimate disposition of all the fractional share rights.

E 21–7
Stock Dividend and Stock
Split: Effects Compared
(L.O. 3)

Uncertain Corporation has the following shareholders' equity:

Share capital, nopar, 20,000 shares outstanding $310,000
Retained earnings.   500,000
  Total shareholders' equity. $810,000

The corporation decided to triple the number of shares currently outstanding (to 60,000 shares) by taking one of the following alternative and independent actions:

a. Issue a 200% (two-for-one) stock dividend (40,000 additional shares) and capitalize retained earnings on the basis of $12 per share.
b. Issue a three-for-one stock split (that is, three new shares issued for each old share replaced).

Required:

1. Give the entry that should be made for each alternative action. If none is necessary, explain why. On the stock split, the old shares are called in, and the new shares are issued to replace them.

2. For each alternative, prepare a schedule that reflects the shareholders' equity immediately after the change. For this requirement, complete the following schedule, which is designed to compare the effects of the alternative actions:

Item	Before Change	After Stock Dividend	After Stock Split
Shares outstanding			
Share capital	$	$	$
Retained earnings	$	$	$
Total shareholders' equity	$	$	$

Be prepared to explain and compare the effects among the columns in the above schedule.

E 21–8
Appropriations and Restrictions of Retained Earnings: Entries (L.O. 4)

TV Corporation carries separate accounts for appropriations and restrictions of retained earnings. One such account is "Reserve for profits invested in operational assets . . . $420,000." Share capital outstanding, 20,000 shares of nopar value common, amounted to $400,000.

The company had bonds payable outstanding of $200,000. The following accounts were also carried: "Bond sinking fund . . . $100,000"; and "Bond sinking fund reserve . . . $100,000."

The board of directors voted a 10% stock dividend and directed that the market value of the shares, $130 per share, be capitalized, using as a basis "the reserves for profits invested in operational assets" to the extent possible.

Required:

Give entries for the following, using preferable titles:

a. To originally establish the reserve related to operational assets.
b. To record the issuance of the stock dividend.
c. To originally establish the bond sinking fund.
d. To originally establish the reserve for the bond sinking fund.
e. To record payment of the bonds, assuming the bond sinking fund and the reserve each have a $180,000 balance at retirement date.

E 21–9
Prepare an Income Statement and Statement of Retained Earnings (L.O. 1, 4)

Using the simplified data below for the year ended December 31, 1994, prepare (1) a single-step income statement and (2) a statement of retained earnings. Assume all amounts are material and are annual data.

Current items (pretax):
a. Sales revenue $800,000
b. Cost of goods sold 320,000
c. Expenses 240,000
d. Extraordinary loss (pretax) 40,000
e. Prior period adjustment—correction of error in recording income
   taxes of a prior year; income tax was understated 4,000
f. Restriction for bond sinking fund (increase) 10,000
g. Dividends declared and paid 60,000
Balances—beginning of period:
h. Retained earnings (unappropriated) 260,000
i. Restriction for bond sinking fund 120,000
Income taxes—assume a 40% average rate.

Average number of common shares outstanding during the year, 40,000.

E 21–10
Sale of Shares, Stock Rights Issued, and Some Lapses: Entries (L.O. 5)

Lytle Corporation has outstanding 50,000 common shares, nopar value. On January 15, 1991, the company announced its decision to sell an additional 25,000 unissued common shares at $15 per share and to give the current shareholders first chance to buy shares proportionally equivalent to the number now held. To facilitate this plan, on February 1, 1991, each shareholder was issued one right for each common share currently held. Two rights must be submitted to acquire one additional share for $15. Rights not exercised lapse on June 30, 1991.

Required:

Give any entry or memorandum that should be made in the accounts of Lytle Corporation on each of the following dates:

January 15, 1991, the date of the announcement.

February 1, 1991, issuance of all rights. At this date, the shares of Lytle Corporation were quoted on the market at $12.50 per share.

June 27, 1991, exercise by current shareholders of 98% of the rights issued.

June 30, 1991, the remaining rights outstanding lapsed.

E 21–11
Employee Stock Purchase
Plan—Compensatory?
Entries
(L.O. 5)

Davis Corporation has a stock purchase plan with the following provisions:

Each full-time employee, with a minimum of one year's service, may acquire from Davis Corporation its common shares, nopar value, through payroll deductions at 10% below the market price on the date selected by the employee for a share purchase (i.e., the exercise date). The exercise decision must be made within one year from the payroll deduction date.

Employee Adam signed a payroll deduction form on January 1, 1993, for $60 per month. At that date, the market price of the shares was $27. Assume a monthly salary of $2,000 and other payroll deductions in the aggregate of 18%. At the end of 1993, Adam requested that shares be purchased equal to the amount accumulated to Adam's credit. At that date, the market price of the shares was $25.

Required:

1. Is this a compensatory plan? If yes, how much should be recorded as additional compensation for Adam? Explain.
2. How many shares will Adam acquire for the 1993 deductions? Show computations.
3. Give entries to record (*a*) one monthly payroll and (*b*) issuance of the shares for the year, assuming unissued shares are used.

E 21–12
Stock Incentive
Plan—Compensatory?
Analysis and Entries
(L.O. 5)

Rex Corporation is authorized to issue unlimited common shares, nopar value, of which 140,000 shares have been issued. The corporation initiated a stock bonus plan during 1991 for designated managers. Each manager will receive stock options to purchase 1,000 Rex common shares, if still employed by the company, any time after two years from date of grant, January 1, 1991. The rights are non-transferable and expire immediately after December 31, 1995. The option price is $20 per share; the market price on the date of grant was $24. The services will be rendered approximately equally over the five-year period ending December 31, 1995.

Required:

1. Is this a non-compensatory plan? Explain.
2. What is the measurement date? Explain.
3. What is the amount of total compensation cost for each manager (e.g., Manager Roe)?
4. Over what period should this compensation cost (for Manager Roe) be assigned as expense? How much should be assigned to 1991 and 1992? Explain.
5. What entry should be made on the date of grant (for Manager Roe)?
6. What entry should be made on December 31, 1991 (for Manager Roe)?
7. Give the entry to record the exercise of the option by Manager Roe on December 31, 1995, when the market price of the common was $80 per share.
8. How much actual "incentive pay" did Manager Roe receive? How much additional compensation expense did Rex Corporation report?

E 21–13
Performance Option
Plan—Measurement Date?
Analysis and Entries
(L.O. 5)

In October 1991, Meno Corporation announced a stock option incentive plan for its six top executives. The plan provided each executive 3,000 stock options for Meno's common shares, nopar value, at a standard option price of $36 per share reduced by the percentage increase in EPS from December 31, 1991, to December 31, 1993. The rights are non-transferable and are exercisable three years after the grant date and prior to five years from the date of grant. Continuing employment is required through to the exercise date, and the service period ends on the first possible exercise date. EPS must increase over the period for the options to be valid.

On January 1, 1992, Executive Smith was granted 3,000 options when the market price was $30 per share. On December 31, 1992, Meno's management believed that EPS would increase and that Executive Smith would exercise his options at the first exercise date. By December 31, 1993, Meno's EPS had increased by 20%. On December 31, 1993, Meno's shares were selling at $40. For simplification, assume total compensation cost at the end of 1992 was estimated to be $24,000.

Executive Smith exercised his option on December 31, 1994, when the market price of the stock was $60 per share.

Required:

1. Is this a compensatory plan? Explain.
2. What date is the measurement date? Explain.
3. What is total compensation cost?
4. What is the service period? Explain.
5. Explain how total compensation cost is allocated to periodic expense in this situation.
6. Give all entries related to Executive Smith's stock option.
7. How much actual "incentive pay" did Executive Smith receive? How much additional compensation expense did Meno Corporation report?

E 21–14
Stock Appreciation Rights:
Analysis, Estimates,
Entries
(L.O. 6)

On January 1, 1991, TP Corporation established a stock appreciation rights plan that offers rights (SARs) to selected executives that can be redeemed for cash equal to the difference between the market price of the company's common shares at the grant date and the market price at the first exercise date. The rights can be exercised three years from the grant date and expire four years from the grant date or when employment is terminated, if earlier. The service period is considered to be three years because exercise is expected (highly probable) to occur on December 31, 1993.

Executive Brown was granted 2,000 SARs on January 1, 1991 (when the common share price was $20), and exercised the rights on December 31, 1993. Relevant market prices at year-end on TP common shares: 1991, $23; 1992, $27; 1993, $30; and 1994, $26.

Required:

1. Answer the following questions:
    a. Is this plan compensatory? _____ Yes _____ No
    b. The measurement date is _____ .
    c. The service period is _____ .
    d. Total compensation cost is $_____ .
    e. Total cash paid by grantor to grantee is $_____ .
2. Give the appropriate journal entries from January 1, 1991, through December 31, 1993.

E 21–15
Stock Incentive
Plan—Lapse of Rights:
Analysis, Entries
(L.O. 5)

Stacy Corporation offers a stock option incentive plan that it granted to six of its top executives. During the second year from date of grant, but prior to the permissible exercise date, one of the six executives resigned and accepted employment with a competitor. In accordance with the provisions of the incentive plan, the stock option for the resigned executive lapsed. At the date of lapse, the relevant account balances for all six executives combined were: deferred compensation expense, $225,000; and executive stock options outstanding, $300,000. The service period extends for three more years, including the second year.

Required:

1. Briefly explain what accounting treatment should be accorded the one sixth of these balances that relate to the one resigned executive.
2. Give all journal entries directly related to the lapsed options.

PROBLEMS

P 21–1
Analysis and Correction of
Shareholders' Equity:
Entries
(L.O. 1)

Careless Corporation was organized on January 1, 1991, and began operations immediately. Unfortunately, the company hired an incompetent bookkeeper. For the years 1991 through 1993, the bookkeeper presented an annual balance sheet that reported only one amount for shareholders' equity: 1991, $137,700; 1992, $156,600; and 1993, $185,000. Also, the condensed income statement reported 1991, net loss, $17,500; 1992, net profit, $12,000; and 1993, net profit, $40,930 (cumulative earnings of $35,430). Based on the $35,430, the president has recommended to the board of directors that a cash dividend of $35,000 be declared and paid during January 1994. The outside director on the board has objected on the basis that the company's financial statements contain major errors. There has never been an audit. You have been engaged to clarify the situation. The single shareholders' equity account, provided by the bookkeeper, appeared as follows:

Shareholders' Equity

1991	Share issue costs	$ 1,300	1991	Common shares, nopar value,	
1991	Net loss	17,500		20,000 shares issued	$160,000
1992	Bought 100 shares from unhappy		1992	Net profit (including a	
	shareholder Doe; shares retired	700		$10,000 land writeup)	22,000
	Depreciation expense*		1992	Common shares, 200 shares	
	(1991, $1,500; 1992, $1,700;			issued	1,800
	1993, $2,300)	5,500			
	Cash shortages*		1993	Common shares, 30 shares	
	(1991, $2,000; 1992, $2,500;			issued	270
	1993, $500)	5,000			
1993	Cash loan to the company		1993	Net profit	40,930
	president	10,000			
		$40,000			$225,000

* Recorded but not shown on the income statement.

Based upon the concerns of the board of directors, you must address three major questions:

Requirement 1:

What amount of retained earnings would be available to support a cash dividend? (Assume the above figures have been found to be arithmetically accurate and that there is no change in income tax.)

Requirement 2:

Based on your calculations in Requirement 1, what journal entries should be made for declaration, and later payment, of the full amount available as a cash dividend?

Requirement 3:

What entry, prior to the dividend entries in Requirement 2, is necessary (*a*) to close the above single shareholders' equity account and (*b*) to record the various components of shareholders' equity in separate accounts? Use the offset method for share issue costs.

P 21–2
Dividends—Common and Preferred, Property and Scrip
(L.O. 2)

The summarized balance sheet at December 31, 1994, for Saxon Corporation is shown below.

Cash	$ 28,000
Receivables	36,000
Inventory	110,000
Long-term investment, 4,000 shares (4%) of Mita	
Corporation, at cost	6,000
Operational assets (net)	80,000
Other assets	10,000
Total	$270,000
Current liabilities	$ 26,000
Bonds payable	50,000
Preferred shares, nopar value, $6, cumulative (200 shares)	25,000
Common shares, nopar (5,000 shares)	100,000
Retained earnings	69,000
Total	$270,000

The dividends on preferred shares are three years in arrears (excluding the current year, 1995). On November 1, 1995, the board of directors of Saxon declared dividends, payment date December 1, as follows:

a. Preferred shares, all dividends in arrears plus the current year dividend; payment to be made by transferring the requisite number of shares of Mita at its current market value of $5 per share.

b. Common shares, $4 per share for the current year, payment to be made by transferring the remainder of the Mita shares and issuing a scrip dividend for the balance. The scrip will earn 10% annual interest from declaration date. The scrip, including interest, will be paid at the end of five months from date of declaration.

Required:

1. Compute the amount of dividends payable on each share class and the amount of the scrip dividend.
2. Give entries to record the transfer of the Mita shares and the issuance of the scrip dividend. Use separate accounts for the common and preferred shares.
3. Give the adjusting entry at December 31, 1995, for the interest on the scrip dividend.
4. Give the entry to record payment of the scrip dividend and interest on April 1, 1996.
5. Prepare the shareholders' equity section of the balance sheet as of December 31, 1995. Assume reported net income of $26,000 for 1995 (does not yet include the interest on the scrip dividend and gain on disposal of Mita shares; assume no change in income tax expense for these items).

P 21–3
Dividends: Cash and Stock, Fractional Shares, Entries
(L.O. 2, 3)

On November 5, 1991, the board of directors of Evers Corporation declared (*a*) a 40% stock dividend on the common shares (i.e., two additional shares of common for each five shares already held) and (*b*) a cash dividend on the preferred shares for one year in arrears and for the current year. The board of directors specified that the average price originally paid in per share of common will be capitalized for the stock dividend. For problem purposes only, assume the declaration and issue (or payment) dates are the same. At November 1, 1991, the records of the corporation showed:

Shareholders' Equity

Preferred shares, nopar value, 70 cents; authorized, unlimited shares; issued, 10,000 shares	$120,000
Common shares, nopar value; authorized, unlimited shares; issued, 15,000 shares	105,000
Retained earnings	160,000

Upon issuance of the stock dividend, 5,000 fractional share rights (for 2,000 shares) were distributed to shareholders. On December 30, 1991, 4,500 fractional share rights were exercised for 1,800 shares. The remaining rights are outstanding to date.

Required:

1. Give entries to record (*a*) issuance of the stock dividend, (*b*) payment of the cash dividend, and (*c*) exercise of the rights.
2. Prepare the shareholders' equity section of the 1991 balance sheet after giving effect to the entries in (1) above and assuming net income for 1991 was $18,000.
3. Give the entry required assuming lapse of the remaining rights on October 30, 1992.

P 21–4
Dividends: Property, Scrip, Fractional Shares, Entries and Reporting
(L.O. 2, 3)

Dawn Corporation records reflect the following data at the end of 1992:

Current assets	$ 167,000
Operational assets (net)	960,000
Other assets	300,000
Long-term investment in AC Corp. (5,000 shares at cost).	5,000
	$1,432,000
Current liabilities	$ 60,000
Long-term liabilities	100,000
Preferred shares, nopar value, $6, cumulative and non-participating; 3,000 shares outstanding	312,000
Common shares, nopar value, 100,000 shares outstanding.	800,000
Retained earnings.	160,000
	$1,432,000

No dividends were declared or paid for 1992. During the subsequent two years, the following transactions affected shareholders' equity:

Year 1993:

Feb. 1 Declared and immediately issued one share of the AC Corporation investment for each preferred share as a property dividend to pay the dividends in arrears from 1992 to date. The current market value of AC was $3.50 per share. In addition, a cash dividend was paid to complete payment of the dividends in arrears.

Oct. 1 Declared and immediately issued scrip dividends amounting to $6 per share on the preferred and $1 per share on the common. Interest on the scrip is 7% per year (maturity date, September 30, 1994).

Dec. 31 Reported 1993 net income was $150,000, including all effects of the above transactions.

Year 1994

Sept. 30 Paid the scrip dividends, including 7% per annum interest for 12 months.

Nov. 1 Declared and issued a stock dividend, payable in common shares to holders of both preferred and common shares. The preferred holders are to receive value equivalent to $6 per share, and the common holders are to receive one share for each five shares held. The value and the amount to be capitalized per share are the market value. The price per common share immediately after the stock dividend was $1.50. Issued the stock dividend in full to the preferred. Fractional share rights for 500 shares (i.e., 2,500 rights) were issued to common shareholders.

Dec. 1 The fractional share rights specified that five such rights could be turned in for one common share. On this basis, 1,800 of the outstanding fractional share rights were turned in. The remaining 700 rights remain outstanding.

Dec. 31 Reported 1994 net income was $95,000, including all effects of the above transactions.

Required:

1. Give the journal entries for each of the above transactions (round to the nearest dollar).
2. Prepare the shareholders' equity section of the balance sheet at December 31, 1994, after recognition of the above transactions.

P 21–5
Retained Earnings—
Appropriations and
Restrictions: Reporting
(L.O. 1, 4)

The following annual data were taken from the records of Yen Corporation at December 31, 1994 (assume all amounts are material; the items in parentheses are credit balances):

Current items, pretax:

a.	Sales revenue	$(450,000)
b.	Cost of goods sold	230,000
c.	Expenses	85,000
d.	Extraordinary loss	30,000
e.	Stock dividend issued	80,000
f.	Cash dividend declared and paid	25,000
g.	Correction of accounting error involving understatement of income tax expense from prior period (not subject to income tax)	8,000
h.	Current restriction for bond sinking fund	10,000
i.	Current appropriation for plant expansion	40,000

Income taxes:
Assume an average income tax rate of 40% on all items except the prior period adjustment.

Balances, January 1, 1994:

j.	Unappropriated retained earnings	$(120,000)
k.	Restriction for bond sinking fund	(20,000)
l.	Appropriation for plant expansion	(60,000)

Required:

1. Prepare a single-step income statement for the year ended December 31, 1994. Disregard EPS.
2. Prepare a statement of retained earnings for the year ended December 31, 1994, that separately discloses each restriction on total retained earnings.
3. Give any entries related to the appropriations and restrictions that would have been made, assuming subdivisions of retained earnings are recorded in separate accounts.

4. Assume Yen Corporation set up a bond sinking fund to pay off the bonds payable at maturity. Also assume the bonds ($200,000 principal) mature when the bond sinking fund has a balance of $194,000 and the restriction for bond sinking fund has a balance of $190,000. Give all related entries to record the bond payment at maturity date (assume all interest has already been paid).

P 21–6

COMPREHENSIVE PROBLEM
♦

Analysis and Correction of Retained Earnings Account
(L.O. 1, 2, 3, 4)

Perkins Corporation is undergoing an audit. The books show an account entitled "surplus," reproduced below, covering a five-year period, January 1, 1992, to December 31, 1996.

Credits

1992–1995	Net income carried to surplus.	$ 800,000
1992	Offset with debit to goodwill—authorized by management	50,000
Jan. 1, 1994	Correction of prior accounting error*	2,000
Jan. 1, 1994	Donation to company—operational asset	11,000
March 31, 1994	Refund of prior years' income taxes due to carryback of a 1993 net operating loss to 1992	9,000
Dec. 31, 1996	Net income, 1996.	170,000
		$1,042,000

* Not included in net income 1992 to 1995.

Debits

1992–1995	Cash dividends declared.	$ 520,000
Dec. 31, 1992	To reserve for bond sinking fund (required annually 1991–1995)	20,000
Dec. 31, 1994	Reserve for bond sinking fund.	20,000
Dec. 31, 1995	Reserve for bond sinking fund.	20,000
Sept. 1, 1996	Fifty percent stock dividend.	250,000
		$ 830,000

Required:

1. The above account is to be closed and replaced with appropriate accounts. Complete a worksheet analysis of the above account to reflect the correct account balances and the corrections needed. It is suggested that the worksheet carry the following columns: (*a*) surplus account per books; (*b*) net income, 1996; (*c*) corrected unappropriated retained earnings, December 31, 1996; and (*d*) columns for debits and credits to any other specific accounts needed.
2. Give the entry or entries to close this account as of December 31, 1996, and to set up appropriate accounts in its place.

(AICPA adapted)

P 21–7
Incentive Stock Plan: Comprehensive Overview, No Complexities, Entries and Reporting
(L.O. 5)

Rye Corporation has a stock option incentive plan for its top managers that includes the following provisions:

a. Each manager that qualifies will receive an option to acquire 10,000 shares of Rye common shares, nopar value, at an option price of $12 per share.
b. The option is non-transferable and, if not exercised, expires after five years from the date of grant.
c. The option cannot be exercised prior to the end of two years from the date of grant and requires continued employment in the company.
d. The stock option is for additional compensation for the year of the grant and the following four years; approximately equal service accrues to each of the five years.

An option was granted to the president on January 1, 1991, at which time the common shares were selling for $20 per share. Assume the option is exercised on December 31, 1995, when the shares are quoted at $45 per share.

At January 1, 1991, 90,000 common shares were outstanding (issued at $2 per share).

Required:

1. Is this a compensatory plan? Explain.
2. What is the measurement date? Explain.
3. Compute the total compensation cost for the option granted to the president.
4. Over what period of time should this total compensation be assigned as expense? Explain.
5. Give the appropriate entries for the option granted to the president at the following dates (if none, explain why):
   a. Date of grant.
   b. Measurement date.
   c. End of each year, starting on December 31, 1991.
   d. Exercise date.
6. Illustrate how the option granted to the president would affect the income statement and balance sheets at the end of 1991 and 1992.
7. What were the amounts of (*a*) total compensation expense recorded, and (*b*) incentive pay earned by the president?

P 21–8
Stock Incentive Plan:
Measurement and Grant
Dates Different,
Comprehensive, Entries
and Reporting
(L.O. 5)

Manford Corporation has unlimited common shares authorized, nopar value, of which 40,000 shares are outstanding. The shares were originally issued for $20 per share. The company has a stock option plan that provides the following:

a. Each qualified manager shall receive, on January 1, an option for a computed number of common shares at a computed option price per share. The computation of the number of option shares and the option price shall be made three years after the option is granted and will be related to the increase in net income over the three-year period. The plan provides additional compensation for qualified managers for services to be performed approximately equally during the years 1991 to 1995.
b. The options are non-transferable and must be exercised not earlier than three years and not later than five years from the date of grant. Employment with the company is required through the exercise date.

On January 1, 1991, an option was granted to J. Dean, the controller. At that date, the common shares were quoted on the market at $50 per share. Assume Dean exercised the option near the end of 1995 when the price of the shares was $90. The following additional information is available:

	Estimates Made December 31, 1991 of What the Amount Would Be on December 31, 1993*	Actual Amount on December 31, 1993
Number of shares optioned	500	510
Option price	$60	$62
Market price per share	$67†	$71

* Estimate at December 31, 1992 same as estimate at December 31, 1991.

† Estimate of future market price, based on actual market price on December 31, 1991.

Required:

1. Is this a compensatory plan? Explain.
2. When is the measurement date? Explain.
3. Over what period should total compensation expense for Dean be assigned?
4. Give appropriate entries (related to Dean) for the following dates (if none, explain why):
   a. Date of grant.
   b. End of 1991 and 1992.
   c. Measurement date.
   d. End of 1993, 1994, and 1995.
   e. Exercise date.
5. Show how Dean's option would affect the income statement and balance sheet for 1992 and 1993.
6. How much actual incentive compensation did Dean earn? How much additional compensation expense did Manford Corporation report?

P 21–9
Stock Incentive Plan: Comprehensive, Dates of Grant and Measurement Different, Entries and Reporting
(L.O. 5)

Huber Corporation is authorized to issue unlimited common shares, nopar value, of which 75,000 shares have been issued at a price of $10 per share. On January 1, 1992, the corporation initiated a stock option plan for its three top managers. The plan provides that each manager will receive an option to purchase, no later than December 31, 1996, 2,000 common shares at a base option price of $48, which will be adjusted for changes in earnings per share (EPS), and requiring continued employment through actual exercise date. The option price is to be established on December 31, 1994, and will be based on changes in EPS. EPS for 1991 was $2. The option price will be established at the end of 1994 as follows:

> The option price per share will be the basic option price of $48 multiplied by the additive inverse of the percentage change (i.e., 1 minus the % of change) in EPS from December 31, 1991 through 1994.

The options are non-transferable and expire on December 31, 1996. The shares were quoted at $45 per share on the market on January 1, 1992. On December 31, 1992, management made what they consider to be realistic estimates that EPS would increase steadily to $3.20 at December 31, 1994, and that the share price would be $46 on that date; this latter estimate was based upon the actual market price on December 31, 1992, which was $46. These estimates were not revised in 1993 because the actual market price of the shares was very close to $46 on December 31, 1993, and EPS expectations remained the same. EPS on December 31, 1994, actually turned out to be $3, and the actual market price of the shares was $47.

The president received the options with the option price unknown on January 1, 1992. The service period was established to be five years (i.e., 1992 through 1996). Assume the president exercised the option on December 31, 1996, when the market price of the shares was $64.

Required:

1. Is this a compensatory plan? Explain.
2. What is the measurement date? Explain.
3. Over what period should total compensation costs for the president be assigned?
4. Give appropriate entries related to the president on the following dates (if none, explain why):
   a. Date of grant.
   b. End of 1992 and 1993.
   c. Measurement date.
   d. End of 1994, 1995, and 1996.
   e. Exercise date.
5. Show how the president's option would affect the income statement and balance sheet for 1993 and 1994.
6. What were the amounts of (a) additional compensation expense reported by the grantor and (b) the actual incentive compensation earned by the grantee?

P 21–10
Stock Appreciation Rights: Analysis, Entries
(L.O. 6)

Delphi Corporation has just employed a new president with the following compensation package: (1) salary, $200,000 per year (minimum employment period, three years); (2) an annual bonus of 10% of the dollar increase in accrual basis income before extraordinary items; and (3) 10,000 stock appreciation rights (SARs) tied to the market price of Delphi's common shares. This problem focuses on the SARs granted to the new president on January 1, 1992, when the market price per share was $30. Four other executives also participate in this SAR plan.

The SAR plan specifies that each SAR will earn for the grantee cash equal to the difference between the market price of Delphi's common shares on the grant date and on the exercise date. The SARs may be exercised at any time after the end of the fourth year from the grant date, and they expire at the end of the fifth year from grant date, or at date of termination of employment, if before the end of the fifth year. The service period is from the grant date to the expected exercise (i.e., vesting) date, December 31, 1995.

The president exercised the SARs on January 4, 1996, when the market price per share was $40. The relevant year-end market prices on Delphi's common shares are: 1992, $33; 1993, $38; 1994, $35; 1995, $40; and January 4, 1996, $40. The accounting period ends December 31.

Required:

1. Respond to the following questions:
   a. Is this plan compensatory? Why?
   b. What is the measurement date? Explain.

  c. What is total compensation cost?
  d. What is the service period? Explain.
  e. How is total compensation expense allocated to annual periodic expense?
2. Give all entries related to the SARs granted to the president from the grant date through the exercise date.

P 21–11

COMPREHENSIVE PROBLEM
◆

An Overview of
Chapters 20 and 21
(L.O. 2, 3, 4, 5)

Howard Corporation is a publicly owned company whose shares are traded on the TSE. At December 31, 1992, Howard had unlimited shares of nopar value common shares authorized, of which 15,000,000 shares were issued.

The shareholders' equity accounts at December 31, 1992, had the following balances:

Common shares (15,000,000 shares)	$230,000,000
Retained earnings	50,000,000

During 1993, Howard had the following transactions:

  a. On February 1, 1993, a distribution of 2,000,000 common shares was completed. The shares were sold for $18 per share, net of issue costs.
  b. On February 15, 1993, Howard issued, at $110 per share, 100,000 of nopar value, $8, cumulative preferred shares with 100,000 detachable warrants. Each warrant contained one right, which with $20 could be exchanged for one common share. On February 15, 1993, the market price for one right was $1.
  c. On March 1, 1993, Howard reacquired and retired 20,000 common shares for $18.50 per share.
  d. On March 15, 1993, when the common shares were trading for $21 per share, a major shareholder donated 10,000 shares, which were retired.
  e. On March 31, 1993, Howard declared a semiannual cash dividend on common shares of 10 cents per share, payable on April 30, 1993, to shareholders of record on April 10, 1993.
  f. On April 15, 1993, when the market price of the rights was $2 each and the market price of the common shares was $22 per share, 30,000 stock rights were exercised.
  g. On April 30, 1993, employees exercised 100,000 options that were granted in 1991 under a non-compensatory stock option plan. Each option entitled the employee to purchase one common share for $20. On April 30, 1993, the market price of the common shares was $23 per share.
  h. On May 31, 1993, when the market price of the common was $23 per share, Howard declared a 5% stock dividend distributable on July 1, 1993, to common shareholders of record on June 1, 1993. On July 1, 1993, immediately after issuance of the dividend shares, the market price of the common was $20.
  i. On June 30, 1993, Howard sold 300,000 common shares. The selling price was $25 per share.
  j. On September 30, 1993, Howard declared a semiannual cash dividend on common shares of 10 cents per share and the yearly dividend on preferred shares, both payable on October 30, 1993, to shareholders of record on October 10, 1993.
  k. On December 31, 1993, the remaining outstanding rights expired.
  l. Net income for 1993 was $25,000,000.

Required:

Prepare a schedule to be used to summarize, for each transaction, the changes in Howard's shareholders' equity accounts for 1993. The columns on this schedule should have the following headings:

  Date of transaction (or beginning date); common—number of shares; common—amount; preferred—number of shares; preferred—amount; common stock warrants—number; common stock warrants—amount; additional contributed capital; retained earnings.

(AICPA adapted)

P 21–12
Quasi Reorganization:
Entries and Reporting
(L.O. 7)

The following account balances were shown on the books of Overton Corporation at December 31, 1991:

Non-cumulative preferred shares, nopar value, $5,	
2,000 shares outstanding	$200,000
Common shares, nopar value, 5,000 shares outstanding	250,000
Retained earnings (deficit)	(45,000)

At a shareholders' meeting which included holders of preferred shares the following actions related to a quasi reorganization were decided upon:

a. All outstanding shares shall be returned in exchange for new shares as follows:
    (1) For each share of the old preferred, one share of new preferred. Purchased for cash at $100 per share, 20 shares of old preferred shares from a dissatisfied shareholder, and the remainder exchanged.
    (2) For each share of the old common, two new common shares.
b. The retained earnings deficit shall be written off against the common share account.

The above actions were approved by Overton's creditors.

During the ensuing year, 1992, the following additional transactions and events were completed.

c. Sold 200 preferred shares at $112 per share.
d. The company issued 1,200 nopar common shares in payment for a patent tentatively valued by the seller at $20,000. (The current market value of common shares was $15.)
e. The company sold 50 common shares at $19 per share, receiving cash. Overton also issued 100, $1,000 bonds at 102; one common share, as a bonus, was given with each bond.
f. At the end of 1992, the board of directors met and was informed that the net income before deductions for bonuses to officers was $100,000. The directors approved the following actions:
    (1) Five hundred common shares shall be issued to the officers as a bonus (at no cost to the officers). The market price of a common share on this date was $16.
    (2) Declared and paid cash dividends (for one year) on the preferred shares outstanding.

Required:

1. Prepare journal entries to record the above transactions, including the quasi reorganization.
2. Prepare the shareholders' equity section of the balance sheet after all of the above transactions were recorded.

P 21–13
Quasi Reorganization: Entries and Reporting (L.O. 7)

During the last five years, Norwood Corporation experienced severe losses. A new president has been employed, who is confident the company can be saved from bankruptcy. Working with an independent public accountant, the new president has proposed a quasi reorganization with the constraints that (a) the capital structure must be changed to eliminate the deficit in retained earnings and (b) it must be approved by the shareholders and creditors. The Norwood board of directors approved the proposal, as did the shareholders and creditors.

Prior to quasi reorganization, Norwood's balance sheet (summarized) reflected the following:

Cash	$ 20,000
Accounts receivable	94,000
Allowance for doubtful accounts	(4,000)
Inventory	150,000
Operational assets	800,000
Accumulated depreciation	(300,000)
Deferred charges	40,000
	$ 800,000
Current liabilities	$ 150,000
Long-term liabilities	240,000
Common shares, nopar; 30,000 shares	500,000
Preferred shares, nopar; 1,000 shares	130,000
Retained earnings, (deficit)	(220,000)
	$ 800,000

The quasi reorganization proposal, as approved by the shareholders and creditors, provided the following:

a. To provide adequately for probable losses on accounts receivable: increase the allowance to $6,000.
b. Write down the inventory to $100,000 because of obsolete and damaged goods.
c. Reduce the book value of the operational assets to $400,000 by increasing accumulated depreciation.

d. With the agreement of the creditors, reduce all liabilities by 5%.

e. Transfer $70,000 from the preferred share account to the deficit account.

f. Transfer any remaining amount needed to reduce the deficit to zero from the common share account.

Required:

1. Give a separate entry for each of the above changes.
2. Prepare a balance sheet immediately after the quasi reorganization.

CASES

C 21–1
Fractional Shares: Analysis
(L.O. 5)

Tudor Corporation made the following entry to record the final disposition of all fractional share rights issued in connection with a small stock dividend:

Fractional share rights, outstanding 3,750		
Common shares (200 shares)	2,000	
Contributed capital, lapsed stock rights	1,250	
Cash	500	

Required:

1. What dispositions were made of the total of the fractional share rights, as evidenced by the above entry? State specifically what the shareholders did with their fractional share rights to dispose of them.
2. On what date would Tudor have known the number of fractional share rights it would have to issue as a part of the stock dividend distribution?
3. How would the above entry be altered if the stock dividend had been large instead of small?

C 21–2
Should the Board of Directors Declare a Dividend?
(L.O. 1, 2)

Drake Company was started in 1983 to manufacture a wide range of plastic products from three basic components. The company was originally owned by 23 shareholders; however, in 1988 the capital structure was expanded considerably, at which time preferred shares were issued. The preferred is non-voting, cumulative, non-participating, nopar, $6. The company has experienced a substantial growth in business over the years. This growth was due to two principal factors: the dynamic management and geographic location. The firm served a rapidly expanding area with relatively few regionally situated competitors.

The December 31, 1993, audited balance sheet showed the following (summarized):

Cash	$ 11,000	Current liabilities	$ 38,000
Other current assets	76,000	Long-term notes payable	60,000
Investment in K Co. shares		Preferred shares, nopar	
(at cost)	30,000	(500 shares)	50,000
Plant and equipment (net).	310,000	Common shares, nopar	
Intangible assets	15,000	(10,000 shares)	150,000
Other assets	8,000	Retained earnings	27,000
	$450,000	Profits invested in plant	125,000
			$450,000

The board of directors has not declared a dividend since organization; instead, the profits are used to expand the company. This decision was based on the fact that the original capital was small and there was a decision to limit the number of shareholders. At the present time, the common shares are held by slightly fewer than 50 individuals. Each of these individuals also owns preferred shares; their total holdings approximate 46% of the outstanding preferred.

The board of directors has been planning to declare a dividend during the early part of 1994, payable June 30. However, the cash position as shown by the balance sheet has raised serious doubts as to the advisability of a dividend in 1994. The president has explained that most of the cash will be needed shortly to pay for inventory already purchased.

The company has a chief accountant but no controller. The board relies on an outside public accountant for advice concerning financial management. The public accountant was asked to advise about the contemplated dividend declaration. Four of the seven members of the board felt very strongly that some kind of dividend must be declared and paid, and that all shareholders "should get something."

Required:

You have been asked to analyze the situation and make whatever dividend proposals that appear to be worthy of consideration by the board. Present amounts to support your recommendations in a form suitable for consideration by the board in reaching a decision. Provide the basis for your proposals, and indicate any preferences that you may have.

C 21–3
Quasi Reorganization
(L.O. 7)

Marks Corporation, a medium-sized manufacturer, has experienced operating losses for the past five years. Although operations for the current year ended also resulted in a loss, several important changes made the fourth quarter a profitable one; as a result, future operations of the company are expected to be profitable.

The treasurer suggested a quasi reorganization to (*a*) eliminate the accumulated deficit of $325,000 in retained earnings, (*b*) write up the $600,000 cost of operating land and buildings to their current market value, and (*c*) set up an asset of $175,000 representing the estimated future tax benefit of the losses accumulated to date.

Required:

1. What is a quasi reorganization?
2. List the conditions under which a quasi reorganization generally would be justified.
3. Discuss the propriety of the treasurer's proposals to:
   a. Eliminate the deficit of $325,000.
   b. Write up the value of the operating land and buildings of $600,000 to their current market value.
   c. Set up an asset of $175,000 representing the future tax benefit of the losses accumulated to date.

(AICPA adapted)

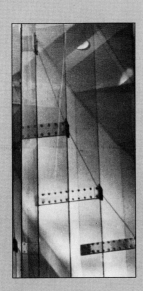

C H A P T E R

22

Earnings per Share

LEARNING OBJECTIVES

◆

After reading this chapter, you will be able to:

1. Explain why financial statement users pay close attention to a company's reported earnings per share (EPS) and why EPS is difficult to interpret.

2. Calculate basic EPS.

3. Calculate fully diluted EPS for firms with complex capital structures.

4. Calculate adjusted EPS and explain when its use is appropriate.

5. Calculate pro forma EPS and explain when its use is appropriate.

1085

◆

Earnings per share (EPS) is a driving force behind common share market price. From the viewpoint of the average investor with no management or employment ties to the company, a publicly traded corporation's reported earnings per share may well be all that matters. More than anything else, EPS appears to move the market price of the company's common shares, spelling profits or losses for the shareholders. Given the impact EPS has on share prices, it should come as no surprise that investors, securities commissions, and other investment regulatory agencies watch this corporate financial statistic closely.

When the CFO (chief financial officer) for a large corporation talks of steps being taken to better manage the company's financial performance, the executive is often referring to:

♦ Different means for establishing the dollar amount of earnings and how these dollars are classified and allocated before they are finally reported as after-tax income. Net income after taxes is the base for EPS computations.

♦ Different techniques for adjusting the net income after taxes and, simultaneously, adjusting the number of shares over which the net income is spread. Adjusting the dollar base and number of shares over which it is spread is the essence of the EPS computation process.

Principles followed in reporting net income components on the income statement were covered in Chapter 4. To an extent, this chapter contains a reprise of that information, presented in conjunction with a discussion of how to apply and evaluate various techniques for computing EPS.

To emphasize the power of EPS computations, consider the waves of forced mergers and hostile takeovers that marked the corporate finance world of the 1980s. Back then, it seemed there were only two types of companies: corporate predators and corporate takeover targets.

To ward off predators, target companies resorted to two basic survival strategies. One approach was to alter EPS by contracting the number of common shares outstanding. This action automatically raised the EPS and caused the market price of the remaining outstanding shares to increase substantially. This increase, it was hoped, would make it too expensive for a predator to pursue a takeover. Alternatively, some takeover target companies took the opposite route. They deliberately diluted their EPS, driving down the market price of the common shares in the process to the point where a predator would be afraid to attempt a takeover. Actually, the banks and other lenders who were financing these takeovers were the ones to back away from such situations. Because the target company's common shares were pledged as collateral for takeover financing, the lower the market price, the less takeover financing capital available.

In implementing the first strategy (contracting the number of shares outstanding and raising EPS), takeover target companies needed to find ways to buy back their shares from the public without incurring the huge debt amounts needed to finance the buy-back. Shearson Lehman Hutton—a major brokerage house and investment banking firm—devised a plan for target companies to use in buying back large blocks of their shares without having to make a cash tender offer to the shareholders. Shearson's plan called for the target company to issue *unbundled stock units* (USUs) in lieu of cash offers.

For each common share surrendered a USU was offered, consisting of:

♦ A bond (at a discount from par value) that paid annual interest equal to the annual dividend paid on the common shares being surrendered. Thus, the shareholder did not forfeit current investment income. Moreover, the issuing company did not commit to any increase in cash outflow.

- One hybrid preferred share (featuring variable dividend payouts), which provided the surrendering shareholder with assurance of additional income equal to any and all future increases in the declared dividends paid on the remaining common shares outstanding. Again, the issuing company did not commit to any extra payout beyond what would have been paid out had the common shares not been bought back.
- A common stock warrant with an exercise price equal to the par value (maturity value) of the bond. Thus, the surrendering shareholder had the option to reacquire shares in the company, at no loss in value, at the bond maturity date, at which time the hostile takeover threat was expected to have passed.

The objective of this manoeuvering was for the number of common shares outstanding to decline substantially, shifting a large portion of the company's equity capitalization away from common to preferred shares and debt capitalization. With the number of common shares outstanding reduced significantly, EPS rises dramatically. If the market price of the shares increases as expected, that is, the price-earnings (PE) ratio remains as it was before issuing the USUs (and overall market conditions do not turn adverse), the takeover attempt will likely be thwarted.

Battling corporate takeovers is but one example of financial situations in which EPS computations play a part. EPS computations are complex, and the accounting rules governing these computations are extensive. Indeed, there are entire textbooks on the subject of EPS and the intricacies involved in calculating them.[1] This text covers the major EPS-related accounting rules and practices and the logic behind them.

◆

FUNDAMENTALS OF EARNINGS PER SHARE

Section 3500 of the *CICA Handbook*, "Earnings per Share," requires that:

> All enterprises, except for the following, should show earnings per share for the current and preceding period in the financial statements covered by the auditor's report:
> *a.* business enterprises which do not have share capital;
> *b.* government owned companies;
> *c.* wholly-owned subsidiaries;
> *d.* companies with few shareholders. (par. 3500.06)

Earnings per share applies only to common shares, the mainstay equity investment medium that corporations use to raise business capital. Millions of investors own common shares either directly, or through an intermediary such as a mutual fund or insurance company, or by participating in employer-sponsored profit sharing or pension programs.

Investors, and the community of brokers, advisors, and analysts who support them, evaluate companies and make decisions to buy, sell, or hold (or sometimes to sell short) based on many factors. Cash flows, future prospects, the state of the economy, the nature of the corporation's competitive market, assessment of the abilities of key employees, and so on, all play a major role. Past performance is viewed as an objective base on which to predict future performance, and its role is crucial. The company's EPS on common shares is a commonly quoted performance statistic, as it relates past performance to the unit (the share) being traded. The relationship between EPS and

---

[1] *APB Opinion No. 15* is the primary U.S. pronouncement governing the computation of EPS for U.S. publicly held corporations. This pronouncement is supplemented by a 186-page interpretation: J. Ball, *Computing Earnings per Share, AICPA, Unofficial Accounting Interpretations of APB Opinion 15. SFAS No. 21,* "Suspension of the Reporting of Earnings per Share and Segment Information by Nonpublic Enterprises" (Norwalk, Conn., April 1978), suspended the EPS reporting requirement for most closely held corporations.

market price is known as the price-earnings (PE) ratio, that is, the number of times the market price exceeds the company's last reported EPS figure. Thus, if a company is reporting earnings of $3.25 per share and the market price of the shares is quoted at 48¾, it means the shares are selling at 15 times earnings ($48.75 ÷ $3.25 = 15).

The significance of PE ratios becomes clear if the same company reported increased earnings per share of $3.50, up 25 cents from the last earnings report. All other factors remaining the same, the shares can be expected to advance in market price to about $52.50, which is a $3.75 increase in price (or $375 profit per 100 shares). At a market price of $52.50, the shares continue to sell at 15 times earnings ($52.50 ÷ $3.50).[2]

The point is that market prices are extremely sensitive to reported EPS figures and earnings trends. Because of the potential profit and loss ramifications, EPS figures must be computed using the exacting procedures specified in the *CICA Handbook* designed to prevent accidental or deliberate overstatement and understatement.

This is not to say that the markets can be "fooled" or manipulated by artificially inflated EPS figures. As we will see in Chapter 24, investors are remarkably sophisticated in discounting earnings increases that are not backed up by real cash flows. They will not be fooled by an increase in earnings that is not caused by an increase in profitable operations. For example, increasing income and EPS by changing depreciation methods will *not* result in an increased market price, regardless of the PE ratio.

At the same time, if a company posts legitimately increased earnings and EPS, the market will react quickly to the implied improved future cash flow prospects, and market price will jump. The incentive for management with stock option plans or bonuses based on stock prices is obvious.

Basic Earnings per Share Calculations

The issuance of common and preferred shares provides a corporation with permanent capital that the company uses to generate economic wealth. This generated wealth is reported in the form of after-tax income available to the shareholders, both common and preferred. This wealth is either paid out to the shareholders or retained by the company for reinvestment and generation of more wealth. However, most preferred shareholders do not fully share in the wealth retained by the company; like bondholders, they are paid a fixed return on their investments, in the form of dividends rather than interest payments. Preferred shares are also similar to bonds in that both are senior securities. In terms of dividend payouts, this means the preferred shareholders have priority over the common shareholders.

EPS, which pertains to common shares only, is therefore calculated based on the total wealth generated by a company during a particular accounting period, reduced by the amount of dividends paid (or to be paid) to the preferred shareholders. Expressed as a formula, **basic EPS** is computed as:

$$Basic\ EPS = \frac{Net\ income\ after\ tax\ -\ Preferred\ dividends}{Weighted\ average\ of\ outstanding\ common\ shares}$$

EPS figures are required for income before discontinued operations and extraordinary items *and* for net income.

If a company has 300,000 (weighted average) common shares outstanding (*weighted average* will be explained shortly), 50,000 shares of nopar, $10 preferred shares

---

[2] Rather than remain constant, PE ratios can be quite elastic. They tend to expand in response to positive developments in the expectation that future earnings will show improvement, and they contract in response to negative developments in the expectation of lower earnings in the future. PE ratios also respond to general market conditions, independently of a given company's earnings outlook. PEs tend to expand during bull markets and contract during bear markets.

outstanding, and has net income after taxes of $2 million, EPS would be $5, computed as follows:

$$\$5 = \frac{\$2,000,000 - \$500,000}{300,000}$$

Cumulative Preferred Dividends In deducting preferred dividends from net income after taxes, one must determine whether the preferred shares are *cumulative* or *non-cumulative,* and whether the board of directors has *declared* the preferred dividend for the year. If the shares are non-cumulative, then preferred dividends are deducted when calculating basic EPS only *if declared.* If the dividends are missed, then the retained earnings are available in subsequent periods for the common shareholders' benefit.

On the other hand, the dividends on *cumulative* preferred shares are deducted in the calculation whether declared or not.[3] Missed dividends on cumulative preferred shares must be made up before retained earnings are available for common shareholders, and they represent a real restriction on the earnings that accrue to common shareholders. Dividends on participating preferred shares are deducted only if declared.

If net income is negative, the methodology discussed would not change. The preferred dividend entitlement would increase the loss per share, and negative EPS would be reported.

Weighted Average Common Shares Outstanding

At times, corporations issue additional common shares, either as public offerings or privately, or in conjunction with the exercise of corporate stock options and warrants to purchase shares. At other times, a corporation may retire blocks of its common shares outstanding. These changes in the number of common shares outstanding must be taken into consideration when calculating EPS for the accounting period in which such changes occur. Weighted average computation techniques are used to accommodate these changes.

To illustrate how the average number of shares outstanding is computed, consider a simple case for a corporation that has the following changes in common shares outstanding during the year 1992 (the firm's fiscal year corresponds to the calendar year):

	Shares	Total Outstanding
January 1, outstanding	10,000	10,000
July 1, issued additional shares	5,000	15,000
October 1, purchased and retired	(2,000)	13,000
December 31, outstanding.		13,000

The average number of shares outstanding for 1992 is computed as follows:

Inclusive Dates	Shares Outstanding	Months Outstanding	Weighted Shares Outstanding
Jan. 1–June 30	10,000	6	60,000
July 1–Sept. 30	15,000	3	45,000
Oct. 1–Dec. 31	13,000	3	39,000
		12	144,000

Average number of shares outstanding: 144,000 ÷ 12 = 12,000.

---

[3] Only this year's cumulative but undeclared dividend is deducted from current period income (or added to current period losses). Prior undeclared cumulative dividends are assumed to have been deducted in prior years.

Stock dividends, stock splits, and *reverse splits* are given special treatment in EPS computations. The new shares they create are subdivisions of previously outstanding shares. Therefore, when stock dividends, stock splits, or reverse splits increase or decrease shares outstanding during the period, computation of the average number of common shares outstanding should give retroactive restatement to the change in capital structure. The computation should not weight the additional shares created by the fraction of the period they were outstanding. This is because there is no infusion of cash or other assets from the shareholders at this time. Hence, the computed average number of shares outstanding is based on the assumption that the additional common shares created by the stock dividend or split were outstanding throughout the reporting period regardless of when the stock dividend or split occurred.

Therefore, all actual shares outstanding prior to the issuance of any common shares from a stock dividend or split are restated retroactively, for the effect of any stock dividends or splits, to year-end equivalent shares outstanding. Then the year-end equivalent shares are weighted by the fraction of the period they were outstanding. Stock dividends and stock splits have the same effect on EPS computations. No distinction is made between them for this purpose.

In reporting EPS for comparative financial statements, prior years' EPS amounts are recomputed based on the current year's capital structure. In other words, all stock dividends or splits are restated retroactively for all prior years reported as though they were outstanding throughout all the periods reported.

Let's consider a couple of examples to make sure we have the basics in hand.[4] For our first example, suppose Clearall Supply Corp. has the following activities related to its common share account during 1992:

	Shares
1. Common shares outstanding, January 1	10,000
2. April 1, sold and issued	1,000
3. June 1, 100% stock dividend	11,000
4. September 1, sold and issued	2,000

The computation of the weighted average number of shares is illustrated in Exhibit 22–1.

In this example, the 100% stock dividend occurred on June 1. Therefore, each share outstanding before that date is restated retroactively to two shares. This restatement enables the corporation and investors to relate earnings for the year to the current capital structure at the year-end date. The shares outstanding after the June 1 stock dividend are not retroactively restated because shares outstanding subsequent to that date already reflect the stock dividend.

Now let's take a slightly more complex example involving several transactions. Suppose Cloverleaf Dairy has the following activities related to its common share account during 1992.

	Shares
1. Common shares outstanding, January 1	100,000
2. February 25, 5% stock dividend	5,000
3. March 21, repurchased and retired	525
4. October 9, sold and issued	10,000
5. November 21. two-for-one stock split	114,475
(100,000 + 5,000 − 525 + 10,000)	

The weighted average number of common shares outstanding to be used in the calculation of earnings per share is shown in Exhibit 22–2.

---

[4] The examples are adapted from J. Ball, *Computing Earnings per Share, AICPA, Unofficial Accounting Interpretations of APB Opinion 15.*

EXHIBIT 22–1 Computation of Weighted Average Number of Common Shares Outstanding when Stock Dividends Occur

Inclusive Dates	Actual Shares Outstanding	Retroactive Restatement for Stock Dividend		Equivalent Shares Outstanding	Months Outstanding		Weighted Shares Outstanding
January 1–March 31	10,000	× 2	=	20,000	× 3	=	60,000
April 1–May 31	11,000	× 2	=	22,000	× 2	=	44,000
June 1–August 31	22,000*		=	22,000	× 3	=	66,000
September 1–December 31	24,000*		=	24,000	× 4	=	96,000
Totals					12		266,000

Weighted average number of shares outstanding: 266,000 ÷ 12 = 22,167.

* These numbers already include the stock dividend.

EXHIBIT 22–2 Computation of the Weighted Average Number of Common Shares Outstanding Involving a Stock Dividend, Stock Split, and Share Retirement

Inclusive Dates	Actual Shares Outstanding	Retroactive Restatement			Equivalent Shares Outstanding	Days Outstanding		Weighted Shares Outstanding
		Stock Dividend	Stock Split					
January 1–February 24	100,000	× 1.05	× 2	=	210,000	× 55	=	11,550,000
February 25–March 20	105,000*		× 2	=	210,000	× 24	=	5,040,000
March 21–October 8	104,475*		× 2	=	208,950	× 202	=	42,207,900
October 9–November 20	114,475*		× 2	=	228,950	× 43	=	9,844,850
November 21–December 31	228,950‡					× 41	=	9,386,950
Totals						365		78,029,700

Weighted average number of common shares outstanding: 78,029,700 ÷ 365 = 213,780.

* Already includes effect of stock dividend.
‡ Already includes effect of stock dividend and stock split.

In Exhibit 22–2, calculations based on days are illustrated. In practice, either days or months can be used. The choice should be consistent over time.

The February 25 stock dividend requires restatement of actual shares outstanding from January 1 through February 24. The November 21 stock split requires restatement of all actual shares outstanding before that date (but not after the date), including the shares restated for the February 25 stock dividend.

Common shares may be issued for cash (etc.) proceeds, or on the conversion of debt or other convertible share classes (e.g., preferred shares). This is generally a straight-forward calculation in the determination of the weighted average number of common shares outstanding. Special consideration is necessary when a conversion takes place between dividend dates (for share conversion) or with no required accrual of interest earned to date (for debt conversion). Under these circumstances, the conversion is assumed to have taken place on the date the dividend or interest obligation ceased.

For example, assume that Silver Foods Corp. had the following capital structure on January 1, 1992:

Preferred Shares, $2.50, nopar, convertible one-for-two into common shares, dividend July 1 and December 31, 5,000 shares outstanding.

Common shares, nopar, 20,000 shares outstanding.

On November 1, 2,000 preferred shares were converted to 4,000 common shares.

In the calculation of weighted average common shares outstanding, the conversion would be included in the calculations as of July 1, the date of the last dividend payment:

Inclusive Dates	Shares Outstanding	Months Outstanding	Weighted Shares Outstanding
January 1–November 1	20,000	6*	120,000
November 1–December 31	24,000	6*	144,000
		12	264,000

Weighted average common shares outstanding 264,000/12 = 22,000.

* 24,000 shares assumed to have been outstanding since July 1, last dividend date.

This provision is meant to ensure that the capital base, shares outstanding, is consistent with earnings measurement. Since the company only paid dividends for six months on the preferred shares converted, they should be shown as common equity for the entire second six months.

Normally, convertible bonds require that interest be paid to the date of conversion, or investors will only convert to common shares directly after an interest date. If this is not the case, then it is appropriate to backdate the conversion to the last interest payment.

The examples just addressed conclude the introductory discussion of earnings per share calculations. Before we consider the more complex issues of convertible securities and options, we need to develop some additional structure. In doing so, our objective is to consider EPS as an accounting measure of management's effective use of the resources supplied by the residual equity claimants. In general, we can say that this measure attempts to be conservative in its presentation. This effectively translates into the interpretation that the reported EPS is the worst case scenario.

CONCEPT REVIEW

1. Why are preferred dividends deducted from net income in the computation of EPS?
2. When a stock dividend is issued, the new number of shares is considered to be outstanding for the entire year in the calculation of EPS. Why?
3. If 100 common shares are issued for cash halfway through the reporting period, what impact does this have on EPS for the period? For the prior period reported?

TYPES OF CAPITAL STRUCTURE FOR EPS CALCULATION PURPOSES
◆

Section 3500 identifies two different types of capital structures and prescribes different EPS presentations for each, as follows:

1. **Simple capital structure**—The shareholders' equity either consists only of common shares or includes no potentially **dilutive securities** that upon conversion or exercise could in the aggregate *dilute* (*decrease*) earnings per common share. For simple capital structures, the *CICA Handbook* prescribes a *single EPS presentation* (amounts assumed):

> Earnings per common share:
> Income before discontinued operations
> and extraordinary items. $1.50
> Extraordinary loss . . . . (.09)
> Loss from discontinued operations . . . . (.02)
>
> Net income $1.39

In the case of a simple capital structure, the resulting EPS figures are called *basic EPS.* Basic EPS must be shown for income before discontinued operations and extraordinary items and for net income. The EPS impact of extraordinary items and discontinued items is often shown separately, as illustrated above.[5]

2. **Complex capital structure**—Complex capital structures constitute *all* capital structures except those described above as simple. A capital structure is not simple if the corporation has outstanding convertible securities or rights that are *potentially dilutive;* potentially dilutive securities are securities that may be converted to common shares and thus cause an increase in the number of outstanding common shares. Dilutive securities that may increase the outstanding common shares include convertible preferred shares, convertible bonds payable, and stock rights, stock options, stock warrants, and other securities that provide for conversion into or purchase of common shares. For *complex capital structures,* Section 3500 prescribes a *dual EPS presentation* that reports the dilutive effects in two sets of EPS amounts (amounts assumed):

	Basic EPS	Fully Diluted EPS
Income before discontinued operations and extraordinary items.	$ 6.40	$2.56
Extraordinary loss.	(1.20)	(.48)
Loss from discontinued operations	(.94)	(.38)
Net income	$ 4.26	$1.70

Fully diluted EPS must be shown for income before discontinued operations and extraordinary items and for net income.

EPS is computed by dividing periodic income attributable to common equity by the average number of common shares outstanding during the period. Depending upon the corporation's capital structure, income and average number of shares must be adjusted for certain items to arrive at fully diluted EPS. Section 3500 provides specific guidelines concerning these adjustments. The basic guideline is that when either the denominator or numerator is changed, the other one must also be changed if there are any related effects.

Fully diluted EPS figures must be presented for companies with complex capital structures if the results are materially different from basic EPS. In the United States, "materially different" has been defined as more than a 3% change from basic. In Canada, materiality is left to professional judgment. The 1989 *Financial Reporting in Canada* survey showed that, of 209 companies with potentially dilutive elements in their capital structure, only 73 disclosed fully diluted EPS. For the rest, the logical assumption is that fully diluted EPS would not be materially less than basic EPS.

COMPUTING EPS WITH A SIMPLE CAPITAL STRUCTURE

A simple capital structure generally is one in which there are common shares only, or common shares and non-convertible preferred shares. The illustrations given in Chapter 3 involved simple capital structures. Exhibit 22–3 shows the computation of EPS

---

[5] Section 3500 of the *CICA Handbook* does not require separate EPS amounts for extraordinary items or discontinued operations because they may be deduced by taking the difference between EPS for income before the items and EPS for net income. We present EPS for all income amounts because the *CICA Handbook* suggests their presentation as a convenience to statement users, and companies usually report all EPS amounts when they have extraordinary gains and losses or gains and losses from discontinued operations.

EXHIBIT 22–3   EPS Computations for a Simple Capital Structure with Non-Convertible Preferred Shares: Framis Corporation

Calculations:
1. For numerator (income): Preferred dividend claim, for the current year only:

$$2,500 \text{ shares} \times \$1.20 \text{ (dividend preference rate)} = \underline{\$3,000}$$

2. For denominator (shares): Computation of weighted average number of common shares outstanding during 1992:

Inclusive Dates	Actual Shares Outstanding	Months Outstanding	Weighted Shares Outstanding
January 1–April 30, shares outstanding. . . .	90,000	× 4	360,000
May 1, sold additional shares	6,000		
May 1–December 31, shares outstanding . . .	96,000	× 8	768,000
Totals.		12	1,128,000

Weighted average number of shares outstanding, 1,128,000 ÷ 12 = $\underline{94,000}$.

Basic Earnings per Common Share:

Basic earnings per common share outstanding:
   Income before extraordinary items:
     ($124,000 − $3,000* = $121,000) ÷ 94,000 shares** $1.29
     Extraordinary gain: (10,000 ÷ 94,000) 10
   Net income: ($134,000 − $3,000* = $131,000) ÷ 94,000 shares $1.39

* Preferred dividend.

** Weighted average common shares outstanding.

for a simple capital structure that has non-convertible preferred shares, based on the following facts for Framis Corporation:

	Shares
1. Capital:	
a. Common shares, nopar, outstanding on January 1, 1992	90,000
b. Common shares, issued and sold May 1	6,000
c. Preferred shares, nopar, $1.20 (cumulative, non-convertible) outstanding on January 1, 1992	2,500
2. Income data for the year ending December 31, 1992:	
a. Net income before extraordinary items	$124,000
b. Extraordinary gain, net of tax	10,000
c. Net income	134,000

If net income for Framis Corp., before extraordinary items, were a negative $124,000 (other facts unchanged), the three basic EPS figures calculated in Exhibit 22–3 would be −$1.35[($124,000 + $3,000) ÷ 94,000], $.10, and −$1.25[($114,000 + 3,000) ÷ 94,000], respectively.

To compute the basic EPS amounts in Exhibit 22–3, two preliminary computations are made—one with respect to the numerator and the other for the denominator.

1. *Numerator—preferred shares dividend claim*—Because EPS relates only to common shares, the dividend claims of any outstanding preferred shares must be recognized in the computation of earnings per common share. That portion of the income for the period that is subject to the period's preferred dividend claim must be subtracted from the numerator.

The facts do not indicate whether Framis Corporation declared the annual $1.20 dividend on the preferred shares. However, because the preferred shares are cumulative,

EXHIBIT 22–4   Overview of EPS Computations

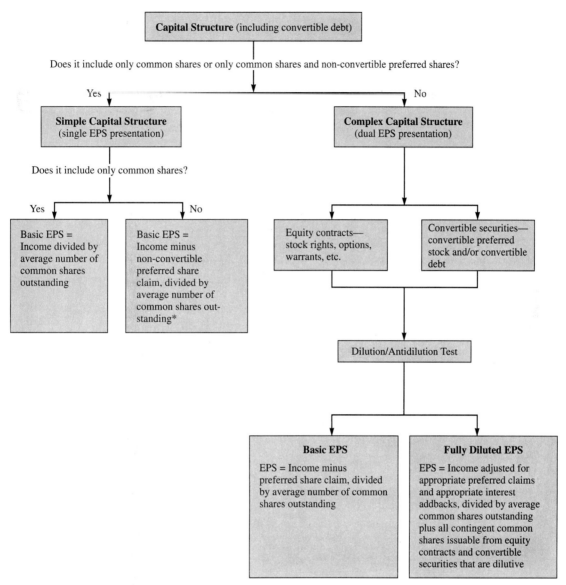

* If the preferred shares are cumulative, deduct the dividends for the current year whether declared or not; if non-cumulative, deduct for current year only if declared during the current year.

declaration is not required. The $3,000 preferred dividend is subtracted from income in calculating basic EPS, or added to a loss.

2. *Denominator—weighted average number of shares outstanding during the year*— EPS relates income of the period to the common shares outstanding during that same period. Therefore, in both simple and complex capital structures, the denominator contains the weighted average number of common shares outstanding during the period when the income was earned. The common shares outstanding are weighted by the fraction of the period during which they were outstanding. If the corporation retires some of its common shares during the period, those shares would be included in the EPS computation only for the fraction of the year they were outstanding.

Exhibit 22–3 presents the computation of the weighted average number of common shares outstanding during 1992. Observe that, in computing the average, the 6,000 shares

EXHIBIT 22-5   Summary of Computation of EPS

Summary of Computation of Basic EPS

Numerator	Denominator
1. Income before discontinued operations and extraordinary items:	
$$\begin{array}{c}\text{Income before}\\\text{discontinued}\\\text{operations and}\\\text{extraordinary items}\end{array} - \begin{array}{c}\text{Dividend claims of}\\\text{preferred shares}^\dagger\end{array}$$	Weighted average number of common shares outstanding
2. Extraordinary items: Extraordinary gain or loss (net of tax)	Same as above.
3. Discontinued operations: Gain or loss (net of tax)	Same as above.
4. Net income: Same as (1) plus or minus extraordinary items and gain or loss from discontinued operations.	Same as above.

Summary of Computation of Fully Diluted EPS*

Numerator	Denominator
1. Income before discontinued operations and extraordinary items:	
$$\begin{array}{c}\text{Income}\\\text{before}\\\text{discontinued}\\\text{operations and}\\\text{extraordinary}\\\text{items}\end{array} - \begin{array}{c}\text{Dividend}\\\text{claims of}\\\textit{non-convertible}\\\text{preferred}\\\text{shares}^\dagger\end{array} + \begin{array}{c}\text{Interest}\\\text{expense}\\\text{(net of tax)}\\\text{on all}\\\text{convertible}\\\text{debt}\end{array} + \begin{array}{c}\text{Interest}\\\text{revenue}\\\text{(net of tax)}\\\text{on proceeds}\\\text{from shares}\\\text{issued under}\\\text{existing}\\\text{options}\end{array}$$	$$\begin{array}{c}\text{Weighted}\\\text{average}\\\text{number}\\\text{of common}\\\text{shares}\\\text{outstanding}\end{array} + \begin{array}{c}\text{All other}\\\text{common}\\\text{shares that}\\\text{would be}\\\text{issued on}\\\text{convertible}\\\text{securities}\\\text{or options}\end{array}$$
2. Extraordinary items: Extraordinary gain or loss (net of tax).	Same as above.
3. Discontinued operations: Gain or loss (net of tax)	Same as above.
4. Net income: Same as (1) plus or minus extraordinary items and gain or loss from discontinued operations.	Same as above.

* Excluding all antidilutive securities.

† If preferred shares are cumulative, subtract the dividends for the current year whether declared or not; if non-cumulative, subtract the dividends for the current year only if declared during the current year.

issued on May 1, 1992, were included only for the eight twelfths of the year they were outstanding during 1992.

COMPUTING EPS WITH A COMPLEX CAPITAL STRUCTURE

◆

Corporations with *complex* capital structures, that is, those that do not meet the definition of a simple capital structure, must present two sets of EPS data with equal prominence on the income statement. Section 3500 describes these two sets as follows:

1. *Basic EPS* is based on the outstanding common shares.
2. *Fully diluted EPS* reflects the maximum dilution of EPS that occurs if all contingent issuances of common shares that would reduce EPS take place at the beginning of the period (or time of issuance of the convertible security, if later).

EXHIBIT 22–6   Basic EPS Computations—Framis Corporation, 1992, Complex Capital Structure

Calculations:
1. For numerator:
   Preferred dividend claim, for current year only, 1992
       2,500 shares × $1.20 (dividend preference rate) = $ 3,000
       1,000 shares × $7 (dividend preference rate)   =   7,000
                                         $10,000

2. For denominator (see Exhibit 22–3):
   Computation of weighted average number of common shares outstanding:

Dates	Shares	Months Outstanding	Weighted Shares Outstanding
January 1–April 30, shares outstanding.	90,000	× 4	360,000
May 1, sold additional shares	6,000		
May 1–December 31, shares outstanding	96,000	× 8	768,000
Totals.		12	1,128,000

Weighted average number of shares outstanding, 1,128,000 ÷ 12 = 94,000.

Basic EPS

Income before extraordinary items: $\dfrac{\$124,000^* - \$3,000^{**} - \$7,000^\dagger}{94,000^\ddagger}$

$= \dfrac{\$114,000}{94,000}$ $= \$1.22$

Extraordinary gain: $\dfrac{\$10,000}{94,000}$ $= \underline{.10}$

Net income: $\dfrac{\$134,000 - \$3,000^{**} - \$7,000^\dagger}{94,000}$ $= \$1.32$

* Income before extraordinary items.

** Dividend claim of non-convertible preferred shares.

† Dividend claim of convertible preferred shares.

‡ Average number of shares outstanding during the year.

Exhibit 22–4 is an overview of EPS computations and complements the explanations that follow. Keep in mind that entities are required to disclose fully diluted EPS only if they are materially different from basic EPS.

The EPS computations for a company with a complex capital structure may be summarized as shown in Exhibit 22–5.

Let's expand on the Framis Corporation example. Suppose Framis has the following additional outstanding securities:

1. Convertible preferred shares, nopar, with a $7 annual dividend per share. The shares are cumulative and each share is convertible into eight shares of common. One thousand shares issued at $108 per share are outstanding over the entire year.
2. Series A convertible bonds, $200,000 outstanding, 8% interest payable annually. Each $1,000 bond is convertible into 30 shares of common. Issued at par and outstanding over the entire year.
3. Series B convertible bonds, $500,000 outstanding, 10% interest payable annually. Each $1,000 bond is convertible into 60 shares of common. Issued at par and outstanding over the entire year.
4. There are outstanding rights to acquire 2,000 common shares at $10 per share.

We assume the after-tax return on temporary investments during the year was 9% and the tax rate was 40 percent.

Basic EPS

The calculation of basic EPS for a complex capital structure is essentially the same as that for a company with a simple capital structure. Since Framis Corp. is now assumed to have 1,000 shares of $7 convertible preferreds outstanding, the preferred dividend claim for these shares must be deducted from income in calculating the basic EPS, as shown in Exhibit 22-6.

Fully Diluted EPS

According to Section 3500 of the *CICA Handbook,* the income figure for calculating **fully diluted EPS** should be the income figure used in the calculation of basic EPS (or adjusted basic, if required) increased by the following:

  i. The amount of dividends applicable to convertible senior shares for the period;
  ii. The amount of interest expensed for the period, after income taxes, on convertible debt; and
  iii. Imputed earnings, after income taxes, on the cash which would have been received on the exercise of the options, warrants and rights at an appropriate rate of return. The appropriate rate of return for imputing earnings must be a matter of judgment in each case and should be disclosed together with the dollar amount of imputed earnings after income taxes (par. 3500.37).

The weighted average common shares outstanding would be increased by the number of shares required to affect the conversion of debt or senior shares or the exercise of warrants and options. The issuance is assumed to take place at the beginning of the year, unless the convertible securities were issued during the year. If they were issued during the year, the conversion is assumed to take place on the issue date.

Options, rights, and warrants that become exercisable more than 10 years past the balance sheet date should not be considered in calculating fully diluted EPS. If options, rights, and so on, have a variety of exercise prices associated with them—varying by date of exercise, for example—the most dilutive alternative must be used.

Exhibit 22-7 first illustrates the preliminary computations required for fully diluted EPS. Each potentially dilutive item is considered individually, and the impact on the EPS numerator and denominator is determined. The individual EPS effect is calculated as follows:

$$\text{Individual EPS effect} = \frac{\text{Effect of assumed conversion on } numerator \text{ of EPS.}}{\text{Effect of assumed conversion on } denominator \text{ of EPS}}$$

$$= \frac{\text{Interest expense or revenue (net of tax) or preferred dividend amount}}{\text{Number of common shares into which the security can be converted/issued}}$$

For example, consider the outstanding stock options (see Exhibit 22-7). If the holders of outstanding options were to have exercised those options at the beginning of 1992, an additional 2,000 common shares would have been outstanding during the period. Thus, 2,000 common shares would be added to the denominator of the calculation. An appropriate adjustment would also have to be made to the numerator to represent the additional income Framis should expect to earn on additional invested capital. Note that the proceeds from the sale of the shares, $20,000, represent a capital transaction and are *not* income.

We could assume that the corporation would use the cash inflow to acquire additional income-generating assets, to retire debt, or to retire common shares. This would

EXHIBIT 22–7   Fully Diluted EPS—Framis Corporation, Complex Capital Structure

Calculations:
1. Stock rights:

For numerator:
$10 (option price) × 2,000 (shares represented) × 9% (after tax rate) . . . . . $ 1,800

For denominator:
Issuable common shares   2,000

Earnings per share effect ($1,800 ÷ 2,000) . . . . $ .90

2. Convertible $7 preferred shares:

For numerator:
Dividends 1,000 shares × $7 . . . . $ 7,000

For denominator:
Issuable common shares on conversion 1,000 × 8   8,000

Earnings per share effect ($7,000 ÷ 8,000) . . . . $ .88

3. Series A convertible bonds:

For numerator:
Interest expense reduction $200,000 × 8%. $16,000
Less income tax expense increase $16,000 × 40%   6,400

Net increase in income had conversion occurred on January 1, 1992 . . . . . . $ 9,600

For denominator:
Issuable common shares on conversion $200,000 ÷ $1,000 × 30 shares   6,000

Earnings per share effect ($9,600 ÷ 6,000) . . . . $ 1.60

4. Series B convertible bonds:

For numerator:
Interest expense reduction $500,000 × 10% $50,000
Less income tax expense increase $50,000 × 40%   20,000

Net increase in income had conversion occurred on January 1, 1992 . . . . . . $30,000

For denominator:
Issuable common shares on conversion $500,000 ÷ 1,000 × 60 shares   30,000

Earnings per share effect ($30,000 ÷ 30,000) . . . . $ 1.00

Test for Dilution/Antidilution for Fully Diluted EPS

	Income	No. of Shares	EPS
Basic EPS (from Exhibit 22–6)	$114,000	94,000	$1.20
Convertible $7 preferred shares	7,000	8,000	
Subtotal.	$121,000	102,000	1.19
Stock rights	1,800	2,000	
Subtotal.	$122,800	104,000	1.18
Series B convertible bonds.	30,000	30,000	
Subtotal.	$152,800	134,000	1.14
Series A convertible bonds.	9,600	6,000	
Subtotal.	$162,400	140,000	1.16*

Note: schedule starts with the most dilutive security.

EXHIBIT 22–7   *(concluded)*

Fully Diluted EPS Calculation

Income before extraordinary
    items:

$$= \frac{\$124{,}000^{**} - \$3{,}000^{**} - \$7{,}000^{**} + \$7{,}000 + \$1{,}800 + \$30{,}000}{94{,}000^{**} + 8{,}000 + 2{,}000 + 30{,}000}$$

$$= \frac{\$152{,}800}{134{,}000} = \$1.14$$

Extraordinary gain:

$$\frac{\$10{,}000}{134{,}000} = \$\ .07$$

Net income:

$$= \frac{\$134{,}000^{**} - \$3{,}000^{**} - \$7{,}000^{**} + \$7{,}000 + \$1{,}800 + \$30{,}000}{94{,}000^{**} + 8{,}000 + 2{,}000 + 30{,}000}$$

$$= \frac{\$162{,}800}{134{,}000} = \$1.21$$

* Antidilutive.

** Carried forward from basic EPS.

argue for the use of a firm-specific return rate in the numerator, such as return on assets, return on equity, or bond interest rates. The *CICA Handbook* only requires use of an "appropriate" rate of return, which should be disclosed.

A popular assumption is that the cash proceeds would be invested in the money market and earn an appropriate interest rate. Of course, interest revenue is subject to tax and the return must be calculated *after* tax. This approach is likely to be conservative in any given case, and thus is consistent with our worst case scenario approach to calculating EPS. It also relies on an objective measure of earnings potential.

In Exhibit 22–7, the $20,000 proceeds are multiplied by the after-tax interest rate on temporary investments (9%). This is likely to be a lower return than could be earned by investing in Framis's own operational assets. The specific EPS of this item, $.90 ($1,800/2,000), is calculated.

If the convertible $7 preferred shares had converted on January 1, 1992, Framis would have avoided a $7,000 dividend claim and thus have had that much more income for the common shareholders. Since dividends are not tax deductible, no tax rate is applied to the $7,000. An additional 8,000 common shares would have been outstanding during the year, which means that this item has an 88 cent ($7,000/8,000) individual EPS effect.

The effect of a January 1, 1992, conversion of Series A convertible bonds has an individual EPS effect of $1.60 ($9,600/6,000). If the bonds had not been outstanding, no interest would have been paid on them, and income would be higher by $9,600 after tax. On the other hand, 6,000 more common shares would have been outstanding for the period.

If the Series B bonds had converted, after-tax interest of $30,000 would have been avoided in exchange for 30,000 common shares, an individual effect of $1 per share. Note that all conversions are assumed to have taken place at the beginning of the current reporting period. If the securities were issued during the period, they would be assumed to have converted on their issuance date.

For example, if $1,000,000 of 9% bonds payable convertible into 500,000 common shares were issued on November 1 of a given year, the calculations for fully diluted EPS would be as follows (a 40% tax rate has been assumed):

Numerator:
Interest avoided — $1,000,000 × 9% × 2/12 . . . . $15,000
Tax benefit (40%) 6,000

Net income effect . . . . $ 9,000

Denominator:
500,000 shares × 2/12 83,333

Individual EPS effect ($9,000/83,333) . . . . $ .108

The conversion assumption rolls the assumed conversion back through the year; the interest or dividend payments are those that would be *avoided*—2 months, in this case.

If the bonds had been outstanding for the whole year, neither the numerator nor denominator effect would be multiplied by two twelfths.

Companies are required to present fully diluted EPS to reveal the lowest amount of EPS the company would report if all its dilutive outstanding equity contracts (e.g., stock rights, options, warrants, etc.) and convertible securities were assumed to be converted to common shares. The purpose is to show the lowest EPS amount the company could report if all those who could convert, did. Determination of this "lowest possible" EPS amount is related to the concept of dilution/antidilution (D/A).

Dilution/Antidilution (D/A)

Dilution/antidilution (D/A) must be considered only with complex capital structures. Dilution means a decrease in EPS results arising from equity contracts or convertible securities. The equity contracts and dilutive securities that cause this effect are called **dilutive securities.** Antidilution means an increase in EPS amounts caused by **antidilutive securities**—equity contracts or convertible securities. Conservatism dictates that we should obtain the maximum dilutive effect on EPS, or look for the worst case scenario. To achieve this, paragraph 3500.34 of the *CICA Handbook* states that

> The calculation of fully diluted earnings per share should exclude any potential conversion of senior shares or debt, exercise of rights, warrants and options or other contingent issuances that would increase earnings per share or decrease a loss per share.

The first step in the D/A test involves ranking the potentially dilutive securities according to their individual EPS effect, from lowest to highest.

It is not entirely clear from Section 3500 of the *CICA Handbook* how the D/A test is to be applied. One alternative is to examine the EPS effect of each item individually. If it is lower than basic EPS, then the item is considered dilutive and included in fully diluted EPS. (In our example, any item with an individual effect of less than basic EPS, $1.20, should be included—$7 preferred shares, stock rights, and Series B bonds would be automatically included.)

The alternative approach is a bottom-line approach, as illustrated in Exhibit 22–7. We calculate the cumulative effect of each item on fully diluted EPS, starting with the most dilutive item (measured individually). Thus, the convertible $7 preferred shares, with an individual EPS of 88 cents, is considered first. Fully diluted EPS is reduced to $1.19. The rights (individual EPS of 90 cents) come second and continue to reduce fully diluted EPS from $1.19 to $1.18. Adding the Series B convertible bonds reduces fully diluted EPS to $1.14. The Series A convertible bonds increase EPS, however, and are considered antidilutive. In this application, the objective is to find the lowest possible fully diluted EPS figure, which is $1.14. The Series A bonds are excluded.

In our example, both D/A methods would result in the same EPS figure—including three dilutive securities and producing fully diluted EPS of $1.14. However, if one potentially dilutive security had an individual EPS of $1.18, the choice of method would become important. Under the "individual" approach, this item would be included because its individual effect is less than basic EPS of $1.20. Under the "bottom-line" approach, however, fully diluted EPS was reduced to $1.14 with the first three items.

Including a \$1.18 security would *increase* this ratio and not succeed in the stated objective of reaching a worst case scenario. Thus, the bottom-line method is preferable.

The final product in Exhibit 22–7 is fully diluted EPS, which must be disclosed along with basic EPS. If there are extraordinary items or gains or losses from discontinued operations, multiple fully diluted EPS ratios must be disclosed. The purpose of fully diluted EPS is to demonstrate the extent to which current earnings levels would be undermined by existing share commitments of the corporation.

CONCEPT REVIEW

1. When does a company have a simple capital structure? What EPS calculations must be disclosed if the capital structure is complex?
2. What is the starting point for fully diluted EPS?
3. When calculating fully diluted EPS, what adjustment is made to the numerator (earnings) for stock options? bonds? preferred shares?
4. What is the purpose of the D/A test?
5. A company has a basic EPS of \$1, and three potentially dilutive securities with individual EPS effects as follows:
   a. Eighty cents.
   b. Ninety-five cents.
   c. \$2.50.
   Which would likely be included in the calculation of fully diluted EPS?

Adjusted Basic EPS

Paragraph 3500.28 of the *CICA Handbook* recommends that "where common shares have been issued on conversion of senior shares or debt during the period, **adjusted basic EPS** should be calculated as though the conversion had taken place at the beginning of the period." Therefore, in calculating the weighted average shares outstanding, the shares that had been issued on conversion would be considered to have been outstanding for the entire 12 months and weighted accordingly.

The income figure (i.e., the numerator) would be increased by:

1. The amount of dividend applicable to the senior shares converted.
2. The amount of interest expensed during the period, after income taxes, on debt converted.

Adjusted basic EPS would be disclosed in the financial statements if the resulting EPS figures are materially different from basic EPS. When disclosed, the adjusted basic EPS should be presented for income both before and after extraordinary items and discontinued operations.

For example, assume that Madison Mines Corporation earned an \$822,000 net income in 1992 and reported the following:

	Number of Shares
1. Common shares, nopar, outstanding on January 1	400,000
2. Common shares, sold for cash on February 1	40,000
3. Common shares, issued on conversion of preferred shares on October 2	100,000
4. Preferred shares, \$8, nopar, each preferred share convertible into 10 common shares, outstanding on January 1	40,000

Net income was \$822,000; dividends are declared quarterly, starting March 31.

Madison Mines Corporation would calculate basic, adjusted, and fully diluted EPS figures, as shown in Exhibit 22–8. The adjusted EPS calculation shows the impact on EPS had the conversion taken place on January 1, not October 1. Fully diluted EPS builds on the adjusted EPS calculation and is necessary since, at year end, 30,000 convertible preferred shares are still outstanding.

EXHIBIT 22–8   EPS Computations—Basic, Adjusted, Fully Diluted: Madison Mines Corp.

Calculations:
1. For numerator (income):
   Preferred dividend claim:

March 31.	40,000 × $8/4	$ 80,000
June 30.	40,000 × $8/4	80,000
Sept. 30	40,000 × $8/4	80,000
Dec. 31.	30,000 × $8/4	60,000
		$300,000

2. For denominator (shares):

	Actual Shares Outstanding	Months Outstanding	Weighted Shares Outstanding
January 1–February 1, shares outstanding.	400,000	1	400,000
February 1, sold shares	40,000		
February 1–October 1, shares outstanding.	440,000	8	3,520,000
October 2, issued shares on conversion	100,000		
October 2–December 31, shares outstanding.	540,000	3	1,620,000
Totals		12	5,540,000

   Weighted average number of shares outstanding 5,540,000 ÷ 12 = 461,667.

3. Converted preferred shares (adjusted):
   For numerator:
   $6 (dividend paid, $8 × ¾) × 10,000 (shares converted) . . . . $ 60,000

   For denominator:
   [10,000 × 10 × ⁹⁄₁₂ (January 1 to October 2)] 75,000

4. Unconverted preferred shares (fully diluted):
   For numerator:
   $8 (dividend) × 30,000 (shares outstanding) $240,000

   For denominator:
   (30,000 × 10) 300,000

   Individual earnings per share effect ($240,000/300,000) . . . . $ .80

Basic EPS calculation:

$$EPS = \frac{\$822,000 - \$300,000}{461,667}$$

$$= \frac{\$522,000}{461,667} = \underline{\$1.13}$$

Adjusted EPS calculation:

$$EPS = \frac{\$522,000^* + \$60,000}{461,667^* + 75,000}$$

$$= \frac{\$582,000}{536,667} = \underline{\$1.08}$$

Fully diluted EPS calculation:

$$EPS = \frac{\$582,000^* + \$240,000}{536,667^* + 300,000}$$

$$= \frac{\$822,000}{836,667} = \underline{\$.98}$$

1103

* Carried down from prior calculation.

Items are included in fully diluted EPS calculations only if they pass the D/A test and reduce reported EPS figures. This is not true of adjusted EPS items, which must be included whether they increase or decrease basic EPS. The rationale behind this requirement is that adjusted EPS is based on a transaction—the conversion of securities or retirement of debt—that has *actually* taken place. Fully diluted EPS considers transactions that *might* take place.

Pro Forma EPS

Where transactions occur after the balance sheet date involving the issue of common shares, the EPS figures previously presented may not be relevant for users' needs. When common shares are issued subsequent to the balance sheet date

   i. for cash where the proceeds are to be used to retire senior shares or debt outstanding at the balance sheet date;

   ii. on the conversion of senior shares or debt outstanding on the balance sheet date; or

   iii. in a reorganization (par. 3500.39)

pro forma basic EPS for the current period using the altered share capital for income before and after extraordinary items and discontinued operations should be disclosed in the financial statements. In addition, if the entity has disclosed fully diluted EPS, then a revised ratio, **pro forma fully diluted EPS,** must also be calculated.

The pro forma EPS figures are calculated as if the common shares (actually issued after the balance sheet date) had been issued at the beginning of the current period, or at the date of issuance of the senior shares or debt, if later. The income figure is increased by

   i. the amount of dividend for the period applicable to the senior shares to be retired or converted; and

   ii. the amount of interest expensed for the period, after income taxes, on the debt to be retired or converted. (par. 3500.40)

Fully diluted EPS would have been calculated for the conversion of senior shares or debt. Pro forma basic EPS would still have to be calculated. However, if the other two situations occur, pro forma fully diluted EPS must be disclosed in addition to pro forma basic unless the subsequent change in capital structure has no material effect on the EPS figures, in which case disclosure may be substituted for the pro forma figures.

For example, let's extend our consideration of Madison Mines Corporation. Assume that after the 1992 fiscal year ended, on January 31, 1993, 100,000 common shares were issued for $1,100,000. The proceeds were used to retire $1,000,000 of 12% debenture bonds payable. The bonds were not convertible and thus did not affect any prior fully diluted EPS calculations. A 40% tax rate has been assumed. Madison would be required to calculate pro forma basic EPS and pro forma fully diluted EPS, as illustrated in Exhibit 22–9.

If the bond had been retired on January 1, 1992, the 12% interest, net of tax, would have been avoided. On the other hand, more shares would have been outstanding. The purpose of these calculations is to show how 1992 results will project into 1993, with a different capital structure.

> *CONCEPT REVIEW*
>
> 1. When is adjusted EPS calculated? What is its purpose?
> 2. What is the starting point in calculating adjusted EPS?
> 3. If bonds are converted to common shares on February 1, how many months of interest are added back to income in the calculation of adjusted EPS?
> 4. When are pro forma EPS ratios calculated? What is their purpose?
> 5. What is the starting point in calculating pro forma basic EPS? Pro forma fully diluted EPS?

EXHIBIT 22-9   EPS Computations—Pro Forma: Madison Mines Corp.

Calculations:
1. For numerator (income):
   Interest avoided $1,000,000 × .12 . . . . $120,000
   Tax effect (40%) 48,000
   Net increase in income . . . . $ 72,000

2. For denominator (shares):
   Shares issued 100,000

Pro forma basic:

$$EPS = \frac{\$522,000^* + \$72,000}{461,667^* + 100,000}$$

$$= \$1.06$$

Pro forma fully diluted:

$$EPS = \frac{\$822,000^* + \$72,000}{836,667^* + 100,000}$$

$$= \$.95$$

* As previously calculated, Exhibit 22–8.

REPORTING EARNINGS PER SHARE
◆

Section 3500 of the *CICA Handbook* recommends that:

> Basic EPS figures should be shown either on the face of the income statement or in a note to the financial statements cross-referenced to the income statements . . . for: (*a*) income before discontinued operations and extraordinary items; (*b*) net income for the period (par. 3500.09 and .11),

and

> Where the effect of potential conversions of senior shares or debt, exercises of rights, warrants and options and contingent issuances on EPS would be materially dilutive, fully diluted EPS figures for "income before discontinued operations and extraordinary items" and "net income for the period," should be disclosed, for the current period, in a note to the financial statements, cross-referenced to the income statement. Such figures should be described as fully diluted. (par. 3500.30)

The *Handbook* does not indicate when potential conversions are "materially dilutive." However, *APB Opinion No. 15* specifies that if the dilution is less than 3% of the basic EPS figure, then fully diluted information need not be presented.

The reporting of EPS is illustrated for Mark's Work Wearhouse, which only reports basic EPS. Labatts, on the other hand, reports both basic and fully diluted EPS. See Exhibits 22–10 and 22–11.

Earnings per share calculations are defined quite differently in the United States versus Canada. There is an increased reporting cost for companies that must comply with both rules (e.g., Canadian public companies that also are listed on American stock exchanges). Users must beware of the potential for a lack of comparability.

Highlights of the U.S. approach are as follows:

◆ The first EPS calculation divides return to common shareholders by the weighted average outstanding common shares. For simple capital structures, this is called *basic EPS*.

EXHIBIT 22–10   Financial Statement Exerpts from Mark's Work Wearhouse, Annual Report, 1989

Consolidated Statement of Earnings

Earnings before extraordinary item:	$1,613	$1,561	$2,155
Extraordinary item	(638)	–	–
Net Earnings	$ 975	$1,561	$2,155
Earnings per Restricted Voting and Class A shares:			
From continuing operations	25¢	17¢	22¢
Before extraordinary item	16¢	16¢	22¢
Net earnings	10¢	16¢	22¢

8. CAPITAL STOCK

The authorized capital stock of the Company is divided into 8,000,000 First Preferred Shares of nopar value; 877,000 Class A Shares of nopar value; and 50,000,000 Restricted Voting Shares of nopar value.

The Class A Shares and Restricted Voting Shares rank equally as to dividends and upon any liquidation, dissolution, or winding up of the Company. The voting rights attached to the Restricted Voting Shares are limited in that the holders thereof are entitled to elect three members of the board while the holders of Class A Shares are entitled to determine the size of the board and to elect the remaining members thereof. Class A Shares are convertible into Restricted Voting Shares on a one for one basis.

The Class A Shares shall have these rights so long as either M.W. Blumes or M.A. Blumes is an officer and director of the Company and the Restricted Voting and Class A Shares controlled by either or both of them aggregate more than 650,000 shares and more than 5% of the total number of outstanding Restricted Voting and Class A Shares.

M.W. Blumes and M.A. Blumes have provided undertakings that they will not directly or indirectly vote any Restricted Voting Shares resulting from the conversion of Class A Shares, nor will they tender any Class A Shares upon any offer made for such shares unless a tender offer on substantially similar terms is made to holders of Restricted Voting Shares.

The issued capital stock of the Company is as follows:

	1987	1988	1989
877,000 Class A Shares	$ 2	$ 2	$ 2
9,094,306 Restricted Voting Shares (1987—9,082,806)	14,541	14,556	14,556
	$14,543	$14,558	$14,558

11,500 Restricted Voting Shares were issued during 1988 pursuant to the exercise of employee stock options.

11,287 Restricted Voting Shares were cancelled during 1987 in settlement of an employee loan balance.

Options to purchase Restricted Voting Shares granted to employees and outstanding as at January 28, 1989, are as follows:

Number of Restricted Voting Shares	Exercise Price	Expiry Date
32,000	$2.92	Dec., 1990
495,000	$1.15	June, 1992

◆ Common stock equivalents (CSEs) include options, other equity contracts, and convertible securities whose effective yield at the time of issuance is less than two thirds of the return on corporate Aa bonds. *Primary EPS* treats these securities as additional outstanding shares if their inclusion reduces basic EPS (i.e., they are dilutive). In making this calculation, the impact conversion would have on income to common shareholders (preferred dividends or interest net of tax) is included in the numerator of the EPS calculation.

◆ Convertible securities that are not common stock equivalents but that are dilutive are included in addition to CSEs in computing *fully diluted EPS.*

◆ The treasury stock method is used to establish the impact of dilutive options in the calculation of primary and fully diluted EPS. Outstanding shares are reduced by using the funds obtained by exercise to purchase shares on the market at the period's average market price (year-end price, if higher, for fully diluted EPS). In Canada, the impact of options is calculated by the imputed earnings assumption. The EPS calculations required to use the treasury stock method are complex and extensive.

A FINAL COMMENT

◆

The reporting of earnings per share figures is highly sensitive, since the financial press pays an inordinate amount of attention to these numbers and their trends over time. Managers often feel considerable pressure to "boost the numbers" because of this outside focus. However, it is difficult to evaluate just what the numbers mean. In particular, the magnitude or trend of EPS may not necessarily indicate the effectiveness with which management uses the resources entrusted to its care.

In particular, a firm's asset structure will change through operations and/or through acquisitions, making comparisons over time difficult at best. It may be more informative to relate return to total capital invested in a return on investment (ROI) calculation, instead of forcing a focus on shares outstanding, which vary in absolute value or size between firms.

Firms can and do engage in activities merely to influence the year's EPS figures. One firm with extensive land holdings used to sell off excess land when necessary so that the gain on sale allowed it to achieve forecast EPS. Using EPS as an important element in a firm's goal structure can contribute to a short-term management attitude that is detrimental to the long-term productivity and financial health of any firm.

Nevertheless, EPS computations are regularly reported and anxiously awaited by shareholders, financial pundits, and management. We must know how these numbers are obtained if we are to be alert to their shortcomings.

SUMMARY OF KEY POINTS

◆

(L.O. 1)   1. Earnings per share computations are an attempt to measure management's effectiveness in using assets to increase the wealth of the residual equity holders through increased earnings.

(L.O. 1)   2. EPS figures are used widely by the financial press, analysts, and investors to determine operating success and help predict future results. Every attempt is made to aid in the predictive power of the ratios, to ensure that they are calculated consistently between companies, and to ensure that they represent conservative ground for projection.

(L.O. 2)   3. The required EPS disclosures are based on whether a firm has a simple or complex capital structure. Simple capital structures do not involve convertible shares or debt, options, rights, or warrants.

(L.O. 2)   4. The EPS calculation divides return to common shareholders by the weighted average of the outstanding common shares. This is called basic EPS.

(L.O. 3)   5. Complex capital structures include debt or senior shares that are convertible into common shares. Companies with outstanding options, rights, or warrants for common shares are also described as having complex capital structures. Such companies must calculate fully diluted EPS.

(L.O. 3)   6. Fully diluted EPS shows the lowest EPS figure possible, taking into account the potential conversions and options. Only those items that are dilutive, that is, that make EPS decline, are included. When calculating fully diluted EPS, earnings attributable to common shareholders (from basic EPS) are increased by the incremental net interest cost or revenue, and/or the preferred dividend avoided. Shares outstanding are increased by the shares that would be issued.

Consolidated Statement of Earnings	**1989**	**1988**
(in millions)		
Net earnings	**$135.1**	$140.6
Net earnings per common share (Note 5):		
Basic	**$ 1.80**	$ 1.92
Fully diluted	**$ 1.60**	$ 1.68

(See accompanying notes.)

5. Net Earnings per Common Share

The number of shares used in calculating net earnings per common share is as follows:

(in millions)	**1989**	**1988**
Basic	74.0	73.4
Fully diluted	90.6	89.8

11. Convertible Debentures

The convertible debentures are reported under the heading of convertible debentures and shareholders' equity on the balance sheet to reflect the permanent nature of this capital. This presentation is supported by the long maturities, the low initial interest rates, an indication by many of the holders of these debentures that they intend to convert in the future, and the Company's intention to ultimately have them converted to equity. The convertible debentures are unsecured obligations and are subordinated to all other indebtedness of the Company.

Particulars of the convertible debentures are as follows:

(in millions)	**1989**	**1988**
1983 adjustable rate debentures to mature June 16, 2003	$ 40.2	$ 41.1
1986 adjustable rate debentures to mature February 28, 2006	124.2	124.6
1987 adjustable rate debentures to mature April 1, 2007	125.0	125.0
	$289.4	$290.7

The 1983 adjustable rate convertible debentures pay a minimum interest rate of 6% and are convertible, at the holder's option, on or before the earlier of the last business day prior to either redemption or June 16, 2003, into common shares of the Company at a conversion price of $11.25 per share unless the Company fixes an interest rate of 6½%, whereupon the conversion price becomes $13.4375 per share. The debentures are redeemable at par plus accrued interest.

The 1986 adjustable rate convertible debentures pay a minimum interest rate of 6% and are convertible, at the holder's option, on or before the earlier of the last business day prior to either redemption or February 27, 2006, into common shares of the Company at an initial conversion price of $17.875 per share until February 28, 1990 and, thereafter, if the Company fixes an interest rate of 7%, at a conversion price of $20.00 per share. The debentures are redeemable at par plus accrued interest after February 28, 1990 and at any time prior to this date, at 106% of par plus accrued interest if at least 85% of the original principal amount of the debentures has been converted.

The 1987 adjustable rate convertible debentures pay a minimum interest rate of 5% and are convertible, at the holder's option, on or before the earlier of the last business day prior to either redemption or March 31, 2007, into common shares of the Company at an initial conversion price of $27.00 per share until April 1, 1992, and, thereafter, if the Company fixes an interest rate of 6%, at a conversion price of $30.00 per share. The debentures are redeemable at par plus accrued interest after April 1, 1992, and at any time prior to this date, at 105% of par plus accrued interest if at least 85% of the original principal amount of the debentures has been converted. On April 1, 2007, the Company has the option to retire any debentures then outstanding by issuing common shares of equivalent fair market value to the debenture holders.

12. Share Capital

Authorized and issued

The authorized capital stock of the Company is as follows:

4,000,000 preferred shares issuable in series, of which 300 consist of a series designated as "Series 1 Preferred Shares."

Common shares of nopar value in unlimited amount.

EXHIBIT 22–11   (*concluded*)

Preferred Shares

During the year, the Company issued by private placement 300 Series 1 Preferred Shares for $150 million. The dividend rate on the shares is fixed at 7.85% per annum, payable quarterly until March 31, 1994. The dividend rate for subsequent periods will be established by negotiation between the Company and the holders of the Series 1 Preferred Shares or, if no agreement is reached, by a bid solicitation procedure involving investment dealers or, if no bids are accepted, by a monthly auction procedure. The shares are redeemable by the Company on or after March 31, 1994, at par plus any accrued and unpaid dividends.

Common Shares

The changes in issued and fully paid common shares of the Company are as follows:

	1989		1988	
(*in millions*)	**Shares**	**Amount**	**Shares**	**Amount**
Issued and outstanding, beginning of year	73.79	$258.0	72.73	$244.2
Issued under employee share purchase and option plans	0.72	13.0	0.64	8.7
Issued as a result of debenture conversions	0.10	1.3	0.40	4.7
Issued under shareholder dividend reinvestment plan and stock dividend election program	0.02	0.4	0.02	0.4
	0.84	14.7	1.06	13.8
Issued and outstanding, end of year	74.63	$272.7	73.79	$258.0

Shares Available for Share Purchase and Option Plans

Details of unissued common shares for allotment to employees under share purchase or option plans as of April 30, 1989, are as follows:

Unissued common shares designated for allotment under By-Law No. 3 (1987).		3,000,000
Less:		
Issued	581,082	
Under option.	120,000	
Reserved for employee share purchase plan maturing in July 1989.	427,329	1,128,411
Shares available for issue		1,871,589

Shares under option to employees under By-Law No. 3 and previous By-Laws as of April 30, 1989, are as follows:

Plan	Number of Shares	Price per Share	Expiry Date
1979 Share option	20,000	$ 5.44	December 1989
1983 Share option	42,000	10.75	October 1993
1984 Share option	8,000	9.71	June 1994
1985 Share option	121,603	13.59	June 1995
1986 Share option	60,500	22.23	December 1996
1987 Share option	90,000	22.68	November 1997
1988 Share option	30,000	22.17	March 1999
	372,103		

Of the 372,103 shares under option there are 51,603 under option to officers of the Company. Under these plans, the individuals are entitled to purchase the shares over periods of up to 10 years.

The following schedule sets out details of the loans to employees for shares purchased:

(*in millions*)	1989	1988
Officers	$16.8	$10.5
Other employees	4.7	3.6
	$21.5	$14.1
Number of shares	1.4	1.2

(L.O. 3)   7. The dilutive/antidilutive (D/A) test involves combining the individual dilutive items sequentially to determine the lowest possible EPS figure.

(L.O. 4)   8. Adjusted basic EPS is required when common shares have been issued on conversion of senior shares or debt during the period. Adjusted basic EPS adjusts basic EPS to reflect the operating results and outstanding shares as though the conversion had taken place at the beginning of the period. If adjusted basic EPS is required, it is used as the starting point for fully diluted EPS.

(L.O. 5)   9. Pro forma EPS figures, both basic and fully diluted, are calculated when companies issue common shares after the balance sheet date and use the proceeds to retire existing debt or senior shares. Pro forma figures are also required if shares are issued after the balance sheet date on the conversion of senior shares or debt, or on a reorganization. The effect of this change in capital structure is worked back through the EPS figures, as required, as though the change took place at the beginning of the period.

REVIEW PROBLEM

◆

Ice King Products Ltd. reported a net income after taxes of $6 million in 1993. Their capital structure included the following as of December 31, 1993:

Long-term debt:
  Bonds payable, due 1997, 12% . . . . $ 5,000,000
  Bonds payable, due 2001, 8%, convertible into common
    shares at the rate of two shares per $100 . . . . $10,000,000

	Number of Shares Outstanding

Shareholders' equity:
  Preferred shares, $4.50, nopar, cumulative,
    convertible into common shares at the rate of two
    common shares for each preferred share   150,000
  Preferred shares, $2.50, nopar, cumulative,
    convertible into common shares at the rate of one
    common share for each preferred share   400,000
  Common shares. 1,500,000

Warrants to purchase common shares:
  100,000 shares at $20, expire in 1997.
  200,000 shares at $52, expire in 1999.

Transactions during the year:
  On August 1, 400,000 common shares were issued on the conversion of 200,000 $4.50 preferred shares.
  On December 1, 100,000 common shares were issued for cash.

Other information:
  Imputed earnings rate, before tax, 10%.
  Tax rate, 25%.
  Quarterly dividends are declared on March 30, June 30, September 30, and December 31.

REVIEW SOLUTION

◆

Basic EPS:

Computations:
1. For numerator (income):

Preferred Dividend Claim

	$4.50 Preferred		**$2.50 Preferred**	
March 30	($4.50/4) × (350,000)	$ 393,750	($2.50/4) × 400,000	$ 250,000
June 30	($4.50/4) × (350,000)	393,750		250,000
September 30	($4.50/4) × (150,000)	168,750		250,000
December 31	($4.50/4) × (150,000)	168,750		250,000
		$1,125,000		$1,000,000

Note: On Aug. 1, 200,000 of the $4.50 preferred shares converted to common. Therefore, before the conversion, 350,000 shares were outstanding (200,000 + 150,000).

2. For denominator (shares):

Weighted Average Number of Common Shares Outstanding during 1993

	Actual Shares Outstanding	Months Outstanding	Weighted Shares Outstanding
January 1–August 1, shares outstanding	1,000,000*	6**	6,000,000
Shares issued August 1	400,000		
August 1–December 1, shares outstanding	1,400,000	5**	7,000,000
Shares issued for cash	100,000		
December 1–December 31, shares outstanding	1,500,000	1	1,500,000
Totals		12	14,500,000

Weighted average shares outstanding: $\dfrac{14,500,000}{12} = 1,208,333.$

Basic Earnings per Common Share

$$EPS = \frac{\$6,000,000 - \$1,125,000 - \$1,000,000}{1,208,333}$$

$$= \frac{\$3,875,000}{1,208,333}$$

$$= \$3.21$$

* By subtraction: (1,500,000 − 100,000 − 400,000).

** Dividend requirement expired on June 30; 400,000 shares asumed to be outstanding from July 1.

Adjusted EPS:

Computations:
1. For numerator (income):

Preferred Dividend Claim Avoided

March 30	($4.50/4) × 200,000	$225,000
June 30	($4.50/4) × 200,000	225,000
		$450,000

2. For denominator (shares):

Additional Shares Outstanding

400,000 × 6/12	200,000

The 400,000 shares were assumed to have been issued on July 1 in the calculation of basic. We are now moving them back from July 1 to January 1.

Adjusted EPS

$$EPS = \frac{\$3,875,000^* + \$450,000}{1,208,333^* + 200,000}$$

$$= \frac{\$4,325,000}{1,408,333}$$

$$= \$3.07$$

* Previously calculated, basic.

Fully Diluted EPS:

Computations:
1. Bonds Payable, 8%:

For numerator ($10,000,000 × .08)(1 − .25)	$600,000
For denominator ($10,000,000 ÷ $100) × 2	200,000
EPS effect ($600,000/200,000)	$3.00

2. Preferred Shares, $4.50:*

For numerator ($4.50 × 150,000)	$675,000
For denominator (2 × 150,000)	300,000
EPS effect ($675,000/300,000)	$2.25

3. Preferred Shares, $2.50:*

For numerator ($2.50 × 400,000)	$1,000,000
For denominator (1 × 400,000)	400,000
EPS effect ($1,000,000/400,000)	$2.50

4. Warrants, $20:

For numerator ($20 × 100,000) (10%) (1 − .25)	$150,000
For denominator (1 × 100,000)	100,000
EPS effect ($150,000/100,000)	$1.50

5. Warrants, $52:

For numerator ($52 × 200,000) (10%) (1 − .25)	$780,000
For denominator (1 × 200,000)	200,000
EPS effect ($780,000/200,000)	$3.90

* Those outstanding at year-end; have not yet converted.

Test for Dilution/Antidilution for Fully Diluted EPS[†]

	Income	No. of Shares	EPS
Adjusted Basic	$4,325,000	1,408,333	$3.07
$20 Warrants	150,000	100,000	
Subtotal	4,475,000	1,508,333	2.96
$4.50 Preferred	675,000	300,000	
Subtotal	5,150,000	1,808,333	2.85
$2.50 Preferred	1,000,000	400,000	
Subtotal	6,150,000	2,208,333	2.79
8% Bonds Payable	600,000	200,000	
Subtotal	6,750,000	2,408,333	2.80*
$52 Warrants	780,000	200,000	
Total	$7,530,000	2,608,333	2.88*

[†] Schedule starts with the most dilutive individual item and works to the least dilutive element.

* Antidilutive. Note that the 8% bonds payable are antidilutive even though their *individual* EPS is lower than adjusted basic EPS.

Fully Diluted EPS Calculation

$$EPS = \frac{\$4,325,000^* + \$150,000 + \$675,000 + \$1,000,000}{1,408,333^* + 100,000 + 300,000 + 400,000}$$

$$= \frac{\$6,150,000}{2,208,333}$$

$$= \$2.79$$

* Previously calculated, adjusted basic.

KEY TERMS

QUESTIONS

1. What is the major difference in EPS computations and reporting between a simple capital structure and a complex capital structure?
2. Explain why non-convertible securities do not cause a complex capital structure while convertible securities do cause a complex capital structure.
3. Why are weighted average common shares used in EPS calculations?
4. If bonds that pay interest on January 1 and July 1 are converted to common shares on October 1 with no further interest paid, when is the conversion assumed to have taken place in the calculation of weighted average common shares outstanding? Why?
5. In the calculation of income attributable to common shareholders for basic EPS, when are dividends on non-cumulative preferred shares deducted? Why?
6. Explain why and when dividends on non-convertible preferred shares must be subtracted from income to compute EPS in both simple and complex capital structures. What about convertible preferred dividends?
7. A company split its common shares two for one on June 30 of its accounting year ended December 31. Before the split, 4,000 common shares were outstanding. How many weighted average common shares should be used in computing EPS? How many shares should be used in computing a comparative EPS amount for the preceding year?
8. Contrast basic EPS and fully diluted EPS.
9. What is the difference between a dilutive security and an antidilutive security? Why is the distinction important in EPS considerations?
10. What is the starting point in the calculation of fully diluted EPS?
11. How is the D/A test applied? Will all items with an individual effect lower than basic, or adjusted basic, EPS always be included?
12. What is added to the numerator in the calculation of fully diluted EPS when options are considered? Convertible bonds? Preferred shares?
13. Nexxus Corp. issued convertible bonds on April 1 of the current fiscal year, which corresponds to the calendar year. When calculating fully diluted EPS, will the conversion be assumed to take place on January 1 or April 1? Why?
14. When is adjusted basic EPS calculated? What is the purpose of adjusted basic EPS?
15. A company had net income of $12.3 million, after an extraordinary loss of $420,000. During the year, holders of $10 million worth of preferred shares converted their investment into common shares. A further $20 million worth of preferred shares converted to common shares two weeks after the end of the fiscal period. How many EPS numbers will the company calculate? State any necessary assumptions.
16. What is the materiality rule in EPS computations?
17. Is the materiality rule in Canada as definitive as it is in the United States?
18. When are pro forma EPS figures calculated? What is their purpose?

EXERCISES

E 22–1
Analyze the Capital Structure: Average Shares, Compute EPS
(L.O. 2)

At the end of 1992 the records of Nickle Corporation reflected the following:

Common shares, nopar value,:	
Outstanding Jan. 1, 1992, 300,000 shares	$1,680,000
Sold and issued April 1, 1992, 2,000 shares	10,000
Issued 10% stock dividend, Sept. 30, 1992, 30,200 shares	151,000
Preferred shares, nopar, 90 cents, non-convertible, non-cumulative, outstanding during year, 20,000 shares	300,000
Retained earnings (after effects of current preferred dividends declared during 1992)	640,000
Bonds payable, 6½%, non-convertible	1,000,000
Income before extraordinary items	182,000
Extraordinary loss (net of tax)	(18,000)
Net income	164,000
Preferred dividends declared	12,000
Average income tax rate, 40%.	

Required:

1. Is this a simple or complex capital structure? Explain.
2. What kind of EPS presentation is required? Explain.
3. Compute the required EPS amounts.
4. Compute the required EPS amounts, assuming the preferred is cumulative.

E 22–2
Analyze the Capital Structure: Average Shares, Compute EPS
(L.O. 2)

The records for Potter Corporation at the end of 1993 reflected the following:

Common shares, nopar, authorized unlimited shares:	
Outstanding at beginning of the year, January 1, 100,000 shares	$200,000
Sold and issued during that year, September 1, 3,000 shares	8,000
Preferred shares, nopar, 90 cents, non-convertible, cumulative, authorized unlimited shares:	
Outstanding during the year, 6,000 shares	65,000
Retained earnings	150,000
Bonds payable, 6½%, non-convertible	400,000
Income before extraordinary items	130,000
Extraordinary gain (net of tax)	20,000
Net income	150,000

Required:

1. Is this a simple or complex capital structure? Explain.
2. What kind of EPS presentation is required? Explain.
3. Compute the required EPS amounts (show computations).
4. Compute the required EPS amounts, assuming the preferred shares are non-cumulative. The current year's dividend has not been declared and the preceding year's dividend was also passed (i.e., not declared).

E 22–3
Compute EPS for Three Years: Stock Dividend and Split
(L.O. 2)

Ramca Corporation's accounting year ends on December 31. During the three most recent years, its common shares outstanding changed as follows:

	1993	1992	1991
Shares outstanding, January 1	150,000	120,000	100,000
Sale of shares, April 1, 1991			20,000
25% stock dividend, July 1, 1992		30,000	
Two-for-one stock split, July 1, 1993	150,000*		
Shares sold, October 1, 1993	50,000		
Shares outstanding, December 31	350,000	150,000	120,000
Net income	$375,000	$330,000	$299,000

* For each share turned in two new shares were issued so that the shares doubled.

Required:

1. For purposes of calculating EPS at the end of each year, for each year independently, determine the number of shares outstanding.
2. For purposes of calculating EPS at the end of 1993, when comparative statements are being prepared on a three-year basis, determine the number of shares outstanding for each year.
3. Compute EPS for each year based on year computations in (2).

E 22–4
Analyze the Capital Structure; Stock Dividend; Compute EPS
(L.O. 2)

At the end of 1992, the records of Alert Corporation showed the following:

Common shares, nopar, authorized unlimited shares:	
Outstanding January 1, 1992, 52,000 shares	$595,000
Retired shares April 1, 1992, 2,000 shares	(22,885)
Issued a 100% stock dividend on December 1, 1992, on outstanding shares (50,000 additional shares).	

Preferred shares:
   Class A, nopar, 60 cents, non-convertible, non-cumulative,
     outstanding 10,000 shares   100,000
   Class B, nopar, 70 cents, non-convertible, cumulative,
     outstanding 20,000 shares   200,000
Retained earnings (no dividends declared in 1992).   570,000
Bonds payable, 7%, non-convertible   120,000
Income before extraordinary items   180,500
Extraordinary gain (net of tax)   10,000
Net income.   190,500
Average income tax rate, 40%.

Required:

1. Is this a simple or complex capital structure? Explain.
2. What kind of EPS presentation is required? Explain.
3. Compute the required EPS amounts (show computations).

E 22–5
Compute EPS: Three
Kinds of Gains and Losses
(L.O. 2, 3)

To illustrate EPS reporting for various combinations of gains and losses, assume 1,000 common shares are outstanding for the five cases given below. No preferred shares are outstanding.

Items	Case A	Case B	Case C	Case D	Case E
Income (loss).	$10,000	$(10,000)	$ 10,000	$(10,000)	$(10,000)
Extraordinary gain (loss)	6,000	(6,000)	(6,000)	6,000	6,000
Discontinued operations, gain (loss)	3,000	(3,000)	(3,000)	3,000	(3,000)
Net income (loss).	$19,000	$(19,000)	$ 1,000	$ (1,000)	$ (7,000)

Assume a complex capital structure and that for fully diluted EPS the number of shares outstanding is 1,500 and that income (loss) amounts above are $2,000 higher for income.

Required:

1. Compute basic EPS for each case.
2. Compute fully diluted EPS for each case.
3. What dilutive elements may be present in the capital structure?

E 22–6
Options and Computation
of EPS
(L.O. 2, 3)

Caball Inc. had a net income of $600,000. During the year in question, 160,000 common shares were outstanding on average. During the year, Caball's common shares sold at an average market price of $50, but at year-end sold for $70. Caball had 20,000 options outstanding to purchase a total of 20,000 shares at $25 for each option exercised. Assume a 10% return, after tax.

Required:

1. Are the options dilutive?
2. Compute fully diluted EPS.

E 22–7
Convertible Bonds and
Calculation of Basic and
Fully Diluted EPS
(L.O. 2, 3)

Shaffer Corporation issued 100, $1,000, 10% convertible bonds in 1989. Each bond is convertible into 100 shares of common. Shaffer's net income for 1991 is $1,824,000 ($3,040,000 before tax). Average common shares outstanding for 1991, considering all factors except convertible bonds, are:

For basic EPS, 1,010,000.

For fully diluted EPS, 1,033,000. (The income effect of the additional shares, excluding the bond, was $25,300 after tax.)

Required:

1. Compute basic EPS.
2. Compute fully diluted EPS.
3. How would you answer (1) and (2) if the bonds were issued July 1, 1991?

E 22–8
Convertible Bonds,
Preferred Shares, Options:
Impact on Fully Diluted
EPS
(L.O. 3)

The Lannifair Corporation has the following items in its capital structure at the end of 1994:

a. Preferred shares, $6, cumulative, nopar, convertible into common shares at the rate of five shares of common for each one preferred share. Shares were outstanding for the entire year. Dividends were declared quarterly. Five thousand shares were outstanding for the whole year.

b. Preferred shares, $6, cumulative, nopar, convertible into common shares at the rate of five shares of common for each one preferred share. Five thousand shares were issued on March 30 of the current year. Dividends were declared quarterly, starting June 30.

c. Options to purchase 200,000 common shares were outstanding for the entire period. The exercise price is $25 per share. The corporation expects to earn 10% before tax.

d. One million dollars of 9½% debentures, issued on November 1 of the current year. Debentures are convertible into 5 common shares for each $100 bond.

e. Ten million dollars of 12% debentures, outstanding for the entire year. Debentures are convertible into a total of 400,000 common shares.

Required:

Calculate the impact on fully diluted EPS for each of the above items, taken individually. The tax rate is 45%. The fiscal year corresponds to the calendar year.

E 22–9
Analyze Capital Structure:
Stock Split, Convertible
Securities, and EPS
Computation
(L.O. 2, 3)

At the end of 1994, the records of Russo Corporation reflected the following:

Common shares, nopar, authorized unlimited shares; issued and outstanding throughout the period to Dec. 1, 1994, 60,000 shares. A stock split was issued Dec. 1, 1994, that doubled outstanding shares.	$840,000
Preferred shares, 50 cents, non-convertible, cumulative, non-participating; shares issued and outstanding during year, 10,000 shares	130,000
Retained earnings (no cash or property dividends declared during year)	570,000
Bonds payable, 10%, issued Jan. 1, 1994, each $1,000 bond is convertible to 60 common shares after the stock split on Dec. 1, 1994 (bonds initially sold at par)	200,000
Income before extraordinary items	86,000
Extraordinary loss (net of tax)	(14,000)
Net income	72,000
Average income tax rate, 30%.	

Required:

1. Is this a simple or complex capital structure? Explain.
2. What kind of EPS presentation is required? Explain.
3. Compute the required EPS amounts (show computations, rounded to two decimal places, and assume all amounts are material).

E 22–10
Analyze Capital Structure:
Non-convertible Preferred,
Stock Rights, and EPS
Computation
(L.O. 2, 3)

The records of Thermal Corporation showed the following as of December 31, 1992:

Common shares, nopar, authorized 400,000 shares; issued and outstanding during 1992, 200,000 shares	$2,300,000
Common share rights outstanding (for 20,000 shares) option price, $15	200,000
Preferred shares, $8, non-convertible, cumulative, authorized 40,000 shares; outstanding during 1992, 10,000 shares	1,400,000
Retained earnings	7,000,000
Net income (no extraordinary items)	2,000,000
After-tax rate of return on net assets	10%

Required:

1. Is this a simple or complex capital structure? Explain.
2. Prepare the required EPS presentation for 1992. Show all computations. Disregard the materiality test.

E 22–11
Analyze Capital Structure: Stock Rights, Preferred Shares, and EPS Computation
(L.O. 2, 3)

At the end of 1992, the records of Johnson Corporation reflected the following:

Common shares, nopar, authorized unlimited number of shares;
  issued and outstanding throughout year, 50,000 shares $580,000
Stock rights outstanding (all year, for 10,000 common shares at
  $15 per share) 100,000
Preferred shares, nopar, $3.50, cumulative, convertible into common share
  for share, authorized 10,000 shares; issued and outstanding
  throughout year, 2,000 shares 100,000
Retained earnings (no dividends declared during the year) 470,000
Bonds payable, 10%, non-convertible 150,000
Income before extraordinary items 85,000
Extraordinary gain (net of tax) 35,000
Net income 120,000
After-tax rate of return on net assets 10%
Average income tax rate, 30%.

Required:

1. Is this a simple or complex capital structure? Explain.
2. What kind of EPS presentation is required? Explain.
3. Compute the required EPS amounts (show computations and assume all amounts are material).

E 22–12
Complex Capital Structure and Reporting EPS
(L.O. 2, 3, 4)

The Ratelli Company reports the following data:

Operating income. . . . .$(1,000,000)
Extraordinary item 2,000,000
Net income . . . .$ 1,000,000

Shares outstanding:

For basic EPS 1,000,000
For adjusted EPS 1,200,000
For fully diluted EPS 1,500,000

Income levels, as calculated:

	Net Income
For basic EPS	$ 100,000
For adjusted EPS	$ 130,000
For fully diluted EPS	$ 200,000

Required:

1. What types of things cause income to differ between basic, adjusted, and fully diluted EPS calculations?
2. What EPS figures would Ratelli report? What are their values?

E 22–13
Analyze Capital Structure: Stock Split, Convertible Securities, EPS Computation
(L.O. 2, 3, 4)

At the end of 1994, Branch Corporation's records reflected the following:

Common shares, nopar, authorized unlimited shares; issued and outstanding
  throughout the period to July 1, 1994, 100,000 shares. A stock split occurred
  on July 1 that doubled outstanding shares. 6,000 shares were issued on
  December 1 when bond holders converted. Interest was paid at the date
  of conversion $1,880,000
Preferred shares, 50 cents, non-convertible, cumulative, non-participating;
  shares issued and outstanding during year, 20,000 shares 260,000
Retained earnings (no cash or property dividends declared during year) 1,140,000
Bonds payable, 10%, issued January 1, 1990; each $1,000 bond is convertible
  to 60* common shares; bonds sold at par 200,000
Income before extraordinary items 272,000
Extraordinary loss (net of tax) 28,000
Net income 244,000
Average tax rate, 30%.
* Sixty shares is the rate of conversion after the stock split.

Required:

1. Is this a simple or complex capital structure? Explain.
2. What kind of EPS presentation is required? Explain.
3. Compute the required EPS amounts (show computations, round to two decimal places, and assume all amounts are material).

E 22–14
Complex Capital Structure and Reporting EPS
(L.O. 2, 3, 5)

The Tripoli Company reported the following information for the year ended December 31, 1992:

Net income . . . . $ 400,000

Shares outstanding:
    For basic EPS 850,000
    For fully diluted EPS 1,900,000

Income:
    For basic EPS . . . . $ 120,000
    For fully diluted EPS 175,000*

* For fully diluted EPS, the $175,000 replaces, rather than adds to, the $120,000.

On January 23, 1993, Tripoli issued 200,000 common shares and used the proceeds to retire $1,000,000 worth of 10% non-convertible bonds payable. The corporate tax rate was 25%.

Required:

1. What EPS figures would Tripoli report?
2. What are their values? Show calculations and ignore materiality concerns.

E 22–15
Complex Capital Structure and Reporting EPS
(L.O. 2, 3, 5)

John Corp. had the following capital structure at the end of 1993:

16% debentures payable, par value $5,000,000, due in 2002 . . . . $5,000,000

Share capital:
  Authorized: 1,000,000, 15 cent, cumulative, nopar value preferred shares,
    convertible into common shares one-for-one, and 2,000,000 common
    shares, nopar value
  Issued and fully paid: 500,000 preferred shares $1,500,000
                  1,740,000 common shares $2,700,000
    (240,000 issued for $1,200,000 seven months after the beginning of the
    most recent fiscal year)

John's net income for the current year before interest and income tax of 45% is $2,500,000.

One month after the end of 1993, John Corp. issued 250,000 common shares and used the proceeds to retire $1,000,000 of the debentures payable.

Required:

Calculate all required EPS disclosures. Show your calculations and ignore materiality concerns.

PROBLEMS

P 22–1
Analyze Capital Structure: Stock Dividend, Convertible Securities
(L.O. 2, 3)

At the end of 1992, the records of Johnson Corporation showed the following:

Common shares, nopar, authorized unlimited number of shares:
  Outstanding Jan. 1, 1992, 200,000 shares $1,650,000
  Shares retired, June 1, 1992, 1,000 shares at a cost of $15,000. Book value . . . . (8,250)
  Stock dividend issued, Nov. 1, 1992, 19,900 shares (10%, one additional
    share for each ten shares outstanding) 398,000
Preferred shares, nopar, $1, non-cumulative, non-convertible;
  issued and outstanding throughout the year, 10,000 shares 275,000
Retained earnings (no cash or property dividends declared during 1992) 942,000
Bonds payable, Series A, 7%, each $1,000 bond is convertible to
  20 common shares after stock dividend (bonds issued at par) 50,000
Bonds payable, Series B, 6%, each $1,000 bond is convertible to
  57 common shares after stock dividend (bonds issued at par) 400,000

Income before extraordinary gain	380,000
Extraordinary gain (net of tax)	15,000
Net income	395,000

Average income tax rate for 1992, 30%.
Both bond series were issued prior to January 1, 1992.

Required:

1. Is this a simple or complex capital structure? Explain.
2. Prepare the EPS presentation with all supporting computations.

P 22–2
Analyze Capital Structure: Stock Rights and Convertible Securities, EPS Computation (L.O. 2, 3)

Jiffie Corporation is developing its EPS presentation at December 31, 1994. The records of the company provide the following information:

Liabilities

Convertible bonds payable, 7% (each $1,000 bond is convertible to 100 common shares)	$150,000

Shareholders' Equity

Common shares, nopar, authorized unlimited number of shares:	
Outstanding Jan. 1, 1994, 59,000 shares	214,000
Sold and issued 10,000 shares on April 1, 1994	40,000
Common share rights outstanding (all year for 4,000 common shares)	16,000
Preferred shares, nopar, 60 cents, cumulative, convertible (each share is convertible into ½ of 1 common share); authorized, unlimited shares; outstanding during 1994, 5,000 shares	65,000
Retained earnings	452,000
Income before extraordinary items	110,000
Extraordinary gain (net of tax)	20,000
Net income	130,000

Additional data:

a. Stock rights—option price, $4 per share; average market price of the common shares during 1994, $6.
b. Convertible bonds—issue price, par.
c. Average income tax rate, 30%.
d. After tax rate of return on net assets, 10%.

Required:

1. Is this a simple or complex capital structure? Explain.
2. What kind of EPS presentation is required? Explain.
3. Prepare the required EPS presentation for 1994. Show all computations.
4. Were there any antidilutive securities? How was this determined?
5. How should antidilutive securities be treated in the computation of EPS? Why?

P 22–3
Complex Capital Structure: Compute EPS for Two Alternatives, Partial Year (L.O. 2, 3)

Falcon Company has a compensatory stock option plan under which options to buy 255,000 common shares were issued in 1991. These options are exercisable during 1992 and 1993 at $3 per share. In 1992, Falcon reported net income of $500,000; the company's capital structure remained unchanged that year.

Outstanding share capital consists of 1 million common shares, which traded at an average price of $20 per share throughout 1992. The company's long-term debt consists of a $2,500,000 bond issue sold at par, which pays 12% annual interest and was outstanding throughout 1992. Falcon has no other indebtedness. Falcon's average income tax rate is 30%. Average return on investment, before tax, was 14%, and the company has a December 31 year-end.

Required:

1. Compute EPS for 1992.
2. Suppose the facts given above are modified as follows: Falcon issued the stock options on July 1, 1992. Compute EPS for 1992. Ignore the materiality rule.

P 22–4
Analyze Capital Structure:
Convertible Bonds Sold at
a Premium and EPS
Computation
(L.O. 2, 3)

At the end of 1993, the records of Mathias Corporation reflected the following information:

Common shares, nopar, authorized 500,000 shares:	
Outstanding Jan. 1, 125,000 shares	$256,000
Sold and issued on Aug. 1, 15,000 shares	30,000
Bonds payable, 8%, convertible.	100,000
Premium on bonds payable	9,200
Retained earnings	900,000
Net income (no extraordinary items)	350,000

The convertible bonds were issued on July 1, 1993, at a premium. Each $1,000 bond is convertible to 30 common shares. Premium amortization related to the bonds during 1993 was $800. The average income tax rate during 1993 was 30%.

Required:

1. Is this a simple or complex capital structure? Explain.
2. Prepare the required EPS presentation for 1993. Show all computations. Disregard the materiality test.

P 22–5
Analyze Capital Structure:
Stock Warrants,
Non-convertible Securities,
and EPS Computation
(L.O. 2, 3)

The records of Crosby Corporation reflected the following data at the end of 1992:

Liabilities	
Bonds payable, 9%, convertible (each $1,000 bond is	
convertible to 40 common shares)	$150,000
Shareholders' Equity	
Common shares, nopar, authorized unlimited shares:	
Outstanding Jan. 1, 1992, 150,000 shares	675,000
Sold and issued on Oct. 1, 1992, 20,000 shares	40,000
Common share warrants (outstanding all year)	
for 6,000 shares.	12,000
Preferred shares, nopar, 30 cents, non-convertible,	
cumulative, authorized unlimited shares, outstanding	
during 1992, 20,000 shares	145,000
Retained earnings	280,000
Income before extraordinary items	170,000
Extraordinary loss (net of tax)	(20,000)
Net income	150,000

Additional data:

a. Stock warrants—option price, $3 per share.
b. Convertible bonds—issue price, par.
c. Average income tax rate, 30%.
d. After-tax rate of return on assets, 10%.

Required:

1. Is this a simple or complex capital structure? Explain.
2. What kind of EPS presentation is required? Explain.
3. Prepare the required EPS presentation for 1992. Show all computations. Disregard the materiality test.
4. Were there any antidilutive securities? How was this determined?
5. How should antidilutive securities be treated in EPS computations? Why?

P 22–6
Analyze Capital Structure:
Stock Dividend,
Convertible Securities,
EPS Computation
(L.O. 2, 3)

At the end of 1995 the records of Luholtz Corporation reflected the following:

Common shares, nopar, authorized 500,000 shares: issued	
and outstanding throughout period, 100,000 shares	$680,000
Stock dividend issued, Dec. 31, 50,000 shares	
(not included in the 100,000 shares above)	340,000
Retained earnings (after effect of dividends)	500,000
Bonds payable, 7%, each $1,000 bond is convertible to	
80 common shares after the stock dividend (bonds issued at par)	100,000

Bonds payable, 8%, each $1,000 bond is convertible to
  90 common shares after the stock dividend (bonds issued at par)   300,000
Income before extraordinary items   210,000
Extraordinary gain   12,000
Net income.   222,000
Average income tax rate, 30%.

Required:

1. Is this a simple or complex capital structure? Explain.
2. What kind of EPS presentation is required? Explain. Disregard the materiality test.
3. Compute the required EPS amounts (show computations, rounded to two decimal places, and assume all amounts are material).

P 22–7
Computing a Loss per Share
(L.O. 2, 3)

Cooper Corporation's balance sheet at December 31, 1994, reported the following:

Accrued interest payable . . . . $ 1,000
Long-term notes payable, 10%, due in 1997   50,000
Bonds payable, 8%, each $1,000 of face value is convertible
  into 90 common shares; bonds mature in 2006   800,000
Preferred shares, nopar, $5, non-convertible, cumulative
  (5,000 shares outstanding at year-end)   250,000
Common shares, 140,000 shares outstanding   700,000
Common share rights outstanding all year entitling holders
  to acquire 40,000 common shares at $9 per share.
Net loss for 1994   125,000

Additional data:

a. During 1994, 1,000 preferred shares were issued at $50 on July 1. Dividends are paid semiannually, on May 31 and November 30.
b. The convertible bonds were issued at par.
c. Income tax rate is 30%.
d. Cooper earned taxable income of $400,000 each year from 1991 to 1993, equal to an after-tax rate of return on net assets of 5%.

Required:

Compute the EPS amount that Cooper should report on the income statement for 1994. Show all computations.

P 22–8
Computation of Average Number of Shares Outstanding and EPS
(L.O. 2, 3)

Zolar Corporation reported 1993 earnings per share of $22,875,000 ÷ 10,500,000 = $2.18 based on the following data:

Net income $22,875,000

Common shares:
  January 1, 1993   12,000,000
  December 31, 1993   9,000,000
Average number of shares outstanding   10,500,000

Upon examination of Zolar's records it is noted that Zolar acquired and retired 4,000,000 shares on April 1, 1993, and issued 1,000,000 shares to satisfy all employee options outstanding on September 30, 1993. No equity securities besides common are outstanding, and Zolar has no convertible securities or other options outstanding.

Required:

1. Is Zolar's EPS calculation correct or not? Explain.
2. Revise the EPS figure if you think it is in error.
3. Suppose the facts above are altered as follows:
   a. An additional 500,000 options allowing holders to buy 500,000 shares at $25 a share are outstanding all of 1993. The appropriate after-tax rate of return is 6%.
   b. In addition to the 500,000 options, Zolar has outstanding 100,000 shares of nopar, $5, cumulative, non-convertible preferred issued in 1988. The dividend was paid in 1993.
   What changes are required in the EPS calculations for basic and fully diluted EPS?

P 22–9
Determination of Capital
Structure: Calculating and
Reporting of EPS
(L.O. 2)

Davidson Corporation had a net operating income from operations of $5.6 million for the year ended December 31, 1994. Davidson also paid flood damages of $1 million, which it disclosed as an extraordinary item of $740,000, after tax. Davidson also reported a $1.23 million after-tax loss on discontinued operations.

Davidson's capital structure consists of:

Preferred: 100,000 shares of nopar, $8, cumulative, non-convertible preferred, issued in 1985. The dividend was declared but was not paid by year-end.

Common: Outstanding January 1, 1994, 4,271,865 shares, nopar, issued at $1 per share. Dividends of 25 cents per share were paid in 1994.
On July 1, 1994, a two-for-one stock split was declared and the shares issued.

Required:

1. What type of capital structure does Davidson have (simple or complex)?
2. Compute and label the relevant EPS figures.
3. Must the EPS figures for the flood damages and discontinued operations be reported?

P 22–10
Computing Basic, Adjusted,
and Fully Diluted EPS
(L.O. 2, 3, 4)

Zorbas Inc. needs to establish its EPS figures for its 1993 reports. The following information is available to Deb Its, Zorbas's controller.

a. Net income $80,000,000. Before tax, $133,340,000.
b. Common shares: 20,000,000 shares authorized, 15,000,000 shares outstanding January 1, 1993.
c. Cumulative, convertible preferred shares: 2,000,000 shares issued August 1, 1988, and outstanding January 1, 1993. Issued at $50 a share with a yearly $4 dividend paid semiannually June 30 and December 31. The shares are convertible on a share-for-share basis adjusted automatically for any stock dividends or splits.
d. March 1, 1993: half the preferred was converted to common.
e. April 1, 1993: Zorbas declared a 10% stock dividend.
f. July 1: 1,000,000 common shares were issued in the acquisition of the Tande Corporation. The share's market value at this time was $15 per share.
g. October 1: Zorbas purchased and retired 600,000 common shares for $700,000.
h. All preferred dividends were declared and paid. Dividends are not prorated to the date of conversion.

Required:

1. Compute basic EPS.
2. Compute adjusted EPS.
3. Compute fully diluted EPS.

P 22–11
EPS Computations:
Complex
(L.O. 2, 3, 4)

The following data relate to Jacobs Inc.:

Year Ended December 31, 1993

From the income statement:
  Net income $10,300,000

From the balance sheet:
  Long-term debt:
    10% convertible debentures, due October 1, 2000 10,000,000
  Shareholders' equity (Note 1)
    Convertible voting preferred shares of nopar value, 20-cent
    cumulative dividend. Authorized 600,000 shares; issued and
    outstanding 600,000.   600,000
    (Liquidation value $22 per share, aggregating $13,200,000.)
    Common shares, nopar, authorized 5,000,000 shares;
    issued and outstanding 3,320,000 13,700,000

Note 1
The 20-cent convertible preferred shares are callable by the company after March 31, 1991, at $53 per share. Each share is convertible into one common share.
Warrants to acquire 500,000 common shares at $60 per share were outstanding at the end of 1993.

Other information:

a. Cash dividends of 12.5 cents per common share were declared and paid each quarter.
b. Ten percent convertible debentures with a principal amount of $10,000,000 due October 1, 2000, were sold for cash at a price of $98 on October 1, 1990. Each $100 debenture is

convertible into two shares of common. Discount is amortized on a straight-line basis. On December 31, 1993, 10,000, $100 bonds with a total face value of $1,000,000 were converted to common shares. Net income properly reflects the transaction, in which the common shares were recorded at market value. Interest was paid to the date of conversion, but the newly issued common shares did not qualify for the December 31 dividend.

c. The 600,000 convertible preferred shares were issued for assets in a purchase transaction of April 1, 1993. The annual dividend on each share of these convertible preferred shares is 20 cents. The dividend was declared and paid on December 15, 1993. Each share is convertible into one common share.

d. Warrants to buy 500,000 common shares at $60 per share for a period of five years were issued along with the convertible preferred shares mentioned in (c).

e. At the end of 1992, 3,320,000 common shares were outstanding. On December 31, 1993, 20,000 shares were issued on the conversion of bonds.

f. A tax rate of 40% is assumed. An appropriate rate of return on assets, before tax, is 12%.

Required:

Calculate all EPS disclosures. Show all calculations and disregard the materiality rule.

P 22–12
Complex EPS
(L.O. 2, 3, 5)

Canax Corp. had the following securities outstanding at its fiscal year-end December 31, 1994:

Long-term debt:	
Notes payable, 14%	$1,500,000
8% convertible debentures	2,500,000
10% convertible debentures	2,500,000
Preferred shares, $5, nopar, cumulative convertible shares; authorized, 100,000 shares; issued, 25,000 shares	3,500,000
Common shares, nopar; authorized, 5,000,000 shares; issued, 500,000 shares	2,000,000

Other information:

a. No dividends were declared in 1994.

b. 1994 net income was $1,000,000.

c. Options are outstanding to purchase 100,000 common shares at $20 per share.

d. Warrants have been issued to purchase 50,000 common shares at $27 per share.

e. The preferred shares are convertible to common at a rate of five for one.

f. Both convertible debentures were issued at par and are convertible at the rate of four shares for each $100 bond.

g. The tax rate is 40%; an appropriate rate of return on assets is 12% before tax.

h. On January 22, 1995, 100,000 common shares were issued. The proceeds were used to retire all the 14% notes payable.

Required:

Calculate all EPS disclosures. Show all calculations and disregard the materiality rule.

P 22–13
Complex EPS
(L.O. 2, 3, 4)

Darren Company had the following capital structure, exclusive of working capital, at December 31, 1993:

Long-term liabilities:	
8% convertible debentures due April 15, 2000	$30,000,000
Other long-term liabilities	20,000,000
Total long-term debt	50,000,000
Shareholders' equity:	
$4, cumulative, convertible preferred shares, nopar, 2,000,000 shares authorized, 1,200,000 outstanding	$24,200,000
Common shares, nopar, 20,000,000 authorized, 6,900,000 outstanding	11,400,000
Retained earnings	56,400,000
Total shareholders' equity	$92,000,000

Additional information:

a. Convertible debentures are convertible at the rate of 10 shares for each $100 debenture until maturity. Convertible preferreds are convertible at the rate of one for four.

b. Dividends on the preferred shares have been paid quarterly on March 31, June 30, September 30, and December 31. Dividends paid on the common were 50 cents per share per quarter.

c. Net income was $8,600,000. The tax rate was 35%. The before-tax rate of return on assets was 12%.

d. Options were outstanding for 200,000 common shares, exercisable in 1995, at a price of $14 per share.

e. Common share transactions during the period were as follows:

Feb. 1   Reacquired and retired 600,000 common shares.
Apr. 30   Preferred shares converted into 250,000 common shares.
          (Preferred shares tendered, 1,000,000.)
Nov. 30   Issued for cash, 400,000 common shares.

Required:

Compute all EPS figures required for 1993 disclosure. Show calculations and ignore materiality concerns.

P 22–14
Complex EPS
(L.O. 2, 3, 4)

The shareholders' equity of Lowella Corp. as of December 31, 1991, the end of the current fiscal year, is as follows:

$1 cumulative preferred shares, nopar, convertible at the rate of three for one, 400,000 shares outstanding	$12,100,000
Common shares, nopar, 9,000,000 shares outstanding	30,000,000
Retained earnings	40,600,000

On August 30, 1991, 100,000 preferred shares were converted to common shares at the rate of three for one.

During 1991, Lowella had 9¼% convertible subordinated debentures outstanding with a face value of $2,000,000. The debentures are due in 1996, at which time they may be converted to common shares or repaid at the option of the holder. The conversion rate is five common shares for each $100 debenture.

The convertible preferred shares had been issued in 1985. Quarterly dividends, on March 31, June 30, September 30, and December 31, have been regularly declared.

On October 31, 1991, Lowella granted options to key employees to purchase 500,000 common shares at a price of $15 per share. The options become exercisable in 1998.

The company's 1991 net income was $9,200,000, after tax at 48%. Lowella earned an after-tax earnings rate of 9% on assets.

On January 6, 1992, Lowella split its common shares two for one. All preferred, debt, and option contracts outstanding were adjusted accordingly.

Required:

What EPS figures does Lowella have to report in 1991? Show calculations and ignore the materiality test.

P 22–15
Pro Forma EPS
Calculations
(L.O. 2, 3, 5)

The Cray Corporation has calculated basic and fully diluted EPS as follows:

$$\text{Basic} = \frac{\$1,000,000 - \$200,000}{1,700,000}$$

$$= \$.47$$

$$\text{Fully diluted} = \frac{\$800,000 + \$200,000 + \$200,000}{3,200,000}$$

$$= \$.38$$

On February 1, following the close of the current fiscal year on January 31, Cray issued common shares on the conversion of all the convertible preferred shares outstanding on January 31.

In the above calculations, the convertible preferred shares had a dividend entitlement of $200,000 and could be converted into 800,000 common shares.

Required:

1. Explain the nature of the numbers used above in basic and fully diluted EPS.
2. Calculate basic and fully diluted pro forma EPS. Does fully diluted EPS change? Explain.

P 22–16

COMPREHENSIVE PROBLEM
♦

Complex EPS
(L.O. 2, 3, 4, 5)

Hyson Limited reported net income before income taxes and after income taxes of $14,000,000 and $5,600,000, respectively. The company reported no extraordinary items in its income statement for the current year ending December 31, 1992. The following information is available:

a. As at January 1, 1992, there were 1,350,000 common shares outstanding.
b. At the beginning of the current year, 200,000 stock warrants, to purchase 200,000 common shares at $15 per share, were outstanding. Thirty thousand of these warrants were exercised on September 1, 1992. The company's estimated rate of return on its investments was 20% before income taxes.
c. An issue of 12% convertible debentures with a principal amount of $20,000,000 has been outstanding for a number of years. Interest payment dates are April 1 and October 1 each year. Each $1,000 debenture is convertible into 30 shares of common. On April 1, 1992, $16,000,000 worth of the outstanding debentures were converted.
d. For a number of years, 8% cumulative redeemable preferred shares in the amount of $10,000,000 have been outstanding. There was no change in this during 1992.
e. On July 1, 1992, 10% non-cumulative convertible preferred shares in the amount of $12,000,000 were issued at face value of $100 per share. Each preferred share is convertible into five shares of common. Dividends totalling $2.50 per share were declared in 1992 on these preferred shares.
f. On January 31, 1993 (before the completion of the 1992 financial statements on February 28, 1993), the common shares were split on the basis of two new shares for each old one.
g. On February 15, 1993, 400,000 common shares were issued for $8,800,000 cash. The proceeds from the sale were used to redeem $8,000,000 of the 8% cumulative redeemable preferred shares at a premium of 10%.

Required:

For the year ended December 31, 1992, compute each of the following:

1. Basic earnings per share.
2. Adjusted basic earnings per share.
3. Fully diluted earnings per share.
4. Pro forma basic earnings per share.
5. Pro forma fully diluted earnings per share.

CASES

C 22–1
Importance of EPS Figures
(L.O. 1)

On July 24, 1990, the Financial Accounting Standards Advisory Council (FASAC) met with the United States SEC Commissioner Philip Lochner and SEC Chief Accountant Edward Coulson to discuss the effect of accounting standards on industry competitiveness. At that meeting, Mr. Dennis Dammerman, senior vice-president for finance of General Electric Company and a member of FASAC, stated, "Chief Executive Officers, right or wrong, get their report card at least once a quarter and it's generally called earnings per share and that report card reflects accounting."

What relevance do you believe this statement has to the competitive strengths of businesses, and why do you think the issue was raised by FASAC?

C 22–2
Analysis of EPS—Loblaw
Companies Limited
(L.O. 1, 2, 3)

Loblaws

Refer to the annual financial report of Loblaw Companies Limited for the year ended December 29, 1990. Determine the following for 1990 and 1989:

a. Weighted average number of shares outstanding.
b. Amount of preferred dividends.
c. Amount available to common shareholders.
d. List the potentially dilutive securities. Why would fully diluted EPS not be disclosed?

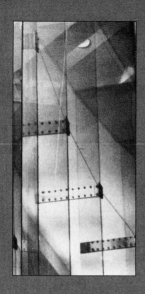

SPECIAL TOPICS

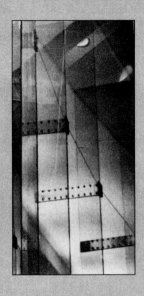

C H A P T E R

23

Statement of Changes in Financial Position

LEARNING
OBJECTIVES

◆

After you have read and studied this chapter, you will be able to:

1. Recognize the usefulness of the statement of changes in financial position, or statement of cash flows.

2. Explain the major provisions of section 1540 of the *CICA Handbook,* "Statement of Changes in Financial Position."

3. Analyze transactions to identify necessary disclosures in the statement of changes in financial position.

4. Prepare a statement of changes in financial position.

5. Prepare a statement of changes in financial position by using a spreadsheet.

6. Prepare a statement of changes in financial position using the T-account approach (refer to Appendix 23A).

◆

INTRODUCTION
◆

In 1989, Rogers Communications Ltd. reported $25.8 million *negative* income, yet generated a *positive* $147.4 million in cash from operations. How could a firm lose that much money, yet generate so much cash? What explained the $173.2 million difference?

The statement of changes in financial position (SCFP), also called a *statement of cash flows,* solved the puzzle. Rogers had recorded a total of $142.6 million in expenses that did not require an outflow of cash, including $82.5 million in depreciation and $16.5 million in tax. They recognized a $25.7 million charge against earnings resulting from writing down the value of a long-term investment, Canadian Home Shopping Network. These items reduced income but did not change the cash balance. Other adjustments were made for items that changed income but affected non-cash assets and liabilities, including payables, receivables, and inventory. The result was a $147.4 million net operating cash inflow.

Investors, creditors, and other interested parties demand cash flow information to project future business cash flows and, therefore, their own cash flows. The SCFP provides information that is not disclosed in the income statement, balance sheet, or footnotes. For example, how much did Telesat Canada spend on satellite construction in 1990? What was Boeing's cash outlay for de Havilland of Canada? How much did Campeau Corporation pay for Federated Department Stores? These amounts are listed on the SCFP.

This chapter discusses the use and preparation of the SCFP. Some of the topics considered in previous chapters are used to illustrate the principles developed in this chapter.

◆

CASH FLOW REPORTING: DEVELOPMENT AND USEFULNESS
◆

The statement of changes in financial position (SCFP), or statement of cash flows (SCF), is a report listing cash inflows and outflows in meaningful categories. The statement explains the change in cash during the period (see Exhibit 23–1).

Firms did not always have to present an SCFP. A brief chronology of events leading to the SCFP follows:

◆ Before 1961: Firms voluntarily disclosed *funds flow statements* that reported sources and uses of working capital (current assets less current liabilities) and that presented partial operating, financing, and investing activity information. Funds flow statements exhibited a variety of titles, format, content, and terminology.
◆ 1961: "Cash Flow Analysis and the Funds Statement," *Accounting Research Study No. 2,* commissioned by the AICPA, recommended that a funds statement be required. The study emphasized that the balance sheet and income statement together did not provide a complete reporting of all changes in resources.
◆ 1963: *APB Opinion No. 3,* "The Statement of Source and Application of Funds," recommended, but did not require, a funds statement.
◆ 1971: *APB Opinion No. 19,* "Reporting Changes in Financial Position," required the *statement of changes in financial position,* a funds statement allowing several "funds" definitions including working capital, cash, and others.[1]
◆ 1974: *CICA Handbook,* section 1540, "Statement of Changes in Financial Position," described, but did not require, the statement; it allowed several definitions of "funds" to be used.

---

[1] Most firms initially chose working capital. The statement explained why working capital increased or decreased during the period, but did not explain the change in cash.

EXHIBIT 23–1 Statement of Changes in Financial Position, Simple Company, Indirect Method

---

SIMPLE COMPANY
Statement of Changes in Financial Position, Indirect Method
For the Year Ended December 31, 1991
(in thousands)

Cash flows from operating activities:

Net income . . . . $ 22

Add (deduct) to reconcile net income to net operating cash inflow:

(*a*) Accounts receivable increase	(8)	
(*b*) Salaries payable increase	2	
(*c*) Depreciation expense.	4	

Net cash inflow from operating activities $20

Cash flows for investing activities:

(*d*) Cash paid for acquisition of plant assets	(30)	
(*e*) Cash received from sale of plant assets.	21	

Net cash outflow for investing activities . . . .   (9)

Cash flows from financing activites:

(*f*) Cash received from long-term debt.	40	
(*g*) Cash paid on long-term debt (principal only).	(46)	
(*h*) Cash paid for common shares retired	(8)	
(*i*) Cash paid for dividends	(11)	
(*j*) Cash received from sale of common shares.	48	

Net cash inflow from financing activites   23

Effect of foreign exchange rates on cash 0*

Net increase in cash and cash equivalents during 1991   34

Cash and cash equivalents, January 1, 1991.   42

Cash and cash equivalents, December 31, 1991 . . . . $76

Note: italic letters refer to later text discussion.

* Effects of foreign currency exchange rate changes are listed for firms with foreign operations or transactions in foreign currencies. The effect of exchange rate changes on foreign currencies held is not a cash flow, but affects the change in the cash balance during the period. Advanced accounting courses discuss foreign currency issues in detail.

- ◆ 1974: Canada Business Corporations Act required disclosure of the SCFP for federally incorporated entities. Revised provincial legislation followed in some jurisdictions.
- ◆ 1985: Revised section 1540 of the *CICA Handbook* did not require a SCFP but did specify that the SCFP report on the change in cash or cash equivalents and classify items as to whether they relate to operating, financing, or investing activities.
- ◆ 1987: *SFAS No. 95*, "Statement of Cash Flows," superseded *APB Opinion No. 19* and required the statement whenever a balance sheet and income statement were reported.[2] Separate disclosure of operating, investing, and financing cash flows was required.

The development of the SCFP is an excellent example of how the accounting profession reacted to suggestions of user groups to improve financial reporting.

The Trend toward Cash Flows

One survey discovered that, between 1980 and 1986, the percentage of 600 surveyed firms defining funds as cash grew from 10% to 66%.[3] Investors and creditors found

---

[2] Exempt are interim reports, and non-profit organizations. *SFAS No. 102,* which amends *SFAS No. 95,* exempts defined benefit pension plans and investment companies subject to certain requirements.

[3] AICPA, *Accounting Trends & Techniques — 1987* (New York, 1987), p. 109. Also, the 1984 edition reflected a three-fold increase in the number of firms categorizing cash flows into operating, investing, and financing from the year before.

cash flow information increasingly valuable for assessing a firm's liquidity and risk.[4] Several organizations, including the Financial Executives Institute, encouraged companies to use the cash-basis format.

Increased Business Risk Beginning in the mid-1970s, a rise in business failures and lawsuits against auditors for not adequately warning of those failures led to an interest in cash flow information. An increasing bankruptcy rate and general economic indicators supported an assessment of a general increase in risk. For example, the average current ratio of surveyed manufacturing firms fell from 2.67 to 1.71 between 1947 and 1979, reflecting a general deterioration in financial condition.[5]

The W. T. Grant bankruptcy case demonstrates the potential usefulness of cash flow information for assessing risk. W. T. Grant, one of the larger retailers in the United States in 1974, filed for bankruptcy in 1975. In 1973, Grant's common shares were selling for 20 times its earnings per share, a high level by historical standards. Grant's income and working capital provided by operations were positive from 1966 through 1974. The company paid regular dividends from 1966 through 1974.

However, during the decade before bankruptcy, the company generated almost no cash from *operations*.[6] Between 1966 and 1974, except for two years in which operating net cash flow was minimal, operations consumed rather than provided cash. The decline in operating cash flows preceded bankruptcy by a decade. Investors who acted on cash flow information rather than on income and other traditional financial ratios avoided losses.[7]

Previous Funds Statements The lack of uniformity in format and content of the SCFP, and the variety of fund definitions contributed to an increased need for standards relating to cash flow information. Working capital is not necessarily correlated with cash flow. A firm with healthy working capital but with large inventories, prepaids, and receivables might be in a weak cash position. The W. T. Grant case is an example.

Differences between Cash and Accrual Accounting Another factor in the trend toward cash flow reporting is the increased complexity of financial accounting principles. Accounting pronouncements on leases, pensions, foreign exchange, tax allocation, and others increase the complexity of financial statements. Determining the relationship between accrual earnings and cash flow is now more difficult for financial statement users.

Accrual accounting matches results (revenues) and efforts (costs). The timing of receipt from sale or of payment for raw materials and labour does not affect the timing of normal revenue and expense recognition. Financial statement users are interested in earnings information because in the long run, profits determine the success of a company. Net income reflects economic changes in financial position rather than immediate cash consequences.

But in the short run, many financial statement users are interested in cash flow. Will the borrower produce sufficient cash to pay liabilities? Business creditors are especially interested in the historical record of cash inflows and outflows. Bankers often require

---

[4] Louis Harris and Associates, *A Study of the Attitudes Toward and an Assessment of the Financial Accounting Standards Board* (Norwalk, Conn., April 1980), p. 13, found 67% of those interviewed rated cash flow information as highly important.

[5] FASB, *Reporting Funds Flows, Liquidity, and Financial Flexibility*, Discussion Memorandum (Norwalk, Conn., 1980), par. 27.

[6] Payments for operating expenses exceeded collections from receivables and other operating sources.

[7] J. Largay and C. Stickney, "Cash Flows, Ratio Analysis, and the W. T. Grant Company Bankruptcy," *Financial Analysts Journal*, July–August 1980, p. 51.

more detailed information than is available in published annual reports.[8] Comparison of earnings versus cash flow is sometimes referred to as an assessment of the *quality* of earnings. High-quality earnings are substantiated by positive cash flows.

Usefulness of Cash Flow Information

Many financial statement users analyse cash flow in making their decisions and recommendations. Some investors avoid companies without **free cash flow**, variously defined but generally connoting cash remaining after covering necessary capital expenditures and debt service payments.[9] Free cash flow can be used to retire shares, pay dividends, expand, acquire other businesses, or invest in debt and equity securities. If free cash flow is negative, the deficiency must be financed with additional debt or equity funding.

The trend of cash flows over several periods allows an assessment of **financial flexibility**, the ability to alter the amount and timing of cash flows to enable a response to unexpected needs and opportunities. For example, a firm able to raise additional capital in the debt and equity markets, to sell non-operating assets, and to increase cash inflows by increasing efficiency and lowering costs is financially flexible. Healthy operating cash flows provide the basis for most other cash flows and imply financial flexibility.

Cash flow information helps users to understand the relationship between income and cash flow and to predict similar cash flows. For example, the trend of net cash inflow from operations is useful for predicting future operating cash flows, in the aggregate and by component. Cash flow information provides feedback about past decisions. What effects are previous investment decisions having on cash flows? How were capital expenditures financed? How much debt was retired?

Cash flow information also helps explain changes in balance sheet accounts. For example, why did long-term debt increase $100,000? There are many possible causes. Did the change involve cash? Cash flow reporting answers these questions and provides information about investing and financing activities.

A study of 491 financial statement users sponsored by the Financial Executives Research Foundation found funds flow information useful for the following purposes:[10]

Assessment by Investors and Creditors of	Uses within the Firm
Ability to finance operations	Cash forecasting
Ability to pay dividends	Monitoring liquidity and changes in financial
Ability to pay interest	position
Cash consequences of deferred taxes	Budgeting
Liquidity	Strategic planning
Ability to adapt to changing conditions	Evaluating operating performance
The quality of earnings	Monitoring working capital and fixed asset
A firm's general performance	investments

THE STATEMENT OF CHANGES IN FINANCIAL POSITION AND REQUIREMENTS OF *CICA HANDBOOK* SECTION 1540

◆

The purpose of the SCFP is to provide relevant information about cash receipts and disbursements. The SCFP is designed to help users assess:

1. The liquidity and solvency of an enterprise.
2. The ability of an enterprise to generate cash from internal sources.

---

[8] "Where's the Cash?" *Forbes,* April 8, 1985.

[9] "Earnings, Schmernings—Look at Cash," *Business Week,* July 24, 1989, p. 57.

[10] Financial Executives Research Foundation, *The Funds Statement: Structure and Use* (New York, 1984).

3. The ability of an organization to repay debt obligations, and to reinvest or make distributions to owners.

By listing cash flows in meaningful categories and disclosing significant non-cash investing and financing activities, the SCFP explains the cash consequences of operations and the changes in balance sheet accounts arising from investing and financing activities.

Exhibit 23–1 presents the SCFP for Simple Company, an example used later to illustrate preparation. Net cash position (cash and highly liquid, short-term securities readily convertible into cash, less short-term bank debt) is the reporting basis for the SCFP.

The SCFP categorizes Simple Company's 1991 cash flows into operating, investing, and financing categories. The reasons *why* cash and cash equivalents increased $34,000 during 1991 is explained by the SCFP. The difference between operating inflows and outflows is **net cash inflow (outflow) from operating activities.** Simple Company generated $20,000 from operations in 1991. This subtotal is an important input into investor assessments of future cash flows. Cash flow from operations is necessary for debt servicing, capital expenditures, dividend payments, and other cash outflows.

Net cash inflow from operating activities is calculated by adjusting net income for items whose cash flow and income effect are not equal. This reconciliation format is called the *indirect method*. For example, depreciation expense reduced income $4,000 but caused no cash outflow. An alternative presentation method for the operations section, called the *direct method*, will be reviewed later in the chapter.

The SCFP in Exhibit 23–1 lists both income *and* net operating cash flow. For Simple, these two amounts are almost equal ($22,000 and $20,000, respectively). For other firms (including Rogers Communications, mentioned previously), they can be vastly different.

Each line-item in the investing and financing sections of the SCFP describes a cash flow. The change in cash for the period from the comparative balance sheets equals the change disclosed in the SCFP. Through the double-entry accounting system, the change in cash is algebraically equal to the net change in all other accounts.

Cash and Cash Equivalents

The assessment of a firm's cash flows is incomplete without considering the *net* cash position. Typically, firms invest a substantial portion of idle cash in cash equivalent securities to earn a return higher than is available from savings accounts. Firms with cash flow shortages routinely borrow from banks on a short-term basis. It is recognized that the components of cash and cash equivalents may vary according to the nature of the industry. In addition to cash itself, the category may include some or all of the company's temporary investments, and, as a reduction in cash, short-term bank debt.

In the United States, the definition includes cash equivalents but excludes bank debt. **Cash equivalents** are strictly defined as investments readily convertible into known amounts of cash that are close to their maturity dates. This would include Treasury bills, notes, and bonds receivable, if the maturity date is not more than three months away. In Canada, the components of temporary investments included in cash are left to professional judgment and thus may include marketable securities and longer term money market investments. The components *must* be disclosed.

According to *Financial Reporting in Canada,* the CICA's 1989 survey of 300 Canadian public companies, 27% defined "funds" as cash, cash equivalents, and short-term borrowings. A further 22% used cash and cash equivalents as the definition. Eleven percent used only cash, and another 17% used only short-term borrowings. Many of these companies would not have balances in all three categories (e.g., a company may well have no cash or temporary investments if it has large current bank debt). However, there does seem to be a reasonable amount of diversity in practice. Ontario Hydro, for example, calls the statement the "Statement of Sources of Cash Used for Investment in Fixed Assets" and uses the change in fixed assets as a fund definition. Several other regulated utilities use this approach, too.

For the remainder of this chapter, we use the term *cash* to describe net cash and cash equivalents less short-term bank debt unless there is a need to distinguish the individual components.

Three Cash Flow Categories

All cash inflows and outflows are classified into one of the following categories:

1. Operating.
2. Investing.
3. Financing.

Classification of cash flows is important for evaluating past cash flows and predicting future flows. The three categories allow the user to distinguish between repetitive on-going activities and long-term strategic changes. An uncategorized list would be less easily understood.

Operating Cash Flows   Operating cash flows are related to the main operations of the firm and are those associated with net income:

Inflows	Outflows
Receipts from customers.[11]	Payments to suppliers.
Interest received.	Payments to employees.
Dividends received.	Interest payments (net of amounts capitalized).
Income tax refunds.	Income and other tax payments associated with ordinary income.
Refunds from suppliers.	
Other receipts related to income producing activities such as revenues received in advance.	Other payments related to income-producing activities, including prepayments and expenses.
	Charitable contributions.
Receipts from lawsuits.	Payments for lawsuit losses.[12]
Insurance proceeds from health, life, and business interruption insurance.	Principal payments on long- and short-term loans from suppliers.[13]
	Payments on operating leases.
	Payments to pension trustees.
	Payments for fines and penalties, and back taxes.

The association of these items with income is the primary criterion for classifying the flows as operating. For example, interest received and paid and dividends received are revenues or expenses. Income tax payments are generally operating cash flows, but may be associated with financing or investing activities. Taxes must be classified with the item that caused the tax.

Many accountants and financial statement users disagree with classifying interest received and paid and dividends received as operating flows. They argue that interest and dividends received result from lending money and investing in shares, which are investing activities. They also argue that interest paid results from incurring debt, a financing activity. However, it seems logical to suggest that these items are most closely associated with income, and this should be the primary criterion for classification.

---

[11] Includes receipts from both short- and long-term receivables from the sale of goods and services.

[12] However, the cost of a successful legal defense of a patent is capitalized to patents and therefore is treated as an investing cash outflow.

[13] Suppliers provide the raw materials for the firm's business. Principal payments are considered a necessary cost of operations, regardless of the term of the loan.

Cash flows from other transactions may appear to be investing or financing flows, but are classified as operating if related to the main business activity. For example, firms in the business of selling long-term assets report the related flows as operating. If a real estate developer acquires land for subdivision, improvement, and resale as individual lots, then the cash payment used to purchase the land is appropriately classified as operational. In this case, the land is similar to inventory in other types of businesses.

Investing Cash Flows   Investing cash flows are related to acquisition or disposal of assets, including investments in securities, real estate, and other ventures. They are generally associated with transactions involving *long-term assets*. This category is important for identifying a firm's growth plans. Capital expenditures and acquisitions of subsidiaries are important strategic decisions for a firm. Following are the typical cash flows under this classification:

Inflows	Outflows
Net proceeds from plant asset sales.	Payments to purchase plant assets.
Proceeds from sales of debt and equity investments.*	Investments in debt and equity securities.*
	Loans made to other parties.
Collections of principal amounts of loans made to other parties.	Payments to purchase real estate.
	Payments for capitalized interest.
Net proceeds from sale of real estate.	
Casualty insurance proceeds (related to involuntary disposal of plant assets).	

* Unless the investment is included in the definition of cash.

The difference between the above cash inflows and outflows is *net cash inflow (outflow) from investing activities*. For example, Simple Company (Exhibit 23–1) received $21,000 from plant asset sales, and paid $30,000 for capital expenditures. The net cash *outflow* for investing activities is $9,000, indicating that Simple Company applied more cash in this area than it received.

Transactions producing extraordinary gains and losses, and gains and losses from discontinued operations, are often associated with investing cash flows. For example, selling assets from discontinued operations produces an investing inflow, shown net of tax on the SCFP. The after-tax accounting gains and losses from extraordinary items and discontinued operations are not cash flows and are excluded from the SCFP. Examples of these disclosures are given in later sections of the chapter.

For most firms, cash flows from purchases and sales of investments in securities are investing cash flows. However, banks and securities dealers carrying, at market, securities in a trading account[14] for resale classify cash flows from purchases and sales of securities as operating.[15] Such securities are inventory to a dealer because they are held for resale and are generally turned over quickly. Cash flows from sales of securities to customers are therefore operational in that business context. These activities also are the principal source of income to the dealer.[16]

Financing Cash Flows   This category describes how the firm obtained capital from creditors (other than suppliers) and investors, and repayments of those amounts. Typically,

---

[14] Securities held in a trading account by a securities dealer are held principally for resale to customers. Both fixed-income and equity securities can be held in a trading account. They are typically held for very short periods of time, sometimes only a few hours.

[15] *SFAS No. 102,* "Statement of Cash Flows—Exemption of Certain Enterprises and Classification of Cash Flows from Certain Securities Acquired for Resale."

[16] Furthermore, cash receipts and payments associated with loans purchased for resale and held for short periods are also classified as operating if the loans are carried at market, or lower of cost or market. If these securities are not held for resale to customers, associated cash flows are classified as investing.

long-term debt or owners' equity accounts are involved. Examples of financing cash flows include:

Inflows	Outflows
Proceeds from share issuance.	Payments to repurchase and retire share capital.
Proceeds from bond issuance.	Payments to retire bonds.
Proceeds from debt for specific investing activities.	Dividends paid to shareholders.
Proceeds from loans from financial institutions.[17]	Principal payments on loans from financial institutions.
	Principal payments on capital leases.
	Principal payments on debt used to purchase productive assets financed by dealers or third parties.

Classification of dividends paid to shareholders is a contentious issue in Canada. Many feel that such dividends are akin to interest payments made to lenders and represent a cost of doing business. According to this line of reasoning, if interest payments are an operating cash flow, so too are dividend payments. On the other hand, operating cash flows are supposed to be related to net income, and dividends are *not* an expense. This has dictated their inclusion in the financing area. Some Canadian companies simply include dividends as a separate, fourth category on the SCFP. (See the Goodyear Tire example in Exhibit 23–3.) According to the 1989 *Financial Reporting in Canada*, 10% included dividends in the operations section, 27% reported the item in a separate category, and the rest generally included dividends in the financing section. In our examples, we will use the financing classification, but it is wise to remember that there is considerable diversity in practice.

The difference between the financing cash inflows and outflows is *net cash inflow (outflow) from financing activities.* For example, Simple Company (Exhibit 23–1) was active in the financing area in 1991. The company sold common shares and incurred new long-term debt for a total $88,000 cash inflow. Simple Company retired long-term debt and common shares and paid dividends to its shareholders. The company netted $23,000 from financing activities.

Disclosure of Non-Cash Activities

Explaining significant investing and financing activities is an important part of the SCFP. Those activities involving cash are disclosed in one of the three cash flow categories in the SCFP. Significant *non-cash* investing and financing activities must be disclosed in a manner that clearly identifies them as non-cash transactions. They may be listed as separate items in the SCFP where they are identified and cross-referenced as non-cash transactions, or disclosed in a note.

Non-cash investing and financing transactions may be completely cash-free or involve a partial cash payment. For example, a debt may be settled in full by issuing common shares, or 30% of the debt may be settled with cash, and the remainder with shares.

Many non-cash transactions are economically similar to cash transactions. For example, settling a $50,000 debt by issuing shares with a $50,000 fair market value has the same effect as issuing the shares for cash and using the proceeds to settle the debt. The non-cash transaction may be disclosed in a schedule or notes as follows:

The Company extinguished $50,000 of long-term debt by issuing shares with a $50,000 fair market value.

Alternatively, the transaction may be listed as a $50,000 financing outflow (debt repayment) and a $50,000 financing inflow (share issuance). The items would be cross-referenced to make it clear that the transactions are interconnected.

---

[17] If the loan is deemed part of the definition of cash (that is, if the loan is short-term) then it does not appear as a separate item in the SCFP. A long-term loan, regardless of purpose, is a financing activity.

The *CICA Handbook* requires only that the transaction be "disclosed," with the two elements of the transaction separated but described in a manner that indicates the nature of their relationship. This allows either method. We will generally include the item as a source and a use of cash on the face of the SCFP in our examples.

If the transaction involves a partial cash payment, the SCFP must identify the cash and non-cash portions. For example, if a plant asset costing $400,000 is acquired by paying $100,000 cash and issuing a $300,000 long-term note, the SCFP would disclose the following:

Investing activities: Acquisition of plant assets; $300,000 financed
  by issuance of long-term note. . . . . ($400,000)
Financing activities: Issuance of long-term note, partial
  payment for plant asset. 300,000

Alternatively, the $300,000 non-cash portion of the transaction could be excluded from the SCFP itself. Under this disclosure alternative, the SCFP discloses the $100,000 cash payment as an investing cash outflow referencing a footnote or supporting schedule. The footnote would appear as follows:

The Company acquired a plant asset; payment consisted of the following:
                 Cost of asset acquired. $400,000
                 Cash paid 100,000
                 Long-term note issued. $300,000

The cash portion is repeated in the note disclosure to emphasize the relationships among the items.

Other common non-cash transactions include:

Bond retirement by issuing shares.
Conversion of bonds to shares.
Conversion of preferred shares to common shares.
Settlement of debt by transferring non-cash assets.
Bond refunding.
Receipt of donated property.
Incurrence of capitalized lease obligations.

Other events, including retained earnings appropriations, and stock dividends and splits, do not affect cash and are not considered significant financial events. These transactions are *not* disclosed on the SCFP.

Gross or Net Cash Flows?

To maximize the information content of cash flow disclosures, gross cash flows should generally be reported. Cash flows are grouped by similar type. For example, in Exhibit 23–1, the $30,000 paid for plant assets may represent several purchases. However, proceeds from bond issuances *cannot* be netted against payments to retire other bond issues. The requirement to report cash flows gross prohibits this type of netting and ensures better cash flow reporting for individual transactions.

Cash Flow per Share

Financial analysts and other users often compute **cash flow per share**, which is defined in many different ways. One common measure of cash flow per share is net operating cash flow divided by the weighted average common shares outstanding during the year.

EXHIBIT 23–2   Disclosure Requirements of Section 1540

The statement of changes in financial position should disclose at least the following items:
a. Cash from operations: the amount of cash from operations should be reconciled to the income statement or the components of cash from operations should be disclosed.
b. Cash flows resulting from discontinued operations.
c. Cash flows resulting from extraordinary items.
d. Outlays for acquisition and proceeds on disposal of assets, by major category, not included in (a), (b) or (c) above.
e. The issue, assumption, redemption, and repayment of debt not included in (a), (b), or (c) above.
f. The issue, redemption, and acquisition of share capital, and
g. The payment of dividends, identifying separately dividends paid by subsidiaries to minority interests.

Source: *CICA Handbook,* par. 1540.12.

In the United States, *SFAS No. 95 prohibits* disclosure of statistics so labeled in financial statements, except for contractually determined cash flow per share values. The FASB believed that allowing cash flow per share to be disclosed would cause confusion between EPS and cash flow per share. Of course, financial statement users are free to compute any statistic from published information.

One difficulty with this number is the potential for faulty conclusions about cash remaining for dividends. The financial press occasionally refers to cash flow per share as the cash available for dividends. Dividends are discretionary and must be determined in the context of long-term strategic cash needs.

The *CICA Handbook* is silent on the issue, which allows Canadian companies to use their judgment in this area. Considerable diversity exists. One example is Halifax Developments Limited, which includes items labelled cash flow from operations and cash flow from operations per share in the Financial Highlights portion of the annual report. The cash flow from operations amount presented is, in fact, *working capital* from operations and is significantly different from its cash counterpart for this company: in 1989, working capital from operations was a negative 1 cent per share, and it was a positive 14 cents in 1988. Cash flow from operations as defined above would have been 6 cents in 1989 and 6 cents in 1988. The figures must be evaluated with care.

Disclosure Requirements of Section 1540

Exhibit 23–2 presents the disclosure requirements for the SCFP. A sample SCFP, for Goodyear Canada Inc., is shown in Exhibit 23–3.

Goodyear's SCFP shows how their cash position, defined as cash and bank indebtedness, improved by $27.7 million during the year, from a negative $31.5 million to a negative $3.8 million. While they reported a net loss for the year, the net effect of the non-cash expenses, principally depreciation and taxes, and the various changes in receivables and payables, meant that operations actually generated a positive $3.9 million in cash flow. Goodyear spent $145.5 million on plant assets, a significant capital investment and a large increase over investment levels in the prior year. The company raised $185.5 million by issuing long-term debt. This accounts for their major activities during the year: operations made a marginal contribution, and a major debt issue was used to finance plant expansion and reduce short-term bank debt.

Notice that the "net change in non-cash working capital," negative $9,281,000, is explained in detail at the end of the SCFP. This removes clutter from the statement itself and serves to improve the understandability of the statement.

EXHIBIT 23-3   Consolidated Statement of Changes in Financial Position, Goodyear Canada Inc. and Subsidiaries, 1989

	Year Ended December 31	
(dollars in thousands)	1989	1988
Cash provided from operations:		
Net income (loss) before extraordinary item	$ (1,835)	$ 2,306
Items not affecting working capital:		
Principally depreciation and deferred taxes	14,991	10,081
Working capital from operations	13,156	12,387
Net change in non-cash working capital (excluding effect of extraordinary item and acquisition of subsidiaries in 1988)	(9,281)	(9,324)
Net effect of extraordinary item in 1988	—	7,505
Cash provided from operations	3,875	10,568
Cash provided from financing activities:		
Increase in long-term debt (net)	185,518	71,034
Increase (decrease) in other long term liabilities (net)	(4,289)	576
Loan payable on acquisition of subsidiaries	—	13,000
Cash provided from financing activities	181,229	84,610
Dividends paid	(3,602)	(3,601)
Cash invested:		
Expenditures for properties and plants	(145,504)	(38,326)
Disposal of properties	723	1,343
Purchase of miscellaneous investments	(8,983)	(4,521)
Acquisition of subsidiaries in 1988 (including bank indebtedness on acquisition of $15,305)	—	(49,778)
Net investment of cash	(153,764)	(91,282)
Increase in cash	27,738	295
Cash at beginning of year	(31,487)	(31,782)
Cash at end of year	$ (3,749)	$(31,487)
Cash at the end of year is represented by:		
Cash	$ 52	$ 51
Bank indebtedness	(3,801)	(31,538)
	$ (3,749)	$(31,487)
Net change in non-cash working capital excluding effect of extraordinary item and acquisition of subsidiaries in 1988:		
Increase (decrease) in current assets:		
Accounts receivable	$ 15,539	$(22,277)
Due from affiliated companies	6,630	21,733
Inventories	18,349	1,590
Prepaid expenses	(1,879)	4,485
Deferred income taxes	506	(1,684)
	39,145	3,847
(Increase) decrease in current liabilities:		
Accounts payable and accrued liabilities	(24,155)	14,311
Due to affiliated companies	(4,029)	(11,174)
Income and other taxes payable	(1,680)	2,340
	(29,864)	5,477
Net increase in non-cash working capital	$ 9,281	$ 9,324

CONCEPT REVIEW

1. Why must the change in cash for a period equal the net sum of the items disclosed in the SCFP?
2. Why are non-cash activities disclosed? How are they disclosed?
3. What is the definition of cash equivalents?
4. What three categories should be used to classify cash flows on the SCFP? Where should dividend payments be classified?

PREPARING THE SCFP
◆

The next several sections of the chapter are devoted to analysing transactions and preparing the SCFP. Learning to prepare the SCFP provides an opportunity to review and integrate your financial accounting knowledge.

Several approaches for preparing the SCFP are used in practice. The objective of each is to identify, through analysis of transactions:

- The operating, investing, and financing cash flows.
- Significant non-cash investing and financing transactions.
- Items that reconcile income and net operating cash flow.

This chapter demonstrates three approaches for preparation:

- A format-free approach, which uses no specific model for determining cash flows.
- A spreadsheet approach.
- A T-account approach (see the chapter appendix).

The spreadsheet and T-account approaches are popular formats for manipulating information. Although the spreadsheet dominates in industry and public accounting, many preparers combine features from several approaches. T-accounts are often used in all three approaches to isolate the effects of transactions on specific accounts during the reporting period.

Simple Company, Format-Free Approach, Indirect Method

Exhibit 23–4 gives the background information leading to the Simple Company SCFP (Exhibit 23–1). This section discusses how to prepare the SCFP using the Simple Company information, under the format-free approach. The format-free approach is appropriate for companies with small numbers of transactions and accounts, and it is useful for explaining transaction analysis. This section reviews the **indirect method** of disclosure for the operations section, which reconciles net income to cash flows from operations.

Sources of Information. To identify amounts for disclosure in the SCFP, information sources are searched for data relating to the period's transactions. Sources include:

1. The income statement, which yields information about non-cash gains and losses, depreciation, and operating expenses helpful in determining operating cash flows. Additional information and the comparative balance sheets are consulted for related data.
2. Additional information, including the retained earnings statement or owners' equity statement, which yields data on transactions such as debt issuance and retirement, share transactions, dividends, and prior period adjustments.
3. The remaining comparative balance sheet account changes not yet explained suggest additional transactions for analysis.

EXHIBIT 23–4   Case Data for Statement of Changes in Financial Position, Simple Company

---

SIMPLE COMPANY
Case Data for Preparing the Statement of Changes in Financial Position
Illustrated in Exhibit 23–1
(in thousands)

1. Income statement for the year ended Dec. 31, 1991:

Sales revenue	$66
Salaries expense	(28)
Depreciation expense	(4)
Administrative and selling expenses (excluding salaries)	(12)
Net income	$22

2. Comparative balance sheets, Dec. 31, 1991:

	Dec. 31	
Items	**1990**	**1991**
Cash (no cash equivalents)	$ 42	$ 76
Accounts receivable	31	39
Plant assets	82	81
Accumulated depreciation	(20)	(14)
Total assets	$135	$182
Salaries payable	$ 3	$ 5
Notes payable, long-term	46	40
Common shares, nopar (shares outstanding, 1990, 70; 1991, 100)	70	108
Contributed capital from share retirement		2
Retained earnings	16	27
Total liabilities and shareholders' equity	$135	$182

3. Additional information:
   a. Plant assets account:
      (1) Purchased plant assets for cash, $30.
      (2) Sold old plant assets for cash, $21; recorded as follows:

Cash	21	
Accumulated depreciation	10	
Plant assets		31

   b. Long-term notes payable account:
      Borrowed cash, $40.
      Payments on note principal, $46.
   c. Bought 10 common shares of Simple Co. for $8 on January 1, 1991. The shares were retired.
   d. Statement of retained earnings:

Balance, Jan. 1, 1991	$ 16
Net income for 1991	22
Cash dividend paid in cash at end of 1991	(11)
Balance, Dec. 31 1991	$ 27

   e. Issued 10 common shares for $48 cash on December 31, 1991.

As cash flows are identified, they are placed into one of the three cash flow categories. For example, if the firm purchased land during the year for $200,000, the cash outflow is placed into the investing activities section. Amounts reconciling income and net operating cash flow are part of the operations section.

Refer to Exhibit 23–4 for information as transactions are analyzed, and to Exhibit 23–1, the Simple Company indirect method SCFP. Also, as transactions are analysed, keep track of the balance sheet account changes that are explained. The income statement accounts are analysed first.

The reconciliation of net income and operating cash flows converts accrual income to cash-basis income. The search is for amounts that explain why net income is not equal to net operating cash flow.

Depreciation expense is an example of a reconciling adjustment. In the Simple Company example, net income is reduced by $4,000 of depreciation expense in 1991. Depreciation is a non-cash expense. However, the indirect method operating section *begins* with net income. In so doing, operating cash flow is understated $4,000 because income is reduced without a related cash outflow. Therefore, the $4,000 is added to net income to remove the effect of the non-cash expense (see Exhibit 23–1).

The following generalization is useful for determining reconciling adjustments:

> If a transaction's effect on *operating* cash flow is not equal to its effect on net income, a reconciling adjustment is needed for the difference.

Transaction Analysis for the Indirect Method SCFP
Income Statement Accounts   (All amounts are in thousands of dollars.)

1. *Sales.* Credit sales ($66) increased accounts receivable, yet accounts receivable increased a net of $8, implying $58 collections on account. Therefore, the net income effect (increase $66) exceeds the operating cash flow effect (increase $58), necessitating an $8 reconciling adjustment. The $8 accounts receivable increase is *subtracted* from net income to remove the excess of accrual revenue over cash received (adjustment (*a*) in Exhibit 23–1).

2. *Salaries expense.* Salaries expense ($28) increased salaries payable, yet salaries payable increased a net of $2, implying $26 of salary payments. Therefore, the net income effect (decrease $28) exceeds the operating cash flow effect (decrease $26). Therefore, the $2 increase in salaries payable is *added* to net income to offset the excess of accrual expense deducted over salary payments made (adjustment (*b*) in Exhibit 23–1).

3. *Depreciation expense.* As discussed above, the $4 expense is *added* to net income (adjustment (*c*) in Exhibit 23–1).

4. *Administrative and selling expenses.* There is no related additional information or balance sheet account, so the cash payments must equal the accrual expense. Therefore, no reconciling adjustment is needed.

Additional Information   No items in additional information affect net income or operating cash flow. Therefore, no other adjustments to net income are required. All income statement accounts now are analysed, and the second source of information is considered.

1. Simple Company purchased plant assets for $30 cash. This is an investing cash outflow.

   Investing outflow (d) in Exhibit 23–1: Cash paid for acquisition of plant assets, ($30).

   Simple company also sold plant assets; the reconstructed entry is illustrated in the additional information, Exhibit 23–4. The $21 proceeds are an investing cash inflow.

   Investing inflow (e) in Exhibit 23–1: Cash received from sale of plant assets, $21.

   The two transactions listed in this item of additional information help explain the changes in accumulated depreciation and plant assets during 1991.

2. Simple Company borrowed $40 cash (financing cash inflow) and paid $46 principal (financing cash outflow) on its long-term notes payable account.

   Financing inflow (f) in Exhibit 23–1: Cash received from long-term debt, $40.
   Financing outflow (g) in Exhibit 23–1: Cash paid on long-term debt (principal only), ($46).

3. The common share repurchase and retirement is a financing outflow. A total of $8 was spent on retiring common shares. On January 1, when the shares were

reacquired and retired, the average carrying value per share was $1 ($70/70 shares). The retirement involves reducing the common share account by $10 ($1 × 10), and increasing the contributed capital from share retirement account by $2 ($10 − $8). The following journal entry describes the transaction:

Common shares.   10
    Contributed capital from share retirement.   2
    Cash.   8

Financing outflow (h) in Exhibit 23–1: Cash paid for common shares retired, ($8).

4. The retained earnings statement reveals $11 in dividends declared and paid in 1991, a financing cash outflow. There is no dividends payable account, meaning all dividends declared are paid.

Financing outflow (i) in Exhibit 23–1: Cash paid for dividends, ($11).

5. The last item is common share issuance for $48, a financing cash inflow.

Financing inflow (j) in Exhibit 23–1: Cash received from sale of
    common shares $48

At this point, all additional information is incorporated and the last information source is considered.

Comparative Balance Sheets   All balance sheet account changes are explained by the transaction analysis. Therefore, there are no further items to disclose in the SCFP. For example, plant assets decreased by $1 in 1991. This is explained by the purchase for $30, and sale of an asset originally costing $31. Accumulated depreciation decreased $6, which equals depreciation expense (increase $4) less the decrease from equipment disposal (decrease $10). The retained earnings $11 increase is explained by net income (increase $22) less dividends ($11).

Completing the SCFP   All cash flows are identified and classified as operating, investing, or financing. To complete the SCFP, the change in cash (increase $34), and the beginning and ending cash balances are entered as shown in Exhibit 23–1. The net increase in cash from the SCFP, $34, agrees with the cash account balance change.

An alternate format for the cash flows from operating activities, the *direct* method, is discussed in the following section.

Simple Company, Format-Free Approach, Direct Method

The investing and financing sections of the indirect and direct method SCFPs are identical. Therefore, this section discusses only the *operating section* of the direct method and uses the Simple Company as an example. The operating section of the **direct method** SCFP seeks to disclose operating cash flows and does not reconcile net income and cash from operations. Instead of "sales," "cash received from customers" is listed; instead of "salaries expense," "payments to employees" is listed. Non-cash expenses, such as depreciation, are simply omitted. See Exhibit 23–5, which displays the Simple Company direct method SCFP.

Transaction Analysis for the Direct Method SCFP
Income Statement Accounts   (All amounts are in thousands of dollars.)

1. *Sales.* Credit sales ($66) increases accounts receivable.

The related cash flow is collections on accounts receivable. This amount can be derived in several ways. If Simple Company's accounting system permits, the total cash receipts

EXHIBIT 23–5   Statement of Changes in Financial Position, Simple Company, Direct Method

SIMPLE COMPANY
Statement of Changes in Financial Position, Direct Method
For the Year Ended December 31, 1991
(in thousands)

Cash flows from operating activities:			
(a)	Cash received from customers	$58	
(b)	Payments to employees	(26)	
(c)	Payments for administrative and selling expenses	(12)	
	Net cash inflow from operating activities		$20
Cash flows for investing activities:			
(d)	Cash paid for acquisition of plant assets	(30)	
(e)	Cash received from sale of plant assets	21	
	Net cash outflow for investing activities		(9)
Cash flows for financing activities:			
(f)	Cash received from long-term debt	40	
(g)	Cash paid on long-term debt (principal only)	(46)	
(h)	Cash paid for common shares retired	(8)	
(i)	Cash paid for dividends	(11)	
(j)	Cash received from sale of common shares	48	
	Net cash inflow from financing activities		23
Effect of foreign exchange rates on cash			0
Net increase in cash and cash equivalents during 1991			34
Cash and cash equivalents, January 1, 1991			42
Cash and cash equivalents, December 31, 1991			$76

Note: Italic letters refer to the text discussion.

amount is obtained from the cash receipts journal. Alternatively, an analysis of accounts receivable reveals collections on account. The T-account below illustrates transactions in summary form, leading to the identification of collections on accounts receivable.

Accounts Receivable

Bal. Jan. 1, 1991	31	Cash collections in 1991 (derived)	58
Sales in 1991	66		
Bal. Dec. 31, 1991	39		

In lieu of the T-account, the following expression allows conversion of the accrual information (sales) to the cash basis (collections on account):[18]

$$\text{Cash collections} = \text{Accrual-basis revenue} \quad \begin{array}{l} + \text{ Decrease in associated receivable} \\ - \text{ Increase in associated receivable} \end{array}$$

Customer collections ($58) = Sales ($66) − Accounts receivable increase ($8)

Operating inflow (a) in Exhibit 23–5: Collections received from customers, $58.

---

[18] These and other expressions facilitate preparation and embody the same logic as the use of the T-account. The emphasis is on the relationships among transactions and account balances, rather than the expression.

2. *Salaries expense.* Salaries expense, $28, is related to salaries payable, which increased $2 during 1991. No additional information applies. The related cash flow is salary payments, determined in two ways as follows:

Salaries Payable

Salary payments (derived) 26	Bal. Jan. 1, 1991	3
	Salaries expense	28
	Bal. Dec. 31, 1991	5

$$\text{Cash payment} = \text{Accrual-basis expense} \begin{array}{l} + \text{ Decrease in associated payable} \\ - \text{ Increase in associated payable} \end{array}$$

Salary payments ($26) = Salaries expense ($28) − Salaries payable increase ($2)

Operating outflow (b) in Exhibit 23–5: Payments to employees, ($26).

3. *Depreciation expense.* Depreciation expense ($4) is not a cash flow; therefore, there is no disclosure in direct method SCFP.
4. *Administrative and selling expenses.* There is no related additional information or balance sheet account. Therefore, the cash and accrual amounts are the same for this expense.

Operating outflow (c) in Exhibit 23–5: Payments for administrative and selling expenses, ($12).

No other adjustments to net income are required. The investing and financing cash flows are identified and entered as under the indirect method.

Comparison of Direct and Indirect Methods

The *CICA Handbook* allows calculation of cash provided by operations to be calculated by reconciliation to the income statement *or* by presenting the components of cash from operations (see Exhibit 23–2, item *a*). The reconciliation, or *indirect* approach, starts with an income figure and lists items for which the income effect and cash flow are *different*. The *direct* approach, on the other hand, shows the cash generated by sales and the cash used for expenses in a direct fashion. The operations section of the SCFP for Simple Company shows net cash flow from operations of $20, irrespective of whether the direct or indirect approach is used. This is worth emphasizing—both methods produce the same net result, but use different methodology. Also note that the investing and financing sections are *identical,* regardless of the method chosen for operations disclosure.

Exhibit 23–6 shows the operations section of Inter-City Gas Corp., using the direct method. Cash receipts for sales and investment revenue are directly disclosed, as are cash disbursements for various categories of operating expenses.

The direct method seems to have several advantages over the indirect method. The indirect method does not report collections from sales and other cash flows that analysts use to assess cash-generating ability. Payments to suppliers and employees, and dividends received from investments, also are not disclosed. Furthermore, under the indirect method, the reconciling adjustments may be misunderstood by financial statement users and confused with cash flows. For example, some users may receive the impression that depreciation is a source of funds. Interpretation problems relating to the SCFP can be tracked back to the reconciliation of net income to operating cash flows. Finally, the direct method reports all three statement categories consistently. Cash flows are presented in all three sections. The user of the indirect method statement receives only indirect information concerning operating cash flows, but direct information for investing and financing activities.

EXHIBIT 23-6   Consolidated Statement of Changes in Financial Position, Inter-City Gas Corporation, 1988

INTER-CITY GAS CORPORATION

Consolidated Statement of Changes in Financial Position

For the Years Ended December 31, 1988, 1987 and 1986

(in millions)	1988	1987	1986
Operations:			
Cash Receipts:			
Receipts from sales	$1,724.5	$1,650.7	$1,517.7
Investment and other income	41.9	63.5	35.1
	1,766.4	1,714.2	1,552.8
Cash Disbursements:			
Purchases and expenses	1,548.4	1,478.1	1,304.2
Interest	117.7	105.9	90.7
Income tax installments	17.1	29.6	17.9
	1,683.2	1,613.6	1,412.8
Cash provided from operations.	$ 83.2	$ 100.6	$ 140.0

At present, most Canadian companies still use the indirect method, likely due to tradition.[19] In the United States, the FASB allows either method to be used, although they have expressed a preference for the direct method. Perhaps Canadian companies will respond to this U.S. lead.

Cash Flow from Operations: Additional Analysis

The operations section is often the most complex area to prepare on the SCFP. Exhibit 23-7 lists the most common reconciliation items for the indirect method.

The T-account is a convenient way to explain the first type of adjustment in Exhibit 23-7. For example, a $4,000 increase in interest payable is shown in the T-account below:

Interest Payable

Interest payments	10,000	Beginning bal	5,000
		Interest expense	14,000
		Ending bal	9,000

The $4,000 payable increase implies that interest expense exceeds interest payments for the year. Income is reduced by the $14,000 interest expense, yet only $10,000 was paid. Therefore, net income understates net operating cash flow by $4,000, and the increase is *added* to net income. Similar logic applies to the other operating working capital accounts.

An example of the second type of adjustment in Exhibit 23-7 is amortization of discount on bonds payable. An example entry amortizing bond discount appears below:

To recognize interest expense and amortize bond discount:

Interest expense	12,000	
Discount on bonds payable		2,000
Cash		10,000

Interest expense reduces income $12,000, yet only $10,000 cash was paid. Therefore, the $2,000 amortization is added to income to make the income effect and the cash flow effect equal. Amortization of bond premium is subtracted.

---

[19] According to *Financial Reporting in Canada, 1989*, 97% of the companies surveyed used the indirect method.

EXHIBIT 23–7   Reconciling Adjustments: Net Income and Net Operating Cash Flows

1. Adjustments for changes in *working capital* accounts related to operations (accounts receivable, inventory, prepaids, interest receivable, accounts payable, interest payable, income taxes payable, short-term payables to suppliers and others):

Change in Account Balance During Year

	Increase	Decrease
Current asset	*Subtract* increase from net income	*Add* decrease to net income
Current liability	*Add* increase to net income	*Subtract* decrease from net income

The following working capital accounts are excluded from this category of adjustments because they are either included in the cash definition or are unrelated to operations: cash, short-term investments, short-term bank debt (the SCFP is explaining the net change in this fund), short-term investments not considered to be cash equivalents (associated cash flows are investing), and dividends payable (associated cash flows are financing activities). *Long-term* payables to suppliers for inventory purchases and other operating activities are *included* in the above type of adjustment.

2. Non-cash expenses, including depreciation, depletion, amortization of intangibles, and amortization of bond discount, are *added* to net income because they do not cause cash to decrease. Net income is reduced by these expenses and thus understates operating cash flow. Also *add* to income: increase in deferred taxes, investment losses from equity-method investments, amortization of premium on bond investments, amortization of discount on bonds payable, unrealized loss on short-term marketable equity securities (LCM method), and dividends received from equity investments.

3. Non-cash revenues, including investment revenue from equity-method investments, are *subtracted* from income because they do not cause cash to increase. Net income is increased by these revenues and thus overstates operating cash flow. Also *subtract* from income: amortization of premium on bonds payable, amortization of discount on bond investments, and decrease in deferred taxes.

4. Non-cash gains are *subtracted* from net income and non-cash losses are *added* back to net income. Examples are gains and losses on disposals of plant assets and bond retirements.

An example of the third type of adjustment in Exhibit 23–7 is revenue recognized under the equity method. For example, assume a firm owned 22% of a company that reported $100,000 in income. The following entry records this transaction:

To record investment revenue:

```
Long-term investment . . . . . . . . . . . . . . . . . . . . .   22,000
    Investment revenue . . . . . . . . . . . . . . . . . . . .            22,000
```

Income is increased by the $22,000 revenue, yet no cash is received. Income therefore overstates net operating cash outflow. To correct the overstatement, the $22,000 revenue is subtracted from income.

A gain on sale of land is an example of the fourth type of adjustment. The following entry is an example:

To record sale of land:

```
Cash . . . . . . . . . . . . . . . . . . . . . . . . . . . . .   200,000
    Land (cost) . . . . . . . . . . . . . . . . . . . . . . . .            150,000
    Gain on sale of land . . . . . . . . . . . . . . . . . . .             50,000
```

The $200,000 proceeds are classified as an investing cash inflow. This cash flow completely explains the cash consequences of the transaction. The gain does not further increase cash flow. Yet income is increased by the $50,000 gain and consequently overstates net operating cash flow by that amount. The gain does not represent cash, nor is it related to operations. Therefore, the $50,000 gain is *subtracted* from net income.

Exhibit 23–7 covers most adjustments needed to complete the reconciliation. In a later section we discuss other, less common, situations.

Additional Examples of Operating Cash Flows—Direct Method   This section provides additional examples of the determination of operating cash flows using the direct method.

Deferred Revenues   Determining the cash receipts related to deferred revenues such as unearned rent revenue is accomplished through transaction analysis with the T-account or with a formula. The analysis follows accrual-basis revenues and expenses as illustrated in the Simple Company example.

$$\text{Cash collections} = \begin{array}{l} \text{Accrual-basis} \\ \text{revenue} \end{array} + \begin{array}{l} \text{Increase in associated} \\ \text{deferred revenue} \end{array}$$
$$- \begin{array}{l} \text{Decrease in associated} \\ \text{deferred revenue} \end{array}$$

For example, assume a firm reported $12,000 in fee revenue and a $2,000 decrease in unearned fee revenue:

$$\begin{array}{l} \text{Fees collected (\$10,000)} \\ \end{array} = \begin{array}{l} \text{Fee revenue} \\ \text{(\$12,000)} \end{array} - \begin{array}{l} \text{Decrease in unearned} \\ \text{fee revenue (\$2,000)} \end{array}$$

Using T-accounts, reconstructing the summary transactions also explains the result:

Unearned Fee Revenue

Decrease	2,000	Fees collected (derived)	10,000
Revenue earned	12,000		

Fees collected are an operating inflow.

Payments for Inventory Purchases   Purchases of inventory are normally made on account. Therefore, accounts payable, cost of goods sold, and inventory are analysed to determine the associated cash flow:

$$\begin{array}{l} \text{Cash paid for} \\ \text{inventory purchases} \end{array} = \begin{array}{l} \text{Cost of} \\ \text{goods sold} \end{array} - \text{Inventory decrease}$$
$$+ \text{Inventory increase}$$
$$- \text{Accounts payable increase}$$
$$+ \text{Accounts payable decrease}$$

An inventory increase implies a cash outflow exceeding cost of goods sold. Therefore, the increase is added. An accounts payable increase implies that purchases exceed payments. Therefore, the increase is subtracted to derive cash payments. Assume that cost of goods sold is $10,000 for the year, accounts payable increased $3,000, and inventory increased $2,000. Payments for inventory purchases is therefore:

$$\begin{array}{l} \text{Cash paid for inventory} \\ \text{purchases (\$9,000)} \end{array} = \begin{array}{l} \text{Cost of goods} \\ \text{sold (\$10,000)} \end{array} + \begin{array}{l} \text{Inventory} \\ \text{increase (\$2,000)} \end{array} - \begin{array}{l} \text{Accounts Payable} \\ \text{increase (\$3,000)} \end{array}$$

Payments for inventory purchases are an operating outflow.

The Spreadsheet Approach

Spreadsheets are frequently used for preparing the SCFP. A spreadsheet is a columnar format for analysing transactions and indentifying SCFP disclosures.

The spreadsheet approach:

- ◆ Provides an organized format for documenting the preparation process for subsequent analysis and review.
- ◆ Facilitates review and evaluation by others.
- ◆ Provides several proofs of accuracy.
- ◆ Formally keeps track of the changes in balance sheet accounts, and ensures that all accounts are explained.

The spreadsheet is the most involved format for preparing the SCFP and a certain amount of practice is required for proficiency. For complicated problems, the benefits of the spreadsheet are worth the extra effort. However no format, spreadsheet or otherwise, eliminates the need to carefully analyse transactions.

The spreadsheet developed for the accounting cycle in Chapter 3, resulting in the income statement and balance sheet, cannot be used for the SCFP. Preparation of the SCFP requires information beyond the ending adjusted ledger account balances.[20] Several different spreadsheet formats are currently in use. The spreadsheet format used in this chapter is concise and allows a simultaneous preparation of both direct and indirect method SCFPs.[21] The format is not a dramatic departure from other spreadsheet formats, however, and can easily be converted.

The spreadsheet and format-free approaches use the same order of information search and logic for identifying disclosure items. The spreadsheet formalizes the process. In many cases, a transaction entry is reconstructed and entered into the spreadsheet to explain changes in account balances. These entries are not recorded in the journals; they are used only for spreadsheet purposes.

Exhibit 23–8 illustrates the complete spreadsheet for the Simple Company. As cash flows are located, they are entered into one of the spreadsheet's cash flow activity sections: inflows are debits (a cash inflow is a debit to cash), outflows are credits (a cash outflow is a credit to cash). The corresponding debit or credit is entered into the appropriate balance sheet or income statement account.

In the operating section, the debit and credit *columns* reflect the reconciliation of income and net operating cash flow. Debit adjustments are added to net income, and credits are subtracted for the reconciliation. Going across *rows*, the debits and credits are adjustments to the accrual revenue or expense yielding the operating cash flow for the direct method.

The investing and financing sections of the spreadsheet are identical for the direct and indirect methods. The process is complete when all balance sheet account balance changes are explained. The information from the three activity sections is transferred to the direct or indirect method SCFP.

The Simple Company Example, Spreadsheet Approach

The explanation for each cash flow and reconciling item mirrors the format-free approach. Refer to Exhibit 23–8 for each spreadsheet entry. The reconciliation

---

[20] If it did not, the SCFP would simply repeat the information in the balance sheet and income statements.

[21] This format is adapted from an article appearing in "Practitioners Forum," *Journal of Accountancy,* May 1990, by W. Collins.

EXHIBIT 23–8   Spreadsheet for Direct and Indirect Method SCFP, Simple Company

SIMPLE COMPANY

Spreadsheet for Direct and Indirect Method SCFP
For the Year Ended December 31, 1991
(in thousands)

Comparative Balance Sheets	December 31, 1990	Dr.	Cr.	December 31, 1991
Cash	$ 42	(m) $ 34		$ 76
Accounts receivable	31	(b) 8		39
Plant assets	82	(f) 30	$ 31 (g)	81
Accumulated depreciation	(20)	(g) 10	4 (d)	(14)
Total assets	$135			$182
Salaries payable	$ 3		2 (c)	$ 5
Notes payable	46	(i) 46	40 (h)	40
Common shares	70	(j) 10	48 (l)	108
Contributed capital on share retirement.	0		2 (j)	2
Retained earnings.	16	(k) 11	22 (a)	27
Total liabilities and owners' equity	$135			$182
Total changes		$149	$149	

Adjustments Leading to SCFP

		Indirect Method Dr.	Indirect Method Cr.	Direct Method (Operations)
Operating activities:				
Net income	$ 22	(a) $ 22		
Sales	66		$ 8 (b)	$58 customer collections
Salary expense	28	(c) 2		$26 salary payments
Depreciation	4	(d) 4		
Administrative and selling.	12		(e)	12 admin. payments
Investing activities:				
Purchase plant assets			30 (f)	
Sale of plant assets		(g) 21		
Financing activities:				
Issue notes payable for cash		(h) 40		
Payments on notes payable.			46 (i)	
Retirement of common shares . . .			8 (j)	
Dividends paid			11 (k)	
Issue common shares		(l) 48	103	
Net cash increase			34 (m)	
		$137	$137	

adjustments for the indirect approach are referenced first because these columns appear before the direct method columns in the spreadsheet. All amounts are in thousands.

(a) The $22 debit (net income, implying cash increase) in the operating section of the indirect method columns begins the reconciliation schedule. Net income is the starting figure for net operating cash flow. The credit partially explains the change in retained earnings.

(b) The $8 debit explains the increase in accounts receivable. In the indirect method columns (the reconciliation), the $8 credit is subtracted from net income. According to Exhibit 23–7, increases in operating current assets are subtracted from net income. The credit also is subtracted from sales to yield cash collected from customers, under the direct method.

(c) The $2 credit explains the increase in salaries payable. The debit (reconciliation columns) increases net income because it is an increase to an operating payable. The direct method column lists the operating cash outflow.

(d) Depreciation affects only the indirect method reconciliation. This spreadsheet entry is the first to reconstruct an actual journal entry. The $4 credit explains part of the accumulated depreciation change, and the debit implies an addition to net income for the reconciliation.

(e) This is not a formal spreadsheet entry because no balance sheet account requires explanation. Administrative and selling expenses were paid entirely in cash. No reconciling item appears, but the direct method column lists the operating cash outflow ($12).

(f) At this point, the operating section is complete; both methods now use only the columns titled "indirect." The $30 debit for the plant asset purchase in this reconstructed journal entry helps explain the change in plant assets. The investing section lists the credit, or cash outflow.

(g) This reconstructed entry records the removal of $10 accumulated depreciation on disposal, removes the $31 original asset cost, and records the $21 investing cash inflow.

(h) The $40 credit of this reconstructed entry records the issuance in long-term note payable. The financing section records the debit, or cash inflow.

(i) The $46 debit of this reconstructed entry records the decrease or principal payment on a long-term note. The financing section records the credit, or cash outflow.

(j) The reconstructed entry to record the reacquisition and retirement of common shares reflects the $10 decrease to common shares and the $2 increase to the contributed capital account. The cash outflow, $8, is listed in the financing section of the spreadsheet.

(k) The reconstructed entry to record dividends paid results in the $11 credit (cash outflow) listed in the financing section.

(l) The share issue is reflected in this reconstructed entry, which explains the remainder of the change in the common shares account and a $48 debit (cash inflow) in the financing section.

(m) This is a balancing entry, not a reconstructed journal entry. At this point, all balance sheet account changes except cash are explained, and all relevant information is exhausted. The $34 debit explains the cash change, and the $34 credit reconciles the cash credit change total with the cash debit change total.

We emphasize that the underlying thought process for preparing the SCFP is not affected by the format chosen. The spreadsheet provides an orderly format for using the information to prepare the SCFP and explain the balance sheet account changes. The three operating cash flows (direct method column) are transferred to the direct method SCFP (see Exhibit 23–5). The three reconciling items (indirect method columns) are transferred to the indirect method SCFP (see Exhibit 23–1). The investing and financing cash flows are transferred to both direct and indirect method SCFPs. Normally, a firm prepares only one SCFP, but both are illustrated here for completeness.

The spreadsheet affords Simple Company several accuracy checks. The changes in all balance sheet accounts are explained. The debit and credit balance sheet change columns agree ($149), although this amount is not a meaningful total except for checking purposes. As mentioned in (*m*), the $34 cash change is a reconciling total. Furthermore, the net operating cash flow ($20) agrees for both methods.

CONCEPT REVIEW

1. Explain why a gain on the sale of equipment is subtracted in the reconciliation of income and operating cash flows.
2. Why are collections of accounts receivable disclosed in the SCFP, direct method, yet not disclosed in the SCFP, indirect method? How can both approaches yield the same operating net cash flow?
3. Why is depreciation added in the reconciliation of net income and net operating cash flow? Why is an accounts receivable increase subtracted?
4. If salaries payable increases during the year, why does this imply that salary expense exceeds salary payments?

ANALYSING MORE COMPLEX SITUATIONS

The purpose of the Simple Company example is to emphasize preparation of a complete SCFP without considering more complicated transactions. In this section, we consider more involved disclosures. We use the same reasoning, however, regardless of the complexity. In the next section, we provide another complete and more complex example.

Dividends When amounts of dividends declared and paid are equal, the financing activities section discloses dividends paid and declared as a cash outflow. Frequently, however, dividends are declared in one period and paid in the next. For example, assume comparative balance sheets disclose the following:

	1991	1992
Dividends payable	$40,000	$60,000

Also, $70,000 of dividends were declared during the year. Using a T-account, we determine dividends paid as follows:

Dividends Payable

	Beginning balance 40,000
	Dividends declared 70,000
Dividends paid (derived) 50,000	
	Ending balance 60,000

Although dividends payable is a current liability, it is not related to operations. Therefore, its change is not shown in the reconciliation of income and operating cash flow. The following disclosure is required:

Financing activities: outflow, dividends paid, $50,000.

1154 V SPECIAL TOPICS

Cumulative Effect of an Accounting Change   An accounting change generally does not affect cash. A change from accelerated depreciation to straight-line depreciation increases retained earnings (retroactive application method) and increases net plant assets, but does not affect cash. Therefore, the adjustment is not reflected on the SCFP since it affects two non-cash balance sheet accounts, plant assets and retained earnings. It does not qualify as a non-cash significant financing activity that would require SCFP disclosure.

Cash Surrender Value of Life Insurance   In Chapter 14 we briefly discussed cash surrender value of life insurance. Cash surrender value increases over the life of an insurance policy. As premiums are paid, a portion is credited to the insured's surrender account. This increasing amount is classified as an investment. Consider the following entry:

To record insurance premium payment:

Cash surrender value of life insurance	2,000	
Life insurance expense	18,000	
Cash		20,000

In this case, $2,000 of the $20,000 premium is applied to the surrender value of the policy. This is reflected on the SCFP as follows:

Direct method, operations: outflow, insurance premiums, $20,000.

Indirect method, operations: reconciliation outflow. Insurance premium applied to surrender value, ($2,000).[22]

Sale of Cash Equivalents   In many cases, selling a cash equivalent security yields face value. No disclosure in the SCFP is warranted because total cash and cash equivalents are not changed by the sale. Further analysis is needed if the sale produces a gain or loss. For example, selling $50,000 (cost) of cash equivalents for $52,000 results in a $2,000 gain. The gain equals the increase in cash and cash equivalents. The impact on the SCFP is as follows:

Direct method, operations: inflow, gain on sale of cash equivalents, $2,000.

Indirect method, operations: no adjustment is necessary because the operating cash effect ($2,000 increase) is reflected in income ($2,000 gain).

Transactions involving only cash and cash equivalents are considered operating activities rather than investment activities.

Sale of Short-Term Investment—Non-Cash Equivalent   The proceeds from the sale of investments are considered an investing cash inflow, and the gain or loss from sale is a reconciliation adjustment. For example, the sale of $24,000 (cost) of short-term investments in common shares for $21,000 is disclosed in the SCFP as follows:

Investing activities: inflow, sale of short-term investments, $21,000.

Indirect method, operations: add back $3,000 loss on sale of investments.

Direct method, operations: the loss is not a cash flow and would not be listed.

Capital Leases   The increase in a lessee's long-term assets and liabilities resulting from lease capitalization is a significant investing and financing activity. Lease payments consist of interest, an operating payment, and principal, a financing payment. For example, assume that on January 1, 1993, a lease requiring five equal annual payments of

---

[22] A completely different disclosure is arguable, considering that the surrender value is an investment:
   Direct and indirect methods, operations: cash outflow, $18,000 insurance premiums; *Investing activities:* outflow, $2,000 increase in cash surrender value. There is no reconciliation adjustment under this treatment.
Most firms probably use the text disclosure, treating the transaction as entirely operating.

$31,656 due each December 31 is capitalized at 10%. The entries and their impact on the SCFP follow.

January 1, 1993—To record capital lease:

```
Leased property . . . . . . . . . . . . . . . . . . . . . . . 120,000
    Lease liability [$31,656 × (PVA, 10%, 5)] . . . . . . . . .        120,000
```

Investing activities: outflow, acquisition of leased assets, financed by lease liability, $120,000.

Financing activities: inflow, long-term lease liability, issued for leased assets, $120,000.

Alternatively, this non-cash significant financial event may be omitted from the SCFP and given note disclosure.

December 31, 1993—To record first lease payment:

```
Interest expense (10% × $120,000) . . . . . . . . . . . .    12,000
Lease liability. . . . . . . . . . . . . . . . . . . . . .    19,656
    Cash . . . . . . . . . . . . . . . . . . . . . . . . .             31,656
```

Indirect method, operations: no adjustment, as the interest payment ($12,000) equals the cash flow for interest, $12,000.

Direct method, operations: outflow, cash payments for interest, $12,000.

Financing activities: outflow, principal payment on capital lease, $19,656.

Income Taxes, Current and Deferred   Income tax expense on income from continuing operations is recorded in income taxes payable and deferred taxes. Changes in these two accounts are listed in Exhibit 23–7 as reconciling adjustments. The following information provides an example of these related accounts and SCFP disclosure:

	1991	1992
From comparative balance sheets:		
Income taxes payable.	$20,000	$27,000
Deferred taxes (long-term)	18,000	23,000
Income tax expense for 1992: $45,000.		
Assume no net reversals of timing differences.		

We reconstruct the entries affecting taxes:

To record income tax expense:

```
Income tax expense . . . . . . . . . . . . . . . . . . . . .    45,000
    Deferred taxes ($23,000 − $18,000) . . . . . . . . . . .            5,000
    Income taxes payable . . . . . . . . . . . . . . . . . .           40,000
```

To record income tax payments:

```
Income taxes payable ($20,000 + $40,000 − $27,000) . . . . . .    33,000
    Cash . . . . . . . . . . . . . . . . . . . . . . . . . .           33,000
```

Income tax expense reduces income $45,000, yet the operating cash outflow is only $33,000. As we indicated in Exhibit 23–7, both the $7,000 income taxes payable increase and $5,000 deferred tax increase are added in the reconciliation of income and net operating cash flow. Together, the two adjustments provide $12,000 of addition adjustments, which explains the difference between income and net operating cash flows. Collapsing the above two entries into one clarifies these conclusions:

Combined entry:

```
Income tax expense . . . . . . . . . . . . . . . . . . . . .    45,000
    Deferred taxes . . . . . . . . . . . . . . . . . . . . .            5,000
    Income taxes payable . . . . . . . . . . . . . . . . . .            7,000
    Cash . . . . . . . . . . . . . . . . . . . . . . . . . .           33,000
```

The combined entry reveals that the deferred taxes and income taxes payable increases completely explain the difference between the accrual account and the tax account. We recommend reconstructing entries whenever the SCFP disclosures are not readily apparent.

The following disclosures are required in the SCFP:

Direct method, operating activities: outflow, tax payments, $33,000.

Indirect method, operating activities: add back, taxes payable increase, $7,000. Deferred tax increase, $5,000.

Equity Method of Accounting for Investments Under the equity method, the investor records its share of investee earnings as an increase to the investment and investment revenue accounts. Dividends received, an operating cash inflow, decrease the investment. For example, assume a firm owns 30% of another company that earned $400,000 and paid $300,000 in dividends the current year. The investor makes the following entries:

To record income:

```
Investment in shares (30% × $400,000) . . . . . . . . . . . . .120,000
    Investment revenue . . . . . . . . . . . . . . . . . . . .        120,000
```

To record dividends received:

```
Cash (30% × $300,000) . . . . . . . . . . . . . . . . . . . . 90,000
    Investment in shares . . . . . . . . . . . . . . . . . .         90,000
```

Investment revenue increases income but not cash. Dividends received are an operating cash inflow. Therefore, we disclose the following:

Direct method, operating activities: inflow, dividends received from investment, $90,000.

Indirect method, operating activities: reconciliation, subtract investment revenue, $120,000. Add back dividends received, $90,000.

The second reconciliation adjustment, $90,000 dividends received, is necessary because net income does not reflect dividends under the equity method, thereby *understating* operating cash inflow. Alternatively, we can make one net adjustment: subtract from net income the excess of investment revenue over dividends, $30,000.

Short- and Long-Term Notes Payable to Banks Some short-term bank debt is classified as part of the cash and cash equivalents definition. Changes in such debt would not be listed in the SCFP. Other short-term loans may be excluded from the definition on the discretion of management, if not considered to be a cash equivalent. Changes in such loans must be included in the SCFP. Principal payments on loans are financing cash flows. Assume that (non-cash-equivalent) short-term notes payable to banks increased from $10,000 to $15,000 during the year, and $25,000 was paid on the account during the year. This implies $30,000 was received from banks during the year. The following disclosures are required:

Financing activities: inflow, short-term borrowings from banks, $30,000.
            outflow, principal payments on short-term borrowings from banks, $25,000.

Accounts Receivable, Bad Debts, and Write-offs We used accounts receivable without adjustments for uncollectible accounts in the Simple Company example. In general, the following disclosures are made for accounts receivable:

Direct method, operating activities: inflow, collections from customers on account, cash.

Indirect method, operating activities: Either (1) adjust net income for the change in *net* accounts receivable or (2) adjust net income for the change in *gross* accounts receivable *before* write-offs, and add bad debt expense back to net income.

The following example illustrates these generalizations; it is another case where transaction analysis is helpful:

	1991	1992
From comparative balance sheets:		
Accounts receivable	$600,000	$175,000
Allowance for doubtful accounts	20,000	35,000

During 1992:
Bad debt expense, $40,000
Accounts written off, $25,000
Collections on account, $1,400,000
Sales on account, $1,000,000

Accounts Receivable

Beginning bal	600,000		
Sales	1,000,000	Collections	1,400,000
		Write-offs	25,000
Ending bal	175,000		

Allowance for Doubtful Accounts

		Beginning bal	20,000
Write-offs	25,000	Bad debt expense	40,000
		Ending bal	35,000

Net accounts receivable, Dec. 31, 1992	$175,000 − $35,000 =	$140,000
Net accounts receivable, Dec. 31, 1991	$600,000 − $20,000 =	580,000
Decrease in net accounts receivable		$440,000

Change in gross accounts receivable before write-offs:

Sales ($1,000,000) − Collections ($1,400,000) = $400,000 decrease

Net income effect:

Sales ($1,000,000) − Bad debt expense ($40,000) = $960,000 increase

Required SCFP disclosures:

Direct method, operating activities: inflow, collections from customers on account, $1,400,000.

Indirect method, operating activities: either (1) add net accounts receivable decrease, $440,000 or (2) add gross accounts receivable decrease, $400,000; and add bad debt expense, $40,000.

Both alternatives under the indirect method yield a net $440,000 adjustment. When this $440,000 adjustment is added to net income, it combines with the $960,000 income effect from transactions involving accounts receivable to yield the $1,400,000 cash inflow.

Extraordinary Items An extraordinary item itself is usually a gain or loss figure that is *different* from the underlying cash flow. The cash flow, if any, associated with the transaction giving rise to the extraordinary item is usually classified as investing or financing. Tax payments (or reductions in payments) resulting from extraordinary items should be netted with the cash flow. In the operations section, the extraordinary gain or loss must be *excluded* from cash from operations. For the indirect method, this is done by starting with "income before extraordinary items" in any disclosures.

For example, assume a company receives $700,000 on the expropriation of a property that had a net book value at the date of expropriation of $370,000. The firm recognizes a $330,000 extraordinary gain and a $70,000 tax provision ($50,000 current, $20,000 deferred). The income statement appears as follows:

Income before extraordinary items (assumed).	$600,000
Extraordinary item, gain on asset expropriation, net of tax of $70,000 of which $20,000 is deferred ($330,000 − $70,000)	260,000
Net income	$860,000

Also assume that deferred taxes increase from $230,000 to $280,000 (credit) during the year.

The following are the SCFP disclosures:

Investing activities: inflow, expropriation of assets, $650,000 ($700,000 − $50,000).

Direct method, operating activities: no disclosure.

Indirect method, operating activities: income before extraordinary items, $600,000, plus increase in deferred taxes due to operations ($280,000 − $230,000 − $20,000), $30,000.

Under the indirect method, we could get the correct numbers by starting with the $860,000 net income and subtracting the $260,000 extraordinary gain to arrive at $600,000, or income before extraordinary items. This is not the preferred disclosure approach. *The indirect method reconciliation should always start with income before extraordinary items.*

In the deferred tax account, some of the increase is caused by the extraordinary item, while some is caused by operations. Under the indirect approach, we have to isolate the portion caused by operations:

Deferred Taxes

Opening balance	230,000
Extraordinary item tax	20,000
Operations tax	30,000
Closing balance	280,000

The worksheet journal entry that reconstructs the transaction is as follows:

Investing activity—Source, property sale ($700,000 − $50,000).	650,000	
Property		370,000
Extraordinary gain		260,000
Deferred taxes		20,000

On the worksheet, the operations section should start with income before extraordinary items; the extraordinary item in the above journal entry should be entered directly to retained earnings.

Discontinued Operations   If a company reports results of discontinued operations, these must be disclosed on the SCFP. First, the cash flow from discontinued operations must be disclosed separately from the cash flow from operations. Second, the company will have disclosed a gain or loss from the sale or closure of the discontinued operations, which generally follows extraordinary item treatment, explained above. Any proceeds from disposition are, of course, investing activities.

For example, Transcanada Pipelines included the following items on its 1989 SCFP (in millions):

Cash generated internally:
   Income from continuing operations. $210.1
   Cash generated from discontinued oil and gas operations . . . 44.4

Investment activities:
  Discontinued oil and gas operations:
   Investment. . . . . (72.1)
   Return on investment 493.5

CONCEPT REVIEW

1. What is the effect on cash and cash equivalents of selling a short-term investment, classed as a cash equivalent, at a $3,000 loss?
2. Explain how transactions giving rise to extraordinary items are disclosed in the SCFP.
3. Explain why dividends received on equity-method investments are added to operations in the indirect method reconciliation.

COMPREHENSIVE EXAMPLE, THE COMPLEX COMPANY

In this section we provide a longer, more involved example of preparing a complete SCFP. Both direct and indirect methods are illustrated. We employ the spreadsheet format and use the concepts developed in previous sections. Exhibit 23–9 furnishes the case data for Complex Company, and Exhibit 23–10 provides the complete spreadsheet for the solution.

We analyse the Complex Company data in the usual order, beginning with the income statement. As you study each entry, refer back to the spreadsheet in Exhibit 23–10.

Income Statement Accounts   Amounts are in thousands of dollars:

(a) $22 Net income before extraordinary items and discontinued operations is entered as the first value in the reconciliation.

(b) *Indirect method:* $3 gross accounts receivable decrease is added to net income. Bad debt expense is a separate adjustment, in (*i*).
Direct method: cash collections exceed sales by $3 because accounts receivable decreased $3 (accrual to cash formula).

(c) *Indirect method:* no adjustment for $1 dividend on short-term investments is necessary because they increase net income by the dividend amount.
Direct method: $1 operating cash inflow.

(d) *Indirect method:* subtract the $3 gain on sale of plant assets.
Both methods: using related additional information, investing cash inflow, sale of plant assets, $15. Relevant changes in accumulated depreciation and plant assets are removed.

(e) *Indirect method:* no adjustment needed because the $2 gain equals the cash increase.
Direct method: $2 operating cash inflow from sale of cash equivalents at a gain.

(f), (g) *Indirect method:* $4 accounts payable increase is added to net income and $7 inventory increase is subtracted.
Direct method: Using the previous formulas for converting accrual information to cash flows, cash payments for purchases equal $45 ($42 − $4 + $7).

(h) *Indirect method:* $8 depreciation is added to net income.

EXHIBIT 23–9   Complex Company: Case Data for Preparing the Statement of Changes in
Financial Position (in Thousands)

Income Statement, Year 1991

Revenues:

Sales and services	$ 96
Dividends (Xenon Corp.)	1
Gain on sale of plant assets	3
Gain on sale of cash equivalents	2

Expenses:

Cost of goods sold	(42)
Depreciation expense	(8)
Bad debt expense	(3)
Interest expense (on bonds)	(5)
Remaining expenses	(13)
Income tax expense (continuing operations)	(9)
Income before extraordinary items and discontinued operations	22
Extraordinary loss, land condemnation, $20 (tax saving, $6)	(14)
Discontinued operations, gain $10 (tax expense, $3)	7
Net income	$ 15

Comparative Balance Sheets, December 31, 1991

Items	Dec. 31, 1990	Dec. 31, 1991
Cash	$ 30	$ 61
Cash equivalents	6	0
Total	36	61
Investment, short-term (shares of Xenon Corp.)	12	17
Accounts receivable	32	29
Allowance for doubtful accounts	(2)	(5)
Inventory	30	37
Prepaid insurance	4	2
Land	60	41
Plant assets	80	96
Accumulated depreciation	(20)	(26)
Other assets (opening balance includes assets for discontinued operations, $13)	35	22
Total assets	$267	$274
Accounts payable	$ 26	$ 30
Interest payable	2	1
Income tax payable	11	4
Notes payable, long-term	0	10
Bonds payable	80	60
Unamortized bond discount	(3)	(2)
Common shares, nopar	100	130
Retained earnings	51	41
Total liabilities and shareholders' equity	$267	$274

Additional Information

a. Sold cash equivalents in January 1991 for $8 cash; none held at end of 1991.
b. Cash borrowed on long-term note at the end of 1991, $10.
c. Statement of Retained Earnings, Year Ended December 31, 1991:

Beginning balance	$ 51
Net income for 1991	15
Cash dividend declared and paid in 1991	(15)
Stock dividend issued in 1991	(10)
Ending balance	$ 41

EXHIBIT 23-9 *(concluded)*

	Plant Asset	Accumulated Depreciation
d. Plant asset account:		
Beginning balance	$ 80	$20 credit
Disposal of asset (for cash, $15)	(14)	(2)
Acquisition of new asset (machine)*	30	
Depreciation		8
Ending balance	$ 96	$ 26 credit

	Bonds	Discount, Unamortized Balance
e. Bonds payable account:		
Beginning balance	$ 80	$3 debit
Discount amortization for 1991		(1)
Bonds retired at end of 1991	(20)	
Ending balance	$ 60	$2

f. Land account:	
Beginning balance	$ 60
Sale due to condemnation (extraordinary loss); cash received in full payment, $40	(60)
Land acquisition (paid cash, $41)	41
Ending balance	$ 41

g. Discontinued operations:

Closed out completely by selling the remaining assets for cash, $23. The $13 cost of these assets is included in the other assets account.

h. Income tax payable account:

Beginning balance		$ 11
Additions for current income taxes:		
Tax on continuing operations	$9	
Extraordinary loss, tax saving	(6)	
Discontinued operations, tax expense	3	
Increase in payable (net)		6
Cash payments made during 1991		(13)
Ending balance		$ 4

* Paid cash $10 and issued common shares in full settlement, $20 (market value).

(*i*) *Indirect method:* $3 bad debt expense is added to net income. Alternatively, the reconciliation adjustments in (*b*) and (*i*) may be combined into one adjustment for the decrease in net accounts receivable: add $6. For the spreadsheet, the separate adjustments may be easier to enter.

(*j*) *Indirect method:* subtract the $1 interest payable decrease, and add the $1 amortization of bond discount.

Direct method: $5 operating cash outflow. A summary entry explains this outflow, and the changes in relevant accounts:

Summary entry for interest

Interest expense		5
Interest payable		1
Unamortized bond discount	1	
Cash (derived)	5	

(*k*) *Indirect method:* add the $2 prepaid insurance decrease.

Direct method: $13 remaining expenses exceed $11 cash payments by the $2 prepaid insurance decrease (accrual to cash formula).

EXHIBIT 23–10   Spreadsheet for Direct and Indirect Method SCFP, Complex Company

COMPLEX COMPANY
Spreadsheet for Direct and Indirect Method SCFP
For the Year Ended December 31, 1991
(in thousands)

Spreadsheet

Comparative Balance Sheets	Dec. 31, 1990	Dr.		Cr.		Dec. 31, 1991
Cash	$ 30	(v)	$ 31			$ 61
Cash equivalents	6			$ 6	(v)	0
Investment in Xenon.	12	(u)	5			17
Accounts receivable	32			3	(b)	29
Allowance for doubtful accounts . .	(2)			3	(i)	(5)
Inventory	30	(g)	7			37
Prepaid insurance	4			2	(k)	2
Land	60	(t)	41	60	(m)	41
Plant assets	80	(r)	30	14	(d)	96
Accumulated depreciation	(20)	(d)	2	8	(h)	(26)
Other assets.	35			13	(n)	22
Total assets	$267					$274
Accounts payable	$ 26			4	(f)	$ 30
Interest payable	2	(j)	1			1
Income tax payable	11	(l)	7			4
Notes payable	0			10	(o)	10
Bonds payable.	80	(s)	20			60
Unamortized bond discount	(3)			1	(j)	(2)
Common shares	100			10	(q)	130
				20	(r)	
Retained earnings	51	(p)	15	22	(a)	41
		(q)	10			
		(m)	14	7	(n)	
Total liabilities and owners' equity	$267					$274
Total changes			$183	$183		

Adjustments Leading to SCFP

		Indirect Method				Direct Method (Operations)
		Dr.		Cr.		
Operating activities						
Net income, before extraordinary items and discontinued operations	$ 22	(a)	$22			
Sales and services	96	(b)	3			$99 customer collections
Dividends	1				(c)	$1 dividends received
Gain on sale of plant asset	3			$ 3	(d)	
Gain on sale of cash equivalents	2				(e)	$2 inflow from cash equiv. sale
Cost of goods sold	42	(f)	4	7	(g)	$45 payments to suppliers
Depreciation	8	(h)	8			
Bad debt expense	3	(i)	3			

EXHIBIT 23–10 *(concluded)*

	Indirect Method		Direct Method (Operations)
	Dr.	Cr.	
Operating activities			
Interest expense	5 (*j*) 1	1 (*j*)	$5 interest payments
Remaining expenses	13 (*k*) 2		$11 payments for other exps.
Income tax expense	9	7 (*l*)	$16 tax payments
Investing activities			
Sale of plant assets	(*d*) 15		
Proceeds from condemnation, net	(*m*) 46		
Proceeds from sale of discontinued assets, net	(*n*) 20		
Purchase of plant assets		30 (*r*)	
Acquisition of land		41 (*t*)	
Purchase of Xenon shares		5 (*u*)	
Financing activities			
Issue common shares	(*r*) 20		
Issue long-term note	(*o*) 10		
Dividend payment		15 (*p*)	
Bond retirement		20 (*s*)	
		109	
Net increase in cash and cash equivalents		25 (*v*)	
	$154	$154	

(*l*) *Indirect method:* subtract the $7 income tax payable decrease.
  Direct method: $16 income tax payment exceeds $9 income tax expense by the $7 income tax payable decrease (accrual to cash formula). All the change in the payable account is assumed to relate to operations, for simplicity.

(*m*) *Both methods:* The $14 extraordinary loss is closed to retained earnings. Using related additional information: net investing cash inflow, proceeds from sale of land due to condemnation ($40 + $6). Tax is added as it is a tax saving from the accounting loss. Original cost of land is removed.

(*n*) *Both methods:* Close the $7 net gain from discontinued operations to retained earnings. Notice that the three income-related adjustments to retained earnings ($22 − $14 + $7) now equal net income ($15). Using related additional information, net investing cash inflow, $20 proceeds from sale of assets from discontinued operations ($23 − $3). Original cost of assets is removed.

Additional Information   The additional information, not yet considered in the above entries, is analysed in order of appearance in Exhibit 23–9.

(*o*) *Both methods:* financing cash inflow, $10 proceeds from issuing long-term note.

(*p*) *Both methods:* financing cash outflow, $15 dividend payments.

(*q*) Stock dividends are not disclosed in the SCFP.

(*r*) *Both methods:* investing cash outflow, $30 acquisition of plant assets, and a financing inflow, $20 on issuance of common shares. Alternatively, the company could elect to use a footnote to the SCFP to describe the non-cash aspects of the acquisition and record the acquisition at $10.

EXHIBIT 23-11   Statement of Changes in Financial Position, Direct Method, Complex Company

---

COMPLEX COMPANY
Statement of Changes in Financial Position, Direct Method
For the Year Ended December 31, 1991
(in thousands)

Cash flows from operating activities:

Cash inflows:

From customers.	$ 99	
From gain on cash equivalents sold	2	
From dividends received on short-term investments.	1	

Cash outflows:

Paid to suppliers (for cost of goods sold)	(45)	
Paid for interest.	(5)	
Paid for income taxes	(16)	
Paid for remaining expenses.	(11)	
Net cash inflow from operating activities.		$ 25

Cash flows from investing activities:

Cash inflows:

From sale of plant assets	15	
From sale of land (condemnation)	46	
From sale of discontinued operations	20	

Cash outflows:

Paid for purchase of investment in Xenon	(5)	
Paid for purchase of land	(41)	
Acquired plant assets (partially financed with common shares, Note A).	(30)	
Net cash inflow from investing activities		5

Cash flows for financing activities:

Cash inflows:

Borrowing on long-term note	10	
Issued common shares (partial payment for plant asset, Note A)	20	

Cash outflows:

Payment on bond principal	(20)	
Paid cash dividend	(15)	
Net cash outflow for financing activities		(5)
Net increase in cash plus cash equivalents during 1991		$ 25
Cash plus cash equivalents, January 1, 1991		36
Cash plus cash equivalents, December 31, 1991.		$ 61

Note A—The company purchased an operational asset (machine); payment was part cash and part the company's unissued common shares as follows:

Cash paid.	$10
Common shares issued	20
Total asset cost recorded	$30

(*s*) *Both methods:* financing cash outflow, $20 payment to retire bonds.

(*t*) *Both methods:* investing cash outflow, $41 payment to acquire land.

Remaining Unexplained Balance Sheet Accounts

(*u*) At this point, all additional information is incorporated, and all balance sheet account changes are explained except the investment in Xenon shares, which increased $5 during 1991. This implies a purchase of additional shares.
Both methods: investing cash outflow, $5 payment to acquire Xenon shares.

(*v*) *Balancing entry:* Cash increased $31 during 1991, and cash equivalents decreased $6. The net increase in cash and cash equivalents is therefore $25. This amount reconciles total cash increases and total cash decreases.

EXHIBIT 23-12 Reconciliation of Net Income to Net Cash Inflow from Operating Activities, Complex Company

COMPLEX COMPANY

**Reconciliation of Net Income to Net Cash Inflow
from Operating Activities
For the Year 1991
(in thousands)**

Net income before extraordinary items and discontinued operations (accrual basis, from income statement).	$22
Add (deduct) to reconcile net income to net cash flow from operating activities:	
Accounts receivable decrease	3
Gain on sale of operational assets	(3)
Inventory increase	(7)
Accounts payable increase	4
Depreciation expense	8
Bad debt expense	3
Interest payable decrease	(1)
Amortization of bond discount	1
Prepaid insurance decrease	2
Income tax payable decrease	(7)
Net cash inflow from operating activities	$25

The spreadsheet is totaled to confirm accuracy. The direct method SCFP is prepared by transferring the operating cash flows in the direct method columns of the spreadsheet to the operating activities section of the SCFP. The investing and financing cash flows are also transferred. The complete direct method SCFP is illustrated in Exhibit 23–11.

The indirect method for the operations section is prepared by transferring the reconciling adjustments from the indirect method columns in the operating section of the spreadsheet. The reconciliation appears in Exhibit 23–12. To prepare the indirect method SCFP, replace the operating section of the direct method SCFP with the reconciliation (not illustrated).

The definition of cash equivalents should be disclosed under both methods.

ISSUES IN CASH FLOW REPORTING

Several studies have focussed on the relative usefulness of cash flow versus accrual information. For example, one study of 98 firms found that cash flow information increases the overall information content of financial statements.[23] Another study found evidence to suggest that in assessing a firm's risk, cash flow variables supply additional information beyond that provided by earnings information alone.[24]

However, other studies have found different results. For example, a study of 290 companies found that operating cash flow data over a five-year period were not a good discriminator between healthy firms and firms that declared bankruptcy.[25] The study found that accrual measures, including traditional financial accounting ratios, are more accurate predictors of business failure.

One reason that firms with poor operating cash flows can survive for an extended period is the willingness of creditors to renegotiate and restructure debt. Massey-

---

[23] R. Bowen, D. Burgstahler, and L. Daley, "The Incremental Information Content of Accrual versus Cash Flows," *Accounting Review,* October 1987, p. 723.

[24] B. Ismail and M. Kim, "On the Association of Cash Flow Variables with Market Risk: Further Evidence," *Accounting Review,* January 1989, p. 125

[25] C. Casey and N. Bartczak, "Cash Flow—It's Not the Bottom Line," *Harvard Business Review,* July–August 1984, p. 60.

Ferguson (now Varity Corp.) and International Harvester (now Navistar) are examples.[26] Also, growing companies often have negative cash flow because they invest heavily in capital expenditures.

Neither accrual nor cash flow information alone is sufficient for a complete understanding of a company's performance. The relationship between revenues and cash inflows, and expenses and cash outflows can be understood only by studying both types of information. As such, the SCFP provides important input to that understanding.

Perhaps the following quotes best reflect the current situation:

> The earnings information will show how well the company is doing at making money. The cash flow information will show how real that money is.[27]

> Furthermore, no one number can accurately and consistently predict performance; many factors affect a company's well-being.[28]

There is considerable disagreement among preparers and users concerning the most appropriate format for the SCFP. Some believe that the indirect method is inconsistent with the requirement to report gross rather than net flows (net operating cash flow is a very aggregate amount). Others believe that the costs of preparing the direct method data exceed the benefits of the disclosure. The controversy has led to diversity among firms' disclosures.

Such controversy and diversity are likely healthy. Users who carefully analyse information presented will not be misled and will be able to make valid comparisons. Forcing decisions on companies leads to a rule-oriented process, in which the role of judgment is downplayed. Companies have the obligation to present information to investors and creditors in the way they believe is the most appropriate.

CONCEPT REVIEW

1. Why is interest received classified as operating?
2. Why are insurance proceeds on involuntary destruction of plant assets classified as investing cash flows?
3. For what decisions would you prefer cash flow information to accrual information?

SUMMARY OF KEY POINTS

◆

(L.O. 1) 1. The trend toward cash flow reporting is influenced by the complexity of GAAP, the perceived low quality of earnings, increased business risk and failure, the need for specific cash flow information, dissatisfaction with previous fund statements, and other factors.

(L.O. 1) 2. Cash flow information is used to predict future cash flows, assess liquidity, assess the ability of a firm to pay dividends and obligations, assess the ability of a firm to adapt to changes in the business environment, assess the quality of earnings, and for other purposes.

(L.O. 2) 3. The SCFP is one of the three major financial statements. Its primary purpose is to report cash flows in meaningful categories.

(L.O. 2) 4. The reporting basis for the SCFP is cash. This must be defined by each company, based on circumstances. It may include, in addition to cash, short-term investments, including cash equivalents, and short-term bank debt.

---

[26] Ibid.

[27] "Are More Chryslers in the Offing?" *Forbes,* February 2, 1981, p. 73.

[28] C. Casey and N. Bartczak, "Cash Flow—It's Not the Bottom Line," *Harvard Business Review,* July–August 1984, p. 60.

(L.O. 2) 5. Cash flows fall into three categories. Operating flows are related to the main activities of the business and are involved in the earnings process. Investing flows describe long-term asset acquisitions and the proceeds from sale of long-term assets. Financing flows describe the sources of short- and long-term financing other than operations, and repayments of short- and long-term liabilities and equities unrelated to operations.

(L.O. 2, 3) 6. There are two allowable methods of reporting cash from operations, the direct and indirect methods. Investing and financing activities are reported in exactly the same way under both methods. The direct method reports the cash inflows from the main classifications of revenues and cash outflows from the main classifications of expenses. In contrast, the indirect method reports operating activities by showing a reconciliation of net income before extraordinary items with net cash flow from operating activities. Examples of adjustments are depreciation and changes in operating working capital accounts.

(L.O. 2, 3) 7. The operating activity sections of both the direct and indirect SCFPs convert accrual income to cash-basis income, the net cash flow from operations.

(L.O. 2, 3) 8. Significant non-cash transactions (e.g., acquiring plant assets by issuing a long-term note) are listed as outflows and inflows on the SCFP, cross-referenced to each other. Alternatively, they may be disclosed in a supplementary schedule to complete the description of significant investing and financing activities.

(L.O. 2, 3) 9. In most cases, gross cash flows are reported, and transactions are not netted against other flows in the same category.

(L.O. 3) 10. There are many approaches to preparing a SCFP. The same objectives apply to all: analyse transactions to identify all cash flows, reconciling items, and non-cash transactions.

(L.O. 4) 11. The format-free approach to preparing the SCFP emphasizes transaction analysis and uses no particular format. Search for transactions in the following order: income statement, additional information, and comparative balance sheets.

(L.O. 5) 12. The spreadsheet is an organized format allowing substantiation of the preparation process, and provides many accuracy checks. Both the direct and indirect method SCFP may be developed with the same spreadsheet.

(L.O. 6) 13. The T-account approach to preparing the SCFP is simple and efficient, and it is useful for shorter problems. It is applicable when there is less need to document the preparation process or review work. (See Appendix 23A.)

REVIEW PROBLEM

◆

The Phillies Company prepared the following information relevant to its 1992 SCFP.

Comparative Balance Sheets

	Dec. 31, 1991	Dec. 31, 1992
Cash	$200,000	$ 62,000
Accounts receivable, net	60,000	80,000
Inventory	12,000	20,000
Prepaids	6,000	10,000
Equipment, net	300,000	500,000
Goodwill	90,000	70,000
Total assets	$668,000	$742,000
Accounts payable	40,000	60,000
Salaries payable	60,000	50,000
Interest payable	6,000	9,000
Income tax payable	12,000	22,000
Mortgage payable	120,000	110,000
Bonds payable	200,000	100,000
Premium on bonds payable	8,000	3,000
Common shares, nopar	150,000	170,000
Retained earnings	72,000	218,000
Total liabilities and owners' equity	$668,000	$742,000

Income Statement Accounts, 1992

Sales	$820,000
Cost of goods sold	380,000
Depreciation expense	100,000
Amortization of goodwill	20,000
Other expenses	46,000
Loss on bond retirement	3,000
Interest expense	22,000
Income tax expense	72,000
Extraordinary gain, excess of insurance proceeds over book value of equipment destroyed, net of $1,000 tax	9,000
Net income	$186,000

Additional Information

1. Phillies declared $40,000 of dividends in 1992.
2. Equipment (cost: $100,000; accumulated depreciation, $60,000) was destroyed by fire. Proceeds from insurance, $50,000. Applicable taxes, $1,000.
3. Bonds were retired on January 1, 1992, at 107.

Required:

Prepare the 1992 SCFP for Phillies, using the direct method. (The optional spreadsheet is used to illustrate the solution. The format-free approach or T-account approach are equally acceptable.)

**REVIEW
SOLUTION**
◆

Spreadsheet

Comparative Balance Sheets	December 31, 1991	Dr.		Cr.		December 31, 1992
Cash	$200,000			138,000	(q)	$ 62,000
Accounts receivable, net	60,000	(b)	20,000			80,000
Inventory	12,000	(c)	8,000			20,000
Prepaids	6,000	(g)	4,000			10,000
Equipment, net	300,000	(h)	60,000	100,000	(e)	500,000
		(n)	340,000	100,000	(h)	
Goodwill	90,000			20,000	(f)	70,000
Total assets	$668,000					$742,000
Accounts payable	$ 40,000			20,000	(d)	$ 60,000
Salaries payable	60,000	(g)	10,000			50,000
Interest payable	6,000			3,000	(i)	9,000
Income tax payable	12,000			10,000	(k)	22,000
Mortgage payable	120,000	(o)	10,000			110,000
Bonds payable	200,000	(l)	100,000			100,000
Premium on bonds payable	8,000	(l)	4,000			3,000
		(j)	1,000			
Common shares, nopar	150,000			20,000	(p)	170,000
Retained earnings	72,000	(m)	40,000	177,000	(a)	218,000
Total liabilities and owners' equity	$668,000			9,000	(h)	$742,000
Total changes			$597,000	$597,000		

Adjustments Leading to SCFP:

		Indirect Method				Direct Method (Operations)
Operating Activities		Dr.		Cr.		
Net income before extraordinary	177,000	(a)	177,000			
Sales	820,000			20,000	(b)	$800,000 customer collections
Cost of goods sold	380,000	(d)	20,000	8,000	(c)	$368,000 supplier payments

Operating Activities		Indirect Method		Direct Method (Operations)
		Dr.	Cr.	
Depreciation expense	100,000	(e) 100,000		
Amortized goodwill	20,000	(f) 20,000		
Other expenses	46,000		14,000 (g)	$60,000 payments
Loss on bond retirement	3,000	(l) 3,000		
Interest expense	22,000	(i) 3,000	1,000 (j)	$20,000 interest payments
Income tax expense	72,000	(k) 10,000		$62,000 tax payments
Investing Activities				
Net insurance proceeds, equipment		(h) 49,000		
Purchase of equipment			340,000 (n)	
Financing Activities				
Retirement of bonds			107,000 (l)	
Dividends paid			40,000 (m)	
Principal payment, mortgage			10,000 (o)	
Issue shares		(p) 20,000		
		402,000		
Net cash decrease		(q) 138,000		
		$540,000	$540,000	

Explanations for spreadsheet entries:

(a) Net income, before extraordinary gain ($186,000 − $9,000).

(b) Accounts receivable increase.

(c) Inventory increase.

(d) Accounts payable increase.

(e) Depreciation expense.

(f) Amortization of goodwill (reduces income but is not a cash flow).

(g) Prepaids increase and salaries payable decrease.

(h) Equipment fire—The gain is closed to retained earnings to include all components of net income in retained earnings. The original cost and accumulated depreciation are removed from the net equipment account. Net proceeds, investing source ($50,000 − $1,000).

(i) Interest payable increase.

(j) Amortization of bond premium in 1992—one half of the premium was removed from the accounts at the beginning of the year upon retirement of one half of the bond issue. The remaining $1,000 decrease in bond premium is amortization.

(k) Increase in income taxes payable.

(l) The loss on the income statement does not represent the amount of cash involved in the transaction and must be removed.

   Entry to record the bond retirement, January 1, 1992:

Bonds payable	. . . .	100,000
Bond premium (½ of $8,000)	. . . .	4,000
Loss on bond retirement	. . . .	3,000
Cash (1.07 × $100,000)	. . . .	107,000

(m) Dividends declared equal dividends paid (no dividends payable account).

(n) There remained a $340,000 unexplained increase in net equipment after all available information was incorporated.

(o) Decrease in mortgage payable implies a principal payment, in the absence of other information.

(p) Increase in common shares implies issuance of additional shares, in the absence of other information.

(q) Net cash decrease, to balance.

PHILLIES COMPANY
Statement of Changes in Financial Position
For the Year Ended December 31, 1992

Cash flows from operating activities:

Collections from customers	$ 800,000	
Payments to suppliers	(368,000)	
Interest payments	(20,000)	
Other payments	(60,000)	
Tax payments	(62,000)	
Net cash inflow from operating activities		$ 290,000

Cash flows for investing activities:

Insurance proceeds—equipment fire	49,000	
Purchase of equipment	(340,000)	
Net cash outflow for investing activities		(291,000)

Cash flows for financing activities:

Bond retirement	(107,000)	
Principal payment, mortgage	(10,000)	
Issue shares	20,000	
Dividends paid	(40,000)	
Net cash outflow for financing activities		(137,000)

Net cash decrease		$(138,000)
Cash and cash equivalents, January 1, 1992		200,000
Cash and cash equivalents, December 31, 1992		$ 62,000

Reconciliation of Net Income and Net Cash Inflow from Operating Activities

Net income before extraordinary item . . . . $ 177,000

Reconciling items:

Accounts receivable increase	(20,000)
Accounts payable increase	20,000
Inventory increase	(8,000)
Depreciation	100,000
Goodwill amortization	20,000
Salaries payable decrease	(10,000)
Prepaids increase	(4,000)
Loss on bond retirement	3,000
Interest payable increase	3,000
Amortization of bond premium	(1,000)
Income taxes payable increase	10,000
Net cash inflow from operating activities	$ 290,000

APPENDIX 23A: *The T-Account Approach to Preparing the SCFP*

The T-account approach to preparation is similar to the spreadsheet approach. The same logic is used, and many of the same entries are found in both approaches. The T-account approach places the entries directly into the accounts themselves. In essence, the T-account approach puts the spreadsheet data and analysis into individual T-accounts rather than into columnar format.

Many accountants find the T-accounts approach easier to use. There are no spreadsheet operations to learn. The T-account approach is more flexible, less formal, and often faster. However, location of errors and review of the preparation process may be more difficult under the T-account approach.

The T-account approach is particularly efficient for shorter and less involved problems, when there are time constraints, or when there is no need to review or retain working papers. Some preparers use T-accounts only for cash, plant assets, and retained earnings and other more "active" accounts, and use the format-free approach for the simpler transactions.

The T-accounts used in this approach are not actual ledger accounts. Rather, they are workspaces in account form used to accumulate the information necessary to prepare the SCFP and to explain all account balance changes. The cash T-account accumulates all changes in cash and is divided into three sections corresponding to the three cash flow categories.

Under the direct method, reconciling items for the operating activities section are placed into a schedule as encountered. The T-accounts are not used for these items. Alternatively, a second cash T-account may be used in addition to the primary cash T-account used for cash flows. This second T-account is the same T-account used in the indirect method.

T-accounts may be set up using the beginning and ending balances for all accounts. Alternatively, only the *change* in the account may be used. We will illustrate both methods and leave it to you to decide which you find easier to follow. The direct method has been illustrated with opening and closing balances; the indirect method, with account balance changes. Both methods produce identical results.

The SCFP is prepared directly from the entries in the cash account. The process is complete when all account balance changes are explained. To illustrate the T-account approach for the direct and indirect methods, we use the information from Exhibit 23–4 for Simple Company.

Lowercase letters indicate the order of the T-account entries. The explanation for each entry parallels those of the format-free and spreadsheet approaches discussed in the chapter, although the letters may not correspond between the different approaches. The same order of information search is used: income statement, additional information, and remaining unexplained balance sheet changes.

T-Accounts for Simple Company, Direct Method

We begin with the income statement. Sales, (*a*), is posted both to accounts receivable and to sales. Customer collections represents the amount that balances accounts receivable. This amount is posted to the cash account. The cash account accumulates all cash flows by category. The explanations for the remaining entries follow the chapter discussion for Simple Company, direct method.

Cash

Jan. 1, 1991, balance	42			
Operating activities:		Operating activities:		
(*b*) Customer collections	58	(*d*) Salary payments		26
		(*f*) Payments for admin. and selling expenses		12
	58			38
Investing activities:		Investing activities:		
(*h*) Sale of plant assets	21	(*g*) Purchase of equipment		30
	21			30
Financing activities:		Financing activities:		
(*i*) Issue long-term note	40	(*j*) Principal payment on note		46
(*m*) Issue shares	48	(*k*) Retire shares		8
		(*l*) Dividend payments		11
	88			65
Dec. 31, 1991, balance	76			

Balance Sheet Accounts

Accounts Receivable

Jan. 1, 1991, balance	31		
(*a*) Sales	66	(*b*) Customer collections	58
Dec. 31, 1991, balance	39		

Plant Assets

Jan. 1, 1991, balance	82		
(*g*) Equipment purchase	30	(*h*) Sale of plant assets	31
Dec. 31, 1991, balance	81		

Accumulated Depreciation

			Jan. 1, 1991, balance	20
(h)	Sale of plant assets	10	(e) Depreciation expense	4
			Dec. 31, 1991, balance	14

Salaries Payable

			Jan. 1, 1991, balance	3
(d)	Salary payments	26	(c) Salary expense	28
			Dec. 31, 1991, balance	5

Notes Payable

			Jan. 1, 1991, balance	46
(j)	Principal payment	46	(i) Issue note	40
			Dec. 31, 1991, balance	40

Common Shares

			Jan. 1, 1991, balance	70
(k)	Retire shares	10	(m) Issue shares	48
			Dec. 31, 1991, balance	108

Contributed Capital from Share Retirement

Jan. 1, 1991, balance	0
(k) Retire shares	2
Dec. 31, 1991, balance	2

Retained Earnings

			Jan. 1, 1991, balance	16
(l)	Dividend payments	11	Net income (to balance)*	22
			Dec. 31, 1991, balance	27

* Alternatively, separate "closing entries" can be made for each income statement account, posting directly to the retained earnings account.

Income Statement Accounts

Sales

(a) Sales	66

Salaries Expense

(c)	Salaries expense	28

Depreciation Expense

(e)	Depreciation expense	4

Administrative and Selling Expense

(f)	Administrative and selling expense	12

The SCFP is prepared by transferring the cash flow information in the cash account to the statement. The complete statement is found in Exhibit 23–5 in the chapter.

T-Accounts for Simple Company, Indirect Method

We again begin with the income statement. The indirect method focusses on the change in operating working capital accounts, non-cash expenses, and other items to determine the operating activities section of the SCFP. The first entry, (a), places net income into the cash account, operating activities section. The next item from the income statement is (b), depreciation expense. Depreciation expense is added back to income. The explanations for the remaining entries follow the chapter discussion for Simple Company, indirect method.

Cash

Jan. 1, 1991, balance	42				
Operating activities:			Operating activities:		
(a) Net income	22		(c) Accounts receivable increase	8	
(b) Depreciation expense	4				
(d) Salaries payable increase	2				
	28			8	
Investing activities:			Investing activities:		
(f) Sale of plant assets	21		(e) Purchase of equipment	30	
	21			30	
Financing activities:			Financing activities:		
(g) Issue long-term note	40		(h) Principal payment on note	46	
(k) Issue shares	48		(i) Retire shares	8	
			(j) Dividend payments	11	
	88			65	
Dec. 31, 1991, balance	76				

Balance Sheet Accounts

Accounts Receivable

Net increase	8		
(c) Increase	8		

Plant Assets

		Net decrease	1	
(e) Equipment purchase	30	(f) Sale of plant assets	31	

Accumulated Depreciation

Net decrease	6			
(f) Sale of plant assets	10	(b) Depreciation expense	4	

Salaries Payable

		Net increase	2	
		(d) Increase	2	

Notes Payable

	Net decrease	6		
(h)	Principal payment	46	(g) Issue note	40

Common Shares

			Net increase	38
(i)	Retire shares	10	(k) Issue shares	48

Contributed Capital from Share Retirement

	Net increase	2
(i) Retire shares		2

Retained Earnings

		Net increase	11
(j) Dividend payments	11	(a) Net income	22

The SCFP is prepared by transferring the cash flow information and income adjustments in the cash account to the statement. The complete statement is found in Exhibit 23–1 in the chapter.

KEY TERMS

Cash equivalents (1134)
Cash flow per share (1138)
Direct method (1144)
Financial flexibility (1133)
Financing cash flows (1136)

Free cash flow (1133)
Indirect method (1141)
Investing cash flows (1136)
Non-cash activities (1137)
Operating cash flows (1135)

QUESTIONS

1. Compare the purposes of the balance sheet, income statement, and statement of changes in financial position.
2. Explain the basic difference between the three activities reported on the SCFP: operating, investing, and financing.
3. List three major cash inflows and three major cash outflows under (a) operating activities, (b) investing activities, and (c) financing activities.
4. Should cash flows be shown gross or net? When may items be combined?
5. Why is the cash basis preferable to working capital for the SCFP?
6. How is cash defined for SCFP purposes? Why is disclosure of the definition so important?
7. Where should dividends paid be classified on the SCFP?
8. Explain the basic difference between the direct and indirect methods of reporting on the SCFP. Use net income, $5,000, sales revenue, $100,000, and an increase of accounts receivable, $10,000, to illustrate the basic difference. Which method provides the most relevant information to investors and creditors?
9. Explain why cash paid during the period for purchases and salaries is not specifically reported on the SCFP, indirect method, as a cash outflow.
10. Explain why a $50,000 increase in inventory during the year must be considered when developing disclosures for operating activities under both the direct and indirect methods.

11. Give an example of a significant non-cash investing and financing event. How is it included in the SCFP?

12. How is a stock dividend reported on the SCFP?

13. Explain why an adjustment must be made (under the indirect approach) to compute cash flow from operating activities for depreciation expense, bad debt expense, and amortization of intangibles (e.g., patents, copyrights, franchises, goodwill, and bond discount or premium).

14. Explain why gains and losses reported on the income statement usually must be omitted (or removed) from operating activities to compute cash flow from operating activities.

15. Feron Corporation's records showed the following: sales, $80,000, and accounts receivable decrease, $10,000, after the write-off of a $3,000 bad debt. Compute the cash inflow from customers.

16. Foley Corporation records showed the following: Purchases, $60,000; increase in accounts payable, $15,000; decrease in inventory, $20,000. Compute the cash paid to suppliers.

17. Why are cash, short-term investments, and short-term bank debt grouped together for purposes of the SCFP even though short-term investments and bank debt are not actually cash?

18. How is an extraordinary item treated on the SCFP? Assume that a firm has net income of $200,000 after an extraordinary loss of $70,000 resulting from fire damange. The $70,000 represented the loss on destruction of fixed assets (net book value, $170,000; insurance proceeds, $100,000).

19. During 1995, ABC Company recorded a decrease of $12,000 in the revenue received in advance account, and a net increase of $50,000 in accounts receivable. Sales were $500,000. How much cash was collected?

20. Discuss an inconsistency in the SCFP in the classification of dividends received and dividends paid.

21. How is a lease payment (after inception) on a capital lease classified in the SCFP?

EXERCISES

E 23–1
SCFP: Terminology,
Format, Requirements
(L.O. 2)

Two lists are given below—key terms and brief descriptions. You are to match the descriptions with the terms by entering one letter in each blank to the left.

Key Terms	Brief Descriptions
_____ 1. Fundamental purpose of the SCFP.	A. Net cash increase (decrease), beginning balance, and ending balance.
_____ 2. Basic components of the SCFP.	B. Cash flows related to obtaining cash to finance the enterprise.
_____ 3. Three reconciling lines at the bottom of the SCFP.	C. Cash flows primarily related to the income statement.
_____ 4. May be disclosed in note disclosure or included in the SCFP itself.	D. A ratio sometimes disclosed in the annual report.
_____ 5. Cash flows from operating activities.	E. Includes highly liquid investments, but not necessarily all short-term investments.
_____ 6. Cash flow per share.	F. Cash flows from three activities: operating, investing, and financing.
_____ 7. SCFP, direct method.	
_____ 8. This amount must agree with the total sources and uses.	G. Add (deduct) to adjust net income to net cash flows.
_____ 9. Cash flows from investing activities.	H. Non-cash investing and financing activities.
_____ 10. This does not appear on the SCFP.	I. Two approaches to develop the SCFP.
_____ 11. SCFP, indirect method.	J. To help investors, creditors, etc., assess future cash flows.
_____ 12. T-account and spreadsheet.	K. Cash flows related to obtaining productive facilities and other non-cash assets.
_____ 13. Cash equivalents.	L. Reports cash flows for each major revenue and expense.
_____ 14. Cash flows from financing activities.	M. Stock dividends.
_____ 15. This item on the SCFP, indirect method, must be clearly identified as a reconciliation.	N. Net increase (decrease) in cash during the period.
	O. Does not report cash flows for revenues and expenses, but reconciles net income with cash flows.

E 23–2
SCFP—Examples of Cash
Inflows and Outflows:
Compare the Direct and
Indirect Methods
(L.O. 2)

A format overview of the SCFP, direct method, is given below with three numbered blank spaces under each cash inflow and outflow—

Operating activities:
  Cash inflows:
    1.
    2.
    3.
  Cash outflows:
    1.
    2.
    3.
Investing activities:
  Cash inflows:
    1.
    2.
    3.
  Cash outflows:
    1.
    2.
    3.
Financing activities:
  Cash inflows
    1.
    2.
    3.
  Cash outflows:
    1.
    2.
    3.

Required:

1. Give major examples in the blank spaces.
2. Assume the indirect method is used instead. Give the format, with three examples, that would be used for operating activities. Be prepared to discuss your examples.

E 23–3
SCFP: Cash Flow Analysis
of Sales
(L.O. 3, 4)

The records of ZZ Company showed sales revenue of $100,000 on the income statement and a change in the balance of accounts receivable. To demonstrate the effect of changes in accounts receivable on cash inflows from customers, five independent cases are used. Complete the following tabulation for each independent case:

Case	Sales Revenue	Accounts Receivable Increase (Decrease)	Computations	Inflow Amount
A	$100,000	$ –0–		
B	100,000	10,000		
C	100,000	(10,000)		
D	100,000	9,000*		
E	100,000	(9,000)*		

* Includes the effect of a $1,000 write-off of an uncollectible account.

E 23–4
SCFP: Cash Flow Analysis
of Cost of Goods Sold
(L.O. 3, 4)

The records of Atlas Company showed cost of goods sold on the income statement of $60,000 and a change in the inventory and accounts payable balances. To demonstrate the effect of these changes on cash outflow for cost of goods sold (i.e., payments to suppliers), eight independent cases are used. Complete the following tabulation for each case:

Case	Cost of Goods Sold	Inventory Increase (Decrease)	Accounts Payable Increase (Decrease)	Computations	Outflow Amount*
A	$60,000	$ –0–	$ –0–		
B	60,000	6,000	–0–		
C	60,000	(6,000)	–0–		
D	60,000	–0–	4,000		
E	60,000	–0–	(4,000)		
F	60,000	6,000	4,000		
G	60,000	(6,000)	(4,000)		
H	60,000	(6,000)	(6,000)		

* This is the amount of cash paid during the current period for past and current purchases.

E 23–5
SCFP: Direct Method: Analysis of Cash Inflows and Outflows
(L.O. 3, 4)

The records of Easie Company provided the following data:

a. Sales revenue, $95,000; accounts receivable decreased, $5,000.
b. Cost of goods sold, $42,000; inventory decreased, $3,000; accounts payable, no change.
c. Wage expense, $16,000; wages payable decreased, $1,500.
d. Depreciation expense; $4,000.
e. Purchased productive asset for $18,000; paid one-third down and gave a two-year, interest-bearing note for the balance.
f. Borrowed $20,000 cash on a note payable.
g. Sold an old operational asset for $3,000 cash; original cost, $10,000, accumulated depreciation, $9,000.
h. Paid a $2,500 note payable (principal).
i. Paid a cash dividend, $4,000.

Required:
For each of the above transactions give (*a*) its SCFP activity (operating, investing, financing) and (*b*) the SCFP (direct method) inflow or outflow amount.

E 23–6
Transaction Analysis, Indirect Method
(L.O. 3, 4)

You are requested by the controller of a large company to determine the appropriate disclosure of the following transactions in the SCFP. Assume all adjusting entries have been recorded.

a. The company wrote off a $2,000 account. During the year, gross accounts receivable increased $50,000, and the allowance for doubtful accounts increased $5,000. All sales ($300,000) are on account.
b. Pension expense is $50,000; the balance of accrued pension cost (cr.) increased $12,000.
c. Deferred tax (cr. balance, long-term) increased $40,000; no net reversals occurred during the year.
d. Ten thousand dollars of interest was capitalized. Interest expense is $50,000. There is no change in interest payable.
e. The company sold short-term investments (cash equivalents) at a $2,000 gain; proceeds, $8,000.
f. The company sold short-term investments (not cash equivalents) at a $2,000 gain; proceeds, $8,000.

Required:
Indicate the complete disclosure of each item in the SCFP under the indirect method.

E 23–7
Cash Flow Categories:
Transaction Analysis
(L.O. 3, 4)

Denton Corporation's balance sheet accounts as of December 31, 1991 and 1992, and information relating to 1992 activities are presented below.

	December 31	
	1992	1991
Assets:		
Cash.	$ 230,000	$ 100,000
Short-term investments.	300,000	—
Accounts receivable (net).	510,000	510,000
Inventory	680,000	600,000
Long-term investments.	200,000	300,000
Plant assets	1,700,000	1,000,000
Accumulated depreciation	(450,000)	(450,000)
Goodwill	90,000	100,000
Total assets	$3,260,000	$2,160,000
Liabilities and shareholders' equity:		
Accounts payable and accrued liabilities	$ 825,000	$ 720,000
Short-term debt to financial institutions	325,000	—
Common shares, nopar.	1,170,000	950,000
Retained earnings	940,000	490,000
Total liabilities and shareholders' equity	$3,260,000	$2,160,000

Information relating to 1992 activities:

♦ Net income for 1992 was $690,000.
♦ Cash dividends of $240,000 were declared and paid in 1992.
♦ Equipment costing $400,000 and having a carrying amount of $150,000 was sold in 1992 for $150,000.
♦ A long-term investment was sold in 1992 for $135,000. There were no other transactions affecting long-term investments in 1992.
♦ Ten thousand common shares were issued in 1992 for $22 per share.
♦ Short-term investments consist of treasury bills maturing on February 15, 1993.

Required:
Determine Denton's 1992:
    1. Net cash from operating activities (indirect method).
    2. Net cash from investing activities.
    3. Net cash from financing activities.

(AICPA adapted)

E 23–8
SCFP: Indirect Method
(L.O. 3, 4)

The following data were provided by the accounting records of SM Company at year-end, December 31, 1993:

Income statement:	
Sales	$ 70,000
Cost of goods sold.	(42,000)
Depreciation expense	(5,000)
Remaining expenses.	(18,000)
Loss on sale of operational assets	(1,000)
Gain on sale of investments (extraordinary)	3,000
Net income	$ 7,000

Comparative balance sheet:

	December 31		Increase (Decrease)
	1992	**1993**	
Debits			
Cash	$ 34,000	$ 33,500	$ (500)
Accounts receivable (net)	12,000	17,000	5,000
Inventory	16,000	14,000	(2,000)
Long-term investments	6,000	—	(6,000)
Operational assets.	80,000	98,000	18,000
Total debits	$148,000	$162,500	$14,500
Credits			
Accumulated depreciation	$ 48,000	$ 39,000	$ (9,000)
Accounts payable	19,000	12,000	(7,000)
Bonds payable.	10,000	30,000	20,000
Common shares, nopar	50,000	55,000	5,000
Retained earnings.	21,000	26,500	5,500
Total credits	$148,000	$162,500	$14,500

Analysis of selected accounts and transactions:

a. Sold operational assets for $6,000 cash; cost, $21,000; two-thirds depreciated.
b. Purchased operational assets for cash, $9,000.
c. Purchased operational assets: exchanged unissued bonds payable of $30,000 in payment.
d. Sold the long-term investments for $9,000 cash, net of tax (assume the gain or loss is an extraordinary item, for illustration only).
e. Purchased and retired shares, $11,500. Shares had originally been issued for $10,000.
f. Retired bonds payable at maturity date by issuing common shares, $10,000.
g. Sold unissued common shares for cash, $5,000.

Required:
Prepare the SCFP, indirect method.

E 23–9
SCFP: Indirect Method
(L.O. 3, 4)

The accounting records of Pall-Mall Company provided the following data:

Income statement for year ended December 31, 1993:

Sales.	$300,000
Cost of goods sold	(180,000)
Depreciation expense	(4,000)
Remaining expenses	(64,000)
Net income	$ 52,000

Comparative balance sheets:

	December 31	
	1992	**1993**
Debits		
Cash	$ 8,000	$ 34,000
Accounts receivable (net)	10,000	18,000
Inventory	20,000	24,000
Investment, long term	4,000	—
Operational assets.	60,000	94,000
Total debits	$102,000	$170,000

	December 31	
	1992	1993
Credits		
Accumulated depreciation	$ 10,000	$ 14,000
Accounts payable	6,000	10,000
Notes payable, short term (nontrade).	8,000	6,000
Notes payable, long term	20,000	36,000
Common shares, nopar	50,000	80,000
Retained earnings.	8,000	24,000
Total credits	$102,000	$170,000

Analysis of selected accounts and transactions:

a. Sold the long-term investment at cost, for cash.

b. Declared and paid a cash dividend of $14,000.

c. Purchased operational assets that cost $34,000; gave a $24,000 long-term note payable and paid $10,000 cash.

d. Paid an $8,000 long-term note payable by issuing common shares; market value, $8,000.

e. Issued a stock dividend, $22,000.

Required:

Prepare the SCFP, indirect method.

E 23–10
SCFP, Indirect Method:
Prepare the Reconciliation
for Operating Activities
(L.O. 3, 4)

The data given below were provided from the accounting records of Darby Company. Prepare the reconciliation of net income with cash flow from operations for inclusion in the SCFP, indirect method.

> Net income (accrual basis), $40,000.
> Depreciation expense, $8,000.
> Decrease in wages payable, $1,200.
> Decrease in trade accounts receivable, $1,800.
> Increase in merchandise inventory, $2,500.
> Amortization of patent, $100.
> Increase in long-term liabilities, $10,000.
> Sale of common shares for cash, $25,000.
> Amortization of premium on bonds payable, $200.
> Accounts payable increase, $4,000.
> Stock dividend issued, $10,000.

E 23–11
SCFP, Indirect Method:
Prepare the Reconciliation
for Operating Activities
(L.O. 3, 4)

The data given below were provided from the accounting records of Sileo Company. Prepare the reconciliation of net income with cash flow from operating activities for inclusion in the SCFP, indirect method.

> Net income (accrual basis), $50,000.
> Depreciation expense, $6,000.
> Increase in wages payable, $1,000.
> Increase in trade accounts receivable, $1,800.
> Decrease in merchandise inventory, $2,300.
> Amortization of patent, $200.
> Decrease in long-term liabilities, $10,000.
> Sale of common shares for cash, $25,000.
> Amortization of discount on bonds payable, $300.

E 23–12
SCFP, Indirect Method:
Individual Transactions
(L.O. 3, 4)

For each of the following *independent* transactions for Needmorecash Corporation, discuss how the transaction would be disclosed and classified in the 1993 SCFP, indirect method.

a. On July 31, 1993, the corporation issued 1,000 common shares in exchange for a $100,000 debenture issued by Needmorecash Corporation five years ago.

b. On December 31, 1993, the corporation paid a stock dividend of 1,000 common shares on its preferred shares outstanding. On the day of the dividend payment, the average book value per common share was $10, and the market price per common share was $100.

c. On June 30, 1993, Needmorecash traded in machinery with a net book value of $250,000. The original cost of the machine was $400,000. The loss on disposal recorded by the corporation was $50,000. In exchange, the corporation acquired a new machine. In addition to the trade-in above, the corporation is required to make six annual payments of $50,000 (plus 10% interest) for the new machine.

d. On October 31, 1993, the corporation paid a $50,000 income tax reassessment relating to the 1991 fiscal period.

e. On December 31, 1993, Needmorecash purchased inventory for $20,000 on account.

E 23–13
SCFP: Indirect Method
(L.O. 3, 4)

Mac MacDonald, the controller of XYZ Corp., has compiled the information needed to prepare the SCFP for the 1992 fiscal year. He has analysed most of the accounts—those he was unsure of, he has described for you. He has asked you to prepare the SCFP based on the following information (indirect method):

1. Purchase of plant equipment.	$320,000
2. Increase in inventory	40,000
3. Declaration of dividends.	70,000
4. Depreciation and amortization expense	129,000
5. Decrease in dividends payable	25,000
6. Increase in deferred taxes	17,000
7. Increase in accounts receivable	9,000
8. Increase in accounts payable.	32,000

Other information:

a. Net income was $420,000 after tax.

b. In 1992, there was a $60,000 gain on the sale of long-term investments. The investments had originally cost $86,000. The gain was not extraordinary.

c. During the year, bonds with a par value of $2,500,000 were exchanged for land, which had been appraised at $2,800,000. The securities experts had predicted that the bonds would have traded at 101 had they been issued for cash; 1/50 of the premium (or discount) was amortized in 1992.

d. A warehouse was constructed on the land in late 1992 at a cost of $1,250,000.

E 23–14
SCFP, Direct Method:
Optional Spreadsheet
(L.O. 3, 5)

Fox Corp. reported the following on its 1993 income statement:

FOX CORP.
Income Statement
For the Year Ended December 31, 1993

Sales	$240,000
Cost of sales	(96,000)
Depreciation	(12,000)
Wage expense.	(44,000)
Income tax expense.	(20,000)
Interest expense	(14,000)
Remaining expenses	(4,600)
Gain on sale of operational asset	6,000
Net income	$ 55,400

Analysis of accounts: (a) purchased an operational asset, $60,000, issued common shares in full payment; (b) purchased a long-term investment for cash, $20,000; (c) paid cash dividend, $20,000; (d) sold an operational asset for $10,000 cash (cost, $36,000; accumulated depreciation, $32,000); and (e) sold common shares, 1,000 shares at $11 per share cash.

Item	Dec. 31, 1992	Analysis		Dec. 31, 1993
		Debit	Credit	
Balance sheet accounts:				
Cash.	$ 39,000			$ 63,800
Accounts receivable (net).	68,000			68,000
Merchandise inventory	156,000			170,000
Investments, long term	—			20,000
Property, plant, and equipment . .	337,000			361,000
Accumulated depreciation	(88,000)			(68,000)
Total	$512,000			$614,800
Accounts payable	$ 42,000			$ 38,000
Wages payable	3,000			1,000
Income taxes payable.	4,000			7,000
Bonds payable	200,000			200,000
Premium on bonds payable	8,000			7,400
Common shares, nopar.	240,000			311,000
Retained earnings	15,000			50,400
Total	$512,000			$614,800

Required:

Prepare the SCFP, direct method. (The solution to this exercise features an optional spreadsheet.)

E 23–15
SCFP, Indirect Method:
Optional Spreadsheet
(L.O. 3, 5)

Hubley Corp. reported the following on its 1993 income statement:

HUBLEY CORP.
Income Statement
For the Year Ended December 31, 1993

Sales	$208,000
Cost of goods sold	(110,000)
Depreciation expense	(16,000)
Patent amortization	(600)
Remaining expenses	(35,400)
Net income	$ 46,000

Analysis of accounts: (*a*) Retired bonds, paid $40,000 cash, (*b*) bought long-term investment, $20,000 cash, (*c*) purchased operational asset, $14,000 cash, (*d*) purchased short-term investment, $6,000 cash, (*e*) paid cash dividend, $8,000, and (*f*) issued common shares, 1,000 shares at $19 cash per share.

Item	Dec. 31, 1992	Analysis		Dec. 31, 1993
		Debit	Credit	
Balance sheet accounts:				
Cash.	$ 30,000			$ 43,000
Investment, short term	—			6,000
Accounts receivable	34,000			42,000
Inventory	20,000			30,000
Investments, long term	—			20,000
Property, plant, and				
equipment (net).	120,000			118,000
Patent (net)	6,000			5,400
Other assets	14,000			14,000
Total	$224,000			$278,400

| Item | Dec. 31, 1992 | Analysis | | Dec. 31, 1993 |
		Debit	Credit	
Accounts payable	24,000			44,000
Accrued expenses payable	—			17,400
Bonds payable	80,000			40,000
Common shares, nopar.	70,000			89,000
Retained earnings	50,000			88,000
Total	$224,000			$278,400

Required:

Prepare the SCFP, indirect method. (The solution to this exercise features an optional spreadsheet.) The short-term investment is not considered to be a cash equivalent.

E 23–16
SCFP, Indirect Method:
Optional Spreadsheet
(L.O. 3, 5)

Shown below are the income statement, comparative balance sheets, and additional information useful in preparing the 1992 SCFP for Sells Company.

Income statement for year ended December 31, 1992:

Net sales		$300,000
Cost of goods sold		80,000
Gross margin		220,000
Depreciation expense	$45,000	
Amortization	2,000	
Other expenses	44,000	
Interest expense	3,000	
Income tax expense	65,000	159,000
Net income		$ 61,000

Comparative balance sheets:	December 31, 1991	December 31, 1992
Cash	$ 16,000	$ 32,000
Accounts receivable	56,000	52,000
Allowance for doubtful accounts	(6,000)	(5,000)
Other receivables	3,000	2,000
Inventory	30,000	32,000
Equipment	80,000	77,000
Accumulated depreciation	(6,000)	(5,000)
Intangibles, net	55,000	53,000
Total assets	$228,000	$238,000
Accounts payable	50,000	60,000
Income taxes payable	70,000	50,000
Interest payable	2,000	1,000
Bonds payable	32,000	—
Discount on bonds payable	(2,000)	—
Common shares, nopar	70,000	80,000
Retained earnings	6,000	47,000
Total liabilities and owners' equity	$228,000	$238,000

Additional information:

a. Dividends of $20,000 were declared in 1992.
b. Equipment costing $66,000 with a book value of $20,000 was sold at book value. New equipment was also purchased; common shares were issued in partial payment.
c. The bonds were retired at book value. $500 of bond discount was amortized in 1992.

Required:

Prepare the 1992 SCFP, indirect method, for Sells Company. (The solution to this exercise features an optional spreadsheet.)

E 23–17
T-Account Preparation of
SCFP, Direct Method
(L.O. 3, 6)

Required:

Using the information from Exercise 23–8, prepare the SCFP, direct method, using the T-account approach.

PROBLEMS

P 23–1
Correcting Erroneous
SCFP
(L.O. 2, 3)

The accountant for Mentor Company prepared the following SCFP and additional information.

MENTOR COMPANY
Statement of Changes in Financial Position
December 31, 1992

Cash inflows:		
Net income (loss)	$(20,000)	
Gain on bond retirement	10,000	
Dividends received on equity method investment	40,000	
Issue shares	60,000	
Total cash inflows.		$ 90,000
Cash outflows:		
Market value of bonds retired	80,000	
Cost of common shares retired.	16,000	
Dividends paid	25,000	
Acquisition of property, plant, and equipment	30,000	
Issuance of bonds for real estate	43,000	
Total cash outflows		194,000
Net cash decrease during 1992		$(104,000)

The accountant was sure that cash decreased $104,000 during 1992, but was not quite sure that all relevant information is incorporated into the statement. Also, the accountant admitted knowing very little about SCFPs. Therefore, the accountant made available the additional information:

Beginning cash balance	$204,000
Depreciation	35,000
Amortization of premium on bonds	5,000
Gain on equipment sale (not extraordinary)	4,000
Stock dividend declared and distributed	20,000
Mentor's share of income from equity method investment.	65,000
Retained earnings appropriation	15,000

The following accounts changed by the amount noted during 1992:

Increased	**Decreased**
Accounts payable, $18,000	Prepaids, $6,000
Revenue received in advance (current liability), $7,000	Inventory, $5,000
Accounts receivable, $20,000	

Required:

Using the above information, prepare a revised SCFP, indirect method. Assume all values are correct in both the statement and additional information. Ignore taxes.

P 23–2
SCFP, Indirect Method:
Individual Transactions
(L.O. 3, 4)

Using the following items and explanations, list all items that would appear on the statement of changes in financial position, indirect method. Use cash plus/minus short-term investments as the definition of funds.

The following items were extracted from the financial statements of Hasbro Co. for the year ended December 31, 1992:

a.	Dec. 31, 1992	Dec. 31, 1991
Property, plant, and equipment (net)	$650,000	$640,000

In 1992, one of the Hasbro Co. factories was destroyed by a fire. The factory's net book value on the day of the fire was $200,000. The company did not have replacement cost insurance and received only $180,000 from the insurance company to replace the totally destroyed factory. By December 31, 1992, a new factory had been built, costing $250,000. Hasbro Co. had to obtain $100,000 by issuing preferred shares with nopar value. The loss from the fire was recorded as an extraordinary item. Depreciation expense of $75,000 was presented on the December 31, 1992, income statement for Hasbro Co.

b.

	Dec. 31, 1992	Dec. 31, 1991
Inventories (lower cost or market)	$ 29,000	$ 50,000

Fortunately, there was no inventory in the factory at the time of the fire; therefore, none was lost. However, one product line, Kilo Puppies, did not sell well in 1992. These were carried at $14,000 in the books. The accountant wrote them off as obsolete inventory.

c.

	Dec. 31, 1992	Dec. 31, 1991
Bonds payable	$100,000	$200,000
Unamortized bond premium	2,000	5,000

During 1992, $1,000 of bond premium was amortized. On December 31, 1992, $100,000 of bonds were retired at 99. At that date, these bonds were carried on the books at 102. Any gain or loss is not extraordinary.

d.

	Dec. 31, 1992	Dec. 31, 1991
Retained earnings	$401,000	$360,000

During the period, cash dividends of $75,000 were declared and paid. A prior period adjustment, representing a $46,000 tax assessment for the year 1982, was paid in 1992 and debited to retained earnings.

e.

	Dec. 31, 1992	Dec. 31, 1991
Deferred tax credits	$ 25,000	$ 19,000

P 23–3
SCFP, Direct Method:
Analysis of Cash Flows
and Reporting
(L.O. 3)

Selected transactions from the records of Dever Company are given below. The annual reporting period ends December 31, 1994. The company uses the direct method. Analyze each transaction and give the following:

Classification of the transaction on the SCFP (operating, investing, financing, or none of these).

Whether a cash inflow or outflow and the amount reported on the SCFP.

Example:
Declared and paid a cash dividend, $10,000.

Response:
Financing activity.
Cash outflow, $10,000.

a. Purchased operational asset (machine) for $30,000; gave a one-year interest-bearing note for $20,000 and paid cash for the difference.
b. Issued 1,000 common shares, nopar, at $25 per share. Received cash $12,000 and a three-year interest-bearing note for $13,000.
c. Cost of goods sold on the income statement, $40,000; inventory increased $10,000 and all purchases are on a strict cash basis.
d. Declared a cash dividend of $8,000 and set up a short-term dividends payable account for $5,000 (to be paid in 1995).
e. Repurchased and retired common shares for $12,000.
f. Sales revenue, $120,000; accounts receivable decreased $8,000 (assumes no allowance account).
g. Salary and wage expense, $30,000; salaries and wages payable increased by $1,000.

h. Depreciation expense, $9,000.

i. Paid a note payable in full, $5,000.

j. Sold an old operational asset for $7,000 cash; original recorded cost, $20,000; accumulated depreciation to date, $18,000.

k. Issued a stock dividend which was debited to retained earnings, $15,000.

l. Sold an investment in land for $35,000; received $10,000 cash and a one-year interest-bearing note for the remainder. The land was orginally recorded in the accounts at $13,000; therefore, a $22,000 gain on sale of land investment was recorded.

m. Received a cash dividend of $3,000 on a long-term investment in the common shares of Z Corporation.

n. Received $11,000 stock dividend on a long-term investment in the common shares of XB Corporation.

o. Interest expense, $9,000; interest payable increased $2,000.

p. Income tax expense, $13,000; income taxes payable decreased $4,000.

q. Interest revenue, $11,000; interest receivable decreased $1,500.

r. Insurance expense, $5,000; prepaid (unexpired) insurance decreased $3,000.

P 23–4
SCFP: Indirect Method
(L.O. 3, 4)

The balance sheet, income statement, and additional information are given below for Supreme Company.

	December 31	
	1991	**1992**
Comparative balance sheets:		
Debits:		
Cash.	$ 40,000	$ 44,900
Accounts receivable (net, no write-offs).	60,000	52,500
Merchandise inventory	180,000	141,600
Prepaid insurance	2,400	1,200
Investments, long term	30,000	—
Land.	10,000	38,400
Operational assets	250,000	259,000
Patent (net)	1,600	1,400
	$574,000	$539,000
Credits:		
Accumulated depreciation	$ 65,000	$ 79,000
Accounts payable.	50,000	53,000
Wages payable	2,000	1,500
Income taxes payable.	9,000	13,400
Bonds payable	100,000	50,000
Premium on bonds payable	5,000	1,700
Common shares, nopar.	315,000	324,000
Retained earnings	28,000	16,400
	$574,000	$539,000
Income statement:		
Sales revenue.		$ 399,100
Cost of goods sold		(224,400)
Depreciation expense.		(14,000)
Patent amortization.		(200)
Bond premium amortization		3,300
Salary expense.		(80,000)
Income tax expense		(18,000)
Interest expense		(7,700)
Remaining expense (includes insurance expense)		(44,000)
Interest revenue		900
Gain on sale of investments (ordinary)		10,000
Net income.		$ 25,000

Analysis of selected accounts and transactions:

a. Purchased operational asset, cost of $9,000; payment by issuing 600 common shares.
b. Payment at maturity date to retire bonds payable, $50,000.
c. Sold the long-term investments for $40,000, net of tax.
d. Error in recording prior years' income taxes; paid during 1992 (a prior period adjustment), $6,600.
e. Purchased land, $28,400; paid cash.
f. Cash dividends declared and paid, $30,000.

Required:

Prepare the SCFP, indirect method.

P 23–5
SCFP: Direct Method
(L.O. 3, 4)

The records of Easy Trading Company provided the following information for the year ended December 31, 1992:

Income statement, 1992:

Sales revenue	$ 80,000
Cost of goods sold	(35,000)
Depreciation expense	(5,000)
Bad debt expense	(1,000)
Insurance expense	(1,000)
Interest expense	(2,000)
Salaries and wages expense	(12,000)
Income tax expense	(3,000)
Remaining expenses	(13,000)
Loss on sale of operational assets	(2,000)
Net income	$ 6,000

	December 31	
	1991	**1992**
Balance sheet:		
Cash	$ 15,000	$ 31,000
Accounts receivable	30,000	28,500
Allowance for doubtful accounts	(1,500)	(2,000)
Inventory	10,000	15,000
Prepaid insurance	2,400	1,400
Operational assets	80,000	81,000
Accumulated depreciation	(20,000)	(16,000)
Land	40,100	81,100
Total	$156,000	$220,000
Accounts payable	$ 10,000	$ 11,000
Wages payable	2,000	1,000
Interest payable	—	1,000
Notes payable, long term	20,000	46,000
Common shares, nopar	100,000	136,000
Retained earnings	24,000	25,000
Total	$156,000	$220,000

Additional information:

a. Wrote off $500 of accounts receivable as uncollectible.
b. Sold operational asset for $4,000 cash (cost, $15,000; accumulated depreciation, $9,000).
c. Issued common shares for $5,000 cash.
d. Declared and paid a cash dividend, $5,000.
e. Purchased land, $20,000 cash.
f. Acquired land for $21,000 and issued common shares as payment in full.
g. Acquired operational assets, cost $16,000; issued a $16,000, three-year interest-bearing note payable.
h. Paid a $10,000 long-term note by issuing common shares to the creditor.
i. Borrowed cash on long-term note, $20,000.

Required:

Prepare the SCFP, direct method.

P 23–6
SCFP: Indirect Method
(L.O. 3, 4)

This problem uses the data given in Problem 23–5. No additional information is needed.

Required:
Prepare the SCFP, indirect method.

P 23–7
SCFP, Indirect Method:
Optional Spreadsheet
(L.O. 3, 5)

The income statement, comparative balance sheets, and additional information for preparing the 1993 SCFP for Mariposa Company appear below (in thousands):

Income statement for year ended December 31, 1993:

Sales	$ 50,000	
Investment revenue, equity method	2,000	
Gain on disposal of building	3,000	
		$ 55,000
Cost of goods sold	15,300	
Depreciation	6,000	
Other expenses	2,000	
Loss on sale of short-term investments	3,000	
Interest expense	13,000	
Income tax expense	7,000	
		46,300
Net income		$ 8,700

	December 31	
	1992	**1993**
Comparative balance sheets:		
Cash	$ 5,000	$ 11,700
Short-term investments	30,000	38,400
Accounts receivable, net	5,000	10,000
Inventory	6,000	9,000
Long-term investment, equity method	12,000	12,600
Land	8,000	10,000
Buildings	40,000	55,000
Accumulated depreciation	(13,000)	(17,000)
Other assets	6,000	6,000
Total assets	$ 99,000	$135,700
Accounts payable	$ 4,000	$ 11,400
Dividends payable	12,000	3,000
Income tax payable	6,000	4,000
Bonds payable	35,000	60,000
Premium on bonds	3,000	2,000
Deferred taxes	1,500	1,800
Preferred shares	12,000	18,000
Common shares	20,500	28,500
Retained earnings	5,000	7,000
Total liabilities and owners' equity	$ 99,000	$135,700

Additional information:

a. Dividends of $6,700 were declared in 1993.
b. Sales of short-term investments during the year resulted in a net $3,000 loss due to increases in interest rates.
c. A building costing $8,000 ($2,000 accumulated depreciation) was sold at a gain.
d. The equity method investment represents a 40% interest in Milbourne Company. The book value of the investment at Dec. 31, 1992 includes goodwill. Amortization of goodwill in 1993 is $300. No shares of Milbourne were purchased or sold during 1993.
e. Bonds were issued during 1993 at 104.

Required:
Prepare the 1993 SCFP, indirect method. (The solution to this problem features an optional spreadsheet.)

P 23–8
SCFP, Direct Method:
Optional Spreadsheet
(L.O. 3, 5)

The records of ABE Company provided the following data for the accounting year ended December 31, 1992:

	December 31	
	1991	**1992**
Comparative balance sheets:		
Debits:		
Cash.	$ 30,000	$ 69,000
Investment, short term (X Co. shares) (not a cash equivalent)	10,000	8,000
Accounts receivable	56,000	86,000
Inventory.	20,000	30,000
Prepaid interest	—	2,000
Land.	60,000	25,000
Machinery	80,000	90,000
Other assets	29,000	39,000
Discount on bonds payable	1,000	900
Total debits	$286,000	$349,900
Credits:		
Allowance for doubtful accounts	$ 6,000	$ 7,000
Accumulated depreciation	20,000	26,900
Accounts payable.	33,000	45,000
Salaries payable	5,000	2,000
Income taxes payable.	2,000	8,000
Bonds payable	70,000	55,000
Common shares, nopar.	100,000	131,000
Preferred shares, nopar.	20,000	30,000
Retained earnings	30,000	45,000
Total credits	$286,000	$349,900

Income statement:

Sales revenue.	$180,000
Cost of goods sold	(90,000)
Depreciation expense.	(6,900)
Bad debt expense.	(1,000)
Salaries	(32,900)
Interest expense	(6,100)
Remaining expenses	(4,000)
Loss on bond retirement	(1,000)
Income tax expense.	(6,700)
Income before extraordinary items	$ 31,400
Extraordinary item, gain on sale of land condemnation (net of tax of $5,400)	12,600
Net income.	$ 44,000

Analysis of selected accounts and transactions:

a. Issued bonds payable for cash, $5,000.
b. Sold land (due to condemnation) for $53,000 cash; book value, $35,000; extraordinary item. Tax provision on the gain is $5,400.
c. Purchased machinery for cash, $10,000.
d. Purchased short-term investments for cash, $2,000.
e. Declared a property dividend on the preferred shares and paid it with a short-term investment (X Company shares); market value and carrying value are the same, $4,000.
f. Prior to maturity date, retired $20,000 bonds payable by issuing common shares; the common shares had a market value of $21,000.
g. Acquired other assets by issuing preferred shares with a market value of $10,000.
h. Statement of retained earnings:

Balance, January 1, 1992	$ 30,000
Net income for 1992	44,000
Dividends paid, cash	(15,000)
Stock dividend issued, common shares.	(10,000)
Property dividend, X Company shares.	(4,000)
Balance, December 31, 1992	$ 45,000

Required:

Prepare the SCFP, direct method. (The solution to this problem features an optional spreadsheet.)

P 23–9
T-Account Preparation:
SCFP, Indirect Method
(L.O. 3, 6)

Required:

Using the information from Problem 23–5, prepare the SCFP, indirect method, using the T-account approach.

P 23–10
SCFP, Indirect Method:
Optional Spreadsheet
(L.O. 3, 5)

The balance sheet, income statement, and analysis of selected accounts of Summer Company are given below.

	December 31	
	1991	1992
Balance sheet:		
Debits:		
Cash plus short-term investments*	$ 80,000	$ 89,800
Accounts receivable (net)	120,000	105,000
Merchandise inventory	360,000	283,200
Prepaid insurance	4,800	2,400
Investments, long-term	60,000	—
Land	20,000	76,800
Plant assets	500,000	518,000
Patent (net)	3,200	2,800
	$1,148,000	$1,078,000
Credits:		
Accumulated depreciation	$ 130,000	$ 158,000
Accounts payable	100,000	106,000
Wages payable	4,000	3,000
Income taxes payable	18,000	26,800
Bonds payable	200,000	100,000
Premium on bonds payable	10,000	3,400
Common shares, nopar	630,000	648,000
Retained earnings	56,000	32,800
	$1,148,000	$1,078,000

Income statement:	
Sales revenue	$ 800,000
Cost of goods sold	(448,800)
Depreciation expense	(28,000)
Patent amortization	(400)
Remaining expenses (including interest)	(292,800)
Gain on sale of long-term investments	20,000
Net income	$ 50,000

* Cash equivalents.

Additional information:

a. Purchased operational asset, cost $18,000; payment by issuing 1,200 common shares.
b. Payment at maturity date to retire bonds payable, $100,000.
c. Sold the long-term investments for $80,000.
d. Purchased land, $56,800; paid cash.
e. Retained earnings statement:

Retained earnings, beginning balance	$ 56,000
Prior period adjustment, income tax, paid in 1992	(13,200)
Net income, 1992	50,000
Cash dividend paid	(60,000)
Ending balance	$ 32,800

Required:

Prepare an SCFP, indirect method. (The solution to this problem features an optional spreadsheet.)

P 23–11

COMPREHENSIVE PROBLEM
◆

SCFP, Direct Method:
Optional Spreadsheet
(L.O. 3, 5)

The 1992 comparative balance sheets and income statement for Gamme Company follow:

	December 31	
	1991	**1992**
Comparative balance sheets:		
Cash	$ 35,000	$ 49,582
Cash equivalent short-term investments	20,000	10,000
Short-term investments in equity securities, LCM, net	8,000	4,000
Accounts receivable	50,000	75,000
Allowance for doubtful accounts	(2,000)	(3,000)
Inventory	120,000	40,000
Prepaid insurance	20,000	30,000
Long-term investment, equity method	40,000	45,000
Land	250,000	350,000
Equipment	100,000	130,000
Leased building	—	75,816
Accumulated depreciation (including leased building)	(50,000)	(80,000)
Intangible assets, net	45,000	35,000
Total assets	$636,000	$761,398
Accounts payable	$ 40,000	$ 70,000
Income tax payable	5,000	8,000
Dividends payable	6,000	12,000
Lease liability, long term	—	63,398
Deferred taxes	20,000	25,000
Mortgage payable	—	80,000
Note payable	—	100,000
Bonds payable	180,000	—
Unamortized bond discount	(12,000)	—
Common shares	300,000	300,000
Retained earnings	97,000	103,000
Total liabilities and owners' equity	$636,000	$761,398

Income statement, 1992:		
Sales		$620,000
Cost of goods sold		400,000
Gross margin		$220,000
Bad debt expense	$(18,000)	
Interest expense	(23,000)	
Depreciation	(42,000)	
Amortization of intangibles	(10,000)	
Other expenses	(85,000)	
Gain on sale of short-term investments	3,000	
Unrealized loss on short-term investments	(1,000)	
Gain on bond retirement	20,000	
Investment revenue	30,000	
Income tax expense (continuing operations)	(23,250)	(149,250)
Income before extraordinary item		$ 70,750
Extraordinary gain, equipment sale, net of $1,750 tax		5,250
Net income		$ 76,000

Additional information about events in 1992:

a. The short-term equity investments cost $10,000 when acquired in 1991. The market value of remaining investments on December 31, 1992, is $4,000. During 1992, investments costing $3,000 were sold for $6,000.

b. Cash equivalents were continually purchased and sold at cost. No gains or losses were incurred.

c. Twenty thousand dollars of accounts receivable were written off in 1992, and $3,000 was collected on an account written off in 1990. All sales are on account.

d. The long-term equity investment represents a 25% interest in Wickens Company. During 1992, Wickens paid $100,000 of dividends and earned $120,000.

e. At the end of 1992, Gamme acquired land for $100,000 by assuming an $80,000 mortgage and paying the balance in cash.

f. Equipment (cost, $20,000; book value, $8,000) was destroyed in a fire. Insurance proceeds were $15,000.

g. Gamme started and completed construction of equipment for its own use in 1992. The cost of the finished equipment, $50,000, includes $5,000 of capitalized interest.

h. Gamme entered into a capital lease on January 1, 1992. The interest rate used to capitalize the lease is 10%. Equal annual payments of $20,000 are due each December 31 for 5 years.

i. The bonds were retired before maturity at a $20,000 gain, before taxes. Discount amortized in 1992: $4,000.

j. There were no net reversals of tax timing differences in 1992.

k. Gamme declared $70,000 of dividends in 1992.

Required:

Prepare the 1992 SCFP for Gamme Company, using the direct method. (The solution to this problem features an optional spreadsheet.)

P 23–12

COMPREHENSIVE PROBLEM
♦

SCFP, Indirect Approach
(L.O. 3, 4)

The following information relates to Acres Company:

Comparative Balance Sheet		December 31		
		1991		**1992**
Cash		$ 8,000		$ 9,000
Accounts receivable.	$19,000		$16,000	
Less: Allowance for doubtful accounts	1,000	18,000	1,000	15,000
Inventory at lower of cost or market		45,000		44,000
Long-term investment, Jones, Inc.				
(equity method)		—		15,000
Long-term investment, Campbell Company:				
Common shares, at cost.		14,000		12,000
Property, plant, and equipment	60,000		74,000	
Less: Accumulated depreciation.	18,000	42,000	19,000	55,000
Total assets.		$127,000		$150,000
Accounts payable.		$ 6,000		$ 11,300
Income taxes payable		2,000		4,000
Deferred income taxes payable, current		2,000		3,000
Current maturity on serial bonds payable		1,000		1,000
Deferred income taxes payable, long term		—		1,000
Serial bonds payable, 5%, maturing in $1,000				
annual series beginning Jan. 1, 1990		22,000		21,000
Premium on serial bonds payable		1,100		1,050
Notes payable, long term		—		4,000
Common shares		48,900		55,000
Retained earnings		44,000		48,650
Total liabilities and equities.		$127,000		$150,000

Income Statement, Year Ended December 31, 1992

Sales revenue		$100,000
Cost of goods sold		65,000
Gross margin		35,000
Operating expenses:		
Depreciation	$ 4,000	
Interest	1,050	
Income taxes:		
Current payable	8,000	
Deferred, current	3,000	
Deferred, long term	1,000	17,050
Operating income		17,950
Investment revenue (Jones, Inc.)		2,700
Income before extraordinary items		20,650
Extraordinary items (assumed extraordinary for problem purposes only):		
Realized gain on sale of investments (net of tax)	3,000	
Loss on sale of machinery (net of tax)	1,000	2,000
Net income		$ 22,650

Analysis of selected accounts and transactions:

a. During 1992, part of the long-term investment in the shares of Campbell Company was sold for $5,000 cash, which is net of tax. The acquisition cost of these shares was $2,000. Assume extraordinary gain or loss (for problem purposes only).

b. During 1992, machinery was sold for $1,000 cash; the cost of this machinery was $5,000; accumulated depreciation to date of disposal was $3,000, which is net of tax. Assume extraordinary gain or loss (for problem purposes only).

c. During 1992, Acres Company purchased machinery for $19,000. The total cost was paid in cash except for $4,000, which was financed by a long-term note payable.

d. Dividends declared and paid during 1992 amounted to $18,000.

e. During 1992, Acres Company issued 500 common shares at $12.20 per share.

f. As a matter of accounting policy, due to the immateriality of the amounts involved, Acres Company amortizes the premium on the serial bonds payable each year on a straight-line basis (an equal amount each year).

g. The investment in Jones, Inc., is 30% of the outstanding voting common shares of Jones, Inc. The investment was made on January 1, 1992, with a cash outlay of $12,900. This was at book value; therefore, no additional depreciation or amortization will be involved.

h. At the end of 1992, Acres recorded $2,700 as its 30% share of Jones's reported net income.

i. During 1992, Jones, Inc., declared and paid cash dividends of $2,000 of which Acres received $600.

Required:

Prepare the SCFP, indirect method.

CASES

C 23–1
SCFP: Direct or Indirect?
(L.O. 1, 2, 3)

There has been considerable debate and disagreement about the relative merits of direct and indirect methods of reporting operational activities on the SCFP. The following quotations from FASB's *SFAS No. 95* suggests the diversity of views:

> The principal advantage of the direct method is that it shows operating cash receipts and payments. Knowledge of the specific sources of operating cash receipts and the purposes for which operating cash payments were made in past periods may be useful in estimating future operating cash flows. The relative amounts of major classes of revenues and expenses and their relationship to other items in the financial statements

are presumed to be more useful than information only about their arithmetic sum—net income—in assessing enterprise performance.

The principal advantage of the indirect method is that it focuses on the differences between net income and net cash flow from operating activities.

Many providers of financial statements have said that it would be costly for their companies to report gross operating cash receipts and payments. They said that they do not presently collect information in a manner that will allow them to determine amounts such as cash received from customers or cash paid to suppliers directly from their accounting systems.

A majority of respondents to the Exposure Draft asked the Board to require use of the direct method. Those respondents, most of whom were commercial lenders, generally said that amounts of operating cash receipts and payments are particulary important in assessing an enterprise's external borrowing needs and its ability to repay borrowings. They indicated that creditors are more exposed to fluctuations in net cash flow from operating activities than to fluctuations in net income and that information on the amounts of operating cash receipts and payments is important in assessing those fluctuations in net cash flow from operating activities. They also pointed out that the direct method is more consistent with the objective of a statement of cash flows—to provide information about cash receipts and cash payments—than the indirect method, which does not report operating cash receipts and payments.

As a basis for your analysis of the two methods, make appropriate check marks on each line in the following overview.

Cash Inflows and Outflows (and Related Changes)	Reported On		
	SCFP		Comparative Balance Sheet
	Direct	Indirect	
1. Cash inflow from sales			
2. Cash inflow from services			
3. Cash inflow from interest			
4. Cash inflow from dividends received			
5. Accounts receivable increase or decrease			
6. Interest receivable increase or decrease			
7. Payments to suppliers (cash purchases)			
8. Inventory increase or decrease			
9. Accounts payable increase or decrease			
10. Payments for salaries and wages			
11. Wages and salaries payable increase or decrease			
12. Payments for income tax			
13. Income taxes payable increase or decrease			
14. Net income			
15. Net cash flow from operating activities			
16. Investing activities			
17. Financing activities			
18. Net increase or decrease in cash during the period			
19. Cash, beginning balance			
20. Cash, ending balance			

Required:

Consider the above comments and your checkoff responses above. (*a*) Prepare an outline of the advantages of each method and (*b*) be prepared to discuss both your outline and your responses in the checkoff overview.

C 23–2
Ethical Considerations:
Interpretation of the SCFP
(L.O. 1, 3)

Honore Company has competed for many years in product lines that recently experienced a great increase in global competition. Honore has no foreign operations and few personnel with experience in international trade. Honore has made few product changes in recent years, and the firm is not actively engaged in product innovation or research and development.

The following information is selected from the company's financial statements and notes, for the period from 1991 to 1993 (in thousands):

	1991	1992	1993
Net income	$50,000	$30,000	$10,000
Net accounts receivable (ending)	40,000	12,000	6,000
Inventory (ending)	19,000	14,000	7,000
Net cash inflow from operations	15,000	7,000	4,500
Capital expenditures	9,000	7,000	6,000
Proceeds from sale of plant assets	15,000	10,000	18,000
Net gain on sales of plant assets, and net extraordinary gains	16,000	12,000	15,000

The company recently negotiated with banks to extend payment terms on short-term loans and has maintained very low levels of accounts payable during this period. It has significant investments in corporate bonds (interest revenue on bonds in 1994 is $3,000). Honore paid no dividends and issued no shares or bonds during this period.

HONORE COMPANY

Statement of Changes in Financial Position
For the Year Ended December 31, 1994

Cash flows from operating activities:		
Net income, before extraordinary loss*	$15,000	
Items reconciling net income and net cash inflow from operating activities:		
Accounts receivable decrease	1,000	
Inventory decrease	1,500	
Dividends received (equity investment)	6,000	
Investment revenue (equity investment)	(10,000)	
Gain on sale of plant assets	(14,000)	
Depreciation, amortization	4,000	
Net cash inflow from operating activities		$ 3,500
Cash flows from investing activities:		
Purchase of plant assets	(4,000)	
Insurance proceeds on building fire	20,000	
Sale of plant assets	29,000	
Purchase of corporate bonds	(5,000)	
Purchase of corporate shares	(10,000)	
Net cash inflow from investing activities		34,000
Cash flows for financing activities:		
Principal payments on short-term notes to financial institutions	(15,000)	
Share repurchase and retirement	(6,000)	
Net cash outflow for financing activities		(21,000)
Net cash increase		16,500
Beginning cash balance		12,000
Ending cash balance		$ 28,500

* There was an extraordinary loss of $8,000 due to a building fire.

Required:

Provide an interpretation of the SCFP in light of Honore's situation. Weigh ethical considerations in terms of company strategy and financial disclosure.

C 23–3
Revise SCFP:
Interpretation
L.O. 1, 2, 3, 4)

The 1989 Consolidated Statements of Changes in Net Borrowings of Torstar Ltd. is presented below. Torstar is involved in various publishing activities, including the *Toronto Star* and Harlequin Romance novels.

TORSTAR LTD.

Consolidated Statements of Changes in Net Borrowings
Years Ended December 31, 1989 and 1988

(thousands of dollars)	1989	1988
Cash was provided by (used in):		
Operations	$ 73,745	$ 108,256
Investment	(93,481)	4,239
Dividends	(32,078)	(30,766)
(Increase) decrease in net borrowings	(51,814)	81,729
Effect of exchange rate changes	2,876	2,121
Net borrowings, beginning of year	(46,403)	(130,253)
Net borrowings, end of year	$ (95,341)	$ (46,403)
Operating activities:		
Income before equity in earnings of		
associated businesses	$ 80,091	$ 75,587
Depreciation	14,042	14,687
Amortization	10,596	11,282
Deferred income taxes	1,080	4,986
Dividends from Southam Inc.	10,860	8,860
(Increase) decrease in non-cash working capital	(18,669)	13,675
Fixed asset additions	(24,874)	(16,455)
Other	619	(4,366)
Cash provided by operations	$ 73,745	$ 108,256
Investment activities:		
Purchase of shares for cancellation	$ (52,141)	—
Investment in Hebdo Mag Inc.	(19,800)	—
Investment in new production facilities	(17,905)	—
Payment under Silhouette acquisition agreement	(3,570)	$ (11,318)
Investment in newspaper operations	(1,025)	(2,095)
Proceeds from discontinued operations	960	5,012
Proceeds from sale of land	—	12,640
Cash (used in) provided by investment activities	$ (93,481)	$ 4,239
Net borrowings represented by:		
Long-term debt	$ 102,815	$ 67,702
Cash and short-term investments net of		
bank indebtedness	(7,474)	(21,299)
	$ 95,341	$ 46,403

Required:

1. Restate the 1989 statement of changes using "cash and short-term investments net of bank indebtedness" as a definition of funds. Include dividends as a financing activity and reclassify any items as you deem appropriate.
2. Comment on the presentation format adopted by Torstar.
3. Comment on the information in the revised statement. Where did Torstar's cash come from? What did they spend it on?

24

Accounting Changes and Error Corrections

LEARNING OBJECTIVES

◆

After you have studied this chapter, you will be able to:

1. Explain the causes of, and reporting issues involved in, accounting changes and error corrections.

2. Describe accounting changes, both changes in accounting principle and changes in estimate, and the proper accounting treatment for each. Describe prior period adjustments and error corrections, and the proper accounting treatment for each.

3. Prepare the required entries and disclosures for the retroactive approach to accounting principle changes and prior period adjustments.

4. Prepare the required entries and disclosures for the current approach to accounting principle changes.

5. Prepare the required entries and disclosures for the prospective approach to accounting principle changes and changes in estimate.

6. Recognize several types of accounting errors and be able to make corrections, including the proper treatment for a prior period adjustment.

7. Prepare financial statements from incomplete records (see Appendix 24A).

◆

INTRODUCTION
◆

For years, General Motors of Canada Limited used a shorter useful life to depreciate plant assets than its competitors. In 1987, the company abruptly increased estimates of useful lives. This change decreased depreciation by $297 million, increasing income, but provided no incremental cash inflow. In similar changes, Baton Broadcasting Inc. increased its 1987 income $770,000 by changing its method of amortizing payments for broadcast licences, and Campbell Resources changed its mineral exploration cost policies, decreasing net income $1.9 million.

Accounting changes often substantially affect the bottom line, but changes made strictly for financial accounting purposes do not necessarily affect cash flows. Accounting changes affect assessments of the quality of earnings. Comparative financial statements, not considered in detail until this chapter, are particularly important for this purpose.

Some observers believe that the major motivation for accounting changes is to achieve a specific reporting objective. These objectives include increased income for better access to capital markets, improved bonuses for management, enhanced compliance with debt covenants, and reduced earnings volatility. But how do accounting changes affect consistency, comparability, and public confidence in the reporting process? Should companies be allowed to restate previously published financial statements for reasons other than errors?

Imagine yourself as an investor examining the 1991 income statement of a prominent engineering and construction company reporting $100 million in construction revenue and a $25 million net income. A year later, you inspect the 1992 report, which discloses a change in the method of accounting for long-term construction contracts. The company retroactively applied the change to the 1991 results reported with the 1992 statements. The change restated 1991 revenue to $40 million and net income to $7 million. Were you misled in 1991? Is it time for you to sell your shares in this company?

This chapter considers the issues underlying accounting changes and methods of reporting. The reporting principles governing accounting changes apply to most of the topics covered in previous chapters of this text. Many accounting methods can be changed, and accounting estimates are always subject to change. This chapter also discusses the rationale for the reporting principles for error corrections and prior period adjustments.

◆

ACCOUNTING CHANGES: REPORTING ISSUES AND APPROACHES
◆

Accounting changes are made for many reasons. New *CICA Handbook* pronouncements often require changes in accounting principle. Firms also change accounting principles to adapt to changing macroeconomic conditions. For example, increased competition may lead to shorter product life cycles and prompt a decision to write off, rather than defer, certain related costs. This type of change helps preserve the relevance of the financial statements. Technological changes and obsolescence cause changes in estimates of the useful lives of plant assets. The significant merger and acquisition activity during the 1980s caused many accounting changes as subsidiary companies adopted the principles of the parent company.

Accounting changes can obscure the impact of net income for casual financial statement users. For example, Cineplex Odeon Corporation reported 1987 earnings of $34.6 million. However, before changes involving estimates of useful life for depreciation expense, income was $32.7 million. The accounting change provided 5.5% of Cineplex's income. This is not a major amount, but it does affect trend analysis and the impression of business success. Critics charge that accounting changes undermine the usefulness and credibility of financial statements because the changes affect reported income, but not the value of the firm.

Before the advent of *CICA Handbook* rules, firms could report accounting changes in several ways. Increases in income caused by accounting changes were often treated as gains in the income statement, while decreases were reported as corrections to retained earnings. Firms sometimes recognized accounting changes that reduced net income in periods of poor operating performance, thus obscuring the impact of an accounting change.

Types of Accounting Change

In an effort to enhance consistency and comparability, confidence in financial reporting, and full disclosure, the CICA developed section 1506 of the *CICA Handbook,* "Accounting Changes." This section narrows reporting alternatives but does not eliminate them.

Section 1506 deals with two types of **accounting changes,** and **correction of error** in previously issued financial statements:

1. *Accounting changes:*
   a. A **change in accounting principle** is a change from one generally accepted accounting principle to another. A change from completed contract to percentage-of-completion for revenue from long-term contracts is an example.
   b. A **change in accounting estimate** is a change from one good faith estimate to another, justified by new information or conditions. A change in the estimated useful life or estimated residual value of a depreciable asset is an example.
2. *Correction of error:*
   Error corrections to rectify accounting errors made in prior periods require special treatment. The discovery and correction in 1993 of overstated depreciation recorded in 1992 is an example. Errors are distinct from estimate changes. Estimate changes result from new information; error corrections require only information known at the time of the error. Error corrections are not accounting changes.

Objectives of Reporting for Accounting Changes and Errors

The essential issue in reporting accounting changes is whether to restate prior period financial statements to reflect the new principle or estimate.

Maintaining consistency is one objective of reporting accounting changes. Financial statement users expect accounting principles and estimates to be consistently applied. Consistency, the conformity of accounting principles and procedures across periods, makes accounting information more useful by facilitating an understanding of information and relationships across time periods and firms. Consistency and comparability are important qualitative characteristics of accounting information, along with relevance, reliability, and understandability. However, accounting changes inherently reduce consistency. In addition, an accounting change may require adjustments to prior management compensation and other arrangements based on net income. Debt covenants involving net income also might be affected by accounting changes.

Comparability, the quality of information enabling users to identify similarities and differences between two sets of reports, is related to consistency. Information is more useful if it can be compared to similar data of the same firm for different time periods, and with similar data from other firms. For example, to determine whether $2,000,000 net income for a firm is a positive result, previous earnings from the same firm and income from other firms are compared.

Consistency is a necessary but insufficient condition for comparability. For example, significant inflation reduces the comparability of revenue even though the same recognition method is consistently used. If different accounting methods are used in consecutive reporting periods, consistency and comparability suffer. Restating previously published financial statements according to the new method preserves consistency.

Another reporting objective is flexibility and adaptability, to promote relevance of policies. Consistency should not prevent positive change. Consistency and comparability do not guarantee relevance and reliability.

A new *CICA Handbook* rule on capital assets or pension costs, for instance, is meant to improve the integrity of the reporting model. But such pronouncements require firms to change their policies and thus simultaneously help and hurt. "And you can't blame the accountants, either, unless you think accountants should stop trying to discover more accurate ways of describing the financial health of a company."[1]

Maintaining public confidence in the financial reporting process is also an important objective. Inconsistent use of accounting principles, disparity between disclosures and underlying firm value, and restatement of previously published financial statements erode confidence. Once published, many users expect that, except for error corrections, financial statements are final. "If companies were forever changing their earnings retroactively, investors would quickly lose whatever faith they once had in financial reports."[2]

Consistency and preserving public confidence in previously published financial statements are conflicting objectives. Allowing the application of a new accounting method to current and future periods only is in conflict with the consistency objective. Restating previously issued financial statements to reflect a new accounting method results in comparative statements based on the same accounting principles, but it is in conflict with the public's expectation that previous financial statements should not be changed.

The Accounting Standards Board concluded that the benefits of consistency and comparability outweigh the benefits of a perceived loss of confidence in the integrity of financial statements. Therefore, when possible, changes in accounting principles should be applied retroactively.

Approaches to Reporting Accounting Changes

The *CICA Handbook* acknowledges three different approaches to the recognition and reporting of accounting changes:

1. Retroactive Approach This reporting method restates all prior financial statements on a comparative basis to conform to the new principle. The **cumulative effect of change in accounting principle** is an adjustment to the current (and comparative) opening retained earnings. The retroactive portion of the change does not affect current income. Error corrections and prior period adjustments affecting prior years' income also use this approach.

For example, assume Ansel Company was formed in 1991. Ansel Company changes its accounting method for long-term construction contracts in 1993 from the completed-contract (CC) method to the percentage-of-completion (PC) method and applies the retroactive approach. Total income before tax actually recognized in 1991 and 1992 under CC was $1,000,000, but under PC would be $2,500,000. Many projects are in process.

Ignoring income taxes, Ansel records the following journal entry:

To record accounting principle change, 1993:

Construction in process inventory 1,500,000
    Retained earnings, adjustment for
      accounting change   1,500,000

The beginning 1993 retained earnings balance is increased by $1,500,000 to reflect earnings under percentage of completion through January 1, 1993, and opening

---

[1] "Solutions, Anyone?" *Forbes,* April 18, 1988, p. 72.

[2] "Add a Dash of Cumulative Catch-up," *Forbes,* June 6, 1983, p. 98.

retained earnings "as restated" are calculated and reported. All relevant account balances in the 1991 and 1992 statements are restated to conform to percentage of completion. Construction-in-process inventory reflects the increased profit recognized on long-term contracts. 1993 income reflects the percentage-of-completion method.

Full retroactive application of any change in accounting policy is required, if it is possible.

Some observers maintain that this approach compromises public confidence in prior financial statements. Users relying on past financial statements observe that previously reported net income has changed. To partially compensate, the financial statements should disclose a description of the change and the effect of the change on all periods presented. Another shortcoming is that certain items are not recognized on the current year's income statement. For example, the retained earnings statement reports the $1,500,000 increase in income from the change to PC. Some view this as an opportunity to manipulate income and would prefer to see the "all-inclusive" approach to income reporting followed, which would report all adjustments on the income statement.

2. Current Approach This reporting method also recognizes the cumulative difference ("catch-up" adjustment) between the expense or revenue under the old and new accounting principles through the beginning of the current period.[3] The retained earnings statement discloses this amount, net of tax effect, as a line item entitled **cumulative effect of change in accounting principle**. The amount is reported as an adjustment to opening retained earnings. Opening retained earnings as restated is calculated and reported. Prior financial statements shown comparatively with the current period are *not* restated.

For example, assume Ansel Company changed its inventory costing method from first-in, first-out (FIFO) to average cost (AC) in 1993 and applied the current approach. Applying AC to years before 1993 results in $500,000 *less* cost of goods sold than was actually recognized under FIFO in those years. Ignoring income taxes, Ansel records the following journal entry:

To record accounting principle change, 1993:

Inventory, opening	500,000	
Retained earnings, adjustment for accounting change . . .		500,000

Opening retained earnings, as restated on January 1, 1993, is calculated and presented in the 1993 annual report, and there is *no* restatement of account balances for 1991 or 1992. That is, prior financial statements are unchanged. Supplemental disclosures describe the change and highlight the fact that the comparatives have not been restated. The 1993 results reflect the AC method. The 1993 statement of retained earnings discloses the total income effect for all prior periods. All account balances are brought up to date. The 1993 ending retained earnings balance reflects the *new* principle.

Clearly, comparability and consistency are not served by this accounting method. Why, then, is it allowed? According to the *CICA Handbook,* par. 1506.13:

> . . . in some circumstances, while the *total* effect of a change in accounting policy on prior periods can be determined, the effect with respect to *specific prior periods may not be reasonably determinable*. . . . In such cases, the retroactive effect of the change in the accounting policy is accounted for as a cumulative adjustment of the opening balance of retained earnings of the period in which the change is made. (emphasis added)

In effect, the Accounting Standards Board requires full retroactive treatment for accounting policy changes *unless it is impossible.* For example, Ansel may be able to re-create the balance in this year's opening inventory using AC, but it may prove

---

[3] Throughout this chapter, the *current* reporting period and the period in which an accounting change or error correction is made are synonymous.

impossible to re-create last year's opening inventory and prior inventory figures due to lack of documentation or excessive cost. In these circumstances, full retroactive restatement is impossible. The CICA recommendations acknowledge this and encourage firms to make their best efforts.

3. Prospective Approach This reporting approach applies revised accounting principles or estimates only to current and future periods affected by the change. Prior financial statements remain unchanged, and no cumulative effect on prior years' income is computed. Estimate changes are the most common example of this treatment. Estimates, by their nature, are subject to error and periodic revision over time. Firms are expected to report financial statements that reflect the most current information.

Prospective treatment is appropriate for:

1. Changes in accounting principle, under certain circumstances.
2. Changes in estimates.

As discussed, a change in accounting principle is to be applied retroactively or as retroactively as possible. A change in principle may be applied *prospectively* if full retroactive restatement is impossible, and even restatement of opening balances and retained earnings *cannot be accomplished*. If no information is available, then the only alternative left is for the company to simply switch from one method to another, although it is hardly desirable. The fact that the change was not made retroactively must be disclosed.

In some instances, the Accounting Standards Board has, on the promulgation of a new standard, specified that prospective application is acceptable. For example, the 1986 pension cost rules and the 1990 capital asset section both allow prospective application. It was obviously thought that benefits of retroactive application would not be worth the cost. Of course, firms may choose to apply these sections retroactively if they wish, but are free to work prospectively.

A company changing prospectively may disclose the effect of the estimate change on current income, if such a revision is unusual, and will repeat unchanged the prior financial statements as comparatives in the current report.

Estimates are necessary for many accounting applications and are based on available information. The prospective approach supports the notion that good-faith estimates using all available information are valid until conditions change. Retroactive application implies a previous error. Estimate changes are more frequent than other accounting changes.[4] Applying the current or retroactive approach would increase confusion and reduce confidence in financial reporting.

The prospective approach maintains consistency by continuing to apply the old estimates to prior periods. Although the current period results reflect the new methods, this is unavoidable.

CONCEPT REVIEW

1. What are the three ways a change in accounting principle can be accounted for? Which is preferable? When is each applicable?
2. How does the current approach maintain some measure of consistency in financial reporting?
3. Why are estimate changes treated prospectively?
4. Explain the major differences between the current and retroactive approaches.

---

[4] Firms have a responsibility to monitor estimates to reflect the most current information.

EXHIBIT 24–1   Summary of Accounting Changes and Reporting Approaches

Type of Accounting Change or Error	Accounting Approach Required	Summary of the Approach	
		Catch-up Adjustment Identified With	Comparative Statements (Results of Prior Year)
Accounting principle changes: *a.* Usual situations.	Retroactive	Retained earnings, a prior period adjustment.	Prior year's results restated to new principle.
b. Able only to restate opening balances.	Current	Opening retained earnings of current period only.	Prior year's results remain unchanged.
c. Unable to restate any balances.	Prospective	Catch-up adjustment not computed or reported.	Prior year's results remain unchanged. New principle applied prospectively.
Changes in accounting estimates.	Prospective	Catch-up adjustment not computed or reported.	Prior year's results remain unchanged. New estimates applied prospectively.
Accounting errors: Those affecting income of prior years.	Retroactive	Retained earnings, a prior period adjustment.	Prior year's results stated correctly.
Prior period adjustment	Retroactive	Retained earnings, a prior period adjustment.	Prior year's results restated.

General Applicability of the Three Approaches

The use of each approach depends on the circumstances. Exhibit 24–1 summarizes the applicability of these approaches.

Exhibit 24–1 indicates that accounting *principle* changes are subject to three accounting approaches: retroactive, current, and prospective. *Estimate* changes always receive prospective treatment. *Errors* affecting prior years' income require a prior period adjustment and are treated retroactively. Errors affecting prior year financial statements (but not prior income) also require restating those financial statements, if presented, but a current year journal entry is not needed. Classic *prior period adjustments* are transactions of the current year specifically related to prior years; retroactive restatement is required.

Changes in accounting principles and estimates, and error discoveries often are made during the current year closing process. The current year results reflect the new principle or estimate for the entire year, because the accounts are not yet closed. Errors affecting current year results also are corrected before the accounts are closed. Entries to record principle changes and error corrections affecting prior years are made *as of the beginning* of the current year.

Cumulative prior years' income effects under the current and retroactive approaches and prior period adjustments are disclosed in the financial statements net of tax. Intraperiod tax allocation is applied to these three items to separate their tax effects from tax on income from continuing operations. Extraordinary items and discontinued operations are handled similarly.

No approach to reporting accounting changes fulfills all reporting objectives. For example, a retroactive change maintains consistency and comparability by restating all financial statements to conform to the new principle and allows adaptation to changing conditions, but it may jeopardize public confidence in financial reporting.

It is not clear which approach provides a more useful income number for predictive purposes, or which approach provides the most useful information. Perhaps it is ironic that this reporting area, which so heavily stresses consistency, allows three different reporting approaches.

Justification for Accounting Changes

Firms should not arbitrarily change accounting principles. Changes should be limited to those that improve financial reporting.

Improved matching of expenses and revenues, enhanced asset valuation, and compliance with a new reporting standard are commonly used justifications. For example, a firm justifies its change from the completed-contract method to the percentage-of-completion method by citing improved reliability of total construction cost estimates. A *CICA Handbook* section containing a new accounting principle, which expresses a preference for a certain accounting principle or rejects a given principle, is sufficient support for a change in accounting principle. In addition, suggestions made in Guidelines published by the CICA, abstracts of issues discussed by the CICA's Emerging Issues Committee, or legislative requirements all justify a change in accounting principle. Often these sources will specify whether the principle should be applied retroactively or prospectively.

The accounting profession has a vested interest in the integrity of financial reporting. When a firm makes an accounting principle change that materially affects the financial statements, it is the auditor's responsibility to ensure that the new principle is in accordance with GAAP and has been properly treated and disclosed. The auditor must exercise judgment in deciding whether the new policy is appropriate for the particular circumstances of the entity. If an acceptable change has been properly treated, there is no adjustment to the audit report. Otherwise, the auditor must qualify the report for lack of conformity with GAAP.[5]

Comparative Statements

Annual reports generally include financial statements for the current year and for one or two previous years for comparative purposes. Comparative financial statements increase the usefulness of annual reports by increasing the quantity of information available and by establishing a base against which the current results can be compared. Trends in earnings and financial ratios can be observed. This dynamic picture is more useful for predictions than single-year statements and indicates whether specific numbers are increasing or decreasing.

Comparative financial statements are required by GAAP,[6] and public companies generally must disclose a five-year summary of key financial data. The Canada Business Corporations Act also requires comparative financial statements. Creditors typically require more than one year's financial statements for credit analysis.

With these fundamentals in mind, we expand our discussion of:

1. Accounting principle changes reported under the retroactive, current, and prospective approaches.
2. Changes in estimate.
3. Prior period adjustments.
4. Error corrections.

REPORTING ACCOUNTING PRINCIPLE CHANGES: RETROACTIVE APPROACH

◆

Accounting principles include methods, techniques, or procedures applied to transactions or information for purposes of measurement, recognition, or disclosure. When a firm makes a change in accounting principle, it substitutes one generally accepted

---

[5] *CICA Handbook*, section 5400, "The Auditors Standard Report" (Toronto, CICA).

[6] *CICA Handbook*, par. 1500.09 (Toronto, CICA).

accounting principle for another. Common examples include changing from FIFO to the weighted-average method, successful efforts to full costing in the oil industry, and from the credit sales method to the aging method of accounting for uncollectible accounts receivable.

Accounting changes include other, less obvious modifications in measurement and reporting.[7] For example, a change in the composition of inventory cost is an accounting change. Hyde Athletic Industries included the following footnote related to a change in inventory accounting in its 1989 annual report:

> In 1989, the Company changed its method of accounting for the costs of inventory by capitalizing certain inventory procurement and other indirect production costs, effective January 1, 1989. Previously, these costs were charged to expense in the period incurred rather than included in cost of sales in the period in which the merchandise was sold. The Company believes that this new method is preferable because it provides a better matching of costs with related revenues.

Although they appear similar to accounting changes, the following are *not* changes in accounting principles that can be applied retroactively. The prospective approach is required for:

1. Initial adoption of an accounting principle for new transactions or transactions that were previously immaterial. For example, immaterial advertising costs were previously expensed but are now capitalized because the advertising program is expanded.
2. Adopting a new accounting principle for a new group of assets or liabilities that are clearly different in substance from those already in existence. For example, a firm adopts the percentage-of-completion method for its first long-term construction contract. Previous construction contracts were short-term.
3. A change from an inappropriate accounting principle to an allowed method. For example, switching from capitalizing research costs to immediate expensing is an error correction.
4. A change in depreciation methods (say, from declining-balance to straight-line) *if based on changed circumstances, experience, or new information*, effective in fiscal years beginning on or after December 1, 1990. Section 3060 of the *CICA Handbook*, "Capital Assets," specifies that the amortization method should be regularly reviewed and, by implication, regularly changed if appropriate. The Accounting Standards Board believed that regular changes were analogous to changes in estimates and should receive prospective treatment. Before this section was issued, a change in depreciation policy was normally treated as a change in policy and given full retroactive restatement. Of course, if a change in depreciation policy is based on something *other* than a change in circumstances, experience, or new information, it should still be applied retroactively. For example, if a firm changes from declining-balance depreciation to straight-line depreciation to conform to a long-standing industry practice, previously ignored, the change would be applied retroactively.

The retroactive approach applies to all accounting principle changes *except* those for which sufficient information is not available. The CICA concluded that requiring accounting changes to be retroactively applied was the only way to maintain the credibility of the financial reporting process.

---

[7] Accounting principles also include methods of application. For example, a change in the application of LCM on an individual item basis to an aggregate basis is an accounting principle change.

EXHIBIT 24-2   Sunset Company Application of Retroactive Approach—Case Information: Change from Average Cost (AC) to FIFO

1. On January 1, 1993, Sunset Company changes its inventory cost method from AC to FIFO for accounting purposes only. The reporting year ends on December 31, and the average income tax rate is 40%.
2. To provide data for the change, a computer generated the following selected data:

	1992		1993—Year of Change	
	FIFO	**AC**	**FIFO**	**AC**
a. Beginning inventory (from prior December 31)	$47,000	$ 45,000	$ 60,000	$50,000
b. Ending inventory.	60,000	50,000	80,000	65,000
c. Income before extraordinary items (after tax).			160,000	176,000*
d. Retained earnings, beginning balance.			86,000	169,000
e. Extraordinary gains (losses), net of tax			3,000	(2,000)
f. Dividends declared and paid			80,000	88,000

* Reflects FIFO policy.

Reporting Guidelines: Retroactive Approach

The following guidelines are applied to accounting principle changes subject to the retroactive approach:

1. Prior financial statements included for comparative purposes are restated to conform to the new accounting principle. All affected account balances are restated. Therefore, all periods presented reflect the new accounting principle.
2. The cumulative income difference between the two methods for prior periods is recorded as an adjustment to the beginning retained earnings balance for the current period, net of tax. The entry to record the cumulative adjustment involves retained earnings and a real (balance sheet) account, and often an income tax account.
3. For *each year* presented in the financial statements, the beginning retained earnings balance is adjusted by the after-tax effect of the change attributable to *prior years* (whether or not presented).
4. The effect of the change on the financial statements of current and prior periods should be disclosed for all periods presented if they are affected by the change. This would include, if appropriate, net income, earnings per share, and working capital.
5. The fact that the prior year's financial statements have been restated must be disclosed.
6. Subsequent financial statements need not repeat the disclosures.

Exhibit 24-2 presents the case data for a change from average cost (AC) to FIFO.

Retroactive Approach: An Example

The change from AC to FIFO, applied retroactively, affects all prior years. The effect on 1992 and 1993 must be determined, as well as the overall change through both years, to fulfill the reporting requirements.

Effect of the accounting change on pretax income:

Through December 31, 1991:

$47,000 (FIFO) − $45,000 (AC) = $2,000 (after tax, $1,200). (FIFO income is higher by $2,000

through December 31, 1991, because $2,000 less cost of goods sold is recognized.)

Through December 31, 1992:

$60,000 (FIFO) − $50,000 (AC) = $10,000 (after tax, $6,000). (FIFO income is higher by $10,000

through December 31, 1992, because $10,000 less cost of goods sold is recognized.)

For 1992:
  Beginning inventory effect:
    FIFO has higher beginning inventory, higher cost of goods sold,
      lower income, $47,000 − $45,000 =   ($2,000)
  Ending inventory effect:
    FIFO has higher ending inventory, lower cost of goods sold,
      higher income, $60,000 − $50,000 =   10,000
  Change to FIFO increases 1992 pretax income $8,000

                                                 (after tax, $4,800)

For 1993:
  Beginning inventory effect:
    FIFO has higher beginning inventory, higher cost of goods sold,
      lower income, $60,000 − $50,000 =   ($10,000)
  Ending inventory effect:
    FIFO has higher ending inventory, lower cost of goods sold,
      higher income, $80,000 − $65,000 =   15,000
  Change to FIFO increases 1993 pretax income $5,000

                                                 (after tax, $3,000)

When computing the cumulative income effect of an inventory change through a particular date (the first two computations above), only the *ending* inventory amounts need be considered. The inventory cost-flow assumptions do not affect purchases, and no beginning inventory existed. The effects through 1991 and 1992 determine the adjustment to the beginning retained earnings balances, shown comparatively. The effect through 1992 is the pretax cumulative difference recognized in 1993, the year of change.

When computing the effect for individual years (the last two computations above), *both* beginning and ending inventories are considered because they both affect cost of goods sold for individual years. These amounts are needed for the footnote describing the income effect for each year presented.

As of January 1, 1993—To record accounting change:

Inventory 10,000
    Deferred income tax ($10,000 × 40%)   4,000
    Retained earnings, adjustment for accounting change   6,000

The total pretax income increase from changing to FIFO for all years before January 1, 1993, is $10,000. This amount is also the difference between ending 1992 inventories under the two methods ($60,000 − $50,000). Sunset made this change only for accounting purposes. Therefore, deferred income tax reflects the expected change in future timing differences. If the change were also made for tax purposes, the $10,000 additional income would trigger an additional $4,000 tax payment, and the entry would credit income tax payable instead of deferred taxes. After the $6,000 increase, beginning 1993 retained earnings reflects FIFO.

Exhibit 24–3 shows the 1992 and 1993 comparative statements. The 1992 statements are restated to reflect FIFO, although they were originally reported under AC.

The comparative statements reflect the new FIFO method, after restating the 1992 results. Net income for 1992 is increased $4,800, and the 1992 balance sheet discloses ending inventory under FIFO, not average cost.

The retained earnings statements for both years contain a cumulative adjustment because income before both 1992 and 1993 is affected by the change. The $1,200 adjustment to the beginning 1992 retained earnings balance accounts for the income effect on all years before 1992. The $6,000 adjustment to the beginning 1993 balance accounts for the income effect on all years before 1993, and equals the amount in the entry to record the accounting change. As such, the $6,000 amount includes the $1,200.

EXHIBIT 24–3   Sunset Company Application of Retroactive Approach: Financial Statements

---

SUNSET COMPANY
Abbreviated Comparative Financial Statements
Change from AC to FIFO

	1992 FIFO Basis	1993 FIFO Basis
Balance sheet:		
Inventory (FIFO)	$ 60,000	$ 80,000
Income statement:		
Income before extraordinary item	$164,800*	$176,000
Extraordinary item, net of tax	3,000	$ (2,000)
Net income	$167,800	$174,000
Earnings per share (100,000 shares):		
Income before extraordinary item	$1.65	$1.76
Extraordinary item	.03	(.02)
Net income	$1.68	$1.74
Retained earnings statement:		
Beginning balance, as previously reported	$ 86,000	$169,000
Add: Cumulative effect of accounting change net of tax of $800, 1992, and $4,000, 1993	1,200	6,000
Beginning balance, as restated	87,200	175,000
Add: Net income (from above)	167,800	174,000
Deduct: Dividends declared and paid	(80,000)	(88,000)
Ending balance	$175,000	$261,000

Note: During 1993, the Company changed from average cost to FIFO for inventory accounting purposes because FIFO more realistically measures net income. The change increased 1992 net income $4,800 (4.8 cents per share). The change increased 1993 net income $3,000 (3 cents per share). The 1992 statements are restated to reflect the change.

---

* $164,800 = $160,000 + $4,800 (after-tax increase in 1992 income due to accounting change).

The 1993 adjustment equals the effect on all years before 1992 ($1,200) plus the effect on 1992 ($4,800). The adjustments in the retained earnings statements thus overlap.

The beginning retained earnings balance is not adjusted if prior years are not affected. For example, assume years 1991 through 1995 are shown comparatively, but only years 1992 through 1995 are affected by a retroactive accounting principle. The beginning retained earnings balances for 1993 to 1995 are adjusted. No retained earnings adjustment is needed for 1992 because 1992 net income is adjusted for the change, and no year before 1992 is affected.

Sunset Company's 1992 retained earnings balance, $175,000, does not equal the beginning 1993 retained earnings balance as previously reported, $169,000, for two reasons:

1. 1992 income now reflects the change to FIFO.
2. The beginning 1992 retained earnings balance is adjusted for prior year effects.

But the $175,000 balance equals the 1993 beginning balance *as restated* in the new comparative figures. In general, the restated ending balance for any year equals the next year's beginning restated balance.

Two retroactive accounting changes are illustrated in the Falconbridge Limited financial statement exerpts that follow.

Consolidated Statement of Retained Earnings

(*in thousands*)

| | Year ended December 31, | | |
	1984	Restated 1983	1982
Retained earnings, beginning of year:			
As previously reported	$307,808	$318,205	$403,459
Adjustments for change in foreign currency			
translation method (note 3)	(8,759)	(7,474)	(4,564)
Adjustments for change in inventory valuation			
method (note 3)	23,745	35,511	28,626
Retained earnings, beginning of year as restated	322,794	346,242	427,521
Earnings (loss)	80,186	(16,593)	(81,279)
	402,980	329,649	346,242
Common share issue expenses	(1,062)	(6,855)	
Retained earnings, end of year	$401,918	$322,794	$346,242

From the notes:

3. Changes in Accounting Policies

   (*a*) Effective January 1, 1984, the Corporation adopted the recommendations of the Canadian Institute of Chartered Accountants for foreign currency translation. This change, from the current/non-current method, was applied retroactively and increased 1984 earnings by $672,000 ($0.09 per share), increased the 1983 loss by $1,285,000 ($0.19 per share) and increased the 1982 loss by $2,910,000 ($0.59 per share).

   (*b*) In June 1984, the Corporation adopted the "first-in, first-out" (FIFO) basis for valuation of inventories because it provides a better matching of costs against revenues and permits inventory costs to be determined more readily. Previously inventory had been valued on the "last-in, first-out" (LIFO) basis. This change was applied retroactively and increased 1984 earnings by $2,121,000 ($0.29 per share), increased the 1983 loss by $11,766,000 ($1.74 per share) and decreased the 1982 loss by $6,885,000 ($1.39 per share).

CONCEPT REVIEW

1. What are the advantages and disadvantages of retroactive restatement following a change in accounting policy?
2. How does a firm decide whether to apply a change retroactively, currently, or prospectively?
3. What decisions do not qualify as a change in policy?
4. Explain how the adjustments to the beginning comparative retained earnings balance are computed under the retroactive approach.
5. What note disclosure is appropriate for the retroactive approach?

REPORTING ACCOUNTING PRINCIPLE CHANGES: CURRENT APPROACH

The current approach applies to accounting principle changes for which it is possible to restate the financial statements as of the beginning of the current year, but it is impossible to restate specific prior periods. The restated opening balances provide evidence of the cumulative income effect up to the current year, but the current approach makes no attempt to associate it with individual years. Thus, a catch-up effect is all that is disclosed.

There is controversy concerning the disposition of the catch-up amount. Some claim that all results of operations *and* business decisions made by the firm during the year should be shown on the income statement. This all-inclusive view of income would dictate recording the effect of the change as a separate component of income, and it is the U.S. approach. Alternatively, the income statement can be viewed principally as a tool to measure current performance. According to this view, the effect of an accounting change on prior periods is not properly included in operating results, but should be presented with the prior income to which it relates: on the retained earnings statement. This is the view adopted by Canadian standards.

Reporting Guidelines: Current Approach

The following reporting guidelines apply to accounting principle changes subject to the *current approach:*

1. Prior financial statements included for comparative purposes remain unchanged.
2. The cumulative income difference between the two methods for prior periods is disclosed as an adjustment to opening retained earnings for the current year only: cumulative effect of change in accounting principle, net of tax. The entry to record the cumulative effect involves a real account (for example, deferred charges or inventory) and often an income tax account.[8]
3. The effect of the new principle on current year's financial statements is disclosed. This would include the effect on net income, earnings per share, and working capital.
4. The fact that comparative financial statements have not been restated must be disclosed.
5. For the current year results, the new principle is applied as of the beginning of the current year. The current year's financial statements reflect the new principle; the prior year's statements reflect the old principle.
6. Future annual reports may repeat the disclosures until the year of change is no longer presented.

Current Approach: An Example

Exhibit 24–4 presents case information for a detailed example of the current approach applied to a change in accounting for long-term contracts from completed contract (CC) to percentage-of-completion (PC). The cumulative income difference before tax, $40,000, also represents the difference in the construction in process inventory balance between the two methods. If the PC method were used during all previous years, the construction in process inventory balance would be $180,000 ($140,000 + $40,000) at the end of 1990. The following entries are made in 1991 to record the accounting change, and income from construction:

As of January 1, 1991—To record accounting change:

Construction in process	40,000	
Deferred income tax ($40,000 × 40%)		16,000
Retained earnings: cumulative effect of change in accounting principle—long-term contracts		24,000

---

[8] If the change also is made for tax purposes, income taxes payable or receivable is recorded, and an amended tax return is filed. If not, a change in deferred income tax is recorded. In most cases, changes may not be made for tax purposes.

EXHIBIT 24-4 Sunrise Company: Change in Revenue Recognition, Long-Term Construction Contracts, Application of Current Approach—Case Information

1. In January 1991, Sunrise Company changes from completed contract (CC) to a percentage-of-completion (PC) for financial reporting purposes only. The new method affects all contracts in progress in 1991. Estimates of percentage of completion were available for January 1 and December 31 of the current year; prior to that, the percentage of completion was not estimable.

2. Sunrise reports 1990 and 1991 results on a comparative basis. Summary financial information for both years is as follows:

	Reported in 1990	1991 Trial Balance Prior to Accounting Change (Completed Contract)
Balance sheet, December 31:		
Assets (not detailed)	$ 700,000	$ 623,400
Construction-in-process inventory	140,000	340,000
Total	$ 840,000	$ 963,400
Liabilities (including deferred income tax)	$ 340,000	$ 282,920
Common shares (100,000 shares)	300,000	300,000
Retained earnings	200,000	380,480
Total	$ 840,000	$ 963,400
Income statement, year ended December 31:		
Revenues	$ 700,000	$ 770,000
Expenses (includes 40% income tax)	(570,000)	(599,520)
Construction income	—	—
Income before extraordinary items	130,000	170,480
Extraordinary gain (loss), net of tax	(6,000)	10,000
Net income	$ 124,000	$ 180,480
Opening retained earnings	76,000	200,000
Closing retained earnings	$ 200,000	$ 380,480
Earnings per share:		
Income before extraordinary items	$1.30	$1.70
Extraordinary gain (loss)	(.06)	.10
Net income	$1.24	$1.80
Contract information:		
PC income earned at January 1		$ 40,000
PC income earned during 1991		70,000

No contracts were completed in 1991. CC is used for tax purposes.

Analysis of the Accounting Change:

1. This is a change in *accounting principle;* the *current approach* must be applied because full retroactive restatement is not possible.
2. Computation of the catch-up adjustment:

Revenue relating to 1990 and prior, PC method	$ 40,000
Catch-up adjustment, net of tax [$40,000 × (100% − 40%)]	$ 24,000

December 31, 1991—To record contract revenue (PC):

| Construction in process | 70,000 | |
| Income from construction | | 70,000 |

The 1991 figures presented for Sunrise already include the tax associated with existing 1991 revenue and expense. Since the accounting policy adopted has resulted in

EXHIBIT 24–5   Sunrise Company: Application of Current Approach: Financial Statements

	1990—No Change	1991—Based on New Principle, PC
Balance sheet:		
Assets	$ 700,000	$ 623,400
Construction in process		
(1991: $340,000 + $40,000 + $70,000)	140,000	450,000
Total	$ 840,000	$1,073,400
Liabilities		
(1991: $282,920 + $16,000 + $28,000)	$ 340,000	$ 326,920
Common shares (100,000 shares)	300,000	300,000
Retained earnings	200,000	446,480
Total	$ 840,000	$1,073,400
Income statement:		
Revenues (1991: $770,000 + $70,000)	$ 700,000	$ 840,000
Expenses (includes 40% income tax)		
(1991: $599,520 + $28,000)	(570,000)	(627,520)
Income before extraordinary items	130,000	212,480
Extraordinary gain (loss), net of tax	(6,000)	10,000
Net income	$ 124,000	$ 222,480
Earnings per share:		
Income before extraordinary items	$1.30	$2.12
Extraordinary items	(.06)	.10
Net income	$1.24	$2.22
Opening retained earnings,		
as previously reported	$ 76,000	$ 200,000
Cumulative effect of change in accounting		
principle—long-term contracts	—	24,000
Opening retained earnings, as restated	$ 76,000	$ 224,000
Net income	124,000	222,480
Closing retained earnings	$ 200,000	$ 446,480

Note: At the beginning of 1991, the company changed from CC to PC to record revenue on long-term construction contracts. In management's opinion, the new method better measures income. The effect of the change on 1991 results is to increase construction income by $70,000 and net income before and after extraordinary items by $42,000, or 42 cents per share. The change in accounting principle was not applied retroactively, as it was not practicable to associate revenue to specific periods prior to 1991.

recording additional revenue, additional tax must be recorded as well.[9] The tax is deferred since it will not be payable until the contract is completed.

December 31, 1991—To record tax provision on construction revenue:

Tax expense 28,000	
Deferred income taxes ($70,000 × .4)	28,000

Exhibit 24–5 illustrates the comparative financial statements and related disclosures. The 1990 statements use the old accounting method (CC) and the 1991 statements use the new method (PC). The ending construction in process balance and construction income for 1990 reflect CC, yet the corresponding 1991 amounts reflect PC. This lack of consistency is mentioned in the notes. The footnote describes the change, its current treatment, and the effect on 1991 income. These disclosures help users understand the change.

---

[9] Another way to analyze the credit to deferred income tax is to consider that the accounting change increased *accounting* income relative to taxable income. Therefore, income tax expense from prior years is increased without any effect to income tax payable. The credit to deferred income tax accounts for this difference.

CONCEPT REVIEW

1. How are the comparative figures affected if the current method is used?
2. What note disclosure is appropriate for the current method?

REPORTING ACCOUNTING PRINCIPLE CHANGES: PROSPECTIVE APPROACH

The prospective approach is used for a change in policy if restatement of prior balances is not determinable. The cumulative income difference between the old and new methods is occasionally impossible, or too costly, to determine. Alternatively, new accounting pronouncements may permit prospective application. In these cases, the reporting requirements are reduced to the following:

1. The fact that the change has not been applied retroactively must be disclosed.
2. The effect of the change on current financial statements should be disclosed.

Generally, firms that change inventory costing methods report only the reduced disclosures because reconstructing inventory layers often is prohibitively expensive or impossible. Past costs and purchase prices necessary to reconstruct inventory often are unavailable. For example, a firm whose annual unit production exceeded unit sales for the last decade requires cost data for 10 years to make the change under the current or retroactive approaches.

To apply the prospective approach, the beginning inventory balance in the current year (under the old method) serves as the base layer or beginning balance for the new method. The current year's financial statements use the new method.

For example, Bombardier Inc. prospectively adopted the revised pension requirements of the *CICA Handbook,* in the year ended January 31, 1988. Prospective treatment was permitted by the *CICA Handbook*. The company made the following note disclosure:

1. Accounting Change.
Effective February 1, 1987, the Corporation changed its method of accounting for pension costs and obligations for its defined benefit pension plans on a prospective basis as required by the new accounting standard issued by the Canadian Institute of Chartered Accountants. The new accounting policy is described in the summary of significant accounting policies.

   As a result of this change, income before extraordinary items and net income decreased by $2,286,000 and $3,658,000, respectively, which represent 4 cents and 6 cents basic income per common share.

REPORTING ACCOUNTING ESTIMATE CHANGES: PROSPECTIVE APPROACH

Financial accounting necessarily uses estimates because future events that affect current measurement and disclosure are not known with certainty. Examples include estimated uncollectible accounts, estimated useful lives and residual values of plant assets, and estimated turnover and mortality in accounting for pensions. Estimates result from judgments that are based on specific assumptions and projections concerning future events. As the anticipated event approaches, the original estimates often can be improved. When estimates are revised, no entry is needed to record the change because prior years are not affected. A change in an estimate not made in good faith or one that did not consider all the relevant information at the time is treated as an error and *must* be corrected retroactively.

Reporting Guidelines: Prospective Approach

The following reporting guidelines apply to prospective treatment:

1. Prior statements shown on a comparative basis are not restated or otherwise affected.
2. "Disclosure of the nature and effect [on the financial statements] on the current period may be desirable for a change in an accounting estimate that is rare or unusual and that may affect the financial results of both current and future periods.... On the other hand, disclosure is usually not necessary for a change in estimate made each period in the course of accounting for normal business activities" (par. 1506.25).
3. The new estimate is applied as of the beginning of the current period, generally based on the book value of the relevant real account remaining at that time. This is the amount to which the new estimates are applied for the current and future years.
4. No entry is made for prior year effects; only the normal current year entry incorporating the new estimate is made.
5. Future years, if affected by the change, continue to use the new estimate.

Estimate Change Affecting Only the Current Year

Assume that during the first two years of Tenaya Company's operations, the actual and estimated uncollectible account receivable rate varied widely as collection experience was gained and credit policies matured. At the end of the third year (1993), Tenaya changed its estimated uncollectible percentage, applied to the ending gross accounts receivable balance, from 2% to 4%. This increase reflects a recent upturn in delinquent accounts.

Tenaya's December 31, 1993, unadjusted trial balance contained the following information:

```
Accounts receivable. . . . . . . . . . . $ 300,000
Allowance for doubtful accounts  . . . .    5,000   (dr. balance)
```

The debit balance in the allowance account reflects the unexpectedly high rate of write-offs. Tenaya records the following entry to recognize uncollectible accounts:

December 31, 1993—To record estimated uncollectible accounts:

```
Bad debt expense (.04 × $300,000) + $5,000. . . . . . . . . . . 17,000
    Allowance for doubtful accounts  . . . . . . . . . . . . .         17,000
```

This entry reflects the estimate change for 1993. A similar change is possible in subsequent years. Under the old estimate, bad debt expense would have been $11,000 [(.02 × $300,000) + $5,000]. Footnote disclosure is optional, as this estimate is made yearly and is part of normal business activities. The following footnote is desirable, however.

In 1993, the Company changed its estimate of uncollectible accounts to provide a better estimate of net realizable accounts receivable. As a result, net income in 1993 declined $4,200, after 30% income tax [.70($17,000 − $11,000)], or 42 cents per share, based on 10,000 shares outstanding.

Estimate Change Affecting Current and Future Years

To illustrate a change in estimate affecting current and future years, assume that equipment with no residual value and a 10-year useful life was purchased by LeMond Company for $120,000 on January 1, 1991. On the basis of new information available during 1995, a 12-year total useful life appears more realistic. In addition, the estimated salvage value is now $8,000. LeMond uses straight-line depreciation.

The book value of the machine on January 1, 1995, represents a new starting point for subsequent depreciation:

Original cost $120,000
Depreciation through December 31, 1994 [($120,000/10) × 4 years]. 48,000
Book value, January 1, 1995 . . . .$ 72,000
Annual depreciation beginning in 1995 [($72,000 − $8,000)/(12 − 4)]. . . . .$ 8,000

December 31, 1995—To record depreciation expense:

Depreciation expense 8,000
    Accumulated depreciation.   8,000

LeMond reports the following in its 1995 comparative financial statements:

	1994	1995
Income statement:		
Depreciation expense	$ 12,000	$ 8,000
Balance sheet:		
Machine.	$120,000	$120,000
Accumulated depreciation	(48,000)	(56,000)*
Net book value	$ 72,000	$ 64,000

* $56,000 = $48,000 + $8,000 (1995 depreciation).

The following footnote accompanies the financial statements:

> In 1995, the company changed its estimate of useful life and residual value on major equipment. This change was made in response to new information about the benefits derived from the machine, and estimated market value. Net income increased $2,800, after 30% tax, [70% × ($12,000 − $8,000)], as a result of the change, or 28 cents per share based on 10,000 shares outstanding.

The 1994 statements reflect the old estimates, and the 1995 statements reflect the new. The inconsistency is unavoidable because conditions changed during ownership and use of the equipment. Future years continue to use the new estimates until either the asset is sold or further new information becomes available.

The 1987 financial statements of Rogers Communications Inc. provide the following example of disclosures for a change in accounting estimate:

> Change in Estimate
> Effective September 1, 1986, the estimate of the useful life for computer software development costs has been reduced from five to three years. This change was made as management believes that technological advances in the computer software industry have reduced the useful life of computer software.
>
> This accounting change has been applied on a prospective basis and the effect of this change is to increase depreciation expense for the year by approximately $1,064,000 and the loss for the year by approximately $511,000 ($0.02 per share).

CONCEPT REVIEW

1. What is the rationale for the prospective approach, as applied to estimate changes? to changes in accounting policy?
2. Explain how book value is used when changing the estimated useful life of a plant asset.
3. If an estimate was not made in good faith, how is the change in estimate treated?

ACCOUNTING CHANGES: AN EVALUATION

Many people believe that all accounting principles should be applied retroactively. They, and others, worry about the effect on comparability. Accounting changes, even those applied retroactively, may cause confusion and reduce the predictive ability of accounting information. For example, one study found that the accuracy of analysts' earnings forecasts declined when accounting changes were made.[10]

Another concern is the endorsement of three approaches to reporting accounting changes. Resulting confusion could dilute public confidence to a greater extent than restatement in all cases. Furthermore, how hard will firms try to reconstruct prior balances if they know there are other options?

Some contend that both the current and retroactive approaches are inappropriate and believe that once an income item is reported, it is final. Except for error corrections, changes should be made only prospectively. Furthermore, they argue that the flexible options available tend to increase the acceptability of changes. The 1990 capital asset standard requiring many changes in depreciation policies to be applied prospectively certainly implies a concern over the nature and frequency of policy changes.

One criticism of the retroactive approach is that the cumulative effect on prior years' income cannot be accurately computed. In many cases particular accounting principles influence operating decisions and pricing. These effects cannot be simulated simply by the arithmetic effect of the new accounting principle on net income.

The variety of reporting approaches reflects a pragmatic response to the availability of information. Retroactive application is the favoured alternative, and clearly is designed to protect consistency. Future deliberations on this issue may consider in greater depth the motivations for making changes. Why do firms choose specific accounting principles, and later make accounting changes?

Motivations for Accounting Changes

Many reasons are advanced to explain initial accounting choices and subsequent changes in principle. Although accounting principles are supposed to be chosen only to improve the reporting model, often other reasons exist.

The following factors are traditionally cited as motivations for accounting choices:

1. To adhere to established firm practice.
2. To conform to industry practice.
3. To minimize accounting costs.
4. To correspond with tax accounting (reduces accounting costs).
5. To maximize income and facilitate capital formation.
6. To report the most advantageous accounting ratios—particularly, rates of return and ratios involving debt.
7. To achieve the closest match between reporting and economic reality (the "best" method).

Researchers are finding that many factors interact to explain accounting choices. Switching accounting methods often is not done to improve accounting measurement or cash flow. For example, why did "entire industries switch from accelerated to straight-line depreciation without changing their tax depreciation methods"?[11]

One theory holds that accounting choices are primarily made to achieve individual or corporate objectives, including increases in bonus compensation, compliance with debt covenants, and reduction in government interference.[12]

---

[10] John Elliot and Donna Philbrick, "Accounting Changes and Earnings Predictability," *The Accounting Review,* January 1990, p. 157.

[11] Ross L. Watts and Jerold L. Zimmerman, "Positive Accounting Theory: A Ten-Year Perspective," *The Accounting Review,* January 1990, p. 132.

[12] Ibid., p. 150.

Many studies of accounting principle choice are consistent with the notion that firms with bonus plans based on earnings choose accounting methods that increase current income.[13] Even if no structured bonus agreement exists, some managers choose techniques and make accounting changes to increase income, because an implicit link exists between income and increased compensation. Furthermore, a study of bonus agreements found that if earnings are not expected to reach the minimum income level necessary to achieve a bonus, managers tend to recognize discretionary losses, including plant asset write-downs.[14] Future years are thus relieved of these losses

Debt convenants can provide another incentive to adopt methods that report higher income. Debt covenants often specify minimum debt:equity ratios. Remember, higher income figures improve equity. Alternatively, some debt covenants require minimum levels of income. For example, Control Data Corporation, which was suffering from a general downturn in the computer industry, was required by its creditors to report positive net earnings for the four quarters ending March 31, 1989, or be in default.[15]

The evidence does not imply unilateral preference for standards that increase net income, however. Studies suggest that larger firms are more likely than smaller firms to want to reduce reported income in an attempt to avoid various regulatory restrictions.[16] Reduced income lessens media exposure and scrutiny by regulators, politicians, and labour unions. Size and prosperity may be a handicap if people believe that big business is bad *per se*.[17]

Income Smoothing

Income smoothing, also known as *earnings management, cooking the books,* and *paper entrepreneurialism,* is the reputed practice of choosing accounting methods and making accounting changes to produce a specified income level or trend. In particular, reducing the volatility of income and reporting relatively gradual and continual increases in income are specific goals. The investing public values a predictable income trend. Investors perceive an erratic earnings trend as more risky than a smooth trend. For example:

> McDonald's numbers, like its food, have long been synonymous with predictability. For 101 consecutive quarters, the burger behemoth reported record results. So last Friday, when second-quarter earnings came in just a penny a share below Wall Street expectations, it was like getting a Big Mac without the pickle.[18]

The French cosmetics company L'Oreal ("I'm worth it") did not like to draw attention to a large increase in earnings:

> This year, for example, when L'Oreal realized that a big capital gain had pushed its 1989 net profit up 43%, it didn't boast. It tried to hide the gain. It announced that net profit had gone up 17.3%—the growth rate before capital gains. Reporters had to hunt through annual report tables to find what many companies would have considered good news.[19]

---

[13] See Chapter 11 in Ross L. Watts and Jerold L. Zimmerman, *Positive Accounting Theory* (Englewood Cliffs, N.J.: Prentice Hall, 1986).

[14] Paul Healy, "The Effect of Bonus Schemes on Accounting Decisions," *Journal of Accounting & Economics,* April 1985, p. 85.

[15] "Control Data Is Considering Asset Sales to Satisfy Bankers' Profit Covenants," *The Wall Street Journal,* April 7, 1989, p. A4.

[16] For example, Mark Zmijewski and Robert Hagerman, "An Income Strategy Approach to the Positive Theory of Accounting Standard Setting/Choice," *Journal of Accounting & Economics,* August 1981, p. 129; and Ross L. Watts and Jerold L. Zimmerman, "Towards a Positive Theory of the Determination of Accounting Standards," *The Accounting Review,* January 1978, p. 112.

[17] "Curse of Big Business," *Barron's,* June 16, 1969.

[18] "McDonald's, Its Profit Predictability Shaken, Should Add Innovation to Menu, Analysts Say," *The Wall Street Journal,* July 26, 1990, p. C2.

[19] "L'Oreal's Preference Is to Shun Publicity," *The Wall Street Journal,* May 11, 1990, p. A7.

Smoothed income provides an additional incentive for making accounting changes. To smooth income, firms seek to increase reported earnings during a downturn and to decrease reported earnings during particularly prosperous times. Excessively high income often invites unfriendly press, government intervention, and increased demand for dividends. Furthermore, large income increases are difficult to sustain.

Firms also attempt to avoid reporting excessively low income. Questions are frequently asked about management's ability when income declines, and there may be reduced access to capital markets and vulnerability to takeover bids.

Considerable evidence suggests that accounting choices and changes are made to smooth earnings to achieve a steadier growth rate.[20] Arbitrarily altering the timing and amount of expenses and revenues recognized, without making an overt accounting change, is another way to smooth income.

Share Prices and Economic Consequences

Many firms seek to avoid the unfavourable economic consequences of lowered earnings and often choose methods which maximize income. Unfavourable economic consequences include lower share prices, higher borrowing costs, non-compliance with debt covenants, and increased governmental interference. However, research suggests that share prices do not react to changes in earnings caused by accounting changes unless there are cash flow effects.

This train of thought suggests that smoothing, per se, is a waste of time because financial statement users are intelligent enough to see through such ploys. Users will react to cash flow effects and will not be fooled by income trends that are not substantiated by cash flows. In spite of the evidence, some firms continue to manage income to avoid earnings reductions, whenever possible. For example, a study of 163 firms found that firms exhibiting financial stress (potential insolvency) made almost twice as many accounting changes as a control group of healthy firms, and over four times as many changes which increased net income or another measure of financial performance and position.[21] Why do they attempt such window dressing? Either they believe the market can be fooled, or there are other complex reasons driving the policy decisions. *In fact, it appears that most accounting policy changes do have some cash flow effects.* Cash flow consequences of an accounting change might include changes in taxes, bonuses, royalties, and other arrangements based on income, and effects on borrowing costs and regulation.

Choice of accounting policies and decisions to voluntarily change those policies are extremely complex. Accountants are just beginning to understand the variables in a firm's internal and external environment that influence choice. It is worthwhile to note that corporate management are sophisticated decision makers. If a particular decision or choice looks irrational to an outsider, the most likely explanation is that the outsider is not aware of critical variables or events.

CONCEPT REVIEW

1. Why might a large company prefer an accounting policy that reduces net income?
2. What impact could a bonus agreement have on choice of accounting policy? Debt covenants requiring minimum equity levels?
3. Why do companies wish to smooth income? If there are no underlying cash flow implications of a change in accounting policy, will investors and creditors be fooled?

---

[20] For example, J. Ronen and S. Sadan, *Smoothing Income Numbers* (Reading, Mass.: Addison-Wesley, 1981), review over 30 studies that investigate the hypothesis that managements attempt to smooth income.

[21] K. B. Schwartz, "Accounting Changes by Corporations Facing Possible Insolvency," *Journal of Accounting, Auditing and Finance,* Fall 1982, p. 32.

PRIOR PERIOD ADJUSTMENTS

◆

Most profit and loss items are disclosed in the income statement. This means that most changes in equity (net assets) are included in income, except those resulting from investments by, and distributions to, owners.

A few items are excluded from income, including:

1. The effect on prior year's income of accounting changes.
2. The effect of an error correction.
3. Certain foreign currency translation adjustments.
4. *Prior period adjustments* (PPAs).

According to section 3600 of the *CICA Handbook,* prior period adjustments are limited to those items that fulfill the following four criteria:

1. Are specifically identified with business activities of particular prior periods.
2. Are not attributable to economic events occurring after the prior period.
3. Depend on determinations by persons other than management or owners.
4. Could not be estimated prior to those determinations. (par. 3600.03)

A lawsuit relating to a prior period, but not settled until the current period, meets these criteria. For example, assume that Terra Ontario Ltd. receives notice in 1992 of a tax assessment for the years 1985 to 1988, inclusive. The tax assessment is the result of a Revenue Canada tax audit, recently completed, and results in Terra Ontario paying $54,000 in full settlement. The criteria for a prior period adjustment are met, and the following journal entry is made:

Retained earnings: effect of tax reassessment, 1985–1988. 54,000
    Cash 54,000

The item labeled "effect of tax reassessment" is shown as an adjustment to opening retained earnings, as previously reported. The tax expense in 1985, 1986, 1987, and 1988 is restated by the amount applicable to each year, if these years are presented in the comparatives. Prior period adjustments would be reported as extraordinary, unusual, or operating items in the restated comparatives, as appropriate. The regular rules for classification of an item as extraordinary would be followed. Lumonics Inc. reported the following prior period adjustment in the 1987 annual report:

LUMONICS INC.

Consolidated Statement of Retained Earnings
(thousands of Canadian dollars)
Year Ended December 31, 1986 and 1987

	1987	1986
Balance, beginning of year:		
As previously reported	$13,575	$17,983
Adjustment of prior years' earnings (Note 11)	(395)	(304)
As restated	13,180	17,679
Net loss for the year	1,697	4,499
Balance, end of year	$11,483	$13,180

11. Prior period adjustment

During the year, the Company concluded an out-of-court settlement with Gordon Gould, Refac International Limited and Patlex Corporation relating to actions against the Company alleging patent infringement in Canada and the United States applicable to the years 1977 to 1986. As a result, the balance of retained earnings at January 1, 1987, has been adjusted by $395,000 (net of income taxes of $295,000) representing the cumulative cost of the settlement as at that date. Of the $395,000, $91,000 (net of income taxes of $69,000) is applicable to 1986 and has been charged to income for that year. The remaining $304,000 is applicable to years prior to January 1, 1986, and the balance of retained earnings at that date has been adjusted accordingly. As at December 31, 1986, deferred income taxes decreased by $295,000 and accounts payable and accrued charges increased by $690,000.

The alternative approach to PPAs follows the all-inclusive approach to income reporting. The item would be shown separately on the income statement, not the statement of retained earnings, and there is no retroactive restatement. This is the U.S. approach. FASB believes that the all-inclusive concept is less confusing than allowing special treatment for some profit and loss items and not for others. To reinforce its stance, the FASB reviewed approximately 6,000 annual reports of the mid-1970s and found that items reported as prior period adjustments were not sufficiently different from items included in net income to warrant special treatment.

CORRECTION OF ACCOUNTING ERRORS

An accounting error occurs when a transaction or event is recorded incorrectly, or is not recorded at all. Errors are caused by the following:

1. Using an inappropriate or unacceptable accounting principle, mistakenly applying GAAP. Changing from an unacceptable accounting principle, or one incorrectly applied, to a generally accepted one is an error correction. For example, if LCM is used to account for an investment when the equity method is appropriate, an error occurs.

2. *Intentionally* using an unrealistic accounting estimate, or being grossly negligent in making estimates. For example, fixing an unrealistic depreciation rate requires an error correction, rather than a change in accounting estimate.

3. Misstating or misclassifying an account balance.

4. Delay in, or failure to recognize, accruals, deferrals, and other transactions. For example, the Hamilton Group Limited made a $314,000 error (12 cents per share) in their 1986 income statement, understating expenses and overstating income in that year. Errors were made in recording the cost of sales and commissions relating to certain sales to customers in China.

5. Arithmetic errors.

6. Fraud or gross negligence in financial reporting.

Material errors are not a common occurrence. Larger firms discover most material errors before completing the financial statements. Smaller firms cannot afford the internal audit staffs found in large companies and are therefore more prone to errors.

The following (shortened and paraphrased) footnote to the 1987 financial statements of Matrix Science Corporation highlights the variety of errors made in practice.

In August 1987, it became known that the Company recorded sales prior to the shipment of goods. It was determined that substantial amounts of credit memorandums, primarily for customer returns, had not been processed in a timely manner. These practices involved the former president, executive vice president, and chief financial officer, who resigned their positions. The results of the ensuing investigation concluded that the sales recording and credit memo practices resulted in the incorrect recording of sales. Accordingly, the financial statements for 1982 through 1986 have been restated.

Classification of Accounting Errors

Accounting and reporting for error corrections depends on:

♦ Whether the error affects prior financial statements.
♦ Whether the error affects prior net income.
♦ Whether the error **counterbalances** (automatically self-corrects) within two accounting periods.
♦ When the error is made and discovered.[22]
♦ The periods presented in the comparative financial statements.

---

[22] In the examples to follow, errors are discovered before closing the books in the year of discovery, and before preparing the financial statements.

To facilitate the discussion, errors are classified as follows:

I. Errors that occur and are discovered in the same accounting period.
II. Errors that occur in one accounting period and are discovered in a later accounting period.
   A. Errors affecting prior financial statements but not income.
   B. Errors affecting prior period net income.
      1. Counterbalancing errors
      2. Non-counterbalancing errors

Errors that Occur and Are Discovered in the Same Accounting Period This type of error does not affect prior financial statements and is corrected (1) by reversing the incorrect entry and then recording the correct entry or (2) by making a single correcting entry designed to correct the account balances. For example, assume that $4,000 cash received in advance is credited to a revenue account as $400:

Initial entry:

Cash 400		
Revenue		400

This could be corrected by reversing the initial entry, and recording the correct version:

Reversing entry:

Revenue 400		
Cash		400

Correct entry:

Cash 4,000		
Unearned revenue		4,000

Alternatively, a correcting entry could be made that, when combined with the incorrect entry, yields the proper ending balances of all affected accounts:[23]

Correcting entry:

Cash 3,600		
Revenue 400		
Unearned revenue		4,000

After this entry, cash and unearned revenue are correctly stated, and revenue is reversed.

Errors Affecting Prior Financial Statements but Not Income This type of error generally involves incorrect classification of permanent or temporary accounts. Neglecting to classify the current portion of a long-term liability as current is an example. Another example is crediting a cash sale to an expense account rather than to revenue. Neither error affects prior years' income, just presentation within the year itself.

Comparative figures that contain errors must be corrected. Applying the retroactive approach to these is not complex because income is not affected. An entry reclassifying any *current* accounts affected is recorded. A footnote discloses the nature of the error, if significant.

Errors Affecting Prior Period Net Income (Counterbalancing) An accounting error counterbalances if it self-corrects over a two-year period. The income for the period of error is misstated, as is the income of the second period, but in the opposite direction. Many

---

[23] Here is a useful way to determine the *correcting* entry: reverse original entry + correct entry = correcting entry.

errors that affect both the income statement and balance sheet are self-correcting over a consecutive two-year period.[24]

For example, assume 1993 ending inventory is overstated $4,000 through an arithmetic error in applying unit costs to inventory items. The error causes the following effects, assuming a 30% tax rate:

	Effect of Error on			
	1993		**1994**	
Ending inventory.	Overstated	$4,000	Unaffected	
Beginning inventory	Unaffected		Overstated	$4,000
Cost of goods sold	Understated	$4,000	Overstated	$4,000
Pretax income	Overstated	$4,000	Understated	$4,000
Income tax expense and income tax payable (30%).	Overstated	$1,200	Understated	$1,200
Net income (70%)	Overstated	$2,800	Understated	$2,800
Ending retained earnings.	Overstated	$2,800	Unaffected	

The inventory error is a counterbalancing error because the overstatement of 1993 income and ending retained earnings is offset by the understatement of 1994 income. Ending 1994 retained earnings is automatically correct, as are all other current (ending 1994) account balances.

The counterbalancing feature does not imply correct financial statements, however. If the 1994 report presents both years comparatively, all the above errors (under- or over-statements) remain, if not corrected. For example, net income for both years is in error. In addition, if the income tax rate changes in 1994, the effects of the error do not completely counterbalance. Assume the tax rate changes to 40% in 1994. Then, in 1994, beginning inventory and pretax income are misstated by $4,000, but income tax expense and payable are now understated and should be $1,600 ($4,000 × 40%). Net income is understated $2,400. Therefore, 1994 ending retained earnings remains overstated $400 ($2,800 overstatement in 1993 − $2,400 understatement in 1994). The $400 is the extra tax that must be paid because the income is earned at a higher tax rate.

Discovery after Self-Correction   Counterbalancing errors that are discovered two or more years after the year of error do not require a correcting entry. For example, if we discovered the above error in 1995 (assume the original 30% tax rate), no correcting entry is required because all relevant 1995 beginning account balances are correct. The ending balances of inventory, income taxes payable, and retained earnings are no longer affected, and the temporary account balances (containing errors) were closed. However, the financial statements for 1993 and 1994, if presented, are restated to reflect the correct amounts.

Discovery before Self-Correction   In contrast, if counterbalancing errors are discovered during the second year of the two-year cycle, a correcting entry in the second year is required. In our example, the error can be corrected in 1994. The entry corrects the beginning 1994 retained earnings balance for the effect of the 1993 error. The following entry is made in 1994 (assuming the original 30% tax rate):

As of January 1, 1994—To correct error made in 1993:

Prior period adjustment, inventory correction	2,800	
Income tax receivable	1,200*	
Inventory.		4,000
* Assuming 1993 income tax has been paid.		

---

[24] Practically all errors eventually counterbalance, but many require more than two years to reverse. For example, a depreciation error on an operational asset self-corrects at disposal. However, a more meaningful classification is achieved when the term is restricted to a two-year cycle.

The prior period adjustment is the after-tax effect of the accounting error on prior period income ($2,800 in our example). It is closed to retained earnings and therefore adjusts the beginning retained earnings balance in the discovery year. The resulting retained earnings balance is error-free. The errors in the 1993–1994 comparative statements are corrected under the retroactive approach. Income tax receivable is debited because the error was made for both accounting and tax purposes. The 1993 tax return would be amended to request a refund.

The accounts involved in counterbalancing errors include inventories, prepayments and deferrals, and accruals. Inventory errors involve omitting, miscounting and misclassifying items, non-recording of purchases, and costing errors. Errors involving prepayments and deferrals are caused by failing to recognize the expirations applicable to the current year. Accrual errors are caused by failing to recognize expense and revenue accruals, which precede cash flows.

Errors Affecting Prior Period Net Income (Non-Counterbalancing) An accounting error is not counterbalancing if it does not automatically self-correct within two consecutive accounting periods. The error continues to affect account balances for a longer period. One or more balance sheet accounts remain in error.

Over- or under-stating depreciation expense is an example of a non-counterbalancing error. The accumulated depreciation and retained earnings balances are in error until corrected or until the asset is sold or fully depreciated.

Another example is immediately expensing a plant asset at purchase. The effects include incorrect asset balances, expense amounts, and retained earnings until corrected or until the asset is sold or fully depreciated. Correcting a non-counterbalancing error usually requires a prior period adjustment.

Reporting Guidelines for Errors Affecting Prior Periods

The previous examples of errors affecting prior net income applied the retroactive approach. Following are the general reporting guidelines for the retroactive approach[25] as applied to errors affecting prior period income:

1. Prior financial statements presented are shown on a restated basis, without error.
2. The cumulative after-tax effect of the error on prior years' income is recorded as a prior period adjustment of the beginning retained earnings balance in the current (discovery) period.[26] The entry also involves all other real accounts with incorrect balances, and often an income tax account.[27]
3. For each year presented in the retained earnings statement, the beginning retained earnings balance is adjusted by the after-tax effect of the error attributable to *prior years* (whether or not presented).
4. The nature of the error, as well as its effect on the financial statements, is disclosed for all periods presented (if affected). The firm must disclose the fact that prior financial statements have been restated.
5. Subsequent financial statements need not repeat the disclosures. (Why continue drawing attention to a corrected error?)

---

[25] There are only minor differences between the retroactive approach as applied to the previously specified accounting changes and to error corrections. In all major respects, they are identical.

[26] There is one exception already illustrated: the discovery of a counterbalancing error after self-correction requires no entry. However, an adjustment to the beginning balance of retained earnings (in the comparative statements) in the discovery year is required. In these cases, a prior period adjustment is needed in the statement, but not the entry.

[27] An accounting error need not necessarily imply a tax error. Furthermore, if an error is made for both accounting and tax, the effects on accounting versus taxable income may be different. For example, if a plant asset is not depreciated, the depreciation errors are not the same for the two systems.

Analysis and Reporting—Example with Comparative Statements

Exhibit 24–6 presents the case data for an example of correcting an error affecting prior years' income, with comparative statements.

The error overstates January 1, 1991, retained earnings by $6,000, the total after-tax effect on 1989 and 1990 income ($10,000 × 60%). This is not a counterbalancing error. The following entry is required for correction:

As of January 1, 1991:

Retained earnings, prior period adjustment, depreciation correction.	6,000	
Income tax receivable (amended return)	4,000	
Accumulated depreciation.		10,000

The entry corrects all account balances stated incorrectly as of January 1, 1991. The prior period adjustment is closed to retained earnings, thus correcting the beginning balance. The comparative statements for 1990 and 1991 are also corrected as shown in Exhibit 24–7.

The 1990 statements reflect the error-free account balances. Depreciation expense, income tax expense, net income, and beginning retained earnings are corrected. Income tax expense is decreased by the tax on overstated pretax income in 1990. The error did not affect 1991.

The adjustments to the beginning retained earnings balances overlap, as in accounting changes under the retroactive approach. The 1991 adjustment ($6,000, the amount from the correcting entry) accounts for both 1989 and 1990 effects, and it therefore *includes* the 1989 adjustment, $3,000. Both adjustments *decrease* retained earnings because income was overstated.

Baton Broadcasting Incorporated provides an example of a prior period adjustment correcting an error:

Consolidated Statement of Retained Earnings

	For the Year Ended August 31	
	1987	**1986**
Balance, beginning of year:		$ 86,775,565
As previously reported	$102,408,895	
Reversal of extraordinary gain		
[note 1(b)]	(3,285,000)	
As restated	99,123,895	
Net income for the year	17,194,040	17,702,969
	116,317,935	104,478,534
Dividends paid	5,520,000	5,354,639
Balance, end of year.	$110,797,935	$ 99,123,895

Excerpt from the notes:

1. (*b*) *Reversal of extraordinary gain*
On August 29, 1986, the Company sold a 10% minority interest in the television operations of CFQC-TV in Saskatoon, Saskatchewan, Canada, for cash consideration of $5 million and recorded an extraordinary gain of $3,285,000 (net of deferred income taxes of $1,215,000). This sale was one of a number of transactions that included the acquisition on that date of a 90% interest in the television operations of CKCK-TV in Regina, Saskatchewan, and that contemplated the disposition of a 10% interest in the television operations of Yorkton and Prince Albert, Saskatchewan. This disposition was not completed, and on February 27, 1987, the Company acquired the remaining 10% interest in the television operations of CKCK-TV, Regina (note 6) and reacquired its 10% interest in the television operations of CFQC-TV, Saskatoon, for $5 million. The Company has determined that the gain recorded in 1986 should be retroactively reversed, since the Company believes that this results in a fairer presentation of the

EXHIBIT 24–6   Emory Company: Case Information, Error Correction

1. The accounting records of Emory Company reflect the following data:

	1990	1991
Sales revenue	$ 450,000	$ 480,000
Cost of goods sold	(300,000)	(310,000)
Depreciation expense	(20,000)	(25,000)
Remaining expenses	(55,000)	(65,000)
Income tax (40% average rate)	(30,000)	(32,000)
Net income (for year ended December 31)	$ 45,000	$ 48,000
Balance in retained earnings, January 1	$ 135,000	$ 165,000
Dividends declared and paid	15,000	17,000

2. During June 1991, the company discovers that *depreciation expense* for 1989 and 1990 was understated each year by $5,000 for both accounting and income tax purposes. Total pretax understatement, $10,000. Assume Emory uses the same depreciation method for accounting and tax purposes, to simplify the example.

EXHIBIT 24–7   Emory Company: Corrected Comparative Income and Retained Earnings Statements

Comparative Income Statements	1990	1991
Sales revenue	$ 450,000	$ 480,000
Cost of goods sold	(300,000)	(310,000)
Depreciation expense	(25,000)*	(25,000)
Remaining expenses	(55,000)	(65,000)
Income tax expense	(28,000)†	(32,000)
Net income	$ 42,000	$ 48,000

Comparative Retained Earnings Statements		
Beginning balance, as previously stated	$ 135,000	$ 165,000
Prior period adjustment, depreciation, net of $2,000 ($5,000 × 40%), and $4,000 ($10,000 × 40%) tax	(3,000)	(6,000)
Beginning balance, as restated	$ 132,000	$ 159,000
Net income	42,000	48,000
Dividends declared and paid	(15,000)	(17,000)
Ending balance	$ 159,000	$ 190,000

Note: Prior period adjustment: In 1991, the company discovered that depreciation expense for 1989 and 1990 was understated. Accordingly, the 1990 statement has been corrected. The error overstated net income $3,000 after tax (3 cents per share, based on 100,000 shares outstanding) in both years.

* $25,000 = $20,000 + $5,000 error correction.

† $28,000 = $30,000 − ($5,000 × 40%).

transaction. Accordingly, the $3,285,000 extraordinary gain (net of deferred income taxes of $1,215,000) recorded in 1986 has been reversed.

CONCEPT REVIEW

1. What criteria must be met for a prior period adjustment?
2. How are comparative statements affected when an error counterbalances in two years?
3. What is the adjustment to the current beginning retained earnings balance called? What does it represent?

Analysis and Correcting Entries

The number of possible errors is potentially unlimited. In this section we provide examples to further illustrate the accounting analysis required. We also introduce the spreadsheet as an analytical tool for correcting several errors simultaneously.

The following five situations for Coe Company include both counterbalancing and non-counterbalancing errors. For each situation, we provide the correcting entry. We ignore income tax effects to concentrate on the analysis required to correct errors.

Situation 1: Error in Both Purchases and Inventory   Coe records a 1991, $2,000 credit purchase in 1992, when paid. Coe does not include the goods in the 1991 ending inventory.

Case A: Coe discovers the error in 1992.

Analysis: In 1991, both purchases and ending inventory are understated by the same amount. Therefore, because they have opposite effects on cost of goods sold and income, 1991 income is correctly stated. However, the ending 1991 inventory and payables balances are understated $2,000. Also, both 1992 beginning inventory and purchases are in error.

Correcting entry in 1992:

Inventory 2,000
    Purchases   2,000

Case B: Coe discovers the error in 1993.

Analysis: Both errors counterbalanced in 1992; therefore, no correcting entry is needed in 1993. Restate 1991 and 1992 comparative financial statements correctly.

Situation 2: Error in Prepaid Expense   Coe acquires a five-year fire insurance policy on January 1, 1991, pays the entire $500 premium, and debits the payment to insurance expense in 1991. Coe does not adjust the expense at the end of 1991.

Case A: Coe discovers the error in 1992.

Analysis: In 1991, insurance expense is overstated, and income is understated, by $400 ($500 expense recognized less $100 correct expense). Also at the end of 1991, both prepaid insurance and retained earnings are understated by $400. By the end of 1992, another $100 expense should be recorded, and the proper balance in the asset is $300.

Correcting entry in 1992:

Prepaid insurance (for 1993–1995). 300
Insurance expense (for 1992) 100
    Retained earnings: prior period adjustment,
      insurance correction.   400

Case B: Coe discovers the error in 1993.

Analysis: The error in beginning 1993 retained earnings is now only $300 because by January 1, 1993, $200 of insurance expense should have been recognized (1991 and 1992), but $500 was recognized. Eventually, this error self-corrects.

Correcting entry in 1993:

Prepaid insurance (1994–1995) 200
Insurance expense (1993) 100
    Retained earnings: prior period adjustment,
      insurance correction.   300

Situation 3: Error in Accrued Expense   Coe fails to record $100 accrued property tax payable for 1991. Coe pays the tax early in 1992 and records an expense at that time.

Case A: Coe discovers the error in 1992.

Analysis: In 1991, property tax expense is understated and income overstated. Also, liabilities are understated, and retained earnings overstated, by $100. Property tax expense for 1992 is overstated by $100. The 1992 payables balance is correct because taxes were paid in 1992.

Correcting entry in 1992:

```
Retained earnings: prior period adjustment,
   property tax correction. . . . . . . . . . . . . . . . . . . . . 100
      Property tax expense . . . . . . . . . . . . . . . . . . . .        100
```

Case B: Coe discovers the error in 1993.

Analysis: The error counterbalanced in 1992 because 1991 income is overstated and 1992 income is understated by the same amount. No correcting entry is needed for 1993.

Situation 4: Error in Revenue Earned but Not Yet Collected   Coe fails to accrue $75 interest receivable earned by the end of 1991. Coe collects the interest in 1992 and records revenue at that time.

Case A: Coe discovers the error in 1992.

Analysis: In 1991, both interest revenue and net income are understated. Receivables and retained earnings are understated. In 1992, interest revenue is overstated. 1992 receivables are correctly stated because the interest *was* collected.

Correcting entry in 1992:

```
Interest revenue. . . . . . . . . . . . . . . . . . . . . . . . . . 75
   Retained earnings: prior period adjustment,
      interest revenue correction. . . . . . . . . . . . . . . . . .        75
```

Case B: Coe discovers the error in 1993.

Analysis: The error counterbalanced in 1992 because 1991 income is understated and 1992 income is overstated by the same amount. No correcting entry is needed in 1993.

Situation 5: Expense Capitalized as as Asset when Incurred   On January 1, 1991, Coe pays $500 for ordinary repairs and debits the machinery account. Depreciation is 10% per year.

Case A: Coe discovers the error in 1992.

Analysis: For 1991, repair expense is understated and depreciation expense overstated. Also, income is overstated by the difference. Assets and retained earnings are overstated by $450 ($500 correct expense − 10% × $500 depreciation recognized).

Correcting entry in 1992:

```
Accumulated depreciation ($500 × 10%). . . . . . . . . . . . . .  50
Retained earnings: prior period adjustment, repair expense . . . . . 450
   Machinery . . . . . . . . . . . . . . . . . . . . . . . . . . .        500
```

Case B: Coe discovers the error in 1993.

Analysis: Retained earnings is overstated $400 because $500 expense should have been recognized but only $100 depreciation is recognized by the end of 1992.

Correcting entry in 1993:

```
Accumulated depreciation ($500 × 10% × 2 years) . . . . . . . . .  100
Retained earnings: prior period adjustment, repair expense  . . . . .  400
      Machinery . . . . . . . . . . . . . . . . . . . . . . . . . . .        500
```

Determining the effect on prior years' income (the prior period adjustment) is crucial to correcting accounting errors.

Spreadsheet Techniques for Correcting Errors

Individual errors can be analysed and corrected without a spreadsheet. However, when errors are numerous and complicated, a spreadsheet approach often is helpful. In addition, several immaterial errors can cause an aggregate material income effect. A spreadsheet facilitates the analysis of errors and their effects as they occur. Errors that cancel each other are easily identified. One compound entry corrects all the errors at the end of the period. In the remainder of this section, we highlight two popular formats for error correction spreadsheets.

Exhibit 24–8 illustrates a case example and the first spreadsheet format useful for (1) computing correct income for each of several periods and (2) providing data for the correcting entries in the year of correction.

The counterbalancing errors are those that self-correct in two years. For example, the 1991 error *a* understates prepaid interest, overstates interest expense, and understates income. The opposite automatically occurs in 1992, counterbalancing the 1991 errors. Each adjacent pair of equal numbers with opposite signs represents a counterbalancing error. No correcting entry is needed for these errors in 1994.

The errors requiring correction in 1994 are (1) those that did not counterbalance because they were discovered in the second year of the cycle (1994) or (2) those that do not counterbalance in two years. These errors are (1) the 1993 errors *a* to *d,* and (2) error *e* for all years (depreciation). For example, the 1993 error *b,* rent revenue collected in advance, overstates 1993 income because rent was recognized as revenue in error. This error is discovered in 1994, requiring the 1993 statements to be restated and the accounts corrected for 1994.

The following 1994 entry corrects these errors:[28]

As of January 1, 1994, correcting entry:

```
Prepaid interest . . . . . . . . . . . . . . . . . . . . . . . . . .  400*
Rent receivable . . . . . . . . . . . . . . . . . . . . . . . . . .  600‡
Retained earnings: prior period adjustment, error correction . . . .  200¶
      Rent revenue collected in advance . . . . . . . . . . . . . .        100**
      Accrued wages payable . . . . . . . . . . . . . . . . . . . .        500†
      Accumulated depreciation . . . . . . . . . . . . . . . . . .        600§
```

* Error *a*, prepaid interest understated at Dec. 31, 1993.

** Error *b*, rent revenue collected in advance understated at Dec. 31, 1993.

† Error *c*, wages payable understated at Dec. 31, 1993.

‡ Error *d*, rent receivable understated at Dec. 31, 1993.

§ Error *e*, accumulated depreciation understated at Dec. 31, 1993 (three years).

¶ The net effect of errors on net income before 1994:

	Prior Income Effect Understatement/Overstatement
1993 interest expense overstated	$ 400
1993 rent revenue overstated	(100)
1993 wage expense understated	(500)
1993 rent revenue understated	600
1991–1993 depreciation expense understated	(600)
Net overstatement of prior years' income	$(200)

---

[28] A separate correcting entry could be made for each error with the same result.

EXHIBIT 24–8 Juniper Company Spreadsheet to Correct Net Income

---

Case Data

1. The first audit of Juniper Company, covering years 1991, 1992, and 1993, discovered the following errors in 1994:

Error	1991	1992	1993
a. Prepaid interest expense (i.e., asset) not recognized at each year-end (the amount was incorrectly expensed when the cash was paid during the year)	$100	$300	$400
b. Rent revenue collected in advance at year-end (the revenue was incorrectly recognized each year when the cash was collected)	300	500	100
c. Wages payable incurred but not recognized by each year-end (was not recognized until paid the next period)	600	800	500
d. Accrued rent revenue (earned but not collected) not recognized at each year-end (the revenue had been earned by year-end but was uncollected; the revenue was incorrectly recognized in the next period when collected)	500	400	600
e. Depreciation expense understated	200	200	200

2. Reported pretax income, uncorrected for the above errors, was, 1991, $5,000; 1992, $7,000; and 1993, $6,000. The accounting year ends December 31.

Spreadsheet to Compute Correct Income at Each Year-End:

	Income		
Item	1991	1992	1993
Reported income (pretax)	$5,000	$7,000	$6,000
Corrections:			
a. Prepaid interest expense not recognized as asset:			
1991	+100	−100	
1992		+300	−300
1993			+400*
b. Rent revenue collected in advance not recognized as liability:			
1991	−300	+300	
1992		−500	+500
1993			−100*
c. Accrued wages not recognized in:			
1991	−600	+600	
1992		−800	+800
1993			−500*
d. Accrued rent revenue not recognized in:			
1991	+500	−500	
1992		+400	−400
1993			+600*
e. Depreciation understated:			
1991	−200*		
1992		−200*	
1993			−200*
Correct income (pretax)	$4,500	$6,500	$6,800

---

* See correcting entry, January 1994.

Four accounts in the correcting entry are involved in the following *correct* entries, during 1994, assuming the errors are discovered early in 1994:

Correct entries in 1994:

Interest expense	400	
Prepaid interest		400
Rent revenue collected in advance	100	
Rent revenue		100

EXHIBIT 24-9   Spreadsheet to Correct Income Statement, Balance Sheet, and Retained Earnings Statement

Case Data

Uncorrected and unadjusted trial balance at December 31, 1992—as shown in first two columns of the spreadsheet.
Additional data:
a. Merchandise inventory, December 31, 1991, overstated, $4,000 (periodic inventory).
b. Prepaid advertising of $2,000 at December 31, 1992, not recorded.
c. Prepaid insurance of $2,000 at December 31, 1992, not recognized because the entire premium, paid on June 1, 1992, was debited to expense.
d. Accrued sales salaries of $1,000 at December 31, 1991, not recorded.
e. Accrued utilities expense of $1,000 at December 31, 1992, not recorded (classify as general expense).
f. No provision was made for doubtful accounts—the amounts should have been 1991, $1,000, and 1992, $3,000 (classify as general expense).
g. Depreciation expense not recorded prior to 1992, $15,000; for 1992, $5,000 (classify as general expense).
h. Cash shortage at end of 1992, $1,000 (classify as general expense).
i. 1992 ending inventory correctly determined, $32,000.

Spreadsheet to Correct Income Statement, Balance Sheet, and Retained Earnings Statement

Account	Uncorrected Trial Balance Debit	Uncorrected Trial Balance Credit	Correcting and Adjusting Entries Debit	Correcting and Adjusting Entries Credit	Income Statement Debit	Income Statement Credit	Retained Earnings Statement Debit	Retained Earnings Statement Credit	Balance Sheet Debit	Balance Sheet Credit
Cash	9,000			(h) 1,000					8,000	
Receivables	20,000								20,000	
Allowance for doubtful accounts . .				(f) 4,000						4,000
Inventory, beginning.	30,000			(a) 4,000	26,000					
Equipment	60,000								60,000	
Accumulated depreciation				(g) 20,000						20,000
Accounts payable		5,000								5,000
Common shares, nopar, 7,500 shares outstanding		76,000								76,000
Retained earnings, beginning . . .		25,000						25,000		
Prior period adjustments:										
Inventory (CGS) correction . . .			(a) 4,000				4,000			
Salary expense correction (1991).			(d) 1,000				1,000			
Bad debt expense correction . . .			(f) 1,000				1,000			
Depreciation expense correction .			(g) 15,000				15,000			
Sales revenue		130,000				130,000				
Purchases.	90,000				90,000					
Selling expenses.	17,000			(b) 2,000	14,000					
				(d) 1,000						
General expenses	10,000		(e) 1,000	(c) 2,000	18,000					
			(f) 3,000							
			(g) 5,000							
			(h) 1,000							
	236,000	236,000								
Prepaid advertising			(b) 2,000						2,000	
Prepaid insurance			(c) 2,000						2,000	
Utilities payable.				(e) 1,000						1,000
Inventory, ending						32,000			32,000	
Net income					14,000			14,000		
Retained earnings balance							18,000			18,000
			35,000	35,000	162,000	162,000	39,000	39,000	124,000	124,000

Accrued wages payable	500	
Cash		500
Cash	600	
Rent receivable		600

Depreciation expense should be recorded for the correct amount in 1994, $200 more than in previous years.

Errors are often discovered during the closing process. Correction requires recasting the incorrect account balances to develop the correct income statement, balance sheet, and retained earnings statement. Exhibit 24–9 shows the second spreadsheet format designed for this purpose.

For example, (a) corrects the overstatement of beginning inventory by reducing beginning inventory and prior years' income. If 1992 beginning inventory is overstated, then 1991 ending inventory also is overstated, as is 1991 income. The debit column is used for prior period adjustments that reduce prior year income. In total, four errors affected prior years' income. (See (a), (d), (f), and (g).) For example, (g) corrects the understatement of prior years' depreciation, which overstated income in prior years.

The entries made in the second set of columns, Correcting and Adjusting Entries, are journalized and posted. The spreadsheet permits a complete analysis before formally recording the adjustments in the accounts.

The discussion of error analysis is extended by considering the preparation of financial statements from incomplete records in the chapter appendix.

SUMMARY OF KEY POINTS

♦

(L.O. 1) 1. Firms change accounting principles and estimates to adapt to changing economic conditions and new accounting standards, to improve financial reporting, and to fulfill other reporting objectives. The accountant must trade off the effect of changes on consistency and public confidence in financial reporting against the need to adapt to changing environments. Financial reporting emphasizes comparability, consistency, and full disclosure.

(L.O. 2) 2. Accounting changes are classified as follows: (a) change in accounting principle, such as a change from completed-contract to percentage-of-completion for long-term construction contracts, and (b) change in estimate, such as a change in the estimated useful life of an operational asset from 20 years to 15 years. An accounting error is an erroneous recording (or omission) of a transaction, but is not classified as an accounting change. A prior period adjustment is an item that specifically relates to a prior period, was not caused by subsequent economic events, depends on the decisions of people other than management or owners, and could not have been estimated earlier.

(L.O. 2) 3. Changes in accounting principle are reported under the retroactive approach. If full retroactive application is impossible, the current approach is used. If that is also impossible, the change is implemented prospectively. Estimate changes are reported under the prospective approach. Both prior period adjustments and errors affecting prior years' income are reported under the retroactive approach.

(L.O. 3) 4. The retroactive approach recognizes the cumulative effect of the change on prior years' income as an adjustment to the beginning balance of retained earnings in the current year. The beginning balance of retained earnings for all years shown comparatively is adjusted by the effect of the change attributable to previous years and prior years' income statements are restated. The impact on the financial statements is disclosed.

(L.O. 4) 5. The current approach recognizes the cumulative effect of the change on prior years' income as an adjustment to opening retained earnings, but comparative financial statements are not restated. The impact on the financial statements is disclosed.

(L.O. 5)   6. Only current and future reporting periods are affected by the prospective approach. No cumulative catch-up amount is recognized. In many cases, an estimate change uses the book value at the beginning of the current year as the starting amount to which new estimates are applied.

(L.O. 6)   7. The net effect of an error in a prior year's financial statements is recorded and reported as a prior period adjustment, an adjustment to the beginning balance of retained earnings. Accounting errors are (a) counterbalancing if they self-correct over two consecutive reporting periods, such as an error in the ending inventory, and (b) non-counterbalancing if they do not self-correct in two reporting periods, such as errors in depreciation.

(L.O. 7)   8. Financial statements can be prepared from incomplete records by an analysis of source documents and other evidence (see Appendix 24A).

REVIEW PROBLEM

◆

The following short cases are independent.

1. Change in Estimated Useful Life and Residual Value

Phelps Company purchases equipment on January 1, 1992, for $36,000 and decides to use the sum-of-years'-digits (SYD) method for depreciation. The equipment has a salvage value of $6,000 and useful life of three years. On July 1, 1993, Phelps decides that the machine has an original total life of four years and $3,000 salvage value.

Required:
What is depreciation in 1993?

2. Retroactive Change in Accounting Principle

Rhein Company changes its method of accounting for long-term construction contracts from the percentage-of-completion method (PC) to the completed-contract method (CC) in 1993. The years affected by the change, and incomes under both methods, appear below (ignore income taxes):

Year	PC	CC
1991	$400	$200
1992	300	150
1993	500	200

Required:
If the financial statements for 1992 and 1993 are shown comparatively, what are the amounts of the effect of change in accounting principle adjustment to the January 1 balance of retained earnings for 1992 and 1993?

3. Prospective Approach to Change in Accounting Principle

Gear Company records depreciation under the SYD method in 1991, the firm's first year of operations. In 1992, the firm decides to change to straight-line (SL) for accounting purposes, based on new information concerning the pattern of asset use. $100,000 of depreciable assets with a 10-year life and no salvage value were acquired at the beginning of 1991. There were no subsequent acquisitions.

Required:
Calculate the 1992 depreciation expense. Why is this accounting policy change applied prospectively?

4. Error Correction and Prior Period Adjustment

Helms Company purchases a delivery truck for $12,000 on January 1, 1992. Helms expects to use the truck only two years and sell it for $4,000. The accountant is instructed to use straight-line depreciation but neglects to record any depreciation in 1992. Rather, the accountant charges the entire cost to delivery expense in 1992. The controller discovers the error late in 1993.

Required:
Provide the 1993 entries to record depreciation and the error correction, and indicate the amounts of the prior period adjustment appearing in the 1992 and 1993 comparative retained earnings statements. The tax rate is 30%. Assume that the tax effect changes taxes payable as an amended return is filed.

5. Error Correction, Prior Period Adjustment, and Comparative Statements
On July 1, 1993, a full year's insurance of $2,400 covering the period July 1, 1993, to June 30, 1994, was paid and debited to insurance expense. Assume:

♦ a calendar-fiscal year.
♦ January 1, 1993, retained earnings is $20,000.
♦ No adjusting entry for insurance is made on December 31, 1993.
♦ Reported net income for 1993 (in error) is $22,800.
♦ Net income for 1994 (assuming error is never discovered) is $30,000.
♦ Net income for 1995 is $40,000.

Required:
a. List the effect of the error on affected accounts, and net income, in 1993 and 1994.
b. Prepare the entry to record the error if discovered in 1993.
c. Prepare the entry to record the error if discovered in 1994, and prepare the 1993 and 1994 comparative retained earnings statements.
d. Prepare the entry (if needed) to record the error if discovered in 1995, and prepare the 1994 and 1995 comparative retained earnings statements.

REVIEW SOLUTION
♦

1. Book value, January 1, 1993 = $36,000 − [($36,000 − $6,000) × ³⁄₆]

$$= \$21,000$$

1993 depreciation = ($21,000 − $3,000) × ³⁄₆ = $9,000

(Three years remain in the asset's useful life on January 1, 1993.)

2. Cumulative effect of change in accounting principle for 1992 retained earnings statement = the effect of the change for all years before 1992 = $200 decrease (dr.) = $400 − $200.

Cumulative effect of change in accounting principle for 1993 retained earnings statement = the effect of the change for all years before 1993 = $350 decrease (dr.) = ($400 + $300) − ($200 + $150).

These amounts decrease the balance of retained earnings as previously reported.

3. Depreciation policies should be reviewed regularly, and the *CICA Handbook* specifies that changes in policy should be applied prospectively if based on new information.

Net book value, beginning of 1992:	
Original cost	$100,000
Accumulated depreciation ($100,000 × ¹⁰⁄₅₅)	(18,180)
	$ 81,820
Depreciation expense, 1992 ($81,820/(10 − 1))	$ 9,091

If SYD had been applied in 1992, depreciation would have been $16,363 ($100,000 × ⁹⁄₅₅). If SL depreciation had been used from the outset, $10,000 ($100,000/10) would have been expensed each year. 1992 results reflect SL depreciation.

4. The 1993 entry to record error correction:

Equipment   12,000
    Retained earnings, prior period adjustment,
      depreciation ($8000) (1 − .30)   5,600
    Income tax payable $8,000 × 30%   2,400
    Accumulated depreciation ($12,000 − $4,000)/2   4,000

1992 income is understated $5,600 ($12,000 erroneous Delivery Expense less $4,000 omitted depreciation, $8000, after tax).

The 1993 entry to record depreciation:

Depreciation expense   4,000
    Accumulated depreciation   4,000

Only the 1993 retained earnings statement reports a prior period adjustment ($5,600 cr.). This is the effect of the error on income before 1993. 1992 does not report a prior period adjustment because years before 1992 are not affected by the error.

5. *a.* Effect of error if not discovered:

	(− = understated;	+ = overstated)
	1993	**1994**
Insurance expense	+ $1,200	− $1,200
Ending prepaid insurance	− 1,200	no effect
Net income	− 1,200	+ 1,200
Ending retained earnings	− 1,200	is now correct

  b. If discover error in 1993:

Prepaid insurance   1,200
    Insurance expense   1,200

  c. If discover error in 1994:

Prepaid insurance   1,200
    Retained earnings, prior period adjustment   1,200

	1993	1994
Retained earnings, Jan. 1, as previously reported . .	$20,000	$42,800[†]
Prior period adjustment	0*	1,200
Retained earnings, Jan. 1, as restated	20,000	44,000
Net income	24,000**	28,800[‡]
Retained earnings, Dec. 31	$44,000	$72,800

* No year before 1993 was affected by error.

** Correct 1993 net income = $22,800 + $1,200 = $24,000.

[†] This balance reflects erroneous 1993 income: $42,800 = $20,000 + $22,800.

[‡] $30,000 erroneous income − $1,200 (1994 income was overstated).

  d. No entry is needed because the error counterbalanced.

	1994	1995
Retained earnings, Jan. 1, as previously reported	$42,800*	$ 72,800[§]
Prior period adjustment	1,200[†]	0
Retained earnings, Jan. 1, as restated	44,000	72,800
Net income	28,800	40,000
Retained earnings, Dec. 31	$72,800	$112,800

* $20,000 + $22,800.

[†] To correct the error's effect on 1993 net income.

[§] Equals the ending adjusted retained earnings from 1994 because by January 1, 1995, the error has counterbalanced.

APPENDIX 24A: *Preparation of Financial Statements from Single-Entry and Other Incomplete Records*

Most businesses maintain a record of all transactions using a double-entry accounting system. However, some small businesses, sole proprietorships, non-profit organizations, and persons acting in a fiduciary capacity as administrators or executors of estates maintain only a single-entry system that records minimum transaction detail. In some cases, only records of cash, accounts receivable, accounts payable, and taxes paid are maintained. Records of operational assets, inventories, expenses, revenues, and other elements usually considered essential in an accounting system are not maintained.

Single-entry records are used for simplicity and are less expensive to maintain than double-entry systems. However, single-entry record keeping usually is inadequate except for low-volume operations. Following are some of the more important disadvantages of single-entry systems:

1. Effective planning and control of business operations are diminished because account balances are unavailable.
2. Single-entry records do not provide a check against clerical errors, as does a double-entry system.
3. Internal transactions, such as depreciation, and other adjusting entries often are not recorded.
4. Omission of information from the financial statements is more likely.
5. Detection of theft and other losses is less likely.

However, the incomplete account record and supplemental transaction data often are the basis for a reasonably complete income statement and balance sheet. The procedures are illustrated in the next set of examples.

Balance Sheet Preparation from Single-Entry Records

Identification and measurement of assets and liabilities are essential to preparing a balance sheet from incomplete records. Canceled checks, receipts, bills of sale, papers transferring title to real estate, and other similar records supply information about the cost of operational assets. Depreciation is based on original cost. The amount of merchandise, supplies, and other inventories on hand is obtained by actual count. If original cost cannot be determined, merchandise and supplies are recorded at current replacement cost.

Similarly, the amounts of notes payable are obtained from source documents, memoranda, correspondence, and consultation with creditors. Invoices from sellers support accounts payable.

Exhibit 24A–1 illustrates preparation of the balance sheet and computation of income from incomplete records. Owner's equity is determined by subtracting total liabilities from total assets. Net income is the difference between beginning and ending owners' equity, adjusted for owner investments and withdrawals.

The following schedule shows the computation of net income when investments or withdrawals occur during the period:

	Computation Where There Was	
	Income	Loss
Owner's equity, end of period	$8,000	$5,500
Owner's equity, beginning of period	7,100	6,300
Change increase (decrease)	900	(800)
Add: Withdrawals during period	1,200	1,000
	2,100	200
Deduct: Additional investments during period	500	300
Income for period	$1,600	
Loss for period		$ (100)

EXHIBIT 24A–1   Preparing a Balance Sheet and Computing Net Income from Incomplete Records

Case Data

1. Brown Company was organized by A. A. Brown on January 1, 1993; on this date the owner invested $4,500 cash in the business. During 1993, no formal records were kept.
2. Additional data for 1993:
    a. December 31, cash on hand and on deposit, $2,345—from count of cash and bank statement.
    b. December 31, merchandise inventory, $1,550—count made by Brown, costed at current replacement cost because purchase invoices were not available.
    c. Office and store equipment acquired on January 1, 1993, $500—from invoice found in the files.
    d. Brown agreed that a depreciation rate of 5% per annum, with no material amount of residual value, was reasonable.
    e. Note receivable, dated December 31, 1993, $50—this note, signed by a customer for goods purchased, was in the files.
    f. December 31, accounts receivable, $90—Brown maintained a charge book that listed four customers as owing a total of $90; Brown was positive that the bills were outstanding. You called the customers for verification.
    g. December 31, accounts payable, $240—the "unpaid invoices" file contained two invoices that totaled to this amount; Brown assured you that they were the only unpaid invoices.

Balance Sheet Prepared from Incomplete Data

BROWN COMPANY
Balance Sheet
At December 31, 1993

Assets			Liabilities		
Current assets:			Current liabilities:		
Cash		$2,345	Accounts payable		$ 240
Accounts receivable		90	Long-term liabilities		None
Notes receivable, trade		50	Total liabilities		240
Merchandise inventory		1,550			
Total current assets		4,035	Owners' Equity		
Property and equipment:			A. A. Brown proprietorship ($4,510 − $240)		4,270
Office and store equipment	$500		Total liabilities and owner's equity		$4,510
Less: Accumulated depreciation	25	475			
Total assets		$4,510			

Income (Loss) Computed

BROWN COMPANY
Computation of Net Loss
For the Year Ended December 31, 1993

Owner's equity, January 1	$4,500
Owner's equity, December 31	4,270
Net loss for period.	$ 230

Income Statement Preparation from Incomplete Data

In some cases, financial statement users request information about the components of net income. Banks and other lenders usually request a statement describing the results of operations. Revenue Canada requires detailed information about taxable revenues and deductible expenses.

It is possible to prepare an itemized income statement from single-entry records and supplemental data without converting to double-entry form. Much of the needed detail is obtained through an analysis of the cash receipts and disbursement records. This process is illustrated in Exhibit 24A–2.

The preceding example (Exhibit 24A–2) suggests the need for a spreadsheet approach to reduce clerical work and minimize errors and omissions. A spreadsheet recognizes each group of transactions in debit-credit form and provides several internal checks for accuracy. Written explanations and computations support the spreadsheet entries. Exhibit 24A–3 illustrates such a spreadsheet designed to develop the income statement and balance sheet.

EXHIBIT 24A–2   Preparing the Income Statement from Incomplete Data

Case Data

	1991			1991
	Jan. 1	Dec. 31		
Account balances:			Analysis of bank statements:	
Accounts and trade notes receivable			Bank overdraft, Jan. 1, 1991	$ 2,800
(no doubtful accounts)	$35,000	$48,000	Deposits during year:	
Inventory (from physical count)	6,900	8,700	Collections on account	42,000
Building and equipment (appraised at			Additional capital contributions	
estimated cost less depreciation)	17,000	17,400	by owner	10,000
Prepaid expenses (from memoranda).	100	110	Checks drawn during year for:	
Accounts payable (from files)	8,100	9,200	Purchases (goods for resale).	26,000
Notes payable (for equipment, from files)		500	Expenses.	6,000
Cash on hand (from cash register)	60	110	Salaries of employees	7,000
Liability for accrued expenses			Withdrawals by owner.	3,000
(from memoranda)	120	150	Purchase of equipment	340

Income Statement Items

1. Sales revenue:

Accounts and trade notes receivable, Dec. 31, 1991	$ 48,000
Cash collected from customers and deposited	42,000
Increase of cash on hand ($110 − $60)	50
Less: Accounts and trade notes receivable, Jan. 1, 1991	(35,000)
Sales revenue for the year, 1991	$ 55,050

2. Purchases:

Accounts and trade notes payable, Dec. 31, 1991	$ 9,200
Payments to creditors for purchases	26,000
Less: Accounts payable, Jan. 1, 1991	(8,100)
Purchases for the year, 1991	$ 27,100

3. Depreciation expense:

Net balance of buildings and equipment, Jan. 1, 1991	$ 17,000
Purchases of equipment during 1991:	
By issue of note payable	500
By cash payment	340
Balance before depreciation	17,840
Less: Net balance on Dec. 31, 1991 (after 1991 depreciation)	(17,400)
Depreciation expense for the year, 1991	$ 440

4. Remaining expenses:

Expenses paid in cash during 1991		$ 6,000
Add: Expenses accrued on Dec. 31, 1991		150
Prepaid expenses on Jan. 1, 1991		100
Total		6,250
Deduct: Expenses accrued on Jan. 1, 1991	$120	
Prepaid expenses on Dec. 31, 1991	110	(230)
Other expenses for the year, 1991		$ 6,020

Income Statement
For Year Ended December 31, 1991

Sales revenue (item 1)		$55,050	
Cost of goods sold:			
Inventory, Jan. 1, 1991 (given)	$ 6,900		
Purchases (item 2)	27,100		
Goods available for sale	34,000		
Less inventory, Dec. 31, 1991 (given)	8,700		
Cost of goods sold		25,300	
Gross margin on sales		29,750	
Less: Expenses:			
Depreciation (item 3)	440		
Other expenses (item 4)	6,020		
Salaries (given)	7,000	13,460	
Net income		$16,290	

EXHIBIT 24A–3   Spreadsheet to Develop Account Balances Based on Incomplete Records

Case Data

1. Main Company has been in business two years and has kept only incomplete records. An accountant prepared a balance sheet at December 31, 1991, and a balance sheet has been completed by "inventorying all assets and liabilities at December 31, 1992." These balance sheet accounts are entered on the spreadsheet.
2. Additional data for 1992, developed in various ways as follows:
    a. Main kept no record of cash receipts and disbursements, but an analysis of canceled checks provided the following summary of payments: accounts payable, $71,000; expenses, $20,700; and purchase of equipment, $3,700. No checks appeared to be outstanding.
    b. Main stated that $100 cash was withdrawn regularly each week from the cash register for personal use. No record was made of these personal withdrawals.
    c. The $5,000 bank loan was for one year, the note was dated July 1, 1992, and 6% interest was deducted from the face amount (cash proceeds, $4,700).
    d. Main stated that equipment listed in the January 1 balance sheet at $900 was sold for $620 cash.
    e. The bank reported that it had credited Main with $4,000 during the year for customers' notes that Main left for collection.
    f. One $400 note on hand December 31, 1992, was past due and appeared worthless. Therefore, this note was not included in the $3,000 notes receivable listed in the December 31, 1992, balance sheet. Assume no allowance for doubtful accounts; bad debts are written off directly to expense because of immateriality.

Spreadsheet to Develop Income Statement (Main Company)

Account	Beginning Balances Jan. 1, 1992	Interim entries Debit	Interim entries Credit	Income Statement	Ending Balances Dec. 31, 1992
Accounts with debit balances:					
Cash	10,000	(c) 4,700 (d) 620 (e) 4,000 (h) 103,280	(a) 95,400 (b) 5,200		22,000
Notes receivable	5,000	(g) 2,400	(e) 4,000 (f) 400		3,000
Accounts receivable	61,000	(i) 112,680	(g) 2,400 (h) 103,280		68,000
Inventories	25,000	(j) 27,000	(j) 25,000		27,000
Prepaid expenses	500	(c) 150 (k) 50	(k) 500		200
Furniture and equipment (net)	10,600	(a) 3,700	(d) 900 (l) 1,000		12,400
Expenses		(a) 20,700 (k) 500 (n) 650	(k) 50 (n) 800	21,000	
Interest expense		(c) 150		150	
Loss on sale of equipment		(d) 280		280	
Loss on worthless note		(f) 400		400	
Depreciation expense		(l) 1,000		1,000	
Purchases		(m) 77,000		77,000	
Net income		(o) 14,850		14,850	
	112,100			114,680	132,600
Accounts with credit balances:					
Bank loan payable			(c) 5,000		5,000
Accounts payable	30,000	(a) 71,000	(m) 77,000		36,000
Accrued expenses payable	800	(n) 800	(n) 650		650
Main, owner's equity	81,300	(b) 5,200	(o) 14,850		90,950
Sales revenue			(i) 112,680	112,680	
Income summary (inventory change)		(j) 25,000	(j) 27,000	2,000	
	112,100	476,110	476,110	114,680	132,600

EXHIBIT 24A–3 *(concluded)*

Explanation of Entries on Spreadsheet (Main Company)

a. To record cash payments shown by analysis of canceled checks.

b. To record Main's cash withdrawals of $100 per week for 52 weeks.

c. To record bank loan of $5,000 less $300 interest of which $150 was prepaid as of December 31, 1992.

d. To record sale of equipment (cost less depreciation, $900) for $620 cash.

e. To record $4,000 notes receivable collected by bank.

f. To record write-off of bad note, $400.

g. To record notes from customers, computed as follows (data taken directly from spreadsheet).

Notes collected.	$ 4,000
Note written off	400
Notes on hand, Dec. 31, 1992	3,000
	7,400
Less: Notes on hand, Jan. 1, 1992	5,000
Notes receivable (received on accounts)	$ 2,400

h. Cash collected from customers (notice that it does not matter whether the collection was at time of sale or on account) is computed as follows from data shown in the cash account on the spreadsheet:

Cash paid out ($95,400 + $5,200)	$100,600
Cash balance, Dec. 31, 1992	22,000
	122,600
Cash collected from all sources other than from customers:	
($4,700 + $620 + $4,000)	9,320
	113,280
Less: Cash balance, Jan. 1, 1992	10,000
Cash collected from customers	$103,280

i. Sales are computed by finding the only "missing entry" in *accounts receivable,* which entry is for sales on account. (Balance in notes receivable has already been reconciled on the spreadsheet.)

Note received on account (item *g*).	$ 2,400
Cash collected from customers (item *h*)	103,280
Ending balance of accounts receivable.	68,000
Total credits and balance	173,680
Less: January 1 balance.	61,000
Total debits for the year (sales revenue)	$112,680

j. To close the January 1 inventory and to record the December 31 inventory (to income summary).

k. To adjust the balance of prepaid expenses and to increase the prepaid expense balance as of December 31 to $200 as given.

l. To set up the depreciation expense for the period. All entries have been made in the furniture and equipment account on the spreadsheet except the 1992 depreciation credit. Depreciation is computed as follows:

Furniture and equipment, Jan. 1, 1992	$ 10,600
Equipment purchased	3,700
	14,300
Less: Equipment sold	900
	13,400
Less: Balance of furniture and equipment, Dec. 31, 1992	12,400
Depreciation expense for the period	$ 1,000

m. Purchases are computed by finding the missing entry in accounts payable on the spreadsheet as follows:

Payments on accounts payable	$ 71,000
Balance of accounts payable, Dec. 31, 1992.	36,000
	107,000
Less: Accounts payable, Jan. 1, 1992	30,000
Purchases for the period	$ 77,000

n. To transfer the beginning balance ($800) of accrued expenses payable to expense and to record accrued expenses payable as of December 31. Note that entry *a* on the spreadsheet transfers all of the expenses paid in cash during 1992 to the expense account. As a result, the beginning and ending balances of accrued expense payable, respectively, are entered in the expense account.

o. To close net income to owner's equity. The net income may be computed by analysing the changes in capital from January 1 to December 31, 1992, as illustrated previously or by extending the balances in the temporary accounts to the Income Statement column and then computing the difference between the debits and credits. One computation serves as a check on the other.

KEY TERMS

QUESTIONS

1. Distinguish among the following: (*a*) change in principle, (*b*) change in estimate, and (*c*) accounting error.
2. What are the three basic ways to account for the effects of accounting changes?
3. How is an accounting error accounted for?
4. Under what circumstances is a change in accounting principle accounted for currently? prospectively? retroactively?
5. Complete the following schedule:

Method of Reflecting the Effect*

	(1) ————	(2) ————	(3) ————
a. Change in estimate	————	————	————
b. Change in principle	————	————	————
c. Correction of error	————	————	————

*Identify these three captions; then enter appropriate checks on each line.

6. Explain the basic difference between a change in principle and an error correction.
7. Why are the effects of a change in depreciation method generally accounted for prospectively when other changes in accounting policy are accounted for retroactively?
8. Accounting changes involve (*a*) principles and (*b*) estimates. Using these letters and the letter (*c*) for error corrections, identify each of the following types of change:
   (1) A lessor discovers while a long-term capital lease term is in progress that an estimated material unguaranteed residual value of the leased property has probably become zero.
   (2) After 5 years of use, an asset originally estimated to have a 15-year life is now to be depreciated on the basis of a 20-year life.
   (3) Because of inability to estimate reliably, a contractor began business using the completed-contract method. Now that reliable estimates can be made, the percentage-of-completion method is adopted.
   (4) Office equipment purchased last year is discovered to have been debited to office expense when acquired. Appropriate accounting is to be applied at the discovery date.
   (5) A company that has been using the FIFO inventory method now is changing to LIFO.
   (6) A company that used 1% of sales to predict its bad debt expense discovers losses are running higher than expected and changes to 2½%.
9. How is the book value of a plant asset at the beginning of the year of a change in estimated life used to account for the change?
10. What factors are likely to explain firms' choice of accounting policies?
11. What is income smoothing and how is it accomplished?
12. What is the difference between a counterbalancing and non-counterbalancing error? Why is the distinction significant in the analysis of errors?
13. Complete the schedule below by entering a plus to indicate overstatement, a minus to indicate understatement, and a zero if no effect.

	Effect of Error on			
	Net Income	**Assets**	**Liabilities**	**Owners' Equity**
a. Ending inventory for 1993 understated:				
1993 financial statements.	————	————	————	————
1994 financial statements.	————	————	————	————
b. Ending inventory for 1994 overstated:				
1994 financial statements.	————	————	————	————
1995 financial statements.	————	————	————	————
c. Failed to record depreciation in 1993:				
1993 financial statements.	————	————	————	————
1994 financial statements.	————	————	————	————
d. Failed to record a liability resulting from revenue collected in advance at end of 1993; instead, credited revenue in full erroneously:				
1993 financial statements.	————	————	————	————
1994 financial statements.	————	————	————	————

14. Give two examples of each of the following types of errors:
   a. Affects the income statement only.
   b. Affects the balance sheet only.
   c. Affects both income statement and balance sheet.
15. A company failed to accrue $12,000 of wages at the end of 1991. Explain (a) why the discovery of the error in 1992, after the issuance of the 1991 statements, requires a correcting entry, and (b) why discovery of the error in 1993, after the issuance of the 1992 statements, does not require a correcting entry.

EXERCISES

E 24–1
Conflicting Issues in Accounting Changes
(L.O. 1)

Consistency and comparability, and the need to maintain public confidence in the financial reporting process (defined as the demand that prior financial statements not be changed except for error), conflict with each other, and the need to make accounting changes.

Required:

Briefly discuss (a) the extent to which the three approaches to accounting changes (retroactive, current, and prospective) fulfill these objectives, and (b) why each is used for changes in accounting principle.

E 24–2
Multiple Choice:
Accounting Changes
(L.O. 2)

1. Which of the following is a change in accounting principle?
   a. Correction of an error using the retroactive approach.
   b. Change from an incorrect method to a correct method.
   c. Change in the application of an accounting principle.
   d. Change in the number of total expected service miles for a truck depreciated under the units-of-output method.
2. Which of the following is a change in accounting principle to be given retroactive treatment?
   a. Change to LIFO for a firm in its second year and that is unable to reconstruct LIFO inventory for the prior year.
   b. Change in depreciation method, based on new information.
   c. Change in years of useful life used in straight-line depreciation.
   d. Change from full costing to the successful efforts method of accounting for natural resources.
3. "Current" accounting treatment is used for which of the following:
   a. Correcting errors and making estimate changes.
   b. Changing inventory cost flow assumptions (FIFO, LIFO) when only opening balances can be reconstructed.
   c. Changing to the completed-contract method of accounting for long-term contracts when prior years can be reconstructed.
   d. Correcting errors affecting prior years' income, but only if those prior years are disclosed on a comparative basis with the current year.
4. A company changed from percentage of completion (PC) to completed contract (CC) for financial accounting purposes during 1992. Prior years' results cannot be reconstructed, but opening balances can be restated.
   a. Beginning January 1, 1992, CC should be used for construction accounting and the difference between the income under the two methods for years before 1992 is disclosed in the 1992 income statement.
   b. Beginning January 1, 1992, CC should be used for construction accounting but no entry is made for the effects of the change on years before 1992.
   c. Beginning January 1, 1992, CC should be used for construction accounting and the difference between the income under the two methods for years before 1992 is an adjustment to the December 31, 1992, retained earnings balance.
   d. Beginning January 1, 1992, CC should be used for construction accounting, and the difference between the income under the two methods for years before 1992 is an adjustment to the January 1, 1992, retained earnings balance.
5. Choose the incorrect statement concerning comparative financial statements.
   a. They are required by GAAP.
   b. They are required by the Canada Business Corporations Act.

     c. The number of statements presented comparatively affects the amount of a cumulative effect of a change in accounting principle reported as an adjustment to opening retained earnings and applied retroactively.

     d. Firms generally do not disclose more than one year because financial statement users already have access to the reports of previous years.

6. One of the advantages of the current type change is:

     a. Consistency is maintained.

     b. Prior years' income effects do not affect retained earnings.

     c. The statements of previous years shown comparatively do not disclose any information about the effect of the change in those previous years.

     d. Prior years' financial statements are not altered.

7. Note disclosures:

     a. Somewhat reduce the loss of comparability inherent in the current treatment of accounting principle changes.

     b. Are required only for the year of a change in accounting principle.

     c. Are never required for changes in estimates.

     d. Always disclose the effect on net income in each individual prior year for a change in accounting principle.

E 24–3
Overview: Types of Accounting Changes and Errors
(L.O. 2, 6)

Analyse each case and enter one letter code under each column (type and approach) to indicate the preferable accounting for each case.

	Type P = Principle E = Estimate AE = Error	Approach C = Current R = Retroactive P = Prospective
Case (Event or Transaction)		
1. Recorded expense, $870; should be $780.	_____	_____
2. Changed useful life of a machine.	_____	_____
3. Changed from FIFO to average cost for inventory. No prior balances can be reconstructed, not even opening balances.	_____	_____
4. Changed from straight-line to accelerated depreciation. No new information is available.	_____	_____
5. Change in residual value of an intangible operational asset.	_____	_____
6. Changed from cash basis to accrual basis in accounting for bad debts; accrual basis could have been used earlier.	_____	_____
7. Changed from percentage-of-completion to completed-contracts for long-term construction. All prior balances can be reconstructed.	_____	_____
8. Changed from LIFO to FIFO for inventory. Only opening balances can be reconstructed.	_____	_____
9. Changed to a new accounting principle required by the *CICA Handbook*.	_____	_____

E 24–4
Change in Resource Exploration Costs: Entries and Reporting
(L.O. 2, 3)

Gunnard Company was formed in 1990 and has a December 31 year-end. Gunnard Company changed from successful efforts (SE) to full costing (FC) for its resource exploration costs in 1991. SE is used for tax purposes. Under FC, all exploration costs are deferred versus under SE, only a portion are deferred. Under both approaches, the deferred cost balance is amortized yearly.

Had FC been used before 1991, a total of $3,200,000 of costs originally written off under SE would have been capitalized. A total of $4,700,000 of such costs were incurred and capitalized under FC in 1991. Gunnard discloses 1990 and 1991 results comparatively in its annual report. The tax rate is 30% in both years.

Resource exploration costs represent a long-term asset, and amortization is charged directly to that account.

Amortization expense for 1990 and 1991 under both methods was as follows:

	SE	FC
1990	$ 40,000	$240,000
1991	200,000	850,000

No amortization has yet been recorded by Gunnard in 1991. Additional information for Gunnard:

	1990	1991
Revenues	$4,400,000	$7,100,000
Expenses other than amortization		
and tax	720,000	2,050,000
Extraordinary loss, after tax.		32,400

Required:

1. Prepare a 1991 comparative income statement using the old policy, successful efforts.
2. Prepare the 1991 entry(ies) for FC amortization, and the accounting change.
3. Prepare the comparative income statements under FC and include disclosures related to the accounting change.

E 24-5
Change in Estimated Useful Life: Entries and Reporting
(L.O. 2, 5)

Stacy Corporation has been depreciating equipment over a 10-year life on a straight-line basis. The equipment, which cost $24,000, was purchased on January 1, 1991. It has an estimated residual value of $6,000. On the basis of experience since acquisition, management has decided to depreciate it over a total life of 14 years instead of 10, with no change in the estimated residual value. The change is to be effective on January 1, 1995. The annual financial statements are prepared on a comparative basis (1994 and 1995 presented); 1994 and 1995 incomes before depreciation were $49,800, and $52,800, respectively. Disregard income tax considerations.

Required:

1. Identify the type of accounting change involved and analyse the effects of the change. Which approach should be used—current, prospective, or retroactive? Explain.
2. Prepare the entry, or entries, to appropriately reflect the change in the accounts for 1995, the year of the change.
3. Illustrate how the change should be reported on the 1995 financial statements, which include 1994 results for comparative purposes (common shares outstanding, 100,000).

E 24-6
Change in Expense Method: Entries and Reporting
(L.O. 2, 3, 4, 5)

Bite Corporation has always deferred product advertising costs and amortized the asset balance on a straight-line basis over the expected life of the related product. The company decided to change to a policy of immediately expensing such costs. The change was adopted at the beginning of 1995. Costs incurred:

Year	Amount	Life Span
1991	$68,000	10 years
1992	40,000	4 years
1993	20,000	5 years
1994	52,000	10 years
1995	45,000	9 years

Required:

1. Identify the type of accounting change involved and analyse the effects of the change. Which approach should be used—current, prospective or retroactive? Explain.
2. Prepare the entry(ies) to appropriately reflect the change in the accounts in 1995, the year of the change, including the entry to record 1995 expenditures. Disregard taxes.
3. Explain how the change should be reported on the 1995 financial statements, which include the 1994 results for comparative purposes.
4. Prepare the entries to reflect the change in the accounts in 1995, including the 1995 expenditures, if only the opening 1995 balance can be reconstructed. What would change in financial statement presentation?
5. Prepare the entries to reflect the change in the accounts in 1995, including the 1995 expenditures, assuming that no restatement of any balances was possible.

E 24-7
Change in Revenue Recognition: Entries
(L.O. 2, 4)

Knowles Sales Company has made an adjustment in revenue recognition policies to more properly reflect the substance of the transactions. Assume it is the end of 1992 and that the accounting period ends on December 31. The books have not been adjusted or closed at the end of 1992.

The change delays revenue recognition on certain types of credit sales from the date of shipment to the date of payment. Under the date of payment method, accounts receivable would still be formally recorded in the books, but all revenue would be deferred. When cash is received, revenue is recognized on the income statement. The following information is available:

Balance, January 1, 1992:
Accounts receivable $320,000
Allowance for doubtful accounts . . . . . . (20,000)

Shipments in 1992 totalled $1,500,000. Of these, $1,200,000 were paid during 1992. $290,000 of the opening balance of accounts receivable was collected.

It is not practicable to restate balances prior to January 1, 1992, as cash receipts records have not been maintained.

Required:

1. Describe the type of accounting change that was involved and briefly explain how it should be accounted for.
2. Give the appropriate journal entry to record the change in 1992, and the entries to record 1992 transactions. Disregard income taxes.

E 24–8
Change from AC to FIFO:
Entries and Reporting
(L.O. 2, 3)

On January 1, 1991, Baker Company decided to change the inventory costing method used from AC to FIFO. The annual reporting period ends on December 31. The average income tax rate is 30%. The following related data were developed.

	AC Basis	FIFO Basis
Beginning inventory, 1990	$ 30,000	$30,000
Ending inventory:		
1990.	40,000	70,000
1991.		76,000
Net income:		
1990: AC basis	80,000	
1991: FIFO basis		90,000
Retained earnings:		
1990 beginning balance	120,000	
Dividends declared and paid:		
1990	64,000	
1991		70,000
Common shares outstanding, 10,000.		

Required:

1. Identify the type of accounting change involved. Which approach should be used—current, prospective, or retroactive? Explain.
2. Give the entry(ies) to record the effect of the change, assuming the change was made only for accounting purposes, not for tax purposes.
3. Complete the following schedule:

	1990	1991
Comparative balance sheet:		
Inventory.	$	$
Retained earnings		
Comparative income statement:		
Net income:		
1990		
1991		
Earnings per share		
Statement of retained earnings:		
Beginning balance, as previously reported		
Cumulative effect of accounting change		
Beginning balance restated		
Net income		
Dividends declared and paid.		
Ending balance		

E 24–9
Errors: Analysis and
Overview
(L.O. 6)

Indicate the effect of the errors and transactions listed below on income for 1991 and 1992. Respond by placing one check mark for 1991 and one for 1992 under the appropriate heading. Each item is independent of the others.

Error	Income—1991 Over-stated	Income—1991 Under-stated	Income—1991 No Effect	Income—1992 Over-stated	Income—1992 Under-stated	Income—1992 No Effect
a. Ending inventory, 1991, overstated.						
b. Depreciation expense, 1992, understated.						
c. Did not recognize the inventory of office supplies at the end of 1991.						
d. Did not amortize goodwill in 1991; normal amortization was recorded in 1992.						
e. Debited the cost of a depreciable asset to an operating expense account on January 1, 1991.						
f. Merchandise purchased on credit in 1991 was neither recorded nor included in 1991 inventory. Recorded and included in 1992; not sold in 1992.						
g. Did not include a large residual value on a depreciable asset, acquired in 1991 (10-year life).						
h. Unpaid wages not accrued at the end of 1991. Paid and expensed in 1992.						
i. Did not record bad debt estimate in 1991. No accounts written off in 1992.						
j. Merchandise purchased on credit in 1991 was not recorded, but was included in the 1991 ending inventory. Recorded in 1992.						
k. Wrote off a bad debt in 1991 (not an error).						
l. Sold merchandise at a profit in 1991 on credit; did not record it as sales revenue until 1992.						
m. Did not recognize interest payable in 1991. Recorded in 1992.						
n. Did not amortize premium on bonds payable in 1991.						
o. Sold common shares; entry not recorded.						

E 24–10
Analysis of Eight Errors:
Correcting Entries and
Correct Pretax Income
(L.O. 6)

The 1991 income statement of Burke Corporation has just been tentatively completed. It reflects pretax income for 1991 of $85,000. The accounts have not been closed for the year ended December 31, 1991. A review of the company's files and records revealed the following errors that have not been corrected:

a. Patent amortization of $3,000 per year was not recorded in 1990 and 1991.
b. The 1989 ending inventory was overstated by $4,000.
c. Machinery acquired on January 1, 1987, at a cost of $26,000 is being depreciated on the straight-line basis over 10 years. The good-faith estimate of its residual value of $6,000 has never been included in the computation of depreciation expense.
d. Accrued wages of $1,500 at December 31, 1990, were not recognized.
e. A $1,000 cash shortage during 1991 was debited to retained earnings.
f. Ordinary repairs on the machinery in (c) above of $7,000, incurred during January 1991, were debited to the machinery account.
g. During 1991, 1,000 common shares were repurchased and retired for $5,000. The common share account was debited for this amount. On average, shares had been issued for $8 per share.

Required:

1. Give the correcting entry, if needed, for each of the above errors. Show computations for each item. Ignore income tax considerations.

2. Compute the correct pretax income amount for 1991. Set up an appropriate schedule that reflects each change and the correct 1991 pretax income.

E 24–11
Analysis of Four Errors:
Correcting Entries and
Correct Pretax Income
(L.O. 6)

Travis Corporation has just completed its financial statements for the reporting year ended December 31, 1995. The pretax income amount is $160,000. The accounts have not been closed for December 31, 1995. Further consideration and review of the records revealed the following items related to the 1995 statements:

a. On January 1, 1991, a machine was acquired that cost $10,000. The estimated useful life was 10 years, and the residual value was $2,000. At the time of acquisition, the full cost of the machine was incorrectly debited to the land account. Use straight-line depreciation.

b. On January 1, 1993, a long-term investment of $18,000 was made by purchasing a $20,000, 8% bond of XT Corporation. The investment account was debited for $18,000. Each year, starting on December 31, 1993, the company has recognized and reported investment revenue on these bonds of $1,600. The bonds mature 10 years from the date of purchase. Assume any amortization would be straight-line and the net method is used to record the investment.

c. The 1994 ending inventory was overstated by $7,000.

d. An $11,000 credit purchase of merchandise occurred on December 18, 1994. Because the merchandise was on hand on December 31, 1994, it was included in the 1994 ending inventory. The purchase was recorded on January 18, 1995, when the invoice was paid.

Required:

1. Prepare any correcting and adjusting entries that should be made on December 31, 1995. Ignore income tax.

2. Compute the correct pretax income for 1995. Set up an appropriate schedule that reflects each change and the correct pretax income, 1995.

E 24–12
Errors: Prior Years'
Adjustments Not
Recorded, Entries to
Correct Current Year
(L.O. 6)

You are auditing the accounts of Sun Merchandising Corporation for the year ended December 31, 1992. You discover that the adjustments made in the previous audit for the year 1991 were not entered in the accounts by Sun's bookkeeper; therefore, the accounts are not in agreement with the audited amounts as of December 31, 1991. The following adjustments were included in the 1991 audit:

a. Invoices for merchandise purchased on credit in December 1991, not entered on the books until payment of $6,000 was made in January 1992; not included in the December 31, 1991, inventory. The company uses a periodic inventory system.

b. Invoices for merchandise received on credit in December 1991 were not recorded in the accounts until payment was made in January 1992; the goods were included in the 1991 ending inventory, $9,000.

c. Allowance for doubtful accounts for 1991 was understated by $1,000 because bad debt expense in 1991 was not recorded.

d. Selling expense for 1991 was not recorded in the accounts until paid in January 1992, $2,500.

e. Accrued wages of $2,000 at December 31, 1991, were not recorded in the accounts until paid in January 1992.

f. Prepaid insurance at December 31, 1991, understated by $300 because this amount was included in 1991 expense. The insurance policy expires on December 31, 1992.

g. Income tax expense for the last part of the year ended December 31, 1991, ($1,200) was not recorded until paid in January 1992.

h. Depreciation of $4,500 was not recorded in 1991.

Required:

You have the uncorrected and unadjusted trial balance dated December 31, 1992. Give the journal entry to collect for each of the above items. Disregard income tax implications.

E 24–13
Analysis of Four Accounts:
Compute Correct Ending
Balances
(L.O. 6, 7)

The accounts and financial statements of Slo Company have never been audited. A preliminary examination has shown numerous errors. Also, the files and supporting documentation are not available in some cases and unclear in others. As a consequence, you have been asked to compute the ending 1992 balances of the four accounts identified below based on the data given. Each item is independent of the others. Show computations.

a. Wage expense, $_____ .
   Data: Amount paid during 1992, $15,000; accrued on December 31, 1991, $1,000; and accrued on December 31, 1992, $2,000.

b. Rent revenue, $_____.

Data: Amount collected during 1992, $8,000; unearned (collected in advance), $500 on December 31, 1991, and $300 on December 31, 1992; earned but not collected, $200 on December 31, 1991, and $600 on December 31, 1992.

c. Sales revenue, $_____.

Data: Cash account, balance, December 31, 1991, $26,000; balance, December 31, 1992, $33,000; and total disbursements for 1992, $39,000. All cash receipts were from customers. Accounts receivable: balance, December 31, 1991, $40,160; and balance, December 31, 1992, $59,000. Accounts written off during 1992 as uncollectible, $960.

d. Purchases (net of cash discounts), $_____.

Data: Accounts payable balance on December 31, 1991, $28,320, and on December 31, 1992, $33,000; payments made on accounts during 1992, $46,000. Credit purchases are recorded net of cash discount whether taken or not.

E 24–14
Incomplete Records:
Worksheet to Develop
Income Statement and
Balance Sheet
(L.O. 7)

On January 2, 1993, Star Retail Company was organized. During 1993, the company paid trade creditors $49,062 in cash and had an ending inventory per count (FIFO basis) of $9,563. Balances available on December 31, 1993, were the following: accounts payable, $16,125; expenses, $2,450 (no depreciation); M. Lane (sole proprietor), capital (representing beginning balance of cash on January 2, 1993), $45,000; accounts receivable, $13,188; and sales, $50,000. There were no withdrawals. All sales and purchases were on credit. The company is not subject to income tax.

Required:

1. Complete a worksheet to develop a correct income statement and balance sheet. Use a format similar to the following:

Accounts	Balance Sheet Jan. 2, 1993	Interim Entries		Income Statement	Balance Sheet Dec. 31, 1993
		Debit	Credit		
Cash					
Accounts receivable					
Purchases					
Expenses					
Accounts payable					
M. Lane, capital					
Sales revenue					
Income summary					
Net gain (loss)					

2. Prepare a proof of the ending cash balance.

PROBLEMS

P 24–1
Multiple Choice:
Accounting Changes
(L.O. 2, 3, 4, 5)

1. Immutable Company changed from the sum-of-years'-digits method (SYD) to the straight-line method (SL) of depreciation in 1992. The change should be applied retroactively. Depreciation under each method for the years affected is as follows:

Year	SYD	SL
1989	$200	$150
1990	240	160
1991	600	450
1992	450	500

Ignoring taxes, Immutable reports which of the following amounts in a cumulative effect of change in accounting principle in 1992?

a. $280 cr.

b. $230 cr.

c. $ 50 dr.

d. $320 dr.

2. Quick Company changed revenue recognition methods for accounting purposes and correctly computed a cumulative effect before tax of $600 (reduces income). The tax rate is 30%. The change affects only accounting income and not taxable income. The entry to record the change in accounting principle includes:
   a. Cr. accounts receivable $420.
   b. Dr. deferred income tax $180.
   c. Dr. income taxes payable $420.
   d. Dr. retained earnings $600.

3. Fido Dog Food Company changed its method of accounting for inventory from AC to FIFO in 1992 for both tax and financial accounting purposes. The 1991 ending inventory was $40,000 under AC, and $55,000 under FIFO. Fido discloses 1991 and 1992 results comparatively. The tax rate is 30%. The entry to record the change in accounting principle includes:
   a. Cr. inventory $15,000.
   b. Dr. retained earnings $10,500.
   c. Cr. deferred taxes $4,500.
   d. Insufficient information.

4. An asset purchased January 1, 1991, costing $10,000 with a 10-year useful life and no salvage value, was depreciated under the straight-line method during its first three years. During 1994, the total useful life was re-estimated to be 17 years. What is depreciation in 1995?
   a. $462.
   b. $412.
   c. $464.
   d. $500.

5. A company made a retroactive accounting change in 1992. Only the net incomes of 1991 and 1992 were affected. Therefore, the comparative retained earnings statements featuring both years disclose which of the following?
   a. A cumulative effect adjusting the January 1, 1991, retained earnings balance.
   b. A cumulative effect adjusting the January 1, 1991 and 1992, retained earnings balances.
   c. A cumulative effect adjusting the January 1, 1992, retained earnings balance.
   d. No cumulative effect.

P 24–2
Change from Completed-Contract to Percentage-of-Completion Method: Entries and Reporting
(L.O. 2, 3, 4, 5)

KLB Corporation has used the completed-contract method to account for its long-term construction contracts since its inception in 1990. On January 1, 1994, management decided to change to the percentage-of-completion method to better reflect operating activities. Completed contract was used for tax purposes, and will continue to be used for tax purposes in the future. The tax rate was 40%. The following data have been assembled:

	Year Ended December 31				
	1990	**1991**	**1992**	**1993**	**1994**
Net income, as reported.	$100,000	$120,000	$150,000	$140,000	$160,000*
CC income, included in above. . .	0	60,000	0	120,000	0
PC income, as calculated	40,000	65,000	50,000	40,000	75,000
Opening retained earnings	10,000	90,000	190,000	320,000	440,000
Dividends	20,000	20,000	20,000	20,000	20,000
Closing retained earnings	90,000	190,000	320,000	440,000	580,000

* Includes PC income, not CC income earnings.

Required:

1. Identify the type of accounting change involved. Which approach should be used—current, prospective, or retroactive? Explain.
2. Give the entry to appropriately reflect the accounting change in 1994, the year of the change. (*Hint:* the entry affects deferred taxes and construction in progress.)
3. Restate the 1994 retained earnings statement, including the 1993 comparative figures.
4. Assume that only the opening balance in 1994 can be restated and that the cumulative effect cannot be allocated to individual years. Recast the 1994 comparative retained earnings statement accordingly.
5. Assume that no balances can be restated. How will the change be reflected in the 1994 financial statements? Explain.

P 24–3
Change in Method of Accounting for Natural Resources: Entries and Reporting
(L.O. 2, 3)

In 1994, Digger Oil Company changed its method of accounting for oil exploration costs from the successful-efforts method (SE) to full-costing (FC) for financial reporting. Digger has been in operation since January 1991.

Pretax income under each method:

	SE	FC
1991	$ 5,000	$15,000
1992	22,000	25,000
1993	25,000	35,000
1994	40,000	60,000

Digger reports the results of years 1992 through 1994 in its 1994 annual report and has a calendar fiscal year. The tax rate is 30%.

Additional information:

	1991	**1992**	**1993**	**1994**
Ending retained earnings (SE basis)	$18,000	$23,000	$31,000	n/a
Dividends declared	9,000	10,400	9,500	$18,000

Required:

1. Prepare the entry in 1994 to record the accounting change. Use "natural resources" as the depletable asset. Assume the difference in accounting for exploration costs accounts for the entire income difference in all years.
2. Prepare the comparative retained earnings statement.

P 24–4
Two Assets—Useful Life and Residual Value Changed: Entries and Reporting
(L.O. 2, 5)

On January 1, 1991, TV Company purchased a machine that cost $78,000. The estimated useful life was 20 years with an estimated residual value of $8,000. Starting on January 1, 1998, the company revised its estimates to 16 years for total life and $9,000 for residual value.

The company also owns a patent that cost $34,000 when acquired on January 1, 1995. It is being amortized over its legal life of 17 years (no residual value). On January 1, 1998, the patent is estimated to have a total useful life of only 13 years (no residual value). The company uses the straight-line method for both of these assets. The annual reporting period ends December 31. Disregard income tax considerations.

Required:

1. What kinds of accounting changes are involved? How should each change be accounted for—current, retroactive, or prospective? Explain.
2. Give all entries required in 1997 and 1998 related to these assets.
3. Show what amounts related to these changes should be reported on the comparative 1998 income statement and balance sheet.

P 24–5
Analysis of Three Accounting Changes, Estimate: Prospective, Current, and Retroactive
(L.O. 2, 3, 4, 5)

During 1994, Sugarland Corporation completed an analysis of its operational assets with the purpose of updating its accounting procedures used to compute inventory costing, depreciation, and amortization each reporting period. The annual reporting period ends December 31. Decisions have been made concerning the three different assets listed below (designated Cases A, B, and C). The indicated accounting changes are to be implemented starting January 1, 1995, the fifth year of operations for this company. Disregard income tax considerations.

Case A

Machine A, acquired on January 1, 1991, at a cost of $60,000, is being depreciated straight-line over an estimated 10-year useful life; residual value is $5,000. On January 1, 1995, the company will start using 20% declining-balance depreciation (with no other changes). The change was based on new information concerning the pattern of asset use.

Required:

1. Identify the type of accounting change and the approach that should be used—current, retroactive, or prospective. Explain.

2. Give the following entries:
   a. Depreciation adjusting entry at the end of 1994.
   b. 1995 entry to record the accounting change in 1995, if any. Explain.
   c. Depreciation adjusting entry at the end of 1995.
3. Explain how the 1994 financial statement amounts are reported in the 1995 comparative statements.

Case B

On January 1, 1995, the company changed from LIFO to FIFO for inventory costing purposes. The ending inventory for 1994: LIFO basis, $12,000; FIFO basis, $17,000. Ending inventory for 1995, FIFO basis, was $19,000. No other balances could be reconstructed.

Required:

1. Identify the type of accounting change and the approach that should be used—current, retroactive, or prospective. Explain.
2. Give the entry to record the catch-up adjustment (i.e., the change effect) in the year of change.
3. Explain:
   a. How the catch-up adjustment (i.e., the change effect) recorded above is reported in the 1995 comparative financial statements.
   b. How the 1994 income statement amounts are reported on the 1995 comparative statements.

Case C

A patent, purchased for $17,000 on January 1, 1991, is being amortized (straight-line) over its legal life of 17 years; there is no residual value. On January 1, 1995, the company decided to change to a more realistic total useful life of 12 years.

Required:

1. Identify the type of accounting change and the approach that should be used—current, retroactive, or prospective. Explain.
2. Compute any catch-up adjustment and give the entry (if any) to record this accounting change in 1995, the year of change. Explain. Give the adjusting entries to record patent amortization for 1994 and 1995.
3. Explain:
   a. How any catch-up adjustment should be reported in the 1995 comparative financial statements.
   b. How the 1994 financial statement amounts are reported in the 1995 comparative statements.

P 24–6
Error—Depreciation,
Income Tax: Correcting
Entries
(L.O. 6)

On January 3, 1991, Young Sales Company purchased a machine that cost $30,000. Although the machine has an estimated useful life of 10 years and an estimated residual value of $6,000, it was debited to expense when acquired. It is now December 1994, and the error has been discovered. The average income tax rate is 30%, and straight-line depreciation is used.

Required:

1. Give the entry to correct the accounts at the end of 1994 assuming the books have not yet been closed for 1994. Also give the adjusting entry for depreciation for 1994. The income tax return was correct and there was no deferred income tax related to this transaction.
2. Assume instead that the income tax return also was incorrect because of this error; therefore, additional income tax must be paid, including a 10% penalty for each year an amount of tax was underpaid, less 10% each year on any amount of tax that was overpaid. Give the entry to correct the accounts, including the income tax effects, at the end of 1994, and the adjusting entry for depreciation for 1994. Round amounts to the nearest dollar.

P 24–7
Error Correction: Entry
and Reporting
(L.O. 6)

In 1994, Arrow Company, a calendar fiscal year company, discovered that depreciation expense was erroneously overstated $1,000 in both 1992 and 1993, for financial reporting purposes. The tax rate is 30%.

Additional information:

	1993	1994
Beginning retained earnings	$18,000	$28,000
Net income (as previously reported, includes error)	16,000	18,000
Dividends declared	6,000	8,000

Required:

1. Record the entry in 1994 to correct the error.
2. Provide the comparative retained earnings statement for 1993 and 1994, including any required footnote disclosure.

P 24–8
Correction of Errors:
Entries and Computation
of Correct Net Income and
Retained Earnings
(L.O. 6)

Victor Wholesale Company was organized as a partnership on January 1, 1991; its five-year existence has involved a steady growth in assets, revenue, and income. The reporting period ends December 31. The 1995 accounts have been adjusted but are not yet closed. Since this is a partnership, it does not pay income tax. The net income for each of the five years was as follows (in thousands):

	1991	1992	1993	1994	1995
Income before extraordinary items	$12	$27	$47	$ 60	$83
Extraordinary item, gain (loss)	—	—	—	(10)	—
Net income	$12	$27	$47	$ 50	$83

Partners' withdrawals through 1994, $100 in total.

The company's records and reports are maintained by the company's bookkeeper. Although a part-time person has assisted in this area for the past two years, numerous problems have arisen with respect to the financial reports prepared for the owners and the local bank. The bank has been the primary source of borrowed funds. The owners currently are making plans (*a*) to expand the business and (*b*) to contract for the construction of a large building to replace the rented space now used. In view of the anticipated financing needs, the company has engaged an outside public accountant to update all of the prior financial statements.

During the March 1996 examination of the 1991 through 1995 financial records, the public accountant discovered the following accounting and reporting errors:

a. A forklift vehicle (used for moving inventory inside the warehouse) that was purchased for $8,500 on January 1, 1993, was debited in full to expense. It has an estimated useful life of eight years and a $500 residual value. The company uses straight-line depreciation.
b. The ending inventory of goods in the warehouse was overstated $10,000 at the end of 1992 due to an arithmetic error. Also, the 1994 ending inventory was overstated by $2,000 for the same reason. The company uses a periodic inventory system and FIFO.
c. Extraordinary repairs of $6,000 were debited in full to repair expense late in December 1993. The equipment repaired was being depreciated over a four-year remaining life, straight-line.
d. Prepaid insurance not recognized at year-end: 1992, $100; 1993, $150; 1994, $160; 1995, $180.
e. Merchandise was purchased on credit (ownership passed) in one year but invoices were recorded as purchases when payments were made in the following year. These items were correctly included in the ending inventory (periodic inventory system). Amounts were as follows: 1991, $700; 1992, $1,000; 1993, $1,200; 1994, $1,400; and 1995, $2,000. The accounts payable are not yet paid for 1995.
f. The company recognized revenue on credit sales only when the cash was collected. Sales revenues related to credit sales that were collected in a subsequent accounting period were as follows: 1991, $4,000; 1992, $7,000; 1993, $10,000; 1994, $14,000; and 1995, $18,000. The receivable is not yet collected for 1995.
g. During 1995, Victor recorded an $800 cash shortage as a debit to retained earnings.
h. Accrued selling expenses were not recorded in the accounts until actually paid: 1991, $2,000; 1992, $2,700; 1993, $3,100; 1994, $4,000; and 1995, $4,400. The payable for 1995 is not yet paid.
i. An allowance for doubtful accounts has never been established. The public accountant made the following estimates of additions to the allowance account (net of write-offs): 1991, $1,600; 1992, $1,200; 1993, $1,200; 1994, $1,700; and 1995, $1,600.

Required:

Ignore income tax considerations.

1. Give all correcting and adjusting entries that should be made on March 31, 1996 (date of discovery of errors and omissions). The 1995 accounts have been adjusted (except when indicated otherwise) but have not yet been closed.
2. Compute net income for 1995. Set up an appropriate schedule that reflects each change.
3. Compute the ending 1995 balance in total partners' capital. There were no withdrawals in 1995. Set up a schedule that reflects each change.

P 24–9
Errors—Set Up Worksheet
to Correct Income:
Correcting Entries
(L.O. 6)

Jackson Company did not recognize all accruals and deferrals in the accounts for a three-year period. In addition, numerous other errors were made in computing pretax income. The income amounts for each of the past three years are given in the tabulation below, along with a list of the items that were not properly recognized and reported. All of these errors were discovered in February 1994 after the 1993 adjusting and closing entries.

Items	1991	1992	1993
a. Reported pretax income (loss)	$4,000	$(3,500)	$10,000
Items not recognized correctly at each year-end:			
b. Accrued wages, not recorded	400	250	300
c. Rent revenue collected in advance, not recorded.	100		200
d. Prepaid insurance, not recognized (was debited to expense) . . .	320	410	120
e. Interest revenue earned but not collected (recognized as revenue when the cash was received)	170	140	
f. Annual depreciation overstated (by year)		1,000	1,200
g. Estimated annual expense for doubtful accounts understated (by year).	170	200	190
h. Goods purchased on credit on Dec. 31 were included in ending inventory; but the purchase was not recorded until payment was made the following year, before discovery date (periodic inventory system)	460	210	150
i. Sales on credit on Dec. 31 not recorded until the following year when the cash was collected, before discovery date; the goods were not included in ending inventory.	290	770	390
j. Ending inventory overstated each year	130	240	290
k. Checks written; not mailed on Dec. 31 as payment on accounts payable; not recorded until the next year	1,100	1,500	1,400*
l. Bad debts that should have been written off each year to allowance for doubtful accounts by year-end (have not been written off to date; not cumulative)	800	950	1,170

* Not yet mailed or recorded for 1993 by discovery date; the checks were mailed after discovery date.

Required:

1. You are to set up a worksheet to correct income for each year. Set up column headings similar to those shown in the tabulation. Key and briefly identify the errors under the first column and enter amounts under the respective years as plus or minus so that the last line will report correct pretax income. All items are pretax and are material in amount. Disregard income tax effects.
2. Give the correcting entry (if any should be made) on date of discovery (i.e., February 1994). For each item, code the entries with the letters given in the above tabulation.

P 24–10
Errors—Worksheet to
Correct Pretax Income:
Entries
(L.O. 6)

L. Long established a retail business in 1991. Early in 1994, Long entered into negotiations with S. Short with the intent to form a partnership. You have been asked by Long and Short to check Long's books for the past three years to help Short evaluate the earnings potential of the business.

The net incomes reported on statements submitted to you were as follows:

	Year Ending Dec. 31		
	1991	**1992**	**1993**
Income, pretax	$9,000	$10,109	$8,840

During the examination of the accounts, you found the data given below:

	For Year Ended Dec. 31		
	1991	**1992**	**1993**
Omissions from the books:			
a. Accrued expenses at end of year	$2,160	$2,094	$4,624
b. Earned (uncollected) revenue at end of year	200	—	—
c. Prepaid expenses at end of year	902	1,210	1,406
d. Unearned revenue (collected in advance) at end of year	—	610	—

	For Year Ended Dec. 31		
	1991	**1992**	**1993**
Goods in transit at end of year omitted from inventory:			
e. Purchase for which the entry had been made (ownership passed)	—	2,610	—
f. Purchase for which the entry had not been made (ownership not passed)	—	—	1,710

Other points requiring consideration:

   g. On January 1, 1993, sold operational equipment for $4,500 that originally cost $5,000 on January 1, 1991. Cash was debited for $4,500 and equipment was credited for $4,500. The asset sold was depreciated in 1991 and 1992 but not 1993 on the basis of a 10-year life and no residual value.

   h. No allowance for bad debts has been set up. An analysis of accounts receivable as of December 31, 1993, indicates that the allowance account should have a balance of $2,000, of which $500 relates to 1991, $700 to 1992, and $800 to 1993.

Required:

1. You have decided to set up a worksheet to correct net income for each of the three years. Use column headings similar to those in the above tabulation and analyse each item separately.
2. Give the correcting entry, if any, for each item that should be made on date of discovery (that is, early January 1994).

                                                                         (AICPA adapted)

P 24–11
Errors—Worksheet to Develop Correct Income Statement and Balance Sheet
(L.O. 6)

The records of Davis Corporation have never been audited. At the end of 1992, the company prepared the following financial statements (summarized):

Income statement:
Sales and service revenue	$ 600,000
Expenses:	
Cost of goods sold	(350,000)
Distribution expenses.	(120,000)
Administrative expenses	(60,000)
Pretax income	$ 70,000
Income taxes	(21,500)
Net income.	$ 48,500

Balance sheet:
Assets:	
Cash.	$ 23,000
Accounts receivable (net)	40,000
Inventory (periodic system)	110,000
Property, plant, and equipment (net)	160,000
Patent	8,000
Other assets	9,000
Total assets.	$ 350,000
Liabilities:	
Accounts payable.	$ 80,000
Income taxes payable	15,000
Notes payable, long-term (8%)	40,000
Total liabilities	$ 135,000
Shareholders' equity	
Common shares, nopar	$ 145,000
Retained earnings (including 1992 net income).	80,000
Dividends declared and paid.	(10,000)
Total shareholders' equity.	$ 215,000
Total liabilities and shareholders' equity.	$ 350,000

The company is negotiating a large loan to finance expansion. The bank has requested that an audit of the company be performed. During the course of the audit, the following facts were determined:

a. The inventory at December 31, 1991, was overstated by $10,000.

b. The inventory at December 31, 1992, was overstated by $20,000.

c. The property, plant, and equipment was underdepreciated in 1991 by $9,000 and in 1992 by $12,000 (report this depreciation as a separate expense).

d. A three-year insurance premium of $900 paid on January 1, 1991, was debited in full to administrative expense at that time.

e. Accrued wages (an element of administrative expense) were not recorded as follows: 1991, $800; and 1992, $1,000.

f. The patent, which originally cost $17,000, is being amortized to administrative expense over a 17-year life (including 1992). Evidence clearly indicates that its economic life will approximate 14 years from date of acquisition.

g. Service revenues earned but not yet collected were not recognized when earned: 1991, $5,000; 1992, $7,500. Revenue is recognized when collection is made.

h. A delivery truck purchased in January 1992, at a cost of $13,000, was debited to distribution expense at that time. The truck has an estimated useful life of 10 years and an estimated residual value of $2,000. The company uses straight-line depreciation (report depreciation on this truck as a distribution expense).

i. Uncollectible account receivable from a bankrupt customer should be, but has not been, written off, $8,500. The balance in the allowance for doubtful accounts is sufficient to cover this bad debt.

Required:

Set up a worksheet to develop corrected amounts for the 1992 income statement and balance sheet. Complete the worksheet and key your entries. Assume the income tax expense amount is correct despite the above terms. *Suggestion:* Set up pairs of columns for Trial Balance, Entries, Income Statement, Retained Earnings, and Balance Sheet. Also, you will need four lines for property, plant, and equipment, six for retained earnings, and three for administrative expense.

P 24–12
Incomplete
Records—Worksheet to
Develop Income Statement
and Balance Sheet
(L.O. 7)

Stanley Company has maintained single-entry records. In applying for a much-needed loan, a set of financial statements was required. An analysis of the records for 1991 provided the following data:

Cash receipts:	
Cash sales	$130,000
Collections on credit sales	43,000
Collections on trade notes	1,000
Purchase allowances	1,500
Miscellaneous revenue	250
Cash payments:	
Cash purchases	84,500
Payments to trade creditors.	34,100
Payment on mortgage on July 1, 1991, plus prepayment of	
one year's interest of $1,020 to July 1, 1992.	4,020
Sales commissions	7,200
Rent expense	2,400
General expenses (including interest)	14,590
Other operating expenses	29,800
Sales returns ($3,000, including $1,000 cash)	1,000
Insurance (renewal three-year premium, April 1)	468
Operational assets purchased.	1,500

	Balances	
	Jan. 1, 1991	**Dec. 31, 1991**
Cash.	$14,100	$10,172
Accounts receivable	13,000	18,000
Trade notes receivable	2,000	1,500
Inventory	10,000	18,400
Prepaid insurance	39	?

	Balances	
	Jan. 1, 1991	Dec. 31, 1991
Prepaid interest expense	600	510
Trade accounts payable.	26,500	23,800
Income taxes payable.	—	1,984
Accrued operating expenses payable	600	400
Operational assets (net)	35,400	33,290
Other assets	11,861	11,861
Common shares	40,000	40,000
Mortgage payable (6%, dated July 1, 1990)	20,000	?

No operational assets were sold during the year.

Required:

Prepare a worksheet to provide data for a detailed income statement for 1991 and a balance sheet at the end of 1991. Show how the amounts for the various entries were developed. *Suggestion:* Set up columns for Balances, January 1, 1991; Interim Entries—Debit and Credit; Income Statement; and Balance Sheet, December 31, 1991.

P 24–13
Incomplete Records:
Analysis to Compute
Income
(L.O. 7)

The following data were taken from the records of Rooster's Sporting Goods Store:

	Balances	
	Jan. 1, 1991	Dec. 31, 1991
Accounts receivable	$ 2,300	$ 3,900
Notes receivable (trade)	1,500	2,000
Interest receivable	90	70
Prepaid interest on notes payable	75	60
Inventory	9,255	10,400
Prepaid expenses (operating).	100	130
Store equipment (net)	8,500	8,600
Other assets	—	500
Accounts payable.	1,700	1,900
Notes payable (trade).	11,000	11,500
Notes payable (equipment)	—	500
Accrued interest payable	40	30
Accrued expenses (operating) payable	170	210
Interest revenue collected in advance	30	40

An analysis of the chequebook, canceled cheques, deposit slips, and bank statements provided the following summary for the year:

Balance, Jan. 1, 1991.		$ 4,200
Cash receipts:		
Cash sales	$23,000	
On accounts receivable.	7,600	
On notes receivable	1,000	
Interest revenue	160	31,760
Cash disbursements:		
Cash purchases	11,800	
On accounts payable	2,400	
On notes payable (trade)	500	
Interest expense	560	
Operating expenses	14,130	
Miscellaneous non-operating expenses	970	
Other assets purchased.	500	
Withdrawals by Rooster	2,400	(33,260)
Balance, Dec. 31, 1991		$ 2,700

Required:

1. Compute income by analysing the changes in the owner's equity account.
2. Prepare a detailed income statement with supporting schedules; show computations.

P 24–14

COMPREHENSIVE PROBLEM
♦

Multiple Accounting
Changes: Entries and
Reporting
(L.O. 2, 3, 4, 5, 6)

For Zealand Company accountants, 1991 was not a good year. The company made several financial accounting changes that year.

First, the company changed the total useful life from 20 years to 13 years on a $350,000 asset purchased January 1, 1988. The asset was originally expected to be sold for $50,000 at the end of its useful life, but that amount was also changed in 1991, to $200,000. Zealand applies the straight-line method of depreciation to this asset.

Second, the company changed from FIFO to LIFO, but is unable to recreate LIFO inventory layers. The FIFO 1991 beginning and ending inventories are $30,000 and $45,000. Under LIFO, the 1991 ending inventory is $35,000. The company expects LIFO to render income numbers more useful for prediction, given inflation.

Third, the company changed its policy for accounting for certain staff training expenses. Previously, the expenses were expensed as incurred. The new policy is to capitalize these costs and amortize them over three years. $100,000 was expensed in 1988, and $60,000 was expensed in 1990. In 1991, expenditures totalled $45,000.

Fourth, an error in amortizing patents was discovered in 1991. Patents costing $510,000 on January 1, 1989, were amortized over their legal life (17 years). The accountant neglected to obtain an estimate of the patents' economic life, which totals only five years.

Additional information: Zealand is a calendar fiscal year company, is subject to a 30% tax rate, and has had 10,000 common shares outstanding since 1986.

	1990	1991
Beginning retained earnings.	.$319,000	
Income before extraordinary items, after tax.	220,000	$325,000*
Extraordinary gain, net of tax.		10,000
Dividends declared	50,000	70,000

*This is the correct reported amount and includes the appropriate amounts related to all the accounting changes.

Required:

1. Record the 1991 entries necessary to make the accounting changes.
2. Prepare the 1990 and 1991 comparative income statement (lower portion) and retained earnings statement, including footnote disclosures for the accounting changes.

CASES

C 24–1
Analysis of Three
Accounting Changes
(L.O. 2, 3)

A business entity may change its method of accounting for certain items. The change may be classified as a change in accounting principle or accounting estimate.

Listed below are three independent, unrelated situations relating to accounting changes.

Situation 1: Able Company determined that the depreciable lives currently used for its operational assets were too long to best match the cost of using the assets with the revenue produced. At the beginning of the current year, the company decided to reduce the depreciable lives of all of its existing operational assets by five years.

Situation 2: On December 31, 1993, Baker Company reviewed its depreciation policies for fixed assets. As a result, they changed from sum-of-the years'-digits to straight-line depreciation. The company recognized that straight-line depreciation has been more widely used in the industry, and wished their statements to be more comparable.

Situation 3: Charlie Company entered into its first long-term construction contract in 1993 and decided to use percentage-of-completion for revenue recognition. Previous construction contracts had spanned less than one year, and the completed-contract method had been used.

Required:

For each of the situations described above, provide the information indicated below.

a. Type of accounting change.
b. Manner of reporting the change under current GAAP including a discussion of how amounts, if any, are computed.
c. Effect of the change on the financial statements, if any.
d. Note disclosures which would be necessary.

(AICPA adapted)

C 24–2
Ethical Considerations:
Accounting Changes
(L.O. 1)

In 1982, RTE Corporation more than doubled its EPS by changing depreciation methods. In justifying the change, the controller said:

> We realized that, compared to our competitors, our conservative method of depreciation might have hurt us with investors because of its negative impact on net earnings. ("Double Standard," *Forbes,* November 22, 1982.)

Although difficult to prove, there is considerable evidence that accounting changes are made for reasons other than improved financial reporting. GAAP is flexible in selecting accounting methods initially and in making subsequent changes.

Required:

Comment on the appropriateness of making accounting changes to fulfill financial reporting objectives. Consider ethics in your response.

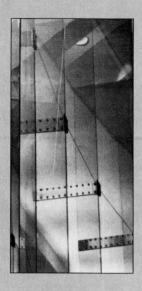

CHAPTER

25

Financial Statement Analysis and Changing Prices

After you have studied this chapter, you will be able to:

1. Explain the importance and limitations of financial statement information in the evaluation of investment opportunities.

2. Perform vertical (within years) and horizontal (across years) comparative percentage analyses.

3. Calculate a number of ratios used in financial statement analysis and interpret the results.

4. Explain the limitations of ratio analysis.

5. Explain the concept of capital market efficiency and what it implies for financial statement analysis.

6. Identify the effects of price changes on historical cost financial statements.

7. Discuss the advantages and disadvantages of general and specific price level adjusted financial statements.

8. Adjust financial statements for general price level changes (historical cost-constant dollar model).

9. Adjust financial statements for specific price level changes (current cost-nominal dollar, and current cost-constant dollar models).

◆

_____

INTRODUCTION
◆

Corporations have been described as a "network of contracts," contracts with individuals and other enterprises. Dealings with other corporate entities include contracts with suppliers, granting credit to customers or borrowers, leasing arrangements, as well as mergers, acquisitions, and the initiation of joint ventures. Before entering into such arrangements, both enterprises should investigate the operational and financial health of their potential customer, supplier, or partner.

The financial statements produced by firms are an important source of information for these decisions. But financial statement data are only a part, often a small part, of the information set used in making these important decisions. Financial statement information must be supplemented with information from other sources such as company management, investment advisors, trade associations, business periodicals, government agencies, and other materials distributed by and about the company. These latter sources are important because they disclose information on a more timely basis than do the published financial statements. For example, unreported litigation and liabilities can threaten the profit potential of a company. Publications such as *The Globe and Mail* and *The Financial Post* provide timely disclosure of such facts.

For instance, a company's obligations to provide health care to employees and particularly retirees were generally not recorded in the financial statements, or the disclosure notes, until recently. In one U.S. example, the buyout price put on a particular company, Armco, dropped by 10%, or $10 million, after last minute negotiations uncovered such a liability. In the early 1980s, when firms did not have to disclose the status of their pension plans (plan assets versus plan liabilities) similar surprises—unrecorded liabilities—also surfaced.[1]

As the conceptual framework points out, there are a number of financial statement users and a myriad of uses for the information contained in the financial statements. Financial institutions examine these statements to ascertain credit risk. Government agencies scrutinize financial reports in regard to excess profits, as they have done with the banking and oil and gas industries, to name a few. Labour unions seek information on the ability of firms to grant wage and work concessions. Communities examine these reports for evidence of good citizenship. Finally, current and potential investors and, in particular, those in the securities industry who advise investors, seek to evaluate the attractiveness of alternative investments.[2]

Decisions relating to businesses are particularly influenced by economic considerations, with earnings, financial position, and cash flows being especially significant factors. Financial statements that span several reporting periods and include selected long-term trend data are relevant sources of economic information. One of the primary objectives of financial statement analysis is to identify and assess major changes in trends, amounts, and relationships. Investigation and evaluation of the reasons underlying those changes are particularly important. Recognition of a turning point may provide an early warning of a significant change in the future success or failure of the business.

Financial statements are organized summaries of the extensive activities of a business. For example, the published financial statements of a large corporation, such as Brascan, CNR, or the Royal Bank of Canada, usually contain from 10 to 15 printed pages, including the supporting notes. It is difficult to imagine the number of transactions, the critical accounting decisions, and the details summarized in these few pages. Summarization inevitably reduces the amount of information available. On the other

_____

[1] Reported in "The Silent Killer," *Forbes,* February 23, 1987, p. 112.

[2] The notion here is to seek undervalued firms and is the basis of "fundamental analysis." See B. Graham, D. Dodd, and S. Cottle, *Security Analysis: Principles and Techniques,* 5th ed. (New York: McGraw-Hill, 1987). Some comments on this approach and an alternative point of view are given later in this chapter.

hand, excessive detail is undesirable because statement users experience time constraints in analysing a mass of data (called information overload).

The analysis and interpretation of financial statements is enhanced if users understand the meaning and purpose of the information. As the *CICA Handbook* states in section 1000, "Financial Statement Concepts," "Users are assumed to have a reasonable understanding of business and economic activities and accounting, together with a willingness to study the information with reasonable diligence." (par. 1000.19)

◆

OVERVIEW OF FINANCIAL STATEMENT ANALYSIS

◆

Financial statement analysis is an organized approach for extracting information from the financial statements that is relevant to the particular decision. The thrust of financial statement analysis in a particular situation should be determined by the decision(s) being contemplated. This chapter considers analytical and interpretative approaches widely used by decision makers.

Analysis and interpretation of financial statements involve the following sequential phases:

1. Examine the auditor's report.
2. Analyse the statement of accounting policies included in the notes to the financial statements.
3. Examine the financial statements as a whole, including notes and supporting schedules.
4. Apply analytical approaches such as:
   a. Comparative statement analysis.
   b. Horizontal and vertical percentage analysis.
   c. Ratio (proportionate) analysis.
5. Search for important supplemental information.

Examine the Auditor's Report

Financial analysts often suggest that in evaluating a financial statement, the first basic step is a careful examination of the auditor's report. This step presumes that the financial statements are audited. If they are not, an analyst should seriously evaluate the statement's credibility. The auditor's report is important because it provides the analyst with an independent and professional opinion about the fairness of the representations in the financial statements. The auditor's report calls attention to all major concerns the auditor has as a result of an intensive examination.

The most favourable auditor's report is an **unqualified (clean) opinion** in which the auditor states that the financial statements present the company's position fairly, in accordance with generally accepted accounting principles. While most statements receive an unqualified opinion, an analyst must still seek out information relevant to the particular questions of interest.

Instead of an unqualified opinion, the auditor can give a *qualified* opinion, an *adverse* opinion, or a *denial* of opinion about the financial statements. Each of these less favourable opinions must include an explanation by the auditor of the factors underlying the decision for the opinion. These unfavourable opinions alert the statement user to major problem areas in the company that should be investigated. An unfavourable auditor's opinion can cause the stock exchanges to stop public trading of the company's shares. Unfavourable opinions are unusual for major firms: *Financial Reporting in Canada* reports no such opinions for the 300 firms covered in its 1989 survey.

An unqualified auditor's report would appear as follows:

Auditor's Report

To the Shareholders of Walsh Corporation:

I have audited the balance sheet of Walsh Corporation as at October 31, 1993, and the statements of income, retained earnings, and changes in financial position for the year then ended. These financial statements are the responsibility of the company's management. My responsibility is to express an opinion on these financial statements based on my audit.

I conducted my audit in accordance with generally accepted auditing standards. Those standards require that I plan and perform an audit to obtain reasonable assurance whether the financial statements are free of material misstatement. An audit includes examining, on a test basis, evidence supporting the amounts and disclosures in the financial statements. An audit also includes assessing the accounting principles used and significant estimates made by management, as well as evaluating the overall financial statement presentation.

In my opinion, these financial statements present fairly, in all material respects, the financial position of the company as at October 31, 1993, and the results of its operations and the changes in its financial position for the year then ended in accordance with generally accepted accounting principles.

Edmonton, Alberta   (signed) C. M. Smith
December 5, 1993   CHARTERED ACCOUNTANT

The important concepts in the auditor's report are explained by the CICA as follows:[3]

"reasonable assurance"

It is not cost effective for the auditor to look at all evidence supporting the amounts and disclosures in the financial statements. The auditor obtains *reasonable* but not absolute assurance. He or she determines what, when, and how much to test on the basis of his or her professional judgment and expertise, with due regard to generally accepted auditing standards.

"material misstatement"

A *material misstatement* is one significant enough to affect the decision of a reader with reasonable knowledge of business and economic activities. Misstatements arise from departures from fact, inappropriate estimates, and omissions of information in relation to the standard of generally accepted accounting principles.

"An audit also includes assessing the accounting principles used and significant estimates made by management, as well as evaluating the overall financial statement presentation."

An audit involves the exercise of professional judgment. The auditor is trained in understanding accounting principles, in evaluating estimates which affect financial statements, and in looking at financial statements from an overall perspective. The auditor must know about the company's business activities, and the environment in which the company operates.

"in my opinion"

The auditor's report is not a statement of fact. It expresses an objective, professional opinion.

"present fairly" and *"in accordance with generally accepted accounting principles"*

These two phrases are linked in the auditor's report. Together they reflect the essential message of fair presentation in the financial statements when measured against the standard of generally accepted accounting principles.

---

[3] CICA, "The New Auditor's Report" (Toronto, 1990).

An example of an unfavourable audit report is as follows:

Auditor's Report

To the Shareholders of Walsh Corporation:

I have audited the balance sheet of Walsh Corporation as at October 31, 1993, and the statements of income, retained earnings and changes in financial position for the year then ended. These financial statements are the responsibility of the company's management. My responsibility is to express an opinion on these financial statements based on my audit.

I conducted my audit in accordance with generally accepted auditing standards. Those standards require that I plan and perform an audit to obtain reasonable assurance whether the financial statements are free of material misstatement. An audit includes examining, on a test basis, evidence supporting the amounts and disclosures in the financial statements. An audit also includes assessing the accounting principles used and significant estimates made by management, as well as evaluating the overall financial statement presentation.

The company's investment in Wilson Company Ltd., its only asset, which is carried at a cost of $10,000,000, has declined in value to an amount of $5,850,000. The loss in the value of this investment, in my opinion, is other than a temporary decline and in such circumstances, generally accepted accounting principles require that the investment be written down to recognize the loss. If this decline in value had been recognized, the investment, net income for the year, and retained earnings would have been reduced by $4,150,000.

In my opinion, because the write-down has not been made for the significant decline in value of the investment described in the preceding paragraph, these financial statements do not present fairly the financial position of the company as at October 31, 1993, and the results of its operations and the changes in its financial position for the year then ended in accordance with generally accepted accounting principles.

Edmonton, Alberta   (signed) C. M. Smith
December 5, 1993   CHARTERED ACCOUNTANT

Analyze the Statement of Accounting Policies

Accounting must accommodate a wide variety of circumstances. Although accounting principles and their implementation are established primarily by the *CICA Handbook* and by precedent, there is considerable room for judgment by the reporting entity and the independent accountant.

Consistent with the full disclosure principle, "Disclosure of Accounting Policies," section 1505 of the *CICA Handbook,* states that "the usefulness of financial statements is enhanced by disclosure of the accounting policies followed by an enterprise" and that such disclosure should be included as an integral part of the financial statements (par. 1505.03–.04). Accounting policies are the specific policies and methods that have been adopted by a company for preparation of its financial statements. The *Handbook* requires that a statement of these policies be provided either as the first note to the financial statements or as a separate summary, called "Summary of Accounting Policies," to which the financial statements are cross-referenced. The summary must disclose all important accounting policies. These policies include selections from among alternative acceptable accounting principles and methods, and use of principles and methods that are peculiar to an industry in which an enterprise operates, even if these are widely followed in that industry. Examples include the basis for consolidated statements, depreciation and amortization methods, inventory costing and valuation approaches used, translation of foreign currencies, revenue recognition on long-term construction contracts, policies for franchising, and leasing arrangements.

The information in the statement of accounting policies is fundamental to understanding, interpreting, and evaluating the information reported in the financial statements. It is particularly useful in evaluating the credibility of the statements and the reliability of the reported earnings, and in comparing data among companies, industries, and reporting periods.

Disclosure issues are considered in more depth in Chapter 26.

Integrative Examination of Financial Statements

After the auditor's opinion and the summary of accounting policies used by the company are examined, the evaluation and interpretive process continue with a careful study of the financial statements in their entirety. This phase of the analysis involves an integrative study of each statement to gain an overall perspective and to identify major strengths and weaknesses. This study also identifies unusual changes and turning points in the trends of sales revenue, expenses, income, asset structure, liabilities, capital structure, and cash flow.

The overall examination should include a review of all of the statements included and their footnotes. Consideration of the notes as a separate activity is not particularly fruitful because a specific note usually is informative only in the context of the specific statement item.

Concurrent with, or subsequent to, the overall examination of the financial statements under review, analysts find it helpful to apply some of the analytical techniques discussed in the next section.

CONCEPT REVIEW

1. Suggest several items beyond those obtainable from a financial report that should be considered when making an investment decision.
2. What are the five steps used in the analysis and interpretation of financial statements?
3. What information is included in the statement of accounting policies?

COMPARATIVE FINANCIAL STATEMENTS AND PERCENTAGE ANALYSIS

Various approaches are used to enhance communication through financial statements:

◆ Ratio analysis.
◆ Graphic presentations and special tabulations.
◆ Subclassifications of information on the statements.
◆ Comparative financial statements.
◆ Percentage analysis.
◆ Supplementary information in separate schedules.
◆ Notes to the statements.

This section considers comparative statements and percentage analysis; the following section discusses ratio analysis.

Comparative Financial Statements

Comparative financial statements present financial information for the current period and one or more past periods in a way that facilitates comparison along several reporting periods. Complete financial statements for the current and one or two immediately preceding periods often are presented in annual reports. In addition, selected financial statement data for several preceding periods may be reported in summary fashion. Firms often include earnings, capital expenditures, dividends, total assets, and working capital in these long-term summaries. The summaries are particularly relevant for financial statement analysis.

The annual financial statements for the current year give only a limited, short-term view of the successes and failures of a company. In contrast, the long-term summaries provide a broad overview of the company's financial past and clues about the firm's future.

Percentage Analysis of Financial Statements

Conversion of financial statement amounts to percentages reveals proportionate relationships that often are difficult to perceive from dollar amounts alone. Conversion of dollar amounts involves dividing one amount by another; the result is expressed as a percentage or ratio.

Analysts and other users typically rely on two variations of percentage analysis, called **vertical analysis** and **horizontal analysis.** *Vertical analysis* (also called *common-size analysis*) expresses each item on a particular financial statement as a percentage of one specific item, called the *base amount.* Vertical analysis emphasizes proportional relationships within each reporting period, rather than between reporting periods.

The base amount (the denominator) for the balance sheet is *total assets,* and each individual asset value (the numerator) is expressed as a percentage of total assets. For the income statement, the base amount is *net revenue.*

Exhibits 25–1 and 25–2 illustrate vertical percentage analysis for the balance sheet and income statement of Cominco Ltd. (Cominco is an integrated natural resource company with three main industry segments: mining and metals, chemicals and fertilizers, and steel and semiconductor manufacturing.) Placing the various items for the two periods side by side in the two columns facilitates comparison. Both the dollar amounts and vertical percentages are given for each reporting year.

A cursory examination of balance sheet percentages shows that Cominco's fixed assets increased as a percentage of total assets (from 61% to 64%). Long-term debt increased from 14% to 17% of total financing sources. Paradoxically, interest costs decreased from 2% to 1% of sales revenue. Percentage analysis often highlights areas for further investigation—interest costs are an example for Cominco. The notes to the financial statements reveal that a major portion of interest incurred was capitalized during the year.

Horizontal analysis involves the use of percentages or ratios to measure the extent that each item changes from one year (the base) to one or more following years. Exhibit 25–3 illustrates the use of horizontal percentage analysis on Cominco's consolidated income statement. The change is calculated by dividing the amount of increase or decrease for each item by the base year amount, 1988, which is the earliest reported period. For example, Cominco's cash and short-term investments increased from $89.5 million in 1988 to $182.7 million in 1989, an increase of 104% [($182.7 − $89.5)/ $89.5 = 1.04]. Horizontal analysis is applied to the balance sheet and to cash flows in exactly the same manner.

Items involving relatively large dollar amounts should be scrutinized more carefully than other items. For example, sales for Cominco involve millions of dollars, but many expenses are much smaller. A minor change in sales can be more significant than a major change in a smaller item. Horizontal analysis should also consider relationships between items. Cominco's sales revenue has declined 4%, while costs of products and distribution have declined 5%, implying that perhaps operating efficiencies have been implemented. Horizontal analysis is not restricted to the two or three years reported in the balance sheet and income statement. Cominco, as is common for many firms, provides a multiyear summary (five years) of selected financial data on page 7 of its annual report.

EXHIBIT 25–1   Cominco Ltd., Vertical Analysis, Balance Sheet

COMINCO LTD.
Comparative Balance Sheet
With Vertical Percentage Analysis
as of December 31, 1989 and 1988
(in thousands)

	1989 Amount	1989 Percent	1988 Amount	1988 Percent
Assets				
Current assets:				
Cash and short-term investments	$ 182,681	7%	$ 89,551	4%
Accounts receivable	242,774	10	249,721	12
Inventories	323,456	13	344,320	16
Prepaid expenses	12,152	—	22,878	1
	761,063	30	706,470	33
Share subscriptions receivable	11,000	—	22,000	1
Investments:				
Associated companies	85,693	4	79,263	4
Other investments	25,709	1	516	—
	111,402	5	79,779	4
Fixed assets:				
Land, buildings and equipment	1,377,857	56	1,120,016	53
Mineral properties and development	201,722	8	172,487	8
	1,579,579	64	1,292,503	61
Other assets	16,877	1	14,230	1
Total assets	$2,479,921	100%	$2,114,982	100%
Liabilities				
Current liabilities:				
Bank loans and notes payable	$ 41,613	2%	$ 799	—
Accounts payable and accrued liabilities	211,562	8	194,928	9%
Income and resource taxes	39,561	2	35,638	2
Long-term debt due within one year	5,189	—	54,094	3
	297,925	12	285,459	14
Long-term debt	421,832	17	289,137	14
Deferred liabilities	93,355	4	101,135	5
Income taxes provided but not currently payable	245,175	10	148,149	7
Minority interests	118,252	5	71,279	3
Shareholders' Equity				
Capital	647,758	26	720,240	34
Earnings reinvested in the business	665,532	26	495,830	23
Cumulative translation adjustment	(9,908)	—	3,753	—
Total shareholders' equity	1,303,382	52	1,219,823	57
Commitments and contingent liabilities	—		—	
Subsequent event	—		—	
Total shareholders' equity and liabilities	$2,479,921	100%	$2,114,982	100%

EXHIBIT 25–2 Cominco Ltd., Vertical Analysis, Income Statement

COMINCO LTD.
Comparative Income Statement
with Vertical Percentage Analysis
Years Ended December 31, 1989 and 1988
(in thousands except per share amounts)

	1989 Amount	1989 Percent	1988 Amount	1988 Percent
Revenue:				
Sales of products and services	$1,591,324	100	$1,660,386	100
Income from investments	18,380	1	7,552	—
Total revenue	1,609,704	101	1,667,938	100
Costs and expenses:				
Costs of products and distribution	1,033,649	65	1,084,643	65
General, administrative and selling	61,696	4	62,157	4
Mineral exploration	30,634	2	29,918	2
Interest	9,782	1	27,317	2
Depreciation, depletion and amortization . . .	69,964	4	72,388	4
Total costs and expenses	1,205,725	76	1,276,423	77
Earnings before the following	403,979	25	391,515	23
Add (deduct):				
Taxes on income including resource taxes . . .	(156,353)	(10)	(157,938)	(9)
Minority interests in net earnings of subsidiary companies.	(46,071)	(3)	(25,780)	(1)
Equity in earnings of associated companies . .	13,060	1	5,675	—
Earnings before extraordinary items	214,615	13	213,472	13
Extraordinary items	—		28,483	2
Net earnings	$ 214,615	13%	$ 241,955	15
Earnings per common share:*				
Basic:				
Earnings before extraordinary items	$ 2.64		$ 2.56	
Net earnings	$ 2.64		$ 2.92	
Fully diluted:				
Earnings before extraordinary items	$ 2.57		$ 2.47	
Net earnings	$ 2.57		$ 2.82	

* No percentage is calculated since amounts are per share.

CONCEPT REVIEW

1. How are the calculations for vertical analysis performed?
2. How are the calculations for horizontal analysis performed?
3. What is the difference in the comparisons made between vertical and horizontal analysis?

RATIO ANALYSIS
◆

Ratio analysis involves measuring the proportional relationship between two single amounts. These amounts may be selected from one financial statement, such as the income statement, or from two statements, such as the balance sheet and income statement. The amounts may represent the balances of two different accounts, the balance of one account and a classification total (such as total assets), or two classification totals.

EXHIBIT 25-3   Cominco Ltd., Horizontal Analysis, Income Statement

COMINCO LTD.

Comparative Income Statement
with Horizontal Percentage Analysis
Years Ended December 31, 1989 and 1988
(in thousands)

	1989		1988
	Amount	Percent	
Revenue:			
Sales of products and services	$1,591,324	(4)%	$1,660,386
Income from investments	18,380	143	7,552
Total revenue	1,609,704	(3)	1,667,938
Costs and expenses:			
Costs of products and distribution	1,033,649	(5)	1,084,643
General, administrative and selling	61,696	—	62,157
Mineral exploration	30,634	2	29,918
Interest	9,782	(64)	27,317
Depreciation, depletion and amortization	69,964	(3)	72,388
Total costs and expenses	1,205,725	(6)	1,276,423
Earnings before the following	403,979	3	391,515
Add (deduct):			
Taxes on income including resource taxes	(156,353)	(1)	(157,938)
Minority interests in net earnings of subsidiary companies.	(46,071)	78	(25,780)
Equity in earnings of associated companies . . .	13,060	130	5,675
Earnings before extraordinary items	214,615	—	213,472
Extraordinary items	—	—	28,483
Net earnings	$ 214,615	(11)	$ 241,955
Earnings per common share:			
Basic:			
Earnings before extraordinary items	$ 2.64	3	$ 2.56
Net earnings	$ 2.64	(10)	$ 2.92
Fully diluted:			
Earnings before extraordinary items.	$ 2.57	4	$ 2.47
Net earnings	$ 2.57	(9)	$ 2.82

As an example, the *current ratio,* which expresses the relationship between current assets and current liabilities, is one way of analysing a company's working capital position. Using Cominco's 1989 balance sheet:

Total current assets	$761.063 million
Total current liabilities	297.925 million
Difference—working capital.	$463.138 million

The amount of working capital, $463.14 million, standing alone, is a useful figure; however, expression as a ratio adds insight to this relationship. The current ratio based on the above amounts is 2.55:

$$\text{Current ratio} = \frac{\text{Current assets}}{\text{Current liabilities}} = \frac{\$761.063}{\$297.925} = 2.55$$

This ratio can also be expressed as 255%, 2.55 to 1, or that there are $2.55 of current assets for each $1 of current liabilities.

Ratio analysis is helpful when the proportional relationship between the selected factors sheds additional light on the interpretation of the individual absolute amounts.

In view of the large number of ratios that could be computed, it is important for analysis purposes to select those amounts that involve relevant relationships and items that are functionally related. For example, the relationship between bad debt expense and credit sales is more meaningful than the relationship between bad debt expense and total sales, which would include cash sales.

Ratios are more helpful if used comparatively, rather than in isolation. Ratios should be compared to those of the same firm but for different time periods, and to those of other firms. Several investment services, Dun & Bradstreet for instance, supply industry data against which to compare the ratios of individual firms. In addition, the *purposes* for which the ratios are to be used must be considered. Investors, managers, and creditors encounter different kinds of problems and decisions. Therefore, different sets of ratios are meaningful to each group. In a later section, the usefulness and limitations of ratio analysis are discussed in more depth.

Because a complete study of ratio analysis is beyond the scope of this text, only representative ratios having general application are discussed.[4] The analyses selected for discussion cover ratios that measure:

1. Liquidity (solvency).
2. Efficiency (activity).
3. Equity position and coverage.
4. Profitability.

The discussion uses the financial statement data for Cominco given in Exhibits 25–1 and 25–2. To assess whether a ratio indicates a favourable or unfavourable condition, the firm's history, industry norms, and other factors must be considered. Such an assessment has not been attempted for Cominco.

Ratios that Measure Liquidity (Solvency)

Ratios in this category are designed to measure a firm's ability to pay its obligations. Ratios often used to measure liquidity are summarized in Exhibit 25–4.

Current ratio   This ratio (previously computed as 2.55 for Cominco) has a long history as an index of short-term liquidity. According to accounting historians, it was the first financial ratio developed.[5] The ratio measures the ability of the business to meet the maturing claims of its creditors from current operating assets. The amount of working capital and the related ratio have a direct impact on the amount of short-term credit that can be obtained. The minimum acceptable current ratio is unique to the industry in which the business operates, and even to the business itself in the light of its operating and financial characteristics. For example, a ratio of 2.11 is adequate in one situation, but too low or too high in another.[6]

The current ratio is only one measure or index of ability to meet short-term obligations and must be interpreted carefully. For example, a high current ratio can result from overstocking inventory, and the ratio is influenced by the inventory cost flow method used. Furthermore, a high current ratio can indicate excess funds that should be invested or used for other purposes.[7]

---

[4] There is no single "generally accepted" method of computing specific ratios or of determining the values to be used in their computation. The formulas presented in this chapter reflect only one approach. For a more detailed list of ratios, see J. Palmer, "Technical Consulting Practice Aid No. 3," in *Financial Ratio Analysis* (New York: AICPA, 1983).

[5] W. Cooper and Y. Ijiri, *Kohler's Dictionary for Accountants,* 6th ed. (Englewood Cliffs, N.J.: Prentice Hall, 1983), p. 146.

[6] A popular rule of thumb is that the current ratio should be at least 2.00. According to this rule, having twice the current assets as current liabilities implies sufficient resources to pay current liabilities as they come due.

[7] The term *fund* is used in a general sense in this chapter and includes cash, cash equivalents, other securities that are readily converted into cash, or, more generally, working capital.

EXHIBIT 25-4 Ratios that Measure Liquidity (Solvency)

Ratio	Formula for Computation	Summary of Significance
1. Current (or working capital) ratio.	$\dfrac{\text{Current assets}}{\text{Current liabilities}}$	Test of short-term liquidity. Indicates ability to meet current obligations from current assets as a going concern. Measure of adequacy of working capital.
2. Acid-test (or quick) ratio.	$\dfrac{\text{Quick assets}}{\text{Current liabilities}}$	A more severe test of immediate liquidity than the current ratio. Tests ability to meet sudden demands upon liquid current assets, particularly cash.
3. Working capital to total assets.	$\dfrac{\text{Working capital}}{\text{Total assets}}$	Indicates relative liquidity of total assets and distribution of resources employed as to liquidity.
4. Defensive-interval ratio.	$\dfrac{\text{Defensive assets}}{\text{Projected daily operational expenditures}}$	The maximum days of operation with present liquid assets.

Acid-Test (or Quick) Ratio This ratio is used as a test of *immediate liquidity* and equals quick assets divided by current liabilities. Quick assets include cash, accounts receivable, short-term notes receivable, and short-term investments in marketable securities. These assets generally represent funds readily available for paying current obligations. Inventories, on the other hand, must be sold and collection made before cash is available for paying obligations. In many cases, particularly for raw materials and work in process inventories, the marketability of the inventory involves considerable uncertainty as to the amount and timing of the ultimate conversion to cash. Also, prepaids generally do not represent liquid resources because they represent claims to goods or services, not to cash.

Traditionally, an acid-test ratio of 1 to 1 (a rule-of-thumb standard) is considered desirable. As with the current ratio, the acid-test ratio for a particular company must be evaluated in terms of industry characteristics and business considerations. Cominco's acid-test ratio for 1989 is:

$$\frac{\text{Quick assets}}{\text{Total current liabilities}} = \frac{\$182,681 + \$242,774}{\$297,925} = 1.43$$

Cominco could liquidate its current debt without requiring additional debt financing, and without relying on the sale of its existing inventory, assuming collection of its receivables in a reasonably short period of time.

Working Capital to Total Assets The ratio of working capital to total assets is a generalized expression of the distribution and liquidity of the assets employed after current liabilities are deducted from current assets. Cominco's working capital to total assets ratio for 1989 is:

$$\frac{\text{Working capital}}{\text{Total assets}} = \frac{\$761,063 - \$297,925}{\$2,479,921} = .19$$

An excessively high ratio might indicate excess cash, inability to collect receivables, or overstocking of inventory, whereas a low ratio indicates a weakness in the current position.

Defensive-Interval Ratio Relating current (or quick) assets to current liabilities presumes these assets are used to pay the existing liabilities. An alternative, favoured in some quarters, is a measure of how long the firm can operate using only its present liquid resources. This measure is the ratio of the firm's defensive assets (quick assets) to projected daily expenditures for production, distribution, and administration. Cominco's defensive-interval ratio for 1989 is:

$$\frac{\text{Defensive assets (quick assets)}}{\text{Projected daily operational expenditures}} = \frac{\$182,681 + \$242,774}{(\$1,033,649 + \$61,696)/365} = 142 \text{ days}$$

Cominco's ratio appears substantial. Operating funds from future operations should arrive before current liquid assets are exhausted. Note that the denominator reflects only operating costs: mineral exploration costs, excluded from the ratio, reflect an activity more likely to be curtailed or eliminated if Cominco encounters severely adverse business conditions.

Ratios that Measure Efficiency (Activity)

Efficiency measures provide another way of evaluating liquidity. In fact, these measures were developed in part to correct for the previously discussed static liquidity measures. More generally, the efficiency measures provide information about how effectively the firm is using its assets. Exhibit 25–5 lists six efficiency ratios.

Accounts Receivable Turnover and Age of Accounts Receivable The ability to quickly convert credit sales (accounts receivable) into cash is an important objective of cash management programs. The balance in trade receivables is related to the credit sales for the period and to the credit terms. The two accounts receivable ratios in Exhibit 25–5 provide important insights into the efficiency of a firm's credit and collection activities. Assuming all Cominco's 1989 sales are on credit, these two ratios are computed as follows:[8]

$$\text{Accounts receivable turnover} = \frac{\text{Net credit sales}}{\text{Average accounts receivable (net)}}$$

$$\frac{\$1,591,324}{(\$242,774 + \$249,721)/2} = \frac{\$1,591,324}{\$\ 246,248} = 6.46 \text{ times}$$

$$\text{Age of accounts receivable} = \frac{365 \text{ days}}{\text{Accounts receivable turnover}}$$

$$= \frac{365}{6.46} = 57 \text{ average days to collect}$$

The numerator of accounts receivable turnover is net credit sales, which encompasses the entire reporting period. Therefore, the denominator uses the *average* accounts receivable, a more representative value for the amount of accounts receivable outstanding during the period than either beginning or ending accounts receivable.

Accounts receivable were generated and collected ("turned over") 6.46 times during 1989. On average, receivables required 57 days to collect—a relatively long term for collection. An age of accounts receivable closer to a month would reflect traditional industry credit terms requiring payment of the net invoice within 30 days of sale to avoid interest charges.[9] Cominco's credit terms may be longer, though, and should be investigated before conclusions are drawn.

---

[8] In many cases, the financial statement user must use total sales for this ratio because the breakdown of sales into cash and credit sales is not available. In the industries in which Cominco operates, cash purchases would be rare.

[9] Some analysts prefer to use 250 (5-day workweek) or 300 (6-day workweek) days as an approximation of the number of business days in the year. Using fewer days would improve Cominco's figure somewhat, but comparative data would demonstrate equivalent trends.

EXHIBIT 25-5   Ratios that Measure Efficiency (Activity)

Ratio	Formula for Computation	Summary of Significance
1. Accounts receivable turnover.	$\dfrac{\text{Net credit sales}}{\text{Average trade receivables (net)}}$	Credit and collection efficiency of trade accounts and notes.
2. Age of accounts receivable.	$\dfrac{365\ (\text{days})}{\text{Accounts receivable turnover}}$	Average number of days to collect trade receivables.
3. Inventory turnover.	$\dfrac{\text{Cost of goods sold}}{\text{Average inventory}}$	Indicates liquidity of inventory. Average number of times inventory was "turned over," or sold, during the period. Indicates possible over- or understocking.
4. Working capital turnover.	$\dfrac{\text{Net sales}}{\text{Average working capital}}$	Indicates the effectiveness with which average working capital was used to generate sales.
5. Asset turnover.	$\dfrac{\text{Net sales}}{\text{Average total assets}}$	Indicates efficiency of asset utilization.
6. Net cash flow to current liabilities.	$\dfrac{\text{Net cash flow from operations}}{\text{Current liabilities}}$	Ability to pay current liabilities.

The example raises computational issues:

♦ Should the total of cash and credit sales, or credit sales only, be used in the computation? Because only credit sales cause accounts receivable, a more stable and meaningful ratio results if only credit sales are used. Otherwise a shift in the proportion of cash to credit sales affects the ratio, even though collection experience is unchanged.

♦ Should the ending balance in receivables or average receivables be used? The *average monthly* receivables balance eliminates seasonal influences. Ideally, the average is determined by adding the 13 monthly balances (January 1 and January 31 through December 31) of trade accounts receivable and then dividing by 13. In the absence of monthly balances, the average of the annual beginning and ending balance is used (with a potentially significant loss of information).

♦ Receivables should be net of the allowance for doubtful accounts. The amounts used in the Cominco example were net amounts.

♦ Trade notes receivable should be included in average receivables.

Inventory Turnover   The inventory turnover ratio expresses the relationship between cost of goods sold and the average inventory balance. Cominco's inventory turnover for 1989 is:

$$\frac{\text{Cost of goods sold}}{\text{Average inventory}} = \frac{\$1,033,649}{(\$323,456 + \$344,320)/2} = 3.1 \text{ times}$$

The result indicates that Cominco turns its inventory into sales about three times a year. Care must be taken when using aggregate financial statement amounts, however. For example, many kinds of inventory in the three operating segments are lumped together in the consolidated balance sheet. Turnover by inventory type would be more meaningful.

Inventory turnover varies across industries and businesses. For example, grocery stores experience high inventory turnover, whereas antique dealers experience just the opposite. The turnover ratio represents an average across all inventory items and does not reflect necessarily the rate for individual items. Thus, a grocery store with an average turnover of 20 will have items on the shelves that have not turned over at all for a three-month period. Furthermore, this ratio is influenced by the inventory costing method used, which also affects comparison among companies. For example, when inventory prices are rising, companies using LIFO will tend to have higher turnover rates than those using other cost flow methods because inventory reflects lower priced goods.

Working Capital Turnover   Working capital has a functional relationship to sales revenue through accounts receivable, inventory, and cash. Therefore, the ratio of sales revenue to working capital is used as a measure of the effectiveness of a company's use of working capital to generate revenue. Cominco's working capital turnover ratio for 1989 is:

$$\frac{\text{Net sales revenue}}{\text{Average working capital}} = \frac{\$1,591,324}{[(\$761,063 - \$297,925) + (\$706,470 - \$285,459)]/2}$$
$$= 3.6 \text{ times}$$

Comparing working capital turnover (3.6) to accounts receivable turnover (6.46) and inventory turnover (3.1) suggests that Cominco does a better job of collecting its receivables than of using inventory to generate sales. Remember that accounts receivable turnover and inventory turnover are components of working capital turnover.

Asset Turnover   This ratio is calculated by dividing net sales by average total assets. The asset turnover ratio extends the idea of efficient use of working capital to all assets. Unfortunately, the ratio is higher (better) for firms using older, more depreciated assets. To the extent the ratio is used to evaluate performance, management is discouraged from replacing older, inefficient assets. Cominco's asset turnover ratio for 1989 is:

$$\frac{\text{Net sales revenue}}{\text{Average total assets}} = \frac{\$1,591,324}{(\$2,479,921 + \$2,114,982)/2} = .69 \text{ times}$$

Cominco is generating approximately 70 cents of sales for each $1.00 of assets employed in the business per year. Because of its limitations, asset turnover should be used with care and only in conjunction with other related measures.

Net Cash Flow to Current Liabilities   This ratio indicates the ability of the firm to cover its current liabilities. It is placed in this category of ratios (efficiency or activity measures) because its numerator is net cash flow from operations, rather than a balance sheet amount. Cominco's net cash flow from operations is $482,037, obtained from its 1989 statement of cash flows (not reproduced here). Therefore, Cominco's net cash flow to current liabilities ratio for 1989 is:

$$\frac{\text{Net cash flow from operations}}{\text{Current liabilities}} = \frac{\$482,037}{\$297,925} = 1.62$$

In 1989, Cominco's operating activities provided 162% of the cash required to liquidate its ending current liabilities.

Ratios that Measure Equity Position and Coverage

The balance sheet reports the two basic sources of funds used by a business: owners' equity and creditors' equity (debt). The relationships between these two different types of equities are measured because they reflect the financial strengths and weaknesses of the business. In particular, the long-term solvency of a business and its potential capacity to generate and obtain investment resources are affected by the proportion of debt to equity. Exhibit 25–6 summarizes five ratios used to measure equity and coverage relationships.

The first two ratios in Exhibit 25–6 focus on the amount of resources provided by creditors as opposed to the amount provided by owners. Because debt and equity capital have significantly different characteristics, the relationship between debt and owners' equity is important. Debt requires the payment of interest at specific intervals. In addition, the principal must be paid at maturity regardless of whether the company

EXHIBIT 25-6   Ratios that Measure Equity Position and Coverage

Ratio	Formula for Computation	Summary of Significance
1. Debt to equity.	$\dfrac{\text{Total liabilities}}{\text{Owners' equity}}$	Measures the balance between resources provided by creditors and resources provided by owners (including retained earnings).
2. Debt to total assets.	$\dfrac{\text{Total liabilities}}{\text{Total assets}}$	Proportion of assets provided by creditors. Extent of leverage.
3. Book value per common share.	$\dfrac{\text{Common shareholders' equity}}{\text{Number of outstanding common shares}}$	Number of dollars of common equity (at book value) per common share outstanding at year-end.
4. Times interest earned.	$\dfrac{\text{Income before taxes and interest}}{\text{Interest charges}}$	Income available to cover interest.
5. Cash flow per share.	$\dfrac{\text{Net cash flow from operations}}{\text{Number of outstanding common shares}}$	Measures cash generated per common share outstanding at year-end.

earned income or incurred a loss. Interest on debt is an expense and is tax deductible. In contrast to debt, owners' equity does not have a maturity date. Dividends are paid only if earnings and cash have accumulated and dividends are declared. A dividend is not an expense and is not tax deductible. Equity ratios are closely monitored by interested parties.

Debt to Equity Ratio   This equity ratio is the most widely used equity ratio because it provides a direct reading of the relationship between debt and owners' equity. Cominco's debt-to-equity ratio for 1989 is:

$$\frac{\text{Total liabilities}}{\text{Owners' equity}} = \frac{\$297,925 + \$421,832 + \$93,355}{\$1,303,382} = .62$$

For every $1 of equity, Cominco has 62 cents in liabilities. Again, care must be taken when interpreting this number. The book value of debt is usually much closer to its market value than are shareholders' equity amounts, which reflect value when the equity was issued and when income was earned. Better measures would rely on current market values. While current market values are available for actively traded securities, they are not easily obtained in most other cases.

The definition of debt must also be carefully considered. Should deferred taxes and the minority interest be included? Many analysts exclude these items, because they do not involve firm obligations to transfer future economic benefits. Others prefer to examine only the relationship between *long-term* debt and equity, as indicative of the permanent capital arrangements.

Debt to Total Assets   This ratio measures the relationship between debt and total assets. Therefore, it represents the percentage of total resources provided by debt holders. Cominco's 1989 ratio is:

$$\frac{\text{Total liabilities}}{\text{Total assets}} = \frac{\$297,925 + \$421,832 + \$93,355}{\$2,479,921} = .33$$

The debt holders provided 33% of the total assets, and the owners (or other deferred claimants) provided the remaining 67%.

Book Value per Common Share Book value per common share is computed by dividing total common shareholders' equity by the number of common shares outstanding at year's end. When more than one share class is outstanding, total shareholders' equity is *allocated* among the various share classes in conformity with the legal and statutory claims that are effective in case of liquidation of the company. Because additional share classes typically are preferred, the usual case requires an allocation based on the rights of the preferred shareholders. Liquidation, cumulative, and participating preferences must be included in the computation.

According to the notes to the financial statements, Cominco has eight different preferred share issues outstanding or subscribed at the end of 1989. The issuance (or subscription) proceeds total $206.042 million. No preferred dividends are in arrears. To calculate the book value of common shares, we should take the total shareholders' equity and subtract the liquidation price of each of the eight preferred share issues. However, this information is not apparent from the disclosure notes. We will assume that the preferred shares would be entitled to their original investment on liquidation. In fact, there may be a significant premium or discount from original issuance price built into a liquidation value.

Computation of book value per share for Cominco at December 31, 1989, is (all figures in thousands except per share amounts):

Total shareholders' equity	$1,303,382
Less: liquidation value of preference shares (assumed value)	(206,042)
Balance applicable to common shareholders	$1,097,340
Common shares outstanding at year-end (from disclosure notes)	79,331.1
Book value per share ($1,097,340/79,331.1)	$13.83

Although often computed, book value per common share has limited usefulness. It has little, if any, correlation to the market value of the common shares ($26 for Cominco on December 31, 1989). Market values reflect investors' expectations of the future cash flows of Cominco, market values of the firm's tangible and intangible assets, and a myriad of other factors to which the stock market reacts. Some investors view with interest shares that have a book value significantly *in excess* of market price because this may suggest a "good buy": the total assets of a business, recorded at cost, have book values considerably below market values, particularly during a period of rising prices.

Times Interest Earned This ratio is computed by dividing income before taxes and interest by interest charges (including capitalized interest). The ratio indicates how many times interest charges are covered by available income. Taxes are paid after interest is deducted; therefore, income before taxes and interest is used in the numerator. Cominco's 1989 interest coverage ratio is:

$$\frac{\text{Income before taxes and interest}}{\text{Interest charges}} = \frac{\$214,615 + \$156,353 + \$9,782}{\$9,782 + \$26,155^*} = 10.6 \text{ times}$$

* Capitalized interest is from the disclosure notes, not reproduced here.

Cominco appears to have no problem covering its interest charges.

Cash Flow per Share As discussed in Chapter 23, various measures of cash flow per share are computed by financial statement users. These measures are receiving increased attention, partly due to the inclusion of the statement of changes in financial position in the annual report. The measure chosen for discussion in this text relates net cash flow from operations to the number of common shares outstanding at year-end. For Cominco, in 1989, this ratio is:

$$\frac{\text{Net cash flow from operations}}{\text{Number of outstanding common shares}} = \frac{\$482,037^*}{79,331.1} = \$6.08 \text{ per share}$$

* From Cominco's statement of cash flows, not reproduced here.

This measure should be interpreted with extreme caution. It represents neither the cash flowing through the firm nor the cash available to the common shareholders. In the United States, FASB has prohibited the publication of this ratio in the financial statements to avoid the potential for misleading conclusions.

Ratios that Measure Profitability

Many investors are more interested in a company's income statement than in its balance sheet. This is because a company can continue to expand, develop, generate high cash inflows, and pay attractive dividends when its long-term earnings record is good and appears likely to be favourable in the future. Consequently, ratio analysis related to profitability is given considerable attention by both investors and creditors. Exhibit 25–7 summarizes several ratios that are widely used to help assess the earnings and cash flow strengths of a business.

Profit Margin on Sales   This ratio is widely used as an index of profitability. It represents the percentage of net sales remaining after all expenses are recognized. However, one significant factor related to profitability, the total amount of assets used to earn income, is given no consideration in the ratio. To illustrate, assume the accounts of a firm showed the following data: income, $20,000; net sales $200,000; and total assets, $1,000,000. In this case the profit margin on sales appears to be quite high at 10% ($20,000/$200,000). However, when earnings performance is measured by the 2% return on total assets ($20,000/$1,000,000), it appears to be low. Thus, the profit margin ratio has value primarily for evaluation of trends and for comparison with industry and competitor statistics.

Cominco's 1989 profit margin on sales is computed as follows:

$$\frac{\text{Income}}{\text{Net sales}} = \frac{\$214,615}{\$1,609,704} = .13$$

Cominco kept (as income) 13% of its sales. The remainder went to cover expenses.

Return on Investment   Many analysts consider return on total assets to be the single most important ratio because it incorporates both earnings and investment. Return on any investment is computed by dividing the income by the investment cost.

The broad concept of return on investment has two important applications for a single business entity:

♦ Evaluating proposed capital additions and other investment decisions on the basis of projected cash flows.[10]
♦ Measuring the annual rate of return earned on the total assets employed during the period; this analysis is based on accrual accounting results (book values) for each accounting period standing alone.

The discussion in this section relates to the latter application. With an income measure in the numerator, return on the investment for a business is computed on the basis of either total assets or owners' equity (ratios 2a and 2b in Exhibit 25–7).

Financial analysts also use the two return ratios together to measure financial **leverage,** also called *trading on the equity.* Financial leverage is the effect of borrowing at a higher or lower rate of interest than the rate of return earned on total assets. To illustrate, if a business can borrow at 8% and earn 12% on the funds borrowed, the financial leverage is *positive.* In contrast, if the borrowing rate is 12% and the earnings rate is 8%, the financial leverage is *negative.* Businesses borrow in anticipation of positive financial leverage.

---

[10] For a fundamental discussion, see H. Bierman and S. Smidt, *The Capital Budgeting Decision,* 7th ed. (New York: Macmillan, 1988), or J. Van Horne, *Financial Management and Policy* (Englewood Cliffs, N.J.: Prentice Hall, 1987).

EXHIBIT 25–7   Ratios that Measure Profitability

Ratio	Formula for Computation	Summary of Significance
1. Profit margin on sales.	$\dfrac{\text{Income*}}{\text{Net sales}}$	Indicates net profitability of each dollar of sales revenue.
2. Return on investment. *a.* On total assets.	$\dfrac{\text{Income plus interest expense (after tax)}}{\text{Average total assets}^{\dagger}}$	Rate earned on *all resources* used. Measures earnings on all investment provided by owners and creditors.
b. On owners' equity.	$\dfrac{\text{Income}}{\text{Average owners' equity}}$	Rate earned on resources provided by owners (excludes creditors). Measures earnings accruing to the owners.
3. Earnings per share, common shares (EPS).	$\dfrac{\text{Income associated with common shares}}{\text{Common shares outstanding}}$	Income earned on each common share. Indicates ability to pay dividends and to grow from within. Discussed in Chapter 22.
4. Price-earnings ratio.	$\dfrac{\text{Market price per share}}{\text{Earnings per share}}$	Reflects the relationship between the latest earnings per share amount and the current market price per share; provides a rough measure of how the market values the company.
5. Dividend payout ratio: *a.* Based on income to common.	$\dfrac{\dfrac{\text{Cash dividends per common share}}{\text{Income less}}}{\text{preferred dividends}}$	Measures the percentage of income that is represented by cash dividends to common.
b. Based on market price of common.	$\dfrac{\text{Cash dividends per common share}}{\text{Market price per share}}$	Provides a rough estimate of the expected rate of return per share.

* Income before extraordinary items, rather than net income, usually is preferable. The inclusion of extraordinary gains and losses is misleading because they are unusual and infrequent.

† Average total assets as used here is also called total liabilities plus owners' equity, total equities, and total investment. These three terms usually refer to the same balance sheet amount.

To illustrate computation of return on total assets, return on owners' equity, and financial leverage, the following data for Cominco is restated for convenience (figures in thousands):

	1989	1988
Balance sheet:		
Total assets	$2,479,921	$2,114,982
Total liabilities*	813,112	675,731
Total shareholders' equity	1,303,382	1,219,823
Preferred equity (from disclosure notes)	206,042	282,589
Income statement:		
Total revenues (pretax)	$1,609,704	$1,667,938
Total expenses (pretax and before		
interest expense)†	1,228,954	1,269,211
Interest expense (pretax)	9,782	27,317
Pretax income.	370,968	371,410
Income tax ($156,353 ÷ 370,968 = 42%)	156,353	157,938
Income before extraordinary items.	214,615	213,472
Extraordinary gain (loss), net of tax	—	28,483
Net income	$ 214,615	$ 241,955

* ($297,925 + $421,832 + $93,355); ($285,459 + $289,137 + $101,135).

† ($1,205,725 − $9,782 + $46,071 − $13,060); ($1,276,423 − $27,317 + $25,780 − $5,675).

Cominco's *return on total assets* for 1989 is:

$$\frac{\text{Income} + \text{Interest expense, net of tax}}{\text{Average total assets}}$$

$$\frac{\$214,615 + \$9,782(1 - .42)}{(\$2,479,921 + \$2,114,982)/2} = 9.6\%$$

Interest expense (net of income tax) is added back to net income because the interest is paid to creditors of the entity. Because the denominator includes the resources provided by both creditors and owners, the numerator must include the return on both types of investment. Income before extraordinary items usually should be used to avoid any distortion due to non-recurring and unusual items.

Return on total assets measures the profitability of the total assets available to the business. It indicates the efficiency with which management used the total available resources to earn income. A more general return on assets (ROA) measure, defined as the ratio of income and average total assets, can be expressed as the product of profit margin on sales and asset turnover:[11]

$$ROA = \text{Return on sales} \times \text{Asset turnover}$$

$$\frac{\text{Income}}{\text{Average total assets}} = \frac{\text{Income}}{\text{Net sales}} \times \frac{\text{Net sales}}{\text{Average total assets}}$$

Therefore, the return on total assets can be increased with a larger profit margin on sales or a larger asset turnover. Increased asset turnover can be accomplished by increasing the turnover of assets such as inventory and accounts receivable.

Cominco's *return on owners equity* for 1989 is:

$$\frac{\text{Income}}{\text{Average shareholders' equity}}$$

$$\frac{\$214,615}{(\$1,303,382 + \$1,219,823)/2} = 17\%$$

Return on owners' equity measures the return that accrues to the shareholders after the interest paid to the creditors is deducted. It does not measure the efficiency with which total resources are used, but rather the residual return to the owners on their investment in the business.

Alternatively, *return on common shareholders' equity* may be calculated as follows:

$$\frac{\text{Income} - \text{Preferred dividends}}{\text{Average common shareholders' equity}}$$

Cominco's statement of retained earnings reports $5,204,000 in preferred dividends declared in 1989. Therefore, return on common equity is calculated as follows (all figures in thousands):

$$\frac{\$214,615 - \$5,204}{((\$1,303,382 - \$206,042) + (\$1,219,823 - \$282,589))/2} = 20.6\%$$

The difference between return on owners' equity and return on total assets is financial leverage. The only difference between these two percentages is the effect of debt. The financial leverage for Cominco in 1989 is a positive 7.4% (17% − 9.6%) based on total shareholders' equity. The 7.4% positive effect in favour of owners' equity resulted because the company earned a higher rate of return on total assets than the after-tax rate of interest paid for borrowed resources. Without debt, the return on total assets and owners' equity is the same.

---

[11] This more general measure does not add back after-tax interest and is presented only to illustrate the disaggregation of return on assets into two other ratios previously discussed.

Earnings per Share   This ratio relates income to the average number of common shares outstanding. It reduces income (or loss) to a per share basis. Cominco's 1989 EPS of $2.64 appears in the income statement (Exhibit 25–2).[12]

Price-Earnings Ratio (P-E Ratio)   This ratio, sometimes called the *multiple,* is frequently used by analysts and investors for evaluating share prices because it relates the earnings of the business to the *current market price* of its shares. This ratio changes each time the market price of the shares changes. Years ago, multiples of 20 or more were not unusual; however, multiples in the range of 5 to 10 currently are more common. The multiple usually should be computed on the basis of EPS before extraordinary items. Cominco's price-earnings ratio for 1989 (based on Cominco's end-of-year market price per common share of about $26) is:

$$\frac{\text{Market price per share}}{\text{Earnings per share}} = \frac{\$26}{\$2.64} = 9.8$$

Cominco's P-E ratio is reasonably high. The primary weakness of this ratio is that the numerator and denominator are measured as of the same date only at the end of the fiscal year. The P-E ratio is often computed during the year with the EPS amount from the most recent financial statements. However, some investment services compensate for this problem to some extent by using a moving quarterly average.

Dividend Payout Ratio   Exhibit 25–7 shows two variations for computing this ratio. The first (5*a*) relates cash dividends declared on common shares during the reporting period to the income *available to common shareholders* for that period. It measures the percentage of income that is distributed as cash dividends. For Cominco, this ratio for 1989 is:

$$\frac{\text{Cash dividends to common}}{\text{Income} - \text{Preferred dividends}} = \frac{\$39,642^*}{\$214,615 - \$5,204^*} = .19$$

* Dividends are taken from Cominco's retained earnings statement, not reproduced here.

The primary weakness of this ratio is the timing mismatch between the numerator (the dividend declaration date) and the denominator (the end of the reporting period).

   The second variation of the ratio (5*b*) relates cash dividends per common share to the ending *market price* of the shares. The ratio gives investors a rough estimate of the return *based on the current market price* of the shares.[13] This ratio for Cominco in 1989 is:

$$\frac{\text{Cash dividends per common share}}{\text{Market price per share}} = \frac{\$39,642/79,331.1}{\$26} = .02$$

Shareholders receiving dividends in 1989 earned roughly 2% on their investment, measured at the end-of-year market price. The primary disadvantage of this ratio is again the timing mismatch between the numerator (the dividend declaration date) and the denominator (the market price date).

CONCEPT REVIEW

1. What are the four classifications of ratios discussed?
2. Name the ratios in each classification. What issue does each try to address?
3. What additional value is obtained by examining these ratios over time and across similar firms?
4. What is financial leverage and how is it calculated?

---

[12] See Chapter 22 for a complete discussion of EPS calculations.

[13] Price appreciation, another component of total return, is not measured by this ratio.

INTERPRETATION AND USE OF RATIOS

◆

Ratio analysis of financial statements is used widely, along with more sophisticated techniques, for making investment and credit decisions. Ratios communicate some aspects of the economic situation of an entity better than the absolute amounts reported in the financial statements. The overriding disadvantage of ratio analyses based on financial statement data is that book values rather than market values are used in the computations. Nevertheless, empirical studies demonstrate that the traditional financial ratios are associated with the process by which share prices are formed.[14]

Financial ratios have been used successfully in prediction models to project whether a business would fail.[15] Thus, it is not surprising that financial analysts and bank lending officers make wide use of ratio analysis in evaluating the future economic prospects of individual companies.

Ratios covering a period of years (as they must, to be very useful) represent average conditions. Therefore, they must be interpreted in the light of the smoothing effect inherent in any average. However, when viewed over an extended period of time, ratios can signal important *turning points*, either favourable or unfavourable, with respect to the future economic prospects for the business. However, one ratio does not always convey a clear message — or even several ratios, whatever their values.

Consequently, a primary problem confronting the statement user relates to the evaluation of a ratio. For example, is an inventory turnover ratio of 12 good or bad? In determining what constitutes a favourable or unfavourable ratio for a particular business, comparisons are necessary:

◆ Compare the actual ratios for the current year with those of preceding years for the company. Comparisons of selected ratios for the company over a period of 5 to 10 years often are included in the published financial statements.

◆ Compare the actual ratios for the company with budgeted or standard ratios developed internally by the company. Unfortunately, this kind of comparison seldom is available to external statement users.

◆ Compare the company's ratios with those of its competitors. Competitors may be of a different size or scope of operation, though, and such comparisons may not be possible or meaningful.

◆ Compare the company's ratios with ratios for the industry in which the company operates.

Industry statistics can be obtained from:

◆ Industry trade associations — Major industries support one or more trade associations that collect and publish financial statistics about the industry.

◆ Bureaus of business research at universities — Many major universities collect, analyse, and publish a wide range of regional statistics on local industries and businesses.

◆ Governmental agencies — Agencies that deal directly with business often publish, or have available as a matter of public record, financial information about industries and individual companies. Statistics Canada collects and publishes a wide variety of data.

◆ Commercial sources, including Dun & Bradstreet and Robert Morris Associates.

---

[14] W. Beaver, P. Kettler, and M. Scholes, "The Association between Market Determined and Accounting Determined Risk Measures," *The Accounting Review,* October 1970, pp. 654–82. For an extension of this work, see W. Beaver and J. Manegold, "The Association between Market-Determined and Accounting-Determined Measures of Systematic Risk: Some Further Evidence," *Journal of Financial and Quantitative Analysis,* June 1975, pp. 231–84.

[15] E. Altman, "Financial Ratios, Discriminant Analysis, and the Prediction of Corporate Bankruptcy," *Journal of Finance,* September 1968, pp. 589–609; E. Deakin, "A Discriminant Analysis of Predictors of Business Failure," *Journal of Accounting Research,* Spring 1972, pp. 167–79; and R. Libby, "Accounting Ratios and the Prediction of Business Failure: Some Behavioral Evidence," *Journal of Accounting Research,* Spring 1975, pp. 150–61.

Despite the wide use of ratio analysis, this technique has a number of limitations. Because of these limitations, ratios must be interpreted with some skepticism. Some of the important limitations are:

- Large percentage changes based on small base values are typically not meaningful. Percentages based on negative base figures need to be carefully considered to avoid misinterpretation.
- Ratios represent average conditions that existed in the *past;* they are based on historical data that incorporate all the peculiarities of the past.
- The method of computing each ratio is not standardized. Therefore, the computations (and, hence, the results) can be influenced by data selection choices. Except for EPS, ratios are not subject to audit or general calculation standards.
- The use of alternative accounting methods affects ratios. For example, there are significant effects on financial statement amounts of such alternatives as FIFO versus LIFO and straight-line versus accelerated depreciation.
- Changes in accounting estimates and principles, not applied retroactively (such as a change from FIFO to AC), affect trends.
- It is necessary to adjust data for the effects of unusual or non-recurring items and extraordinary items where material.
- When the data on which ratios are based are historical book values, they reflect neither price level effects nor current market values. The failure to adjust historical values for inflation can destroy meaningful comparisons. The techniques needed to adjust for price level changes are explored in depth later in this chapter.
- Comparisons among companies are difficult. Each company has different operating characteristics such as product lines, methods of operation, size, methods of financing, and geographical location.
- The **efficient market theory** states that other investors have the same data available and can compute the same ratios. Studies have shown that the market very quickly absorbs publicly available information.[16] As a result, it is extremely difficult to consistently earn above-average returns on share investments by relying only on publicly available information. Thus, excessive reliance on ratio analysis, or any analysis based upon publicly available information, must consider this limitation.

Can fundamental (including ratio) analysis, as advocated in Graham, Dodd, and Cottle (see footnote 2) be used to discover undervalued investments? Or does market efficiency make this impossible? Let's consider this issue in greater detail.

The Capital Market Approach

Fundamental analysis attempts to identify under- (or over-) valued shares by establishing the share's *intrinsic* value: the value justified by the economic characteristics of the company. The characteristics include the dividend record, earnings history, financial strength (as evidenced by ratio analysis), and other factors available in the public record. The analysis extends to private information not generally available, including the health of key employees and future business prospects. While any knowledge related to the *riskiness* of a particular investment is considered, there is no formal means of evaluating risk. An investment portfolio is assembled based on the presumption that one can make better decisions than other investors.

Alternatively, those who support the **capital market approach** relate the expected return on any investment to the risk level assumed if the investment is purchased. The *expected return,* measured by the ratio of expected dividends plus price appreciation

---

[16] For a summary of this evidence, see W. Beaver, *Financial Reporting: An Accounting Revolution* (Englewood Cliffs, N.J.: Prentice Hall, 1981); and T. Dyckman and D. Morse, *Efficient Capital Markets and Accounting: A Critical Analysis* (Englewood Cliffs, N.J.: Prentice Hall, 1986). An interesting example of an inefficiency in the market is documented in G. Foster, "Briloff and the Capital Market," *Journal of Accounting Research,* Spring 1979, pp. 262–74.

to the security's price at the start of the period, is higher if the risk is also higher. Risk, in turn, can be conceptualized as the potential variability in return. Risk is composed of two components, **systematic risk** and **unsystematic risk.** Systematic risk is the average expected change in a security's return for a unit change in the return on the total market of securities. This measure of the security risk is known as its *beta,* a relative risk measure.

To illustrate, we will consider a share traded on the Toronto Stock Exchange (TSE) with a beta of 2. If a measure of the TSE market's return (e.g., the TSE 300 composite index) rises (falls) by 10%, then the share is expected to rise (fall), on average, by 20% ($2 \times .10$). The important fact is that the risk measure is related to the change in a portfolio of all the market investments.

The second aspect of risk is the unsystematic portion, which does not vary in any predictable way. Unsystematic risk is random. But the investor is fortunate because this risk can be overcome (diversified away) by creating an investment portfolio that will average out the random element. Moreover, it is easy to create a well-diversified portfolio. If the portfolio is of sufficient size and represents major markets, 10 investments selected across different industries are generally sufficient. The investor need only consider the beta to evaluate the risk being assumed.

Capital market efficiency proponents believe the attempt to find under- or overvalued investments using fundamental analysis and charting share prices is a fruitless exercise. The issue of concern should be, instead, how the riskiness of the particular investment interacts with the risk of the investor's current portfolio.

The debate between these alternative approaches continues. We believe that the truth lies somewhere between the extremes. While capital market analysis has given us a better understanding and measure of how risks should be evaluated, additional work needs to be done. Moreover, not all investments are traded in well-functioning markets. Highly efficient markets rely in part on those who analyse financial information in search of bargains (fundamental analysis). Many important investment decisions rely on additional data beyond that contained in financial reports. Specific decisions, such as granting credit, place different weight on financial data compared to a straight equity investment.[17]

Financial statement evaluation should be thought of in a broader context, namely, as an integral part of "an information system designed to provide firm-related data for decision makers."[18] Investors need to search for information to supplement the financial statements. Hearsay is hazardous. Investors should seek objective data concerning the company—its operations, policies, competitive position, the quality of the management, and other non-quantitative information. Brokerage firms and security analysts typically gather and disseminate this type of information. Companies listed with the stock exchanges file periodic reports, which are publicly available and which provide considerable information not included in the annual financial statements. Investment decisions should be based on this full range of information, not on a particular subset.

CONCEPT REVIEW

1. What are the major limitations to ratio analysis?
2. What is fundamental analysis and why is it done?
3. What is the capital markets approach and what does it imply about fundamental analysis?

---

[17] J. Patton, "Ratio Analysis and Efficient Markets in Introductory Financial Accounting," *The Accounting Review,* July 1982, pp. 626–30.

[18] See B. Lev, *Financial Statement Analysis: A New Approach* (Englewood Cliffs, N.J.: Prentice Hall, 1974); and G. Foster, *Financial Statement Analysis* (Englewood Cliffs, N.J.: Prentice Hall, 1986).

FINANCIAL REPORTING AND CHANGING PRICES

◆

When developing an accounting model, three critical choices must be made:

1. What *costing basis* will be measured? The major choice is between *historical cost* (HC) and some measure of *current cost* (CC). CC can be defined as present value, exit or sales price, or current entry or replacement cost.
2. What will be the *measuring unit?* The alternatives are the *nominal dollar* (ND) or the *constant dollar* (CD).
3. What *capital maintenance* concept is appropriate? The alternatives are *financial capital* or *productive capacity.*

These decisions can be combined in a variety of ways, producing various accounting measurement models. The first two choices, the costing basis and measuring unit, combine to produce the alternative accounting measurement models described in Exhibit 25–8. Our traditional model is the HC/ND alternative. We will examine each of the models in the material that follows.

The accounting profession has consistently endorsed historical cost (HC) as the basis for financial statements. Section 1000 of the *CICA Handbook* states that

> financial statements are prepared primarily using the historical cost basis of measurement whereby transactions and events are recognized in financial statements at the amount of cash or cash equivalents paid or received or the fair value ascribed to them when they took place. (par. 1000.53)

HC statements are reliable because they are based on objectively verifiable information. However, critics charge that HC statements fail to reflect current and relevant information when prices change. Some financial analysts make adjustments for changing prices when performing some of the analyses we discussed in the preceding part of this chapter.

Traditional financial statements are constructed under the assumption that the dollar is a stable unit of money measurement. This unit is called the **nominal dollar** (ND), one that is not adjusted for changing purchasing power. Traditional financial statements are stated in nominal dollar terms. The stable monetary unit assumption ignores inflation, which erodes the purchasing power of the dollar.[19] Consequently, financial statements combine assets and liabilities measured in units of different purchasing power. For example, assume that total assets include equipment purchased in 1980 and buildings constructed in 1990. How do you interpret the dollar amount of total assets?

Constant dollars (CD), or dollars of constant purchasing power, result from adjusting nominal dollars for inflation. For example, assume that you invest $1,000 in a bank account at the beginning of the year. The bank account pays 5% interest. During the year, the inflation rate also is 5%. At the end of the year your account is worth $1,050. Your account increased 50 nominal dollars. However, its value in CDs is unchanged. The purchasing power of $1,050 at the end of the year is equivalent to that of $1,000 at the beginning of the year [$1,000(1.05) = $1,050]. You cannot purchase any more goods and services at the end of the year than you could at the beginning. The interest you earned exactly offset the effects of inflation on your purchasing power.

Both specific price increases and general price increases (inflation) tend to result in an overstatement of reported income because expenses do not reflect the cost of replacing inventory and plant assets consumed in operations. Assume that a $40,000 plant asset purchased several years ago now costs $160,000 to replace. Note that the asset may have an increased replacement cost due to general inflation, or due to specific conditions that drove up the price of that specific asset (supply problems, for example). HC/ND depreciation understates the value of the services used up during the year and

---

[19] Because inflation has been pervasive, our discussions illustrate rising prices. However, the concepts discussed also apply to times of generally declining prices—deflation.

EXHIBIT 25-8   Four Models for Financial Reporting

Costing Basis	Measurement Unit	
	Nominal Dollars	Constant Dollars
Historical cost	Historical cost/Nominal dollar (HC/ND)	Historical cost/Constant dollar (HC/CD)
Current cost	Current cost/Nominal dollar (CC/ND)	Current cost/Constant dollar (CC/CD)

thus does not provide adequate matching. Income is overstated. If the company distributes all its HC earnings, it is not retaining sufficient funds for eventual replacement of capacity.

One source estimates that at least a fourth of all major firms paid dividends exceeding inflation-adjusted earnings in the late 1970s.[20] CN Railway System's 1985 earnings dropped from $118 million to a loss of $548 million, after adjusting for current costs, and BC Telephone's $98 million HC income turned into a $123 million loss when converted to a current cost basis!

Capital Maintenance

What income measurement is more useful to investors and creditors? This problem highlights the importance of the third attribute of an accounting measurement model, the **capital maintenance concept.** Capital maintenance defines capital and, by inference, income. The two alternatives are **financial capital** and **productive capacity .** This additional attribute makes the grid of financial reporting models shown in Exhibit 25–8 three dimensional. Each of the four models could be designed to reflect financial capital or productive capacity. The GAAP model uses financial capital.

Financial capital defines capital as the dollar (or constant dollar) investment in the entity. Increases in value over and above the financial capital are income. Productive capacity measures capital as the physical assets of the corporation. If the value of those assets were to increase, then the value of *capital* increases and no distributable income is earned until physical capital can be replaced.

As an example, assume that Holden Corporation was formed in early 1991, with $100,000 of invested capital, all of which was used to buy inventory. On the last day of the year, the inventory was sold for $140,000. On this date, the replacement cost of the inventory was $130,000. Inflation was 6% during the year. How much income did Holden earn during 1991? Another way to ask this question is, how much could Holden distribute in dividends without impairment of its capital base?

The alternative income measurements are as follows:

1. *Financial capital measured in dollars: $40,000* ($140,000 − $100,000). At year-end, Holden's assets have increased from $100,000 to $140,000. If they distributed $40,000 in dividends, the company would be left with their original financial capital intact. This is the approach our GAAP model uses. Unfortunately, $100,000 at the end of the year would not represent the same purchasing power as at the beginning of the year, nor would it be adequate to replace this inventory.

2. *Financial capital measured in purchasing power: $34,000* [$140,000 − ($100,000 × 1.06)]. At year-end, Holden must have $106,000 in equity to have the same purchasing power as was implicit in the opening equity investment. Value increments over this level are considered income, available for dividend distribution.

---

[20] "Living Off Capital," *Forbes,* November 10, 1980, p. 232.

3. *Productive capacity measured in dollars or constant dollars: $10,000* ($140,000 − $130,000). Holden must have $130,000 at year-end to replace the inventory necessary to stay in business. If they distribute more than $10,000, they will have to borrow just to maintain their current size. Therefore, the only amount considered distributable income is the excess of proceeds over replacement cost, or the *trading gain,* of $10,000. At year-end, capital is stated in dollar figures as $130,000, versus $100,000 at the beginning of the year. While the dollar amount has increased, physical capital has not—capital represents the same constant level of inventory investment.

Productive capacity may be measured in dollars or constant dollars. In this example, the results would be identical since the sale took place at the end of the year.

While productive capacity capital maintenance appears very appealing, it has certain problems associated with it. For instance, it assumes that Holden will want to maintain existing inventory levels, or buy more of this particular product. It produces results that are counterintuitive if the replacement cost of inventory declines. Financial capital has remained the GAAP choice for hundreds of years for good reason.

In the discussion that follows, we will focus on the issues of measurement unit and costing basis. Capital maintenance is inherent in a discussion of the components of income.

General Price-Level Changes—Inflation

The prices of most goods and services change over time. Supply and demand, quality differences, acquisition and production costs, and government regulations are factors that affect prices. However, the prices of *specific* goods and services are not necessarily interrelated. For example, automobile prices have generally increased while consumer electronics prices have declined. Although real estate prices in general have increased over the last decade, certain locales have experienced significant declines, while others have seen steeply higher prices. Real estate prices fluctuate according to supply and demand factors, and the strength of the local economy.

General price-level (GPL) indices were created to provide a measure of the *general* change in prices. A GPL index is a weighted average of the prices of a representative group of goods and services. The average is set to a base number (e.g., 100) for a particular year. The average for all other years is measured in relation to the base year. Increases in GPL indices define inflation; decreases define deflation.

For example, the **Consumer Price Index (CPI),** published monthly by Statistics Canada, is based on the prices of food, clothing, housing, fuel, drugs, transportation costs, health care, and other goods and services for everyday living. The base year (1986) weighted average is set to 100. Other GPL indices in wide use are the Gross National Product Implicit Price Deflator (GNPIPD) and the Wholesale Price Index. The CPI does not measure inflation in the business economy, but it is available on a timely basis and is widely reported, so it is used for financial statement calculations. The GNPIPD may also be used.[21]

The CPI for a representative period is displayed in Exhibit 25–9. For example, in 1977 the group of goods used in the CPI cost only 51.3% of the cost in 1986. The inflation rate for a period is the percentage change in the CPI. Inflation in 1980, a year of very high inflation by Canadian standards, was 10.2%

$$\frac{CPI\ (1980)\ -\ CPI\ (1979)}{CPI\ (1979)} = \frac{67.2\ -\ 61.0}{61.0} = 10.2\%$$

---

[21] No GPL index is perfectly appropriate for all individuals or businesses because each purchases a different mix of products and services. There is some disagreement about the items included in the CPI—a person purchasing some other mix of goods and services does not experience inflation so defined.

EXHIBIT 25-9   Consumer Price Index

Year	Annual Average CPI	Annual Inflation Rate	Year	Annual Average CPI	Annual Inflation Rate
1976	47.5	7.5	1983	88.5	5.7
1977	51.3	8.0	1984	92.4	4.4
1978	55.9	9.0	1985	96.0	3.9
1979	61.0	9.1	1986	100.0	4.2
1980	67.2	10.2	1987	104.4	4.4
1981	75.5	12.4	1988	108.6	4
1982	83.7	10.9	1989	114.0	5
			1990	119.5	4.8

Although inflation rates in Canada are low relative to those of many other countries, the compound effect is quite substantial over a period of years. From 1976 through 1989, the CPI increased a total of 140% [(114.0 − 47.5)/47.5]. Furthermore, many corporations have significant operations in countries experiencing much higher inflation rates. The effects of inflation on financial statements can be substantial, and an appreciation of those effects is integral to your understanding of the accounting model.

GPL indices and general purchasing power are inversely related. As inflation increases, general purchasing power decreases. For example, in 1989 the purchasing power of the dollar was only 59% of that in 1980 (67.2/114.0). Inflation is an important factor in lending decisions. During inflation, creditors lend current dollars and are repaid future, inflated dollars that are worth less than those originally lent. Therefore, the interest rate must include a component to compensate for this loss. During highly inflationary times, *most* of the interest paid is a compensation for inflation.

Restatement of HC/ND Amounts to Constant Dollars   Many believe that HC statements restated to dollars of constant purchasing power improve comparability and relevance. The following formula incorporating GPL indices converts historical cost/nominal dollar (HC/ND) amounts to historical cost/constant dollar (HC/CD) amounts:

$$\text{HC/CD amount (non-monetary item)} = \text{HC/ND amount} \times \frac{\text{GPL index at end of period}}{\text{GPL index at transaction date}}$$

More generally, amounts are presently stated in terms of the denominator GPL index and are restated to the numerator GPL index. For example, equipment purchased for $100,000 when the GPL index was 200 is equivalent to $125,000 at the end of a year in which the GPL index is 250:[22]

$$\$125,000 = \$100,000(250/200)$$

This does not imply that the replacement cost of the equipment is $125,000. That is a specific price. Rather, the purchasing power sacrifice made to purchase the equipment for $100,000 when the GPL index was 200 is identical to a sacrifice of $125,000 when the GPL index is 250. HC/CD restatement is not a departure from historical cost. The restatement only adjusts for changes in the *measuring unit*. Converting financial statement elements to CDs increases comparability because all amounts reflect the same purchasing power.

Monetary and Non-Monetary Items   Financial statement elements are classified as **monetary items** or **non-monetary items.** Monetary assets are money or claims to receive a fixed amount of money. Monetary liabilities are obligations to pay fixed amounts of

---

[22] Throughout this chapter, we use assumed GPL indices rather than actual CPI indices.

dollars. These amounts do not change as market prices change. Non-monetary items are not stated in fixed dollar amounts.

Monetary items include cash, accounts receivable and payable, bonds payable, and most other liabilities. For example, a $4,000 account payable is a claim on exactly $4,000 cash, regardless of inflation during the term of the payable. Neither inflation nor deflation affects the number of dollars to be received or paid for a monetary item, although inflation erodes the purchasing power of these dollars. Restatement of monetary items to end-of-year CDs is not necessary because they are already stated in end-of-year dollars.

Items not classified as monetary are non-monetary items.[23] The number of dollars commanded by non-monetary items changes. Non-monetary items include inventories, operational assets, investments in shares, some liabilities, and share capital (equity) outstanding. For example, a $4,000 estimated warranty liability will probably cost more or less than $4,000 to service as the price of parts and labour changes. The value of temporary investments in common shares fluctuates daily. All non-monetary items must be restated to CDs, as in the equipment example above. All revenues, expenses, gains, and losses reported on the income statement are considered non-monetary items.

Purchasing Power Gains and Losses   During inflation or deflation, holders of monetary items incur a **purchasing power gain or loss.** For example, if you hold $10,000 cash during a period in which the GPL increases 10%, you incur a $1,000 purchasing power loss. Your $10,000 can buy fewer goods or services at the end of the year because prices in general increased. For your purchasing power to remain the same, you must hold $11,000 at the end of the period [$10,000(1.10)]. The purchasing power loss is stated in end-of-period dollars.

If you *owe* $10,000 rather than hold $10,000 cash, then you experience a $1,000 purchasing power gain; this happens because a smaller purchasing power sacrifice is required at the end of the year to extinguish the liability. Income statements restated for inflation include the net purchasing power gain or loss, and thus ensure that the purchasing power of financial capital is maintained.

The magnitude of purchasing power gains and losses depends on the amount of monetary items held, and the rate of inflation. Relative to many other countries, inflation in Canada has been moderate. For example, Brazil's compounded inflation rate between 1985 and 1990 was 1,000,000%. On average, items costing $1 in 1985 cost $10,000 in 1990.[24] However, many Brazilians benefitted from this hyperinflation. For example, the real cost of payments on mortgages became negligible and reflected enormous purchasing power gains from holding monetary liabilities: "By the end, he was paying the equivalent of a mere $6.50 per month. 'It was costing them more than that to send me the mortgage bill.'"[25]

Exhibit 25–10 shows the computation of a purchasing power loss using both monetary assets and liabilities. Perk Company began 1992 with a positive net monetary asset position and increased its holdings of net monetary assets during a period of inflation. Its purchasing power was eroded in 1992 because its actual net monetary asset amount ($25,000) was less than that required to maintain its ability to buy goods and services ($28,364). The increase in net monetary items during 1992 is the result of income-producing activities, as well as investing and financing activities that affected monetary items. The increase is restated to ending constant dollars by the ratio 240/220 because the changes in monetary items are assumed to occur evenly during 1992.

---

[23] The distinction is not always easily made. Bonds payable expected to be extinguished early are non-monetary because their value fluctuates as interest rates change. Bonds held to maturity are monetary because the maturity amount is fixed.

[24] "Brazil's Efforts to Curb Inflation Face Hurdle. A Lot of People Like It," *The Wall Street Journal*, March 29, 1991, p. A1.

[25] Ibid.

EXHIBIT 25-10   Perk Company Computation of Purchasing Power Loss

	January 1, 1992	December 31, 1992
Monetary assets	$20,000	$40,000
Monetary liabilities	10,000	15,000
Net monetary assets	$10,000	$25,000

General price level indices:

January 1, 1992	200
Average, 1992	220
December 31, 1992	240

Changes in monetary items occurred evenly throughout 1992.

Computation of purchasing power loss:

	Nominal Dollars	Restatement Ratio	Constant Dollars*
Net monetary assets, January 1, 1992	$10,000	240/200	$12,000
Increase in net monetary assets, 1992	15,000	240/220	16,364
Net monetary assets required at December 31, 1992, to keep pace with inflation			28,364
Net monetary assets, December 31, 1992	$25,000		25,000
Purchasing power loss, 1992			$ 3,364

* At December 31, 1992.

Specific Price Changes

Although inflation and specific price changes are often correlated, many accountants maintain that financial statements restated for changes in specific prices yield information more relevant for predicting income and cash flow. The result of specific price restatement is a measure of current value, which is a departure from historical cost.

The current value of an asset is its value at the present time, and depends on the expected disposition of the item. Three alternative measures of current value are: (1) **present value,** (2) **exit value,** and (3) **entry value** (current cost or replacement cost).

An asset's *present value* is the discounted amount of its expected future net cash receipts. This amount is a measure of the true economic value of the asset. Although theoretically appealing, uncertainty of cash flows, interaction among assets, and the need to specify the discount rate render this alternative impractical in most situations.

If the firm plans to sell the asset, its *exit value* is another potential measure of current value. The net amount a firm expects to realize from the sale of an asset through normal sale channels is its net realizable value. Published price lists and offers from buyers are reliable sources of exit values for assets.

The CICA adopted entry value as the most appropriate measure of current value. The *entry value* of an asset is an estimate of its **current cost** (CC) or **replacement cost** in its present condition: *the cost to purchase or produce the item.* Entry and exit value often differ substantially. Use of entry value is consistent with the going concern assumption and the need to replace assets periodically.

During the time a firm holds or uses an asset, unrealized changes in current cost, also called holding gains or losses, occur, measured by the change in CC. For example, if land purchased for $40,000 at the beginning of the year has a current cost of $60,000 at the end of the year, the unrealized holding gain is $20,000, the increase in CC. This gain usually is not equal to the effect of inflation. If inflation is 10%, the restated HC of the land at year-end is $44,000 ($40,000 × 1.10), while the CC of the land is $60,000.

Is the holding gain income or an increase in capital? Choice of capital maintenance concept will dictate the answer to this question. If financial capital maintenance is chosen, the holding gain will be considered income. If productive capacity is chosen, it is capital.

Current invoice prices, vendor price lists, and standard manufacturing costs provide direct price information to determine current cost. **Specific price indices** also are employed. Firms can use externally published specific price indices covering their specialized asset categories or develop indices internally. For example, the CC of lumber is estimated by applying industry price indices, which measure the change in lumber costs, to the historical cost of the lumber. The use of specific indices is less costly than obtaining the direct price of each individual item, but it is also more error prone.

CONCEPT REVIEW

1. What three decisions have to be made to define an accounting measurement model?
2. Describe financial capital and productive capacity capital maintenance.
3. Why are both specific and general price changes considered when financial statements are adjusted for price changes?
4. Explain what a GPL-adjusted amount for land owned for several years means. Is this amount the CC of land?
5. Explain why a person owing a monetary liability during inflation experiences a purchasing power gain.

ALTERNATIVE MODELS OF ACCOUNTING FOR CHANGING PRICES
◆

There are several ways to adjust financial statements for price changes. One issue is whether to maintain the HC basis or to report CC. The second question is whether NDs or CDs are more appropriate. These alternatives combine to form the four accounting models for financial reporting listed in Exhibit 25–8. Finally, capital maintenance must be determined.

The *HC/ND* model, required by GAAP for primary financial statements, does not adjust for price-level changes. The *HC/CD* model retains HC as the costing basis, but restates amounts to constant dollars by using the GPL restatement ratio. The *CC/ND* model reports CCs without adjusting for changes in the purchasing power of the dollar. The *CC/CD* model also reports CCs but in dollars of constant purchasing power. GPL adjustments reflect changes in the value of the dollar and are appropriate for both HC and CC bases.

The following basic example of the four models emphasizes the advantages and disadvantages of each. In later sections, we give expanded illustrations of the HC/CD and CC/CD models.

1. Aido Company purchases inventory costing $8,000 on January 1, 1992. The GPL index is 120 on this date.
2. Aido sells the inventory on December 31, 1992, for $13,000. On this date the cost to replace the inventory is $11,000 and the GPL index is 150. Assume no other expenses or transactions.

Historical Cost/Nominal Dollar

The 1992 HC/ND (GAAP) income statement, which uses financial capital, for Aido follows:

Sales	$13,000
Cost of goods sold	8,000
Net income	$ 5,000

Aido must replace inventory to stay in business, assuming no major changes in operations or markets. The $13,000 cash received from sales pays for the $11,000 CC of inventory and leaves $2,000 for dividends. If Aido had distributed all $5,000 of HC income, it would have to reduce permanent capital or borrow to replace the inventory. Under these assumptions, the HC/ND model, using financial capital, overstates distributable income, the amount that is distributable without eroding capital. The use of HC depreciation would also overstate distributable income, by understating the amount of resources that must be retained for eventual replacement of plant assets.

If Aido continued to hold the inventory at the end of 1992, the balance sheet would disclose $8,000 of inventory. This amount understates current value. On a larger scale, this undervaluation can seriously affect assessments of firm value or future cash flow. In addition, the balance sheet may report assets measured in dollars of different purchasing power. The income statement also reflects this problem. Net income is the difference between sales, measured when the GPL was 150, and cost of goods sold, measured when the GPL was 120. Net income is difficult to interpret under these conditions.

Finally, price increases distort rates of return involving plant assets. The HC model understates the current cost of the denominator, average total assets. The use of HC depreciation overstates the numerator. Both factors serve to overstate the ratios. A study of companies disclosing CD and CC information found that average return on investment (operating income divided by net assets) based on HC/ND was 14.3% in 1981. However, it was only 2.9% and 2.5% on the HC/CD and CC/CD bases.[26]

Historical Cost/Constant Dollar

The 1992 HC/CD income statement for Aido follows:

Sales	$13,000	
Cost of goods sold	10,000	$8,000(150/120)
Net income	$ 3,000	

This reporting basis maintains HC; it changes only the measuring unit and reports financial statements in dollars that have the same purchasing power. The adjustment for the GPL change between the purchase and sale of inventory results in restating inventory to $10,000. This amount is equivalent in purchasing power to the $8,000 spent when the inventory was purchased. Sales occurred at the end of 1992, and thus the sales amount is correctly stated.

Net income, measured in CDs, is less than income under HC/ND because HC/CD cost of goods sold reflects the increase in the GPL index. This method will preserve Aido's financial capital measured in constant dollars. To the extent that inflation and specific price level changes are correlated, HC/CD income is an improvement over HC/ND, but does not necessarily reflect distributable income, since inflation adjustments are an imperfect substitute for specific price level changes.

If Aido had continued to hold the inventory at the end of 1992, the GPL-adjusted balance sheet would disclose $10,000 of inventory. This amount is closer to CC ($11,000) than is the $8,000 amount reported under HC/ND but it does *not* represent its CC. Ten thousand dollars is the amount the inventory must generate in revenue for Aido to maintain its purchasing power. All non-monetary balance sheet items are adjusted to the ending GPL index, resulting in a common measuring unit that improves comparability and understandability. Monetary items automatically reflect the ending GPL index, without adjustment.

HC/CD maintains the historical cost basis and is significantly less costly than either CC model because GPL indices are readily available and relatively easy to apply. The

---

[26] K. Evans and R. Freeman, "*Statement 33* Disclosures Confirm Profit Illusion in Primary Statements," *FASB Viewpoints* (Norwalk, Conn.: FASB, June 1983).

model is objective and reliable, eliminates the effect of inflation, and can reduce the incentive to use accounting methods that partially compensate for inflation, such as LIFO and accelerated depreciation. Furthermore, the net purchasing power gain or loss is reported as an element of income (illustrated in a later comprehensive example), to disclose the economic effect of holding monetary items during inflation. Aido held no monetary assets or liabilities during the year, so its purchasing power gain or loss is zero.

Current Cost/Nominal Dollar

This model is better understood by using a two-period example with the following information:

1. Aido Company purchases inventory on January 1, 1991, for $6,000, when the GPL index was 100.
2. At January 1, 1992, Aido still holds the inventory. On this date, the CC of the inventory is $8,000 and the GPL index 120.
3. Aido sells the inventory on December 31, 1992, for $13,000. On this date the CC to replace the inventory is $11,000 and the GPL index 150. Assume no other expenses or transactions.

Information item 1 adds to the data originally given; the rest remains unchanged. The 1991 and 1992 CC/ND income statements for Aido follow:

	1991	1992
Sales . . . . $	0	$13,000
Cost of goods sold at CC	0	11,000
CC operating income	0	2,000
Realized holding gain	0	5,000[†]
Realized income	0	7,000
Unrealized holding gain (loss)	2,000*	(2,000)[§]
CC net income . . . . $	$2,000	$ 5,000

* $8,000 − $6,000, the increase in CC during 1991.

[†] $11,000 − $6,000, the realized increase in CC during the period the inventory was held (1991 and 1992).

[§] The portion of the realized holding gain recognized in 1991.

The holding gain in 1991 is unrealized because the inventory was not sold.[27] This income statement incorporates financial capital and recognizes the increase in value of the inventory as income. If productive capacity is used, holding gains and losses are reported as changes in owners' equity. Under this alternative view, the holding gains do not increase value of the firm because the inventory must be replaced.

CC *operating income* for 1992, $2,000, is the amount earned by operations that can be distributed without eroding capital for inventory replacement. This amount is the trading gain, or the real increase in value of the firm, the value added by the sale of inventory. CC operating income reflects the CC of expenses and sales and is useful for predicting future CC operating income. If productive capacity is used as a capital maintenance concept, CC operating income is considered to be net income.

The $5,000 realized holding gain represents the majority of the HC/ND profit margin of $7,000 ($13,000 − $6,000) in 1992. The CC/ND model separates total 1992 income into distributable operating income and holding gain. The entire holding

---

[27] For assets acquired during the year, beginning CC equals HC at acquisition. For assets sold during the year, ending CC is the CC on the date sold.

gain is realized in 1992 because the inventory was sold in this period. The portion of the 1992 realized holding gain recognized in 1991 is subtracted in 1992 to avoid double counting.

Total realized income is the sum of realized holding gain and CC operating income. This amount equals HC/ND income ($2,000 + $5,000 = $7,000).

The 1991 balance sheet reports $8,000 of inventory at CC. If Aido had continued to hold the inventory at the end of 1992, the balance sheet would report the inventory at $11,000 (CC). All other assets and liabilities would reflect CC.

CC/ND is appealing because it uses specific prices rather than GPL indices. Proponents of the CC/ND model argue that CC/ND income is an improved basis for predicting income and cash flows, for computing income tax, for determining dividends, and for use in wage negotiations.

The high cost and questionable reliability of CC estimates are disadvantages of the CC models. The CICA defines the CC of plant assets as the cost of acquiring the service potential provided by existing assets.[28] But reliable markets for used assets might not exist and the current value for some assets only can be estimated. Also, management may not intend to replace the assets.

For example, Imperial Oil included the following comments in their 1982 annual report:

> The CICA approach calculates a replacement cost for property, plant, and equipment required to maintain productive capacity. While productive capacity in some segments of the business is deliberately being reduced to respond to markets, in others it is being increased. Therefore, it becomes difficult, if not impossible, to develop a valid investment base for productive capacity on which to calculate depreciation. Imperial believes that a large and diversified company's investments are not made to replace existing productive capacity but rather to invest in segments of the business where market needs match the company's strengths.
>
> For example, the petroleum industry is currently faced with an excess of refinery capacity. The task of determining which assets will be required to maintain today's productive capacity, and which company will own those assets, cannot be done with any degree of certainty or validity. Including all refinery assets results in an excessive adjustment to the depreciation expense. However, at present there is no objective basis on which a portion of the investment can be excluded.

Considerable judgment is required to estimate CC for many assets. Adjustments are made for differences in useful life, output capacity, and operating costs. Many firms use external specific price indices to estimate CCs. A study of these indices found that CC is often overstated, perhaps underestimating CC/ND earnings.[29]

Unfortunately, CC/ND models fail to separate the effects of inflation from the total change in CC. For example, Aido's wealth did not really increase by $2,000 in 1991—the general purchasing power of the dollar declined that year. The income statements can reflect dollars of several different purchasing power levels and the gain or loss from holding monetary items during the period is not reflected. However, current cost models can be modified to adjust for the changing purchasing power of the dollar. The next section briefly illustrates the resulting CC/CD model.

Current Cost/Constant Dollar

This model combines both general and specific price changes and combines the advantages of both CC and CD approaches.

---

[28] *CICA Handbook,* section 4510, "Reporting the Effects of Changing Prices" (Toronto: CICA), par. 4510.33–.35.

[29] K. Shriver, "An Empirical Examination of the Potential Measurement Error in Current Cost Data," *The Accounting Review,* January 1987.

To illustrate this model, we go back to the original one-period example (1992 only). The 1992 CC/CD income statement for Aido follows:

Sales.	$13,000
Cost of goods sold at CC	11,000
CC operating income.	2,000
Realized holding gain, net of inflation	1,000*
CC net income	$ 3,000

* Computation of holding gain, net of inflation:

	CC/ND	CC/CD
Current cost of goods sold, in year-end CD	$11,000	$11,000
Historical cost of goods sold, ND; CD ($8,000 × 150/120)	8,000	10,000
Increase in CC of inventory, ND; CD . . .	$ 3,000	$ 1,000

This model adjusts CC for inflation and reports the holding gain in CDs. The realized holding gain before inflation is $3,000 ($11,000 − $8,000). However, after adjusting inventory for inflation to $10,000 [$8,000(150/120)], only $1,000 of inflation-adjusted holding gain remains. The general price level increased 25% [(150 − 120)/120] during 1992. Inflation accounts for $2,000 of the increase in CC [.25($8,000)]. In this example, the specific price of inventory increased faster than the general rate of inflation because CC increased after removing the effects of inflation.

Notice that the sales and cost of goods sold figures have not changed from the CC/ND to the CC/CD model. This is because, in this simple example, the sale took place on December 31, and thus the sale and estimate of CC on the sale date are already in end of period dollars.

If Aido had continued to hold the inventory at the end of 1992, the balance sheet would report $11,000 of inventory at CC. The balance sheet reports assets at CC, measured in end-of-period CDs.

The CC/CD model has many of the same advantages and disadvantages as the CC/ND model, especially with respect to capital maintenance. In addition, all financial statement items are stated in terms of the same purchasing power, enhancing comparability. We give a comprehensive example of this model in a later section.

History and Usefulness of Price-Level–Adjusted Financial Statements

Accounting for price changes has been one of the most controversial issues in the history of the profession. A brief chronology of important events pertaining to this issue follows:

1918 Livingston Middleditch, Jr., "Should Accounts Reflect the Changing Value of the Dollar?" *Journal of Accountancy* 25 (February 1918), pp. 114–20—the controversy starts!

1936 Henry W. Sweeney, *Stabilized Accounting* (New York: Harper & Bros., 1936)—this was the first book on the subject; it explains "Constant Dollar Accounting."

1963 "Reporting the Financial Effects of Price-Level Changes," *Accounting Research Study No. 6* (New York: AICPA, 1963)—recommended supplementary disclosure of the effects of price level changes.

1969 "Financial Statements Restated for General Price-Level Changes," *Accounting Principles Board Statement No. 3* (New York: AICPA, 1969)—recommended supplementary disclosure of financial statements for general price level changes.

1975 "Accounting for Changes in the General Purchasing Power of Money," *Exposure Draft* (Toronto: CICA, 1975)—provided a comprehensive approach to GPL adjustment but was never enacted because current cost disclosures were considered more relevant.

1976   "Current Value Accounting," *Discussion Paper* (Toronto: CICA, 1976)—provided a concise explanation of the different alternatives, together with a brief overview and preliminary position with respect to current value accounting.

1976   "Disclosures of Certain Replacement Cost Data," *Accounting Series Release No. 190* (Washington, D.C.: SEC, 1976)—required supplementary general price-level disclosures about inventories and operational assets for large "listed" companies.

1979   "Current Cost Accounting," *Exposure Draft* (Toronto: CICA, 1979)—draft recommendations for reporting effects of changing prices on enterprises' financial statements.

1979   "Financial Reporting and Changing Prices," *Statement of Financial Accounting Standards No. 33* (Norwalk, Conn.: FASB, 1979)—required large companies to disclose supplementary information about the effects of changing prices.

1981   "Reporting the Effects of Changing Prices," *Reexposure Draft* (of "Current Cost Accounting") (Toronto: CICA, 1981)—called for supplementary disclosure.

1982   *CICA Handbook,* section 4510, "Reporting the Effects of Changing Prices" (Toronto: CICA, 1982)—Large public companies were called on to present prescribed information about the results of changing prices in the annual report. The disclosures were voluntary, as no qualified audit report resulted from non-compliance.

1986   "Financial Reporting and Changing Prices," *Statement of Financial Accounting Standards No. 89* (Norwalk, Conn.: FASB, 1986)—supersedes the nine prior FASB Standards on this topic. Supplementary disclosure of price change effects is "recommended, but not required."

1990   J. Hanna, D. Kennedy, and G. Richardson, *Reporting the Effects of Changing Prices: A Review of the Experience with Section 4510* (Toronto: CICA, 1990)—a review of 4510 disclosures and the attitudes of preparers and users to the information. The study recommended withdrawal of section 4510.

1991   "Reporting the Effects of Changing Prices—Proposed Withdrawal of Section 4510," *Exposure Draft* (Toronto: CICA, 1991)—4510 to be removed from the *Handbook.*

Few firms chose to comply with the 1982 voluntary section 4510, which was not covered by the audit report. In 1983, only 23% of the 321 companies targeted by section 4510 provided the supplementary information. By 1988, no one was providing the information in section 4510 format, although *Financial Reporting in Canada, 1989* reported that two companies among those surveyed included some inflation-adjusted data in the disclosure notes. For all intents and purposes, supplementary data on changing prices were and are not GAAP in Canada.

Several factors contributed to this lack of compliance. The section was adopted in 1982, after the rate of inflation had peaked. The rate of inflation declined significantly during the 1980s and has remained low. Interest in the disclosures subsided as inflation declined.

A CICA report on initial experience with 4510 reviewed the objections that companies frequently raised:[30]

> A common comment by companies of all types was that preparation of the recommended data was complex and involved numerous assumptions, approximations and estimates that could produce misleading results. Based on premises such as this, some companies concluded that presentation of the data would be inappropriate because results would not be comparable between enterprises, the costs incurred in preparation of the data would not be matched by the benefits and users would not understand the information disclosed. In the words of one company that presented a detailed explanation of its reasons for not complying, "the recommendations fail to meet the objectives of simplicity, uniformity and understandability."

---

[30] *Reporting the Effect of Changing Prices: A Report on First Year's Experience with 4510 of the CICA Handbook* (Toronto: CICA, 1984), p. 18.

Lack of understanding is a significant problem. Few companies prepare such data for internal use, and thus few see the value of it for users seeking insight into how the business operates. One study into this problem reported the following:[31]

> Very few Canadian companies prepare formal price-adjusted accounting reports for internal use by management. Most financial executives believe that such reports are not useful; they are complex, costly and not easily understood, and price adjusted reports are not requested or understood by operating or executive managers....
>
> The fact that the vast majority of Canadian managers perceived little advantage to preparing price-adjusted accounting reports for their own use may help to explain why Canadian companies have been slow to report the effects of changing price levels in external financial reports.

The 1990 CICA-sponsored review of section 4510 confirmed these conclusions. The study found that while financial analysts preferred some disclosure of changing prices information to no disclosure at all, they found section 4510 data of limited usefulness. Preparers generally considered the issue of changing prices unimportant.[32]

In response to this widespread dissatisfaction, the CICA Accounting Standards Board suggested withdrawal of section 4510 in 1991. Suggestions for alternative disclosures include the following:[33]

(i) parenthetical balance sheet or footnote disclosure of "current value" where historical cost and current value differ significantly, supplemented by disclosure of the methods used to determine current value;

(ii) funds flow statement disclosures of the impact of changing prices portraying management's view as to cash flow available for dividends after providing for the replacement of productive capacity at current costs;

(iii) constant dollar historical cost reporting, either full or partial; and

(iv) management commentary on the past, present and likely future impact of inflation on the enterprise's operating cash flows, including quantitative disclosures as appropriate.

The lack of interest in price-level disclosures is due, in part, to lack of understanding. If significant inflation rates return, the long process of developing pronouncements to effectively address price-level changes may have to be repeated. Accounting systems will have to be recreated, and the continuity of data will be lost. Standard setters will undoubtedly continue to consider the complex issues surrounding the financial statement effects of price changes.

CONCEPT REVIEW

1. Why is the denominator of the GPL restatement ratio equal to the GPL at transaction date?
2. How does CC operating income allow for maintenance of physical capital?
3. Prepare an argument against requiring price-level adjusted financial statements.
4. Why were section 4510 disclosures not generally accepted?

---

[31] J. Waterhouse, "Reporting Non-Historical Accounting Data to Canadian Managers," *Study Paper No. 5* (Toronto: Canadian Certified General Accountants Research Foundation, 1984), preface.

[32] J. Hanna, D. Kennedy, and G. Richardson, *Reporting the Effects of Changing Prices: A Review of the Experience with Section 4510* (Toronto: CICA, 1991).

[33] "Proposed Withdrawal of Accounting Recommendations; Reporting the Effects of Changing Prices, Section 4510," *Exposure Draft* (Toronto: CICA, 1991), par. 08. These suggestions come from the CICA study authored by J. Hanna, D. Kennedy, and G. Richardson.

COMPREHENSIVE ILLUSTRATION: HC/CD FINANCIAL STATEMENTS

◆

Preparation of complete HC/CD financial statements requires (1) restating all non-monetary items to the GPL index at the end of the year and (2) computing the purchasing power gain or loss on monetary items. The purchasing power gain or loss is a component of HC/CD earnings.

HC/CD statements can be prepared as of any date. We will use the end-of-year GPL as the measure of CDs because it is the most current and requires no adjustment for monetary items. The alternative, average-of-year GPL, alleviates the need to adjust many revenue and expense items that occur evenly throughout the year.

Monetary items are restated in the following situations: (1) rolling-forward HC/CD statements of prior years to current year CDs[34] and (2) restating HC/CD statements to the average GPL index for the year. Restating monetary items does not imply that their fixed value has changed. Rather, *any* CD statement reflects the GPL index as of the statement date. We do not illustrate these two cases because they do not change the procedures. However, the end-of-chapter material gives examples.

Exhibit 25–11 provides the HC/ND (GAAP) financial statements, GPL indices, and additional data to illustrate preparation of HC/CD statements for Phog Company. These data support Exhibits 25–12 through 25–14.

Exhibit 25–11 classifies each financial statement item as monetary (M) or non-monetary (NM) to facilitate computation of the purchasing power gain or loss. The summary of transactions indicates the transaction dates to enable restatement to the ending 1991 GPL.

HC/CD Balance Sheet   Exhibit 25–12 presents the HC/CD balance sheet. The objective of restating the HC/ND balance sheet for GPL changes is to report HC assets, liabilities, and owners' equity at their CD equivalents. *Note that the CD restatement ratios are rounded to three decimal places before multiplication.*

Monetary Items   Because monetary items are correctly stated in terms of the December 31, 1991, GPL index, their HC/ND and HC/CD amounts are the same.

Non-monetary Items   The restatement ratio for each non-monetary item uses the ending 1991 GPL index (159) as the numerator and the GPL index at transaction date as the denominator. For example, Phog purchased ending inventory evenly during the fourth quarter when the GPL index was 157. Therefore, the restatement ratio is 159/157.

Phog first issued common shares on January 1, 1986, when the GPL index was 127. Phog subsequently issued additional shares on September 30, 1991, when the GPL index was 154. The two issuances are restated separately, as shown in Exhibit 25–12.

HC/CD retained earnings is a balancing amount in Exhibit 25–12. Exhibit 25–14 illustrating the restated income and retained earnings statements proves the ending $63,693 balance.

Purchasing Power Gain or Loss   We next compute the net purchasing power gain or loss because it is a component of the HC/CD income statement. Phog reported $60,000 of monetary assets ($36,000 cash and $24,000 accounts receivable) and $40,000 of monetary liabilities (accounts payable) at the beginning of 1991 (refer to Exhibit 25–11). Therefore, Phog started 1991 in a $20,000 net monetary asset position. During the year, Phog completed transactions that increased and decreased its monetary assets and liabilities.

---

[34] Comparative financial statements are restated to the ending GPL index of the most recent year using the restatement ratio: Ending GPL index for most recent year/Ending GPL index for the year reported comparatively.

General Price Level Indices and Ratios

Date	GPL Index	CD Restatement Ratio
Jan. 1, 1986	127	159/127
Mar. 31, 1987	138	159/138
Dec. 31, 1990	147	159/147
Mar. 31, 1991	149	159/149
June 30, 1991	151	159/151
Sept. 30, 1991	154	159/154
Dec. 31, 1991	159	159/159

Period		
Average, 4th quarter, 1990	146	159/146
Average, 4th quarter, 1991	157	159/157
Average, full year, 1991	152*	159/152

Summary of Transactions During 1991

a. Sales of $144,000 were made evenly during the year (assume all on credit).
b. Purchases of $85,000 were made evenly during the year (assume all on credit).
c. The equipment is depreciated 4% per year with no residual value; the equipment was bought on January 1, 1986, when the GPL index was 127.
d. The long-term investment in common shares of Smith Company was acquired for $25,000 on March 31, 1987, when the GPL index was 138. On December 30, 1991, when the GPL index was 159, half of these shares (i.e., cost of $12,500) were sold for $15,000 cash.
e. General expenses (including interest) of $20,000 were accrued and paid evenly during the year.
f. Collections on accounts receivable, $135,000, were made evenly during the year.
g. Payments on accounts payable, $80,000, were made evenly during the year.
h. A $10,000 cash dividend was declared at midyear when the GPL index was 151. It was paid one month later.
i. The parking garage was acquired January 1, 1991, when the GPL index was 147; issued 12% note payable in payment, $50,000; interest paid quarterly.
j. The parking garage is depreciated 4% per year with no residual value.
k. Issued common shares for cash on September 30, 1991, when the GPL index was 154; cash received, $60,000. The initial $100,000 of common shares were issued on January 1, 1986, when the GPL index was 127.
l. Income tax of $10,000 was accrued evenly during the year. For instructional convenience, assume that all of it will be paid in 1992.
m. The December 31, 1991, inventory was $25,000 (FIFO basis; LCM = cost).
n. Ending 1990 retained earnings on an HC/CD basis is $43,619.

**Comparative Balance Sheets,
HC, at December 31, 1991**

		1991	1990
	Assets		
M	Cash	$136,000	$ 36,000
M	Accounts receivable (net)	33,000	24,000
NM	Inventory (FIFO)	25,000	20,000
NM	Investment in common shares of Smith Co.	12,500	25,000
NM	Equipment	100,000	100,000
NM	Accumulated depreciation, equipment	(24,000)	(20,000)
NM	Parking garage	50,000	—
NM	Accumulated depreciation, parking garage	(2,000)	—
	Total assets	$330,500	$185,000
	Liabilities		
M	Accounts payable	$ 45,000	$ 40,000
M	Income tax payable	10,000	—
M	Note payable, 12%	50,000	—
	Shareholders' Equity		
NM	Common shares, nopar	160,000	100,000
NM	Retained earnings	65,500	45,000
	Total liabilities and shareholders' equity	$330,500	$185,000

EXHIBIT 25–11 *(concluded)*

Income Statement,
HC, for the Year Ended December 31, 1991
(All Items are NM)

Sales revenue	$144,000
Gain on sale of investment	2,500
Total revenues and gains	146,500
Cost of goods sold†	80,000
General expenses (including interest)	20,000
Depreciation expense, equipment	4,000
Depreciation expense, garage	2,000
Income tax expense	10,000
Total expenses	116,000
Net income	$ 30,500

Statement of Retained Earnings,
HC, for the Year Ended December 31, 1991
(All Items Are NM)

Beginning balance, January 1, 1991	$ 45,000
Add: Net income for 1991	30,500
Deduct: Dividends declared during 1991	(10,000)
Ending balance, December 31, 1991	$ 65,500

M = Monetary item.

NM = Non-monetary item.

* (147 + 149 + 151 + 154 + 159) ÷ 5 = 152.

† Cost of goods sold (FIFO):

Inventory, beginning	$ 20,000
Purchases (all on credit)	85,000
Goods available for sale	105,000
Inventory, ending	(25,000)
Cost of goods sold	$ 80,000

The beginning net monetary asset amount, plus the increases and minus the decreases in HC/ND net monetary assets that occurred during the year, equals the ending HC/ND net monetary asset (or net monetary liability) amount. Exhibit 25–13 shows that the ending HC/ND net monetary asset amount is $64,000. To determine the effect of inflation on purchasing power, we compare this amount to its counterpart restated for inflation.

The GPL-adjusted ending net monetary asset amount is computed by restating the beginning HC/ND net monetary balance and all changes in monetary items during the year to the ending GPL index.[35] These adjustments are performed individually because the changes in monetary items did not occur simultaneously. Sales of goods and services, operational assets, and common shares, whether for cash or on account, cause net monetary assets to increase. In contrast, purchases, expenses, declaration of dividends, and acquisition of non-monetary assets, whether for cash or on account, cause net monetary assets to decrease.

Exhibit 25–13 shows that the GPL-adjusted counterpart to the ending HC/ND net monetary assets equals $64,264. If Phog held $64,264 in net monetary assets at year-end, its position kept pace with inflation. But monetary items, by definition, cannot keep pace with inflation because they are fixed in amount. Phog has only $64,000 of

---

[35] This is why income statement items are classified as non-monetary. If the accounts affected by revenue and expense recognition are monetary (such as cash, accounts receivable), then they are considered in the purchasing power gain or loss. If not, they do not affect the purchasing power gain or loss (e.g., depreciation).

EXHIBIT 25–12 Phog Company HC/CD Restated Balance Sheet

Summary of Acquisition Dates and GPL Index Values for Non-Monetary Items

a. Ending 1991 inventory was acquired evenly throughout the fourth quarter; GPL index, 157.

b. Investment in common shares of Smith Company was acquired March 31, 1987; GPL index, 138.

c. Equipment was acquired on January 1, 1986; GPL index, 127.

d. Accumulated depreciation, equipment, restated on same basis as related asset account.

e. Parking garage was acquired on January 1, 1991; GPL index, 147.

f. Accumulated depreciation, parking garage, restated on same basis as related asset account.

g. Original issue of common shares, $100,000, on January 1, 1986; GPL index, 127. Subsequent issuance of common shares, $60,000, on September 30, 1991; GPL index, 154.

HC/CD Balance Sheet
At December 31, 1991

	HC/ND	CD Restatement Ratio*	HC/CD
Assets			
Cash	$136,000	Monetary	$136,000
Accounts receivable (net)	33,000	Monetary	33,000
Inventory	25,000	159/157	25,325
Investment in common shares of Smith Company	12,500	159/138	14,400
Equipment	100,000	159/127	125,200
Accumulated depreciation, equipment	(24,000)	159/127	(30,048)
Parking garage	50,000	159/147	54,100
Accumulated depreciation, parking garage	(2,000)	159/147	(2,164)
Total assets	$330,500		$355,813
Liabilities			
Accounts payable	$ 45,000	Monetary	$ 45,000
Income tax payable	10,000	Monetary	10,000
Note payable, 12%	50,000	Monetary	50,000
Shareholders' Equity			
Common shares, nopar	160,000	†	187,120
Retained earnings	65,500	Bal. amt.	63,693
Total liabilities and shareholders' equity	$330,500		$355,813

* The CD restatement ratios are rounded to three decimals before multiplication.

† Original common share restatement (GPL index at issuance, 127):

$100,000 × (159/127) $125,200

1991 common share issuance restatement (GPL index at issuance, 154).

$60,000 × (159/154) 61,920

Common shares restated in CDs $187,120

net monetary assets. Hence, Phog incurred a $264 purchasing power loss in 1991. This amount is placed in the HC/CD income statement to follow.

In general, maintaining a net monetary asset position during inflation results in a purchasing power loss; holding a net monetary liability position produces a gain during inflation. If the restated ending net monetary asset balance exceeds the actual net monetary asset balance (Phog's situation), a purchasing power loss occurs. Suppose Phog had a net monetary liability position at the beginning and end of 1991. If the restated ending net monetary liability balance exceeds the actual ending net monetary liability balance, a purchasing power gain occurs. Here, the company has less net monetary debt than if its position kept pace with inflation.

HC/CD Income Statement   The objective of restating the HC income statement for GPL changes is to report the HC revenues, expenses, gains, and losses at their ending 1991 CD equivalents. The restatement process is the same as that applied to the balance sheet. Exhibit 25–14 illustrates the procedure.

EXHIBIT 25-13   Phog Company Purchasing Power Loss for Year Ended December 31, 1991

	HC/ND	CD Restatement Ratio	HC/CD
Net monetary items—increases (decreases):			
1. Total beginning net monetary assets	$ 20,000*	159/147	$ 21,640
2. Increases in net montary assets during 1991 from:			
Sales revenue	144,000	159/152	150,624
Sale of investment	15,000	159/159	15,000
Sale and issuance of common shares	60,000	159/154	61,920
3. Decreases in net monetary assets during 1991 from:			
Purchases	(85,000)	159/152	(88,910)
General expenses (including interest)	(20,000)	159/152	(20,920)
Income tax expense	(10,000)	159/152	(10,460)
Cash dividends declared†	(10,000)	159/151	(10,530)
Parking garage acquisition	(50,000)	159/147	(54,100)
4. Total ending net monetary assets:			
HC	$ 64,000‡		
HC/CD			$ 64,264
5. Purchasing power gain (loss) on net monetary items; to income statement, ($64,000 − $64,264); a positive remainder is a gain and a negative remainder is a loss			$ (264)

* Computation from 1990 balance sheet: Cash ($36,000) + Accounts receivable ($24,000) − Accounts payable ($40,000) = $20,000 (may be positive or negative; positive in this case).

† Declaration date, not payment date, is relevant to the CD restatement of dividends because on declaration date, the entity incurs a monetary liability and, hence, decreases net monetary assets. Subsequent payment has no effect on net monetary assets because payment involves monetary items only (i.e., dr. dividends payable; cr. cash).

‡ Computation from 1991 balance sheet: Cash ($136,000) + Accounts receivable ($33,000) − Accounts payable ($45,000) − Income tax payable ($10,000) − Note payable ($50,000) = $64,000 (may be positive or negative; positive in this case). This exhibit demonstrates that usually it is unnecessary to compute the purchasing power gain (loss) on each separate monetary item; rather, they can be combined as shown.

For example, sales were recognized evenly during 1991. Therefore, the restatement ratio is the ending GPL index divided by the average GPL index value for the year.[36] To restate the gain on sale of investment, the components of the HC/ND entry recording the gain are restated as shown in the first note (*) to Exhibit 25–14. The HC/CD amount of the investment is restated by the ratio of 159/138 because the GPL index at date of acquisition, March 31, 1987, was 138. The resulting HC/CD gain of $600 is the increase in the value of the investment account after restating the amounts to a CD basis.

Cost of goods sold requires multiple HC/CD restatements as shown in the second note (†) of Exhibit 25–14. Based on the FIFO assumption, Phog acquired the beginning inventory during the fourth quarter of the preceding year when the average GPL index was 146. Therefore, it is restated by the CD ratio 159/146. Because the purchases were made evenly during 1991, the average GPL index of 152 is used. Based on the FIFO assumption, Phog acquired ending inventory evenly during the fourth quarter of 1991 when the average GPL index was 157. This amount is restated by the ratio, 159/157.

If Phog used LIFO, the denominators of the GPL restatement ratios applied to beginning and ending inventory are the GPL indices for the purchase dates. In some cases, those dates are in the distant past. If Phog used the average cost method for

---

[36] Items that experience numerous transactions during the reporting period, such as sales revenue, often are assumed to occur evenly throughout the period. This assumption provides a practical basis for using an average GPL index value for the denominator in the restatement ratio.

EXHIBIT 25–14   Phog Company HC/CD Restated Income Statement and Statement of Retained Earnings for Year Ended December 31, 1991

HC/CD Income Statement
For the Year Ended December 31, 1991

	HC/ND	CD Restatement Ratio	HC/CD
Sales revenue	$144,000	159/152	$150,624
Gain on sale of investment	2,500	*	600
Total revenues and gains	146,500		151,224
Cost of goods sold	80,000	†	85,365
General expenses (including interest)	20,000	159/152	20,920
Depreciation expense, equipment	4,000	159/127	5,008
Depreciation expense, garage	2,000	159/147	2,164
Income tax expense	10,000	159/152	10,460
Total expenses	116,000		123,917
Net income	$ 30,500		
HC/CD income before purchasing power loss on net monetary items			27,307
Purchasing power loss on net monetary items			(264)
HC/CD income			$ 27,043

HC/CD Retained Earnings Statement
For the Year Ended December 31, 1991

	HC/CD
Beginning balance January 1, 1991, HC/CD balance from prior year ($43,619 × 159/147)	$ 47,180
Add: Net income for 1991 (above)	27,043
Deduct: Dividends, 1991 ($10,000 × 159/151)	(10,530)
Ending balance, December 31, 1991	$ 63,693

* Entry to record sale of investment (Dec. 31, 1991):

Cash	15,000		159/159	15,000
Investment in common shares ($25,000 ÷ 2)		12,500	159/138	14,400
Gain on sale of investment		2,500	Bal. amt.	600

† Cost of goods sold:

Inventory, beginning	$ 20,000	159/146	$ 21,780
Purchases	85,000	159/152	88,910
Goods available for sale	105,000		110,690
Inventory, ending	(25,000)	159/157	(25,325)
Cost of goods sold	$ 80,000		$85,365

inventory, the denominators of the CD ratios for beginning and ending inventory are the average GPL indices for 1990 and 1991, respectively. Purchases are not affected by the inventory cost flow method.

The restatement ratios for general expenses and income tax expense reflect the average GPL index (152) because these expenses occur evenly during the year. Restated depreciation expense is computed separately because the two plant assets were acquired on different dates. The restatement ratios reflect the acquisition dates (127 and 147, respectively).

HC/CD Retained Earnings Statement   Exhibit 25–14 also illustrates this statement. The ending 1990 *HC/CD* retained earnings amount, $43,619, is restated to reflect the GPL index at December 31, 1991. That amount represents the ending balance resulting from the GPL-restatement process in 1990. The ratio 159/147 restates that amount to the end-of-1991 CDs. Next, HC/CD net income is added. Then dividends are restated by using the mid-year GPL index (151) because dividends were declared in the middle of the year. The ending balance, $63,693, provides proof of the retained earnings balancing amount used in the balance sheet (Exhibit 25–12).

Recap   The HC/CD statements report higher total assets and lower retained earnings and income, relative to the HC/ND statements. Total assets increased on a CD basis because the GPL index increased. This effect is most pronounced for equipment and other older assets.

Restatement of revenues and expenses caused HC/CD earnings to fall below HC/ND earnings because expenses increased more than revenues and gains as a result of GPL restatement. The HC/ND cost of goods sold and depreciation are significantly less than the restated amounts. In addition, restatement reduced the gain on sale of investment, and the purchasing power loss decreased HC/CD earnings.

The HC/CD balance sheet most likely does not reflect the current value of a firm's assets, nor does the HC/CD income statement typically reflect the real increase in wealth, after providing for capital maintenance. While HC/CD earnings are adjusted for changes in purchasing power, they do not consider specific price changes. Hence the need for CC/CD statements. We turn to these in our final example.

COMPREHENSIVE ILLUSTRATION: CC/CD FINANCIAL STATEMENTS

◆

Objectives of the CC/CD Model   The objective of the CC/CD balance sheet is to report the lower of (1) CC or (2) net recoverable amount of each asset or asset group measured in constant dollars.[37] This objective is consistent with conservatism. The objective of the CC/CD income statement is to report current cost income in CDs.

Current Cost   The CICA defines CC in terms of reacquiring existing assets:

Inventory: CC is the cost of purchasing or producing an inventory item, including an overhead allowance.

Plant assets: CC is the cost of acquiring the same service potential as measured by operating costs and physical output capacity of existing assets. The following measurement alternatives are allowed: (1) cost of a new asset having the same service potential as the used asset when it was new, less depreciation, (2) cost of a used asset of the same age and condition, and (3) cost of a new asset with different service potential, adjusted for the difference in service potential due to differences in life, output capacity, nature of service, and operating costs, less depreciation.

Price quotations for individual assets, specific price indices for groups of similar assets, and standard manufacturing costs are used to compute CC. If the recoverable amount—that is, the net realizable value or value in use—is lower than current cost, then it should be used instead of current cost.

Overview   Comprehensive CC/CD statements include an income statement, retained earnings statement, and balance sheet. Preparation of CC/CD financial statements involves measurement of the CC of each financial statement item and restatement of all such CC amounts to end-of-period CDs. The purchasing power gain or loss is reported as a component of earnings, as in HC/CD statements, because it represents the change in economic purchasing power from holding monetary items. Thus, the comprehensive

---

[37] The net recoverable amount of an asset is the net cash amount expected to be recoverable from use or sale.

CC/CD model includes amounts included in other measurement models. In addition, the change in the CC (the holding gains) of non-monetary items, net of inflation, is reported as a component of CC/CD comprehensive income. This amount, along with the purchasing power gain or loss, must be computed before completing the income statement.

For our example, we supplement Exhibit 25–11 from the previous HC/CD Phog Company example with CC information presented in Exhibit 25–15.

CC/CD Balance Sheet   Exhibit 25–16 presents the CC/CD balance sheet stated in CDs at December 31, 1991. The reported amounts of monetary items agree with the HC/CD balance sheet because they are correctly stated at ending CDs. The ending CCs for non-monetary items are given in Exhibit 25–15. In a real situation, a considerable amount of effort is required to estimate these values. For example, we used a specific price level index to determine the CC of equipment, which increased from $175,000 to $196,000 during 1991. These amounts reflect the condition and utility of the equipment at those dates.

The accumulated depreciation amounts reflect the percentage of depreciation recognized for HC/ND. The equipment is depreciated 24% ($24,000 HC depreciation/ $100,000 HC). Therefore, $47,040 [.24($196,000)] of accumulated depreciation, based on CC, is reported at December 31, 1991. For the parking garage, the amounts are as follows: 4% depreciated ($2,000/$50,000); $2,240 accumulated depreciation based on CC [.04($56,000)].

The CC/CD amount for common shares is the HC/ND amount restated to end-of-period dollars, which agrees with the amount in the HC/CD balance sheet. The share capital account, representing a previous cash investment, has no specific price. Retained earnings is computed as a balancing amount, which we verify after deriving CC/CD earnings.

Change in CC of Non-Monetary Items, Net of Inflation   Non-monetary items are affected by two types of price changes: (1) general inflation and (2) specific price changes. The CC/CD statements are stated in terms of CDs. Therefore, the holding gains or losses reported in CC/CD earnings are the changes in specific prices of non-monetary items *after* removing the effects of GPL changes. Exhibit 25–17 shows how to separate these two effects.

Our previous discussion of the four models for financial reporting included an example of this computation applied to inventory (see the CC/CD example). Exhibit 25–17 illustrates the same computation. The reasoning underlying the computations is similar to that of the purchasing power gain or loss on net monetary assets. Changes in the CC amount of each non-monetary asset are analysed using the beginning balance, additions, and deductions during the period to derive the ending balance.

For inventory, the total increase in nominal CC during the year is the difference between (1) the actual ending CC amount ($26,000) and (2) the computed ending CC nominal amount ($19,500). This total nominal CC increase is $6,500. The *CC at transaction date* column in the exhibit supplies the computed ending nominal CC amount, which would also be actual ending CC amount if specific price changes remained constant.

The nominal CC increase then is separated into an inflation effect, and a specific price change effect. By restating each amount in the *CC at transaction date* column to ending CDs, we derive the ending CC amount expected, in CDs ($21,135). The effect of inflation during the period is therefore the difference between this restated figure ($21,135), and the computed ending nominal CC amount ($19,500). This difference, $1,635, is that part of the total $6,500 CC increase attributable to inflation. Therefore, the remainder, $4,865, is the increase in CC exclusive of inflation, the "real" holding gain. The increase in specific prices of inventory exceeded inflation.

EXHIBIT 25–15   Phog Company CC Information for CC/CD Restated Financial Statements

Item	Source of CC Data	Current Cost
December 31, 1990:		(in CDs of Jan. 1, 1991)
Assets (beginning balances):		
Inventory	From prior period, 1990.	$ 20,500
Investment in common shares of Smith Company.	From prior period, 1990.	33,000
Equipment	From prior period, 1990.	175,000
Retained earnings (credit)	From prior period, 1990.	97,822
December 31, 1991:		(in CDs of Dec. 31, 1991)
Assets (ending balances):		
Inventory	Suppliers' price lists	$ 26,000
Investment in common shares of Smith Company.	Quoted market price	15,000
Equipment (acquired January 1, 1986)	Indexed, specific	196,000
Parking garage (acquired January 1, 1991)	Professional appraisal.	56,000
During 1991 (revenues and expenses occurred evenly throughout the year):		(in Average CDs of 1991)
Sales revenue	HC, Exhibit 25–11	$144,000
Cost of goods sold	Suppliers' price lists on day of sale	86,000
General expenses (including interest).	HC, Exhibit 25–11	20,000
Income tax expense	HC, Exhibit 25–11	10,000
Depreciation expense, equipment	(($175,000 + $196,000) ÷ 2) × .04.	7,420
Depreciation expense, parking garage	(($50,000 + $56,000) ÷ 2) × .04.	2,120

Note: HC/ND transaction and financial statement data and GPL indices are given in Exhibit 25–11.

EXHIBIT 25–16   Phog Company CC/CD Balance Sheet at December 31, 1991

		Source (Exhibit)	CC/CD (in CDs of Dec. 31, 1991)
Balance Sheet CC/CD as at December 31, 1991			
Assets			
M	Cash	25–11	$136,000
M	Accounts receivable (net)	25–11	33,000
NM	Inventory	25–15	26,000
NM	Investment in common shares of Smith Co.	25–15	15,000
NM	Equipment	25–15	196,000
NM	Accumulated depreciation, equipment	calc.*	(47,040)
NM	Parking garage	25–15	56,000
NM	Accumulated depreciation, parking garage	calc.†	(2,240)
	Total assets		$412,720
Liabilities			
M	Accounts payable	25–11	$ 45,000
M	Income tax payable	25–11	10,000
M	Note payable, 12%.	25–11	50,000
Shareholders' Equity			
NM	Common shares, nopar	25–12	187,120
NM	Retained earnings	Bal. amt.	120,600
	Total liabilities and shareholders' equity		$412,720

M = monetary item.

NM = non-monetary item.

* $196,000 × 24%

† $56,000 × 4%

EXHIBIT 25–17   Phog Company Change in CC of Non-Monetary Items, Net of Inflation

Non-Monetary Assets	Source	CC at Transaction Date (1)	Restated to CDs (2)	CC at Dec. 31, 1991 (3)
Inventory				
Beginning balance	25–15	$ 20,500	159/147 = $ 22,181	
Add—purchases during 1991 (HC)	25–14	85,000	159/152 = 88,910	
Deduct—cost of goods sold for 1991 (CC)	25–15	(86,000)	159/152 = (89,956)	
1. Ending inv. at CC at transaction dates.		$ 19,500		
2. Ending inv. at CC restated to CDs.			$ 21,135	
3. Ending inventory at year-end CC.	25–15			$ 26,000

Changes in CC during 1991

Total increase (decrease) in CC (3 − 1). . . . . $26,000 − $19,500 = $ 6,500

Change in CC due to inflation (2 − 1) . . . . $21,135 − $19,500 = $ 1,635
Change in CC, net of inflation (3 − 2) . . . . $26,000 − $21,135 = $ 4,865

Non-Monetary Assets	Source	CC at Transaction Date (1)	Restated to CDs (2)	CC at Dec. 31, 1991 (3)
Investment in Common Shares of Smith Co.				
Beginning balance	25–15	$ 33,000	159/147 = $ 35,706	
Add—acquisitions—none				
Deduct—sale on Dec. 30, 1991, at CC when sold	25–11	(15,000)	159/159 = (15,000)	
1. Ending balance at CC at transaction dates.		$ 18,000		
2. Ending balance at CC restated to CDs.			$ 20,706	
3. Ending balance at year-end CC.	25–15			$ 15,000

Changes in CC during 1991

Total increase (decrease) in CC (3 − 1). . . . . $15,000 − $18,000 = $(3,000)

Change in CC due to inflation (2 − 1) . . . . $20,706 − $18,000 = $ 2,706
Change in CC, net of inflation (3 − 2) . . . . $15,000 − $20,706 = $(5,706)

Non-Monetary Assets	Source	CC at Transaction Date (1)	Restated to CDs (2)	CC at Dec. 31, 1991 (3)
Equipment				
Beginning balance (net of depreciation) ($175,000 × (1 − .20))	calc.	$140,000	159/147 = $151,480	
Add—acquisitions—none				
Deduct—depreciation during 1991	25–15	(7,420)	159/152 = (7,761)	
1. Ending balance at CC at transaction dates.		$132,580		
2. Ending balance at CC restated to CDs.			$143,719	
3. Ending balance at year-end CC.	25–15			$148,960

Changes in CC during 1991

Total increase (decrease) in CC (3 − 1). . . . . $148,960 − $132,580 = $16,380

Change in CC due to inflation (2 − 1) . . . . $143,719 − $132,580 = $11,139
Change in CC, net of inflation (3 − 2) . . . . $148,960 − $143,719 = $ 5,241

EXHIBIT 25–17   *(concluded)*

Non-Monetary Assets	Source	CC at Transaction Date (1)	Restated to CDs (2)	CC at Dec. 31, 1991 (3)
Parking Garage				
Beginning balance (net of depreciation)	25–15	$ –0–	$ –0–	
Add—acquisition on Jan. 1, 1991, CC at acquisition date	25–11	50,000	159/147 = 54,100	
Deduct—depreciation during 1991	25–15	(2,120)	159/152 = (2,218)	
1. Ending balance at CC at transaction dates.		$ 47,880		
2. Ending balance at CC restated to CDs.			$ 51,882	
3. Ending balance at year-end CC.	25–15			$ 53,760

Changes in CC during 1991

Total increase (decrease) in CC (3 – 1). . . . . $53,760 – $47,880 = $ 5,880

Change in CC due to inflation (2 – 1) . . . . $51,882 – $47,880 = $ 4,002
Change in CC, net of inflation (3 – 2) . . . . $53,760 – $51,882 = $ 1,878

EXHIBIT 25–18   Phog Company CC/CD Income Statement for Year Ended December 31, 1991

Income Statement CC/CD
For the Year Ended December 31, 1991

	Source (Exhibit)	CC Nominal Dollars	CD Restatement Ratio	CC/CD (in CDs of Dec. 31, 1991
Revenues and gains:				
Sales revenue	25–14	$144,000	159/152	$150,624
Expenses and losses:				
Cost of goods sold	25–15	86,000	159/152	(89,956)
General expenses (including interest).	25–14	20,000	159/152	(20,920)
Depreciation expense, equipment	25–15	7,420	159/152	(7,761)
Depreciation expense, parking garage	25–15	2,120	159/152	(2,218)
Income tax expense	25–14	10,000	159/152	(10,460)
CC/CD income from continuing operations.				19,309
Purchasing power gain (loss) on net monetary items.	25–13			(264)
Total change in CC of non-monetary items	below		$25,760	
Change in CC of NM items due to general inflation.	below		19,482	
Change in CC of NM items, net of general inflation	below			6,278
CD/CD comprehensive income				$ 25,323

Summary of Non-Monetary Price Changes, from Exhibit 25–17:

Non-Monetary Asset	Change in CC Total	Change in CC due to General Inflation	Change in CC net of General Inflation
Inventory	$ 6,500	$ 1,635	$ 4,865
Investment in common shares of Smith Co..	(3,000)	2,706	(5,706)
Equipment.	16,380	11,139	5,241
Parking garage.	5,880	4,002	1,878
Total	$25,760	$19,482	$ 6,278

CC depreciation, a component of the computed ending nominal CC amount for plant assets, is computed using the following formula (see Exhibit 25–15):

CC depreciation = Average CC during period × Depreciation rate based on HC

EXHIBIT 25–19 Phog Company CC/CD Retained Earnings Statement

	CC/CD (in CDs of Dec. 31, 1991)
Retained Earnings Statement CC/CD **For the Year Ended December 31, 1991**	
Retained earnings, January 1, 1991 (from prior year, Exhibit 25–15; $97,822 × 159/147)	$105,807
Add: CC/CD income (Exhibit 25–18)	25,323
Deduct: CC/CD dividends 1991 ($10,000 × 159/151)	(10,530)
CC/CD retained earnings, December 31, 1991	$120,600

$$\text{For equipment,} \atop \text{CC depreciation} = (\$175,000 + \$196,000)/2 \times 4\%$$

$$= \$7,420$$

$$\text{For parking garage,} \atop \text{CC depreciation} = (\$50,000 + \$56,000)/2 \times 4\%$$

$$= \$2,120$$

This formula bases CC depreciation on the *average* CC associated with the period. The parking garage was purchased in 1991. Therefore, its beginning CC equals its purchase price. CC depreciation expense as computed above reflects average 1991 CDs. Therefore, these amounts are restated to ending CDs on the income statement, and for computing the change in CC net of inflation.

The remaining computations for the investment in common shares, equipment, and the parking garage follow the format applied to inventory. Both the equipment and parking garage experienced CC changes in excess of inflation. However, the CC of the investment in common shares declined in 1991 from $33,000 to $30,000 (half the investment shares were sold on December 30, 1991). Because the GPL increased during 1991, the change in CC, net of general inflation, was negative $5,706.

At the bottom of Exhibit 25–18, we aggregate the total change in CC of non-monetary assets, the change in CC due to inflation, and the change in CC net of inflation. For Phog Company during 1991, the total change in CC, net of general inflation, is $6,278. This amount is carried to the HC/CD income statement.

We include this net holding gain in earnings because we have applied financial capital, and thus the holding gains represent a distributable value increase. Under productive capacity, holding gains do not represent distributable income and are a permanent part of equity.

CC/CD Income Statement and Retained Earnings Statement   Our last step is to prepare the CC/CD income and retained earning statements. The purchasing power loss is carried from the HC/CD income statement. The CC/CD income statement is presented in Exhibit 25–18, and the CC/CD retained earnings statement in Exhibit 25–19.

Sales revenue, general expenses, and income tax expense are reported at the amounts appearing in the HC/CD income statement because these amounts involve only monetary assets. Cost of goods sold and depreciation expense involve non-monetary assets. Supplier price lists were used to determine the CC cost of goods sold (see Exhibit 25–15). Depreciation expense is based on the HC rate applied to the average CC of depreciable assets, as illustrated in the previous section.

No gain on sale of the investment in common shares of Smith Company is reported because the sale proceeds ($15,000) was equal to the CC of the investment at the date of sale. The CC of marketable common shares is the quoted market price of the shares. However, Phog suffered a $5,706 holding loss on the investment, the decline in CC measured in ending CDs. This amount is part of the aggregate change in CC of non-monetary items, net of inflation.

All the CC revenue and expense items are multiplied by the CD restatement ratio, 159/152, to restate each item from average 1991 dollars to CDs of December 31, 1991.

Income from continuing operations for Phog ($19,309) is the difference between CC revenues and CC expenses. The remaining two items contributing to comprehensive CC/CD income are the purchasing power loss, taken from Exhibit 25–13, and the increase in CC of non-monetary items, net of inflation.

The beginning CC balance in retained earnings ($97,822) is restated to ending CDs. Comprehensive CC/CD income is added to it and restated dividends are deducted. The result is ending CC/CD retained earnings, stated in terms of ending CDs. This amount proves the balancing amount presented in the balance sheet.

Recap   CC/CD income from continuing operations is useful for (1) assessing the future net cash flows of an enterprise and (2) predicting distributable income because it deducts the CCs of assets consumed in production.

The increase or decrease in the CCs of non-monetary assets held represents a change in the value of the firm. Information on changes in CCs is one basis for assessing future cash flows.

The separation of CC/CD income into its operating and holding components is useful for many kinds of analysis, as operating and holding activities are inherently different.

The CC/CD balance sheet presents assets, liabilities, and shareholders' equity at CC. This gives users an estimate of the amount required currently to replace the entity's assets in their present condition. It also helps investors and others to estimate the value of a company. However, reliable CC information is difficult to develop and may not be worth its cost. The controversy about the usefulness of price-level–adjusted information continues.

CICA-SUGGESTED DISCLOSURE REQUIREMENTS FOR CHANGING PRICES

Section 4510 of the *CICA Handbook* required disclosure of the following information in a supplementary note to the financial statements:

Related to the income statement:

1. *Current cost: cost of goods sold and depreciation.* These are the only two income statement items that need be restated, presumably because they are the most affected by inflation and/or specific price changes.
2. *Historical cost income tax,* both current and deferred. Inclusion of this item should highlight the portion of "real" income that is paid in tax.
3. *Income on a current cost basis.* This represents historical cost income, before extraordinary items, adjusted for the current cost of COGS and depreciation.
4. *Purchasing power gain or loss,* from holding net monetary items.
5. *Increase in current cost during the year* (holding gains), from property, plant, and equipment, and inventory. The change in CC must be calculated once in nominal dollars, and once in constant dollars, so that the "real" change, and the portion due to inflation, is apparent.
6. *Financing adjustment.* The financing adjustment is calculated by multiplying the total increase in CC, or just the realized portion, by the percentage of the enterprise's capital structure that is provided by debt. For instance, if a firm with total changes in CC of $20,000 is financed 25% by debt, the financing adjustment is $5,000. The financing adjustment is considered to be the portion of CC increases that lenders, not owners, would finance, and thus it could be distributed to shareholders with no capital impairment. It may be included in income.

Related to the balance sheet:

7. *Current cost of inventory and property, plant, and equipment.* These are the only two balance sheet categories that must be restated.
8. *Net assets (shareholder's equity),* after the restatement of assets.

Other:

9. *Management explanations* of the impact of inflation on their operation.

We refer you to section 4510 for examples of the minimum disclosure recommendations. Our comprehensive illustration exceeds the minimum for most items.

CONCEPT REVIEW

1. Why are monetary items not adjusted to the ending GPL index?
2. Why is the purchasing power gain or loss included in both HC/CD and CC/CD earnings?
3. Explain how to compute the change in the CC of an asset, net of inflation. Why is this amount included as a component of CC/CD earnings?

SUMMARY OF KEY POINTS

(L.O. 1) 1. A primary objective of financial statement analysis is to identify and assess major changes in trends, amounts, and relationships.

(L.O. 1) 2. Important initial steps in financial statement analysis include careful examination of the auditor's report for any departures from GAAP and evaluation of accounting policies.

(L.O. 2) 3. Horizontal analysis is particularly useful in revealing trends. However, it is important to be sure that changed circumstances do not render the comparisons inappropriate.

(L.O. 3) 4. Ratios can be usefully segmented into those related to liquidity, efficiency, coverage, and profitability. Several ratios should be examined in each category before conclusions are attempted. Implications for ratios in the other categories should also be checked.

(L.O. 4) 5. Great care should be exercised before drawing conclusions from either earnings per share or cash flow per share data.

(L.O. 4) 6. The major disadvantage of ratio analysis is that the values used are almost always book values rather than market values. Company comparisons are also hazardous due to different business conditions and accounting techniques in use.

(L.O. 5) 7. To the extent capital markets are efficient, the information contained in ratios should be already reflected in market prices.

(L.O. 5) 8. Any serious analysis of a firm should search beyond the financial reports (e.g., in the press, with security analysts) for additional information. Financial statement evaluation is an integral part of a broader information system designed to provide data for decisions.

(L.O. 6) 9. The alleged effects of price-level changes on historical cost financial statements include overstatement of earnings and assets, and capital erosion.

(L.O. 7) 10. There are two types of price-level changes: general and specific. Changes in general price level indices measure inflation; specific prices and indices measure the change in the price of specific goods and services. Restating historical cost amounts for changes in GPL indices results in reports measured in dollars of constant purchasing power.

(L.O. 7) 11. Monetary items are cash or claims to cash and obligations to pay cash, fixed in dollar amount. Holding monetary items during times of general price-level changes results in a purchasing power gain or loss. This amount is a component of price-level–adjusted earnings.

(L.O. 7) 12. Non-monetary items do not carry fixed dollar amounts. Holding gains and losses, resulting from holding non-monetary items during times of specific price-level changes, are included in earnings adjusted for specific price changes if financial capital is used as a capital maintenance concept. If productive capacity is considered appropriate, holding gains and losses are considered part of capital and are excluded from income.

(L.O. 7) 13. The CICA recommends CC, the cost to replace an asset in its present condition and utility, as the appropriate measure of current value and for computing specific price changes. CC estimates, however, are often unreliable and costly.

(L.O. 7) 14. Three alternative models for adjusting financial statements for price-level changes are proposed: historical cost/constant dollar (HC/CD), current cost/nominal dollar (CC/ND), and current cost/constant dollar (CC/CD).

(L.O. 8) 15. The HC/CD model adjusts financial statement items to dollars of constant purchasing power, maintains the HC basis, and uses financial capital as a capital maintenance concept.

(L.O. 9) 16. The CC/ND model reports all financial statement items at CC, without adjusting for GPL changes. The CC/CD adjusts for GPL changes. The CC models separate earnings into operating (distributable) and holding components, allowing analysis of productive capacity maintenance and income generation. This separation may improve prediction of earnings and cash flows and prevent capital erosion.

(L.O. 8, 9) 17. The CICA recommended supplementary disclosure of price-level–adjusted financial statement information. The suggested disclosures emphasized the CC/CD model but opted for piecemeal disclosures. The disclosures did not gain general acceptance due to the perceived lack of reliability and poor cost/benefit trade-offs.

REVIEW PROBLEM

This review problem consists of two unrelated parts, A and B.

Part A

This part is based on the 1989 balance sheet and income statement for Dofasco Inc.

1. Calculate the following 1989 ratios for Dofasco:
   a. Current ratio.
   b. Inventory turnover.
   c. Accounts receivable turnover.
   d. Debt to equity.
   e. Times interest earned.
   f. Profit margin on sales and gross profit margin.
   g. Return on assets and equity.
2. What conclusions would you draw from this analysis?
3. What additional data would you like to have before rendering an opinion concerning the health of this company:
   a. From the company's annual report?
   b. From other sources?

DOFASCO INC.

Consolidated Balance Sheet

For the Years Ended December 31, 1989 and 1988

(in millions)

	1989	1988
Current Assets		
Cash and short term investments.	$ 140.7	$ 91.5
Accounts receivable	447.4	520.6
Inventories	1,151.2	1,077.0
	$1,739.3	$1,689.1

	1989	1988
Current Liabilities		
Accounts payable and accrued charges	$ 555.7	$ 496.4
Income and other taxes payable	56.5	31.4
Dividends payable	19.6	18.0
Current requirements on long term debt	172.0	52.2
	803.8	598.0
Working capital	$ 935.5	$1,091.1
Fixed and Other Assets		
Fixed assets	$3,213.3	$3,143.2
Investments at equity	107.1	8.7
Investments at cost and other assets	31.1	31.2
	3,351.5	3,183.1
Capital employed	$4,287.0	$4,274.2
Long-Term Liabilities		
Long term debt	$1,027.3	$1,134.2
Accruals for:		
Relining blast furnaces	129.0	104.2
Net pension and other post-employment benefits . . .	180.4	187.5
Income tax allocations relating to future years	658.9	693.6
Minority interest	32.6	34.7
	2,028.2	2,154.2
Net assets	$2,258.8	$2,120.0
Shareholders' Equity		
Represented by:		
Preferred shares	$ 340.7	$ 341.2
Common shares	501.1	471.9
Dividends distributable in common shares	8.0	6.0
Retained earnings	1,409.0	1,300.9
	$2,258.8	$2,120.0

DOFASCO INC.

Consolidated Income Statement
For the Year Ended December 31, 1989
(in millions)

	1989
Revenues:	
Sales	$3,908.3
Interest and other income	33.6
	3,941.9
Expenses:	
Cost of sales (before the following items):	3,160.2
Depreciation and amortization	242.1
Employees' profit sharing	52.4
Interest on long term debt	131.8
	3,586.5
Income before income taxes	355.4
Income taxes (33%)	116.7
	238.7
Income from equity investments	20.3
Income from continuing operations	259.0
Estimated cost of closing mining properties net of income taxes	
of $31 million	41.1
Net income for year	$ 217.9

Part B

Quality Transport Company transfers freight from its home office in Moncton, New Brunswick, to cities throughout Canada. Thus, it is a service-oriented enterprise and has no merchandise inventory. On January 1, 1991, the HC balance sheet of Quality Transport was as follows:

QUALITY TRANSPORT COMPANY
Balance Sheet
January 1, 1991

Assets

Cash and receivables	$12,000
Trucks	80,000
Accumulated depreciation	(–0–)
	$92,000

Liabilities and Owners' Equity

Current liabilities	$10,000
Long-term liabilities.	30,000
Owners' equity	52,000
	$92,000

Assume for simplicity that all revenues and all expenses occur evenly during the year. The trucks are new on January 1, 1991, are expected to remain in service for five years, and will be depreciated on a straight-line basis with no estimated residual value. GPL indices were 100 at January 1, 1991, 102 at February 15, 1991, 104 for average of 1991, and 108 at December 31, 1991. Current cost (CC) of the trucks at December 31, 1991, was $88,000 before deducting accumulated depreciation.

Historical cost (HC) transactions for 1991 included the following:

1. Payment on February 15, 1991, of the $10,000 beginning balance of current liabilities.
2. Service revenue of $100,000, of which $70,000 is collected in cash.
3. Depreciation of $16,000.
4. Other expenses (including interest) of $75,000, of which $35,000 is unpaid at December 31, 1991. The $35,000 of liabilities are current.

Required (round all CD restatement ratios to three decimals before multiplication):

1. Prepare the CC/CD (CDs as of December 31, 1991) balance sheet of Quality Transport Company at December 31, 1991.
2. Prepare the CC/CD (CDs as of December 31, 1991) income statement for Quality Transport Company for the year ended December 31, 1991.

REVIEW
SOLUTION
◆

Part A

1. Dofasco ratios:
   a. Current ratio:

$$\frac{\$1,739.3}{\$803.8} = 2.16$$

   b. Inventory turnover:

$$\frac{\$3,160.2}{(\$1,151.2 + \$1,077)/2} = 2.83$$

   c. Accounts receivable turnover:

$$\frac{\$3,908.3}{(\$447.4 + \$520.6)/2} = 8.08$$

$d.$ Debt to equity:

$$\frac{\$803.8 + \$1,027.3 + \$129 + \$180.4}{\$2,258.8} = .95$$

$e.$ Times interest earned:

$$\frac{\$259 + \$116.7 + \$131.8}{\$131.8} = 3.85$$

$f.$ Profit margin on sales:

$$\frac{\$259}{\$3,908.3} = 6.6\%$$

Gross profit margin:

$$\frac{\$3,908.3 - \$3,160.2}{\$3,908.3} = 19\%$$

$g.$ Return on assets:

$$\frac{\$259 + \$131.8(1 - .33)}{(\$1,739.3 + \$3,351.5) + (\$1,689.1 + \$3,183.1)/2} = 7\%$$

Return on equity:

$$\frac{\$259}{(\$2,258.8 + \$2,120)/2} = 11.8\%$$

2. One would conclude that:
   Dofasco's inventory turnover is low, although this may be typical for the industry. They collect their receivables far more quickly, although this is not as high a ratio as a 30-day collection period would produce.
   The debt-to-equity ratio is fairly high—about half of Dofasco's financing is provided by debt. Interest coverage is adequate, but hardly at Cominco's level. Leverage is working to the advantage of Dofasco's shareholders. A return on assets of 7% was parlayed into a return on equity of close to 12%.
   Overall, no particular danger signals arise from this ratio analysis.
3. Here are some suggestions for additional information. The list is not exhaustive. From the company's annual report:
   $a.$ The auditor's report.
   $b.$ Data from the five-year summary so trends can be observed (horizontal analysis).
   $c.$ The president's letter, which may give some clue to the potential future profitability of the firm.
   $d.$ The statement of changes in financial position, to indicate whether cash flows are healthy.
   $e.$ The footnotes, to tell us the accounting principles used and explain the items on the statements as well as give more detail.
   From other sources:
   $f.$ Strength of the industry and of Dofasco's customers.
   $g.$ Quality of its management, employee talent, marketing network, R&D activities.
   $h.$ Reputation for quality, ability to meet deadlines, flexibility of manufacturing operations.

Part B

1.

QUALITY TRANSPORT COMPANY
CC/CD Balance Sheet
At December 31, 1991

Cash and receivables	$ 62,000*	Current liabilities	
Trucks	88,000	($10,000 − $10,000 + $35,000)	$ 35,000
Accumulated depreciation		Long-term liabilities	30,000
($88,000 ÷ 5)	(17,600)	Owners' equity (balancing amount) . . .	67,400**
Total	$132,400	Total	$132,400

* ($12,000 + $100,000 − $10,000 − $40,000)

** ($52,000 × 108/100 = $56,160) + $11,240

2.

QUALITY TRANSPORT COMPANY
CC/CD Income Statement
For the Year Ended December 31, 1991

Service revenue ($100,000 × 108/104)	$103,800
Expenses:	
Depreciation ($16,800* × 108/104)	(17,438)
Other ($75,000 × 108/104)	(77,850)
Operating income.	8,512
Purchasing power gain on net monetary items (see computation below)	1,290
Increase in current cost of trucks (see computation below) $7,200	
Increase due to general inflation (see computation below) . . . . (5,762)	
Excess of CC over inflation (see computation below).	1,438
CC/CD comprehensive income	$ 11,240

* ($80,000 + $88,000) ÷ 2 = $84,000; $84,000 ÷ 5 = $16,800.

QUALITY TRANSPORT COMPANY
Purchasing Power Gain (Loss) on Net Monetary Items
For the Year Ended December 31, 1991

		CD Restatement	
Monetary Items—Increases (Decreases)	HC	Ratio	HC/CD
Total beginning net monetary assets ($12,000 − $40,000).	$(28,000)	108/100	$(30,240)
Increases during 1991 from:			
Sales revenue.	100,000	108/104	103,800
Decreases during 1991 from:			
Other expenses.	(75,000)	108/104	(77,850)
Total ending net monetary assets:			
HC ($62,000 − $65,000)	$ (3,000)		
GPL restated.			$ (4,290)
Purchasing power gain on net monetary items [−$3,000 − (−$4,290)].			$ 1,290

QUALITY TRANSPORT COMPANY
Change in the CC of Trucks
For the Year Ended December 31, 1991

	CC at Transaction Date	CD Restatement Ratio	CC/CD (in CDs of Dec. 31, 1991)	CC at Dec. 31, 1991
Beginning balance (net of depreciation)	$ 80,000	108/100	$ 86,400	
Additions—none	—		—	
Deductions—depreciation during 1991. .	(16,800)	108/104	(17,438)	
Ending balance at CC at transaction date	$ 63,200			
Ending balance at CC restated to CD . .			$ 68,962	
Ending balance at year-end CC ($88,000 − $17,600)				$70,400
Changes in CC during 1991: Total increase ($70,400 − $63,200) . . .			$ 7,200	
Change in CC due to inflation ($68,962 − $63,200)			$ 5,762	
Change in CC net of inflation ($70,400 − $68,962)			$ 1,438	

KEY TERMS

Capital maintenance concept (1284)
Capital market approach (1281)
Constant dollar (1283)
Consumer Price Index (CPI) (1285)
Current cost (1288)
Efficient market theory (1281)
Entry value (1288)
Exit value (1288)
Financial capital maintenance (1284)
Fundamental analysis (1281)
General price level (1285)
Horizontal analysis (1265)
Leverage (1276)

Monetary items (1286)
Nominal dollar (1283)
Non-monetary items (1286)
Present value (1288)
Productive capacity maintenance (1284)
Purchasing power gain or loss (1287)
Ratio analysis (1267)
Replacement cost (1288)
Specific price index (1289)
Systematic risk (1282)
Unqualified (clean) opinion (1261)
Unsystematic risk (1282)
Vertical analysis (1265)

QUESTIONS

1. Why is the past financial record of a company important to statement users? What is meant by a turning point?
2. Explain why financial analysts and others, in analysing financial statements, examine the auditor's report and the summary of accounting policies.
3. Explain why the notes to the financial statements should be read carefully when analysing financial statements. Why are five-year summaries considered important to statement users?
4. Distinguish between vertical and horizontal analyses. Briefly explain the importance of each.
5. What is meant by ratio analysis? Why is it important in the analysis of financial statements?
6. Distinguish between the current ratio and the quick ratio. What purpose does each serve?
7. Current assets and current liabilities for two companies with the same amount of working capital are summarized below. Evaluate their relative liquidity positions.

	X Company	Y Company
Current assets	$300,000	$900,000
Current liabilities	100,000	700,000
Working capital	$200,000	$200,000

8. X Corporation's receivables average age is 24.3 days. Interpret this figure. What is the accounts receivable turnover ratio? What does it reveal?

9. Y Corporation has an inventory turnover of 9; interpret this figure.

10. Explain and illustrate the effect of financial leverage.

11. Compute and explain the meaning of the book value per common share of the Craft Manufacturing Company, assuming the following data are available:

Preferred shares, nopar, $6, cumulative, non-participating, 200 shares issued
  and outstanding, liquidation value is $100 per share . . . . $ 20,000
Common shares, nopar, 10,000 shares issued and outstanding   100,000
Retained earnings   7,000
(Three years' dividends in arrears on preferred shares including current year.)

12. Explain the circumstances where a company has debt financing and the leverage factor is (a) positive, (b) negative, and (c) zero.

13. Explain the return on assets employed. Why is it a fundamental measure of profitability?

14. What is meant by the multiple? Why is it considered important?

15. What are the principal limitations in using ratios?

16. What is the price phenomenon known as inflation? What is the opposite phenomenon called? How would each affect you if you received an equal amount from an educational trust fund set up by your parents 20 years ago?

17. "When prices are going up, they all go up; when they drop, they all drop." Comment on this statement.

18. What indices measure changes in the general purchasing power of the Canadian dollar? What index is normally used for preparation of CD financial statements?

19. Among sales, cost of goods sold, salaries, and depreciation expense, during a period of rapidly changing prices, which would most nearly be at the current price under the conventional historical cost (HC) model and which would not be on a current price basis? Give reasons for your response.

20. When prices are changing rapidly, why may financial statements prepared on the HC basis be deficient in some respects?

21. Under the CD restatement approach, financial statement items are classified as monetary or non-monetary. Briefly, by which criterion can these two categories be distinguished?

22. Indicate, with explanations where necesssary, whether the following items are monetary or non-monetary: (a) shares held as investments, (b) bonds held as investments, (c) deposits in banks, (d) merchandise inventory, (e) accounts and notes receivable, (f) machinery and equipment, (g) accounts and notes payable, (h) preferred shares, (i) retained earnings, and (j) deferred credit related to income taxes.

23. During its most recent accounting period, Crouse Company had a larger balance of cash and receivables than monetary liabilities; general prices rose steadily. Would this condition cause a purchasing power gain or loss on net monetary items?

24. If prices rise steadily over an extended period of time, indicate whether the following items would cause a purchasing power gain, a purchasing power loss, or neither purchasing power gain nor loss on net monetary items:
   a. Maintaining a balance in a chequing account.
   b. Owing bonds payable.
   c. Owning land.
   d. Amortizing goodwill.

25. A company begins the fiscal year with a $10,000 net monetary asset position, has an even outflow of monetary assets of $25,000 during the year, and ends the year with a net monetary liability position of $15,000. If the GPL index is 120 at the beginning of the year, 125 on average for the year, and 132 at the end of the year, what is the purchasing power gain or loss during the year?

26. "The HC/CD accounting model changes the unit of measure but retains the attribute measured relative to the conventional accounting model, whereas CC/CD changes both the attribute measured and the unit of measurement." Evaluate this statement.

27. What are the advantages and disadvantages of CC/CD reporting in relation to HC/CD reporting?

28. How does the recognition of increases or decreases in the CC of non-monetary assets under the CC/CD model affect the ability of an entity to "manipulate its earnings" by selling selected assets that have increased or decreased in value?

29. How does the net realizable value, or recoverable amount, of an asset affect current cost accounting?
30. The current cost of land is $50,000 on January 1, 1991, and $55,000 on December 31, 1991. If the GPL index was 100 and 110 on January 1 and December 31, respectively, what was the increase in the current cost of land, net of inflation, during 1991 (stated in dollars as of December 31, 1991)?
31. Assume that in question 30 the GPL index remained unchanged during 1991; it was 100 on January 1, 1991 and December 31, 1991. What was the increase in the current cost of land, net of inflation, during 1991 (stated in dollars as of December 31, 1991)?

EXERCISES

E 25–1
Horizontal and Vertical Analysis: Income Statement (L.O. 2)

Beathard Trading Company's income statements (condensed) for two years are shown below.

	December 31	
	1990	**1991**
Gross sales	$ 272,700	$ 303,000
Returns	(2,700)	(3,000)
	270,000	300,000
Cost of goods sold	(135,000)	(180,000)
Gross margin	135,000	120,000
Expenses:		
Selling	(67,500)	(69,000)
Administrative (including income taxes)	(37,800)	(33,000)
Interest (net of interest revenue)	(2,700)	3,000
Net income before extraordinary items	27,000	21,000
Extraordinary gain (loss), net of tax	5,400	(3,000)
Net income	$ 32,400	$ 18,000
Common shares outstanding	10,000	10,000

Required:

1. Prepare a multiple-step comparative income statement including a vertical percentage analysis. Round to the nearest percent.
2. Prepare a single-step income statement, including horizontal percentage analysis. Round to the nearest percent.

E 25–2
Horizontal and Vertical Analysis: Balance Sheet (L.O. 2)

Levy Company's balance sheet (condensed and unclassified) for two years is shown below.

	December 31	
	1990	**1991**
Cash	$ 12,000	$ 26,000
Accounts receivable (net)	20,000	19,000
Inventory (FIFO, LCM)	32,000	40,000
Prepaid expenses	2,000	1,000
Funds and investments (at cost)	18,000	22,000
Plant assets	120,000	126,000
Accumulated depreciation	(28,000)	(45,000)
Intangible assets	4,000	11,000
Total	$180,000	$200,000
Accounts payable	$ 30,000	$ 15,000
Remaining current liabilities	10,000	10,000
Long-term mortgage payable	40,000	33,000
Common shares, nopar	70,000	100,000
Retained earnings	30,000	42,000
Total	$180,000	$200,000

Required:

1. Prepare a comparative balance sheet in good form, including a vertical percentage analysis. Round to the nearest percent.
2. Prepare a comparative balance sheet in good form, including a horizontal percentage analysis. Round to the nearest percent.

E 25–3
Ratio Analysis of Current Assets: Significance
(L.O. 3)

The condensed financial information given below was taken from the annual financial statements of Cohlan Corporation:

	1990	1991	1992
Current assets (including inventory)	$ 200,000	$ 240,000	$ 280,000
Current liabilities	150,000	160,000	140,000
Cash sales	800,000	780,000	820,000
Credit sales	200,000	280,000	250,000
Cost of goods sold	560,000	585,000	600,000
Inventory (ending)	120,000	140,000	100,000
Quick assets	80,000	80,000	112,000
Accounts receivable (net)	60,000	64,000	61,000
Total assets (net)	1,000,000	1,200,000	1,400,000

Required:

1. Based on the above data, calculate the following ratios for 1991 and 1992; use 365 days for computation purposes. Round to one decimal point (e.g., ratios, 5.2 and percents, 8.4%). Also, briefly explain the significance of each ratio listed. Use the following format:

Ratio	1991	1992	Significance

a. Current ratio.
b. Acid-test ratio.
c. Working capital to total assets.
d. Accounts receivable turnover.
e. Age of accounts receivable.
f. Merchandise inventory turnover.
g. Working capital turnover.

2. Evaluate the overall results of the computations, including trends.

E 25–4
Ratio Analysis, Inventory and Receivables—Assess Results
(L.O. 3)

The following information was taken from the financial statements of Infante Company:

	1990	1991	1992
Sales—cash	$190,000	$200,000	$220,000
Sales—credit	100,000	120,000	130,000
Average receivables	25,000	34,000	50,000
Average inventory	60,000	70,000	80,000
Cost of goods sold	180,000	190,000	200,000

Required:

1. Prepare a ratio analysis of (*a*) inventory and (*b*) receivables. Use 365 days. Credit terms are 2/10, n/30. Round to one decimal place and even days. Also, briefly explain the significance of each ratio. Use the following format:

Year	Ratio	Significance

2. Assess possible impacts of trends that your analysis indicates relative to (*a*) inventory and (*b*) receivables.

E 25–5
Compute Book Value per Share: Common and Preferred Shares
(L.O. 3)

Mandarich Manufacturing Corporation's balance sheet showed, as of December 31, 1993:

Total liabilities	$100,000
Preferred shares, nopar, $3, 4,000 shares outstanding	240,000
Common shares, nopar, 30,000 shares outstanding	360,000
Retained earnings	90,000

Required:

Compute the book value per common share assuming:

1. None of the preferred shares have been issued.

2. Preferred is non-cumulative and non-participating; liquidation preference value of preferred is $50 per share.
3. Preferred is cumulative and non-participating; three years' dividends in arrears, including current year; liquidation value of preferred is $50 per share.
4. Preferred has a liquidation value of $60 per share and is non-cumulative and non-participating.
5. Preferred has a liquidation value of $60 per share and is non-cumulative and non-participating, and the retained earnings account shows a deficit of $30,000, instead of the $90,000 credit balance shown above.

E 25–6
Compute and Explain Profitability Ratios
(L.O. 3)

The 1992 comparative financial statements for Testaverde Corporation reported:

	1990	1991	1992
Sales revenue.	$12,000,000	$13,000,000	$14,000,000
Net income.	100,000	120,000	100,000
Interest expense, net of income tax	10,000	12,000	20,000
Shareholders' equity	1,400,000	1,450,000	1,460,000
Total assets.	3,500,000	3,500,000	3,700,000
Market value per share	$66	$72	$44
Common shares outstanding	20,000	20,000	25,000

Required:

1. Based on the above financial data, compute the following ratios for 1991 and 1992: (*a*) profit margin, (*b*) return on total assets, (*c*) return on owners' equity, (*d*) the leverage factor, (*e*) EPS, and (*f*) price-earnings ratio. Carry computations to two decimal places (e.g., ratios, 5.22 and percents 8.43%.)
2. As an investor in the common shares of Testaverde, which ratio would you prefer as a single measure of profitability? Why?
3. Explain any significant trends that appear to be developing.

E 25–7
Compute and Assess Profitability Ratios for Five Years
(L.O. 3)

The following data relate to the Peete Printing Company:

	1988	1989	1990	1991	1992
Net income.	$ 12,000	$ 15,000	$ 25,000	$ 30,000	$ 40,000
Interest expense (net of tax)	1,000	1,200	2,000	2,200	3,000
Sales revenue.	120,000	140,000	180,000	230,000	260,000
Total assets.	50,000	72,000	110,000	160,000	190,000
Total liabilities	25,000	30,000	40,000	70,000	80,000

Required:

1. For each of the five years, compute the (*a*) profit margin, (*b*) return on owners' equity, (*c*) return on total assets, and (*d*) financial leverage factor. Round to the nearest percentage.
2. Based on (1), assess the five-year trend of earnings reflected in the income statement.

E 25–8
Compute and Summarize Significance of Ratios of Liquidity, Efficiency, Equity, and Profitability
(L.O. 3)

O'Brien Corporation's 1990 and 1991 balance sheets and 1991 income statement are as follows (in thousands):

	December 31			
	1990		1991	
Balance sheet:				
Cash.	$ 10		$ 19	
Investments (short term)	2		3	
Accounts receivable (net of allowance)	22		18	
Inventory (FIFO, LCM)	30		36	
Prepaid expenses.	3		2	
Funds and investments	30		30	
Plant assets (net of accumulated depreciation)	80		70	
Accounts payable.		$ 21		$ 9
Accrued liabilities		1		2
Note payable, long-term.		40		40
Common shares, nopar (60,000 shares outstanding)		75		75
Retained earnings (including 1991 income)		40		52
Totals	$177	$177	$178	$178

Income statement (1991):

Sales revenue (⅓ on credit)	$153
Investment revenue	6
Cost of goods sold	(70)
Distribution expense	(20)
Administrative expense	(15)
Interest expense	(4)
Income tax expense (40%)	(20)
Net income	$ 30
Dividends declared and paid ($.30 per share)	$ 18
Market price per common share	$ 8
Cash flow from operations	$ 28

Required:

For each requirement, use a format similar to the following (example given):

Ratio	Formula	Computation	Significance
1. Current ratio	Current assets ÷ Current liabilities	$\dfrac{\$78}{\$11} = 7.1$	Short-term liquidity; adequacy of working capital

Note: Round ratios to one decimal place (3.5); round percentages to the nearest percent (35%).

1. Compute the 1991 ratios that measure liquidity position (as given in Exhibit 25–4 and in the same order).
2. Compute the 1991 ratios that measure efficiency (as given in Exhibit 25–5 and in the same order).
3. Compute the 1991 ratios that measure equity position and coverage (as given in Exhibit 25–6 and in the same order).
4. Compute the 1991 ratios that measure profitability (as given in Exhibit 25–7 and in the same order).

E 25–9
Four Financial Reporting Models
(L.O. 6, 7)

Nicky Company purchased land for $200,000 on January 1, 1990. Near the end of 1990, Nicky received several offers from other firms to purchase the land. The bids are all within $1,000 of the average $250,000 bid. Other, similar plots of land in the vicinity have sold for amounts very close to $250,000 in the recent past. Nicky decided not to sell. General price-level indices are as follows: January 1, 1990, 100; December 31, 1990, 110.

Required:

Discuss how each of the four models for financial reporting discussed in the text (HC/ND, HC/CD, CC/ND, CC/CD) would report the above information. Include income statement and balance sheet effects in your discussion, as well as general advantages and disadvantages of each approach.

E 25–10
Prepare HC/CD Balance Sheet and Income Statement
(L.O. 8)

Banner Corporation is completing its fifth year of operations (1993). Comparative balance sheets (HC basis) at year-end 1992 and 1993 are as follows:

	December 31 1992	December 31 1993
Cash and receivables	$250,000	$325,000
Inventories	187,500	162,500
Future plant site	62,500	62,500
Fixtures	210,000	270,000
Accumulated depreciation	(50,000)	(74,000)
	$660,000	$746,000

	December 31	
	1992	**1993**
Current liabilities	$ 75,000	$137,500
Long-term liabilities.	150,000	125,000
Share capital	400,000	400,000
Retained earnings	35,000	83,500
	$660,000	$746,000

The income statement (HC basis) for the year ended December 31, 1993, follows:

Sales revenue		$1,000,000
Cost of goods sold:		
Beginning inventory	$187,500	
Purchases	625,000	
Goods available	812,500	
Ending inventory	162,500	
Cost of goods sold		650,000
Gross margin		350,000
Expenses:		
Operating expenses, except depreciation	120,000	
Depreciation expense	24,000	144,000
Income before taxes		206,000
Income tax expense		87,500
Net income		$ 118,500

A dividend of $70,000 was declared at year-end. At midyear, additional fixtures costing $60,000 were purchased: $3,000 of depreciation was charged on the new fixtures in 1993. Inventories are on a FIFO basis. When the share capital was issued at various times, the average GPL index was 130.312. The original fixtures of $210,000 and the future plant site were acquired during the first year of operations when the relevant GPL index was 120. Other GPL index data are as follows: Dec. 31, 1993, 163.8; Dec. 31, 1992, 150; average for 1993, 157.5; average for 1992, 146.25.

Assume the beginning inventory was acquired at average 1992 prices. Purchases, sales, operating expense, and income taxes occurred or accrued evenly throughout the year.

Required:

Round all CD restatement ratios to three decimals before multiplication.

1. Prepare an HC/CD balance sheet as of December 31, 1993, and an HC/CD income statement for 1993. Determine the purchasing power gain or loss on net monetary items and present a separate schedule detailing its computation.
2. Prepare the 1993 HC/CD retained earnings statement.

E 25–11
Analysis of GPL Index
Numbers: Investment
(L.O. 7, 8)

Becker Corporation sold one third of its long-term investment in the common shares of another company (carried at cost) and made the entry shown in column A below:

	Column A	Column B
Cash	62,000	62,000
Investment in shares	50,000	57,500
Gain on sale of investment	12,000	4,500

In preparing HC/CD statements, the transaction of column A was restated as shown in column B.

Required:

Round restatement ratios to five decimal places before multiplication.

1. If the GPL index was 138 when the transaction recorded above occurred, at what level was it when the shares were acquired? Show computations.
2. Assume the remaining two thirds of the shares are sold later for $120,000 when the GPL index is 147. Give entries paralleling those above in columns A and B.
3. If the share prices and GPL index values given were unchanged, what other factors, if any, would cause entries reflected in columns A and B to differ at the time of either the first or second sale?

E 25–12
HC/CD of Individual Items on the Balance Sheet and Income Statement
(L.O. 8)

Bertrand Company is preparing financial statements on the HC/CD basis. Selected data are as follows:

1. GPL index data: Jan. 1, 1987, 115; Dec. 31, 1987, 120; June 30, 1988, 126; Dec. 31, 1990, 168; Average for 1991, 174; Dec. 31, 1991, 180.
2. Property, plant, and equipment acquisition and depreciation data:
   a. Land acquired January 1, 1987, at a cost of $90,000.
   b. Building acquired December 31, 1987, at a cost of $120,000; by year-end, 1990 and 1991, respectively, accumulated depreciation on the building amounted to $44,000 and $48,000.
   c. Equipment costing $168,000 was acquired June 30, 1988; by December 31, 1990, accumulated depreciation amounted to $109,200; depreciation recorded for 1991 was $8,400.
   d. New equipment, added during 1991 at a time when the index was at an average value for the year, cost $58,000; depreciation recorded on this new equipment for 1991 amounted to $4,350.
3. Monetary items: At the start of 1991, total monetary assets amounted to $120,000, while total monetary liabilities amounted to $180,000. At the end of 1991, total monetary assets amounted to $140,000, while total monetary liabilities were $190,000.

Required:

Use the numbers below for identification and compute the amounts for each numbered item. Round CD restatement ratios to five decimal places before multiplication.

A. On the HC/CD balance sheet as of December 31, 1991, carrying values for each would be:
   1. Land.
   2. Building (gross amount).
   3. Accumulated depreciation—building.
   4. Original equipment (gross amount).
   5. New equipment (gross amount).
   6. Accumulated depreciation on equipment (original).
   7. Accumulated depreciation on equipment (new).
   8. Total monetary assets.
   9. Total monetary liabilities.
B. On the HC/CD income statement for the year ended December 31, 1991, amounts reported would be:
   10. Depreciation expense (original equipment).
   11. Depreciation expense (new equipment).
   12. Depreciation expense (building).
   13. Sales revenue (if sales of $400,000 were made evenly throughout 1991).

E 25–13
Analytical; Purchasing Power Gain or Loss on Monetary Items
(L.O. 7, 8)

An incomplete computation of purchasing power gain or loss on net monetary items is given below.

	HC	HC/CD
Total beginning excess of monetary assets over monetary liabilities	$121,000	$132,000
Increases during the year:		
Sales revenue	$287,500	$300,000
Sale of common shares	106,200	108,000
Total increases	$393,700	$408,000
Decreases during the year:		
Purchases	$197,800	$206,400
Expenses	33,120	34,560
Cash dividend declared	20,000	20,000
Total decreases	$250,920	$260,960

Additional data: Sales, purchases, and expenses occurred evenly throughout the year. The GPL index at year-end was 120.

Required:

Support each answer; show how it was derived.

1. What was the index value when the period began?
2. What was the average index value for the year?
3. What was the index value when the shares were sold?
4. Assuming prices rose steadily, when was the dividend declared?

5. What was the purchasing power gain or loss on net monetary items?

E 25–14
CC/CD: Analysis of Inventory and Cost of Goods Sold
(L.O. 9)

The following information is available regarding the inventory of Spruce Corporation:

	HC	CC (at transaction or balance date)
January 1, 1993, balance.	$ 90,000	$100,000
Purchases during 1993.	600,000	600,000
December 31, 1993, balance	164,000	190,000

Purchases were made evenly during 1993. Merchandise that sold evenly during 1993 had an average current cost of $50 per unit (10,800 units sold). GPL index information during 1993: January 1, 1993, 100; average for 1993, 115; December 31, 1993, 132.

Required:

Round ratios to three decimal places before multiplication.

1. Set up and complete a schedule of inventory changes in the current cost (CC) of inventory and compute (*a*) total increase in CC, (*b*) increase in CC, due to general inflation, and (*c*) decrease in CC, net of general inflation. Suggestion: set up three column headings: CC at transaction or balance date, CC restatement ratio, and CC/CD (in CDs as of Dec. 31, 1993). Also, indicate what items would be reported on the CC/CD financial statements.
2. Assume the CC/CD income from continuing operations is $80,000 and the purchasing power loss on net monetary items is $24,000. Complete the HC/CD income statement for Spruce Corporation.

E 25–15
CC/CD: Analysis of Equipment
(L.O. 9)

Wood Company acquired equipment on January 1, 1988, at a cost of $100,000. On December 31, 1990, the current cost of the equipment was $140,000, and on December 31, 1991, the current cost was $170,000. Both current cost amounts are estimated before deducting associated accumulated depreciation. The equipment is being depreciated on a straight-line basis over a 10-year period with no residual value. GPL index data are as follows: January 1, 1988, 105; December 31, 1990, 120; December 31, 1991, 128; 1991 average, 124.

Required:

Round all CD restatement ratios to three decimal places before multiplication.

1. Compute the CC of the equipment, net of accumulated depreciation, on December 31, 1990, and December 31, 1991.
2. Compute CC depreciation expense for 1991.
3. Compute for equipment (*a*) the total change in CC during 1991 and (*b*) the change in CC due to general inflation during 1991. Set up captions for CC at transaction or balance date, CD restatement ratio, and CC/CD (in Dec. 31, 1991 CDs).
4. Assume the CC/CD income from continuing operations is $95,000 and the purchasing power loss on net monetary items is $11,000. Complete the HC/CD income statement for Wood Company.

E 25–16
CC/CD: Analysis of Changes in Land Costs
(L.O. 9)

Waco Development Corporation acquired land on January 1, 1987, for $1,000,000. On June 30, 1993, half of the land was sold for $1,600,000. The following current cost data regarding the land are available:

	CC of Land	GPL Index
January 1, 1993	$2,800,000	150
June 30, 1993		162
1993—average.		160
December 31, 1993	1,700,000*	171

* After sale of land.

Required:

Round all CD restatement ratios to three decimal places.

1. Compute for land the 1993 change in CC as follows: (*a*) total, (*b*) due to general inflation, and (*c*) net of general inflation (*in average CDs of 1993*). Set up column headings for: CC at transaction or balance date, CD restatement ratio, and CC/CD (in average CDs).
2. Assume the CC/CD income from continuing operations is $1,600,000 and that the purchasing power loss on net monetary items is $30,000. Complete the HC/CD income statement for Waco Development Corporation.

PROBLEMS

P 25–1
Overview of Ratios
(L.O. 3)

Below are columns listing commonly used ratios (third column), ratio formulas (fourth column), and significance—key words (last column). For each commonly used ratio, identify its formula by entering the appropriate letter in the first column and identify its significance by entering the appropriate number in the second column.

The current ratio is given as an example. Use each letter and number only once.

Matching		Commonly Used Ratio	Basic Formula	Significance— Key Words
Formula	Signifi- cance			
H	10	Net cash flow to current liabilities	A. $\dfrac{\text{Income}}{\text{Average owners' equity}}$	1. Profitability of each sales dollar.
		Current ratio	B. $\dfrac{365\ \text{days}}{\text{Receivable turnover}}$	2. Proportion of assets provided by owners.
		Book value per common share	C. $\dfrac{\text{Net sales}}{\text{Average total assets}}$	3. Test of current liquidity.
		Defensive-interval ratio	D. $\dfrac{\text{Market price per share}}{\text{Earnings per share}}$	4. Rate of return on all resources used.
		Profit margin	E. $\dfrac{\text{Cost of goods sold}}{\text{Average inventory}}$	5. Rough estimate of the expected rate of cash return per share based on market value.
		Dividend payout ratio, based on income	F. $\dfrac{\text{Current assets}}{\text{Current liabilities}}$	6. Credit and collection efficiency.
		Age of accounts receivable	G. $\dfrac{\text{Defensive assets (quick assets)}}{\text{Projected daily operational expense}}$	7. Efficiency in use of total assets.
		Debt to total assets	H. $\dfrac{\text{Net cash flow from operations}}{\text{Current liabilities}}$	8. Percentage of income that is paid out in cash dividends.
		Inventory turnover	I. $\dfrac{\text{Cash dividends per share}}{\text{Market price per share}}$	9. Rough measure of how long the firm could operate using only its present liquid resources.
		Accounts receivable turnover	J. $\dfrac{\text{Income}}{\text{Net sales}}$	10. Ability to pay current liabilities.
		Working capital turnover	K. $\dfrac{\text{Net credit sales}}{\text{Average trade receivables}}$	11. Effectiveness of use of working capital to generate sales.
		Return on owners' equity	L. $\dfrac{\text{Cash dividends per share}}{\text{Earnings per share}}$	12. Proportion of assets provided by creditors.
		Cash flow per share	M. $\dfrac{\text{Net cash flow from operations}}{\text{Outstanding common shares}}$	13. Severe test of immediate liquidity.
		Working capital to total assets	N. $\dfrac{\text{Income before taxes and interest}}{\text{Interest charges}}$	14. Income available to cover interest.

Matching		Commonly Used Ratio	Basic Formula	Significance— Key Words
Formula	Signifi-cance			
		Times interest earned	O. $\dfrac{\text{Total liabilities}}{\text{Total assets}}$	15. Number of dollars of common equity per share.
		Debt to equity	P. $\dfrac{\text{Working capital}}{\text{Total assets}}$	16. Relationship between earnings per share and market price.
		Earnings per share	Q. $\dfrac{\text{Income plus interest expense net of tax}}{\text{Average total assets}}$	17. Times average inventory was sold.
		Acid-test ratio	R. $\dfrac{\text{Net sales}}{\text{Average working capital}}$	18. Relationship between debt and resources provided by owners.
		Dividend payout ratio—market	S. $\dfrac{\text{Owners' equity}}{\text{Total assets}}$	19. Relative investment in current assets to total assets.
		Return on total assets	T. $\dfrac{\text{Income associated with common shares}}{\text{Common shares outstanding}}$	20. Average number of days to collect trade receivables.
		Asset turnover	U. $\dfrac{\text{Quick assets}}{\text{Current liabilities}}$	21. Rate of return on resources provided by owners.
		Price-earnings ratio	V. $\dfrac{\text{Total liabilities}}{\text{Owners' equity}}$	22. Income earned on each common share.
		Owners' equity to total assets	W. $\dfrac{\text{Common share equity}}{\text{Outstanding common shares}}$	23. Cash generated per share.

P 25–2

Compute and Assess Current Position Ratios for Three Years

(L.O. 3)

The following information was taken from the annual financial statements of Sabo Corporation:

	1990	1991	1992
Current assets:			
Cash	$ 17,500	$ 11,000	$ 7,000
Short-term investments	45,000	30,000	25,000
Trade receivables	180,000	170,000	165,000
Less: Allowance for doubtful accounts	(5,000)	(6,000)	(5,000)
Notes receivable (non-trade)	120,000	125,000	88,000
Inventory	290,000	350,000	445,000
Prepaid expenses	12,500	10,000	10,000
Total	$ 660,000	$ 690,000	$ 735,000
Current liabilities:			
Trade payables	$ 75,000	$ 138,000	$ 196,000
Notes payable	90,000	72,000	60,000
Accrued wages payable	72,000	46,000	52,000
Income taxes payable	19,000	23,000	24,000
Deferred rent revenue	2,000	2,000	2,000
Accrued liabilities	17,000	19,000	16,000
Total	$ 275,000	$ 300,000	$ 350,000
Additional data:			
Cash sales	$3,300,000	$3,500,000	$3,200,000
Credit sales	1,500,000	1,700,000	1,800,000
Cost of goods sold	2,700,000	2,900,000	3,180,000
Operating expenses	1,000,000	1,200,000	1,350,000
Total assets (net)	6,400,000	7,100,000	7,700,000
Cash from operations	640,000	620,000	640,000

Required:

1. Compute the ratios that measure liquidity and efficiency for 1990, 1991, and 1992. Round to one decimal place (e.g., ratios, 5.2; and percents, 8.4%).
2. Set up and complete a tabulation similar to the one below to indicate the usefulness of the results derived in (1) (an example is provided for the current ratio):

Ratio	Computed Ratio			Significance and Assessment
	1990	**1991**	**1992**	
1. Current ratio.	2.4	2.3	2.1	Test of adequacy of working capital. Consistent decrease — unfavourable
2. Etc.				

P 25–3
Compute and Evaluate Ratios
(L.O. 3)

The financial statements of Larkin Manufacturing Company for a three-year period:

	1990	1991	1992
Total assets.	$2,000,000	$2,040,000	$1,940,000
Total current assets	368,000	450,000	480,000
Total current liabilities	230,000	150,000	150,000
Operational assets (net).	1,248,000	1,257,600	1,260,000
Total liabilities	1,090,000	1,110,000	900,000
Common shares, nopar (6,000 shares)	600,000	600,000	700,000
Retained earnings.	310,000	330,000	340,000
Sales revenue (net)	6,600,000	7,000,000	7,100,000
Net income (after tax).	50,000	70,000	40,000
Interest expense (net of tax).	34,000	38,000	30,000

Required:

Round to one decimal place.

1. Based on the above data, compute the following ratios to measure liquidity position for each year.
   a. Current ratio.
   b. Working capital turnover.
   Evaluate the current position. What additional information do you need to adequately evaluate the current position? Explain.
2. Based on the above data, compute the following ratios to measure the equity position:
   a. Debt to equity.
   b. Debt to total assets.
   c. Book value per common share.
   Evaluate the equity position. What additional information do you need to adequately evaluate the equity position? Explain.
3. Based on the above data, compute the following ratios to measure profitability results and leverage:
   a. Profit margin on sales.
   b. Return on total average assets.
   c. Return on average owners' equity.
   d. Financial leverage.
   Evaluate the operating results and financial leverage.

P 25–4
Compute, Interpret, and Evaluate Three Equity Ratios
(L.O. 3)

The balance sheet for two similar companies reflected the following:

	Company A	Company B
Current liabilities	$ 30,000	$ 30,000
Long-term liabilities (10%)	30,000	230,000
Shareholders' equity:		
Common shares, nopar (outstanding, 34,000; 9,200 shares)	190,000	50,000
Preferred shares, nopar (outstanding, 5,000; 2,000 shares).	50,000	20,000

	Company A	Company B
Retained earnings.	60,000	30,000
Net income, included in the above retained earnings amount (less taxes, 40%)	50,000	20,000
Cash flow from operations.	32,000	26,000

Required:

1. Compute the ratios listed in the chapter that evaluate the equity position. Interpret the results.
2. Compute the leverage factor for each company. The average interest rate on total liabilities is 10% for both companies.
3. Interpret and evaluate the situation for each company.

P 25–5
Ratios to Measure Profitability: Evaluate Implications
(L.O. 3)

The following annual data were taken from the records of McKeon Trading Corporation:

	1989	1990	1991	1992	1993
Sales revenue	$400,000	$420,000	$450,000	$440,000	$490,000
Net income	15,000	16,000	20,000	5,000	40,000
Total assets	200,000*	220,000	230,000	240,000	250,000
Owners' equity	100,000*	110,000	120,000	115,000	140,000
Market price per common share	20	20	33	14	60
Dividends per common share	4	4	4	1	5
Shares outstanding	4,000	4,000	4,000	3,900	3,800
Interest expense (net of tax)	$ 4,000	$ 4,500	$ 4,600	$ 5,000	$ 4,100

* The beginning balance was the same as this year-end balance.

Required:

Compute ratios to measure profitability for the years 1990, 1991, 1992, and 1993. Immediately following each ratio, evaluate and comment on the results (e.g., trends, problems, and favourable/unfavourable implications).

P 25–6
Leverage—Sell Share Capital versus Debt: Analysis
(L.O. 3)

Boggs Corporation is considering building a second plant at a cost of $600,000. Management is considering two alternatives to obtain the funds: (*a*) sell additional common shares or (*b*) issue $600,000, five-year bonds payable at 10% interest. Management believes that the bonds can be sold at par for $600,000 and the shares at $10 per share.

The balance sheet (before the new financing) reflected the following:

Liabilities	None
Common shares, nopar (40,000 shares)	$300,000
Retained earnings	100,000
Average income for past several years (net of tax) . . .	30,000

The average income tax rate is 40%. Average dividends per share have been 50 cents per share per year. Expected increase in pretax income (excluding interest expense) from the new plant, $100,000 per year.

Required:

1. Prepare an analysis to show (*a*) expected income after the addition, (*b*) cash flows from the company to prospective owners of the new capital, and (*c*) the leverage advantage or disadvantage to the present shareholders of issuing the bonds to obtain the financing.
2. What are the principal arguments for and against issuing the bonds, as opposed to selling the common shares?

P 25–7
Prepare HC/CD Balance Sheet, Income Statement, and Retained Earnings Statement
(L.O. 8)

The items reflected in the September 30 trial balance given below were acquired when the relevant GPL index was 105.0 except for share capital, which was 105.2377.

Cash	$ 27,235	
Land	79,085	
Accounts payable		$ 2,570
Share capital		100,000
Retained earnings		3,750
	$106,320	$106,320

The following transactions occurred during the first quarter of the current accounting year.

Date	GPL Index	Date
Oct. 1	110	Purchased machinery costing $9,600 on account.
15	120	Paid for machinery purchased on October 1.
31	135	Billed customers for services rendered, $8,000.
Nov. 15	140	Paid $1,230 of the initial liability balance.
30	145	Collected half of the billed revenue.
Dec. 10	150	Paid general expense of $5,700.
31	160	Recorded three months' depreciation on machinery, which has a five-year life with no residual value.

Required:

1. Enter the initial balances and then record the transactions for the first quarter directly into ledger accounts; also include, in parentheses, the GPL index number prevailing when each transaction occurred.

2. As of the close of the quarter, prepare the balance sheet and income statement on the HC basis and the HC/CD (CDs as of December 31) basis using the GPL index number procedures illustrated in the chapter. Show calculation of the purchasing power gain or loss on net monetary items. Prepare a statement of retained earnings at HC and HC/CD (the HC/CD beginning balance is $6,058). No average index value for the period is given. Therefore, it will be necessary to apply to each transaction a specific CD restatement ratio. For example, if a $360 transaction occurred when the index was 120, in December 31 terms, this would convert to $360 × 160/120 = $480. Round all calculations to the nearest dollar.

P 25-8
Overview of HC/CD: Six Analytical Questions (L.O. 7, 8)

Select the best answer in each of the following. Justify your choices.

1. A company was formed on January 1, 1990. Selected balances from its HC balance sheet at December 31, 1990, were as follows:

Accounts receivable . . . . $ 70,000
Accounts payable.   60,000
Long-term debt. 110,000
Common shares   100,000

At what amounts should these selected accounts be shown in an HC/CD (CDs as of December 31, 1990) balance sheet at December 31, 1990, if the general price level index was 100 at December 31, 1989, and 110 at December 31, 1990?

	Accounts Receivable	Accounts Payable	Long-Term Debt	Common Shares
a.	$70,000	$60,000	$110,000	$100,000
b.	70,000	60,000	110,000	110,000
c.	70,000	60,000	121,000	110,000
d.	77,000	66,000	121,000	110,000

2. Baker Company reported sales of $2,000,000 in 1990 and $3,000,000 in 1991 made evenly throughout each year. The GPL index during 1989 remained constant at 100, and at the end of 1990 and 1991 it was 102 and 104, respectively. What should Baker report as sales revenue for 1991, restated in CDs (in CDs as of the end of 1991)?
   a. $3,000,000.   *c.* $3,058,821.
   b. $3,029,126.   *d.* $3,120,000.

3. On January 2, 1991, the Mannix Corporation mortgaged one of its properties as collateral for a $1,000,000, 12% five-year loan. The mortgage note payable was interest-bearing, and the interest rate was realistic. During 1991, the GPL increased evenly, resulting in a 5% rise for the year.

   In preparing an HC/CD (CDs as of the end of 1991) balance sheet at the end of 1991, at what amount should Mannix report the five-year mortgage note?
   a. $950,000.   *c.* $1,025,000.
   b. $1,000,000.   *d.* $1,050,000.

4. The HC balance sheet of Post Company showed the original cost of depreciable assets as $5,000,000 at December 31, 1989, and $6,000,000 at December 31, 1990. These asset costs are being depreciated on a straight-line basis over a 10-year period with no residual value. Acquisitions of $1,000,000 were made on January 1, 1990. A full year's depreciation was taken in the year of acquisition.

Post presents HC/CD financial statements as supplemental information to its HC financial statements. The December 31, 1989, depreciable assets balance (before accumulated depreciation) restated to reflect December 31, 1990, purchasing power was $5,800,000. What amount of depreciation expense should be shown in the HC/CD (CDs as of December 31, 1990) income statement for 1990 if the GPL index was 100 at December 31, 1989, and 110 at December 31, 1990?

a. $600,000.   c. $670,000.
b. $660,000.   d. $690,000.

5. If a constant unit of measure during a period of inflation is used, the general purchasing power of the dollar in which some expenses are measured (for assets systematically allocated among several accounting periods) may differ significantly from the general purchasing power of the dollar in which revenue is measured. Which of the following accounting procedures minimizes this effect?

a. Allowance method of accounting for bad debts.
b. Income tax allocation.
c. Accelerated depreciation.
d. Valuing inventory at the LCM.

6. Land was purchased for $20,000 when the GPL index was 115. When the index was 138, the land was sold for $25,000. Ignoring taxes on the transaction, the landowner, for having bought and sold the land, is economically (i.e., in terms of purchasing power):

a. Worse off.
b. Better off.
c. In the same position.

(AICPA adapted)

P 25–9
HC/CD Overview: Six
Analytical Questions
(L.O. 7, 8)

Select the best answer in each of the following. Justify your choices. For (1) to (4) below, use the following GPL data (round CD restatement ratios to three decimals): Dec. 31, 1989, 165; Mar. 31, 1990, 171; June 3, 1990, 175; Sept. 30, 1990, 180; Dec. 31, 1990, 186; Mar. 31, 1991, 190; June 30, 1991, 194; Sept. 30, 1991, 198; Dec. 31, 1991, 201.

1. On January 1, 1990, P Corporation had as its only asset $14,000 in cash (no liabilities). On March 31, 1990, P Corporation paid $10,000 for a machine that will have a 10-year life and no residual value. On September 30, 1990, P Corporation purchased merchandise inventory on account for $2,000. At an even rate during the three months ended December 31, 1990, P Corporation paid off the $2,000 on the inventory and sold half the inventory for $1,300 cash. If these are the only transactions P Corporation entered into during 1990, the company will report for 1990 (in terms of CDs as of Dec. 31, 1990) a purchasing power gain or loss on net monetary items of:

a. Loss of $730.   c. Gain of $730.
b. Loss of $852.   d. Gain of $852.

2. Assume that P Corporation's January 1, 1990, owners' equity consisted of share capital of $14,000. On its HC/CD (CDs as of Dec. 31, 1990) income statement for the year ended December 31, 1990, P Corporation will report net income (loss)—ignoring the purchasing power gain or loss on net monetary items—of:

a. $(552).   c. $(510).
b. $(528).   d. $(506).

3. On its December 31, 1990, HC/CD (CDs as of Dec. 31, 1990) balance sheet P Corporation will report cash of:

a. $3,300.   c. $2,570.
b. $4,160.   d. $5,808.

4. You are in the process of preparing the 1991, HC/CD financial statements (assume that you have been given the necessary transaction data involving revenues and expenses for 1991). In particular, you are now "rolling foward" the January 1, 1991, HC balance sheet in order to obtain the January 1, 1991, HC/CD owners' equity balance stated in December 31, 1991, dollars—as a test of the accuracy of your other HC/CD restatements. Assuming that the

beginning cash balance arose on the beginning date, the correct January 1, 1991, owners' equity stated in December 31, 1991, dollars would be:

a. $14,394.   d. $15,950.

b. $14,644.   e. None of the above.

c. $15,554.

5. Under HC/CD reporting, purchasing power gains are earned during inflation on:

a. Net monetary assets.   c. Non-monetary assets.

b. Net monetary liabilities.   d. Non-monetary liabilities.

6. Which of the following items is a non-monetary item?

a. Marketable securities—bonds to be held to maturity.

b. Accounts receivable.

c. Accounts payable.

d. Preferred shares stated at liquidation value.

e. Unearned revenue.

P 25-10
HC/CD Financial
Statements
(L.O. 8)

Wagner Company prepared the following comparative balance sheets (HC basis) at the close of its 10th year of operations (1991):

	December 31	
	1990	1991
Cash	$ 75,000	$ 101,000
Receivables (net)	215,000	195,000
Inventory	135,000	127,000
Land	150,000	150,000
Building.	240,000	240,000
Accumulated depreciation, building	(56,000)	(64,000)
Machinery	225,000	280,000
Accumulated depreciation, machinery	(115,000)	(137,500)
Total	$ 869,000	$ 891,500
Current liabilities	$ 124,000	$ 137,000
Long-term liabilities.	75,000	81,000
Bonds payable.	60,000	60,000
Common shares	350,000	350,000
Retained earnings.	260,000*	263,500
Total	$ 869,000	$ 891,500

* At HC/CD on this date, $277,070.

The common shares were issued and the land was bought in 1982, when the GPL index was 104. The building was acquired early in 1984 when the GPL index was 107; it has an estimated 30-year life and no residual value and is depreciated on a straight-line basis. Machinery is depreciated 10% per year on cost with no residual value. The first machine was bought at a cost of $50,000 in 1983 when the GPL index was 106; a second machine was acquired for $100,000 in 1985 when the index was 108.5; a third machine was bought in 1989 when the index was 117. A full year's depreciation is taken in the year of acquisition unless the purchase is at year-end. At year-end 1991, machinery costing $55,000 was acquired.

On January 2, 1991, an $85,000 dividend was declared and paid when the GPL index was 121. Assume the beginning inventory was acquired when the GPL index was 107; the ending inventory should be restated to CDs on the assumption the index was 125 when it was bought.

Sales, operating expenses, income taxes, and purchases occurred evenly during 1991. Relevent GPL index data (aside from that already given) are as follows: Dec. 31, 1990, 121; Dec. 31, 1991, 127; average for 1991, 125. The income statement (HC basis) for the year 1991 was as follows:

Sales revenue		$1,275,000
Cost of goods sold:		
Inventory, January 1.	$135,000	
Purchases.	850,000	
Goods available	985,000	
Inventory, December 31	127,000	
Cost of goods sold		858,000
Gross margin		417,000

Expenses:
Operating (excluding depreciation). 210,000
Depreciation, building. 8,000
Depreciation, machinery. 22,500   240,500

Income before taxes. 176,500
Income tax expense 88,000

Net income . . . . $ 88,500

Required:

Prepare an income statement for 1991 and a balance sheet as of December 31, 1991, on an HC/CD (CDs as of December 31, 1991) basis. Round all CD restatement ratios to three decimals before multiplication. Show computations of the purchasing power gain or loss on net monetary items. Prepare a proof of retained earnings.

P 25–11
CC/CD: Analyse Fleet of Trucks—Income Statement (L.O. 9)

Brown Hauling Company maintains a fleet of trucks for use in its business. Information regarding the acquisition dates and cost of these trucks is provided below:

Total Cost	Date Acquired	GPL Index
$80,000	January 1, 1988	100
60,000	January 1, 1989	115
50,000	June 30, 1990	125

Trucks are depreciated on a straight-line basis over a five-year life with residual value estimated to be zero. The acquisition on June 30, 1990, was depreciated for one-half year in 1990.

A schedule of the current cost of the trucks (before deducting accumulated depreciation) is given below as of January 1, 1991, and December 31, 1991:

Trucks Acquired In	CC on Jan. 1, 1991	CC on Dec. 31, 1991
1988.	$100,000	$125,000
1989.	80,000	90,000
1990.	60,000	80,000

Additional GPL index data are as follows: January 1, 1991, 130; 1991 average, 135; December 31, 1991, 140.

Required:

Round all CD restatement ratios to three decimal places before multiplication.

1. Compute the current cost of the trucks, net of accumulated depreciation, on January 1, 1991, and December 31, 1991.
2. Compute 1991 depreciation expense for the trucks on a current cost basis.
3. Prepare a schedule that shows (*a*) the total 1991 change in CC, (*b*) change in CC, due to general inflation, and (*c*) change in CC, net of general inflation (in CDs as of Dec. 31, 1991). Set up column headings for CC at transaction or balance date, CD restatement ratio, and CC/CD.
4. Assume the CC/CD income from continuing operations is $150,000 and the purchasing power loss on net monetary items is $12,000. Complete the HC/CD income statement for Brown Company.

P 25–12
CC/CD: Analysis of Inventory—Income Statement (L.O. 9)

The following information regarding the historical and current cost of Control Corporation's inventory is available:

	HC	CC*
January 1, 1990, inventory.	$ 10,000	$ 10,000
1990 purchases	100,000	100,000
1990 cost of goods sold	80,000	90,000
December 31, 1990, inventory	30,000	50,000
1991 purchases	120,000	120,000
1991 cost of goods sold	95,000	115,000
December 31, 1991, inventory	55,000	75,000

* Current cost at transaction or balance date.

GPL index data are as follows: January 1, 1990, 110; 1990 average, 118; December 31, 1990, 125; 1991 average, 132; December 31, 1991, 140. Sales and purchases occurred evenly during 1990 and 1991.

Required:

Round all CD restatement ratios to three decimal places before multiplication.

1. Prepare a schedule of the total 1990 change in CC, change in CC due to general inflation, and change in CC, net of general inflation (in average CDs of 1990) for inventory. (Set up three column headings: CC at transaction or balance date, CD restatement ratio, and CC/CD.)
2. Assume the CC/CD income from continuing operations is $80,000 and that the purchasing power loss on net monetary items is $10,000. Complete the CC/CD income statement for 1990 for Control Company.
3. Prepare a schedule of the total 1991 change in CC, change in CC due to general inflation, and change in CC, net of general inflation (in average CDs of 1991) for inventory. (Set up three column headings: CC at transaction or balance date, CD restatement ratio, and CC/CD.)
4. Assume the CC/CD income from continuing operations is $90,000 and that the purchasing power gain on net monetary items is $7,000. Complete the CC/CD income statement for 1991 for Control Company.
5. Does the cost flow assumption used for inventory (i.e., LIFO, FIFO) affect the computation of changes in current cost? Explain.

P 25–13

COMPREHENSIVE PROBLEM
◆

CC/CD—Prepare Financial
Statements
(L.O. 8, 9)

Palmer Company prepared the following comparative balance sheet (HC basis) at the close of its 10th year of operations (1991):

	December 31	
	1990	**1991**
Cash	$ 60,000	$ 101,000
Receivables (net)	175,000	195,000
Inventory	135,000	127,000
Land	150,000	150,000
Building	240,000	240,000
Accumulated depreciation, building	(48,000)	(56,000)
Machinery	280,000	280,000
Accumulated depreciation, machinery	(196,000)	(224,000)
Total	$ 796,000	$ 813,000
Current liabilities	$ 124,000	$ 137,000
Long-term liabilities	75,000	81,000
Bonds payable	60,000	60,000
Common shares	350,000	350,000
Retained earnings	187,000	185,000
Total	$ 796,000	$ 813,000

The common shares were issued, and the land was bought in 1982, when the GPL index was 104. The building was acquired late in 1984 when the GPL index was 107; it has an estimated 30-year life and no residual value and is depreciated on a straight-line basis. Machinery is depreciated 10% per year on cost with no residual value. The machinery was purchased late in 1983 when the GPL index was 106.

On January 2, 1991, an $85,000 dividend was declared and paid. Sales, operating expenses, income taxes, and purchases occurred evenly during 1991. Relevant GPL index data (aside from that already given) are as follows: Dec. 31, 1990, 121; Dec. 31, 1991, 127; average for 1991, 125.

The income statement (HC basis) for the year 1991 was as follows:

Sales revenue		$1,275,000
Cost of goods sold:		
Inventory, January 1	$135,000	
Purchases	850,000	
Goods available	985,000	
Inventory, December 31	127,000	
Cost of goods sold		858,000
Gross margin		417,000

Expenses:
Operating, excluding depreciation   210,000
Depreciation, building.   8,000
Depreciation, machinery.   28,000   246,000

Income before taxes   171,000
Income tax expense   88,000

Net income . . . . $ 83,000

Current cost data are as follows:

	December 31	
	1990	**1991**
Non-monetary assets (in CDs as of the balance sheet date):		
Inventory	$ 160,000	$135,000
Land	185,000	200,000
Building	270,000	270,000
Accumulated depreciation, building	(54,000)	(63,000)
Machinery	300,000	330,000
Accumulated depreciation, machinery	(210,000)	(264,000)
Retained earnings (credit) from prior period	220,000	
Expenses (in average of CDs of 1991):		
Cost of goods sold		$897,000
Depreciation expense, building		9,000
Depreciation expense, machinery		31,500
Sales revenue and all other expenses		Same as HC

Required:

Round all CD restatement ratios to three decimals.

1. Prepare the CC/CD (CDs as of Dec. 31, 1991) balance sheet for the company at December 31, 1991.
2. Prepare the single-step CC/CD (CDs as of Dec. 31, 1991) income statement for the company for the year ended December 31, 1991, with all supporting computations.
3. Prove the accuracy of the CC/CD ending balance of retained earnings.

P 25–14

COMPREHENSIVE PROBLEM
♦

CC/ND and CC/CD
Financial Statements
(L.O. 8, 9)

On December 31, 1992, the Rerun Company is formed by investors who contribute $250,000 in return for nopar common shares. This capital is used to purchase 18,000 video tape movies for $25 per tape. The Rerun Company purchased a parcel of land at a cost of $70,000 for a future building site that is financed by a five-year note payable. The Rerun Company's balance sheet on December 31, 1992, is as follows:

Cash . . . . $ 50,000
Inventories   450,000
Land   70,000

Total assets $570,000

Note payable . . . . $ 70,000
Nopar common shares.   500,000

Total equities $570,000

During 1993, the company sold 4,000 tapes in the first half of the year and 8,000 tapes in the July to December half of the year for a total of 12,000 tapes at $45 each. The sales occurred evenly over their respective halves of the year. The Rerun Company purchased 14,000 more tapes on September 30, 1993, at a cost of $28 each. The inventory is accounted for on a first-in, first-out basis. The other expenses were incurred at an even rate throughout the year. The Rerun

Company had the following income statement for the year ending December 31, 1993, and balance sheet as at December 31, 1993:

Revenues	$ 540,000
Cost of goods sold	(300,000)
Other expenses	(80,000)
Net income	$ 160,000
Cash	$ 118,000
Inventories	542,000
Land	70,000
Total assets	$ 730,000
Note payable	$ 70,000
Common shares, nopar	500,000
Retained earnings	160,000
Total equities	$ 730,000

Other information:

a. The replacement cost of the inventory remained at $25 per tape until June 30, 1993, when it increased to $28 per tape. On December 31, 1993, the replacement cost increased to $30 per tape. The Rerun Company will be selling the tapes at $52 each during 1994.

b. The replacement cost of the land had increased to $86,000 by December 31, 1993.

c. The relevant index of general purchasing level increased steadily throughout 1993 as follows:

December 31, 1992	100
March 31, 1993, and first half average	110
June 30, 1993	120
September 30, 1993, and second half average	130
December 31, 1993	140

Required:

1. Assume that the Rerun Company adopts current value accounting using current entry prices and productive capacity maintenance (i.e., excludes holding gains from the income statement; they are a separate component of equity). Prepare an income statement for the year ending December 31, 1993, and a balance sheet as at December 31, 1993, for the Rerun Company.

2. Assume that the Rerun Company adopts general price-level accounting based on historical costs. Calculate for inclusion in the Rerun Company's financial statements for 1993 restated in dollars of December 31, 1993, purchasing power, the following amounts:

   a. Revenues.

   b. Purchases.

   c. Purchasing power gain or loss.

   d. December 31, 1993, inventories.

   e. Land.

   f. Note payable.

   g. Nopar common shares.

   Financial statements are not required.

[SMA adapted]

CASES

C 25–1
Recommend Which Company's Shares Should Be Purchased: Ratio Analysis
(L.O. 3)

Investor Ng is considering investing $100,000 cash in the common shares of either Company A or Company B. The two companies are in the same industry, but in different regions of the country. The following summarized data were taken from the annual audited financial statements (in thousands):

	Company A	Company B
Income statement:		
Sales revenue	$ 4,000	$ 9,400
Cost of goods sold	(2,160)	(5,640)
Operating expenses	(500)	(1,710)
Interest expense	(90)	(350)
Income tax expense	(500)	(680)
Extraordinary gain (loss), net of tax	(110)	350
Net income	$ 640	$ 1,370

	Company A	Company B
Balance sheet:		
Current assets.	$ 1,000	$ 4,000
Fixed assets.	4,500	19,000
Accumulated depreciation	(1,500)	(7,000)
Investments, long term (cost)	400	100
Other assets	600	7,900
Total	$ 5,000	$24,000
Current liabilities	$ 900	$ 2,000
Long-term liabilities.	100	1,800
Share capital		
(outstanding shares, 3,000; 18,000)	3,000	18,000
Retained earnings.	1,000	2,200
Total	$ 5,000	$24,000
Additional data for current year:		
Quick assets	$ 400	$ 500
Average income tax rate	42%	40%

After examining the data given above, Investor Ng has expressed a strong preference for Company B because (*a*) it is larger, (*b*) it has almost five times as much in total assets, (*c*) net income as a percentage of sales is virtually identical, and (*d*) it earned more than twice as much. Ng has asked you to confirm the soundness of his tentative decision by analysing the data available.

Because the only information now available to you is given above, a comparative analysis of the current position, equity position, operating results, and financial leverage seems appropriate as a start.

Required:

1. Prepare your analysis and support it with comments related to each value.
2. Based only upon your analysis, prepare your recommendation to Ng, which is limited to consideration of these two companies. Give a brief to-the-point summary of the basis for your recommendation.

C 25–2
What Investors Want from
the Annual Report
(L.O. 1, 5)

This case is adapted from an article by Ned Reynolds, senior vice-president in the financial relations division of Hill & Knowlton Inc., in *The Wall Street Journal*, January 18, 1988. The article posed a provocative issue.

American companies spend an estimated $2 billion a year on annual reports to shareholders. But their message often falls on deaf ears, research suggests.

A survey conducted by Hill & Knowlton Inc. asked a sample of individual investors where they got their best investment information. Only 3% named the annual report—1% less than those who cited friends and relatives.

The author correctly states that companies traditionally view the annual report as an opportunity to radiate optimism, not to report failings. The author then suggested,

But since the October market crash, which dealt investor confidence a severe blow, companies need to think seriously about enlisting the annual report as a natural way of getting investors to trust them.

The Hill & Knowlton survey asked questions about how investors rate the credibility of annual reports. Comments received, such as the following, presented a bleak view:

◆ "Annual reports hide too much. They don't tell the entire truth."
◆ "They are not dependable."
◆ "The annual report is little more than a piece of advertising."
◆ "I think annuals are much too biased."
◆ "I believe they lie in these reports."

Author Reynolds then states that,

nonetheless, the annual report is the best shot a publicly held company has all year to speak directly to investors. The report is a powerful platform for management to persuade investors to buy or hold the company's stock. That's exactly what an annual report should be doing if it is earning its keep.

To succeed, an annual report must answer the investor's gut question: "What's in it for me?"—a question that ought to be displayed on the wall of every preparer of annual reports.

The research findings pinpointed the investors' complaints about annual reports:

a. **Credibility.** Investors complain that annual reports are too promotional. The reports play down negatives, investors say, and present only management's viewpoint. Some investors distrust what they read in annual reports.

b. **Business segments.** Annual reports often fail to adequately show or explain information about a company's various business segments, investors say.

c. **Detail.** Contrary to a common view, the majority of investors do not believe annual reports are too detailed. In fact, investors are eager for more facts in reports—provided they are relevant.

d. **The future.** Investors believe annual reports fail to tell them what management is doing to build the shareholder's investment.

e. **Clarity.** Investors criticize companies for using stilted wording and "technicalese" in their annual reports. They want to hear from companies in clear, straightforward language.

The author concludes the article as follows:

> It is unlikely that during the October market debacle investors cooly scrutinized company annual reports before calling their brokers. But perhaps many investors might think twice about unloading their positions if management seizes the opportunity in its next annual report to foster an underlying sense of confidence by credibly answering that essential question: "What's in it for me?"

Required:

1. Be prepared to suggest ways that might be used by companies to resolve each of the five complaints.
2. Prepare notes to support your suggestions.

C 25–3
HC versus HC/CD
Financial Statements
(L.O. 6, 7)

A number of companies have presented HC/CD statements as supplements to conventional historical cost basis statements. Knowing that you have studied accounting, a friend, who owns common shares in several companies, drops their latest annual reports before you with a look that hovers between dismay and bewilderment.

Your friend begins "I used to think that I understood a little about these reports, but now that the companies have all gone to this price-level accounting, the only things clear to me are the nice pictures of company employees and products!" Upon inquiry, you find that the following points bother your friend:

a. Most of the companies reported higher net income on their HC statements than on their HC/CD statements, while at the same time the latter statements showed the assets to be larger in amount.

b. Some of the companies reported purchasing power gains on net monetary liabilities concurrent with operating gains; others reported general purchasing power losses on net monetary assets concurrent with operating gains; yet all of the companies were subject to the same degree of general inflation.

c. The comparative statements, prepared on an HC/CD basis, showed that the amount of cash reported for last year had changed. Your friend wonders whether the companies discovered overages or shortages of cash or are somehow "juggling the figures."

d. Your friend realizes that the prices of most things are rising and wonders whether the increased values of certain assets on the HC/CD statements represent what the items are worth. At the same time, your friend noticed that some assets are carried at identical amounts on both sets of statements (i.e., both HC and HC/CD statements).

Required:

1. Explain the specifics that are confusing your friend in such a way that a knowledgeable non-accountant can understand them.
2. To cope with the effects of price changes, aside from HC/CD statements, what alternative accounting models could be used? Describe them briefly and cite some of their pros and cons.
3. What is your assessment of the usefulness of HC/CD financial statements? Give reasons for your answer.

C 25–4
Analysis of CC
Disclosures, Alcan
(L.O. 6, 7)

Excerpts from the 1984 Alcan current cost disclosures are reproduced below.

Consolidated Statement of Income
For the year ended December 31, 1984

(in millions of U.S. dollars)	Historical Cost, as Reported		Current Cost Basis, in Average 1984 dollars	
	1984	**1983**	**1984**	**1983**
Sales and operating revenues	$5,467	$5,208	$5,467	$5,409
Cost of sales and operating expenses	4,214	4,188	4,242	4,410
Depreciation expense	250	238	409	465
Selling, research, and administrative expenses	442	433	442	450
Interest	244	255	244	265
Other (income) and expenses—net	(71)	(65)	(75)	(73)
	$5,079	$5,049	$5,262	$5,517
Income (loss) before income taxes and other items	$ 388	$ 159	$ 205	$ (108)
Income taxes	151	73	151	75
Equity (income) loss and minority interests	21	28	10	15
Income (loss) before income tax recovery	216	58	44	(198)
Income tax recovery applicable to prior years' losses	37	15	37	15
Net income (loss)	$ 253	$ 73	$ 81	$ (183)

Schedule of Consolidated Assets
As at December 31, 1984

(in millions of U.S. dollars)	Historical Cost, as Reported		Current Cost Basis, in Average 1984 Dollars	
	1984	**1983**	**1984**	**1983**
Inventory	$1,512	$1,448	$1,559	$1,627
Property, plant, and equipment—net	3,600	3,550	6,501	6,860
Net assets (common shareholders' equity)	2,916	2,799	5,990	6,242

Supplementary Information
As at December 31, 1984

(in millions of U.S. dollars)	In Average 1984 Dollars	
	1984	**1983**
Increase in current cost amounts of inventory and property, plant, and equipment based on:		
General inflation	$316	$315
Specific prices	171	334
Difference	$145	$(19)
General purchasing power gain on net monetary liabilities	$ 53	$ 64

Required:
1. Explain the meaning of each of the following items:
   a. Income (loss) before taxes and other items on a current cost basis.
   b. Current cost of inventory; property, plant, and equipment; and net assets (schedule of consolidated assets).
   c. Increase in current costs of inventory and property, plant, and equipment.
   d. General purchasing power gain.
2. Comment on Alcan's 1984 operating performance on a current cost basis, compared to their 1983 results.

C 25–5
HC/CD versus CC/CD
(L.O. 6, 7)

Checker Corporation, a manufacturer with large investments in property, plant, and equipment, began operations in 1940. The company's history has been one of expansion in sales, production, and physical facilities. Recently, some concern has been expressed that the HC financial statements do not provide sufficient information for decisions by investors. After consideration of proposals for various types of supplementary financial statements to be included in the 1992 annual report, management has decided to present an HC/CD balance sheet as of December 31, 1992, and an HC/CD income statement and retained earnings statement for 1992.

Required:

1. Why should Checker's HC financial statements be restated for changes in the general price level (GPL)?
2. Distinguish between HC/CD financial statements and CC/CD financial statements.
3. Distinguish between monetary and non-monetary assets and liabilities as the terms are used in the HC/CD reporting model. Give examples of each.
4. Outline the procedures Checker should follow in preparing the proposed HC/CD statements.
5. Indicate the major similarities and differences between the proposed HC/CD statements and the corresponding HC statements.
6. Assuming that in the future Checker will want to present comparative HC/CD statements, can the 1992 HC/CD statements be presented in 1993 without adjustment? Explain.

(AICPA adapted)

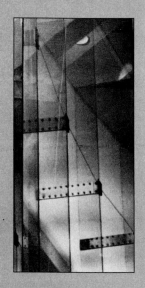

C H A P T E R

26

Special Topics: Disclosure, Interim Reporting, and Segment Reporting

LEARNING
OBJECTIVES
◆

After you have studied this chapter, you will be able to:

1. Explain the problem of standards overload and some actions that might be undertaken to relieve the problem.

2. Explain the information overload issue.

3. Discuss the rationale for, and components of, the summary of significant accounting policies disclosure note and other required disclosure notes to the financial statements.

4. Explain the alternative concepts that might be applied in designing interim reports and prepare appropriate disclosures.

5. Discuss the rationale for segment reporting and prepare the required disclosures.

◆

INTRODUCTION
◆

I magine you run a successful small business. You produce and sell a variety of souvenirs for your university or college, and others like it in your geographical area. You either produce or subcontract to have produced T-shirts, key chains, tie clasps, coffee cups, and other similar products, which you sell to a number of outlets in the area. As your business grows and you find you need additional capital, you go to your bank and apply for a loan. The loan officer at the bank asks that you submit financial statements for your business, and of course, the loan officer indicates they must be prepared in accordance with generally accepted accounting principles.

Consider all of the pronouncements with which you must comply if your financial statements are going to be in accordance with GAAP. Notice that your text authors have written over 1,300 pages of text in attempting to explain the application of these various rules and standards. You may begin to wonder whether it's worth the effort for your small business to even attempt to comply with all the standards the various policy-making bodies have established. Indeed, the cost to you of total compliance with the rules of GAAP may seem greater than the loan you wish to obtain!

This, in a nutshell, is the problem of *standards overload*. Standards overload is a term sometimes used by firms to describe the financial reporting burden they face to comply with current accounting standards. A related, and many ways very similar, issue is called *information overload*. This is a view of the problem from the perspective of the user of the statements. Under this perspective, the concern is that much of the information reported is of little or no use, and that valuable information is obscured by the presentation of data that the user does not need.

This chapter considers the standards overload problem, the related information overload problem, and the trade-off involved between full disclosure and standards and information overload. The chapter also reviews issues of reporting that are treated differently for large, widely held firms versus non-public companies, and several specific reporting issues.

◆

STANDARDS OVERLOAD AND FULL DISCLOSURE
◆

Generally, GAAP rules and standards apply equally to all reporting companies, regardless of the size of the reporting entity.[1] The financial burden or cost that firms incur in complying with these rules and standards gives rise to what has been termed the standards overload problem.

The issue then is, should all the standards, practices, and disclosures of GAAP apply equally to all firms regardless of size, ownership structure, and type of business? More specifically, should small or closely held companies be required to comply with the same GAAP as large, widely held, national corporations?

This issue is controversial. The Accounting Standards Board has, in some instances, limited the applicability of standards to publicly held companies. One example is segment reporting, discussed in detail in this chapter.

Now, consider this issue from what might be the opposite perspective. Accountants have long recognized that it is extremely difficult, if not impossible, to present all the information essential for decision making in a balance sheet, income statement, statement of changes in financial position, and retained earnings statement. Diverse types of

---

[1] Firms that are not required to present financial statements to public investors or creditors (because they are privately held and/or creditors do not require financial statements) can use measurement standards and procedures that are not GAAP. Creditors such as banks sometimes will require the firm to submit financial statements prepared in accordance with GAAP measurement rules, but will not require as much overall disclosure as would otherwise be required under GAAP.

EXHIBIT 26-1   Types and Sources of Information Useful for Investment, Credit, and Other Decisions

Recognition and Measurement in Financial Statements of Business Enterprises

◄———————————All Information Useful for Investment, Credit, and Similar Decisions———————————►

◄————————————————Financial Reporting————————————————►

◄————————Area Directly Affected by Existing Standards————————►

◄—————Basic Financial Statements—————►

Scope of Recognition
◄—and Measurement—►
Concepts Statement

Financial Statements	Notes to Financial Statements (& parenthetical disclosures)	Supplementary Information	Other Means of Financial Reporting	Other Information
◆ Balance sheet	Examples:	Examples:	Examples:	Examples:
◆ Income statement	◆ Accounting policies	◆ Current cost disclosures (section 4510)	◆ Management discussion and analysis	◆ Analysts' reports
◆ Statement of changes in financial position	◆ Contingencies		◆ Letters to shareholders	◆ Economic statistics
◆ Statement of retained earnings	◆ Inventory methods	◆ Oil and gas reserves information		◆ News articles about company
	◆ Number of shares outstanding			
	◆ Alternative measures (market values of items carried at historical cost)			

Source: Adapted from FASB, *Statement of Financial Accounting Concepts, No. 5.* (New York, 1984).

information are used in investment, credit, and similar decisions. A basic framework outlining different types of information is presented in Exhibit 26-1.

Many individuals in the business community and in the accounting profession are concerned about the ever-increasing number and complexity of authoritative accounting pronouncements. Some of this concern focusses on the perception that smaller companies find the cost of compliance with the standards greater than the benefits. This is essentially the **standards overload** argument; the CICA might be requiring accounting practices that are too costly for smaller firms. At other times, even major corporations get concerned and express resistance to complex standards. For example, many firms, both large and small, have expressed concerns about the cost and difficulty of implementing standards such as pension accounting, foreign currency, and current cost disclosures, to name a few. The arguments often have an **information overload** flavour: firms argue that they could provide information at some considerable cost, but that it would be of little, if any, value to the statement user. Such arguments must be considered seriously by standard setters, as rules that do not cross the cost/benefit threshold are doomed to failure. Widespread non-compliance with current cost disclosure requirements in the 1980s, followed by the suspension of those rules, illustrates this fact.

In Chapter 2 we discussed the concepts underpinning financial reporting. The primary objective of financial reporting is to provide present and potential investors, creditors, and other users with information that is useful in making resource allocation decisions. The financial statements of the reporting entity are a primary source of information. Many different users groups desire information about the firm, and different groups may desire different information. *General purpose financial statements* prepared in conformity with generally accepted accounting principles are the most cost-effective way to provide the desired information to all the various user groups. In our attempt to make such statements as useful as possible, ensuring they are informative in a wide range of decision settings, the tendency has been to require disclosure of virtually any piece of information that may be of interest to some set of users of financial statements. Some view the result as information overload.

The **full disclosure principle** calls for the disclosure of any financial information that is potentially significant enough to influence the judgment of an informed reader. This requirement is subject to a cost-benefit evaluation, but making such an evaluation is often very difficult. Standard setters often hear (from firms that must comply with standards) that the costs of implementing standards are high. More difficult to determine are the benefits of the required disclosures to users. This has been explained as follows:

> The criterion of cost/benefit effectiveness is a difficult one to use. This is partly because it is almost always so difficult to attach figures to all of the wide variety of benefits (and to a lesser extent of costs) of adopting one accounting practice or accounting standard rather than another. Most of the figures, even if they could be computed, are marginal in the sense that they are additions to benefits or costs that have already been achieved or incurred and that will continue whatever action is taken. Moreover, the chief beneficiaries of accounting standards or reporting practices are generally the users of financial statements (although the benefits obtained by preparers should not be underestimated), yet most of the costs of securing these benefits for the users fall upon other groups, such as the preparers, the standard setters, regulatory agencies, and so on.[2]

Until a method is developed to better measure and quantify the benefits of disclosure, standard setters will continue to be subject to the argument that requiring various disclosures results in information overload.

There has been a substantial increase in disclosure requirements during the past two decades. Most of the standards issued during this period have required various disclosure notes in addition to providing guidance on accepted methods of measurement. This trend is likely to continue, although perhaps less rapidly than in recent years. There are many reasons for the increased disclosure requirements. Perhaps most important is what appears to be the ever-increasing complexity of business transactions and the difficulty of distilling them into rather simple accounting transactions. Think about the complex financial instruments that have been used in recent years, primarily to finance business acquisitions and mergers. These instruments often have many of the characteristics of both debt and equity. To date, GAAP requires that they must be reported as one or the other on the balance sheet. Information in the disclosure notes is a way to provide readers with more detailed information on the specific debt versus equity characteristics of the financial instruments.

A related cause of increased disclosure is rooted in the desire by many in society and government to better monitor and control the activities of large public corporations. Government regulations require increased disclosure regarding items like insider trading transactions, environmental issues, and illegal activities. Many of these requirements are issued by the relevant securities commissions, but the accounting profession must implement and respond to these requirements.

CONCEPT REVIEW

1. Define standards overload. Why is it a problem? What are some possible solutions for the problem?
2. Define information overload. How does it relate to the full disclosure principle?

---

[2] *Corporate Reporting: Its Future Evolution* (Toronto: CICA, 1980), p. 63.

NOTES TO FINANCIAL STATEMENTS

◆

The notes are an integral part of the financial statements. They are audited by an external auditor and must be presented if the statements are to be complete. Notes provide descriptive explanations regarding various items included (and not included) in the body of the statements that are deemed to be potentially meaningful to users. Unlike the purely quantitative balance sheet, income statement, and SCFP, information can be provided in qualitative terms. Readers can then make their own assessment of the potential quantitative ramifications of the information presented. Notes sometimes take on a complex and highly technical nature. In many instances, they provide invaluable information.

The first note usually found in a set of financial statements is a general disclosure of accounting policies. Information is included on the accounting policies, standards, and procedures used to prepare the financial statements. Disclosure of this information is required, although it may be in a separate summary, cross-referenced to the financial statements.

Summary of Significant Accounting Policies

Knowledge of the various accounting policies used in generating a set of financial statements is essential when developing an understanding of the specific figures presented in the statements. Knowing, for example, that a firm is using the LIFO method of inventory valuation rather than the FIFO method provides the reader with a basis for interpreting both the inventory value and the cost of goods sold amount found in the financial statements.

Section 1505 of the *CICA Handbook,* "Disclosure of Accounting Policies," requires disclosure of accounting policies used by the firm. The policies used are those that are judged by management to be the most appropriate in order to fairly present the financial position, cash flows, and results of operations in accordance with GAAP. Accounting policies include specific accounting principles and the methods of applying these principles. In general, disclosure should encompass important judgments as to principles relating to revenue recognition and allocation of asset costs to current and future periods. More specifically, the disclosures must include those accounting principles and methods that involve:

◆ A selection from existing acceptable alternatives.
◆ Principles and methods particular to the industry.

The information may be presented as the first note to the financial statements, or in a separate summary of significant accounting policies section. The specific items found in this disclosure note will vary from firm to firm. An example of such a disclosure is found in Exhibit 26–2. Let's look more closely at the specific disclosures made by Cineplex Odeon.

Cineplex Odeon discusses its policies for cost deferral and revenue recognition in some depth. Costs eligible for deferral are disclosed. The revenue recognition criteria are clearly explained, both for admissions and for film distribution agreements. In the summary of significant accounting policies section, Cineplex Odeon provides a description of the procedures used, but not actual dollar figures. Dollar value disclosures are generally found in subsequent notes.

Cineplex also discusses amortization policies: they use straight-line depreciation for their major asset groups. Specific rates, by group, are disclosed. They also use straight-line amortization, over 40 years, for goodwill. Other disclosures include their policies for consolidation and foreign currency translation, and some information concerning the computation of earnings per share. In the first paragraph, U.S. GAAP is referred to. Cineplex must comply with the disclosure requirements of the U.S. SEC, as they

EXHIBIT 26–2   Summary of Significant Accounting Policies, Cineplex Odeon, December 31, 1989

Summary of Significant Accounting Policies

The consolidated financial statements are prepared in accordance with accounting principles generally accepted in Canada, which, except as described in note 19, conform in all material respects with accounting principles generally accepted in the United States. A summary of significant accounting policies is set out below.

Principles of Consolidation: The consolidated financial statements include the accounts of the Corporation, its majority-owned subsidiaries and its 51% interest in the Film House Partnership. Intercompany accounts and transactions have been eliminated.

Property, Equipment, and Leaseholds: Property, equipment, and leaseholds are stated at cost. Depreciation and amortization are calculated using the following methods and annual rates:

Buildings	2.5% straight-line
Projection equipment	5.0% straight-line
Other equipment	6.7% straight-line
Leaseholds	Straight-line over the lease term plus renewal options

Inventories: Inventories are stated at the lower of cost (first-in, first-out basis) and net realizable value.

Distribution Costs: Costs incurred in preparing specific films for distribution for all media exploitation are stated at the lower of cost and net realizable value. Distribution costs are amortized using the individual-film-forecast computation method. The individual-film-forecast computation method amortizes costs in the same ratio that current gross revenues bear to anticipated total gross revenues.

Deferred Charges: Deferred charges, which include bank financing charges, long-term prepaid rent, theatre opening costs, and organization expenses, are stated at cost and are being amortized based on a straight-line basis over one to five years, with the exception of bank financing charges, which are amortized over the term of the related debt.

Revenue Recognition: (A) Admissions—Revenue from the exhibition of motion pictures and live theatre is recognized on the dates of exhibition.

(B) Distribution—Film rentals from theatrical exhibition are recorded on the date of exhibition. Revenue from television and similar licensing agreements is recorded when all of the following conditions have been met: (*i*) the license period has commenced, (*ii*) the sale price for each film is known, (*iii*) the related film costs are known or reasonably determinable, (*iv*) collectibility of the full license fee is reasonably assured, (*v*) the film has been accepted by the licensee in accordance with the conditions of the license agreement, and (*vi*) the film is available to the licensee.

(C) Development income—Income earned from development activities is accounted for using the percentage of completion method.

Goodwill: Goodwill represents the excess of the purchase price of certain businesses over the fair value of the net assets acquired and is being amortized on a straight-line basis, principally over a period of 40 years.

Foreign Currency Translation: Assets and liabilities denominated in a currency other than the U.S. dollar are translated to the U.S. dollar equivalent at exchange rates in effect at the balance sheet date.* The resulting gains or losses are accumulated in a separate component of shareholders' equity under the caption "Translation adjustment." Revenue and expense items are translated at average exchange rates prevailing during the year.

Earnings Per Share: Basic earnings per share are calculated using the weighted daily average number of common shares and subordinate restricted voting shares outstanding.

Fully diluted earnings per share are calculated under the assumption that all preference shares and stock options outstanding during the year had been exercised at the beginning of the year, or when granted.

*Cineplex Odeon is a Canadian company that prepares its reports in U.S. dollars, on the basis that U.S. dollar data are more useful to the financial statement users, investors, and creditors. This is acceptable under Canadian GAAP.

have debt and/or shares that trade publicly in the United States. They reconcile their Canadian GAAP statements, required by law since they are incorporated in Canada, with U.S. GAAP in a subsequent note.

Different firms will discuss different items in the summary of significant accounting policies section. In general, the information contained in the summary is invaluable to the reader in interpreting the amounts reported in the financial statements.

Other Notes to Financial Statements

Following the summary of significant accounting policies, there are a number of required disclosures in the notes to the financial statements. Many are disclosures required by various accounting standards covered earlier in this text. The specific requirements of the standards were covered with the relevant topic.

In general, notes can fulfill the following functions:

1. Provide Detail   If detail is included on the face of a financial statement itself, the resulting clutter may reduce the understandability of the statement. Thus, details concerning accounts receivable, inventory, fixed assets, debt, and share capital are usually found in the notes.

Consider the following notes from Cineplex Odeon's December 31, 1989, financial statements:

4. Cash

Cash includes an amount of $11,086,000 which is to be used only for theatre expansion in the Corporation's U.K. subsidiary and cash held in escrow from the sale of the Live Entertainment division in the amount of $26,461,000. The escrow funds were released subsequent to the year end.

7. Property, equipment and leaseholds

	December 31, 1989	December 31, 1988
Land	$ 58,243,000	$ 60,216,000
Buildings	92,449,000	92,057,000
Equipment	185,287,000	144,402,000
Leaseholds (including capital leases)	651,342,000	594,414,000
Other	10,670,000	—
	997,991,000	891,089,000
Less accumulated depreciation and amortization	105,615,000	66,253,000
	$892,376,000	$824,836,000

The net book value of assets held under capital leases at December 31, 1989, was $14,015,000 ($15,081,000 at December 31, 1988), net of accumulated amortization of $3,341,000 ($2,665,000 in 1988).

11. Long-term debt

	December 31, 1989	December 31, 1988
(A) Bank credit facilities of $235,000,000 of which $175,000,000 is non-revolving	$229,800,000	$229,626,000
(B) Bank credit facility of $85,000,000 Canadian dollar revolving/term	—	67,000,000
(C) Bank credit facility of $70,000,000 fixed term	—	70,000,000
(D) Bank credit facilities of $325,000,000 revolving/term	320,768,000	261,227,000
(E) Bank credit facility of £30,000,000 Sterling revolving/term	—	—
(F) Various mortgages (with interest at rates from 9.00% to 10.64%)	29,645,000	37,186,000
(G) Other debt	7,443,000	8,242,000
	587,656,000	673,281,000
Less: Current Portion	9,541,000	9,437,000
	$578,115,000	$663,844,000

This information is included in the notes to simplify balance sheet presentation.

2. Explain Transactions The nature of major acquisitions or disposals during the year must be disclosed in the notes to the financial statements to comply with various accounting standards. Transactions involving share capital or other ownership interests, including stock options, are also described in the notes.

For example, Cineplex Odeon's notes include the following:

2. Acquisitions

During the three years ended December 31, 1989, the Corporation made the following significant acquisitions:

(A) In June 1987, the Corporation purchased all the issued and outstanding shares of The Walter Reade Organization, Inc., a New York-based theatre exhibition company. The purchase price was approximately $32,280,000 payable partially in cash and partially with 652,742 common shares of the Corporation.

(B) In December 1987, the Corporation purchased the net assets of the Washington Circle Theatres, a Delaware-based theatre exhibition company. The purchase price was approximately $51,000,000, being $46,375,000 cash, including acquisition costs and the present value of other purchase consideration of approximately $4,625,000.

(C) In May 1988, the Corporation acquired all of the outstanding shares of the Maybox Movie Centre Limited, located in the United Kingdom, from the Maybox Group Plc and a group of private investors for consideration of approximately £5,500,000, which included a cash payment of £1,800,000 and the assumption of £3,700,000 in liabilities. The purchase price was allocated to fixed assets in the amount of £5,000,000 and to goodwill in the amount of £500,000.

The above transactions have been accounted for using the purchase method. The results of operations of the acquired companies are included in the income statement of the Corporation from the respective dates of acquisition.

9. Loss on investments
(A) The Corporation's investment in MCA INC. was sold in 1989 for net proceeds of approximately $8,811,000, resulting in a net loss of $394,000.

(B) During 1989, the Corporation fully provided for certain investments in the amount of $7,000,000 which reduced their carrying value to nil.

(C) The Corporation fully provided for its investment in its equity accounted New Visions joint venture during the year in the amount of $7,759,000, which reduced the carrying value to nil.

5. Other income and expenses (excerpts)
In December 1989, Garth Drabinsky and Myron Gottlieb, the former Chairman and Vice-Chairman of the Board of Directors, resigned from the Corporation. Under the terms of employment agreements which had been entered into with the Corporation during 1989, Messrs. Drabinsky and Gottlieb received payments aggregating $6,806,000 ($8,000,000 Cdn.). In addition, further severance costs were recorded in the amount of $1,870,000 relating to other senior executives and employees. This amount includes accrued severance expected to be incurred in 1990 as the Corporation curtails its expansion program and concentrates on its core exhibition business in major markets.

On December 14, 1989, the Corporation sold the assets of its Live Entertainment division, which included the Canadian production of "The Phantom of the Opera," to Messrs. Drabinsky and Gottlieb. The total purchase price amounted to $76,679,000 and resulted in a gain of $19,850,000. Certain liabilities were also assumed on the sale which were applied against the purchase price resulting in proceeds to the Corporation in the amount of $56,609,000, of which $26,461,000 was held in escrow at December 31, 1989. These funds were received subsequent to the year end and are being used to fund ongoing operations and necessary capital expenditures. The remainder of the proceeds were applied to retire a short-term secured borrowing and to fund employee termination costs.

13. Capital stock (excerpts)
Stock options with respect to common shares of the Corporation have been granted to certain officers and employees. On May 13, 1988, all outstanding options granted at a price in excess of $11.00 (Cdn.) were cancelled and

reissued at $11.00 (Cdn.) per share, representing the market price at the time subject to the terms and conditions set forth in the original option agreements. All options outstanding at December 31, 1989, were granted at per share prices of $8.375 (Cdn.) to $15.125 (Cdn.) and expire between November 23, 1990, and December 2, 1994.

	December 31, 1989	December 31, 1988
Options outstanding beginning of year	3,401,500	2,287,400
Additional options granted	657,000	1,443,500
Less options exercised	152,000	280,650
Less options terminated, cancelled or expired	1,181,125	48,750
Options outstanding end of year	2,725,375	3,401,500

The results of these transactions are fully reflected in the financial statements, but are explained in the notes to help analysis.

3. Explain Unrecorded Items   Some contracts or business arrangements are not recorded in the financial statements even though they are important to an understanding of the entity's financial position or results of operations. These items are disclosed in the notes. Lawsuits are an example; they cannot be recorded until the outcome is known and the dollar amount ascertainable. Fixed contracts to buy or sell products are another example: they will affect future cash flow, but not current operations.

Events that take place between the end of the fiscal year and the date of the auditor's report, if significant, must also be disclosed as **subsequent events.** Subsequent events do not reflect conditions at the balance sheet date and therefore cannot be recognized. They must be disclosed to keep financial statement users fully informed.

Varity Corporation (the continuation of Massey Fergusson) reported the following in the notes to the 1990 financial statements:

15. Contingent liabilities and commitments
(*a*) MCC related matters
(*i*) In connection with the financial failure of Massey Combines Corporation ("MCC"), which was placed in receivership in March, 1988, various parties in Canada and the United States have commenced, or announced their intentions to commence, actions or proceedings against the Company with respect to the termination of employment and loss of certain employee benefits. Such benefits include severance and termination payments, unfunded pension liabilities, disability benefits, and health and insurance benefits of employees and retirees, including employees who retired from the employ of the Company prior to the establishment of MCC. In 1989, the Company completed a settlement agreement with one of the claimant groups providing for the restoration of health and life insurance benefits.

The ultimate determination of the remaining claims is not free from doubt and may be affected by various factors, such as recent amendments to relevant legislation, the absence of judicial consideration of these issues, and the intrinsic uncertainties of litigation. While the aggregate amounts claimed are substantial, the Company believes that it has reasonable defences to the remaining claims and that the outcome of these claims will not have a material adverse effect on its financial position.

(*ii*) The Company has assumed MCC's obligations to the Governments of Canada and Ontario to create and maintain specified levels of permanent jobs to an eventual level of 1,500 such jobs through May 1, 1993, or to pay to the Governments penalties which the Company believes would aggregate Cdn. $30,000 for each job that is not maintained. The Governments have made claims (aggregating Canadian $13.2 million) based on their determination of the level of jobs maintained at May 1, 1989. The Company believes that the agreement affords the Company opportunities and remedies to cure the shortfall and that its failure, if any, to satisfy the job covenant would not have a material adverse effect on its financial position.

(b) Capital expenditure programs

Approved capital expenditure programs outstanding at January 31, 1990, were $73.7 million, including capital commitments of approximately $48.8 million.

(c) Discounted obligations

The Company has contingent liabilities relating to notes receivable discounted, bills guaranteed and similar obligations amounting to $98.8 million and $77.5 million at January 31, 1990 and 1989, respectively, which include finance company receivables sold to third parties on a recourse basis.

Canadian Pacific-Limited reported the following subsequent event in the financial statements for the year ended December 31, 1989:

25. Subsequent event

On January 24, 1990, the Corporation announced that it had successfully completed its tender offer for all of the issued and outstanding shares of Soo Line Corporation it did not already own. As a result of the tender offer, the Corporation now owns 96% of the outstanding Soo Line shares. It is expected that the tender offer will be followed by a merger of a wholly owned subsidiary of the Corporation with Soo Line, following which the shares not tendered under the offer will be acquired at the offer price.

Based on the offer price of U.S. $21.50 per share, the cost to the Corporation will be approximately U.S. $95 million.

The acquisition is not expected to have a significant effect on the Corporation's results of operations or financial position.

None of the above transactions should or could be recognized in the financial statements. They provide important information to users, however, and are essential disclosures.

4. Provide New Information   Many important pieces of information cannot be incorporated into a financial statement, due to the nature of the item or the nature of the financial statement itself. The information is still crucial for decision making. Examples include:

1. Assets pledged as collateral for long-term debt.
2. Pension fund assets and pension fund liabilities. While these do not have to be recorded on the balance sheet, they are required in the notes.
3. Information about lines of business and geographical spread of operations. *Segment disclosure* is discussed later in the chapter.
4. Non-arm's-length transactions. Data on *related party transactions,* also discussed later in this chapter, may be significant in evaluating risk and profitability.

Consider the long-term debt note contained in the 1989 financial statements of Campbell Resources Inc. (amounts are in thousands):

5. Long-term debt

	1989	1988
Term loan (a)	$ 8,222	$11,511
Revolving term loan (b)	9,000	2,980
Notes payable (c)	1,200	1,600
Convertible debenture (d)	1,500	1,500
Province of Quebec (e)	955	872
	20,877	18,463
Less current portion	6,194	4,714
	$14,683	$13,749

(a) The term loan as well as bank indebtedness are secured by substantially all of the assets of the Company and its subsidiary, Camchib Mines Inc. The loan is repayable in instalments to 1992 and bears interest at prime plus 1½%.

(b) The revolving term loan is secured by the inventory and receivables of Meston. The loan is repayable by October 1992 and bears interest at prime plus 1%.

(c) Notes payable bear interest at 10%, are repayable in annual instalments to 1992, and are secured in part by the inventory and receivables of Meston.

(d) The convertible debenture is unsecured, matures on April 1, 1992, bears interest at 7%, and is convertible into 828,947 common shares.

(e) The Province of Quebec loan is repayable from profits, as defined, from the Cedar Bay mine and bears interest at 5%.

The estimated principal repayments over the next five years are:

1990	$6,194
1991	7,029
1992	6,699
1993	nil
1994	nil

Interest on long-term debt was as follows:

1989	$2,504
1988	1,865
1987	2,014

The Company had no unusued short-term lines of credit with banks at December 31, 1989 (1988—$24,000).

In two separate transactions, the Company is in the process of negotiating two debt facilities for a possible aggregate amount of $37 million to replace and supplement its existing term and revolving term loans.

The information in this note leaves the reader with a far better understanding of the terms, security, cost, and sources of long-term debt.

5. Other Notes   The above classification is not meant to be exhaustive. Companies prepare notes under a myriad of circumstances. Notes are prepared to explain most complex business arrangements and any accounting issues that arise, such as changes in policies, and so forth. Claims of information overload are quite understandable at times! Take a few moments, after reading this chapter, to review the full notes to the financial statements for Loblaw Companies Limited.

SPECIAL TRANSACTIONS AND EVENTS

Some transactions and events are sufficiently unusual and sensitive that they create especially difficult reporting problems for the firm. Three specific examples are:

1. Related party transactions.
2. Errors and irregularities.
3. Illegal acts.

The accountant has the problem of balancing the rights of the reporting entity and the rights of the potential users of the financial statements.

Related Party Transactions   When a firm engages in transactions where one of the transacting parties has the ability to significantly influence the policies of the other, or when a non-transacting third party has the ability to influence the actions of the transacting parties, the transaction is termed a **related party transaction**. Such transactions cannot be assumed to be carried out at arm's length as the conditions for a competitive free market interaction may not be present. Examples of related parties include the following (this list is not exhaustive):

1. A firm and its principal owners, management, and members of families of owners or management.
2. A parent firm.
3. Subsidiaries of a common parent firm.
4. Parties related by means of share ownership when the share ownership results in the ability to exercise significant influence over the investee.

CICA Handbook section 3840, "Related Party Transactions," requires the following disclosures:

1. A description of the nature of the relationship(s) involved.
2. A description of the transaction, including transactions in which no amounts or nominal amounts were involved, for each period for which income statements are presented.
3. The dollar amounts of transactions for each period for which income statements are presented.
4. Any amounts due to or from related parties as of the balance sheet date, and the terms and manner of settlement planned.

Two examples of related party disclosure notes are found in Exhibit 26–3.

Errors and Irregularities In Chapter 24 we discussed accounting for errors. *Errors* are defined as "incorrect recording and reporting of the facts about the business that existed at the time an event or transaction was recorded." They are essentially unintentional mistakes. Irregularities are *intentional* distortions of the financial statements. Both errors and irregularities should be corrected when they are detected.

In many ways irregularities are more serious problems than errors because they involve an attempt by owners and/or management to deceive readers of financial statements. An auditor must bring questionable activities to the attention of appropriate company officials, perhaps the board of directors, and decide whether disclosure is required. An auditor might find it necessary to withdraw from an audit if the company did not take corrective action, since an auditor must be able to rely on the good faith of management to complete an audit investigation.

Illegal Acts Items such as illegal political contributions, bribes, kickbacks, and other violations of any country's statutes and regulations constitute **illegal acts**. In the United States, Congress enacted the Foreign Corrupt Practices Act of 1977 largely to stop these illegal acts and to require their disclosure when discovered. Under this legislation, the auditor must ensure complete disclosure of relevant information when an illegal act is discovered. For example, if the auditor discovers that revenue is the result of an illegal act such as a bribe, the amount must be disclosed, along with all known facts about the bribe. In Canada, there is no such legislation. The auditor would proceed as for the discovery of an irregularity, bringing the matter to the attention of appropriate company officials and contemplating disclosure. These items are very serious because of the violation of laws or regulation.

Fraudulent Financial Reporting

While rare, there are from time to time instances of *fraudulent financial reporting,* defined as "intentional or reckless reporting, whether act or omission, that results in materially misleading financial statements." Fraudulent financial reporting can generally be traced to the existence of conditions in either the internal environment of the firm, such as poor internal control, or to the external environment, such as industry or overall business conditions. Extreme pressures on management, such as a major decline in

EXHIBIT 26–3   Related Party Disclosures

Taken from the notes to the financial statements of Campbell Resources Inc. at December 31, 1989:

10. Related Party Transactions

(*a*) In January 1987, a commission of $204,000 was paid to a company owned by a director of the Company for services rendered in connection with a bank refinancing.

(*b*) In December 1987, the Company purchased royalty interests in the Joe Mann property for approximately $2.5 million from a principal shareholder of the Company.

(*c*) A trucking company, of which a director of the Company is an officer and shareholder, provides transportation services to the Company. During 1989, approximately $1,678,000 (1988–$2,151,000; 1987–$1,673,000) was paid in respect of such services.

(*d*) Included in accrued liabilities is an amount payable to Northgate Exploration Limited, a principal shareholder, of $1,500,000 bearing interest at prime plus 2%.

Taken from the notes to the financial statements of Kerr Addison Mines Limited at December 31, 1987:

11. Related party transactions

The company is related to Noranda Inc. and its affiliated companies ("the Noranda Group"). Details of significant transactions with the Noranda Group for the years 1987 and 1986 are set out below:

(*i*) Canadian Electrolytic Zinc ("CEZ")—

The company's portion of zinc concentrate purchased on the company's behalf by CEZ from the Noranda Group amounted to approximately $11,275,000 (1986—$7,000,000).

(*ii*) Marketing and administrative services—

The Noranda Group markets substantially all of the company's production and renders technical and administrative services to the company. During the year marketing fees were $315,000 (1986—$251,000) and fees for technical and administrative services were $126,000 (1986—$123,000).

Copper and zinc concentrates and gold bullion sales by the company to Noranda Inc. during 1987 amounted to approximately $79,373,000 (1986—$47,216,000).

(*iii*) Short-term securities—

The company participates in a short-term investment pool with the Noranda Group. The pool is operated to provide participating companies with the opportunity to invest or borrow funds on a short-term demand basis within the Noranda Group. During 1987, the company incurred interest on net borrowings amounting to $1,656,000 (1986—interest earned of $669,000). At December 31, 1987, the company's deposit in the pool was $3,660,000 (1986—$6,100,000).

During 1987 the company invested $200,000,000 in common shares of an affiliated company; $100,000,000 of these shares were subsequently sold at cost to other affiliated companies. Dividends on the shares amounted to $4,639,000. At December 31, 1987, the cost of the shares, which approximates market value, is included in short-term securities.

During 1987, the company invested in short-term debt securities issued by certain affiliated companies. Interest on these investments amounted to $112,000. At December 31, 1987, the investment in such short-term securities totalled $34,727,000.

revenue, unrealistic profit or other performance goals, or bonus plans that depend on short-term performance, can also lead to fraudulent financial reporting.

The opportunity for management to engage in fraudulent financial reporting is present when:

◆ The board of directors or an audit committee of the board does not carefully review the reporting process.
◆ The firm has engaged in unusual or complicated transactions.
◆ Poor systems of internal control are in place.

♦ Internal audit staffs are small or poorly trained and underfunded.
♦ There is extensive need for judgment in making accounting estimates.

The ethical climate or culture of an organization can either contribute to or inhibit fraudulent financial reporting. The attitude of top management toward issues of honesty and truthful reporting can influence the actions of other managers in the organization who are in positions to engage in fraudulent reporting.

The accounting profession is faced with a problem, first, of trying to prevent fraudulent financial reporting and, second, of determining responsibility when it occurs. Auditors' responsibility to detect fraudulent reporting is not fully resolved. The accounting profession is of the opinion that it is not the responsibility of the auditor to detect fraud, beyond what can be detected with the diligent application of generally accepted auditing standards and of GAAP. In litigation, however, the auditor is often included among the parties being sued. The issue revolves around what the auditor should have detected in the audit, and what is beyond the scope of detection through normal procedures. The legal system will continue to play a leading role in the resolution of this issue.

CONCEPT REVIEW

1. Describe what financial statement users might expect to find in a summary of significant accounting policies. Why is it important?
2. What disclosure is required for a related party transaction?
3. What should an auditor do if an illegal act is discovered?

INTERIM REPORTS
♦

The fiscal year is the accounting period that is required for financial reporting. Annual financial statements, however, simply are not timely information for many investors. Users of financial statements often cannot wait until after the end of the fiscal year of the firm to make decisions. Interim information, the **interim report**, is presented by firms to provide more timely data. Usually such information is presented on a quarterly basis, although nothing prevents a firm from reporting more frequently.

Reporting more frequently than on a fiscal year basis gives rise to a new set of financial reporting problems. For example, a retailer generally does a very large percentage of its volume in the Christmas holiday season. It is often the results of this quarter that determine whether the firm will make a profit. In preparing quarterly reports for such a firm, the accountant must decide which costs to expense in the other three quarters, and what costs are most appropriately capitalized and expensed in the Christmas quarter.

The *CICA Handbook,* section 1750, "Interim Financial Reporting to Shareholders," was issued in 1971 to provide guidance on how to prepare interim financial reports, if a firm should decide to prepare them. *Section 1750 does not require firms to prepare interim financial statements.* Public companies are required to produce the information under stock exchange regulations.

Interim financial reports do not need to include a complete set of financial statements. Such reports can consist of only summarized financial data. If a firm elects to present only summarized financial data, the following should be reported, as a minimum:

1. A summary disclosing separately:
   a. Sales or gross revenue.
   b. Investment income.
   c. Amount charged for depreciation, depletion, and amortization.

      d. Interest expense.

      e. Income taxes.

      f. Income or loss before discontinued operations and extraordinary items.

      g. Discontinued operations and related income taxes.

      h. Income or loss before extraordinary items.

      i. Extraordinary items and related income taxes.

      j. Net income or loss for the period.

2. Basic and fully diluted earnings per share figures, calculated and presented in accordance with section 3500 of the *CICA Handbook,* "Earnings per Share."

3. Information as to significant changes in financial position such as in working capital, fixed assets, long-term liabilities, or shareholders' equity. This information can often be provided by a statement of changes in financial position together with other information for any changes that are not disclosed in that statement. In some cases this information can be provided in an alternative form, such as a statement of changes in net assets.

4. Information concerning:

      a. Changes in accounting principles or practices or in their method of application.

      b. Discontinued operations.

      c. Extraordinary items, if the descriptive titles of the items do not disclose their nature.

      d. Subsequent events.

      e. Other matters, not previously reported to shareholders as part of the annual financial statements, such as changes in contingencies or commitments, or issue or expiry of convertible securities, rights, warrants, or options.

Underlying Concepts of Interim Reporting   Preparing interim reports presents difficulties because of a number of factors:

1. Seasonality of revenues, costs, and expenses.
2. Major costs that occur only in one interim period but benefit other interim periods within the same reporting year.
3. Seasonality of production activities.
4. Extraordinary items and accounting changes that occur in one interim period.
5. Selection of appropriate income tax rates for each interim period.

To systematically deal with these potential problems, there are two opposing views on how to treat the interim period.

1. **Discrete view.** Each interim period is viewed as a basic reporting period. It stands alone and separate without considering it as a part of a longer (i.e., annual) reporting period. Under this view, revenue and expense recognition, accruals, and deferrals for the interim period follow the same principles and procedures as for an annual period, and there would be no "interim-period" allocations. An expense incurred in one interim period usually would not be allocated to other interim periods.

2. **Integral view.** Each interim period is viewed as an inseparable part of the annual reporting period. Under this view, revenue and expense recognition and deferrals and accruals are affected by judgments made at the end of each interim period about the results of operations for the remainder of the reporting period. Thus, an expense incurred in one interim period may be allocated among other interim periods within the reporting year.

Section 1750 of the *CICA Handbook* generally adopts the integral view, but points out that "interim financial reports should present information with respect to the results of a specified period rather than a proration of expected results for the annual period." In the United States, *APB Opinion No. 28* also requires use of the integral view but makes a few practical concessions.

Guidelines for Preparing Interim Financial Reports

The following guidelines are appropriate for preparing interim reports:

1. In general, the accounting principles and practices used by the firm in preparing its annual financial statements should be used for interim reports, with certain modifications (discussed below).
2. Revenue from products and services sold should be recognized as earned during the interim period on the same basis as followed for the annual period.
3. Costs and expenses for interim periods are classified as follows:
   a. Costs that are *directly associated* with interim revenue are reported in the interim period.
   b. Costs and expenses that are *not directly associated* with interim revenue must be allocated to interim periods on a reasonable basis. If it is not possible to allocate these costs, they must be expensed in the interim period.

Costs Directly Associated with Revenue   Costs directly associated with revenue, such as cost of goods sold, wages, salaries, fringe benefits, and warranties, should be expensed in the interim period in which the related revenue is recognized.

Costs Not Directly Associated with Revenue   All costs not directly associated with revenue should be accounted and reported for interim periods as follows:

1. Recognize as expense in the interim period in which incurred, or allocate among interim periods based on an estimate of time expired, benefit received, or activity associated with the periods.
2. Arbitrary allocation of such costs should not be made. If any costs cannot be reasonably allocated, they should be assigned to the interim period in which they were incurred.
3. Gains and losses that arise in any interim period, similar to those that would not be deferred at year-end, should be recognized in the interim period in which they arise.

Other Issues   Income tax expense for an interim period is affected by the overall tax status of the corporation. Many companies pay tax on a two-rate system, where the first level of earnings attracts tax at a low rate, and earnings above this level are taxed at a higher rate. The tax assigned to interim periods may be based on either (1) an estimate of the yearly total *combined* effective tax rate or (2) "low tax" earnings that may be assigned evenly to interim periods. Similar problems arise with assigning the benefit of taxes saved as the result of a tax loss carry-forward from a previous year, or when some interim periods show income, and others, losses. The policies chosen to deal with these issues should be internally consistent and disclosed.

Unusual or infrequently occurring items and extraordinary items should be recognized in the interim period in which they occur. Similarly, contingent losses not directly associated with revenue (and the related liabilities) should be recognized in the interim period in which they occur. Accounting changes are accounted for and reported in essentially the same manner as discussed in Chapter 24 for annual reporting periods.

Interim Reporting Illustrated

Assume the following data are for the first quarter (ended March 31, 1994) for the Interim Corporation:

Selected Items	Amount
Sales of products and services.	$500,000
Interest revenue	1,000
Extraordinary loss	15,000
Correction of 1993 accounting error (credit).	6,000
Cost of goods sold	241,000

EXHIBIT 26–4 Interim (Quarterly) Income Statement and Statement of Retained Earnings for Interim Corporation

INTERIM CORPORATION
Income Statement
For the Quarter Ending March 31, 1994

Revenues:	
Sales of products and services	$500,000
Interest revenue	1,000
Total revenue	501,000
Expenses:	
Cost of goods sold	241,000
Salaries and wages	89,000
Depreciation expense	12,000
Inventory decline, LCM	–0–
Advertising expense	9,000
Contributions	6,000
Property tax expense	3,000
Shipping expense	7,000
Unusual loss	4,000
Income tax expense	39,000
Total expenses	410,000
Income before extraordinary item	91,000
Extraordinary loss (net of $4,500 income tax)	10,500
Net income	$ 80,500
Earnings per share (30,000 common shares outstanding):	
Income before extraordinary items ($91,000/30,000 shares)	$ 3.03
Extraordinary loss ($10,500/30,000)	(.35)
Net income ($80,500/30,000)	$ 2.68

INTERIM CORPORATION
Statement of Retained Earnings
For Quarter Ending March 31, 1994

Beginning balance, as previously reported	$100,000
Prior period adjustment, error correction [6,000 × (1 − .3)]	4,200
Beginning balance, as restated	$104,200
Net income	80,500
Ending balance	$184,700

Selected Items (continued)	Amount
Operating assets, cost (10-year remaining useful life, no residual value, straight-line)	480,000
Salary and wage expense	89,000
Inventory allowance change, LCM (temporary)	4,000
Advertising expense (benefits first and second quarters equally)	18,000
Annual property tax for 1994 (estimated)	12,000
Contribution to United Fund for 1994 (charity)	6,000
Shipping supplies expense	7,000
Unusual loss	4,000
Estimated average income tax rate, 30%; Reporting period ends December 31; 30,000 common shares outstanding.	

Exhibit 26–4 illustrates the quarterly interim statement amounts needed to meet reporting requirements. It is important to notice the distinctions that are maintained

between costs directly related to interim revenue and all other costs not directly related to interim revenue. Both sales of products and interest revenue are direct and thus recognized in full in the interim period. Cost of goods sold and salaries and wages are recognized in full since they relate directly to the revenues recognized. Depreciation expense is computed as [$480,000 × $^3/_{120}$], or $12,000 for the quarter. There is no recognition of the inventory decline since it is viewed as temporary. Had it been viewed as permanent, the full amount of the decline would have been expensed in the current interim period. Advertising expense is allocated over the two periods expected to benefit from this item. Similarly, the property tax item is allocated over the four quarters; [$12,000 × ($^1/_4$)] equals $3,000 allocated to each quarter. The charitable contribution is accrued as expense for the quarter since it is not related to operations and there is no reasonable basis for allocation. Finally, the shipping expense and unusual loss are both accrued as expenses in the current quarter. The estimate of the annual tax rate is used to estimate income tax expense for the interim period.

An example of an interim financial statement is found in Exhibit 26–5. This interim report exceeds the minimum requirements of section 1750, as it includes a balance sheet. Other information, including a management commentary on results, was included in the information sent to shareholders.

Interim reporting standards are in the stage of infancy. While section 1750 provides some guidance, much remains to be done. One view is that, as information processing costs continue to decrease, there will be an increasing demand for interim financial reporting. A related issue will be the auditor's role in interim reporting. Most auditors are reluctant to express an opinion on interim financial statements because the information is subjective and involves more estimation and allocation than in annual reports. On the other hand, it seems likely that users of financial statements will expect the auditor to provide assurance that the published data are accurate and in accordance with generally accepted accounting principles. There is little question that interim reports are taking on increased importance and are a significant source of information for investors.

CONCEPT REVIEW

1. Explain the difference between the "discrete view" and the "integral view" of accounting measurement in interim reporting.
2. Suppose a firm that owns and operates a ski resort is preparing to issue a second quarter interim report. The firm has just completed a $100,000 advertising campaign, which it expects to generate revenues in the third and fourth quarters. How would this item be accounted for under the discrete view? How would it be accounted for under the integral view? Suggest two methods to allocate the expense to the third and fourth quarters.

SEGMENT REPORTING

Many large firms engage in more than one line of business. Indeed, even smaller corporations diversify their operations into more than one industry. In the past, investors seeking to assess the relative attractiveness of an investment in a diversified company were faced with the difficult task of analysing and interpreting company financial reports that reported only aggregated data with no information on the performance of its various lines of business.

Suppose you are an investor analysing Steinberg Inc. as a possible investment. Steinberg operates a chain of retail food stores and is involved in processing and wholesaling foodstuffs. They also operate self-service department stores in Ontario and Quebec, and they have a real estate operation. Their real estate activities include acquisition, development, operation, and management of various properties, primarily in Ontario and Quebec.

EXHIBIT 26–5   Interim Financial Statements, Canadian Utilities Limited, for the Nine Months
Ended September 30, 1990 (Unaudited)

Consolidated Statement of Earnings and Retained Earnings

	Nine Months Ended September 30	
(in thousands, except earnings per share)	1990	1989 (Restated)
Revenues	$ 835,136	$ 850,922
Operating expenses:		
Natural gas supply.	179,933	200,155
Operation and maintenance	297,442	292,693
Depreciation and depletion	84,935	75,897
Taxes—other than income.	49,002	48,226
Taxes—income	61,857	70,383
	$ 673,169	$ 687,354
Operating income	161,967	163,568
Allowance for funds used during construction	23,077	18,339
Other income	3,631	3,671
Earnings before financing charges	188,675	185,578
Interest expense.	92,029	78,988
Dividends on preferred shares	31,599	31,696
	$ 123,628	$ 110,684
Earnings attributable to Class A and Class B shares	$ 65,047	$ 74,894
Retained earnings at beginning of period:		
As previously reported.	453,201	422,893
Adjustment of prior years' earnings	(4,479)	—
	$ 513,769	$ 497,787
Dividends on Class A and Class B shares.	60,709	59,766
Retained earnings at end of period.	$ 453,060	$ 438,021
Earnings per Class A and Class B share	$ 1.09	$ 1.26

Consolidated Balance Sheet

	September 30	
(in thousands)	1990	1989 (Restated)
Assets		
Current Assets:		
Cash	$ 3,093	$ 1,514
Accounts receivable.	90,834	88,965
Income taxes recoverable	19,770	14,825
Materials and supplies.	37,226	27,889
Natural gas stored.	20,123	14,666
Prepaid expenses	9,471	5,501
	180,517	153,360
Investments	20,655	26,475
Property, plant, and equipment	2,846,008	2,637,658
Deferred expenses.	26,959	23,440
	$3,074,139	$2,840,933
Liabilities and Capitalization		
Current liabilities:		
Due to bank.	$ 13,329	$ 22,414
Accounts payable and accrued liabilities	125,281	107,051
Other taxes payable	10,243	8,652
Dividends payable	4,973	4,982
Long-term debt—current maturities	24,058	36,958
	177,884	180,057

EXHIBIT 26–5   *(continued)*

(in thousands)	September 30	
	1990	**1989 (Restated)**
Liabilities and Capitalization		
Deferred credits:		
Contributions for extensions to plant.	$ 262,282	$ 244,392
Deferred income taxes.	31,961	28,589
Other.	16,377	22,591
	310,620	295,572
Capitalization:		
Notes payable	140,411	150,869
Long-term debt	1,006,919	786,948
Preferred shares.	552,727	556,948
Class A and Class B shareholders' equity.	885,578	870,539
	2,585,635	2,365,304
	$3,074,139	$2,840,933

Consolidated Statement of Changes in Cash Position

(in thousands)	Nine Months Ended September 30	
	1990	**1989 (Restated)**
Cash provided from operations:		
Earnings attributable to Class A and Class B shares	$ 65,047	$ 74,894
Depreciation and depletion	84,935	75,897
Other.	10,955	9,271
Allowance for funds used during construction—		
shareholders' equity	(9,215)	(7,369)
Decrease in working capital	12,696	10,839
	164,418	163,532
Dividends:		
Class A and Class B shares	60,709	59,766
	103,709	103,766
Financing:		
Increase in notes payable	48,588	115,169
Issue of long-term debt	125,000	
Reduction in long-term debt	(38,509)	(23,452)
Contributions for extensions to plant.	15,444	17,446
Other.	(18,486)	(5,570)
	132,037	103,593
Total cash for investment	235,746	207,359
Investment:		
Capital expenditures	237,730	225,225
Allowance for funds used during construction—		
shareholders' equity	(9,215)	(7,369)
	228,515	217,856
Purchase (disposal) of investments.	(4,479)	6,481
Disposition of property, plant and equipment	162	(820)
Increase (decrease) in deferred expenses	5,655	(1,561)
	229,853	221,956
Increase (decrease) in cash*	$ 5,893	$ (14,597)

Notes to Consolidated Financial Statements

Note 1: The figures in this interim report are unaudited.

Note 2: There are 35,573,905 (1989–35,473,497) Class A non-voting shares and 23,944,669 (1989—24,045,077) Class B common shares outstanding on September 30, 1990.

EXHIBIT 26-5   *(concluded)*

Note 3: Due to the seasonal nature of the Company's operations and the timing of rate case decisions, the consolidated statements of earnings and retained earnings for the nine months ended September 30, 1990, and September 30, 1989, are not necessarily comparable or indicative of operations on an annual basis.

Note 4: The Company is proposing to distribute one half of its investment in its wholly owned oil and gas subsidiary to its Class A and Class B shareholders. The proposal will be implemented by a Plan of Arrangement contingent upon directors', shareholders', court and regulatory approvals, and an advance income tax ruling. The distribution of the shares will result in a charge to retained earnings of approximately $66 million, including the costs of the arrangement. Following the distribution the Company will use the equity method to account for its remaining investment.

Note 5: The Public Utilities Board, by an order dated August 2, 1989, directed the Company's subsidiary, Canadian Western Natural Gas Company Limited, to file a submission for a general rate application covering the years 1989, 1990, and 1991. A final decision was issued by the Board on July 27, 1990. The impact on 1989 earnings was a reduction of $4,479,000, an amount considered by management to be significant enough to restate the previously reported earnings for that year. Earnings for the nine months ended September 30, 1989, decreased by $3,166,000 from the amount previously reported.

Note 6: Certain of the 1989 figures have been reclassified to conform with the consolidated financial statement presentation adopted in 1990.

Degree Days	Edmonton and Calgary Nine Months Ended September 30		
	1990	1989	Normal
EDMONTON	3,021	3,532	3,513
CALGARY	2,987	3,455	3,347

DEGREE DAYS: The number of degrees by which daily mean temperature falls below 18 degrees C. One degree day is counted for each degree of deficiency for each day on which such a deficiency occurs. For example, if the mean temperature for a day was 10 degrees C, then there were eight degree days during that 24-hour period.

* "Long-term debt—current maturities" and cash are excluded from working capital. Cash is defined as "cash" less "due to bank."

Supply and demand for these major products and services react differently during good and bad economic times. For example, consumers must buy groceries during economic bad times, but might be more inclined to buy house brands if they were less expensive. To a lesser extent, they must also continue to buy consumer durables, sold at department stores. However, during a recession they are more likely to delay such purchases if at all possible. Finally, the real estate market is known to be volatile, and property values are likely to decline when the economy is weak. Thus, the status of the economy is most important when assessing the prospects for real estate profitability, and it is least important for the food segment.

Stated differently, each of the businesses discussed above possesses different risk characteristics. Investors who know the relative proportions of company resources committed to operations in the various businesses are likely to be able to make more informed decisions than investors who know only aggregate data for the company.

This line of reasoning is the basis for section 1700 of the *CICA Handbook,* "Segmented Information," issued by the CICA in 1979. Only public companies and life insurance companies are required to disclose segmented information, for **industry and geographic segments.** An industry segment of a business is a subdivision of the business that derives revenue from individual products or services that are significant parts of the business. In addition, segment reporting applies to operations in other geographic areas, if they account for 10% or more of company revenue or identifiable assets.

Industry Segments

Section 1700 leaves the definition of reportable industry and geographic segments up to management. First, segments are identified and, second, management must decide which of the segments are reportable.

In general, an *industry* classification would proceed as follows:

1. Identify the individual products or services from which the enterprise derives its revenue.
2. Group those products or services by industry lines into industry segments. The nature of the product, production process, and markets must be considered.

A **reportable segment** for industry must meet at least *one* of the following criteria:

1. Revenue is 10% or more of the combined revenue segments of the entity.
2. The absolute amount of operating profit or loss is 10% or more of the greater, in absolute amount, of, respectively:
   a. The combined operating profit of all industry segments of the entity that earned an operating profit.
   b. The combined operating loss of all industry segments of the entity that incurred an operating loss.
3. Identifiable assets are 10% or more of the combined identifiable assets of all industry segments of the entity.

Of course, any industry segment, regardless of size, can be designated significant and therefore reportable.

When an enterprise has a dominant industry segment, this fact should be disclosed together with a general description of the products and services from which revenue is derived.

Required Disclosures   A general description of the products and services from which each reportable industry segment derives its revenue should be provided. Disclosure of the following data should be made for each reportable industry segment and, in aggregate, for the remainder of the enterprise's industry segments:

1. Segment revenue derived from sales to customers outside the enterprise.
2. Segment revenue derived from inter-segment sales or transfers and the basis of accounting therefor.
3. Segment operating profit or loss; the amount of depreciation, amortization, and depletion expense; and any unusual items included in determining segment operating profit or loss.
4. Total carrying amount of identifiable assets at the end of the fiscal year and the amount of capital expenditure for the period.

A reconciliation of the aggregate segment revenue, aggregate segment operating profit or loss, and aggregate identifiable assets to the sales, net income, and total assets reported in the financial statements of the enterprise should be provided.

Segment revenue includes all product and service sales to unaffiliated customers (i.e., customers from outside the enterprise), inter-segment sales, and interest on segment trade receivables. It does not include interest revenue on loans to other segments.

Segment operating gain or loss is segment revenue (as defined above) less all segment operating expenses. Operating expenses for a segment include:

1. Operating expenses that are directly related to a segment's revenue.
2. Operating expenses incurred by the company that can be allocated on a reasonable basis to the segment(s) for whose benefit those expenses were incurred.

None of the following should be added or deducted in computing the operating income or loss of a segment: (1) company revenues not derived from the segment, (2) general company expenses, (3) interest expenses, (4) income taxes, (5) equity in income of unconsolidated subsidiaries or other equity investees, (6) extraordinary items, and (7) minority interests in income.

Identifiable assets include the tangible and intangible indentifiable assets of the segment that are used exclusively by the segment or jointly by two or more segments, allocated on a reasonable basis. Asset valuation accounts, such as allowance for doubtful accounts and accumulated depreciation, also must be included. Assets that cannot be included are those used for general company purposes and loans or advances to other segments.

Geographic Segments

Investors need information on geographic segments to help assess risk and potential. Investments in North America, the Middle East, Soviet Bloc countries, Hong Kong, and/or Third World countries have radically different risk characteristics.

The determination of a geographic segment is, again, a management responsibility. Factors to consider, outside of pure geography, include the proximity of operations, whether operations in areas are related, and the nature of the economic and political risks in each location. It's often not as easy as it seems: Are Canada and the United States one geographic segment or two? England and France? France and Germany? Answers are firm-specific.

Once a firm has identified its geographic segments, it then must determine which of the segments are *reportable*. Significant—or reportable—geographic segments are those that account for:

1. Ten percent or more of the revenue generated from customers outside the enterprise.
2. Ten percent or more of the total assets of the enterprise.

Disclosure The disclosure required for a reportable geographic segment closely parallels that required for an industry segment, but is less extensive. Section 1700.44 provides that

> The location of each reportable foreign geographic segment should be disclosed.
> Disclosure of the following data should be made for each reportable foreign geographic segment, in total for all other foreign geographic segments when they are in the aggregate identified as significant and for the domestic geographic segment:
>
> (a) segment revenue derived from sales to customers outside the enterprise;
> (b) segment revenue derived from sales or transfers between geographic segments and the basis of accounting therefor;
> (c) segment operating profit or loss or, where appropriate, some other measure of profitability (information as to after-tax profitability may be more appropriate when the tax structure applicable to the reportable foreign geographic segment is substantially different from that experienced by the enterprise's domestic operation); and
> (d) total carrying amount of identifiable assets at the end of the fiscal year.
>
> A reconciliation of the aggregate segment revenue, aggregate measure of profitability and aggregate identifiable assets to the sales, net income and total assets reported in the financial statements of the enterprise should be provided.

In addition, paragraph 1700.46 requires disclosure of the amount of export sales, when sales of products and services by an enterprise's domestic operations to foreign customers are significant.

Exhibit 26–6 provides an example of segmented information from the Steinberg Inc. 1988 annual report. Notice that most of the sales volume takes place in the food retailing segment. Although the volume in this segment has increased over the prior year, it is less profitable in the current year. The general merchandise segment continues to show a net loss, although the magnitude of losses has decreased with only a marginal increase in revenue. This suggests some improvements in operating efficiency.

EXHIBIT 26-6   Steinberg Inc., 1988 Segment Reporting Note

Results by Business Segment

(thousands of dollars)	Food Retailing, Wholesaling, and Processing		General Merchandise Retailing		Real Estate		Consolidated	
	1988	1987	1988	1987	1988	1987	1988	1987
Sales and operating revenue:								
Outside customers	$4,326,842	$4,238,769	$202,424	$ 198,828	$ 55,419	$ 53,758	$4,584,685	$4,491,355
Inter-segment	—	—	—	—	22,914	24,967	—	—
Total	4,326,842	4,238,769	202,424	198,828	78,333	78,725	4,584,685	4,491,355
Earnings (loss) before the following	50,677	74,315	(5,807)	(12,255)	35,436	43,086	80,306	105,146
Corporate expenses, including interest expense, special charge and unusual items and income taxes, less other income							97,317	38,220
Net earnings (loss)							$ (17,011)	$ 66,926
Assets:								
Identifiable by segment.	1,025,008	1,008,186	51,376	59,264	263,052	237,187	1,339,436	1,304,637
Corporate							137,883	114,561
Investment in affiliates.							47,314	50,155
Total							$1,524,633	$1,469,353
Additions to fixed assets—net . . .	137,577	122,264	2,216	1,659	29,945	5,574	169,738	129,497
Depreciation.	52,366	41,332	1,802	1,975	6,631	8,621	60,799	51,928

Note: Food retailing, wholesaling and processing—merchandises a complete range of food and non-food products, through warehouses, supermarkets, limited assortment stores and restaurants. General merchandise retailing—operation of self-service department stores in Quebec and Ontario. Real estate—acquisition, development, operation and management of real estate, principally in Quebec and Ontario, with certain land held for future development in the United States. Inter-segment transactions are shown on the basis of accounting used for internal accounting purposes.

Results by Geographic Area

(thousands of dollars)	Canada		United States		Consolidated	
	1988	1987	1988	1987	1988	1987
Sales and operating revenue	$3,684,231	$3,576,103	$900,454	$915,252	$4,584,685	$4,491,355
Earnings before the following	54,913	69,217	25,393	35,929	80,306	105,146
Corporate expenses, including interest expense, special charge and unusual items and income taxes, less other income					97,317	38,220
Net earnings (loss)					$ (17,011)	$ 66,926
Assets:						
Identifiable	1,004,782	981,408	334,654	323,229	1,339,436	1,304,637
Corporate					137,883	114,561
Investment in affiliates.					47,314	50,155
Total					$1,524,633	$1,469,353
Additions to fixed assets—net	136,336	94,054	33,402	35,443	169,738	129,497
Depreciation.	52,009	42,688	8,790	9,240	60,799	51,928

The real estate division appears to be extremely profitable, as a percentage of revenues. Note that a significant portion of its revenues are inter-segment, which implies that Steinberg owns properties in which it has retail operations. This affects any assessment of risk inherent in the real estate segment.

Geographically, Canada and the United States have been treated as two distinct segments. Earnings data indicate that U.S. operations are far more profitable than

EXHIBIT 26–7   Boeing Company, 1989 Segment Reporting Note

Financial information by segment for the three years ended December 31, 1989, is summarized below. Revenues consist of sales plus other income applicable to the respective segments. Corporate income consists principally of interest income from corporate investments. Corporate expense consists of interest on debt and other general corporate expenses. Corporate assets consist principally of cash and short-term investments.

	Year ended December 31		
(in millions)	1989	1988	1987
Revenues:			
Commercial transportation products and services. . . .	$14,305	$11,369	$ 9,827
Military transportation products and related systems . .	3,962	3,668	3,979
Missiles and space.	1,467	1,457	1,063
Other industries.	542	468	636
Operating revenues	20,276	16,962	15,505
Corporate income	347	378	308
Total revenues.	$20,623	$17,340	$15,813
Operating profit:			
Commercial transportation products and services. . . .	$ 1,165	$ 585	$ 352
Military transportation products and related systems . .	(559)	(95)	60
Missiles and space.	85	124	119
Other industries.	26	(28)	(34)
Operating profit	717	586	497
Corporate income	347	378	308
Corporate expense	(142)	(144)	(147)
Earnings before taxes	$ 922	$ 820	$ 658
Identifiable assets at December 31:			
Commercial transportation products and services. . . .	$ 6,675	$ 4,558	$ 5,170
Military transportation products and related systems . .	3,367	2,923	2,846
Missiles and space.	911	684	548
Other industries.	329	319	362
	11,282	8,484	8,926
Corporate.	1,996	4,124	3,640
Consolidated assets	$13,278	$12,608	$12,566
Depreciation:			
Commercial transportation products and services. . . .	$ 242	$ 243	$ 218
Military transportation products and related systems . .	208	188	170
Missiles and space.	72	52	42
Capital expenditures, net:			
Commercial transportation products and services. . . .	$ 612	$ 326	$ 286
Military transportation products and related systems . .	506	241	316
Missiles and space.	155	62	72

Canadian operations, where the bulk of Steinberg's volume is concentrated. It is not possible to determine from this disclosure what kind of activity—food, general merchandise, or real estate—is being carried out in the United States, although the information is available elsewhere in the annual report.

A final sample of segment reporting is found in Exhibit 26–7. This exhibit contains excerpts from the note to the 1989 Boeing financial statements. It is interesting to see that Boeing uses category of customer (i.e., commercial or government) to develop its segments. Both the "commercial transportation" and the "military transportation" segments are basically producing and marketing aircraft and related products. However, much of the marketing effort, opportunity for profit, and, indeed, the risk undertaken by the company differs between these two markets.

CONCEPT REVIEW

1. Why might users of financial statements find segment reporting useful? How might it affect their decision making?
2. The apparel segment of a diversified company has a loss of $12 million. Five other segments have operating profits (losses) of $34 million, ($57 million), $48 million, $15 million and ($73 million). Based only on this information, does this segment have to be reported as a segment? Why or why not?

SUMMARY OF KEY POINTS

(L.O. 1, 2)   1. Two related concepts or arguments support a decrease in the amount of information disclosed in financial statements. First, *standards overload* argues there are too many complex and costly-to-implement standards. The costly standards place an unfair (or at least uneconomic) financial burden on some firms, primarily smaller firms. The related notion of *information overload* essentially argues that so much marginally useful information is disclosed that important information is obscured.

(L.O. 1, 2)   2. The offsetting notion to the above two concepts is the principle of *full disclosure.* This principle calls for the disclosure of any financial information that is potentially of sufficient significance so as to influence the judgment of an informed reader.

(L.O. 3)   3. The notes to the financial statements are an integral part of the statements. Financial statements are incomplete if they do not contain the appropriate note disclosures.

(L.O. 3)   4. Firms must include in the financial statements a summary of significant accounting policies. The disclosure must include the selections made from existing acceptable alternatives and the principles and methods of accounting measurement particular to the industry.

(L.O. 3)   5. There are special disclosure requirements for related party transactions and errors and irregularities.

(L.O. 4)   6. Interim reports are not required. If they are presented, however, they should be prepared using the same accounting policies used for annual reports. The interim report can contain a summary of information less complete than an annual financial statement. The information that must be presented if an interim report is prepared is specified in section 1750 of the *CICA Handbook.*

(L.O. 4)   7. Use of the integral view is required in preparing interim reports. This view allocates items between interim periods that are not normally allocated across fiscal periods in annual financial statements.

(L.O. 5)   8. Publicly held firms operating in multiple businesses and/or in multiple geographic areas report various information on the activities of segments meeting qualifying criteria. Principally, the information relates to sales, assets, some measure of profit, and, for industry segments, capital expenditures and depreciation. Management identifies industry and geographic segments which may be reportable.

(L.O. 5)   9. If one or more of the following criteria are met by an industry segment, it must be reported as a separate segment: (*a*) segment revenue is 10% or more of the combined revenue of the firm; (*b*) segment assets are 10% or more of the combined assets for the firm, or (*c*) the absolute amount of the operating profit or loss of a segment is 10% or more of the greater of the absolute total of all industry segment operating profits and the absolute total of all industry segment operating losses. A geographic segment is reportable if it meets the test of either (*a*) or (*b*).

REVIEW PROBLEM

The following situations are independent.

1. Ryan Royalty Lines (RRL) sold an apartment building to its parent company, Ryan Holding Corp (RHC), in 1992, for net proceeds of $20 million. The proceeds were to be paid to RRL over the next 10 years out of cash flow from the apartment building,

and the outstanding debt bore market interest rates. RRL also leased space at market prices to three other subsidiaries of RHC during 1992. Rent receivable from these parties, three months in arrears at year-end, totalled $137,500.

Required:

Draft related party transactions notes to the RRL 1992 financial statements.

2. During the course of the 1992 audit of RRL, the auditor discovered a payment made to an individual building inspector in the province of Ontario in the amount of $50,000. RRL included the amount under "Building Costs" for an apartment building under construction in Ontario in 1992. When asked, management of RRL indicated that the payment was made to "expedite construction."

Required:

Discuss the steps the auditor should take in relation to this expenditure.

3. RRL has asked how each of the following items should be reported in its interim report for the first quarter of fiscal year 1993, which runs from July 1, 1992, to September 30, 1992.
   a. Advertising expense of $120,000. The rental complex advertises heavily once a year, over the summer, as most leases come due on September 1. All quarters benefit equally.
   b. Power cost of $540,000. Power bills in the summer months run 25% higher than normal due to air-conditioning costs in apartment buildings.
   c. RRL pays tax as follows:
      1. On the first $200,000 of annual income, 25%.
      2. On any remaining income, 45%.
      Projected net income for the 1993 fiscal year is $500,000.
   d. Rental income for the first three months of 1993 totalled $620,000 of which $40,000 was unpaid at September 30, 1992.
   e. The company president and CEO was fired on July 15, 1992, resulting in a severance payment of $200,000.
   f. The net realizable value of short-term investments was $70,000 lower than cost on September 30, 1992, due to generally depressed stock market conditions, which analysts expected to reverse by December 1992.

4. RRL has operations in construction, management services, rental properties, and retail sales. Data concerning these operation are as follows (in thousands):

	Sales to Outsiders	Inter-Segment Sales	Total Sales	Profits (Losses)	Identifiable Assets
Construction	$ 500	$1,500	$2,000	$ 800	$ 400
Management services	100	125	225	50	40
Rental properties	1,800	700	2,500	(600)	1,500
Retail sales	500	—	500	(50)	160
	$2,900	$2,325	$5,225	$ 200	$2,100

Required:

Identify the reportable segments, and outline the required disclosures for industry segments.

REVIEW SOLUTION

◆

1. During 1992, RRL engaged in related party transactions as follows:
   a. RRL sold an apartment building to its parent corporation, Ryan Holding Corporation (RHC), for net proceeds of $20 million, resulting in an accounting gain of xxx. The $20 million proceeds is still outstanding at year-end, bears market interest rates, and is repayable over 20 years.
   b. RRL has rental revenue from related parties in the amount of $550,000 ($137,500 × 4) for the year 1992, of which $137,500 was receivable at year-end.

2. The auditor should:
   a. Bring the matter to the attention of the audit committee and/or board of directors. This appears to be an illegal act, and their reaction will be critical to the auditor. They should be prepared to disclose the item, cooperate in legal investigation, and take steps to ensure that it does not happen again.
   b. If there is an unsatisfactory response from the board, the auditor must consider resigning from the engagement.
   c. The auditor should get legal advice concerning any responsibility to report the transaction, as information obtained during an audit is highly confidential.

3. a. The advertising expense benefits all interim periods and may be allocated ¼ to each interim quarter.
   b. Air conditioning expense of $108,000 is an expense of the summer quarter ($540,000/1.25 = $432,000; $540,000 − $432,000 = $108,000).
   c. The average expected tax rate for fiscal year 1993 is:

$$.25 \times \tfrac{2}{5}{}^* = .10$$
$$.45 \times \tfrac{3}{5}{}^* = \underline{.27}$$
$$\underline{\underline{.37}}$$

   * $200,000/$500,000; $300,000/$500,000

   This rate should be applied to each quarter.

   Alternatively, some portion of the $200,000 low tax rate earnings may be allocated to each quarter.
   d. Rental income of $620,000 should be reported as earned in the first quarter (subject, of course, to an allowance for doubtful accounts).
   e. This unusual event should be reported in its entirety in the summer quarter.
   f. Since the decline will reverse before year-end, no write-down need be recorded.

4. Reportable segments are as follows:
   a. Based on total sales: Construction ($2,000/$5,225) = 38%
                                  Rental properties ($2,500/$5,225) = 48%
   Management services and Rental properties each accounts for less than 10% of total sales.
   b. Based on profit/loss: Construction [$800/($800 + $50)] = 94%
                                  Rental properties [$600/($800 + $50)] = 70.5%

   Other segments account for less than 10% of the absolute value of the profit pool, which is greater than the absolute value of the loss pool.
   c. Based on assets: Construction ($400/$2,100) = 19%
                                  Rental properties ($1,500/$2,100) = 71%

   Other segments account for less than 10% of total assets.

   Required disclosures are as follows:
   a. Segment revenue derived from outside customers, inter-segment sales, and a reconciliation to total sales.
   b. Segment operating profit or loss, reconciled to net income.
   c. Segment identifiable assets, reconciled to total assets.
   d. Capital expenditure and depreciation by segment.

KEY TERMS

Discrete view, interim reporting (1353)
Full disclosure principle (1342)
Geographic segment (1359)
Illegal acts (1350)
Industry segment (1359)
Information overload (1351)

Integral view, interim reporting   (1353)
Interim reports (1352)
Related party transaction (1349)
Reportable segment (1360)
Standards overload (1341)
Subsequent events (1347)

QUESTIONS

1. What is standards overload? Why is it a problem?
2. What is information overload? Why is it a problem?
3. What is the full disclosure principle? Why have note disclosures increased substantially over the past decade?
4. Why are notes to the financial statements prepared?
5. What is a subsequent event? Why is it not recorded in the statements?
6. What are the accounting policies of a company? What, if any, are the requirements for disclosing information about accounting policies?
7. When are parties "related" for accounting purposes?
8. What must a firm disclose about related party transactions?
9. What is an illegal act? What must an auditor do if an illegal act is encountered?
10. Is interim reporting required by public companies? Non-public companies?
11. What is interim reporting? Why is it potentially important?
12. What is the difference between the discrete view and the integral view of interim financial reporting periods?
13. Should income statement items that are separately classified, such as extraordinary items, be prorated over interim reporting periods, or recognized in a single interim period?
14. List the minimum information that should be included in an interim financial report.
15. What is the basic rationale for requiring segment reporting? What are the arguments against segment reporting?
16. Segmented information must be presented for industry and geographic segments. Are these independent of each other? When might they be? When might they not be?
17. What is the difference, if any, between the terms industry segment and reportable segment? Explain how each is determined.
18. Explain the following terms: identifiable assets, intersegment sales, and common cost.
19. Briefly describe the alternative tests for determining a reportable industry segment.
20. How are the requirements for the determination of reportable industry segments different from reportable geographic segments? The reporting requirements?

EXERCISES

E 26–1
Interim Reporting
(L.O. 4)

In January 1992, management of Clip Inc. estimates that its year-end bonus to executives will be $500,000 for 1992. The amount paid in 1991 was $440,000. The final determination of the amount to be paid is made at the conclusion of the fiscal year and is based on total income for the year and the share price at year-end.

Required:
Determine the amount, if any, of bonus expense that should be reflected in Clip's quarterly income statement for the three months ending March 31, 1992. Justify and explain your answer.

E 26–2
Interim Reporting
(L.O. 4)

In September 1991 Crystal Mountain Ski Resorts (CMSR) spent $300,000 advertising for the coming ski season. The ski season lasts from October through the following March, with business expected to be spread evenly over this period. The fiscal year for CMSR ends March 31, 1992.

Required:
Determine the amount of expense that should be included in CMSR's interim financial statements for September 30, and for December 31, 1991. Justify and explain your answer.

E 26–3
Interim Reporting
(L.O. 4)

The Proctor Company reported income before income taxes of $100,000 and $150,000 in the first two quarters of 1992. Management's estimate of the annual effective tax rate was 35% at the end of the first quarter, and 30% at the end of the second quarter.

Required:
Determine the income tax expense for the first two quarters of 1992.

E 26–4
Segment Reporting:
Geographic Segments
(L.O. 5)

Montgomery Company operates in one industry segment, but has operations throughout the world, as follows:

	Sales	Identifiable Assets
Mexico	$16,000,000	$ 2,000,000
Brazil	2,000,000	500,000
Argentina	5,000,000	1,500,000
Uruguay	4,000,000	1,200,000
England	13,000,000	1,100,000
France	19,000,000	25,000,000
United States	14,500,000	40,000,000
Canadian domestic sales	40,000,000	120,000,000

Additional information:

a. Canadian domestic sales include sales of $14,000,000 to U.S. federal government agencies.
b. U.S. sales include $2,000,000 to Brazil.

Required:

Determine the reportable geographic segments if the distinction is based only on sales and/or assets. Be prepared to discuss your decisions.

E 26–5
Segments: Prepare
Disclosures
(L.O. 5)

Big Company has two segments of its operations that qualify as reportable industry segments. The revenues of the specialty products segment approximate 11% of total revenues, and the identifiable net assets of the services segment approximate 17% of total identifiable assets.

Relevant pretax data for 1992 are as follows (in thousands):

	Specialty	Services	Company*
Revenues.	$1,350	$ 975	$9,760†
Direct expenses.	800	400	6,000
Companywide expenses (allocable)			1,800†
General company expenses (not allocable).			1,385
Identifiable assets‡ (net of depreciation)	250	1,200	5,600
Income tax rate, 40%.			

* Excludes the segment amounts.

† Allocate on the basis of direct expense ratios.

‡ None used jointly.

Required:

1. Prepare the segmented income statement for the company. Use three columns: Specialty Segment, Services Segment, and Total Company. Show computations.
2. Show what amounts should be reported for identifiable assets for each segment and the total company.

E 26–6
Identify Reportable
Segments: Give Basis
(L.O. 5)

ACR Corporation has expanded rapidly, and industry segment reporting has become an accounting issue. The following situations are under consideration (in millions):

Situation	Revenues	Operating Profit	Identifiable Assets
1. Product Group A	$28	$5	$15
2. Foreign Operation—SA	27	4	14
3. Foreign Operation—ME	28	6	16
4. Product Group B.	29	4	15
5. Product Group C.	30	7	13

Additional data (in millions):

a. Combined operating profit of all industry segments
   (no operating losses) . . . . $ 50
b. Combined identifiable assets of all industry segments   160
c. Combined revenue of all segments of the entity   300

Required:

Select those segments that ACR Corporation should designate as reportable segments. Explain the basis for your decision in each situation.

E 26-7
Interim Reporting:
Application of Guidelines
(L.O. 4)

In the context of interim reporting, items may be (*a*) recognized in the interim statements of the current interim period, (*b*) recognized in the current interim period but require special disclosure, (*c*) deferred in their entirety (i.e., not recognized until some later interim period, or not at all), or (*d*) amortized or accrued (i.e., recognized partly in the current interim period and partly in subsequent interim periods). A number of items are listed below that require a decision as to how they should be incorporated on interim statements. You are to match the letters given above with the numbered items given below to indicate how each item should be incorporated on the interim statements.

1. Salaries allocable to services rendered during the current period.
2. Inventories estimated by use of the gross margin method.
3. Temporary declines in market value of inventories.
4. Short-term investment gains from recoveries of market value of shares held (not in excess of previously recognized market declines).
5. Materials and wages allocable to products sold this period.
6. Costs benefiting two or more interim periods.
7. Quantity discounts allowed to customers based upon annual volume of their purchases.
8. Contingencies and other uncertainties which may affect fairness of presentation.
9. Income tax on income of first quarter where total income for the first quarter only puts company in a "low tax" bracket; subsequent operations are expected to be sufficiently profitable that by end of second quarter, and thereafter, taxable income of company will be in a higher bracket.

E 26-8
Industry Segment
Disclosure
(L.O. 5)

Operating profit and loss figures for the seven industries in which the Sheets Company operates are as follows:

	1992 Operating Profit (Loss)
Industry 1	$1,075,000
Industry 2	200,000
Industry 3	550,000
Industry 4	(208,000)
Industry 5	(18,000)
Industry 6	5,000
Industry 7	(2,000)
	$1,602,000

Required:

Identify those industries that meet the operating profit or loss criteria to be a reportable segment for 1992.

PROBLEMS

P 26-1
Segment Reporting
(L.O. 5)

Study the industry segment data as abstracted from the 1990 FMC Corporation annual report presented below.

FMC Corporation Industry Segment Data

(*in millions*)	Year Ended December 31				
	1990	**1989**	**1988**	**1987**	**1986**
Sales:					
Industrial chemicals	$1,029.6	$ 975.9	$ 914.0	$ 876.8	$ 835.1
Performance chemicals	594.4	565.6	521.0	478.1	477.9
Precious metals.	187.7	190.2	175.7	133.3	86.3
Defense systems	1,067.2	900.3	945.7	1,020.3	971.1
Machinery and equipment	845.5	783.0	734.1	634.1	645.4
Eliminations	(2.2)	(0.5)	(3.6)	(3.5)	(13.1)
Total.	$3,722.2	$3,414.5	$3,286.9	$3,139.1	$3,002.7

(in millions)	**1990**	**1989**	**1988**	**1987**	**1986**
			Year Ended December 31		
Income (loss) before taxes:					
Industrial chemicals	$ 106.9	$ 137.7	$ 146.9	$ 141.9	$ 138.6
Performance chemicals	84.8	88.0	76.8	44.2	39.8
Precious metals*	81.3	100.9	93.3	55.3	29.7
Defense systems	96.8	47.3	54.2	88.9	123.5
Machinery and equipment	52.0	28.3	11.7	13.0	(3.2)
Operating profit	421.8	402.2	382.9	343.3	328.4
Net interest expense	(128.1)	(133.7)	(148.4)	(184.9)	(130.8)
Gain on FMC Gold Company					
sale of stock.	—	—	—	94.7	—
Corporate and other	(101.8)	(86.2)	(84.7)	(94.7)	(76.6)
Unusual items	19.5	36.0	39.7	43.0	71.6
Total.	$ 211.4	$ 218.3	$ 189.5	$ 201.4	$ 192.6
Identifiable assets:					
Industrial chemicals	$1,048.3	$ 931.5	$ 842.3	$ 846.4	$ 830.9
Performance chemicals	420.9	397.4	391.2	392.0	420.2
Precious metals.	157.4	99.3	102.5	96.8	93.0
Defense systems	444.7	502.9	492.4	478.9	535.4
Machinery and equipment	495.2	459.3	450.8	462.2	423.0
Eliminations	—	—	(0.1)	(0.1)	(0.3)
Subtotal	2,566.5	2,390.4	2,279.1	2,276.2	2,302.2
Corporate and other	392.7	428.6	469.7	318.9	383.6
Total.	$2,959.2	$2,819.0	$2,748.8	$2,595.1	$2,685.8

* Includes 100% of FMC Gold Company's income before income taxes of $49.0 million in 1990, $60.7 million in 1989, $82.7 million in 1988, $65.1 million in 1987, and $26.8 million in 1986 and the effects of the FMC Corporation hedging program. Minority shareholder interests since the initial public offering in June 1987 are included in Corporate and other.

Required:

1. For the 1990 data, evaluate the reportable segment criteria for each of the six segments to determine why each was designated reportable.
2. For 1990, which segment earned the largest return on assets? Which segment reported the largest return on sales?
3. Suppose the precious metals segment operating profit were reduced by $49.0 million. Would this continue to be a reportable segment? Why or why not?
4. If FMC had additional businesses, none of which by itself required reporting as a segment, how would the above industry segment data report be changed?

P 26–2
Segment Reporting
(L.O. 5)

The segmented information for Redpath Industries Ltd. for 1988 is as follows:

Redpath Industries Ltd.

Segmented Information The Company operates primarily in three industry segments—sugar, automotive products, and industrial and construction products. The sugar segment refines and distributes consumer, institutional and industrial sugars. The automotive products segment manufactures and sells various automotive components to original equipment manufacturers. The industrial and construction products segment manufactures and sells plastic and metal products designed for use in manufacturing, housing and other construction. Operations by industry segment and geographic segment are as presented below in millions of dollars:

Industry Segments

	Sales to Third Parties		Operating Income		Total Assets	
	1988	**1987**	**1988**	**1987**	**1988**	**1987**
Sugar.	$381.6	$410.3	$35.5	$42.3	$225.7	$194.3
Automotive products	175.9	140.2	25.4	16.2	114.9	104.1
Industrial and						
construction products . . .	148.0	108.9	11.7	10.7	113.4	70.8
Other	.9	.8	(3.2)	(4.6)	35.1	47.0
	$706.4	$660.2	$69.4	$64.6	$489.1	$416.2

	Capital Expenditures		Depreciation and Amortization	
	1988	**1987**	**1988**	**1987**
Sugar.	$ 15.0	$ 12.6	$ 4.8	$ 4.7
Automotive products	18.4	17.8	7.3	6.4
Industrial and construction products . . .	9.3	6.0	6.5	3.3
Other	.2	.1	(.3)	1.2
	$ 42.9	$ 36.5	$18.3	$ 15.6

Geographic Segments

	Sales to Third Parties		Operating Income		Total Assets	
	1988	**1987**	**1988**	**1987**	**1988**	**1987**
Canada.	$283.6	$267.1	$39.1	$37.1	$202.9	$188.7
United States.	421.8	392.3	30.1	27.6	281.9	223.8
Other	1.0	.8	.2	(.1)	4.3	3.7
	$706.4	$660.2	$69.4	$64.6	$489.1	$416.2

Canadian operations include export sales of $44,081,000 ($47,466,000 in 1987).

Required:

1. Explain how Redpath would have approached identification of its reportable segments. Why would the North American operations—Canada and the United States—have been reported separately under geographic segments?
2. Complete the following schedule:

	Sales		Operating Income		Total Assets	
	1988 %	**1987 %**	**1988 %**	**1987 %**	**1988 %**	**1987 %**
Sugar						
Automotive products						
Industrial and construction products						

Canada
United States

What does this information tell you?

3. What conclusions would you draw from the capital expenditures information?
4. Critique Redpath's segmented information. In what ways, if any, do they exceed requirements? Is there any information you would have expected to see?

P 26–3
Interim Reporting
(L.O. 4)

The following description deals with the principles of interim financial reporting.

> Interim financial information is essential to provide investors and others with timely information as to the progress of the enterprise. The usefulness of such information rests on the relationship that it has to the annual results of operations. Accordingly, the conclusion is that each interim period should be viewed primarily as an integral part of an annual period.
>
> In general, the results for each interim period should be based on the accounting principles and practices used by an enterprise in the preparation of its latest annual financial statements unless a change in an accounting practice or policy has been adopted in the current year. However, the conclusion is that certain accounting principles and practices followed for annual reporting purposes may require modification at interim reporting dates so that the reported results for the interim period may better relate to the results of operations for the annual period.

Required:

Below are six independent cases on how accounting facts might be reported on a company's interim financial reports. State whether the proposed method would be acceptable under generally accepted accounting principles applicable to interim financial data. Support your answer with a brief explanation.

a. Cup Company management was reasonably certain it would have an employee strike in the third quarter. As a result, it shipped heavily during the second quarter but plans to defer recognition of the sales in excess of normal sales. The deferred sales will be recognized as sales in the third quarter, when the strike is in progress. Management thinks this is more nearly representative of normal second and third quarter operations.

b. Glass Company takes a physical inventory at year-end for annual financial statement purposes. Inventory and cost of sales reported in interim quarterly statements are based on estimated gross profit rates, because a physical inventory would result in a temporary shutdown of operations. Glass Company has reliable perpetual inventory records.

c. Taylor Company is planning to report one fourth of its annual pension expense each quarter.

d. Temple Company wrote down inventory to reflect lower of cost or market in the first quarter of 1992. At year-end the market exceeds the original acquisition cost of this inventory. Consequently, management plans to write the inventory back up to its original cost as a year-end adjustment.

e. Tall Company realized a large gain on the sale of investments at the beginning of the second quarter. The company wants to report one third of the gain in each of the remaining quarters.

f. Dill Company has estimated its annual audit fee. Dill management plans to prorate this expense equally over the four quarters.

(CMA adapted)

P 26–4
Interim Reporting
(L.O. 4)

The Dunn Manufacturing Company, a corporation listed on the Toronto Stock Exchange, budgeted activities for 1992 as follows:

	Amount	Units
Net sales	$ 6,000,000	1,000,000
Cost of goods sold	(3,600,000)	
Gross margin	$ 2,400,000	
Selling, general, and administrative expenses	(1,400,000)	
Operating earnings	$ 1,000,000	
Non-operating revenues and expenses	0	
Earnings before income taxes	$ 1,000,000	
Estimated income taxes (current and deferred)	(350,000)	
Net earnings	$ 650,000	
Earnings per common share	$ 6.50	

Dunn has operated profitably for many years. It has experienced a seasonal pattern of sales volume and production similar to the following, forecast for 1992. Sales volume is expected to follow a quarterly pattern of 10%, 20%, 35%, 35%, respectively, because of the seasonality of the industry. Also, due to production and storage capacity limitations, it is expected that production will follow a pattern of 20%, 25%, 30%, 25%, respectively, during the four quarters of 1992.

At the conclusion of the first quarter of 1992, the controller of Dunn has prepared and issued the following interim report for public release:

	Amount	Units
Net sales	$ 600,000	100,000
Cost of goods sold	(360,000)	
Gross margin	$ 240,000	
Selling, general, and administrative expenses	(275,000)	
Operating loss	$ (35,000)	
Loss from warehouse fire	(175,000)	
Loss before income taxes	$(210,000)	
Estimated income taxes	0	
Net loss	$(210,000)	
Loss per common share	$ (2.10)	

The following additional information is available for the first quarter just completed, but was not included in the public information released:

a. The company uses a standard cost system in which standards are set at currently attainable levels on an annual basis. At the end of the first quarter there was underapplied fixed factory overhead (volume variance) of $50,000 that was treated as an asset at the end of the quarter. Production during the quarter was 200,000 units, of which 100,000 were sold and expensed.

b. The selling, general, and administrative expenses were budgeted on a basis of $900,000 fixed expenses for the year plus 50 cents variable expenses per unit of sales.

c. Assume that the warehouse fire loss met the conditions of an extraordinary loss. The warehouse had a depreciated cost of $400,000; $225,000 was recovered from insurance on the warehouse. No other gains or losses are anticipated this year from similar events or transactions, nor has Dunn had any similar losses in preceding years. Assume that the full loss will be deductible as an ordinary loss for income tax purposes.

d. The effective income tax rate, for federal and provincial taxes combined, is expected to average 35% of earnings before income taxes during 1992. There are no permanent differences between pretax accounting income and taxable income.

e. Earnings per share were computed on the basis of 100,000 common shares outstanding. Dunn has only one share class outstanding, no long-term debt outstanding, and no stock option plan.

Required:

1. Without reference to the specific situation described previously, what are the standards of disclosure for interim financial data (published interim financial reports) for publicly traded companies? Explain.

2. Identify the weaknesses in form and content of Dunn's interim report without reference to the additional information.

3. Redraft the interim report, with reference to the above information.

P 26–5
Interim Reporting
(L.O. 4)

Excerpts from the interim report of AGF Growth Fund, a mutual fund that invests in bonds and shares, are as follows:

Statements of Income and Expenses, Change in Net Assets, and Realized Gain on Sale of Investments

For the six months ended March 31, 1991 (with comparative figures for the six months ended March 31, 1990) (unaudited).

	1991	1990
Income:		
Dividends	$1,233,068	$1,014,901
Interest	801,999	146,617
	2,035,067	1,161,518
Expenses:		
Management fee	1,216,489	878,451
Shareholder servicing	355,979	310,438
Annual and quarterly reports	42,161	63,177
Audit fees	11,948	14,587
Custodian fees and bank charges	5,001	8,568
Interest	24,979	117,887
Legal fees	19,178	23,360
Directors' fees	2,732	2,125
Other	—	1,585
	1,678,467	1,420,178
Income (loss) before income taxes	356,600	(258,660)
Foreign withholding taxes	1,415	—
Net income (loss) for the period	$ 355,185	$ (258,660)
Net income (loss) per share (based on average number of shares outstanding)	2.8¢	(2.8)¢

Required:

1. What items on the income statement have likely been allocated? Would revenue items have been a problem?

2. How would audit fees likely have been allocated?
3. What conclusions would you draw from the interim report in relation to the comparatives? What additional information would you like to see for this mutual fund?
4. Would you prefer the statements to be audited? Discuss both sides of the issue.

P 26–6
Segmented Information
(L.O. 5)

Canabold Corp. operates a worldwide business from a Canadian head office and base of operations. Management has grouped the company's operations into geographic areas and assembled supporting data for the current year as follows:

	Sales to Outside Customers	Sales to Other Geographic Areas	Operating Profit	Identifiable Assets
Canada.	$ 46,000	$ 38,000	$ 20,000	$ 108,000
Pacific Rim.	72,000	—	28,000	68,000
France	432,000	104,000	86,000	540,000
Germany.	54,000	36,000	24,000	110,000
South America	60,000	—	22,000	72,000
Total.	$664,000	$178,000	$180,000	$ 898,000

The current year's consolidated financial statements yielded the following:

Revenues.	$ 700,000
Net income before tax.	$ 100,000
Income tax	44,000
Net income	$ 56,000
Total assets.	$1,130,000

Additional information:

a. The consolidated income statement showed investment income of $36,000.
b. General corporate expenses were $80,000, and assets not allocable to geographic areas amounted to $232,000.

Required:

1. Which geographic segments are reportable?
2. Prepare the disclosure note required for geographic segments.

CASES

C 26–1
Standards Overload
(L.O. 1, 2)

Several authors have addressed the question of whether small business enterprises should have their own set of generally accepted accounting principles rather than be required to comply with all the recommendations presently in the *CICA Handbook*. The writers reason that many current accounting principles seem to be geared to large businesses and that small enterprises should not be asked to implement recommendations that do not justify their costs by relevance or resulting benefits.

Required:

1. Give the arguments for (*a*) having one set of generally accepted accounting principles for all sizes of businesses and (*b*) small businesses having their own set of generally accepted accounting principles.
2. Indicate which accounting sections now included in the *CICA Handbook* must be applied to small business enterprises yet may not be of relevance to them. State why you believe these sections may not be relevant or beneficial.

(CICA adapted)

C 26–2
Standards Overload
(L.O. 1, 2)

Recently, on learning of a new *CICA Handbook* recommendation, a company controller exclaimed to the company's auditor,

> Another of your accounting standards! You CAs are always issuing rules for us to follow, and we don't need a tenth of them! Information is an economic commodity: left alone, the market would determine what information is needed, as it does for other commodities. Therefore, your standards amount to interference in the marketplace. You've made so many rules, and they cost so much, that you've overdone it. Canadian business and the economy in general can't bear the cost much longer.

Required:

Discuss the issues raised by the controller.

(CICA adapted)

C 26–3
Interim Financial
Reporting
(L.O. 4)

In today's rapidly changing financial markets, financial statement users are demanding more information, released more promptly than in the past. Accordingly, the CICA is conducting a research project to review the *CICA Handbook* section, "Interim Financial Reporting to Shareholders," and to recommend revisions to this section. You have agreed to join the study group. At the first meeting two study-group members are engaged in a lively discussion; one is a CA and controller of an international public company while the other is a senior financial analyst in a securities firm.

> Financial analyst: My review of the *CICA Handbook* leads me to conclude that the objectives of interim reporting should be the same as those of annual reporting.
> Controller: I disagree. Interim reports are aimed at different users, serve different purposes, and must be published more quickly than annual reports. It follows that the underlying objectives should also differ.
> Financial analyst: Regardless of the content of interim reports, the interim operating results should be measured on the same basis as the annual results because the interim period is an integral part of the annual period.
> Controller: I agree that there is a measurement problem for interim reporting, but I don't see a simple solution. For example, I find it difficult to make interim estimates for various expenses given the cyclical nature of our business. After all, the interim period is only a portion of the annual period.

Required:

Prepare a memo for the study group discussing the main issues raised in the preceding conversation.

(CICA adapted)

C 26–4
Segmented Information
(L.O. 5)

Ermine Oil Limited is a fully integrated Canadian oil company. Ermine commenced as a petroleum exploration company and was very successful in its oil field discoveries. In order to attain market security and improve profits, Ermine was forced to embark on a program of vertical integration. It first acquired a refining division and then marketing and transportation divisions. From the beginning, management appreciated the integrated nature of the business, and production was transferred between divisions at standard cost. The management control system recognized the exploration, refining, and transportation divisions as cost centres and the marketing division as a revenue centre. While the exploration, refining, and transportation divisions did make external sales, historically, none of these divisions' external sales accounted for 10% of Ermine's total sales. However, in the last fiscal year, due to unusual world market conditions, the transportation division's sales accounted for 11% of Ermine's total sales. Over 90% of Ermine's sales were within Canada, with the balance spread over many countries worldwide. Ermine did not feel it was necessary to disclose segmented information in its annual financial statements.

Beluga Petroleum Limited was similar to Ermine in size and also in scope of operations except that, in addition, it had a chemical division. However, Beluga was a subsidiary of a foreign oil company and its divisions were each organized as profit centres with products transferred between divisions at world market prices. Each division purchased and sold products extensively to outside companies. In addition, about 15% of Beluga's sales were export, almost exclusively to the United States. In its annual financial statements, Beluga showed segmented information by the five divisions (exploration, refining, transportation, chemical, and marketing) and sales were divided between domestic and export operations.

Required:

Discuss how both Ermine and Beluga could report differently with respect to disclosure of segmented information, and yet be in accordance with generally accepted accounting principles.

(SMA adapted)

C 26–5
Segmented Information
(L.O. 5)

Many financial analysts and professional accountants argue that firms should report segment data, while many managers argue strongly against such disclosures.

Required:

1. Outline the reasons for requiring financial reporting by segments.
2. Outline the reasons against requiring financial reporting by segments.
3. Outline the accounting difficulties in implementing segment reporting.

C 26–6
Interim Information
(L.O. 4)

The unaudited quarterly financial statements issued by many corporations are prepared on the same basis as annual statements, with some minor exceptions.

Required:

1. What are some areas where there would be a difference between the basis used to prepare interim statements as opposed to annual statements?
2. Why are there problems in using interim statements to predict annual income?
3. How might quarterly income be affected by the behaviour of costs incurred in a repairs and maintenance of manufacturing equipment account?

Loblaw Companies Limited 1990 Annual Report

FINANCIAL REPORT

MANAGEMENT DISCUSSION AND ANALYSIS

1990 was a year of steady improvement in operating performance, similar in this respect to the preceding year. Control of assets employed and of interest expense amplified this solid growth in operating income to produce a good increase in bottom line results. Return on common shareholders' equity was 14.6 percent for the year as compared to 11.7 percent in 1989.

RESULTS OF OPERATIONS

(in millions)

		Retail	Wholesale	Total	Operating Income
Eastern	1989	$2,570	$1,418	$3,988	$ 90
Canada	1990	$2,597	$1,615	$4,212	$104
Western	1989	$1,197	$1,453	$2,650	$ 67
Canada	1990	$1,446	$1,446	$2,892	$ 75
United	1989	$1,258	$ 38	$1,296	$ 34
States	1990	$1,277	$ 36	$1,313	$ 36
Total	1989	$5,025	$2,909	$7,934	$191
	1990	$5,320	$3,097	$8,417	$215

(Note: For an understanding of the geographic areas covered by Eastern Canadian Operations, Western Canadian Operations and United States' Operations, please refer to the map on page 3.)

Sales increased by 6.1 percent in 1990 which compares to a 9.2 percent increase in the previous year, after the 1989 increase is adjusted for the effects of the divested operations in New Orleans and exchange rate fluctuations.

In Eastern Canada, sales increased by 5.6 percent in 1990 and 7.6 percent in 1989. In this segment of the business, retail sales grew by 1.1 percent in 1990 and 5.7 percent in 1989. New corporate stores have been added in both years. In 1990, 324,000 sq. ft. of new retail stores were added to the business, in addition to expansions of existing stores. However total retail footage declined by 2.5 percent during the year as a result primarily of franchising as well as some downsizing and store closures. During 1989 corporate retail footage increased by 2.0 percent and increases in sales per foot were slightly ahead of inflation, reflecting an asset base which is improving in terms of sales generating capacity. In 1990 increases in sales per foot were slightly below inflation, reflecting the impact of the weakened economy in the region. Wholesale sales in Eastern Canada increased by 13.9 percent in 1990 and 11.2 percent in 1989. The number of sq. ft. in stores

operated by franchisees grew by 3.7 percent in 1990 and 2.8 percent in 1989. Growth in franchise business was a major contributor to overall wholesale volume increases and a substantial portion of this growth was as a result of the conversion of Fortino's and no frills corporate stores to franchise stores.

In Western Canada, sales increased in 1990 by 9.1 percent compared to a 13.2 percent increase in 1989. In this segment of the business, retail sales grew by 20.8 percent in 1990 and 21.9 percent in 1989. Seven new Real Canadian Superstores opened since the fall of 1988 account for three quarters of the retail sales growth in 1989 and almost 90 percent of it in 1990. Wholesale sales declined by 0.5 percent in 1990 after increasing by 7.0 percent in 1989. During the year the supply to several major customers which were providing an inadequate return was discontinued.

In Canada, food inflation (for "food purchased at stores") was 4.2 percent in 1990 and 2.3 percent in 1989. Generally, gross margins have not been increasing and it is reasonable to attribute the balance of the sales increases in Eastern and Western Canada to tonnage growth.

In the United States, sales adjusted for divested operations increased by 1.3 percent in 1990 and 6.3 percent in 1989. General food price inflation, as measured by the "food-at-home" component of the U.S. Consumer Price Index was 6.6 percent in 1990 and 6.5 percent in 1989. However in 1990 this index was not representative of National Tea. Actual tonnage increased about 1.0 percent indicating that there was very little impact of inflation on sales in 1990.

In 1991, the accounting for the Canadian goods and services tax will reduce reported sales by 1-2 percent, but is not expected to have a material impact on operating income.

Operating income in 1990 increased by 12.6 percent to $214.5 million from $190.5 million in the previous year. The previous year's increase was 18.9 percent.

In Eastern Canada, operating income increased by 15.6 percent after increasing by 18.4 percent in 1989. Management is pleased that the business is achieving this income leverage off sales improvements and also finds the year over year improvement significant. The 1989 result was achieved in part through gross margin increases.

MANAGEMENT DISCUSSION AND ANALYSIS

In 1990 gross margins have declined slightly as a percent of sales and improvements in operating profits are attributable to cost reductions in various areas, most notably administration, distribution and advertising expense. The rate of growth in operating income is expected to be more modest in 1991 but is still expected to exceed the rate of growth in sales.

In Western Canada operating income increased by 11.9 percent in 1990 compared with a 19.6 percent improvement in 1989. In both years the major factor in operating income growth was the new Real Canadian Superstore volume. In 1990 expense ratios declined as these stores matured and there were fewer new store openings. Wholesale profits declined in 1990 largely as a result of decreasing volume. Operating income is expected to continue to grow in Western Canada next year at a similar rate.

Operating income in the United States improved from $34 million in 1989 to $36 million in 1990. This 5.9 percent improvement in 1990 compares to a 54.5 percent improvement in operating income from continuing operations in the previous year. The improvement in both years is largely attributable to improved gross margins as new and acquired stores mature. Operating income is expected to grow in the United States at between 5 and 10 percent next year.

Income from the sale of capital assets was $5.2 million less in 1990 than in 1989. Inflation was not considered to be a significant factor in operating income increases in either year.

Interest expense decreased $15.5 million from $79.6 million in 1989 to $64.1 million in 1990. Lower average debt levels accounted for approximately half of this reduction in interest expense. Lower effective interest rates achieved through interest rate management, more than offset the impact of higher short term market interest rates in 1990 and accounted for the balance of the decrease in interest expense. Positive cash flow in 1991 should result in further interest reductions next year.

Earnings before income taxes increased from $110.9 million last year to $150.4 million in the current year, giving a year over year increase of 35.6 percent. This compares to an increase of 29.0 percent in the previous year if the effect of the unusual charge against income is excluded from the 1988 results.

The *effective income tax rate* for the year increased from 34.7 percent last year to 36.2 percent this year. This trend of rate increase is expected to continue as the proportion of earnings subject to higher Canadian tax rates rises.

Earnings before extraordinary items was $96.0 million in 1990 versus $70.2 million in 1989 and *earnings per share* rose from $.80 to $1.10.

OPERATING INCOME AND
INTEREST EXPENSE
(in millions)

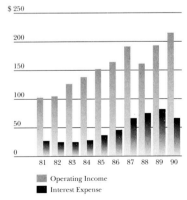

■ Operating Income
■ Interest Expense

MANAGEMENT DISCUSSION AND ANALYSIS

FINANCIAL CONDITION

The financial condition of the business is being impacted by two major trends. First, capital spending has declined following the growth of the mid to late 1980's. Second, and partially related to the first, the current focus of the business is on improving asset effectiveness.

Considering the first trend, expenditures on fixed assets were $171.2 million in 1990 and $165.7 million in 1989 after averaging $215 million in the five preceeding years.

Considering the second trend, it often takes a period of months or years for a new store to reach its maximum contribution level. Therefore as the percentage of very new assets declines, the business is generating more profits and cash related to its maturing asset base. *Cash flow from operations* was $252.4 million in 1990 and $259.3 million in 1989, beginning to exceed fixed asset expenditures by substantial amounts.

Considering further the second trend of improving asset effectiveness, an important aspect of generating strong cash flow from operations is management of working capital. The Company attempts to maintain its net investment in the non-cash elements of working capital (the principal components of which are accounts receivable, inventories, accounts payable and accrued liabilities) at the minimum necessary for effective operation. For 1989 the average ratio of these elements of non-cash working capital to sales was 0.6 percent. In 1990 this ratio declined to 0.5 percent, reflecting continued efforts to control this investment. In 1990 *cash provided from working capital* was $50.7 million, representing the third consecutive year in which this has been a source rather than a use of cash. Continuing efforts to improve the ratio of this investment to sales should result in working capital being either a source or a minimal use of cash next year.

The above factors combined to produce a net positive *cash flow before financing and dividends* of $109.1 million in 1990 and $31.7 million in 1989. (It should be noted when comparing these numbers that in 1989, $76.8 million was invested in the acquisition of the minority interest in Kelly, Douglas & Company, Limited.)

At year end, *cash* (cash and short term investments net of bank advances and notes payable) was $31.2 million, a $15.0 million increase from last year. Short term *liquidity* requirements are met during the year through a $500 million commercial paper program. The Company's short term commercial paper is rated R-1 low/A-1. Financial instruments are used to manage the interest rate on the underlying commercial paper borrowings. At year end 1990, approximately $45 million of 1991 short term borrowing requirements had been fixed at the rate of 10.8 percent.

CASH FLOW FROM OPERATIONS
AND FIXED ASSET EXPENDITURES
(in millions)

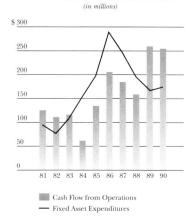

■ Cash Flow from Operations
— Fixed Asset Expenditures

MANAGEMENT DISCUSSION AND ANALYSIS

Total debt declined by $76.0 million in 1990. Of this, $56.2 million was a decrease in *long term debt* (excluding capital leases) and included repayment of the $35 million 12.5 percent debenture and the U.S.$13.0 million term loan. With the debt repayments, the weighted average interest rate on fixed rate long term debt (excluding capital lease obligations) declined from last year at 10.6 percent to 10.5 percent in 1990 and the weighted average term to maturity (measured both on the basis of maturity date and on the earlier of maturity and first retraction date) was 10.1 and 5.2 years respectively in 1990 compared to 9.8 and 5.6 years respectively in 1989. Total debt also decreased in 1989 when $60 million of new perpetual preferred shares were issued.

Shareholders' equity increased by $66.3 million after increasing by $94.9 million in 1989. In 1989, $60 million in new perpetual preferred shares were issued and $55 million in retractable preferred shares were replaced with an equivalent amount of perpetual preferred shares.

Loblaw strives to create shareholder value through common share appreciation reflecting historical earnings per share growth and growth potential. The Company's dividend policy is to pay out *dividends* on common shares amounting to approximately 20 percent of the prior year's earnings per share.

Reduced debt levels and an increase in shareholders' equity have resulted in an improvement in the *debt: equity ratio* from .74:1 in 1989 to .58:1 in 1990. These ratios are better than the Company's internal guideline of maintaining a debt:equity ratio of less than 1:1.

During 1990, enhancements were made to benefits payable under some of the Company's pension plans. As a result, the value of accrued pension benefits increased from $286.4 million in 1989 to $343.8 million in 1990.

FUTURE PROSPECTS

Fixed asset expenditures are expected to be approximately $190 million next year and the cash required is expected to be generated through operations. About half of this investment will be made in Eastern Canada and United States' operations will spend about one-sixth, with about one-third going into Western Canada. This weighting of expenditures is similar to 1990. Approximately 80 percent will be spent on corporate stores versus about 70 percent in 1990. Projects already begun, and which the Company is effectively committed to complete, total approximately $72 million of the anticipated 1991 expenditure.

The Company is an aggressive competitor in the food distribution business. Its strategies often involve penetration of new markets such as has taken place in the past two years in Calgary and Vancouver and in the past year in Gatineau, Quebec. It is willing to experiment with new store formats and expand its operations through focused acquisitions when opportunities arise. While these strategies increase short term *risk*, management believes they are essential to long term security and growth.

Management also follows certain strategies to reduce risk: operating in geographically diverse areas to minimize exposure to regional economies and demographics; operating in both the wholesale and retail sectors of the food distribution industry to minimize exposure to shifts in the balance of economic power between these two major components of the industry; following a policy of owning its real estate whenever possible to preserve operating flexibility and position the Company to benefit from any real estate appreciation; and developing powerful corporate brands (no name™, President's Choice™, G•R•E•E•N™) to enhance customer loyalty and provide some insulation from national brand pricing. All these strategies reduce risk.

RETAIL AND WHOLESALE OPERATIONS

Retail sales consist of sales to consumers through corporate stores operated by Loblaw Companies Limited. Wholesale sales consist of sales and service fees to franchised independent stores and independent accounts but exclude sales to corporate stores or other inter-company sales.

The following charts illustrate the makeup and trends in Loblaw Companies Limited when viewed from a retail and wholesale perspective.

RETAIL OPERATIONS	1990		1989		1988	
CORPORATE STORES	Stores	Sq. Ft.	Stores	Sq. Ft.	Stores	Sq. Ft.
		(in millions)		*(in millions)*		*(in millions)*
Beginning of year	334	11.3	311	10.6	361	11.3
Opened	18	.8	55	1.2	21	1.2
Closed	(20)	(.5)	(18)	(.2)	(58)	(1.7)
Franchised						
Transfer to:	(20)	(.3)	(22)	(.4)	(18)	(.3)
Transfer from:	17	.1	8	.1	5	.1
End of year	329	11.4	334	11.3	311	10.6
Average store size *(in thousands)*		34.7 sq. ft.		33.9 sq. ft.		34.1 sq. ft.
Analysis by size						
More than 60,000 sq. ft.	43		40		33	
40,000 - 60,000 sq. ft.	50		48		44	
20,000 - 39,999 sq. ft.	140		148		154	
10,000 - 19,999 sq. ft.	59		64		68	
Less than 10,000 sq. ft.	37		34		12	
	329		334		311	
RETAIL SALES *(in millions)*	$5,320		$5,025		$4,921	
Annual average sales per gross sq. ft.	$475		$458		$440	

WHOLESALE OPERATIONS	1990		1989		1988	
FRANCHISED INDEPENDENT STORES	Stores	Sq. Ft.	Stores	Sq. Ft.	Stores	Sq. Ft.
		(in millions)		*(in millions)*		*(in millions)*
Beginning of year	1,289	7.3	1,183	6.8	1,354	9.1
Opened	76	.3	174	.7	148	.6
Closed	(102)	(.4)	(82)	(.5)	(332)	(3.1)
Corporate						
Transfer from:	20	.3	22	.4	18	.3
Transfer to:	(17)	(.1)	(8)	(.1)	(5)	(.1)
End of year	1,266	7.4	1,289	7.3	1,183	6.8
Warehouses	54		54		52	
Cash & carry units	53		54		53	
Independent accounts	11,839		12,337		10,114	
WHOLESALE SALES *(in millions)*	$3,097		$2,909		$3,387	

RESPONSIBILITY FOR FINANCIAL REPORTING

The management of Loblaw Companies Limited is responsible for the preparation and integrity of the financial statements and related financial information of the Company. The financial statements and other financial information in this report have been prepared by the management of the Company in accordance with generally accepted accounting principles and, where necessary, utilizing management's judgements and best estimates.

To help fulfill its responsibility and to assure integrity of financial reporting, management maintains a system of internal controls encompassing all financial records. These controls, which include a comprehensive budgeting system and timely periodic reporting of financial information, provide reasonable assurance that assets are safeguarded and transactions and events are properly recorded. To augment the internal control systems, the Company maintains a program of internal audits coordinated with the external auditors.

Ultimate responsibility for financial statements to shareholders rests with the Board of Directors. An audit committee of non-management directors is appointed by the Board to oversee the fulfillment by management of its responsibilities in the preparation of financial statements and financial control of operations. The audit committee reviews financial statements with management and reports to the directors prior to the approval of the audited financial statements for publication.

Peat Marwick Thorne, independent auditors appointed by the shareholders, review the financial statements in detail and meet separately with both the audit committee and management to discuss their findings, including the fairness of financial reporting and the results of their review of internal controls. The shareholders' auditors report directly to shareholders and their report also appears on this page.

Richard J. Currie
President

David K. Bragg
Senior Vice President,
Planning and Control

John W. Thompson
Senior Vice President,
Finance and Administration

AUDITORS' REPORT

To the Shareholders of Loblaw Companies Limited
We have audited the consolidated balance sheets of Loblaw Companies Limited as at December 29, 1990 and December 30, 1989 and the consolidated statements of earnings, retained earnings and cash flow for the 52 week periods then ended. These consolidated financial statements are the responsibility of the Company's management. Our responsibility is to express an opinion on these consolidated financial statements based on our audits.

We conducted our audits in accordance with generally accepted auditing standards. Those standards require that we plan and perform the audits to obtain reasonable assurance whether the consolidated financial statements are free of material misstatement. An audit includes examining, on a test basis, evidence supporting the amounts and disclosures in the financial statements. An

audit also includes assessing the accounting principles used and significant estimates made by management, as well as evaluating the overall consolidated financial statement presentation.

In our opinion, these consolidated financial statements present fairly, in all material respects, the financial position of the Company as at December 29, 1990 and December 30, 1989 and the results of its operations and the changes in its financial postion for the periods then ended in accordance with generally accepted accounting principles.

Peat Marwick Thorne
Chartered Accountants
March 4, 1991
Toronto, Canada

KPMG Peat Marwick Thorne

26

CONSOLIDATED STATEMENT OF EARNINGS
52 Weeks Ended December 29, 1990

(in millions of dollars)	1990	1989	1988
SALES — Canada	$7,103.9	$6,638.2	$6,044.3
— United States	1,312.7	1,295.7	2,263.3
	8,416.6	7,933.9	8,307.6
OPERATING EXPENSES			
Cost of sales, selling and administrative expenses	8,097.1	7,643.3	8,049.8
Depreciation	105.0	100.1	97.6
	8,202.1	7,743.4	8,147.4
OPERATING INCOME	214.5	190.5	160.2
Interest — Long term debt	54.7	59.2	62.8
— Short term debt	9.4	20.4	11.4
	64.1	79.6	74.2
Unusual item (note 2)			21.5
Earnings before income taxes	150.4	110.9	64.5
Income taxes (note 3)	54.4	38.5	19.4
Earnings before minority interest	96.0	72.4	45.1
Minority interest		2.2	4.3
EARNINGS BEFORE EXTRAORDINARY ITEMS	96.0	70.2	40.8
Extraordinary items (note 4)			(14.6)
NET EARNINGS FOR THE PERIOD	$ 96.0	$ 70.2	$ 26.2
PER COMMON SHARE			
Earnings before extraordinary items	$1.10	$.80	$.41
Extraordinary items			(.20)
Net earnings	$1.10	$.80	$.21

CONSOLIDATED STATEMENT OF RETAINED EARNINGS
52 Weeks Ended December 29, 1990

(in millions of dollars)	1990	1989	1988
RETAINED EARNINGS, BEGINNING OF PERIOD	$ 433.9	$ 390.4	$ 395.7
Net earnings for the period	96.0	70.2	26.2
	529.9	460.6	421.9
Dividends declared			
Preferred shares	16.3	12.2	11.3
Common shares, per share — 20¢			
(1989—20¢, 1988—20¢)	14.5	14.5	14.4
Premium on redemption of common shares			5.8
	30.8	26.7	31.5
RETAINED EARNINGS, END OF PERIOD	$ 499.1	$ 433.9	$ 390.4

27

CONSOLIDATED BALANCE SHEET
As at December 29, 1990

(in millions of dollars)	1990	1989	1988
ASSETS			
CURRENT ASSETS			
Cash and short term investments	$ 31.2	$ 24.5	$ 23.5
Accounts receivable	137.9	139.6	168.6
Inventories	621.5	579.6	555.0
Prepaid expenses and other assets	16.5	16.8	18.1
	807.1	760.5	765.2
INVESTMENTS (note 5)	123.5	131.6	117.5
FIXED ASSETS (note 6)	1,077.7	1,044.4	1,052.4
GOODWILL	58.2	69.7	35.7
OTHER ASSETS	35.8	33.4	33.1
	$2,102.3	$2,039.6	$2,003.9
LIABILITIES			
CURRENT LIABILITIES			
Bank advances and notes payable		$ 8.3	$ 63.4
Accounts payable	$ 513.2	490.6	412.1
Accrued liabilities	208.1	177.5	191.1
Dividends payable	3.7		
Taxes payable	27.3	2.9	13.0
Long term debt payable within one year (note 7)	4.2	47.1	4.7
	756.5	726.4	684.3
LONG TERM DEBT (note 7)	469.2	494.0	554.7
OTHER LIABILITIES	20.9	26.8	34.9
DEFERRED INCOME TAXES	43.4	46.4	37.2
MINORITY INTEREST IN SUBSIDIARIES			41.7
	1,290.0	1,293.6	1,352.8
SHAREHOLDERS' EQUITY			
CAPITAL STOCK (note 8)			
Preferred shares	223.5	224.3	164.8
Common shares	110.6	108.9	108.2
	334.1	333.2	273.0
CONTRIBUTED SURPLUS	8.8	9.0	9.0
RETAINED EARNINGS	499.1	433.9	390.4
FOREIGN CURRENCY TRANSLATION ADJUSTMENT	(29.7)	(30.1)	(21.3)
	812.3	746.0	651.1
	$2,102.3	$2,039.6	$2,003.9

APPROVED BY THE BOARD

W. Galen Weston
Director

Richard J. Currie
Director

CONSOLIDATED CASH FLOW STATEMENT

52 Weeks Ended December 29, 1990

(in millions of dollars)	1990	1989	1988
OPERATIONS			
Earnings before minority interest	$ 96.0	$ 72.4	$ 45.1
Depreciation	105.0	100.1	97.6
Deferred income taxes	(4.2)	9.6	(1.6)
Other	4.9	4.4	14.9
	201.7	186.5	156.0
Provided from working capital	50.7	72.8	2.4
Cash flow from operations	252.4	259.3	158.4
INVESTMENT			
Purchase of fixed assets	(171.2)	(165.7)	(192.0)
Proceeds from sale of fixed assets	21.9	47.1	36.3
Gain on sale of fixed assets included in operations	(3.7)	(8.9)	(13.5)
Acquisition of subsidiary companies (note 9)		(76.8)	(42.2)
Disposition of subsidiary company			148.4
Decrease (increase) in investments in franchisees	4.4	(11.7)	(2.8)
Net decrease (increase) in other items	5.3	(11.6)	(24.6)
	(143.3)	(227.6)	(90.4)
Net cash in before financing and dividends	109.1	31.7	68.0
FINANCING			
Long term debt — Borrowings		3.0	8.0
— Repayments	(67.7)	(11.7)	(14.2)
Capital stock — Issued	1.7	115.7	1.2
— Redeemed	(.8)	(55.6)	(1.6)
Other			(6.0)
	(66.8)	51.4	(12.6)
DIVIDENDS			
To shareholders	(27.3)	(26.5)	(25.7)
To minority shareholders in subsidiary companies		(.5)	(.9)
	(27.3)	(27.0)	(26.6)
INCREASE IN CASH	15.0	56.1	28.8
Cash at beginning of period	16.2	(39.9)	(68.7)
CASH AT END OF PERIOD	$ 31.2	$ 16.2	$ (39.9)

Cash is defined as cash and short term investments net of bank advances and notes payable.

NOTES TO CONSOLIDATED FINANCIAL STATEMENTS
52 Weeks Ended December 29, 1990

(Narrative and tabular amounts in millions of dollars except Capital Stock note)

1. SUMMARY OF SIGNIFICANT ACCOUNTING POLICIES

a) Basis of consolidation

The consolidated financial statements include the accounts of the Company and all subsidiaries. The effective interest of Loblaw Companies Limited in the equity share capital of principal subsidiaries is 100%. Kelly, Douglas & Company, Limited formerly an 85% owned subsidiary, became a 100% owned subsidiary June 18, 1989.

b) Cash offsetting

Cash balances for which the Company has a right of offset are used to reduce reported short term borrowings. In addition, the Company has $195.7 (1989 - $157.1) in short term investments held by its United States subsidiaries of which $164.5 (1989 - $157.1) is used to offset short term borrowings in Canada. The $13.5 (1989 - $12.9) income from these investments is included as a reduction of interest expense.

c) Inventories

Retail store inventories are stated at the lower of cost and net realizable value less normal profit margin. All other inventories are stated at the lower of cost and net realizable value.

d) Fixed assets

Fixed assets are stated at cost, including capitalized interest. Interest capitalized during the year amounts to $3.4 (1989 - $4.1). Depreciation is recorded principally on a straight line basis to amortize the cost of these assets over their estimated useful lives.

Estimated useful lives range from twenty to thirty-five years for buildings and three to eleven years for equipment and fixtures. Leasehold improvements are depreciated over the lesser of the applicable useful life and term of the lease.

e) Translation of foreign currencies

Foreign currency balances are translated at a rate approximating the current rate at each year end. The net difference on translation of the Company's equity in United States subsidiaries is included in a separate category of shareholders' equity on the balance sheet, to be recognized in earnings in proportion to any reduction of the net investment. Revenues and expenses are translated at a rate approximating the average rate for the year.

f) Goodwill

Goodwill reflects the excess of the cost of investments in subsidiaries over the fair value of the underlying net tangible assets acquired at the dates of acquisition. Goodwill is being amortized on a straight line basis determined for each acquisition over the estimated life of the benefit, to a maximum period of 40 years. The weighted average amortization period is 27 years.

2. UNUSUAL ITEM

There are no unusual items in 1990 and 1989. The unusual item of $21.5 in 1988 consists of the costs of downsizing and remerchandising combination stores in Eastern Canada.

3. INCOME TAXES

The Company's effective income tax rate is made up as follows:

	1990	1989	1988
Combined basic Canadian federal and provincial income tax rate	44.5%	44.1%	47.3%
Lower tax rate on capital gains	(.2)	(1.3)	(3.7)
Impact of operating in foreign countries with lower effective tax rates	(7.1)	(8.2)	(12.9)
Other (including adjustment of prior years' estimates)	(1.0)	.1	(.6)
	36.2%	34.7%	30.1%

4. EXTRAORDINARY ITEMS

There are no extraordinary items in 1990 and 1989. Extraordinary items in 1988 consist of a provision for loss on planned disposition of the substantial portion of the New Orleans division, $(16.7), net of income tax recovery of $8.6; and the gain on disposition of Peter J. Schmitt Co., Inc., $2.1, net of income tax recovery of $.2.

5. INVESTMENTS (AT COST)

	1990	1989	1988
Secured loans and advances	$ 30.8	$ 30.6	$ 28.5
Capital lease receivables	30.7	30.9	30.6
Investments in franchisees	39.4	43.8	32.1
Long term receivables	15.3	14.2	18.2
Sundry investments	7.3	12.1	8.1
	$123.5	$131.6	$117.5

Notes to Consolidated Financial Statements

6. Fixed Assets

		1990				1989	1988
	Cost	Accumulated Depreciation	Net	Cost	Accumulated Depreciation	Net	Net
Properties held for development	$ 5.8		$ 5.8	$ 8.7		$ 8.7	$ 18.2
Land	224.1		224.1	209.5		209.5	194.0
Buildings	578.5	$110.5	468.0	523.5	$ 91.7	431.8	421.5
Equipment and fixtures	644.3	393.6	250.7	602.3	351.2	251.1	265.7
Leasehold improvements	151.0	71.3	79.7	144.4	64.0	80.4	78.1
	1,603.7	575.4	1,028.3	1,488.4	506.9	981.5	977.5
Buildings and equipment under capital leases	82.1	32.7	49.4	91.1	28.2	62.9	74.9
	$1,685.8	$608.1	$1,077.7	$1,579.5	$535.1	$1,044.4	$1,052.4

7. Long Term Debt

	1990	1989	1988
Debentures			
12 1/2 %, repaid 1990		$ 35.0	$ 35.0
Series 2, 12 1/4 %, due 1994	$ 35.0	35.0	35.0
Series 3, 11 5/8 %, due 1992	50.0	50.0	50.0
Series 4, 11 %, due 1995	40.0	40.0	40.0
Series 5, 10 %, due 2006	50.0	50.0	50.0
Series 6, 9 3/4 %, due 2001	75.0	75.0	75.0
Series 7, 10 %, due 2001	75.0	75.0	75.0
Series 8, 10 %, due 2007	60.7	65.5	65.5
Term loan at LIBOR plus 3/8 % — 3/4 %, repaid December, 1990 (U.S. $13.0)		15.5	15.8
Mortgages at a weighted average interest rate of 10.53 %, due 1991 — 2002 (including U.S. $1.7)	12.3	13.0	14.0
Other long term debt at a weighted average interest rate of 9.71 %, due 1991 — 1997	3.1	3.3	10.2
Capital lease obligations at a weighted average interest rate of 12.41 % due 1991 — 2012	72.3	83.8	93.9
	473.4	541.1	559.4
Less payable within one year	4.2	47.1	4.7
	$469.2	$494.0	$554.7

The Series 5 and Series 6 debentures are retractable annually commencing 1996 and 1993 respectively. The Series 7 debentures are retractable in 1991 and 1996. Current intentions are to reset the interest rate on the Series 7 debentures in 1991 which will encourage renewal until 1996. The five year schedule of repayments of long term debt, at the earlier of maturity or first retraction date, excluding the Series 7 debentures is as follows:

1991 - $4.2; 1992 - $54.4; 1993 - $80.1; 1994 - $40.2; 1995 - $46.5.

NOTES TO CONSOLIDATED FINANCIAL STATEMENTS

8. CAPITAL STOCK

	Number of shares issued			Paid-up-capital *(in millions of dollars)*		
	1990	*1989*	*1988*	*1990*	*1989*	*1988*
First preferred shares						
First series	439,652	439,652	439,652	$ 22.0	$ 22.0	$ 22.0
Second series	307,273	316,660	326,010	10.1	10.4	10.8
	746,925	756,312	765,662			
Second preferred shares						
First series			300,000			30.0
Second series			250,000			25.0
Third series	3,000,000	3,000,000	3,000,000	75.0	75.0	75.0
Fourth series	120	120		60.0	60.0	
Fifth series	110	110		55.0	55.0	
	3,000,230	3,000,230	3,550,000			
Junior preferred shares	14,125	18,955	20,980	1.4	1.9	2.0
Total preferred shares				223.5	224.3	164.8
Common shares	72,621,007	72,255,301	72,111,000	110.6	108.9	108.2
Total capital stock				$334.1	$333.2	$273.0

SHARE DESCRIPTION:

First preferred shares (authorized - 1,000,000)
First series — $2.40 cumulative dividend redeemable at $50.

Second series — $3.70 cumulative dividend redeemable at $70. In each fiscal year the Company is obligated to apply $400,000 to the purchase of these shares for cancellation, provided that such shares are available at a price not exceeding $67. During 1990, the Company purchased 9,387 (1989 - 9,350) of these shares for cancellation at a cost of $415,561 (1989 - $401,919). The premium of $105,789 (1989-$93,369) on these purchases has been deducted from contributed surplus.

Second preferred shares

First series — cumulative dividend with floating rate, redeemed at $100 on December 15, 1989.

Second series — cumulative dividend with floating rate, redeemed at $100 on December 15, 1989.

Third series — $1.825 cumulative dividend redeemable at $25, retractable at the option of the holder on September 1, 1993.

Fourth series — cumulative dividend with a fixed rate of 7.75% to March 1, 1995 and a floating rate thereafter, redeemable at par on or after March 1, 1995. These shares were issued December 13, 1989 by way of a private placement.

Fifth series — cumulative dividend with a fixed rate of 7.75% to March 1, 1995 and a floating rate thereafter, redeemable at par on or after March 1, 1992. These shares were issued December 15, 1989 by way of a private placement.

Junior preferred shares

First series — $9.00 cumulative dividend, converted into common shares in 1990. (4,830 convertible into 203,368 common shares in 1989).

Second series — $12.00 cumulative dividend, converted into common shares in 1989.

Third series — cumulative dividend with floating rate equal to two-thirds of average bank prime rate plus 3/4%, redeemable after August 6, 1992 at $100, 6,975 convertible into 186,000 common shares, (6,975 convertible into 186,000 common shares in 1989).

Fourth series — cumulative dividend with floating rate equal to two-thirds of average bank prime rate plus 3/4%, redeemable after May 16, 1993 at $100, 7,150 convertible into 112,157 common shares, (7,150 convertible into 112,157 common shares in 1989).

Common shares
In 1990 the Company issued 203,368 (1989 - 64,000) common shares for a consideration of $483,000 (1989 - $202,500) on conversion of 4,830 junior preferred shares.

In 1990 the Company issued 162,338 (1989 - 80,301) common shares for cash of $1,211,845 (1989 - $484,585) on exercise of employee stock options.

As at December 29, 1990, there were outstanding stock options, which were granted at the market price on the day preceding the grant, to purchase 2,611,953 common shares at prices ranging from $3.00 to $18.50 with a weighted average price of $11.71. Options expire on dates ranging from October 7, 1991 to December 13, 1997, with 204,000 expiring in 1991.

The exercise of the conversion privileges and stock options would not materially dilute earnings per share.

9. ACQUISITIONS

There were no acquisitions in 1990. During 1989, the Company purchased the 15.04% minority interest of Kelly, Douglas & Company, Limited and in 1988 acquired four former Super Carnaval stores and purchased Fortino's Supermarket Ltd.

These transactions have been accounted for using the purchase method with the results of operations included in these financial statements since the dates of acquisitions. Details of the acquisitions are as follows:

	1989 Kelly, Douglas Minority Interest	1988 Super Carnaval and Fortino's
Working capital		$ (6.2)
Fixed assets	$ 7.3	34.5
Goodwill	26.6	30.2
Long term debt		(16.3)
Minority interest	42.9	
Cash consideration	$76.8	$ 42.2

10. PENSIONS

Current actuarial estimates indicate that the present value of accrued pension benefits is $343.8 (1989 - $286.4) and the value of pension fund assets is $299.7 (1989 - $295.3). In addition, a subsidiary is a participant in union-sponsored multiemployer pension plans. The share of these plans' unfunded vested liabilities allocable to the subsidiary, for which it may be contingently liable, is not determinable by the plans' administrators.

11. OTHER INFORMATION

a) Segmented information

The Company's only significant activity is food distribution. Geographically segmented information is as follows:

	Canada			United States		
	1990	1989	1988	1990	1989	1988
Operating income	$ 178.5	$ 157.0	$ 131.8	$ 36.0	$ 33.5	$ 28.4
Total assets	$1,735.6	$1,671.0	$1,605.3	$366.7	$368.6	$398.6

b) Contingent liabilities and commitments

Endorsements and guarantees in the normal course of business amount to $37.8. Gross rentals under leases assigned at the time of sale of United States divisions for which the Company is contingently liable, amount to $46.0.

In addition to various claims arising in the normal course of business, legal actions concerning the rights and obligations associated with the class A shares of the Company's subsidiary, Westfair Foods Ltd., were commenced in January, 1989. Under an Alberta court decision rendered in the first quarter of this year, Westfair has been directed to purchase these shares, of which there are approximately 30,000 in the hands of minority shareholders, at a value to be independently determined in further proceedings. An appeal of this decision was heard in February, 1991 by the Alberta Court of Appeal and Westfair is currently awaiting the decision. The potential liability arising from an adverse decision is not determinable. Management continues to believe that the appeal ultimately will be successful.

Commitments for net operating lease payments total $596 ($721 gross, net of $125 of expected sub-lease income). Net payments for each of the next five years are as follows:
1991 - $86; 1992 - $78; 1993 - $68; 1994 - $54;
1995 - $44; thereafter to 2023 - $266.

c) Related parties

The Company's majority shareholder, George Weston Limited and its subsidiaries are related parties. It is the Company's policy to conduct all transactions with related parties on normal trade terms. The magnitude of these transactions and balances is not considered significant to the Company.

TEN YEAR SUMMARY

EARNINGS STATEMENT

($ millions)	1990	1989	1988	1987	1986	1985	1984	1983	1982	1981
Sales — Canada	7,104	6,638	6,044	5,689	5,098	4,668	4,394	4,121	3,847	3,513
— United States	1,313	1,296	2,264	2,942	2,741	2,263	2,025	1,970	2,374	2,282
Total	8,417	7,934	8,308	8,631	7,839	6,931	6,419	6,091	6,221	5,795
Trading profit*	320	291	258	290	249	225	205	190	173	166
Depreciation	105	100	98	100	86	73	67	62	58	53
Operating income	215	191	160	190	163	152	138	128	115	113
Interest	64	80	74	64	45	36	29	26	26	29
Income taxes	54	39	19	48	39	44	44	46	39	37
Minority interest		2	4	4	5	4	3	4	4	6
Earnings before extraordinary items	96	70	41	74	74	67	61	52	45	41
Extraordinary items			(15)				3	1	(6)	12
Net earnings	96	70	26	74	74	67	64	53	39	53
PER COMMON SHARE *(dollars)*										
Earnings before extraordinary items	1.10	.80	.41	.87	.91	.85	.77	.66	.54	.49
Net earnings	1.10	.80	.21	.87	.91	.85	.81	.66	.46	.66
Dividends — declared	.20	.20	.20	.195	.175	.155	.135	.118	.105	.085
— year end rate	.20	.20	.20	.20	.18	.16	.14	.12	.11	.09
RETURN ON SALES *(percent)*										
Operating income	2.5	2.4	1.9	2.2	2.1	2.2	2.1	2.1	1.9	1.9
Earnings before income taxes	1.8	1.4	.8	1.5	1.5	1.7	1.7	1.7	1.4	1.4
Earnings before extraordinary items	1.1	.9	.5	.9	.9	1.0	1.0	.9	.7	.7
EARNINGS RATIOS** *(percent)*										
Return on common equity	14.6	11.7	5.9	12.5	14.6	15.6	16.3	16.3	15.3	16.3
Return on capital employed	15.8	13.8	11.2	13.6	14.3	17.0	18.1	18.6	17.5	18.0

*Trading profit is defined as operating income before depreciation.

**Earnings ratios have been computed as follows:

Return on common equity — Earnings before extraordinary items less preferred dividends divided by average common share capital, retained earnings, foreign currency translation adjustment and the applicable portion of contributed surplus.

Return on capital employed — Operating income divided by average total assets less non-interest bearing debt.

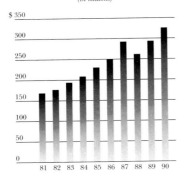

TRADING PROFIT*
(in millions)

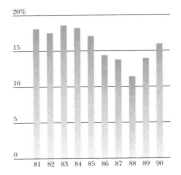

RETURN ON CAPITAL EMPLOYED

Financial Position

($ millions)	*1990*	*1989*	*1988*	*1987*	*1986*	*1985*	*1984*	*1983*	*1982*	*1981*
Current assets	807	761	765	983	940	753	624	581	575	531
Current liabilities	756	727	684	843	739	627	495	470	479	433
Working capital	51	34	81	140	201	126	129	111	96	98
Fixed assets (net)	1,078	1,044	1,052	1,057	932	688	577	508	494	459
Total assets	2,102	2,040	2,004	2,214	1,978	1,530	1,264	1,151	1,111	1,034
Long term debt	473	541	559	588	518	342	251	219	226	193
Total debt	473	549	623	686	569	390	283	233	253	220
Retained earnings	499	434	390	396	348	295	245	198	159	134
Shareholders' equity	812	746	651	690	655	521	466	413	344	317
Average capital employed	1,360	1,379	1,433	1,393	1,141	893	761	692	657	628
Per Common Share *(dollars)*										
Book value	7.99	7.10	6.62	7.12	6.68	5.85	5.09	4.33	3.69	3.34
Price range — high	18⅞	15¼	13⅛	16⅞	14	12⅛	9¾	7⅜	5⅛	4½
— low	13⅝	10¼	9⅞	9	11	8	6½	4⅝	2¾	2½
Financial Ratios *(xx:1)*										
Working capital	1.07	1.05	1.12	1.17	1.27	1.20	1.26	1.24	1.20	1.23
Total debt to equity	.58	.74	.96	.99	.87	.75	.61	.56	.74	.70

Changes in Financial Position

($ millions)										
Cash flow from operations	252	259	158	182	204	132	60	117	110	123
Purchase of fixed assets	171	166	192	248	290	193	150	104	72	99
Per Common Share *(dollars)*										
Cash flow from operations	3.48	3.59	2.19	2.54	2.86	1.85	.84	1.65	1.55	1.80
Financial Ratios *(xx:1)*										
Cash flow from operations to long term debt	.53	.48	.28	.31	.39	.39	.24	.53	.49	.64
Interest coverage on total debt	3.35	2.39	2.16	3.00	3.62	4.17	4.72	4.86	4.35	3.80

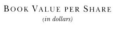

Book Value per Share
(in dollars)

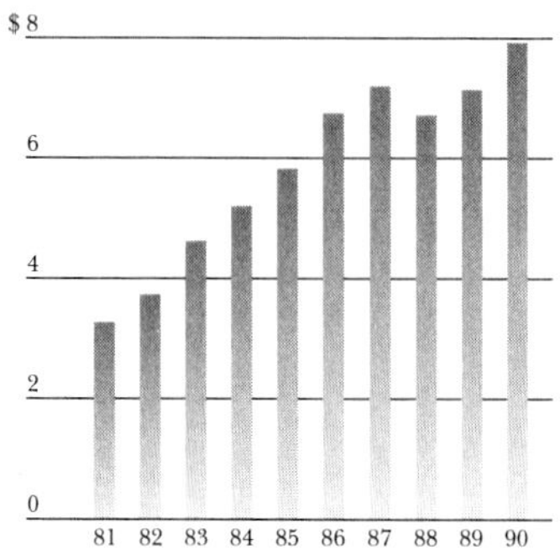

Common Share Price Range
(in dollars)

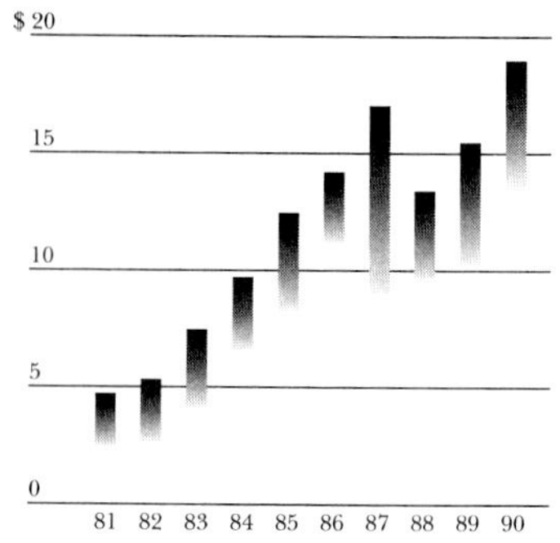

CORPORATE STRUCTURE

LOBLAW COMPANIES LIMITED

DIRECTORS

W. Galen Weston, OC
Chairman and President
George Weston Limited

Richard J. Currie
President, Loblaw
Companies Limited

Camilla Dalglish
Corporate Director

Charles M. Humphrys*
Management Consultant

Robert H. Kidd*
Senior Vice President and
Chief Financial Officer
George Weston Limited

Roger A. Lindsay
Executive Vice President
Wittington Investments,
Limited

Arthur H. Mingay*
Former Chairman
Canada Trust

David A. Nichol
Executive Vice President
Loblaw Companies
Limited

Shirley E. Robertson*
Homemaker,
Professional Photographer

*member - Audit Committee

HONORARY CHAIRMAN
George C. Metcalf

CORPORATE OFFICERS

W. Galen Weston, OC
Chairman of the Board

Richard J. Currie
President

Raymond J. Addington
Executive Vice President

Brian Y. Davidson
Executive Vice President

David A. Nichol
Executive Vice President

David M. Williams
Executive Vice President

David K. Bragg
Senior Vice President,
Planning and Control

Stewart E. Green
Senior Vice President
and Secretary

John W. Thompson
Senior Vice President,
Finance and
Administration

Roy R. Conliffe
Vice President,
Labour Relations

Glenn D. Leroux
Vice President,
Risk Management

John N. McCullough
Vice President,
General Counsel

Richard P. Mavrinac
Vice President, Taxation

Donald G. Reid
Vice President, Treasurer

Stephen A. Smith
Vice President,
Controller

Randy W. Bowes
Assistant Vice President,
Computer Audit Services

Barbara T. Cook
Assistant Controller

Marjorie E. Kyle
Assistant Vice President,
Systems and Internal Control

Louise M. Lacchin
Assistant Treasurer

Dorothy M. Leamen
Assistant Secretary

▲

CENTRAL CANADA
GROCERS INC.
(Toronto, Ontario)
David M. Williams
President

NATIONAL TEA CO.
(Rosemont, Illinois)
Sheldon V. Durtsche
Chairman

Harold A. Seitz
President

LOBLAW
INTERNATIONAL
MERCHANTS
(Toronto, Ontario)
David A. Nichol
President

INTERSAVE BUYING
& MERCHANDISING
SERVICES
(Toronto, Ontario)
Brian Y. Davidson
Chairman

Douglas N. Lunau
President, Intersave
Canada

Harry DeMuth
President, Intersave
U.S.A.

KELLY, DOUGLAS &
COMPANY, LIMITED
(Vancouver,
British Columbia)
Raymond J. Addington
Chairman

Serge K. Darkazanli
President

ATLANTIC
WHOLESALERS LTD.
(Sackville,
New Brunswick)
Albert F. Rose
President

▲   ▲

FORTINO'S
SUPERMARKET LTD.
(Hamilton, Ontario)
John Fortino
President

HASTY MARKET
INC.
(Toronto, Ontario)
Neil M. Walker
President

IPCF
PROPERTIES INC.
(Toronto, Ontario)
Stanley B. Swartzman
President

LOBLAWS
SUPERMARKETS
LIMITED
(Toronto, Ontario)
David T. Stewart
President

WESTFAIR FOODS LTD.
(Calgary, Alberta)
Raymond J. Addington
Chairman

Serge K. Darkazanli
President

NATIONAL GROCERS
CO. LTD.
(Toronto, Ontario)
David M. Williams
President

ZEHRMART INC.
(Cambridge, Ontario)
Grant J. Heimpel
President

The average age and years of
service of the Officers and
operating Presidents are 47
and 15 years respectively.

INDEX

◆